The Transformation of Work in the New Economy

Sociological Readings

Robert Perrucci
Carolyn C. Perrucci
Purdue University

OXFORD
UNIVERSITY PRESS

OXFORD
UNIVERSITY PRESS

Oxford University Press, Inc., publishes works that further Oxford University's objective of excellence in research, scholarship, and education.

Oxford New York
Auckland Cape Town Dar es Salaam Hong Kong Karachi
Kuala Lumpur Madrid Melbourne Mexico City Nairobi
New Delhi Shanghai Taipei Toronto

With offices in
Argentina Austria Brazil Chile Czech Republic France Greece
Guatemala Hungary Italy Japan Poland Portugal Singapore
South Korea Switzerland Thailand Turkey Ukraine Vietnam

First published in 2007 by Roxbury Publishing Company
Published by Oxford University Press, Inc.
198 Madison Avenue, New York, New York 10016
http://www.oup.com

Library of Congress Cataloging-in-Publication Data available

ISBN 978-0-19-533081-6

Dedication

We dedicate this book to our mothers,
Kathleen McGraw Cummings and Inez Mucci Perrucci.
Their lifetimes of paid and unpaid work taught us much about life and work.

Contents

       Sanford M. Jacoby
       A description of working conditions and labor-management relations dur-
       ing early industrialization and the factory system in the United States.

       Harry Braverman
       A critical examination of how Scientific Management in the early twentieth
       century sought to apply the methods of science to expand management con-
       trol of labor.

       Richard Edwards
       Discussion of the forms of control used to convert the potential to work into
       actual work and of how bureaucratic control has come to replace close su-
       pervision and technical control.

       Karl Marx
       Karl Marx's classic mid-nineteenth century critical analysis of how capital-
       ism contributes to the alienation of workers from their product, their work,
       their coworkers, and themselves.

       Dan Clawson
       Examines how the idea of globalization as broadly beneficial trade relations
       has changed to neoliberal globalization based on markets and limited gov-
       ernment regulation.

About the Editors

Robert Perrucci is Professor of Sociology at Purdue University. His research and teaching interests have focused on work and organizations, and inequality and political economy. He recently completed a four-year research project, funded by the Alfred P. Sloan Foundation, focusing on the impact of shift work on workers, their families, and community activities. He has also directed a number of large-scale research projects funded by the National Science Foundation, and the National Institute of Mental Health. He has authored or edited 15 books, and has published extensively in the leading journals in sociology and related disciplines. He is former editor of *The American Sociologist* and *Social Problems*, and co-editor (with Jo Ann Miller) of *Contemporary Sociology*. He has held elected positions as President of the Society for the Study of Social Problems, and the North Central Sociological Association, and Chair of the Organizations and Occupations section of the American Sociological Association.

Carolyn Cummings Perrucci is Professor of Sociology at Purdue University where she has enjoyed a 40-year career teaching in the areas of gender, work and family, and conducting research focusing on gender and socioeconomic achievement, social impacts of plant closings, the economic status of retirees, and graduate educational attainment. Dr. Perrucci is co-editor of *Marriage and the Family: A Critical Analysis and Proposals for Change* and *Women in the Scientific Professions*. She is co-author of *Plant Closings: International Context and Social Costs,* which won the Outstanding Scholarly Achievement Award of the North Central Sociological Association. She has also authored over 40 articles in the leading journals in sociology and related disciplines. She has served as elected Chair of the Section on Sex and Gender, and member of the governing council of the American Sociological Association. Currently she is elected Chair of the Division of Youth, Aging and the Life Course, and is a member of the Board of Directors of the Society for the Study of Social Problems. ✦

About the Contributors

David Bacon received his firsthand education in the global economy as a farm worker and twenty years as a union organizer. As an associate editor for Pacific News Service he has published many articles about border workers and their labor struggles.

Donald L. Barlett and his colleague James B. Steele are America's most widely acclaimed investigative team. They have worked together for three decades, first at the *Philadelphia Inquirer,* and, since 1997, as editors at large for *Time.* They are the coauthors of six books, including *America: What Went Wrong?* They are the only two journalists in history to have won two Pulitzer Prizes and two National Magazine Awards.

Stephen R. Barley is Charles M. Pigott Professor of Management Science and Engineering and Co-Director of the Center for Work, Technology and Organization in School of Engineering at Stanford University.

Penny Edgell Becker is associate professor of sociology at the University of Minnesota. She has studied the links between religious culture, decision-making, and conflict, and how religious ideals shape social inclusion and exclusion along lines of gender, family status, and race. Her publications include two books, *Culture and Conflict in Congregations,* and *Religion and Family in a Changing Society,* and articles that appear in leading journals.

Edna Bonacich is professor of sociology and ethnic studies at the University of California, Riverside. Her work focuses on issues surrounding race, class, and labor. She has written two books on the apparel industry, *Global Production: The Apparel Industry in the Pacific Rim* (a co-edited and co-authored volume published by Temple University Press) and (with Richard Appelbaum) *Behind the Label: Inequality in the Los Angeles Apparel Industry.*

James T. Bond is Vice President for Research and Director of Work-Life Research at the Families and Work Institute. He provides technical advice on research design and data analysis to all major research for the Institute's work-life research program. Included in this area are the National Study for the Changing Workforce and the Business Work-Life Study.

Robert L. Brannon's interests are in the sociology of work, occupations and professions, as well as medical sociology and the sociology of education. He wrote *Intensifying Care* on the health care industry and the reorganization of nursing labor.

Harry Braverman, 1920–1976, is best known for his 1974 book *Labor and Monopoly Capital.* This work attracted a generation of scholars interested in the sociology of work, and the role of skills and control in the capitalist workplace.

April Brayfield is an associate professor of sociology at Tulane University in New Orleans. Her research interests include work-family issues, including attitudes toward women's employment. Currently, she is investigating childrearing values and societal beliefs about young children in Hungary.

Bennett Cherry is associate professor of Management and Organizational Behavior at California State University-San Marcos. His major areas of research include emerging entrepreneurs, service delivery strategy, interpersonal trust development in traditional and non-traditional environments, and humility in leadership.

Dan Clawson teaches sociology at the University of Massachusetts-Amherst, where he is also president of the faculty union, the Massachusetts Society of Professors (affiliated with the National Education Association). His most recent book is *The Next Upsurge: Labor and the New Social Movements* (Cornell University Press 2003). He is one of the co-editors of a forthcoming book entitled *Public Sociology*, concerning efforts to connect academic work to larger publics. His current project, with Naomi Gerstl, examines overtime and extended hours, and the ways workers do or do not contest those hours.

Peter Dicken is professor of economic geography, University of Manchester, UK. He has published extensively on international economic activities, including two books with P. E. Lloyd, *Modern Western Society* (1981), and *Location in Space: Theoretical Perspectives in Economic Geography* (1990).

Richard Edwards is an economist and is dean of the college of liberal arts and sciences at the University of Kentucky, Lexington. He has published widely on work and labor markets.

Barbara Ehrenreich is the author of numerous books, including the New York Times bestseller, *The Worst Years of Our Lives*, as well as *Blood Rites* and *Fear of Falling*, which was nominated for a National Book Critics Circle Award.

Sarah Beth Estes is assistant professor of sociology at the University of Arkansas at Little Rock where she directs the gender studies program. In her research she has examined how workplace family accommodations are related to parenting, children's well-being, and the division of domestic labor.

Jill Andresky Fraser is a well-known financial journalist who has reported on corporate America, investment strategies, personal finance, public policy, and workplace issues. As finance editor of *Inc.* Magazine, she has spent more than a decade advising entrepreneurs about how best to handle personal and corporate financial challenges.

Kathleen Gerson is professor of sociology at New York University. Her research and writing focus on the connections between gender, work, and family change in contemporary societies. Her books include *Hard Choices: How Women Decide About Work, Career, and Motherhood* (1985), *No Man's Land: Men's Changing Commitments to Family and Work* (1993), and *The Time Divide: Work, Family, and Gender Inequality* (with Jerry A. Jacobs, 2004).

Jennifer L. Glass is professor of sociology at the University of Iowa. Her research and publications are in the areas of sex and gender, work and labor markets, family, and mental health.

David M. Gordon (deceased) was Dorothy H. Hirshon Professor of Economics and Director of the Center for Economic Policy Analysis at the New School for Social Research. He wrote, with Samuel Bowles and Thomas Weisskopf, *After the Wasteland: A Democratic Economics for the Year 2000*, and *Beyond the Wasteland: A Democratic Alternative to Economic Decline*.

Janet C. Gornick is associate professor of political science at the Graduate Center and at Baruch College, at the City University of New York. She has written extensively on family policy and gender equality.

Laurie Graham is assistant professor of Organizational Leadership and Supervision with a joint appointment in Women's Studies at Purdue University. Her research interests include workplace health and safety issues and conflict management.

Markus Groth is a senior lecturer in organizational behavior at the Australian Graduate School of Management in Sydney, Australia. His research interests include service management, customer-employee interactions, and the role of emotions in service delivery. His published work has appeared in the *Journal of Applied Psychology, Personnel Psychology, Journal of Management,* and *Academy of Management Executive.*

Barbara A. Gutek holds the Eller Chair in Women and Leadership and is professor in the Department of Management and Policy, Eller College of Management, University of Arizona. She is the author of over 100 books and articles. In 1994, she received two awards from the American Psychological Association and an award from the Women in Management Division of the Academy of Management. Her book with T. Walsh, *The Brave New Society Strategy,* was selected one of the 30 best business books of the year 2000 by Soundview, publishers of Business Executive Summaries.

Richard Hogan is associate professor of sociology and American Studies at Purdue University. In addition to race, class, and gender inequality, he also studies social theory, social history, social movements, and community studies, focusing on local and local-national political struggles in the Nineteenth and Twentieth Century United States.

Jerry A. Jacobs is Merriam Term Professor of Sociology at the University of Pennsylvania. He has served as Editor of the American Sociological Review and the President of the Eastern Sociological Society. His research has addressed a number of aspects of women's employment, including authority, earnings, working conditions, part-time work, and entry into male-dominated occupations.

Sanford M. Jacoby is Howard Noble Professor of Management in the Anderson School of Management at the University of California-Los Angeles. He is author of five books and numerous articles on management, labor markets, and workplace history. His latest book is *The Embedded Corporation: Corporate Governance and Employment Relations in Japan and the United States.*

Arne L. Kalleberg is professor of sociology at the University of North Carolina at Chapel Hill. He has written more than 90 articles and chapters and has coauthored or coedited six books dealing with topics related to the sociology of work, organizations, occupations and industries, labor markets, and social stratification.

Stacy S. Kim is a senior research associate at the Families and Work Institute. She is involved in research on the work-family needs of low-wage workers, the Ask the Children Survey Series, and continuing analysis of the National Study of the Changing Workforce and the Business Work-Life Study. She also provides technical assistance to users of the public-use data files of the National Study of the Changing Workforce.

N. R. Kleinfield is a *New York Times* writer who is winner of the 2002 Jesse Leventhol Prize for Deadline News reporting by an individual.

Gideon Kunda is associate professor in the Department of Labor Studies at Tel Aviv University.

Robin Leidner is associate professor of sociology at the University of Pennsylvania. She has published in the areas of work and labor markets, sex and gender, and cultural sociology.

Frank Levy is Daniel Rose Professor of Urban Economics at the Massachusetts Institute of Technology. His books include *Teaching the New Basic Skills* (with Richard Murnane) and *New Dollars and Dreams: American Incomes and Economic Change.*

Marta Lopez is a Program Associate at the Families and Work Institute, based in New York City. One of the projects in which she has participated includes partnering with the National Latino Children's Institute to organize a conference that brought together the nation's top experts on early childhood education, community organizing, resource development and demographics.

Stephanie Luce is an assistant professor at the Labor Center, University of Massachusetts-Amherst. She is author of *Fighting for a Living Wage* and coauthor with Robert Pollin of *The Living Wage: Building a Fair Economy*.

Karl Marx (1818–1883), was a philosopher, social scientist, historian, and revolutionary, and arguably the most influential socialist thinker in the 19th century. He is widely recognized for his extensive scholarship on the political economy of capitalism.

David J. Maume, Jr. is professor of sociology and Director, Kunz Center for the Study of Work & Family at the University of Cincinnati. In addition to studying labor market inequality, he is also studying temporal differences in the intensification of work and gender differences in limiting work efforts because of family responsibilities.

Sue Falter Mennino is an assistant professor in the Department of Sociology at Loyola University, New Orleans. She has authored several articles dealing with the relationship between gender as a social structure and work/family issues. Her research interests include fathers and job-family balance.

Marcia K. Meyers is associate professor of Social Work and Public Affairs at the University of Washington, and an affiliate of the Social Indicators Survey Center at Columbia University. Dr. Meyers' research focuses on public policies and programs for vulnerable populations, with a particular focus on issues of poverty, inequality, and policy implementation. Current research projects examine the impact of U.S. state policy regimes on the labor force participation of mothers, on inequality in access to early childhood education and care, and on disposable income.

Phyllis Moen holds the McKnight Presidential Chair in Sociology at the University of Minnesota. She studies occupational careers, gender, families, and well-being over the life course, including the frequently obsolete social, cultural, and policy ecologies in which lives play out. She has published numerous books, including *It's About Time: Couples and Careers* (2003), and *The Career Mystique: Cracks in the American Dream* (2005) with Patricia Roehling.

Philip Moss is associate professor and Chair of the Department of Policy and Planning at the University of Massachusetts at Lowell. He has done research on labor markets, regional economic development, changes in racial and gender employment opportunities, employment policy, and immigration.

Richard J. Murnane is Julian W. and William Foss Thompson Professor of Education and Society at Harvard University. His books include *Who Will Teach? Politics That Matter* and coauthor with Frank Levy of *Teaching the New Basic Skills*.

Richard M. Pfeffer was a scholar, lawyer, and political activist until his death in 2002. Relatively early in his career, to learn more about factory work he got a job as a $4.00-an-hour forklift operator, and recorded his observations and conclusions in the well-known *Working for Capitalism* (1979).

Nestor Rodriguez is professor and chair in the Department of Sociology at the University of Houston. His areas of research include international migration, political sociology, and global studies. He is co-editor with Cecilia Menjivar of *When States Kill: Latin America, the U.S., and Technologies of Terror,* University of Texas Press, 2005.

Mark V. Roehling is associate professor in the Department of Labor and Industrial Relations at Michigan State University. His research interests are in the area of employer-employee relations, including psychological contracts and the changing nature of the employment relationship.

Patricia V. Roehling has been with Hope College since 1987 and is currently department chair. Since 1997, she has been conducting research in the area of work and family, in which she became interested during a two-year leave from Hope College (1997–99) when she worked as Director of Research at the Cornell Employment and Family Career Institute.

Jackie Rogers is professor of sociology and Director of Women's Studies Program at Lehigh University. Her publications are in the area of women's studies, and work and labor markets.

Beth A. Rubin is professor of management and adjunct professor of sociology at the University of North Carolina-Charlotte. Rubin publishes on economic and workplace transformation, labor unions, homelessness and social policy and social theory in leading academic journals. Her current research is on organizational commitment in the context of the new economy, inequality and industrial restructuring, organizational and workplace restructuring and time in organizations, the latter of which is represented in the forthcoming book, *Research in the Sociology of Work: Workplace Temporalities,* that Rubin is editing.

James B. Steele and his colleague Donald L. Barlett are America's most widely acclaimed investigative team. They have worked together for three decades, first at the *Philadelphia Inquirer,* and, since 1997, as editors at large for *Time.* They are the coauthors of six books, including *America: What Went Wrong?* They are the only two journalists in history to have won two Pulitzer Prizes and two National Magazine Awards.

Charles Tilly is Joesph L. Buttenwieser Professor of Social Science at Columbia University. He has held teaching and research appointments at University of Delaware, Harvard University, Massachusetts Institute of Technology, University of Toronto, University of Michigan, and the New School for Social Research.

Chris Tilly, University Professor of Regional Economic and Social Development at the University of Massachusetts-Lowell, studies inequality, low-wage work, and social movements. His books include *Glass Ceilings and Bottomless Pits: Women's Work, Women's Poverty* (with Randy Albelda) and *Stories Employers Tell: Race, Skill, and Hiring in America* (with Philip Moss).

Louis Uchitelle has been an award-winning *New York Times* economic writer since 1980. He has taught at Columbia University and was a visiting scholar at the Russell Sage Foundation in New York in 2002–2003.

Steven P. Vallas is professor and chair of Sociology and Anthropology at George Mason University. Most of his research in the sociology of work has concerned the ways in which new technologies and new organizational forms have transformed the managerial regimes within both traditional and highly science-intensive industries. He has written widely on post-Fordism, team systems, and (more recently) on the nature of knowledge work. His current research focuses on the ways in which cultural orientations and identities impact the occupational aspirations of minority and immigrant youth.

Jerry L. Van Hoy is associate professor of sociology and Co-Director of the Program in Law & Social Thought at the University of Toledo. His research focuses on the work practices of lawyers. In particular, he is interested in attorneys who work in entrepreneurial, mass production settings. His current research and publications focus on the social and cultural organization of plaintiffs' personal injury lawyers.

Earl Wysong is professor of sociology at Indiana University-Kokomo. His current research interests include class analysis, organizations, intergenerational mobility, and worker access to family friendly workplace benefits. With Robert Perrucci, he is co-author of a forthcoming new edition of *The New Class Society: Goodbye American Dream?*

Shoshana Zuboff is Benjamin and Lillian Hertzberg Professor of business administration at Harvard University. She has published widely on the subject of information technology in the workplace, and on the history and future of work. ✦

Acknowledgements

We are indebted to Claude Teweles, the publisher at Roxbury, for initiating this project and encouraging us through its completion. The anonymous reviews by the following colleagues of several versions of the proposed book were extremely valuable: Michael Aguilera (*University of Oregon*), Beverly Burris (*University of New Mexico*), William Canak (*Middle Tennessee University*), Carol Caronna (*Towson University*), Scott Fitzgerald (*Indiana University*), Melissa Fry (*University of Arizona*), Michael Handel (*University of Wisconson-Madison*), Kevin Leicht (*University of Iowa*), Nancy Marshall (*Wellesley College*), Peter Meiksins (*Cleveland State University*), Chris Prendergast (*Illinois Wesleyan University*), Robert Rothman (*University of Delaware*), Joyce Rothschild (*Virginia Tech University*), Ken Spenner (*Duke University*), Thomas Steiger (*Indiana State University*), Charles Varano (*University of Sacramento*), Frank Weed (*University of Texas-Arlington*), and Monika D. Wood (*Armstrong Atlantic State University*).

We also thank Jim Ballinger and Scott Carter at Roxbury for working with us on this project. Our work on this project was aided by the contributions of Kristopher Morgan, Beth Williford, and Melissa Young-Spillers. ◆

Introduction

Work and the New Economy

The first great transformation of work occurred with the industrial revolution and the rise of the factory system in the middle of the eighteenth century. The settled agricultural societies of the seventeenth and eighteenth centuries were composed of large landholders, small farmers, peasants who were tied to the land, artisans, and a small merchant class. The division of labor was based on products (farmer, cobbler, baker), and a guild system of independent artisans regulated work. The agricultural/artisanal/guild society started to unravel with the appearance of the merchant capitalist, who used his capital to provide raw materials and tools to artisans who first worked out of their homes (cottage industry) and then in small shops where several artisans were employed by the merchant entrepreneur. This marked the beginning of task specialization and the artisan as an employee. Artisans no longer made the entire product; now the making of the product was divided into component tasks performed by a number of workers.

The discovery of new energy sources in the form of water, steam, and electric power made possible the creation of the factory, a centralized place of production that brought workers to the raw materials and machinery. The factory system was associated with a new worker, who worked regularly scheduled hours for a fixed rate of pay under the control of the factory owner.

The factory system, which appeared in England around 1750, represented a new social organization of work that historians have called the industrial revolution. Some of the earliest sociological classics were produced by scholars who were trying to understand the significance of the transformation of agricultural society and the emergence of industrial society. Karl Marx (1818–1883) and Max Weber (1864–1920) provided the most comprehensive analyses of the emerging industrial order, and many of their insights are still studied by contemporary social scientists.

Marx's analysis of the industrial order focused on the appearance of two new historical figures: the *bourgeoisie*, or capitalist owners of the means of production, and the *proletariat*, or workers who sell their labor power. For Marx, the bourgeoisie and the proletariat represented one propertied class and one propertyless class, locked in a continual struggle in their interdependent relationship; this struggle would shape the future of industrial society. Workers had no choice but to sell their labor power to the owners, and their work, according to Marx, was a form of *alienated labor*. Workers under industrial capitalism are alienated from the means of production (they no longer own the tools, as artisans did), from the product of their own labor (they work on a small part of a total product), and from fellow workers (they are separated by fragmented work and by competition). In addition, workers under capitalism experience *exploitation*, in that the value of their labor to the capitalist is worth more than the cost of reproducing their labor (their wage).

Weber looked at the industrial revolution and saw both the decline of traditional ways of thinking in commerce and government and the rise of rational analysis of human action, influenced by science. He referred to this as the "march of rationality," which he believed was influencing all areas of social life, particularly in the large bureaucratic organizations in which work took place under bureaucratic control. The bureaucratic form of organization had specific characteristics: there was a clearly ordered hierarchy of positions (the organizational chart); every position had defined activities (precise division of labor); there were written rules and regulations (reduced ambiguity); positions were filled on the basis of expertise (universalistic standards); and impersonality characterized work relationships (relationships without anger or emotion). Weber believed that the bureaucratic organization is superior to all other forms of organization because it leads to greater calculability of actions and outcomes, greater precision in planning, and greater speed in achieving objectives. For many contemporary sociologists, the bureaucratic organization also can become an "iron cage" that limits human potential and produces many unanticipated negative outcomes (DiMaggio and Powell 1983).

Weber's prediction about the trend toward greater rationalization of work would be confirmed in the United States in the research of Frederick W. Taylor (1880–1920), who sought to develop a "science of work" in order to increase efficiency and productivity. Taylor's research and recommendations for organizational practices were reported in his book *The Principles of Scientific Management* (1911). This collection of ideas about how to study and rationalize the labor process came to be called *Taylorism*, the scientific study of workers' tasks and the scientific selection of workers that would replace the arbitrary decisions of managers. Taylor believed that the appli-

cation of his principles would lead to greater harmony between labor and management because both work effort and the pay received for work would be the result of scientific analysis. Many of Taylor's principles of scientific management would be adopted by Henry Ford's mass production technologies, which would come to be known as *Fordism*.

This book is about the second great transformation of work that has been unfolding during our lifetime. Beginning in the 1970s, we can observe dramatic changes in the U.S. economy and the world of work that may truly be called *transformative*. There have been major changes in the things that we produce (sharp decline in manufacturing), the way that we produce them (computer-based production), the people who are part of the labor force (many more women workers and foreign workers), the relations between workers and their employing organizations (end of lifetime employment), and the family and social life of workers (family life changes with two working parents). We refer to all of these changes as the *new economy*, which emphasizes (a) a new computer-based production technology, which has changed what we produce and how we produce it; (b) telecommunications technologies, which have made it possible to coordinate spatially dispersed global production and delivery of goods and services; (c) new ways of organizing work, which have reduced job security and increased control of both blue- and white-collar workers; and (d) the changing composition of the U.S. labor force, which now has a greater number of women and workers from around the world.

The new economy is also characterized by a rapid pace of change, requiring adaptations not just across age generations but within one's lifetime. The 35-year-old production worker who has lost her or his job in consumer electronics because the plant moved overseas cannot simply wait for another electronics plant to open. That industry no longer exists in the United States. With another 30 working years ahead, this displaced worker will probably have to move into a service job, where the pay will be lower and there will be no health insurance or retirement program. Family life will be transformed as dual-earner families emerge to maintain an adequate standard of living. Things will be even harder for the single mother with one or two children and a job in retail sales or food service. Family life in dual-earner and single-parent families will be greatly affected by the spillover of work schedules into family schedules.

Organization of the Book

This book is organized into five major parts containing a total of 40 chapters. Part I provides a historical context for the new economy, acquainting readers with some of the dominant practices and issues in the workplace for most of the twentieth century that preceded the new economy. In Chapter 1 we get a picture of factory life in the early decades of the 1900s, with particular attention to the role of the foreman as the dominant figure in the lives of workers. In Chapter 2 we learn about the long-standing concern of employers in the factory system about how to control the pace and quality of work. In the preindustrial system, artisans and craft workers worked alone or in small shops and generally controlled when they worked, how they did their work, and how much they produced. The industrial factory system introduced patterns of external control of workers, and "scientific management" was one of the prominent theories of the day about how managers could exercise greater control over work. Chapter 3 expands the discussion of control, contrasting personal control (close supervision), technical control (assembly line), and the emerging "modern" form of bureaucratic control. Finally, in Chapter 4 we have a classic discussion of alienated labor that was put forward during early industrialization. The interesting question is whether or not alienated labor is still a characteristic of the new economy.

Part II, composed of three sections, introduces the reader to the new economy and the three social forces and related conditions that have helped to define and shape it and that have transformed work and the workplace. Section A looks at *globalization* and the emphasis on global production and international competition. In the global economy, companies can no longer be viewed as *national* companies but rather as *multinational* companies. They may produce parts for their products in many different countries, employ workers from around the globe, import materials from worldwide suppliers, and sell their products wherever they find a market. As this section was being written, Dell computer announced that it would build a plant in India and employ 10,000 Indian workers in order to penetrate the Indian computer market. In the old economy, Dell would still have tried to penetrate the Indian market but would have made the computers in the United States and shipped the finished product to India. The chapters in Section A examine the impact of globalization on job loss in the United States and on the use of foreign workers.

Section B deals with the role of technology in enabling a global production system and in shaping the way that work is organized, controlled, and rewarded. Four chapters examine how computer-based technology and telecommunications have played a role in transforming work in the new economy. Section C contains three chapters describing the way that factories and offices have changed in order to give employers more flexibility in deciding the number of workers they need and type of workforce they will use. These chapters provide an understanding of how a new social contract between employers and employees is being created with the use of temporary employees, part-time workers, and outside contractors.

Part III shifts attention to the everyday experiences of workers in a variety of settings. Section A examines questions about income and opportunities for employees in the new economy. Attention is focused on those workers who are most vulnerable because of their limited power in the labor market, especially women and workers of color. Section B shifts attention to professionals, that group of workers who have traditionally had strong labor market power because of their education, skills, and relative scarcity. The three chapters in this section look at the fields of franchise law, computer specialization, and nursing to see how much freedom and control their practitioners have over their work in the new economy. Section C looks at work on the factory floor. Even though the manufacturing sector has declined in the United States, it still has a large number of employees, and they are facing new corporate strategies to get them to work harder and smarter. Workers may no longer face managers espousing Scientific Management principles and old-style Taylorism, but they now face new systems of work teams and worker participation that may have the same old objectives of working harder and smarter. Finally, Section D turns to service work, the fastest growing sector of the economy. One of the three chapters provides an overview of service work, and two chapters discuss service work in two corporations that have become household names—McDonald's and Wal-Mart.

In Part IV we have four chapters that deal with the connections between work and family life. These chapters take a fresh look at a major feature of the new economy, namely, the sharp increase in women's labor force participation and the growth of dual-earner families. About 50 percent of the labor force is now female, and almost two-thirds of all women over 18 are working. One theme dealt with in these chapters is the increased time demands on workers and parents, and the need to consider changes in public policy to deal with greater work and family stress. A second theme focuses on how dual-earner families are dealing with the work-family balancing act. Do parents share more responsibilities at home? Do they scale back on work commitments? A final theme is concerned with the role of supportive workplace cultures, so-called family-friendly policies, in reducing negative job-to-home spillover.

Finally, Part V consists of two sections and seven chapters that are oriented toward emerging issues in the workplace. Section A focuses on work-family policies that can improve both organizational performance and healthy family functioning. One chapter compares policies in the United States with those of other industrialized countries. Other chapters look at specific employer policies like flextime and child care, and the need for federal policies to ensure a more family-friendly workplace. Section B looks at policies that go beyond family issues to focus on the income needs of low-wage workers, the need for better health care policies, and the future role of the labor movement in protecting the most vulnerable workers in the new economy.

Reference

Paul J. Dimaggio and Walter W. Powell. 1983. "The Iron Cage Revisited: Institutional Isomorphism and Collective Rationality in Organizational Fields," *American Sociological Review*, 48: 147–160. ✦

Part I

Historical Background for the New Economy

In the aftermath of World War II, the U.S. economy was the largest and most dominant in the world. This dominance was due in part to the fact that the war was fought on the soil of other industrialized nations such as Japan, Germany, France, England, and the Soviet Union, leaving their industrial infrastructures severely damaged. For two decades, from the 1950s to the 1970s, the domestic U.S. economy flourished, with the labor force enjoying high levels of employment and sustained wage growth. This was the period in which the United States was being hailed as a "middle-class" society, with expanding opportunities for workers across the occupational structure. In the period from 1947 to 1979, family income wage growth for the lowest quintile of Americans was 120 percent, exceeding the family income growth of the top 20 percent of Americans (94 percent) and the next top 20 percent (114 percent). Contrast this with the period of the new economy (1979–1999), when family income growth of the lowest quintile was –1 percent, while the top quintile enjoyed a 42 percent gain in family income.

The four chapters in Part I provide a glimpse of working conditions in the United States during the first half of the twentieth century, during the period preceding World War II (although Chapter 3 deals with conditions after World War II). This was a time of considerable conflict between labor and management, and workers experienced a variety of efforts aimed at controlling them in order to increase productivity and employer profits. In the decades after World War II, a combination of economic growth and strong labor unions led to a new accord between labor and management. In return for reduced conflict, in the form of no-strike agreements, labor received a promise of job security, wage growth, and work rules that protected workers' rights. This new accord—some called it a *social contract*—worked as long as U.S. corporations enjoyed near dominance in the world economy and growing profits that flowed from that dominance.

The chapters in this unit may serve as a basis for comparison with some of what follows with regard to the new economy. What changes can you detect in work between the pre- and post-1970 period? ◆

1

The Way It Was: Factory Labor Before 1915

Sanford M. Jacoby

Jacoby focuses our attention on the conditions of employment in the early factory system in the United States. This serves as a reference point for readers considering how the workplace has and has not changed since the early twentieth century. The factory system was a new way of organizing work that displaced production in small shops by craft workers. Before the factory system, the division of labor was closely associated with specific skills and products, resulting in bakers, tailors, shoemakers, weavers, wood carvers, brewers, and the like. With the factory system came a more finely graded division of labor, with products broken down into component parts, each of which was done by a different worker.

Jacoby discusses the broad powers of the foreman, who was responsible for recruiting and hiring workers, setting wage rates, and supervising work. This type of close personal power led to many unfair practices and also to the emergence of trade unionism as an organized response to curb the foreman's arbitrary exercise of power.

At the beginning of the nineteenth century, most commodities in the United States were produced either in the workshops of artisans or at home. Skilled tradesmen—carpenters, cobblers, potters—crafted their wares in small shops, owned by merchants or master craftsmen, that had not yet been significantly affected by machine methods. Goods made at home were usually consumed there, although in urban areas the putting-out system was common: Merchants distributed raw materials and tools to household workers, who then wove the cloth or made the shoes and returned the finished product to the merchants for distribution and sale. By the end of the century, however, everything had changed: Most commodities were now manufactured in factories, which were enormous agglomerations of machinery and men.

America's first factories were New England's textile mills, which supplanted home methods of production between 1790 and 1840. These early mills shared a number of features that distinguished the factory system from other modes of production: a reliance on power-driven machinery; the integration of different production processes at a single site; an elaborate division of labor; and finally, new methods of administration based on the overseer or foreman.

The overseer was the key figure in the early New England mills. Large mills employed a number of them, each in charge of a room full of machinery and workers. Although there was an agent who dealt with the mill's owners, the overseer did most of the work of maintaining mechanical and human order. In addition to tending machines, he selected the workers, assigned them to their tasks, and made sure that they labored diligently. Indeed, one advantage of the textile factories was that they permitted more effective labor supervision than was previously possible. Under the putting-out system, merchants could manipulate only the piece prices they paid; effort was controlled by the worker, who could take anywhere from two days to two weeks to turn in his goods. But in the factory, workers had less discretion over their work pace and methods. As one Rhode Island merchant wrote in 1809, "We have several hundred pieces now out weaving, but a hundred looms in families will not weave so much cloth as ten at least constantly employed under the immediate inspection of a workman."[1]

Until the 1840s, the factory system was limited chiefly to the textile industry. By

1880, it had become the dominant production mode in most manufacturing industries. As Carroll D. Wright observed in his introduction to the census of manufactures for 1880:

> Of the nearly three millions of people employed in mechanical industries of this country at least four-fifths are working under the factory system. Some of the other [than textiles] remarkable instances of the application of this system are to be found in the manufacture of boots and shoes, of watches, musical instruments, clothing, agricultural implements, metallic goods generally, firearms, carriages and wagons, wooden goods, rubber goods, and even the slaughtering of hogs. Most of these industries have been brought under the factory system during the past thirty years.

Despite this dramatic growth, the factory did not immediately displace older organizational forms. In the iron and steel industry, rural forges and small foundries coexisted during the 1860s and 1870s with giant rail mills employing more than a thousand workers. Similarly, although steam-powered machinery provided the impetus to establish shoe factories in the 1850s, certain types of women's shoes and slippers were manufactured on a putting-out basis until the end of the century.[2]

Older methods persisted in yet another way. Many of the industries that shifted to the factory system after 1850 continued to depend on techniques from the earlier period. In these industries, the factory was often no more than a congeries of artisanal workshops which had been mechanized and enlarged. A steady infusion of craft skills was still required, particularly when the factory turned out small batches of an unstandardized product. As a result, proprietors in these industries were content to let their foremen and skilled workers make most of the decisions about the timing and manner of production.[3] . . .

The foreman exercised his authority within limits set by the skilled workers, who guarded their autonomy in production through a multitude of working rules that governed methods of shop organization and through what one historian has called the craftsman's "moral code." The code included output quotas set by the workers to protect themselves from overexertion, as well as an ethos of manly defiance to any foreman who tried to subvert traditional shop rules.[4]

Foremen had their own moral code, one which owed a great deal to the skilled worker's shop culture. They were arrogant, proud, conservative men, mindful of the position to which their skill and knowledge had elevated them. Often they wore white shirts to work and seated themselves at raised desks in the middle of the shop floor. But despite their former status as skilled workers, most foremen were strenuously antiunion. They were well aware that their authority depended on severing ties to their pasts. As one observer noted, "They spurn the rungs by which they did ascend."[5]

By the 1880s, winds of change were beginning to erode the power of foremen and skilled workers over production management. The new industries, such as electrical machinery and chemicals, were based on a technology that had little continuity with artisanal techniques. The older industries, like iron and steel, had mechanized to the point where craft skills were no longer essential to production. After the introduction of continuous flow methods in steel manufacturing, the foreman was left with little authority. Most production decisions were now made by engineers and metallurgists. Among skilled steelworkers, who had once been "strong, even arrogant in their indispensability," the "strong sense of independence disappeared." In machine-paced industries like textiles, the overseer was forced to share authority with an increasing number of specialists equal or superior in rank: the chief engineer, the chief electrician, and the supervisors of piping and the waste house. Other than making occasional repairs or inspecting goods to insure their quality, the overseer had fewer and fewer responsibilities in production. In textiles, as in steel and other industries, most of the foreman's tasks were related to employing and supervising labor. Here, however, the methods of the 1850s persisted, with little modification.[6]

I. Foremen in Control, 1880–1915

Whereas the foreman's degree of control over production varied by industry, his authority in employment matters was uniform across industries. Whether in a machine shop or on the assembly line, the foreman was given free rein in hiring, paying, and supervising workers. To the worker, the foreman was a despot—rarely benevolent—who made and interpreted employment policy as he saw fit. Any checks on the foreman's power emanated from the workers he supervised, not from the proprietor.

Recruiting and Hiring

The foreman's control over employment began literally at the factory gates. On mornings when the firm was hiring—a fact advertised by signs hung outside the plant, by newspaper ads, or by word of mouth—a crowd gathered in front of the factory, and the foreman picked out those workers who appeared suitable or had managed to get near the front. At one Philadelphia factory, the foreman tossed apples into the throng; if a man caught an apple, he got the job. Foremen could be less arbitrary. For instance, they frequently hired their friends, the relatives of those already employed, and even their own relatives: "Oftentimes he [the foreman] is connected by blood ties with those who come under his control and he will inevitably be swayed by considerations of previous friendship no matter how hard he may strive not to be." New foremen might dismiss current employees to make room for their friends and relatives, as occurred in a Lawrence textile mill during the 1880s. The overseers "made changes very freely in the departments committed to them, and the result was that for several months a feeling of great insecurity prevailed among the hands."[7]

In addition to blood ties, foremen relied on ethnic stereotypes to determine who would get a job and which job they would get. The Irish and Germans were considered good skilled workers, while Poles and "Hunkies" were thought to be suited for heavy labor. Jews were said to be dexterous, Rumanians dishonest, Slovaks stupid, and Italians "so susceptible to the opposite sex that they could not be satisfactorily employed." When an investigator in the steel mills asked for a job on a blast furnace, he was told "only Hunkies work on those jobs, they're too damn dirty and too damn hot for a white man."[8]

To get a job, workers often resorted to bribing the foreman with whiskey, cigars, or cash, a practice that one study found to be "exceedingly common" in Ohio's factories. The study included an affidavit from an immigrant worker who, to get a factory job, had paid the foreman a five-dollar bribe. Several days later the foreman told the man that he would be fired unless he paid another five dollars right away, because someone else had just paid ten dollars for a similar job.[9]

Assignment to a job was determined in large part by favoritism or ethnic prejudice. The foreman had little interest in or knowledge of an employee's previous work experience. If a newly hired employee proved unsatisfactory, he was easily replaced by someone else. Although intradepartmental promotions occurred, transfers and promotions between departments were rare, as were definite lines of promotion (except on skilled work). The foreman had a parochial view of the factory and was reluctant to give up his best workers to another foreman. . . .

Although direct recruitment was common during the nineteenth century, it was not usually done by the foreman. Instead, employers either sent their own special recruiters to the New York docks to secure immigrant workers or else relied on private agencies like the American Emigrant Company, which kept scouts in several foreign ports to recruit emigrating workers. After the 1890s, however, immigration flows had become large enough and cyclically sensitive enough to meet industrial demand. Consequently, direct recruitment was rare, except in sectors like construction and the railroads, where work was seasonal and labor requirements for certain projects could run into the thousands.[10]

During the heyday of mass immigration, employers recruited through the immigrants' own informal network: Newcomers to America headed for areas where their countrymen, often men from the same European villages, had found jobs. As more men of a given nationality arrived, benefit societies were organized, priests appeared, and wives and children were sent for. Gradually a new ethnic community developed in the area. The news that a company was seeking help was transmitted to friends and relatives in the old country; sometimes, tickets were purchased for them. Letters might also warn of a shortage of jobs.[11]

Wages and Effort

The foreman also had considerable power in determining the wages of the workers he hired, whether for piecework or daywork. As a result, different individuals doing the same job were often paid very different rates. Because top management monitored labor costs but not the wage determination process, the foreman had an incentive to hire individuals at the lowest rate possible. It was common practice for a foreman "to beat the applicant down from the wage he states he wishes to the lowest which the interviewer believes he can be induced to accept." Moreover, by being secretive about wage rates and production records, foremen could play favorites, varying the day rate or assigning workers to jobs where piece rates were loose. Since each foreman ran his shop autonomously, rate variations across departments were also common. In their report on the stove industry, Frey and Commons found that "molding [piece] prices were far from equal on similar work in the same shop or district."[12]

Despite—or perhaps because of—the latitude they gave him in determining rates, the firm's owners expected the foreman to hold down labor costs. This meant paying a wage no greater than the "going rate" for a particular job. But it also meant keeping effort levels up in order to reduce unit costs. When the going rate rose, effort became the key variable to be manipulated by the foreman. The methods used by foremen to maintain or increase effort levels were known collectively as the "drive system": close supervision, abuse, profanity, and threats. Informal rules regulating such work behavior as rest periods were arbitrarily and harshly enforced. Workers were constantly urged to move faster and work harder. Sumner Slichter defined the drive system as "the policy of obtaining efficiency not by rewarding merit, not by seeking to interest men in their work . . . but by putting pressure on them to turn out a large output. The dominating note of the drive policy is to inspire the worker with awe and fear of the management, and having developed fear among them, to take advantage of it."[13]

Driving was more prevalent with day work, where the effort wage was indeterminate. But it occurred with straight piecework too, when foremen sought to prevent workers from restricting output. An official of the machinists complained that "in many cases the rapidity with which the workingmen have been driven under the piecework and similar systems have been the means of driving the mechanics to the insane asylum." Under the bonus wage systems that began to appear after 1890, wages did not rise in proportion to output. Thus, unit labor costs fell with additional production, creating an incentive for the foreman to drive his men even harder and arousing the unions' anger over these new "scientific" payment plans.[14]

The drive system depended, ultimately, on fear of unemployment to ensure obedience to the foreman. Workers were more submissive when jobs were scarce, as was often the case before World War I. A discharge was usually devastating, since few workers had savings to cushion the hardships of unemployment and only meager relief was available. On the other hand, a tight labor market tended to undermine the foreman's authority, forcing him to rely more heavily on discharges to maintain discipline. Data from a metalworking plant illustrate this point. In 1914, a depressed year, the plant had 225 dismissals, many of them for "unadaptability" or "slow work"; this suggests that workers who could not keep up to standard were fired during hard times. By 1916, when the economy had improved and workers could afford to be feisty, the number of dismissals rose to 467, and a relatively large number of workers were fired for "insubordination," "troublemaking," and "positive misconduct." But whether times were tough or easy, the foreman was free to fire anyone as he saw fit, and discharges were meted out liberally. One critic of this system told the story of an assistant superintendent making his rounds through the shop: "Bill," he said to the foreman, "has anyone been fired from this shop today?" "No," the foreman meekly replied. "Well, then, fire a couple of 'em!" barked the assistant superintendent, in a voice that carried. "It'll put the fear of God in their hearts."[15]

Employment Security

Employment instability involved more than high dismissal rates. In its cyclical and seasonal forms, unemployment regularly touched a large portion of the working class. Between 1854 and 1914, recessions or depressions occurred every three or four years, with about twenty-five of these sixty years spent in contraction. In Massachusetts, unemployment was high even during relatively prosperous periods such as 1900–1906, when about one in every five of the state's manufacturing workers was unemployed for at least part of each year. Even Massachusetts' trade union members, a relatively skilled group, were not immune to job loss. An average of 29 percent of these workers had a spell of joblessness each year between 1890 and 1916. The amount of time spent in unemployment was considerable: In 1890 and again in 1900, over 40 percent of the nation's unemployed were jobless for more than four months.[16] . . .

However, the existence of widespread unemployment is not by itself an indication of the impermanence of the employment relationship. Had there been some understanding that laid-off workers would be recalled when needed, periodic unemployment need not have severed the relationship. But few firms made systematic attempts to rehire their workers after layoffs. For example, statistics from a large Chicago metalworking plant, whose records distinguished between new hires and rehires, reveal that only 8 percent of all new hires during the 1908–1910 period were rehires of workers who had been laid off during the depression that began late in 1907. Average industrial rehire rates were probably much lower. Of course, rehiring was more common in seasonal industries, since layoffs and their durations were more predictable. Even here, however, reemployment was by no means guaranteed. A government study of seven dressmaking establishments found that from 32 percent to 75 percent of those employed during the spring busy season were rehired after the summer lull.[17]

In addition to rehiring, mechanisms to maintain the employment relationship during downturns included guaranteed employment plans and work-sharing arrangements. By 1920, only 15 companies had employment guarantee plans. Work-sharing plans, though more prevalent, were usually initiated by trade unions in cooperation with unionized employers. Employers in nonunion firms maintained that work-sharing was cumbersome and inefficient.[18]

Few workers had anything resembling equity in their jobs. When layoffs came, it was the rare employer who ordered his foremen to reduce the work force systematically. Employment security was determined by the same arbitrary criteria as hiring. Bribes were a common means of ensuring job security. Shortly after the turn of the century, a group of Lithuanian workers in a rubber factory were forced to hand over a regular portion of their wages to the foreman as a sort of unemployment insurance. In other shops, according to an article in *Engineering Magazine*, everyone had to "pay some sort of tribute to his foreman. The tribute is usually in the form of money or service, but there are cases where the tribute is of a nature which cannot be mentioned in an open paper."[19]

In short, prior to World War I employment for most manufacturing workers was unstable, unpredictable, and frequently unjust. The worker's economic success and job satisfaction depended on a highly personal relationship with his foreman, with management and "the company" playing only a minor role. A foreman interviewed in 1920 noted that "before the war, most workmen worked where they did not so much because of the company they worked for but because of the foreman. To them the foreman represented the company, and workers in the barroom and other hangouts didn't talk so much about this company or that company as they did about this foreman or that foreman they had worked for." There was an implicit system of employment here, but it was not bureaucratic. Foremen had many favors to offer those whom they had befriended or those who had bought their friendship. Personal ties and loyalty counted for much, although later reformers were horrified by the particularism and brutality that infused the drive system. Those changes that made employment practices more rational, stable, and equitable were not a managerial innovation; rather, they were imposed from below.[20]

II. The Union Response

Trade unionism helped to curb the foreman's arbitrary exercise of power and gave the skilled worker some control over the terms of his employment. The trade union ensured that strict rules and equitable procedures would govern allocative decisions. While only a minority of all workers belonged to unions, those unions were a persistent reminder that the employer's authority, and that of his agents, could be circumscribed through collective action.[21]

Prior to the 1880s, local trade unions unilaterally adopted working rules or "legislation" that governed wages and working conditions for union members. Enforcement depended upon members' refusing—under threat of punishment by the union—to obey any order that contravened the union's rules. But after 1880, as the unions and their national organizations grew more powerful, the status of these rules changed from unilateral group codes to contractual and bargained restrictions on the employer and his foremen. These contracts were extensive documents that strictly regulated work methods and effort norms as well as such issues as apprenticeship standards and wage scales. An 1889 Memorandum of Agreement for members of the Amalgamated Association of Iron, Steel and Tin Workers at the Homestead Works contained fifty-eight pages of "footnotes" defining work rules for union members.[22]

Hiring

Controlling access to a trade was a fundamental element of the unions' power, and regulating apprenticeship standards was an important method for effecting this control. By limiting the number of apprentices or by lengthening the time required to become a journeyman, the union ensured that there would not be an over-supply of men in the trade and thus that the living standards to which union members were accustomed would not deteriorate. Moreover, by overseeing the training process, the union made certain that persons entering the trade were exposed to the virtues of unionism and had absorbed its moral code.

By the turn of the century, however, the apprenticeship system was fading out in many occupations where an ever finer division of labor reduced the demand for versatile craftsmen who knew all the "secrets" of a trade. The ratio of apprentices to the total number employed in manufacturing steadily declined, from 1:33 in 1860 to 1:88 in 1900. In testimony to Congress in 1901, Samuel Gompers noted that "the apprenticeship system is not so generally in vogue now as formerly. The introduction of new machinery . . . and the division and subdivision of labor have rendered a high class of skill, in which workmen have whole work, scarcely necessary (except the demand for the highest skill in a particular branch)."[23]

Nevertheless, the unions had other ways to bolster their control. One important mechanism was the closed or preferential shop, which restricted the foreman's discretion to hire whomever he chose and enhanced the demand for union labor. This protected union members against discrimination in hiring and guaranteed that vacancies would be filled by them. In some trades, the closed shop led to more restrictive union admissions policies so that a fixed number of potential vacancies could be divided among a smaller body of members. Some unions required that the foreman apply to a union hiring hall when in need of labor; this practice allowed the union to dispense jobs to the workers of its choice. Such arrangements also allowed unions to provide employment for older members and to prohibit the use of tests and other screening devices deemed objectionable. But basically they were a powerful demonstration to the worker that his well-being was best served by allegiance to the union rather than to his foreman.[24]

Wages and Effort

In their approach to wage determination, trade unions sought to protect not only absolute wage levels but also relative and effort wages. The central feature of this approach was the so-called standard rate, which all union members were supposed to receive. Reflecting the principle of equal pay for equal work, the standard rate ruled out all incentive wage systems under which earnings did not rise in proportion to output and effort, as well as all payment systems which "graded" workers: that is, classified them by some criterion such as merit or competence or sometimes even seniority. (One union said that seniority allowed the employer to get "first class service from a man getting less than a first class wage.") The unions' strong emphasis on the standard rate was based on the premise that

foremen would always prefer to deal with individuals and that grading was the surest way to divide and conquer.

The unions were opposed to grading on other grounds as well. First, they argued that grading was unnecessary since apprenticeship standards insured that all journeymen were equally competent. Second, they feared that grouping workers by competence would undercut the standard rate and lead inevitably to the substitution of relatively cheap labor for higher priced men. Third, they believed that grading encouraged specialization within the trade, thereby lessening the demand for all-around craftsmen and eroding wage levels. Finally, they viewed grading and other meritocratic wage determination methods as an affront to their egalitarianism and their insistence on occupational autonomy. When the United Typothetae, an employers' association, proposed a graded wage system in 1887, the Typographical Union replied that "it would be impossible to satisfactorily grade all workmen except by an elaborate system of examination which would be appalling to undertake."[25]

In practice, however, the unions permitted the payment of different rates for the various steps within a trade and for especially skilled or dangerous work. Among machinists and molders, for example, journeymen who had recently advanced from apprenticeship could be paid wages below the standard rate. Other unions allowed grading by skill, but only if the different grades were nonsubstitutable. The photoengravers permitted half-tone etchers to be paid more than line-etchers, but the latter—however capable—were never permitted to do half-tone work.[26]

The standard rate represented a level of well-being for which union members had fought and to which they felt entitled. Consequently, organized workers viewed wage cuts as a threat to their living standards and stood ready to strike in defense of the standard rate. As early as 1870, textile manufacturers in Fall River, and then coal operators in Ohio's Hocking Valley, deliberately provoked strikes by cutting the wages of their unionized workers, hoping to break the unions in the ensuing disputes.[27]

Unions were equally concerned about how hard members had to work to receive their pay. To check the foreman's driving and to protect the effort wage, skilled workers made effective use of "the stint," the deliberate restriction of output. In many instances, the union specified output limits in the trade agreement and imposed fines on pieceworkers whose earnings were excessive. Typically, however, union members policed themselves. Skilled workers who restricted their output did not think of themselves as Luddites but instead as "sober and trustworthy masters of the trade" whose stinting demonstrated "unselfish brotherhood."[28]

While the stint was also used to deter foremen from playing favorites in assigning piecework jobs, the unions had other ways to limit favoritism. For example, in 1896 the molders demanded that piece rates be listed in a price-book, so as to prevent foremen from paying different rates for similar work. In one stovemaking shop, both the foreman and a union representative were given keys to the locker in which the price-book was kept. In the Chicago meatpacking industry, the cattle butchers devised a detailed system of promotion lines governed by seniority that was intended to curtail favoritism in job allocation and to create a sense of equity among the union's members. Foremen and other managers were strongly opposed to the practice. As John R. Commons observed, "These rules of promotion do not find favor with the superintendents, who contend that forced promotion takes a man away from work he does well."[29]

Elsewhere, promotion lines were devised primarily to enhance the prospects of a shop's incumbent workers. During the 1870s, unskilled helpers in the steel industry demanded that they be given preference over outsiders whenever a skilled position became vacant. By the late 1880s, the steelworkers' union had adopted rules calling for promotion lines governed by seniority. "We endeavor," said the union, "to prevent men from learning the skilled posi-

tions before they have served in the minor ones. If they are permitted to learn the skilled jobs, it would necessarily mean that those holding the minor positions would have no opportunity for improvement."[30]

Security

In an effort to reduce unemployment, trade unions adopted rules regulating manning levels and working hours, as well as output quotas. Workers in seasonal industries like construction were encouraged to slow down as the slack season approached. While such strictures may have had some stabilizing effect on the demand for union labor, they could not prevent periodic outbreaks of unemployment. When layoffs threatened, the unions attempted to mitigate the impact of unemployment through work-sharing and through seniority rules.

Work-sharing was practiced by a variety of unions—the needle trades, the boot and shoe workers, the machinists, the coal miners—and took a variety of forms. Groups of workers might alternate shifts of a week or less. Alternatively, some union shops closed early or shut down for a day or two each week. In industries such as brewing, the employers and the union made joint arrangements to share the work; in other trades, the unions unilaterally withdrew their members on certain days of the week.[31]

A few unions responded to downturns with rules requiring that layoffs be made in accordance with reverse seniority. This was less common than work-sharing, in part because employment was so volatile in many industries that seniority rules would have divided the union into two groups, those who had steady jobs and those who did not. Further, seniority layoffs were unsuited to those trades with a tradition of mobility, where few workers remained with an employer for any length of time. Hence, some of the first unions to rely on seniority layoffs were found on the railroads and in newspaper printing, industries in which employment was relatively stable and workers were attached to their employer rather than to their trade. The first written agreement recognizing seniority as a factor in layoffs was signed by railroad workers in 1875; fifteen years later the typographers adopted their famous "priority law," which required that layoffs be made in strict accordance with seniority.[32]

Another cushion against the shock of unemployment was the requirement that advance notice be given of impending layoffs. Innocuous as this rule may seem, employers were under no obligation to give notice, and unprepared workers often suffered. A shopman on the Baltimore & Ohio railroad recalled, "Our boss was always afraid to tell you there was going to be a layoff. I have seen McSweeney write on the door with a piece of chalk, 'No work tomorrow.' He waited so long that he could not get around to tell the men in time."[33]

Whether the unions chose seniority or work-sharing, their regulations undermined one of the foreman's chief prerogatives under the drive system—determining the incidence of layoffs. Neither scheme allowed foremen to discriminate against union members or to pit workers against each other in a struggle to retain their jobs. Indeed, the printing and railroad unions became interested in seniority-based layoffs at a time when both industries were experiencing an increase in favoritism, nepotism, and, especially, discrimination against union members.[34]

The strongest protection the unions devised against unfair treatment were the restrictions they imposed on the foreman's power to discipline and discharge. These restrictions were of two types. In some industries, the union followed a craft tradition of unilaterally promulgating rules with respect to discipline and dismissal. That is, the *union* determined standards of behavior; fined or expelled members who fell below these standards; and provided its own internal grievance procedure. The closed shop was critical to the operation of these systems: Only if union membership was a prerequisite of employment could the union secure compliance with its rules. For example, the milkwagon drivers' union agreed in its contracts to fine or suspend any member proved guilty of "drunken-

ness, or dishonesty, incompetency, smoking or drinking while on duty." Moreover—and this is key—the company agreed to dismiss anyone whom the union expelled. Hence, a union member's job security depended less on his relation to any single employer or foreman than on his standing in the union, which controlled access to future employment via the closed shop.[35]. . .

These disciplinary provisions, together with the closed shop and seniority rules, undermined the fundamental assumption of the drive system: that employment was a relationship of indefinite duration terminable at the employer's will. The unions held the alternative concept that employment was a permanent relationship between the union (a set of workers) and the employer (a set of jobs). In the building trades, this set of jobs spanned establishment boundaries; on the railroads, and in the printing, metalworking, and needle trades, these jobs were found within a single firm. In either case, the union behaved as if it owned this set of jobs: With the closed shop, only union men could fill the jobs; under work-sharing, the jobs could not be dissolved. The union's various security mechanisms kept the employer from turning to the open market to fill vacancies. Moreover, through its allocative, wage, and dismissal practices, the union embedded the employment relationship in a web of impersonal, equitable rules. Indeed, by 1915 the unions had come very close to creating a bureaucratic employment system for their mostly skilled members.

III. The Less Skilled

The unskilled worker dissatisfied with his job had few options. He could complain to higher officials, but they invariably supported the foreman in any dispute. Daniel McCallum, president of the Erie Railroad, justified this practice by asserting that "obedience cannot be enforced where the foreman is interfered with by a superior officer giving orders directly to his subordinates." More was involved here than the application of a military model to industry. As one economist perceptively observed, managers feared that any show of liberality would "give the workmen exaggerated notions of their rights and management desires to keep the workers' minds off their rights." In the early 1900s a group of nineteen unskilled rubber workers presented their employer with signed affidavits that described how they had been forced to bribe a foreman to retain their jobs. All nineteen were fired within two weeks.[36]

Occasionally the unskilled were able to establish their own workplace organizations, which regulated employment in much the same way as the craft unions did. During the 1880s, the Knights of Labor included local assemblies made up of less skilled workers who banded together to press for higher wages and to protect themselves from arbitrary foremen. Some of the locals even achieved the closed shop and a seniority-based layoff system. But unskilled workers had relatively little bargaining power and were rarely able to sustain sizable, stable organizations.

The absence of organization did not, however, deter them from engaging in militant activity. In steel, for instance, pitched battles were fought at Cleveland (1899), East Chicago (1905), McKees Rocks (1909), and Bethlehem (1910), with the unskilled, immigrant work force on one side and the militia and police on the other. The particularly violent strike at McKees Rocks was touched off when the company fired a group of workers who had protested pay practices and fee-charging by the company's foremen. But these strikes, while spectacular, were sporadic and seldom successful.[37]

Limitation of output was a somewhat more effective means of checking the foreman. The Commissioner of Labor's 1904 report on *Regulation and Restriction of Output* found that stints and slowdowns were "enforced in nonunion establishments" and were widely accepted "among all wage earners." But lacking the discipline provided by a union, and sundered by ethnic conflicts and language barriers that stymied cooperation, unskilled workers—even those belonging to assemblies of the Knights of Labor—had less success with this method than did their skilled counterparts.[38]

Because his actions were so ineffectual, the unskilled worker seeking higher wages or better working conditions usually had no alternative but to quit. Data from the 1900s and 1910s show labor turnover levels that were extraordinarily high by modern standards, especially among less skilled workers. Many companies experienced monthly separation rates in excess of 10 percent. In one Milwaukee engine factory, whose experience was typical of other factories, the separation rates for unskilled and semiskilled workers in 1912 were three times as high as the rates for skilled workers in the tool and pattern department. A government official termed labor turnover "the individualistic strike": Just as the number of strikes by skilled trade unionists tended to increase during a recovery period, so did the number of quits by the less skilled.[39]

High turnover rates also reflected the immigrant backgrounds of the unskilled. Almost two-thirds of the immigrants arriving in the United States between 1870 and 1910 were unskilled, and they became the backbone of the manufacturing labor force. Around the turn of the century, when the foreign-born constituted nearly one-quarter of the labor force, they represented about half of all unskilled laborers in manufacturing. Foreign-born workers accounted for 58 percent of all workers in iron and steel manufacturing, 61 percent in meatpacking, 62 percent in bituminous coal mining, and 69 percent in the cotton mills.[40]

While it is well-known that immigration flows were large and cyclically sensitive, it is less well-known that emigration flows followed the same pattern. Between 1870 and 1914, one person left the United States for every three that arrived. While emigration decreased and immigration increased during good years, the annual proportion of emigrants to immigrants never fell below 20 percent. Emigration rose during depressed years, as recent immigrants—the first to lose their jobs—decided to return home. Ninety percent of the Bulgarians who made up most of the unskilled labor force in an Illinois steel mill had left town by the end of the 1908 depression. That year, immigration fell, and the national proportion of emigrants to immigrants rose to 75 percent. Although more immigrants stayed than left, the large backflow contributed to the instability of the unskilled labor force and to high rates of turnover.[41]

Immigrants often came to the United States with no intention of permanently settling here. Many were single men or married men with families back home. This was true of about half of the unskilled Italian laborers living in Buffalo in 1905, and of four in five of the nation's immigrant steelworkers. These men came to make their "stake," planning to return to Europe to buy land, open shops, or pay off debts. The transience of the immigrant labor force was part of an older European pattern of peasant mobility. In Italy, landless day laborers roamed from place to place looking for work, often spending weeks or months away from home. Slovaks worked seasonally on their plots and then supplemented their incomes as roving peddlers; Polish peasants went to Germany. The fact that many immigrant workers viewed their stay in the United States as temporary made it difficult to organize them into unions. A strike just lengthened the time a man was away from home and family, while the prospect of returning home made one's privations more bearable.[42]

Finally, quitting was a form of resistance to the rigors of factory life. Here there was a continuity of experience among the early New England textile workers, their French-Canadian and Irish replacements, and the southeastern Europeans who filled the factories after 1880. Each group brought to the factories a preindustrial work ethic that was attuned to the seasons, migratory, and uncomfortable with industrial discipline. Ellen Collins quit the mill at Lowell in the 1840s complaining about her "obedience to the ding-dong of the bell—just as though we were so many living machines." During the 1870s, managers of New England textile mills complained that absenteeism and quits made it difficult to run their machines on the hottest summer days. One manufacturer said in 1878 that "our mill operatives are much like other people and take their frequent holidays for pleasure and visiting." Forty years later, the quit rate at a Connecticut silk mill quadrupled during the hot summer months of 1915. Thus, each group successively went through the process of internalizing factory discipline; this was one of the props to high turnover before 1920.[43] . . .

IV. A Market of Movement

Because the employment relationship was one of weak attachment on both sides, the industrial labor market prior to 1915 was a market of movement, characterized by high rates of mobility. Indeed, the few available company records indicate a pattern of continuously high turnover rates before World War I. The earliest turnover data come from the New England textile industry of the 1830s and 1840s, and they show that the young Yankee women who worked in the mills were an unstable labor force. Most were unmarried and could return to their parents' farms if they were dissatisfied or if work was scarce. But the immigrants who began to replace native workers in the 1850s had high turnover rates too. A study of 151 Scottish weavers recruited by Lyman Mills in 1853 found that nearly 80 percent of the women had left the firm within three years.[44]

A similar picture emerges in other companies, especially those employing relatively more men. A Massachusetts firm that manufactured textile machinery recruited large numbers of French-Canadians between 1860 and 1890. But "so rapid was the turnover" that, of every three workers hired, only one stayed with the firm. Rates of persistence were also very low at the Boston Manufacturing Company. For quinquennial periods between 1850 and 1865, only 10–12 percent of the male workers employed at the beginning of a period were still working for the firm five years later.[45]

Nineteenth-century employers sometimes complained about what one of them called "the nomadic system of employing men." Employers often responded to high quit rates by withholding the wages of those who left without prior notice, a practice that also deterred strikes. When a Massachusetts mill owner was asked in the 1870s to explain these wage forfeitures, he replied, "If a mill did not keep back workers' wages, it would simply awake to find all its hands gone by the morning."[46]

The better records available for the first two decades of the twentieth century show continuing high levels of turnover throughout the manufacturing sector. But because the overall data are so fragmentary, especially for the nineteenth century, some other source of information is needed to gauge labor turnover levels. . . .

Discussion Questions

1. How did the skill level of workers influence their relationship with the foreman and with the trade union movement?

2. Are there examples of close supervision and broad personal power in the workplace today?

Excerpted from Sanford M. Jacoby, "The Way It Was: Factory Labor Before 1915," in *Employing Bureaucracy* (New York: Columbia University Press, 1985), pp. 13–37. Reprinted by permission of the author.

Endnotes

1. Samuel Batchelder, *Introduction and Early Progress of the Cotton Manufacture in the United States* (Boston, 1863), passim; Stephen Marglin, "What Do Bosses Do? The Origins and Functions of Hierarchy in Capitalist Production," *Review of Radical Political Economics* (Summer 1974), 6:33–60; Caroline F. Ware, *The Early New England Cotton Manufacture* (Boston, 1931), pp. 23, 50–51, 263–266; Howard M. Gitelman, "The Waltham System and the Coming of the Irish," *Labor History* (Fall 1967), 8:227–253; Hannah Josephson, *The Golden Threads: New England's Mill Girls* (New York, 1949), pp. 220–221; Thomas Dublin, *Women at Work: The Transformation of Work and Community in Lowell, Massachusetts, 1826–1860* (New York, 1979).

2. Carroll D. Wright, "The Factory System of the United States," U.S. Bureau of the Census, *Report of the United States at the Tenth Census* (Washington, D.C., 1883), p. 548; Victor S. Clark, *History of Manufactures in the United States* (Washington, D.C., 1929), 3:15–16, 76–80, 473; Daniel Nelson, *Managers and Workers: Origins of the New Factory System in the United States, 1880–1920* (Madison, Wis., 1975), p. 4.

3. The authority of the foreman and the skilled worker, said Frederick W. Taylor, come from "knowledge handed down to them by word of mouth. . . . This mass of rule-of-thumb or traditional knowledge may be said to be the principal asset or possession of every tradesman." *The Principles of Scientific Management* (New York, 1912), pp. 31–32.

4. George S. Gibb, *The Whitesmiths of Taunton: A History of Reed and Barton, 1824–1843* (Cambridge, Mass., 1943), pp. 282–286; Clawson, *Bureaucracy*, pp. 126–130; Nelson, *Managers and Workers*, p. 40; Montgomery, "Workers' Control," p. 491.

5. Alexander Hamilton Church, "The Twelve Principles of Efficiency: The Eleventh Principle—Written Standard Practice Instructions," *The Engineering Magazine* (June 1911), 41:445; Gibb, *Whitesmiths*, p. 184; Ordway Tead, "The Importance of Being a Foreman," *Industrial Management* (June 1917), 53:353.

6. David Brody, *Steelworkers in America: The Nonunion Era* (New York, 1969), p. 85; "The Characteristics of a Foreman," *The Engineering Magazine* (February 1909), 36:847; Evelyn H. Knowlton, *Pepperell's Progress: History of a Cotton Textile Company, 1844–1945* (Cambridge, Mass., 1948), pp. 159–161.

7. Joseph H. Willits, "Steadying Employment," *The Annals* (May 1916), vol. 65, suppl., p. 72; H. Keith Trask, "The Problem of the Minor Executive," *The Engineering Magazine* (January 1910), 38:501; "Fall River, Lowell, and Lawrence," Massachusetts Bureau of the Statistics of Labor, *Thirteenth Annual Report* (Boston, 1882), p. 381.

8. Brody, *Steelworkers*, p. 120; Virginia Yans-McLaughlin, *Family and Community: Italian Immigrants in Buffalo, 1880–1930* (1977; reprint, Urbana, Ill., 1982), p. 43; Arthur Hanko, "Reducing Foreign Labor Turnover," *Industrial Management* (May 1921), 61:351.

9. Fred H. Rindge, Jr., "From Boss to Foreman," *Industrial Management* (July 1917), 53:508–509; C. J. Morrison, "Short-Sighted Methods in Dealing With Labor," *The Engineering Magazine* (January 1914), 46:568.

10. Charlotte Erickson, *American Industry and the European Immigrant, 1860–1885* (Cambridge, Mass., 1957), pp. 17–28, 67–87; Brody, *Steel-*

workers, p. 109; Don D. Lescohier, "Working Conditions," in J. R. Commons et al., *History of Labor in the United States* (New York, 1935), 3:188; Isaac A. Hourwich, *Immigration and Labor* (New York, 1912), pp. 93–101; Harry Jerome, *Migration and Business Cycles* (New York, 1926).

11. Yans-McLaughlin, *Italian Immigrants*, pp. 59–64, 72–73; William I. Thomas and Florian Znaniecki, *The Polish Peasant in Europe and America*, abridged by Eli Zaretsky (1918; reprint, Urbana, Ill., 1984), pp. 139–255.

12. Sumner H. Slichter, *The Turnover of Factory Labor* (1919; reprint, New York, 1921), p. 319; Dwight T. Farnham, "Adjusting the Employment Department to the Rest of the Plant," *Industrial Management* (September 1919), 58:202; Commission of Inquiry, Interchurch World Movement, *Report on the Steel Strike of 1919* (New York, 1920), p. 139; Nelson, *Managers and Workers*, pp. 44–45; John P. Frey and John R. Commons, "Conciliation in the Stove Industry," U.S. Bureau of Labor Statistics (BLS) Bulletin No. 62 (Washington, D.C., 1906), p. 128.

13. John R. Commons, "Labor Conditions in Meat Packing and the Recent Strike," *Quarterly Journal of Economics* (November 1904), 19:8; Nelson, *Managers and Workers*, p. 43; Slichter, *Turnover*, p. 202.

14. Lloyd Ulman, *The Rise of the National Trade Union* (Cambridge, Mass., 1955), p. 549.

15. Philip Klein, *The Burden of Unemployment* (New York, 1923), pp. 13–37; Paul F. Brissenden and Emil Frankel, *Labor Turnover in Industry: A Statistical Analysis* (New York, 1922), pp. 80–81; Slichter, *Turnover*, p. 184; *Industrial Relations* (also known as *Bloomfield's Labor Digest*) (May 12, 1923), 15:1530.

16. Alexander Keyssar, "Men Out of Work: A Social History of Unemployment in Massachusetts, 1870–1916" (Ph.D. dissertation, Harvard University, 1977), pp. 43, 72, 76–77, 79, 107; Robert A. Gordon, *Business Fluctuations* (New York, 1961), p. 251.

17. Slichter, *Turnover*, pp. 126–127, 129.

18. Keyssar, "Out of Work," p. 129; "How to Meet Hard Times: A Program for the Prevention and Relief of Abnormal Unemployment," Mayor's Committee on Unemployment, City of New York (New York, 1917), p. 24; "Guaranteed Wages: Report to the President by the Advisory Board," Office of War Mobilization and Reconversion and Office of Temporary Controls (Washington, D.C., 1947), app. C, pp. 290, 293.

19. Keyssar, "Out of Work," p. 153; Morrison, "Short-Sighted," p. 568.

20. *Industrial Relations* (December 11, 1920), 5:484.

21. At its pre-Wagner Act peak in 1920, the proportion of nonagricultural employees who belonged to unions was 18.5 percent. Leo Wolman, *Ebb and Flow in Trade Unions* (New York, 1936), pp. 172–193.

22. F. W. Hilbert, "Trade-Union Agreements in the Iron Molders' Union," in Jacob H. Hollander and George E. Barnett, *Studies in American Trade Unionism* (London, 1906), pp. 221–260; Bruno Ramirez, When Workers Fight: The Politics of Industrial Relations in the Progressive Era, 1898–1916 (Westport, Conn., 1978), pp. 17–48; Brody, *Steelworkers*, p. 52.

23. James M. Motley, *Apprenticeship in American Trade Unions* (Baltimore, 1907); Paul H. Douglas, *American Apprenticeship and Industrial Education* (New York, 1921), p. 74; "Testimony of Samuel Gompers," in U.S. Industrial Commission, *Report on the Relations and Conditions of Capital and Labor* (Washington, D.C., 1901), 7:620.

24. Sumner H. Slichter, *Union Policies and Industrial Management* (Washington, D.C., 1941), p. 63; "Gompers," p. 603; Sanford M. Jacoby and Daniel J. B. Mitchell, "Development of Contractual Features of the Union-Management Relationship," *Labor Law Journal* (August 1982), 33:515; Howard T. Lewis, "The Economic Basis of the Fight for the Closed Shop," *Journal of Political Economy* (November 1912), 20:928–952; D. P. Smelser, *Unemployment and American Trade Unions* (Baltimore, 1919), pp. 57–74.

25. Sidney and Beatrice Webb, *Industrial Democracy* (1897; reprint, London, 1920), pp. 279–323; David A. McCabe, *The Standard Rate in American Trade Unions* (Baltimore, 1912), pp. 101–111; William H. Buckler, "The Minimum Wage in the Machinists' Union," in Hollander and Barnett, *Studies*, pp. 111–151.

26. Ulman, *National Trade Union*, pp. 483–484.

27. Montgomery, "Workers' Control," p. 496.

28. "Regulation and Restriction of Output," Eleventh Special Report of the U.S. Commissioner of Labor (Washington, D.C., 1904); Slichter, *Union Policies*, pp. 166–167; Montgomery, "Workers' Control," p. 491; G. G. Groat, *An Introduction to the Study of Organized Labor in America* (1916; reprint, New York, 1926), pp. 358–365. Unions also practiced output limitation as a way to stave off unemployment. Smelser, *Unemployment*, pp. 46–50.

29. Ulman, *National Trade Union*, pp. 542–543; Frey and Commons, "Stove Industry," pp. 128, 157; Commons, "Meat Packing," p. 17.

30. Quoted in Bernard L. Elbaum, "Industrial Relations and Uneven Development: Wage Structure and Industrial Organization in the British and U.S. Iron and Steel Industries, 1870–1970" (Ph.D. dissertation, Harvard University, 1982), p. 171.

31. Keyssar, "Out of Work," p. 107; Mayor's Committee, "Hard Times," p. 24; Commons, "Meat Packing," p. 15; Smelser, *Unemployment*, pp. 109–129.

32. Selig Perlman, *A History of Trade Unionism in the United States* (New York, 1923), pp. 181–182.

33. Slichter, *Union Policies*, p. 104; "Gompers," p. 832.

34. Dan Mater, "The Development and Operation of the Railroad Seniority System," *Journal of Business* (October 1940), 13:6–29; Robert K. Burns, "Daily Newspapers," in Harry A. Millis, ed., *How Collective Bargaining Works* (New York, 1942), p. 86.

35. David E. Feller, "A General Theory of the Collective Bargaining Agreement," *California Law Review* (May 1974), 61:728–731; "Restriction of Output," p. 21; "Collective Bargaining Agreement of the Milk Wagon Drivers' Union, Local 753, International Brotherhood of Teamsters, Chicago, Illinois, May 1924," in Slichter Papers, Littauer Library, Harvard University.

36. McCallum quoted in Richard Edwards, *Contested Terrain: The Transformation of the Workplace in the Twentieth Century* (New York, 1979), p. 31; Slichter, *Turnover*, p. 387; Keyssar, "Out of Work," p. 153.

37. Montgomery, "Workers' Control," p. 489; Perlman, *History*, pp. 98–99, 116; Brody, *Steelworkers*, pp. 138–139.

38. "Restriction of Output," pp. 22, 29; Montgomery, "Workers' Control," p. 499. Also see Stanley B. Mathewson, *Restriction of Output Among Unorganized Workers* (New York, 1931).

39. Brissenden and Frankel, *Labor Turnover*, pp. 41, 48; Slichter, *Turnover*, pp. 57–69; William B. Wilson, "Labor Program of the Department of Labor," BLS Bulletin No. 247 (1918), p. 166. At a large metalworking plant, the number of quits rose from 581 in 1914, a depressed year, to 3,035 in 1916. The plant's proportion of quits due to "dissatisfaction" rose from 27 percent in 1914 to 34 percent in 1915, the beginning of the recovery; by 1916, these accounted for 64 percent of all quits. Slichter, *Turnover*, p. 180.

40. Stanley Lebergott, *Manpower in Economic Growth: The American Record Since 1800* (New York, 1964), p. 28; Hourwich, *Immigration*, p. 503; Walter Fogel, "Immigrants and the Labor Market: Historical Perspectives and Current Issues," in D. G. Papademetriou and M. J. Miller, eds., *The Unavoidable Issue: U.S. Immigration Policy in the 1980s* (Philadelphia, 1983), p. 73.

41. Ulman, *National Trade Union*, p. 9; Jerome, *Migration*, p. 106; Federated American Engineering Societies, *Waste in Industry* (New York, 1921), p. 300; Brody, *Steelworkers*, pp. 105–106.

42. Yans-McLaughlin, *Italian Immigrants*, pp. 26–30, 49, 78; Brody, *Steelworkers*, pp. 97–98; Stephen Hickey, "The Shaping of the German Labor Movement: Miners in the Ruhr," in Richard J. Evans, ed., *Society and Politics in Wilhelmine Germany* (New York, 1978), pp. 215–240.

43. Herbert Gutman, *Work, Culture and Society in Industrializing America* (New York, 1976), p. 28; Massachusetts Bureau of Statistics of Labor, *Tenth Annual Report* (Boston, 1978), cited in Daniel T. Rodgers, *The Work Ethic in Industrializing America, 1850–1920* (Chicago, 1978), p. 162; Slichter, *Turnover*, p. 184.

44. Ware, *Cotton Manufacture*, pp. 224–226; Norman Ware, *The Industrial Worker, 1840–1860* (Boston, 1924), p. 149; Ray Ginger, "Labor in a Massachusetts Cotton Mill: 1853–1860," *Business History Review* (March 1954), 28:84, 87.

45. Thomas R. Navin, *The Whitin Machine Works Since 1831: A Textile Machinery Company in an Industrial Village* (Cambridge, Mass., 1950), pp. 160–161; Howard M. Gitelman, *Workingmen of Waltham: Mobility in American Urban Industrial Development, 1850–1890* (Baltimore, 1974), p. 71.

46. Rodgers, *Work Ethic*, p. 164. In an 1853 case involving a weaver who quit without giving prior notice, a Maine court said that, "The only valuable protection which the manufacturer can provide against such liability to loss and against what are in these days denominated 'strikes,' is to make an agreement with his laborers that if they willfully leave their machines and his employment without notice, all or a certain amount of wages that may be due to them shall be forfeited." *Harmon v. Salmon Falls Mfg. Co.*, 35 Me. 450 (1853). ✦

2

Scientific Management

Harry Braverman

Industrialization created a new class of workers who labored for wages in large industrial plants, who followed the rhythms of the clock, and who were directed by close supervisors. They were the working class. Scientific Management was developed by Frederick Winslow Taylor as a science of control over the labor process. It was designed to address the question of how to transform the potential to work into actual work.

Although Taylor was born into a wealthy Philadelphia family and was preparing to attend Harvard and make a career in law, he was attracted to industrial administration and began a craft apprenticeship in the firm of a family friend. Taylor's experiences as a "gang boss" (supervisor) in a lathe department led him to discover that workers under his supervision had their own ideas about what was a "fair day's work" and about how they should do their work. Moreover, they socialized new workers into their work group-based standards and effectively resisted management. Taylor was determined to break this system of worker control and embarked on a program of studying the labor process. In this chapter, Harry Braverman analyzes the Scientific Management movement and argues that its essence was an effort at "de-skilling" workers and placing greater control over the conception and execution of work in the hands of managers.

The classical economists were the first to approach the problems of the organization of labor within capitalist relations of production from a theoretical point of view.

They may thus be called the first management experts, and their work was continued in the latter part of the Industrial Revolution by such men as Andrew Ure and Charles Babbage. Between these men and the next step, the comprehensive formulation of management theory in the late nineteenth and early twentieth centuries, there lies a gap of more than half a century during which there was an enormous growth in the size of enterprises, the beginnings of the monopolistic organization of industry, and the purposive and systematic application of science to production. The scientific management movement initiated by Frederick Winslow Taylor in the last decades of the nineteenth century was brought into being by these forces. Logically, Taylorism belongs to the chain of development of management methods and the organization of labor, and not to the development of technology, in which its role was minor.[i]

Scientific management, so-called, is an attempt to apply the methods of science to the increasingly complex problems of the control of labor in rapidly growing capitalist enterprises. It lacks the characteristics of a true science because its assumptions reflect nothing more than the outlook of the capitalist with regard to the conditions of production. It starts, despite occasional protestations to the contrary, not from the human point of view but from the capitalist point of view, from the point of view of the management of a refractory work force in a setting of antagonistic social relations. It does not attempt to discover and confront the cause of this condition, but accepts it as an inexorable given, a "natural" condition. It investigates not labor in general, but the adaptation of labor to the needs of capital. It enters the workplace not as the representative of science, but as the representative of management masquerading in the trappings of science.

A comprehensive and detailed outline of the principles of Taylorism is essential to our narrative, not because of the things for which it is popularly known—stopwatch, speed-up, etc.—but because behind these commonplaces there lies a theory which is nothing less than the explicit verbalization of the capitalist mode of production. But before I begin this presentation, a number of introductory remarks are required to clarify the role of the Taylor school in the development of management theory.

* * *

It is impossible to overestimate the importance of the scientific management movement in the shaping of the modern corporation and indeed all institutions of capitalist society which carry on labor processes. The popular notion that Taylorism has been "superseded" by later schools of industrial psychology or "human relations," that it "failed"—because of Taylor's amateurish and naive views of human motivation or because it brought about a storm of labor opposition or because Taylor and various successors antagonized workers and sometimes management as well—or that it is "outmoded" because certain Taylorian specifics like functional foremanship or his incentive-pay schemes have been discarded for more sophisticated methods: all these represent a woeful misreading of the actual dynamics of the development of management.

Taylor dealt with the fundamentals of the organization of the labor process and of control over it. The later schools of Hugo Münsterberg, Elton Mayo, and others of this type dealt primarily with the adjustment of the worker to the ongoing production process as that process was designed by the industrial engineer. The successors to Taylor are to be found in engineering and work design, and in top management; the successors to Münsterberg and Mayo are to be found in personnel departments and schools of industrial psychology and sociology. Work itself is organized according to Taylorian principles, while personnel departments and academics have busied themselves with the selection, training, manipulation, pacification, and adjustment of "manpower" to suit the work processes so organized. Taylorism dominates the world of production; the practitioners of "human relations" and "industrial psychology" are the maintenance crew for the human machinery. If Taylorism does not exist as a sep-

arate school today, that is because, apart from the bad odor of the name, it is no longer the property of a faction, since its fundamental teachings have become the bedrock of all work design.[ii] Peter F. Drucker, who has the advantage of considerable direct experience as a management consultant, is emphatic on this score:

> Personnel Administration and Human Relations are the things talked about and written about whenever the management of worker and work is being discussed. They are the things the Personnel Department concerns itself with. But they are not the concepts that underlie the actual management of worker and work in American industry. This concept is Scientific Management. Scientific Management focuses on the work. Its core is the organized study of work, the analysis of work into its simplest elements and the systematic improvement of the worker's performance of each of these elements. Scientific Management has both basic concepts and easily applicable tools and techniques. And it has no difficulty proving the contribution it makes; its results in the form of higher output are visible and readily measurable.
>
> Indeed, Scientific Management is all but a systematic philosophy of worker and work. Altogether it may well be the most powerful as well as the most lasting contribution America has made to Western thought since the Federalist Papers.[3]

The use of experimental methods in the study of work did not begin with Taylor; in fact, the self-use of such methods by the craftsman is part of the very practice of a craft. But the study of work by or on behalf of those who manage it rather than those who perform it seems to have come to the fore only with the capitalist epoch; indeed, very little basis for it could have existed before. The earliest references to the study of work correspond to the beginnings of the capitalist era. . . . The publication of management manuals, the discussions of the problems of management, and the increasingly sophisticated approach taken in practice in the second half of the nineteenth century lend support to the conclusion of the historians of the scientific management movement that Taylor was the culmination of a pre-existing trend: "What Taylor did was not to invent something quite new, but to synthesize and present as a reasonably coherent whole ideas which had been germinating and gathering force in Great Britain and the United States throughout the nineteenth century. He gave to a disconnected series of initiatives and experiments a philosophy and a title."[4]

Taylor has little in common with those physiologists or psychologists who have attempted, before or after him, to gather information about human capacities in a spirit of scientific interest. Such records and estimates as he did produce are crude in the extreme, and this has made it easy for such critics as Georges Friedmann to poke holes in his various "experiments" (most of which were not intended as experiments at all, but as forcible and hyperbolic demonstrations). Friedmann treats Taylorism as though it were a "science of work," where in reality it is intended to be a *science of the management of others' work* under capitalist conditions.[5] It is not the "best way" to do work "in general" that Taylor was seeking, as Friedmann seems to assume, but an answer to the specific problem of how best to control alienated labor—that is to say, labor power that is bought and sold.

The second distinctive feature of Taylor's thought was his concept of control. Control has been the essential feature of management throughout its history, but with Taylor it assumed unprecedented dimensions. The stages of management control over labor before Taylor had included, progressively: the gathering together of the workers in a workshop and the dictation of the length of the working day; the supervision of workers to ensure diligent, intense, or uninterrupted application; the enforcement of rules against distractions (talking, smoking, leaving the workplace, etc.) that were thought to interfere with application; the setting of production minimums; etc. A worker is under management control when subjected to these rules, or to any of their

extensions and variations. But Taylor raised the concept of control to an entirely new plane when he asserted as an *absolute necessity for adequate management the dictation to the worker of the precise manner in which work is to be performed.* That management had the right to "control" labor was generally assumed before Taylor, but in practice this right usually meant only the general setting of tasks, with little direct interference in the worker's mode of performing them. Taylor's contribution was to overturn this practice and replace it by its opposite. Management, he insisted, could be only a limited and frustrated undertaking so long as it left to the worker any decision about the work. His "system" was simply a means for management to achieve control of the actual mode of performance of every labor activity, from the simplest to the most complicated. To this end, he pioneered a far greater revolution in the division of labor than any that had gone before.

Taylor created a simple line of reasoning and advanced it with a logic and clarity, a naive openness, and an evangelical zeal which soon won him a strong following among capitalists and managers. His work began in the 1880s but it was not until the 1890s that he began to lecture, read papers, and publish results. His own engineering training was limited, but his grasp of shop practice was superior, since he had served a four-year combination apprenticeship in two trades, those of patternmaker and machinist. The spread of the Taylor approach was not limited to the United States and Britain; within a short time it became popular in all industrial countries. In France it was called, in the absence of a suitable word for management, "l'organisation scientifique du travail" (later changed, when the reaction against Taylorism set in, to "l'organisation rationnelle du travail"). In Germany it was known simply as *rationalization;* the German corporations were probably ahead of everyone else in the practice of this technique, even before World War I.[6]

Taylor was the scion of a well-to-do Philadelphia family. After preparing for Harvard at Exeter he suddenly dropped out, apparently in rebellion against his father, who was directing Taylor toward his own profession, the law. He then took the step, extraordinary for anyone of his class, of starting a craft apprenticeship in a firm whose owners were social acquaintances of his parents. When he had completed his apprenticeship, he took a job at common labor in the Midvale Steel Works, also owned by friends of his family and technologically one of the most advanced companies in the steel industry. Within a few months he had passed through jobs as clerk and journeyman machinist, and was appointed gang boss in charge of the lathe department.

In his psychic makeup, Taylor was an exaggerated example of the obsessive-compulsive personality: from his youth he had counted his steps, measured the time for his various activities, and analyzed his motions in a search for "efficiency." Even when he had risen to importance and fame, he was still something of a figure of fun, and his appearance on the shop floor produced smiles. The picture of his personality that emerges from a study recently done by Sudhir Kakar justifies calling him, at the very least, a neurotic crank.[7] These traits fitted him perfectly for his role as the prophet of modern capitalist management, since that which is neurotic in the individual is, in capitalism, normal and socially desirable for the functioning of society.

Shortly after Taylor became gang boss, he entered upon a struggle with the machinists under him. Because this struggle was a classic instance of the manner in which the antagonistic relations of production express themselves in the workplace, not only in Taylor's time but before and after, and since Taylor drew from this experience the conclusions that were to shape his subsequent thinking, it is necessary to quote at length here from his description of the events.[iii] The following account, one of several he gave of the battle, is taken from his testimony, a quarter-century later, before a Special Committee of the U.S. House of Representatives:

Now, the machine shop of the Midvale Steel Works was a piecework shop. All the work practically was done on piecework, and it ran night and day—five nights in the week and six days. Two sets of men came on, one to run the machines at night and the other to run them in the daytime.

We who were the workmen of that shop had the quantity output carefully agreed upon for everything that was turned out in the shop. We limited the output to about, I should think, one-third of what we could very well have done. We felt justified in doing this, owing to the piecework system—that is, owing to the necessity for soldiering under the piecework system—which I pointed out yesterday.

As soon as I became gang boss the men who were working under me and who, of course, knew that I was onto the whole game of soldiering or deliberately restricting output, came to me at once and said, "Now, Fred, you are not going to be a damn piecework hog, are you?"

I said, "If you fellows mean you are afraid I am going to try to get a larger output from these lathes," I said, "Yes; I do propose to get more work out." I said, "You must remember I have been square with you fellows up to now and worked with you. I have not broken a single rate. I have been on your side of the fence. But now I have accepted a job under the management of this company and I am on the other side of the fence, and I will tell you perfectly frankly that I am going to try to get a bigger output from those lathes." They answered, "Then, you are going to be a damned hog."

I said, "Well, if you fellows put it that way, all right." They said, "We warn you, Fred, if you try to bust any of these rates, we will have you over the fence in six weeks." I said, "That is all right; I will tell you fellows again frankly that I propose to try to get a bigger output off these machines."

Now, that was the beginning of a piecework fight that lasted for nearly three years, as I remember it—two or three years—in which I was doing everything in my power to increase the output of the shop, while the men were absolutely determined that the output should not be increased. Anyone who has been through such a fight knows and dreads the meanness of it and the bitterness of it. I believe that if I had been an older man—a man of more experience—I should have hardly gone into such a fight as this—deliberately attempting to force the men to do something they did not propose to do.

We fought on the management's side with all the usual methods, and the workmen fought on their side with all their usual methods. I began by going to the management and telling them perfectly plainly, even before I accepted the gang boss-ship, what would happen. I said, "Now these men will show you, and show you conclusively, that, in the first place, I know nothing about my business; and that in the second place, I am a liar, and you are being fooled, and they will bring any amount of evidence to prove these facts beyond a shadow of a doubt." I said to the management, "The only thing I ask you, and I must have your firm promise, is that when I say a thing is so you will take my word against the word of any 20 men or any 50 men in the shop." I said, "If you won't do that, I won't lift my finger toward increasing the output of this shop." They agreed to it and stuck to it, although many times they were on the verge of believing I was both incompetent and untruthful.

Now, I think it perhaps desirable to show the way in which that fight was conducted.

I began, of course, by directing some one man to do more work than he had done before, and then I got on the lathe myself and showed him that it could be done. In spite of this, he went ahead and turned out exactly the same old output and refused to adopt better methods or to work quicker until finally I laid him off and got another man in his place. This new man—I could not blame him in the least under the circumstances—turned right around and joined the other fellows and refused to do any

more work than the rest. After trying this policy for a while and failing to get any results I said distinctly to the fellows, "Now, I am a mechanic; I am a machinist. I do not want to take the next step, because it will be contrary to what you and I look upon as our interest as machinists, but I will take it if you fellows won't compromise with me and get more work off of these lathes, but I warn you if I have to take this step it will be a durned mean one." I took it.

I hunted up some especially intelligent laborers who were competent men, but who had not had the opportunity of learning a trade, and I deliberately taught these men how to run a lathe and how to work right and fast. Every one of these laborers promised me, "Now, if you will teach me the machinist's trade, when I learn to run a lathe I will do a fair day's work," and every solitary man, when I had taught them their trade, one after another turned right around and joined the rest of the fellows and refused to work one bit faster.

That looked as if I were up against a stone wall, and for a time I was up against a stone wall. I did not blame even these laborers in my heart, my sympathy was with them all of the time, but I am telling you the facts as they then existed in the machine shops of this country, and in truth, as they still exist.

When I had trained enough of these laborers so that they could run the lathes, I went to them and said, "Now, you men to whom I have taught a trade are in a totally different position from the machinists who were running these lathes before you came here. Every one of you agreed to do a certain thing for me if I taught you a trade, and now not one of you will keep his word. I did not break my word with you, but every one of you has broken his word with me. Now, I have not any mercy on you; I have not the slightest hesitation in treating you entirely differently from the machinists." I said, "I know that very heavy social pressure has been put upon you outside the works to keep you from carrying out your agreement with me, and it is very difficult for you to stand out against this pressure, but you ought not to have made your bargain with me if you did not intend to keep your end of it. Now, I am going to cut your rate in two tomorrow and you are going to work for half price from now on. But all you will have to do is to turn out a fair day's work and you can earn better wages than you have been earning."

These men, of course, went to the management, and protested that I was a tyrant, and a nigger driver, and for a long time they stood right by the rest of the men in the shop and refused to increase their output a particle. Finally, they all of a sudden gave right in and did a fair day's work. . . .

The issue here turned on the work content of a day's labor power, which Taylor defines in the phrase "a fair day's work." To this term he gave a crude physiological interpretation: all the work a worker can do without injury to his health, at a pace that can be sustained throughout a working lifetime. (In practice, he tended to define this level of activity at an extreme limit, choosing a pace that only a few could maintain, and then only under strain.) Why a "fair day's work" should be defined as a physiological maximum is never made clear. In attempting to give concrete meaning to the abstraction "fairness," it would make just as much if not more sense to express a fair day's work as the amount of labor necessary to add to the product a value equal to the worker's pay; under such conditions, of course, profit would be impossible. The phrase "a fair day's work" must therefore be regarded as inherently meaningless, and filled with such content as the adversaries in the purchase-sale relationship try to give it.

Taylor set as his objective the maximum or "optimum" that can he obtained from a day's labor power. "On the part of the men," he said in his first book, "the greatest obstacle to the attainment of this standard is the slow pace which they adopt, or the loafing or 'soldiering,' marking time, as it is called." In each of his later expositions of his system, he begins with this same point, under-scoring it heavily.[8] The causes of this soldiering he breaks into two parts: "This loafing or soldiering proceeds from two causes. First, from the natural instinct and tendency of men to take it easy, which may be called *natural soldiering*. Second, from more intricate second thought and reasoning caused by their relations with other men, which may be called systematic soldiering." The first of these he quickly puts aside, to concentrate on the second: "The natural laziness of men is serious, but by far the greatest evil from which both workmen and employers are suffering is the *systematic soldiering* which is almost universal under all the ordinary schemes of management and which results from a careful study on the part of the workmen of what they think will promote their best interests.". . .

The conclusions which Taylor drew from the baptism by fire he received in the Midvale struggle may be summarized as follows: Workers who are controlled only by general orders and discipline are not adequately controlled, because they retain their grip on the actual processes of labor. So long as they control the labor process itself, they will thwart efforts to realize to the full the potential inherent in their labor power. To change this situation, control over the labor process must pass into the hands of management, not only in a formal sense but by the control and dictation of each step of the process, including its mode of performance. In pursuit of this end, no pains are too great, no efforts excessive, because the results will repay all efforts and expenses lavished on this demanding and costly endeavor.[iv]. . .

As we have already seen from Taylor's belief in the universal prevalence and in fact inevitability of "soldiering," he did not recommend reliance upon the "initiative" of workers. Such a course, he felt, leads to the surrender of control: "As was usual then, and in fact as is still usual in most of the shops in this country, the shop was really run by the workmen and not by the bosses. The workmen together had carefully planned just how fast each job should be done." In his Midvale battle, Taylor pointed out, he had located the source of the trouble in the "ignorance of the management as to what really constitutes a proper day's work for a workman." He had "fully realized that, although he was foreman of the shop, the combined knowledge and skill of the workmen who were under him was certainly ten times as great as his own."[9] This, then, was the source of the trouble and the starting point of scientific management.

We may illustrate the Taylorian solution to this dilemma in the same manner that Taylor often did: by using his story of his work for the Bethlehem Steel Company in supervising the moving of pig iron by hand. This story has the advantage of being the most detailed and circumstantial he set down, and also of dealing with a type of work so simple that anyone can visualize it without special technical preparation. We extract it here from Taylor's *The Principles of Scientific Management:*

> One of the first pieces of work undertaken by us, when the writer started to introduce scientific management into the Bethlehem Steel Company, was to handle pig iron on task work. The opening of the Spanish War found some 80,000 tons of pig iron placed in small piles in an open field adjoining the works. Prices for pig iron had been so low that it could not be sold at a profit, and therefore had been stored. With the opening of the Spanish War the price of pig iron rose, and this large accumulation of iron was sold. This gave us a good opportunity to show the workmen, as well as the owners and managers of the works, on a fairly large scale the advantages of task work over the old-fashioned day work and piece work, in doing a very elementary class of work.
>
> The Bethlehem Steel Company had five blast furnaces, the product of which had been handled by a pig-iron gang for many years. This gang, at this time, consisted of about 75 men. They were good, average pig-iron handlers, were under an excellent foreman who himself had been a pig-iron handler, and the work was done, on the whole, about as fast and as cheaply as it was anywhere else at that time.
>
> A railroad switch was run out into the field, right along the edge of the piles of pig iron. An inclined plank was placed against the side of a car, and each man picked up from his pile a pig of iron weighing about 92 pounds, walked up the inclined plank and dropped it on the end of the car.
>
> We found that this gang were loading on the average about 12½ long tons per man per day. We were surprised to find, after studying the matter, that a first-class pig-iron handler ought to handle between 47 and 48 long tons per day, instead of 12½ tons. This task seemed to us so very large that we were obliged to go over our work several times before we were absolutely sure that we were right. Once we were sure, however, that 47 tons was a proper day's work for a first-class pig-iron handler, the task which faced us as managers under the modern scientific plan was clearly before us. It was our duty to see that the 80,000 tons of pig iron was loaded on to the cars at the rate of 47 tons per man per day, in place of 12½ tons, at which rate the work was then being done. And it was further our duty to see that this work was done without bringing on a strike among the men, without any quarrel with the men, and to see that the men were happier and better contented when loading at the new rate of 47 tons than they were when loading at the old rate of 12½ tons.
>
> Our first step was the scientific selection of the workman. In dealing with workmen under this type of management, it is an inflexible rule to talk to and deal with only one man at a time, since each workman has his own special abilities and limitations, and since we are not dealing with men in masses, but are trying to develop each individual man to his highest state of efficiency and prosperity. Our first step was to find the proper workman to begin with. We therefore carefully watched and studied these 75 men for three or four days, at the end of which time we had picked out four men who appeared to be physically

able to handle pig iron at the rate of 47 tons per day. A careful study was then made of each of these men. We looked up their history as far back as practicable and thorough inquiries were made as to the character, habits, and the ambition of each of them. Finally we selected one from among the four as the most likely man to start with. He was a little Pennsylvania Dutchman who had been observed to trot back home for a mile or so after his work in the evening, about as fresh as he was when he came trotting down to work in the morning. We found that upon wages of $1.15 a day he had succeeded in buying a small plot of ground, and that he was engaged in putting up the walls of a little house for himself in the morning before starting to work and at night after leaving. He also had the reputation of being exceedingly "close," that is, of placing a very high value on a dollar. As one man whom we talked to about him said, "A penny looks about the size of a cartwheel to him." This man we will call Schmidt.

The task before us, then, narrowed itself down to getting Schmidt to handle 47 tons of pig iron per day and making him glad to do it. This was done as follows. Schmidt was called out from among the gang of pig-iron handlers and talked to somewhat in this way:

"Schmidt, are you a high-priced man?"

"Vell, I don't know vat you mean."

"Oh yes, you do. What I want to know is whether you are a high-priced man or not."

"Vell, I don't know vat you mean."

"Oh, come now, you answer my questions. What I want to find out is whether you are a high-priced man or one of these cheap fellows here. What I want to find out is whether you want to earn $1.85 a day or whether you are satisfied with $1.15, just the same as all those cheap fellows are getting."

"Did I vant $1.85 a day? Vas dot a high-priced man? Vell, yes, I vas a high-priced man."

"Oh, you're aggravating me. Of course you want $1.85 a day—every one

wants it! You know perfectly well that that has very little to do with your being a high-priced man. For goodness' sake answer my questions, and don't waste any more of my time. Now come over here. You see that pile of pig iron?"

"Yes"

"You see that car?"

"Yes."

"Well, if you are a high-priced man, you will load that pig iron on that car tomorrow for $1.85. Now do wake up and answer my question. Tell me whether you are a high-priced man or not."

"Vell—did I got $1.85 for loading dot pig iron on dot car tomorrow?"

"Yes, of course you do, and you get $1.85 for loading a pile like that every day right through the year. That is what a high-priced man does, and you know it just as well as I do."

"Vell, dot's all right. I could load dot pig iron on the car tomorrow for $1.85, and I get it every day, don't I?"

"Certainly you do—certainly you do."

"Vell, den, I vas a high-priced man."

"Now, hold on, hold on. You know just as well as I do that a high-priced man has to do exactly as he's told from morning till night. You have seen this man here before, haven't you?"

"No, I never saw him."

"Well, if you are a high-priced man, you will do exactly as this man tells you tomorrow, from morning till night. When he tells you to pick up a pig and walk, you pick it up and you walk, and when he tells you to sit down and rest, you sit down. You do that right straight through the day. And what's more, no back talk. Now a high-priced man does just what he's told to do, and no back talk. Do you understand that? When this man tells you to walk, you walk; when he tells you to sit down, you sit down, and you don't talk back at him. Now you come on to work here tomorrow morning and I'll know before night whether you are really a high-priced man or not."

This seems to be rather rough talk. And indeed it would be if applied to an educated mechanic, or even and intelligent laborer. With a man of the mentally sluggish type of Schmidt it is appropriate and not unkind, since it is effective in fixing his attention on the high wages which he wants and away from what, if it were called to his attention, he probably would consider impossibly hard work. . . .

Schmidt started to work, and all day long, and at regular intervals, was told by the man who stood over him with a watch, "Now pick up a pig and walk. Now sit down and rest. Now walk—now rest," etc. He worked when he was told to work, and rested when he was told to rest, and at half-past five in the afternoon had his 47½ tons loaded on the car. And he practically never failed to work at this pace and do the task that was set him during the three years that the writer was at Bethlehem. And throughout this time he averaged a little more than $1.85 per day, whereas before he had never received over $1.15 per day, which was the ruling rate of wages at that time in Bethlehem. That is, he received 60 per cent higher wages than were paid to other men who were not working on task work. One man after another was picked out and trained to handle pig iron at the rate of 47½ tons per day until all of the pig iron was handled at this rate, and the men were receiving 60 per cent more wages than other workmen around them.[10]

The merit of this tale is its clarity in illustrating the pivot upon which all modern management turns: the control over work through the control over the *decisions that are made in the course of work*. Since, in the case of pig-iron handling, the only decisions to be made were those having to do with a time sequence, Taylor simply dictated that timing and the results at the end of the day added up to his planned day-task. . . .

Taylor spent his lifetime in expounding the principles of control enunciated here, and in applying them directly to many other tasks: shoveling loose materials, lumbering, inspecting ball bearings, etc., but particularly to the machinist's trade. He believed that the forms of control he advocated could be applied not only to simple labor, but to labor in its most complex forms, without exception, and in fact it was in machine shops, bricklaying, and other such sites for the practice of well-developed crafts that he and his immediate successors achieved their most striking results.

From earliest times to the Industrial Revolution the craft or skilled trade was the basic unit, the elementary cell of the labor process. In each craft, the worker was presumed to be the master of a body of traditional knowledge, and methods and procedures were left to his or her discretion. In each such worker reposed the accumulated knowledge of materials and processes by which production was accomplished in the craft. The potter, tanner, smith, weaver, carpenter, baker, miller, glassmaker, cobbler, etc., each representing a branch of the social division of labor, was a repository of human technique for the labor processes of that branch. The worker combined, in mind and body, the concepts and physical dexterities of the specialty: technique, understood in this way, is, as has often been observed, the predecessor and progenitor of science. The most important and widespread of all crafts was, and throughout the world remains to this day, that of farmer. The farming family combines its craft with the rude practice of a number of others, including those of the smith, mason, carpenter, butcher, miller, and baker, etc. The apprenticeships required in traditional crafts ranged from three to seven years, and for the farmer of course extends beyond this to include most of childhood, adolescence, and young adulthood. In view of the knowledge to be assimilated, the dexterities to be gained, and the fact that the craftsman, like the professional, was required to master a specialty and become the best judge of the manner of its application to specific production problems, the years of apprenticeship were generally needed and were employed in a learning process that extended well into the journeyman decades. Of these trades, that of the machinist was in Taylor's day among the most recent, and certainly the most important to modern industry.

As I have already pointed out, Taylor was not primarily concerned with the advance of technology (which, as we shall see, offers other means for direct control over the labor process). He did make significant contributions to the technical knowledge of machine-shop practice (high-speed tool steel, in particular), but these were chiefly by-products of his effort to study this practice with an eye to systematizing and classifying it. His concern was with the control of labor at any given level of technology, and he tackled his own trade with a boldness and energy which astonished his contemporaries and set the pattern for industrial engineers, work designers, and office managers from that day on. And in tackling machine-shop work, he had set himself a prodigious task.

The machinist of Taylor's day started with the shop drawing, and turned, milled, bored, drilled, planed, shaped, ground, filed, and otherwise machine- and hand-processed the proper stock to the desired shape as specified in the drawing. The range of decisions to be made in the course of the process is—unlike the case of a simple job, such as the handling of pig iron—by its very nature enormous. Even for the lathe alone, disregarding all collateral tasks such as the choice of stock, handling, centering and chucking the work, layout and measuring, order of cuts, and considering only the operation of turning itself, the range of possibilities is huge. Taylor himself worked with twelve variables, including the hardness of the metal, the material of the cutting tool, the thickness of the shaving, the shape of the cutting tool, the use of a coolant during cutting, the depth of the cut, the frequency of regrinding cutting tools as they became dulled, the lip and clearance angles of the tool, the smoothness of cutting or absence of chatter, the diameter of the stock being turned, the pressure of the chip or shaving on the cutting surface of the tool, and the speeds, feeds, and pulling power of the machine.[11] Each of these variables is subject to broad choice, ranging from a few possibilities in the selection and use of a coolant, to a very great number of effective choices in all matters having to do with thickness, shape, depth, duration, speed, etc. Twelve variables, each subject to a large number of

choices, will yield in their possible combinations and permutations astronomical figures, as Taylor soon realized. But upon these decisions of the machinist depended not just the accuracy and finish of the product, but also the pace of production. Nothing daunted, Taylor set out to gather into management's hands all the basic information bearing on these processes. He began a series of experiments at the Midvale Steel Company, in the fall of 1880, which lasted twenty-six years, recording the results of between 30,000 and 50,000 tests, and cutting up more than 800,000 pounds of iron and steel on ten different machine tools reserved for his experimental use.[v] His greatest difficulty, he reported, was not testing the many variations, but holding eleven variables constant while altering the conditions of the twelfth. The data were systematized, correlated, and reduced to practical form in the shape of what he called a "slide rule" which would determine the optimum combination of choices for each step in the machining process.[12] His machinists thenceforth were required to work in accordance with instructions derived from these experimental data, rather than from their own knowledge, experience, or tradition. This was the Taylor approach in its first systematic application to a complex labor process. Since the principles upon which it is based are fundamental to all advanced work design or industrial engineering today, it is important to examine them in detail. And since Taylor has been virtually alone in giving clear expression to principles which are seldom now publicly acknowledged, it is best to examine them with the aid of Taylor's own forthright formulations.

First Principle

"The managers assume . . . the burden of gathering together all of the traditional knowledge which in the past has been possessed by the workmen and then of classifying, tabulating, and reducing this knowledge to rules, laws, and formulae. . . ."[13] We have seen the illustrations of this in the cases of the lathe machinist and the pig-iron handler. The great disparity between these activities, and the different orders of knowledge that may be collected about them, illustrate that for Taylor—as for managers today—no task is either so simple or so complex that it may not be studied with the object of collecting in the hands of management at least as much information as is known by the worker who performs it regularly, and very likely more. This brings to an end the situation in which "Employers derive their knowledge of how much of a given class of work can be done in a day from either their own experience, which has frequently grown hazy with age, from casual and unsystematic observation of their men, or at best from records which are kept, showing the quickest time in which each job has been done."[14] It enables management to discover and enforce those speedier methods and shortcuts which workers themselves, in the practice of their trades or tasks, learn or improvise, and use at their own discretion only. Such an experimental approach also brings into being new methods such as can be devised only through the means of systematic study.

This first principle we may call the *dissociation of the labor process from the skills of the workers*. The labor process is to be rendered independent of craft, tradition, and the workers' knowledge. Henceforth it is to depend not at all upon the abilities of workers, but entirely upon the practices of management.

Second Principle

"All possible brain work should be removed from the shop and centered in the planning or laying-out department. . . ."[15] Since this is the key to scientific management, as Taylor well understood, he was especially emphatic on this point and it is important to examine the principle thoroughly.

In the human, as we have seen, the essential feature that makes for a labor capacity superior to that of the animal is the combination of execution with a conception of the thing to be done. But as human labor becomes a social rather than an individual phenomenon, it is possible—unlike in the instance of animals where the motive force, instinct, is inseparable from action—to divorce conception from execution. This dehumanization of the labor process, in which workers are reduced almost to the level of labor in its animal form, while purposeless and unthinkable in the case of the self-organized and self-motivated social labor of a community of producers, becomes crucial for the management of purchased labor. For if the workers' execution is guided by their own conception, it is not possible, as we have seen, to enforce upon them either the methodological efficiency or the working pace desired by capital. The capitalist therefore learns from the start to take advantage of this aspect of human labor power, and to break the unity of the labor process.

This should be called the principle of the *separation of conception from execution*, rather than by its more common name of the separation of mental and manual labor (even though it is similar to the latter, and in practice often identical). This is because mental labor, labor done primarily in the brain, is also subjected to the same principle of separation of conception from execution: mental labor is first separated from manual labor and, as we shall see, is then itself subdivided rigorously according to the same rule.

The first implication of this principle is that Taylor's "science of work" is never to be developed by the worker, always by management. This notion, apparently so "natural" and undebatable today, was in fact vigorously discussed in Taylor's day, a fact which shows how far we have traveled along the road of transforming all ideas about the labor process in less than a century, and how completely Taylor's hotly contested assumptions have entered into the conventional outlook within a short space of time. . . .

Third Principle

The essential idea of "the ordinary types of management," Taylor said, "is that each workman has become more skilled in his own trade than it is possible for any one in the management to be, and that, therefore, the details of how the work shall best be done must be left to him." But, by contrast: "Perhaps the most prominent single element in modern scientific management is the task idea. The work of every workman is fully planned out by the management at least one day in advance, and each man receives in most cases complete written instructions, describing in detail the task which he is to accomplish, as well as the means to be used in doing the work. . . . This task specifies not only what is to be done, but how it is to be done and the exact time allowed for doing it. . . . Scientific management consists very largely in preparing for and carrying out these tasks."[16]

In this principle it is not the written instruction card that is important.[vi] Taylor had no need for such a card with Schmidt, nor did he use one in many other instances. Rather, the essential element is the systematic pre-planning and pre-calculation of all elements of the labor process, which now no longer exists as a process in the imagination of the worker but only as a process in the imagination of a special management staff. Thus, if the first principle is the gathering and development of knowledge of labor processes, and the second is the concentration of this knowledge as the exclusive province of management—together with its essential converse, the absence of such knowledge among the workers—then the third is the *use of this monopoly over knowledge to control each step of the labor process and its mode of execution.*

As capitalist industrial, office, and market practices developed in accordance with this principle, it eventually became part of accepted routine and custom, all the more so as the increasingly scientific character of most processes, which grew in complexity while the worker was not allowed to partake of this growth, made it ever more difficult for the workers to understand the processes in which they functioned. But in the beginning, as Taylor well understood, an abrupt psychological wrench was required.[vii] We have seen in the simple Schmidt case the means employed, both in the selection of a single worker as a starting point and in the way in which he was reoriented to the new conditions of work. In the more complex conditions of the machine shop, Taylor gave this part of the responsibility to the foremen. It is essential, he said of the gang bosses, to "nerve and brace them up to the point of insisting that the workmen shall carry out the orders exactly as specified on the instruction cards. This is a difficult task at first, as the workmen have been accustomed for years to do the details of the work to suit themselves, and many of them are intimate friends of the bosses and believe they know quite as much about their business as the latter."[17]

* * *

Modern management came into being on the basis of these principles. It arose as theoretical construct and as systematic practice, moreover, in the very period during which the transformation of labor from processes based on skill to processes based upon science was attaining its most rapid tempo. Its role was to render conscious and systematic, the formerly unconscious tendency of capitalist production. It was to ensure that as craft declined, the worker would sink to the level of general and undifferentiated labor power, adaptable to a large range of simple tasks, while as science grew, it would be concentrated in the hands of management.

Discussion Questions

1. Some critics of Braverman's analysis of scientific management believe that he underestimates the power of workers to resist efforts by management to control the labor process. Do you agree? If so,

what are some of the ways that workers can resist control?

2. Do you see any contemporary examples of Taylor's efforts to develop a science of work?

Excerpted from Harry Braverman, "Scientific Management," in *Labor and Monopoly Capital* (New York: Monthly Review Press, 1974, pp. 85–123). Copyright © 1974 by MRPress. Reprinted by permission of Monthly Review Foundation.

Footnotes

i. It is important to grasp this point, because from it flows the universal application of Taylorism to work in its various forms and stages of development, regardless of the nature of the technology employed. Scientific management, says Peter F. Drucker, "was not concerned with technology. Indeed, it took tools and techniques largely as given."[1]

ii. "As a separate movement," says George Soule, "it virtually disappeared in the great depression of the 1930's, but by that time knowledge of it had become widespread in industry and its methods and philosophy were commonplaces in many schools of engineering and business management."[2] In other words, Taylorism is "outmoded" or "superseded" only in the sense that a sect which has become generalized and broadly accepted disappears as a sect.

iii. Extracts of considerable length from Taylor's several writings will appear in this chapter. This is because Taylor is still the most useful source for any study of scientific management. In the storms of opposition that followed Taylorism, few ventured to put the case so baldly as did Taylor, in his naive assumption that all reasonable people, including workers, would see the supreme rationality of his argument and accede to it. What he avows openly are the now-unacknowledged private assumptions of management. On the other hand, most of the academic commentators on Taylor are of limited usefulness, since everything that is so clear in Taylor becomes blurred or misunderstood. Kakar's book is a useful exception, despite his conventional conclusion that "with Taylor's ends there is no quarrel."

iv. Clearly, this last conclusion depends on Adam Smith's well-known principle that the division of labor is limited by the extent of the market, and Taylorism cannot become generalized in any industry or applicable in particular situations until the scale of production is adequate to support the efforts and costs involved in "rationalizing" it. It is for this reason above all that Taylorism coincides with the growth of production and its concentration in ever larger corporate units in the latter part of the nineteenth and in the twentieth centuries.

v. Friedmann so far forgets this enormous machine-shop project at one point that he says: "This failure to appreciate the psychological factors in work is at least partially explained by the nature of the jobs to which Taylor exclusively confined his observations: handlers of pig iron, shovel-laborers, and navvies."[18] He was led to this error by his marked tendency to side with the psychological and sociological schools of "human relations" and work adjustment which came after Taylor, and which he always attempts to counterpose to Taylorism, although, as we have pointed out, they operate on different levels. In general, Friedmann, with all his knowledge of work processes, suffers from a confusion of viewpoints, writing sometimes as a socialist concerned about the trends in capitalist work organization, but more often as though the various forms of capitalist management and personnel administration represent scrupulous efforts to find a universal answer to problems of work.

vi. This despite the fact that for a time written instruction cards were a fetish among managers. The vogue for such cards passed as work tasks became so simplified and repetitive as to render the cards in most cases unnecessary. But the concept behind them remains: it is the concept of the direct action of management to determine the process, with the worker functioning as the mediating and closely governed instrument. This is the significance of Lillian Gilbreth's definition of the instruction card as "a self-producer of a predetermined product."[19] The worker as producer is ignored; management becomes the producer, and its plans and instructions bring the product into existence. This same instruction card inspired in Alfred Marshall, however, the curious opinion that from it, workers could learn how production is carried on: such a card, "whenever it comes into the hands of a thoughtful man, may suggest to him something of the purposes and methods of those who have constructed it."[20] The worker, in Marshall's notion, having given up technical knowledge of the craft, is now to pick up the far more complex technical knowledge of modern industry from his task card, as a paleontologist reconstructs the entire animal from a fragment of a bone!

vii. One must not suppose from this that such a psychological shift in relations between worker and manager is entirely a thing of the past. On the contrary, it is constantly being recapitulated in the evolution of new occupations as they are brought into being by the development of industry and trade, and are then routinized and subjugated to management control. As this tendency has attacked office, technical, and "educated" occupations, sociologists have spoken of it as "bureaucratization," an evasive and unfortunate use of Weberian terminology, a terminology which often reflects its users' view that this form of government over work is endemic to "large-scale" or "complex" enterprises, whereas it is better understood as the specific product of the capitalist organization of work, and reflects not primarily scale but social antagonisms.

Endnotes

1. Peter F. Drucker, "Work and Tools," in Melvin Kranzberg and William H. Davenport, eds., *Technology and Culture* (New York, 1972), pp. 192–93.
2. George Soule, *Economic Forces in American History* (New York, 1952), p. 241.
3. Peter F. Drucker, *The Practice of Management* (New York, 1954), p. 280.
4. Lyndall Urwick and E. F. L. Brech, *The Making of Scientific Management*, 3 vols. (London, 1945, 1946, 1948), vol. I, p. 17.
5. See Georges Friedmann, *Industrial Society* (Glencoe, Ill., 1964), esp. pp. 51–65.
6. Lyndall Urwick, *The Meaning of Rationalisation* (London, 1929), pp. 13–16.
7. Kakar, *Frederick Taylor*, pp. 17–27, 52–54.
8. Frederick W. Taylor, "Shop Management," in *Scientific Management*, p. 30. See also Taylor's *The Principles of Scientific Management* (New York, 1967), pp. 13–14; and Taylor's *Testimony in Scientific Management*, p. 8.
9. Ibid., pp. 48–49, 53.
10. Ibid., pp. 41–47.
11. *The Principles of Scientific Management*, pp. 107–109.
12. *The Principles of Scientific Management*, p. 111.
13. Ibid., p. 36.
14. Ibid., p. 22.
15. "Shop Management," pp. 98–99.
16. *The Principles of Scientific Management*, pp. 63, 69.
17. "Shop Management," p. 108.
18. Friedman, *Industrial Society*, p. 63.
19. Lillian Gilbreth, *The Psychology of Management* (1914), in *The Writings of the Gilbreths*, William R. Spriegel and Clark E. Myers, eds. (Homewood, Ill., 1953), p. 404.
20. Alfred Marshall, *Industry and Trade* (London, 1919, 1932), pp. 391–393. ✦

3

Bureaucratic Control

Richard Edwards

Chapters 1 and 2 dealt with the question of control over the labor process. How have workers typically maintained controls over their work? How has management tried to exercise greater control over workers? In this chapter, Edwards undertakes a systematic examination of the meaning of control in the workplace and identifies three of its most prominent concrete examples: personal control, technical control, and bureaucratic control. Edwards examines the conditions that have led to change in systems of control. He devotes most of his discussion to bureaucratic control, which "rests on the principle of embedding control in the social structure or social relationships of the workplace."

The Dimensions of Control

How much work gets done every hour or every day emerges as a result of the struggle between workers and capitalists. . . . Each side seeks to tip the balance and influence or determine the outcome with the weapons at its disposal. On one side, the workers use hidden or open resistance to protect themselves against the constant pressure for speed-up; on the other side, capitalists employ a variety of sophisticated or brutal devices for tipping the balance their way. But this is not exactly an equal fight, for employers retain their power to hire and fire, and on this foundation they have developed various methods of control by which to organize, shape, and affect the workers' exertions.

Control in this sense differs from coordination, a term that appears more frequently in popular literature describing what managers do, and it may be useful at the outset to distinguish the two. Coordination is required, of course, in all social production, since the product of such production is by definition the result of labor by many persons. Hence, whether a pair of shoes is produced in a Moroccan cobbler's shop, a Chinese commune, or an American factory, it is an inherent technical characteristic of the production process that the persons cutting and tanning the leather must mesh their efforts with those who sew the leather, those who attach the heels, and others. Without such coordinations, production would be haphazard, wasteful, and—where products more complex than shoes are involved—probably impossible as well. Hence, coordination of social production is essential.

Coordination may be achieved in a variety of ways, however, and the differences are crucial. Coordination may be achieved by tradition—through long-established ways of doing the work and the passing on of these trade secrets from master to apprentices. Or it may be achieved directly by the producers themselves, as occurs when the members of a cooperative or commune discuss their parts in the production process to ensure that their tasks are harmonized. As the scale of production increases, workers may designate one member (or even choose someone from the outside) to act as a full-time coordinator of their interests, thus establishing a manager. As long as the managerial staff, no matter how large, remains accountable to the producers themselves, we may properly speak of their efforts as "coordination" or "administration."

A different type of coordination characterizes capitalist workplaces, however; in capitalist production, labor power is purchased, and with that purchase—as with the purchase of every commodity in a capitalist economy—goes the right to designate the use (consumption) of the object bought.

Hence there is a presumption, indeed a contractual right backed by legal force, for the capitalist, as owner of the purchased labor power, to direct its use. A corollary presumption (again backed by legal force) follows: that the workers whose labor power has been purchased have no right to participate in the conception and planning of production. Coordination occurs in capitalist production as it must inevitably occur in all social production, but it necessarily takes the specific form of top-down coordination, for the exercise of which the top (capitalists) must be able to control the bottom (workers). In analyzing capitalist production, then, it is more appropriate to speak of control than of coordination, although of course, control is a means of coordination.

"Control" is here defined as the ability of capitalists and/or managers to obtain desired work behavior from workers. Such ability exists in greater or lesser degrees, depending upon the relative strength of workers and their bosses. As long as capitalist production continues, control exists to some degree, and the crucial questions are: to what degree? how is control obtained? and how does control lead to or inhibit resistance on a wider scale? At one extreme, capitalists try to avoid strikes, sit-downs, and other militant actions that stop production; but equally important to their success, they attempt to extract, day by day, greater amounts of labor for a given amount of labor power.

In what follows, the *system of control* (in other words, the social relations of production within the firm) are thought of as a way in which three elements are coordinated:

1. Direction, or a mechanism or method by which the employer directs work tasks, specifying what needs to be done, in what order, with what degree of precision or accuracy, and in what period of time.

2. Evaluation, or a procedure whereby the employer supervises and evaluates to correct mistakes or other failures in production, to assess each worker's performance, and to identify individual workers or group of workers who are not performing work tasks adequately.

3. Discipline, or an apparatus that the employer uses to discipline and reward workers, in order to elicit cooperation and enforce compliance with the capitalist's direction of the labor process.

The Types of Control

Systems of control in the firm have undergone dramatic changes in response to changes in the firm's size, operations, and environment and in the workers' success in imposing their own goals at the workplace. The new forms did not emerge as sharp, discrete discontinuities in historical evolution, but neither were they simply points in a smooth and inevitable evolution. Rather, each transformation occurred as a resolution of intensifying conflict and contradiction in the firm's operations. Pressures built up, making the old forms of control untenable. The period of increasing tension was followed by a relatively rapid process of discovery, experimentation, and implementation, in which new systems of control were substituted for the older, more primitive ones. Once instituted, these new relations tend to persist until they no longer effectively contain worker resistance or until further changes occur in the firm's operations.

In the nineteenth century, most businesses were small and were subject to the relatively tight discipline of substantial competition in product markets. The typical firm had few resources and little energy to invest in creating more sophisticated management structures. A single entrepreneur, usually flanked by a small coterie of foremen and managers, ruled the firm. These bosses exercised power personally, intervening in the labor process often to exhort workers, bully and threaten them, reward good performance, hire and fire on the spot, favor loyal workers, and generally act as despots, benevolent or otherwise. They had a direct stake in translating labor power into labor, and they combined both incentives and sanctions in an idiosyncratic and unsystematic mix. There was little structure to the way power was exercised, and workers were often treated arbitrarily. Since workforces were small and the boss was both close and powerful, workers had limited success when they tried to oppose his rule. This system of "simple" control survives today in the small-business sector of the American economy, where it has necessarily been amended by the passage of time and by the borrowings of management practices from the more advanced corporate sector, but it retains its essential principles and mode of operation. . . .

Large firms developed methods of organization that are more formalized and more consciously contrived than simple control; they are "structural" forms of control. Two possibilities existed: more formal, consciously contrived controls could be embedded in either the physical structure of the labor process (producing "technical" control) or in its social structure (producing "bureaucratic" control). In time, employers used both, for they found that the new systems made control more institutional and hence less visible to workers, and they also provided a means for capitalists to control the "intermediate layers," those extended lines of supervision and power.

Technical control emerged from employers' experiences in attempting to control the production (or blue-collar) operations of the firm. The assembly line came to be the classic image, but the actual application of technical control was much broader. Machinery itself directed the labor process and set the pace. For a time, employers had the best of two worlds. Inside the firm, technical control turned the tide of conflict in their favor, reducing workers to attendants of prepaced machinery; externally, the system strengthened the employer's hands by expanding the number of potential substitute workers. But as factory workers in the late 1930s struck back with sit-downs, their action exposed the deep dangers to employers in thus linking all workers' labor together in one technical apparatus. The conflict at the workplace propelled labor into its "giant step," the CIO.

These forces have produced today a second type of work organization. Whereas simple control persists in the small firms of the industrial periphery, in large firms, especially those in the mass-production industries, work is subject to technical control. The system is mutually administered by management and (as a junior partner) unions. . . .

There exists a third method for organizing work, and it too appeared in the large firms. This system, bureaucratic control, rests on the principle of embedding control in the social structure or the social relations of the workplace. The defining feature of bureaucratic control is the institutionalization of hierarchical power. "Rule of law"—the firm's law—replaces "rule by supervisor command" in the direction of work, the procedures for evaluating workers' performance, and the exercise of the firm's sanctions and rewards; supervisors and workers alike become subject to the dictates of "company policy." Work becomes highly stratified; each job is given its distinct title and description; and impersonal rules govern promotion. "Stick with the corporation," the worker is told, "and you can ascend up the ladder." The company promises the workers a *career.* . . .

Bureaucratic control, like technical control, differs from the simple forms of control in that it grows out of the formal structure of the firm, rather than simply emanating from the personal relationships between workers and bosses. But while technical control is embedded in the physical and technological aspects of production and is built into the design of machines and the industrial architecture of the plant, bureaucratic control is embedded in the social and organizational structure of the firm and is built into job categories, work rules, promotion procedures, discipline, wage scales, definitions of responsibilities, and the like. Bureaucratic control establishes the impersonal force of "company rules" or "company policy" as the basis for control.

In its most fundamental aspect, bureaucratic control institutionalized the exercise of hierarchical power within the firm. The definition and direction of work tasks, the evaluation of worker performances, and the distribution of rewards and imposition of punishments all came to depend upon established rules and procedures, elaborately and systematically laid out.

Bureaucratic control attempted to routinize all of the functions of management in the way that technical control had routinized the first function. Capitalists were to retain overall control of the enterprise's operations through their power to establish the rules and procedures. But once the goals and structure were set, the management process was to proceed without need of, and (except in exceptional circumstances) without benefit of, the conscious intervention or the personal power of foremen, supervisors, or capitalists.

Bureaucratic control first emerged in firms such as IBM and Polaroid, where management enjoyed a virtually free hand to introduce the new relations from the top down. Management saw bureaucratic control as a way of avoiding unions and as a basis for labor-management relations that was an alternative to the dual power, collective-bargaining model that had emerged from the 1930s. For management, bureaucratic control eliminated the weakness of technical control.

In most firms the new form of control did not necessitate a sharp break with past practice. Rather, the new procedures were introduced piecemeal, more in response to actual problems than as part of a master plan. Moreover, the new form of control could never completely eliminate prior forms. The shift to bureaucratic control was therefore a shift towards relatively greater dependence on this organizational method, and bureaucratic control came to exist alongside and be reinforced by elements of hierarchical and technical control. Bureaucratic control became the predominant system of control, giving shape and logic to the firm's organization, but it

did not completely eliminate elements of other systems of control.

As we shall see later, a different (though in some ways parallel) development occurred in firms where unions already existed. Here, the inadequacy of technical control and the subsequent bargaining between unions and management led to a modification of technical control that pushed it towards bureaucratization. Management sought to use bureaucratic control to limit the impact of the unions, to draw them into joint disciplining of workers, and to regain some of its lost initiative. Unions turned to bureaucratization of the workplace to codify and thereby defend their negotiated gains. This dynamic led to quite different results, however. Most notably, management retained many more prerogatives where unionism was excluded than where joint administration was accepted.

Even though it was by no means a new invention, bureaucratic control constituted the most important change wrought by the modern corporation in the labor process. Just as technical control had emerged from the factory floor to be applied not only to blue-collar but also to lower-level white-collar work, so now bureaucratic control appeared first in the office and was later applied to production work. The new system transcended its white-collar origins and, in the corporations discussed below—IBM, AT&T, U.S. Steel, Polaroid, GE, and others—came to organize manual as well as mental work. This was the "managerial revolution" of the modern corporation. Technical control is now seen to be but half—and the lesser half at that—of the full story of the transformation of the workplace in the twentieth century.

Bureaucratic Control in Operation

The Polaroid Corporation, best known for its instant photography, provides a detailed case history of sophisticated bureaucratic control. The corporation was large enough to rank 230 on *Fortune*'s 1977 list of top industrial corporations. In 1975, despite the worst layoffs in Polaroid's history, it employed over nine thousand persons.[i]

Polaroid's major activity is manufacturing, and in this respect it is typical of big business in general. While the hobbyist and family-snapshot uses of Polaroid's products provide most of the company's sales, its cameras have also proved useful for many industrial needs, most notably in issuing identification cards. To meet these demands, Polaroid itself manufactures the equipment and supplies sold under its brand.

Polaroid activities also extend beyond manufacturing. Until the still-unfolding and quite shaky effort by Kodak to challenge Polaroid, the corporation had the instant-photography market entirely to itself. As a result, Polaroid carries out all those activities that monopolistic, multinational firms find necessary to maximize their profits. For example, the company makes a large sales effort; rather than relying on the market to generate demand, it has pursued an aggressive and costly advertising strategy. Similarly, it maintains a huge research and development program to devise new products, partly to attract new consumer dollars and partly to defend itself from competition. In addition to its basic manufacturing force, Polaroid employs a substantial number of workers in sales, research, legal, and other tasks. In 1977, 45 percent of the firm's workforce (4,879 employees) were classified as production workers; another 23 percent (2,523 workers) were engaged in office work; and 32 percent (3,509 employees) were assigned to supervisory, research, and other professional jobs.

Polaroid is thus a middle-sized manufacturing giant, with considerable market power, international operations, an active sales effort, and a large production staff. In all these respects, it is typical of "smoke-stack America." Its employees are not unionized.

Polaroid's system of control is built on a finely graded division and stratification of workers. The divisions run both hierarchically (creating higher and lower positions) and laterally. They tend to break up the homogeneity of the firm's workforce, creating many seemingly separate strata, lines of work, and focuses for job identity.

The workforce at Polaroid (as elsewhere) is divided into two different groups: those supervisory and professional employees who are exempt from the provisions of the Fair Labor Standards Act and the production workers who, in Polaroid's terminology, are "nonexempt." The exempt employees (numbering 3,016 in September, 1975) are paid on a salaried basis and are subject to a separate set of compensation procedures. The nonexempt workers (some 6,397 strong in September, 1975) are paid on an hourly basis.

Two points of importance emerge from a comparison of these groups. First, despite superficial distinctions in procedures, pay scales, methods of evaluation, and the like, there are no essential differences in the way Polaroid controls the two groups. Both are enmeshed within a highly articulated bureaucratic control system. Second, the existence of two groups with superficial and formalistic distinctions, and with real differences in pay and power, creates an important division among Polaroid workers. Thus a first step is taken in the divide-and-conquer strategy.

But the stratification of workers into separate groups and subgroups goes much further than division into salaried and nonsalaried status. The nonsalaried employees are first divided into "job families"—eighteen groups of jobs such as "general clerical," "metal trades," or "chemical mixing and processing" that are "similar in nature and involve similar skills." Within every job family, the proliferation of job titles permits a far more fertile basis for distinguishing each worker from his or her co-workers. The Materials Control and Movement job family, for example, includes a Section Leader, a Materials Aide, and some fifteen other job titles. General Clerical-Administrative has roughly thirty-five titles. Overall, the company has about three hundred job titles for its hourly staff alone. Polaroid thereby takes a second and somewhat larger step toward making each job slot appear individual or distinct.

Then there is the pay scheme. Each individual job is assigned a "Polaroid Classification Value" (PCV)—a designation in yet another, and subordinate, classification scheme. In Polaroid's theory, as many as twenty or twenty-five PCV levels are possible, although only fourteen were actually in use in 1975.

With eighteen different job families, three hundred job titles, and fourteen different pay grades, not to mention the dichotomy between salaried and hourly workers, it might appear that Polaroid had gone far enough in dividing and redividing its workers. Not so: each job is now further positioned along the pay scale so that for any given job (or PCV value), seven distinct pay steps are possible, from entry-level through 5 percent increments to top pay for the job. Thus are established many more distinct slots. Of course, workers are not so conveniently arranged as to ensure that no slots are overpopulated, but taking just the job titles and pay steps and ignoring the job families classification, Polaroid has created roughly 2,100 (300 times 7) individual slots for its 6,397 hourly workers. And that leaves out a number of ancillary means of further subdividing workers—the seniority bonus, "special pay" status, the incentive bonus, and so on.

The salaried or exempt employee compensation scheme at Polaroid is similar, in all essentials, to that for hourly workers. Employees are grouped into ten grades, each of which is subdivided further into nine steps. Organizationally, salaried employees are divided among the various branches (engineering, marketing, and so on) of the company.

The consequences of this highly stratified job structure extend far beyond the amount of money each worker receives, though wage differentials are by no means trivial. Most importantly, the narrow categorization of workers lays the basis for differences in job autonomy, power over other workers, working conditions, and chances for job placement or being laid off.

The point is simply that bureaucratic control makes possible a vastly greater stratification of the firm's workforce. Stratification is no longer limited by the firm's ability either to divide delegated power or to find technologically rooted differences. Now *social* or *organizational* distinctions (always supplemented, of course, by differences both in power and in technical function) both become the basis for ranking and advancement. . . .

Supervising and Evaluating Workers' Performance

When it comes to the monitoring and evaluating function, bureaucratic control again marked a departure from previous practice. The vehicle for supervision remained, of course, the foremen, supervisors, and managers who together constituted the supervisory staff. But the new system drastically transformed their role and power.

The new method of evaluation was built on two elements. First, it introduced the principle that the workers should be evaluated on the basis of what was contained in the job descriptions. And second, those who were formally charged with the responsibility of evaluating—foremen, supervisors, and managers—were themselves subjected to bureaucratic control; that is, they were directed and supervised in how to evaluate their subordinates by the job descriptions for their own jobs.

Polaroid appraises every worker's performance on a regular schedule. Undoubtedly, supervisors on the job constantly monitor, assess, and reprimand or praise workers as production occurs. But more formally, at least once a year supervisors must evaluate each employee's performance. The bureaucratic direction of work provides the structure for evaluation, since workers are evaluated on the tasks and duties laid out in the job description. Although the significance of any particular task or the severity of the assessment undoubtedly varies with the supervisor, the job description provides a limited, explicit, and controlled basis for rating each worker's performance. Just as the job descriptions are known to both worker and boss, so too is the evaluation. Evaluation is an open process, with the final supervisor's rating available for the worker's inspection.

The content as well as the form of Polaroid's evaluation provides insight into its control system. Each worker is rated in each of four equally important categories on a seven-point scale; the seven levels are defined as performance appropriate to each of the seven pay steps built into every job classification. Of the four categories, the fourth ("skill and job knowledge") measures whether the employee is capable of doing the assigned job. One category treats the quantity of work done. The remaining two categories—"quality" (meaning the worker's dependability and thoroughness) and "work habits and personal characteristics"—are concerned with work behavior rather than with the actual production achieved. A separate category in the evaluation checks up on attendance and punctuality. Here mere judgments are not enough, and the form demands more precise information: a space is left for percentages and frequencies. The main concern seems to be not measuring output but instead checking compliance with the rules. . . .

Eliciting Cooperation and Enforcing Compliance

As a system of power, bureaucratic control must also provide for rewards and sanctions, a channel or structure in which management can "maintain [the] discipline of employees," to borrow the language of the International Harvester workers' contract. Here again, bureaucratic control represented something new.

In line with the general logic of bureaucratic control, reprimand, suspension, dismissal, and other punishments became fixed penalties for specified categories of offenses. Punishment flowed from the established organizational rules and procedures. Sanctions were still applied by the foremen and supervisors, of course, but their application was subject to review by both higher levels of supervision and the grievance machinery. Punishment, like other elements of control, became embedded in the organizational structure of the bureaucratic firm.

But perhaps even more important was the institutionalizing of *positive* incentives under bureaucratic control. Not only was "bad" behavior punished, but "proper" behavior was rewarded.

In the entrepreneurial firm, positive incentives derived from the workers' personal ties to the entrepreneur. But both hierarchical and technical control relied almost exclusively on negative sanctions, for the firm was too large for personal ties to be decisive, and other potential incentives (promotion policies, higher pay) were haphazard, erratic, and subject to favoritism. No established career ladders existed, for example, to promise regular promotion to good workers. Wage differentials in fact were often set by foremen, who used their power to classify workers or measure output arbitrarily.

Bureaucratic control brought an organizational logic to the systematic dispensation of higher pay, promotion, more responsibility, access to better or cleaner or less dangerous working conditions, better health benefits, longer vacations, assignment to work stations with more status or comfort, and the other privileges that corporations now bestow on favored employees. Positive incentives greatly heightened the workers' sense of the mobility *within the firm* that lay in front of them.

These aspects of the new system can be easily seen at Polaroid. The company's power to hire and fire underlies its ability to get purchased labor power transformed into labor done. This power comes into play in a couple of ways. Insubordination and other explicit "violations of company rules and of accepted codes of proper behavior" (to use the company's language) can trigger immediate dismissal. Dismissal also threatens workers who get poor evaluations. The company states that the evaluations are designed to weed out mediocrity and, of course, mediocre job performance is determined by how faithfully the worker fulfills the job descriptions. In addition to periodic reviews—new employees after three months, other workers at least once a year—both old and new workers are on almost continuous probation. So the penalty for failing to comply with stated performance standards is evident.

Yet, even though bureaucratic control at Polaroid continues the historic capitalist right to deprive workers of their livelihood, this right has been reshaped by the bureaucratic form. Exceptional violations aside, workers can be dismissed only if they continue to "misbehave" after receiving written warnings specifying the improper behavior. Moreover, higher supervisory approval is required and any grievance can be appealed. Even the process of dismissal has become subject to the rule of (company) law.

Bureaucratic control has brought even greater change by introducing elaborate positive rewards to elicit cooperation from the workers. At Polaroid, the structure of rewards begins with the seven pay steps within each job. Each of these steps represents a 5 percent increment over the previous level. Once hired into a particular job, the worker is expected to pass through the first two ("learning") steps over a period of months. What is actually to be learned is not so much job skills as "work habits, attendance, attitude, and other personal characteristics" that Polaroid deems necessary for dependable performance. Moreover, the learning may occur more on the side of the company (learning whether the new worker has acquired the proper work habits through prior schooling or jobs) than on the part of the employee.

As the worker demonstrates mastery of the normal work routine, he or she moves up into the middle three ("experienced") pay steps. At these levels, the company expects that work "quality can be relied on," that the worker is "reliable," and that "good attendance [has been] established"; or more simply, that "personal characteristics are appropriate to the job." Progress is by no means automatic, but the worker who tries reasonably hard, makes little trouble, and is an average performer moves, in time, through these steps. . . .

The Institutionalization of Power

Above all else, bureaucratic control institutionalized the exercise of capitalist power, making power appear to emanate from the formal organization itself. Hierarchical relations were transformed from relations between (unequally powerful) people to relations between jobholders or relations between jobs themselves, abstracted from the specific people or the concrete work tasks involved. "Rule of law"—the firm's law—replaced rule by supervisor command. And indeed, the replacement was not illusory: To the extent that firms were successful in imposing bureaucratic control, the method, extent, and intensity of sanctions imposed on recalcitrant workers were specified by organizational rules. Foremen, supervisors, and managers were to apply such regulations, not formulate them, and in so doing, they objectively participated in the exercise of organizational, not personal, power.

By establishing the overall structure, management retained control of the enterprise's operations. Once the goals and structure had been established, the system could operate under its own steam. Of course, work activities could never be completely specified in advance by job descriptions; new situations continually arose for which prior regulations were not appropriate. Moreover, the workers' continual resistance to regulations meant that a rule, once promulgated, was not necessarily followed. Yet the ability to establish rules provided the capitalists with the power to determine the terrain, to set the basic conditions around which the struggle was to be fought. That power was decisive. As workers were isolated from each other, and as the system was made distinct from the bosses who supervise it, the basic capitalist-worker relation tended to shrink from sight. The capitalist's power was effectively embedded in the firm's organization.

Such a structural view of control goes a long way towards clearing up the issue of whether bureaucratic organization is an effective control device or not. Popular opinion strongly suggests that "bureaucracy" is wasteful, slow, and ineffective. Expert opinion often agrees. Alvin Gouldner, for example, noted that while bureaucratic rules specify the minimum level of acceptable performance, the rules also detail how little the worker can do and still remain secure. Still other observers, most notably Max Weber, saw bureaucracy as the most highly developed and purest form of rational authority.

Yet both popular opinion and expert insight miss what is essential here. The core corporations survive and prosper on their ability to organize the routine, normal efforts of workers, not on their ability to elicit peak performances. The entrepreneurial firm often depends on exceptional efforts, and the workers on occasion may put forth such efforts because of their personal ties to the capitalist or as an expression of their interest in keeping the firm in business. But the large firm generally has no claim on such efforts and (aside from virtuoso performances in the executive offices) has little interest in them. Instead, it seeks to raise as high as possible the standard for minimal acceptable performance. . . . Michael Crozier has observed that,

> people have power over other people insofar as the latter's behavior is narrowly limited by rules [or other constraints] whereas their own behavior is not . . . the predictability of one's behavior is the sure test of one's own inferiority.

Bureaucratic control made workers' behavior more predictable, and predictability brought with it greater control for the corporation.

Thus while bureaucratic control may in certain cases give up the prospect of exceptional performance, it instead achieves for the firm a high level of standard performance. Management's control is less than perfect, but compared to realistic alternatives, it is considerable. It is so considerable, in fact, that virtually all large corporations use it.

Understanding control in this sense also permits us to distinguish between workers' self-direction and autonomy. Several investigators have confused the lack of immediate external controls (self-direction) with the freedom to make decisions in one's own interest (autonomy). From the firm's perspective, all that is required is that workers perform according to the enterprise's criteria. Whether they do so because they have internalized the descriptions of their jobs (and hence want to perform well), or because it is in the worker's own self-interest, is immaterial to the enterprise. It is not immaterial, however, in deciding whether workers have autonomy in their jobs. Alienated labor—workers forced to work according to the capitalist's criteria—is alienated no less because it has internalized these criteria, and its consequences are no less damaging to the workers.

The 'Good' Worker

Bureaucratic control has not only transformed relations among the various strata of workers and between workers and their employers, but it has also altered the attributes that the firm expects of, and rewards in, its workers. It brought with it a new image of the "good" worker.

In previous control systems, there was little direct connection between personal attributes and control. Employers in all systems undoubtedly rewarded hard workers more than those who soldiered on the job, but the point is that the behavior demands arose directly from production and not from the control system itself. In entrepreneurial control, the personality of the capitalist set the tone, and, aside from a general deference to the employer's power, no generalization can be made about what was required. In hierarchical control, capitalists placed primary reliance on negative sanctions to discipline workers; workers needed to obey the boss and be sufficiently deferential, but the required behavior varied greatly according to the particular fore-man, the circumstances of employment, and so forth. In technical control, the system forced workers to respond to machine pacing, but it left them relatively free from other demands on their behavior. In all these cases, bosses demanded that employees work regularly and that they defer to their superiors. But beyond that, no particular attributes were systematically reinforced, and foremen rewarded and punished worker behavior arbitrarily and idiosyncratically.

Thus, while severe in regulating output-related behavior, these earlier systems of control left considerable leeway or tolerance for the workers to express other behavior to create their own ambience or culture in the workplace. There existed a certain breathing space inside prebureaucratic control. In some cases the workers' culture resulted in weekly observance of the unofficial holiday Blue Monday, in other instances it resulted in bullying and routine displays of aggression, ethnic identifications, formation of informal groups that restricted output or punished overzealous foremen, exaggerated male chauvinism, and patterns of humor, anger, and other ways of expressing the workers' identity. Most importantly, the workplace culture tended to build on an image of "them" and "us," in which workers were clearly distinguished from bosses. Workers brought many of these cultural patterns with them from their communities, of course, but the point is that the workplace organization made room for such elements.

With the imposition of bureaucratic control, much of that changed. The new organization of work produced change in required behavior comparable to the changes wrought by the coming of the factory. Particular work traits and patterns of interaction associated with bureaucratic control were rewarded, and in general the system intruded more insistently on the development of the worker's behavior and personality. The breathing space was reduced. Symptomatically, under bureaucratic control the workplace culture tends to express less of the workers and more of the firm. Working-class orientations and patterns of interacting yield to more bureaucratic, so-called middle-class ways. The notion of a family ("the IBM family") that includes both management and workers resurrects a concept not relevant since the entrepreneurial firm. The workers begin to use the first person plural differently; "we" now means "we the firm," not "we the workers." The workers' ability to create a workday culture begins to fade, just as, on a grander level, the working class loses its ability to make its own class culture.

Bureaucratic control tends to be a much more totalitarian system—totalitarian in the sense of involving the total behavior of the worker. In bureaucratic control, workers owe not only a hard day's work to the corporation but also their demeanor and affections. . . .

Bureaucratic control thus establishes an explicit structure around which broader struggles in the political arena may coalesce. These struggles provide an immediate avenue for improving the conditions of wage labor, and they may have more revolutionary consequences by linking workplace struggle with class conflict in society at large. For bureaucratic control is merely the latest form in which capitalist development socializes the process of production; by constructing formal rights and responsibilities, capitalists have abolished the individual capitalist's responsibility for working conditions and replaced it with social accountability. Thus does modern control resolve the problem of local conflict only at the cost of raising it to a more general level.

Discussion Questions

1. What forms of control in the workplace have you observed or directly experienced?

2. What are the potential costs and benefits of each form of control for workers and management?

3. Some analysts have written about "hegemonic control," whereby workers are so identified with the goals and values of the company that they essentially control themselves for the benefit of the employer. Is this possible?

Excerpted from Richard Edwards, "Bureaucratic Control," in *Contested Terrain* (New York: Basic Books, 1979, pp. 92–95, 130–162). Copyright ©1979 by Basic Books. Reprinted by permission of Basic Books, a member of Perseus Books, L.L.C.

Footnote

i.   All data, quotations, and other material on Polaroid, unless otherwise noted, are taken from conversations and internal documents the corporation readily provided. Indeed, it is a mark of the sophistication of Polaroid's management and of the success of its version of bureaucratic control that the company showed little hesitation in making this information available. Some of the details (e.g., the number of job families) may have changed since the interviews, but these changes in no way affect the essentials. ✦

4
Alienated Labour

Karl Marx

Karl Marx's analysis of early industrial society was based on the belief that capitalism introduced a major distortion of natural work arrangements. Drawing upon idyllic notions of the autonomous artisan producing things that had use value, Marx saw private ownership of the means of production and workers producing things for market exchange as a severing of the bond between the worker and work. Under capitalism and wage labor, the things that are produced do not belong to the worker; and because of the extreme division of labor, the worker no longer identifies with the product. In addition, workers sell their skill and ability to work to the owner of the means of production and thereby become a commodity, like a pair of shoes. Thus, workers under industrial capitalism are alienated in four ways: from their product, from the work process, from coworkers, and from themselves.

We have proceeded from the premises of political economy. We have accepted its language and its laws. We presupposed private property, the separation of labour, capital and land, and of wages, profit of capital and rent of land—likewise division of labour, competition, the concept of exchange-value, etc. On the basis of political economy itself, in its own words, we have shown that the worker sinks to the level of a commodity and becomes indeed the most wretched of commodities; that the wretchedness of the worker is in inverse proportion to the power and magnitude of his production; that the necessary result of competition is the accumulation of capital in a few hands, and thus the restoration of monopoly in a more terrible form; that finally the distinction between capitalist and land-rentier, like that between the tiller of the soil and the factory-worker, disappears and that the whole of society must fall apart into the two classes—the property-*owners* and the propertyless *workers*. . . .

. . . [W]e have to grasp the essential connection between private property, avarice, and the separation of labour, capital and landed property; between exchange and competition, value and the devaluation of men, monopoly and competition, etc.; the connection between this whole estrangement and the *money*-system. . . .

We proceed from an *actual* economic fact.

The worker becomes all the poorer the more wealth he produces, the more his production increases in power and range. The worker becomes an ever cheaper commodity the more commodities he creates. With the *increasing value* of the world of things proceeds in direct proportion the *devaluation* of the world of men. Labour produces not only commodities: it produces itself and the worker as a *commodity*—and does so in the proportion in which it produces commodities generally.

This fact expresses merely that the object which labour produces—labour's product—confronts it as *something alien*, as a *power independent* of the producer. The product of labour is labour which has been congealed in an object, which has become material: it is the *objectification* of labour. Labour's realization is its objectification. In the conditions dealt with by political economy this realization of labour appears as *loss of reality* for the workers: objectification as *loss of the object* and *object-bondage*: appropriation as *estrangement*, as *alienation*.

So much does labour's realization appear as loss of reality that the worker loses reality to the point of starving to death. So much does objectification appear as loss of the object that the worker is robbed of the objects most necessary not only for his life but for his work. Indeed, labour itself becomes an object which he can get hold of only with the greatest effort and with the most irregular interruptions. So much does the appropriation of the object appear as estrangement that the more objects the worker produces the fewer can he possess and the more he falls under the dominion of his product, capital. . . .

Political economy conceals the alienation inherent in the nature of labour by not considering the direct relationship between the worker (labour) *and production.* It is true that labour produces for the rich wonderful things—but for the worker it produces privation. It produces palaces—but for the worker, hovels. It produces beauty—but for the worker, deformity. It replaces labour by machines—but some of the workers it throws back to a barbarous type of labour, and the other workers it turns into machines. It produces intelligence—but for the worker idiocy, cretinism.

The direct relationship of labour to its produce is the relationship of the worker to the objects of his production. The relationship of the man of means to the objects of production and to production itself is only a *consequence* of this first relationship—and confirms it. We shall consider this other aspect later.

When we ask, then, what is the essential relationship of labour we are asking about the relationship of the *worker* to production.

Till now we have been considering the estrangement, the alienation of the worker only in one of its aspects, i.e., the worker's *relationship to the products of his labour.* But the estrangement is manifested not only in the result but in the *act of production*—within the *producing activity* itself. How would the worker come to face the product of his activity as a stranger, were it not that in the very act of production he was estranging himself from himself? The product is after all but the summary of the activity, of production. If then the product of labour is alienation, production itself must be active alienation, the alienation of activity, the activity of alienation. In the estrangement of the object of labour is merely summarized the estrangement, the alienation, in the activity of labour itself.

What, then, constitutes the alienation of labour?

First, the fact that labour is *external* to the worker, i.e., it does not belong to his essential being; that in his work, therefore, he does not affirm himself but denies himself, does not feel content but unhappy, does not develop freely his physical and mental energy but mortifies his body and ruins his mind. The worker therefore only feels himself outside his work, and in his work feels outside himself. He is at home when he is not working, and when he is not working he is not at home. His labour is therefore not voluntary, but coerced; it is *forced labour.* It is therefore not the satisfaction of a need; it is merely a *means* to satisfy needs external to it. Its alien character emerges clearly in the fact that as soon as no physical or other compulsion exists, labour is shunned like the plague. External labour, labour in which man alienates himself, is a labour of self-sacrifice, of mortification. Lastly, the external character of labour for the worker appears in the fact that it is not his own, but someone else's, that it does not belong to him, that in it he belongs, not to himself, but to another. Just as in religion the spontaneous activity of the human imagination, of the human brain and the human heart, operates independently of the individual— that is, operates on him as an alien, divine or diabolical activity—in the same way the worker's activity is not his spontaneous activity. It belongs to another; it is the loss of his self.

As a result, therefore, man (the worker) no longer feels himself to be freely active in any but his animal functions—eating, drinking, procreating, or at most in his dwelling and in dressing-up, etc.; and in his human functions he no longer feels himself to be anything but an animal. What is animal becomes human and what is human becomes animal.

Certainly eating, drinking, procreating, etc., are also genuinely human functions. But in the abstraction which separates them from the sphere of all other human activities and turns them into sole and ultimate ends, they are animal.

We have considered the act of alienation of practical human activity, labour, in two of its aspects. (1) The relation of the worker to the *product of labour* as an alien object exercising power over him. This relation is at the same time the relation to the sensuous external world, to the objects of nature as an alien world antagonistically opposed to him. (2) The relation of labour to the *act of production* within the *labour* process. This relation is the relation of the worker to his own activity as an alien activity not belonging to him; it is activity as suffering, strength as weakness, begetting as emasculating, the worker's *own* physical and mental energy, his personal life or what is life other than activity—as an activity which is turned against him, neither depends on nor belongs to him. Here we have [*self-alienation*] as we had previously the [*alienation*] of the thing.

We have yet a third aspect of [*alienated*] *labour* to deduce from the two already considered.

Man is a species being, not only because in practice and in theory he adopts the species as his object (his own as well as those of other things), but—and this is only another way of expressing it—but also because he treats himself as the actual, living species; because he treats himself as a *universal* and therefore a free being. . . .

In estranging from man (1) nature, and (2) himself, his own active functions, his life-activity, estranged labour estranges the *species* from man. It turns for him the *life of the species* into a means of individual life. First it estranges the life of the species and individual life, and secondly it makes individual life in its abstract form the purpose of the life of the species, likewise in its abstract and estranged form. . . .

It is just in the working-up of the objective world, therefore, that man first really proves himself to be a *species being*. This production is his active species life. Through and because of this production, nature appears as *his* work and his reality. The object of labour is, therefore, the *objectification of man's species life:* for he duplicates himself not only, as in consciousness, intellectually, but also actively, in reality, and therefore he contemplates himself in a world that he has created. In tearing away from man the object of his production, therefore, estranged labour tears from him his *species life*, his real species objectivity, and transforms his advantage over animals into the disadvantage that his inorganic body, nature, is taken from him.

Similarly, in degrading spontaneous activity, free activity, to a means, estranged labour makes man's species life a means to his physical existence.

The consciousness which man has of his species is thus transformed by estrangement in such a way that the species life becomes for him a means.

Estranged labour turns thus:

(3) *Man's species being,* both nature and his spiritual species property, into a being *alien* to him, into a *means* to his *individual existence*. It estranges man's own body from him, as it does external nature and his spiritual essence, his *human* being.

(4) An immediate consequence of the fact that man is estranged from the product of his labour, from his life-activity, from his species being is the **alienation of man** from *man*. If a man is confronted by himself, he is confronted by the *other* man. What applies to a man's relation to his work, to the product of his labour and to himself, also holds of a man's relation to the other man, and to the other man's labour and object of labour.

In fact, the proposition that man's species nature is alienated from him means that one man is alienated from the other, as each of them is from man's essential nature.

The alienation of man, and in fact every relationship in which man stands to himself, is first realized and expressed in the relationship in which a man stands to other men.

Hence within the relationship of alienated labour each man views the other in accordance with the standard and the position in which he finds himself as a worker.

We took our departure from a fact of political economy—the alienation of the worker and his production. We have formulated the concept of this fact—*estranged, alienated* labour. We have analysed this concept—hence analysing merely a fact of political economy.

Let us now see, further, how in real life the concept of estranged, alienated labour must express and present itself.

If the product of labour is alien to me, if it confronts me as an alien power, to whom, then, does it belong?

If my own activity does not belong to me, if it is an alien, a coerced activity, to whom, then, does it belong?

To a being *other* than me.

Who is this being?

The *gods?* To be sure, in the earliest times the principal production (for example, the building of temples, etc., in Egypt, India and Mexico) appears to be in the service of the gods, and the product belongs to the gods. However, the gods on their own were never the lords of labour. No more was *nature*. And what a contradiction it would be if, the more man subjugated nature by his labour and the more the miracles of the gods were rendered superfluous by the miracles of industry, the more man were to renounce the joy of production and the enjoyment of the produce in favour of these powers.

The *alien* being, to whom labour and the produce of labour belongs, in whose service labour is done and for whose benefit the produce of labour is provided, can only be *man* himself.

If the product of labour does not belong to the worker, if it confronts him as an alien power, this can only be because it belongs to *some other man than the worker.* If the worker's activity is a torment to him, to another it must be *delight* and his life's joy. Not the gods, not nature, but only man himself can be this alien power over man.

We must bear in mind the above-stated proposition that man's relation to himself only becomes *objective* and *real* for him through his relation to the other man. Thus, if the product of his labour, his labour *objectified*, is for him an *alien*, hostile, powerful object independent of him, then his position towards it is such that someone else is master of this object, someone who is alien, hostile, powerful, and independent of him. If his own activity is to him an unfree activity, then he is treating it as activity performed in the service, under the dominion, the coercion and the yoke of another man.

Every self-alienation of man from himself and from nature appears in the relation in which he places himself and nature to men other than and differentiated from himself. For this reason religious self-estrangement necessarily appears in the relationship of the layman to the priest, or again to a mediator, etc., since we are here dealing with the intellectual world. In the real practical world self-estrangement can only become manifest through the real practical relationship to other men. The medium through which alienation takes place is itself *practical*. Thus through alienated labour man not only engenders his relationship to the object and to the act of production as to powers that are alien and hostile to him; he also engenders the relationship in which other men stand to his production and to his product, and the relationship in which he stands to these other men. Just as he begets his own production as the loss of his reality, as his punishment; just as he begets his own product as a loss, as a product not belonging to him; so he begets the dominion of the one who does not produce over production and over the product. Just as he estranges from himself his own activity, so he confers to the stranger activity which is not his own.

Till now we have only considered this relationship from the standpoint of the worker and later we shall be considering it also from the standpoint of the non-worker.

Through *alienated labour*, then, the worker produces the relationship to this labour of a man alien to labour and standing outside it. The relationship of the worker to labour engenders the relation to it of the capitalist, or whatever one chooses to call the master of labour. *Private property* is thus the product, the result, the necessary consequence, of *alienated labour*, of the external relation of the worker to nature and to himself.

Private property thus results by analysis from the concept of *alienated labour*—i.e., of *alienated man*, of estranged labour, of estranged life, of estranged man.

True, it is as a result of the *movement of private property* that we have obtained the concept of *alienated labour* (of *alienated life*) from political economy. But on analysis of this concept it becomes clear that though private property appears to be the source, the cause of alienated labour, it is really its consequence, just as the gods *in the beginning* are not the cause but the effect of man's intellectual confusion. Later this relationship becomes reciprocal.

Only at the very culmination of the development of private property does this, its secret, re-emerge, namely, that on the one hand it is the *product* of alienated labour, and that secondly it is the *means* by which labour alienates itself, the *realization of this alienation.* . . .

Discussion Questions

1. Some contemporary sociologists view Marx's discussion of alienation as a very pessimistic perspective. Others say that Marx viewed work as inherently pleasing and rewarding. What do you think about Marx's view of alienated labor?

2. Can you apply Marx's idea of alienation to a personal work experience or to occupations that differ in their level of skill and education (e.g., nursing, bank manager, skilled carpenter).

3. Discuss changes in the occupational structure since Marx's time that may require a revision of his ideas on alienation.

Excerpted from Karl Marx, "Estranged Labor," in *Economic and Philosophical Manuscripts of 1844* (New York: International Publishers, 1964). Used by permission. ◆

Part II

How Globalization, Technology, and Organization Affect Work

The central argument of this book is that beginning around 1970 the main features of the U.S. economy started to change so substantially that we call it the *new economy*. Moreover, we argue further that the new ways of producing goods and services are *transforming* the world of work. Each of the three sections in this unit focuses on one of the three social forces that constitute the new economy: globalization, technology, and organization.

Section A deals with the globalization of production and all that it entails, such as the global context for the location of production and the decline of national corporations and rise of multinational corporations. Globalization, as in activities of international trade and foreign investment, is not new. There have always been elements of a world economic system in relations among developed economies, and especially between powerful states and colonial territories. Globalization in the new economy places unregulated international production, distribution, and consumption at center stage in the world economy. One result is that governments are pressured to expand global free markets, unfettered by regulation, and a second result is that multinational corporations have

dismissed any sense of obligation to their employees, their local communities, or their nations. Chapter 5 refers to this feature of the new economy as *neoliberal globalization*.

In Section B, the focus turns to the role of microelectronic technology as the "great growling engine of change" (Chapter 10). The chapters in this section look at the broad (macro) effects of technology in terms of altering spatial and temporal production practices and the individual-level (micro) effects on workers as they carry out day-to-day activities. There is also a chapter on middle-level (meso) effects of technology in changing needs for different jobs and skills and in the pay levels for different types of work.

Section C looks at the new economy in terms of the way that work organizations are changing their contractual relationships with workers by introducing more part-time and temporary employees, to whom they have minimal obligations. In addition, large corporations are changing their internal structures by reducing production workers and expanding supervisory personnel in order to maintain or expand productivity with fewer employees. ◆

5

Neoliberal Globalization

Dan Clawson

Globalization is a term that is invoked frequently in today's world to describe everything from international trade, to the global spread of Hollywood films, to immigration, and to terrorism. For some, it is the source of many of today's problems, such as unemployment, poverty, and increasing inequality among people and nations. For others, it is the solution to many problems that could be remedied by increased international trade and free markets. Clawson discusses what we might call *normal globalization* as the interaction between nations, businesses, and groups of people that can contribute to mutually beneficial outcomes for all. He distinguishes this from *neoliberal globalization*, which is a set of policies emphasizing greater reliance on the market and a reduced role for government in regulating the economy and in assisting those most harmed by rapid economic change. Some observers of global economic development applaud neoliberal policies like the North American Free Trade Agreement (NAFTA), which encourages less-regulated trade between the United States, Mexico, and Canada. They argue that NAFTA will be win-win, creating more trade and more jobs on both sides of the border. Critics of NAFTA point to loss of U.S. jobs as many manufacturing plants transferred production to countries with lower wages, nonunion workers, and weaker environmental and worker protections.

Clawson examines the political forces behind neoliberal globalization and identifies the winners and losers in a global context. He also discusses the uneven effects of globalization across different U.S. industries and employment sectors.

Forces and processes associated with globalization fundamentally shape the world we live in. No account of labor's current weakness and potential regeneration can neglect the topic. In the United States from 1899 through 1963, import content as a proportion of finished manufacture was never more than 3 percent; in 1971 it was still only 9 percent. Today the value of manufactured imports is equal to 69 percent of the sector's GDP. Not only is world trade more important, but the technical and cost barriers to world interactions are dramatically lower than they once were. The cost of a three-minute New York–to–London telephone call fell from $188 in 1940 to $31 in 1970 to $3 in 1990 to under half a dollar in 2002.[1] When we ask how the world of today differs from that of the 1930s, globalization is clearly one of the most consequential differences.

But what is "globalization"? Is it sharing music and ideas, enjoying foods from around the world, and utilizing the World Wide Web? By that standard, most people in the United States would endorse globalization. Is it taking steps to address global warming and adopting policies that show concern for every person on earth? The most vocal advocates of "globalization" would oppose such policies. Or does "globalization" mean that business and profit must be all-determining, that any law that helps workers or the environment must be abolished?

Business and conservative advocates have seized control of the term "globalization." The debate is usually framed as "globalization: yes or no?" with those opposed to "globalization" cast as modern-day equivalents of flat-earthers, people putting their heads in the sand in hopes that doing so will stop "progress." But, despite what Thomas Friedman of the *New York Times* would have us believe, the meaningful debate is not about whether or not this is and will be one world—at least since Columbus, *that's* been settled—but rather what will be the terms of engagement, who will control the process, for what ends will it be pursued, and by whose standards will it be evaluated? Are we seeking global justice or the worldwide triumph of business neoliberal policies?

Neoliberal policies—that is, those that promote reliance on the market and a questioning of government—have been thoroughly integrated into the institutions regulating globalization, so much so that it is often difficult to think about globalization separate from its neoliberal variant. In the United States neoliberal policies are advocated by both Republicans and New Democrats. The alternative viewpoint—usually called "anti-globalization" by business and the media—promotes global justice for workers and the environment. The contest between these two competing visions can be divided into three stages: business's mobilization and increasing triumph from the 1970s to the late 1990s, the post-Seattle period (1999–2001) when global justice forces began to redefine the debate, and post-9/11 when everything has been in abeyance.

An old joke tells of a man returning a broken rake to his neighbor. In his defense he argues (1) I never really borrowed it, (2) besides, it was broken when I got it, and (3) anyway, there's nothing wrong with it. Advocates of neoliberal globalization argue in similarly contradictory ways: First, that globalization is a neutral, inevitable, unstoppable process which has nothing to do with politics or human will. Second, that these are desirable policies, the only ones that can guarantee our country's prosperity, and that business and conservatives deserve a lot of credit for introducing them. Third, well, maybe these policies aren't so good for most people in the United States, but they are needed to aid the underdeveloped world. Every one of these business claims is demonstrably wrong.

The structure of this chapter differs somewhat from that of the others, because the political-economic framework both created labor's difficulties and must be changed if labor is to advance. Policies that may initially seem to have nothing to do with labor actually structure the options and determine what is possible. More background is therefore needed in order to understand the challenge labor and its allies face, and the sorts of approaches that need to be considered to develop solutions. The first half of the chapter considers and refutes each of the three arguments made by the advocates of a business-driven globalization policy. The last half of the chapter considers three of the options labor can take to advance workers' interests: capital controls, international labor standards, or building cross-national labor solidarity.

Inevitable and Apolitical?

Business apologists claim that globalization in its current form just happened; no one pushed for it, no one sought to shape policies to promote their self-interest or class interest. According to Thomas Friedman: "I feel about globalization a lot like I feel about the dawn. Generally speaking, I think it's a good thing that the sun comes up every morning. . . . But even if I didn't much care for the dawn there isn't much I could do about it."[2] Because globalization is an inevitable accompaniment of modernization and economic development, no one should try to fight it. The only debate is how to adapt to it.

But there are alternatives to the neoliberal framework of globalization through commercialization; consider the (fully global) Internet. Because it's a spectacular success, companies today are of course attempting to take it over and shape it to their purposes, but the Internet and World Wide Web are global but not (yet) neoliberal. Key steps in the development process were pushed by researchers, university-based personnel, and idealists. Its creators relied on public rather than corporate funding, and their aim was to facilitate communication and connect people with one another, not to enrich themselves. The Internet and the Web are powerful forces bringing people together globally. By no means can the Internet be said to be open to all on equal terms, but once plugged in to the Internet there are few limits to where someone can go. Anyone may not only receive messages, but post them to others. A person with little wealth or power can create a web site accessed by tens of thousands around the world. This model of globalization contrasts sharply with the World Trade Organization (WTO) model that all decisions must be made in terms of what is best for business.

Much of the debate about globalization "presupposes an 'original condition,' a starting-point for the process, in which the world is made up of distinct and self-sufficient national economies, each under the jurisdiction of an independent nation-state." But movements of goods, people, and ideas go back many thousands of years, at least since modern people swept out of Africa some sixty thousand years ago. Although the term "globalization" is new, the phenomena to which it refers have long been discussed and studied. "States have always had to respond to and been constrained by external actors. Their autonomy in terms of their real capacity to formulate and implement public policy has almost invariably fallen short of their formal claims to sovereign national power."[3] People living in small or weak states have no trouble understanding this: the intellectuals and workers of Panama or Nicaragua (or for that matter the Netherlands) are under no illusion that their states or economies are, ever were, or possibly could be autonomous and self-sufficient. However, both intellectuals and ordinary citizens in hegemonic states, such as the United States, or former hegemonic states, such as Great Britain, have much more difficulty understanding or remembering this, and may become angry or engage in victim-bashing when events force them to recognize the limits to sovereignty.

The implicit argument—rarely made explicit, because once it's brought into the open its ludicrous character is almost self-evident—is that "globalization" requires that local democracy be abolished in favor of decision making by unelected bodies such as the WTO (dominated by representatives from the world's richest countries acting on behalf of the most powerful businesses). Neither these organizations nor globalization in its neoliberal form appeared through some magical, apolitical, technological imperative. As Frances Fox Piven, Leo Panitch, and others have emphasized, globalization is a politically instituted process. "As *The Economist* [perhaps the world's leading business magazine] put it recently, those 'who demand that the trend of global integration be halted and reversed, are frightening precisely because, *given the will, governments could do it.*' "[4]

It's taken many years for business and its political allies to build the neoliberal version of globalization; each step in the process required a new set of decisions. One key element was dismantling capital controls; the United States pushed hard for this to be the policy of both national governments and the International Monetary Fund.[5] Perhaps the most crucial neoliberal step was the creation of the World Trade Organization. In 1994, business neoliberals thought that GATT (the General Agreement on Tariffs and Trade) wasn't strong enough, because it applied only to trade in goods and because it had weak and ineffective mechanisms for resolving disputes between nations. So they strengthened their particular version of globalization by creating the WTO, which covered trade in services as well as goods, and they instituted new rules requiring member nations to accept its jurisdiction and obey its decisions. Countries that fail to do so promptly are subject to fines and trade sanctions imposed by the WTO: When the WTO investigates disputes and imposes penalties, the decision is made by a totally unrepresentative body meeting in secret, with the deliberations not open to the public even after the fact.

The WTO not only rules on tariffs, but also on "nontariff barriers to trade," that is, any governmental policy (at whatever level:

federal, state, local) that limits "free" trade. When the United States passed regulations requiring that fishing nets be modified to reduce the likelihood that they would ensnare (and thus drown) endangered sea turtles, the WTO ruled that this was a "nontariff barrier to trade" and the United States was forced to abandon the regulation (and the sea turtles). The Ethyl Corporation has sued Canada, arguing Canada has no right to ban a harmful gasoline additive; Metalclad has sued Mexico, arguing Mexico has no right to deny Metalclad a permit for a toxic waste disposal site; and the United States has argued France has no right to ban entry to hormone-treated beef.[6] Neither the creation of the WTO, nor such rules and rulings, are inevitable.

For workers, unions, and environmentalists, such treaties pose serious problems. Neoliberals act as if we must either operate on these rules or entirely cut ourselves off from the world economy, thus eliminating coffee and bananas from our diet, and never hearing records or seeing films produced outside our borders. Such a claim, implicit in much of what neoliberals say, is ludicrous. Because WTO decisions are made out of the public spotlight, through the workings of bodies whose officials are not politically accountable (or even recognized by the public), it may seem that the neoliberal version of globalization is the only possibility. But the fact that a decision is hidden, or the alternatives are never presented or debated, does not mean that the decision is technically necessary or inevitable. Quite the reverse: the decision must be made in secret precisely because it could not withstand public scrutiny.

Good for the United States?

Forced to admit that the neoliberal variant of globalization is by no means inevitable, but instead a politically instituted process, proponents of the neoliberal variant of globalization have a fallback position: Even if globalization isn't inevitable, we should support it because it's good policy. Globalization, Thomas Friedman tells us,

"is the engine of greater long-term prosperity for every country that plugs into the globalization system."[7] Neoliberals say that we must therefore abolish all impediments to the free market and accept complete free trade both inside the United States and with all the rest of the world. (Not quite all: neoliberals make exceptions for corporate welfare, tax breaks, and export subsidies.) Otherwise, they say, our nation's economy will stagnate, consumers will pay inflated prices, incomes will go down, and everyone will suffer.

If "prosperity" refers to conditions for most of the population, this is simply wrong. Neoliberal globalization has been good for profits and wealthy individuals, but for few others. This can be seen by comparing two periods: the welfare state (or Keynesian or social democratic) policies that prevailed in the 1950s and 1960s, and the increasing neoliberalism of 1973 to the present. From the end of World War II to the early 1970s, the United States, most European countries, and most of the Global South (also called "the underdeveloped countries" or "the Third World") pursued at least mildly social democratic policies involving strong government intervention in the economy. In much of the world—although notably not in the United States—key industries were nationalized. Social welfare systems were created or expanded. And typically a compromise, or at least modus vivendi, was reached between the labor movement and the capitalist class, a compromise that extended to both company and government-level policies. For example, Richard Nixon, a conservative Republican, announced that "we are all Keynesians now," a statement that was consistent with his economic policies—which included support for creating the Environmental Protection Agency, the Occupational Safety and Health Administration, wage-price controls, and what was in effect a proposal for a guaranteed annual income. Business generally accepted these policies both because of the strength of unions and because, given a relatively closed economy, business relied on increasing working-class incomes to support the growth of a mass-based consumer economy.

Before 1973, governments regulated transfers of capital or currency from one country to another (the so-called Bretton Woods system).[8] Such regulation is needed in order to maintain a strong welfare system, protect the environment, and pursue most other people-oriented goals. Suppose a megabillion dollar corporation can say, "We moved our official headquarters to the Bahamas (although we only have four employees there), and we now count all our profits as coming from there; therefore we have no U.S. profits and don't need to pay any taxes." (Not so long ago this would have been illegal; today it is an increasingly common corporate tactic.) If there are no controls on a corporation's ability to move its capital from one country to another, it can (on paper) claim that all its profits come from whatever country will give it the lowest tax rates.

Since the early 1970s, the United States and most other countries have increasingly adopted neoliberal policies, deregulating both their national economies and all international economic exchanges. Government intervention in the economy has been drastically reduced. As president, Ronald Reagan declared that government was not the solution, government was the problem. In Europe, nationalized industries have been sold; in the United States, regulated industries have been deregulated, and government services have been contracted out to private firms. In this way, a market logic comes to dominate even the provision of government services. The market, rather than strengthened international institutions, becomes the force regulating global activity, with FedEx and UPS as the new post office and a host of private banks and securities firms in place of an effective global regulatory institution. Social welfare programs have been curtailed everywhere, since their cost has increased and their benefits (to business) decreased.[9]

These policy changes, made with relatively little public awareness, much less debate, have had profound consequences. Once, foreign currency exchange was about paying for trade (or tourism); now it's mostly about speculation. "It is estimated that, in 1971, just before the collapse of the Bretton Woods fixed exchange rate system, about 90 percent of all foreign exchange transactions were for the finance of trade and long-term investment, and only about 10 percent were speculative. Today, those percentages are reversed, with well over 90 percent of all transactions being speculative."[10] This dramatically increases the amount of money involved, which no longer bears any meaningful relation to the actual flow of goods and services. The effects of that reverberate throughout the economy, strengthening the hand of those who want to restructure other institutions. As a consequence "international financial pressures are felt by small and medium sized firms operating in the home market, and not only by large companies operating internationally."[11]

Neoliberals would have us believe that these post-1973 policies have produced economic success, and that if we want to increase economic performance we need to further extend and strengthen neoliberal globalization, But in fact the economic record is quite clear: from 1945 to 1973, the "bad old days" of currency controls, capital controls, strong unions, frequent strikes, and government regulation, the economy boomed and prosperity was widely shared. During the period of neoliberal globalization, on the other hand, the economy has stagnated and inequality increased. In the United States, using constant 1999 dollars for all comparisons, from 1949 to 1973 average family income more than doubled, from $19,515 to $41,935; moreover, incomes during this period became more equal, so those at the bottom benefited even more. In the next quarter-century, from 1973 to 1999, incomes went up much more slowly, and much of the increase was because so many more married women were working. Moreover, incomes during this period became substantially more unequal, with the largest gains going to those at the very top. If incomes had increased as fast in the neoliberal period as they did during the welfare state period, the average 1999 family would have had an income of $97,623 instead of the actual average of $48,950. It takes some nerve for neoliberals to claim their policies are necessary for economic success.[12]

Help the World's Poor?

If the neoliberal version of globalization is not inevitable, and if it has a poor economic record in the United States, perhaps it nonetheless helps promote development in Africa, Asia, and Latin America. Maybe the U.S. economy has been stagnating precisely because globalization is promoting the development of the Global South. Such thinking makes sense only if we assume that there is a fixed quantity of production and wealth; in such a zero-sum world, a gain for any group must be counterbalanced by an equal loss for some other group. For more than twenty years, as U.S. wages stagnated, such views have become more widespread, entrenched, and a part of accepted common sense.

But that's not how capitalism operates. Even Marx recognized—and celebrated—capitalism's enormous productivity, and the liberatory potential of these increases in production. Over 150 years ago he described what sounds like the globalization of today:

> The bourgeoisie cannot exist without constantly revolutionising the instruments of production, and thereby the relations of production, and with them the whole relations of society. . . . The need of a constantly expanding market for its products chases the bourgeoisie over the whole surface of the globe. . . . The bourgeoisie has through its exploitation of the world-market given a cosmopolitan character to production and consumption in every country. . . . All old-established national industries have been destroyed or are daily being destroyed. . . . The intellectual creations of individual nations become common property. . . . From the numerous national and local literatures, there arises a world literature. . . . [The bourgeoisie]

has created enormous cities, has greatly increased the urban population as compared with the rural, and has thus rescued considerable part of the population from the idiocy of rural life. . . . The bourgeoisie, during its rule of scarce one hundred years, has created more massive and more colossal productive forces than have all preceding generations together.[13]

Remarkable as U.S. growth was in the post-1945 period, the economic development of the Global South during this same period was still more incredible. "In statistical terms, the Third World's economic achievements of the three decades 1950–80 are a story without parallel in world development history."[14] The South's record during this period surpassed that of Europe during the nineteenth century from 1820 to 1900. "The South did this in half the time at twice the growth rates" and did so despite having a population five times as large as that of Europe in the nineteenth century.

Economic growth of this kind is not simply a statistical abstraction; consider some of what it meant for people's lives. In Brazil, from negligible levels in 1950, by 1980 76 percent of all households had radios, 55 percent had televisions, 50 percent had refrigerators, and 22 percent had automobiles. Or consider literacy. Europe's literacy rate is estimated to have been below 25 percent in 1850 and below 50 percent in 1900.

> The corresponding level of literacy in the South was about 30 per cent in 1950. By the 1980s, however, it had risen to 50 per cent in Africa, 70 per cent in Asia and 80 per cent in Latin America. More significantly, despite all the shortcomings both in the data and in the quality of education imparted in developing countries, the North-South educational gap narrowed spectacularly during these decades of relative prosperity.[15]

Public health also improved dramatically, with life expectancy in the Global South increasing "from around forty years in 1950 to sixty years by the mid 1980s," an extra twenty years of life for the average person.

One of the reasons for the economic development of the Global South was that those who dominated U.S. and European business and politics wanted to forestall revolution or the appeal of so-called Communist parties. More than a third of the world's population was in this "Communist" bloc, which had a major presence in Europe (Eastern Europe, Russia) and Asia (China, parts of Korea and Vietnam), a minor presence in the Americas (Cuba), and, in one variant or another, substantial political appeal in much of the rest of the world. Communist parties were significant political forces in France and Italy. At one point or another over a forty-year span an impressive list of countries accepted aid from, or maintained friendly relations with, China or the Soviet Union. Competition with the Communist bloc constrained the United States to see that benefits were widely distributed to the Global South's population; anything less would have weakened the United States in its competition with the Communists. As Robert McNamara explained:

> Too little, too late, is history's most fitting epitaph for regimes that have fallen in the face of the cries of the landless, unemployed, marginalised and oppressed, pushed to despair. As such, there must be policies designed specifically to reduce the poverty of the poorest 40 per cent of the population in developing countries. This is not just the principled thing to do, it is also the prudent thing to do. Social justice is not only a moral obligation, it is also a political imperative.[16]

For most of the Global South the explosive economic growth of the post-1945 period of social democracy ended under the impact of neoliberal policies, although rapid growth continued in Asia. "In Latin America, after a sustained rise in the previous three decades, per capita incomes fell by 10 percent in the 1980s. In Sub-Saharan Africa, per capita incomes fell on average by as much as 25 per cent during the same period."[17]

The political (and economic) conclusion from this is crucially important but—remarkably—seems to be almost completely missing from the conventional wisdom of globalization discourse: economic prosperity for one region (whether North or South) does not come at the expense of the other. Rather, the same set of social democratic policies brought economic growth to both North and South, and the neoliberal policies that have created stagnation for average workers in the North have also created hardship in the South. Rather than a trade-off between workers of the two regions, the policies that benefit one also aid the other. For economic policy, the conflict is not so much that between the Global North and South, but rather that between capitalists and workers.

How Damaging Is Neoliberal Globalization?

Neoliberal claims about the origins and benefits of globalization don't hold up, and the neoliberal form of globalization hurts workers both North and South. But just how significant is globalization for workers and unions? Many commentators argue that the effects of globalization overwhelm most other factors and are (almost?) all-determining. These analysts seem to imply either that there isn't much labor can do, or that labor needs to focus almost all its energy on addressing globalization.

Once again we need to analytically separate globalization (the worldwide spread of ideas and economic development, based on interchange and interaction) from neoliberalism (the abolition of government regulation and all other barriers to the unchecked rule of business and the market). Most people support globalization and oppose neoliberalism, so business and its allies have tried to blend the two and insist that to have globalization we must also have neoliberalism. If labor is to develop a response (the focus of the last half of this chapter), it needs to determine the source and seriousness of the problem.

Even without neoliberalism, globalization would have significant effects on the U.S. economy, but neoliberalism is far more important. Globalization is, of course, one of the factors that has helped strengthen neoliberalism and maintain it in place. The combination of globalization and neoliberalism has devastated manufacturing unions. But neoliberalism, even without globalization, has had similar effects on many other sectors of the labor movement. At this point it may not be possible to disentangle neoliberalism and globalization, but the independent effects of globalization per se may not be the primary issue. There's every reason to believe that the effects of globalization will spread to new areas of employment. Despite that, outside of manufacturing much of U.S. employment is not particularly vulnerable to being moved elsewhere, but is vulnerable to other forms of neoliberal policy such as privatization, deregulation, and contracting out.

The effects of globalization are of course uneven: for some industries it is devastating and inescapable, for others it has little or no direct impact. Consider Table 5.1, which gives a tentative assessment of the relative impact of globalization on various sources of employment, and the number of employees in each area. The table uses broad categories which are useful for a first approximation, although there is wide variation within some categories. In manufacturing, for example, the garment industry is largely based outside the United States, but the tobacco consumed here is manufactured almost exclusively inside this country; the auto industry is somewhere in between. Within the business services category computers and data processing are vulnerable to globalization, but temporary help is not. Moreover, globalization can exercise a substantial effect on an industry by means of a change of ownership, the importation of another country's labor practices, and so on, even if employment in the sector stays almost exclusively U.S.-based. (This is probably true for the communications industry, for example.)

It's important to remember that at issue is the extent to which employment, not the employer, must be based in the United States. Foreign firms can purchase U.S. hotels, but if the hotels are in the United States, so must be the employment. Similarly, the issue is not the country of origin of the employee: a large fraction of private household workers may have been born outside the borders of the

Table 5.1

Vulnerability of the U.S. Economy to Globalization, by Sector

Employment sector	Number of sector employees (in millions)	Total for category (in millions)
Highly vulnerable (imports more than 50% of domestic)		18.9
Manufacturing	18.4	
Mining	0.5	
Somewhat vulnerable (imports 15–20%)		7.7
Transportation	4.4	
Agriculture	3.3	
Minimally vulnerable (imports less than 5%)		93.3
Communications	1.6	
Public utilities	0.9	
Finance, insurance, and real estate	7.5	
Hotels	1.9	
Personal services	1.3	
Auto repair	1.2	
Business services	9.7	
Amusement and recreation services	1.8	
Health services	10.1	
Legal, educational, and social services	6.5	
Wholesale trade	7.1	
Retail trade	23.1	
Government (federal, state, and local)	20.6	
Total employment accounted for in table		119.9
Total U.S. employment		135.2

Source: *Statistical Abstract of the United States 2001*, calculated from tables 609, 641, 1283, and 1306. No major employment category had imports between 21 and 49 percent or between 6 and 14 percent.

United States, but the work itself must be performed here. Responsive unions should be able to organize U.S.-based workers, whatever their country of origin, and whatever the nationality of their employer.

Not only is two-thirds of employment (by this calculation) relatively insulated from globalization, but that is even more true of the fastest-growing jobs. Of the thirty occupations with the largest job growth, I would classify only four as vulnerable to globalization: systems analysts, database administrators and computer support specialists, computer engineers, and hand packers and packagers. Job growth for these four occupations from 1996 to 2006 was projected to be 1.2 million. Excluding general managers and top executives as not relevant to a union analysis, the other twenty-five occupations with the largest job growth all appear to be relatively insulated from the pressures of globalization. These occupations include (from most to least job growth) cashiers, registered nurses, retail salespersons, truck drivers, home health aides, teacher aides and educational assistants, nursing aides (including orderlies and attendants), receptionists and information clerks, secondary-school teachers, child care workers, clerical supervisors and managers, marketing and sales supervisors, maintenance repairers, food counter and fountain workers, special education teachers, food preparation workers, guards, general office clerks, waiters and waitresses, social workers, adjustment clerks, short-order and fast food cooks, personal and home care aides, food service and lodging managers, and medical assistants. Job growth for these occupations was projected to be 6.9 million.[18]

Globalization has been devastating in the manufacturing sector, especially in the old-line industrial unions that had some of the best wages and benefits and sometimes provided a model of progressive labor militance. Given this, employers can routinely threaten that if workers vote for a union, the owners will close the plant and move it abroad, and this is a powerful weapon in the assault on unions. Kate Bronfenbrenner's study, conducted for the NAFTA Labor Secretariat, showed that in manufacturing, where it is particularly credible to threaten closure and plant relocation, employers threatened closure in 62 percent of all union organizing campaigns, and unions won only 23 percent of the manufacturing campaigns where employers threatened closure.[19]

But even in relatively immobile industries such as construction, health care, education, and retail, employers threatened to close in 36 percent of campaigns. Employers routinely threatened "that the employer might go out of business or have to contract out work if the union succeeded in its collective bargaining goals." Globalization alone simply cannot explain the decline of union membership or the growth of contracted-out labor. For example, from 1975 to 1999 the number of members of the vulnerable-to-globalization auto workers/steel workers, and machinists declined 42.5 percent (from 2.9 million to 1.7 million). But leading construction unions, which are relatively immune to the (direct) effects of globalization, declined just as fast as the auto, steel, and machinist unions: by 47.7 percent over the 1975 to 1999 period (from 1.6 million to under 0.9 million).[20]

There are alternatives to the neoliberal form of globalization. . . . There are no easy solutions, however, because neoliberal assumptions have been structured into the institutional fabric of economics, politics, intellectual life, and popular discourse. That means the transition from the current regime to something else is likely to be difficult.

A solution seemingly requires one of four things, all equally unlikely:

1. Impose codes of conduct to hold corporations to standards enforced by monitoring and publicity

2. Control capital, creating policies that discourage corporations from leaving the country, and thus make it possible to enforce U.S.-specific labor standards and to establish effective fiscal policy

3. Regulate labor conditions internationally through some official agency such

as the United Nations or World Trade Organization

4. Develop global class solidarity, either with a single world union for each industry, or with strong alliances between unions around the world

In practice, unions are pursuing all four, some mix of all is likely to be needed, success on one makes it easier to succeed on the others, and it seems exceptionally difficult to win a significant victory in any of these areas. Advance on any of these fronts will require a strong social movement; absent a movement the likelihood is that neoliberal globalization will become even more firmly entrenched. . . .

Discussion Questions

1. Is it possible to slow down or stop globalization? If government leaders wanted to discourage globalization, what could they do?

2. What have you read or heard about antiglobalization movements? Google "Battle in Seattle" and discuss the results.

Endnotes

1. Jonathan Perraton, David Goldblatt, David Held, and Anthony McGrew, "The Globalisation of Economic Activity," *New Political Economy* 2 (1997): 261, 262. This is an excellent overview packed with useful data. Their book version contains much more complete information; see David Held, Anthony McGrew, David Goldblatt, and Jonathan Perraton, *Global Transformations: Politics, Economics, and Culture* (Stanford, CA: Stanford University Press, 1999). Air transport costs also fell, although not nearly as rapidly. Data for today's imports are 1999 data from *Statistical Abstract of the United States 2001*, tables 641 and 1306.

2. Thomas L. Friedman, *The Lexus and the Olive Tree: Understanding Globalization*, rev. ed. (New York: Anchor Books, 2000), pp. xxi–xxii.

3. "Original condition" quotation from Hugo Radice, "Taking Globalisation Seriously," in *Socialist Register 1999: Global Capitalism versus Democracy*, ed. Leo Panitch and Colin Leys (New York: Monthly Review Press, 1999), p. 3. For previous work on the general topic see, for example, the voluminous literatures on multinational corporations, on "modernization" and "development," on imperialism, colonialism, international relations, etc. Constraints to autonomy quotation from Jonathan Perraton, David Goldblatt, David Held, and Anthony McGrew, "The Globalisation of Economic Activity," *New Political Economy* 2 (1997): 259.

4. Piven, "Globalization, American Politics, and Welfare Policy," *Annals of the American Academy of Political and Social Science* 577 (2001): 26–37; Piven and Richard A. Cloward, "Power Repertoires and Globalization," *Politics and Society* 28 (2000): 413–30; Leo Panitch, "The New Imperial State," *New Left Review* 2 (2000): 5–20; and Panitch, "Reflections on Strategy for Labour," in *Working Classes: Global Realities: Socialist Register 2001*, ed. Leo Panitch and Colin Leys (New York: Monthly Review Press, 2000), pp. 367–92. *Economist*, October 7, 1995, p. 16, quoted in James Crotty and Gerald Epstein, "In Defence of Capital Controls," in *Socialist Register 1996: Are There Alternatives?* ed. Leo Panitch (New York: Monthly Review Press, 1996), p. 144; emphasis theirs.

5. Crotty and Epstein, op. cit., pp. 126–27.

6. Naomi Klein, "Reclaiming the Commons," *New Left Review*, May–June 2001, pp. 87–88. The Multilateral Agreement on Investment (MAI) was intended to be a further step in quietly building the neoliberal version of globalization. Originally to be completed by 1997, it had to be repeatedly postponed because of difficulties securing its passage; that is, it was part of a political struggle, by no means an inevitability. Its passage would have drastically restricted the ability to regulate business, and would have required that many existing regulations be repealed. See the excellent article by Elissa Braunstein and Gerald Epstein, "Creating International Credit Rules and the Multilateral Agreement on Investment: What Are the Alternatives?" in *Global Instability: The Political Economy of World Economic Governance*, ed. Jonathan Michie and John Grieve Smith (New York: Routledge, 1999), pp. 113–33.

7. Friedman, op. cit., p. 442.

8. See Fred Block's wonderful *The Origins of International Economic Disorder* (Berkeley: University of California Press, 1977).

9. The costs (to business) of a strong welfare system increase because to compete globally firms "need" workers to be as desperate and low-wage as possible; the benefits decrease since the funds transferred to the less affluent may be spent on imports. See John O'Connor, "From

Welfare Rights to Welfare Fights" (Ph.D. diss., University of Massachusetts, Amherst, 2002).

10. John Eatwell, "The International Origins of Unemployment," in *Managing the Global Economy*, ed. Jonathan Michie and John Grieve Smith (New York: Oxford University Press, 1995), p. 277. See also Crotty and Epstein, op. cit., p. 132.

11. Eatwell, op. cit., p. 279.

12. Probably the best data on and discussion of this are in Frank Levy, *The New Dollars and Dreams: American Incomes and Economic Change* (New York: Russell Sage Foundation, 1998), from which these figures are taken. Levy provides data for 1949 (p. 27), and 1973 and 1996 (p. 50); pp. 40–41 provide data on the equality of distribution over this period. I calculated the 1999 hypothetical using data from table 669 of the *Statistical Abstract of the United States: 2001*. Growth rates and increases in income were still higher in Europe and Japan. From 1973 to 1996, incomes for the bottom 40 percent of the population declined, but for the top 20 percent incomes increased by $20,900 or 37.4 percent, raising the Gini Coefficient from .356 to .425. Similar changes took place in Thatcher's Britain. All "average" comparisons are made using median family incomes.

13. Karl Marx and Frederick Engels, *The Communist Manifesto* (1848), in *Selected Works* (Moscow: Progress Publishers, 1970), pp. 38–40.

14. Ajit Singh and Ann Zammit, "Employment and Unemployment, North and South," in Michie

and Grieve, op. cit., p. 102, the source of much of the following information; more generally, the article is highly recommended.

15. David Denslow Jr. and William G. Tyler, *Perspectives on Poverty and Income Inequality in Brazil: An Analysis of the Changes During the 1970s*, World Bank Staff Working Papers No. 601 (Washington, D.C.: The World Bank, 1983), table A-1. These figures conceal huge urban-rural differences; in rural areas, only 15 percent had a television and 13 percent a refrigerator, but these were increases from 1.6 percent and 3.2 percent in 1970, not to mention 1950. Quotation from Singh and Zammit, op. cit., p. 102.

16. Eric Toussaint, *Your Money or Your Life! The Tyranny of Global Finance*, trans. Raghu Krishnan (London: Pluto Press, 1999), p. 125. Toussaint cites Robert S. McNamara, *One Hundred Countries, Two Billion People* (New York: Praeger, 1973).

17. Singh and Zammit, op. cit., p. 93.

18. *Statistical Abstract of the United States 1999*, p. 427, table 676; again the classification by degree of vulnerability to globalization is my own.

19. This and the following data on threats of closure come from Kate Bronfenbrenner, "Organizing in the NAFTA Environment: How Companies Use Free Trade to Stop Unions," *New Labor Forum* 1 (1997): 51–60. The quotation is from page 56.

20. Data from *Directory of U.S. Labor Organizations*, ed. Court Gifford (Washington, D.C.: Bureau of National Affairs, 2000), pp. 250–51. ✦

6

Global Economy and Privileged Class

Robert Perrucci and Earl Wysong

One of the most important consequences of the new economy is the way it has changed the occupational structure, eliminating manufacturing jobs in the auto, rubber, steel, and textile industries and expanding a wide array of service jobs in lower-wage sectors of restaurant, hotel, and hospital maintenance employees. This chapter continues the examination of globalization that was introduced in chapter 5. The authors look at the global economy and ask: "Cui bono?" Or "Who benefits?" Their answer is that people in the privileged classes (owners, upper-level managers, upper-level professionals) have benefited at the expense of the working classes. The new global economy began going full steam ahead in the mid-1970s, and for the next 30 years U.S. corporations closed or reduced production in domestic plants and shipped production and jobs overseas. They also eliminated many middle-management and white-collar jobs while outsourcing many of these jobs to workers in other countries. The result was the loss of millions of relatively high-wage jobs in manufacturing and management and the creation of millions of low-wage jobs in the service sector. As a consequence, there was a shrinking of the middle class, which had once enjoyed secure jobs with growing wages and benefits. With the erosion of the middle class, American society is left with a two-class structure of 20 percent in the privileged class, with high wages and benefits and job security, and 80 percent in the working class,

with insecure jobs, modest-to-low wages, no benefits, and no prospects for upward growth.

* * *

Allowing the defenders of privilege to monopolize the term "globalization" for their own vision too easily allows them to portray themselves as agents of an impersonal process and to paint advocates of global justice as narrow specialists or naive opponents of technological progress.

—Salih Booker and William Minter, *Nation*, July 9, 2001

In 2001, record layoffs led to the worst U.S. job market since the recession of 1990–91. In the period from January to June, 2001, U.S. companies announced 652,510 layoffs. From manufacturing to high-tech, workers lost jobs at the fastest rate in years. Although the 2001 job cuts were dramatic, they were merely the latest chapter in what has been a long story for U.S. workers. Twenty years earlier we followed 850 workers through what has since become an all-too-familiar pattern for millions of workers.

On December 1, 1982, an RCA television cabinet-making factory in Monticello, Indiana closed its doors and shut down production. Monticello, a town of five thousand people in White County (population twenty-three thousand), had been the home of RCA since 1946. The closing displaced 850 workers who were members of Local 3154 of The United Brotherhood of Carpenters and Joiners. Officials at RCA cited the high manufacturing costs and foreign competition as key factors leading to the closing.

Reactions of displaced workers from RCA were varied, with most expressing either a general sense of despair or a feeling of confidence that they would survive. One worker was hopeful, stating: "Losing one's job is a serious jolt to your attitude of security, preservation, and well-being. However, I feel strongly that we must look forward to hope and faith in our country and its people. Deep inside I want to believe that tough times won't last, but tough people do. This will mean a lot of sacrifice, determination, and change in those people affected by losing one's job." Less hopeful views are revealed in the following remarks:

We are down to rock bottom and will probably have to sell the house to live or exist until I find a job here or somewhere else. I have been everywhere looking in Cass, White, and Carroll counties. We have had no help except when the electric company was going to shut off the utilities in March and the Trustee [County Welfare] paid that $141. My sister-in-law helps us sometimes with money she's saved back or with food she canned last summer. The factories have the young. I've been to all the factories. (Personal interviews with RCA workers.)

Whether the personal response to the closing was faith, fear, or anger, the common objective experience of the displaced workers was that they had been "dumped" from the "middle class." These displaced factory workers viewed themselves as middle class because of their wages and their lifestyles (home ownership, cars, vacations). Most had worked at RCA for two decades or more. They had good wages, health care benefits, and a pension program. They owned their homes (with mortgages), cars, recreational vehicles, boats, and all the household appliances associated with middle-class membership. All the trappings of the American Dream were threatened as their seemingly stable jobs and secure incomes disappeared. In the space of a few months these workers and their families joined the growing new working class—the 80 percent of Americans without stable resources for living.

The severity of this jolt to their sense of well-being and their "downward slide" is also revealed in the bleak picture displaced workers have of their future and the futures of their children: "I'm afraid it will be years before I get up the courage to buy a car, appliance, or anything on a long-term note,

regardless of how good the pay is in a new job"; "I have a National Honor Society daughter with one more year of high school. If she can't get aid there's no way she can go to college." (Personal interviews with RCA workers.)

The experiences of the 850 RCA workers from Monticello, Indiana, were part of a national wave of plant closings that swept across the land two decades ago. According to a study commissioned by the U.S. Congress, between the late 1970s and mid-1980s more than 11 million workers lost jobs because of plant shutdowns, relocation of facilities to other countries, or layoffs. Most of these displaced workers were in manufacturing. Subsequent displaced worker surveys commissioned by the Bureau of Labor Statistics estimated that between 1986 and 1991 another 12 million workers were displaced, but now they were predominantly from the service sector (about 7.9 million).[1] When these displaced workers found new jobs, it was often in industry sectors where wages were significantly lower than what they had earned and jobs were often part-time and lacked health insurance and other benefits.

Beginning in the mid-1970s and continuing to the present, the American class structure was being reshaped from the layer-cakelike "middle-class" society into the double-diamond structure with the top diamond being the privileged class and the bottom diamond the working class. The first step in this reshaping was a privileged-class-led attack on higher-wage unionized workers, eliminating their jobs in the auto industries, steel mills, rubber plants, and textile mills. The reshaping continued through the late 1980s to the mid-1990s, when the strategy was expanded to include not only plant closings and relocations, but "restructuring and downsizing" strategies as well, often directed at eliminating white-collar jobs.

The rush to downsize in some of America's largest and most prestigious corporations became so widespread in the 1990s that a new occupation was needed to handle the casualties. The "outplacement professional" was created to put the best corporate face on a decision to downsize, that is, to terminate large numbers of employees—as many as ten thousand. The job of these new public relations types is to get the general public to accept downsizing as the normal way of life for corporations that have to survive in the competitive global economy. Their job is also to assist the downsized middle managers to manage their anger and to get on with their lives.

The *Human Resources Development Handbook* of the American Management Association provides the operating philosophy for the outplacement professional: "Unnecessary personnel must be separated from the company if the organization is to continue as a viable business entity. To do otherwise in today's globally competitive world would be totally unjustified and might well be a threat to the company's future survival."[2]

The privileged 20 percent of the population are hard at work telling the other 80 percent about the harsh realities of the changing global economy. "Lifetime employment" is out. The goal is "lifetime employability," which workers try to attain by accumulating skills and being dedicated and committed employees. Even Japan's highly touted commitment to lifetime employment (in some firms) is apparently unraveling, as reported in a prominent feature article in the *New York Times*.[3] It should be no surprise that an elite media organization like the *Times*, whose upper-level employees belong to the privileged class, should join in disseminating the myth of the global economy as the "hidden hand" behind the downsizing of America. The casualties of plant closings and downsizings are encouraged to see their plight as part of the "natural laws" of economics.

This enormous transformation of the U.S. economy over a thirty-year period has been described by political leaders and media as the inevitable and therefore normal workings of the emerging global economy. Some, like former president Reagan, even applauded the changes as a historic opportunity to revitalize the economy. In a 1985 report to Congress, he stated, "The progression of an economy such as Amer-

ica's from the agricultural to manufacturing to services is a natural change. The move from an industrial society toward a postindustrial service economy has been one of the greatest changes to affect the developed world since the Industrial Revolution."[4]

A contrasting view posits that the transformation of the U.S. economy is not the result of natural economic laws or the "hidden hand" of global economic markets but, rather, the result of calculated actions by multinational corporations to expand their profits and power. When corporations decide to close plants and move them overseas where they can find cheap labor and fewer government regulations, they do so to enhance profits and not simply as a response to the demands of global competition. In many cases, the U.S. multinationals themselves are the global competition that puts pressure on other U.S. workers to work harder, faster, and for lower wages and fewer benefits.

The Global Economy and Class Structure

Markets, which in mainstream ideology are as natural as gravity, have frequently been created and deepened through coercive state action—ranging from enclosures (the privatization of common lands) in Britain hundreds of years ago to NAFTA's eviction of Mexican peasants from their land today.

—Doug Henwood, *In These Times*, September 30, 1996

Discussion about the new global economy by mainstream media reporters and business leaders generally focuses on three topics. First is the appearance of many new producers of quality goods in parts of the world that are normally viewed as less developed. Advances in computer-based production systems have allowed many countries in Southeast Asia and Latin America to produce goods that compete with those of more advanced industrial economies in Western Europe and North America. Second is the development of telecommunications systems that permit rapid economic transactions around the globe and the coordination of economic activities in locations separated by thousands of miles. The combination of advances in computer-based production and telecommunications makes it possible for large firms, especially multinationals, to decentralize their production and locate facilities around the globe. Third is the existence of an international division of labor that makes it possible for corporations to employ engineers, technicians, or production workers from anywhere in the world. This gives corporations great flexibility when negotiating with their domestic workforce over wages and benefits. These changes in how we produce things and who produces them have resulted in expanded imports and exports and an enlarged role for trade in the world economy. Leading this expansion has been increased foreign investments around the world by the richer nations. It is estimated that two-thirds of international financial transactions have taken place within and between Europe, the United States, and Japan.[5]

The changes just noted are often used as evidence of a "new global economy" *out there* constraining the actions of all corporations to be competitive if they hope to survive. One concrete indicator of this global economy *out there* is the rising level of international trade between the United States and other nations. In the 1960s, the United States was the dominant exporter of goods and services, while the imports of foreign products played a small part in the U.S. economy. Throughout the 1970s foreign imports claimed an increasing share, and by 1981 the United States "was importing almost 26 percent of its cars, 25 percent of its steel, 60 percent of its televisions, tape recorders, radios, and phonographs, 43 percent of its calculators, 27 percent of its metal-forming machine tools, 35 percent of its textile machinery, and 53 percent of its numerically controlled machine tools."[6] Imports from developing nations went

from \$3.6 billion in 1970 to \$30 billion in 1980.

Throughout the 1980s, the United States became a debtor nation in terms of the balance between what we exported to the rest of the world and what we import. By 2000, the U.S. trade deficit indicated that the import of goods and services exceeded exports by \$370 billion. This is the largest deficit since the previous high in 1987 of \$153.4 billion. But what do these trade figures tell us? On the surface, they appear to be a function of the operation of the global economy, because the figures indicate that we have an \$81.3 billion deficit with Japan, \$83.8 billion with China, and \$24.9 billion with Mexico.[7] It appears that Japanese, Chinese, and Mexican companies are doing a better job of producing goods than the United States and thus we import products rather than producing them ourselves. But is this the correct conclusion? The answer lies in how you count imports and exports.

Trade deficit figures are based on balance of payment statistics, which tally the dollar value of U.S. exports to other countries and the dollar value of foreign exports to the United States; if the dollar value of Chinese exports to the United States exceeds the dollar value of U.S. exports to China, the United States has a trade deficit with China. This would appear to mean that Chinese companies are producing the goods being exported to the United States. But that is not necessarily the case. According to the procedures followed in calculating trade deficits, "the U.S. balance of payments statistics are intended to capture the total amount of transactions between U.S. *residents* and *residents* of the rest of the world."[8] If "resident" simply identifies the geographical location of the source of an import, then some unknown portion of the \$49.7 billion U.S. trade deficit with China could be from U.S.-owned firms that are producing goods in China and exporting them to the United States. Those U.S. firms are residents of China, and their exports are counted as Chinese exports to the United States.

Thus, the global economy that is *out there* forcing U.S. firms to keep wages low so we can be more competitive might actually be made up of U.S. firms that have located production plants in countries other than the United States. Such actions may be of great benefit to the U.S. multinational firms that produce goods around the world and export them to the U.S. market. Such actions may also benefit U.S. consumers, who pay less for goods produced in low-wage areas. But what about the U.S. worker in a manufacturing plant whose wages have not increased in twenty years because of the need to compete with "foreign companies"? What about the worker who may never get a job in manufacturing because U.S. firms have been opening plants in other countries rather than in the United States? As the comic strip character Pogo put it: "We have met the enemy and it is us."

American multinational corporations' foreign investments have changed the emphasis in the economy from manufacturing to service. This shift has changed the occupational structure by eliminating high-wage manufacturing jobs and creating a two-tiered system of service jobs. There have been big winners and big losers in this social and economic transformation. The losers have been the three out of four Americans who work for wages—wages that have been declining since 1973; these American workers constitute the new working class. The big winners have been the privileged classes, for whom jobs and incomes have expanded at the same time that everyone else was in decline. Corporate executives, managers, scientists, engineers, doctors, corporate lawyers, accountants, computer programmers, financial consultants, health care professionals, and media professionals have all registered substantial gains in income and wealth in the last thirty years. And the changes that have produced the "big losers" and "big winners" have been facilitated by the legislative actions of the federal government and elected officials of both political parties, whose incomes, pensions, health care, and associated "perks" have also grown handsomely in the past two decades.

This chapter demonstrates that the privileged classes have benefited at the expense of the working classes. The profits of corporations and stockholders have expanded because fewer workers produce more goods and services for lower wages. The profits of corporations are distributed to executives, managers, and professionals in higher salaries and benefits because they are able either to extract more work from workers while paying them less, or to justify inequality by providing distracting entertainment for the less fortunate, or control them if necessary. The privileged class is able to maintain its position of advantage because its members control the jobs and incomes of other Americans. They also control the mass media and education, which are the instruments of ideological domination. If all of this is not enough, they also control the means of violence (military, national guard, police, and the investigative and security apparatus) that are used to deal with large-scale dissent.

Creating the Global Economy: The Path to Corporate Profits

We have entered the era of Empire, a "supranational" center consisting of networks of transnational corporations and advanced capitalist nations led by the one remaining superpower, the United States.

—Michael Hardt and Antonio Negri, *Empire*, 2000

When World War II ended in 1945, all but one of the industrial nations involved had experienced widespread destruction of their industrial system and the infrastructure that is necessary for a healthy economy to provide sufficient food, shelter, and clothing for its people. Although all nations that participated in the war suffered terrible human losses, the United States alone emerged with its economic system stronger than it was at the start of the war.

For nearly thirty years following World War II, the United States dominated the world economy through its control of three-fourths of the world's invested capital and two-thirds of its industrial capacity. At the close of the war, there was concern in the United States that the high levels of production, profits, and employment stimulated by war mobilization could not be sustained. The specter of a return to the stagnation and unemployment experienced only a decade earlier during the Great Depression led to the search for a new economic and political system that would maintain the economic, military, and political dominance of the United States.

The postwar geopolitical-economic policy of the United States was designed to provide extensive foreign assistance to stimulate the recovery of Western Europe. This policy would stimulate U.S. investment in Europe and provide the capital for countries to buy U.S. agricultural and industrial products. The policy was also designed to "fight" the creation of socialist governments and socialist policies in Western Europe, governments that might not be sympathetic to U.S. capital, trade, and influence. The foreign assistance policy known as the Marshall Plan was instituted to provide $22 billion in aid over a four-year period and to bring together European nations into a global economic system dominated by the United States.[9]

This system was the basis for U.S. growth and prosperity during the 1950s, the 1960s, and the early 1970s. By the mid-1970s, steady improvements in the war-torn economies of Western Europe and Asia had produced important shifts in the balance of economic power among industrialized nations. The U.S. gross national product was now less than twice that of the Soviet Union (in 1950 it was more than three times), less than four times that of Germany (down from nine times in 1950), and less than three times that of Japan (twelve times in 1950). With many nations joining the United States in the production of the world's goods, the U.S. rate of growth slowed. As England, France, Germany, and Japan produced goods for domestic consumption, there was less need to import ag-

ricultural and industrial products from the United States.

The profits of U.S. corporations from the domestic economy were in a steady decline through the late 1960s and into the 1970s. In the early 1960s the annual rate of return on investment was 15.5 percent. In the late 1960s it was 12.7 percent. In the early 1970s it was 10 percent, and after 1975 it slipped below 10 percent, where it remained.

The privileged classes in the United States were concerned about declining profits. This affected their accumulation of wealth from stocks, bonds, dividends, and other investments. It affected corporate, managerial, and professional salaries indirectly, through the high rate of inflation that eroded the purchasing power of consumption capital (i.e., salaries) and the real value of investment capital (i.e., value of stocks, bonds, etc.). To account for the U.S. decline, business leaders and the national media listed the usual suspects.

The leading "explanation" was that U.S. products could not compete in the global economy because of the power of organized labor. This power was reflected in the high labor costs that made products less competitive and in cost-of-living adjustments that increased wages at the rate of inflation (which was sometimes at double digits). Union control of work rules also made it difficult for management to adopt new innovations to increase productivity and reduce dependence on labor.

Next on the list was the American worker, who was claimed to have embraced a declining work ethic, resulting in products of lower quality and higher cost. U.S. workers were portrayed as too content and secure and thus unwilling to compete with the ambitious workers of the rapidly developing economies.

The third suspect was the wide array of new regulations on business that had been adopted by the federal government to protect workers and the environment. Corporate executives complained about the increased cost of doing business that came from meeting the workplace standards of the Occupational Safety and Health Administration (OSHA) or the air and water pollution standards of the Environmental Protection Agency (EPA).

The explanations business leaders put forth for declining profits—selfish unions, lazy workers, and government regulations were said to make American products less competitive in the global economy. They provided the rationale for an attack on unions and on workers' wages and helped to justify massive plant closings and capital flight to low-wage areas. They also served to put the government on the defensive for its failure to be sensitive to the "excessive" costs that federal regulations impose on business.

What was rarely discussed in the business pages of the *New York Times* or the *Wall Street Journal* was the failure of corporate management in major U.S. firms to respond to the increasing competition to the once U.S.-dominated production of autos, steel, textiles, and electronics. In the early 1960s, imports of foreign products played a small part in the American economy, but by 1980 things had changed. In the early 1960s, imports accounted for less than 10 percent of the U.S. market, but by 1980 more than 70 percent of all the goods produced in the United States were actively competing with foreign-made goods.[10]

American corporations failed to follow the well-established management approach to the loss of market share, competitive advantage, and profits. Instead of pursuing long-term solutions, like investing in more efficient technology, new plants, research and development, and new markets, corporate executives chose to follow short-term strategies that would make the bottom line of profits the primary goal. The way was open for increased foreign investment, mergers, and downsizing.

When Your Dog Bites You

With industrial jobs shrinking in the United States, and so much of what we buy, from clothing to electronics to auto-

mobiles, now made abroad, a common perception is that "globalized" production is a primary cause of falling living standards for American workers.

—Richard B. DuBoff, *Dollars and Sense,*
September–October 1997

While corporate profits from the domestic U.S. economy were declining steadily from the mid-1970s, investment by U.S. corporations abroad showed continued growth. The share of corporate profits from direct foreign investment increased through the 1970s, as did the amount of U.S. direct investment abroad. In 1970, direct investment by U.S. firms abroad was $75 billion, and it rose to $167 billion in 1978. In the 1980–85 period it remained below $400 billion, but thereafter increased gradually each year, reaching $716 billion in 1994. The 100 largest U.S. multinational corporations reported foreign revenue in 1994 that ranged from 30 to 70 percent of their total revenue: IBM had 62 percent of total revenue from foreign sources; Eastman Kodak 52 percent; Colgate-Palmolive 68 percent; and Johnson and Johnson, Coca Cola, Pepsi, and Procter and Gamble each 50 percent.[11]

American multinational corporations sought to maintain their profit margins by increasing investments in affiliates abroad. This strategy may have kept stockholders happy, and maintained the price of corporate stocks on Wall Street, but it would result in deindustrialization—the use of corporate capital for foreign investment, mergers, and acquisitions rather than for investment in domestic operations.[12] Instead of investing in the U.S. auto, steel, and textile industries, companies were closing plants at an unprecedented rate and using the capital to open production facilities in other countries. By 1994, U.S. companies employed 5.4 million people abroad, more than 4 million of whom worked in manufacturing.[13] Thus, millions of U.S. manufacturing workers who were displaced in the 1980s by plant closings saw their jobs shifted to foreign production facilities. Although most criticism of U.S. investment abroad is reserved for low-wage countries like Mexico and Thailand, the biggest share of manufacturing investment abroad is in Germany and Japan—hardly low-wage countries. The United States has large trade deficits with Japan and Western Europe, where the hourly wages in manufacturing are 15–25 percent higher than in the United States.[14] This fact challenges the argument made by multinational corporations that if they did not shift production abroad, they would probably lose the sale of that product.

The movement of U.S. production facilities to foreign countries in the 1980s and 1990s was not simply the result of a search for another home where they could once again be productive and competitive. It appeared as if RCA closed its plant in Monticello, Indiana, because its high-wage workers made it impossible to compete with televisions being produced in Southeast Asia. Saddened by having to leave its home in Indiana of thirty-five years, RCA would have to search for another home where, it was hoped, the company could stay at least another thirty-five years, if not longer. Not likely. Plants did not close in the 1980s to find other homes; the closures were the first step in the creation of the homeless and stateless multinational corporation— an entity without ties to place, or allegiances to people, communities, or nations.

Thus, the rash of plant closings in the 1970s and 1980s began as apparent responses to economic crises of declining profits and increased global competition. As such, they appeared to be rational management decisions to protect stockholder investments and the future of individual firms. Although things may have started in this way, it soon became apparent that what was being created was the *spatially decentered firm:* a company that could produce a product with components manufactured in a half-dozen different plants around the globe and then assembled at a single location for distribution and sale. Although spatially decentered, the new transnational firm was also centralized in its decision making, allowing it to coordinate

decisions about international investment. The new firm and its global production system were made possible by significant advances in computer-assisted design and manufacturing that made it unnecessary to produce a product at a single location. They were also made possible by advances in telecommunications that enabled management at corporate headquarters to coordinate research, development, design, manufacturing, and sales decisions at various sites scattered around the world.

The homeless and stateless multinational firm is able to move its product as quickly as it can spot a competitive advantage associated with low wages, cheaper raw materials, advantageous monetary exchange rates, more sympathetic governments, or proximity to markets. This encourages foreign investment because it expands the options of corporations in their choice of where to locate, and it makes them less vulnerable to pressure from workers regarding wages and benefits.

The advantages of the multinational firm and foreign investments are also a product of the U.S. tax code. In addition to providing the largest firms with numerous ways to delay, defer, and avoid taxes, corporate profits made on overseas investments are taxed at a much lower rate than profits from domestic operations. Thus, as foreign investments by U.S. firms increased over the last two decades, the share of total taxes paid by corporations declined. In the 1960s, corporations in the United States paid about 25 percent of all federal income taxes, and in 1991 it was down to 9.2 percent. A 1993 study by the General Accounting Office reported that more than 40 percent of corporations with assets of more than $250 million either paid no income tax or paid less than $ 100,000.[15] Another study of 250 of the nation's largest corporations reported that in 1998, twenty-four of the corporations received tax rebates totaling $1.3 billion, despite reporting U.S. profits before taxes of $12.0 billion. A total of forty-one corporations paid less than zero federal income tax in at least one year from 1996 to 1998, despite reporting a total of

$25.8 billion in pretax profits.[16] In testimony before the Committee on the Budget of the U.S. House of Representatives, Ralph Nader reported that in fiscal year 1999 corporations received $76 billion in tax exclusions, exemptions, deductions, credits, and so forth, and that the estimates for the years 2000–2004 will reach $394 billion in corporate tax subsidies.[17]

Creating the New Working Class

They call this "global competitiveness," but that's globaloney. Call it by its real name: Class War.

—Jim Hightower, *Dollars and Sense*,
November–December 1997

When the large multinational firm closes its U.S. facilities and invests in other firms abroad or opens new facilities abroad, the major losers are the production workers who have been displaced and the communities with lower tax revenues and increased costs stemming from expanded efforts to attract new businesses. But this does not mean that the firms are losers, for they are growing and expanding operations elsewhere. This growth creates the need for new employees in finance, management, computer operations, information systems, and clerical work. The total picture is one of shrinking production plants and expanding corporate headquarters; shrinking blue-collar employee rolls and two-tiered expansion of high-wage professional-managerial and low-wage clerical positions.

Having been extraordinarily successful in closing U.S. plants, shifting investment and production abroad, and cutting both labor and labor costs (both the number of production workers and their wage-benefit packages), major corporations now turned their attention to saving money by cutting white-collar employees. In the 1990s, there were no longer headlines about "plant closings," "capital flight," or "deindustrialization." The new strategy was "downsizing," "rightsizing," "reengineering," or how to get the same amount of work done

with fewer middle managers and clerical workers.

When Sears, Roebuck and Company announced that it could cut 50,000 jobs in the 1990s (while still employing 300,000 people) its stock climbed 4 percent on the New York Stock Exchange. The day Xerox announced a planned cut of 10,000 employees, its stock climbed 7 percent. Eliminating jobs was suddenly linked with cutting corporate waste and increasing profits. Hardly a month could pass without an announcement by a major corporation of its downsizing plan. Tenneco Incorporated would cut 11,000 of its 29,000 employees. Delta Airlines would eliminate 18,800 jobs, Eastman Kodak would keep pace by eliminating 16,800 employees, and AT&T announced 40,000 downsized jobs, bringing its total of job cuts since 1986 to 125,000. Not to be outdone, IBM cut 180,000 jobs between 1987 and 1994. The practice continues into the new century; as reported in the *New York Times* (July 13, 2001), Motorola, Inc., announced on July 12, 2001, that it would cut 30,000 jobs in 2001. On that same day, although it reported an operating loss in the second quarter of eleven cents per share, Motorola stock rose by 16 percent.

Even the upscale, more prestigious banking industry joined in the rush to become "lean and mean." A total of ten bank mergers announced in 1995 would result in 32,400 jobs lost because of the new "efficiencies" that come with mergers. Even banks that were already successful in introducing "efficiencies" were not immune to continued pressure for more. Between 1985 and 1995, Chase Manhattan's assets grew by 38 percent (from $87.7 billion to $121.2 billion), and its workforce was reduced 28 percent, from 44,450 to 33,500 employees. Yet when Chase was "swallowed" by Chemical Banking Corporation in a merger, both banks announced further reductions totaling 12,000 people.

Job loss in the 1990s appeared to hit hardest at those who were better educated (some college or more) and better paid ($40,000 or more). Job loss aimed at production workers in the 1980s was "explained" by the pressures of global competition and the opportunities to produce in areas with lower-wage workers. The "explanation" for the 1990s downsizing was either new technology or redesign of the organization. Some middle managers and supervisors were replaced by new computer systems that provide surveillance of clerical workers and data entry jobs. These same computer systems also eliminate the need for many middle managers responsible for collecting, processing, and analyzing data used by upper-level decision makers.

Redesign of organizations was achieved by eliminating middle levels within an organization and shifting work both upward and downward. The downward shift of work is often accompanied by new corporate plans to "empower" lower-level workers with new forms of participation and opportunities for career development. All of this redesign reduced administrative costs and increased the workload for continuing employees.

Investors, who may have been tentative about the potential of profiting from the deindustrialization of the 1980s because it eroded the country's role as a manufacturing power, were apparently delighted by downsizing. During the 1990s and continuing beyond 2000, the stock market skyrocketed from below 3,000 points on the Dow Jones Industrial Average to 10,478 in mid-July 2001—an increase of almost 250 percent. The big institutional investors apparently anticipate that increasing profits would follow the broadly based actions of cutting the workforce.

Downsizing is often viewed by corporations as a rational response to the demands of competition and thereby a way to better serve their investors and ultimately their own employees. Alan Downs, in his book *Corporate Executions*, challenges four prevailing myths that justify the publicly announced layoffs of millions of workers.[18] First, downsizing firms do not necessarily wind up with a smaller workforce. Often, downsizing is followed by the hiring of new workers. Second, Downs questions the belief that downsized workers are often the least productive because their expertise is obsolete: According to his findings, increased productivity does not necessarily follow downsizing. Third, jobs lost to downsizing are not replaced with higher-skill, better-paying jobs. Fourth, the claim that companies become more profitable after downsizing, and that workers thereby benefit, is only half true—many companies that downsize do report higher corporate profits and, as discussed earlier, often achieve higher valuations of their corporate stock. But there is no evidence that these profits are being passed along to employees in the form of higher wages and benefits.

After challenging these four myths, Downs concludes that the "ugly truth" of downsizing is that it is an expression of corporate self-interest to lower wages and increase profits. This view is shared by David Gordon, who documents the growth of executive, administrative, and managerial positions and compensation during the period when "downsizing" was at its highest.[19] Gordon describes bureaucratic "bloat" as part of a corporate strategy to reduce the wages of production workers and increase and intensify the level of managerial supervision. Slow wage growth for production workers and top-heavy corporate bureaucracies reinforce each other, and the combination produces a massive shift of money out of wages and into executive compensation and profits. This "wage squeeze" occurred not only in manufacturing (because of global competition) but also in mining, construction, transportation, and retail trade.[20] Although it is to be expected that foreign competition will have an impact on wages in manufacturing, it should not affect the nontrade sector to the same extent. Thus, the "wage squeeze" since the mid-1970s that increased income and wealth inequality in the United States is probably the result of a general assault on workers' wages and benefits rather than a response to global competition.

The impact of these corporate decisions on the working class was hidden from public view by the steady growth of new jobs in the latter part of the 1990s, and by the relatively low rate of unemployment. In his second term in office, President Clinton made frequent mention of the high rate of job creation (without mentioning that they were primarily low-wage service jobs) and the historically low unemployment rate. Unfortunately, the official rate of unemployment can hide the real facts about the nation's economic health. For example, an unemployment rate of 4.2 percent in 1999 excludes part-time workers who want full-time work, and discouraged workers who have given up looking. If these workers are added to the unemployed we have an "underemployment rate" of 7.5 percent, or about 10.5 million workers. The official unemployment rate also hides the fact that unemployment for Black Americans was 8.0 percent in 1999, or that in urban areas there were pockets of unemployment that approached 25 percent.[21]

Thus, the result of more than a decade of plant closings and shifting investment abroad, and less than a decade of downsizing America's largest corporations, has been the creation of a protected privileged class and a working class with very different conditions of employment and job security. The three major segments of the working class are core workers, temporary workers, and contingent workers.

Core Workers

Core workers are employees possessing the skills, knowledge, or experience that are essential to the operation of the firm. Their income levels place them in the "comfort class." They are essential for the firm, regardless of how well it might be doing from the standpoint of profits and growth; they are simply needed for the firm's continuity. Being in the core is not the same as being in a particular occupational group. A firm may employ many engineers and scientists, only some of whom might be considered to be in the core. Skilled blue-collar workers may also be in the core. Core employees have the greatest job security with their employing organizations; they also have skills and experiences that can be "traded" in the external labor market if their firm should

experience an unforeseen financial crisis. Finally, core employees enjoy their protected positions precisely because there are other employees just like them who are considered temporary.

Temporary Workers

The employment of temporary workers is linked to the economic ups and downs that a firm faces. When sales are increasing, product demand is high, and profits match those of comparable firms, the employment of temporary workers is secure. When inventories increase, or sales decline sharply, production is cut back, and temporary employees are laid off or fired. The temporary workers' relationship to the firm is a day-to-day matter. There is no tacit commitment to these employees about job security and no sense that they "belong to the family."

A good example of the role of temporary workers is revealed in the so-called transplants—the Japanese auto firms like Toyota, Nissan, and Honda that have located assembly plants in Kentucky, Ohio, Michigan, Illinois, Indiana, and Tennessee. Each of these firms employs between two thousand and three thousand American workers in their plants, and they have made explicit no-layoff commitments to workers in return for high work expectations (also as a way to discourage unionization). However, in a typical plant employing 2,000 production workers, the no-layoff commitment was made to 1,200 hires at start-up time; the other 800 hires were classified as temporary. Thus, when there is a need to cut production because of weak sales or excessive inventory, the layoffs come from the pool of temporary workers rather than from the core workers. Sometimes these temporary workers are not even directly employed by the firm but are hired through temporary help agencies like Manpower. Employment through temporary help agencies doubled between 1982 and 1989, and doubled again between 1989 and 1999.[22] These temporary workers are actually contingent workers.

Contingent Workers

Workers in nonstandard employment arrangements (part time, temporary, independent contractors) are often described as contingent workers. Some of these workers, as noted earlier, are employees of an agency that contracts with a firm for their services. About one in four persons in the labor force is a contingent worker, that is, a temporary or part-time worker.[23] These workers can be clerk-typists, secretaries, engineers, computer specialists, lawyers, or managers. They are paid by the temp agency and do not have access to a company's benefit package of retirement or insurance programs. Many of the professionals and specialists who work for large firms via temp firms are often the same persons who were downsized by those same companies. The following experience of a downsized worker is an ironic example of how the contingent workforce is created.

> John Kelley, 48, had worked for Pacific Telesis for 23 years when the company fired·him in a downsizing last December. Two weeks later, a company that contracts out engineers to PacTel offered him a freelance job.
>
> "Who would I work for?" Kelley asked.
>
> "Edna Rogers," answered the caller.
>
> Kelley burst out laughing. Rogers was the supervisor who had just fired him. "That was my job," he explained. "You're trying to replace me with myself."[24]

These three groups of workers fit into the bottom part of the double-diamond class structure, and it is only the core workers who have even the slightest chance to make it into the privileged class. Core workers with potential to move up generally have the credentials, skills, or social capital to have long-term job security, or to start their own business, and therefore the possibility of having substantial consumption capital (a good salary) and capital for investment purposes. Let us now consider how the privileged class holds on to its advantaged position in the double-diamond class structure.

Care and Feeding of the Privileged Class

The federal government of 1997 is a very different creature from that of, say, 1977—more egregiously corrupt and sycophantic toward wealth, more glaringly repressive, and even less responsive to the needs of low- and middle-income people.

—Barbara Ehrenreich, *Nation*, November 17, 1997

Most people who are in the privileged class are born there, as the sons, daughters, and relatives of highly paid executives, professionals, and business owners. Of course, they do not view their "achievements" that way. As one comic once said of former President George Bush, "He woke up on second base and thought he'd hit a double." But some members of the privileged class have earned their places, whether by means of exceptional talent, academic distinctions, or years of hard work in transforming a small business into a major corporation. Regardless of how much effort was needed to get where they are, however, members of the privileged class work very hard to stay where they are. Holding on to their wealth, power, and privilege requires an organized effort by businessmen, doctors, lawyers, engineers, scientists, and assorted political officials. This effort is often cited to convince the nonprivileged 80 percent of Americans that the privileged are deserving of their "rewards" and that, in general, what people get out of life is in direct proportion to what they put in. This effort is also used to dominate the political process so that governmental policies, and the rules for making policy, will protect and advance the interests of the privileged class.

However, before examining the organized effort of the privileged class to protect its privilege, it is first necessary to examine how members of the privileged class convince one another that they are deserving. Even sons and daughters from the wealthiest families need to develop biographical "accounts" or "stories" indicating they are deserving. This may involve accounts of how they worked their way up the ladder in the family business, starting as a clerk but quickly revealing a grasp of the complexities of the business and obtaining recognition from others of their exceptional talent.

Even without the biographical accounts used by the privileged class to justify exceptional rewards, justification for high income is built into the structure of the organizations they join. In every organization—whether an industrial firm, bank, university, movie studio, law firm, or hospital—there are multiple and distinct "ladders" that locate one's position in the organization. New employees get on one of these ladders based on their educational credentials and work experience. There are ladders for unskilled employees, for skilled workers, and for professional and technical people with specialized knowledge. Each ladder has its own distinct "floor" and "ceiling" in terms of what can be expected regarding salary, benefits, and associated perks. In every organization, there is typically only one ladder that can put you in the privileged class, and this usually involves an advanced technical or administrative career line. This career line can start at entry levels of $70,000–80,000 annual compensation, with no upper limit beyond what the traffic will bear. These are the career ladders leading to upper executive positions providing high levels of consumption capital and opportunities for investment capital.

Claiming Turf

Many young attorneys, business school graduates, scientists, engineers, doctors, economists, and other professionals would like to get entry-level positions on these upper-level career ladders. In fact, there are probably many people who are qualified for entry positions in terms of their educational credentials and work experiences. So how are people selected from among the large number of qualified applicants for such desirable career opportunities? The

answer is simple: Once credential qualifications and experience are used to define the pool of eligible applicants, the choice of who gets the job depends on the applicants' social capital. We define social capital as the social ties that people have with members of their college, fraternity or sorority, ethnic group, or religious group. People get jobs through their social networks, which provide them with information about job openings and with references valuable to those doing the hiring.[25] These social networks are usually composed of persons with similar social backgrounds. A recent study examined the social backgrounds of persons in the highest positions in corporations, the executive branch of the federal government, and the military. Although there is increased diversity among leaders today compared with 1950 with respect to gender, ethnicity, and race, the "core group continues to be wealthy white Christian males, most of whom are still from the upper third of the social ladder. They have been filtered through a handful of elite schools of law, business, public policy, and international relations."[26]

A good illustration of how social capital works is found in a study of 545 top position holders in powerful organizations in the United States.[27] Ten institutional sectors were studied, including *Fortune* 500 industrial corporations, *Fortune* 300 nonindustrial corporations, labor unions, political parties, voluntary organizations, mass media, Congress, political appointees in the federal government, and federal civil servants. Within each sector, fifty top position holders were interviewed—persons who may be considered "elites in the institutional sectors that have broad impact on policy making and political processes in the U.S."[28] Although we have no information on the incomes and wealth of the 545 elites, it is very likely they would fit our definition as members of the privileged class.

Table 6.1 provides some of the findings from this study, which identify the ethnic-religious composition of elites and their distribution across different institutional sectors. As can be seen from the first line of the table, 43 percent of all the elites in the study were WASPs (Protestants with ancestry from the British Isles), 19.5 percent were Protestants from elsewhere in Europe, 8.5 percent were Irish Catholics, 8.7 percent were Catholics from elsewhere in Europe, 11.3 percent were Jews, and 3.9 percent were minorities (non-Whites and Hispanics). The second line indicates the percentage of the national population of men born before 1932 from different ethnic-religious backgrounds. The third line indicates the percent of the national population of college-educated men born before 1932 of each ethnic background. A comparison of line (1) with lines (2) and (3) shows the extent to which each ethnic-religious group may be overrepresented or underrepresented among the elites. Thus, WASPs and Jews are overrepresented among elites relative to their composition in the general population. The elite representation of other Protestants and Irish Catholics is comparable to their representation in the national population; and other Catholics and minorities are underrepresented among elites.

More interesting for our purposes are the overrepresentation and underrepresentation of elites in different institutional sectors. Overrepresentation would suggest the operation of social ties operating to get positions for persons with the same ethnic-religious background. White Anglo-Saxon Protestants are greatly overrepresented in business and in Congress. Irish Catholics are very overrepresented in labor and politics. Jews are sharply overrepresented in mass media, voluntary organizations, and federal civil service. This ethnic-religious overrepresentation indicates that social capital may be used to get access to career ladders leading to the privileged class. Moreover, there appears to be ethnic-religious specialization in the institutional sectors that they "colonize." People help to get jobs for relatives and friends, whether the job is for a Mexican immigrant in a Los Angeles sweat shop or a young Ivy League graduate in a Wall Street law firm. Parents invest their capital in an Ivy League education for a son or daughter, who then uses the social capital of family or school ties to enter a career path into the privileged class.

Securing Turf

After obtaining positions on career ladders that will make them members of the privileged class, our entry-level managers, attorneys, and faculty become aware of the

Table 6.1
Ethnic Representation Among Elites

	WASPs	Other Protestants	Irish Catholics	Other Catholics	Jews	Minorities	Probably WASPs
1. Overall elite	43.0	19.5	8.5	8.7	11.3	3.9	5.0
2. Men born before 1932	22.9	22.5	4.2	17.2	2.9	14.4	13.4
3. College-educated men born before 1932	31.0	19.8	6.0	15.5	8.9	5.2	10.3
4. Institutional sectors							
Business	57.3	22.1	5.3	6.1	6.9	0.0	2.3
Labor	23.9	15.2	37.0	13.0	4.3	2.2	4.3
Politcal parties	44.0	18.0	14.0	4.0	8.0	4.0	8.0
Voluntary organizations	32.7	13.5	1.9	7.7	17.3	19.2	7.7
Mass media	37.1	11.3	4.8	9.7	25.8	0.0	11.3
Congress	53.4	19.0	6.9	8.6	3.4	3.4	5.2
Political appointments	39.4	28.8	1.5	13.6	10.6	3.0	3.0
Civil service	35.8	22.6	9.4	9.4	15.1	3.8	3.8

Source: Alba and Moore (1982), table I.

very high incomes enjoyed by their senior colleagues. One response to these high salaries is to feel that they are unjustified and to exclaim, "Why should the President of the university make $300,000 a year when some of our professors with twenty years experience are making $60,000?" A second response is to recognize that the president's salary is used to justify the $230,000 salaries of the executive vice presidents, which in turn justify the $150,000 salaries of the deans, which in turn justify the $120,000 salaries of senior professors in selected fields. People in positions of power in organizations work together to justify their high salaries by creating beliefs about the need to be competitive in the market or to risk losing valuable people.

The second response is the typical one for people involved in career ladders that promise access to the privileged class. This response might be called symbiotic greed, where the parties are locked together in a mutually beneficial relationship. As the salary of the president rises, so do the salaries of all the others who are on the privileged-class career ladder. The rub is that only a small proportion of all the managers, attorneys, or faculty are on that career ladder, even though they may share the same educational credentials and work experience. This is a form of misguided self-interest, wherein low-level employees support the high salary of their superiors because of the belief that they may one day also have such a high salary.

Although it may seem surprising, members of the privileged class often feel that their incomes are far below what they deserve, or they feel relatively deprived in comparison to those above them in the income hierarchy. A recent story in the *New York Times* ("Well-Off but Still Pressed, Doctor Could Use Tax Cut")[29] provided thinly veiled support for President Bush's tax cut along with a sympathetic story of a surgeon earning $300,000 a year who says he does not feel rich. The good doctor, who lives in a $667,000 four-bedroom house with a pool, frets about his retirement, college tuition, and the anticipated cost of future weddings for his five daughters. More-

over, he is pained by the appearance of the new high-tech millionaires driving around in Porsches. The good doctor's wife exclaims, "We don't have the luxuries that you would think in this bracket," as she describes shopping at cheaper grocery stores and clipping coupons. The message of the article is that there are rich people and super rich people, and both would benefit from a tax cut. In short, you can never have too much money!

Now to the organized effort by businessmen, doctors, lawyers, and the like to protect the interests of the privileged class. This effort is revealed in three ways: (1) Members of the privileged class hold upper-level positions in all the major institutions of American society. These institutions control enormous resources that can be used to shape public awareness, the political process, and the nation's policy agenda. (2) The organizations to which the privileged class belong form associations in order to hire lobbyists, contribute to political campaigns, and shape legislation in their interests. (3) The members of the privileged class who are in professional occupations, like medicine and law, are represented by powerful professional associations that protect their members against any efforts by other groups to encroach on their "turf." Thus, the American Medical Association (AMA) makes sure that state legislatures continue to give doctors a monopoly over what they do by preventing nurses, or pharmacists, or chiropractors, or holistic practitioners from providing certain types of care to clients. Similarly, the American Bar Association acts to prevent paralegals from competing with lawyers in handling wills, estates, or certain types of litigation.

Not every segment of the privileged class is unified on all issues. Doctors are not pleased with the actions of attorneys when they vigorously pursue malpractice suits against doctors and hospitals. The AMA has urged Congress to pass legislation limiting the dollar amount of damages that might be awarded in malpractice claims. Lawyers resist such efforts because they make their living from obtaining 30 percent of the damage awards made to persons suing doctors or hospitals. Similarly, the banking industry and the large industrial corporations may differ on whether they would like to see the Federal Reserve Board raise or lower interest rates. Some sectors of the business community may support giving China special trade concessions, while others may be opposed.

Despite the differences and disagreements over specific policies by members of the privileged class, they are unified in their support for the rules of the game as they are currently played: The privileged class is unified in its view of how the political process should operate. Individuals and organizations should be free to lobby members of Congress on matters of interest to them. Individuals and organizations should be free to contribute money to political action committees and to political parties. And above all else, privileged-class members agree that business should be able to operate in a free and unregulated environment and that the country runs just fine with a two-party system.

Then there are the really big policy issues, where the "payoffs" are substantial to almost all segments of the privileged class. The North American Free Trade Agreement (NAFTA) and the General Agreement on Tariffs and Trade (GATT) were supported by Presidents Reagan, Bush, and Clinton and by a bipartisan majority of both houses of Congress. The new President George W. Bush took office in 2001 and proceeded to promote the so-called Free Trade Area for the Americas (FTAA), which would extend NAFTA throughout the Western Hemisphere. Taken together, NAFTA and FTAA represent the effort of the international privileged class to have countries in the Americas adopt economic policies to attract foreign investment, encourage "free trade," and restrict government efforts to protect the rights of workers. These agreements promise to advance the global economy and the continued pursuit of profits across the globe by multinational corporations.

The privileged class in the United States achieved major victories in the 1980s through their efforts to reduce government spending on a variety of social programs that benefit the working class. Using the scare tactics of budget deficits and the national debt, the privileged class supported a balanced budget agreement that required the president and Congress to reduce spending on welfare, education, Medicare, and Medicaid. In the 1990s, the privileged class turned its attention to the global economy by devising ways to protect opportunities for investment and profit around the globe. The main way to achieve this was to make it easy for large corporations to circle the globe in search of the best opportunities and thereby threaten workers everywhere so as to keep their wages and benefit demands at low levels. Facing the oft-repeated threat that there are "other" workers willing to do the same work for less money, the American working class has lived with declining earnings and disappearing health benefits and employer-provided pensions. And all this occurred during an eight-year economic recovery and a booming stock market!

During the 1990s, major U.S. and foreign corporations joined forces to lobby Washington policy makers to relax federal policies on international trade. This included granting most-favored nation trading status to China (with whom we have a high trade deficit) and passing the North American Free Trade Agreement, which eliminated trade barriers between the United States, Canada, and Mexico. Before the passage of NAFTA, the United States had a $1 billion trade surplus with Mexico, but the year following NAFTA that surplus had become a $16.2 billion deficit.[30]

To garner public support for free trade, President Clinton frequently pointed out that for every $1 billion in goods and services we export to other countries, we create 20,000 jobs at home. This may be true, but the problem is that it also works in reverse: for every $1 billion of goods that we import, we lose 20,000 jobs. And, as indicated earlier in this chapter, in 2000 the United States had a trade deficit of $370 billion with other countries.

Despite claims by officials in Canada, Mexico, and the United States that NAFTA has been a success, an analysis of the impact of NAFTA seven years after its adoption indicates that 766,000 actual and potential jobs have been eliminated in the United States "between 1994 and 2000 because of the rapid growth in the U.S. export deficit with Mexico and Canada."[31] Thus, we lose many more jobs than we create with our free-trade policies. But free trade is not about jobs; it is about profits for corporations and the privileged class.

Defending Turf

In February 1998 the *New York Times* published a two-page open letter to the Congress of the United States, entitled "A Time for American Leadership on Key Global Issues."[32] The letter expresses concern about "a dangerous drift toward disengagement from the responsibilities of global leadership." Congress is asked to approve new fast-track negotiating authority, which would extend NAFTA-like agreements to other countries in Latin America and around the globe, and to support the International Monetary Fund bailout of failed banks in Southeast Asia (although it failed to mention the benefit to U.S. banks and financial institutions that are heavily invested in those economies).

Signatories to this letter include two former presidents (Jimmy Carter and Gerald Ford), 42 former public officials (secretaries of defense, treasury, commerce, and state; CIA directors, national security advisers; U.S. senators), and eighty-eight corporate presidents and CEOs (of AT&T, Boeing, Amoco, Chase Manhattan Bank, IBM, Time Warner, Bank America, etc.). Many of the former public officials now work as lobbyists for the U.S. and foreign multinationals that "feed at the public trough" via tax loopholes and federal subsidies.

Why would these 132 members of the privileged class spend $100,000 for this two-page ad in the "Times"? Surely not to influence members of Congress. Corporations and the privileged class have more effective ways of doing that, such as the $3 million in campaign contributions by Philip Morris or the $2.5 million that

Chiquita Brands CEO Carl Linder gave to both political parties from 1993 to 1996. Perhaps the ad was designed to convince the working class to support fast-track legislation. Probably not. The circulation of the *New York Times* is about 1.6 million, and very few of those readers are from the working class. The most likely targets of the ad were the nationally scattered members of the privileged class that the elite leaders wanted to mobilize at the grass roots. The ad was designed to get the millions of privileged doctors, lawyers, journalists, managers, scientists, stock brokers, and media executives to mobilize public opinion through the hundreds of professional and business associations that represent their interests. The privileged class constitutes 20 percent of the population (about 14 million families), and when mobilized, it can represent a potent political force.

Opposition to the privileged-class agenda on the global economy is fragmented, and operates with limited resources. Critics of NAFTA and the GATT, like Ralph Nader and Jesse Jackson, can hardly stand up to the National Association of Manufacturers or the U.S. Chambers of Commerce. The opposition to NAFTA and the GATT voiced by reactionary populists Ross Perot and Pat Buchanan, who appeared to be "traitors" to the interests of the privileged class, was dealt with swiftly and sharply by the major media. Perot was given the persona of a quirky, eccentric millionaire who was trying to buy the presidency because he had nothing better to do with his time and money. Buchanan was vilified as a crypto-racist, anti-Semite, and general all-around loose cannon.

The attacks on Perot and Buchanan by academics and political commentators on media talk shows should not be surprising. Elite universities and the major media are controlled by the wealthy and corporate elite who are at the top of the privileged class. The major networks of ABC, CBS, NBC, Fox, and Turner Broadcasting determine what the overwhelming majority of Americans will receive as news and entertainment. Two of the major networks are owned by major multinational firms, and institutional investors control substantial percentages of stock in the networks.

Is it any wonder, therefore, that efforts to attack the status quo are immediately marginalized or co-opted? An example of this process was revealed during the Republican presidential primary in early 1996. Pat Buchanan was making his usual bombastic attacks on immigration, NAFTA, and the GATT when he suddenly started lobbing some grenades at the corporate elite while yelling about "corporate greed." Here are a few samples, from speeches made in February of 1996: "When AT&T lops off 40,000 jobs, the executioner that does it, he's a big hero on the cover of one of these magazines, and AT&T stock soars"; "Mr. Dole put the interest of the big banks—Citibank, Chase Manhattan, Goldman Sachs—ahead of the American People."[33]

When it appeared that Buchanan's reactionary populist attack on the corporate elite was striking a responsive chord among people on the campaign trail, the *New York Times* decided to take the extraordinary step of publishing a seven-part series, called "The Downsizing of America," which ran from March 3 through March 9, 1996. Some might call this a major public service by the *Times*, designed to inform Americans about an important issue. Others might say it was a clever effort to take the issue out of Buchanan's hands and to shape it and frame it in ways that would deflect the criticisms and attacks on the corporate elite. The *Times* series did not point an accusing finger at corporate America for the loss of millions of jobs. If anything, the series made the reader either feel sorry for everyone, including the "guilt-ridden" managers who had to fire workers ("Guilt of the Firing Squads"), or to blame everyone, including downsized workers. In an extraordinary example of blaming the victim, consider the following "explanation" for downsizing. "The conundrum is that what companies do to make themselves secure is precisely what makes their workers feel insecure. And because workers are heavily represented among the 38 million Americans who own mutual funds, they unwittingly contribute to the very pressure from Wall Street that could take away their salaries even as it improves their investment income."[34]

The *New York Times* series did not help its readers to understand who benefits from downsizing, but it did help to defuse the issue and to take it out of the hands of those who might be critical of corporate America. It is an example of the pacification of everyday life.

Resistance to the Global Economy

The rules created by NAFTA are imbalanced; they encourage capital mobility by extending trinational protection to investors while protections for workers and the environment are left to national governments. . . . One result has been a rise in inequality and insecurity among working people.

—Jeff Faux, *Nation*, May 28, 2001

In this chapter we have tried to provide a glimpse of the meaning of the bogeyman global economy. The term has been used to threaten workers and unions and to convince everyone that they must work harder if they want to keep their jobs. The global economy is presented as if it is *out there* and beyond the control of the corporations, which must continually change corporate strategies in order to survive in the fiercely competitive global economy. It is probably more accurate to view the current global economy as an accelerated version of what U.S. financial and industrial corporations have been doing since the end of World War II—roaming the globe in search of profits. The big change is that since the 1980s, U.S. firms have found it easier to invest overseas. They have used this new opportunity to create new international agreements like NAFTA and FTAA that attack organized labor and threaten workers to keep their wage demands to a minimum. In this view, the global economy is composed primarily of U.S. companies investing abroad and exporting their products to the United States (as the largest consumer market in the world) and other countries. These multinational corporations have an interest in creating the fiction that the global economy is some abstract social development driven by "natural laws" of economics, when it is actually the product of the deliberate actions of 100 or so major corporations.

There has been growing popular opposition to the international accords that are creating the new global economy. In December of 1999 the so-called Battle in Seattle signaled the growing resistance to globalization. Tens of thousands protested against the World Trade Organization's "free trade" agenda that would threaten U.S. workers' jobs and wages, and provide little protection against environmental damage. Protesters were confronted by police using pepper spray and tear gas to prevent disruption of the WTO meeting.[35] On April 20–22, 2001, the Third Summit Meeting of the Americas took place in Quebec City, Canada. Heads of state from thirty-four countries in the Americas (Cuba was excluded) assembled for negotiations on the so-called Free Trade Agreement for the Americas. Once again, tens of thousands demonstrated against this new effort to make it easier for international finance capital and multinational corporations to control the global economy.[36]

The resistance that took place in Seattle and Quebec City (as well as in Washington, D.C., and Davos, Switzerland) reveals the operation of the Alternative Power Network. Groups representing labor, environmentalists, anti-sweatshop campaigns, and human rights activists came together to challenge the international agreements that provide few protections for working people throughout the Americas. They are calling for trade agreements that protect the rights of workers to a living wage, regulations on the behavior of multinational corporations and international finance capital, and consideration of environmental protections consistent with economic and social development.

The problem posed by the global economy is that it has increased the influence of large corporations over the daily lives of most Americans. This influence is revealed in corporate control over job growth and job loss, media control of information, and the role of big money in the world of national politics. At the same time that this growing influence is revealed on a daily basis, it has become increasingly clear that the major corporations have abandoned any sense of allegiance to, or special responsibilities toward, American workers and their communities.

This volatile mix of increasing influence and decreasing responsibility has produced the double-diamond class structure, where one in five Americans is doing very well indeed, enjoying the protection that comes with high income, wealth, and social contacts. Meanwhile, the remaining four out of five Americans are exploited and excluded.

Discussion Questions

1. Some scholars argue that inequality will often be accepted as long as there is opportunity for upward mobility for the younger generation. Do you agree?

2. Do you think that a two-class society is more politically unstable than a five- or six-class society?

3. What is the role of higher education with regard to globalization?

From Robert Perrucci and Earl Wysong, "Global Economy and Privileged Class," in *The New Class Society: Goodbye American Dream?* 2nd ed. (Lanham, MD: Rowman and Littlefield, 2003, pp. 91–118). Used by permission.

Endnotes

1. Office of Technology Assessment, *Technology and Structural Unemployment* (Washington, D.C.: Congress of the United States, 1986); Thomas S. Moore, *The Disposable Work Force* (New York: Aldine de Gruyter, 1996).
2. Joel Bleifuss, "The Terminators," *In These Times*, March 4, 1996, 12–13.
3. Sheryl Wu Dunn, "When Lifetime Jobs Die Prematurely: Downsizing Comes to Japan, Fraying Old Workplace Ties," *New York Times*, June 12, 1996.

4. John Miller and Ramon Castellblanch, "Does Manufacturing Matter?" *Dollars and Sense,* October 1988.

5. Noam Chomsky, *The Common Good* (Monroe, Me.: Common Courage Press, 2000).

6. Robert B. Reich, *The Next American Frontier* (New York: Times Books, 1983).

7. U.S. Bureau of the Census, Foreign Trade Division, Washington, D.C. 20233, 2000.

8. John Pomery, "Running Deficits with the Rest of the World—Part 1," *Focus on Economic Issues,* Purdue University (Fall 1987). (Emphasis added.)

9. For an extended discussion, see Michael Stohl and Harry R. Targ, *Global Political Economy in the 1980s* (Cambridge, Mass.: Schenkman, 1982).

10. Reich, *Next American Frontier.*

11. "The 100 Largest U.S. Multinationals," *Forbes,* July 17, 1995, 274–76.

12. Barry Bluestone and Bennett Harrison, *The Deindustrialization of America* (New York: Basic Books, 1982).

13. Louis Uchitelle, "U.S. Corporations Expanding Abroad at a Quicker Pace." *New York Times,* July 25, 1998.

14. David M. Gordon, *Fat and Mean: The Corporate Squeeze of Working Americans and the Myth of Managerial Downsizing* (New York: Free Press, 1996).

15. Richard J. Barnet and John Cavanagh, *Global Dreams: Imperial Corporations and the New World Order* (New York: Simon and Schuster, 1994).

16. Robert S. McIntyre, "Testimony on Corporate Welfare," U.S. House of Representatives Committee on the Budget, June 30, 1999. On the Internet at <http://www. ctj.org/html/corpwelf .htm> (visited June 25, 2001).

17. Ralph Nader, "Testimony on Corporate Welfare," U.S. House of Representatives Committee on the Budget, June 30, 1999. On the Internet at <www.nader.org/releases/63099 .html> (visited June 25, 2001).

18. Alan Downs, *Corporate Executions* (New York: AMACOM, 1995).

19. See Gordon, *Fat and Mean,* chap. 2.

20. Ibid., 191.

21. Lawrence Mishel, Jared Bernstein, and John Schmitt, *The State of Working America 2000– 2001* (Ithaca, N.Y.: Cornell University Press, 2001), 220; Marc Breslow, "Job Stats: Too Good to Be True," *Dollars and Sense,* September–October 1996, 51.

22. Mishel et al., op cit., 252.

23. Chris Tilly, *Half a Job: Bad and Good Part-Time Jobs in a Changing Labor Market* (Philadelphia: Temple University Press, 1996); Kevin D. Henson, *Just a Temp* (Philadelphia: Temple University Press, 1996).

24. Ann Monroe, "Getting Rid of the Gray," *Mother Jones,* July–August 1996, 29.

25. Mark Granovetter, *Getting a Job: A Study of Contacts and Careers* (Cambridge: Harvard University Press, 1974).

26. Richard L. Zweigenhaft and G. William Domhoff, *Diversity in the Power Elite: Have Women and Minorities Reached the Top?* (New Haven: Yale University Press, 1998), 6.

27. Richard D. Alba and Gwen Moore, "Ethnicity in the American Elite," *American Sociological Review* 47 (June 1982): 373–83.

28. Ibid., 374.

29. Jim Yardley, "Well-Off but Still Pressed, Doctor Could Use Tax Cut," *New York Times,* April 7, 2001: 1, A8.

30. Richard W. Stevenson, "U.S. to Report to Congress NAFTA Benefits Are Modest," *New York Times,* July 11, 1997.

31. Robert E. Scott, "NAFTA's Hidden Costs," *Economic Policy Institute,* Washington, D.C., May 21, 2001.

32. *New York Times,* February 11, 1998.

33. Francis X. Clines, "Fueled by Success, Buchanan Revels in Rapid-Fire Oratory," *New York Times,* February 15, 1996.

34. Louis Uchitelle and N. R. Kleinfield, "On Battlefield of Business, Millions of Casualties," *New York Times,* March 3, 1996.

35. Jim Phillips, "What Happens After Seattle?" *Dollars and Sense,* January–February 2000, 15–16, 31–32.

36. David Moberg, "Tear Down the Walls: The Movement Is Becoming More Global," *In These Times,* May 28, 2000, 11–14. ✦

7

The Price of Jobs Lost

Louis Uchitelle and
N. R. Kleinfield

In 1996, the *New York Times* published a nine-part, front-page series of articles on the dramatic changes that were taking place in the U.S. occupational structure. That series, entitled *The Downsizing of America*, was eventually published in a book of the same title, and this chapter, written by two *Times* reporters, is drawn from that book. Although the *New York Times* was a decade late in acknowledging the massive job loss that started in the mid-1970s with blue-collar workers, the loss of management jobs in the 1990s got their attention. The *Times* series put a front-page face on the tens of millions of workers who were the victims of plant closings, downsizings, and outsourcing of jobs to plants and workers in other countries. This chapter describes two waves of job loss. The first took place in the early 1980s, when the so-called "Rust Belt" factories in the auto, rubber, and steel industries were shutting down and eliminating millions of unionized manufacturing jobs paying about $30,000 per year (in 1994 dollars). The second wave took place in the early 1990s and hit the better-educated and better-paid white-collar workers across many industry sectors, including manufacturing, wholesale and retail trade, and public and private services.

Drive along the asphalt river of Interstate 95 across the Rhode Island border and into the pristine confines of Connecticut. Stop at that first tourist information center with its sheaves of brochures promising lazy delights. What could anyone possibly guess of

Steven A. Holthausen, the portly man behind the counter who dispenses the answers?

Certainly not that for two decades he was a loan officer whose salary had risen to $1,000 a week. Not that he survived three bank mergers only to be told, upon returning from a family vacation, that he no longer had his job. Not that his wife kicked him out and his children shunned him. Not that he slid to the bottom step of the economic ladder, pumping gas at a station owned by a former bank customer, being a guinea pig in a drug test and driving a car for a salesman who had lost his license for drunkenness. Not that, at *51*, he makes do on $1,000 a month as a tourist guide, a quarter of his earlier salary. And not that he is worried that his modest job is itself fragile, and that he may have to work next as a clerk in a brother's liquor store.

That, however, is his condensed story, and its true grimness lies in the simple fact that it is no longer at all extraordinary in America. "I did not realize on that day I was fired how big a price I would have to pay," Mr. Holthausen said in a near whisper.

More than 43 million jobs have been erased in the United States since 1979, according to a *New York Times* analysis of Labor Department numbers. Many of the losses come from the normal churning as stores fail and factories move. And far more jobs have been created than lost over that period. But increasingly the jobs that are disappearing are those of higher-paid, white-collar workers, many at large corporations, women as well as men, many at the peak of their careers. Like a clicking odometer on a speeding car, the number twirls higher nearly each day.

Peek into the living rooms of America and see how many are touched:

Nearly three-quarters of all households have had a close encounter with layoffs since 1980, according to a new poll by *The New York Times*. In one-third of all households, a family member has lost a job, and nearly 40 percent more know a relative, friend, or neighbor who was laid off.

One in 10 adults—or about 19 million people, a number matching the adult population of New York and New Jersey combined—acknowledged that a lost job in their household had precipitated a major crisis in their lives, according to the *Times* poll.

While permanent layoffs have been symptomatic of most recessions, now they are occurring in the same large numbers even during an economic recovery that has lasted five years and even at companies that are doing well.

In a reversal from the early 1980s, workers with at least some college education make up the majority of people whose jobs were eliminated, outnumbering those with no more than high school educations. And better-paid workers—those earning at least $50,000—account for twice the share of the lost jobs that they did in the 1980s.

Roughly 50 percent more people, about 3 million, are affected by layoffs each year than the 2 million victims of violent crimes (reported murders, rapes, robberies, and aggravated assaults). But while crime bromides get easily served up—more police, stiffer jail sentences—no one has come up with any broadly agreed upon antidotes to this problem. And until Patrick J. Buchanan made the issue part of the presidential campaign, it seldom surfaced in political debate.

Yet this is not a saga about rampant unemployment, like the Great Depression, but one about an emerging redefinition of employment. There has been a net increase of 27 million jobs in America since 1979, enough to easily absorb all the laid-off workers plus the new people beginning careers, and the national unemployment rate is low. The sting is in the nature of the replacement work. Whereas twenty-five years ago the vast majority of the people who were laid off found jobs that paid as well as their old ones, Labor Department numbers show that now only about 35 percent of laid-off, full-time workers end up in equally remunerative or better-paid jobs. Compounding this frustration are stagnant wages and an increasingly unequal distribution of wealth. Adjusted for inflation, the median wage is nearly three percent below what it was in 1979. Average household income climbed 10 percent between 1979 and 1994, but 97 percent of the gain went to the richest 20 percent.

The result is the most acute job insecurity since the Depression. And this in turn has produced an unrelenting angst that is shattering people's notions of work and self and the very promise of tomorrow, even as President Clinton proclaims in his State of the Union Message that the economy is "the healthiest it has been in three decades" and even as the stock market had rocketed to 81 new highs in the year ending March 1, 1996.

Driving much of the job loss are several familiar and intensifying stresses bearing down upon companies: stunning technological progress that lets machines replace hands and minds; efficient and wily competitors here and abroad; the ease of contracting out work; and the stern insistence of Wall Street on elevating profits even if it means casting off people. Cutting the payroll has appeal for gasping companies that resort to it as triage and to soundly profitable companies that try it as preventative medicine against a complicated future. The conundrum is that what companies do to make themselves secure is precisely what makes their workers feel insecure. And because workers are heavily represented among the 38 million Americans who own mutual funds, they unwittingly contribute to the very pressure from Wall Street that could take away their salaries even as it improves their investment income.

The job apprehension has intruded everywhere, diluting self-worth, splintering families, fragmenting communities, altering the chemistry of workplaces, roiling political agendas and rubbing salt on the very soul of the country. Dispossessed workers like Steven Holthausen are finding themselves on anguished journeys they never imagined, as if being forced to live the American dream of higher possibilities in reverse.

Many Americans have reacted by downsizing their expectations of material comforts and the sweetness of the future. In a nation where it used to be a given that children would do better than their parents, half of those polled by *The Times* thought it unlikely that today's youth would attain a higher standard of living than they have. What is striking is that this gloom may be even more emphatic among prosperous and well-educated Americans. A *Times* survey of the 1970 graduating class at Bucknell University, a college known as an educator of successful engineers and middle managers, found that nearly two-thirds doubted that today's children would live better. White-collar, middle-class Americans in mass numbers are coming to understand first hand the chronic insecurity on which the working class and the poor are experts.

All of this is causing a pronounced withdrawal from community and civic life. Visit Dayton, Ohio, a city fabled for its civic cohesion, and see the detritus. When Vinnie Russo left his job at National Cash Register and went to another city, the eighty-five boys of Pack 530 lost their cubmaster, and they still don't have a new one. Many people are too tired, frustrated or busy for activities they used to enjoy, like church choir.

The effects billow beyond community participation. People find themselves sifting for convenient scapegoats on which to turn their anger, and are adopting harsher views toward those more needy than themselves.

Those who have not lost their jobs and their identities, and do not expect to, are also being traumatized. The witnesses, the people who stay employed but sit next to empty desks and wilting ferns, are grappling with the guilt that psychologists label survivor's syndrome. At Chemical Bank, a department of fifteen was downsized to just one woman. She sobbed for two days over her vanished colleagues. Why them? Why not me?

The intact workers are scrambling to adjust. They are calculating the best angles to job security, including working harder and shrewder, and discounting the notion that a paycheck is an entitlement. The majority of people polled by *The Times* said they would work more hours, take fewer vacation days, or accept lesser benefits to keep their jobs.

Even the most apparent winners are being singed. A generation of corporate managers have terminated huge numbers of people, and these firing-squad veterans are fumbling for ways to shush their consciences. Richard A. Baumbusch was a manager at CBS in 1985 when a colleague came to him for advice: Should he buy a house? Mr. Baumbusch knew the man's job was doomed, yet felt bound by his corporate duty to remain silent. The man bought the house, then lost his job. Ten years have passed, but Mr. Baumbusch cannot forget.

One factor making this period so traumatic is that since the Second World War people have expected that their lives and those of their children would steadily improve. "It's important to recall that throughout American history, discontent has always had less to do with material well-being than with expectations and anxiety," said David Herbert Donald, a social historian at Harvard. "You read that 40,000 people are laid off at AT&T and a shiver goes down your back that says, 'That could be me,' even if the fear is exaggerated. What we are reacting against is the end of a predictable kind of life, just as the people who left the predictable rhythms of the farm in the 1880s felt such a loss of control once they were in the cities." As the clangor from politicians over the jobs issue has begun to be heard, aspirants to public office may find an audience in that group of households in which a lost job produced a major crisis.

The *Times* poll revealed something of their signature. Only 28 percent, versus 44 percent of the entire population, say they are as well off as they imagined at this juncture of their lives. The vast majority feel the country is going in the wrong direction, and they are more pessimistic about the economy. They are more likely than the overall population to be divorced or separated. They are better educated. Politically, they are more apt to label themselves liberal. They are more likely to favor national health insurance, and to say that curbing government programs like Medicare, Medicaid, and welfare is a misguided idea. And more than 63 percent, compared with 47 percent in the whole population, want the government to do something about job losses.

Wherever one turns one encounters the scents and sounds of this sobering new climate. Ask Ann Landers. Last year, when she adopted a stone-hearted view in her column to a laid-off worker, lecturing him that he had a "negative attitude," she was swamped by 6,000 venomous letters, one of the largest responses to any of her columns. "They were really giving me the dickens," Ms. Landers said. "This is the real world, girl. Now I am trying to be supportive." People run into acquaintances and don't ask how their job is, but whether they still have it. Surf the Internet or flick on the comedy channels and take in the macabre jokes. Sales clerk: "What size are you?" Customer: "I'm not sure. I used to be a 42 Regular. But that was before I was downsized." Wife: "But why'd they fire you?" Husband: "They said something about the company making too much money. If the business tanks, they said they'd call me back." Such graveyard humor is pervasive in Scott Adams's popular comic strip, *Dilbert*, about a 1990s computer engineer who quakes under a gruff and hectoring boss. In one strip, Dilbert competes with Zimbu, a monkey, for a job, and loses. In another, the boss informs Dilbert that he is about to become involved in all aspects of the company's production. "Dear Lord," Dilbert realizes. "You've fired all the secretaries." Raw material arrives daily in the form of E-mail from demoralized workers.

In an effort to somehow cauterize the emotional damage of the dismissals, managers have introduced a euphemistic layoff-speak. Employees are "downsized," "separated," "severed," "unassigned." They are told that their jobs "are not going forward." The word *downsize* didn't even enter the language until the early 1970s, when it was coined by the auto industry to refer to the shrinking of cars. Starting in 1982, it was applied to humans and entered in the college edition of the American Heritage Dictionary.

Meanwhile, the word *layoff* has taken a fresh meaning. In the past, it meant a sour but temporary interruption in one's job. Work was slow, so a factory shift would be laid off. But stay by the phone—the job will resume three weeks or three months from now when business picks up. Today, layoff means a permanent, irrevocable goodbye.

A Portrait of the Victims

Imagine the downsized posed shoulder to shoulder for an annual portrait, some sort of dysfunctional graduation picture. Mostly young, male, blue-collar workers dominated the glossies of the 1980s. Now, white-collar people stare out from every row. Many more of them are women and those whose hair flashes with gray. Instead of factory clothes, far more wear adornment appropriate for carpeted offices.

At his office in the Labor Department's Bureau of Labor Statistics, Thomas Nardone, an associate commissioner, keeps a chart that tracks the correlation between income and layoffs. In the 1980s, the chart shows, the higher the income, the less frequent the layoffs. Now the two lines rise in tandem. Blue-collar workers constituted the bulk of the layoffs in the 1980s, but as companies have slashed their costs more deeply, and as technology has obviated the need for office workers and middle managers, the concentricity of the layoffs opened up in the 1990s to include white-collar people. Whereas those with no more than high school educations used to be hardest hit, now it is frequently people with college degrees, even advanced degrees.

The job insecurity reaches beyond corporations. Government is also scaling back, although not as drastically as corporations, erasing many of the jobs that historically elevated the poor. Between 1979 and 1993, 454,000 public service jobs vanished. Academia is contributing to the dislocation by paring its rolls and increasingly leaving college teachers in jeopardy by denying them tenure. Doctors, once leading the way along the smug path to American bounty, are succumbing to the cost-containment convulsions in health care.

What so many middle-class workers are experiencing for the first time is achingly familiar to poorer people. Job security never seemed to apply to them. Indeed, those at the lower end of the economic ladder are slipping even further. Rene Brown is a thrice-downsized woman who is still in her forties. Since the start of the 1980s she has been downsized out of an $8.50-an-hour job at a meatpacking plant, a $7.25-an-hour job in a bank mailroom, and a $4.75-an-hour job loading newspapers. She now earns $4.25 cleaning office buildings in Baltimore. Ms. Brown, who is married without children, has done this menial work for three years, without a raise. She is annoyed that, despite a high school diploma and a year of community college, she cannot find a way back up the income ladder. If her wage were only higher, she said, it would "make the humiliation of this job at least endurable."

The poor are losing out in another way. The newly pinched middle class has grown increasingly intolerant of having its tax dollars applied to social programs benefiting the disadvantaged.

What Happened

People, of course, always lost their jobs. In the nineteenth and early twentieth centuries, it didn't take much; job security was not yet an American concept. Indeed, the nature of work was changing drastically a hundred years ago, just as it has been today. Tens of millions of Americans migrated from farms and rural communities to the new work growing up around urban centers. Millions of new jobs materialized, for example, in the auto industry, in highway construction, in the expanding network of railroads and commuter lines and, above all, in the shift from cumbersome steam-powered equipment to sophisticated factory machinery powered by electricity. That shift ushered in mass production. The giant department store and the big retail chain also appeared in this era, elbowing out smaller enterprises. The advertising industry was born and office jobs mushroomed.

Huge fortunes were amassed overnight and mansions appeared along the beaches of Newport. Poverty, child labor, twelve-hour days, and unhealthy working conditions were huge problems, of course. And there was also a lot of insecurity, as workers discovered that the familiar guarantees of life on the farm and in their small towns were gone. Skilled craftsmen who once thought they were masters of their own destiny awoke—like middle managers today—to discover that their talents were suddenly redundant. But there was a saving grace: A worker forced off a job much more often than not found himself in another that paid as well or better, if not right away, then within a year or two. Indeed, the incomes of most Americans kept rising, and millions of families, for the first time, acquired the multitude of inexpensive consumer goods made possible by mass production.

The Great Depression brought a temporary halt to this progress, but the Second World War ushered in an unprecedented era of economic growth. Demand for workers soared. The postwar years led many people to the succoring belief that they had an almost divine right to a very particular American dream entailing a home, a secure job, and a raise every year. An unwritten social contract, codified in part by strong labor unions, came into being, under which managers and workers pledged their loyalty to one another. Leaving a job became a major decision, one made more often by the workers than their bosses. And if a worker left, or was fired, the odds of landing another job at similar or better pay were very much in the worker's favor. "We had a vision then that life was good, and a conviction you could make it even better," said Michael Piore, an economist and historian at the Massachusetts Institute of Technology. "Now that conviction is gone."

The booming economic growth that fed this optimism slackened in the early 1970s, and the American economy has remained stuck at a lower volume. Not since the middle of the nineteenth century, in fact, has the economy grown so slowly for so long; even the Depression, while far more devastating, lasted only a decade. The vigor that had lifted so many families to higher incomes subsided. There were many reasons.

Intensified competition from foreign producers with lower labor costs—and from American companies offering low wages—withered the demand for workers with pretensions of earning even fifteen or twenty dollars an hour. Adding to the burden, the steady and pronounced progress of technology kept taking tasks from human beings and giving them to machines, undermining the bedrock notion of mass employment. Whereas the General Motors Corporation employed 500,000 people at its peak in the 1970s, twenty years later it can make just as many cars with 315,000 workers. Computer programs rather than lawyers prepare divorce papers. If 1,000 movie extras are needed, the studio hires only 100 and a computer spits out clones for the rest. Behind every ATM flutter the ghosts of three human tellers. Cutbacks in military spending and mergers that shrunk two companies into one also helped to make American workers less and less needed.

By the late 1970s, the convergence of these trends prompted companies to sanction large-scale layoffs. At first, the job losses occurred largely in beleaguered smokestack industries. Now the most modern and prosperous industries like telecommunications and electronics are shedding jobs regularly—companies like Sun Microsystems, Pacific Telesis, and IBM. Media companies, including *The New York Times*, are also doing so. Labor Department statistics show that more than 36 million jobs were eliminated between 1979 and 1993, and an analysis by *The New York Times* puts the number at 43 million through 1995.[i] Many of the jobs would disappear in any age, when a store closes or an old product like the typewriter yields to a new one like the computer. What distinguishes this age are three phenomena: white-collar workers are big victims; large corporations now account for many of the layoffs; and a large percentage of the jobs are lost to "outsourcing"—contracting work to another company, usually within the United States.

Far more jobs are being added than lost. But many of the new jobs are in small companies that offer scant benefits and less pay, and many are part-time positions with no benefits at all. Often, the laid off get only temporary work, tackling tasks once performed by full-timers. The country's largest employer, renting out 767,000 substitute workers each year, is Manpower Inc., the temporary-help agency. In this game of musical jobs, people making $150,000 resurrect themselves making $50,000 sometimes as self-employed consultants or contractors. Those making $50,000 reappear earning $25,000. And these jobs are discovered often after much time, misery, and personal humiliation.

The Rationale for Cutting

Most chief executives and some economists view this interlude as an unavoidable and even healthy period during which efficiency is created out of inefficiency. They herald the downsizings, messy as they are, as necessary to compete in a global economy. The argument is that some workers must be sacrificed to salvage the organization.

Sears, Roebuck and Company felt its very existence threatened in a world of too many stores and too many ways for people to buy what Sears sold for less. Cost cutting, in the form of 50,000 eliminated jobs in the 1990s, was part of the response. "I felt lousy about it," Arthur C. Martinez, Sears's chairman, said. "But I was trying to balance that with the other 300,000 employees left, and balance it with the thousands of workers in our supplier community, and with 125,000 retirees who look to Sears for their pensions, and with the needs of our shareholders." At the Newport News, Virginia, shipyard of Tenneco Inc., a diversified manufacturer, 11,000 out of 29,000 jobs have been shed since 1990, largely because of technological efficiencies like automated welding. It's also true that the Pentagon is buying fewer ships. Dana G. Mead, Tenneco's chairman, boasts that Newport News is now as efficient as any shipyard in the world. Four workers operating robots can cut all the ribs of a tanker, a task that had required twenty-one and took longer. "We put in automation to get more competitive," Mr. Mead said, adding that the change won important tanker and submarine contracts. "Then how many workers you build back depends on the rate the commercial business grows, and what the Navy decides to build."

Robert E. Allen, the AT&T chairman who has recently been turned into something of a symbol of corporate avarice for authorizing the elimination of 40,000 jobs, said that intensifying competition left him without choices. He said that with the Baby Bells free to invade AT&T's long-distance stronghold, AT&T's bloated staff of middle managers is no longer affordable. "The easy thing would be to rest on our laurels and say we are doing pretty well, let's just ride it out. The initiative we took is to get ahead of the game a little bit." Also intrinsic to the new message is that the lion's share of raises and bonuses must be channeled to those judged most talented and diligent. This new standard of "pay for performance" has made a growing divide among incomes a hallmark of the layoff era. In essence, a new notion of growth and job creation has emerged in which, rather than an expanding economy benefiting all, only the stellar performers—or those providentially in the right careers—come out ahead.

At the same time, some layoffs seem rooted in economic fashion. An unforgiving Wall Street has given its signals of approval—rising stock prices—to companies that take the meat-ax to their costs. The day Sears announced it was discarding 50,000 jobs, its stock climbed nearly 4 percent. The day Xerox said it would prune 10,000 jobs, its stock surged 7 percent. And thus business has been thrust into a cycle where it is keener about pleasing investors than workers.

How this all plays out is a matter of debate. Some contend that through these adjustments American companies will recapture their past dominance in world markets and once again be in a position to deliver higher income to most workers. Others predict that creating such fungible workforces will leave businesses with dispirited and disloyal employees who will be less productive. And many economists and chief executives think the job shuffling may be a permanent fixture, always with us, as if the nation had caught a chronic, rasping cough.

The Hardest Hit

The tally of jobs eliminated in the 1990s—123,000 at AT&T, 18,800 at Delta Airlines, 16,800 at Eastman Kodak—has the eerie feel of battlefield casualty counts. And like waves of strung-out veterans, the psychically frazzled downsized workers are infecting their families, friends, and communities with their grief, fear, and anger. The metabolic changes taking place in the country are only beginning to be understood, but there is no missing the deep imprint on the life of Steven Holthausen, the loan officer turned tourist guide. His high-velocity slide has caused him to go into his soul with calipers. He is suffused with anger, much of it toward himself. Why, he berates himself over and over, did he give so many evenings and weekends to his employer? Why didn't he see that his job was doomed? And then when the dismal news came that July day in 1990, he took it as he felt an executive should, coolly accepting the unfeeling reality of modern economics. Accepting it, that is, until he learned that his duties had been assumed by a 22-year-old at a fraction of his pay.

Once laid off, he not only withdrew from work, he withdrew from sight. He had been co-chairman of the trustees of a church in Westbrook, Connecticut, as well as vice chairman of the police advisory board. He left both posts. No longer a banker, he felt he had lost the requisite dignity to participate in civic activities. "You feel the community has lost its respect for you," he said. For almost a year, Mr. Holthausen scraped by on severance pay, on meager commissions earned as a freelance mortgage broker and on unemployment insurance. The fact that the unemployment pay was taxed made him resent the government. If the federal budget were balanced by scaling back spending, he reasoned, less of his skimpy income would be taken from him. Accordingly, Mr. Holthausen voted for Ross

Perot in 1992, warming to his pledge to cure the deficit. He now considers himself a budget-balancing Republican, although he has yet to settle on a candidate.

He lives alone with his torments in a humble apartment owned by a brother. He sat stock still as he ruminated on the tatters of his family. Even while he was a banker, tensions underlay the marriage. When he was fired, the couple sought therapy. At the sessions, he beseeched his wife to help him regain his shattered confidence. He found her unsympathetic. Six months later, she ordered him out. Soon after, she filed for divorce and, after years of not working, found a job as a medical secretary. His two teenage children avoided him. Their view, he felt, was that he must have shortcomings or he would not be jobless. Recently, Mr. Holthausen said, his daughter, a high school senior, has become more empathetic after seeing the parents of classmates go through similar ordeals.

"The anger that I feel right now is that I lost both my family and my job," he said. "That is not where I wanted to be at this point in my life." In a society in which identity is so directly quantified by work, the psychological fall involved in losing a job is leading many to stress-induced illnesses. "What makes it so hard for people is very often these situations come about very suddenly," said Dr. Gerd Fenchel, the head of the Washington Square Institute for Psychotherapy and Mental Health in New York, who has seen his caseload swell with downsized workers. "We have a diagnosis called posttraumatic stress syndrome that applies to this. It leaves a trace that people can't get rid of. I'm seeing a lady who for years was employed by an organization and was well liked but was fired. She has been in depression for two years. Her expression now is, 'If the Lord calls, I'm ready.'"

The impact of job loss on marriages varies. The divorce rate, according to several studies, is as much as 50 percent higher than the national average in families where one earner, usually the man, has lost a job and cannot quickly find an equivalent one. Often the wife loses patience. On the other hand, many families where both husband and wife are employed seem to be drawing closer to muster their energies against the common enemy of job insecurity.

The effect on community unity seems more straightforward. In city after city, downsized people are withdrawing from the civic activities that held communities together. Sociologists report that involvement has tumbled at PTAs, Rotary clubs, Kiwanis clubs, town meetings, and church suppers. Bowling leagues are unraveling, even though more people are bowling than ever. The reason is they are visiting alleys not as part of corporate or community leagues, but singly or with a friend. "The 'we' has become a 'me,' or at least a narrower 'we,'" said Robert D. Putnam, a Harvard professor who has documented this contracting participation. He fingers downsizing as a culprit, although not as insidious as television.

In some communities, downsizing has spawned a distrust of big companies headquartered locally for generations, and that has translated into a greater reluctance to support projects favored by those companies. In Cincinnati, for example, the prominent corporate fathers—Procter & Gamble, General Electric, Cincinnati Milacron, Federated Department Stores—once got their way in civic affairs. But recent stands by the corporations—in support of a new arts center, two new sports stadiums, and a shift to a strong mayor-led government—have faced strenuous opposition: And some connect that to bitterness about downsizing. "Loss of trust on the job level extends into the community," said Dennis Sullivan, a former president of Cincinnati Bell. Many citizens are investing less of their energies in organizations promoting civic good and more in narrower groups directly concerned with business. Joseph Kramer, vice president of the Greater Cincinnati Chamber of Commerce, notices that trend and worries about it. "What is lost," he said, "is broader concern about the community."

At the same time, the job insecurity is unleashing a "floating anger that is attaching itself to all sorts of targets as a form of scapegoating," said Daniel Yankelovich, president of DYG Inc., a polling firm. Polls have shown this anger directed at targets as diverse as immigrants, blacks, women, government, corporations, welfare recipients, computers, the very rich, and capitalism itself. Some experts say that part of the growth in membership of so-called hate groups is traceable to disaffected downsized workers. The floating anger is also influencing people's attitude toward politics. Pollsters say it is making centrist politics harder to practice and making people less faithful to any one party, less likely to vote, and more willing to entertain the idea of a third party. But at the same time, according to the *Times* poll, those who have gone through a traumatizing layoff are more likely to say that curbing government programs like Medicare, Medicaid, and welfare is a misguided idea, and that the government should do something to halt the loss of jobs.

Adapting to New Times

The downsizing has set off unmistakable currents of adjustment. Increasing numbers of families are scaling back their lifestyles. Two-thirds of those in the *Times* poll said that in recent years queasiness about their economic future had compelled them to curtail their day-to-day spending. One-fifth said the cuts had been "severe."

Many of the dispossessed are stepping up their involvement in new networks rooted in job pursuit. There are assemblages like "Xerox-ex" for laid-off Xerox workers and "Out of the Blue" for former IBM employees. There are age-specific groups like the 40 Plus Club in New York for people over 40 who have lost jobs. And there are arrangements like the job-seekers club at the Trinity Episcopal Church in Princeton, New Jersey.

Some are fulfilling dreams by initiating their own businesses and otherwise tapping into some new inner serenity. After twice losing jobs at computer companies in six years, Marilyn Collins, a 52-year-old computer systems expert, got fed up feeling she was "dispensable" and joined her husband in the small New York direct-mail consultancy he had founded. Since her arrival, the once marginal business has flourished.

Eighteen months ago, Kenneth Russell, 41, quit his aerospace engineer's job at Northrop just ahead of a sure layoff. He and his wife, a nurse, sold their home in Palmdale, California, and moved to Arlington, South Dakota. They make pottery. The corporate life meant income of $110,000. The pottery life netted $15,000 last year (this year is going much better). "It is fantastic," he said. "We have much better friends, because there is no inordinate competition between people as there was in the corporate stuff. There are no false pretenses, you don't have to try to impress anyone. It is very real.". . .

To find Mark Featherstone in the small hours of a Monday morning, it is necessary to journey to the nearly deserted cafeteria of the Willow Creek Community Church in South Barrington, Illinois. Mr. Featherstone is a 37-year-old software engineer at Motorola. He has no explicit reason for thinking his job is in jeopardy—Motorola has in fact been adding jobs—but rather than this buoying him, he still feels cornered. Thus he was here at a "Dads Group," rooting for the emotional sustenance he used to get at work. He said he was seeking "a peace within myself instead of the rush of the job." The church has watched its membership grow rapidly, in large measure because of job insecurity. Mr. Featherstone likes his work, but feels the company constantly demands more of him. Every day in the papers, he reads headlines about layoffs, and he waits for the day that the type spells out Motorola. Three years ago, Motorola instituted a point system to rate its software engineers, a now commonplace management tool. Mr. Featherstone finds the rating system stressful. "They are putting a number on everyone," he said. "Everyone may be doing a good job, but someone has to be in the bottom ten percent of the ratings. If there are layoffs, they would be the ones.". . .

Discussion Questions

1. Does this chapter help you understand the reasons why corporations started downsizing? Was it competition from foreign companies? Was it desire for greater profits?

2. Does this chapter make you want to get involved in a social movement to protect jobs?

3. Why are some jobs and industry sectors better protected against downsizing?

Reprinted from Louis Uchitelle and N. R. Kleinfield, "The Price of Jobs Lost," in *The Downsizing of America* (New York: New York Times Books, 1996, pp. 3–36). Used by permission.

Footnote

i. The Bureau of Labor Statistics conducts surveys on job displacement of adults 20 and over every other year, generally in January or February, and asks about prior years. To compensate for varying recall accuracy, overlapping surveys have been combined into a single consistent series by *The New York Times* using a moving-average technique. 1994 and 1995 figures are *New York Times* projections based on past trends and annual figures for unemployment and the labor force. Survey results and estimates based on them are subject to sampling error, which may be substantial for small states and demographic groups. ✦

8

Grapes and Green Onions

David Bacon

In 1994, the U.S. Congress passed the North American Free Trade Agreement (NAFTA), which was supported by President Bill Clinton, his labor secretary Robert Reich, and a majority of congressional Democrats and Republicans. Most analyses of the impact of NAFTA have focused on U.S. manufacturing plants that closed their operations in states like Michigan, Indiana, and Ohio and opened plants across the border in Mexico, where they found lower-wage, nonunion workers. This chapter looks at the impact of NAFTA on agricultural workers in the Southwest, along the U.S.-Mexico border. NAFTA made it possible for U.S. companies to import grapes from Mexico and Chile and for U.S. grape growers to plant across the border in Mexico. Both practices had negative effects on workers and their unions.

This chapter is about how NAFTA affected the lives of José Castillo and his wife Ingracia and other agricultural workers on both sides of the border. NAFTA dropped restrictions on importing Mexican grapes into the United States, but the law was supposed to provide assistance to American workers who lost their jobs because of the new competition from foreign producers. Grape workers like the Castillos found that many workers harmed by the new competition from imports didn't qualify for protection under NAFTA. The law was supposed to protect workers displaced by foreign competition, but the fine print in the NAFTA law says something else. As the saying goes: "The devil is in the details!"

The Castillos Lose Their Union

NAFTA [North American Free Trade Agreement] repeatedly plunged a knife into José Castillo's heart.

He felt its first thrust on almost the same day the treaty took effect. He lost his job.

That New Year's Day, in 1994, the Zapatistas took up arms in southern Mexico, denouncing NAFTA's marginalization of poor Mayan farmers in the Lacandon jungle. Video cameras closed in on their ski masks and ancient rifles, uplinking to satellites a new iconography of the underside of the global economy. Three thousand miles north, on the desert fringe of southern California, Castillo and a thousand other Mexican farmworkers were also being pushed to the social margins. They offered an equally haunting icon of the impact of free trade, but unemployed Mexicans in California have less media appeal. No one from the *Times* or CNN noticed.

NAFTA then inflicted a second wound: its promised benefits failed to materialize. According to U.S. president Bill Clinton and labor secretary Robert Reich, a safety net—including retraining and extended unemployment benefits—was ready to catch the unfortunate few whose out-of-date skills made their jobs expendable. José Castillo and his wife, Ingracia, found this promise to be like the hot wind that blows around their home in the Coachella Valley—elusive, empty, and incapable of sustaining life.

But the third thrust was the cruelest. To understand this, you must know that José and Ingracia are veterans of the union wars that swept the California fields for three decades. They are the ones called *de hueso Colorado*—all the way "to the marrow of their bones"—they are Chavistas, followers of César Chávez.

They lost their union.

"I felt like I lost my child." Ingracia's voice aches at the memory of the change that turned their world inside out and threatened the meaning that their struggle for dignity had given to their lives. Their story is part of the real history of NAFTA, about its consequences for working people on both sides of the border.

* * *

Because the Coachella Valley is so far south, only a couple of hours north of Mexico, its grape harvest comes in at the beginning of the season, in late May. By bringing their grapes into supermarkets before anyone else, valley growers always commanded premium prices; during the early 1990s, they were accustomed to receiving twenty dollars or more for a twenty-two-pound box in May. By July, when the harvest moved north to the San Joaquin Valley, the price usually dropped by half.

General Augusto Pinochet was the first to threaten that privileged position. Looking for exports to revive Chile's economy after the 1973 fascist coup, he discovered a winter market in his patron country. Even today, supermarket shelves in the United States are filled with Chilean grapes when the Coachella harvest starts.

But the real blow to the Coachella growers came from Mexico. U.S. ranchers like Delano's Jack Pandol, who began growing grapes in Chile under Pinochet, later began planting in the Sonoran Desert, south of Arizona. The year after NAFTA dropped restrictions on importing Mexican grapes into the United States, 7 million boxes flooded across the border. Coachella Valley's harvest was 10 million boxes that same season, only slightly more than the Mexican imports. And, to make matters worse for Coachella growers, the Mexican harvest starts at the same time. Their profitable position vanished overnight.

Since NAFTA, hardly any new fields of grapes have been planted anywhere in the Coachella Valley. Heaps of dry dead vines, their roots torn from the earth, point at the sun—sentinels of a dying industry.

The Bluestone Farming Company was one of the first to start tearing up its grapes. On January 6, 1994, Bluestone sent a letter to the Castillos and hundreds of other workers, informing them that the company was quitting the business of growing table grapes. By that time, however, the company was only a shell of its former self, a far cry from the days when its huge vineyards, spreading out across the desert, belonged to Lionel Steinberg.

Steinberg's enterprise, the David Freedman Company—or simply Freedman, as workers called it—is legendary in the United Farm Workers Union (UFW). It was one of the world's largest grape growers through the 1960s and 1970s, and it became the early home of the union.

While other grape growers fought the UFW with everything from lawyers to the gloved fists of strikebreakers to bullets, Steinberg was the exception. Perhaps ironically, his different attitude made him a very wealthy man.

By 1970, grape growers in California had been squeezed for five years by the UFW's fight for union recognition and its first grape boycott, a social movement that had become a symbol of economic justice in the minds of millions of people. The boycott had spread across the country, keeping growers' grapes locked up in coolers instead of filling supermarket shelves.

Steinberg broke ranks with the other growers and signed the first contract ending the historic grape strike, which had begun in 1965. Other growers followed suit. But when those same growers signed sweetheart contracts with the Teamsters union in 1973, in an effort to break the UFW, the farmworkers struck again. The renewed boycott once more squeezed off the sales of table grapes.

Steinberg, however, stayed with the UFW. Socially conscious consumers were trained to look for boxes of Freedman grapes, with the UFW's black eagle stamped prominently on the side. Steinberg sold when no one else could, and he got a higher price.

* * *

In 1973, the Castillos were strikers. But a decade earlier, when the union began, they had not been Chavistas. After coming north from Mexico at the beginning of the 1960s, José Castillo became a seasonal laborer. Like most farmworkers of that era, he was unemployed and hungry much of the year.

But then he got a job as a year-round permanent employee on the big grape ranch of Mr. Karahadian.

With a dream of stability seeming closer to reality, he went back to Mexicali, a hundred miles south across the border. There, he married Ingracia, a woman from his home state of Jalisco, and then brought her back to the vineyards in the desert. Mr. Karahadian rented a house to them on the company ranch, a privilege commonly granted to permanent employees. And, in return, the Castillos were loyal workers.

"Those were hard times. We never had any breaks," Ingracia says. "I remember that I would bring food to work hidden in my clothes, and I would eat a little when I thought no one was looking. Today there's cold water to drink when we work, but in those days there was nothing. When women wanted to go to the bathroom, we'd just have to go find a place to hide ourselves in the vines. These were all things we had to battle for—time to eat, water to drink, bathrooms. We never had unemployment insurance before. We just had to work and work and work. As soon as one job ended, I had to find another one right away."

In June of 1965, the first grape strike started in Coachella. Filipino workers across the valley walked out, seeking to raise wages from $1.10 an hour to $1.25. When the harvest moved north into the San Joaquin Valley around Delano, the Mexican workers organized by César Chávez and Dolores Huerta agreed to join the fight. The two streams of migrants—the old Filipino *manongs* (a term of respect because of their age), who had been organizing field labor upheavals since the 1920s, and the vast wave of Mexican workers who had been flooding California fields since the 1940s—came together, and the United Farm Workers union was born.

"I remember that I was very afraid," Ingracia recalls. "We were so green then. I'll never forget it. We were working in a field on Fifty-Seventh Avenue, which is just a dirt road. When the organizers first showed up and started talking to us from the road, we went running into the field so that we wouldn't be able to hear what they were

saying, about how good the union was. We went running into the vines. We didn't want to have anything to do with the union."

This, of course, made Mr. Karahadian very happy, and he told his workers to run and hide whenever the organizers showed up. But as the strikes ground on, year after year, Karahadian's losses began to temper his enthusiasm for fighting the union.

José remembers: "In 1970, Karahadian couldn't sell his grapes because of the boycott. One morning, very early, he came out and told us he wanted to talk to us. We were all at the labor camp. At that time, we were all still very against the union, because we were with him. We always believed whatever the boss told us. 'Don't sign anything. I'm with you. You're with me.'

"But when the boycott beat him, he said, 'I don't want to go broke. I'm going to sign with Chávez. You have four days. If you don't sign within those four days, you'll be out of here.' From that time onward, we saw how he had used us, and we never believed him again. First he'd hidden us inside his vines, and then he'd just made us a meal on a plate on the table."

In the three years that followed, the Castillos and the other grape workers in the valley realized that the union organizers had been right: the union was good for the workers. They might have been drawn in by the growers' involuntary defeat, but once they learned how to make the union work, they discovered that their contracts provided benefits, job security, and a newfound freedom from discrimination.

Despite the UFW's tumultuous history of strikes and boycotts, most grape workers had only those three years of UFW contracts by which to judge the union. Yet it was enough to win their loyalty for the two decades of struggle that were to come.

When the UFW grape contracts expired in 1973, "one night, Mr. Karahadian signed with the Teamsters," Castillo explains. "The next morning, he told us, '*Senores*, I'm with the Teamsters now, and for me it's the better choice. You have four days to sign up.' But this time, a worker at the ranch named Hilario stood up, and he said to Karahadian, 'If you've made what's the best choice for you, well, we have too.' And he pulled a great big union flag out from under his shirt, and that's how the strike started there. And so Karahadian threw us off his property, into the street."

The Castillos took their children to stay with José's mother in Mexicali. Ingracia and her sister pulled their crew out on strike, in a scene made famous in the UFW's film *Fighting for Our Lives.* By the time the strike reached Delano in midsummer, it was one of the largest farmworker strikes in U.S. history. The Teamsters union, still two decades away from reform under Ron Carey, furnished goons who beat up strikers on the picket lines. In rural, grower-dominated counties, the sheriffs either looked on approvingly or arrested strikers and carted them off to jail. Ingracia still remembers vividly a priest telling her that her own arrest was an act of conscience and that God was on the side of the poor.

But when Juan de la Cruz and Nagi Daifullah were gunned down on the picket line, César Chávez called off the strike. The union sent some of the strikers to reorganize the grape boycott in cities across the United States and Canada, but most went back to the fields to find work, having spent months on the picket lines. And they discovered the unpleasant reality of the blacklist.

For grape workers like the Castillos, Freedman was the only company where the union still had the right to dispatch workers to the job—and it was the only company that would hire them. For twenty-one years, that right kept them employed—José as a permanent worker, Ingracia as a seasonal one—and provided stability for their family. It helped them buy a house in a pleasant neighborhood in Coachella. Their children went to college, a rare achievement for farmworkers.

It was the blacklist that made Freedman the vibrant heart of the union.

The workers at Freedman, despite their many skirmishes with Steinberg over work rules and grievances, looked at the company almost as if it were their own. "All the people who had the consciousness that the union was a good thing were concentrated there," José asserts. "And with that consciousness, Freedman was very well organized. Lots of workers would tell us it was the best place to be. It had the best benefits, and it had job security. In other companies, if you weren't working, you were afraid to even leave the house to go on an errand, because they might call you to give you work. In Freedman, we knew when we were going in to work and when we would leave. We didn't have to please anyone today to get work tomorrow."

When Governor Jerry Brown signed California's Agricultural Labor Relations Act in 1975, the vote at Freedman to decide whether or not workers wanted the union was a celebration, whereas at most other companies it was like a war. More than nine hundred workers voted for the UFW at Freedman. Only fourteen voted against it.

* * *

As the years passed, Steinberg's son, Billy, left farming and went to Hollywood to become a songwriter. Lionel finally sold most of the ranch to new investors, including Prudential Insurance, who renamed it Bluestone Farming Company.

When Bluestone closed, the Freedman workers applied for benefits under the NAFTA-related Trade Adjustment Assistance (TAA) program. A bone thrown to workers during the debate over the treaty, NAFTA-TAA extends unemployment benefits and pays for retraining for workers who can demonstrate that NAFTA cost them their jobs.

Hundreds of workers at Bluestone depended on getting seasonal work every year thinning and picking grapes and pruning, tying, and girdling the vines. But the California Employment Development Department (EDD) ruled that, out of the entire workforce, only forty-three people were eligible for benefits—everyone except the permanent year-round workers was disqualified. José got a little extra money as a result, but not much.

EDD's rationale was that the company's layoff notice was dated January 7, a few days before the seasonal crews would have been called to begin pruning vines. Because they were on layoff and not yet actively working at the time of the notice, EDD held that they didn't qualify. Ingracia and hundreds of other workers received no benefit at all from NAFTA-TAA, although no one—not EDD, the U.S. Labor Department, or even the company itself—disputes that Mexican grape imports allowed under NAFTA caused the company to close.

EDD will not discuss the case, but its claim of confidentiality seems an odd objection. The EDD office does virtually nothing to let workers know that the program even exists. The workers laid off from Bluestone had to discover it for themselves, and they subsequently took on the burden of collecting money and buying radio time to ask potentially eligible workers to come forward and apply through the union.

In Coachella, José Castillo was unemployed for a year after being laid off. He applied at all the other grape companies but never got a call. He finally found work at a golf course.

Ingracia was hired, with a number of other Chavistas from Bluestone, by Bagdasarian, a big nonunion grape grower. But when the supervisor of their crew found out that they were all ex-Freedman workers, their jobs suddenly disappeared.

According to Gus Romero, the UFW representative in the valley at the time, "The safety net just wasn't there to catch them."

* * *

In fact, EDD seemed much more interested in holding down the number of claims, to avoid embarrassing California governor Pete Wilson. The governor, of course, had claimed that NAFTA would produce hundreds of thousands of jobs, although his administration's own statistics were proving the opposite.

Wilson wasn't the only public official facing embarrassment. Many congressional representatives, including some liberal Democrats, had been wooed and won by the same job promises. While the agreement was being debated, corporate executives of companies belonging to USA•NAFTA, the business coalition formed to back the agreement, walked the halls of Congress,

wearing red, white, and blue neckties. They made extravagant claims that U.S. exports to Mexico would add 100,000 jobs in its first year alone. Yet even these boosters could document only 535 U.S. jobs actually created by the agreement in 1994, a figure also cited in "NAFTA's First Year: Lessons for the Hemisphere," a December 1994 report edited by Sarah Anderson et al., sponsored by the Alliance for Responsible Trade, the Citizens Trade Campaign, and the Trade Research Consortium.

Except for NAFTA's boosters, everyone else also documents a hemorrhaging of jobs. In the first year of the treaty, the U.S. Department of Labor received claims for NAFTA-TAA from 34,799 workers, including those from Bluestone. In only the first five months of 1995, another 34,000 applied. These applications had to be certified both by the U.S. Department of Labor and by state unemployment offices. Like EDD, the Department of Labor had a vested interest in keeping the numbers of certified claims low, since President Clinton had also promised thousands of new jobs in order to get the treaty through Congress.

In California, 3,457 workers applied for NAFTA-TAA in the year and a half after the treaty went into effect. This number is very low, in the opinion of many employment experts, because most workers who lose their jobs are not aware of the program. The unemployment office and employers themselves do little to publicize it. Unless workers have a union, few are knowledgeable enough to apply. Further, the applications of people like the seasonal workers at Bluestone simply aren't counted.

Nevertheless, of the 3,457 laid-off California workers who did apply during that period, only 914 were certified by the U.S. Department of Labor.

California's experience was echoed in Kingstree, South Carolina, when Baxter International laid off 830 workers after sending their jobs out of the country. The Department of Labor certified the claims of 120 of those workers, agreeing that their jobs had gone to Mexico. But it asserted that the rest of the jobs had gone to Asia, and it therefore rejected the claims of 610 workers.

In Eatonstown, New Jersey, fifty workers at Allied Signal lost their jobs in March 1994. When they applied for NAFTA-TAA, they were also rejected, even though some of them had actually been sent to train their counterparts at the company's plant in Monterrey, Mexico, and Mexican managers had been trained in New Jersey. Allied Signal workers had reason to be bitter. The CEO of their company, Lawrence Bossidy, was the chair of USA•NAFTA. While NAFTA was being debated on the floor of Congress, Bossidy had directly denied, on television, any intention of moving Allied Signal jobs south.

The production of many well-known manufactured items shifted to Mexico in 1994. The list includes KeyTronic computer keyboards (277 jobs lost in Washington), Matsushita televisions (295 jobs in Illinois), Nintendo games (136 jobs in Washington), Oxford shirts (435 jobs in Georgia), Sara Lee sweatshirts (245 jobs in Georgia), Woolrich sportswear (500 jobs in Pennsylvania and Colorado), and Zenith televisions (430 jobs in Missouri). California companies certified by the U.S. Department of Labor for NAFTA-related layoffs include Formglas, Canon Business Machines, Xentek, Baltimore Aircoil, A&W Brands, ITT Cannon, Kyocera International, American Metal Products, Plantronics, Bluestone, Hughes Aircraft, and Amphenol.

And one other—Boscovich Farms.

* * *

South of Riverside, in Perris, the workers at Boscovich had to fight their way into the NAFTA-TAA program. No one keeps count of all the farmworkers who have, for whatever reason, lost their jobs. But only Bluestone and Boscovich workers applied for NAFTA-TAA—because they had an organization to help them. At Bluestone, workers had the UFW. Boscovich farmworkers never had a union. But they did have the Hermandad Mexicana Nacional, the Mexican National Brotherhood, a grassroots community organization that fights for civil rights and social services.

Over the years, some of the 170 Boscovich workers who cultivated and picked green onions in the Perris Valley had participated in community campaigns organized by the Hermandad. The biggest had been the fight with the city council to rename the town library after César Chávez.

On January 17, 1995, all the Boscovich workers received letters saying that the company was ending its operations in Perris and was laying them off. They knew that the Hermandad office was the place to go.

In the local newspaper, Phil Boscovich, vice president of Boscovich Farms, blamed the water district, claiming that it was taking back land for the Domenigoni Valley Reservoir, land that had been leased by the company. The district, according to Boscovich, wouldn't guarantee a continued flow of water to irrigate the land that was left.

Workers knew, however, that Boscovich, with offices in Oxnard, California, also farmed in Arizona and in the Sonoran Desert below the border. "We got really suspicious," recalls Luz Maria Ayala, who directs the Hermandad's Perris office, "when we saw irrigation pumps being taken out at night and driven away on trucks."

In 1993, Ayala had traveled to Washington, D.C., with a delegation led by legendary civil rights leader Bert Corona, to lobby against NAFTA. She understood the effect the treaty would have and anticipated that she would see its results in her own community. She didn't have to wait long.

Ayala, her husband, Antonio (a fellow Hermandad coordinator), and Jesus González, a retired Boscovich worker, decided to follow the trucks. Their search led them to San Luis Rao Colorado, a small farmworker town at the eastern edge of the Mexicali Valley, just across the border from Arizona's Gila River Valley. There, they found onion packing sheds—and workers who told them about Boscovich's operations. Armed with that information, Ayala went to the U.S. Department of Labor. Eventually, Boscovich personnel manager John Bautista admitted that the lost production had gone to Mexico, and the Department of Labor agreed.

Even then, the Boscovich workers had to fight against the EDD office in nearby Hemet, which they say mistreated them. "EDD never told anyone about TAA," Ayala says. "They think that because farmworkers are immigrants from Mexico, we have no right to unemployment [benefits]. If we hadn't fought for TAA, if we hadn't made our own investigation, we would have received nothing."

But Ayala explains that the fight was about more than TAA. "We're trying to wake people up, to make them more conscious, so there'll be a change. We're Mexicans and immigrants, but we live here now. We have to take care of this country. No one else is doing it."

Children in the Fields

From a distance, Muranaka Farms' green onion field, in the heart of the Mexicali Valley, looks almost festive. Dozens of large colored sheets are strung between pieces of iron rebar, providing shelter from the sun and rippling in the morning breeze. The soft conversations of hundreds of people, sitting in the rows next to great piles of scallions, fill the air. The vegetable's pungent scent is everywhere.

Small toddlers wander among the seated workers, some of the children nursing on baby bottles and others, their faces smeared with dirt, chewing on the onions. A few sleep in the rows or in little makeshift beds of blankets in the vegetable bins.

A closer look reveals that the toddlers are not the only children in this field. As the morning sun illuminates the faces of the workers, it reveals dozens of young girls and boys. By rough count, perhaps a quarter of the workers here are anywhere from six or seven years old to fifteen or sixteen. The crew foreman, who doesn't want to reveal his name, says it's normal for his three-hundred-person crew to be made up of families, including many kids. He says they work for Muranaka Farms.

The year is 1996. NAFTA has been in effect for more than a year.

This field is where Muranaka transferred its onion harvest, after shutting down its operation near Oxnard and Coachella. The surrounding valley here is dotted with other farms, also runaways from southern California.

Gema López Limón moves slowly down the rows. She has a slight limp, which makes her steps careful and deliberate. She is a stranger to the families seated here in the dirt, but she's obviously not a very threatening one.

She stops next to María, a child who is working alongside her mother, and talks to her softly. María is twelve years old. "My grandmother told me this year that we didn't have enough money for me to go to school," she explains. "At first, I stayed home to take care of my little sister, but it was boring, and sometimes I was scared being by ourselves all day. So I came to work here. We need the money."

López takes careful note of what María says. López is a well-known investigator of child labor in Mexico, a professor in the school of education at the Autonomous University of Baja California in Mexicali. She has an easy way with children. They talk to her as if she is a relative, or someone who has just come over from the next field.

López moves on down the row.

Honorina Ruiz is six years old. She sits in front of a pile of green onions in the same field. She notices Lopez coming toward her, but she keeps working, grabbing onions from the top of her pile to make a bunch. In a little gesture of self-consciousness, she pulls her sweater away from her face.

Her hands are very quick. She lines up eight or nine onions, straightening out their roots and tails. Then she knocks the dirt off, puts a rubber band around them, and adds the bunch to those already in the box beside her. She's too shy to say more than her name, but she's obviously proud to be able to perform a task at which her brother Rigoberto, at thirteen, working near her, already excels.

Lopez talks to Honorina's mother for a few minutes and then moves on again.

In another onion field about a mile away, Lopez finds another crew. Here Lorena, also twelve, works in an even larger group of five hundred people. She's here with her sisters Lupe and Cynthia; her mother, Maria; and her little brother Agustín, who at four years old is too young to work. Lorena says she's been coming to the fields every year for seven years, beginning at the same age as Honorina. "I finished first grade in primary school," she tells Lopez, "but then I left." Her mother adds that she tried to send Lorena back to school, "but what I can earn here by myself isn't enough for us to live on, so she had to come help us.". . .

Child labor is not legal in Mexico, any more than it is in the United States. Article 123 of the Mexican Constitution proclaims that children under the age of fourteen may not work and limits the work time of those between the ages of fourteen and sixteen to six hours a day. Article 22 of the Federal Labor Law also prohibits the employment of children younger than fourteen and permits those between fourteen and sixteen to work only by special permission, if they have already completed their mandatory education.

But according to Lopez, child labor is growing, as a result of the country's succes-sive economic crises and the rise in export-oriented agriculture. Joint ventures between Mexican and U.S. growers, producing for the U.S., European, and Japanese markets, "are achieving greater competi-tiveness at the cost of children working in the fields," she observes. "We're creating a workforce without education, condemned to the lowest wages and to periods of great unemployment.". . .

Discussion Questions

1. Why do you think there was such strong support for NAFTA among both Democrats and Republicans?

2. What position did U.S. labor unions, like the AFL-CIO, take on NAFTA.

3. Google NAFTA to find reports on job loss and job gain due to NAFTA.

Reprinted from David Bacon, "Grapes and Green On-ions," in *Children of NAFTA* (Berkeley and Los Angeles: University of California Press, 2004, pp. 19–32). Used by permission. ✦

9

'Workers Wanted': Employer Recruitment of Immigrant Labor

Nestor Rodriguez

The new economy brings with it the possibility that U.S. corporations can employ workers from around the globe to produce goods and services. This is done by moving plants to low-wage countries in Central America or Southeast Asia and employing predominantly women from the local labor market. It is also done by outsourcing jobs to workers in other countries, such as U.S. firms employing computer analysts in India or setting up call centers for customer service operations. The foreign workers do not come to the United States, but they take the jobs done formerly by American workers. In this chapter the author describes another feature of the new economy, which involves recruiting immigrants to work in the United States. The author discusses why employers are attracted to immigrant labor and the collaboration between large U.S. farms and the U.S. and Mexican governments, which created the Bracero Program in the early 1960s. This private-public cooperation, which continues today, is largely responsible for the creation of the politically volatile issue of the United States having an estimated 10 million illegal immigrant workers employed on U.S. farms and in U.S. factories, restaurants, and retail stores. Supporters of such immigration argue that migrant workers are filling the jobs that U.S. workers have rejected because of the working conditions and low wages. However, opponents argue that the solution is to raise wages instead of hiring migrant labor, which only further depresses wages for many jobs and serves to worsen working conditions for all workers.

In the surge in immigration research in the United States since the 1980s, with few exceptions,[1] studies on foreign migrant workers usually have given scant attention to employers (Chavez, 1992; Lopez-Garza, 2001; Rodriguez, 1986), as if these economic actors play only secondary roles in the social incorporation of foreign workers. Yet employers play important, if not critical, roles in the development of immigrant labor streams, ranging from passive hirer to central organizer. Regardless of their level of action, all employers function as gatekeepers to the labor market. The act of hiring, by itself, can produce manifest and latent effects that resonate throughout the international social structures of immigrant labor.

One popular image of employers of immigrant labor is that they are motivated wholly by the pursuit of profit to seek the cheapest labor, especially in labor-intensive industries of cutthroat competition and low profit margins (Hamilton & Chinchilla, 2001; Su & Martorell, 2001). A broader, economic perspective looks at the market pressures on capitalistic enterprises to hold down the cost of variable capital (Piore, 1979). Yet the advantage of immigrant labor for employers often consists of more than just a lower wage bill. According to Burawoy (1976), foreign migrant labor is a major advantage to employers because the costs of the production and reproduction of this labor is borne abroad by another social system. In this international arrangement, employers of migrant labor not only pay a lower wage bill but also avoid the tax liability for maintaining the institutional resources (educational, health care, housing, etc.) necessary to produce and reproduce migrant labor.

In the following four sections, I elaborate on the role of U.S. employers in recruiting and hiring immigrant labor. First, I explain in more detail the various advantages that employers gain from the recruitment and hiring of immigrant labor. Secondly, I review the Bracero Program as a case study of large-scale collaboration between the U.S. federal government, the Mexican government, and large farmers to import Mexican workers temporarily for harvest work. Thirdly, I focus on the demand for low wage immigrant labor in the context of economic restructuring that began in the 1970s. In this discussion, I address issues of labor market segmentation and the strategies of employers in the primary and secondary labor markets to recruit foreign workers. Finally, I end the discussion by addressing the structural pressures that drive U.S. employers to seek foreign-born labor and the ambivalence of the federal government toward this form of labor.

Advantages Drawn From the Hiring of Immigrant Labor

Many employers are willing to pay immigrant labor the prevailing wage level, or at least the federal minimum wage, if they can gain another major economic advantage. This advantage is acquiring a self-regulating and self-sustaining labor supply, that is, a labor supply that is self-recruiting, self-training, and self-disciplining (Browning & Rodriguez, 1985; Hagan, 1994; Rodriguez, 1986). This arrangement is similar to the benefits of outsourcing work but without actually having to contract with an external firm. The employer simply turns over the responsibilities of the labor process to the immigrant workforce, whose members organize and operate the work process through internal social networks and hierarchies. This labor arrangement develops in workplaces with work crews that have strong kinship or compatriot bonds (Hagan, 1994; Hamilton & Chinchilla, 2001; Repak, 1995).[2] In these work crews, internal social networks facilitate recruitment and job training, and age and other status

hierarchies facilitate discipline among the workers. The end result is that the employer saves on the costs of managing and maintaining a labor force, as the labor cost is reduced mainly to paying for work performed. But this advantage is derived only when immigrant labor is hired in groups, which enables internal networks to develop and provide the internal mechanisms of labor management and control. As immigrant workers are increasingly hired in groups, employers create a reserved labor market for immigrant labor (Piore, 1979).

Employers may also be attracted to immigrant labor for cultural reasons. In ethnic enterprises, employers may seek immigrant workers who are skilled in the cultural knowledge and customs used in the workplace (Gordon, Edwards, & Reich, 1982). This often means seeking immigrant workers who have had experience in the type of work performed in the ethnic workplace and who are fluent in the ethnic language, because oral language is often the repository of traditional culture (Portes & Rumbaut, 1996). Examples of this abound in Mexican bakeries in southwestern U.S. cities. In these ethnic businesses, the bakers are often immigrants from Mexico. As workers in the second immigrant generation increasingly speak English and seek mainstream jobs (Portes & Rumbaut, 1996; Waldinger & Lichter, 2003), ethnic employers are increasingly pressured to look for workers among the first immigrant generation. Ethnic employers derive a second cultural advantage from immigrant workers because these workers speak the language of ethnic customers. Examples of this can be found in such ethnic businesses as Latino or Asian music shops and herbal stores, in which the customers are often immigrants.

U.S. employers in low paying workplaces also obtain a spatial advantage from Latin American immigrant labor. The proximity of Mexico and Central America provides U.S. employers with a constant supply of low wage immigrant labor. This is a major advantage whose significance may escape observers because it is so commonplace. To grasp this significance, one only has to ask what low wage U.S. labor markets would look like if the huge reservoir of Latin American migrant labor was not so spatially accessible to U.S. employers (e.g., if the countries south of the United States were advanced industrial societies or if Mexico and the rest of Latin America were a faraway region).

To grasp this hypothetical situation, one can consider the case of China. Chinese farmers represent the largest single workforce in the world. With an income that is only slightly above that of African farmers (The World Bank, 1995), they have developed strong migration tendencies. In the past decade, an estimated 100 million Chinese peasants have migrated to Chinese cities (Zhang, 2001). Annually, several thousand Chinese workers enter the United States, with or without visas, but because of spatial barriers, China has not become a massive source of migrant labor for the U.S. labor market, as Mexico has been for decades. The spatial advantage of Latin American immigrant labor for U.S. employers of low wage labor is readily evident even after the passage in 1986 of the Immigration Reform and Control Act (IRCA), which introduced into federal law sanctions against employers who hired undocumented workers and intensified border enforcement. Across many U.S. labor markets, a surplus of Latin American immigrant labor literally pours out into the streets—and this labor supply is renewed daily.

A fourth advantage that some employers draw from immigrant labor has a political nature: the advantage of employing immigrant workers restricted by illegal status, by lack of work authorization, or by a specific employer, in the case of legal temporary workers. Such immigrants often are easily controlled and exploited, offering little or no resistance in the face of poor and even illegal working conditions (Browning & Rodriguez, 1985). Employers unilaterally decide on the work conditions (wages, work schedules, work pace, health and safety standards, etc.), and unauthorized immigrant workers must accept them or go without work. There is no negotiation, and

worker protests are rare. Although some may view this as an economic situation of immigrant labor, it is actually a political condition that develops from government action or more precisely, inaction. Because the federal government defines eligibility for work authorization, it can keep an undocumented immigrant labor force politically (and legally) vulnerable by not providing it with legal protection, through a guest-worker program or other form of legalization. The political advantage of hiring tractable immigrant workers becomes clearer when viewed against the historical background of class relations between capital and labor in the workplace (Gordon et al., 1982). When viewed from this perspective, tractable immigrant labor represents a major gain for employers in the class struggle over working conditions.

In addition to paying scant attention to how employers influence the incorporation of immigrant labor in U.S. society, many studies of foreign-born workers ignore the role of the state in this process, beyond the realm of offering new visa policies for immigrant workers. In this regard, even the recent work of Waldinger and Lichter (2003), which gives an excellent description of employer functions in the labor-market incorporation of immigrant workers, remains silent. In the following section, I examine a large-scale, temporary labor importation program enacted in the mid 1900s in which the U.S. government played a leading role in designing and implementing the program.

The Bracero Program

A private-public collaboration between large U.S. farmers and the U.S. and Mexican governments designed and implemented the Bracero Program of imported Mexican agricultural workers, which lasted from 1942 to 1964. On paper, Mexican *braceros* were contracted, and thus they were not technically employees, but in reality, they had every bit of a proletarian experience, which was made even more rigid by the regimentation of the program (Galarza,

1964). With the exception of a brief labor importation program during World War I, in no other migrant labor stream before or after the Bracero Program has the U.S. government played such a prominent role in recruiting foreign migrant labor for the large-scale restructuring of a workforce. Some scholars (Barrera, 1979; Galarza, 1964; Massey, Durand, & Malone, 2002; Samora, 1971) now consider the government-supported Bracero Program to have played a major role in stimulating large influxes of undocumented migrants, initiating the patterns of Mexican undocumented immigration that have characterized U.S. society since the late 20th century.

The Bracero Program was originally organized as a wartime measure to replenish the agricultural workforce that had lost workers to the armed forces and to wartime industries in the cities (Calavita, 1992; Craig, 1971). In response to requests from large farmers in California, Texas, and Arizona and a few railroad companies, the U.S. government sought and obtained a labor import agreement with the Mexican government in 1942. The program operated as follows. After receiving an order for braceros from U.S. officials in Mexico City, the Mexican government directed pools of potential workers to recruitment centers in Mexico where U.S. and Mexican agents made final selections and listed braceros for specific farmers in the United States. The U.S. government paid for the transportation of braceros to their work destinations, with only a $5 contribution made by the U.S. employers for each of the workers (Calavita, 1992).

According to Calavita (1992), the implementation of the Bracero Program in the United States involved multilayered federal coordination. Initially, overall coordination of the program was the responsibility of the Agricultural Department, but it was the State Department that negotiated the agreement with the Mexican government. The Farm Security Administration was responsible for recruiting and contracting with the braceros, after the employment service certified the employers' need for them. The Immigration and Naturalization Service (INS) supervised the arrival and departure of the braceros. In 1942, the program started when 4,203 braceros arrived to work for their U.S. employers. By the termination of the program in 1964, 4.9 million braceros had gone through the program (Barrera, 1979).

The actions of U.S. federal agencies facilitated the economic and spatial advantages of Mexican migrant labor for U.S. employers. For the agricultural employers, a much-desired economic advantage was to have a large supply of workers to keep wages down. From this perspective, a labor shortage did not mean too few workers but too few workers to keep wages down to the lowest possible levels (Reisler, 1976). Bracero labor allowed agricultural employers to reduce some operating costs by about 50%. In beet farming, for example, employers reduced harvest costs from $32 per acre to $13 after hiring bracero workers (Galarza, 1977). Moreover, U.S. policy makers and employers realized the benefit of hiring braceros without their families. The American Farm Bureau Federation found that bracero labor could "fill . . . seasonal peaks and return home . . . without creating difficult social problems" (Galarza, 1977, p. 32) that result when families come along. The federal government facilitated the spatial advantage for employers when it underwrote most of the millions of dollars it cost to transport braceros to their U.S. work sites. This advantage was further increased for employers when U.S. government agents arrested thousands of undocumented workers for illegal entry into the United States and then converted these arrested migrants into bracero workers for U.S. farmers.

Employers of bracero labor also gained major political benefits from the government-supported labor import program. Through the bracero labor supply, these employers avoided hiring native labor, which often went through organizing cycles. This advantage probably was also a motivation for agricultural employers to pressure the federal government to implement the Bracero Program. Large farmers in California, who were the primary supporters of the Bracero Program, had experienced labor strife for decades before the implementation of the program (Reisler, 1976). In the 1910s, the labor movement in California agriculture became more active after the Industrial Workers of the World (IWW) started organizing migrant farm workers. The IWW took class struggle as a given and organized under the principle that "the working class and the employing class have nothing in common" (Pelling, 1960, p. 111). In the 1930s, the communist-led Cannery and Agricultural Workers' Industrial Union called strikes that involved thousands of farm workers and put at risk crops valued in the millions of dollars (Chacon, 1980). With increased organizing of Mexican farm workers, the labor movement conducted more than 140 strikes in the California agricultural fields during the 1930s (Reisler, 1976). Therefore, in the early 1940s, California farmers saw the Bracero Program as heaven sent. The agreement with the Mexican government stipulated that braceros could not be used as strikebreakers, but this did not stop some California farmers from using them in this manner (Galarza, 1977).

The continuation of the Bracero Program after the end of World War II demonstrated that its attraction for U.S. employers was more than just the replacement of labor lost to the war effort. It had become a preferred labor supply of large agricultural employers and some railroad corporations. One large agricultural employer described the attitude toward bracero labor as follows: "We used to own our slaves, now we rent them from the U.S. government" (Moquin & Van Doren, 1971, p. 344). When World War II ended in 1945, a total of 168,000 braceros had been imported into the United States for temporary work, but 4.7 million more would be imported by the end of the program in 1964. Importation of braceros would peak in the period from 1956 to 1960, when more than 400,000 workers were imported annually (Barrera, 1979).

After federal agencies initiated the Bracero Program in 1942, Congress enacted Public Law 45 in 1943 to provide the legal machinery for the program. This law provided for the continuation of the program until 1948, yet when the termination date arrived, the importation of braceros continued after the State Department negotiated a new agreement with Mexico. According to Calavita (1992), this signified a de facto extension in which Congress permitted the executive branch to act on an issue on which it would not legislate. Congressional endorsement for this administrative strategy was given in December 1947 in a hearing of the House Committee on Agriculture, when key federal officials stated their intention to continue the bracero importations (Calavita, 1992). Congressional members who were concerned about the impact on domestic labor did not have the votes to stop this decision. Until Congress again formalized the Bracero Program in 1951 through Public Law 78, bracero importations continued through several short-term administrative and Congressional measures in which the interests of large agricultural employers were protected. With no Congressional oversight to worry about and with a favorable regulatory atmosphere, the employers of braceros had a labor program that was tailor made for their needs from 1948 to 1951 (Craig, 1971).

During this interim, between the end of the first phase of the Bracero Program and its formal reinstatement by Congress in 1951, agricultural employers gained two important advantages in the bilateral bracero negotiations. One advantage was that labor contracts were changed from contracts between the U.S. and Mexican governments to contracts between agricultural employers and the bracero workers (Calavita, 1992). The second advantage was that agricultural employers could hire undocumented workers who were arrested and legalized by the INS ("dried out") as braceros (Calavita, 1992; Galarza, 1964). This second agreement greatly facilitated the spatial advantage of bracero labor for agricultural employers. For years, employers of braceros had sought recruitment centers in nearby Mexican border towns, but the Mexican government had refused on the grounds that it would create a labor rush to the northern Mexican border. Being able to contract braceros inside the United States thus reduced transportation costs and lessened the need to deal with the Mexican regulatory agency in Mexico. According to Calavita (1992), between 1947 and 1949, approximately 75,000 braceros were imported and 142,000 were legalized and contracted in the United States. In 1950, fewer than 20,000 were imported and more than 96,000 were turned over to agricultural employers after being arrested by the INS for illegal entry. In January 1954, when the Mexican government stalled over a question of wage levels in negotiations over the Bracero Program, the U.S. government responded by emptying out its immigrant detention centers in Southern California and converting the released undocumented migrants into braceros, as well as converting into braceros other undocumented migrants delivered by their agricultural employers (Galarza, 1964).

When Congress passed Public Law 78 in 1951, the Department of Labor was placed in charge of the program, and the contracting arrangement reverted to government to government, much to the satisfaction of the Mexican government (Calavita, 1992). In response to increasing criticism over the impact of the program on domestic labor, Public Law 78 was written in a way that required the Bracero Program to be reviewed and reauthorized periodically. In the period from 1953 to 1959, Congress extended Public Law 78 with little difficulty, but after 1959, opposition to the law mounted (Craig, 1971). Labor groups and some national policy planners had always opposed the law on the grounds that it maintained poor working conditions and lessened the ability of domestic labor to organize, but in 1960, agricultural employers also criticized the law for placing too many requirements on employers after the program was placed under the supervision of the Department of Labor. In the late 1950s, for example, the Department of Labor issued new policies concerning the housing, wages, and transportation of braceros. Department of Labor agencies acted to enforce the new policies

and closed down hundreds of bracero units temporarily or permanently (Craig, 1971). Although not necessarily taking an anti-bracero stance, the Department of Labor increasingly enacted policies in support of the domestic agricultural labor force. After the House Agricultural Committee passed a 2-year extension of Public Law 78 in 1963, the full House of Representatives voted not to extend the Bracero Program (Craig, 1971).

The end of the Bracero Program in 1964 did not terminate the employment of Mexican foreign workers in the workplaces of U.S. agribusiness; the undocumented worker replaced the bracero worker. This change was not dramatic because braceros and undocumented workers had often labored side by side (Galarza, 1964). Indeed, to the extent that the Bracero Program stimulated the development of massive undocumented immigration, the undocumented worker can be seen as the natural outcome of the government-supported bracero labor system. The Bracero Program enhanced the image of the United States as a major employment source to millions of Mexican workers, and when U.S. agents converted undocumented workers into braceros, it also created the image of another avenue through which Mexican workers could enter U.S. workplaces. Government statistics roughly demonstrate that as the number of imported braceros increased, the number of illegal migrants apprehended by the INS (which some take as a rough indicator of the trend of undocumented immigration) also increased during the first half of the Bracero Program (Calavita, 1992, pp. 217–218).

Less than a decade after the end of the Bracero Program, the U.S. economy underwent a dramatic change that fundamentally altered the accord between capital and labor that had been established in the 1930s and 1940s (Cleaver, 1979). In this accord, peace was maintained between corporate employers and their workforces through negotiations that linked wage increases and other worker benefits to increases in productivity and cost-of-living arrangements. If the costs of production increased, business owners and managers simply raised prices to maintain profits (Harrison & Bluestone, 1988). The next section discusses the desire of U.S. employers to hire foreign workers as the country passed into a new era in which economic development became increasingly dependent on global strategies.

'The Great U-Turn' and the Segmented Labor Market

Reacting to a falling rate of profit, business leaders in the 1970s moved the U.S. economy into a dramatic restructuring phase that was soon supported by governmental policies. Economists Harrison and Bluestone (1988) characterized this transition as "The Great U-Turn," involving corporate warfare against organized labor, a change in investment patterns from manufacturing to financial markets, and federal policies that supported the corporate sector and weakened the power of organized labor. In The Great U-Turn, corporations were "merged and acquired, downsized, deindustrialized, multi-nationalized, automated, streamlined, and restructured" (Harrison & Bluestone, 1988, p. 22). The consequences for labor included job losses, wage and benefits reductions, expansion of part-time and temporary employment, an emerging two-tier wage system, and labor market polarization (Harrison & Bluestone, 1988).

According to Sassen-Koob (1984), labor polarization resulted from the new demand for skilled and unskilled labor of restructured urban labor markets. Especially in larger metropolitan areas, concentrations of highly and poorly paid jobs emerged as large domestic and international corporations and advanced service businesses produced agglomerated economies of professional service firms, such as legal, financial, managerial, technical, and so forth. The large corporations and the professional service firms produced demands for both specialized skills and expertise and, directly and indirectly, for low wage

labor. A direct demand for dead-end, low wage labor was produced when jobs were downgraded for informal industrial homework or when production jobs were offered at low wages. An indirect demand for low wage jobs was created when the concentration of high salary professional and other specialized workers produced a market for low wage services to support their gentrified consumption patterns (Sassen-Koob, 1984). These services include home cleaners, dog walkers, yard workers, car parking attendants, restaurant and coffee shop workers, and a host of other low wage service workers. As Sassen-Koob (1984) explains, economic restructuring in the U.S. urban system created new growth trends that played an important role in attracting immigrant labor from peripheral countries to the United States. From this viewpoint, the incorporation of immigrant labor into low wage job markets in the United States cannot be understood simply as a survival strategy of foreign workers fleeing economic decline in their home countries. On the contrary, the incorporation must be understood as a growth phenomenon of a new capitalistic arrangement of business development in domestic and global contexts (Sassen-Koob, 1984). Census data indicated that by 2000 the new capitalistic arrangement included a larger proportion of professional and other skilled foreign workers as well (Mosisa, 2002).

From the late 1960s to the mid 1980s, a number of studies in low income areas in northern and midwestern U.S. cities produced theoretical models to explain poverty and unemployment in local labor markets (Baron & Hymer, 1967; Gordon, 1972; Gordon et al., 1982). The studies, which were conducted from nonconventional economic perspectives, separately concluded that labor markets were divided into sectors that differed fundamentally in such characteristics as skill and income levels, the quality of supervision and management, and the possibilities for worker advancement (Gordon, 1972). For some theorists, labor market segmentation emerged from structural constraints or social antagonisms based on race, gender, or class within the larger economy (Bonacich, 2001; Edwards, Reich, & Gordon, 1975). For other theorists, labor market segmentation resulted from deep class contradictions in the historical development of capitalism, especially since the early 20th century (Gordon et al., 1982). One popular theory that emerged from these conceptualizations was the dual labor market theory. This theory viewed the labor market as segmented into primary and secondary markets of skilled, high paying, stable jobs and unskilled, low paying, temporary jobs, respectively (Gordon, 1972; Piore, 1979). In the primary labor market, the employer is often an organization, such as a company, firm, or agency, but in the secondary labor market, the employer is often an individual. Internal labor markets, bureaucratic regulations, and contractual agreements often direct the management of labor in the primary labor market, but in the secondary labor market, the personal values and customs of the employer shape the operating normative system. Although dual labor market theory was eventually reworked into a historical perspective of labor segmentation (Gordon et al., 1982), it contributed the handy classification of primary and secondary labor markets to distinguish broadly between jobs in the core and peripheral sectors of the economy (Hodson & Sullivan, 1990).

Whether theorists characterized labor market segmentation as a dual labor market, segmented work, or a split labor market, the analytical conclusions were the same: Neoclassical economic theory, which looks at labor market behavior in terms of supply and demand, marginal productivity, and human capital, could not account for major social divisions in labor markets (Gordon, 1972; Piore, 1979). At play, according to nonconventional theorists, were reflective actors (employers) attempting to derive economic gain within a matrix of qualitatively different work opportunities and worker social statuses (Bonacich, 2001; Stone, 1975).

In the models of economic segmentation, the employer emerges as an especially critical starting and end point for the mus-

tering of workforces in the secondary labor market. In contrast to employers in the primary labor market who often must follow established company policies, employers in the secondary labor market have greater room to maneuver in organizing a workforce (Gordon, 1972). Indeed, employers in the secondary labor market often organize their workforce informally outside the realm of government regulation and keep employment records off the books by paying workers in cash, thereby gaining an extra economic advantage by not paying into governmental social programs for workers. This is a significant advantage for small employers with limited capital outlays, for whom small sums of money determine the difference between business survival and collapse.

Foreign Labor Policies for the Primary Labor Market

Employers in different sectors of the segmented labor market have affected the current record-setting immigration wave into the United States in different ways. Indeed, one could argue that the segmented labor market is a major social force generating a segmented immigration of legal and unauthorized workers into the U.S. economy. Employers in the primary labor market have acted to acquire foreign workers by lobbying the U.S. Congress to increase the number of permanent and temporary work visas. One half of the 34,000 visas set aside for employment-based immigration from the eastern hemisphere in 1965 were for professionals (and their spouses and children) with scientific or artistic skills whose work would benefit the national welfare, and one half was for qualified immigrants, who could perform skilled or unskilled labor (Usdansky & Espenshade, 2001). Admittedly, these were small numbers, coming as they did, just 2 years after organized labor had successfully lobbied to shut down the Bracero Program. In 1970, workers accounted for just more than half (55%) of the 34,000 employment-based visa allotment, their spouses and children accounting for the rest (Usdansky & Espenshade,

2001). Reacting to corporate demands, Congress made it easier for employers to use foreign labor in the mid- and late 1970s when it increased the employment-based visa allotment from 34,000 to 58,000 and the worldwide immigration cap to 290,000 (Usdansky & Espenshade, 2001; U.S. Immigration and Naturalization Service, 2000, Appendix 1). In 1986, with the passage of IRCA, Congress made available a large supply of newly legalized immigrant workers for employers. In addition to introducing employer sanctions, IRCA provided amnesty and legalization for 2.7 million immigrant workers and their foreign-born spouses and children. About 900,000 of these immigrants were legalized through the efforts of agricultural employers, who lobbied Congress for a special provision for seasonal agricultural workers to circumvent the 5-year residency requirement for amnesty (U.S. Bureau of the Census, 1989, Table 298). Although many of the immigrants legalized through IRCA had unskilled backgrounds, a segment of this population had participated in professional and technical occupations (Borjas & Tienda, 1993).

The Immigration Act of 1990 significantly increased the allotment of employment-based visas as it increased the total immigrant visa allotment to 700,000 for the period from 1992 to 1994 and to 675,000 beginning in 1995 (U.S. Immigration and Naturalization Service, 2000). Employment-based visas were increased to 140,000 for workers, spouses, and children, with the specification that the number of unskilled workers would not exceed 10,000. The Immigration Act of 1990 also significantly increased the use of temporary skilled labor. As a response to pressure from corporate employers, the 1990 Act created the temporary, 3-year H-1B visa (renewable for 3 more years) for work in skilled occupations and capped this nonimmigrant visa category at 65,000 (U.S. Immigration and Naturalization Service, 2000). The 1990 Act also capped the H-2B visas for nonagricultural temporary workers (less than 1 year) at 66,000 and created three additional visa categories for scientists, educators, and other skilled and religious workers.

In the dynamic economy of high-tech industries, employers saw the H-1B visa as a means to quickly access a highly skilled labor force without going through the lengthy, bureaucratic process of acquiring workers through employment-based immigration and without testing the U.S. labor market for native workers. The H-1B visa provided the means for employers to bring foreign-skilled workers (computer programmers, engineers, etc.) into corporate offices within months. As capital investment in high-tech industries accelerated in the 1990s, the corporate demand for H-1B visas grew more intense. Congress responded generously and in 1998, passed the American Competitiveness and Workforce Act, raising the ceiling for H-1B visas for 3 years, to 115,000 in 1999 and 2000 and to 107,500 in 2001 (U.S. Immigration and Naturalization Service, 2000). When numerical limits were reached earlier than expected and new corporate demands exceeded the expanded caps, in 2000, Congress passed the American Competitiveness in the Twenty-First Century Act and increased the H-1B visa cap to 195,000 for 3 years, with unlimited H-1B visas for nonprofit research institutions (Lowell, 2001).

Corporate employers were not alone in lobbying Congress for more H-1B visas. Probusiness interest groups, libertarians, immigration lawyers, and other advocates of immigration also lobbied Congress in support of H-1B visas and even in support of repealing the annual caps. In a report titled *The H-1B Straightjacket*, analysts of the Cato Institute argued that "Congress should return to U.S. employers the ability to fill gaps in their workforce with qualified foreign national professionals rapidly, subject to minimal regulation, and unhampered by artificially low numerical quotas" (Masters & Ruthizer, 2000, p. 1). According to Bach (2001), who served as executive associate commissioner of the INS in the Clinton administration, all parties involved in the issue made unsubstantiated claims about labor market conditions or about the labor force impacts of H-1B workers because the federal government did not have a reliable count of the H-1B visas issued. When the statistical branch of the INS analyzed a representative sample of H-1B visa holders authorized for the fiscal year 2000, the results showed that the three largest occupational categories supported by the visas were computer-related occupations (55%); architecture, engineering, and surveying (15%), including computer and information systems technicians; and administrative specialization (8.5%), including accountants and management systems analysts (Bach, 2001). The analysis of the sample also showed that the H-1B workers were headed to occupations that paid below the average $50,000 a year projected by employers; in the most popular occupations, the pay ranged from $33,500 to $54,000. Workers from India represented about 43% of the H-1B visas issued for the fiscal year 2000 and 51 % of the H-1B workers requesting a time extension (Bach, 2001).

The short history of the H-1B visas suggests that the corporate sector has found these visas to be an alternative avenue to skilled labor. Considering the results of the INS survey, it is logical to think that corporate employers were motivated to seek H-1B workers partly to save on salaries.

Recruiting Immigrant Labor Into the Secondary Labor Market

For obvious reasons, employers in the secondary sector of the labor market do not lobby the government for foreign workers. Indeed, IRCA introduced the category of authorized workers and introduced legal measures to penalize employers who hired unauthorized workers (U.S. Immigration and Naturalization Service, 2000). Yet employers in the secondary sector of the labor market are a major employment source for immigrant labor, especially for undocumented workers, as they are for native-born racial minorities and women. It is likely that on a yearly basis, employers in the secondary labor market employ as many immigrant workers as are employed in the primary labor market. The most recent U.S. government estimate is that the undocumented immigrant population grew by 350,000 annually in the 1990s, which is more than the annual allotments of H-1B visas (currently set to the original quota of 65,000 annually; U.S. Department of Homeland Security, 2003). Given that the undocumented worker population grows through continual immigration but that H-1B visa holders can renew their visas only once, one can logically hypothesize that the number of undocumented workers in the secondary labor market exceeds the number of H-1B and employment-based immigrant workers, especially because the number of H-1B visas can fluctuate by almost 300% and because only about half of the 140,000 employment-based visas actually go to workers (the remainder go to their spouses and children).

How do employers circulate such a large volume of labor through the secondary labor market? To answer this question, one must understand the dynamic nature of the secondary labor market. It is not a market where workers settle in for long spells of employment in secure jobs. Quite the opposite. Not bound by government regulations, union contracts, or internal career ladders, the secondary labor market is a labor whirlpool that attracts and ejects large quantities of workers on a regular basis. In the most labor-concentrated industries of the secondary labor market (e.g., agricultural workplaces, downtown office cleaning companies, construction firms), in which work tasks have short duration, employers often select new work crews on a frequent if not daily basis (Harris, 1995). The substitutability of lower skilled labor in the secondary sector of the labor market also makes workers highly expendable and promotes their mobility across the market. Given the lower skill range of this labor market sector, employers prefer to hire new workers than to invest in those who do not rise to expectations. From the perspective of workers, given the inferior conditions of the secondary labor market, there is no desire to hold on to specific jobs for a long time, especially after gaining initial entry into the labor market. All jobs are interchangeable, and workers often move around looking for those that may have a particular advantage (e.g., pay a little more, offer better work hours, are closer to home; Gordon, 1972). All of these conditions maintain the dynamism of the secondary sector of the labor market.

A number of studies have described the different ways employers recruit immigrant workers, often undocumented, into the secondary labor market (Chavez, 1992; Hagan, 1994; Hamilton & Chinchilla, 2001; Hondagneu-Sotelo, 1994; Kempadoo & Doezema, 1998; Kwong, 1997; Menjivar, 2000; Rodriguez, 1986; Waldinger & Lichter, 2003). According to these studies, the recruitment modes include the following: employers find and recruit immigrant workers in day-labor pools, hire immigrant workers when they approach workplaces to ask for work, hire immigrant workers introduced and recommended by other workers, contact labor recruiters or smugglers to procure immigrant workers, indenture immigrant workers by paying the smuggling fare, ask immigrant employees to recruit immigrant workers, and visit community and commercial areas frequented by immigrants to locate and recruit workers. Research also reveals a number of interesting interactions between how employers recruit and hire immigrants and characteristics of immigrant workers or their workplaces. For example, the hiring of immigrant women for household work seems to occur by recruitment through social networks among both female employers and female workers (Hagan, 1994). Indentured employment is a pattern among Chinese immigrant workers who must pay large smuggling fees and among immigrant women working in bars and nightclubs (Kwong, 1997; Kempadoo & Doezema, 1998). Casual employers often rely on day-labor pools to recruit immigrant workers, whereas large employers often rely on labor recruiters or self-recruitment among immigrant employees to maintain immigrant workforces (Rodriguez, 1986).

Although it is commonly perceived to be a labor supply for the secondary labor market, undocumented migrant labor is also recruited into the primary labor market (Hagan, 1994; Rodriguez, 1986). It has only been since the passage of IRCA in 1986 that the hiring of this labor was made a federal violation. Before the enactment of IRCA, employers in the primary labor market routinely hired undocumented workers. After the passage of IRCA, some employers in the primary labor market continued to bring undocumented workers into their workplaces. Some did so unknowingly, believing their immigrant employees to be authorized workers, but others did so by outsourcing work to other firms (such as building maintenance companies) or by meeting the letter, but not the spirit of the law, when they hired immigrant workers with questionable work authorization permits (Hagan, 1994).

Discussion and Conclusion

I have described how employers, often with government support, have played major roles in the growth of immigrant labor in the U.S. economy. Even if employers did nothing else in terms of labor recruitment than just hire immigrant workers who appeared at their workplaces, this still would give employers the critical role of gatekeepers to the labor market. If employers do not hire them, that is, if immigrant workers cannot access U.S. labor markets, then much of the immigration we see today would collapse. It also would mean the collapse of transnational communities that sustain this immigration. But the opposite has happened. Many U.S. employers in the primary and secondary labor markets have developed a penchant for foreign workers, and as a consequence, transnational structures of immigration have emerged and expanded across U.S. localities. By the early 21st century, the foreign born constituted 13% of the 140 million workers in the U.S. labor force (Mosisa, 2002).

Although employers may hail the often-assumed superior characteristics of immigrant workers (e.g., they work harder, are more disciplined, have greater labor force commitment), there is a deeper motivation that drives employers to seek these workers. This motivation is the capitalistic imperative to keep down the costs of production. This is what drives employers to immigrant labor: the various cost-cutting advantages that this labor represents. But before one assumes that this labor is readily abundant, it is necessary to recognize its restrictions within the political boundaries of nation states. Capital has always been freer than labor to migrate across nation-state borders in search of markets. As the cases of the Bracero Program and H-1B visas demonstrate, U.S. employers in the primary labor market have found it necessary to obtain the collaboration of the federal government to access an international labor supply. On the other hand, through autonomous migration, undocumented workers have made themselves abundantly accessible for many employers in the secondary labor market, as well as for some employers in the primary labor market. The cost of this success, however, has been high. Hundreds of undocumented immigrants die annually trying to cross into the United States (Eschbach, Hagan, & Rodriguez, 2003), and among those who succeed, the reward is usually employment on the lowest rungs of the labor market and a life of concealment.

The federal government has taken an ambivalent, and often inconsistent, approach to the employment of immigrant labor. Rather than maintaining a stable policy for legal labor immigration, the federal government has used short-term policies to supplement employment-based immigration through a number of programs, such as legalizing workers through IRCA and recruiting foreign-skill labor through H-1B visas. Some employers plausibly can argue that the H-1B visa quotas represent levels of political will more than the labor needs of employers. Indeed, this would explain the dramatic fluctuations of H-1B visa allotments (e.g., by two thirds between fiscal years 2003 and 2004) without a corresponding fluctuation in the economic cycle. In this regard, the statement of Bach (2001) seems very appropriate: the allocations of H-1B visas are based more on perceptions (and persuasions) of employers and policy makers than on data. It is likely that the U.S. Congress, which is sensitive to shifting attitudes among electorates, will face strong political opposition in any attempt to shape a policy for high levels of skilled-labor importation that is more than temporary. The announcement in early 2004 by President Bush of a plan to develop a broad, long-term program of labor importation received strong opposition from within his own political party.

Another level at which the immigration-policy ambivalence of the federal government becomes evident concerns the actions of the government toward undocumented immigrant labor. By law, the federal government must act to prevent illegal immigration and the employment of workers who do not have work authorization. In border areas, since the 1990s, the federal government has carried out this responsibility through massive campaigns to arrest and deport undocumented immigrants. But in interior regions of the country, there is little indication that the federal government is attempting to arrest undocumented immigrants or locate their employers in a systematic way. To illustrate this point, when the federal government does launch coordinated operations in the interior of the country to arrest undocumented immigrant workers (e.g., Operation Tarmac in 2002 and the Wal-Mart raids in 2003), it makes national headlines, partly because of its infrequency. Another illustration of the ambivalence of the federal government toward undocumented immigrants is the way in which federal law protects certain rights of undocumented immigrants (e.g., the right for undocumented immigrants to receive emergency medical treatment, the right to file claims against abusive employers, the right for undocumented children to attend public schools).

Although not often highlighted in the immigration research literature, employers have played a critical role in anchoring immigration trends to the U.S. labor market through formal and informal means. For employers in the primary labor market, the federal government has been a critical ally in opening the door to foreign workers. In recent years, the results have been dramatic: From 1996 to 2000, foreign-born workers accounted for almost half of the net growth of the U.S. labor force (Tossi, 2002). The imbalance between world economic development and population growth keeps increasing the number of workers who turn to international migration to find jobs through governmental programs or autonomous action. Although the growth rates of the U.S. labor force are projected to decrease in coming decades, the competitive pressures of capitalism and ongoing economic restructuring are likely to keep employers focused on the advantages offered by immigrant labor.

Discussion Questions

1. Why do U.S. firms in foreign countries hire a predominantly female workforce?

2. Although the wages of workers in U.S. plants overseas are low compared with U.S. standards, is it possible that they are doing well by local standards?

3. If there are so many illegal workers employed in U.S. businesses, why doesn't the Immigration and Naturalization Service identify such workers and fine their employers for breaking the law?

Nestor Rodriguez, " 'Workers Wanted': Employer Recruitment of Immigrant Labor" (*Work and Occupations* 31, November 2004), pp. 453–473. Copyright © 2004 by Sage Publications, Inc. Reprinted by permission of Sage Publications, Inc.

Endnotes

1. One notable exception is Waldinger and Lichter's book published in 2003, *How the Other Half Works: Immigration and the Social Organization of Labor.* These authors devote a whole chapter to employers and give extensive entries in the index under the heading of "employers."

2. It is interesting that Waldinger and Lichter (2003) report that in their Los Angeles study of immigrant labor, employers were hesitant to hire kin because, among other things, it could affect the motivation among the workers. It is likely that employer confidence in the self-direction of immigrant labor, including kin, has to be gained over time, as reported by Hagan (1994).

References

Bach, R. L. (2001). New dilemmas of policy-making in transnational labor markets. In W. A. Cornelius, T. J. Espenshade, & I. Salehyan (Eds.), *The international migration of the highly skilled: Demand, supply, and development consequences in sending and receiving countries* (pp. 113–130). San Diego: University of California at San Diego, Center for Comparative Immigration Studies.

Baron, H. & Hymer, B. (1967). *The negro in the Chicago labor market.* Chicago: Chicago Urban League.

Barrera, M. (1979). *Race and class in the southwest: A theory of racial inequality.* Notre Dame, IN: University of Notre Dame Press.

Bonacich, E. A. (2001). Theory of ethnic antagonism: The split labor market. In D. B. Grusky (Ed.), *Social stratification: Class, race & gender* (pp. 555–568). Boulder, CO: Westview.

Borjas, G. J., & Tienda, M. (1993). The employment and wages of legalized immigrants. *International Migration Review, 27*(4), 712–747.

Browning, H. L., & Rodriguez, N. (1985). The migration of Mexican indocumentados as a settlement process: Implications for work. In G. J. Borjas & M. Tienda (Eds.), *Hispanics in the U.S. economy* (pp. 277–297). Orlando, FL: Academic Press.

Burawoy, M. (1976). The functions and reproduction of migrant labor: Comparative materials from southern Africa and the United States. *American Journal of Sociology, 87,* 1050–1087.

Calavita, K. (1992). *Inside the state: The Bracero Program, immigration, and the I.N.S.* New York: Routledge.

Chacon, R. D. (1980). The 1933 San Joaquin Valley cotton strike: Strikebreaking activities in California agriculture. In M. Barrera, A. Camarillo, & F. Hernandez (Eds.), *Work, family, sex roles, language* (pp. 33–70). Berkeley, CA: Tonatiuh-Quinto Sol International.

Chavez, L. R. (1992). *Shadowed lives: Undocumented immigrants in American society.* New York: Harcourt Brace.

Cleaver, H. (1979). *Reading capital politically.* Austin: University of Texas Press.

Craig, R. B. (1971). *The Bracero Program: Interest groups and foreign policy.* Austin: University of Texas Press.

Edwards, R. C., Reich, M., & Gordon, D. M. (Eds.). (1975). *Labor market segmentation.* Lexington, MA: D.C. Heath.

Eschbach, K., Hagan, J., & Rodriguez, N. (2003). Deaths during undocumented migration: Policy implications in the new era of homeland security. *Defense of the Alien, 26,* 37–52.

Galarza. E. (1964). *Merchants of labor: The Mexican bracero story.* Santa Barbara, CA: McNally & Loftin.

Galarza, E. (1977). *Farmworkers and agri-business in California, 1947–1960.* Notre Dame, IN: University of Notre Dame Press.

Gordon, D. M. (1972). *Theories of poverty and underemployment: Orthodox, radical, and dual labor market perspectives.* Lexington, MA: D.C. Heath.

Gordon, D. M., Edwards, R., & Reich, M. (1982). *Segmented work,, divided workers: The historical transformation of labor in the United States.* UK: Cambridge University Press.

Hagan, J. M. (1994). *Deciding to be legal: A Maya community in Houston.* Philadelphia: Temple University Press.

Hamilton, N., & Chinchilla, N. S. (2001). *Seeking community in a global city: Guatemalans and Salvadorans in Los Angeles.* Philadelphia: Temple University Press.

Harris, N. (1995). *The new untouchables: Immigration and the new world worker.* New York: Penguin.

Harrison, B., & Bluestone, B. (1988). *The great U-turn: Corporate restructuring and the polarizing of America.* New York: Basic Books.

Hodson, R., & Sullivan, T. A. (1990). *The social organization of work.* Belmont, CA: Wadsworth.

Hondagneu-Sotelo, P. (1994). *Gendered transitions: Mexican experiences of immigration.* Berkeley: University of California Press.

Kempadoo, K., & Doezema, J. (Eds.). (1998). *Global sex workers: Rights, resistance, and redefinition.* New York: Routledge.

Kwong, P. (1997). *Forbidden workers: Illegal Chinese immigrants and American labor.* New York: The New Press.

Lopez-Garza, M. (2001). A study of the informal economy and Latina/o immigrants in the greater LosAngeles. In M. Lopez-Garza & D. R. Diaz (Eds.), *Asian and Latino immigrants in a restructuring economy: The metamorphosis of southern California* (pp. 141–168). Palo Alto, CA: Stanford University Press.

Lowell, B. L. (2001). The foreign temporary workforce and shortages in information technology. In W. A. Cornelius, T. J. Espenshade, & I. Salehyan (Eds.), *The international migration of the highly skilled: Demand, supply, and development consequences in sending and receiving countries* (pp. 131–160). San Diego: University of California at San Diego, Center for Comparative Immigration Studies.

Massey, D. S., Durand, J., & Malone, N. J. (2002). *Beyond smoke and mirrors: Mexican immigration in an era of economic integration.* New York: Russell Sage.

Masters, S. B., & Ruthizer, T. (2000). The H-1B straightjacket: Why Congress should repeal the cap on foreign-born highly skilled workers. *Cato Institute, Center for Trade Policy Studies.* Retrieved June 10, 2004, from <www.cato.org>.

Menjivar, C. (2000). *Fragmented ties: Salvadoran immigrant networks in America.* Berkeley: University of California Press.

Moquin, W., & Van Doren, C. (Eds.). (1971). *A documentary history of the Mexican Americans.* New York: Praeger.

Mosisa, A. T. (2002). The role of foreign-born workers in the U.S. economy. *Monthly Labor Review, 125*(5), 3–14.

Pelling, H. (1960). *American labor.* Chicago: The University of Chicago Press.

Piore, M. J. (1979). *Birds of passage: Migrant labor and industrial societies.* UK: Cambridge University Press.

Portes, A., & Rumbaut, R. G. (1996). *Immigrant America: A portrait* (2nd ed.). Berkeley: University of California Press.

Reisler, M. (1976). *By the sweat of their brow: Mexican immigrant labor in the United States.* Westport, CT: Greenwood.

Repak, T. A. (1995). *Waiting on Washington: Central American workers in the nation's capital.* Philadelphia: Temple University Press.

Rodriguez, N. (1986). Chicano-indocumentado work relations: Findings of the Texas indocumentado study. In T. Mindiola, Jr. & M. Martinez (Eds.), *Chicano-Mexicano relations* (pp. 72–83). Houston, TX: University of Houston-University Park, Mexican American Studies Program, Mexican American Studies.

Samora, J. (1971). *Los mojados: The wetback story.* Notre Dame, IN: University of Notre Dame Press.

Sassen-Koob, S. (!984). The new labor demand in global cities. In M. P. Smith (Ed.), *Cities in transformation: Class, capital, and the state* (pp. 139–171). Beverly Hills, CA: Sage.

Stone, K. (1975). The origins of job structure in the steel industry. In R. C. Edwards, M. Reich, & D. M. Gordon (Eds.), *Labor market segmentation* (pp. 27–84). Lexington.MA: D.C. Heath.

Su, J. A., & Martorell, C. (2001). Exploitation and abuse in the garment industry: The case of the Thai slave-labor compound in El Monte. In M. Lopez-Garza & D. R. Diaz (Eds.), *Asian and Latino immigrants in a restructuring economy: The metamorphosis of southern California* (pp. 21–45). Palo Alto, CA: Stanford University Press.

Tossi, M. (2002). A century of change: The US labor force, 1950–2050. *Monthly Labor Review, 125*(5), 15–28.

Usdansky, M. L., & Espenshade, T. J. (2001). The evolution of U.S. policy toward employment-based immigrants and temporary workers: The H-1B debate in historical perspective. In W. A. Cornelius, T. J. Espenshade, & I. Salehyan (Eds.), *The international migration of the highly skilled: Demand, supply, and development consequences in sending and receiving countries* (pp. 23–53). San Diego: University of California at San Diego, Center for Comparative Immigration Studies.

U.S. Bureau of the Census. (1989). *Statistical abstract of the United States.* Washington, DC: U.S. Government Printing Office.

U.S. Department of Homeland Security. (2003). *Yearbook of immigration statistics, 2002.* Washington, DC: U.S. Government Printing Office.

U.S. Immigration and Naturalization Service. (2000). *Statistical yearbook of the Immigration and Naturalization Service, 1998.* Washington, DC: U.S. Government Printing Office.

Waldinger, R., & Lichter, M. I. (2003). *How the other half works: Immigration and the social organization of labor.* Berkeley: University of California Press.

The World Bank. (1995). *Workers in an integrating world.* UK: Oxford University Press.

Zhang, L. (2001). *Strangers in the city: Reconfigurations of space, power, and social networks within China's floating population.* Palo Alto, CA: Stanford University Press. ✦

10

Technology: The 'Great Growling Engine of Change'

Peter Dicken

Without recent advances in computer-based production systems and telecommunications technology, we could not have created the *new economy*, which is the subject of this book. In this chapter, Peter Dicken invites the reader to see technology as the engine of change and discusses technology in terms of four broad change-related types: small-scale incremental innovation; radical innovations that affect specific products or processes; far-reaching changes in technology that give rise to new economic sectors, like biotechnology; and large-scale revolutionary changes, such as the computer, that transform products and styles of production and management that affect almost every branch of the economy.

Dicken identifies the main features of technological change that have been responsible for the globalization of economic activity. He also cautions readers not to adopt a "deterministic" view of technology that assumes that new technology will inevitably be adopted and produce a particular outcome. A nondeterministic view of technology says that the choice of whether to use a new technology is usually a political choice based on a struggle between those who believe they will benefit and those who believe they will be harmed.

Technology and Economic Transformation

Technological change is at the heart of the process of economic growth and economic development. As Joseph Schumpeter (1943, p. 83) pointed out many years ago, 'the fundamental impulse that sets and keeps the capitalist engine in motion comes from the new consumers' goods, the new methods of production or transportation, the new markets, the new forces of industrial organization that capitalist enterprise creates'. Technological change is the 'prime motor of capitalism'; the 'great growling engine of change' (Toffler, 1971); the 'fundamental force in shaping the patterns of transformation of the economy' (Freeman, 1988); the 'chronic disturber of comparative advantage' (Chesnais, 1986). Although technologies, in the form of inventions and innovations, originate in specific places, they are no longer confined to such places. Innovations spread or diffuse with great rapidity under current conditions. Indeed, one of the most significant sets of innovations is in the sphere of communications, which itself facilitates such technological diffusion. As we shall see, however, this does not signal the 'death of distance' or 'the end of geography'. Indeed, there continues to be a pronounced geography of knowledge creation and a strong geographical localization of innovative activity.

Technology is, without doubt, one of the most important contributory factors underlying the internationalization and globalization of economic activity:

Technological change, through its impact on the economics of production and on the flow of information, is a principal factor determining the structure of industry on a national scale. This has now become true on a global scale.

Long-term technological trends and recent advances are reconfiguring the location, ownership, and management of various types of productive activity among countries and regions. The increasing ease with which technical and market knowledge, capital, physical artefacts, and managerial control can be extended around the globe has made possible the integration of economic activity in many widely separated locations. In doing so, technological advance has facilitated the rapid growth of the multinational corporation with subsidiaries in many countries but business strategies determined by headquarters in a single nation. (Brooks and Guile, 1987, p. 2)

However, in looking specifically at technology in this chapter, we need to beware of adopting a position of technological determinism. It is all too easy to be seduced by the notion that technology 'causes' a specific set of changes, makes particular structures and arrangements 'inevitable' or that the path of technological change is linear and sequential. Technology in, and of, itself does not cause particular kinds of change. In one sense, then, technology is an enabling or facilitating agent: it makes possible new structures, new organizational and geographical arrangements of economic activities, new products and new processes, while not making particular outcomes inevitable. But in certain circumstances technology may, indeed, be more of an imperative. In a highly competitive environment, once a particular technology is in use by one firm, then its adoption by others may become virtually essential to ensure competitive survival. More generally, as Freeman (1982, p. 169) points out, for business firms 'not to innovate is to die'.

In this chapter we focus only on certain aspects of technology and technological change: those which specifically influence the processes of internationalization and globalization of economic activity. The chapter is divided into four major parts:

- First, some of the broad characteristics of technological change are discussed in order to identify the key technologies and their evolution over time.

- Second, we focus on the 'space shrinking' technologies of transport and communication which are obviously central to the processes of internationalization and globalization.

- Third, we look at technological changes in both products and processes and explore the extent to which totally new forms of production technology and organization are occurring.

- Fourth, we focus explicitly on the geography of innovation, in particular on the tendency of innovative activity and knowledge creation to be geographically localized in 'technology districts'.

The Process of Technological Change: An Evolutionary Perspective[1]

Technological change is a form of learning: of how to solve specific problems in a highly diverse, and often volatile, environment. It is, however, more than a narrowly 'technical' process. Technology is also not independent or autonomous; it does not have a life of its own. Technology is a social process which is socially and institutionally embedded. It is created and adopted (or not) by human agency: individuals, organizations, societies. The ways in which technologies are used—even their very creation—are conditioned by their social and their economic context. In effect, from the viewpoint taken here, this means the values and motivations of capitalist business enterprises operating within an intensely competitive system. Choices and uses of technologies, therefore, are influenced by the drive for profit, capital accumulation and investment, increased market share and so on.

A Typology of Technological Change

Freeman and Perez (1988) identify four broad types of technological change, each of which is progressively more significant:

- *Incremental innovations:* the small-scale, progressive modification of existing products and processes:

  They may often occur, not so much as the result of any deliberate research and development activity, but as the outcome of inventions and improvements suggested by engineers and others directly engaged in the production process, or as a result of initiatives and proposals by users ('learning by doing' and 'learning by using'). . . . Although their combined effect is extremely important in the growth of productivity, no single incremental innovation has dramatic effects, and they may sometimes pass unnoticed and unrecorded. (Freeman and Perez, 1988, p. 46)

- *Radical innovations:* discontinuous events which may drastically change existing products or processes. A single radical innovation will not, however, have a widespread effect on the economic system; 'its economic impact remains relatively small and localized unless a whole cluster of radical innovations are linked together in the rise of new industries and services, such as the synthetic materials industry or the semiconductor industry' (Freeman, 1987, p. 129).

- *Changes of 'technology system':* 'these are far-reaching changes in technology, affecting several branches of the economy, as well as giving rise to entirely new sectors. They are based on a combination of radical and incremental innovations, together with organizational and managerial innovations affecting more than one or a few firms' (Freeman and Perez, 1988, p. 46). Freeman (1987) suggests that the following five 'generic' technologies have created such new technology systems:

1) information technology.

2) biotechnology.

3) materials technology.

4) energy technology.

5) space technology.

- *Changes in the techno-economic paradigm:* the truly large-scale revolutionary changes which are

  the 'creative gales of destruction' that are at the heart of Schumpeter's long wave theory. They represent those new technology systems which have such pervasive effects on the economy as a whole that they change the 'style' of production and management throughout the system. The introduction of electric power or steam power or the electronic computer are examples of such deep-going transformations. A change of this kind carries with it many clusters of radical and incremental innovations, and may eventually embody several new technology systems. Not only does this fourth type of technological change lead to the emergence of a new range of products, services, systems and industries in its own right—it also affects directly or indirectly almost every other branch of the economy . . . the changes involved go beyond specific product or process technologies and affect the input cost structure and conditions of production and distribution throughout the system. (Freeman, 1987, p. 130)

Information Technology: A Key Generic Technology[2]

. . . The first of the five 'generic' technologies referred to above is information technology (IT). 'The contemporary change of paradigm may be seen as a shift from a technology based primarily on cheap inputs of energy to one predominantly based on cheap inputs of information derived from advances in microelectronic and telecommunications technology' (Freeman, 1988, p. 10). Information technology, therefore, is the new techno-economic paradigm around which the next wave of technological and economic changes will cluster. But, as Hall and Preston (1988, p. 30) point out, information technology in itself is nothing new: 'for thousands of years, since the first cave paintings and the invention of writing humans have used tools and techniques to collect, generate and record data'. Consequently, they identify three main phases of information technology:

- Simple pictorial representation and written language, evolving eventually into printing: its basic elements were paper, writing instruments, ink and printing presses.

- Mechanical, electromechanical and early electronic technologies which developed during the late nineteenth and early twentieth centuries: the basic elements were the telephone, typewriter, gramophone/phonograph, camera, tabulating machine, radio and television.

- Microelectronic technologies, which emerged only in the second half of the twentieth century: the basic elements are computers, robots and other information-handling production equipment, and office equipment (including facsimile machines). Hall and Preston regard the first of these as 'old IT'; the second and third together as 'new IT'. They then employ a further term 'convergent IT' to refer to the newest advances of the 1970s and 1980s, whereby computers and telecommunications became integrated into a single system of information processing and exchange.

It is this quality of the convergence of two initially distinct technologies which is of the greatest importance for developments in today's (and tomorrow's) global economy. It is this kind of information technology which is most significant for the processes of internationalization and globalization of economic activities. When we use the term 'information technology' or 'IT' in this and the following chapters it is the convergent IT which is involved. . . .

The 'Space-Shrinking' Technologies[3]

A fundamental prerequisite of the evolution of international production and of the transnational corporation [TNC] is the development of technologies which overcome the frictions of space and time. The most important of such enabling technologies— and the most obvious—are the technologies of transport and communications. Neither of these technologies can be regarded as the cause of international production or of the TNC; rather, they make such phenomena feasible. But without them, today's complex global economic system simply could not exist. Indeed, both the geographical and organizational scale at which any human activity can occur is directly related to the available media of transport and communication. Similarly, the degree of geographical specialization—the spatial division of labour—is constrained by these media.

Transport and communication technologies perform two distinct, though closely related and complementary roles:

- *Transport systems* are the means by which materials, products and other tangible entities (including people) are transferred from place to place.

- *Communication systems* are the means by which information is transmitted from place to place in the form of ideas, instructions, images and so on.

For most of human history, transport and communications were effectively one and the same. Prior to the invention of electric technology in the nineteenth century, information could move only at the same speed, and over the same distance, as the prevailing transport system would allow. Electric technology broke that link, making it increasingly necessary to treat transport and communication as separate, though intimately related, technologies. Developments in both have transformed our world, permitting unprecedented mobility of materials and products and a globalization of markets.

Major Developments in Transport Technology

In terms of the time it takes to get from one part of the world to another there is no doubt that the world has 'shrunk' dramatically. . . . For most of human history, the speed and efficiency of transport were staggeringly low and the costs of overcoming the friction of distance prohibitively high. Movement over land was especially slow and difficult before the development of the railways. Indeed, even as late as the early nineteenth century, the means of transport were not really very different from those prevailing in biblical times. The major breakthrough came with two closely associated innovations: the application of steam power as a means of propulsion and the use of iron and steel for trains and railway tracks and for oceangoing vessels. These, coupled with the linking together of overland and ocean transport and the cutting of the canals at Suez and Panama, greatly telescoped geographical distance at a global scale. The railway and the steamship introduced a new, and much enlarged, scale of human activity. The flow of materials and products was enormously enhanced and the possibilities of geographical specialization were greatly stimulated. Such innovations were a major factor in the massive expansion in the global economic system during the nineteenth century.

The twentieth century, and especially the past few decades, has seen an acceleration of this process of global shrinkage. In economic terms, the most important developments have been the introduction of commercial jet aircraft, the development of much larger ocean-going vessels (superfreighters) and the introduction of containerization, which greatly simplifies transhipment from one mode of transport to another and increases the security of shipments. Of these, it is the jet aircraft which has had the most pervasive influence, particularly in the development of the TNC. It is no coincidence that the take-off of TNC

growth and the (more literal) take-off of commercial jets both occurred during the 1950s. As a consequence in terms of time, New York is now closer to Tokyo than it was to Philadelphia in the days of the thirteen colonies. . . .

However, although the world has shrunk in relative terms, we need to be aware that . . . such shrinkage is highly uneven. The technological developments in transport (and in communications) tend to be geographically concentrated. What the geographer Donald Janelle called *time-space convergence* affects some places more than others. While the world's leading national economies and the world's major cities are being pulled closer together others—less industrialized countries or smaller towns and rural areas—are, in effect, being left behind. . . .

Major Developments in Communications Technology

Both the time and relative cost of transporting materials, products and people have fallen dramatically as the result of technological innovations in the transport media. However, such developments have depended, to a considerable degree, on parallel developments in communications technology. In the nineteenth century, for example, neither rail nor ocean transport could have developed as they did without the innovation of the electric telegraph and, later, the oceanic cable. Only with the ability to transmit information at great speed—for example to co-ordinate flows of commodities on a global scale—could the potential of the transport technologies be fully realized. Similarly, the far more complex global transport system of the present day depends fundamentally on telecommunications technology.

The communications media are, however, fundamentally significant in their own right. Indeed, as implied in our earlier discussion of the central role of information technology, communications technologies should now be regarded as the key technology transforming relationships at the global scale. 'The new telecommunications technologies are the electronic high-ways of the informational age, equivalent to the role played by railway systems in the process of industrialization' (Henderson and Castells, 1987, p. 6).

Transmission channels: Satellites and optical fibres. Global communications systems have been transformed radically during the past twenty or thirty years through a whole cluster of significant innovations in information technology. Probably the most important catalyst to enhanced global communications was the development of satellite technology. . . .

Satellite technology, together with a whole host of other communications technologies, is making possible quite re-markable levels of global communication of conventional messages and also the transmission of data. In this respect, the key element is the linking together of computer technologies with information-transmission technologies over vast distances. It has become possible for a message to be transmitted in one location and received in another on the other side of the world virtually simultaneously. Consequently,

> communications costs are becoming increasingly insensitive to distance. The crucial fact is the economics of satellite communication. Within the beam of a satellite it makes no difference to costs whether you are transmitting for five hundred miles or five thousand miles. The message goes from the earth station up twenty-two thousand three hundred miles to the satellite and down again twenty-two thousand three hundred miles. It makes no difference whether the two points on earth are close together or far apart. . . . The important point about satellites is that their existence sets a limit on the extent to which costs are a function of distance. Many other technologies may compete with satellites, but in the end, satellite communication will ultimately be cheaper. Whatever that distance, it makes no difference how much further one communicates, the costs will be the same. Under those circumstances, the cost of access to any particular data base or in-formation service becomes largely independent of its location. That does not make it free nor even necessarily cheap. There are costs for compiling the data and costs for manipulating it. (de Sola Pool, 1981, pp. 162–63)

Satellite communications are now being challenged by a new technology: optical fibre cables. Optical fibre systems have a very large carrying capacity, and transmit information at very high speed and with a high signal strength. 'Each hair-like strand can now accommodate up to 60,000 simultaneous telephone calls (as opposed to 6–7,000 for a much wider coaxial cable)' (Graham and Marvin, 1996, p. 18). . . .

Nevertheless, only the very large organization, whether business or government, yet has the resources to utilize fully the new communications technologies. For the TNC, however, they have become essential to its operations.[4] All TNCs operate immense international telecommunications networks. They are the major users of international leased telecommunications networks, which permit them to transmit their internal communications at great speed to other parts of their international corporate network. . . . It is the possession of such instantaneous global communication systems that enables the TNC to operate globally, whether it is engaged in manufacturing, resource exploitation or business services. . . .

Summary

Technological developments in communications media have transformed space-time relationships between all parts of the world. Of course, not all places are equally affected. Consistent with the nature of the time-space convergence process, as defined by Janelle, is its inherent geographical unevenness. In general, the places which benefit most from innovations in the communications media are the 'important' places. New investments in communications technology are market related; they go to where the returns are likely to be high. The cumulative effect is to reinforce both certain communications routes at the global scale and to enhance the significance of the nodes (cities/countries) on those routes. For example, although developing countries contain around 75 per cent of the world's population they have only around 12 per cent of the world's telephone lines. 'A new geography of rich and poor is emerging with the poor now those deprived of access to . . . communications technology' (Batty and Barr, 1994, p. 711). There is an additional factor which limits the universal spread of new communications technologies. In virtually all countries of the world, governments regulate the communications industries within their borders. Today, however, there is a strong trend towards the deregulation of telecommunications in several countries. Within this geographically uneven communications surface there is also a social dimension. Not everybody—whether they are business firms or private individuals—has equal access. Despite the general decline in communications costs driven by technological change, the costs of usage are far from trivial.

Nevertheless, although we need to beware of the hype which surrounds the 'information revolution', there is no doubt that epochal changes are occurring through the development of digital technologies:

> The rapid advance of digital systems, based on the 'ones and zeros' of binary computer language, is sweeping away the remaining differences between data processing and telephony, and leading to the dawn of a new information age, epitomized by the explosive growth of the Internet and internal corporate intranets. . . . Digital technology has made it possible to convert text, sound, graphics and moving images into coded digital messages which can be combined, stored, manipulated and transmitted quickly, efficiently, and in large volumes over wired and wireless networks without loss of quality. As a result, electronic commerce and the multimedia revolution are driving the computing and telecommunications worlds into ever-closer competition and cooperation. 'The coming era of digital

personal communications is an era of converging technologies, converging products, converging media and converging industries.' (*The Financial Times*, 5 March 1997)

Technological Changes in Products and Processes

When thinking of 'products' most of us tend to think of consumer products. But, for industry as a whole, most products are themselves intermediate in nature; they form the inputs to subsequent stages in the production chain. Bearing in mind this intricate relationship between product and process, however, it is useful to look at them separately in the first instance. . . .

The Production Process and Technology

In today's intensely competitive global environment product innovation alone is inadequate as a basis for a firm's survival and profitability. Firms must endeavour to operate the production process as efficiently as possible. Recent developments in technology—and, especially, in information technology—are having profound effects upon production processes in all economic sectors. Three major, and closely interrelated, decisions are involved in the production process (Smith, 1981):

- The *technique* to be adopted. This decision concerns both the particular technology used and also the way in which the various inputs or factors of production are combined. It is almost always possible to vary the precise combination of, say, labour and capital according to their relative availability and cost. However, there are limits to such substitution of factors. Some production processes are intrinsically more capital intensive than others and *vice versa*. Closely related to the question of technique is that of

- The *scale of production*. In general, the average cost of production tends to decline as the volume of production increases. The extent of such economies of scale varies considerably from one industry to another. They are much greater, for example, in automobile production than in the manufacture of fashion garments. Technique and scale are, themselves, closely related. . . .

- *Location.* The choice of location cannot be considered in isolation from scale and technique. Different scales of operation may require different locations to give access to markets of different sizes. . . . Different techniques will favour different locations, as firms tend to gravitate toward cheap sources of the inputs required in the largest quantities, and location itself can influence the combination of inputs and hence the technique adopted. (Smith, 1981, pp. 23–24)

Clearly, therefore, a firm which is seeking to reduce its production costs or to increase its efficiency and productivity can seek such economies at different points in the production process. It can attempt to purchase lower-cost inputs. In the case of material inputs this increasingly involves a shift to supplies in developing countries. In the case of labour, a relatively immobile factor of production, the search for lower costs may involve the physical relocation of production to a cheap labour location.

Flexibility: The World 'After Fordism'

This point leads us to consider the major recent developments that have been occurring in the technology of production processes and, particularly, those associated with the new techno-economic paradigm of information technology. Most technological developments in production processes are, as we observed earlier, gradual and incremental: the result of 'learning by doing' and of 'learning by using'. But periods of radical transformation of the production process have occurred throughout history.

We are now in the midst of such a radical transformation.

Over the long timescale of the development of industrialization, the production process has developed through a series of stages each of which represents increasing efforts to mechanize and to control more closely the nature and speed of work. The stages generally identified are:

- *Manufacture:* the collecting together of labour into workshops and the division of the labour process into specific tasks.

- *Machinofacture:* the application of mechanical processes and power through machinery in factories. Further division of labour.

- *Scientific management* ('Taylorism'): the subjection of the work process to scientific study in the late nineteenth century. This enhanced the fineness of the division of labour into specific tasks together with increased control and supervision.

- *'Fordism':* the development of assembly-line processes which controlled the pace of production and permitted the production of large volumes of standardized products.

- *'After-Fordism':* the development of new flexible production systems based upon the deep application of information technologies. . . .

The Fordist system was characterized by very large-scale production units using assembly-line manufacturing techniques and producing large volumes of standardized products for mass market consumption. It was a type of production especially characteristic of particular industrial sectors, notably automobiles. Not all sectors, nor all production processes, lent themselves to such a system of mass production but it was seen to be the main characteristic. . . . Many now argue that this Fordist system of production (and its associated organizational structures) entered a period of 'crisis' from about the mid-1970s and that it has been replaced by new modes of production.

The most important characteristic of this new system is claimed to be flexibility: of the production process itself, of its organization within the factory and of the organization of relationships between customer and supplier firms.

The key to production flexibility lies in the use of *information technologies* in machines and operations. These permit more sophisticated control over the production process. With the increasing sophistication of automated processes and, especially, the new flexibility of electronically controlled technology, far-reaching changes in the process of production need not necessarily be associated with increased scale of production. Indeed, one of the major results of the new electronic and computer-aided production technology is that it permits rapid switching from one part of a process to another and allows the tailoring of production to the requirements of individual customers. "Traditional" automation is geared to high-volume standardized production; the newer 'flexible manufacturing systems' are quite different:

> Flexible automation's greatest potential for radical change lies in its capacity to manufacture goods cheaply in small volumes. . . . In the past batch manufacturing required machines dedicated to a single task. These machines had to be either rebuilt or replaced at the time of product change. Flexible manufacturing brings a degree of diversity to manufacturing never before available. Different products can be made on the same line at will. . . . The strategic implications for the manufacturer are truly staggering. Under hard automation the greatest economies were realised only at the most massive scales. But flexible automation makes similar economies available at a wide range of scales. A flexible automation system can turn out a small batch or even a single copy of a product as efficiently as a production line designed to turn out a million identical items. (Bylinsky, 1983, pp. 53–54)

What does this all mean in terms of the broader question of what comes 'after-Fordism'? There are strongly opposed interpretations of the nature of Fordism itself (for example, the extent to which it really constituted an all-embracing system of production, even in its heyday) and of what it is being replaced by.[5] Is it a variant on Fordism, 'neo-Fordism', in which automated control systems are applied within a Fordist structure? Or is it a totally new 'post-Fordism', in which the new technologies create quite different forms of production organization? It is a debate which stretches way beyond the bounds of technology and technological change into the realms of the social organization of production, of the ways in which the state regulates economic activity, and the nature of consumption and markets. . . .

Flexible specialization: The rebirth of craft-based production? Some assert unequivocally that flexible specialization is becoming the norm; the dominant style of production displacing Fordism. This is the 'post-Fordist' view which sees the hegemony of Fordism as being replaced by a new regime of flexible production and smaller organizational units. It is the viewpoint most closely associated with the work of Piore and Sabel whose 1984 book, *The Second Industrial Divide*, triggered off much of the 'after-Fordist' debate. As we have seen, Fordism was associated overwhelmingly with very large, vertically integrated firms producing standardized goods at very large volumes to benefit from economies of scale in production and selling to mass consumer markets. Piore and Sabel's interpretation of the development of flexible production technologies is that it leads to the resurgence of small, independent entrepreneurial firms emancipated from the tyrannies of mass production by the new flexibility which permits small-scale operations to serve small (perhaps local) markets. . . .

This craft-based, 'flex-spec' interpretation of the changes in the production system also sees it as heralding a process of reskilling of labour as opposed to the relatively low skills characteristic of Fordism. The deintegration of the production system also goes hand-in-hand with a deintegrated organizational structure which then develops as horizontal networks of inter-related, specialist firms. . . .

Conclusion

The aim of this chapter has been to identify some of those features of technological change which are most important in the internationalization and globalization of economic activity. Technological change is at the dynamic heart of economic growth and development; it is fundamental to the evolution of a global economic system. We focused on four specific aspects of technological change.

First, we explored the process of technological change as an evolutionary process in which much change is gradual and incremental, often unnoticed but none the less extremely significant. But there are periodic radical transformations of existing technologies—revolutionary developments in clusters of technologies—which dramatically alter not only products and processes in one industry but which also pervade the entire socioeconomic system. These are the shifts in the technoeconomic paradigm which seem to be associated with the long waves of economic change.

Second, we concentrated on what is undoubtedly the major technological driving force today: the convergence of two initially distinct technologies—computer technology and communications technology—into a single, though complex, strand: information technology. IT is transforming both the technologies of transport and communication and also the technologies of products and processes. IT is capable of spreading into all sectors of the economy and to all types and sizes of organization but it is still the very large business organization, particularly the TNC, which is reaping the greatest benefits.

Third, we argued that the claim that we are shifting from one hegemonic (Fordist) system to another hegemonic (post-Fordist) system is far too sweeping and simplistic to capture the complex reality of a world based upon increased flexibility of production and organization. There are a number of alternatives to Fordism which, although they are all based upon the new flexibilities, take on rather different forms. We need to recognize the existence of such diversity. Part of that diversity is related to the fourth focus of the chapter: the strongly localized nature of innovation and technological change. The path-dependent nature of technological change and the social conditions within which such change occurs give major importance to the *geography* of the process.

In concluding this chapter, then, we should again remind ourselves that technological change, in itself, is not deterministic. We must not assume that a particular technology will lead inevitably and irrevocably to a particular outcome. More realistically

> A frontier of new possibilities has been defined: a frontier which identifies the types of new products and services that can be made available. That frontier is itself a product of past choices. . . . Specific choices within the frontier of technological possibilities are not the product of technological change; they are, rather, the product of those who make the choices within the frontier of possibilities. *Technology does not drive choice; choice drives technology.* (Borrus, quoted in Cohen and Zysman, 1987, p. 183, emphasis added)

Discussion Questions

1. What might have been some of the political forces that favored development of the auto industry over development of a mass transportation system?

2. Can you think of a technology that has potential value but has not been developed and adopted?

3. What past technological innovation has had the greatest impact on American

society? The internal combustion engine? The telephone? Air travel?

Endnotes

1. This kind of perspective on technological change is based upon the work of Perez (1985), Freeman (1982; 1987), Dosi et al. (1988). See also Metcalfe and Diliso (1996).
2. Useful general introductions to information technology can be found in Forester (1985; 1987). More advanced treatments are provided by Freeman (1987), Hall and Preston (1988), Hepworth (1989), Castells (1996).
3. For broad-ranging discussions of these technologies, see Hall and Preston (1988), Brunn and Leinbach (1991), Castells (1996), Graham and Marvin (1996).
4. These data are from Baylin (1996).
5. There is a huge literature on this subject. Important contributions are provided by Piore and Sabel (1984), Blackburn, Coombs and Green (1985), Gertler (1988), Coombs and Jones (1989), Kenney and Florida (1989), Schoenberger (1988a, 1989), Sayer and Walker (1992), Amin (1994), Ruigrok and van Tulder (1995).

References

Amin, A. (ed) (1994) *Post-Fordism: A Reader*, Blackwell, Oxford.

Batty, M. and Barr, R. (1994) The electronic frontier: Exploring and mapping cyberspace, *Futures*, Vol. 26, pp. 699–712.

Baylin, F. (1996) *World Satellite Yearbook* (4th edition), Baylin Publications, Boulder, CO.

Blackburn, P., Coombs, R. and Green, K. (1985) *Technology, Economic Growth and the Labour Process*, Macmillan, London.

Brooks, H.E. and Guile, B.R. (1987) Overview, in B.R. Guile and H.E. Brooks (eds) *Technology and Global Industry: Companies and Nations in the World Economy*, National Academy Press, Washington, DC, pp. 1–15.

Brunn, S.D. and Leinbach, T.R. (eds) (1991) *Collapsing Space and Time: Geographic Aspects of Communication and Information*, HarperCollins, New York.

Bylinsky, G. (1983) The race to the automatic factory, *Fortune*, 21 February, pp. 52–64.

Castells, M. (1996) *The Rise of the Network Society*, Volume 1, Blackwell, Oxford.

Chesnais, F. (1986) Science, technology and competitiveness, *Science Technology Industry Review*, Vol. 1, pp. 85–129.

Cohen, S.S. and Zysman, J. (1987) *Manufacturing Matters: The Myth of the Post-Industrial Economy*, Basic Books, New York.

Coombs, R. and Jones, B. (1989) Alternative successors to Fordism, in H. Ernste and C. Jaeger (eds) *Information Society and Spatial Structure*, Belhaven Press, London, Chapter 8.

de Sola Pool, I. (1981) International aspects of telecommunications policy, in ML. Moss (ed) *Telecommunications and Productivity*, Addison-Wesley, Reading, MA, Chapter 7.

Dosi, G., Freeman, C., Nelson, R., Silverberg, G. and Soete, L. (eds) (1988) *Technical Change and Economic Theory*, Pinter, London.

Forester, T. (ed) (1985) *The Information Technology Revolution*, Blackwell, Oxford.

——. (1987) *High-Tech Society: The Story of the Information Technology Revolution*, Blackwell, Oxford.

Freeman, C. (1982) *The Economics of Industrial Innovation*, Pinter, London.

——. (1987) The challenge of new technologies, in OECD, *Interdependence and Cooperation in Tomorrow's World*, OECD, Paris, pp. 123–56.

——. (1988) Introduction, in G. Dosi, C. Freeman, R. Nelson, G. Silverberg and L. Soete (eds) *Technical Change and Economic Theory*, Pinter, London.

Freeman, C. and Perez, C. (1988) Structural crises of adjustment, business cycles and investment behaviour, in G. Dosi, C. Freeman, R. Nelson,

Gertler, M. (1988) *The Limits to Flexibility: Comments on the Post-Fordist Vision of Production and Its Geography*, Transactions, Institute of British Geographers, Vol.13, pp. 419–32.

Graham, S. and Marvin, S. (1996) *Telecommunications and the City: Electronic Spaces, Urban Places*, Routledge, London.

Hall, P. and Preston, P. (1988) *The Carrier Wave: New Information Technology and the Geography of Innovation, 1846–2003*, Unwin Hyman, London.

Henderson, J. and Castells, M. (eds) (1987) *Global Restructuring and Territorial Development*, Sage, London.

Hepworth, M. (1989) *Geography of the Information Economy*, Belhaven, London.

Kenney, M. and Florida, R. (1989) Japan's role in a post-Fordist age, *Futures*, Vol. 21, pp. 136–51.

Metcalfe, J.S. and Diliso, N. (1996) Innovation, capabilities and knowledge: the epistemic connection, in J. de la Mothe and G. Paquet (eds) *Evolutionary Economics and the New International Political Economy*, Pinter, London, Chapter 3.

Perez, C. (1985) Microelectronics, long waves and world structural change, *World Development*, Vol. 13, pp.441–63.

Piore, M.J. and Sabel, C.F. (1984) *The Second Industrial Divide: Possibilities for Prosperity*, Basic Books, New York.

Ruigrok, W and van Tulder, IL (1995) *The Logic of International Restructuring*, Routledge, London.

Sabel, C.F. (1989) Flexible specialization and the re-emergence of regional economies, in P. Hirst and J. Zeitlin (eds) *Reversing Industrial Decline: Industrial Structure and Policy in Britain and Her Competitors*, Berg, Oxford, Chapter 1.

Sayer, A. and Walker, R. (1992) Beyond Fordism and flexibility, in A. Sayer and R. Walker, *The New Social Economy*, Blackwell, Oxford, Chapter 5.

Schoenberger, E. (1988) From Fordism to flexible accumulation: Technology, competitive strategies and international location, *Environment and Planning D: Society and Space*, Vol. 6, pp. 245–62.

——. (1989) Thinking about flexibility: A response to Gertler, *Transactions, Institute of British Geographers*, Vol. 14, pp. 98–108.

Schumpeter, J. (1943) *Capitalism, Socialism and Democracy*, Allen & Unwin, London.

Smith, D.M. (1981) *Industrial Location: An Industrial-Geographical Analysis* (2nd edition), Wiley, New York.

Toffler, A. (1971) *Future Shock*, Pan, London. ✦

11

Worker Skills and Computer-Mediated Work

Shoshana Zuboff

Without a doubt, the part of mankind which has advanced intellectually is quite under the spell of technology. Its charms are twofold. On the one hand, there is the enticement of increasingly comfortable living standards; on the other, there is a reduction in the amount of work which is necessary to do.... The irresistible pull toward technological development ... is caused, we should remember, by the unconscious and deep-rooted desire to free ourselves from the material oppression of the material world.

—Folkert Wilken,
The Liberation of Capital

The Body's Virtuosity at Work

The new economy, with its emphasis on computer-based work, has elevated so-called "knowledge workers" and "symbol analysts" to center stage in the workplace. Left behind, backstage, with the decline of Rust Belt manufacturing, are the blue-collar manual workers whose physical work and skill has rarely been viewed as based on special intelligence. It is hard to believe today that these craft/construction workers were once referred to as *blue-collar aristocrats.*

The rise of the knowledge worker as a privileged employee has led some scholars to question the very meaning of "skill" and why it is that some types of work are believed to be mental in nature, but other types of work are viewed as manual. Some critics of skill have gone so far as to assert that it probably takes more skill to drive a car on the Dan Ryan in Chicago than it does to fly a 747. How is the work of a waitress or a carpenter any less based on complex spatial and mathematical calculations than the work of a computer programmer? Is it possible that college-based computer graduates just have a better public relations agent?

This chapter examines how the introduction of computers into industrial work affects the experience-based skills of workers. The author contrasts the nature of action-centered physical skills with intellective skill that is based on abstract thought. The author asks the reader to consider how computer-mediated work affects how workers think about their work and themselves.

In the older pulp and paper mills of Piney Wood and Tiger Creek, where a highly experienced work force was making the transition to a new computer-based technology, operators had many ways of using their bodies to achieve precise knowledge. One man judged the condition of paper coming off a dry roller by the sensitivity of his hair to electricity in the atmosphere around the machine. Another could judge the moisture content of a roll of pulp by a quick slap of his hand. Immediacy was the mode in which things were known; it provided a feeling of certainty, of knowing "what's going on." One worker in Piney Wood described how it felt to be removed from the physical presence of the process equipment and asked to perform his tasks from a computerized control room:

> It is very different now.... It is hard to get used to not being out there with the process. I miss it a lot. I miss being able to see it. You can see when the pulp runs over a vat. You know what's happening.

The worker's capacity "to know" has been lodged in sentience and displayed in action. The physical presence of the process equipment has been the setting that corresponded to this knowledge, which could, in turn, be displayed only in that context. As long as the action context remained intact, it was possible for knowledge to remain implicit. In this sense, the worker knew a great deal, but very little of that knowledge was ever articulated, written down, or made explicit in any fashion. Instead, operators went about their business, displaying their know-how and rarely attempting to translate that knowledge into terms that were publicly accessible. This is what managers mean when they speak of the "art" involved in operating these plants. As one manager at Piney Wood described it:

> There are a lot of operators working here who cannot verbally give a description of some piece of the process. I can ask them what is going on at the far end of the plant, and they can't tell me, but they can draw it for me. By taking away this physical contact that he understands, it's like we have taken away his blueprint. He can't verbalize his way around the process.

In this regard, the pulp and paper mills embody a historical sweep that is unavailable in many other forms of work. Unlike other continuous-process industries, such as oil refining or chemical production, the pulp-and-paper-making process has not yet yielded a full scientific explication. This has retarded the spread of automation and also has worked to preserve the integrity of a certain amount of craft know-how among those operators with lengthy experience in the industry. Like other continuous-process operations, the technological environment in these mills has created work that was more mediated by equipment and dependent upon indirect data than, say, work on an assembly line. However, discrete instrumentation typically was located on or close to the actual operating equipment, allowing the operator to combine data from an instrument reading with data from his or her own senses. Most workers believed that they "knew" what was going on at any particular moment because of what they saw and felt, and they used past experience to relate these perceptions to a set of likely consequences. The required sequences and routines necessary to control certain parts

of the process and to make proper adjustments for achieving the best results represented a form of knowledge that the worker displayed in action as a continual reflection of this sentient involvement. Acquired experience made it possible to relate current conditions to past events; thus, an operator's competence increased as the passing of time enabled him or her to experience the action possibilities of a wide variety of operating conditions.

In Piney Wood and Tiger Creek, the technology change did not mean simply trading one form of instrumentation for another. Because the traditional basis of competence, like skilled work in most industries, was still heavily dependent upon sentient involvement, information technology was experienced as a radical departure from the taken-for-granted approach to daily work. In this sense, workers' experiences in these mills bridge two manufacturing domains. They not only illustrate the next phase of technological change within the continuous-process industries but also foreshadow the dilemmas that will emerge in other industrial organizations (for example, batch and assembly-line production) with the transition from machine to computer mediation.

When a process engineer attempts to construct a set of algorithms that will be the basis for automating some portion of the production process, he or she first interviews those individuals who currently perform the tasks that will be automated. The process engineer must learn the detail of their actions in order to translate their practice into the terms of a mathematical model. The algorithms in such a model explicate, rationalize, and institutionalize know-how. In the course of these interviews, the process engineer is likely to run up against the limits of implicit knowledge. A worker may perform competently yet be unable to communicate the structure of his or her actions. As one engineer discovered:

> There are operators who can run the paper machine with tremendous efficiency, but they cannot describe to you how they do it. They have built-in ac-

tions and senses that they are not aware of. One operation required pulling two levers simultaneously, and they were not conscious of the fact that they were pulling two levers. They said they were pulling one. The operators run the mill, but they don't understand how. There are operators who know exactly what to do, but they cannot tell you how they do it.

Though every operator with similar responsibilities performs the same functions, each will perform them in a unique way, fashioned according to a personal interpretation of what works best. A process engineer contrasted the personal rendering of skill with the impersonal but consistently optimal performance of the computer:

> There is no question that the computer takes the human factor out of running the machine. Each new person who comes on shift will make their own distinct changes, according to their sense of what is the best setting. In contrast, the computer runs exactly the same way all the time. Each operator thinks he does a better job, each one thinks he has a better intimate understanding of the equipment than another operator. But none of them can compete with the computer.

These comments describe a particular quality of skill that I refer to as action-centered. Four components of *action-centered* skill are highlighted in the experiences of these workers:

1. *Sentience.* Action-centered skill is based upon sentient information derived from physical cues.

2. *Action-dependence.* Action-centered skill is developed in physical performance. Although in principle it may be made explicit in language, it typically remains unexplicated—implicit in action.

3. *Context-dependence.* Action-centered skill only has meaning within the context in which its associated physical activities can occur.

4. *Personalism.* It is the individual body that takes in the situation and an individual's actions that display the required competence. There is a felt linkage between the knower and the known. The implicit quality of knowledge provides it with a sense of interiority, much like physical experience.

The Dissociation of Sentience and Knowledge

Computerization brings about an essential change in the way the worker can know the world and, with it, a crisis of confidence in the possibility of certain knowledge. For the workers of Piney Wood and Tiger Creek, achieving a sense of knowing the world was rarely problematical in their conventional environments. Certain knowledge was conveyed through the immediacy of their sensory experience. Instead of Descartes's "I think, therefore I am," these workers might say, "I see, I touch, I smell, I hear; therefore, I know." Their capacity to trust their knowledge was reflected in the assumption of its validity. In the precomputerized environment, belief was a seamless extension of sensory experience.

As the medium of knowing was transformed by computerization, the placid unity of experience and knowledge was disturbed. Accomplishing work depended upon the ability to manipulate symbolic, electronically presented data. Instead of using their bodies as instruments of *acting-on* equipment and materials, the task relationship became mediated by the information system. Operators had to work through the medium of what I will call the "data interface," represented most visibly by the computer terminals they monitored from central control rooms. The workers in this transition were at first overwhelmed with the feeling that they could no longer see or touch their work, as if it has been made both invisible and intangible by computer mediation.

> It's just different getting this information in the control room. The man in

here can't see. Out there you can look around until you find something.

The chlorine has overflowed, and it's all over the third floor. You see, this is what I mean . . . it's all over the floor, but you can't see it. You have to remember how to get into the system to do something about it. Before you could see it and you knew what was happening—you just knew.

The hardest thing for us operators is not to have the physical part. I can chew pulp and tell you its physical properties. We knew things from experience. Now we have to try and figure out what is happening. The hardest part is to give up that physical control.

In a world in which skills were honed over long years of physical experience, work was associated with concrete objects and the cues they provided. A worker's sense of occupational identity was deeply marked by his or her understanding of and attachment to discrete tangible entities, such as a piece of operating equipment. Years of service meant continued opportunities to master new objects. It was the immediate knowledge one could gain of these tangible objects that engendered feelings of competence and control. For workers, the new computer-mediated relationship to work often felt like being yanked away from a world that could be known because it could be sensed.

Our operators did their job by feeling a pipe—"Is it hot?" We can't just tell them it's 150 degrees. They have to believe it.

With computerization I am further away from my job than I have ever been before. I used to listen to the sounds the boiler makes and know just how it was running. I could look at the fire in the furnace and tell by its color how it was burning. I knew what kinds of adjustments were needed by the shades of color I saw. A lot of the men also said that there were smells that told you different things about how it was running. I feel uncomfortable being away from these sights and smells. Now I only have numbers to go by. I am scared of that

boiler, and I feel that I should be closer to it in order to control it.

It is as if one's job had vanished into a two-dimensional space of abstractions, where digital symbols replace a concrete reality. Workers reiterated a spontaneous emotional response countless times—defined by feelings of loss of control, of vulnerability, and of frustration. It was sharpened with a sense of crisis and a need for steeling oneself with courage and not a little adrenaline in order to meet the challenge. It was shot through with the bewilderment of a man suddenly blind, groping with his hands outstretched in a vast, unfamiliar space. "We are in uncharted water now," they said. "We have to control our operations blind." This oft-repeated metaphor spoke of being robbed of one's senses and plunged into darkness. The tangible world had always been thick with landmarks; it was difficult to cast off from these familiar moorings with only abstractions as guides.

One operator described learning to work with the new computer system in Tiger Creek's pulping area. "The difficulty," he said, "is not being able to touch things." As he spoke, his hands shot out before him and he wiggled all his fingers, as if to emphasize the sense of incompleteness and loss. He continued:

When I go out and touch something, I know what will happen. There is a fear of not being out on the floor watching things. It is like turning your back in a dark alley. You don't know what is behind you; you don't know what might be happening. It all becomes remote from you, and it makes you feel vulnerable. It was like being a new operator all over again. Today I push buttons instead of opening valves on the digester. If I push the wrong button, will I screw up? Will anything happen?

Many other descriptions conveyed a similar feeling:

With the change to the computer it's like driving down the highway with your lights out and someone else pushing the accelerator. It's like flying an airplane and taking all the instruments out so you can't see.

It's like if you had an airplane and you put pieces over each instrument to hide it. Then, if something went wrong, you have to uncover the right one in a split second.

Doing my job through the computer, it feels different. It is like you are riding a big, powerful horse, but someone is sitting behind you on the saddle holding the reins, and you just have to be on that ride and hold on. You see what is coming, but you can't do anything to control it. You can't steer yourself left and right; you can't control that horse that you are on. You have got to do whatever the guy behind you holding the reins wants you to do. Well, I would rather be holding the reins than have someone behind me holding the reins.

The feeling of being in control and the willingness to be held accountable require a reservoir of critical judgment with which to initiate informed action. In the past, operators like those at Piney Wood derived their critical judgment from their "gut feel" of the production process. Becoming a "good" operator—the kind that workers and managers alike refer to as an "artist" and invest with the authority of expertise—required the years of experience to develop a finely nuanced, felt sense of the equipment, the product, and the overall process. With computerization, many managers acknowledged that operators had lost their ability "to feel the machine." Without considering the new skill implications of this loss, many managers feared it would eliminate the kind of critical judgment that would have allowed operators to take action based upon an understanding that reached beyond the computer system.

Piney Wood's plant manager, as he presided over the massive technology conversion, asked himself what the loss of such art might mean:

In the digester area, we used to have guys doing it who had an art. After we put the computers in, when they went down we could go to manual backup.

People remembered how to run the digesters. Now if we try to go back, they can't remember what to do. They have lost the feel for it. We are really stuck now without the computer; we can't successfully operate that unit without it. If you are watching a screen, do you see the same things you would if you were there, face-to-face with the process and the equipment? I am concerned we are losing the art and skills that are not replenishable.

There were many operators who agreed. In one area of Piney Wood, the crew leader explained it this way:

The new people are not going to understand, see, or feel as well as the old guys. Something is wrong with this fan, for example. You may not know what; you just feel it in your feet. The sound, the tone, the volume, the vibrations . . . the computer will control it, but you will have lost something, too. It's a trade-off. The computer can't feel what is going on out there. The new operators will need to have more written down, because they will not know it in their guts. I can't understand how new people coming in are ever going to learn how to run a pulp mill. They are not going to know what is going on. They will only learn what these computers tell them.

Sam Gimbel was a young production coordinator in Piney Wood. Though trained as a chemical engineer, he had been particularly close to the operators whom he managed. He had shepherded them through the technology conversion and construction of the new control room, and worked closely with them as they grappled with new ways of operating:

We are losing the context where hands-on experience makes sense. If you don't have actual experience, you have to believe everything the computer says, and you can't beat it at its own game. You can't stand up to it. And yet who will have the experience to make these kinds of judgments? It will surely be a different world. You lose the checkpoints in reality to know if you are doing it right;

therefore, how will anyone be able to confront the computer information?

Piney Wood's management had approached the technology conversion with the following message: "We are simply providing you with new tools to do your job. Your job is to operate the equipment, and this is a new tool to operate the equipment with." Managers repeatedly made statements such as, "We told them this was a tool just like a hammer or a wrench." One manager even went so far as to say, "We hoped they wouldn't figure out that the terminal we were giving them was really a computer."

As experience with the new operating conditions began to accumulate, many managers began to see that treating the computer system like a physical object, "just another tool," could lead to chronic suboptimization of the technology's potential. A powerhouse worker with over twenty-five years of experience had developed a special way of kicking the boiler in order to make it function smoothly. He used the same approach with the terminal; if he hit a certain button on the keyboard, a particular reading would change in the desired direction, but he did not know why or how. Piney Wood's powerhouse manager put it this way:

> The guy who kicks the boiler is the same guy who mashes the button a certain way just to make the line go down. This person will never optimize the process. He will use too much chemical and too high pressure. He will never make you money because he doesn't understand the problem.

Just as the digester operators had lost their ability to cook manually, other workers throughout the mill felt equally powerless:

> In the old way, you had control over the job. The computer now tells you what to do. There is more responsibility but less control. We lost a boiler that was on computer control. We just had to sit there and stare. We were all shook up.

> Sometimes I am amazed when I realize that we stare at the screen even when it has gone down. You get in the habit and you just keep staring even if there is nothing there.

Ironically, as managers and operators across the mill watched the level of artistry decline, the senior technical designers continued to assume that manual skills would provide the necessary backup to their systems.

The problem was even more acute in Cedar Bluff, where most of the work force lacked the experience base from which felt sense and critical judgment are developed. Managers at Cedar Bluff engaged in a quiet debate as to how much of a problem this lack of experience would ultimately be. On one side of the argument were the "old-timers"—managers with years of experience in the industry:

> I like to smell and feel the pulp sometimes. It can be slick, it can be slimy, it can be all different consistencies. These are the artistic aspects of making pulp that the computer doesn't know about. Some of the operators have been picking up these aspects, but there are so many numbers so readily accessible, we have to shortcut it at times and solve more problems from the office. The information is so good and rapid we have to use it. . . . You have got to be able to recognize when you can run things from the office and when you have to go and look. Yet, I recognize that I am not as good a pulp maker as the people who trained me, and the new operators are not as good as I am. They are better managers and planners. I am very happy with the new managers, but not with the new pulp makers.

The younger engineers, schooled in computer-based analytic techniques, had little patience with anxious laments over the loss of the art of pulp making. They were relentlessly confident that a good computer model could reproduce anything that operators knew from experience—only better. Here is how the process engineers articulated the argument:

Computer analysis lets us see the effects of many variables and their interactions. This is a picture of truth that we could not have achieved before. It is superior to the experience-based knowledge of an operator. You might say that truth replaces knowledge.

People who have this analytic power do not need to have been around to know what is going on. All you need is to be able to formulate a model and perform the necessary confirmation checks. With the right model you can manage the system just fine.

Most Cedar Bluff managers agreed that the computer system made it possible to do a better job running the plant with an inexperienced work force than otherwise would have been possible, though some wondered whether the levels of expertise would ever be as high as among workers with hands-on exposure to the pulping process. Yet even as managers argued over the essentiality of action-centered skill, technology was irreversibly altering the context in which the operators performed. The opportunities to develop such skills were becoming increasingly rare as the action context was paved over by the data highway.

Many of Cedar Bluff's managers believed that the traditional knowledge of the pulp mill worker would actually inhibit the development of creativity and flexibility. Under the new technological conditions, the young operators would develop their capacity to "know better" than the systems with which they worked as they struggled with the complexities of the new technology and the data it provided. The data interface would replace the physical equipment as the primary arena for learning.

Yet as months passed, other managers observed a disturbing pattern of interactions between the operators and the computer system. Some believed that the highly computerized task environment resulted in a greater than usual bifurcation of skills. One group of operators would use the information systems to learn an extraordinary amount about the process, while another group would make itself an appendage to the system, mechanically carrying out the computer's directives. These managers complained that the computer system was becoming a crutch that prevented many operators from developing a superior knowledge of the process. One "old-timer" provided an example:

> When there is a shift change and new operators come on, the good operator will take the process from the computer, put it on manual, make certain changes that the operator thinks are necessary, and then gives it back to the computer. The average operator will come in, see this thing on automatic control, and leave it with the computer. Sometimes that operator won't even realize that things are getting bad or getting worse. They should have known better, but they didn't.

Most Cedar Bluff operators spoke enthusiastically about the convenience of the computer interface, and some freely admitted what they perceived to be a dependence on the computer system:

> The computer provides your hands. I don't think I could work in a conventional mill. This is so much more convenient. You have so much control without having to go out to the equipment and adjust things.

> We can't run this mill manually. There are too many controls, and it is too complex. The average person can only run four or five variables at once in a manual mode, and the automatic system runs it all. If the computer goes down, we have to sit back and wait. We sit and we stare at the screens and we hope something pipes in.

Many managers observed with growing alarm the things that occurred when operators neither enjoyed the traditional sources of critical judgment nor had developed enough new knowledge for informed action.

> In a conventional mill, you have to go and look at the equipment because you cannot get enough data in the control room. Here, you get all the data you

need. The computer becomes a substitute tool. It replaces all the sensual data instead of being an addition. We had another experience with the feedwater pumps, which supply water to the boiler to make steam. There was a power outage. Something in the computer canceled the alarm. The operator had a lot of trouble and did not look at the readout of the water level and never got an alarm. The tank ran empty, the pumps tripped. The pump finally tore up because there was no water feeding it.

We have so much data from the computer, I find that hard drives out soft. Operators are tempted not to tour the plant. They just sit at the computer and watch for alarms. One weekend I found a tank overflowing in digesting. I went to the operator and told him, and he said, "It can't be; the computer says my level is fine." I am afraid of what happens if we trust the computer too much.

At least since the introduction of the moving assembly line in Ford's Highland Park plant, it has been second nature for managers to use technology to delimit worker discretion and, in this process, to concentrate knowledge within the managerial domain. The special dilemmas raised by information technology require managers to reconsider these assumptions. When information and control technology is used to turn the worker into "just another mechanical variable," one immediate result is the withdrawal of the worker's commitment to and accountability for the work. This lack of care requires additional managerial vigilance and leads to a need for increased automatic control. As this dynamic unfolds, it no longer seems shocking to contemplate an image of work laced with stupefaction and passivity, in which the human being is a hapless bystander at the margins of productive activity. One young operator in Cedar Bluff discussed his prior job as a bank clerk. I asked him if his two employment experiences had anything in common. "Yes," he said, "in both cases you punch the buttons and watch it happen."

As automation intensifies, information technology becomes the receptacle for larger and larger portions of the organization's operating intelligence. Algorithms become the functional equivalent of a once diffuse know-how, and the action context in which know-how can be developed and sustained vanishes. Because many managers assume that more technology means a diminished need for human operating skill, they may recognize the waning of worker know-how without becoming concerned enough to chart a different course. Left unchallenged, these systems become more potent, as they are invested with an escalating degree of authority. Technical experts temporarily serve as resources, but once their knowledge has been depleted, and converted into systematic rules for decision making, their usefulness is attenuated. The analysts and engineers, who construct programs and models, have the capacity to manipulate data and, presumably, to make discoveries. Ultimately, they will become the most important human presence to offer any counterpoint to the growing density and opacity of the automated systems.

There is an alternative, one that involves understanding this technological change as an occasion for developing a new set of skills—skills that are able to exploit the informating capacity of the technology and to become a new source of critical judgment. In order to assess the likelihood of this alternative—the forces that will drive organizations in this direction and those that will impede them—we first have to understand the nature of these new skills. What can the experiences of workers in these three mills teach us about the emerging requirements for competence at the data interface?

From Action-Centered to Intellective Skill

The pulp and paper mills reveal the shift in the grounds of knowledge associated with a technology that informates. Men and women accustomed to an intimate physical association with the production process found themselves removed from the action. Now they had to know and to do based upon their ability to understand and manipulate electronic data. In Piney Wood, a $200 million investment in technology was radically altering every phase of mill life. Managers believed they were merely "upgrading" in order to modernize production and to improve productivity. Tiger Creek was undergoing a similar modernization process. In both cases, informating dynamics tended to unfold as an unintended and undermanaged consequence of these efforts. Cedar Bluff had been designed with a technological infrastructure based on integrated information and control systems. In that organization, managers were somewhat more self-conscious about using the informating capacity of the technology as the basis for developing new operating skills.

The experiences of the skilled workers in these mills provide a frame of reference for a general appraisal of the forms of knowledge that are required in an informated environment. My contention is that the skill demands that can be deciphered from their experiences have relevance for a wider range of organizational settings in both manufacturing and service sectors. . . . This joint appraisal will help to unravel the intrinsic and the contingent aspects of change and to gauge the generalizations that follow from the dilemmas of transformation described here.

A fundamental quality of this technological transformation, as it is experienced by workers and observed by their managers, involves a reorientation of the means by which one can have a palpable effect upon the world. Immediate physical responses must be replaced by an abstract thought process in which options are considered, and choices are made and then translated into the terms of the information system. For many, physical action is restricted to the play of fingers on the terminal keyboard. As one operator put it, "Your past physical mobility must be translated into a mental thought process." A Cedar Bluff manager with prior experience in pulping contemplates the distinct capacities that

had become necessary in a highly computerized environment:

> In 1953 we put operation and control as close together as possible. We did a lot of localizing so that when you made a change you could watch the change, actually see the motor start up. With the evolution of computer technology, you centralize controls and move away from the actual physical process. If you don't have an understanding of what is happening and how all the pieces interact, it is more difficult. You need a new learning capability, because when you operate with the computer, you can't see what is happening. There is a difference in the mental and conceptual capabilities you need—you have to do things in your mind.

When operators in Piney Wood and Tiger Creek discuss their traditional skills, they speak of knowing things by habit and association. They talk about "cause-and-effect" knowledge and being able to see the things to which they must respond. They refer to "folk medicine" and knowledge that you don't even know you have until it is suddenly displayed in the ability to take a decisive action and make something work.

In plants like Piney Wood and Tiger Creek, where operators have relied upon action-centered skill, management must convince the operator to leave behind a world in which things were immediately known, comprehensively sensed, and able to be acted upon directly, in order to embrace a world that is dominated by objective data, is removed from the action context, and requires a qualitatively different kind of response. In this new world, personal interpretations of how to make things happen count for little. The worker who has relied upon an intimate knowledge of a piece of equipment—the operators talk about having "pet knobs" or knowing just where to kick a machine to make it hum—feels adrift. To be effective, he or she must now trade immediate knowledge for a more explicit understanding of the science that undergirds the operation. One Piney Wood manager described it this way:

The workers have an intuitive feel of what the process needs to be. Someone in the process will listen to things, and that is their information. All of their senses are supplying data. But once they are in the control room, all they have to do is look at the screen. Things are concentrated right in front of you. You don't have sensory feedback. You have to draw inferences by watching the data, so you must understand the theory behind it. In the long run, you would like people who can take data and draw broad conclusions from it. They must be more scientific.

Many managers are not optimistic about the ability of experienced workers to trade their embodied knowledge for a more explicit, "scientific" inference.

The operators today know if I do "x," then "y" will happen. But they don't understand the real logic of the system. Their cause-and-effect reasoning comes from their experience. Once we put things under automatic control and ask them to relate to the process using the computer, their personal judgments about how to relate to equipment go by the wayside. We are saying your intuition is no longer valuable. Now you must understand the whole process and the theory behind it.

Now a new kind of learning must begin. It is slow and scary, and many workers are timid, not wanting to appear foolish and incompetent. Hammers and wrenches have been replaced by numbers and buttons. An operator with thirty years of service in the Piney Wood Mill described his experience in the computer-mediated environment:

Anytime you mash a button you should have in mind exactly what is going to happen. You need to have in your mind where it is at, what it is doing, and why it is doing it. Out there in the plant, you can know things just by habit. You can know them without knowing that you know them. In here you have to watch the numbers, whereas out there you have to watch the actual process.

"You need to have in your mind where it is at"—it is a simple phrase, but deceptive. What it takes to have things "in your mind" is far different from the knowledge associated with action-centered skill.

This does not imply that action-centered skills exist independent of cognitive activity. Rather, it means that the processes of learning, remembering, and displaying action-centered skills do not necessarily require that the knowledge they contain be made explicit. Physical cues do not require inference; learning in an action-centered context is more likely to be analogical than analytical. In contrast, the abstract cues available through the data interface do require explicit inferential reasoning, particularly in the early phases of the learning process. It is necessary to reason out the meaning of those cues—what is their relation to each other and to the world "out there"?

It is also necessary to understand the procedures according to which these abstract cues can be manipulated to result in the desired effects. Procedural reasoning means having an understanding of the internal structure of the information system and its functional capacities. This makes it possible both to operate skillfully through the system and to use the system as a source of learning and feedback. For example, one operation might require sixteen control actions spread across four groups of variables. The operator must first think about what has to be done. Second, he or she must know how data elements (abstract cues) correspond to actual processes and their systemic relations. Third, the operator must have a conception of the information system itself, in order to know how actions taken at the information interface can result in appropriate outcomes. Fourth, having decided what to do and executed that command, he or she must scan new data and check for results. Each of these processes folds back upon a kind of thinking that can stand independent from the physical context. An operator summed it up this way:

Before computers, we didn't have to think as much, just react. You just knew what to do because it was physically there. Now, the most important thing to learn is to think before you do something, to think about what you are planning to do. You have to know which variables are the most critical and therefore what to be most cautious about, what to spend time thinking about before you take action.

The vital element here is that these workers feel a stark difference in the forms of knowledge they must now use. Their experience of competence has been radically altered. "We never got paid to have ideas," said one Tiger Creek worker. "We got paid to work." Work was the exertion that could be known by its material results. The fact that a material world must be created required physical exertion. Most of the operators believed that some people in society are paid to "think," but they were not among them. They knew themselves to be the ones who gave their bodies in effort and skill, and through their bodies, they made things. Accustomed to gauging their integrity in intimate measures of strain and sweat, these workers find that information technology has challenged their assumptions and thrown them into turmoil. There was a gradual dawning that the rules of the game had changed. For some, this created panic; they did not believe in their ability to think in this new way and were afraid of being revealed as incompetent.

Such feelings are no mere accident of personality, but the sedimentation of long years of conditioned learning about who does the "thinking"—a boundary that is not meant to be crossed. As a Tiger Creek manager observed:

> Currently, managers make all the decisions. . . . Operators don't want to hear about alternatives. They have been trained to *do*, not to *think*. There is a fear of being punished if you think. This translates into a fear of the new technology.

In each control room, a tale is told about one or two old-timers who, though they knew more about the process than anyone else, "just up and quit" when they heard the new technology was coming. From one plant to another, reports of these cases were remarkably similar:

> He felt that because he had never graduated high school, he would never be able to keep up with this new stuff. We tried to tell him different, but he just wouldn't listen.

Despite the anxiety of change, those who left were not the majority. Most men and women need their jobs and will do whatever it takes to keep them. Beyond this, there were many who were honestly intrigued with the opportunity this change offered. They seemed to get pulled in gradually, observing their own experiences and savoring with secret surprise each new bit of evidence of their unexpected abilities. They discussed the newness and strangeness of having to act upon the world by exerting a more strictly intellectual effort. Under the gentle stimulus of a researcher's questions, they thought about this new kind of thinking. What does it feel like? Here are the observations of an operator who spent twenty years in one of the most manually intensive parts of the Tiger Creek Mill, which had recently been computerized:

> If something is happening, if something is going wrong, you don't go down and fix it. Instead, you stay up here and think about the sequence, and you think about how you want to affect the sequence. You get it done through your thinking. But dealing with information instead of things is very . . . well, very intriguing. I am very aware of the need for my mental involvement now. I am always wondering: Where am I at? What is happening? It all occurs in your mind now.

Another operator discussed the same experience but added an additional dimension. After describing the demand for thinking and mental involvement, he observed:

Things occur to me now that never would have occurred to me before. With all of this information in front of me, I begin to think about how to do the job better. And, being freed from all that manual activity, you really have time to look at things, to think about them, and to anticipate.

As information technology restructures the work situation, it abstracts thought from action. Absorption, immediacy, and organic responsiveness are superseded by distance, coolness, and remoteness. Such distance brings an opportunity for reflection. There was little doubt in these workers' minds that the logic of their jobs had been fundamentally altered. As another worker from Tiger Creek summed it up, "Sitting in this room and just thinking has become part of my job. It's the technology that lets me do these things."

The thinking this operator refers to is of a different quality from the thinking that attended the display of action-centered skills. It combines abstraction, explicit inference, and procedural reasoning. Taken together, these elements make possible a new set of competencies that I call intellective skills. As long as the new technology signals only deskilling—the diminished importance of action-centered skills—there will be little probability of developing critical judgment at the data interface. To rekindle such judgment, though on a new, more abstract footing, a reskilling process is required. Mas-

tery in a computer-mediated environment depends upon developing intellective skills. . . .

Discussion Questions

1. The dominant view of intelligence is that it is revealed through language-based and math-based abilities, so universities recruit students with the highest SAT and GRE scores and companies hire graduates with the highest GPA scores (and increasingly, companies are also asking for SAT scores). But what about interpersonal intelligence and so-called "street smarts," which help people to get along with others and be successful in managing group-based projects? The test score smartest-person-on-the-block may not be able to convince anyone to follow his/her lead or take their advice. What do you think?

2. Develop a list of skills and apply them to a wide variety of jobs. In what way is a physician more skilled than a nurse or a chef?

3. Can you apply Zuboff's distinction between mental and manual work to your own experience?

12

'They Used to Use a Ball and Chain': Technology's Impact on the Workplace

Jill Andresky Fraser

It sometimes seems that everyone has a personal computer, a laptop, a cell phone, an Ipod, a Black-Berry, and any other piece of electronic Internet-linked gadget that some computer engineer can dream up. We often think about this electronic bazaar as a part of our leisure life, but consider what it might mean when all this electronic technology becomes a part of the standard equipment on your job.

This chapter examines how electronic technology in the workplace can become oppressive, narrowing the space between work and nonwork lives. Originally designed to increase office efficiency, electronic technology can also be used to expand daily working hours by keeping people working when they might otherwise be relaxing. Now you can be reached for work when you are on a commuter train, in a hotel room when traveling, driving in a car, flying around the globe, or relaxing at home on the weekend. In addition, employee monitoring has been elevated to a normal workplace practice designed to raise productivity, especially among the growing pool of contingent temporary workers.

We've all got the cell phones, the beepers, the laptops. "I bring mine back and forth between my home and office every day," commented Phyllis, a finance officer with one of the nation's large retail chains. "Everybody does it—you feel like you always need to be accessible. Even when you're on vacation, you've got to be accessible. You've got to be prepared to check in all the time." She sighed, then concluded, "All those pieces of equipment are a big reason we're working harder."

Today's new technologies, for all their ability to lighten routine job tasks, lower business costs, and boost performance levels, are inextricably linked to contemporary overwork patterns. As many people's work lives seem to be moving inexorably toward a "24/7" vision of round-the-clock, ever-increasing productivity, they could hardly meet their employers' rising expectations without a ready arsenal of workplace tools—Internet-linked computers, personal digital assistants, cell phones, pagers, laptops, and even e-mail-receptive watches—at home as well as at the office.

Technology has done more than simply *facilitate* the current trend of working longer and harder. It may, indeed, have exacerbated patterns of overwork and job stress by broadening many white-collar staffers' (and their employers') definitions of "on the job" to include areas far beyond the traditional confines of their office space.

Technological developments, meanwhile, have permitted corporations to extend their control over employees to an oppressive degree: all in the interest of keeping men and women at maximum productive efficiency, whether they find themselves in their cars or commuter trains, hotel rooms, or even master bedrooms. White-collar staffers themselves have responded by using the Internet to vent their hostilities and anxieties about deteriorating conditions, as well as, increasingly, to mobilize resistance to "sweatshop" trends.

Technology Encourages Job Spill

When I set up an Internet discussion site to explore issues like these relating to work and technology, here's how "tickler" responded: "I had two phone lines (local and toll free (at home, 2 voicemails, email, and the rest . . . [and] was besieged with the usual crap of being assaulted during the evening, nights, weekends, and the like."[1] Those images of "siege" and "assault" are apt, since many people feel as though the office is invading their home front—an invasion facilitated by the introduction of at least some of these pieces of electronic equipment into the house, the car, or another personal space.

White-collar workers increasingly find themselves somewhere in the vast space that looms between "just checking in with the office" and "just having one or two things to finish up," whether it's during their after-dinner hours, commuting time, weekends with the family, sick days, vacations, or holidays. Workloads inevitably increase: according to a study of people who spent five hours or more each week on the Internet, 25 percent of them reported that they were working harder at home without any reduction at the office.[2]

Despite workers' complaints about excessive job demands, however, more and more workplace gadgets keep showing up outside the office. As they do, they blur the old lines between home and office. In 1997 more than one quarter of American families owned pagers—twice as high as the year earlier—and more than one third of U.S. households owned cellular telephones.[3] That same year, 3.6 million households purchased fax machines, 14 million bought notebook computers, and a whopping 31 million bought personal computers.[4]

The trend only accelerated. By the year 1998, two thirds of all households had cellular phones; just about half of them had pagers.[5] Market researchers projected "home market" sales of personal computers and related consumer electronic appliances at about 35 million units during that same year.[6]

Many, if not all, of these tools can be used by families for personal matters, too, as when children swap homework assignments by fax or surf the Internet for fun. But for large numbers of people, one significant result of having these workplace technologies at home was greater access to work, clients, colleagues, the office. The flip side was that the business world now had greater, round-the-clock access to its workers.

By the late nineties, it was estimated that 7 million Americans regularly checked their business e-mails from outside the office.[7] At more and more workplaces, such checking became an unspoken requirement of many people's jobs. America Online, for example, "occasionally announces e-mail-free weekends, usually around a holiday, when employees are not expected to check e-mail. On all other weekends, of course, they are expected to check their e-mail."[8]

What about when they're on the road? The many Americans who find themselves traveling for their jobs—and 32 percent do, at least occasionally[9]—have been robbed by high-tech equipment of whatever personal downtime they once might have cherished: in the quiet of an airplane (where, now able to plug their laptop computers into new "Empower" jacks, they never run out of battery power and so can never doze off or idly leaf through a magazine); in airport lobbies (where Internet-access kiosks allow them to check e-mail accounts, while frequent flier clubs provide faxes, copiers, dataports, and the like); in rental cars (where rental cell phones and beepers are usually available, along with cars and adapters that can turn cigarette lighters into sources of power for portable computers); or in hotel rooms (which increasingly provide the same range of office-electronics comforts that their customers have come to rely upon in their homes and workplaces).[10]

One could say, simply, that all this new technology has increased the capabilities and outputs of business travelers. Or an observer of the current corporate scene could view new workplace gadgets from a different, darker perspective: as instruments designed to eliminate human inefficiency or "personal downtime," all in the interest of creating an optimally productive white-collar work machine. Whether these work machines (that is, business travelers) return home more stressed out than they were when they left the office scarcely matters in this new business-world order.

Here's how "technoid," another visitor to my Internet chat room, described the *way* technology had ratcheted up the demands on his travel time. "When I travel to another country, someone from a local office always escorts me with a cell phone. This means I'd have problems to fix at the customer site, problems they'd call in on the phone, and problems in e-mail when I got back to the hotel."[11] All those mobile pieces of electronics allowed "technoid"'s employer to keep him working at what the company deemed an appropriate level of efficiency, "10–12 hour days, and they'll always ask you to work seven days a week." He added, "If a customer canceled meetings or I finished early, they'd always have more meetings lined up to replace the time so that I couldn't go home early."

Perhaps business travelers should expect to perform business tasks whether they're in the air or on the ground; after all, they are on their employers' payroll. But until recently, most vacationers were freed from similar constraints, unless they were such high-level executives that their companies simply could not function without them, even for a few days.

Thanks to the democratization of workplace technologies, however, that's no longer the case. One recent survey of "messaging technology" found that 53 percent of all those who owned pagers *had* been paged during a vacation. Meanwhile, 41 percent of those who owned cell phones had used them to call their offices while on vacation; another 32 percent who had access to the Internet while on vacation had checked their e-mail; and 34 percent had checked their office answering machine or voice-mail account while on vacation.[12]

"Yes, people feel good about the stock market going up. Yes, some people are taking better vacations and they've got more money to spend on them," Zachary, a long-time employee of Citicorp told me. But the trade-off wasn't worth it, he explained. "If you've got to be on call during the whole vacation—if you've got to check in with the office through the voice mail and the e-mail, and everyone out there can reach you if they need you—then you're worse off." He quipped, "It's kind of like, people have the money to buy toys, but they're so busy with work that they don't have the time to play with them.". . .

Elsewhere, signs of the "you can't get away from it all" times abound, often tied to some type of technology. One was a recent advertising campaign from Sheraton Hotels of New York that boasted "everything you've always wanted in an office. In a hotel room." The traveler's fantasy list that appeared in this ad included "HP fax/copier/printers, data ports and more." Also noteworthy was an article that appeared in *Gourmet* magazine's typically pleasure-oriented "Travel Journal." It focused on such devices to stay "linked-up, logged-on and tuned-in" as "OFFICE Pro by Kluge," a portable mini-office/computer center masquerading as a piece of luggage which enables travelers to carry their laptops, batteries, diskettes, power cords, personal digital assistants, cell phones, papers, and files, along with their clothing.[13]

If we can, as we increasingly do, take our offices and workloads along with us wherever we go, this is clearly a mixed blessing at best. As one business observer, writing in the *Harvard Business Review*, put it: "What those tools have done . . . is help to extend the working day: in effect, they have created a portable assembly line for the 1990s that 'allows' white-collar workers to remain on-line in planes, trains, cars and at home. So much for the liberating technologies of the Information Age."[14]

The Negative Impact on Work Conditions

Physical discomforts tied to inescapable office technologies abound. Eye strain, wrist strain, and back strain are all common complaints among those who spend long hours at their computers, whether at the office or at home. So are stress-related headaches, especially for corporate staffers who carry pagers, beepers, or cell phones in their pockets, handbags, or briefcases which enable them to stay "on call" at the office virtually twenty-four hours each day. . . .

If new technologies have contributed to workers' stress by changing the settings in which white-collar employees perform their jobs (and the conditions under which they perform them), these tools have also, for many people, changed the *pace* of work.

Electronic mail, currently used by an estimated 82 million American workers, has played a key role in the corporate speedup. Since e-mails are frequently slapdash and ungrammatical, one might expect them to be taken less seriously than other forms of business communication. Yet perhaps because of the involvement of the computer in their transmittance (or because their very sloppiness conveys the impression that their authors were too busy to worry about dotting every *i* and crossing their *t*'s), they seem to carry much more weight than the same messages would if conveyed via telephone or some other method.

They're a huge source of job stress in corporate America. Remember "tickler"'s description of feeling besieged by work? One survey found that 28 percent of today's "message users" feel more pressure to respond quickly to work-related messages than they used to feel five years ago. An estimated 24 million Americans suffer from so-called message overload.[15] And that problem will likely continue to worsen, since market researchers predict that by the year 2001, 135 million Americans will have e-mail access.[16]

The concept of message overload would sound all too familiar to Jimmy, a consultant on international sales, who was interviewed by Arlie Russell Hochschild for her recent book *The Time Bind*. He described the following: "I'm gone for a couple of hours, and I have twenty electronic messages on my computer when I get back. People are working weekends; you can see by the dates. They send things Friday at 10 p.m., Saturday mornings at 9 a.m., Sundays at 9 p.m. Of the twenty messages on my machine, I have to do something about twelve of them. My head spins."[17]

Within many corporations, there seems no electronic end in sight. A Silicon Valley executive complained that he received about one hundred e-mails every single day. "On average, it takes one minute per e-mail to answer. I don't have 100 minutes a day however." Another added, "There will be ten e-mails between the time you pack your briefcase and lock the door" to head home from the office.[18]

When one looks beyond e-mails, the problem only intensifies. A 1998 survey by Pitney Bowes found that the average office employee sent or received 190 messages *every single day*, including faxes, traditional letters, telephone calls, and electronic messages. By 1999 this volume had spiraled even higher, to 201 messages daily.[19] Nearly half of the people surveyed reported being interrupted by six or more messages every single hour they spent in their offices. One of every four people complained about being "distracted" or "very distracted" by these various interruptions.

No wonder white-collar workers complain about job stress.

It's also not too hard to figure out why people frequently check in with their voice-mail and e-mail accounts when they're not at the office: they're just trying to keep the message landslide from burying them alive. The analogy to an assembly line seems all too apt. At the same time that corporate men and women feel *more* pressure to respond—and more quickly than ever—to office communications, their work pace has picked up as well, in part because they keep receiving increasing numbers of communiqués that demand prompt attention.

Craig Brod, a clinical psychologist, coined the term "techno-stress" back in 1984 to describe these and other experiences he observed in people adapting to new technologies at the workplace and elsewhere. "For the manager, as for the clerical worker," he wrote, "a key element of technostress is a distorted sense of time. Days, hours and minutes take on new meaning as time is compressed and accelerated. Recognition of what is humanly possible fades." Among the many results, he argued, was people's "tendency to push themselves harder than ever to match the efficiency and tirelessness of the computer."[20]

Technological innovations are speeding up the work pace in other, even more fundamental ways as well. In her provocative study *The Electronic Sweatshop*, Barbara Garson explored how corporate employers had begun using what she called "a combination of twentieth-century technology and nineteenth-century scientific management . . . [to turn] the Office of the Future into the factory of the past." At first, she added, "this affected clerks and switchboard operators, then secretaries, bank tellers and service workers. The primary targets now are professionals and managers." To Garson, the objective of these changes was simply "to make white-collar workers cheaper to train, easier to replace, less skilled, less expensive and less special."[21]

Garson examined the ways that new technologies had begun to affect a wide range of white-collar professionals, including investment advisers and social workers. Her study of airline reservation clerks illustrates the patterns she uncovered: "American Airlines had divided the two-minute reservation conversation into segments—opening, sales pitch, probe and close—and provided a set of interchangeable conversation modules for each segment. An acceptable conversation could now be put together like a mix-and-match outfit or a Chinese dinner—one from column A, two from column B. On one level, it's obvious why this is considered efficient," she explained. "In industry, production is routinely arranged so that the bulk of the work can be done with a minimum of skill. The more an airline can standardize the reservation conversation, the less they need to depend on the agents' experience and judgment. This should make the agents cheaper and more interchangeable."[22] . . .

From a vantage point ten years after Garson's study, it now appears that white-collar workers can be sorted into three basic categories: those whose jobs have been "reengineered" by technology, somewhat along the lines described above; those who are increasingly being replaced by technology (as when nearly 180,000 bank tellers were replaced by ATMs between 1983 and 1993);[23] and those whose work lives appear—at least for now—to be resistant to such changes, typically because of the high levels of skill, experience, or creativity their jobs require.

That third category is small and shrinking, seemingly before our eyes. That's because new technological advances have pushed computer and other electronic capabilities far beyond the realm most people would have imagined possible even a decade ago. At the same time, the business world has displayed an insatiable appetite for all those advances that can be translated into productivity measures (often by facilitating human resources cutbacks).

In his book *The End of Work*, Jeremy Rifkin warns of the unprecedented problems the United States will increasingly come to face as the result of "technological displacement." Rifkin predicts that the trend, now seen in all three traditional sectors of the economy (agriculture, manufacturing, and service), will eventually affect hundreds of millions of people. Already, he argues, "most Americans feel trapped by the new lean-production practices and sophisticated new automation technologies, not knowing if or when the re-engineering drive will reach into their own office or workstation, plucking them from what they once thought was a secure job and casting them into the reserve army of contingent workers, or, worse yet, the unemployment line."[24] . . .

Monitoring and Controlling the Workforce

The *New York Times,* Xerox Corporation, and Edward Jones & Company, the brokerage firm, do not appear at first glance to have much in common.

But all three captured headlines in 1999 for firing groups of employees after catching them in the act of some type of electronic no-no. At the *Times,* "inappropriate and offensive" e-mails led to the termination of more than twenty employees from its Norfolk, Virginia, payroll-processing center; at Xerox, Web surfing nailed forty staffers (some of whom had used office access to the Internet to visit pornography sites).[25]

Here's another way that technology has helped worsen work life: by providing corporations with an arsenal of new, and continually improving, tools with which to supervise their employees' activity and output. For white-collar workers, who have traditionally enjoyed greater latitude than their blue-collar brethren (themselves regulated by tools such as time cards and assembly-line monitors), this is yet another feature of the corporate "sweatshop."

Two business-software packages gained popularity during the late 1990s. The "Investigator" program, sold by WinWhatWhere Corporation, can be installed by a company in any or all of its desktop computers in order to record how many keys are stroked, mouses clicked, and commands entered by each employee during a day. Its users include Exxon Mobil Corporation, Delta Air Lines, and Ernst & Young LLP. "Desktop Surveillance," which marketed itself as the "software equivalent of a video surveillance camera on the desktop," allows employers to view, in real time or playback, whatever tasks their staffers are performing on the computer.[26]

While some people might argue that these monitors are not all that different from the time records long maintained by high-end professionals such as lawyers and accountants, the comparison is anything but apt. These software packages were designed to be installed and operated within someone's computer without him or her being aware of that fact. "Investigator" can do far more than indicate productivity: its corporate users can adjust the software program so that anytime a staffer types an "alert" word (such as boss or union), the document in which it appears is automatically e-mailed to the appropriate supervisor. Some so-called keystroke loggers keep such comprehensive records of computer activity that an employer can read every single thing a person types at the office—whether or not he actually stores it in his desktop computer's hard drive, prints it out, sends it to someone via e-mail, or decides to discard it instead.[27]

And software packages like these represented only one part of a trend. "Back in the fifteenth century, they used to use a ball and chain, and now they use technology," one public relations executive complained to me. Some corporations have programmed their internal computer networks and security systems to make it possible for anyone within their organization to track the movements of anyone else at any time. That can include the exact moment each person starts work, leaves the office, or vacates his or her desk for a trip out to lunch or to the rest room.

One manager who begged me not to mention her company (or even her industry) told me about a time when supervisors had figured out that two of her colleagues were having an affair, because they could track electronically the exact timing of each of their movements into and out of the building in which they worked. One of the pair was eventually fired—not, she assured me, because of the affair, but because of his lack of productivity.

The justification for electronic monitoring is as old as the industrial age itself: greater efficiency. After all, business operations can be much more productive when coworkers and supervisors know how to track people down at any point in the workday. What's unusual about today's monitors, though, is their target: initiatives like these strip white-collar workers of their traditional perquisites (most importantly, a degree of independence). The message not so subtly being conveyed by their employers is this: We need everyone to work harder and longer but can't trust *you* to do it unless we start watching more closely . . . and if we find out that you're not working as we expect, we'll replace you.

In a disturbing article written for *PC Week*, Bill Machrone, then the vice president of technology for Ziff-Davis, compared many of today's corporate employers to Santa Claus ("he knows when you are sleeping, he knows. . ."). As Machrone explained, "He or she may not be able to pry into your personal life, but when you're at work, there's little you can do in the office that can't be monitored."[28]

Employee monitoring, like other deteriorating-workplace trends, continues to pick up steam, owing to the business world's seemingly endless quest to raise productivity regardless of the toll exacted upon working men and women. Back in 1993, for example, a survey by *Macworld* magazine found that nearly 22 percent of the companies surveyed engaged in electronic monitoring of their workforce. (Less than one third of those companies bothered to inform their staffers.) Nearly 30 percent of them justified the practice by citing a desire to "monitor work flow."[29] The American Management Association estimated that by 1999 45 percent of American corporations were monitoring their employees' e-mails. But that's not all. When video surveillance, phone-call tracking, electronic monitoring of computer work, and other types of supervision were counted in as well, a whopping 67 percent of companies acknowledged the practice. *Business Week* termed it "Big Brother at Work."[30] . . .

White-Collar Protests in Cyberspace

. . . To someone seeking to understand the experience of work, as well as employees' attitudes about it, in today's hard-driving corporations, there may be no better way to begin than by exploring the Internet.

Indeed, the Net has surfaced in recent years as a virtual town meeting hall where growing numbers of people interact and share their work-related complaints and anxieties.

The big draw for them, of course, is the cloak of anonymity provided by e-mail addresses and cyber-aliases. It's true that this cloak can be penetrated through extraordinary measures, as when hackers or employers intrude themselves into computer correspondence that once seemed private. But consider the real-world alternatives for those white-collar workers who may fear that layoffs, workload reorganizations, or even their own replacement by temporary staffers are just around the corner, *any corner*. Those conversational venues that are closer to home (the traditional watercooler gripe session, stress management seminars, or a host of mental health services paid for, and potentially monitored, by employers) often seem fraught with far greater risks of personal exposure than anything cyberspace can offer.

Given the variety of forces conspiring against them, today's white-collar workers may indeed be afraid to challenge their employers about their workloads or express their resentments face-to-face. But a tour of work-related Internet sites reveals a working population that is angry, exhausted, sometimes crude, and almost invariably frustrated by conditions on the job. "All jobs are bad," commented one anonymous visitor to <www.disgruntled.com>, a slick monthly Internet magazine whose focus on the dysfunctional world of work drew on average about three thousand "page views" each day from visitors.[31] . . .

Calls for corporate sabotage abounded at <www.disgruntled.com>, as elsewhere in cyberspace. "If your readers want to think about revenge . . . they need to think about stealing equipment, destroying or corrupting important files, blowing the whistle on illicit practices, and selling proprietary information to competitors."[32]

It's highly unlikely that most white-collar workers would actually carry out these threats. During my own research, not a single man or woman whom I interviewed acknowledged committing any act, even a petty one, of sabotage. (In fact, the consistency with which people seemed surprised or offended by my questions on this subject demonstrated how closely they still identified with notions such as self-responsibility, personal integrity, and their status within the corporate hierarchy, even when they felt betrayed or otherwise misused by an employer.) Still, the electronic conversations that appear in work-related chat rooms and other websites makes it clear that, if nothing else, these Internet threats provide over-stressed workers with a valuable opportunity to play out their collective revenge fantasies.

The growing pool of contingent white-collar workers are among the most vocal workplace critics on the Internet. Most are practically invisible and almost certainly interchangeable within the corporate world. The Internet gives them an opportunity to articulate their resentments in an electronic forum in which their status is the same as everyone else's and their voices can be as easily heard. . . .

Group therapy in cyberspace is a big part of the appeal of work-related websites for such people. In an era in which newspapers and other old-media venues continually trumpet the signs and success stories of economic prosperity, the cynicism that flourishes across the Internet comes as a relief. Net surfers seek comrades who can convince them that they're not the only ones for whom the world of work has become something in between a hassle and hell.

But what they find on the Internet varies. The "greedy" employer, the stupid employer, the abusive employer: hostility to the corporation, or to the top management that many people view as synonymous with the corporation, are basic themes.[33] At one site among many, web visitors can find "Bad Managers" (which describes itself as reporting on "true life horror stories of software development cowboys"), where one message continuously blinks across the right-hand corner of the screen: "You are not alone. Is your boss giving you the Hump? You are not alone."

One reason these sites have quickly gained popularity is because many "hyper-link" their web pages to each other. That enables visitors to identify and travel easily between a vast selection of electronic hot spots that share their antiwork perspectives. Some of these antiemployer or workplace-support messages turn out to be marketing ploys by entrepreneurial individuals or companies. Their goal, fairly simple to identify, is to attract more and more unhappy workers to their websites and thereby lock in revenues from either advertising or merchandising sales. Fairly typical of the genre is <www.jobhater.com>, which mainly sells T-shirts that enable unhappy workers to broadcast their woes.

At the other end of the spectrum are activist sites that attempt to rally Internet visitors into getting involved with some type of organized group, running the gamut from existing trade unions to self-help groups of, say, downsized employees. And somewhere in between are electronic chat rooms and websites that basically exist to help working people air and share their grievances.

In the late-1990s business boom, accompanied as it has been by ever more difficult and demanding workplace conditions, one trend seems clear: the number of antiwork websites, as well as their legions of visitors, seem to be endlessly proliferating. Current listings, as I write these words, run the gamut from "The Official Anti-Nike Site" and "The Disgruntled Ex-Burger King Employees Page" to "Working Stiff," <www.dinosaurclub.com> (aimed specifically at downsized, middle-aged executives) and "TempSlave." There's even a site called <www.nynexsucks.com>, whose allure for unhappy employees (as well as customers) proved so powerful that it continued to receive active electronic postings long after NYNEX had merged with Bell Atlantic.

The long-term implications of this trend remain uncertain. Even electronic communication may, like so many other technological advances, be subtly contributing to the spread of today's white-collar "sweat-shops." While cyberspace camaraderie, and all those rants and raves about work that dot the e-waves, may help over-stressed workers release some steam, the Internet may—by pacifying some people and intimidating others through the implicit message that work life is tough for everyone these days—rob many white-collar workers of the strength to resist excessive employer demands.

Discussion Questions

1. How does electronic technology raise the specter of Big Brother in the workplace?

2. How can workers develop their own strategies of resistance to workplace monitoring?

3. Have you ever experienced intrusive technology in your life?

4. Can you think of some useful ways to use electronic monitoring in the workplace?

Endnotes

1. Excerpted from correspondence from "tickler," May 6, 1999, on <http://alex.bla-bla.com/bla/go.cfm?goto=3644>.
2. Survey conducted by Stanford Institute for the Quantitative Study of Society. Cited in John Markoff, "A Newer, Lonelier Crowd Emerges in Internet Study," *New York Times*, February 16, 2000, A1.
3. Amy Harmon, "Plugged-in Nation Goes on Vacations in a New Territory," *New York Times*, July 13, 1997, section 1, 1.
4. The respective sources for these statistics, all cited by Data Analysis Group at its website, <http:www.cif1.com>, are "1999 Industry Outlook-Forecast: Consumer," Appliance Manufacturer/CEMA, January 1, 1999, 92; "1998 Buyers Guide," Presentations, December 1, 1997, A10; EDN, April 1, 1990, 80.
5. Ownership statistics come from Dataquest, a division of Gartner-Croup. According to Census Bureau projections, there were 102,118,600 households in the United States during 1999.
6. Statistics from EDN, see citation in note 4 above.
7. 1997 estimate provided by IDC Corporation, cited in Harmon, 14.
8. Katie Hafner, "For the Well Connected, All the World's an Office," *New York Times*, March 30. 2000, G1.
9. Cited in Sue Shellenharger, "Business Travelers Reshape Work Plans in Rush to Get Home," *Wall Street Journal*, March 18, 1998, B1.
10. Tom Mainelli, "Working While You're Away," *Smart Computing*, February 1998, 79; Patricia J. Bell, "Travel Journal: Taking the High-Tech Road," *Gourmet*, March 1998, 72.
11. Excerpted from correspondence from "technoid," April 20, 1999, on <http://alex.bla-bla com/bla/go.cfm?goto=3644>.
12. Statistics from the "Casio PhoneMate Report: Managing Messages in a Wired World," research conducted by Yankelovich Partners, March 10–22, 1998.
13. Bell.
14. Technology and the 24 Hour Day," *Harvard Business Review*, November–December 1996, 85.
15. "Casio PhoneMate Report."
16. Inter@ctive Week/Forrester Research. August 10, 1998, 39, cited by Data Analysis Group, <http://www.cif Econ>.
17. Arlie Russell Hochschild, *The Time Bind: When Work Becomes Home and Home Becomes Work* (New York: Metropolitan Books, 1997), 129.
18. Christopher Grimes, "As 'Bandwidth' Goes By, Tech Workers in Silicon Valley Coin Timely Phrase," *Wall Street Journal*, June 8, 1999, B4A.
19. "Messaging Practices in the Knowledge Economy," Pitney Bowes survey released on June 21, 1999; Tammy Reiss, "You've Got Mail, and Mail, and Mail. . . ," *Business Week*, July 20, 1998, 6.
20. Craig Brod, *TechnoStress: The Human Cost of the Computer Revolution* (Reading, Mass.: Addison-Wesley Publishing, 1984, 68–69, 41.
21. Barbara Garson, *The Electronic Sweatshop: How Computers Are Transforming the Office of the Future into the Factory of the Past* (New York: Penguin Books, 1988), 10.
22. Ibid., 60.
23. Jeremy Rifkin, *The End of Work: The Decline of the Global Labor Force and the Dawn of the Post-Market Era* (New York: G. P. Putnam's Sons, 1995), 144.
24. Ibid., 194.
25. Nick Wingfield, "More Companies Monitor Employees' E-Mail," *Wall Street Journal*, December 2, 1999, B8.
26. "A Different Type of Computer Monitor," *New York Times*, August 27, 1998; Michael J. McCarthy, "Thinking Out Loud: You Assumed 'Erase' Wiped Out That Rant Against the Boss? Nope!" *Wall Street Journal*, March 7, 2000, A1.
27. McCarthy, A1.
28. Bill Machrone, "The Depersonalization Continues," *PC Week*, September 2, 1996, 63.

29. Cited in Daniel S. Levine, *Disgruntled: The Darker Side of the World of Work* (New York: Berkley Boulevard Books, 1998), 118–19.
30. Statistics based upon an American Management Association survey of 1,054 member companies, cited in "Upfront: The Big Picture," *Business Week*, May 31, 1999, 8.
31. Founded in 1995 by financial journalist Daniel Levine, <www.disgruntled.com> combined a raucous and irreverent style with relentless, often well-researched criticisms of the workplace. Its revenue-producing ventures included the sale of advertising, antiwork T-shirts, and a range of books, among them a published collection of articles and letters excerpted from the website. In his "memo from the boss" to new visitors, Levine wrote, "We work because we need food, shelter, clothing and anything that numbs the pain of work itself. If it weren't for the fact that the only thing that sucks worse than work is being unemployed, who'd do it." The Internet magazine ceased publication in early 2000.
32. <http://www.disgruntled.com/anonymous1297.html>.
33. Mike France and Joann Muller, "A Site for Soreheads," *Business Week*, April 12, 1999, 86–90. ✦

13

How Computers Change Work and Pay

Frank Levy and
Richard J. Murnane

Almost everyone today has had enough experience with computers to speculate about the many ways in which they can affect work. We have all noticed the disappearance or decline of occupations like the telephone operator, bank teller, retail clerk, and travel agent, who have been replaced by friendly electronic telephone voices and customer-based checkout machines. We have also noticed the growing demand for computer programmers, information technology managers, medical technology assistants, and local geek shops to help the computer challenged.

In this chapter we are asked to approach the question of how computers impact work by focusing on four questions. First, regarding the fear of job loss, how did computers affect overall employment figures? Second, what jobs are in greater demand because of computers and what jobs are needed less? Third, what jobs win and lose in the contest for better wages? And fourth, what kind of skills are upgraded and downgraded because of computers?

Designing Airplanes

In November 1962 Boeing launched the 727, a 131-passenger jetliner designed to operate out of small airports with short runways. The roll-out completed an eighty-one-month development process during which more than 5,000 engineers worked with thousands of pounds of blueprints to design an aircraft that included more than 100,000 parts.[1] The airplane's complexity meant that no one person could guarantee the blueprints' internal consistency and so the second step in the design process was the construction of a full-scale model to ensure that the components fit—that proper space had been left for the aircraft's seats, hydraulic lines, air conditioning ducts, and other components.

When the model was completed and blueprints had been corrected, design engineers translated blueprint specifications into settings for stamping presses, turning lathes and the other machine tools that would fabricate the 727's parts. The translation resulted in many small errors and the parts often fit imperfectly. Assembly workers had to adjust the parts by hand, using metal shims to fill in small gaps. A manager familiar with the process estimated that a 727 weighing forty-four tons typically contained a half-ton of shims.

Thirty-two years later, in April 1994, Boeing rolled out the 777, a 305-passenger plane designed to carry passengers up to 6000 miles. Although much larger and more complex than the 727, the 777's development cycle was shorter by twenty-nine months. The explanation was no secret: the 777 was the first commercial jet to be completely designed using computers! Using CATIA, computer-assisted design and manufacturing software developed by the French engineering company Dassault Systèmes, engineers designed components on computer screens rather than on paper. The software's power was its ability to integrate individual views into a three-dimensional visualization. The virtual model substituted for a physical mock-up in checking plans for internal consistency. Once engineers had corrected the plans, CATIA produced the digital settings for the computer-numerically-controlled (CNC) machine tools that would fabricate the 777's parts.

Boeing purchased the CATIA system as part of an effort to pursue several competitive strategies. One was to compete better by increasing design speed. Being first to

market confers an advantage in many industries but it is particularly important in
civilian aircraft, where two large producers—Boeing and Airbus—vie for a limited
number of orders. Boeing's adoption of
CATIA eliminated the need for mock-up
models and reduced the time required to
correct plans and to set up machine tools.
The result was a 36 percent reduction in the
length of Boeing's development cycle.

A second competitive strategy facilitated
by CATIA was improved product quality.
The digital settings that CATIA produced
for CNC machine tools made it possible to
produce parts that fit together well and so
the 777's assembly required far fewer hand
adjustments and shims. According to Boeing, "[T]he first 777 was just .023 of an
inch—about the thickness of a playing
card—within perfect alignment while most
airplane parts line up to within a half inch
of each other."[2]

Since CATIA reduced design time, its use
made it possible for Boeing to compete by
offering product variety. It could provide
configurations tailored to customers' specifications without long design delays.

The digital machine tool settings produced by CATIA facilitated another Boeing
competitive strategy: the ability to outsource production with less regard to distance. . . . [C]omputerization made it possible to outsource call center work. Similarly,
CATIA facilitated the outsourcing of blue-
collar manufacturing work. Once CATIA
produced the digital machine tool settings,
the machine tools themselves could be located anywhere since Boeing knew the
parts would fit when brought to a common
assembly point. Boeing used this ability to
locate production in Italy, the United Kingdom, Japan, and other countries, in part to
attract foreign customers and in part to reduce production costs. (In retailing, a similar conquering of geography occurs as
firms like Amazon.com and LandsEnd.com
use single websites to reach widely dispersed customers and use computerized
shipping to deliver orders in acceptably
short times.[3])

None of these strategies was new. Fifty
years ago Boeing wanted to bring high-

quality planes to market as soon as possible
and to tailor specifications to customers'
preferences. What was new—what computers had changed—was the cost of pursuing
the strategies. Fifty years ago, bringing aircraft to market sooner without compromising quality would have involved paying vast
amounts of overtime. The adoption of computer-based design tools and computer-
driven production tools dramatically lowered the cost of achieving these goals.

If we take a step back from aircraft production, we see how the Boeing-CATIA
story illustrates a final computer-supported
strategy—the creation of new, information-
intensive products including CATIA itself,
an important revenue source for Dassault
Systèmes. CATIA, CDs, cell phones, DVDs,
geo-positioning devices, the modern echo-
cardiograph machine, the Eurex Trading
network, complex financial derivatives,
and the Palm Pilot are all successful products that computers have made possible.

Why Jobs Change

As the Boeing-CATIA example illustrates, computers change work through a
three-step process. The first step occurred
when Boeing purchased CATIA to pursue
particular competitive strategies that were
impractical without computers. To take advantage of CATIA's capabilities, Boeing next
had to reorganize work, using computers to
substitute for humans in carrying out some
tasks and to complement humans in carrying out others. In the process's final step,
the reorganization of work changed both
Boeing's job mix and the skills needed to do
many jobs. Engineers now had to create designs on computer screens rather than
drafting boards. The labor hours required
to build a full-scale mock-up were no longer needed and the number of hours spent
hand-fitting parts was sharply reduced.
Some jobs that had been previously located
in the United States were moved offshore.

The same three-step process characterizes almost every new application of computers. Firms adopt computers to gain a
particular competitive advantage. Real-

izing computers' potential requires reorganizing work. As computers proliferate in the workplace, the jobs they create, destroy, and change are the byproduct of this work reorganization. Since computers are present in a large and growing number of American work places, they are catalyzing dramatic change in the nature of work. We turn to these changes.

Four Ways to Think About Work

When we ask how computers are changing work, we have several specifics in mind.

1. *Employment*. With all the prophecies that computers would create mass unemployment, why didn't it happen?

2. *The economy's mix of jobs*. As computers have substituted for humans in carrying out some tasks and complemented humans in tackling others, what kinds of jobs have grown in importance, and what kinds of jobs have declined?

3. *Wages*. What are the wage trends for different kinds of workers, and what do these trends tell us the about the changing content of work?

4. *Worker skills*. Which skills are of rising importance in the economy and which skills face diminishing demand? The answer to this question involves changes in the economy's mix of jobs but also the changing nature of work within jobs.

Employment

As this book goes to press [2004], the economy continues in a post-bubble recession, but the current unemployment rate is nothing like the fear of mass unemployment expressed in the Ad Hoc Committee's 1964 memo to President Lyndon Johnson. Moreover, if we focus on the unemployment rate per se, we will miss the economy's strong job-creation performance as computer use soared.

When the Ad Hoc Committee drafted its memo, mainframe computers were a commercial reality and special-purpose computers—for example, computers that control machine tools—were on the horizon. Had computers created large-scale unemployment, we should have seen the first signs by the end of the 1960s. In fact, the opposite occurred. For much of the 1970s and 1980s, the labor force grew explosively as the largest baby-boom cohorts turned twenty-one and women of all ages moved into paid work. The fast growth in the number of potential workers meant that the number of jobs had to grow rapidly to keep unemployment from rising. In 1969, a boom year, unemployment stood at 3.5 percent. In 2000, another boom year, unemployment stood at 4.0 percent. In the intervening thirty-one years, the number of employed persons had grown from 83 million to 135 million—clearly not the picture the Ad Hoc Committee had expected.[4]

We have made reference to Herbert Simon's 1960 essay, "The Corporation; Will It Be Managed by Machines?" In this essay, Simon explained why predictions of mass unemployment would prove to be wrong. Borrowing from international trade theory Simon invoked David Ricardo's historic principle of comparative advantage. Simon began from the premise that society can always find uses for additional output (consider today's unfulfilled demand for health care). Under this premise, computers and humans will both be used in producing this output, each in those tasks for which they have a comparative advantage. As Simon wrote:

> If computers are a thousand times faster than bookkeepers in doing arithmetic, but only one hundred times faster than stenographers in taking dictation, we shall expect the number of bookkeepers per thousand employees to decrease but the number of stenographers to increase. Similarly, if computers are a hundred times faster than executives in making investment decisions, but only ten times faster in handling employee grievances (the quality of the decisions being held constant), then

computers will be employed in making investment decisions, while executives will be employed in handling grievances. (25)

Note that in Simon's examples (as in Ricardo's original formulation), computers are absolutely more efficient than humans in both tasks but employing humans is still worthwhile in tasks in which they have a *comparative* (that is, relative) advantage. As we know, our current situation is not this extreme since humans are absolutely more efficient than computers in understanding speech, interpreting visual images, and in a host of other activities requiring recognition of complex patterns. At the same time, Simon does not rule out that the adoption of computers may cause painful adjustments or that workers displaced by computers may regain employment only at lower wages, at least in the short run.

The story Simon describes has played out with many different technologies. When the combine harvester came into widespread use in the 1920s, it displaced manual labor and created substantial rural unemployment. Over the longer run, most farm workers became reemployed through either of two channels.

In the first channel, greater efficiency in agriculture meant that farm products could be sold at lower prices, and so consumers could increase the amounts they purchased. Workers were rehired to help produce the larger levels of output now demanded by consumers.

In the past twenty years, this channel has characterized "back-office" jobs in the securities industry. Consider the entry-level accountants who keep the books for mutual funds and compute the Net Asset Value per share (NAV) that appears in daily newspaper stock tables. Over two decades, the computerization of their job has allowed the average accountant to keep records for four mutual funds instead of one or two. Had the number of mutual funds stayed constant, the accountants' greater productivity would have meant fewer accounting jobs. But over the same period, the number of mutual funds expanded from 500 to 5,000 and the number of mutual fund accountants significantly increased. The growth in the number of mutual funds stemmed, in part, from the decline in the cost of running a mutual fund as computers lowered the costs of record keeping, trade execution, and other back-office functions.[5]

The second, more important channel of reemployment was the movement of displaced workers into other, expanding industries. In the first half of the twentieth century, large numbers of displaced agricultural workers moved into manufacturing jobs. Similarly, beginning in the 1970s, displaced manufacturing workers moved into service jobs. These moves can be painful and can involve significant cuts in pay and benefits, but they avoid long-term unemployment.[6]

Under both channels, the economy produces more goods and services per person. In the agricultural example, the mechanical harvester allows the same amount of farm product to be produced with fewer farm laborers. Depending on demand, the displaced laborers produce either additional farm products or additional output in the industries to which they moved. This additional output is no economists' fantasy. In 1947, the median U.S. family income stood at $20,400 (in year-2001 dollars).[7] By 1964, it had risen to $31,773. The growing purchasing power largely reflected increased output per worker stemming from technological improvements and a more educated workforce. Over the long run, we can pay ourselves only what we produce, and it was the higher output per worker that permitted family incomes to rise.

Today, median family income stands at about $51,000, and a significant fraction of recent income gains has been spent on computer-related products: cell phones, advanced medical treatments, CDs, DVDs, and so on. These purchases, in turn, increased employment in those occupations in which labor had a comparative advantage.

In sum, plenty of evidence supports Simon's argument that computerized work does not lead to mass unemployment. But

Simon also made clear that computerization could sharply alter the economy's mix of jobs. We turn next to this topic.

The Mix of Jobs

How do computers affect the economy's job mix? Most predictions have fallen into one of two schools. The first is that computers will do low-level, routine work, so that people have to move into higher-skilled work to survive. The second is that computers will largely do high-level work, leaving most people no alternative but menial jobs.

Peter Drucker, the management theorist, has been an enthusiastic member of the first school. In Drucker's mind, computerization subsumes routine work, and so the real danger is a shortage of trained managers to direct what computers should do. Writer Jeremy Rifkin is a member of the second school. In *The End of Work*, Rifkin argues that the economy's requirements for high-level knowledge workers can never compensate for the number of jobs computers will eliminate. The result will be a large concentration of workers in low-level dead-end jobs. Apparent support for this prediction comes from the U.S. Bureau of Labor Statistics, which projects that food preparation and serving workers—a low-paying occupation requiring little training—will gain more jobs in the decade from 2000 to 2010 than any other occupation.[8]

In his 1960 essay Herbert Simon made a set of predictions about the job mix in a typical corporation in 1985. Simon's predictions were closer to Drucker's than to Rifkin's, but they were also highly nuanced. While Simon did not lay out an explicit cognitive framework, something like the [following] was implicit in the predictions he made for a variety of occupational categories.

- Blue-collar workers: "There will be a few vestigial 'workmen'—probably a smaller part of the total labor force than today—who will be part of in-line production, primarily doing tasks requiring relatively flexible eye-brain-hand coordination." (37)

- Machine maintenance workers (people we now call technicians): "There will be a substantial number of men whose task it is to keep the system operating by preventative and remedial maintenance." (37)

- Clerical workers: "The same kinds of technical developments that lead toward the automatic factory are bringing about an even more rapid revolution—and perhaps eventually a more complete one—in large-scale clerical operations. . . . We can conjecture that by 1985, the departments of a company concerned with major clerical functions—accounting, processing of customers' orders, inventory and production control, purchasing and the like—will have reached an even higher level of automation than most factories." (26)

- Salespeople: "I have little basis for conjecture on this point. If we think that buying decisions are not going to be made much more objectively than they have in the past, then we might conclude the automation of the salesman's role will proceed less rapidly than the automation of many other jobs. If so, selling will account for a larger fraction of total employment." (37)

- Managers: "There will be a substantial number of men at professional levels, responsible for the design of product, for the design of productive process, and for general management. We have still not faced the question of how far automation will go in these areas, and hence we cannot say very firmly whether such occupations will be a larger or smaller part of the whole." (38)

Note how some of Simon's predictions made in 1960 run counter to predictions made by business analysts in the 1990s. Simon's emphasis on managers goes against the precepts of re-engineering in which information technology would eliminate layers of managers. His qualified emphasis on salespeople runs counter to predictions that e-commerce would dramatically reduce the number of salespeople.

Were Simon's predictions accurate? It is time to look at the numbers. To see what actually happened to occupations, we first present the 1969 occupational structure for adult workers (Figure 13.1). Data for the figure come from the U.S. Census Bureau, which classifies workers into roughly 400 occupational titles, including the following: Managers [in] Marketing, Advertising, and Public Relations; Administrators [in] Education and Related Fields; Funeral Directors; and Buyers [in] Wholesale and Retail Trade, Except Farm Products. To make these data comprehensible, Figure 13.1 groups the detailed occupational titles into seven broad categories arrayed from left to right in order of increasing average earnings.[9]

The category "Professional Occupations" in Figure 13.1 includes teachers, ministers, doctors, engineers, and other white-collar jobs typically requiring college or post-college education. "Blue-Collar Workers" includes skilled craftsmen, assembly line workers, day laborers, and similar workers, most of whom work in industrial settings and have not completed college.[10] The category "Service Workers" includes janitors, cafeteria servers and waiters, policemen, firemen, childcare workers, and others who deal with people face to face; many of these jobs do not require a college degree (policemen are now an exception in many jurisdictions but were not so in 1969).

The variety of occupations in each category blurs the meaning of the category's average earnings. Service workers on average earn less than blue-collar workers, but the highest paid service workers—policemen and firemen—earn more than many blue-collar workers and many sales workers as well. Nonetheless, the figure gives a reasonable overview of the U.S. occupational structure.

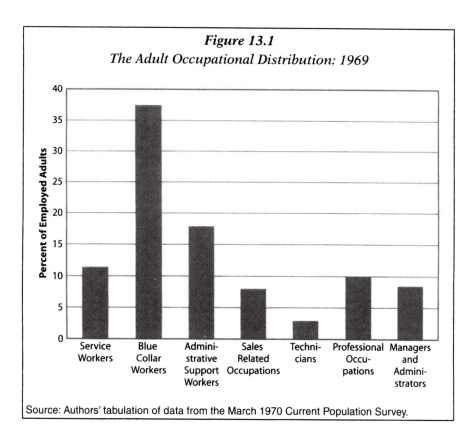

Figure 13.1
The Adult Occupational Distribution: 1969

Source: Authors' tabulation of data from the March 1970 Current Population Survey.

Figure 13.2 shows how these occupational groupings changed in relative size between 1969 and 1999, a period when computers of all kinds permeated the economy. (We chose 1999 instead of a later year as the end point of our comparison in order to compare two business-cycle peak years.) Reading the figure from left to right, we learn the following:

- Service Workers grew modestly from 11.6 percent of all workers in 1969 to 13.9 percent in 1999.

- Blue Collar Workers and Administrative Support Workers both declined. Together, these two occupational groups employed 56 percent of all adult workers in 1969, falling to 39 percent of all adult workers in 1999.

- Sales Related Occupations ranging from McDonald's clerks to stockbrokers to real estate agents grew from 8

percent to 12 percent of all adults—from one adult worker in every twelve to one in every eight.[11]

- Technicians increased from 4.2 percent to 5.4 percent of all adult workers.

- Professional Occupations—engineers, teachers, scientists, lawyers—increased from 10 percent to 13 percent—from one worker in ten to one in eight.

- Managers and Administrators increased from 8 percent to 14 percent—from one adult worker in twelve to one in every seven.

This hollowing out of the occupational structure is broadly consistent with Simon's predictions including his general expectation of more "face-to-face interaction." With one exception, it is also consistent with Peter Drucker's view of the world—that the growth would be in jobs re-

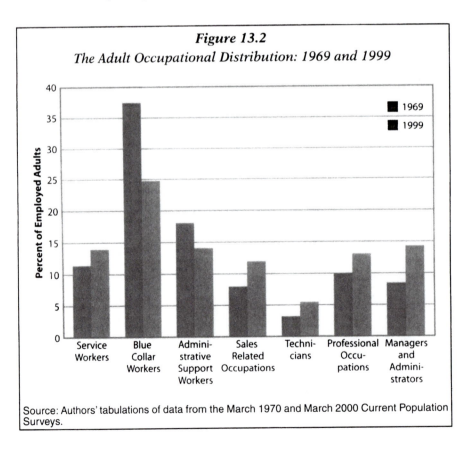

Figure 13.2
The Adult Occupational Distribution: 1969 and 1999

Source: Authors' tabulations of data from the March 1970 and March 2000 Current Population Surveys.

quiring more education. The exception is the modest growth of Service Workers at the bottom of the pay distribution.

To see why trends in Service Workers are difficult to predict, consider the statement that computers are best at doing routine jobs. In casual conversation, a security guard has a routine job: he or she walks the same beat every night looking for suspicious activity. But from a cognitive perspective, a security guard's job is exceedingly complex.[12] The core of the job—identifying suspicious activity—begins with the perception of large quantities of visual and aural information. This information must be processed using pattern recognition that requires substantial contextual knowledge. In casual conversation, "routine" means "repetitive." In software terms, however, "routine" means "expressible in rules." Determining whether a person is a potential burglar or a worker staying late is not easily encoded in rules.

A security guard is not paid well because most humans can do the job—that is, the potential supply of workers is large. But that does not mean the job is easy to program. The distinction between "easy for humans to do" and "easy to program computers to do" helps to explain why routine service workers—cafeteria workers, janitors—have not been replaced by computers and why the fraction of adults in service work has grown (see Figure 13.2).[13]

More generally, the theory implicit in Simon's 1960 essay . . . provides a coherent story about why occupations changed as they did:

- The growing number of Service Workers (janitors, cafeteria workers, security guards) reflects the inability to describe human optical recognition and many physical movements in sets of rules.

- The growth of Sales Occupations (fast food clerks through bond traders) stems in part from the way that an increased flow of new products—driven by computers—increases the need for selling, and in part from the inability of rules to describe the exchange of com-

plex information that salesmanship requires.

- The growth of Professional, Managerial and Technical occupations reflects the inability to express high end cognitive activities in rules: formulating and solving new problems, exercising good judgment in the face of uncertainty, creating new products and services. The competitive strategies listed earlier—strategies driven by computers—have increased demand for these activities.

- In contrast, many Blue Collar and Administrative Support jobs can be described in rules, and this accounts in large part for the decline in these two categories through both direct substitution and computer-assisted outsourcing.

The result is a picture in which the number of menial jobs is growing, but the general shift of occupations is toward higher-end jobs. While computers are not responsible for all of these changes, they do play a major role in bringing them about.[14]

Before leaving this picture, we have one loose end to consider—the Bureau of Labor Statistics (BLS) projection that food preparation and serving workers will be the occupation with the largest job growth over the next decade. How can this BLS projection square with the general shift of occupations toward higher-skilled jobs shown in Figure 13.2?

The answer becomes clear once we put the projection into context. In the year 2000 there were more food preparation and food servers in the economy (about 2.2 million) than there were lawyers (681,000), doctors (598,000), or electrical engineers (450,000). But these head-to-head comparisons tell us little since food preparation and serving workers are counted under one occupational title while jobs requiring significant education tend to be divided into many occupations (e.g., electrical engineering is one of sixteen major engineering occupations classified in BLS statistics).

The shift that Jeremy Rifkin feared, a "deskilled" occupational structure, requires that the total number of low-skilled jobs (janitors plus security guards plus food preparation and service workers, etc.) increases more than the *total* number of higher-skilled jobs (lawyers plus doctors plus electrical engineers plus mechanical engineers, and so on). These totals are the kind of occupational categories displayed in figure 13.2, where the food preparation and service workers are included in Service Occupations. Once we move from individual job titles to occupational categories, the evidence of deskilling disappears. Between 1969 and 1999, the number of adults employed as Service Workers grew from 11.6 percent to 13.9 percent of the adult work force, but Managers, Administrators, Professional Workers, and Technicians taken together—the highest paid categories—grew from 23 percent to 33 percent.

The Distribution of Wages

In a healthy economy, demands for different kinds of workers are changing all the time—so quickly that it is easy for specific kinds of workers to find themselves in shortage or surplus. In the labor market, as in any other competitive market, the best indicators of shortages and surpluses are changes in prices—in this case, wages. When workers with particular attributes are in surplus, their real wages (net of inflation) fall. Real wages rise for workers in shortage. For the period we are examining, the best wage data comes from the decennial U.S. Census and its companion survey, the monthly Current Population Survey. Based on these data, Figures 13.3 and 13.4 show trends over the period 1973–2001 in the average wages of male and female workers with different educational attainments.

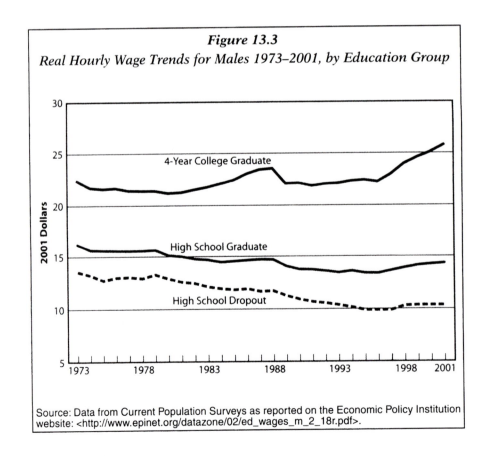

Figure 13.3
Real Hourly Wage Trends for Males 1973–2001, by Education Group

Source: Data from Current Population Surveys as reported on the Economic Policy Institution website: <http://www.epinet.org/datazone/02/ed_wages_m_2_18r.pdf>.

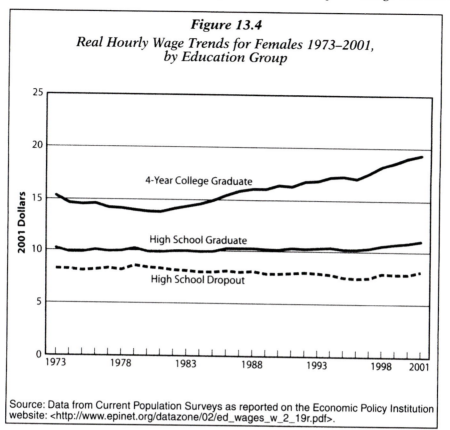

Figure 13.4

*Real Hourly Wage Trends for Females 1973–2001,
by Education Group*

Source: Data from Current Population Surveys as reported on the Economic Policy Institution website: <http://www.epinet.org/datazone/02/ed_wages_w_2_19r.pdf>.

In 1996 the average real wage of male college graduates was almost identical to its value in 1973, an indication that demand kept up with the supply of college-educated workers. Then in the strong economy of the late 1990s, the real wage of male college graduates grew markedly. In contrast, the average real wage of male high school graduates fell by almost $3.00 per hour between 1973 and 1996, and the average wage of male dropouts fell by almost $4.66 per hour during this period. While the strong economy of the late 1990s allowed these groups to recover some part of the earnings decline, hourly wages in 2001 were still markedly below 1973 wages for these groups.

The pattern of wage stability and recent wage growth among college graduates and long-run wage decline among high school graduates could have come from changes in the demand for workers with different educational attainments or from changes in their supply. The data point to changes in demand. During this period, the number of male college graduates was growing *faster* than the number of male high school graduates and dropouts. Had demand been stable, the faster growing group would have experienced declining wages. That, of course, is not what happened—real wages of male college graduates rose in the two decades after 1980. The changing occupational structure was creating new demand for college graduates that outstripped their fast-growing supply. Applying the same logic, the real wages of male high school graduates and male dropouts were falling because demand for these workers was growing even more slowly than their slow-growing supply.[15]

Women's wages tell a broadly similar story. As with men, the number of employed female college graduates grew faster during these years than the number of employed female high school graduates and dropouts. Yet as shown in Figure 13.4, the average wage of female college graduates increased quite sharply while the average wage of female high school graduates and school dropouts did not grow.

We are beginning to fill in the blanks about how computers are changing work. On the labor market's demand side, the share of menial jobs has increased modestly, but the largest job growth has been in occupations requiring significant education. On the labor market's supply side, the number of college graduates has been growing faster than the number of high school graduates and dropouts. Yet the rising wages of college graduates indicate demand is outstripping their supply. Conversely, the declining wages of male high school graduates and dropouts, despite the slow growth of these groups, indicate they will end up in jobs that no longer pay enough to support families.

College graduates have fared better than high school graduates in the changing U.S. labor market because they are more likely to have the skills needed to do the tasks that are part of high-wage jobs. We turn now to a description of these tasks.

Worker Skills and the New Nature of Work

Today virtually all public schools operate under mandates to prepare all students to master skills defined in state standards. Private corporations spend an average of $800 per employee on training each year.[16] Much of this effort is devoted to preparing people to work productively in the computerized workplace. If the effort is to make sense, the nation needs to understand what tasks humans will do at their work and the skills they will need to carry out these tasks effectively.

We already have some answers. We have established that computers have a comparative advantage over people in carrying out tasks requiring the execution of rules, but people have the comparative advantage in

recognizing complex patterns. We have also seen how complex pattern recognition is critical in two quite different kinds of tasks—optical recognition and physical movement (security guards, Simon's "few vestigial 'workmen'") and tasks involving higher-order cognitive skills. As a next step we can usefully divide these higher order tasks into two broad groups. The first are tasks that involve solving new problems—problems that cannot be solved by applying well-understood rules. The second are tasks that require explanation, negotiation, persuasion, and other forms of intense human interaction. We will call these two sets of tasks, respectively, tasks requiring expert thinking and tasks requiring complex communication.

In joint work with David Autor of MIT's Department of Economics, we have shown that tasks requiring expert thinking and complex communication are two of five broad kinds of tasks carried out by the U.S. labor force:[17]

- Expert thinking: solving problems for which there are no rule-based solutions. Examples include diagnosing the illness of a patient whose symptoms seem strange, creating a good tasting dish from the ingredients that are fresh in the market that morning, repairing an auto that does not run well but that the computer diagnostics indicate has no problem. By definition, these are not tasks that computers can be programmed to do. While computers cannot substitute for humans in these tasks, they can complement humans in performing them by making information more readily available.

- Complex communication: interacting with humans to acquire information, to explain it, or to persuade others of its implications for action. Examples include a manager motivating the people whose work she supervises, a biology teacher explaining how cells divide, an engineer describing why a new design for a DVD player is an advance over previous designs.

• Routine cognitive tasks: mental tasks that are well described by logical rules. Examples include maintaining expense reports, filing new information provided by insurance customers, and evaluating applications for mortgages. Because these tasks can be accomplished by following a set of rules, they are prime candidates for computerization.

• Routine manual tasks: physical tasks that can be well described using rules. Examples include installing windshields on new vehicles in automobile assembly plants, and counting and packaging pills into containers in pharmaceutical firms. Since these tasks can be defined in terms of a set of movements to be carried out over and over in exactly the same way, they are also candidates for computerization.

• Nonroutine manual tasks: physical tasks that cannot be well described as following a set of If-Then-Do rules because they require optical recognition and fine muscle control, that have proven extremely difficult for computers to carry out. Examples include driving a truck, cleaning a building, and setting gems in engagement rings. Computers do not complement human effort in carrying out most such tasks. As a result, computerization should have little effect on the percentage of the work force engaged in these tasks.

Earlier in this chapter, we saw how the nation's occupational distribution has changed in the period from 1969 to 1999. In the same way, we can look for changes in the nature of the tasks that comprise this work. While the Census does not ask about the content of work, a second survey does—the U.S. Department of Labor's Dictionary of Occupational Titles (DOT).

The DOT is a compilation of 12,000 detailed occupational descriptions, each containing professional observers' ratings of the training time required for the occupation, the occupation's physical and cogni-

tive requirements, and other characteristics. Because an occupation's details can vary across work sites, each occupation is rated across many workers in multiple sites and the DOT provides an average of the ratings.

The DOT offers far from perfect data. Updates are infrequent, and so it is difficult to track changes in tasks that occur within occupations. Nonetheless, the DOT allows an approximate translation of changes in the economy's distribution of occupations into changes in the kind of tasks that people perform in the workplace.[18] Figure 13.5 displays the trend for each of these five types of tasks. Each trend reflects changes in the numbers of people employed in occupations emphasizing that task. To facilitate comparisons, the importance of each task in the U.S. economy is set to zero in 1969, our baseline year. The value in each subsequent year represents the percentile change in the importance of each type of task in the economy.[19]

A quick look at the figure shows that, consistent with our expectations, tasks requiring pattern recognition grew in frequency while rules-based tasks declined. Complex communication is important in management, teaching, and sales occupations among others. As the occupational structure evolved toward these particular occupations, the frequency of tasks requiring complex communication grew steadily during the 1970s, 1980s, and 1990s. The frequency of tasks requiring expert thinking—tasks that involved solving new problems—followed a similar growth path.

For rules-based tasks where computers can substitute for humans, the picture is one of decline. The share of the labor force employed in occupations that emphasized routine cognitive tasks remained quite steady during the 1970s and then declined quite precipitously over the next two decades. The pattern for routine manual tasks—tasks that might be subsumed by automation—is roughly similar: a slight rise during the 1970s and a steady decline in the subsequent two decades. The share of the labor force working in occupations

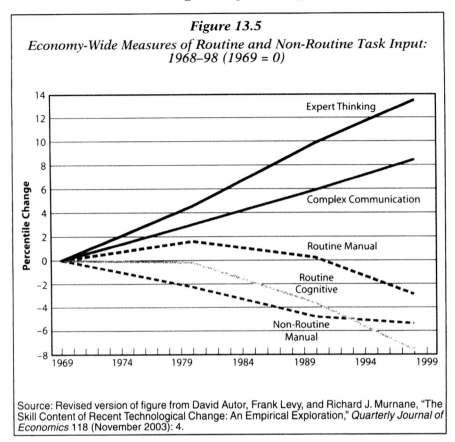

Figure 13.5
*Economy-Wide Measures of Routine and Non-Routine Task Input:
1968–98 (1969 = 0)*

Source: Revised version of figure from David Autor, Frank Levy, and Richard J. Murnane, "The Skill Content of Recent Technological Change: An Empirical Exploration," *Quarterly Journal of Economics* 118 (November 2003): 4.

that emphasize nonroutine manual tasks declined throughout the period. This reflects in part the movement of manufacturing jobs offshore.

The data in Figures 13.2 (occupations) and 13.5 (tasks) are consistent with our description of computers' economic impacts. But this correlation does not prove causation—the trend in both figures could have been caused by other factors. To make a stronger case, we must increase the level of detail to look at changes within industries. If our argument is right—if the adoption of computers shifts work away from routine tasks and toward tasks requiring expert thinking and complex communication—it should be observable when we look within industries. Specifically, we can ask: are those industries that invested most heavily in computers the industries where we see the greatest changes in task structure?

The answer is yes. In Figure 13.6 the left of each pair of bars describes the average change in task frequency within industries over the period 1980 to 1998.[20] The height of the right bar in each pair is an estimate of the change in task frequency that would have occurred had there been no increase in computer use. A comparison of the bars in each pair illustrates that changes in task frequency have been concentrated in the industries experiencing the most rapid increases in computer use. This pattern is particularly striking for routine cognitive tasks. The percentage of the labor force employed in jobs that consisted primarily of carrying out routine cognitive tasks declined substantially over these years. The figure shows that in the absence of changes in computer use, the estimated percentage of the labor force working at routine cognitive tasks would have increased. The amount of routine information processing taking place in the economy grew substantially over these years, but increasingly this work was carried out by computers instead of by people.[21]

The case for the link between computerization and task change is strengthened by looking specifically at the changes in tasks performed by high school graduates. Since 1970, industries that invested heavily in computers shifted their workforces away from high school graduates and toward college graduates. This comes as no surprise. On average, college graduates are better suited than high school graduates for jobs like product design, technical trouble shooting, and managing—all tasks requiring expert thinking and complex communi-

cation. But if high school graduates in computer-intensive industries also saw their jobs shift toward these two kinds of tasks, it would be additional evidence of how deep computerization has reached into the workplace.

In fact, this has been the case. In the technical work with David Autor, we show that the past twenty years have seen increases in the percentage of high school graduates working at jobs that emphasize complex communication and substantial declines in the percentages of high school graduates working at jobs that emphasized routine cognitive or routine manual tasks. Consistent with our theory, these changes were concentrated in industries that experienced the greatest growth in computer usage. . . .

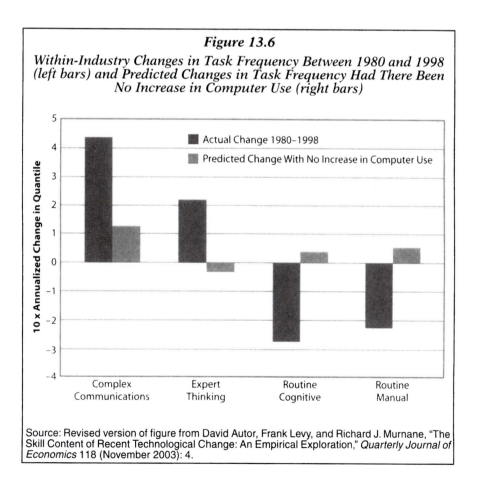

Figure 13.6

Within-Industry Changes in Task Frequency Between 1980 and 1998 (left bars) and Predicted Changes in Task Frequency Had There Been No Increase in Computer Use (right bars)

Source: Revised version of figure from David Autor, Frank Levy, and Richard J. Murnane, "The Skill Content of Recent Technological Change: An Empirical Exploration," *Quarterly Journal of Economics* 118 (November 2003): 4.

Tasks and Skills

In this chapter we have provided a variety of evidence showing how computerization has altered the tasks that American workers perform in their jobs. Declining portions of the labor force are engaged in jobs that consist primarily of routine cognitive work and routine manual work—the types of tasks that are easiest to program computers to do. Growing proportions of the nation's labor force are engaged in jobs that emphasize expert thinking or complex communication—tasks that computers cannot do.

If the set of products and services produced in the economy did not change, there would be less and less good work for humans to do as advances in computerization increased the possibilities for substitution. Such a trend, however, would run directly counter to the profit motive. A task, once computerized, is potentially easy to replicate and so invites intense competition. The response to the competition is a constant drive to use advances in computer technology to develop new products and services—cell phones, DVDs, broad-band Internet, computer-assisted surgery, financial derivatives, sensors in cars—the list is endless. This drive to develop, produce, and market new products relies on the human ability to manage and solve analytical problems and communicate new information, and so it keeps expert thinking and complex communication in strong demand. . . .

Discussion Questions

1. What is your desired job and how do you think it is affected by computers?

2. What advice would you give to a high school student about how to prepare for today's world of work?

3. What do you think are the chances of a revolt against computers and the development of a modern Luddite movement? Google "Luddite" if necessary.

Endnotes

1. Kark Sabbagh, *21st-century Jet: The Making and Marketing of the Boeing 777* (New York Scribner, 1996), 58–59.
2. See <http://www.boeing.com/commercial/777 family/compute/index.html>.
3. See Frances Cairncross, *The Death of Distance: How the Communications Revolution Will Change Our Lives* (Cambridge: Harvard Business School Press, 1997).
4. A larger fraction of the entire population was working in the year 2000 than in 1969, but the unemployment rate is defined as:

$$\frac{(\text{number of people looking for work})}{(\text{number of people looking for work} + \text{number of people working})}$$

and this statistic could be equal in the two years because the number of people working and the number of people looking for work had both risen.
5. Another factor contributing to the growth in the number of mutual funds was the replacement of defined benefit pension plans (fully managed by employers) by 401K plans.
6. These stories should be abstracted from temporary unemployment due to fluctuations in the business cycle.
7. That is, 50 percent of all families had higher incomes and 50 percent had lower incomes. The figure refers to all U.S. families regardless of age, the number of earners, etc.
8. Daniel E. Hecker, "Occupational Employment Projections to 2010," *Monthly Labor Review* 57, no. 84 (2001): p. 80, table 4.
9. The calculations that underlie figures 13.1 and 13.2 were done using the March supplements to the 1970 and 2000 Current Population Series. We included farmers and members of the armed forces in the total number of adult workers, but did not form separate categories for these very small groups.
10. Most blue-collar occupations are in manufacturing and construction but some—telephone repairmen, airline and bus mechanics—are found in service industries.
11. A more detailed analysis of sales employment shows a slight decline during the 1990s, but the thirty-year trend is strongly positive.
12. For a thoughtful discussion of the many definitions that the term "skill" can take, see Paul Attewell, "What Is Skill?" *Work and Occupation* 17, no. 4 (1990): 422-48.

13. It is also true that these face-to-face jobs must be performed where the customers are and so cannot be outsourced to other countries.
14. See Autor, Levy, and Murnane, "The Skill Content of Recent Technological Change," for evidence on the role of computers in bringing about these economic changes.
15. Over the past thirty years, the average U.S. wage grew very slowly, a reflection of slow-growing productivity. If the average wage had grown faster, high school graduates might have seen their wages hold steady or increase modestly while college graduates would have seen their wages increase rapidly.
16. The dollar figure on per-employee expenditures on training per year is taken from the following American Association for Training and Development website: <http://www.astd.org/virtual_community/library/tfaq.html>.
17. This work is detailed in Autor, Levy, and Murnane, "The Skill Content of Recent Technological Change."
18. A complete translation would also include changes in tasks that occur within occupations. See ibid, for a detailed description of the use we made of the data from the Dictionary of Occupational Titles.
19. See ibid, for a detailed description of the metric used on the vertical axis in figure 13.5.
20. For a detailed description of the methodology used in all the statistical work described in this chapter, including this test, see ibid.
21. To simplify exposition, we did not include in figure 13.6 the two bars displaying changes in nonroutine manual tasks. The two bars both have negative heights of –0.90, showing that over this period the percentage of the labor force working at nonroutine manual tasks fell, but that the decline was no more pronounced in computer-intensive industries than in other industries. ✦

14

Flexible Firms and Labor Market Segmentation: Effects of Workplace Restructuring on Jobs and Workers

Arne L. Kalleberg

The new economy offers expanded opportunities for corporations across every sector of our economy. The invention of new food products, pharmaceutical drugs, clothing fabrics, household appliances, and medical diagnostic tools, to name but a few, offer companies new markets and the chance for expanded profits. New services in the areas of personal finance, health care, and online shopping have stimulated the growth of new businesses and new occupations. Advances in telecommunications and transportation have offered companies new customer markets worldwide for their goods and services.

However, with new opportunities has come increased competition with many new global producers of goods and services. In the 1950s and 1960s, the U.S. auto industry had little fear of foreign competition, but Toyota and Honda have changed all that. One way that companies are dealing with greater competition is by restructuring their workforces to provide greater flexibility in the type of workers they hire and in their work arrangements. This chapter looks at the use of part-time employment, nonstandard work arrangements like temporary workers, and the use of independent contractors as some of the new strategies employers are using to achieve greater flexibility and reduce labor costs.

Social and economic changes in all industrial societies during the past quarter century have underscored the need for organizations to have greater flexibility in their production processes and employment systems in order to adapt quickly to rapid developments in technology, greater diversity in labor markets, growing international and price competition in product markets, and corporate financial restructuring in capital markets (see, for example, Boyer, 1987; Piore & Sabel, 1984; Vallas, 1999).

Employers have responded to these changes by seeking two main kinds of organizational flexibility. First, functional or internal flexibility refers to the ability of employers to redeploy workers from one task to another. This is often accomplished by the use of "high performance work organizations" that empower workers to participate in decision making, enable them to work in teams, and enhance their commitment to the organization by, among other things, linking their compensation to organizational performance (see Appelbaum & Batt, 1994; Gittleman, 1999; Osterman, 2000; Wood, 1999).

Second, numerical or external flexibility refers to the organization's ability to adjust the size of its workforce to fluctuations in demand by using workers who are not their regular, full-time employees. (Organizations can also obtain numerical flexibility by asking or requiring their regular, full-time employees to work overtime.) An organization's externalized workforce includes several kinds of nonstandard employment relations (see Table 14.2). Organizations can limit the duration of employment through the use of part-time and (especially) short-term temporary workers who (a) are often viewed as being disposable and can be recruited and selected quickly, (b) may be used when the organization does not have the authorization to hire, and (c) often cost less than regular, full-time employees. These workers are on the company payroll but have relatively weak ties to the organization, are generally hired for finite periods on an as-needed basis, and, at least in the United States, typically receive no or few benefits. In addition, organizations can obtain numerical flexibility and often reduce costs by externalizing administrative control through the use of temporary help agency or contract workers. These workers are considered to be employees of the temporary agency or contract company, not the client organization. They include both high skilled (e.g., consultants and independent professionals) and low skilled (e.g., clericals, food service) workers.

There is some disagreement about the extent to which organizations have adopted one or both of these forms of flexibility. Although some evidence suggests that the use of high performance work organizations has diffused considerably (Osterman, 2000), writers have not always agreed on how best to measure these practices and longitudinal data on organizations' practices of adoption are scarce. Moreover, support for the productionist view that there has been a decline in Fordism and a rise of alternatives such as flexible specialization is arguably less powerful with regard to the service sector that dominates the advanced countries (see, for example, Frenkel, Korczynski, Shire, & Tam, 1999). With regard to numerical flexibility, the evidence is

fairly clear that there has been an increase in some forms of nonstandard work arrangements such as temporary help agency employment and probably contractors (see the review in Kalleberg, 2000), although the prevalence of these arrangements varies across industries: For example, the use of agency temporaries is relatively high in manufacturing, whereas the use of short-term temporaries is higher in services (Houseman, 2001). Writers also disagree about the extent to which nonstandard work arrangements represent a fundamental change in the institutions underlying employment relations (see, for example, Cappelli, 1999, and Jacoby, 1999).

In any event, it appears that employers frequently benefit from adopting flexible work practices and employment systems: Organizations adopting high performance work practices have been shown to often experience improvements in productivity and performance (Appelbaum, Bailey, Berg, & Kalleberg, 2000), and some organizations have been able to save on labor costs by using temporary and part-time workers and thus have enjoyed greater profits. Subcontracting and outsourcing nonessential functions have also enabled some organizations to concentrate more on their core competences and thereby to use their resources more efficiently. However, attempts to increase flexibility also have a "dark side" in the form of negative consequences for some organizations and employees, and these effects have been less documented. The flip side of flexibility is insecurity and there has been a general increase in job insecurity in the workforce. Moreover, employers' attempts to achieve flexibility have led to increased segmentation of their workforces into core and periphery components, creating a division between organizational insiders and outsiders. Organizational outsiders are heterogeneous and include both highly skilled, well-paid workers as well as low skilled, low-paid workers.

In this article, I discuss some key ways in which employers have sought to restructure their workforces in an attempt to become more flexible and some of the consequences of such restructuring for workers. I argue that U.S. employers' use of numerical and functional flexibility strategies has led to a division between organizational insiders (standard employment relations) and outsiders (who have nonstandard work arrangements). The consequences of working in nonstandard employment relations differ depending on workers' individual and collective control over skills and other valued resources. I illustrate some of my main points using data from recent U.S. national surveys of establishments and labor force participants.

The Search for Numerical and Functional Flexibility

Most studies of organizational flexibility have focused on either functional or numerical flexibility, although some have considered explicitly the interplay between them and have sought to explain how organizations are able to obtain simultaneously these seemingly contradictory forms of flexibility (see the review in Kalleberg, 2001). Writers have used various labels to refer to models of organizations' labor utilization strategies that combine numerical and functional flexibility; perhaps the most influential is the dualistic model of the flexible firm proposed by John Atkinson (1984, 1987). His "core-periphery" or "micro dual labor market" model (Pollert, 1988, p. 283; Harrison, 1994) has been the subject of lively and often critical debate (e.g., Hakim, 1990; Hunter, McGregor, MacInnes, & Sproull, 1993; Pollert, 1988; Procter, Rowlinson, McArdle, Hassard, & Forrester, 1994).

The core-periphery model offered managers and government policy makers a framework for identifying the main practices on which they should focus in order to obtain both functional and numerical flexibility. Managers were urged to internalize part of their workforces (the core, regular, permanent workers who are highly trained, skilled, and committed to the organization, attributes that are thought to be needed for

functional flexibility) at the same time as they externalize other activities and/or persons by means of transactional contracts. Segmenting the organization's workforce into fixed and variable components is assumed to achieve cost effectiveness, as the numerically flexible, nonstandard, peripheral workers are used to buffer or protect the regular, core labor force from fluctuations in demand. This segmentation is believed to avoid the morale problems engendered by laying off regular employees and the disequilibria (and illegalities in some countries) associated with treating regular workers differently. This model has been thought to be especially applicable to the United States and United Kingdom, where labor laws leave employers relatively free to choose and vary their employment contracts, compared with many other European countries (Hakim, 1990).

Several assumptions of the core-periphery model have been the subject of considerable empirical research, particularly the idea that organizations use both functional and numerical flexibility simultaneously. Although there is little hard, direct systematic evidence on this assumption, some research has examined it indirectly. A number of studies have found a negative or no relationship between functional and numerical flexibility within establishments, suggesting that there are conflicts and other problems that make the two kinds of flexibility incompatible (Cappelli, 1995; Gittleman, 1999), for example, segmenting workforces could well divide loyalty and diminish cooperation and teamwork.

Other studies have found that patterns of internalization and externalization may coexist within the same organization (Lautsch, 1996). A recent (1996) study of high performance and flexible staffing practices based on a representative sample of establishments in the United States (the Second National Organizations Survey—see Kalleberg, Knoke, & Marsden, 1999) provides information on establishments' simultaneous use of numerical and functional flexibility practices. Table 14.1 cross-classifies establishments by their use of these two flexibility strategies. Nearly three quarters

(72% = 479/669) of establishments used some combination of numerical flexibility strategies such as direct hire temporaries, temporary help agencies, or contract companies. The columns of the table indicate the number of establishments that use from 0 to 4 high performance work practices (i.e., teams, offline committees, multitasking, performance incentives—see Kalleberg, Marsden, Reynolds, & Knoke, 2002). If we consider establishments that use two or more of these practices as functionally flexible, then 42% (281/669) fit this description; if we use one or more practices as the criterion, then two thirds (67% = 447/669) are in this category. Cross-classifying establishments by their use of both numerical and functional flexibility indicates that 36% (242/669) use both forms of flexibility (using two or more high performance work practices as the criterion of functional flexibility), whereas about half (333/669) use numerical flexibility strategies as well as at least one high performance work practice. These data provide suggestive evidence that between one third and one half of U.S. establishments have adopted some form of core-periphery labor utilization strategy.

Moreover, more than half of the participants in the same survey agreed or strongly agreed with the statement, "Your human resource management strategy divides the workforce into permanent and nonpermanent employees."

Organizational Insiders and Outsiders: Standard Versus Nonstandard Employment Relations

Employers' search for the two kinds of flexibility has led to a polarization between organizational insiders versus outsiders. One useful way of representing this is the division between standard and nonstandard work arrangements. Table 14.2 defines these types of employment relations and Table 14.3 presents the distributions of the labor force among these types of work arrangements in the United States in 1995 and 1997.

Standard work arrangements refer to regular, full-time jobs with a single employer. Having a standard work arrangement is usually regarded as a necessary condition for being located in the core of the organization, although it is probably not a sufficient condition because most writers assume that core workers do more than simply work full-time on open-ended contracts; for example, they are also assumed to be involved in decision making and otherwise be well integrated into the organization.

Nonstandard employment relations are generally located in the organization's periphery, including temporary work (both direct-hire temporaries and employees of

Table 14.1
Models of Labor Utilization (1996 National Organizations Survey)

Type of Staffing Arrangement	No. of High Performance Work Practices					
	0	1	2	3	4	
Full-time only Only full-time and part-time	76	75	25	12	2	190
Full-time/full-time and part-time and direct-hire temporaries Full-time/full-time and part-time and employment intermediaries Full-time/full-time and part-time and direct-hire temporaries and employment intermediaries	146	91	154	70	18	479
Number of establishments (weighted)	222	166	179	82	20	669

Table 14.2

Characteristics of Standard and Nonstandard Work Arrangements

			Dimension of Work Arrangements			
Type of Work Arrangement	Who is the de jure employer?	Who is the de facto employer?	Assumption of continued employment by de jure employer?	Assumption of continued employment by de facto employer?	Who directs work?	Hours of Work
Standard	organization A	organization A	yes	yes	organization A	full-time
Part-time	organization A	organization A	sometimes	sometimes	organization A	part-time
On-call/day labor	organization A	organization A	no	no	organization A	full-time or part-time
Short-term temporary	organization A	organization A	no	no	organization A	full-time or part-time
Temporary help agency	THA agency	organization A	sometimes	no	organization A	full-time or part-time
Contract company[a]	contract company	organization A	yes	no	contract company	full-time or part-time
Independent contracting, self-employment	self	client(s)	yes	no	self	full-time or part-time

a. Contract company employees may have a standard work arrangement with their de jure employer (the contract company), but from the point of view of Organization A, their work arrangements are nonstandard.

Table 14.3

Distribution of Workers Across Work Arrangements in the United States 1995 and 1997

	1995			1997		
Type of Work Arrangement	Male	Female	Number (Weighted)	Male	Female	Number (Weighted)
Standard (regular full-time)	69.2[a]	61.1	79,232,748	70.7	62.3	83,173,388
Regular part-time	7.7	21.9	17,222,418	7.5	21.9	17,654,592
Day labor	.1	0	109,278	0	0	27,035
On-call (regular hours)[b]	1.2	1.6	1,701,224	.5	.6	705,882
On-call (without regular hours)	—	—	—	.8	1	1,121,605
Short-term temporary	3.9	3.5	4,510,980	3.4	2.8	3,924,647
Temporary help agency	.8	1.1	1,170,876	.9	1.2	1,288,398
Contract company	1.7	.9	1,619,654	1.7	.9	1,639,150
Independent contractor (W&S)	.9	.9	1,125,179	.7	.8	975,576
Independent contractor (self-employed)	7.6	3.9	7,114,850	7.7	4	7,455,704
Self-employed (other)	6.7	5	7,174,467	6	4.3	6,495,478
Total	**65,214,948**	**55,766,726**	**120,981,674**	**66,765,743**	**57,695,712**	**124,461,455**

a. These figures are percentages.
b. On-call category in 1995 does not distinguish between those with and without regular hours.

Source: Current Population Survey Supplements, February 1995 and 1997.

temporary agencies) and contractors (both employees of contract companies and independent contractors). Part-timers may be located in either the organization's core or periphery.

Table 14.3 indicates that in the mid- to late-1990s, about 70% of men and about 60% of women in the United States worked in standard arrangements.[1] (These percentages represented about 80 million jobs in 1995 and 83 million jobs in 1997.) The biggest category of nonstandard jobs for women was regular part-time jobs (about 22%[2]), whereas for men it was self-employment (about 14% of men were self-employed, either as independent contractors or in other forms of self-employment). Overall, though, the sexes' distributions across employment relations are quite similar, with an index of dissimilarity of about 15% in both 1995 and 1997.

The creation of a dualism between organizational insiders and outsiders is intimately related to employers' search for numerical and functional flexibility. Bennett Harrison (1994, p. 196) argued that the flexibility of large firms depends fundamentally on the perpetuation of contingent work (part-time, part-year, temporary, and contract work), which he argued that American companies were deliberately creating (p. 205). The insiders that Harrison describes are full-time, relatively secure core workers with fringe benefits, training, and promotional opportunities; the outsiders are often contingent workers. Employees who occupy an organization's periphery may be employees of other organizations that are connected to the focal organization by means of networks (see also Heckscher, 2000).

Much of the writing on organizational flexibility (especially functional flexibility) has focused on the "survivors" of the restructuring process, who have experienced enhanced autonomy and control, and has neglected the contradictions in the meaning of flexibility for different groups who have been increasingly marginalized as a result of the growth in segmentation and polarization that has accompanied this flexibility (Goldthorpe, 1984; Harrison,

1994; Vallas, 1999). Many lower-level, often contingent workers are likely to continue to be governed by the logic of Fordist employment relations, which sees them as disposable, a concern earlier expressed by Atkinson (1984), who worried that an increased use of a core-periphery model would mean that "an individual's pay, security and career opportunities will increasingly be secured at the expense of the employment conditions of others, often women, more of whom will find themselves permanently relegated in dead-end, insecure and low paid jobs" (p. 31).

Worker Control and Nonstandard Work Arrangements

Workers differ in the extent to which they are able to benefit from the growth in nonstandard work arrangements. Whether or not workers are able to take advantage of the opportunities presented by these work arrangements depends on the degree to which they can exercise individual or collective control over their skills or otherwise obtain market power by collective forms of control such as unionization and professional associations. Workers with portable skills and autonomy/control over their work are likely to be employable in a variety of organizations and thus are also likely to have relatively stable employment in the occupation (through structures such as occupational internal labor markets), if not with a given employer.

Sociologists have suggested some mechanisms that lead to the differences in the control that workers have over their jobs. For example, Sorensen (1996) argued that agency and monitoring problems enable some workers to establish closed employment relations and to obtain rents or higher than market wages, whereas open employment relations are subject to competitive market forces and do not provide rents. Wright (1997) also suggested that autonomous workers receive higher wages due to a "loyalty rent" that is paid to induce their cooperation and effort. Similarly, efficiency wage theory in economics assumes that employers pay wage premia to workers in closed employment relations to induce them to avoid shirking or to reciprocate as part of a gift exchange (Akerlof, 1984). The premium that firms pay above market clearing levels is assumed to be the difference between closed and open employment relations. Closed employment relations pay high wages because workers have high autonomy/control over their work, and so it is difficult for managers to monitor their work and to detect whether they are shirking. By contrast, in open employment relations, workers are often closely supervised and monitored (e.g., Neal, 1993).

Table 14.4 cross-classifies the core-periphery distinction with the degree of control that workers have over their skills and their market situation. The two-by-two representation in Table 14.4 is intended only to illustrate the nature of the relationship between these dimensions of labor market segmentation; differences in degree of worker control, as well as the core vs. periphery nature of the employment relationship, are more complex than shown in this table.

The division between an organization's core and periphery is distinct from the degree of control that workers have over their skills and market situation. Some core workers have considerable control over their skills and autonomy over their work, whereas some periphery workers have relatively little control. However, there are also workers in the periphery of the organization who have considerable control and autonomy over their work: These workers do not have high levels of security within a particular firm; temporary workers, independent contractors, and other peripheral workers—even highly skilled ones—face job insecurities and instabilities due to their weak ties to their client organizations. Nevertheless, some of these peripheral workers have skills that are in high de-

Table 14.4
Dimensions of Labor Market Segmentation

Relationship to Employer	Degree of Worker Control	
	High	Low
Core	High firm-specific skills; high security with employer Example: autonomous jobs in standard employment relations	Low skills; low security with employer Example: regular part-time, routine jobs
Periphery	Highly portable skills; effective occupational association; high security with an occupation Examples: high-skilled independent contractors and consultants High-skilled temporary help agency employees	Nontransferable skills; weak occupational association; low security with employer or occupation Examples: short-term hires in routine jobs Low-skill temporary help agency employees

mand, so they are highly employable and should have little trouble obtaining highly rewarded employment elsewhere. Examples include highly skilled temporary help agency employees such as nurses and computer programmers, as well as sought-after consultants in specialized areas such as software design and the knowledge workers in the bank divisions described by Royal and Althauser (2003). Workers with high control over their skills and market situations are thus found both in firm internal labor markets (in the core of the firm) as well as in occupational internal labor markets that span firms and provide opportunities to move from one firm to another via networks of organizations and strategic alliances. Finally, some workers who might be classified in the core of the organization have few skills and relatively low security but have few opportunities to move elsewhere either. An example is regular, full-time jobs in fast-food establishments, which provide little security and opportunity for advancement.

Heterogeneity in Open Versus Closed Types of Work Arrangements

Occupational differences are a reasonable (albeit imperfect) indicator of variations in worker autonomy/control and skills. Table 14.5 presents the distribution of occupational groups within standard and the various types of nonstandard work arrangements in the United States in 1997, separately for men and women. Table 14.5 shows that there is considerable heteroge-

Table 14.5
Percentage of Nonstandard Workers in Each Major Occupational Group in 1997

	Regular Full-Time	Regular Part-Time	On-Call (regular hours)	On-Call (w/o reg. hours)	Short-Term Temp.	Temp. Help Agency	Contract Co.	Indep. Cont. (WS)	Indep. Cont. (SE)	Self-Emp. (other)	All Workers
Males											
Managerial	14.9	3.6	6.5	1.0	13.9	4.6	11.0	13.6	24.1	26.1	14.9
Professional	13.2	10.6	7.3	11.8	18.5	9.5	21.4	17.7	15.4	14.7	13.5
Technical	3.4	2.6	7.0	.9	3.0	8.1	6.0	1.4	.7	1.0	3.1
Sales	9.7	15.0	4.9	1.5	4.7	1.6	3.6	32.5	14.5	21.8	11.0
Administrative, clerical	6.4	9.7	2.8	5.2	5.8	13.9	4.0	3.4	.8	.6	5.9
Private household	.0	.1		.1				1.8			.0
Protective service	3.1	2.0	6.8	.5	3.1	1.8	11.5		.4		2.6
Service	6.2	24.1	8.1	7.4	5.8	6.1	5.8	2.1	1.9	2.5	7.2
Craft and repair	19.6	7.1	30.5	27.6	18.5	10.4	24.8	12.8	26.8	11.4	18.6
Machine operatives	9.2	2.9	4.8	3.0	8.9	21.3	1.8	.4	1.5	1.4	7.4
Transport operatives	7.3	5.5	11.1	19.3	7.7	7.8	5.8	7.0	6.1	2.4	6.9
Laborers	4.9	13.9	9.2	14.4	6.8	12.0	2.6	4.4	.9	.7	5.3
Farming, forestry, fishing	2.1	2.9	.9	7.3	3.3	2.9	1.8	2.8	7.0	17.3	3.6
	100.0	100.0	100.0	100.0	100.0	100.0	100.0	100.0	100.0	100.0	100.0
Females											
Managerial	16.6	4.7	3.9	1.4	15.7	8.8	12.1	6.7	17.8	21.0	13.6
Professional	19.3	13.5	22.5	38.2	21.3	4.3	23.1	14.2	24.2	10.1	17.9
Technical	4.0	3.2	9.8	1.4	3.3	3.9	5.9		.9	.3	3.5
Sales	10.1	19.2	19.0	6.1	6.8	1.7	2.9	32.6	19.1	18.9	12.9
Administrative, clerical	26.6	24.1	10.7	14.7	26.8	50.4	11.1	12.4	9.1	13.0	24.6
Private household	.6	1.9	3.1	7.7	2.5	.3	1.1	18.4	1.9		1.2
Protective service	.6	.6	1.7	1.0	1.0	.3	6.2	.1	.1		.6
Service	10.8	26.1	22.6	19.5	9.7	9.3	27.6	14.9	18.1	22.2	15.4
Craft and repair	2.2	.9	.7	.9	2.7	1.0	4.3	.5	3.0	1.3	1.9
Machine operatives	6.4	1.9	.4	1.4	6.5	13.6	2.3		2.4	2.1	4.9
Transport operatives	.8	1.3	.6	2.1	.7		2.4		.9	.2	.9
Laborers	1.5	2.0	2.7	4.9	2.4	5.8	.9		.1	.3	1.6
Farming, forestry, fishing	.4	.5	2.2	.6	.5	.6		.2	2.3	10.6	1.0
	100.0	100.0	100.0	100.0	100.0	100.0	100.0	100.0	100.0	100.0	100.0

Note: All figures are percentages.

neity in occupational membership within a given type of work arrangement, and this varies for men and women.

For example, temporary help agency employment includes workers in high- as well as low-skilled occupations: about 22% of men and 17% of women employed by temporary help agencies work in managerial, professional, or technical occupations, whereas more than one quarter of men and more than half of women who are employed by temporary help agencies work as machine or transport operatives and administrative or clerical workers, respectively. These high- and low-skilled occupations are likely to vary considerably in their employability and so will be found in both primary and secondary labor markets. This division into high- and low-end occupations also illustrates the polarization of the temporary help supply industry that has been observed in cities such as Chicago (see Peck & Theodore, 1998).

Moreover, independent contractors are found in both high- and low-skilled occupations: More than 40% of self-employed independent contractors (both men and women) are in managerial or professional occupations, whereas more than one quarter of men and nearly one fifth of women who are self-employed independent contractors work in craft and sales occupations, respectively. Whereas some independent contractors may actually be employees who are misclassified by their employers to avoid payment of various taxes and benefits (e.g., Morgan, 1998), others are highly valued and relatively well-paid consultants. Although the latter group may be peripheral labor in the sense of being exposed to the open labor market, they are a privileged group of workers who have scarce skills and should thus properly be regarded as part of the primary sector (e.g., Pollert, 1988, p. 290).

In addition, there is considerable occupational variation in regular part-time work. About one quarter of women and men who are in regular part-time positions work in service occupations, and another quarter of women are in administrative and clerical occupations. At the same time,

about 14% of women and about 11% of men who work in regular part-time positions are employed in professional occupations. This is consistent with the notion that there is a duality within part-time employment (see Tilly, 1996).

Finally, there is also considerable occupational variation among regular full-time employees: More than one third of women and nearly 30% of men classified as regular full-time workers are employed in managerial or professional occupations, whereas about 20% of men and more than one quarter of women are in semi-skilled or unskilled and clerical occupations, respectively.

These occupational differences also underscore the differences in women's and men's situations even when they are classified within the same nonstandard employment arrangement. For example, the modal temporary help agency occupation for women is secretaries, whereas for men it is nonconstruction laborers; self-employed men are most often managers and administrators (not elsewhere classified), whereas for women it is bookkeepers.

Consequences for Labor Market Inequality

Both dimensions of labor market segmentation discussed above—the distinction between standard and nonstandard employment relations, as well as differences in the degree of worker control—are needed to explain adequately the heightened labor market and social duality between advantaged and disadvantaged labor force members. Employers' search for flexibility has resulted in a more diverse set of employment relations and a more differentiated labor market than previously (cf. Herzenberg, Alic, & Wial, 1998). This diversity in employment relations has implications for inequality in labor market outcomes. Moreover, occupational differences in skills (level and portability) and autonomy over work and schedule suggest the importance for inequality of worker control over skill development and acquisition. In this section, I provide suggestive evidence that differences in both standard and nonstandard employment relations, as well as occupations, have distinct effects on inequality.

Table 14.6 shows the relationship between various standard/nonstandard work arrangements and several indicators of job quality in 1997: the proportion of workers in these arrangements that do not receive health insurance and retirement benefits, and the proportion who are in the bottom 20% of the wage distribution (see also Kalleberg, Reskin, & Hudson, 2000).

Every nonstandard work arrangement is more likely to be associated with these three bad job characteristics than standard work arrangements. At the same time, workers in certain nonstandard work arrangements—particularly self-employment (both independent contracting and other forms of self-employment) and contract-company employment—have jobs that are not all that bad. Although workers in these nonstandard arrangements were less likely to have fringe benefits than workers in standard arrangements, many earned higher wages than regular full-time workers in standard jobs (results not shown). Moreover, relatively few workers in these particular nonstandard arrangements expressed a preference for standard jobs (see Kalleberg et al., 1997). The heterogeneity within some nonstandard work arrangements is seen in the overrepresentation of some workers—such as self-employed women—in both the low- and high-wage groups (results not shown).

On the other hand, male and female temporary-help agency employees, on-call workers and day laborers, and part-time workers are consistently more likely than workers in the other nonstandard arrangements to have low pay and to lack insurance and pension benefits (an exception is "other" self-employed women, who are the most likely group of women to have jobs with low wages). Moreover, most workers in these arrangements (especially temporary-help agency employees and on-call workers and day laborers) prefer standard, full-time employment (Kalleberg et al., 1997). In view of these findings, the explosive growth of the temporary-help industry, in particular, makes the strong negative effect of employment in temporary-help agencies on job quality a matter of concern in the United States. As suggested above, there are also differences in job quality within some of these categories of nonstandard work (results not shown). Thus, the wages of temporary help agency employees differ considerably: Temporary help agency

Table 14.6
Quality of Nonstandard Work Arrangements in the United States, 1997

| | Dimension of Job Quality | | | | | |
| | % No Employer Health Care | | % No Employer Pension | | % Low Wages | |
Type of Work Arrangement	Male	Female	Male	Female	Male	Female
Standard (regular full-time)	29	33	39	39	10	15
Regular part-time	84	82	87	78	51	43
On-call workers	79	94	86	85	30	33
Short-term temporary	45	46	57	52	16	22
Temporary help agency	94	95	96	96	24	33
Contract company	45	66	57	77	13	25
Independent contractor (self-employed)	60	72	60	61	15	31
Self-employed (other)	47	65	51	62	20	49
Total	39	49	47	52	15	24

Source: Current Population Survey Supplement, February 1997.

nurses, for example, earn wages that are typically higher than nurses who are regular employees of a hospital, whereas auto supply workers who are employees of temporary agencies typically earn less than regular employees (see Houseman, Kalleberg, & Erickcek, in press).

In addition, there are occupational differences in wages as well as receipt of these kinds of fringe benefits when the type of work arrangement is controlled. Thus, Kalleberg, Reskin, and Hudson (2000) found that women operatives, sales workers, and service workers—nearly one third of all women—experience significantly more bad job characteristics than do female managers. Men and women in more complex (and thus more highly skilled and autonomous) occupations are less likely to obtain low wages and more likely to obtain health insurance and pension benefits from their jobs. Moreover, within part-time workers, men and women in low-skill occupations (and low-end service and sales occupations in particular) earn less and receive fewer health and fringe benefits than members of other occupations (analysis not shown), which provides further support for the idea that there is a duality within part-time employment (Tilly, 1996).

Conclusions

Organizations have differed in their responses to pressures to become more flexible: Some have taken the "high road" and adopted high performance work organizations and functional flexibility, whereas others have taken a "low road" and sought to cut costs by treating workers as disposable. A sizeable number of organizations have adopted a mixed strategy and tried to obtain both forms of flexibility simultaneously by protecting a core of functionally flexible workers with a buffer of numerically flexible workers.

These flexible employer strategies have helped to generate great diversity in employment relations, and there has been a proliferation of nonstandard work arrangements. These arrangements represent a po-

tential source of both employment flexibility and uncertainty for employers as well as workers. Nonstandard employment relations are attractive to employers because they may often reduce employment costs in addition to enhancing flexibility. On the other hand, in some cases the use of nonstandard workers may create conflicts with regular employees and thereby diminish cooperation and teamwork.

Whether workers are able to benefit from the growth of nonstandard work arrangements depends on their degree of control over resources such as portable skills. Some workers—such as those employed by the bank divisions studied by Royal and Althauser (2003)—have highly portable skills and hence considerable control over their employment situations, as the bank tried to retain them using sophisticated human resource management strategies. These workers participate in occupational internal labor markets, which are likely to become increasingly important as bases for career progression. Other nonstandard workers, such as those in part-time and temporary positions, may be less likely to exercise much control over their employment situations and thus often are in bad jobs that pay less and do not provide fringe benefits (e.g., Kalleberg, Reskin, & Hudson, 2000).

More research is needed on each of the links in the argument presented in this chapter. Relatively few longitudinal data are available on the trends in organizations' adoption of each type of flexibility, much less on the extent to which these employment systems are used simultaneously. The establishment may not be as useful as the firm for studying organizational flexibility because firms may often obtain flexibility by dividing work differently among various establishments, as is the case with profit as opposed to cost centers. To the extent that organizations obtain functional and numerical flexibility by means of their relations to other organizations in networks—as is the case in subcontracting relations or linkages to temporary help firms—the most appropriate unit of analysis may be neither the firm nor the establishment but the network defined by the relationships among the organizations and the labor market intermediaries from which they recruit their workers and subcontract some of their functions.

We also know relatively little about the inequalities associated with membership in core and periphery parts of organizations. Studies are particularly needed of inequalities within as well as between firms, of patterns of mobility between core and periphery sectors, and of differences among temporary help agency workers, independent contractors, and other categories of nonstandard workers. It is particularly important to collect data on factors that differentiate occupations within particular kinds of employment relationships, such as autonomy/control and skill portability. Analyses of the portion of inequality that is attributable to employer strategies (such as the creation of nonstandard work arrangements) as opposed to occupational differences (such as the growth of service sector occupations) would help to identify likely points of intervention that might be useful for reducing inequalities in job-related rewards. For example, if inequality is mainly due to employer strategies, then policies designed to discourage the use of contingent workers might be helpful in creating more good jobs. If, on the other hand, inequality results mainly from differences in skill portability, this suggests that attention might more profitably be paid to strengthening institutions that span organizations and enhance worker power such as unions and occupational associations.

My focus in this article has been on the United States, yet cross-national research on flexibility and labor market segmentation is sparse. Comparative research is essential for understanding the effects of workplace restructuring on jobs and workers. Much of the research on organizational flexibility has tended to be firm-centered, which may reflect the very deregulated labor markets and employment relations characteristic of the United States and United Kingdom, where most studies have been carried out. Extending the discussion of organizational flexibility to other coun-

tries underscores the importance of considering explicitly the role of the state (e.g., laws and regulations governing trade union influence, employment protection, and the operation of temporary help agencies) and of economic, social, and political institutions in shaping employers' labor utilization strategies. Organizations in all industrial countries need to be flexible to respond to competition, technological changes, and changes in labor force composition, although the types of flexible labor utilization strategies that organizations are likely to adopt will depend on their country's institutional context. For example, whether organizations are apt to use numerical flexibility strategies depends on their country's regulatory regime, such as the amount of protection given to regular, permanent workers and the existence of laws that limit the use of temporary help agencies to certain kinds of work. Moreover, the likelihood that organizations will adopt functionally flexible labor utilization strategies depends on the existence of institutions that help employers spread the risk of long-term training, development, and innovation in work design, as well as on a high level of trust between managers and workers (see the discussion in Kalleberg, 2001, pp. 493–495).

Understanding the nature and consequences of workplace restructuring for labor market segmentation is a potentially fruitful area for cross-national research and of collaboration between sociologists and economists. The ways in which institutions affect the operation of markets is becoming increasingly urgent given the growing importance of diversity in employment relations for issues ranging from labor market stratification to individuals' work experiences, family relations, and patterns of gender inequality.

Discussion Questions

1. How do you think new flexible work arrangements might affect day-to-day work relationships among employees when they are a mix of regular, part-

time, and temporary workers, as well as outside contractors?

2. How would you feel being a temporary employee? Would it make you work harder or would you be more laid back?

3. Would the existence of temporary employees put greater pressure on regular employees?

Endnotes

1. Contract company employees and on-call employees with regular hours could also be considered to have standard employment relations with their employers.

2. This figure underestimates the percentage of part-time jobs in the economy, because a person could also work part-time in any of the other nonstandard arrangements. Table 14.3 defines regular part-time jobs as those that are not classified in any of the other nonstandard work arrangements.

References

Akerlof, G. A. (1984). Gift exchange and efficiency-wage theory: Four views. *The American Economic Review*, 74, 79–83.

Appelbaum, E., Bailey, T., Berg, P., & Kalleberg, A. L. (2000). *Manufacturing advantage: Why high-performance work systems pay off*. Ithaca, NY: Cornell University Press.

Appelbaum, E., & Batt, R. (1994). *The new American workplace: Transforming work systems in the United States*. Ithaca, NY: ILR Press.

Atkinson, J. (1984). Manpower strategies for flexible organizations. *Personnel Management*, 76(8), 28–31.

——. (1987). Flexibility or fragmentation? The United Kingdom labour market in the eighties. *Labour and Society*, 12, 87–105.

Boyer, R. (1987). Labor flexibilities: Many forms, uncertain effects. *Labour and Society*, 72, 107–129.

Cappelli, P. (1995). Rethinking employment. *British Journal of Industrial Relations*, 33, 563–602.

——. (1999). *The new deal at work*. Boston, MA: Harvard Business School Press.

Frenkel, S. J., Korczynski, M., Shire, K. A., & Tam, M. (1999). *On the front line: Organization of work in the information economy*. Ithaca, NY: ILR/Cornell University Press.

Gittleman, M. (1999). *Flexible working practices: Where are they found and what are their labour market implications?* Paris, France: OECD Employment Outlook.

Goldthorpe, J. H. (1984). The end of convergence: Corporatist and dualist tendencies in modern Western societies. In J. H. Goldthorpe (Ed.), *Order and conflict in contemporary capitalism* (pp. 315–343). New York: Oxford University Press.

Hakim, C. (1990). Core and periphery in employers' workforce strategies: Evidence from the 1987 E.L.U.S. survey. *Work, Employment and Society*, 4, 157–188.

Harrison, B. (1994). *Lean and mean: The changing landscape of corporate power in the age of flexibility*. New York: Basic Books.

Heckscher, C. (2000). HR strategy and nonstandard work: Dualism versus true mobility. In F. Carre, M. A. Ferber, L. Golden, & S. A. Herzenberg (Eds.), *Nonstandard work: The nature and challenges of changing employment arrangements* (pp. 267–290). Champaign, IL: Industrial Relations Research Association.

Herzenberg, S. A., Alic, J. A., & Wial, H. (1998). *New rules for a new economy: Employment and opportunity in postindustrial America*. Ithaca, NY: ILR/Cornell University Press.

Houseman, S. N. (2001). Why employers use flexible staffing arrangements: Evidence from an establishment survey. *Industrial and Labor Relations Review*, 55(1), 149–170.

Houseman, S. N., Kalleberg, A. L., & Erickcek, G. (in press). The role of temporary agency employment in tight labor markets. *Industrial and Labor Relations Review*.

Hunter, L., McGregor, A., MacInnes, I., & Sproull, A. (1993). The "flexible firm": Strategy and segmentation. *British Journal of Industrial Relations*, 31, 383–407.

Jacoby, S. (1999). Are career jobs headed for extinction? *California Management Review*, 42(1), 123–145.

Kalleberg, A. L. (2000). Nonstandard employment relations: Part-time, temporary, and contract work. *Annual Review of Sociology*, 26, 341–365.

——. (2001). Organizing flexibility: The flexible firm in a new century. *British Journal of Industrial Relations*, 39, 479–504.

Kalleberg, A. L., Knoke, D., & Marsden, P. V. (1999). The 1996 National Organizations Survey [machine readable data file]. University of Minnesota [producer] Inter-University Consortium for Political and Social Research (ICPSR) [distributor].

Kalleberg, A. L., Marsden, P. V., Reynolds, J., & Knoke, D. (2002). Beyond the core: High performance work practices in U.S. organizations. Unpublished paper, University of North Carolina at Chapel Hill.

Kalleberg, A. L., Rasell, E., Cassirer, N., Reskin, B. R., Hudson, K., Webster, D., Appelbaum, E., & Spalter-Roth, R. M. (1997). *Nonstandard work, substandard jobs: Flexible work arrangements in the U.S.* Washington, DC: Economic Policy Institute.

Kalleberg, A. L., Reskin, B. F., & Hudson, K. (2000). Bad jobs in America: Standard and nonstandard employment relations and job quality in the United States. *American Sociological Review*, 65, 256–278.

Lautsch, B. A. (1996). Institutionalizing uncertainty. Paper presented at the annual meeting of the Academy of Management, Cincinnati, August.

Morgan, D. L. (1998). The tax consequences of characterizing workers as employees vs. independent contractors. In Employee? Common law employee? Leased employee? Independent contractor? Who's in the workforce? (Section E). Chicago, IL: American Bar Association, Center for Continuing Legal Education.

Neal, D. (1993). Supervision and wages across industries. *Review of Economics and Statistics*, 75, 409–417.

Osterman, P. (2000). Work organization in an age of restructuring: Trends in diffusion and effects on employee welfare. *Industrial and Labor Relations Review*, 53, 179–196.

Peck, J., & Theodore, N. N. (1998). The business of contingent work: Growth and restructuring in Chicago's temporary employment industry. *Work, Employment and Society*, 12(4), 655–674.

Piore, M., & Sabel, C. F. (1984). *The second industrial divide: Possibilities for prosperity*. New York: Basic Books.

Pollert, A. (1988). The "flexible firm": Fixation or fact? *Work, Employment and Society*, 2, 281–316.

Procter, S. J., Rowlinson, M., McArdle, L., Hassard, J., & Forrester, P. (1994). Flexibility, politics and strategy: In defence of the model of the flexible firm. *Work, Employment and Society*, 8, 221–242.

Royal, C., & Althauser, R. (2003). The labor markets of knowledge workers: Investment bankers' careers in the wake of corporate restructuring. *Work and Occupations*, 30(2).

Sorensen, A. B. (1996). The structural basis of social inequality. *American Journal of Sociology*, 101, 1333–1365.

Tilly, C. (1996). *Half a job: Bad and good part-time jobs in a changing labor market*. Philadelphia: Temple University Press.

Vallas, S. P. (1999). Rethinking post-Fordism: The meaning of workplace flexibility. *Sociological Theory*, 17(1), 68–101.

Wood, S. (1999). Human resource management and performance. *International Journal of Management Reviews*, 1, 367–413.

Wright, E. O. (1997). *Class counts: Comparative studies in class analysis*. Cambridge: Cambridge University Press. ✦

15

Bureaucratic Bloat

David M. Gordon

In Chapter 7, we learned about the "downsizing" of corporate middle managers in the early 1990s. In 1994, well-known corporations announced plans to eliminate jobs: General Motors (69,650), Sears, Roebuck (50,000), I.B.M. (38,500), AT&T (33,525), Boeing (31,000), and the list continues. Together, they eliminated over 200,000 middle managers and technical professionals. But before we start feeling sorry for these white-collar casualties, the author of this chapter tells us, "not so fast." David Gordon (now deceased) tells us that when we consider the total picture of laid-off production workers and laid-off managers at the end of the downsizing era (post 1994), there is actually a higher percentage of managers in corporate America than there was before downsizing. As the author states: "Lots of managers can be laid off, resulting in evidence of substantial *gross* job turnover, but lots of managers can also be rehired at similar positions at the same or other companies, potentially producing no *net* change or even a *net* increase in managerial employment."

Thus, the image of "lean and mean" corporations was true only for production workers. Corporate bureaucracies continued to grow, supporting the argument put forward in Chapter 6 that members of the privileged classes are the biggest beneficiaries of the new economy.

More than a decade ago *The New York Times* hosted a small roundtable on "The Ailing Economy," subsequently publishing extracts from the discussion.[1] Participants included Felix Rohatyn, senior partner in the Wall Street firm Lazard Frères and a major economic policy adviser in centrist Democratic Party circles; and Walter B. Wriston, then chairman of Citicorp and Citibank and a member of Ronald Reagan's Economic Policy Advisory Board. I also joined in the conversation. Moderated by the late *Times'* economics columnist Leonard Silk, we roamed widely over the economy's problems in the early 1980s and various prescriptions for their solution.

At one point in the discussion, talking about some of the structural sources of stagnant productivity in the U.S. economy, we turned to the huge size of U.S. corporate bureaucracies. I cited some recent management consultant studies that had suggested that as many as 50 percent of corporate managerial and supervisory personnel were redundant.[2] We could apparently trim huge chunks of fat off the top and middle layers of those corporations, this seemed to imply, and the corporations would be able to function just as effectively at much lower cost.

One might have expected the participants from the business sector to rise to the bait, defending the citadels of U.S. capitalism. But they scarcely batted an eyelash. "I wouldn't know" if expenditures for executive personnel are "wasted," Walter Wriston replied. "The chances are half of it is," he joked. "[Figuring out] which half is the difficult problem."[3]

I call it the "bureaucratic burden"—the massive size and cost of the managerial and supervisory apparatus of private U.S. corporations. It's one of the most stunning features of the U.S. economy.

The political right has mastered the rhetoric art of blaming the federal government for the size and wastefulness of its bureaucracies. Far less attention is paid to the size and wastefulness of private corporate bureaucracies. The bureaucratic burden in the United States is gargantuan, especially when compared to other leading economies such as Germany and Japan. It's a huge mountain range in our economic landscape that has long been covered by clouds. This chapter attempts to penetrate the cloud cover and map the terrain. Having provided that mapping, it then explodes the widespread myth that in the 1990s, after a decade of "downsizing," U.S. corporations have pared their bureaucracies and are now slim and trim—free of fat and waste.

Top-Heavy Corporations

I got my first peek at this topography in the mid-1970s. Colleagues and I had just begun some outreach educational work with local union officials and rank-and-file workers. We were trying different ways of engaging workers about pressing economic issues. Since these first discussions came on the heels of the sharp recession of 1973–75 and in the throes of that strange new phenomenon called "stagflation," we expected that the workers in our classes would steer the conversations toward problems of job security and inflation. Much to our surprise they were more interested in talking about problems they were constantly experiencing with their bosses on the job. They complained that their supervisors were always on their case, that bureaucratic harassment was a daily burden. They inveighed against speed-up, hostility, petty aggravations, capricious threats and punishments, and—perhaps most bitterly—crude, arrogant and often gratuitous exercises of power. Their catalogues of complaints were both eloquent and acute.

We were nonplussed. We had no idea whether these were the common and enduring laments of similarly situated workers at any time and place, or whether their urgency perhaps followed from a recent intensification of bureaucratic supervision on the job. I don't know to this day whether and when I might have paid attention to the bureaucratic burden if I hadn't been sitting in union halls in the mid-1970s, chewing on stale jelly doughnuts, listening to workers' grumbling about their continuing hassles with their employers.

The problem has remained hidden from public scrutiny for most of the intervening two decades. For at least some of the public, the first whiff of smoke came during the

mid- and late-1980s when critics began to excoriate the soaring and often astronomic salaries of chief executives in U.S. corporations. During the 1980s, according to data developed by the British weekly *The Economist*, after-tax CEO annual salaries increased by two-thirds after adjusting for inflation—while production workers' real hourly take-home pay was declining by seven percent.[4] By 1994, taking it from the top, Michael D. Eisner of Walt Disney was reaping a total harvest of $203.0 million, including company stock gains, while second-ranked Sanford I. Weill of Travelers was earning a total remuneration of "only" $53.1 million.[5] Respondents to a 1991 *Industry Week* survey about soaring CEO salaries were not spare with their criticisms: according to the magazine's summary, respondents called top executive pay levels "way out of line," "disgraceful," "embarrassing," "infuriating," and "sickening."[6] Sometime populist presidential candidate Bill Clinton charged in 1992 that "American CEOs were paying themselves 100 times more than their workers."[7] By the early 1990s, writes Derek Bok, former president of Harvard University, "almost everyone seemed to agree that executive pay had reached unseemly heights."[8]

But CEO salaries are only the tip of the iceberg. We need to peer below the surface and assess the size and cost of the entire corporate administrative apparatus—not just the millions paid to the top corporate guns. The key question, in the end, is the *relative* size of U.S. corporations' bureaucracies, in comparison to the numbers of employees they control. We need to gauge how much of that bureaucracy is dedicated to bossing people and whether that's an efficient or effective allocation of resources. And we need to be more than a little skeptical about the widespread impression that corporations have recently pared their managerial ranks, that through "downsizing" they have sliced away at the layers of flab at the top and middle of their bureaucratic hierarchies. "Downsizing" has certainly been taking place since the 1980s in many U.S. corporations. *But the weight of the bureaucratic burden has actually been growing, not contracting, through the mid-1990s.*

The easiest gauge of the size of this corporate behemoth—partly because the data are consistently available back to World War II—comes from official government surveys of business establishments. In 1994, according to the U.S. Bureau of Labor Statistics, 17.3 million private nonfarm employees worked in nonproduction and supervisory jobs[9]—mostly, as we shall see, as managers and supervisors at all levels of the corporate hierarchy. . . . This was almost as many employees as those working in the entire public sector, in all occupations at all levels of government including federal, state, and local. It was close to as many people living in the states of Texas or New York. It roughly equaled the national populations of Australia, Ghana, or Saudi Arabia.[10] Stretched out head-to-toe, all these supervisory employees would reach more than three-quarters of the way around the earth's equator.[11]

At least as imposing is the amount of money we pay to cover the salaries and benefits of these millions of employees. In 1994 supervisory employees in the private nonfarm sector were paid $1.3 trillion in total compensation.[12] This accounted for almost a quarter of all national income received by all income recipients. Twenty cents of every dollar we paid for goods and services went to cover the salaries and benefits of supervisory employees. This is as if, when we pay $5.00 for a sixpack of beer, $1.00 goes to cover the costs of the bureaucratic burden. Or when we pay $20,000 for a new car, we are pouring $4,000 into the managerial tank.

And this doesn't even include the costs of supporting these supervisory employees. Think of all the equipment and supplies purchased to provision these armies of bureaucratic employees. And think of the secretaries and assistants whose sole function is to serve this officer corps of 17 million. If we can assume that at least some of these bureaucratic personnel are unnecessary, then some of the desk chairs and paper clips and computers and secretaries mobilized to support them may constitute unnecessary expenditures as well.

Even ignoring these additional support costs, the tithe we pay for supervisory compensation dwarfs many other expenditure categories about which various groups have been publicly wringing their hands in recent years.[13] In 1994, for example, supervisory compensation was *four* times the total federal bill for Social Security payments—a tab which critics like Wall Street investment banker Peter Peterson have charged is bankrupting our future.[14] It was more than four times as large as total federal expenditures for national defense, a burden on which the peace movement has aimed its non-violent ire for decades. It was more than *fifty* times the payments providing Aid for Dependent Children (AFDC), or welfare, the scapegoated public assistance program over which Republicans and Democrats alike have been sharpening their scalpels. . . .

It is difficult to be very precise about the specific jobs performed by these more than 17 million supervisory employees. The surveys of business establishments from which these figures are drawn provide no further detail about occupation, allowing no breakdown within the nonproduction/supervisory classification. We are simply told from the instructions for the establishment surveys that enterprise respondents should include in this grouping all employees "engaged in the following activities: executive, purchasing, finance, accounting, legal, personnel, cafeteria, medical, professional and technical activities, sales, advertising, credit collection, and in the installation and servicing of own products, routine office functions, and factory supervision *(above working supervisor's level)*."[15] These instructions make it sound, indeed, as if a wide variety of occupational functions may be covered, especially including professional and technical activities.[16]

But some quick detective work suggests otherwise, appearing to confirm this initial reckoning of the scale of the bureaucratic burden. We can look to the Bureau of Labor Statistics' surveys of households, which provide much more detailed occupational breakdowns, for some important clues. Data for 1993 were the most recent raw data available to me at the time of writing.

In 1993, according to the same establishment data we've already plumbed, 17.1 million supervisory employees worked in the private nonfarm sector. According to the household surveys for the same year, there were 16.6 million private nonfarm employees who worked as wage-and-salary employees in various occupations labeled as either "managers" or "supervisors."[17] (These totals exclude the self-employed, those who work for themselves rather than for a corporation.) So when we count "supervisory" workers from the establishment surveys or "managers" and "supervisors" from the household surveys, we arrive at roughly comparable measures of the size of the bureaucratic burden. Some who are tallied as "nonproduction and supervisory" employees in the establishment surveys, given the survey instructions, are obviously not managers and supervisors. At the same time, however, those surveys do not include those "at the working supervisors level." These two effects seem roughly to cancel each other out. When we get a more direct tally of managers and supervisors from the detailed occupational definitions of the household surveys, the totals are almost exactly equivalent.

And what did these 16.6 million managerial and supervisory employees do? Somewhat more than three-fifths worked as managers and a little less than two-fifths as supervisors.

Among the managers, the bulk—4.1 million out of 10.7 million—were all-purpose managers in the catch-all "not elsewhere classified" category. More than six million worked as "supervisors" in one sector or another. About 1.3 million worked as supervisors of blue-collar "production occupations," for example, and another 340,000 worked as clerical supervisors.

Still, even these tabulations from the household surveys are only estimates, based on approximate categories from government surveys. They could potentially be off the mark as measures of the full extent of managerial and supervisory employment

in either of two possible directions. They could *over*estimate the extent of supervision if large numbers of employees categorized as managers are not actually and actively involved in supervision. Or they could *under*estimate the bureaucratic burden if many other kinds of employees, not officially categorized in these government data as managers or supervisors, *also* engage in substantial supervision as an important part of their activities.

We have one important body of data that can help us assess these possible distortions in the official series. Through some pioneering studies spearheaded by Wisconsin sociologist Erik Olin Wright, we can glimpse the actual extent of supervision by U.S. employees regardless of their primary occupational categorization. In nationally representative surveys conceived and organized by Wright and replicated in the United States in both 1980 and 1991, respondents were asked directly about their positions and roles on their jobs. Several different questions aimed at highlighting occupational responsibilities from a number of different angles. Referring to their present or most recent jobs, participants were asked whether or not they were engaged in supervising others, whether or not their position was considered to be managerial or supervisory, and what kinds of authority they exercised over others. We can compare impressions from these data—afforded by what I shall be labeling for short as the Class Structure Surveys—with estimates from the official government sources already reviewed. The more recent data from the 1991 survey are the most relevant for this discussion.[18]

- In 1991, according to government establishment surveys, 19.1 percent of private nonfarm employees worked in nonproduction or supervisory jobs. But in the 1991 Class Structure Survey, almost exactly double this proportion—fully 38.9 percent of all private nonfarm workers—reported that they "supervise the work of other employees or tell other employees what work to do." This would amount to roughly 35 million employees in the private non-farm sector who report direct supervisory responsibility.

- In the 1991 household surveys, 18.7 percent of private nonfarm workers were categorized as in either managerial or supervisory occupations. But in the 1991 Class Structure Survey, 36.3 percent report that their position within their business or organization was "managerial" or "supervisory." Of these 36 percent, roughly half worked in "supervisory" jobs and the other half at various levels of the "managerial" hierarchy.

- One of the main tests of how many "bosses" are sprinkled through the occupational category is how many employees can discipline or even fire another employee. In the 1991 Class Structure Survey, 27.7 percent of private nonfarm employees reported that they had the authority to directly "discipline a subordinate because of poor work or misconduct."

Why are these estimates of managerial and supervisory employment so much higher than the estimates we derive from official government sources? The Class Structure Surveys were carefully structured and weighted so that they were effectively representative of the characteristics of the population revealed in other official government surveys.[19] Consequently the differences do not appear to flow from biases in the construction of the actual surveys.

One possibility, of course, is that when asked direct questions about their role on the job, people might tend to exaggerate their importance and attribute greater authority to their own positions than they actually have. This source of bias is probably relatively minor in the Class Structure Survey, however, because estimates of managerial and supervisory responsibilities based on very different kinds of questions within the survey fall within a fairly narrow range—and all considerably higher than

the estimates from official government sources.

More important as an explanation of the discrepancy between the two kinds of information, apparently, is precisely that many people besides those working in jobs officially categorized as "managers" and "supervisors" *also* have substantial supervisory responsibilities.

Table 15.1 compiles the percent of private nonfarm employees in different occupational categories in the 1991 U.S. Class Structure Survey—as those categories are conventionally defined in standard government censuses—who report that their present (or most recent) job is best described as a "managerial or supervisory position." As the table shows, substantial numbers of workers outside the explicit occupational categories of managers and supervisors also have such responsibilities within their firms' hierarchies. Someone trained as a lawyer who is running a corporate division, for example, may get tabulated in the government surveys as a "professional" but would be captured in the Class Structure Survey as someone who also exercises managerial responsibility.

This would suggest, in short, that we can rely on the kinds of official government sources reported initially—such as the percent of employees in supervisory jobs esti-

---

Table 15.1

Supervisory Responsibilities Across the Occupations, 1991

(Percent in various private nonfarm occupations with 'managerial' or 'supervisory' responsibilities)

Managers	79.6%
Technicians or supervisors	59.0
Professionals	29.1
Clerical or sales workers	16.4
Skilled workers	12.0
Semiskilled workers	8.1
Unskilled workers	2.2
All employees	35.5

Sources and Notes: Author's own calculations from the Class Structure Survey for the United States, 1991. Sample is for all nongovernment employees not in farm occupations.

mated from the establishment data—as *minimum* estimates of the scope of the bureaucratic burden in the United States. It would appear that there are many more people in other occupational categories than "managers" and "supervisors" *who have direct supervisory responsibility* than there are people in jobs categorized as "managers" and "supervisors" *who do not actually perform such supervisory roles.* Yes, it is certainly true that many, perhaps most of these cadres do not spend every working hour directly supervising others. But the fact that they spend at least some of their time directing subordinates means that the corporate structures in which they work are predicated upon those supervisory functions, that their supervisory and managerial responsibilities are an essential aspect of their jobs. We shall apparently not be engaged in false advertising if we conclude that the legions of bosses and supervisors in the United States corporations are plenteous indeed—even if we rely on the relatively more restrictive occupational data which tabulate only managers and supervisors and ignore those in other occupational categories who also have supervisory responsibilities.

How is it possible that so many people spend at least some of their time directing others? The basic principle is simple. If a labor-management system relies on hierarchical principles for managing and supervising its frontline employees on the shop and office floors—as does that in the United States—then it needs more than just the front-line supervisors who directly oversee these production and nonsupervisory workers. Who keeps the supervisors honest? What guarantees that those supervisors won't be in cahoots with their charges? In such a hierarchy, you need supervisors to supervise the supervisors . . . and supervisors above them . . . and managers to watch the higher-level supervisors . . . and higher-level managers to watch the lower-level managers. A pyramid takes shape in which every level of supervision from the bottom on up is essential to the operations of the entire enterprise.

We get some feel for this pyramiding effect from a classic article in 1970 by Elinor Langer about her brief career as a customer sales representative in the New York Telephone Company:[20]

> [My supervisor] is the supervisor of five women. She reports to a Manager who manages four supervisors (about twenty women) and he reports to the District Supervisor along with two other managers. . . . A job identical in rank to that of the district supervisor is held by four other men in Southern Manhattan alone. They report to the Chief of the Southern Division, himself a soldier in an army of division chiefs.

And thus is the bureaucratic burden formed. Layer upon layer rises from the base of the corporation, each layer spread with officers checking on their subordinates. In the Class Structure Survey for 1991, for example, we find that of those employees with supervisory responsibilities, roughly one quarter supervise someone who also has "people working under them"—suggesting an average span of supervision within the supervisory ranks of something like one to three or four. In his study of the size and structure of corporate management for the American Management Association, business analyst Robert M. Tomasko infers from his own case studies an estimate that is consistent with this mapping of the managerial hierarchy. Although front-line supervisors oversee larger numbers, he writes, "in middle-management ranks, the pyramid commonly narrows to 3, 4, or 5 people reporting to a manager, and [as a result] the number of management layers increases."[21]

Robert H. Hayes and Steven C. Wheelwright, from the Harvard and Stanford business schools respectively, analyze this general tendency in U.S. corporations organized on the basis of top-down authority:[22]

> As the scale of a production unit increases, so does the workforce required to operate it. The larger the workforce, the more supervisors, coordinators, and managers are required. Since managers usually feel that the number of people

reporting to them ought to be less than some maximum number (generally 8 to 12), organizations tend to grow like pyramids: as the base of the pyramid (representing the number of workers) grows, so does the number of layers of managers—each of whom probably requires at least one support person (a secretary, assistant, etc.). As the number of layers in the management hierarchy grows, communication and coordination becomes more difficult, so additional support personnel are required. For example, whereas a 200-person workforce would normally have at most three organizational levels above the workers, a 2000-person workforce typically has four or five levels.

Tomasko echoes this analysis: "Big seems to breed bigger. As total employment increases, so does the number of management layers required to keep things under control."[23]

The pattern is quite general. No one can be trusted. Everyone must be watched. And everyone must be paid more than those below them on the hierarchical ladder. For this, we spent $1.3 trillion in 1994.

Who's Fat and Who's Not

It could be, of course, that this massive bureaucratic burden is part of the cost of doing business in a sophisticated, increasingly globalized economy. Perhaps it is inevitable that we need legions of managers and supervisors to oversee complex production systems, spur product and process innovations, conquer markets at home and abroad, and plan for the future. Maybe we need such a large corps of corporate officers if we are to win the war for global economic supremacy.

When I first started studying the bureaucratic burden in the late 1970s, I didn't know how seriously to take the kinds of consultant reports of redundant managers to which I alluded at the beginning of the chapter. Some observers seemed to find layers of fat in U.S. management, but fat is partly in the eye and mind of the beholder.

What kinds of effective standards should one use to judge whether a corporate bureaucracy is too small, too big, or just the right size?

One obvious approach would be to compare the size of the bureaucratic burden across U.S. firms, stacking relatively more successful firms up against their less successful competitors, an approach I pursue somewhat later on. Another obvious strategy would essay international comparisons. By the early 1980s, it was widely perceived that large corporations in other leading economies such as Germany and Japan were competing at least as effectively in global markets as U.S. firms. Were their bureaucratic armies as massive as ours?

It is this kind of international standard, indeed, which has helped fuel spreading public anger about stratospheric CEO salaries in the United States. Many observers have noted that top-level managers in the United States earn far more than they do abroad. A 1991 survey found, for example, that chief executive officers in large U.S. corporations on average received almost exactly twice the total compensation of their counterparts in either Japan or Germany.[24] Are corporate honchos really twice as smart or productive or creative in the United States as corporate bosses elsewhere?

It turns out that international comparisons of the bureaucratic burden reveal similar patterns.

There are no direct analogues for other economies to the U.S. data on nonproduction and supervisory employment. But the International Labour Organization (ILO) has made possible some direct cross-country explorations of a similar kind of category. ILO compilations provide international data for the number and relative proportions of employees in "administrative and managerial" occupations.[25] Although individual countries' definitions of occupational categories vary substantially, the ILO has devoted considerable effort to fitting the respective nations' census data into standardized occupational definitions across countries. Overlaying the ILO figures with U.S. data, we find that "administrative and managerial" occupations in the ILO data correspond precisely to the category of "executive, administrative, and managerial" occupations in the BLS household surveys, or the group I've been calling "managers" for short.[26] The ILO data therefore allow us to compare the relative proportions of managers across countries but not the relative numbers of other employees in job slots called "supervisors." This will provide at least a start in gauging the relative size of the managerial armies in the United States.

   ... And because the employment share of supervisory workers is highly sensitive to the business cycle, let's focus on 1989, the most recent year in which these advanced economies were more or less at their business cycle peaks. With the ILO data, we can compare nine of those twelve countries; data for 1989 are not available for France, Italy, and the United Kingdom.

   Figure 15.1 presents the percent of nonfarm employment in administrative and managerial occupations for the United States and for these other eight advanced economies.[28] The data in the graph suggest some fairly dramatic patterns.

- The bureaucratic burden in the United States was the highest among the nine countries. Thirteen percent of total nonfarm employment in the United States worked in administrative and managerial occupations in 1989.

- Canada also stands out as another economy weighted with a heavy proportion of managerial employees. Canada and the United States along with the United Kingdom are considered the three advanced economies with the most "conflictual" systems of labor-management relations. This provides a first strong hint that among the developed countries top-heavy corporate

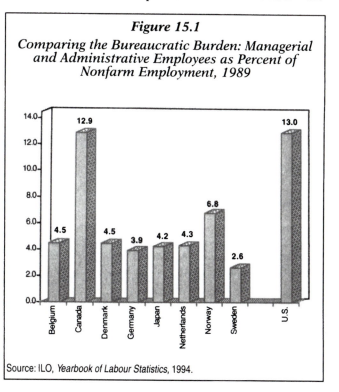

Figure 15.1

Comparing the Bureaucratic Burden: Managerial and Administrative Employees as Percent of Nonfarm Employment, 1989

Source: ILO, *Yearbook of Labour Statistics*, 1994.

bureaucracies are associated with adversarial labor relations.

- Following that lead further, we can look at the managerial proportions for three other economies that are widely regarded as representing much more "cooperative" approaches to corporate organization and labor management—Germany, Japan, and Sweden.[29] In 1989 the relative size of the U.S. bureaucratic burden had reached more than three times the levels in Japan and Germany and more than four times the percentage in Sweden. (This portrait would not differ markedly if we used the most recent available data instead of those for 1989. In 1993, for example, the U.S. percentage was 13.2 and the Japanese share was 4.1.)

- Except for the United States and Canada, there is a striking consistency in the size of the bureaucratic burden across the other economies. Sweden is the lowest at 2.6 percent and Norway the highest at 6.8, but all the others fall in a narrow band between 3.9 and 4.5 percent. The average for the seven economies not including the United States and Canada is 4.4 percent—almost exactly one-third of the U.S. proportion. By these standards, the U.S. pattern is obviously atypical. . . .

Gaining Weight

Why should U.S. corporations be so top-heavy compared to their major international competitors? Is there method to the fatness, a sound strategy behind the bloat? The answer to these questions is complex.

But one preliminary step toward such an answer is relatively straightforward. By placing the bureaucratic burden in historical perspective, we can at least determine whether U.S. corporations have always been so top-heavy or whether their massive scale is of relatively recent origin.

Let us return to the data for private nonfarm supervisory employees for the United States. One of the advantages of this measure of the bureaucratic burden is that we have continuous data, relying on fairly consistent definitions, since World War II.

In 1994, as we have already seen, there were somewhat more than 17 million supervisory employees in the private nonfarm sector. In 1948, there were only 4.7 million. In raw numbers, it would appear, there was tremendous growth in the cadres of managers and supervisors over the postwar period, an increase of roughly 360 percent.

Overall employment was increasing rapidly as well, of course, so just looking at the raw numbers doesn't tell us very much. It makes much more sense to look at the *relative* size of the bureaucratic burden, tracing the ratio of nonproduction and supervisory employment to total employment in the private nonfarm sector.

Figure 15.2 presents this measure of the bureaucratic burden. It shows that in 1948 it began at a postwar low of 12 percent of all private nonfarm employees working in supervisory jobs. It increased substantially as the postwar period progressed, leveling off at roughly 19 percent in the 1980s. At that point almost one in five private nonfarm wage-and-salary employees were employed in this category, working mostly, as we have already seen, as managers and supervisors of one sort or another.

The trends revealed by international comparisons show a similar pattern. Here, with the ILO data, we can only go back as far as 1960. Table 15.2 traces changes in the bureaucratic burden over the decades since 1960 for the United States and for Germany, Japan, Sweden—the three countries I listed earlier as representing relatively more cooperative approaches to labor rela-

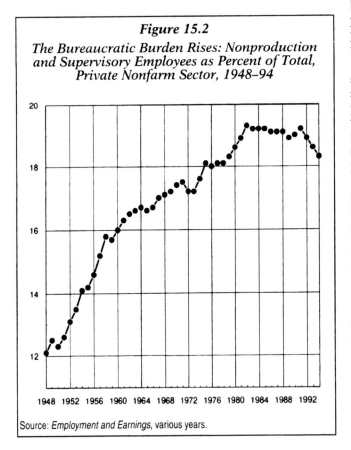

Figure 15.2

The Bureaucratic Burden Rises: Nonproduction and Supervisory Employees as Percent of Total, Private Nonfarm Sector, 1948–94

Source: *Employment and Earnings*, various years.

tions—allowing us to glimpse when and how the huge gap between the United States and the other three countries, revealed above in Figure 15.1, actually emerged. The final row of the table calculates the ratio of the U.S. bureaucratic burden to the (unweighted) average of the other three economies.

In 1960 the United States had the highest share of administrative and managerial employees, but the gap was not particularly pronounced. Then the bureaucratic burden in the United States began to grow quite steadily and rapidly. At the same time, the administrative and managerial share in the other three countries remained relatively flat. In Sweden it scarcely changed; in Germany it remained quite low until a bit of growth in the 1980s; and in Japan it actually increased some through 1980 and then declined. In no other country do we find anything like the U.S. pattern of steady expansion, much less the massive levels to which the U.S. bureaucratic burden eventually expanded. The ratio between the U.S. share and the average for the other three grew consistently throughout, but increased most rapidly during the 1970s and 1980s.

A single slice of comparison helps underscore the story told by the data in the table. In 1960, the percentage of administrative and managerial employment in the United States was only about 1.5 times its level in Japan. By 1989, it had increased to more than three times the Japanese level. In 1960, by international standards, U.S. corporations were heavy. By 1989, they had become obese.

Can we be more precise about the trajectory along which U.S. corporations put on so much weight? If we look back at the trends portrayed for the United States in Figure 15.2 more closely, it appears that there are two phases in the general rise of the bureaucratic burden. The share of supervisory employees fluctuates fairly sharply with the business cycle, rising in recessions when relatively more production

Table 15.2
Taking on Weight: Administrative and Managerial Employees as Percent of Nonfarm Employment

	1960	1970	1980	1989
Germany	2.6	2.5	2.8	3.9
Japan	3.9	5.9	5.2	4.2
Sweden	2.1	2.6	2.9	2.6
U.S.	6.6	8.7	11.4	13.0
Ratio, U.S. to average of other three	**2.3**	**2.4**	**3.1**	**3.6**

Sources and Notes: International Labour Organization, *Yearbook of Labour Statistics*, various years. Figure for 1960 for Germany is actually for 1961.

workers tend to be laid off. Taking those fluctuations into account, two fairly distinct periods emerge from the numbers.

In the first phase, the share of supervisory employees grew very rapidly through the late 1950s and then somewhat more slowly during the 1960s. This was the period during which the foundations of modern U.S. managerial structures were laid. Many corporations, especially in key manufacturing sectors such as auto and steel, had accommodated to life with labor unions by the early 1950s. But the entire premise of the postwar "accord" between corporations and their workers, as some of us have called it, was that corporations continued to control decisions about production and that workers, even if unionized, had no rights to interfere.[30] The corporations were running the show, they knew it, and they constructed a corporate bureaucracy to exercise their prerogatives. . . . The postwar system of corporate control was in place and, for a time, it was working.

Two features of this first phase were crucial. First, the instruments and structures of top-down corporate power were established, with managers and supervisors reasserting their control over basic investment and production decisions in a booming economy. Second, the very boom itself enabled workers to share at least partly in the harvest—with rising real wages, enhanced job security, and improving working conditions. The labor-management system relied upon and reinforced corporate control over the workforce, but workers received a reward—reflected in their weekly paychecks—for their acquiescence to the new structures of control.

A second phase then appears to have emerged after the early 1970s. The growth of the bureaucratic burden accelerated once again. . . .

Through the 1970s . . . the relative size of corporate bureaucracies continued to grow. By the mid-1980s, the paunch was protruding. Peter Drucker concluded in the 1980s: "Middle managements today tend to be overstaffed to the point of obesity. . . . A good many businesses, large and small, [have become] equally bureaucratic and equally suffer from gross overweight around the midriff."[31] Looking back at the same period, Barry Bluestone and Irving Bluestone concur: "by the beginning of the 1970s, and surely by the 1980s, bureaucratic firms were too bloated with middle-level managers to be efficient and much too burdened by rules and regulations to dance fast enough to keep up with foreign competition."[32] After John Welch became CEO of General Electric in the early 1980s, he observed that the company had reached the point "where we were hiring people [just] to read reports of people who had been hired to write reports."[33] . . .

If U.S. corporations were already suffering by the mid-1980s "from gross overweight around the midriff," in Drucker's words, should we conclude that they had solved their problems once the bureaucratic burden reached a more or less level plateau? Let's assume for the moment that the corporate world was indeed top-heavy. If so, concluding that they had solved their problems after 1983 would be like saying that a fat man of 350 pounds no longer suffered from obesity because he had stopped gaining weight. A fat corporation would still be a fat corporation.

What About 'Downsizing'?

The story doesn't end with the 1980s. Corporate "downsizing" has become a watchword of the 1990s. We've read that corporations are becoming "lean and mean," that they're dramatically reducing their managerial staffs, that they've gone on a crash diet. Most astounding, as the news has been presented by the media, is that the scalpel has cut out managers as well as production workers. "After years of layoffs," *Business Week* reported in 1992, "the specter of downward mobility is haunting legions of once-secure managers and professionals. . . . As corporate stalwarts such as General Motors, United Technologies, and IBM join in a long list of downsizing companies, the economic trajectories of thousands of white-collar workers are plunging."[34] A relatively early study by the American Management Association sounded the theme: "There is a consensus that middle managers and technical professionals—the exempt employees who fill the boxes on the organization charts between line management and officers—are among the hardest hit in this leaner, meaner business climate."[35]

It is true that many managers and supervisors have been laid off in recent years, especially during the recent recession. Between 1990 and 1992, the total number of private nonfarm supervisory employees fell by 240,000—hardly a trivial number. "Downsizing" as a term and phenomenon had become familiar to many by the mid-1980s—witness Robert Tomasko's book bearing that title, published in 1987.[36] And media reports—of the thousands laid off at IBM, the tens of thousands elsewhere—have continued since the 1990–91 recession. Typically, a new term was invented to refer to the victims of these excisions. "Just as the last decade was defined by yuppies and their flamboyant material excesses," *Business Week* wrote in 1992, "the 1990s may come to be the age of 'dumpies'—downwardly mobile professionals—and their struggle to stay in the upper end of the middle class."[37]

But all these stories do not by themselves establish that the problem of corporate top-heaviness is being addressed. They do not even establish, indeed, that the weight of the bureaucratic burden itself is being reduced. Hundreds of thousands of production employees have also been fired or laid off in recent years alongside the reductions at higher levels of the hierarchy. The story of the bureaucratic burden, as I've been recounting it in this chapter, is primarily a story of *relative* overweight, of the proportion of total employment in managerial and supervisory jobs and not simply their absolute mass.

What matters most, in short, is whether or not corporate "downsizing" in the past several years has actually reduced the bureaucratic burden itself.

In looking more closely at changes over a small number of years, the establishment data do not serve us as well as they did in Figure 15.2 because, as noted above, there are no further detailed occupational breakdowns within the category of nonproduction and supervisory employees. To explore the impact of "downsizing" since the late 1980s, we can get a more finely-grained picture if we concentrate on the occupational data in the household surveys, where specific tabulations of "executive, administrative, and managerial" employees as well as a range of supervisory occupations are provided.

Here, we can concentrate on employment changes from the business cycle peak of 1989 to 1994, the period during which stories of downsizing have been most widely reported. What happened to the managerial employment share over those years?

The household survey data suggest that the requiem for middle management has been premature. In 1989, according to the official published tabulations, "executive, administrative, and managerial" workers (excluding managers in public administration) accounted for 12.6 percent of total nonfarm employment. (This number includes only managers and does not yet consider the several million employees in various supervisory jobs.) Between 1989 and 1994, employment in this category accounted for almost one-quarter of total net employment growth, rising from 14.3 million in 1989 to 15.7 million in 1994.[38] As a result, the share of private managers in total nonfarm employment *increased over those five years by 5 percent over its 1989*

level, from 12.6 percent to 13.2 percent, rather than declining as the recurring and sometimes sensational stories have appeared to imply. During the recession there was some net reduction in managerial ranks, but since then, during the recovery, proportionately more managers have been hired back than other occupational groupings. Many managers have lost their jobs, but many have been rehired as managers and many others have joined the managerial ranks for the first time. For all of the talk of "downsizing," there were more managers in 1994 than there were in 1989 before the "downsizing" began.

And these trends appear to be continuing beyond 1994. As I write, the most recent available detailed occupational data cover the second quarter of 1995.[39] By then, the percent of private "executive, administrative and managerial" employees in total nonfarm employment had increased further still, from 13.2 percent in 1994 to 13.6 percent. Dating the recovery from 1991, total nonfarm employment had increased to the second quarter of 1995 by 7.4 million—a jobs expansion for which President Clinton wishes his economic policies would receive a little more credit. Growth of private managerial employment accounted for almost two million of these jobs. This surge in managerial employment amounted to more than a quarter of the total net jobs expansion during this period, *or more than double the managerial share at the beginning of the recovery.*

Figures 15.3 and 15.4 highlight these trends. Figure 15.3 shows the percentage of managers in total private nonfarm employment in 1989 and the second quarter of 1995. Figure 15.4 concentrates on the change in employment over the period of the recovery. The left-hand bar shows the share of managers in nonfarm employment in 1991. The right-hand bar displays the growth in managerial employment over the recovery as a percent of the total growth in nonfarm employment. If bloated corporate management has been put on a crash diet in the United States, you can't tell it from these scales.

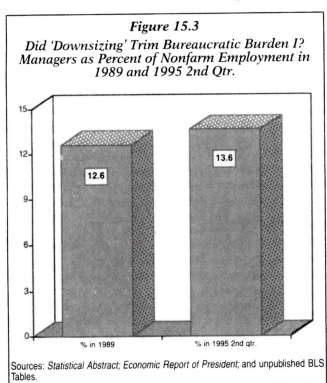

Figure 15.3

*Did 'Downsizing' Trim Bureaucratic Burden I?
Managers as Percent of Nonfarm Employment in
1989 and 1995 2nd Qtr.*

Sources: *Statistical Abstract; Economic Report of President;* and unpublished BLS Tables.

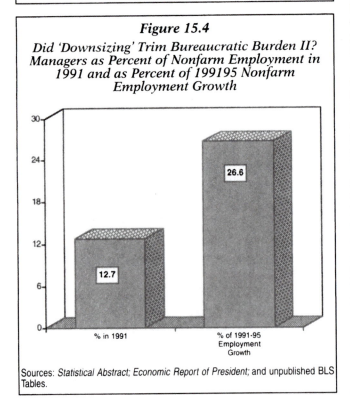

Figure 15.4

*Did 'Downsizing' Trim Bureaucratic Burden II?
Managers as Percent of Nonfarm Employment in
1991 and as Percent of 199195 Nonfarm
Employment Growth*

Sources: *Statistical Abstract; Economic Report of President;* and unpublished BLS Tables.

The story remains the same when we expand our focus not only to managers but also to those with supervisory responsibility. During the period of "downsizing" the percentage of supervisors in total nonfarm employment remained roughly constant. In 1989, 16.1 percent of total nonfarm employees worked as private managers and in the full range of supervisory occupations. By the second quarter of 1995, that percentage had increased to 16.8 percent.[40] Some may believe that U.S. corporations have become "leaner." In fact, they are even top-heavier than before.[41] . . .

Nor, apparently, would we find a different story if we concentrated on the largest corporations. Here, we can turn to annual surveys by the American Management Association (AMA) of a sample of its membership, which is concentrated among "major" U.S. firms, especially those whose earnings place them in the top 2 percent of corporations.

The AMA has conducted surveys of what it calls "downsizing," of actual workforce reductions, since 1989. If the media reports were accurate, we would expect to find a rising percentage of managerial cutbacks over that period. But "middle management" reductions as a percent of total downsizing actually fell over the period, from 23.6 percent to 18.5 percent between 1989 and 1990 and 1993 and 1994. If we add supervisory jobs to middle management, then the proportion of the total reductions in those two categories remained about constant.[42]

The AMA argues that over the whole period of their surveys, workplace reductions have hit middle management disproportionately, that "middle managers in particular continue to bear the brunt of corporate reductions." This would be true if, as they claim, the share of middle managerial jobs in the recent layoffs was higher than their share of total employment in the corporate sample at the beginning of the period.

But they're looking *only* at reductions, not at net employment changes. Like many who have overreacted to the "downsizing" trends, the AMA fails in its study to keep track of the critical distinction between *net* and *gross* changes in employment. Lots of managers can be laid off, resulting in evidence of substantial gross job turnover, but lots of managers can also be rehired at similar positions in the same or other companies, potentially producing no *net* change or even a *net* increase in managerial employment. If workplace reductions at the middle managerial level are offset by job expansions in those same job categories, then the bureaucratic burden would not be affected. The aggregate numbers on the expanding managerial employment share cited above suggest that this is exactly what's been happening—that new managerial positions have been opening up to compensate for those eliminated.

And Labor Department studies of displaced workers precisely confirm this pattern. The most recent study, released in July 1995, allows us to look at workers displaced in 1991 and 1992 and to trace where they ended up as of February 1994.[43] In these studies, displaced workers are defined as those employees twenty years and older "who lost or left a job because their plant or company closed or moved, there was insufficient work for them to do, or their positions or shifts were abolished."[44] Their definition closely corresponds, in other words, to what most people have in mind when they write or talk about "downsizing."

According to their studies, to be sure, large numbers of displacements occurred among managers in 1991 and 1992. But for the bureaucratic burden to have been reduced displacement rates for managers would need to have been larger than for other occupational categories. And they weren't. "By the early 1990s," the BLS report concludes, "job loss had become more common among white-collar workers than it had been a decade earlier . . . ; however, even this higher figure was low relative to that for blue-collar workers."[45] Looking just at the category of managers rather than at all white-collar workers, we also find that the managerial displacement rate was lower than the average for all blue-collar workers.

But these data look only at the displacement side of the equation. What happened to all those managers after they lost their jobs? Two findings from the BLS study are especially useful in reconciling people's impressions of widescale managerial layoffs with the evidence of an actual increase in the managerial share of employment:

- Among those workers displaced in 1991 and 1992, managers had the highest rate of reemployment by February 1994 of *any* occupational grouping: Among managers displaced in 1991 and 1992, 80.6 percent were employed in February 1994 while, for example, only 74.8 percent of craft workers and 68.8 percent of other blue-collar workers had jobs in that month.

- Most of those reemployed managers landed on their feet as managerial or professional workers. (The data don't classify the occupation of reemployment for managers alone.) The rates of reemployment in the same occupational category were considerably higher for those with "managerial and professional specialty" and "technical, sales, and administrative support" workers than in most other categories. Almost three-fifths of managers and professionals were reemployed in February 1994 as managers and professionals, for example, while less than half of those in service occupations wound up in the same kinds of jobs.

If the reports of the decimation of corporate managerial ranks have been gravely exaggerated, why have they seemed so credible?

One possible explanation is that the media, and especially business journalists, report *about* and *for* the top strata of the occupational ladder. When managers are laid off, it's big news. When business eliminates the jobs of workers on the shop and office floor, it's small news. The media appear to pay disproportionate attention to downsizing toward the top rungs of the occupational hierarchy because these workers are disproportionately their friends and relatives and readers and listeners.

These kinds of exaggerated accounts have appeared before. In the sharp recession of 1979–82, hundreds of thousands of workers lost their jobs, including many middle-level managers and supervisors. It was widely reported, Mark Green and John F. Berry observed in their 1985 book, "that middle managers lost jobs in record numbers during the economic recessions of the early 1980s." Just like the more recent period. "But aside from the considerable anecdotal evidence in magazines and newspapers chronicling the gutting of middle management," they continued, "what statistical proof is there of this widespread cutback of middle managers? The answer is, there isn't any."[46] What they meant is that the bureaucratic burden hadn't declined, just as it hasn't declined during the more recent period.

A second possible reason that the effects of "downsizing" on managerial hierarchies have been exaggerated is that most observers, like the AMA, have failed to keep track of the distinction between *net* and *gross* changes in employment. They trumpet the announcements of managerial layoffs when they occur. But they fail even to notice the widespread hiring of managers in other firms. They wince when long-time managers lose their jobs. But they probably don't even know about the thousands of workers who previously had other kinds of jobs who have now climbed into the managerial ranks. Among displaced workers actually employed as managers and professionals in February 1994, for example, a total of 45 percent—close to 250,000 workers—came from occupational backgrounds outside the managerial and professional sphere.[47]

Another reason that "downsizing" stories have paid such disproportionate attention to the fates of mid-level managers, apparently, is that those who have fallen from the ranks have fallen hard. Columbia University anthropologist Katherine S. Newman traced the trajectories of many of these "fallen" managers during the mid-1980s. The personal stories are wrenching. "Middle-aged managers who have lost their jobs," she writes, "carry indelible memories of the day they were 'let go.' It is a central scene in the drama of downward mobility."[48]

"Downsized" managers, indeed, fall quite far. Managerial employment is a ticket to affluence in the U.S. economy. As a useful study by Stephen J. Rose of the National Commission for Employment Policy shows, those men who worked at least eight out of ten years as managers during the 1980s earned 68 percent more than the average earnings for all male workers. But, strikingly, those managers who were *unable* to maintain their position at that occupational rung, those who worked less than eight of the ten years as managers in the 1980s, suffered the biggest relative earnings dropoff, compared with those who stayed on the managerial ladder, of employees in any occupational grouping.[49] As Anthony Carnevale summarizes Rose's findings, "There is both more risk and more gain in managerial jobs."[50] And the risks involve more than just material losses. Newman concludes:[51]

> The distress that refugees from the managerial milieu feel is only partly a matter of income loss, or the destruction of a lifestyle. It is fundamentally the pain of being evaluated and found wanting. To be a downwardly mobile executive is first to discover that you are not as good a person as you thought you were and then to end up not sure who or what you really are.

The business pages have been especially sensitive to this distress.

You can only fool people for so long. Eventually, just as I was completing this manuscript, some in the business press were finally waking up and recognizing the facts. In Fall 1995 the *Wall Street Journal* published a front-page story which finally paid more attention to the facts than the fantasies of "downsizing." "Despite years of relentless downsizing, 'right-sizing' and re-engineering in corporate America, all aimed in part at shedding excess bureaucracy," the *Journal* acknowledged, "reports of middle management's demise are proving much exaggerated."[52] Even "corporate giants," among whom the most dramatic reports of managerial layoffs had been reported, "have more managers per 100 employees today than they did in 1993." And smaller companies appear to have been employing managers with a vengeance. Those running smaller, growing companies, according to one business analyst quoted by the *Journal*, "are some of the most control-oriented people out there. They add bureaucracy to their businesses in order to maintain control." Many managers have been laid off in corporate restructuring, the *Journal* concluded, but they've found managerial work elsewhere. "There is so much opportunity [for managers] in the marketplace," one "downsized" executive reported, "it's incredible."

There is one more reason not to take the widespread reports of "lean" corporations too seriously. If U.S. firms were actually addressing their problems of obesity in any kind of systematic way, we would find substantial evidence of *coherent strategies* underlying managerial cutbacks when and where they have actually occurred.

But the evidence seems to suggest the opposite. In general, U.S. corporations have been slicing their workforces in piecemeal and often shotgun fashion, rarely acting upon clear and considered strategies for changing their ways of doing business.

This was beginning to become evident, to some at least, from the start. In Tomasko's 1987 book, for example, he warned:

The consequences of top-heavy organizational structures are already well known. . . . But the equally destructive consequences of deep, across-the-board cutbacks, sometimes happening wave after wave, are only beginning to become apparent. These consequences include diminished employee commitment to their companies; bitter personal trauma inflicted when the reductions were implemented with concern only for their economic impact, ignoring their psychological impact; and creation of corporate environments that are risk-averse and innovation-fearing. These harder-to-quantify problems may return to haunt many businesses.

The pattern has continued. "Most organizations downsize poorly," contends Kim Cameron of the University of Michigan School of Business Administration, who has closely studied the phenomenon. "Productivity suffers, morale suffers, innovation gets squashed and companies get less flexible and less competitive."[53] In general, economists James R. Emshoff and Teri E. Demlinger report, downsizing has not been "part of a thoughtful strategy to redesign the whole corporate structure and culture. Instead it's an almost panicked reaction to pressures and problems, administered with the sheeplike justification that everyone else is doing the same thing."[54] In his recent study of restructuring corporations, former *New York Times* reporter Hedrick Smith concurs. "In corporate America today," Smith concludes from his travels around the country, "downsizing is like dieting: Everyone is doing it, so people try it again and again, even though few achieve the desired results. As one wag put it, the fixation with downsizing has become the new 'corporate anorexia.'"[55]

Surveys conducted by the American Management Association in 1994 highlight the superficial and shotgun character of most corporate "downsizing" efforts.[56] Only a third of corporations reported that their downsizing efforts had actually resulted in productivity gains; fully 30 percent reported that productivity had declined. A vast majority of companies surveyed reported that their restructuring efforts had placed a high priority on changing corporate culture, but less than a quarter reported that these results were "very successful." Far from generating uniform improvements in performance, one of the surveys concluded, "the surest after-effect of downsizing is a negative impact on employee morale"; 83 percent of corporations which had downsized between 1989 and 1991 reported that "employee morale had declined in 1994."[57]

In their panic, in their herding behavior, corporations have been swinging their machetes wildly. More often than not, Cameron concludes, downsizing occurs by brute force. "That's like throwing a hand grenade into a crowded room—you don't know which 25 percent you are going to kill."[58] Many more production employees than managers and supervisors have been hit by the grenades.

* * *

And so we end the chapter where we began. Corporate bureaucracies have grown to massive size. Walter Wriston jokes that half of those bureaucratic employees may be redundant; "[figuring out] which half is the difficult problem."

The media have reported widely that corporate downsizing has begun to attack this problem of overweight. But the share of managers in total employment has been increasing since the reports of downsizing began, not decreasing. And corporate downsizers haven't known "which 25 percent [they] are going to kill."

The same basic questions echo through the entire discussion: Why do we spend $1.3 trillion to cover the costs of the bureaucratic burden? Isn't this too big a price to pay?

Discussion Questions

1. The United States has the highest percentage of managerial and administrative employees among nine industrialized countries. What could be some of the reasons for the differences among countries?

2. If the work of many managers involves supervising the work of others, why would the United States use so many more managers than other countries?

Reprinted from David M. Gordon, "The Bureaucratic Burden" in *Fat and Mean* (New York: Free Press, 1996, pp. 33–60).

Endnotes

1. "The Ailing Economy: Diagnoses and Prescriptions," *New York Times*, April 4, 1982, p. 4E.
2. Some of these early studies are reported in Mark Green and John F. Berry, *The Challenge of Hidden Profits: Reducing Corporate Bureaucracy and Waste* (New York: William Morrow, 1985).
3. "The Ailing Economy," p. 4E.
4. Based on an analysis of *The Economist* data in Lawrence Mishel and Jared Bernstein, *The State of Working America 1994–95* (Armonk, NY: M.E. Sharpe, 1994), Table 3.52. Figure for production workers' real hourly take-home pay from series on real spendable hourly earnings presented in Chapter 1.
5. "Paychecks of Americas 800 Top Chief Executives," *Forbes*, May 23, 1994, pp. 190–191, 172–173.
6. Joani Nelson-Horchler, "CEO Pay," *Industry Week*, April 15, 1991, p. 13.
7. Bill Clinton and Al Gore, *Putting People First: How We Can All Change America* (New York: Books, 1992), p. 5.
8. Derek Bok, *The Cost of Talent: How Executives and Professionals Are Paid and How It Affects* (New York: The Free Press, 1993), p. 95.
9. *Employment and Earnings*, January 1995, Tables 48–49.
10. Total government employment from *Employment and Earnings*, January 1995, Table 48. State and county populations from *Statistical Abstract*, 1993, Tables 31, 1375.
11. Based on median height of about 5'7"–5'8"for weighted combination of men and women, ages 36–64. *Statistical Abstracts*, 1993, Table 216.
12. Data for total compensation paid to nonproduction and supervisory employees are not directly available. But I have been able to estimate it from standard government sources by making a few reasonable assumptions: One begins with hourly earnings received by private nonfarm production and supervisory (P&NS) employees [*Employment and Earnings*, January 1995, Table B-2]. Then, assuming that the ratio of earnings to compensation is the same for these employees as for all private nonfarm employees [*National Income and Produce Accounts*, Tables 6.4–6.5R] one extrapolates average hourly compensation for private nonfarm production and nonsupervisory employees. (This seems a fairly reasonable assumption,

since many P&NS workers are unionized and enjoy healthy benefits. But, if anything . . . it probably slightly overstates P&NS compensation which ends up understating nonproduction and supervisory [NP&S] compensation, giving me a conservative estimate of the numbers reported in the text.) Then assuming that private nonfarm P&NS workers have the same average weekly hours worked as all private nonfarm employees and work all paid overtime hours reported in the manufacturing sect or [*Employment and Earnings* Table B-2), we can get an estimate of total annual hours worked by private nonfarm P&NS workers. (The assumption about average weekly hours seems reasonable—once again because many P&NS workers are unionized and therefore enjoy limits on straight-time hours. But, as with the ratio of earnings to compensation, this assumption is probably a slight underestimate of the NP&S compensation estimates.) Then, multiplying hours by conservative hourly compensation, we get an estimate of total private nonfarm P&NS annual compensation. Subtracting this from total private nonfarm compensation (*National Income and Product Accounts*, Table 6-5), the residual provides an estimate of total private nonfarm nonproduction and supervisory employee compensation.

13. All figures for these comparisons come from the *National Income and Product Accounts*.

14. See Peter G. Peterson and Neil Howe, *On Borrowed Time: How the Grab in Entitlement Spending Threatens America's Future* (New York: ICS Press, 1988).

15. Bureau of Labor Statistics, Handbook of Methods, Bulletin 2282, April 1988, p. 77 [emphasis in the original].

16. It is largely for this reason, indeed, that some economists have recently criticized reliance on these establishment survey categories. . . . It is exactly for this reason that I continually check conclusions drawn from the establishment data against the more detailed breakdowns available in the BLS household surveys.

17. These data for the household surveys are based on the author's own tabulations from the Current Population Surveys microdata samples for March 1993, including only private nonfarm wage-and-salary employees. For this tabulation I include all those from the general category of "executive, administrative, and managerial" and all those in specific categories, scattered throughout the census occupational codes, designated as one kind of "supervisor" or another.

18. All the following data are based on the author's own tabulations from the 1991 U.S. survey organized under the auspices of Erik Olin Wright's Comparative Project on Class Structure and Class Consciousness. The survey was conducted by the Survey Research Center of the University of California-Berkeley under the direction of Michael Hout, Erik Olin Wright,

and Martin Sanchez-Jankowski. For an introductory background to the data and their methodological purposes, see Erik Olin Wright, *Classes* (London: Verso Books, 1985). For a more recent discussion, including both a discussion of the survey methodology and an overview of the results from the 1991 survey see Erik Olin Wright, *Class Counts: Comparative Studies in Class Analysis* (New York: Cambridge University Press, 1996), especially Ch. 2.

19. See the detailed discussion of the representative character of the surveys in Wright, *Class Counts*, Ch. 2.

20. Elinor Langer, "The Women of the Telephone Company," *New York Review of Books*, March 12, 1970, p. 16.

21. Robert M. Tomasko, *Downsizing: Reshaping the Corporation for the Future* (New York: American Management Association, 1987), p. 21.

22. Robert H. Hayes and Steven C. Wheelwright, *Restoring Our Competitive Edge: Competing Through Manufacturing* (New York: John Wiley & Sons, 1984), pp. 62–63.

23. Tomasko, *Downsizing*, p. 14.

24. Towers Perrin, Inc., "1991 Worldwide Total Remuneration," 1991, p. 12.

25. International Labour Organization, *Yearbook of Labor Statistics, 1994* (Geneva: ILO, 1994), Table 3.

26. In 1989, there were 14.8 million "administrative and managerial" employees tallied for the United States in the ILO compilation. This exactly equaled the total number of "executive, administrative, and managerial" employees identified in the BLS tabulations from the 1989 Household surveys (*Employment and Earnings*, January 1990).

27. The Swedish percentage is an approximation. 1984 was the last year in which administration and managerial employment are separated from clerical employment. To estimate the 1989 percent, the 1984 share of administrative, managerial, clerical, and related workers was applied to composite category for 1989 in order to estimate the number of managerial and administrative employees: that number was then calculated as a percent of total nonfarm employment. Although this is an approximation, it is unlikely to distort the figure presented in the graph very much since these shares had been fairly stable in Sweden in previous years.

28. For a useful presentation of these three alternative models, see Eileen Appelbaum and Rosemary Batt, *The New American Workplace: Transforming Work Systems in the United States* (Ithaca NY: Cornell University ILR Press, 1994), Ch. 3.

29. For an account of this dynamic in the period of the postwar boom see Bowles, Gordon, and Weisskopf, *After the Waste Land*, Chapter 5.

30. See Bowles, Gordon, and Weisskopf, *After the Waste Land*, Chapter 5 for documentation of

these features of the "limited capital-labor accord.

31. Quoted in Green and Berry, *The Challenge of Hidden Profits*, p. 49.

32. Barry Bluestone and Irving Bluestone, *Negotiating the Future: A Labor Perspective on American Business* (New York: Basic Books, 1992), p. 131.

33. Tomasko, *Downsizing*.

34. Bruce Nussbaum, "Downward Mobility: Corporate Castoffs Are Struggling Just to Stay in the Middle Class," *Business Week*, March 23, 1992, p. 57.

35. Cited in Amacom Briefing & Surveys, *Responsible Reductions in Force: An American Management Association Research Report on Downsizing and Outplacement* (New York: American Management Association, 1987), p. 55.

36. Tomasko, *Downsizing*.

37. Nussbaum, "Downward Mobility," p. 57.

38. U.S. Bureau of Labor Statistics, "Employment in Perspective: Earnings and Job Growth," Report No. 877. August 1994, Table 2: and *Employment and Earnings*, January 1990, January 1995.

39. U.S. Bureau of Labor Statistics. "Employed and experienced unemployed persons by detailed occupation, . . . 2nd Quarter 1995" unpublished tables, 1995.

40. *Employment and Earnings*, January 1990; BLS "Employed and experienced unemployed persons, . . . 2nd Quarter 1995." Two extrapolative assumptions needed to be made for this comparison. First, I assumed that the portion of the total category of "sales supervisors and proprietors" who worked as nonfarm private sales supervisory wage-and-salary employees was the same in 1989 and the second quarter of 1995 as it had been in tabulations from the 1993 CPS. Second, I assumed that the percentage of personal service employees working as supervisors was the same in 1989 as in the published data for 1994.

41. For a careful and useful study of some other ways in which the term "lean and mean" may make sense, see Bennett Harrison, *Lean and Mean: The Changing Landscape of Corporate Power in the Age of Flexibility* (New York: Basic Books, 1994).

42. American Management Association, "1994 AMA Survey on Downsizing," News Release, November 1994.

43. Jennifer M. Gardner, "Worker Displacement: A Decade of Change," *U.S. Bureau of Labor Statistics*, Report No. 2464, July 1995.

44. Gardner, "Work Displacement," Appendix A.

45. Ibid., 4. Following data citations are from Tables 3, D-5, and D-7 respectively.

46. Green and Berry, *The Challenge of Hidden Profits*, p. 46.

47. Gardner, "Worker Displacement," Table D-7.

48. Katherine S. Newman, *Falling From Grace: The Experience of Downward Mobility in the American Middle Class* (New York: The Free Press, 1988), p. 48.

49. Stephen J. Rose, *Declining Job Security and the Professionalization of Opportunity* (Washington, D.C.: National Commission for Employment Policy, May 1995), Research Report No. 95-04, Table A-3.

50. Anthony Carnevale, "Preface," in Stephen J. Rose, *Declining Job Security and the Professionalization of Opportunity*, p. vi.

51. Newman, *Falling From Grace*, p. 94.

52. Alex Markels, "Restructuring Alters Middle-Manager Role But Leaves It Robust," *Wall Street Journal*, September 25, 1995, p. A1.

53. Quoted in Mary Lord, "Where You Can't Get Fired," *U.S. News & World Report*, January 14, 1991, p. 48.

54. James R. Emshoff and Teri E. Demlinger, *The New Rules of the Game* (New York: HarperCollins, 1991), p. x.

55. Hedrick Smith, *Rethinking America* (New York: Random House, 1995), p. 410.

56. Survey results summarized in *The Editor*, "Corporate Surveys Can't Find a Productivity Revolution, Either," *Challenge*, November-December 1995, 31–34.

57. Survey quote from Smith, *Rethinking America*, p. 411; results on morale from "Corporate Surveys Can't Find a Productivity Revolution," p. 32.

58. Quoted in Lord, "Where You Can't Get Fired," p. 48. ✦

16
Just a Temp

Jackie Rogers

One of the more dramatic symbols of the new economy is the *temporary worker,* a new category of worker who is and is not an employee. The temp and the temporary-help industry provide corporations with the maximum flexibility of a one-sided employment contract. Since temps actually work for the temp agency, the corporation where they work doesn't have to worry about providing health insurance, a pension plan, or other benefits. Corporations hire and fire temps at a moment's notice, adding them when there is an increase in production orders and eliminating them when the demand declines. One of the editors of your textbook remembers interviewing a temp worker who was wrestling with the question of whether she was eligible to be a member of the company softball team. Some of her co-workers wanted her to play, but others said no, because she might not be working there as the season progressed and the team might be stuck without someone to fill her position. This chapter looks at the temp worker through the eyes of the temporary employee. It provides a grim picture of the temp as a person and a nonperson.

Both sociologists and management theorists seem to agree that the world of work is changing in the United States. Whether that world is changing for better or for worse is up for debate. One way in which the work world is changing is through increasing "flexibilization" of labor. Flexible strategies run the gamut from increasing the range of workers' skills, to rotating jobs, to decreasing employer obligation through the use of temporary and contract workers. Joan Acker (1992) cautions that changes in the organization of work often result in a polarization of skill, security, and autonomy and that this polarization is inflected by race, class, and gender.

This study looks at the ways in which workers experience temporary employment, one of several strategies employers use to increase their flexibility. So on one level, this is an ethnographic account of the daily struggles of temporary workers; however, it also analyzes the social organization of temporary work as it shapes those experiences and struggles.

How do workers experience temporary work?

How does the organization of temporary work empower or constrain workers?

In what ways is gender embedded in the organization of temporary work?

What are the implications of the increasing use of temporary workers for social equality?

As more and more people in the United States find themselves in temporary work arrangements, a sociological understanding of these arrangements becomes more imperative.

Both the popular press and human resource management texts discuss the boom in temporary employment (see, for example, Castro, 1993; Morrow, 1993). These sources relate how companies are finding temporary workers to be a less expensive alternative to increasing their staffs, especially because access to such workers has become relatively easy with the proliferation of temporary agencies (National Association of Temporary Services, 1992). Parker (1994) demonstrates how temporary-help firms' public relations efforts portray temporary work as an exchange beneficial to both the employer and the temporary employee. Therefore, the reader should keep in mind that this study is set against a dominant discourse of flexibility and cost reduction that largely reflects employers' realities and interests. This study seeks to establish a new discourse that places the worker at the center of inquiry.

Temporary Employment and the Contingent Economy

Temporary clerical workers are part of what is called the *contingent economy*. The term contingent economy covers a diverse array of work arrangements, including part-time employment, temporary employment, employee leasing, job sharing, and domestic day work (Polivka & Nardone, 1989). The growth in this sector has outpaced overall employment growth, demonstrating that this phenomenon is less cyclical than in the past and more incorporated into usual business strategies. For example, temporary employment has grown at three times the rate of overall U.S. employment since 1982 (Callaghan & Hartmann, 1991) and currently stands at approximately 1.4 million (Senate Committee on Labor and Human Resources, 1993). This is about 1% of the U.S. workforce, but the proportion of temporary workers is predicted to continue growing. Indeed, noncyclical (i.e., does not rise and fall with recession and recovery periods) continued growth of the temporary workforce was cited in the 1993 congressional subcommittee meetings on contingent labor (Senate Committee on Labor and Human Resources, 1993). By 1989, between 25% and 30% of the American workforce could be classified as contingent workers (Belous, 1989). Yet social scientists have only recently attempted to understand this growing phenomenon.

Certain segments of the contingent economy have received more attention than others. For example, there seems to be a fair amount of attention to part-time work (Beechey & Perkins, 1987; Negrey, 1993; Tilly, 1990), whereas other portions of the contingent economy, such as temporary work, remain relatively unexamined.

Managerial and Labor Perspectives on Temporary Employment

Research about temporary employment to date can be categorized into two dominant streams, the managerial perspective and the labor perspective. Congressional hearings on temporary employment in 1988 and 1993 (House Committee on Government Operations, 1988; Senate Committee on Labor and Human Resources, 1993) reveal this same distinction, with business leaders, managers, and the temporary industry generally championing the former view while workers, social reformers, and some labor leaders champion the latter. For its proponents, temporary employment is a functional phenomenon or a market exchange. It allows the flexibility necessary for competition in the global marketplace. In fact, a term previously reserved for money-saving inventory control systems has been adopted to describe this new workforce: "just-in-time." When managers speak in terms of flexibility and just-in-time, they seldom ask, "flexible for whom?" or "just in time for whom?" The worker is conceptualized as a work input and is managed in much the same way as inventory or machines. This attitude is revealed in one simple statement, "In fact, in certain cases, [contingent labor] may be the most important control mechanism that management has in the short run, given that management often can treat labor as a variable cost while other costs usually are fixed" (Belous, 1989).

Such an understanding of temporary employment reveals a managerial bias that obfuscates the realities of those not in the position to manage or control their work. There is a parallel here between managerial postures of temporary work and Taylor's discussion of scientific management. Braverman's (1974) criticism of Taylor's notion of a fair day's work illustrates this point: "Why a 'fair day's work' should be defined as a physiological maximum is never made clear" (p. 97). In other words, a fair day's work for whom? Taylor's work was conducted purely from a managerial perspective without the least concern for the realities of the worker. Callaghan and Hartmann (1991) begin to expose the bias in a managerial perspective:

If, however, the impetus for change [to contingent employment] is only to meet the evolving needs of the work environment, then we would not expect to see the lower wages and lack of fringe benefits which are currently part of the price of being a contingent worker. (p. 1)

In contrast to the managerial perspective, the labor perspective has provided a much more illuminating analysis of the situation of temporary workers. The congressional hearings in 1988 and 1993 brought many economic and legal labor issues to the forefront. On the whole, contingent workers:

- are paid less;
- have fewer fringe, health, and retirement benefits;
- are unlikely to be unionized;
- have little or no long-term security;
- have a more difficult time qualifying for unemployment and workers' compensation;
- often "slip through the cracks" with regard to labor legislation, specifically OSHA, ERISA, and Wage & Hours Standards (House Committee on Government Operations, 1988; Senate Committee on Labor and Human Resources, 1993).

Callaghan and Hartmann (1991) identify several alarming trends in contingent employment. Recent increases in contingent employment have occurred at the expense of workers who would otherwise prefer to be employed full-time. Thus employers are not merely accommodating workers' desires for greater flexibility. The phenomenon appears to be employer-driven rather than worker-driven, as employer-demand variables are better predictors of growth in temporary employment than labor-supply variables (Golden & Appelbaum, 1992). As a result, contingent workers experience uncertainty regarding the duration or regularity of their work and are unlikely to receive on-the-job training or to be considered for promotional opportunities. Callaghan and Hartmann (1991) summarize:

Low wages and a lack of benefits result in economic hardship and poverty for contingent workers more often than for other workers. Involuntary part-time workers have a poverty rate of 16.5 percent, which is slightly higher than unemployed people who are out of work and seeking a job (15.3 percent), and much higher than for full-time workers (2.7 percent). (p. 15)

Finally, Callaghan and Hartmann (1991) offer a precautionary note regarding the extent to which temporary employment has become "business as usual." They view the change in temporary employment to a noncyclical phenomenon as evidence that employers are avoiding "long-term commitments, wage growth, and substantial fringe benefits" as well as occupational safety and health protections (p. 28).

Labor perspectives such as those given in the 1988 and 1993 congressional hearings and those given by Callaghan and Hartmann (1991) provide a substantial, but incomplete, picture of temporary work. In addition to the material consequences of temporary jobs cited by labor perspective advocates, temporaries experience the social and interpersonal consequences of their work. This area in the literature is underdeveloped. We need an understanding of the day-to-day challenges contingent workers face and how they deal with those challenges in order to round out a labor perspective, which focuses mainly on economic drawbacks and legal loopholes in contingent work arrangements.

Race, Gender, and the Contingent Workforce

Callaghan and Hartmann (1991) and Tilly (1990) have demonstrated the overrepresentation of women and people of color in various sectors of the contingent economy. Women and African American[1] workers are overrepresented in the temporary workforce. For example, a survey by the National Association of Temporary Services (1992) estimates that 80% of member-agency temporaries are female,[2] and Belous (1989) estimates that more than 64% of the entire temporary workforce is female, and more than 20% is Black. The corresponding figures for the general workforce are 45% and 10%, respectively. Thus the problems associated with temporary employment are disproportionately the problems of women and African Americans. And the numbers of Americans being introduced to these working arrangements is increasing every year.

Many social scientists have demonstrated that men and women often perform different work. Cynthia Cockburn (1985) tells us that "women may push the buttons but they may not meddle with the works" (p. 12). Furthermore, men tend to be located in capital-intensive jobs, whereas women tend to be located in labor-intensive jobs (Acker, 1990; West, 1990); part-time work (which has been shown to intensify the labor process) is largely gendered as female (Beechey & Perkins, 1987; West, 1990).

At the occupational level, many have detailed the persistence of occupational segregation and the male-female wage gap (Reskin & Roos, 1990; Sokoloff, 1992) and Black-White wage gap (Sokoloff, 1992) within and across occupations. Job queues and labor queues are influenced by a broad array of factors, ranging from job autonomy and working conditions to sex composition of a job and gender ideology of employers (Milkman, 1987).

Race/ethnicity and gender are also implicated in the structuring of the secondary labor market (Amott & Matthaei, 1991).

Jobs in the secondary labor market are marked by low wages, poor working conditions, little stability or opportunity for advancement, and minimal benefits, if any. Furthermore, these labor markets are a primary mechanism in reproducing racial/ethnic and gender inequality, although they do not do so in isolation from other social institutions.

Smith (1993) and Acker (1992) build upon the notion that gender is implicated in the structuring of labor markets by examining how gender affects the organization of "flexible" work arrangements. Not all flexible labor strategies are created equal. Smith characterizes some as "enabling" (those that upgrade labor processes and employment relationships) and others as "restrictive" (those that downgrade labor processes and employment relationships). In manufacturing, gender ideology largely delineates the contingent from the permanent jobs, as women's jobs are turned into temporary or part-time jobs in order to support a "core" of male workers. Smith points to institutional foundations of gender inequalities that occur when an entire sector, such as clerical work, is increasingly organized as contingent. Thus, to fully understand the effect of contingent work on the workers, gender and race must be part of the analysis. To help organize such an analysis, I have employed the concept of alienation.

Alienation: A Contested Term

Alienation is a complex concept, the terms of which are often contested by social scientists. Nevertheless, alienation can be a useful heuristic device for understanding temporary workers' experiences. As I use the term, alienation signals a lack of control, a certain powerlessness felt by the individual and derived from the structure of social relations. It is the lack of power to direct one's work, to maintain satisfactory work relationships and to create a self-definition rather than have it imposed.

Some of the literature on alienation characterizes it as a subjective psychological or emotional state to manage (see Kohn & Schooler, 1983; Rizzo, House, & Lirtzman, 1970; Seeman, 1959) and as highly individualistic in orientation. In contrast, Marxist interpretations view alienation as an outgrowth of the social relations of capitalist production, sometimes seemingly removing the individual from analysis entirely. These two orientations are not mutually exclusive.

One can employ the concept of alienation in such a way that it attends to individual psychological and emotional states and broader structural factors related to the organization of capitalist production. Such a concept of alienation would link individuals' experiences of alienation to the way in which their work is organized as alienating. Israel (1971) suggests a useful application of alienation to demonstrate a series of social relations "that present a link between the sociological and the psychological conditions" (p. 15). Analysis must be structural as well as subjective. Schmitt and Moody (1994) suggest the concept of alienation is a useful tool of social criticism when its use demonstrates how social organization exacerbates alienation *when it need not.* Therefore, the alienating aspects of temporary employment are contrasted to more traditionally organized work, which in itself may be considerably alienating.

In integrating experience and structure in the discussion of alienation and clerical temporary work, I follow three broad Marxist categories: alienation from work, alienation from others, and alienation from self. I will address each of these aspects of alienation more closely in the empirical sections on alienation that follow.

Furthermore, as Schmitt and Moody (1994) note, any discussion of alienation is incomplete without examining resistance as well. In examining resistance, we glean a more accurate understanding of the ways temporary workers attempt to shape their own world in the face of enormous constraints. Attention to resistance reveals the contested character of the temporary worker's terrain. Temporary work is not a mutual exchange between employer and worker.

Some feminist writings on women and work (Bookman & Morgan, 1988; Ward, 1990) implement a broad view of women's resistance that includes more subtle forms of resistance than are usually considered in more traditional studies of work. Forms of resistance range from subtle (crying and "female" problems; Ong, 1987) to overt (those means traditionally labeled resistance, such as sabotage and union organizing; Bookman & Morgan, 1988). I will follow a broad conceptualization of resistance to include both subtle and overt forms. This is particularly important when studying work that affords little opportunity for traditionally conceived worker resistance, particularly unionization. Because temporary work separates temporary workers from each other, temporary workers from "regular" workers, and temporary workers from union workers,[3] unionization for temporary workers is unlikely at this time. This broad conception of resistance also creates space to explore the contradictory nature of much resistance. Resistance in one realm may make workers complicit in their own subordination in another realm (Ong, 1987), or it may reinforce damaging stereotypes. Nevertheless, temporary workers do resist, sometimes effectively and sometimes not. In this chapter, I will explore the multitude of ways temporary workers resist, attempting to understand this resistance in light of the constraints temporary work places on that resistance.

Method

This research is based on in-depth interviews with 13 women who have been employed[4] as temporary clerical workers and with the branch managers of two temporary-services firms in Los Angeles. I obtained the interviews through a variety of sources: responses to a letter of introduction given to the workers at a temporary agency I work through,[5] personal contact with other temporaries while working as a temporary, responses to a flier posted at a local gym requesting interviews, and referrals from friends and previous interview subjects (snowballing). Collecting data from such diverse means is preferable to relying solely on self-selection or on the personal recommendation of the temporary agency personnel. In this way, I avoided drawing solely on people who "have an axe to grind," who are comfortable responding to a letter written on university letterhead, or whom the agency wishes to represent them.

The data represent a diverse group of respondents, including subjects from 23 to 60 years old, both married and single women, high school as well as college graduates, and two African American women, two Latino women, one Filipino woman, and eight White women. In addition, the respondents' experience with temporary work ranges from several months to over 10 years and includes experiences with over 20 different temporary agencies; most have worked through at least two temporary agencies.

Each semistructured interview lasted between 1 and 2 hours and followed three trajectories:

1. the relationship of the worker to her work,

2. the relationship of the worker to others in the workplace, and

3. the feelings of the worker about herself in relation to her work.

The interviews with the branch managers focused on the business of temporary employment, relationships with clients, and relationships with temporary workers. Using interview guides structured around these themes lends consistency to the interviews while still affording flexibility in following interesting topics. All names and places in the text are pseudonyms.

I transcribed each interview and employed both methodological and theoretical memo writing, open coding, axial coding, and selective coding (Strauss, 1987) in the development of an emergent theory (Glaser & Strauss, 1967). In this case, the emergent theory corresponded closely to the sociological concept of alienation; therefore, I employed the concept of alienation as the underlying theme of analysis, fleshing out the ways in which alienating experiences are related to the organization of temporary work.

Alienation From Work

In the classical Marxist depiction, alienation from work has at least two components. Workers are alienated not just from the product of their work, but from the work process as well: "alienation shows itself not only in the result, but also in the act of production, inside productive activity itself" (McLellan, 1977, p. 80). With temporary work, labor is twice alienated from its product. The worker's labor belongs not only to the company for whom she works, but also to the temporary agency that receives a fee for her services. For example, the company that hires a temporary may pay the agency $10 an hour for her services; however, the temporary worker may only receive $7 an hour. Thus, the alienation Marx depicted is taken one step further through the subcontracting relationship that exists in temporary employment.

More important for this analysis is the fact that temporary workers also are alienated from the labor process. This type of alienation is characterized by temporaries' lack of control over their work, their lack of control over the conditions of their work, and their lack of understanding of the purpose of their work. Certainly, these conditions are not unique to temporary employment. As Braverman (1974) illustrated, clerical work has become degraded in much the same manner as factory work through the separation of conception and execution.

> Typists, mail sorters, telephone operators, stock clerks, receptionists, payroll and timekeeping clerks, shipping and receiving clerks are subjected to routines, more or less mechanized according to current possibilities, that strip them of their former grasp of even a lim-

ited amount of office information, divest them of the need or ability to understand and decide, and make of them so many mechanical eyes, fingers, and voices whose functioning is, insofar as possible, predetermined by both rules and machinery. (p. 340)

To an even greater extent than the workers Braverman described, clerical temporaries are seldom provided with enough information for them to understand the purpose of the work that they perform. Little time is invested in instruction regarding the task to be performed, particularly for short-term assignments. When asked about their tasks, the temporaries I interviewed were seldom able to describe the purpose of their work. One woman who was doing temporary work after losing her "permanent" job stated:

I still don't know what it was that I was doing. I just sat there and entered, I think they were coordinates or something. It's some kind of program that builds a building. They just gave me the coordinates to punch in. (Julie Grovers, 30-year-old White woman)

Another temporary described the purpose of her filing "hundreds of boxes" over a period of 3 to 4 weeks:

For some reason they were redoing all their files because they changed something, they changed the districts or something like that. Whatever, I don't really know. (Irene Pedersen, 25-year-old White woman)

The temporary nature of the work deprives the temporary worker of even the most limited realization of the finished product of her work. This happens even on longer-term assignments, because once the work is finished, the temporary moves on to another assignment. Seldom do temporaries complete subsequent stages of a project, which would provide them with a sense of continuity. In fact, one temporary described a situation in which the speedy completion of her work resulted in the termination of the assignment, rather than progression to the next phase of the project.

She had estimated that this job would take 3 days. Well it turns out that my partner and I worked quickly together. The woman that hired us was surprised that a 3-day job got finished in a day. And she goes, that's fantastic, here's your reward, I'll cut the assignment short. I mean you're told it's going to be a 3-day assignment and you arrange your schedule, but it gets pulled from you. (Cheryl Hansen, 23-year-old White woman)

Later, reflecting on that experience and its lack of purpose, Cheryl said, "It's not like you're in there to clean up, it's not like you're in there to say well, 'I think that we need to improve this, and I think we need to improve that.' "

Thus, while clerical work has wrested understanding from the hands of workers, temporary work has done so more dramatically. This analysis can be taken further if one looks at the labor process more closely. For temporaries, alienation from work is partially due to the organization of clerical work. However, the particular organization of temporary work exacerbates the situation. First, the work is often the least desirable of all the clerical work. Temporaries consistently report being assigned to "shit work," "scut work," or "dreg work." They expressed an awareness that this particular type of work was allocated to temporaries over "regular" employees: "You end up doing the stuff that nobody else wants to do, or has time to do. And when I worked at that bank, I ended up doing. . . . It was just too monotonous, too boring" (Jean Masters, 34-year-old African American woman).

In many cases, temporaries described long periods of monotonous filing, stuffing envelopes, copying, or even proofreading address labels. They described their work as monotonous, mindless, and even robotic. One temporary who once had to work 23 consecutive hours offered this explanation for the monotony and intensity of her work:

It's because you are a temp. They sort of look at you as a sort of disposable factor. You're in there, you get all the dirty work, because nobody wants to do the filing or the xeroxing for 2 hours at a time. Nobody wants to do any of this stuff so you get it. (Cheryl Hansen)

Another woman describes her experience at a bank:

I worked in a bank and stuffed envelopes for 5 days straight. It was terrible, it was so monotonous. He delegated me these huge boxes of stuff, so like I would only have to go to him 2 days later. I'd just go to him when I ran out of stuff to stuff. (Sarah Tilton, 26-year-old White woman)

Others described work being piled on them in a never-ending fashion. One woman described her temporary work experience in a manner reminiscent of the sorcerer's apprentice in the Disney movie, *Fantasia.* Just as Mickey Mouse is confronted by an army of uncontrollable brooms, Irene is confronted by her own uncontrollable workload:

All I could do was come home and think about these boxes piling up. And then I remember one day, I had just finished filing like all these *fuckin' boxes* and this humongous UPS truck comes in, or whatever it was, this truck with this man, he just unloaded like 50 more. So it was almost like I didn't do anything! So yeah, I had a lot of anxiety about these boxes. (Irene Pedersen)

Although temporaries often perform their tasks at an intensified rate when compared with regular employees, there is a second, contradictory tendency in the work experience of temporaries. They are often left for long periods of time without any work to do.

You know, you're hired as a receptionist and the phone rings like twice. . . . I had a temp job I think for 2 weeks. I was covering for a secretary and the bosses were all out of town, but they needed somebody just to be there and to cover the phones. (Ludy Martinez, 36-year-old Filipino woman)

Fifty percent of the time, there was absolutely very little to do, with just answering the phone or taking messages. (Ellen Lanford, 38-year-old White woman)

Often, the difference between feast and famine lies in the nature of the assignment. According to the interviews, feast conditions usually occur when temporaries are brought in to complete a special assignment (for example, a company might be recoding all its files; rather than have regular employees perform this work, they hire three temps for 2 weeks) and famine conditions usually occur when a temporary is brought in to substitute for a regular employee.

However, temporaries in substitute positions occasionally do report being assigned projects that have been sitting around the office. For example, one company wanted to use this temporary's time efficiently by having her complete a filing project while she was substituting for the receptionist.

Oh my Lord, this woman wanted me to work. You're doing the phone, OK. You're filing. And it's not like next to each other. The phones are right here, and the filing cabinet is all the way in Siberia . . . the job was too much. Using you, not paying you. They want you to do this, to do that . . . the inventory, the filing, the telephone. I was doing so many things. What else? What else? (Shari Jensen, 31-year-old African American woman)

In addition, substitute temporaries can be assigned to help out everyone in the office in the absence of a regular employee. Work is intensified by increasing the number of supervisors one must serve: "It's like you know when I got here and you said I'm working for two people. Well, I'm working for four" (Ludy Martinez).

In summary, temporary workers are alienated from the product of their work as well as from the labor process. They have little control over their work and often experience periods of intense labor or a complete lack of activity. Quite often, temporaries have little understanding of the purpose of their work, and they are seldom around to see the finished product because they are, after all, "only temporary."

Alienation From Others

Alienation from others derives from the relational characteristics particular to temporary clerical employment. Temporary workers are structurally constrained from forming satisfactory relationships in the workplace. There are several factors unique to temporary employment that foster alienation from others. The transitory relationship of the temporary to both the agency and the companies she works for engenders social isolation. First, temporaries are isolated from other temporaries employed by the same agency. Temporaries from the same agency rarely know each other unless the assignment happens to require the placement of two individuals at a single location. For example, Katie Hallaway, a 60-year-old White woman, reported attending a "holiday party" for the temporaries given by the agency; the only person she knew was the woman who sent her on assignments.

The only in-person contact most temporaries report with the agency is for the initial application and on subsequent paydays. One woman even reported faxing her time cards and receiving her paycheck through the mail, the only contact with the temporary agency being the initial application. Therefore, temporaries find it difficult to form lasting relationships with agency personnel. In addition, several of the women I interviewed identified turnover in the agencies as problematic for them.

> At the agency, they changed faces too many times. I mean, the only person who was stable there was their marketing person. It's great if they know you, but then the next thing you know every couple months, they change supervisors on you. (Jean Masters)

> The agencies have massive turnover too. And it was amazing because they would jump from agency to agency. You get

somebody different like every 2 months. (Ludy Martinez)

Further complicating the ability to form relationships with the agency is the fact that nearly all of the women I interviewed used multiple agencies to ensure that they would have enough work to pay their bills. Several of them used more than five agencies: "I used, oh I don't know, eight agencies for some reason. You know, sometimes I even took it personal. It's like, is it me? You don't have anything for *me* or you just don't have anything?" (Shari Jensen).

Second, temporary employees are socially isolated from regular employees at the worksite. The transitory nature of temporary work discourages all but the necessary social interaction. Temporary workers felt that their coworkers did not think they were worth getting to know on a personal level.

> That's what can be really hard. Because most people don't really wanna get to know the temps . . . because they figure you're not worth the investment. You're not gonna be there that long. That was probably one of the biggest frustrations. People just don't want to get to know you. (Ludy Martinez)

> You know, as a matter of how much they were interested in knowing about me . . . more often than not, they wouldn't ask any questions. Or they'd be too busy or not interested. (Ellen Lanford)

> I think since they don't see you as being permanent they sort of dismiss you as being expendable, like you're not worth it. I don't know . . . I find that now even as a permanent worker I create a distance between myself and temps, you know. It's like you don't want to get too close to them because you know they're leaving. (Carol Ketchum, 29-year-old White woman)

Temporaries reported being left to do their work while regular employees socialized. One temporary mentioned that other employees would go out for drinks while she stayed at the office and worked. I asked her if she ever got invited along and she responded,

> Well, it's like a small community, everybody has their friends, and to break into that circle of friends is . . . when you're just about ready to break into the circle of friends, they actually invite you out on a Friday night for drinks with everybody else . . . you leave. (Cheryl Hansen)

This particular type of social isolation is not unique to short-term assignments. One temporary relayed the following story about a temporary job where she and others had worked for several months.

> And there was no Christmas present for you under the tree like the rest of the company would get. . . . There were some places where it was just blatant, just terribly blatant. Whenever there was going to be a company party or something, the temps had to stay and work. You know cover the phones so the regular people got to go. You could tell where the second-class citizenship started. (Ludy Martinez)

Third, in cases where the workload is extremely heavy and monotonous, actual physical isolation accompanies and exacerbates social isolation. Often, work takes place in an unobtrusive location where temporaries cannot easily be seen. Arlene Kaplan Daniels (1987) described the different types of "invisible work" that women perform as volunteers or domestic workers. Temporary work, although paid work, is invisible in that it is often undervalued and performed behind the scenes.

The nature of the tasks and the intensity of much of the work, which several women characterized as "grunt work," often resulted in temporaries being relegated to the "back office," out of the sight of visitors and other workers.

> They kind of separated us from the permanent employees. But I didn't care, it was only temporary. (Linda Mejia, 31-year-old Latino woman)

> She was really gung ho about giving me all this grunt work to do, and I spent the entire time back there typing in things

while she was pigging out on Doritos and what not. And I think I was really supposed to be answering the phones all the time, but she ended up doing the phones and I ended up back there typing and stuff. (Irene Pedersen)

> I had this little room to myself. I brought in my walkman and listened to tapes all day. . . . I was very removed. I mean I didn't deal with anyone because I was there for 1 week and I had to report to one person who delegated the work to me. There was no interaction whatsoever. (Sarah Tilton)

Sometimes, temporaries who are hired to do office work are used for more personal services, which more directly resemble women's unpaid work in the home.

> I mean the job that I just left . . . they had temps taking the bosses' cars to car washes. And one temp was going shopping for the boss's Christmas party at his house. (Ludy Martinez)

> People just take advantage of you and they get in that habit. They say, "Let's go out for a drink and have her still work, she's happy." It's kind of like being a housewife I guess. It might start off being appreciated, but then after a while if you keep doing it, it's taken for granted. (Cheryl Hansen)

Finally, the low status of the temporary clerical worker and the gender of the worker engenders nonperson treatment. Even when temporaries are physically visible, they are assigned the role of nonperson, an interactionally invisible role. Goffman (1959, p. 151) described the discrepant role of a nonperson as someone who is present during a performance, and may actually be part of the team, but who is considered "not there" by both the performers and the audience. The role of nonperson is usually reserved for those of low status, such as waiters or children (I would also add women to Goffman's gender-blind approach).

As a nonperson, the temporary employee is treated much like a waiter or a child. This treatment occurs particularly when they are given tasks to perform inconspicuously in conspicuous places. For example, the temporaries I spoke with reported working in well-trafficked hallways, behind the receptionist while she answered phones, at filing cabinets in the way of other employees, and in a conference room while a meeting was proceeding. In all these cases, interaction was kept to a minimum. The temp is interactionally invisible.

> I could tell she'd been temping for years. She knew when to shut up. She knew when to be invisible. She knew when to make herself known. And it was like, yes, she had been a servant in a master's house before. (Ludy Martinez)

> This woman came out of her office and said [about the temporary worker sitting there], "I didn't want *HER!* I told the agency not *HER.* No, send her home." (Bernice Katz, 36-year-old White woman)

> The guy who was in charge of the office was also not very . . . he kind of didn't treat me like I was a person. He was like, well, he didn't treat me like a human being. He was condescending to me. He would tell me, "Oh, type that up," and not talk to me like I was a human with a brain, like I was a machine, and that I was a woman, lower than he was. He didn't talk to me. He never formally talked to me and said, "You're going to be here today and my name is so and so." (Irene Pedersen)

> I don't object to getting coffee for someone, but what I do object to is . . . "Coffee!" [points, snaps fingers]. And I've gotten that. I just thought, "OK if I was the vice president would you have done that?" See what I don't like in this whole thing is that you're really looked on as low class. . . . You're just in another world. (Cheryl Hansen)

Temporary workers are alienated from others because they have no longevity on which to base satisfactory relationships, because they are sometimes physically isolated from other employees, and because their low status in the workplace engenders nonperson treatment.

Alienation From Self

The temporary employee is also alienated from herself through her labor. This type of alienation occurs through emotional labor and identity struggles. Arlie Hochschild (1983) revealed the costs of emotional labor that women perform as flight attendants: "The worker can become estranged or alienated from an aspect of self—either the body or the margins of the soul—that is *used* to do the work" (p. 7). As she further points out, women are overrepresented in jobs that require this type of emotional labor, particularly in the service sector. Temporary clerical employees experience similar demands for emotional labor in their assignments (Henson, in press).

The agency relationship creates a greater need for emotional labor in two ways. First, the temporary worker actually has two jobs: one as a clerical worker at the hiring company and another as a representative of the temporary agency. Temporary workers are highly aware that they are considered representatives of the temporary agency that sent them on the assignment, even though they may work through several other agencies. They are also aware that their job may depend upon their accommodation of the clients.

> You need flexibility . . . and a strong ego. And calm, I mean you're being hired to be calming, not enervating. And that's what a lot of times would be commented on . . . that you're just so calm. (Ellen Lanford)

> I don't usually have a problem with anybody. Usually, I do well with adjusting. She's the type of person that probably needed a 2-month vacation because she was too nervous. You know and because of that you had to either tune her out or you got involved in that same nervous attitude. (Jean Masters)

> I think you need to be first of all, very friendly. And very nice, and very, well you have to be I think very, very easy-going. Because you're not going to stay in one place. Today you're here, the next

day you're . . . you know. You always gotta be nice, I think. (Shari Jensen)

The temporary workers' perceptions accurately reflect what I was told by the temporary agency representatives when I asked what qualities were important for a temporary.

> Friendly, friendly. That always works. Happy, um, helpful. Based on personality if I get a friendly applicant I think has a great personality and they're warm and they're fuzzy and they're friendly. Warm and fuzzy is always a good quality. If they're warm and fuzzy I may choose that over technical ability. If I can tell a client, you know what I've got someone who's hard-working, she's willing to try, she's got a great personality, she'll mesh with the people in the office . . . as opposed to someone who types 102 words a minute and is very stoic and has no personality. I'd rather send the warm and fuzzy that types 40 or 50 words a minute. As long as they can get the job done, I think that works better in the long run. (Sandy Mathers, a 28-year-old African American woman)

Second, temporary workers feel the need to perform emotional labor to secure future assignments. This ranges from putting on a happy face for the agency to tolerating abusive work situations. Temporaries are instructed to maintain a pleasant demeanor in the face of conflict at the work location and to report problems with the assignment to the agency only. For example, temporaries report taking the blame for mistakes they did not make.

> I know my boss has blamed me on this assignment for a lot of things that he's misplaced, that he's screwed up, and he goes, "Well, you see, Sarah didn't get it in on time" or "Sarah lost it." And it's really embarrassing because he asks me in front of people like, "Sarah, where did you put this?" And I know full well that he didn't give it to me. This has happened 3 days in a row now. After awhile you just go, "Well, you know, I'm just really sorry. I guess I just really screwed up." (Sarah Tilton)

They also report taking abusive comments without responding. The following incident occurred when one woman's "boss" could not get the copier to work.

> So I said [in a child's voice], "Oh gosh, do you want me to give it a shot?" And he goes to me, like I am a little girl, "Well, I really don't think you can make it work." So I looked around and pushed the "ON" button. And he threw a fit. He called me a smart this and an f'n that. (Sarah Tilton)

> If they treat you badly on the job . . . I have never figured out what to do. Because I'm afraid if I complain to the agency they'll just pull me off the assignment and then I have to wait for the next one and you never know when that's gonna come. . . . If I complained they'd just think I was a complainer. I knew this was a great account for them. (Cindy Carson, 38-year-old White woman)

Emotional labor is a significant component of temporary work. Temporary workers are required to use emotional labor to gain favor with the agency and to manage difficult situations on the job.

The second way temporary workers are self-alienated arises because of the organization of temporary work as something that is brief and intermittent, and it is also related to the low status of the temporary worker both as a temp and as a woman. Here alienation from self arises from the worker's inability to satisfactorily create a self-definition (Schmitt & Moody, 1994). Aspects of their identity are imposed from the outside, and these often conflict with the worker's ideas about who she is.

The women I interviewed reported consistently that when people did interact with them, they did so on a very superficial level and often resorted to employing negative stereotypes of temps in their interactions.[6] Women's responses to these negative stereotypes repeatedly took the form of identity struggles and identity manipulation.

> You just felt like a moron. And if you weren't thinking like a moron, you weren't going to get the job done. So you have

to train yourself to be a moron, and then you feel like you're becoming a moron. But it's in your best interest to be a moron. (Irene Pedersen)

There were some days when I thought this is ludicrous. I am so miserable. I can't believe I'm however many years old and I am making 9,000 copies of this script or something. I have two master's degrees. (Ellen Lanford)

Another woman volunteered to bring in a computer book for her supervisor, who was having trouble with a complicated software package. The following account reveals frustration with being stereotyped:

He asked why I had this book. I go, "Because it's on my machine at home." His expression was just so, I mean he was really blown away. Did anybody bother to ask me? I mean it's on my resume. People look at me and say you must not really be that capable . . . because I'm a temp. (Sarah Tilton)

Other temporaries report changing their behavior and their dress from assignment to assignment to fit into the image required. One woman who used to work full-time in an insurance office reported that she often had to "dress down." So rather than wear her suits from her previous job, she went to Kmart and bought what she felt were unobtrusive and nonthreatening clothes.

That temps must manipulate their identity became evident throughout the interviews. When asked what qualities were important in a temp, Cheryl Hansen summarized:

I think you have to have a pretty strong personality so that you can be *adaptable* and you really have to be *political*. I mean you have to be very *pliable* so that you can just automatically just *mold* to any situation. It just sort of demands that you *blend* in.

Another form of identity struggle concerns the substitution of "the temp" for one's name. I found that not only do employers call temporaries "the temp" or "the temporary," but women frequently report

self-naming as "the temp." One woman even used a different name in her temporary assignments so that she could be remembered. Although her name was not unusual, she found that it helped to provide people with a simple way to remember her name, even if it wasn't her real name: "All you do is introduce yourself as 'Jill, as in Jack and . . . ' and people never forget. So that's the name I use when I'm temping." (Sarah Tilton).

Women report changing their voices, their names, their personalities, and even their histories on a regular basis. In fact, temporary agencies encourage identity manipulation by telling temporaries how to dress, how to act, and how to "sell" themselves to the client.

She would really go so far as to tell us, "On this job, please do not smoke, or please do not wear those kinds of clothes, because these are not those kinds of people. So if that makes a difference to you, if you have to dress like that, then don't take this assignment please." (Ludy Martinez)

Before each assignment they give you instructions on how to dress for that company, whether it's very conservative and wear a suit or casual, wear nice slacks and a blouse or whatever. (Bernice Katz)

One woman with a college education reported denying anything more than a high school diploma in order to feel like she could get along in her assignments. She quickly learned to keep her education and aspirations "under wraps," as she put it.

If I told them, people would look at me like I had an attitude. And if I ever expressed a desire to go on to something else, they sort of squashed you down. So I keep that under wraps. (Cheryl Hansen)

They saw my resume, which has two master's degrees, and they said take all that stuff out. That's going to scare people. You're never going to get work that way. Just put the secretarial experience you have down. So that's what I did. I rewrote my resume for them because they felt they could pitch me better. (Ellen Lanford)

Thus temporaries tend to keep their "other" self out of the workplace. Just as "a grocer who dreams is offensive to the buyer because such a grocer is not wholly a grocer" (Sartre, 1966, p. 102), the temp must be wholly a temp or she is offensive.

Resistance to Alienation

Although temporaries regularly experienced alienation from work, from others, and from themselves, they actively resisted alienation in a variety of ways. As used here, the concept of resistance encompasses a broad range of strategies, going beyond worker organization (Ward, 1990) to include more subtle forms such as reminding oneself that "It's only temporary" as well as more overt forms such as leaving an assignment and even sabotage. It is also important to recognize that resistance often occurs in a context of constraint that shapes what modes of resistance are employed. Resistance can be more or less effective and can even bring contradictory results, such as reproducing stereotypes about temporary workers. However, the fact remains that temporary workers do not merely experience alienation, they actively resist it.

Resistance to Alienation From Work

Some temporaries employed strategies to minimize or resist alienation. In the case of monotonous work, they reported shifting their interest from the tasks that they were performing to the objects on which they performed the task or to other aspects of the work environment. In the Los Angeles entertainment industry, temps have an advantage in this aspect. One temporary worker who was filing studio memorabilia for 4 months found a lot of interest in the old pictures and scripts that she was filing.

We were handling a lot of neat things, like original scripts and stills and things

from some of these television shows like *Dr. Kildare, I Spy, I Spy* with Bill Cosby. Oh, *Get Smart, Get Smart*. We were handling the original scripts and that was pretty exciting. (Bernice Katz)

Another temporary described her favorite assignment as one in which the monotony was broken by watching celebrities come in and out of the offices at her worksite.

Yeah, I still think that the movie company comes to mind. 'Cause I found it intriguing and interesting and I had never been exposed to anything in the entertainment business. And I ran into Marilou Henner one day. That was good. (Carol Ketchum)

Even in nonentertainment companies, temporaries find some interest in their work to alleviate the monotony. For example, one woman who was doing transcriptions found interest in the content of the material she was transcribing.

It's like piecework. That's when I would make a game of it. You know it's like sewing machine work. You sit there and you do it. You get paid by the hour. You take a break. You have to be able to do spelling. And you can get kind of interested in some of what you're doing. I was doing these transcriptions of death row inmates. And I was sitting there saying "Oh my God!" Same thing with personal injury cases. But then the other stuff could be just incredibly dull. You just sort of get through. (Ludy Martinez)

In cases of too little work, temporaries found their greatest latitude for resistance. Although they could not control the flow of work coming to them because temporaries (especially on the shorter-term assignments) typically do not possess enough organizationally specific knowledge to seek additional work tasks, they could surreptitiously control the use of their time at the worksite. So rather than sitting and staring at the wall, some temporaries "cruised," slept, or did other work.

I realized that I tended to be real fast, and rather than slow myself down and socialize, I could work real fast and take a lot of breaks. I call it cruising. (Carol Ketchum)

Very bored! I'm telling you . . . I used to sleep there. Yes there's nothing to do. I always bring my book. When I get sick and tired of reading, I sleep. And I wake up and take the phone calls. Sometimes, OK, you're not supposed to make phone calls, but what am I gonna do with 8 hours? OK, you can only read so much. After that, you sleep. You're going to wake up because it's not in your bed. OK. And then after that, you make some calls. (Shari Jensen)

There were times when somebody, another office worker, would say listen you really can't be reading. And so I'd put my book away and I wouldn't read and I would just do whatever. Sometimes I would play computer games if I felt I could get away with it. Depending on how much supervision I had, if I felt comfortable working on my own stuff. I just can't sit and not do anything. And oftentimes I would hide what I was doing under something associated with work. But I also felt responsible to the temp agency. . . . I didn't want anybody complaining about me back to the temp agency. (Ellen Lanford)

Although the work was alienating, the temporaries I interviewed strategized to find interest in or have control over their work. In cases where temporaries had too little work, their resistance might be misinterpreted to reinforce stereotypes of temporaries as "flaky" or lazy. However, when viewed from the temporary's perspective and in the context of the organization of temporary work, these actions represent temporary workers' resistance to otherwise alienating forms of labor.

Resistance to Alienation From Others

One way temporaries resist social isolation is by taking longer-term assignments when available. Temporaries felt that at least part of their isolation came from the transitory nature of temporary work. Seeking out less transitory assignments

(i.e., a duration of several months) was one effective way to combat social isolation. However, as mentioned earlier, a long assignment does not guarantee social integration.

Basically when you work long-term assignments, after a while everything gets to be yours so to speak. You know where you're going every day. You know, maybe you're working through the agency, but you're going through one agency so that's all you have to deal with. (Jean Masters)

A second way I found that temporaries resisted social isolation was through restricting their work to one or two agencies. Although turnover in the agencies, or lack of available assignments, can limit the effectiveness of this strategy, one woman got around the problem by following her representative to a new agency. In addition, temporaries often work very hard at maintaining relationships with agency personnel. For example, frequent phone calls and "check-ins" help the agency get to know a temporary. This relationship work, a type of emotional labor, often serves an economic purpose as well, because some temporaries feel that an agency is more likely to give them more work if they know them better.

I do think that being known to them helps. I mean there are temps who sign up with an agency and never call them again . . . it doesn't work that way. You've got to be a presence. When I went out of town I sent them postcards and I was a presence, even when I'm not there. It helped. The people they know, the people who show the real desire to work, are the ones who get the jobs. (Bernice Katz)

Temporaries resisted nonperson treatment in two ways. The first was to remind oneself that "it's only temporary" and that one should not take things personally. Here's what Ellen Lanford did when someone treated her poorly.

I would just shut down and I would do the work and I would be in my own space in my head. I'd be writing my own story in my head. Because when someone treats me badly I know that they've got their own problems. . . . I mean I'm a temp, I have nothing to do with any of their problems, and so I don't let that stuff bother me.

In fact, Ellen is able to use her status as a temporary to reject internalizing any poor treatment that does occur. However, not all temporaries frame their experiences in this way. Each assignment may be temporary; however, for the worker, temporary work may be not-so-temporary and may go on long after a particular assignment has ended.

Others resist nonperson treatment more directly through office sabotage. Carol Ketchum felt that she was not considered for a permanent job opening because she was a temp, even though she had already been doing the job for a month: "I wondered . . . if they didn't like me or whatever. So I got back at them, this is an entertainment company, by stealing one of their screenplays. I showed them" [laughs].

On several occasions, Bernice Katz had an assignment end abruptly and was not informed by either the agency or the client so that she could seek additional work elsewhere. Bernice was resentful of the way she was treated and told me what she did.

> I had a little revenge with it too because they had these cabinets that you locked, and I had the key, you know. While I was there another employee had given it to me. And in it I stored things, my coffee cup, a couple of work tools. So I locked it and there I had the key with me. So they had to break their cabinet open. I was not gonna go all the way back there just to give them their key back. They had made such a big deal about don't lose the key, I guess they had to break it. Which is fine with me.

Once again, temporaries' resistance offers contradictions. The relationship work that temporaries use to combat social isolation is a form of emotional labor that engenders alienation from self. There is also the possibility that more overt acts of resistance, such as stealing a screenplay, can be used to justify both the marginal position of temporary workers and even greater social control of temporaries via the agency. For that reason, I was concerned that portraying some acts of resistance would reveal temporaries' "secrets." However, I emphasize again that all acts of resistance must be placed in the context of women's struggles to survive and derive a sense of control over otherwise alienating work.

Resistance to Alienation From Self

Temporaries resist emotional labor through seeking out assignments that are less likely to require emotional labor. "Back office" jobs such as filing are less likely to require emotional labor on the job than "front office" jobs such as executive secretary or receptionist. For example, Shari preferred filing jobs to receptionist jobs because filing jobs can often be done with minimal contact or supervision. After telling me about a bad experience with a supervisor, Shari Jensen told me that she came to prefer filing assignments because everyone left her alone to do her own work: "I like computer filing. That was my favorite because, you know, nobody told me what to do. I used to start there at 7 a.m. Nobody bothers you."

Temporaries also resist emotional labor by leaving an agency or an assignment. Although this option is not often used and is dependent upon the worker's financial circumstances, it does often represent an effective immediate strategy. Temporaries may actually walk out of an assignment, but it is more likely that they will just tell the agency that they are not available for further assignments. Here again, the worker can invoke her status as temporary to her advantage. In areas with an abundance of temporary agencies, this may represent a more effective strategy than in areas where temporary agencies are few, because the worker has more agencies available to her.

Another way temporaries resist alienation from self is by reminding themselves that they are not "just a temp." Interestingly this is the opposite of the strategy of claiming "just a temp" or "it's only temporary" in order to get by.

> It's important to keep in mind why you're doing it, because if you're treated badly you can have something to hold onto and keep your self-esteem up. Try to be assertive if you're called "the temp" or if you're picked on. Try to be clear about what your skills are and keep your long-term goals in mind. (Carol Ketchum)

> I was happy to redefine in my mind that I was only there temporarily, and to let everyone know that I was only there temporarily . . . and let everyone know that that wasn't my life. (Irene Pedersen)

This response works most easily for temps who have something "going on the side," but it can work in other cases as well. Temporaries may do this by using skills that coworkers were not aware that they possessed as a way of setting themselves apart from "just temps." For example, both Linda Mejia and Ludy Martinez surprised coworkers and supervisors with their ability to speak two or more languages. Cheryl Hansen and Jean Masters showed they were capable of using complicated computer software from previous job experience and education. As a result, each of these women was given additional job duties that made her feel better about her work and herself. It is a way to reject the negative stereotypes about temporary workers. The women I interviewed often reported that they were not like the "bad temps" we all hear stories about. In fact, they often told me that employers or agencies told them "bad temp" stories as well.

> The agencies don't really like it when you flake out that way and don't show up. They told me about these people. In fact, when I first signed up, they warned me about this kind of thing. And I'm there, like, "No, people really do that?" They're like, "Yeah." They've had people just flake out. They didn't feel like going to work that day, or had an audition that day. (Bernice Katz)

> I think they expected a less competent person. I think they expected someone who wasn't . . . they definitely expected a less competent person from a temp agency. I think that's the stereotype. (Sarah Tilton)

> Nothing surprises me in this industry any longer. Applicants when they don't show, when they have excuses. And then we're dealing with people and human nature. And you would think that these are responsible adults we're hiring, but not all the time. . . . They don't show up, they're 2 hours late, they leave for lunch and don't come back. (Sandy Mathers)

Temporaries who compare themselves favorably with "bad temps" are successful in resisting internalizing the negative identity themselves; however, this does leave the broader stereotypes intact. They are, in effect, stereotyping other temps. Although this may not be in their best interest in the long run, it reaffirms their sense of self today, even if they receive neither additional compensation nor permanent employment from the use of these special skills. In addition, the "bad temp" stories coming from the agency or the client seem to operate as a mechanism of social control, reinforcing temporaries' marginality. It serves as a warning and conveys expectations about what is deviant.

Constraints on Resistance

Even though temporary workers found room for resistance at the worksite, this resistance occurs within a context of constraint. The constraint on resistance is largely due to temporary workers' marginal position in the workforce. Temporary workers' relationships with the agencies is one of dependence. Temporaries feel they must please the agency in order to continue to receive assignments. This often means tempering or forgoing one's resistance to alienation. Bernice was asked to take an assignment at a company where she had previously had a bad experience.

Oh, I said, put it this way. If they really needed someone and I didn't have a job that day. . . . I mean it's a job for the day. But it's not my first choice. . . . So I did it and they were pleased with me. (Bernice Katz)

Once Ludy complained about being overworked on an assignment. She told me about the agency's response.

It was just you know, they said, "If you're not *happy* on that assignment, well we'll take you off and put somebody else on." And if I couldn't afford it, then I'd just stay there. But I noticed that most agencies, even when they knew I was being taken advantage of, they wouldn't go to bat for you. . . . They very often wimped out. They wanted to keep the accounts or whatever, "Just accommodate them." What does that mean, "accommodate them"? (Ludy Martinez)

Cindy Carson was angry when the paychecks were delayed, and "stomped" out of the office when she learned she could not get her check until the next day: "And I stomped out of the office. And I thought, 'OK, I guess when this assignment ends that'll be the end of me.' I figured I'd be canned or something just for expressing myself. I'm not sure."

Indeed, temporary employees' perceptions of their position vis-à-vis the temporary agency are confirmed by my interviews with temporary agency personnel. Both agency representatives expressed an unwillingness to continue relationships with temporaries they considered "flaky" or bothersome. Joe Harcum, a branch manager, said he is less likely to place someone who "won't work with him." Similarly, Sandy Mathers told what happened when a temp does something that displeases the agency or the client: "You don't get too many opportunities to do that. One strike. I give just one strike. After the first one, that's it for me."

For some temporary workers, dependence appeared to be less of a factor. They actually felt empowered to resist, stating that they could leave their agency and use other agencies instead. Indeed, at least in Los Angeles, the proliferation of agencies seems to offer some chance for temporaries to break the dependency relationship. "And I said if she ever screamed at me, I'm out of there. And she did it once. And that's when I thought, I mean you don't pay me enough. . . . I'm not permanent. So I left." (Linda Mejia)

However, these measures are tempered by the financial constraints each temporary faces individually. One temporary worker summarized:

In a way you have to be better than the regular people. You have to behave better. You have to be more on time. You have to not take personal calls. You have to be more straight and narrow because you're a temp. They can dump you tomorrow. . . . I've seen other secretaries sitting and knitting on the phone. If you could figure out how much these people can get away with that might be acceptable for you. Usually it wasn't because they'd get back to the agency and that could jeopardize your getting an assignment when you really needed it or something like that. (Ludy Martinez)

Shari Jensen told me what happened after a particularly bad work experience. Although Shari supports herself, she shares an apartment with her mother and sister who also work. Breaking the relationship with one temporary agency did not pose a great financial threat to her, even though she consequently went several weeks without finding work.

I called the agency and told them what happened. So what, you're not gonna give me another assignment. Am I gonna die? No, I'm not gonna die. I will survive. So and after that, they never gave me another assignment. I don't care. I knew they were gonna do that but I don't care.

In addition, leaving one agency means greater reliance on other agencies (since many temporary workers use more than one) or cultivating relationships with new temporary agencies. Jean Masters initially fought a pay decrease, but eventually ended up taking the cut and going to a different agency.

> I went from $17 to $12. It was too hard to get a job that was even $13 an hour then. And then they wanted to cut me down from that to $11. Think I was getting like $12. Know whatever it was that I fought it. In those cases with unemployment, if someone called you for an assignment you had to have a really good reason not to accept that assignment, otherwise unemployment will cut you off. So basically you had to accept the job. But when they wanted to go to that second pay cut, I fought it. You know, because if I accepted it, that means I'd have to accept jobs from now on at that pay scale.

Even though temporary workers manage to resist alienation from work in a variety of ways, this resistance occurs within a context of constraint that includes the availability of work at other agencies and the temporary worker's financial situation. Although resistance occurs in a variety of ways, it is more likely to occur surreptitiously than overtly. Modes of resistance are shaped by the organization of temporary work and can have contradictory and unintended results. Nevertheless, temporary work should be described as a struggle rather than an exchange.

Conclusion

These experiences, related by the women I interviewed, increase the understanding of the everyday experiences and struggles of temporary clerical employment. This research adds another dimension to labor studies that focus on the economic and legal issues of temporary employment. The comments of the women I interviewed demonstrate an astute understanding of the ways in which temporary workers are alienated, not only from their work, but from themselves and others. My analysis, along with the voices of the workers, poses a challenge to managerial analyses by asking, "What are the human costs of flexibil-ity and who bears those costs?" Unfortunately, the answer is that the temporary worker bears the costs in the form of alienation from work, alienation from others, and alienation from self.

Examining the organization of temporary work in conjunction with these experiences provides understanding of the structural basis for this alienation. This structural basis is found not only in the capitalist work relations from which temporary work arises, but also in women's often marginal position in the labor market. Despite overwhelming constraints, women do resist alienation in its various forms, with results that range from favorable to contradictory. It is clear that temporary work should be characterized in more conflictual than consensual terms.

The implications of the alienating effects of temporary employment for the organization of work in the United States should not be understated, especially considering the demographic composition of this group of workers. Recall that groups that are already marginalized in this society, such as women and African Americans, are overrepresented in the temporary workforce. Temporary work as it is now organized serves to reproduce and reinforce marginality. With nearly one third of the U.S. workforce (Belous, 1989) employed in work characterized as contingent, these implications are serious.

Finally, as management consultants continue to espouse the benefits of temporary employment for business, even in times of economic recovery, the phenomenon of temporary employment is expected to grow. As temporary employment of all kinds grows, so does the number of us who will be incorporated into working arrangements similar to those analyzed in this study. We must ask ourselves if this is a wave of the future that we want to ride.

Discussion Questions

1. Analyze the position of the temporary worker using Marx's discussion of alienation in Chapter 4.

2. Are there other jobs that are like temp work, even though they are not called that?

3. Can you think of reasons why someone would want to be a temp worker?

4. Have you had any direct or indirect experience with temporary workers?

Endnotes

1. Unfortunately, the available data do not include adequate racial/ethnic breakdowns. The figures here only indicate percentages for White and Black workers.

2. Keep in mind that the agencies that compose the National Association of Temporary Services largely focus on temporary clerical work, where the proportion of women is considerably higher than in temporary industrial work. Belous's (1989) figures include all temporary workers.

3. Recall the 1994 Teamsters strike, in which the increasing use of contingent workers was one of the main issues. Currently, union leaders seem to oppose contingent work (House Committee on Government Operations, 1988) because it threatens what remaining power unions do have in the United States.

4. Of the women interviewed, five were not currently working as temporaries when I interviewed them; however, they had worked as a temporary in me past 2 years. Having the input of both current and previous temporary workers decreases the likelihood that my data are unbalanced in favor of those who are staying with temporary work for one reason or another. It is also quite common for people to move in and out of temporary work over a period of time; therefore, these interviews help capture that experience as well.

5. I have worked on and off as a temporary employee in the Los Angeles area over the past 3 years. My interest in temporary work came before my employment as a temporary worker. My experience as a temporary worker has helped me to formulate effective questions, to gain access to interview subjects, and to have better rapport with my interview subjects.

6. There have been several excellent examples of the stereotypes associated with temporary employees that have appeared on television or in films. For example, in a recent episode of NBC's new drama series, *ER*, a temporary employee sat filing her nails while chaos ensued all around her. She then interrupted emergency surgery to have her time card signed. Most of the stereotypes the women I interviewed encountered portrayed temporaries as incompetent and unintelligent.

References

Acker, J. (1990, June). Hierarchies, jobs, bodies: A theory of gendered organizations. *Gender and Society*, 4, 139–158.

———. (1992). The future of women and work: Ending the twentieth century. *Sociological Perspectives*, 35(1), 53–68.

Amott, T., & Matthaei, J. (1991). *Race, gender, and work: A multicultural economic history of women in the United States*. Boston: South End Press.

Beechey, V., & Perkins, T. (1987). *A matter of hours: Part-time work and the labor market*. Minneapolis: University of Minnesota Press.

Belous, R. (1989). *The contingent economy: The growth of the temporary, part-time and subcontracted workforce*. Washington, DC: National Planning Association.

Bookman, A., & Morgan, S. (1988). *Women and the politics of empowerment*. Philadelphia: Temple University Press.

Braverman, H. (1974). *Labor and monopoly capital: The degradation of work in the twentieth century*. New York: Monthly Review Press.

Callaghan, P., & Hartmann, H. (1991). *Contingent work*. Washington, DC: Economic Policy Institute.

Castro, J. (1993, March 29). Disposable workers. *Time* Magazine, pp. 43–47.

Cockburn, C. (1985). *Machinery of dominance: Women, men, and technical know-how*. Boston: Northeastern University Press.

Daniels, A. K. (1987). Invisible work. *Social Problems*, 54(5), 403–415.

Glaser, B., & Strauss, A. (1967). *The discovery of grounded theory*. Chicago: Aldine.

Goffman, E. (1959). *The presentation of self in everyday life*. New York: Doubleday.

Golden, L., & Appelbaum, E. (1992). What was driving the 1982–88 boom in temporary employment—Preferences of workers or decisions and power of employers? *American Journal of Economics and Society*, 51(4), 473–494.

Henson, K. D. (in press). *Just a temp: The disenfranchised worker*. Philadelphia: Temple University Press.

Hochschild, A. R. (1983). *The managed heart: Commercialization of human feeling*. Berkeley: University of California Press.

House Committee on Government Operations, 100th Congress. (1988). *Rising use of part-time and temporary workers: Who benefits & who loses?* Washington, DC: Government Printing Office.

Israel, J. (1971). *Alienation from Marx to modern sociology*. Boston: Allyn & Bacon.

Kohn, M., & Schooler, C. (1983). *Work and personality: An inquiry into the impact of social stratification.* Norwood, NJ: Ablex.

McLellan, D. (1977). *Karl Marx: Selected writings.* New York: Oxford University Press.

Milkman, R. (1987). *Gender at work: The dynamics of job segregation by sex during World War II.* Chicago: University of Illinois Press.

Morrow, L. (1993, March 29). The temping of America. *Time* Magazine, pp. 40–41.

National Association of Temporary Services. (1992). *Report on the temporary help services industry.* New York: DRI/McGraw Hill.

Negrey, C. (1993). *Gender, time, and reduced work.* Albany: State University of New York Press.

Ong, A. (1987). *Spirits of resistance and capitalist discipline: Factory women in Malaysia.* Albany: State University of New York Press.

Parker, R. E. (1994). *Flesh peddlers and warm bodies: The temporary help industry and its workers.* New Brunswick, NJ: Rutgers University Press.

Polivka, A., & Nardone, T. (1989, December). On the definition of contingent work. *Monthly Labor Review,* pp. 9–16.

Reskin, B., & Roos, P. (1990). *Job queues, gender queues.* Philadelphia: Temple University Press.

Rizzo, J., House, R. J., & Lirtzman, S. I. (1970). Role conflict and ambiguity in complex organizations. *Administrative Science Quarterly,* 15, 150–163.

Sartre, J.-P. (1966). *Being and nothingness.* New York: Washington Square Press.

Schmitt, R., & Moody, T. E. (1994). *Alienation and social criticism.* Atlantic Highlands, NJ: Humanities Press.

Seeman, M. (1959). On the meaning of alienation. *American Sociological Review,* 26, 753–758.

Senate Committee on Labor and Human Resources, 103rd Congress. (1993). *Toward a disposable workforce: The increasing use of "contingent labor."* Washington, DC: Government Printing Office.

Smith, V. (1993). Flexibility in work and employment: The impact on women. In *Research in the sociology of organizations* (pp. 195–216). Greenwich, CT: JAI Press.

Sokoloff, N. (1992). *Black women and White women in the professions.* New York: Routledge.

Strauss, A. L. (1987). *Qualitative analysis for social scientists.* New York: Cambridge University Press.

Tilly, C. (1990). *Short hours, short shrift.* Washington, DC: Economic Policy Institute.

Ward, K. (1990). *Women workers and global restructuring.* Ithaca, NY: BLR Press.

West, J. (1990). Gender and the labor process. In D. Knights & H. Willmott (Eds.), *Labor process theory* (pp. 244–273). London: Macmillan. ✦

Part III

The Changing Face of Work

Part III is composed of four sections, each analyzing changes in a particular category of work. The first section concerns changes in general labor force participation and promotion opportunities for white and black women and black men in comparison with white men. The second section considers changes in three professional-level occupations, ranging from the male-dominated field of law to the female-dominated field of nursing. The third section three focuses on the experiences of workers on the factory floor, including the efforts by management to introduce work teams to enhance performance. The fourth section focuses on the growing area of service work.

Section A.
Income and Opportunities

As noted in previous chapters, the new economy is characterized in part by a loss of production plants in the United States, growth of jobs overseas, and growth of low-wage jobs in the service sector at home. It is largely these service jobs that show a demand for women and minority workers. Once in the labor force, however, these workers experience inequality in income and promotion opportunities.

Race and gender differences (in comparison to white men) result in part from which workers are being compared. When all workers are the basis for analysis, the race and gender differences, or gaps, according to Richard Hogan and Caroyln Perrucci, are maximized. This is because the comparison is between workers who are more likely to work part-time (e.g., women) with those who are more likely to work full-time (men). When only full-time, year-round workers are the basis for race and gender analysis, the differences decrease.

A frequently used explanation for race and gender differences in income and promotion is called the *human capital approach*. Here the focus is on the extent to which a worker has invested in himself/herself through formal education and on-the-job experience that builds skills and knowledge. Chris Tilly and Charles Tilly critique this approach and offer an alternative approach in which they take into account factors such as workers' preferences, networks, bargaining, and inertia.

The chapter by Philip Moss and Chris Tilly concerns racial differences in obtaining an entry-level job in an urban area. Interview data indicate that employers tend to believe that young black urban men lack relevant skills related to interaction with customers.

In the final chapter in this section, David Maume takes a different, structural approach to account for race and gender differences in promotion into managerial responsibilities. Specifically, he examines and documents the effects of the relative concentration of women and minorities in their first jobs on their subsequent promotions.

Section B. Professional Work

In the study of work and occupations, occupations are conceptualized as being more or less professionally based on a commonly agreed-upon set of criteria. These criteria include having a systematic body of theory behind skills; having the sanction of the professional community through education, training, licensing, and certification; having a code of ethics to define appropriate and inappropriate behavior for those in the profession; and having a professional culture of language, symbols, and norms of their own, plus a lifetime commitment to the work. In this section, we consider three professions—law, technical professions, and nursing—and the ways in which each is changing in the new economy.

In the first chapter, Jerry Van Hoy presents findings from a case study of a time-honored profession—the law. He maintains that there has been a "McDonaldization" of an important segment of the law, which he calls franchise law. In franchise law firms, attorneys work under tight centralized control in the provision of standardized services. They also work for relatively low salaries because of the glut of lawyers on the market.

Second, Stephen Barley and Gideon Kunda present an ethnography of another occupation near the top of the occupational hierarchy, college-educated technical professionals. As we have seen, prior to the 1980s, such professionals could expect long-term employment security, with a good salary and fringe benefits such as health insurance and a pension, in exchange for which they would work hard and be loyal to their employer. Due to downsizing and outsourcing, however,

these workers now are contingent workers, employed as "itinerant experts" moving from firm to firm for short-term contract work, which carries no benefits.

The third chapter, by Robert Brannon, traces changes in the health-care industry in recent decades of cost containment by focusing on unsuccessful attempts by the leaders of the nursing occupation to further professionalize. Having shifted the credentialing of nurses from hospital training programs to two-year college degree programs in the 1970s and 1980s, nursing educators and administrators promoted a change on hospital wards from "team nursing," in which there was a hierarchy of personnel consisting of registered nurses, licensed practical nurses, and nurse's aides, to a displacement of many of the auxiliaries, largely black women, and reunification of nursing tasks under the responsibility of the RNs.

Section C. Life on the Factory Floor

Although the proportion of the labor force employed in manufacturing has declined in the new economy, it is still the workplace for almost 20 million machine operators, assemblers, and inspectors. Manufacturing is a high-risk work setting, exposing workers to conditions that affect their health and safety. Each year, thousands of workers die in industrial accidents, and tens of thousands experience work-related illnesses and disability. In the new economy, manufacturing employment has become risky because of greater job insecurity, little wage growth, and declining worker benefits such as health insurance and pensions.

The first chapter in this section looks at one of the new ways of organizing work in the new economy, requiring greater participation of employees in work teams. Steven Vallas reports on the difficulties associated with an effort to introduce new work arrangements in four manufacturing plants.

The second chapter, by Laurie Graham, describes her experiences working in a Japanese automobile plant in the United States, focusing specifically on new management efforts to improve worker productivity and quality. The final chapter, by Richard Pfeffer, describes his first two weeks in a factory job. It provides interesting raw material for considering questions raised in the two previous chapters about teamwork and worker commitment.

Section D. Service Work

In the history of the United States, the economy has changed from agrarian to industrial to service based. Service work, defined as work that "does not produce either a tangible durable product or foodstuffs" (Gutek, Cherry, and Groth 1999), is a broad category ranging from law, which was discussed above as a profession; to the women's professions of nursing, elementary-school teaching, librarianship, and social work; to fast food and retail operations.

In the first chapter in this section, the authors analyze research on service delivery, organizing their review around the service provider, the customer, and the physical and social environment in which they interact. In doing so, they note that a higher proportion of women than men work in service jobs, and that women are also the primary consumers of services. Most research, however, fails to focus on either the gender of the provider or the customer.

The chapters by Robin Leidner and Barbara Ehrenreich present case studies of the work of two frontline service providers, one a counter clerk in a fast food establishment (McDonald's) and the other an "associate" in a large retail establishment (Wal-Mart). In McDonald's, most of the work is low-paid, low status, and part-time, giving workers little autonomy, unpredictable hours of work, and no fringe benefits. Workers conform to the McDonald's way because of socialization into company norms, very close supervision, individual and group incentives, peer pressure, and pressure from customers. Work as an associate at Wal-Mart is also low-paid and low status and, although full-time, too low paid for a single individual to live on for very long. ✦

17

Gender, Race, and Income Gaps

Richard Hogan and
Carolyn Perrucci

This chapter notes the marked increase in the labor force participation of women in the new economy and addresses the lack of scholars' agreement on several key issues regarding the relative income of whites, blacks, men, and women. Is there a race or gender difference (gap) in income? How big is it? Is it getting larger or smaller? Why? The authors provide a basis for understanding the size and relative stability of race and gender gaps in income over time.

Boraas and Rodgers (2003:9) report that "women earned approximately 77 percent as much as men did in 1999." This sounds about right. Scholars and journalists have been throwing around comparable figures, suggesting that the gender gap has declined of late, from around 72 to around 77 percent of male earnings. Slowly but surely women are narrowing the gap. In contrast, the racial gap is, according to some (Cancio et. al. 1996; Hogan and Perrucci 1998), increasing or, at least, no longer declining (following some initial progress right after the equal opportunity legislation of 1964).

Consequently, it appears that women are closing the gender gap while the racial gap remains. The fact that white women, in general, are now earning more than black men indicates the extent to which a combination of gender progress and racial stagnation characterize the postmodern era (roughly 1972 to the present).

We are skeptical. We do not deny that women, both white and black, have made some progress in narrowing the earnings gaps that separate them from the lofty heights of white male earnings, but we think that the magnitude of the change has been exaggerated. Similarly, we recognize the difference between racial and gender inequality and the fact that some white females have (in 2004) overtaken some black males in their progress toward narrowing the earnings gaps. Much of the apparent progress, however, is due to the fact that women, particularly middle class white women, have increased their labor force participation over the last three decades. That, combined with the fact that women were so far behind to begin with, explains much of the apparent progress. At the same time, however, two stubborn facts remain. First, black women continue to be the truly disadvantaged, suffering the disadvantages of race and gender. Second, the progress of white women, in particular, is largely due to the declining value of real wages in the postindustrial or postmodern era. It is not that women are doing so well but that men are faring so poorly, as only the rich get richer while the middle class continues to decline.

Before turning to problems and possibilities for the future, however, we must first clearly define what we mean by the race and gender gap and estimate, as best as we can, the current state of gender and racial inequality. Then we can turn to trends in the last three decades before returning to a critical analysis of the situation we are in and the prospects for the future.

The Size of the Race and Gender Gaps: What Is Being Compared?

The size of the race and gender income gaps varies dramatically depending on which populations are compared and

Table 17.1

Median and Mean Income in 2004 for Men and Women, Fifteen Years or Older, Who Worked Full Time, Year Round and Reported Income (with female proportion of male income in parenthesis)

Men		Women	
Median	Mean	Median	Mean
$41,667	$56,475	$32,101 (.77)	$39,930 (.71)
N=60,095		N=42,333	

Source: U.S. Census Bureau, Current Population Survey, 2005 Annual Social and Economic Supplement: <http://pubdb3.census.gov/macro/032005/perinc/new01_037.htm> (males); <http://pubdb3.census.gov/macro/032005/perinc/new01_046.htm> (females).

Table 17.2

Median and Mean Income in 2004 for Full-time, Year-Round Non-Hispanic White and Black, Male and Female Workers Reporting Income (with proportion of white male income in parenthesis)

	White Male	White Female	Black Male	Black Female
Median	$46,986	$34,878 (.74)	$31,732 (.68)	$29,145 (.62)
Mean	$62,755	$42,504 (.68)	$40,078 (.64)	$33,831 (.54)
N	41,977	29,121	5,681	5,960

Source: U.S. Census Bureau, Current Population Survey, 2005 Annual Social and Economic Supplement: <http://pubdb3.census.gov/macro/032005/perinc/new01_040.htm> (white male), <http://pubdb3.census.gov/macro/032005/perinc/new01_049.htm> (white female), <http://pubdb3.census.gov/macro/032005/perinc/new01_042.htm> (black male), and <http://pubdb3.census.gov/macro/032005/perinc/new01_051.htm> (black female).

which measures of income are used. The Current Population Survey (CPS) data for 2005, which is based on a national sample of households, indicates that the median (midpoint) income for women age fifteen and over who were working full-time, year-round (fifty weeks or more) was 77% of comparable male income (U.S. Census 2005a). Thus, we might consider 77% to represent the overall gender income gap, which means that women earn $0.77 for every $1.00 a man earns.

As seen in Table 17.1, however, when we compare average (mean) wealth, women report only 71% of male income. The gender gap increases due to the effect of "positive outliers"—men who earn far more than average, even among men. These high earning males increase average income to over $56,000 (compared to median wealth of less than $42,000). The fact that there are fewer extremely well paid workers among the women (see Hogan, Perrucci, and Behringer forthcoming) is indicated by the relatively modest increase in mean ($39,930) versus median ($32,101) female income. Since the lack of super-high earners is characteristic of what has been termed the "glass ceiling" (Allessio and Andrzejewshi 2000), we feel that 71% (based on mean differences) is a more valid measure of the gender gap, because it takes into account both the general distribution of income and the extreme values of that distribution (the "positive outliers").

We are, however, still not satisfied, because this figure combines white and black males, whose incomes are quite divergent, and white and black females, whose incomes are much closer, thereby offering a very low estimate of the gender gap. Using the same CPS figures to compare women and blacks to white men, one sees, in Table 17.2, that white women report only 74% of median and 68% of mean white male income. Black men report a race gap of 68% (median) and 64% (mean), while black women report 62% and 54% (respectively). Thus, the gender gap, the percentage of average white male income reported by white females, is 68%. The comparable racial gap is 64%, but the compounded racial and gender gap (54% for black women) is substantially greater.

This estimate of the race and gender income gap is still conservative, however, since it ignores the extent to which blacks and females have irregular employment histories. When one compares full-time, year-round workers, this yields a biased estimate of racial and gender gaps, because it does not take into account the fact that white males, black males, white females, and black females have different rates of labor force participation as full-time, year-round workers. If one includes all workers, one incorporates the fact that black men and women and, particularly, white women are less likely to have stable employment careers.

Table 17.3 reports mean income for all workers, including part-time or seasonal workers. Here the gender gap (for white females) is 55% (for median and mean income). The racial gap (for black males) is somewhat smaller: 64% (or 68% of median white male income), due to the higher rate of black men employed in full-time, year-round work. The compound race and gender gap (for black females) is 48% (or 52% of median white male income). On balance, including part-time or seasonal workers increases the gender gap by thirteen points (.68 in Table 17.2 versus .55 in Table 17.3; the difference is .74 versus .55 or 19 points for median income). This has no effect on the racial gap (for black males), but increases the compound gap (for black women) by six points (ten points for median income).

Contrary to the initial claim that women earn 77 cents for each dol-

lar earned by men, we find that the mean for black women is 48 cents, and, for white women, 55 cents for each dollar of white male earnings. Our preferred estimate of the gender gap uses mean rather than median earnings, in order to incorporate the "glass ceiling" of merely high but not spectacular earnings, as opposed to the extraordinary earnings of some white men. These white men are the positive outliers who raise the average far beyond the median income figure. Also, we compare white and black women and black men to white men, so that we can incorporate the qualitatively different types of inequality represented by race, gender, and their combined effects (Behringer, Hogan, and Perrucci 2004). Even more important, we compare, in Table 17.3, average earnings for all workers, including part-time and temporary workers, since part of the disadvantage of gender (for white women, in particular) is the burden of the double shift and the irregular employment career of the caregiver (Hochschild 1989). As seen in Table 17.4, 58% of white men, but only 39% of white women, report full-time, year-round employment in 2004. For black men, it is 56%; for black women, 47%. Thus black men and

---

Table 17.3

Median and Mean Income in 2004 for Non-Hispanic White and Black, Male and Female Workers Reporting Income (with proportion of white male income in parenthesis)

	White Male	White Female	Black Male	Black Female
Median	$33,652	$18,379 (.55)	$22,714 (.68)	$17,383 (.52)
Mean	$46,868	$25,979 (.55)	$29,880 (.64)	$22,581 (.48)
N	72,768	74,810	10,074	12,621

Source: U.S. Census Bureau, Current Population Survey, 2005 Annual Social and Economic Supplement: <http://pubdb3.census.gov/macro/032005/perinc/new01_013.htm> (white male), <http://pubdb3.census.gov/macro/032005/perinc/new01_022.htm> (white female), <http://pubdb3.census.gov/macro/032005/perinc/new01_015.htm> (black male), and <http://pubdb3.census.gov/macro/032005/perinc/new01_024.htm> (black female).

Table 17.4

Percent of Non-Hispanic White and Black, Male and Female Workers Reporting Income in Full-time, Year-Round Employment in 2004

White Male	White Female	Black Male	Black Female
58%	39%	56%	47%
N= 72,768	N=74,810	N=10,074	N=12,621

Source: U.S. Census Bureau, Current Population Survey, 2005 Annual Social and Economic Supplement (see Tables 17.2 and 17.3).

Table 17.5

Mean Income for Non-Hispanic White and Black, Male and Female Workers Reporting Income (Number in Thousands), in 2003 Dollars, Selected Years From 1955–2001 (With Proportion of White Male Income for Blacks and Women Reported in Parenthesis)

Year	White Male	White Female	Black Male	Black Female
2004a	$46,868	$25,979 (.55)	$29,880 (.64)	$22,581 (.48)
	N= 72,768	N=74,810	N=10,074	N=12,621
1999	$46,697	$24,207 (.52)	$29,032 (.62)	$21,765 (.47)
	N=71,553	N=75,158	N=10,317	N=12,383
1994	$40,334	$20,981 (.52)	$24,817 (.62)	$18,353 (.46)
	N=70,919	N=73,665	N=9,199	N=11,450
1989	$39,765	$19,474 (.50)	$23,133 (.58)	$16,747 (.42)
	N=69,558	N=72,509	N=8,806	N=10,577
1984	$34,925	$16,519 (.47)	$20,419 (.58)	$14,527 (.42)
	N=67,126	N=69,497	N=7,851	N=9,460
1979	$35,487	$14,332 (.40)	$21,754 (.61)	$13,254 (.37)
	N=65,506	N=66,447	N=7,288	N=8,533
1974	$33,842	$13,813 (.41)	$20,616 (.61)	$12,266 (.36)
	N=60,397	N=49,757	N=6,409	N=6,779

Source: U.S. Census Bureau, Historical Income Tables, <http://www.census.gov/hhes/income/histinc/p03.html>. a2004 means are in 2004 (current) dollars (see Table 17.3); all others are in 2003 (constant) dollars.

gap are less affected than the gender gap by the convention of comparing only full-time, year-round workers.

The Stability of the Racial and Gender Income Gaps

Table 17.5 presents mean income for white and black men and women, including part-time and seasonal workers, from 1974 to 2004. The 2004 figures are reproduced from Table 17.3 (in 2004 dollars). All other figures are reported in 2003 (constant) dollars. For white and black females and for black males, each mean is accompanied by its relation (proportion) to white male income for the same year. Thus we can compare earnings gaps from 1974 to 2004, presented, to save time and space, in five-year intervals.

As seen in Table 17.5, the gender gap (white female mean earnings/white male mean earnings) declined from .41 in 1974 to .55 in 2004. The racial gap for black men declined from .61 to .64, and the compounded race and gender gap declined from .36 to .48. Clearly, the substantial gender gap declined much more rapidly than the somewhat smaller racial gap, simply because women's income increased more rapidly than men's.

Mean income (in 2003 dollars) for white men increased 38% between 1974 and 1999 (from $33,842 to $46,697) but stagnated thereafter. The major increases were in the late 1980s (14%), just before the savings and loan crash of 1989, and in the late 1990s (16%), just before the election of George W. Bush in 2000. For black men, mean income increased 45% in these three decades, increasing most dramatically in the late 1980s (13%) and the late 1990s

even black women are more likely than white women to work full-time, year-round, which explains why the racial gap and even the compounded race and gender

(17%), more or less paralleling the boom and bust cycles experienced by their white counterparts.

Mean income for white women increased 88% during these three decades. For black women, the increase was 84%. Unlike their male counterparts, white women made substantial gains (15%) and black women reported modest gains (10%) in the early 1980s (during the recession, when both white and black males experienced declining income). White women also experienced substantial growth in earnings (18%) during the boom years of the late 1980s (as did black women, who claimed a 15% increase), but comparable growth in white male earnings resulted in only modest decline in the gender gap (3%) and no change in the compound race and gender gap (which remained at .42 between 1984 and 1989). A similar pattern emerges in the boom years of the late 1990s. Ultimately, then, progress in reducing the gender gap was most impressive when male earnings were declining, particularly in the early 1980s.

The income growth reported above is linked to the U.S. economy (as indicated by Gross Domestic Product (GDP) in 2000 dollars), which experienced steady growth, an increase of 149% between 1974 and 2004, despite the downturns near the beginning of each decade (U.S. Bureau of Economic Analysis 2005). In fact, the overall economy performed much better than did the wages and salaries of workers, yielding the now familiar experience of steadily falling "real" wages. Additionally, well-paying manufacturing positions were replaced with less remunerative and less stable employment, with limited if any benefits (Hogan 2003: 45–48).

Nevertheless, the economic standing of men declined more rapidly than the status of women, who were also experiencing decline. Earnings growth for white women (88%) and black women (84%) lagged behind growth in GDP (149%) for these three decades, but not nearly so far behind as were white men (38%) and black men (45%). In fact, in the early 1980s white female earnings increased 15% while GDP increased only 12%, in this period of relatively slow economic growth, in which women, white and black made considerable progress in narrowing the earnings gap.

Female labor force participation was facilitated by the shift from manufacturing to service jobs, and the replacement of highly paid men with lowly paid women in corporate downsizing and cost-cutting efforts (Hogan and Perrucci 1998:530). Even in 2003 women were still ghettoized in the service, sales, and office occupations. U.S. Department of Labor (2005) statistics indicate that just over 29% of white men worked in service, sales, and office occupations in 2003, compared to nearly 55% of white women, 38% of black men, and just over 59% of black women (U.S. Department of Labor 2005). Clearly, the turn toward a service and sales economy created employment opportunities for women, which dovetailed nicely with corporate efforts to reduce payroll and benefits costs by hiring women, including black women.

Female labor force participation increased dramatically between 1974 and 2004. As was indicated in Table 17.5, white men still outnumbered white women in the 1974 labor force, but they were surpassed by 1979. As seen in Table 17.6, female representation in the full-time, year-round paid labor force increased fairly dramatically between 1974 and 2004, from 28% to 40% of all white female workers and from 28% to 47% for black females.[1] Although white males still predominate numerically in the full-time, year-round labor market, and blacks are still a numerical minority, females have sharply increased their representation in the full-time, year-round labor force.

In fact, the gender gap in representation in the labor force has declined as dramatically as the income gap, yielding direct and indirect effects. The indirect effects are, perhaps, most important, since it is the ability of women to enter occupations and particularly management and supervisorial positions that seems to have the greatest effect in breaking down barriers to pay and promotion advances (Cohen, Broshak, and

Haveman 1998; Cotter, De Flore, Hermsen, Marstellar-Kowalewski, and Vanneman 1997; Reskin and McBrier 2000).

Of course, the employment opportunities resulting from increasing demand for marginal workers were mostly limited to the younger cohort of workers, who were able to operate the computers and to accommodate the demands of the modern office. For the older cohorts, who were approaching retirement in the 1990s, this new economy was, in some sense, beyond their grasp. They suffered racial and gender gaps in employment and retirement income that were still rooted in an industrial past, within which their cohort had labored, back in the days when men, especially black men, worked in the South or in Northern factories and women, especially black women, worked in the home as housewives or domestic servants.

Looking Toward the Future

The postmodern service economy has, in some sense, liberated women, particularly middle class white women, from unpaid domestic labor and the suburban ennui of "the problem that has no name" (Friedan 1963). It has, however, been characterized by stagnant real wages, unstable employment, declining health and retirement benefits, speculative frenzies, welfare for the wealthy, and fiscal crises, both public and private (Hogan 2003 and 2005; Calavita and Pontell, 1992; Morris and Western 2001). Rather than dwelling on the nightmare of the present, however, we might consider some possible futures, suggested by other scholars.

The failure of liberalism is clear. Morris and Western (2001) point to unsuccessful efforts to raise the minimum wage and to the continuing decline of union membership. To this we might add the failure to provide affordable healthcare and the inability to offer a viable alternative to the privatization schemes of the conservative plan for changing the current system of Social Security. The failure of liberalism is, in short, the death of the New Deal coalition of big labor, big capital, and big government. The new social movements and new liberals (such as Clinton) have accepted the death of industrial unionism without considering the new face of unionism, including efforts to or-

Table 17.6

Percent of White and Black, Male and Female Workers Reporting Income (Number in Thousands) in Full-time, Year-Round Employment From 1974–2004

Year	White Male	White Female	Black Male	Black Female
2004	59%	40%	56%	47%
	N=85,112	N=84,366	N=12,272	N=14,931
1999	60%	39%	56%	47%
	N=81,911	N=83,690	N=10,317	N=12,383
1994	57%	35%	52%	40%
	N=78,220	N=80,045	N=9,199	N=11,450
1989	58%	34%	49%	38%
	N=75,858	N=77,933	N=8,806	N=10,577
1984	54%	30%	44%	35%
	N=72,162	N=73,977	N=7,851	N=9,460
1979	55%	27%	46%	30%
	N=69,247	N=69,839	N=7,288	N=8,533
1974	55%	28%	44%	28%
	N=63,388	N=52,038	N=6,409	N=6,779

Source: U.S. Census Bureau, Historical Income Tables (see note 1), <http://www.census.gov/hhes/income/histinc/p03.html> (total), <http://www.census.gov/hhes/income/histinc/p36b.html> (full-time black), and <http://www.census.gov/hhes/income/histinc/p36w.html> (full-time white); see Tables 17.2 and 17.3 (black male and female 2004 total and full-time), <http://pubdb3.census.gov/macro/032005/perinc/new01_012.htm> (white male 2004 total), <http://pubdb3.census.gov/macro/032005/perinc/new01_039.htm> (white male 2004 full-time), <http://pubdb3.census.gov/macro/032005/perinc/new01_021.htm> (white female 2004 total), and <http://pubdb3 .census.gov/macro/032005/perinc/new01_048.htm (white female 2004 full-time).

ganize health care workers and other black female constituencies, who might benefit from unionization drives and whose unionization might revitalize the labor movement (Milkman and Voss 2004).

Social democratic alternatives (Esping-Andersen 2001) are attractive to academics, but it is not clear that Joe Sixpack is ready to embrace the idea that public sector investments in education, training, childcare, and family services will produce multiplier effects in the postmodern service economy. The problem with private sector alternatives is that these require service workers whose wages are even lower than the entry level jobs that might attract young mothers. In Southern California, for example, Latina workers free upper middle class women for minimum wage employment. In Scandanavia, this is more problematic.

Of course, here in the U.S. we can continue to use immigrant workers to provide the low-cost service work in restaurants and housekeeping, lawn and garden services. This might continue to be a viable alternative to the more traditional conservative defense of family: the Italian model of protecting women and children from poverty (Casper, McLanahan, and Garfinkle 1994). The problem with the American plan is twofold. On the one hand, the conservative governing coalition is divided on the immigrant issue, with Homeland Security anti-immigrant interests opposing business class split-labor-market interests (Bonacich 2001). On the other hand, the Latinos (and Latinas) are revolting. Perhaps middle class white women will have their consciousness raised by their domestic servants. This did not happen to any marked extent among suffragists, in 1903 (Karaditor 1981, chapter Seven), or during the Civil Rights Movement, in 1955 (Morris 1984:49–50). Perhaps the third time is the charm.

Discussion Questions

1. The authors calculate race and gender income gaps in two ways. Which method do you think is more illuminating? Why?

2. How do you think the race and gender gap might differ across occupations?

3. Have you ever experienced being paid less because of your race or gender? Paid more?

Reprinted from Richard Hogan and Carolyn Perrucci, "Gender, Race, and Income Gaps." Unpublished manuscript, 2006.

Endnote

1. The U.S. Census Bureau, Historical Income Tables, do not distinguish Hispanic from Non-Hispanic Whites among full-time, year-round workers, prior to 1987. Thus Table 17.6 includes Hispanics among white males and females, which is why the *N*s differ from Table 17.5.

References

Allessio, John and Julie Andrzejewshi. 2000. "Unveiling the Hidden Glass Ceiling: An Analysis of the Cohort Effect Claim." *American Sociological Review* 65:311–15.

Behringer, Autumn, Richard Hogan and Carolyn C. Perrucci. 2004. "Disentangling Disadvantage: Race, Gender, Class and Occupational Effects in the Employment Earnings of Older U.S. Workers." *International Journal of Contemporary Sociology* 41:147–162.

Bonacich, Edna. 2001. "A Theory of Ethnic Antagonism: The Split Labor Market." Pp. 555–568 in David Grusky (ed.), *Social Stratification: Class, Race, & Gender in Sociological Perspective*. Boulder, CO: Westview Press.

Boraas, Stephanie and William M. Rodgers III. 2003. "How Does Gender Play a Role in the Earnings Gap? An Update. *Monthly Labor Review* (March):9–15.

Calavita, Kitty and Henry N. Pontell. 1992. "The Savings and Loan Crisis." Pp. 233–258 in *Corporate and Governmental Deviance*, M. David Erman and Richard J. Lundman (eds.). New York: Oxford University Press.

Cancio, Silvia A., T. David Evans, and David J. Maume, Jr. 1996. "Reconsidering the Declining Significance of Race: Racial Differences in Early Career Wages." *American Sociological Review* 61:541–56.

Casper, Lynne M., Sara S. McLanahan and Irwin Garfinkle. 1994. "The Gender-Poverty Gap: What We Can Learn From Other Countries." *American Sociological Review* 59:594–605.

Cohen, Lisa E., Joseph P. Broshak and Heather A. Haveman. 1998. "And Then There Were More?

The Effects of Organizational Sex Composition on the Hiring and Promotion of Managers." *American Sociological Review* 63:711–27.

Cotter, David A., JoAnn DeFiore, Joan M. Hermsen, Brenda Marstellar-Kowalewski and Reeve Vanneman. 1997. "All Women Benefit: The Macro-Level Effect of Occupational Integration on Gender Earnings Equality." *American Sociological Review* 62:714–34.

Epsing-Andersen, Gøsta. 2001. "Social Foundations of Postindustrial Economies." Pp. 830–845 in David Grusky (ed.), *Social Stratification: Class, Race, & Gender in Sociological Perspective*. Boulder, CO: Westview Press.

Friedan, Betty. 1963. *The Feminine Mystique*. New York: Dell.

Hochschild, Alie, with Anne Machung. 1989. *The Second Shift*. New York: Avon Books.

Hogan, Richard. 2003. *The Failure of Planning: Permitting Sprawl in San Diego Suburbs, 1970–1999*. Columbus: Ohio State University Press.

——. 2005. "Political Opportunity and Capitalist Crisis." Pp. 161–176 in *Economic Opportunities and Political Contention in Comparative Perspective*, edited by Charles Tilly and Maria Kousis. Boulder, CO: Paradigm Publishers.

Hogan, Richard and Carolyn C. Perrucci. 1998. "Producing and Reproducing Class and Status Differences: Racial and Gender Gaps in U.S. Employment and Retirement Income." *Social Problems* 45:528–49.

Hogan, Richard, Carolyn C. Perrucci and Autumn Behringer. 2005. "Enduring Inequality: Gender and Employment Income in Late Career." *Sociological Spectrum* 25:53–77.

——. forthcoming. "Gender, Educational Credentials, and Employment Income in Late Career." *International Journal of the Humanities*.

Kraditor, Aileen S. *The Ideas of the Woman Suffrage Movement/1890–1920*. New York: W.W. Norton.

Milkman, Ruth and Kim Voss. 2004. "Introduction." Pp. 1–16 in Ruth Milkman and Kim Voss (Eds.), *Rebuilding Labor: Organizing and Organizers in the New Labor Movement*. Ithaca, NY: Cornell University Press.

Morris, Aldon D. 1984. *The Origins of the Civil Rights Movement: Black Communities Organizing for Change*. New York: Free Press.

Morris, Martina and Bruce Western. 2001. "Inequality in Earnings: Trends and Implications." Pp. 875–880 in David Grusky (ed.), *Social Stratification: Class, Race, & Gender in Sociological Perspective*. Boulder, CO: Westview Press.

Reskin, Barbara F. and Debra Branch McBrier. 2000. "Why Not Ascription? Organizations' Employment of Male and Female Managers." *American Sociological Review* 65:210–33.

U.S. Bureau of Economic Analysis. 2005. *Gross Domestic Product*. Retrieved from: <http://www.bea.gov>.

U.S. Census Bureau. 2005a. *Current Population Survey, Annual Demographic Survey, March Supplement*. Retrieved from: <http://pubdb3.census.gov/macro/032005/perinc/new01_012[-51].htm>.

——. 2005b. *Current Population Survey, Historical Income Tables—People*. Retrieved from <http://www.census.gov.hhes/income/histinc/p03.html>.

U.S. Department of Labor, Bureau of Labor Statistics. 2005. *Household Data Annual Averages, Employed Persons by Occupation, Race, Hispanic or Latino Ethnicity, and Sex*. Retrieved from: <http://www.bls.gov/cps/cpsaat10.pdf>. ✦

18

Inequality at Work: Wages and Promotion

Chris Tilly and Charles Tilly

Chris Tilly and Charles Tilly build on the Hogan and Perrucci chapter to consider a model for both promotion and compensation, the latter being a broader concept than income in that it includes wages, benefits, and nonmonetary perquisites. They present and critique the human capital approach, commonly used by economists and some sociologists, to account for variation in compensation and promotion. They then present an alternative approach that includes workers' preferences, networks, bargaining, and inertia.

Beyond Human Capital Theory

What determines wage levels? Without doubt, the theory of wage determination that has enjoyed the greatest acceptance is human capital theory. More productive workers get paid more, human capital (abilities and skills) largely determines productivity, and there is much variation in the extent to which people are endowed with and invest in human capital. But human capital theory leaves much unexplained. Standard human capital research uses regression analysis to discover how much of the variation in wages among individuals can be explained by differences in human capital. Table 18.1, adapted from Erica

Groshen (1991), shows typical results from such research.

Without getting into technical details, note that a person's education and age are the human capital variables. Age imperfectly represents workforce experience, as well as captures any wisdom accumulated through aging itself. The square of age is included because mathematically this allows the positive impact of age on earnings to level off and even become negative with increasing age (which indeed it does). Table 18.1 reveals that the standard human capital variables only account for about one-quarter of the variation in wage levels among individuals. Taking account of each individual's occupation, industry, race, sex, and whether they are unionized doubles this but still leaves 49 percent of the variation unaccounted for.

More detailed studies highlight that pesky 49 percent, finding large wage differences even among similar jobs in similar workplaces within local areas. Langton and Pfeffer (1994) cited a number of such studies:

- John Dunlop (1957) found that in Boston, truck drivers hauling scrap metal earned $1.27 an hour, whereas truck drivers who carried magazines received $2.49 an hour, almost 100 percent more—despite belonging to the same union.

- Donald Treiman and Heidi Hartmann (1981, Table 12) pointed out that the U.S. Bureau of Labor Statistics's Area Wage Surveys (now renamed Occupational Compensation Surveys) typically turn up wide variations in the wages paid to narrowly defined jobs within specific metropolitan areas. Table 18.2 illustrates this variation, showing the ratio of highest to lowest wages found in six jobs in the Atlanta, Detroit, and Los Angeles metropolitan areas in the early 1990s. If we consider the full range of wages for a given job in a given city, the highest-paying businesses pay up to four times as much as the lowest—and only rarely pay less than twice as much. Even when we throw out the highest one-quarter and lowest one-quarter of wages, focusing on the "middle range," the highest wage in this range is typically 30 percent or more above the lowest, and in some cases is twice as great. Not surprisingly, registered nurses, with their readily transferable, certified skills, show the least variation. Janitors show the most variation: Given the limited skill required for this job, their pay will depend far more on the specific institutional setting in which they are employed. Variation in other forms of compensation is even greater (U.S. Bureau of Labor Statistics 1991): In the Atlanta area, the number of paid holidays for production workers spanned from zero to sixteen; office workers' hours of vacation after five years of service extended from zero weeks to eight!

• Jonathan Leonard (1989) found that [wage differences] are present even within the electronics industry in two California counties. The highest-paying firm paid twice as much, or more, as the lowest-paying firm for secretar-ies, janitors, stock clerks, and production supervisors.

All of this unexplained variation does not in itself sink a human capital model of earnings (Baker, Jensen & Murphy 1988). Unexplained differences in wages can always be attributed to unobserved differences in ability, and hence productivity. But a more satisfactory response is to seek to build richer models of compensation and other rewards. In our framework, this quest starts by considering compensation as only one form of incentive among several.

Incentive Systems

Incentive systems combine compensation with coercion and commitment. . . .

A producing organization's relative concentration on commitment, compensation, and coercion significantly affects its operation. In general, emphasis on commitment maintains the organization, emphasis on compensation enhances short-run effectiveness, and emphasis on coercion enhances short-run control over members. In parallel, these three emphases offer particular leverage for attaining objectives of quality, efficiency, and power respectively. Organizations relying heavily on commitment generally sacrifice short-run control over their members but gain long-term allegiance. Conversely, organizations whose powerholders seek long-term control over members tend to choose contracts stressing commitment and coercion over those stressing compensation, whereas those seeking a one-time effort and no further involvement do it all with cash. No one could run a hospital with the kinds of cash-on-the-spot transactions that work perfectly well in street vending.

A combination of history, culture, productive logic, and embeddedness in other social structures accounts for the location of different activities with respect to commitment, compensation, and coercion, which in

---

Table 18.1

The Percentage of Wage Variation Among Individuals Accounted for by Human Capital and Other Variables, United States, 1986

Explanatory Variables	Percent of Wage Variation Explained
Years of education, Age, Age^2	26%
Years of education, Age, Age^2, Occupation	42%
Years of education, Age, Age^2, Occupation, Race, Sex, Union status	48%
Years of education, Age, Age^2, Occupation, Race, Sex, Union status, Industry	51%

Notes: Sample includes all people aged 18–54 employed for wages and salaries in nonagricultural industries in the United States. Dependent variable is log(hourly earnings). Occupation and Industry denote dummy variables at the two-digit level.

Source: Data from Erica Groshen, "Five Reasons Why Wages Vary Among Employers," *Industrial Relations* 30 (1991):350–381, Table 1.

turn affects the position of those activities on the scales of monetization and time-discipline. Thus far in this mapping exercise, we have emphasized productive logic. But the enormous importance of history, culture, and embeddedness becomes clear in making international comparisons and in tracking change over time.

Compared to the United States, Japanese work contracts tend to rely more on commitment, whereas volatile labor relations in South Korea reflect attempted coercion by both employers and workers. One reflection of such variation is the span of control—the number of workers per manager. Coercion correlates with more intense supervision, hence fewer workers per manager. Figure 18.1, calculated from the work of David Gordon, tabulates the span of control for sixteen industrialized nations. Among these nations, the United States imposes the heaviest management control, with about one manager per six workers. The hand of management is far lighter in Japan, with a manager for every sixteen workers. But the most laid-back countries of all are Italy, Sweden, and Switzerland, all with 25 workers or more per manager. Surely the require-

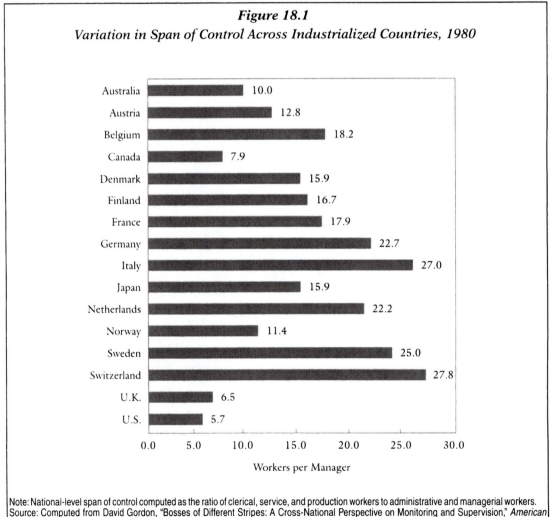

Figure 18.1

Variation in Span of Control Across Industrialized Countries, 1980

Country	Workers per Manager
Australia	10.0
Austria	12.8
Belgium	18.2
Canada	7.9
Denmark	15.9
Finland	16.7
France	17.9
Germany	22.7
Italy	27.0
Japan	15.9
Netherlands	22.2
Norway	11.4
Sweden	25.0
Switzerland	27.8
U.K.	6.5
U.S.	5.7

Note: National-level span of control computed as the ratio of clerical, service, and production workers to administrative and managerial workers.
Source: Computed from David Gordon, "Bosses of Different Stripes: A Cross-National Perspective on Monitoring and Supervision," *American Economic Review* 84(2) (1994):375–379 (Figure 1).

ments for producing Fords, Toyotas, Fiats, and Volvos do not differ this greatly! Nor does the mix of productive activities across the sixteen countries vary so widely. Instead, these patterns reflect the historical paths labor relations have taken in the sixteen countries and the norms and other shared understandings the march along these historical paths has trod out. Gordon (1994) found that the span of control is highly correlated with worker bargaining power and a strong welfare state. . . .

Levels of Compensation

. . . Table 18.2 shows the median annual earnings of men and women working full-time year-round in these occupations. Although the occupational breakdown is not as detailed as the one we examined earlier, mineworkers are still visible as "extractive occupations," and their pay is quite handsome for manual work. Textile operatives (who are predominantly women) are approximated in Table 18.2 by female machine operators, who earn on average less than half as much as the overwhelmingly male miners. Health care workers' pay straddles that of the two industrial groups: Doctors earn far more than miners, nurses about as much as miners, whereas women health service workers receive about the same yearly pay as their machine operator counterparts.

Looking beyond these particular groups of workers, certain regularities emerge. Within occupations, supervisors earn more than other workers. Women earn less than men in *every* occupation, without exception, for which reliable estimates for both sexes were available. The differences often yawn wide. Moreover, within each broad occupational category, the higher the percentage of women in the job, the lower tends to be the pay that both men *and* women receive in that job.

. . . [A] combination of productivity, preferences, networks, bargaining, and inertia sets these pay scales. In particular, compensation of workers in labor markets varies as a function of nine main variables:

1. Market power of the firm.

2. Amount of capital per worker in the firm.

3. Extent of the worker's discretionary control over the firm's capital.

4. Impact of the worker's performance on the firm's aggregate performance.

5. Substitutability of that impact.

6. Worker's membership in favored ascriptive categories.

7. Worker's network proximity to others scoring high on items 3, 4, 5, and 6.

8. the nature of institutions regulating compensation in the firm, industry, or occupation.

9. Inertial effect of earlier configurations with respect to 1–8.

Thus we find very high compensation (wages, benefits, and nonmonetary perquisites) for a worker belonging to a privileged demographic group (men, for example) in an oligopolistic, heavily capitalized firm; who disposes of expensive machinery or other assets; whose expertise in using that machinery or those assets is both hard to reproduce and crucial to the firm's profitability; who is closely connected with other workers (including managers) having nonsubstitutable expertise and extensive discretionary control of capital; who benefits from the intercession of a union, professional organization, or government bureaucracy; and whose job has historically been blessed by these advantages. Conversely, we find low compensation for a member of a less-favored demographic group working in a weakly capitalized firm exposed to competition, who is easily replaced, has little access to the firm's capital, remains distant from its crucial handlers of capital, enjoys no institutional protections, and has a job long marked by this set of curses.

Specific examples illustrate the theory. Textile machine operators, who are predominantly women, easily replaced, working in a moderately capitalized industry facing sharp competition, earn far less than overwhelmingly male miners, with harder-to-replace skills, working with more capital in a more concentrated industry—and represented by a powerful, though shrinking, union. Looking beyond cotton and coal, note that managers, who exercise considerable discretion over the use of capital and contribute substantially to a firm's performance, are the highest-paid workers, although certain professionals with valuable, specialized knowledge and the protection

Table 18.2
Who's Getting Paid: Total Annual Earnings of Men and Women Who Worked Full-Time, Year-Round, and Percent Female, by Selected Occupations, United States, 1992

	Median Annual Earnings of:		
	Men	Women	Percent Female
Total	30,538	21,440	41%
Executive, administrative, managerial	42,509	27,945	41
Professional	44,015	31,261	48
Engineers	47,765	41,955	6
Physicians and other health diagnosing	87,224	52,233	18
Registered nurses and other health assessment and treating	41,418	36,006	85
Technical	33,092	24,681	46
Health technologists and technicians, except licensed practical nurses	34,413	22,949	70
Licensed practical nurses	—	22,936	94
Other technical workers	33,328	27,030	30
Sales	31,346	17,924	38
Supervisors and proprietors, salaried	33,888	19,872	33
Cashiers	14,230	11,928	73
Administrative support, including clerical	27,186	20,321	77
Supervisors	38,099	26,599	61
Secretaries, stenographers, typists	—	20,614	98
Service	20,606	12,931	51
Private household	—	9,668	89
Police and firefighters	36,136	—	8
Health service	17,291	15,243	88
Precision production, craft, repair	28,923	19,045	8
Automobile mechanics	20,933	—	1
Extractive occupations	37,977	—	2
Precision production	30,817	17,481	19
Operators, fabricators, laborers	23,005	16,609	23
Machine operators and tenders	23,315	15,019	36
Motor vehicle operators	25,566	17,436	7
Farming, forestry, and fishing	14,897	10,079	11
Farm operators and managers	15,294	12,801	11
Other farm occupations	12,213	—	15

Notes: More recent editions of this publication do not include this information. Percent female is for full-time, year-round workers. Median earnings for technical Workers as a whole imputed by authors.

Source: U.S. Department of Commerce, *Money Income of Households, Families, and Persons in the United States, 1992* (Washington, D.C.: U.S. Printing Office, 1993).

of a professional association, also gain high earnings. The substitutability concern means that physicians or lawyers must be well paid even when their contributions to firm performance are limited since the earnings must be sufficient to win them away from other jobs available to them. Secretaries of important decisionmakers earn more than other secretaries with equal skills both because of their heightened impact on the firm's functioning and because of their network position. Market power, capital per capita, and regulatory institutions offer a partial explanation of the fact that high-paying and low-paying firms and industries exist, even for jobs and workers who appear identical in all observable characteristics.

. . . The standard economic theory stresses *productivity*-based determinants of pay: capital per worker, discretionary control over capital, and the worker's impact on firm performance. But preferences, networks, bargaining, and inertia insistently place their thumbs on the scale. *Preferences* account for part of the pay differences among ascriptive categories. Not all: We know, for example, that most of the difference between women's and men's wages results from the fact that women and men work in different jobs. But in fact, as Table 18.2 documents, women do earn less than men even within the same occupation (and—though this cannot be determined from the table—even after controlling for differences in human capital). Furthermore, as advocates of comparable worth are wont to point out, the fact that "women's" jobs pay less than "men's" jobs surely reflects the preferences and perceptions of employers, embodying judgments deeply ingrained in culture. Similar invidious distinctions trail other ascriptive traits. In nineteenth-century California, rural construction, which was carried out by a Chinese workforce, was viewed as unskilled, whereas urban construction, which employed white men, was considered skilled (Johnson 1989).

Ascriptive characteristics do not matter equally in all settings. Jeffrey Pfeffer (1977), for example, discovered that the im-

pact of socioeconomic origins on salary was greater in staff rather than line positions, in smaller organizations, and in financial businesses relative to manufacturing ones. "The results," he concluded, "are consistent with the hypothesis that the use of ascriptive characteristics will increase to the extent performance is difficult to evaluate or to the extent linkage in a high socioeconomic status network is itself an important determinant of performance" (p. 553).

Moreover, the effects of ascriptive characteristics spill over to both productivity and networks. When they find themselves an unwelcome minority, women construction workers may be less productive—not because they are less able, but because resentful male coworkers may refuse to train and cooperate with them and may even sabotage their work. The connection with *networks* is even more decisive. Social networks segregate, to some extent, by ascriptive characteristics. Networks, in turn, determine who is likely to get what jobs . . . as well as what other workers will be network-linked to a given employee. Thus, much difference in wages by demographic group reflects the working of networks in matching and promotion rather than worker productivity or employer wage discrimination.

Indeed, networks affect the job one is able to find, the pay level for a given job, and in some cases the entire system of compensation. It is tempting to suppose that finding a job through a contact brings a wage advantage. But the wage effect, of course, depends on to whom the network connects a job searcher. Luis Falcón and Edwin Melendez (1996), studying workers in Boston, discovered that although non-Latino whites who found their jobs through contacts received higher wages than those who did not, blacks and to a lesser extent Latinos actually paid a penalty—in wages, hours, and/or benefits—for finding a job via networks. Networks bend compensation most when they are powerful enough to alter the system of compensation. The New England fishing industry, for instance, bifurcates into "kinship" fishing vessels, whose Italian and Portuguese immigrant crews are linked by strong family and kinship ties, and "capitalist" boats, whose Yankee, Norwegian and other non-Mediterranean owners hire from the labor market at large. Kinship vessels pay crew members according to an income-sharing system whereas capitalist fishing boats pay market wages (Doeringer, Moss & Terkla 1986).

Compensation differences among New England fishing vessels point as well to the fundamental role of *bargaining* in setting pay. A wide variety of institutions condition and structure bargaining. Although family ties may be the most important such institutions aboard fishing vessels, unions and civil service systems play the same role in other industries. Wage tribunals in Australia or France's sectoral bargaining—in which agreements between unions and employer associations are binding on all employers in a given sector whether or not they were a party to the agreement—exert highly visible influence on compensation. But even in the notoriously flexible, unregulated labor market of the United States, tens of millions of workers have wages set by unions, minimum wage laws (federal, state, and local), or prevailing wage laws. Bargaining generates wage patterns that diverge markedly from those predicted by a "pure" market model. Within the unionized sector of the United States, steady patterns of wage growth, little affected by shifts to labor demand, have long alternated with sharp, dramatic adjustments. Such adjustments took place in the early 1920s, early 1960s, and early 1980s; in each case employers seem to have suddenly realized that their bargaining power had increased (Mitchell 1986).

Bargaining mediates the effect of the firm's market power on wages. Although greater market power denotes greater ability to pay, only the bargaining process can determine whether that ability will actually translate into higher wages. Among businesses in concentrated industries, unionization correlates with lower profits: Evidently unions compel oligopolies to share their windfalls (Freeman & Medoff 1984).

And even in work contracts untouched by unions or government regulations, norms of fairness inevitably emerge. Alfred Marshall (1925: 213, cited in Solow 1990) declared about a century ago that

> the basis of the notion that there should be given "a fair day's wage for a fair day's work" is that every man who is up to the usual standard of efficiency of his trade in his own neighborhood, and exerts himself honestly, ought to be paid for his work at the usual rate for his trade and neighborhood; so that he may be able to live in that way to which he and his neighbors in rank of life have been accustomed.

Notions of fairness blossom particularly within internal labor markets, and Paul Pigors and Charles Myers (1981: 362, cited in Solow 1990) described the consequences: "Wage and salary differentials are a mark of social status in almost every organization. If they do not correspond to the relative significance of jobs, as employees view them, the employee's sense of justice is outraged." But although conceptions of fairness are universal, their content varies across regions and countries and changes over time.

Finally, *inertia* slows change in compensation, prolonging wage patterns well beyond the factors that initially gave rise to them. Just as the best predictor of who will hold a job today is who held it yesterday, the best predictor of today's wage is yesterday's wage. Longitudinal studies of wages paid to individuals over their tenure with particular employers find strong serial correlation: The wage in each period is tightly correlated with the wage in the previous period (Baker & Holmstrom 1995). Nominal wage cuts, common in the United States during the 1910s and 1920s, have become extremely rare, although arguably the increasing use of bonuses and profit sharing creates ways for compensation to fluctuate downward as well as upward. When firms seek to cut wages, they typically lower wages for new hires—not incumbent workers. Norms of fairness surely play an important part in the downward rigidity of wages: Opinion surveys in the United States demonstrate a powerful public antipathy for nominal wage cuts (Jacoby & Mitchell 1990; Kahneman, Knetch & Thaler 1986). Nothing new there: Marshall, quoted previously, continued his statement by adding, "And further, the popular notion of fairness demands that [the worker] should be paid this rate ungrudgingly; that his time should not be taken up in fighting for it, and that he should not be worried by constant attempts to screw his pay down by indirect means" (1925: 213, cited by Solow 1990). . . .

Promotion and Mobility

In addition to compensation, the other major reward offered by firms is promotion. Promotion marks one particular form of job mobility. Mobility matters to employers, who depend on job-to-job movement to provide training and motivate workers. It matters also to workers, who use mobility to gain advancement. Most people find promotion rewarding not only because it brings increased perquisites and pay, but also because recognition, deference, power, and greater proximity to capital are gratifying in themselves. In the United States, many hold long-term jobs. The median tenure of a 45–54-year-old man with his current employer was over 12 years in 1991. At the same time, however, U.S. workers experience surprisingly vigorous occupational churning. Ten percent of the workforce (including eight percent of those aged over 25) change occupations each year (U.S. Bureau of Labor Statistics 1992). This combination of statistics points to multiple models of job mobility.

Three main patterns of mobility predominate. Craft workers, such as plumbers or computer programmers, move, at times rapidly, from job to job but consistently ply a particular skilled trade and may rise formally or informally within the ranks of that trade. Secondary workers bounce from employer to employer, and often occupation to occupation, without accumulating significant skills. Employers utilizing secondary

labor markets often experience annual turnover rates of 200 to 300 percent among "permanent" workers (Chris Tilly 1996). Finally, within salaried and industrial internal labor markets, workers advance with a particular employer through promotion. The rules for internal advancement typically turn on seniority (for blue-collar and some lower level white-collar jobs) or merit (for managerial and professional jobs).

Mapping Mobility

. . . A grid of mobility and training sheds considerable light on variation in other dimensions of work and labor markets (Figure 18.2). We classify work contracts by the degree to which training takes place within a given work contract and by a mobility spectrum from turnover, through stagnation, to promotion. (The latter axis oversimplifies since certain "up or out" work contracts combine promotion and turnover but foreclose stagnation.)

A number of regularities emerge. First, mobility and training correlate: Most work contracts—and particularly most contracts within labor markets—fall on the diagonal running from turnover and extra-contractual training to promotion and internal training. Craft, unskilled, and temporary workers huddle in the turnover/outside-contract corner. Managers, military officers, and clergy hobnob in the opposite corner, where promotion and in-house training predominate. Criminals and semi-skilled workers loiter closer to a stagnant mobility pattern, where slaves and small family business employees—both trained primarily within their contracts—stand shackled by bonds of coercion and commitment. Housewives and professionals fall between the two poles.

The groupings at the two ends of the diagonal differ in other ways as well. They correspond to external and internal labor markets. In the one case, the key social relations that embed the work contract tend to fall outside the firm or other productive organization; in the other case, many of these social relations fall within. Although the proverbial CEO-who-started-as-a-file-clerk

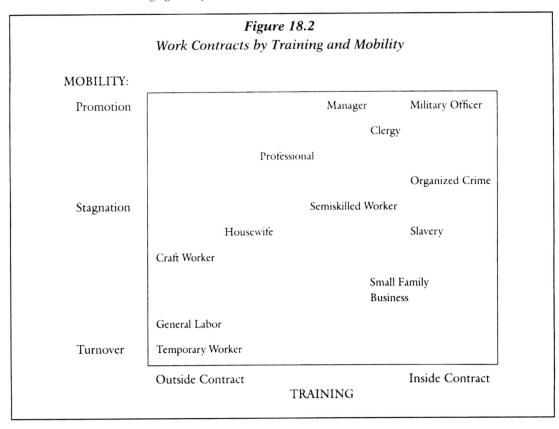

Figure 18.2
Work Contracts by Training and Mobility

travels the length of the diagonal, more commonly careers stay within a relatively small section of the training-mobility plane. Today's fast-food chains, for example, commonly concentrate the great bulk of their workers in the diagram's lower left corner—outside recruitment and high turnover—but keep an eye out for the occasional worker who has the personal style and social characteristics to enter a promotion ladder as a potential manager.

The split workforce adopted by fast-food chains, in fact, is widespread in labor markets. Although the mix of high-turnover and promotion-ladder jobs varies widely across businesses, most large firms create at least two district internal labor markets. One consists of low-ceiling or dead-end jobs whose entrants work under close supervision with little hope of advancement within the firm, the other of hierarchically arranged jobs whose occupants, much more closely screened for compatibility

with the firm's high officers, enter directly into the firm's system of command, patronage, information, promotion, and solidarity. We might call the first a **turnover pool,** the second a **command pool.** Even where the entry-level jobs differ little in direct compensation or intrinsic difficulty, the two pools commonly contrast dramatically in dress, demeanor, perquisites, class origin, race, ethnicity, gender, and citizenship. Such arrangements create a bifurcated power structure within the firm.

Businesses do their best to mobilize compensation and coercion to direct the turnover pool, and commitment to motivate the command pool. . . . Nonetheless, incentives once more vary systematically across this plane. Commitment grows in importance as one moves from turnover to promotion and from external to internal training. (Craft workers and professionals, who substitute commitment to craft or profession for commitment to firm, constitute the major exception.) Compensation looms larger as one moves in the opposite direction; in the absence of long-term attachments craft and temporary workers are motivated primarily by short-term pecuniary rewards. Coercion is used most extensively in stagnant or high-turnover work contracts, then held in reserve for the policing of unruly craft and professional workers.

Describing only two classes of pools oversimplifies: More generally, the segmentation of internal labor markets forms a continuum from pools containing nothing but command jobs to other pools containing nothing but dead-end jobs. Incentives vary accordingly, spanning a spectrum from loyalty to direct surveillance. Compensation likewise varies accordingly, with long-term salary, nonmonetary perquisites, and pensions more common at the loyalty end of the continuum, hourly wages with minimum benefits and perquisites more common at the surveillance end. The differential assignment of workers to segments of internal labor markets by race, ethnicity, citizenship, class origin, and gender therefore produces systematic differences in compensation across those categories as well.

The same logic that distinguishes command from promotion pools within firms also accounts for variation among firms and industries. Firms and industries differ greatly in the extent to which employers and workers (in combination, sometimes with state officials or labor unions) bargain out different combinations of incentive systems, routines of labor recruitment, compensation, and allocation of jobs among command and turnover pools. Broadly speaking, the same conditions that produce high compensation—capital intensivity, workers' discretionary control over capital, high and unsubstitutable impact of worker performance on aggregate performance, worker membership in favored ascriptive groups, network proximity of workers to other high-impact workers, firm market power, and strong institutional protections for compensation—also favor loyalty systems, worker control of recruitment, and extensive command pools.

But the character of the pools themselves also varies across firms and industries. Even in turnover pools, on the whole heavily capitalized firms and industries offer higher wages, more extensive benefits, and greater job security to their workers than do those having low ratios of capital per worker. Since workers in such industries, on the average, enjoy greater capacity to organize and greater leverage in bargaining (Conell 1980, 1989; Hanagan 1989), employers are more inclined to preempt their unionization and collective action by providing company unions and paternalistic welfare programs. These tendencies have given rise to the distinction between "core" and "peripheral" industries.

Explaining Promotion Patterns

Differences among firms and industries in patterns of internal promotion raise three questions about internal labor markets. First, what determines the extent to which a given organization fills higher-status jobs via promotion, and *which* jobs do they fill by promotion? Data gathered by George Baker, Michael Gibbs, and Bengt Holmstrom (1994, Table II) illustrate the question. The medium-sized U.S. service firm they studied had eight levels of employment. The percentage of jobs filled from inside at each level, ranked from lowest to highest, was:

Level 1	1%
Level 2	73%
Level 3	70%
Level 4	75%
Levels 5–8:	90%

Why fill three-quarters of level 2–4 jobs internally, rather than 1 percent or 90 percent? Why fill a higher proportion of jobs by promotion at the upper levels of the organization?

Productive logic provides a starting point. Firms use promotion more where firm-specific knowledge requirements are greater and where screening and evaluation of outside candidates are difficult. Imbuing workers with firm-specific knowledge is costly, and businesses seek to husband that investment once it is made. Promotion ladders also give employers an opportunity to assess worker abilities and separate the wheat from the chaff.

Firms are also more likely to promote when they rely more on commitment rather than other incentive systems (though the choice of incentive system and job-filling mechanism are—conceptually— simultaneous). Hiroshi Ishida and colleagues (1995), studying large Japanese and American financial sector firms, found that among college graduates entering the companies, initial promotions were essentially automatic. In the Japanese company, nearly every employee was promoted to deputy section chief, and about 90 percent attained the rank of section chief. However, promotion to deputy section chief required at least ten years of seniority (most were promoted after thirteen years) or reaching the age of 33. Neither the universality of the promotions nor the uniformity of their timing can be readily explained by learning or screening processes. Instead, they constitute encouragements for loyalty.

For Japanese corporations, which offer lifetime employment for some classes of employees, loyalty may trump skill. At many companies, job applicants with previous experience and job-related skills are actually *disadvantaged*, since "Japanese companies prefer to hire motivated but inexperienced students and provide on-the-job training" (Ishida et al. 1995: 7). Loyalty considerations, along with firm-specific knowledge and screening, help explain why promotion from within is more common at higher levels of a firm's hierarchy.

The history and current configuration of bargaining also alters the degree of reliance on promotion. Workers and their organizations press for opportunities for upward mobility. In the U.S. hospital industry, in which the boundaries among job strata have been virtually impermeable, unions have bargained to establish education and training programs. Managers' response to proposals such as these depends in part on productivity costs and benefits but also on their assessment of the extent to which promotion can serve to co-opt workers (as opposed to giving workers the opportunity to infiltrate management!). More generally, businesses take worker expectations and desires into account when designing or redesigning mobility systems. They may design promotion systems to satisfy those expectations—or to forestall them. Illustrating the latter case, increasing numbers of U.S. businesses, including manufacturers, are conducting initial hires through temporary help agencies, then screening the temporary employees for possible promotion to permanent employment. This device heads off new hires' claims on benefits or even on continued employment during the screening period. . . .

Discrimination based on preferences and perceptions can radically reshape promotion ladders, particularly when the beneficiaries of the discrimination are disposed to defend their claims. Railroads in the southern United States at the beginning of the twentieth century hired African-Americans for the midlevel jobs of brakeman and fireman but barred their advancement to conductor or engineer. This peculiarity prevented southern railroads from creating seniority-based promotion ladders, which had become standard on other North American railroads. White-dominated unions not only defended the promotion bar, but fought to drive blacks from the midlevel jobs as well (Sundstrom 1990).

Detailed patterns of discrimination in promotion can be quite varied, depending on institutional history and needs. In one Pittsburgh insurance company, part-timers are forbidden to bid for full-time jobs; managers explained to Chris Tilly (1996) that this provision was designed to attract only people who wanted long-term part-time work. On the other hand, in numerous grocery stores—and in the U.S. Postal Service—virtually every worker must enter through a part-time position.

Once promotion ladders have been established, precedent freezes them in place. Since changing the rules for promotion can spark confusion and resentment in an incumbent workforce, firms generally alter ladders only when major shifts in the environment require it. A Boston insurance company official told Chris Tilly,

> Typically, [the company's] culture was that we hired at the entry level, and moved people up at a steady rate—not extremely rapid. . . . But that's beginning to change . . . particularly in a couple of areas—financial, data processing. We're really having to fight for a highly skilled labor supply. It would take too much time to promote from within—our needs are growing and changing too rapidly. So we . . . are bringing in more MBAs at midstream. This does cause problems in employee relations . . . MBAs hired in at grade 14 or 15 have the same attitude as people at the *bottom*— "I've been here a couple of years, where's my promotion?" The old-style managers say, "We've already given you a break, we've given you an opportunity that we and your co-workers never had." We have no plan yet for how to handle this problem—it's sink or swim. The good ones [MBAs] move up to 16 or 17. That creates some resentment below. Or, they get frustrated and leave. (Chris Tilly 1989)

A third and final question is who—in categorical terms—follows promotion paths. Who moves up depends on worker knowledge—but in this case, less on firm-specific skills than on groups' differential access to credentials and general job-related skills. Networks and discrimination (which may be at work both in the promotion process itself and in the mentoring and training that sets the stage for promotion) also loom large. For example, the "glass ceiling" confronting women in U.S. corporations is well-known. In the large corporation studied by Rosabeth Kanter, "male" and "female" jobs differed systematically in the mobility chances they offered. For women, therefore,

> mobility was so rare and the chance for social contact so great in office jobs that strong peer networks easily developed. It was also easier for the women to support a culture devaluing hierarchical success because of tradition and because they had few women upward in

the hierarchy with whom to identify. Then, the distribution of men and women throughout the organization also shaped the psychological filter through which these women viewed promotion. As a woman rose in Indsco, she was likely to find fewer and fewer female peers, whereas men found a male peer group at every level of the system. So concern about "leaving friends" and the social discomforts of a promotion were often expressed by women in the clerical ranks; men in management had no such problem. (Kanter 1977: 151; see also Epstein 1981)

Similar mobility problems beset members of racial and ethnic minorities within large firms.

Networks bulk particularly large in the determination of upward mobility within internal labor markets. The importance of networks for promotion varies inversely with the formality of promotion procedures. Pyramid selling marks one extreme—networks alone create the opportunity to rise within the organization—but the same pattern holds across other types of business as well. Shirley Mark (1990) reported that engineers in high technology firms move upward by participating in the formation of project groups—an informal process structured by networks of acquaintance that disproportionately exclude Asian-American engineers. A similar process marginalized women in the advertising firm studied by Herminia Ibarra (1992). Jomills Braddock and James McPartland (1987) found that jobs filled by promotion from within are more likely to have white employees if the employer approaches employees directly to offer the job or to solicit applications for the job; they are less likely to have white employees if a written job description is posted or circulated. A portion of the exclusion commonly attributed to discriminatory attitudes thus results instead from network segregation. In addition to networks and discrimination, access to promotion also turns crucially on explicit or implicit bargains among powerful actors, often embodied in policies such as seniority and affirmative action.

The End of Internal Labor Markets?

Ironically, as researchers developed taxonomies of U.S. labor market segments over the last two decades, the labor market began to change in ways that render these taxonomies obsolete. The portion of the workforce fitting an industrial profile—long-term, rule-bound subordinate employment—has shrunk, for reasons including a shift of employment from manufacturing to services and employers' responses to heightened global competition (Harrison & Bluestone 1988; Albelda & Tilly 1994). More generally, U.S. employers have widely shifted away from internal labor markets in both their industrial and salaried varieties, toward a system relying far more on external educational institutions for training, combined with greatly increased mobility among firms. This widespread externalization results in part from the rapid growth of institutions for adult and continuing education, in part from firms' attempts to "get lean" and stay "poised for contraction" (Appelbaum 1987; Noyelle 1987; Carré, duRivage & Tilly 1995). Workers' heightened mobility takes the voluntary form of job-hopping but also the involuntary form of downsizing. Although some growing job groups fit the pattern of secondary or craft segments, others combine features of various segments in new ways.

As AT&T geared up to lay off an estimated 40,000 workers in early 1996 Vice President for Human Resources James Meadows told the *New York Times*, "People need to look at themselves as self-employed, as vendors who come to this company to sell their skills." He added, "In AT&T, we have to promote the whole concept of the workforce being contingent, though most of the contingent workers are inside of our walls." Instead of jobs, people increasingly have "projects" or "fields of work," he remarked, leading to a society that is increasingly "jobless but not workless" (Andrews 1996: D10). Meadows's statement holds that employment has de-

volved from jobs toward contracts—and in the limit, is tending toward individual transactions. Large-scale surveys reveal a similar shift in attitudes and expectations. Workers and managers alike rate employees' commitment to their current employer, and employers' commitment to their current workers, far lower than in earlier decades (Cappelli 1995). Even that most long-term of employers, the United States Postal Service, has expanded noncareer part-time jobs and created a "transitional" workforce as they automated and outsourced mail-sorting systems.

Are jobs in the United States really becoming less permanent? Yes and no. Jobs are becoming less permanent for men, particularly older and less-educated men, and more permanent for women (Farber 1995; Rose 1995, 1996). When these changes are combined, the net effect is no detectable trend (Farber 1995, though some measures do show an overall decrease in tenure; see Swinnerton & Wial 1995). However, this netting out does not necessarily imply that the changes are neutral. Arguably, women's growing tenure reflects a shift in labor supply—women are more likely to choose to stay at jobs rather than quitting. But men's declining tenure presumably primarily reflects a shift in labor demand—meaning that employers are more likely to lay off or fire workers or shut down. For the purposes of assessing the opportunities available to workers, the shift in labor demand is the decisive element.

Evidence from the Census Bureau's Displaced Worker Survey (DWS) also suggests reduced opportunity for long-duration jobs (Farber 1996). The DWS focuses on an extreme set of events: permanent layoffs. Displacement rates in 1991–93, nominally years of recovery from a mild recession, were higher than during the deep recession years of 1981–83. In turn, displacement rates for the 1980–92 period as a whole exceeded job loss rates during 1968–79, according to research based on the Panel Study of Income Dynamics (Boisjoly, Duncan & Smeeding 1994). Between these two periods, the percentage of people laid off increased by one-third, and the percentage fired doubled.

Do shortening job durations harm workers' interests? Some in the business press have argued that frequent job changes facilitate ongoing learning and advancement or have argued that rather than viewing shorter tenure as a setback, it should simply be seen as a change in the patterns and rules of job-holding. Journalists have introduced us to beneficiaries of mobility from one short-term job to another, such as 25-year-old temporary worker Jayson Elliot, who comments, "I don't want a job. I would never take one" (Flynn 1996). Providing some scholarly support for a benign view is the flexible specialization literature launched by Piore and Sabel (1984). Flexible specialization theorists argue that smaller firms and more volatile employment herald a return to craft forms of organization, marked by attachment to a trade, rather than a firm, with possibilities of advancement within that trade.

However, an instructive counterpoint to high-tech temp Elliot is provided by the words of temporary manual labor pool workers in the Carolinas. The Carolina Alliance for Fair Employment held a workshop with such temporary workers in 1994 and asked each participant to supply four words to describe how he/she felt about his/her work life (Gardner & McAllister 1995). Although the list yielded a few positive terms (qualified, hopeful, capable, competent), the bulk were negative: discouraged (five times), unimportant (twice), sad, bad, unpredictable, abused, rough, angry, disappointed, disgusted, tired of looking, expendable, on the outside, insecure, used, underpaid, aggravated, no future, pressured, threatened, unhappy, out of place, depressed, could be better, sucks, demanding, hate, stinks, poor, unfair, tired, and overworked!

Although temporary work marks one extreme in impermanence, Jencks, Perman, and Rainwater (1988) found that in general, a 10 percent increase in the expected risk of job loss in the next two years reduces the job's rating as much as a 10 percent pay cut. And although the earnings penalty associated with job changes was lower in the 1980s than in the 1970s, it remained a penalty. Even among job-changers who stayed within the same occupation, men who changed employers at most once during the 1980s earned 11 percent more per year than those who changed two or three times; the corresponding earnings premium among women was 32 percent (Rose 1995). The preponderance of the evidence indicates that most workers experience shorter-term employment as a contraction of employment opportunity.

Closely related to the issue of permanence is the question of mobility over time. Overall wage mobility decreased between the 1970s and early 1990s (Buchinsky & Hunt 1996). What's more, *downward* mobility has become markedly more common in the United States. Tracing the trajectories of individual prime-age adults, Stephen Rose (1994) found that about one-fifth experienced declines of five percent or more in real earnings over the decade of the 1970s; that proportion rose to one-third during the 1980s. As in some of the other indicators, men and women crisscrossed: Men's likelihood of losing annual earnings increased, whereas women became less likely to lose. However, in terms of *hourly wages* (factoring out the effect of changes in weeks and hours worked, which enter into annual earnings), both groups became more likely to experience declines in the later decade.

What heightened the probability of downward mobility? Rose accounts for half of men's greater probability of an earnings drop by the increased frequency of job changes. But data about other firm-level changes suggest a more complex picture. Although the frequency of job *changes* increased, the benefits of job *stability* decreased at the same time. The payoff to accumulating seniority with a single employer, long a standard feature of compensation, diminished sharply during the 1980s (Chauvin 1994; Marcotte 1994). Employers also significantly decreased the amount of formal training they provided in order to qualify employees for jobs (Constantine & Neumark 1994). And new forms of work organization have removed layers of management and folded unskilled blue-collar jobs into multifunctional teams, taking out rungs in traditional job ladders (Cappelli 1993; Cappelli & O'Shaughnessy 1995). In short, the possibilities of upward mobility with a particular employer contracted, but the opportunities for ascent via movement from job to job have not offset this contraction.

The new "casualization" of labor attachment marks not only the United States, but also France, Italy, Japan, and other countries. The apparent convergence of these countries may be deceptive, however. In France and Italy, employers have shifted to less formal employment and subcontracting in large part to fend off the worker militancy of the late 1960s and early 1970s as well as to evade strict government and union regulations restricting discharge. U.S. employers, pressed by growing global and domestic competition, have acted more to blunt worker *expectations* of long-term employment than to dodge specific rules. Japanese expansion of nonregular employment initially represented employers' attempts to cope with a labor shortage by absorbing more women, students, and hundreds of thousands of illegal workers and later responded to a sharp recession induced by currency fluctuation. Although some have argued that the economies of Japan and Germany are now gravitating toward U.S.-style low-commitment labor markets (*Economist* 1996), such predictions seem premature.

Is this the end of internal labor markets in the United States? Clearly, the old internal labor market model is dissolving, especially for men. The U.S. business press has embraced the notion that there is a new career model founded on interemployer movement. In this "employability" model, much like a craft labor market, employers' commitment to workers is not continued employment, but provision of skills that render the worker more employable. But at present, although job-hopping surely offers new opportunities to some, on the average sustained attachment to a single employer still offers the greatest payoff to men and

women alike. U.S. workers will strive to find ways to shield themselves from labor market insecurity, as workers everywhere have always done. Although workers have lost bargaining power due to decreased unionization and intensified product market competition, their power—and particularly their ability to rally the state as a sometime ally—is still to be reckoned with.

Given all of this, the labor market situation in the United States in the late 1990s looks like a transitional phase, not a stable new system. It is difficult to predict the final outcome. The reconstruction of some sort of within-firm internal labor markets is one possibility, though not the strongest one. Alternatively, worker security can be rebuilt based on a state-provided or required "safety net" of benefits portable from job to job, or new forms of unionization or other worker organization that impose standards for worker mobility across firms in an industry or geographic area—or some combination of these elements. What is certain is that in any new system, mechanisms of incentive and mobility will, as always, be shaped by productivity, preferences, networks, bargaining, and inertia. What is also certain is that the new system will be hammered out through contention among workers, employers, and the state.

Discussion Questions

1. To what extent do you think the Tillys' approach to accounting for variation in compensation and promotion is an improvement over the human capital approach?

2. What factors should be considered by employers when deciding on promotion and wages?

Reprinted with permission from Chris Tilly and Charles Tilly, *Work Under Capitalism*. Westview Press, a Division of Harper Collins Publishers, 1998.

References

Albelda, Randy & Chris Tilly. (1994): "Towards a Broader Vision: Race, Gender, and Labor Market

Segmentation in the Social Structure of Accumulation Framework," in David M. Kotz, Terrence McDonough & Michael Reich, eds., *Social Structures of Accumulation*. Cambridge: Cambridge University Press, 212–230.

Andrews, Edmund L. (1996): "Don't Go Away Mad, Just Go Away: Can AT&T Be the Nice Guy as It Cuts 40,000 Jobs?" *New York Times*, February 13, D1, D10.

Appelbaum, Eileen. (1987): "Restructuring Work: Temporary, Part-Time, and At-Home Employment," in Heidi I. Hartmann, ed., *Computer Chips and Paper Clips: Technology and Women's Employment*. Vol. II: Case Studies and Policy Perspectives (Washington, D.C.: National Academy Press).

Baker, George & Bengt Holmstrom. (1995): "Internal Labor Markets: Too Many Theories, Too Few Facts," *American Economic Review. Papers and Proceedings* 85: 255–259.

Baker, George, Michael Gibbs, and Bengt Holmstrom. (1994): "The Internal Economics of the Firm: Evidence From Personnel Data," *Quarterly Journal of Economics* 109: 881–919.

Baker, George P., Michael C. Jensen, & Kevin J. Murphy. (1988): "Compensation and Incentives: Practice vs. Theory," *Journal of Finance* 43: 593–616.

Boisjoly, Johanne, Greg J. Duncan, & Timothy Smeeding. (1994): "Have Highly Skilled Workers Fallen From Grace? The Shifting Burdens of Involuntary Job Losses From 1968 to 1992." Mimeo, University of Quebec, Rimouski.

Braddock, Jomills Henry II and James M. McPartland. (1987): "How Minorities Continue to Be Excluded From Equal Employment Opportunities: Research on Labor Market and Institutional Barriers," *Journal of Social Issues* 43: 5–39.

Buchinsky, Moshe & Jennifer Hunt. (1996): "Wage Mobility in the United States." Working Paper 5455. National Bureau of Economic Research, Cambridge, Massachusetts.

Cappelli, Peter. (1993): Are Skill Requirements Rising? Evidence for Production and Clerical Workers," *Industrial and Labor Relations Review* 46: 515–530.

——. (1995): "Rethinking Employment," *British Journal of Industrial Relations* 33: 563–602.

Cappelli, Peter & K. C. O'Shaughnessy. (1995): "Skill and Wage Change in Corporate Headquarters, 1986–1992." National Center on the Educational Quality of the Workforce, University of Pennsylvania, Philadelphia.

Carré, Francoise, Virginia L. duRivage, & Chris Tilly. (1995): "Piecing Together the Fragmented Workplace: Unions and Public Policy on Flexible Employment," in Lawrence G. Flood, ed., *Unions and Public Policy*. Westport, Conn.: Greenwood Press, 13–37.

Chauvin, Keith. (1994): "Firm-Specific Wage Growth and Changes in the Labor Market for Managers," *Managerial and Decision Economics* 15: 21–37.

Conell, Carol. (1980): "The Impact of Union Sponsorship on Strikes in Nineteenth-Century Massachusetts." Doctoral dissertation in sociology, University of Michigan.

——. (1989): "The Local Roots of Solidarity: Organization and Action in Late Nineteenth-Century Massachusetts," *Theory and Society* 17: 365–402.

Constantine, Jill M. & David Neumark. (1994): "Training and the Growth of Wage Inequality." Working Paper, National Center on the Educational Quality of the Workforce, University of Pennsylvania, Philadelphia.

Doeringer, Peter B., Philip I. Moss, & David G. Terkla. (1986): "Capitalism and Kinship: Do Institutions Matter in the Labor Market?" *Industrial and Labor Relations Review* 40: 48–60.

Dunlop, John. (1957): "The Task of Contemporary Wage Theory," in John Dunlop, ed., *The Theory of Wage Determination*. London & New York: Macmillan & St. Martin's Press, 3–27.

Economist. (1996): "Stakeholder Capitalism: Unhappy Families," February 10: 23–25.

Epstein, Cynthia Fuchs. (1981): *Women in Law*. New York: Basic Books.

Falcón, Luis & Edwin Melendez. (1996): "The Role of Social Networks in the Labor Market Outcomes of Latinos, Blacks, and Non-Hispanic Whites." Paper presented at Multi-City Study of Urban Inequality Conference on "Residential Segregation, Social Capital, and Labor Markets," Russell Sage Foundation, New York City, February 8–9.

Farber, Henry S. (1995): "Are Lifetime Jobs Disappearing? Job Duration in the United States: 1973–1993." Working Paper 341, Industrial Relations Section, Princeton University, Princeton, N.J.

Flynn, Laurie J. (1996): "For Some, Steady Job Isn't the End of the Road." *New York Times*, May 20, D8.

Freeman, Richard B. & James L. Medoff. (1984): *What Do Unions Do?* New York: Basic Books.

Gardner, Florence & Jean McAllister. (1995): "Temporary Workers: Flexible or Disposable?" *Poverty & Race* (newsletter of the Poverty & Race Research Action Council) (November/December): 9–14.

Gordon, David. (1994): "Bosses of Different Stripes: A Cross-National Perspective on Monitoring and Supervision." *American Economic Review* 84(2): 375–379.

Groshen, Erica. (1991): "Five Reasons Why Wages Vary Among Employees," *Industrial Relations* 30: 350–381.

Hanagan, Michael. (1989): "Solidary Logics: Introduction," *Theory and Society* 17: 309–328.

Harrison, Bennett & Barry Bluestone. (1988): *The Great U-Turn: Corporate Restructuring and the Polarizing of America*. New York: Basic Books.

Ibarra, Herminia. (1992): "Homophyly and Differential Returns: Sex Differences in Network

Structure and Access in an Advertising Firm." *Administrative Science Quarterly* 37: 442–47.

Ishida, Hiroshi, Seymour Spilerman & Kuo-Hsien Su. (1995): "Educated Credentials and Promotion Prospects in a Japanese and an American Organization." Working Paper 92, Center on Japanese Economy and Business, Columbia University, New York, N.Y.

Jacoby, Stanford & Daniel J. B. Mitchell. (1990): "Sticky Stories: Economic Explanations of Employment and Wage Rigidity," *American Economic Review, Papers and Proceedings* 80: 33–37.

Jencks, Christopher, Lauri Perman, & Lee Rainwater. (1988): "What Is a Good Job? A New Measure of Labor-Market Success," *American Journal of Sociology* 93: 1322–1357.

Johnson, Mark. (1989): "Capital Accumulation and Wage Rates: The Development of the California Labor Market in the Nineteenth Century," *Review of Radical Political Economics* 21(3): 76–81.

Kahneman, Daniel, Jack L. Knetch, & Richard Thaler. (1986): "Fairness as a Constraint on Profit-Seeking: Entitlements in the Market," *American Economic Review* 76: 728–741.

Kanter, Rosabeth. (1977): *Men and Women of the Corporation.* New York: Basic Books.

Langton, Nancy & Jeffrey Pfeffer. (1994): "Paying the Professor: Sources of Salary Variation in Academic Labor Markets," *American Sociological Review* 59: 236–256.

Leonard, Jonathan. (1989): "Wage Structure and Dynamics in the Electronics Industry," *Industrial Relations* 30: 392–395.

Marcotte, Dave. (1994): "Evidence of a Fall in the Wage Premium for Job Security." Working Paper, Center for Governmental Studies, Northern Illinois University, De Kalb, Illinois.

Mark, Shirley. (1990): "Asian-American Engineers in the Massachusetts High Technology Industry: Are Glass Ceilings a Reality?" Master of City Planning thesis, Department of Urban Studies and Planning, Massachusetts Institute of Technology, Cambridge, Mass.

Marshall, Alfred. (1925): "A Fair Rate of Wages," in A. C. Pigou, ed., *Memorials of Alfred Marshall.* New York: Macmillan.

Mitchell, Daniel J. B. (1986): "Union vs. Nonunion Wage Norm Shifts," *American Economic Review* 76(2): 249–252.

Novelle, Thierry. (1987): *Beyond Industrial Dualism.* Boulder: Westview Press.

Pfeffer, Jeffrey. (1977): "Toward an Examination of Stratification in Organizations," *Administrative Science Quarterly* 22: 553–567.

Pigors, Paul and Charles Myers (1981): *Personnel Administration.* McGraw-Hill.

Piore, Michael & Charles Sabel. (1984): *The Second Industrial Divide: Possibilities for Prosperity.* New York: Basic Books.

Rose, Stephen J. (1994): *On Shaky Ground: Rising Fears About Income and Earnings.* Research Report 94-02. Washington, D.C.: National Commission on Employment Policy.

——. (1995): *Declining Job Security and the Professionalization of Opportunity.* Research Report 95-04. Washington, D.C.: National Commission on Employment Policy.

——. (1996): "The Truth About Social Mobility." *Challenge* (May-June): 4–8.

Solow, Robert M. (1990): *The Labor Market as a Social Institution.* Oxford: Blackwell.

Sundstrom, William A. (1990): "Half a Career: Discrimination and Railroad Internal Labor Markets," *Industrial Relations* 29: 423–440.

Swinnerton, Kenneth A. & Howard Wial. (1995): "Is Job Stability Declining in the U.S. Economy?" *Industrial and Labor Relations Review,* 48: 293–304.

Tilly, Chris. (1989): "Half a Job: How U.S. Firms Use Part-Time Employment," Ph.D. dissertation, Departments of Economics and Urban Studies and Planning, M.I.T., Cambridge.

Tilly, Chris. (1996): *Half a Job: Bad and Good Part-Time Jobs in a Changing Labor Market.* Philadelphia: Temple University Press.

Treiman, Donald & Heidi I. Hartmann, eds. (1981): *Women, Work, and Wages: Equal Pay for Jobs of Equal Value.* Washington, D.C.: National Academy Press.

U.S. Bureau of Statistics. (1991): *Area Wage Survey: Atlanta, Georgia, Metropolitan Area, May 1991,* Bulletin 3060-14.

——. (1992): "Employee Tenure and Occupational Mobility in the Early 1990s," *Bureau of Labor Statistics News,* June 26.

19
'Soft' Skills and Race

*Philip Moss and
Chris Tilly*

Philip Moss and Chris Tilly use interview data to explain the difficulty black men experience in getting hired for entry-level jobs in urban settings. They identify "soft skills" that employers want in employees, skills related to "emotional labor" and "motivation," which they perceive that young urban black men lack. The authors then propose several solutions that range from broad national policies to reduce unemployment to a variety of firm-based programs.

The Black/White gap in hourly wages of young men in the United States, after narrowing for decades, began to widen in the mid-1970s, a period that also saw a growing racial gap in male employment rates (Bound & Freeman, 1992; Juhn, Murphy, & Pierce, 1991). Skill upgrading constitutes one source of growing racial inequality in employment and earnings. There is substantial evidence of skill upgrading in U.S. jobs, which has resulted from both compositional shifts and upgrading of requirements within specific jobs (Osterman, 1995). Indeed, Ferguson (1993) showed that an increasing payoff to basic math and reading skills can explain much of the racial wage divergence for men.

The growth of "soft" or social skills is a factor that has been neglected in research on the racial gap in labor market outcomes, despite the fact that employer surveys have repeatedly identified such skills as the most

important hiring criterion for entry-level jobs (Capelli, 1995). In this study, therefore, we examined the relationship between employer racial attitudes and their hiring practices, with special attention given to their use of soft skills. We defined soft skills as skills, abilities, and traits that pertain to personality, attitude, and behavior rather than to formal or technical knowledge. Based on 56 face-to-face interviews with employers, we sought to learn how employment gatekeepers conceived of soft skills in relation to hiring Black men for entry-level jobs.

According to our findings, employers reported an increasing need for soft skills—driven, they said, by heightened competitive pressure—and they rated Black men poorly in terms of such skills. Thus, the heightened competition that propels current business restructuring appears to contribute to increased labor market inequality by race.

Skills and the Racial Gap

Research on the labor market issues facing Black men shows that shifts in labor demand have contributed substantially to their worsening situation, but the nature of these demand shifts remains unclear (Moss & Tilly, 1991). As noted above, rising demand for skills could help explain the growing racial differential in both wages and employment rates. Black men lag behind their White counterparts in educational attainment (Bound & Freeman, 1992), in standardized tests administered in the public schools (Jencks, 1991), and in tests measured in national data sets, such as the Armed Forces Qualifying Test (AFQT) (Ferguson, 1993; O'Neill, 1990). If Blacks lag behind in skills, increasing demand for skills will put them at an increasing disadvantage. Bound and Freeman investigated this possibility with educational attainment but concluded that the equalizing effects of Black/White convergence in educational attainment should be greater than the disequalizing effects of a rising payoff to education. On the other hand, Ferguson

(1993) found that a rising premium on basic skills, as measured by the AFQT, could explain much—perhaps all—of the increase in the Black/White male wage difference between 1980 and 1988.

These studies leave a number of questions unanswered. Some authors argue that defining job requirements in terms of individual knowledge greatly oversimplifies the requisites for successful job performance (Darrah, 1994; Vallas, 1990). In particular, Darrah noted that in most work contexts, successful performance depends crucially on a set of relationships with other workers and managers. In service settings, relationships with customers are also critical. And as noted above, employers assign soft-skill traits like attitude or personality paramount importance in hiring decisions (Capelli, 1995). Holzer's (1996) employer survey found decreased representation of Black men in jobs whose tasks required hard skills (such as reading and arithmetic) but also in jobs whose tasks called for soft skills (such as interaction with customers face to face or by telephone). Thus, soft skills—captured neither by educational attainment nor by standardized test scores—are important, both in their own right and in facilitating the learning and exercise of hard skills.

Because employer assessments of the soft skills of current or potential workers are inevitably subjective, racial discrimination can enter into such assessments. Becker (1957) offered a helpful distinction among forms of discrimination originating with customers, coworkers, and employers. Phelps (1972) and Arrow (1972a, 1972b, 1973) moved beyond Becker's notion of a "taste for discrimination" (a distaste for contact with members of a given group) by suggesting that employers may engage in statistical discrimination. That is, given the impossibility of measuring individual productivity in advance, employers may discriminate against whole classes of people based on (correct or incorrect) perceptions of the mean productivity (or variation in productivity) for these classes.

Research in social psychology and organizational demography (Tsui, Egan, & O'Reilly, 1992) has added richness to these relatively austere economic models of discrimination. Such research builds on the similarity-attraction hypothesis (positing that people use demographic traits to infer similarity in attitudes, which is an important basis for attraction) and on self-categorization theory (holding, likewise, that people rely on traits to define groups from which they draw positive self-identity). Surveys consistently find an expressed preference for coworkers who are homogeneous by race and other characteristics (Shellenbarger, 1993; Tajfel & Turner, 1986), and in fact homogeneous groups outperform other groups along some dimensions (Jackson, 1991). Similarly, racial and other demographic differences in a superior-subordinate pair are linked to discomfort and less favorable performance evaluations of the subordinate (Ford, Kraiger, & Schectman, 1986; Greenhaus, Parasuraman, & Wormley, 1990; Kraiger & Ford, 1985; Sackett & DuBois, 1991; Tsui & O'Reilly, 1989). Thus, a taste for discrimination appears to be anchored deeply in individuals' self-definition and attraction to others and has measurable effects in actual work settings.

Kirschenman and Neckerman's (1991; Neckerman & Kirschenman, 1991) qualitative study provided direct evidence on employer perceptions of racial groups. Based upon face-to-face interviews with employers in Chicago and its surrounding suburbs, they found that employers used race as a primary distinction while making recruiting, screening, and hiring decisions. They reported that Chicago employers rated Blacks, and particularly Black men, worse than Whites and Latinos, both in terms of basic hard skills and in terms of soft skills such as work ethic. Waldinger (1993) reported similar findings from interviews with employers in the hotel and restaurant industries in Los Angeles.

Given the stress employers place on soft skills, it is important to explore more fully employer perceptions of the soft skills of Black men. We extended previous qualitative research by interviewing employers in additional cities and a broad range of industries. Most important, we investigated in more detail how and why employers formed negative assessments of the soft skills of Black men and why employers sought increased levels of soft skills in entry-level jobs.

Method and Data

We conducted 66 face-to-face, open-ended interviews with 75 employer representatives at 56 organizations in 1991 and 1992. The 66 interviews included 6 revisits to organizations, and 4 separate interviews of a second person during visits to organizations. We spoke to multiple respondents in about one third of the organizations.

Although our interviews were open-ended, they were structured to generate comparable data across interviewees. The same 46-item instrument was used in all 56 initial interviews. Probes and follow-up questions depended on the responses to these 46 questions, and follow-up interviews varied in focus. We maintained a consistent tone of professional yet friendly, nonjudgmental interest throughout all interviews.

We spoke to employers in the Los Angeles and Detroit metropolitan areas.[1] We chose firms from four industries: auto parts manufacturers, retail clothing stores, insurance companies, and the public sector (somewhat expansively defined to include some public utilities and private hospitals, as well as local government agencies). This cross-section of industries included a range of entry-level jobs available to workers with a high school education or less. Within each industry, we sampled both suburban and central city establishments of varying size. Where possible, we included Black-owned businesses in the sample.[2]

Thus, our sample was designed to capture differing social and demographic contexts (by metro area and central city/suburb), different skill needs, employment practices, and market conditions (by industry and firm size), and differing commitments to Black employment (by race of owner among smaller businesses). How-ever, analysis in this article primarily identifies *common* themes across these categories. In particular, although the two metropolitan areas offered contrasting environments (Kirschenman, Moss, & Tilly, 1996; Moss & Tilly, 1995a), we found little inter-area difference in the employer characteristics under study and primarily report pooled results.

Interviews gathered information on the largest category of entry-level jobs requiring no more than a high school degree at each organization—a category we call the *sample job*.[3] Questions fall into five sections: general background on the respondent and company; skill levels and needs for the job in question; the recruitment/ screening/hiring process and criteria; area business climate and company location decisions; and evaluation of different racial, ethnic, and gender groups as employees. (A copy of the instrument is available from the authors on request.) Table 19.1 includes a profile of some of the basic characteristics of the sampled firms.[4] In another article (Moss & Tilly, 1995a), we described the variety of barriers to Black men that emerged in the interviews.

In the next section of this article, we briefly report on changes in the demand for soft skills in each of the four industries we sampled. Following that, we explore how employers perceived the soft skills of Black men, and then we offer conclusions and implications for policy.[5]

Several caveats should be offered. Although proportions are reported in the findings, these are purely indicative and should not be interpreted as sample estimates of a larger population. Although many respondents spoke openly about race, a substantial minority were visibly cautious. Many of our findings rely on retrospective evaluation by informants of change over time; such evaluations must be interpreted with some caution. Finally, all interviews were conducted during the early stages of recovery from a nationwide recession, which surely affected employer perceptions of the labor market.

The Growing Importance of Soft Skills

Again, we defined soft skills as skills, abilities, and traits that pertain to personality, attitude, and behavior rather than to formal or technical knowledge.[6] Two clusters of soft skills were important to the employers surveyed. The first, *interaction*, involves ability to interact with customers, coworkers, and supervisors. This cluster includes friendliness, teamwork, ability to fit in, and appropriate affect, grooming, and attire. The interaction category is related to concepts of *emotional labor* (Hochschild, 1983; Wharton, 1993) and *nurturant social skills* (England, 1992; Kilbourne, England, & Beron, 1994). A second cluster, *motivation*, takes in characteristics such as enthusiasm, positive work attitude, commitment, dependability, and willingness to learn. We distinguish both from hard skills, including skills in math, reading, and writing; knowledge of particular job procedures; "brightness"; ability to learn; educational attainment; and physical strength.

Interaction and motivation skills differ from one another, and in much of our analysis, we distinguish between the two. However, we grouped them together under the rubric of soft skills because employers often subsumed both in terms like *attitude* and because many employers viewed both as more immutable than hard skills. Of course, soft skills are in part culturally defined, and therefore employer assessments of soft skills will be confounded by differences in culture and by racial stereotyping. Indeed, the word *skills* is to some extent a misnomer, although employers most definitely conceptualize these attributes as contributing to individual productivity differences.

We asked almost all interviewees to identify the most important qualities they looked for when hiring entry-level workers. As Table 19.2 shows, interaction skills were by far the most important qualification in retail.[7] Motivation and hard skills received roughly equal emphasis in auto parts and insurance. Only in the public sector were

hard skills mentioned most often. Overall, 86% of respondents included soft skills in their list of the most important hiring criteria, and almost half mentioned soft skills first in that list (Table 19.3).[8]

Employers reported that requirements for both hard and soft skills have recently been rising. Here, and wherever we asked retrospective questions, we asked respondents to discuss changes over the last 5 to

Table 19.1
Characteristics of the 58 Sites

Variable	Proportion (%) or Mean
Industry	
Auto parts manufacturing	33
Retail clothing	29
Insurance	14
Public sector	24
Location	
Inner city	47
Rest of city	12
Suburban	24
Mixed	17
Relocated in last 10 years or so	14
If so, when relocated	1977
Other background firm characteristics	
Any part of firm unionized	39
Sample job unionized	37
Minority-owned	11
Mean firm size	1,795
Employment rising	16
Employment falling	51
Sample job entry wage	$6.54
Rising competition in product market	59
Employee demographics	
Black	32
Latino	27
Of color	64
Female	50
Normalized employee demographics (index)[a]	
Black	1.9
Latino	0.8

a. To normalize the proportions of employees who were Black and Latino, we divided by the proportions of the metropolitan population who were Black and Latino, respectively. A normalized index of 1.0 means that the proportion of a group in the workplace matches that in the population; a higher index signifies overrepresentation of the group in that workplace.

10 years *that affected the sample job* (the largest category of entry-level jobs requiring no more than a high school education). Although more employers (50%) reported hard-skill upgrading, the number citing increased requirements for soft skills was not far behind (43%).[9] Furthermore, although 1 employer in 10 described *falling* hard-skill requirements, not one respondent reported decreasing soft-skill needs. Soft-skill increases were reported most often in retail (65%) and insurance (63%), but less frequently in auto parts (26%) and the public sector (29%).[10]

Based on a large, representative survey, Osterman (1995) confirmed that behavioral traits were important hiring criteria for blue-collar jobs (one of the two top criteria in 82% of cases, and the top criterion in about half). However, he found that, among the 40% of employers reporting rising blue-collar job complexity, only one in seven cited increased demand for interpersonal skills or responsibility.[11]

Respondents in all four industries stated that competitive pressures have led to growing soft-skill needs (Moss & Tilly, 1996).[12] For instance, auto makers are pushing their suppliers to cut costs and increase quality. In response, many of the parts manufacturers are escalating basic and technical skill requirements. Some, however, are demanding more soft skills as well. For instance, a human resource manager at an alloy casting plant told us:

> Hiring used to be based on 90% experience, 10% attitude or work ethic. I find that changing . . . due to the [emphasis on] teamwork and total quality. Attitudes and people getting along with one another . . .—this is a big part now. I would almost say it's 50% to 60% being experience and the other 40% being attitude, work ethic, teamwork.

In retail clothing, heightened emphasis on customer service—again, spurred by intensified competition—has led companies to screen more carefully for soft skills when hiring sales clerks. One discount clothing chain has adopted the slogan "fast, fun, and friendly." According to a regional personnel representative for the chain, this means that now

> I tell my . . . personnel managers, "If they don't smile, don't hire them." I don't care how well-educated they are, how well-versed they are in retail, if they

Table 19.2
Most Important Qualities Looked for in Entry-Level Employees

Industry	Frequency With Which Each Category Was Mentioned (Percent)		
	Hard Skills	Interaction	Motivation
Auto parts manufacturing	58	32	63
Retail clothing	22	78	39
Insurance	67	67	78
Public sector	100	60	60

Note: Informants typically mentioned more than one desired quality.

Table 19.3
Skill Needs in Sample Jobs at the 58 Sites

Variable	Proportion (%)
Education, hard skills	
High school graduates as proportion of sample job workforce	70[a]
Require high school	17
Require basic literacy or math	83
Job entails SPC or other precise measurement of output	29
Soft skills	
Soft skills first in list among most important hiring criteria	47
Soft skills among most important hiring criteria	86
Changes in skill requirements	
Overall skill requirements rising	64
Hard skill requirements rising	50
Soft skill requirements rising	43
Overall skill requirements falling	3
Hard skill requirements falling	10
Soft skill requirements falling	0

a. This percentage is the mean of percentages reported at individual sites.

can't smile, they're not going to make a customer feel welcome. And we don't want them in our store.

On the other hand, respondents reported declining hard skill needs among sales clerks, due to optical scanning equipment and computerized cash registers.

Insurance companies increasingly demand computer literacy among their clerical workers. In addition, financial deregulation has heightened competition, leading insurers to adopt several strategies: downsizing, reorganization of work, and greater stress on customer service. As one human resource manager put it, "on a scale of 1 to 10 it [customer relations] is a 9.999. . . . There is much more emphasis now being placed on it."

Finally, in the public sector, budget cuts have combined with political demands for greater productivity and quality of service. In our public sector interviews, two thirds of respondents reported that they were looking for more skilled people. Although some of these respondents noted a greater need for some basic or technical skill, all mentioned a need for greater customer skills—in jobs ranging from clerk-typist to hospital housekeeper.

Soft Skills and Race in the Eyes of Employers

The emphasis employers place on soft skills disadvantages Black male job applicants. This is because many employers see Black men as lacking in precisely the skills they consider increasingly important. Indeed, in our sample, the employers placing the greatest emphasis on soft skills were those most likely to have negative views of Black men as workers.[13] The views employers hold of Black men in this regard were partly stereotype, partly cultural gap, and partly an accurate perception of the skills that many less educated Black men bring to the labor market.

To demonstrate the connection between soft skills and race in the eyes of employers, we examine in turn each of the two major soft-skill areas that our interviews highlighted: interaction and motivation. Then we address how and why employers form their perceptions of Black men. Finally, we provide evidence for the importance of the pre-employment interview—the main tool employers use to assess the soft skills of applicants—which poses particular barriers for Black applicants.

Interaction Skills

Employers voiced two main sets of concerns about the ability of Black men to interact effectively with customers and co-workers. First, a substantial minority of respondents—32%—described Black men as defensive, hostile, or having a difficult "attitude." The content of these comments ranged widely. A Latino store manager in a Black area of Los Angeles, who hires mostly Latinos, flatly stated, "You know, a lot of people are afraid, they [Black men] project a certain image that makes you back off. . . . They're really scary." When asked, "How much of that do you think is perception, how much do you think is actually reality?" he responded, "I think 80% is reality. 80% of it's factual."

Other respondents stated that managers see Black men as difficult to control. For example, the Black female personnel manager of a Detroit retail store commented,

Employers are sometimes intimidated by an uneducated Black male to come in. Their appearance really isn't up to par, their language, how they go about an interview. Whereas females Black or White, most people do feel, "I could control this person.". . . A lot of times people are physically intimidated by Black men. . . . The majority of our employers are not Black. And if you think that person may be a problem, [that] young Black men normally are bad, or [that] the ones in this area [are], you say, "I'm not going to hire that person, because I don't want trouble."

A White female personnel official from a Los Angeles public sector department offered a related perspective, laying part of the blame with White supervisors:

There's kind of a being cool attitude that comes with walking down the street a certain way and wearing your colors or challenging those who look at you wrong, and they come to work with an awful lot of that baggage. And they have a very difficult time not looking for prejudice. If a supervisor gives him an instruction, they immediately look to see if it's meant, if it's said different to them because they're Black. Or if something goes wrong in the workforce, they have a tendency to blame the race, their being Black. . . . And I also think that part of the problem is that the supervisors and managers of these people have their own sets of expectations and their own sets of goals that don't address the diversity of these people, and it's kind of like, well, hell, if they're going to come work for me, they're going to damn well do it my way. . . . And my own personal feeling is that a lot of these young Black men who are being tough scare some of their supervisors. And so rather than address their behavior problems and deal with the issues, they will back away until they can find a way to get rid of them. We have a tendency to fear what we're not real familiar with.

Although a few respondents provided this level of detail, most of the negative responses were far briefer: "a lot of Black males have a chip on their shoulder," or "I get a strong sense of, with Black males at times of a hostility, of 'I deserve so and so, this belongs to me.'"

Our questions probed primarily for generalizations, but some respondents noted variation within race and gender categories. Even the store manager who described Black men as "really scary" added, "You know, there's a lot of Black males that are nice; they usually project a different image. They don't want to project the same image as gangsters."

In addition to negative views of the demeanor of Black men, we found that many retail employers saw the racial composition of employment itself as an issue for customers. The Black male personnel manager of a large retail store located in a Detroit-area suburban mall stated that because the labor market area is 90% Black, "we are forced to have an Affirmative Action program for nonminorities in this particular store." In fact, the store has shifted away from walk-in applications to in-store or mail recruiting from the store's customer base. Given that the mall sits in an integrated suburb of Detroit, his statement implies a fear that an all-Black workforce would erode the White suburban customer base.

In subsequent interviews, we asked retail informants explicitly about attempts to keep the racial mix of store employees similar to that of customers. Seven of the 10 retail informants whom we asked, responded that this was indeed a management concern. Not all of them approved of the customer attitudes to which they were responding. For example, a White female personnel manager at a Los Angeles store said,

> At [a store she was posted at previously] we had a lot of customer complaints because it's primarily White, and we were always getting complaints that there were all Black employees and it's because they were Black. That would be the first thing the customer would bring up was "Black." It was because they were Black that they didn't do their job right.

Nonetheless, this informant and others—Black, White, and Latino alike—viewed the goal of race-matching staff with customers as a legitimate management objective.

Motivation

Forty percent of respondents voiced perceptions of Black men as unmotivated employees. Once again, comments varied widely in substance. A Latino female personnel officer of a Los Angeles retail distribution warehouse, whose workforce is 72% Latino and only 6% Black, stated, "Black men are lazy. . . . Who is going to turn over? The uneducated Black." The White male owner of a small Detroit area plastic parts plant (46% Black, 54% White) said that in his experience, Black men "just don't care—like everybody owes them." "Black kids don't want to work," was the opinion of a White male owner of a small auto parts rebuilding shop in Los Angeles, whose workforce was entirely Hispanic female. "Black men are not responsible," added a Latina female personnel supervisor for a Los Angeles auto parts manufacturer located next to a major Black area but with a workforce that was 85% Latino and less than 1% Black.

This is still a minority viewpoint. The majority of respondents stated that they saw no differences in work ethic by race, although surely, in some cases, they were simply proffering the socially approved response. As in the case of interaction, some respondents discussed variation within race/gender categories. A number of employers invoked such variation to dismiss racial differences:

> We have problem employees, who choose not to come to work as often as others, but that cuts across all racial lines, you know, so no, I wouldn't say that's the case as a blanket statement. We have problem people, but they're just problem people. Some of them happen to be Black and some of them happen to be White, but I wouldn't say it's any better or worse in any one group or the other.

Other managers attributed apparent racial differences to class or neighborhood effects. Yet others noted distinctions within racial groups but still rated Black employees lower on average. For example, in a Los Angeles area discount store where the main workforce was Latino, the manager opined:

> I think the Hispanic people have a very serious work ethic. I have a lot of respect for them. They take pride in what they do. Some of the Black folks that I've worked with do, but I'd say a majority of them are just there putting in the time and kind of playing around.

In fact, although only a minority of respondents questioned the work ethic of Blacks, a substantial majority agreed with the idea that immigrants have a stronger work ethic than native-born workers—81% of Detroit respondents who ventured an opinion on this agreed, and 88% of Los Angeles respondents. This bodes ill for less-skilled Black workers, particularly in Los Angeles, because they increasingly compete with immigrant workers for jobs.

Table 19.4 summarizes the proportions of employers expressing negative views of the soft skills of Black men, broken down by firm characteristics. The data suggest that Los Angeles employers, those located in the inner city, those with fewer than 100 employees, and those not owned by minorities are more likely to state such negative views. However, these results should not be over interpreted, given the small sample sizes and nonrandom sample. Furthermore, differences in the probability of stating negative views do not necessarily correspond to differences in the probability of holding or acting on the views. Consequently, the key finding reported in this table is that negative assessments of Black men's soft skills appear in all categories of employers.

How and Why Employers Form These Perceptions

Employers indicated that they based their perceptions of Black men on experiences with past and present employees, on impressions of applicants, and on more general impressions from the media and from experiences outside work.[14] About half of respondents referred to their own employees, sometimes arguing that the immediacy of these observations rendered them objective. Stated a store manager,

> I think [Black men] feel things should be given to them and not earned. And because of that, they don't earn the right to keep jobs. Now that may be, you know, someone would say I may have an attitude problem, but that, I just look at pure facts. I mean with the people that I've had work for me.

In a few cases, employers drew inferences from differences across sites:

Table 19.4
Percentage of Employers Expressing Negative Views of Black Men's Soft Skills, by Firm Characteristics

	Percentage of Employers Expressing a Negative View of Black Men as Employees, in Terms of:			
	Interaction (%)	Motivation (%)	Either (%)	Sample Size (N)
All employers	32	40	53	57
By metro area				
Detroit	23	31	44	31
Los Angeles	39	48	61	26
By location				
Inner city	46	46	68	28
Rest of city	33	33	50	6
Suburb	0	21	21	14
Mixed	33	56	60	9
By firm size				
<100 employees	33	50	67	12
100 or more	31	38	50	45
By ownership				
Nonminority-owned	32	44	57	50
Minority-owned	17	17	17	6

Manufacturing human resource manager: The big problem with the inner-city male is transportation and to some degree the motivation to work. I have been in organizations in Glendale on the other side of the city, and our stability there was not as high.

Store manager: I was at Culver City before I went to this store, and it seems like we had a very high turnover in that area, and it was a very, very busy store, and it was probably 95% Black. And I think there is a different work ethic.

A much smaller number described the applicant pool as a basis for assessments about Black men. In a number of cases, informants pleaded ignorance due to a lack of Black applicants: "It's hard for us to say [why Black men do poorly in the labor market], because we don't have a large enough community, so we don't interview very many Blacks, and we don't reject many Blacks."

Other employers, especially those in White or Hispanic areas, referred to contact with Blacks outside the workplace. A White male insurance manager outside Detroit reported:

I am involved and attend an urban church, and we attend there working with the homeless and the retarded and people of that nature, [and] unless something is done to help these Black males, it is just a sorry situation.

Although no respondent specifically cited the media as a source for their impressions of Black men, the impact of the media was evident, as in these two comments by White Detroit area manufacturing managers:

Manager 1: We have a lot guys out there with cocaine in their pocket and Uzis in the trunk.

Manager 2: I think a lot of [the difficulty Black men face in the labor market] is based on their inability to complete schooling early on, for whatever reason. I don't know a lot of the statistics of the Black race but I do see that. I think that is a good fact. . . . It's going to take unfortunately a heck of a long time to fully eliminate discrimination. We hear about it in the news still, and it's a shame.

Those managers who spoke at length often wove together information from a wide variety of personal experiences inside and outside the workplace, combined with general knowledge shaped by the media. For instance, the White owner of a small manufacturing shop in a Los Angeles suburb related:

[Forty years ago in Los Angeles] the workforce was Caucasian, and the lower end of the workforce, the labor end, was Black. . . . Through civil rights and so forth, the Black community elevated themselves into positions that weren't there [previously]. . . . As that workforce disappeared and the great migration from the Latin countries [took place], it became a Latino environment. We put an ad in the paper, we would have had very few Caucasian applicants. Even very few Black applicants.

It seems that the Black kids maybe just don't want to work. . . . Why should they take an entry-level job when they can make more on some sort of welfare, unemployment, or dealing drugs? We have a lot of poor people in the city, a lot of homeless, people asking for money. . . . I was in the L.A. airport a while back and a Black man walks up to me and says "hey man, I need five bucks." It is a "gimme" attitude. I can remember as a kid a man coming into my father's store and saying, "I need money, can I sweep the floors for 50 cents?" But that is not the way it is anymore, now it's "can you spare a quarter" or "can you spare a dollar." Nobody wants to work for it.

Even more important than how employers form their perceptions of Black men is why they hold these views. We argue that the negative views are a complicated combination of stereotypes, realities, and conflicting cultures. The evidence that stereotypes are involved is straightforward. On the one hand, some respondents voiced clearly stereotypical attitudes: "Black men are lazy. . . . They've got no respect for anyone"; and "I'm no doctor . . . but I'm convinced, having dealt with grievance and unrest . . . that Black men, and to some extent Black women, do not deal with stress physically as well as some other races."

On the other hand, certain managers charged that other managers harbored stereotypical views:

People have a tendency to look toward, even if they don't voice it, they deal with their stereotypes. It's easy to identify someone as a female or identify someone as a Black male or a White male. And so whatever it is that they have of their expectations of those people, they will project that.

In particular, some managers claimed that their peers engaged in statistical discrimination or generalized from a visible but unrepresentative subset of Black men:

I think that many employers may feel that because of the large numbers of Black males who are in prison and have problems, that there is a tendency for those who are out and in the workforce to do mischievous things. That's unfortunate.

And one informant, a Black female manager at a Detroit area utility, contended that employers hold Blacks to a different standard than Whites:

When Blacks and Hispanics and whomever come into the work group, and they are not part of the majority, then one thing they need to know is that they cannot always do what they see others doing, and that is key. That is a lesson that needs to be taught. I think the rules aren't always the same, and it may not always be intentional. A lot is institutional and lot of it is people just not understanding others.

We believe that the perceptions stated by employers contain an element of reality as well. We have no independent way of verifying the statements employers made. However, some comments offered substantial detail and specificity, and some referred to "objective" measures such as absenteeism. More convincing, a variety of other research, including ethnography (Anderson, 1990; Wilson, 1987), surveys (Wilson, 1987), and focus groups (Jobs for the Future, 1995), reports that many young Black men in U.S. inner cities really do act "tough" and that they really are skeptical of what legitimate jobs offer and find other alternatives attractive. Wilson (1987), for instance, concluded that poor neighborhoods generated less opportunity to develop interaction skills and motivation. Anderson (1990) cautioned, however, that although young, inner-city Black men may lag in the skills most sought by employers, they possess a wealth of other soft skills needed to survive and thrive in dangerous environments.

Wilson (1987) argued that soft-skill problems are the product of poor neighborhoods; a number of our informants argued instead that such skills—and particularly motivation—are endogenous to the workplace and labor market. As a Black human resource official of a Detroit-area insurer expressed it,

> I think business drives the work ethic. . . . If business is lax . . . then people have casual attitudes about their jobs. . . . You are one thing up to the point of entering the business world, but then you are something else. I'm not the same person I was 15 years ago. I had to take on certain thoughts and attitudes whether I liked it or not.

Several others agreed that motivation is more a function of management than of the workforce. When asked about racial differences in the work ethic, a White male manager of contracted public-sector workers mused,

> I think it's how you motivate each group. Two or three years ago, I would have probably said, well, the Black race isn't as motivated as the Oriental or the Hispanic. But I've seen that if you motivate, that you have to motivate each group differently.

A White male public-sector human resource official added that work ethic may vary by job:

> If I take security, or I take the basic labor jobs, I'm not so sure that when they were Caucasian-dominated 20 years ago, that people weren't leaning on a shovel and goldbricking. Many times, the classifications we normally associate with being more lazy or finding ways to avoid work, are the entry-level, lower skilled ones. And now those happen to be dominated by Blacks and to a lesser extent Hispanics right now.

A small number of informants also argued that workers can be trained to relate well to customers. Even a store manager who commented that "it does take a certain kind of person" to be "fast, fun, and friendly," added, "but if you work with a person, I think that you could pretty much [get them to] be fast, fun, and friendly."

The ability of employers to shape work attitudes is strikingly evident in the contrast between two department store distribution warehouses located in the same Latino neighborhood in the Los Angeles area. In one case, personnel officials complained sarcastically about employees' laziness, their propensity for theft, the presence of "gang bangers" wearing their gang colors, and even the poor personal hygiene of the workforce. Turnover in this warehouse stands at 25%, even after personnel beefed up screening to select more stable employees. In the second warehouse, however, turnover is 2%. Although this warehouse also employs large numbers of present and past gang members, managers have successfully imposed a dress code that bans the wearing of colors. The key to the remarkably low turnover, according to the vice president for human resources, "is simply locating your operation in an area where you don't have an awful lot of competition, and what competition you do have, you meet or exceed all pay and benefits they offer." And indeed, this warehouse pays its entry-level workers from 50 cents to $2.50 more per hour than its competitor. The contrast suggests that efficiency wage models (Akerlof & Yellen, 1986) help to explain worker attitude and effort.

In addition to stereotype and reality, interviewees spoke of cultural gaps between young Black men and their supervisors, coworkers, and customers—especially as an explanation of difficulties in interaction. A Black human resource manager at an insurance company described the problems of cultural translation:

> I think that, as I attend executive meetings, and in many cases, I'm the only Black man there, the cultural diversity and the strangeness that different people bring to one another—oftentimes people aren't prepared to receive what another person may be prepared to offer. And I think that through that lack of communication, a lot of times things are misunderstood. When problems occur, if I work for you and you had a

problem with me, you may not know how to approach me and vice versa, I may not know how to approach you.

White respondents also referred to "a difference in understanding," but were more likely to pose it as a failure of the Black men themselves: "[Young Black men] don't present themselves well to the employer, just because they don't know, they don't realize how they're communicating, or not communicating." This conforms with the view, expressed in focus groups by young, inner-city Black and Latino men, that code switching—being able to present oneself and communicate in ways acceptable to majority White culture—is the most important skill needed to find and keep a job (Jobs for the Future, 1995).

A Latina personnel official for a retail chain placed responsibility on both sides of the divide:

> I think [high Black male turnover] has a lot to do with the Black male culture. It's very, very difficult for the White male manager to relate to that. There isn't a lot of understanding. There isn't a lot of nurturing. There isn't a lot of openness going in either direction. . . . I mean, the way you walk could turn somebody off, could turn a manager off.

She and her boss, a non-Latino White man, had recently been through a management diversity training, and expressed new awareness of these issues:

> *He:* We do a little diversity test on that, how we perceive the Black male to be and how they really are.
>
> *She:* It's amazing we all have the same, you know, the consensus was right there on the board.
>
> *He:* We're trying to teach [managers] that it's a very good business decision to do that [hire minorities] because it's going to be a matter of necessity that we attract and retain various minority groups. . . . [Diversity training is] about teaching them to value [the other official's name] as a Hispanic individual and some of the cultural things about that, that she feels most close to. It's go-

ing to teach them that [she] may have a different set of values on certain issues than we do, appreciate and understand it.

In short, they claim that appropriate training can help close cultural gaps. On a related note, several auto parts manufacturers averred that the movement toward a team approach and employee involvement has reduced racial tensions by increasing communication among different skill and occupational groups.

The Importance of the Pre-employment Interview

Most of our respondents identified the pre-employment interview as the most important source of information about a job applicant. The proportion rating the interview most important amounted to 81% of auto parts respondents, 82% of those in retail, 87.5% of those in insurance, and 80% of the small number of public sector units not subject to civil service hiring procedures. In a typical comment, a retail personnel official remarked that in hiring sales staff, "The individual presentation is probably the most important source of information and the most important qualities are their apparent ability to relate to the interviewer and have that extend to relating to customers."

The growing stress on soft skills would lead one to expect growing reliance on the interview to assess these characteristics. Indeed, although we did not specifically ask about it, a few respondents did project an increasingly important role for the interview. The central and potentially growing role of the interview is bad news for Black men, because the interviewing process incorporates racial bias (Stone, Stone, & Dipboye, 1992).

Although some respondents spoke proudly of their ability to assess an applicant via interview, others acknowledged some discomfort with the subjectivity involved. "I hate to say this, but a lot of it is gut feeling," stated the personnel director in an auto parts manufacturer in Detroit. A public sector human resource official in

Los Angeles commented: "Woven into that [the interview assessment] is all of the individual interviewer prejudices, how they see the job, how they evaluate the candidate and how they present it. You cannot get away from that."

In general, public sector agencies place much less emphasis on personal interviews to screen candidates. A major Detroit area local government no longer conducts pre-employment interviews at all, according to an official, because interviews were not really used in hiring decisions and could have been interpreted as discriminatory. He argued that private-sector reliance on the interview is indeed discriminatory:

> The phenomenon [of discrimination] is very much linked up with that compunction [sic] of the private sector with wanting to press the meat before they hire you. There is all kinds of ways that discrimination happens. A lot of it is unconscious. We are past the point where on a mass basis, people are doing overt discrimination intentionally, but we still have it out there. . . . [People] don't examine their practices and question whether the impact of what they do is in fact racist.

Conclusions

We find that due to competitive pressure, employers are demanding more soft skills, even in low-skill jobs. Soft skills include interaction and motivation, and employers are valuing both more highly. However, many managers perceive Black men as possessing fewer soft skills, along both dimensions. Thus, the same increases in competitive pressure that drive corporate downsizing and restructuring are contributing to widening racial inequality in labor market outcomes.

Employers base their perceptions of Black men on assessments of current or past employees and applicants, as well as interaction outside the workplace, and media images of Blacks. Three factors underlie negative evaluations of Black men as workers: racial stereotypes, cultural differ-ences between employers and young Black men, and actual skill differences. The actual skill differences themselves are in part endogenous to the work situation. Moreover, in a work world characterized by increasing levels of interaction, racially biased attitudes held by customers or coworkers of other racial groups can themselves lead to lower measured productivity—that is, productivity differences can be the direct result of discrimination.

Our findings suggest some potential avenues for improvement of Black men's labor market experience—including both public policy and private, company-level policy. Several types of public policy can affect the demand for Black male labor. At the macrolevel, policies to reduce unemployment will aid Black men, who stand at the end of hiring queues (Freeman, 1989, 1990). The nearly double-digit unemployment rates in Detroit and Los Angeles at the time of our interviews were reflected in employer use of screening—rather than training—to obtain the worker skills they needed. But when labor markets are tighter, employers cannot be as selective. At the microlevel, affirmative action policies can spur employer efforts to hire Blacks, and minority contracting requirements and assistance for community economic development can help to sustain businesses that are committed to hiring Blacks and other disadvantaged groups.

Public policy can also act on the supply side, through training and support services for young, inner-city Black men. Based on our findings, there should be a high payoff to programs that teach code switching to assist inner-city Blacks in bridging the cultural divide with employers.

Company policies can also affect both demand and supply of labor. Demand-side policies would heighten business receptivity to young, less educated Black men. In this regard, several respondents touted diversity training. Others spoke about the importance of learning to manage in a way that elicits motivation. A number of managers reported that team-based management methods also help resolve difficulties in interaction. Minority contracting by private-sector customers, such as the Big Three automakers, extends beyond the reach of governmental minority contracting. Two Detroit area auto parts manufacturers that are minority contractors expounded to us at length about their efforts to hire and retain Black employees at every level. Employers can also create supply-side impacts by training less skilled Black men, for example, through school-to-work transition programs.

At least two goals can fuel these company-level policies. To some extent, companies undertake them to enhance their public image—a not insubstantial issue in cities like Detroit and Los Angeles, where racial and ethnic conflict shape local politics. But companies also seek to incorporate inner-city Black men—along with other disadvantaged groups—in order to tap a growing workforce that is ignored or underused by many employers (Johnston & Packer, 1987).

In addition, the renewed national policy dialogue on skills offers some potentially positive elements. The 1991 Secretary's Commission on Achieving Necessary Skills (SCANS) and subsequent efforts to promote national skill standards (Bailey & Merritt, 1994) have highlighted the importance of soft skills—but they have also emphasized that these are indeed skills that can be learned rather than simply innate qualities. The SCANS report, for example, identified *interpersonal skills* as one of five main competencies. To the extent that employers accept this view (for which there is considerable evidence; see Capelli, 1995), they may be more willing to train for such skills rather than simply screening for them.

To guide public and company-level policy, additional research is called for, on two tracks.[15] First, additional evidence is needed to corroborate or refute the patterns we identified. Such evidence could emerge from replication of the study on larger, more representative samples (as we are doing now) and from other methodologies (large-scale surveys, focus groups, and other approaches to studying employers and their prospective workers). Second, to

the extent that our conclusions are valid, they call out for further exploration of how employer stereotypes are formed and modified, how White employers and Black employees actually differ along cultural dimensions such as values and language, and to what extent worker and/or manager retraining can bridge these gaps. These broader questions call not just for added empirical work, but for a more complete theorization of the role of race in organizations (Ferdman, 1992; Nkomo, 1992). With answers to these questions, we can seek to modify the effects of trends that are otherwise likely to spell growing disadvantage for Black men.

Discussion Questions

1. The concept "emotional labor" was first coined by Arlie Hochschild to refer to work done predominantly by women, rather than Blacks. Describe some possible jobs to which this concept would apply.

2. Soft skills seem to be more important in service sector jobs than other jobs. Do you agree?

3. Have you ever worked in a job that required "soft skills"? If so, were you aware that such skills were required for the job before you were hired?

Philip Moss and Chris Tilly, " 'Soft' Skills and Race: An Investigation of Black Men's Employment Problems" (*Work and Occupations*, August 1996), pp. 252–276. Copyright ©1996 by Sage Publications, Inc. Reprinted by permission of Sage Publications, Inc.

Endnotes

1. We chose these cities primarily to conduct research in parallel with household surveys on labor market dynamics and other issues, oversampling communities of color, that have recently been undertaken in these cities (Johnson, Oliver, & Bobo, 1994). Both were cities in recession at the time of the study: over 1991–1992, unemployment averaged 9.1% in the Detroit metropolitan area and 8.8% in Los Angeles.

2. The sample was drawn from the Yellow Pages in each city, business directories, and more idiosyncratic sources such as suggestions from academic, business, community, and union contacts. Because the goal was an initial, small study focused on qualitative findings, we sought variety without requiring statistical reliability. At sampled companies, initial contact was made with the highest-ranking personnel official who had detailed knowledge of the hiring process. Interviews were typically conducted with this person or a deputy. Interviews typically lasted about 1.25 hours, and were taped and transcribed for analysis.

3. Typical occupations discussed within each industry were as follows. Auto parts manufacturing: mainly unskilled and semiskilled machine operators, although relatively skilled machinist jobs were discussed in a small number of cases. Retail clothing: cashier, clerk. Insurance: clerical jobs including data entry, file clerk, and customer service representative (in many companies these jobs were being combined). Public sector: this industry had the most varied set of occupations, including manual blue-collar, service, and clerical jobs.

4. Although the sample included 56 firms, Table 19.1 reports on 58 sites, because at one retailer, we gathered separate information on store, office, and warehouse sites. Across 49 variables, a mean of 1.8 observations out of the 58 sites had missing values. Most had no missing values; the highest number of missing values was 10. Where proportions are reported in this article, they omit missing values.

5. In another article (Moss & Tilly, 1995b), we reported results of regression analysis on these data.

6. One difficulty is that when employers discussed "speech" or "communication skills," they tended to combine hard skills such as knowledge of grammar with soft skills such as use of affectively or culturally appropriate speech. In this analysis, we counted references to spoken communication skills as soft skills; excluding them does not substantially alter the quantitative or qualitative findings we report.

7. Given small sample sizes, these differences in proportions should be interpreted with some caution.

8. Although soft skills are highly sought, certain soft skills may not be highly rewarded. For instance, England, Herbert, Kilbourne, Reid, and Megdal (1994) reported that occupations involving "nurturance" offered lower wages, even after controlling for gender composition.

9. Reported rises in hard skills and reported rises in soft skills were positively correlated, with $r = 0.24$.

10. Detroit employers viewed soft skills as less important and were less likely to report increases in soft skills than their Los Angeles counterparts. However, these differences were quite small after taking into account the somewhat different industry mixes of the samples in the two metropolitan areas.

11. Possible reasons for this discrepancy include the fact that Osterman limited his sample to firms employing 50 or more, that he coded open-ended responses in a way that excluded multiple types of skill changes, and that the "blue collar" category omits the service and clerical jobs that characterized much of our sample. Of course, it is also quite possible that the industries we sampled are not fully representative of U.S. employment, or that the operations managers surveyed by Osterman have different perceptions of skill changes than the human resource managers we interviewed.

12. We discuss qualitative findings about growing demands for soft skills at more length in Moss and Tilly, 1996.

13. The correlations between variables indicating the importance of soft skills and negative perceptions of Black men were generally small (ranging from 0.01 to 0.25) but positive, with one exception: there was a negative correlation between negative perceptions of Black men other than those related to interaction or motivation, and the placement of soft skills first on the list of the most important qualities for an entry-level job.

14. We did not directly ask employers to state the basis for their perceptions, but as they discussed the perceptions, these patterns emerged.

15. We are indebted to two anonymous referees for suggesting these directions for future research.

References

Akerlof, G. A., & Yellen, J. L. (1986). *Efficiency wage models of the labor market.* Cambridge: Cambridge University Press.

Anderson, E. (1990). *Streetwise: Race, class, and change in an urban community.* Chicago: University of Chicago Press.

Arrow, K. (1972a). Models of job discrimination. In A. H. Pascal (Ed.), *Racial discrimination in economic life* (pp. 83–102). Lexington, MA: Lexington Books.

——. (1972b). Some mathematical models of race in the labor market. In A. H. Pascal (Ed.), *Racial discrimination in economic life* (pp. 187–204). Lexington, MA: Lexington Books.

——. (1973). The theory of discrimination. In O. A. Ashenfelter & A. Rees (Eds.), *Discrimination in labor markets* (pp. 3–33). Princeton, NJ: Princeton University Press.

Bailey, T., & Merritt, D. (1994). *Making sense of industry-based skills standards.* Mimeo, Institute for Education and the Economy, Columbia University, New York.

Becker, G. S. (1957). *The economics of discrimination.* Chicago: University of Chicago Press.

Bound, J., & Freeman, R. B. (1992). What went wrong? The erosion of the relative earnings and employment of young Black men in the 1980s. *Quarterly Journal of Economics, 107*(1), 201–232.

Capelli, P. (1995). Is the "skills gap" really about attitudes? *California Management Review, 37*(4), 108–124.

Darrah, C. (1994). Skill requirements at work: Rhetoric vs. reality. *Work and Occupations, 21,* 64–84.

England, P. (1992). *Comparable worth: Theories and evidence.* New York: Aldine de Gruyter.

England, P., Herbert, M. S., Kilbourne, B. S., Reid, L. L., & Megdal, L. M. (1994). The gendered valuation of occupations and skills: Earnings in 1980 census occupations. *Social Forces, 73*(1), 65–99.

Ferdman, B. M. (1992) The dynamics of ethnic diversity in organizations: Toward integrative models. In K. Kelley (Ed.), *Issues, theory, and research in industrial/organizational psychology* (pp. 339–384). New York: Elsevier.

Ferguson, R. (1993). *New evidence on the growing value of skill and consequences for racial disparity and returns to schooling* (Paper H-93-10, Malcom Wiener Center for Social Policy). Boston, MA: John F. Kennedy School of Government, Harvard University.

Ford, J. K., Kraiger, K., & Schectman, S. L. (1986). Study of race effects in objective indices and subjective evaluations of performance: A meta-analysis of performance criteria. *Psychological Bulletin, 99,* 330–337.

Freeman, R. B. (1989). *Help wanted: Disadvantaged youths in a labor shortage economy.* Mimeo, National Bureau of Economic Research.

Freeman, R. B. (1990). *Labor market tightness and the mismatch between demand and supply of less educated young men in the United States in the 1980s.* Mimeo, National Bureau of Economic Research.

Greenhaus, J. H., Parasuraman, J., & Wormley, W. M. (1990). Effects of race on organizational experiences, job performance evaluations, and career outcomes. *Academy of Management Journal, 33*(1), 64–86.

Hochschild, A. R. (1983). *The managed heart: Commercialization of human feeling.* Berkeley: University of California Press.

Holzer, H. (1996). *What employers want: Job prospects for less-educated workers.* New York: Russell Sage Foundation.

Jackson, S. E. (1991). Team composition in organizational settings: Issues in managing an increasingly diverse workforce. In S. Worchel, W. Wood, & J. Simpson (Eds.), *Group process and productivity* (pp. 138–173). Newbury Park, CA: Sage.

Jencks, C. (1991). Is the American underclass growing? In C. Jencks & P. E. Peterson (Eds.), *The urban underclass* (pp. 28–100). Washington, DC: Brookings Institution.

Jobs for the Future. (1995). Information from focus groups of young, inner city men of color, for work in progress. Unpublished manuscripts. Boston, MA: Author, for the Annie E. Casey Foundation.

Johnson, J. H., Jr., Oliver, M. L., & Bobo, L. (1994). Understanding the contours of deepening urban inequality: Theoretical underpinnings and research design of a multi-city study. *Urban Geography, 15*(1), 77–89.

Johnston, W. B. & Packer, A. H. (1987). *Workforce 2000: Work and workers for the 21st century.* Indianapolis, IN: Hudson Institute.

Juhn, C., Murphy, K. M., & Pierce, B. (1991). Accounting for the slowdown in Black-White wage convergence. In M. H. Kosters (Ed.), *Workers and their wages: Changing patterns in the United States.* Washington, DC: AEI Press.

Kilbourne, B. S., England, P., & Beron, K. (1994). Effects of changing individual, occupational, and industrial characteristics on changes in earnings: Intersections of race and gender. *Social Forces, 72,* 1149–1176.

Kirschenman, J., Moss, P., & Tilly, C. (1996). *Space as a signal, space as a barrier: How employers map and use space in four metropolitan labor markets* (Working Paper No. 89). New York: Russell Sage Foundation.

Kirschenman, J., & Neckerman, K. M. (1991). "We'd love to hire them, but . . .: The meaning of race for employers. In C. Jencks & P. E. Peterson (Eds.), *The urban underclass* (pp. 203–232). Washington, DC: Brookings Institution.

Kraiger, K., & Ford, J. K. (1985). A meta-analysis of race effects in performance ratings. *Journal of Applied Psychology, 70,* 56–65.

Moss, P., & Tilly, C. (1991). *Why Black men are doing worse in the labor market: A review of supply-side and demand-side explanations* (Monograph). New York: Social Science Research Council.

——. (1995a). *Raised hurdles for Black men: Evidence from employer interviews* (Working Paper No. 81). New York: Russell Sage Foundation.

——. (1995b). Skills and race in hiring: Quantitative findings from face-to-face interviews. *Eastern Economic Journal, 21,* 357–374.

——. (1996). *Growing demand for "soft" skills in four industries: Evidence from in-depth employer interviews* (Working Paper No. 93). New York: Russell Sage Foundation.

Neckerman, K. M., & Kirschenman, J. (1991). Hiring strategies, racial bias, and inner-city workers. *Social Problems, 38*(4), 801–815.

Nkomo, S. M. (1992). The emperor has no clothes: Rewriting "Race in Organizations." *Academy of Management Review, 17*(3), 487–513.

O'Neill, J. (1990). The role of human capital in earnings differences between Black and White men. *The Journal of Economic Perspectives, 4*(4), 25–46.

Osterman, P. (1995). Skill, training, and work organization in American establishments. *Industrial Relations, 34*(2), 125–146.

Phelps, E. (1972). The statistical theory of racism and sexism. *American Economic Review, 62,* 659–661.

Sackett, P. R., & DuBois, C. L. Z. (1991). Rater-ratee effects on performance evaluation: Challenging meta-analytic conclusions. *Journal of Applied Psychology, 76*(6), 873–877.

Secretary's Commission on Achieving Necessary Skills. (1991). *What work requires of schools: A SCANS report for America 2000.* Washington, DC: U.S. Department of Labor.

Shellenbarger, S. (1993, September 3). Work-force study finds loyalty is weak, divisions of race and gender are deep. *Wall Street Journal,* p. B1.

Stone, E. R., Stone, D. L., & Dipboye, R. L. (1992). Stigmas in organizations: Race, handicaps, and physical unattractiveness. In K. Kelley (Ed.), *Issues, theory, and research in industrial/organizational psychology* (pp. 385–457). New York: Elsevier.

Tajfel, H., & Turner, J. C. (1986). The social identity theory of intergroup behavior. In S. Worchel & W. G. Austin (Eds.), *Psychology of intergroup relations* (pp. 7–24). Chicago: Nelson-Hall.

Tsui, A. S., Egan, T. D., & O'Reilly, C. A., III. (1992). Being different: Relational demography and organizational attachment. *Administrative Science Quarterly, 37,* 549–579.

Tsui, A. S., & O'Reilly, C. A. (1989). Beyond simple demographic effects: The importance of relational demography in superior-subordinate dyads. *Academy of Management Journal, 32,* 402–423.

Vallas, S. (1990). The concept of skill: A critical review. *Work and Occupations, 17,* 379–398.

Waldinger, R. (1993). *Who makes the beds? Who washes the dishes? Black/immigrant competition reassessed* (Working Paper 246). Los Angeles: Institute of Industrial Relations, University of California at Los Angeles.

Wharton, A. (1993). The affective consequences of service work: Managing emotions on the job. *Work and Occupations, 20*(2), 205–232.

Wilson, W. J. (1987). *The truly disadvantaged.* Chicago: University of Chicago Press. ◆

20

Glass Ceilings and Glass Escalators

David J. Maume, Jr.

David Maume addresses the question of how likely promotion into a professional occupation with managerial responsibilities can be determined by a structural factor like gender composition, which is not an individual characteristic. To do this, he focuses on the gender and racial segregation of workers' initial job; that is, the extent to which women and blacks are concentrated in specific initial jobs. He shows that the effect of gender segregation on promotions to management differ for men and women. He also shows that the effect of the percentage of blacks in initial jobs works differently for men and women. Finally, he shows how the speed of promotion varies by gender and race.

White women, Black women, and Black men are disproportionately excluded from supervisory authority, resulting in lower pay for these groups (Kanter, 1977; Kluegel, 1978; Reskin & Ross, 1995; Wolf & Fligstein, 1979). Increased representation of minority groups in managerial positions is a necessary condition for achieving parity in work rewards.

Women have made some inroads into management. In 1970, 18% of managers were women; by 1990, two in five were women (Reskin & Ross, 1995). Olson and Frieze's (1987) survey of the literature found small gender differences in starting salaries of master of business administration (MBA) graduates. Jacobs (1992) found that the ratio of women's to men's earnings among managers increased from 56.9% to 61.1% between 1969 and 1987.

For Blacks, evidence of progress is mixed. The proportion of Black men in management increased from 1.3% to 6.7% between 1940 and 1970 (Farley & Allen, 1987) but fell back to 6.3% by 1984 (Jaynes & Williams, 1989). Black women showed a similar pattern, with an overall increase from .7% to 5.2% between 1940 and 1984 (Jaynes & Williams, 1989). Because Black men and Black women constitute only a small fraction of all managers, Blacks' rate of entry into management exceeded that for Whites in the 1970s (Nkomo & Cox, 1990, p. 39). Given that one of the most controversial figures in sociology predicts a convergence of Black and White mobility chances (Wilson, 1980, 1989), these figures bear on important theoretical and policy questions regarding the status of African Americans in U.S. society.

Despite some progress, White women, Black women, and Black men continue to face barriers within corporations. Business magazines have documented the almost total absence of these groups from top positions within large firms (e.g., see Cordtz, 1994). The term *glass ceiling* suggests that despite their increased presence in corporations, White women, Black women, and Black men fail to attain top managerial positions in the firm.

Numerous studies indicate that women and men are allocated to different positions when entering a firm (Bielby & Baron, 1986; Kanter, 1977; Reskin, 1988; Tomaskovic-Devey, 1993). Moreover, race and sex segregation account for substantial portions of the pay gap between White men and other groups (Baron & Newman, 1990; England, Farkas, Kilbourne, & Dou, 1988; England, Herbert, Kilbourne, Reid, & Megdal, 1994; Jacobs & Steinberg, 1990; Kilbourne, England, Farkas, Beron, & Weir, 1994; Sorenson, 1989; Tomaskovic-Devey, 1993). Despite the value of these studies, their reliance on cross-sectional samples precludes an examination of career changes. Examining the impact of segregation on economic rewards at a single point in time cannot explicate the sorting process that maintains and exacerbates inequality over time. By definition, careers take place over time as individuals move between jobs, and movement from nonsupervisory to supervisory positions is often associated with income growth and career development.

Case studies and interview data suggest that segregation affects the chances of receiving a promotion (e.g., see Kanter, 1977; Williams, 1992). Although informative, these studies are subject to the criticism that they rely on relatively small (and possibly unique) samples. To draw the attention of policy makers, studies of inequality often must obtain representative samples of the labor force. A few studies do show a segregation effect on movement to a higher pay grade but with samples from a single firm (Hartmann, 1987; Paulin & Mellor, 1996) or from the public sector (DiPrete & Soule, 1988; Steinberg, Haignere, & Chertos, 1990). Samples from a single firm may not generalize to the labor force as a whole, however. In addition, economists contend that because government employers need not make a profit to survive, they will adopt pay and promotion policies that differ from those in the private sector (Filer, 1990).

I am unaware of a longitudinal study providing robust statistical evidence of the association between occupational segregation and managerial mobility using a representative sample of the labor force. That is the purpose of this article. Using the Panel Study of Income Dynamics (PSID), I estimate a discrete-time hazard rate model to examine the managerial transitions of U.S. workers. Results from this analysis will assess the degree of similarity (or dissimilarity) between White men and other groups in the speed and process of ascending to managerial positions. Findings from this article will also bear on the enduring controversy of a declining significance of race. Below, I review prior research to develop testable hypotheses regarding race and gender differences in managerial promotions.

Occupational Segregation and Managerial Promotions

Whereas most studies fail to investigate the process of advancement to managerial positions, wage growth is an important correlate of authority mobility. Thus, this section reviews the sociological arguments linking occupational segregation with earnings. Most of the segregation literature is concerned with gender segregation. After an extended discussion of gender segregation, this section will conclude with a brief review of racial segregation.

Gender Segregation and Careers

Reskin and Roos (1990) provide a useful way to conceptualize segregation. They contend that workers rank jobs in terms of their desirability and rewards, whereas employers rank workers in terms of their skills and commitment to work. Men and women hold similar evaluations of jobs, but for discriminatory reasons, employers rank men ahead of women in the labor queue. Thus, the labor queue is essentially a gender queue, and sex segregation across jobs reflects stereotypical notions about the kinds of work that are appropriate for men and women. Reskin and Roos then draw on case studies to illuminate the process of redefining the sex type of jobs. Women move into "male" jobs either because market conditions force employers to reach down into the labor queue to hire women, or because men reevaluate and vacate jobs, thereby creating openings for women.

Although Reskin and Roos (1990) set out to explain changes in the sex type of jobs, their discussion reveals several ways in which men maintain their privileged position in the labor queue (see also Acker, 1990; Baron & Newman, 1990; Reskin, 1988). First, social closure processes describe the means by which men resist attempts at job integration. Through administrative rules and requirements for skill and experience, men effectively limit the pool of women competing for what may be considered the better jobs in the economy.

By segregating women into female-typed jobs, men are free to compete among themselves for higher paying jobs that offer better career opportunities (Cockburn, 1991; Tomaskovic-Devey, 1993). Those who do enter male-dominated occupations are harassed and isolated, which limits their effectiveness (Kanter, 1977) and drives some out of the job (Jacobs, 1989). Furthermore, the social closure argument contends that women are confined to short promotion ladders in which the few available supervisory opportunities are supervising other women doing routine work (Kanter, 1977).

Related to the social closure explanation is the status composition perspective, which contends that occupations with large numbers of female incumbents are devalued in the eyes of the organization. The jobs women hold are viewed as peripheral to the mission of the firm and require skills easily learned in the home. Steinberg (1990) clearly demonstrates the impact of status composition processes in her analysis of comparable worth job evaluation schemes. She found that women received fewer points for the skills used in their jobs compared with the skills in men's jobs, resulting in women's lower pay. In addition, employers provide fewer training opportunities to women in female-typed occupations (Acker, 1990; Baron & Newman, 1990; Bielby & Baron, 1986; Cockburn, 1991; Reskin, 1988; Tomaskovic-Devey, 1993). We may expect that low pay coupled with the denial of opportunity to grow professionally will result in stagnant career profiles.

Yet, these studies do not address the impact of occupational segregation on managerial promotions. Rather, Kanter (1977) provides a point of departure for understanding how the gender composition of an occupation affects the process of becoming a manager. Kanter found that much of what managers do is create and convey information. To accomplish their goals, effective managers must build rapport and secure the cooperation of diverse units in the firm. Managers prefer to interact with those who share their background and life experiences so as to build alliances and to reduce the chances of miscommunication. Be-

cause women are perceived as different, they are often overlooked when filling managerial positions.

In chapter 6 of her classic work, Kanter (1977) contends that opportunity is a characteristic of jobs, not people. In doing so, Kanter incorporates the perspectives above. She found evidence of social closure when talented women with career ambitions were shunted off to clerical and office jobs to work beside other women. Once in these positions, Kanter described how the organization failed to train women, develop their skills, or give them visible jobs that would enhance their mobility. She found that most women in sex-typical jobs fail to move out of them. She was also interested, however, in the few instances when secretaries received promotions to management positions. She found that in their previous clerical jobs, women had not received the training or job assignments needed for competence in their managerial roles. Women's subsequent failure as managers was viewed by the organization as further proof of women's inability to manage. This crowding of women into sex-typical office jobs illustrates status composition processes. The firm's neglect of these women led to stalled careers for most and ineffective performance in higher level jobs for the few who were promoted.

Although Kanter (1977) provides some valuable insights, her study does not examine gender differences in mobility using a multivariate framework. Her results suggest that segregation is largely responsible for women's lack of authority mobility, but without controls for human capital and other factors, we cannot definitively conclude that this is the case. Others have examined the relative impact of demographic, human capital, and job-related factors in exercising authority on the job. Reskin and Ross (1995), for example, found that percentage of women present in the occupation determined the amount of discretionary authority. Their sample was restricted to those workers who had already attained managerial status, however. Thus, they did not examine gender differences in the process of entering management and the impact of segregation on this process. Similarly, Jacobs (1992) drew samples of managers from two national data sets and examined gender differences in earnings, working conditions, and attitudes. Jacobs found that from 1969 to 1987, the gender gap in wages closed slightly, whereas the authority gap remained the same. Nevertheless, Jacobs does not examine the impact of occupational segregation on transitions into management. Finally, Wolf and Fligstein (1979) found that occupation type (i.e., whether the job is female typed or not) affected supervisory authority in a general sample of workers. Unfortunately, their sample was cross-sectional (which precluded a study of career effects) and taken in 1975 (just as women were beginning to enter the ranks of management).

Although there is little work on the impact of occupational segregation on promotions into management, the literature suggests a negative effect. If men monopolize the best positions in the economy and female-typed jobs are devalued within organizations, then the chances that women will receive a managerial promotion should decline with percentage of women present in the occupation. However, the impact of segregation may itself vary by gender, with men possibly benefiting from employment in female-dominated occupations, as suggested by Williams (1992, 1995).

Williams (1992) interviewed nurses, teachers, librarians, and social workers. She found that the construction of a male identity was problematic in these positions. Many men were viewed as deviants because they worked in occupations that required nurturing skills that women are believed to possess uniquely (England et al., 1994). In particular, clients preferred women to men for teaching their children, dispensing advice to welfare mothers, or giving sponge baths to patients. This preference was often expressed to supervisors, who resolved the situation by moving men to managerial positions and out of contact with the organization's clients.

Coworkers also assumed that men were temporarily doing women's work and were looking to move up. On one hand, many women welcomed male colleagues because they thought it might raise the status of the profession. On the other hand, they also partly agreed with clients who regarded these jobs as proper places of employment for women but not men. The prevailing assumption was that men are less capable than women of performing nurturing tasks and better suited to instrumental tasks, such as organizational planning and delegating authority. Moreover, men's underrepresentation in these female professions also worked to their advantage. Because of the scarcity of male coworkers, men often bonded with their male supervisors. Sharing similar interests in so-called male activities (e.g., golf, home and car maintenance, etc.) resulted in the formation of mentoring relationships that fostered men's transitions into management.

Williams (1992, 1995) found that to improve workplace morale and customer relations, organizations promoted men in female-dominated occupations, a phenomenon she called the "glass escalator." Williams also found that some men recognized the existence of the glass escalator, with some admitting that they opted for careers in female-dominated occupations because they provided a stepping stone to management status. Although Williams's argument is provocative, it is based on interviews with 76 men and 23 women in four semi-professions. There are no multivariate studies testing the predictive power of the glass escalator argument in a general sample of workers. This article provides such a test.

To summarize the argument thus far, there is much research showing that how an occupation is viewed by the organization varies with gender composition. As occupations become more "female," they are increasingly viewed as depositories for female entrants into the firm. In these occupations, women find that their skills are overlooked and that they are denied training opportunities. These dynamics result in lower pay and failure to attain managerial positions. But for men, increasing representation of women in an occupation poses problems for the organization's clients and may disrupt workplace morale. To alleviate these strains, men are more likely to move to managerial positions as women's presence in the origin job increases. Based on the literature cited above, the first hypothesis tested is as follows:

Hypothesis 1: Percentage of workers who are female in the origin occupation will negatively affect women's chances of moving into managerial positions but positively affect men's promotion chances.

Racial Segregation and Careers

Whereas the topic of racial segregation has drawn much less attention than gender segregation (Tomaskovic-Devey, 1993), there are indications in the literature that similar processes are at work. For example, there is little doubt that White men seek to exclude Black women and Black men as competitors for prestigious jobs, as suggested, by the social closure argument (for a review, see Wilson, 1980). One way to minimize encroachment into privileged positions is to channel Black women and Black men into "racialized" jobs. That is, Black executives tend to be placed in liaison jobs linking the company to the Black community or to advocates for Black equality (Collins, 1983, 1993; Jones, 1986). In the public sector, this results in the concentration of Black women and Black men in agencies with Black clients, such as social welfare or corrections (Collins, 1993). In the private sector, Blacks are hired to market products to the Black community or run affirmative action programs (Collins, 1993). The problem with these assignments was summarized nicely by one of Jones's (1986) informants:

Too often Black managers are channeled into The Relations as I call them—the community relations, the public relations, the personnel relations. These may be important functions, but they are not the gut functions that make the business grow or bring in revenues. And they are not the jobs that prepare an executive to be a CEO. (p. 89)

If this experience is typical, the channeling of Black workers into racialized jobs reserves the more visible and revenue-producing jobs (sales, marketing, product development, etc.) for Whites. Moreover, the impact of segregation will be magnified if there is evidence that the firm neglects or devalues jobs that are increasingly associated with minorities, as the status composition perspective suggests. Indeed, two studies found that supervisor ratings of job complexity and skill requisites were lower when the job was held by large numbers of Blacks (Braddock & McPartland, 1987; Greenhaus, Parasuraman, & Wormley, 1990).

These findings suggest a segregation effect in that Black women and Black men are hired into and then allowed to languish in racialized jobs. There is also evidence that the percentage of Blacks in a job reduces earnings (Baron & Newman, 1990; Tomaskovic-Devey, 1993). Unfortunately, the evidence linking racial segregation with managerial transitions is sketchy at best. Paulin and Mellor (1996) found that percentage of minority workers in a job reduced the chances of moving to a higher pay grade, but the sample was drawn from a single firm, and the process of entering management was not examined. Another study looked at racial composition on promotions, but the sample consisted of current managers and did not assess how segregation affected movement into supervisory positions (Greenhaus et al., 1990).

Because of the lack of research on the subject, this article will examine the promotion effect of racial composition in the origin occupation. Unlike Williams's (1992) discussion of the glass escalator, which posits that men move upward after working in female-typed jobs, there is no research indicating that Whites will similarly benefit from working in Black-dominated jobs. Thus, the devaluing effects of placement in a minority-typed occupation should affect all incumbents, suggesting the following hypothesis:

Hypothesis 2: Percentage of Black workers in the origin occupation will negatively affect the chances of entering management.

Testing the Hypotheses

Research suggests that employers evaluate worker characteristics differently depending on the gender of the incumbent (Acker, 1990; Reskin, 1988). For example, having a spouse or young children may signal stability in men but a potential work disruption in women (Rosenfeld, 1980). For this reason, the models will be analyzed separately by gender. Hypothesis 1 will be confirmed if the sign on the gender composition variable is positive for men and negative for women. Unfortunately, there were too few Blacks entering management to reliably estimate promotion models by race. Thus, Blacks and Whites will be pooled in gender-specific models that control for the race of the respondent. Hypothesis 2 will be supported if percentage of Black workers in the origin occupation is negative for men and women alike. Such a finding would suggest that rising levels of racial segregation reduce mobility chances for all workers.

In addition to the mobility effects of race and sex segregation in the origin occupation, this article examines the significance of the race coefficient in predicting managerial promotions. Wilson's (1980, 1989) "declining significance of race" thesis suggests that expanded educational opportunities and the passage of antidiscrimination legislation have created unprecedented mobility opportunities for African Americans. Wilson claims that family background and social class are better determinants of access to good jobs than is racial identity per se. If Wilson is correct, the race effect on entering management should be insignificant.

Yet, if the race effect on managerial mobility proves to be significant, Wilson would reject the assertion that such a finding contradicts his thesis. Wilson (1989) contends that racial comparisons that include older Blacks are biased because older Blacks suffered discrimination in the past, which depresses their current rewards compared with Whites. Wilson goes on to assert that analyses limited to younger and better educated Blacks should show a convergence in mobility opportunities with their White counterparts. For this reason, supplemental analyses will examine the impact of race on managerial mobility among a sample of workers who entered the labor market after the passage of antidiscrimination legislation and who have attained success in school. Wilson's argument will receive support if race insignificantly predicts mobility chances in this subset of workers (see Cancio, Evans, & Maume, 1996, for an elaboration of this approach in testing Wilson's argument).

Data, Design, and Measures

Data

Data for this study come from the PSID, a representative, longitudinal survey (Institute for Social Research, 1992) in which year-to-year attrition rates are low. The PSID originated in 1968, collecting information on all members of 5,000 families to determine changes in the fortunes of American families. The sample selected for this article consists of Black and White adults between the ages of 18 and 62 in 1981. Hispanics were excluded from the analysis because there were not enough Hispanics included in the early years of the PSID.[1]

Selection into the initial sample in 1981 was conditional on several factors. First, individuals were included if they were working for an employer in a nonmanagerial occupation (to examine transitions into management). Second, exclusively self-employed individuals were deleted from the sample because the concept of a managerial promotion is inappropriate when the individual is both the boss and a worker. Third, members of the armed forces were excluded because they do not participate in a labor market.

Analytic Design

By comparing respondents' occupations across survey years, the analyst can detect movement into managerial positions. The PSID changed the wording on important variables (e.g., employer and job tenure) in 1989; to remain consistent across all years of the study, work histories were examined through the 1988 survey year. Thus, this article examines job changes over the calendar years 1981 to 1987. A discrete-time hazard rate model is used to model career experiences (Allison, 1984; Teachman, 1983). The strategy in event history analysis is to estimate the probability of receiving a managerial promotion for each person year of exposure to the risk of experiencing the event. This entails treating each year as if it were a sample and pooling the seven samples of workers at risk of moving into management.

Workers were defined as being at risk for receiving a managerial promotion if they worked in a nonmanagerial job and were paid by an employer. Beginning in 1981, workers were followed until they experienced a career transition, such as a managerial promotion, or a move to unemployment or self-employment (see below). At this point, the worker is no longer in the risk set and is dropped from the analysis. Thus, the number of cases contributing to the pooled data set decreases each year. Respondents excluded from the initial sample in 1981 (i.e., nonworking respondents or those exclusively self-employed) could enter the risk set in later years if they met the selection criteria (i.e., worked in a nonmanagerial job for an employer for pay). Like those selected in 1981, these workers remained in the risk set until they experienced a career transition. The total number of person years in the 1981 to 1987 pooled data set was 8,534 men and 7,778 women.

After pooling the 7 years of observations, the analyst specifies a logistic regression equation, which models the log odds of entering a management position between $year_t$ and $year_{t+1}$. Because tenure is controlled, the model estimates the log odds of receiving a promotion given the failure to have been promoted at an earlier duration. Results from this model approximate a discrete-time hazard rate model, which easily accommodates time-varying covariates (Allison, 1984; Teachman, 1983).

The Dependent Variable: Entry Into Management

At the beginning of any $year_t$, all workers in the risk set worked for an employer in a nonmanagerial occupation, as classified by the Census Bureau's 1970 three-digit standard occupation classification codes. In $year_{t+1}$, workers who worked in managerial positions (i.e., occupation codes 201 through 245) received a 1 on a binary variable signifying entry into a management occupation; all other workers received a 0. Conceptualizing managerial promotions in this way raises two methodological issues.

First, in the past, the Census Bureau treated many job titles as technical or sales positions, although they involved managerial duties. In 1970 (and in 1980), the Census Bureau reserved the term *manager* for professional occupations (U.S. Bureau of the Census, 1980). For example, branch managers at a bank were coded as managers, whereas branch managers at shoe stores were coded as sales positions. Thus, by defining managerial transitions with census occupational definitions, this article is implicitly examining moves into professional occupations that have management duties. For our purposes, this coding scheme is advantageous in that this article attempts to model what is popularly meant by the term *glass ceiling*—that is, movement into positions at the apex of the occupational hierarchy.[2]

A second measurement issue is that besides receiving a managerial promotion, workers can move to several alternative destinations, including unemployment, withdrawal from the labor force, or self-employment. In addition, workers can receive salary promotions without changing jobs. It is possible to give each of these destinations scores of 1 on separate binary dependent variables and analyze these transitions using a competing-risks model (Hachen, 1988). The challenge for the analyst is to define mutually exclusive destination states on the dependent variable with enough cases in each destination to sustain a rigorous analysis. To simplify matters, then, this article will only analyze entry into a management position on the belief that such moves represent unique career transitions with significant effects on later achievement (Harlan, 1989). Elsewhere, I analyze career transitions resulting in salary increases or job exits (Maume, 1999).

Occupational Segregation

Both the Current Population Survey (CPS) and the PSID use census-defined standard occupation classification codes at the three-digit level of detail. The 1981 CPS provided information on the demographic composition of occupations (Institute for Social Research, 1982). Percentage of female workers and percentage of Black workers in each occupation were calculated, and the values merged onto the occupations held by PSID respondents.

Readers are no doubt aware that jobs are grouped into occupations. That is, the term *job* describes an actual position in a firm or industry; the term *occupation* is defined as a collection of jobs that have similar skill requirements and duties. Whereas occupations are abstract labels to describe locations in the economy, jobs are specific activities that people perform. When studying sex segregation in the economy, there is a concern that analyses of occupational segregation (rather than job segregation) may be misleading. Indeed, some sex-integrated occupations (e.g., retail sales clerk) consist of many sex-segregated jobs (e.g., men selling golf clubs and women selling earrings). Quantitative research clearly shows lower levels of sex segregation measured at the occupation level compared with segregation measured at the job level (for a review, see Tomaskovic-Devey, 1993).

For practical reasons, analysts will continue to study inequality using occupation data because most data sets lack information on specific jobs. This does not mean, however, that occupation-level analyses are without merit. Indeed, Stone (1995, pp. 417–419) provides two compelling reasons for using occupation to study sex segrega-

tion. First, Stone draws from Reskin and Roos (1990), who assert that sex segregation is maintained by institutional and attitudinal processes. Institutional factors refer to actions men take to protect specific jobs against female encroachment (similar to the social closure perspective reviewed above). At the larger level of occupations, however, people form attitudes and stereotypes about work that is appropriate for men and women. Inevitably, women's work is devalued in terms of status, pay, and career potential (similar to the status composition perspective). Because knowledge of specific jobs is limited, people develop career aspirations and make choices with occupations in mind. Studying segregation at the occupation level, therefore, reveals much about attitudinal forces that define the sex typicality of groups of jobs and the impact this has on individual careers.

Second, Stone (1995) contends that when comparing results from analyses of sex segregation at the job level to those at the occupation level, there are more similarities than differences. For example, Jacobs and Lim (1995) compared 56 countries to examine trends in occupational segregation and found similar results at different levels of aggregation. In research on wage inequality, results from job level analyses found that segregation accounts for approximately one half of the gender gap in wages (Tomaskovic-Devey, 1993), whereas analyses using occupation data attribute one third of the wage gap to segregation (England et al., 1988, 1994; Sorenson, 1989). Whereas analyses using detailed data should show larger effects, Stone concludes that results from analyses using occupation-level data will parallel those using job-level data. Therefore, if this study finds significant composition effects on managerial mobility, the effects are probably smaller than would be the case if segregation had been measured at the job level.

Additional Predictors

A worker's family situation was controlled in this article with two binary variables; marital status (1 = married), and the presence of a preschool-age child in the family. In addition, because Rosenbaum (1979) found that older workers are less likely to receive a promotion, the age of the respondent was controlled. Obviously, better educated respondents enjoy greater opportunities in the labor market, so a binary measure of the attainment of a college diploma was controlled (the PSID lacks a ratio measure of educational attainment). In addition, work attachment may affect the chances of entry into management; thus, the models include a control for hours worked during the year.

Workplace factors may also affect the rate of entry into management. For example, controls were introduced for a worker's tenure in the current job and real hourly wage.[3] Kanter (1977) and Rosenbaum (1979) both contend that companies locate star performers early in their careers and promote them; thus, employer tenure should be negatively related to the chances of promotion into management. Similarly, if companies reward individuals they want to promote to management (Kanter, 1977), the origin wage may positively influence such moves.[4]

Because movement within the occupational structure is more likely to be short distance than long distance (Blau & Duncan, 1967), the type of occupation in year *t* is controlled. Specifically, workers in professional and in sales/clerical positions received scores of 1 on separate binary variables; the reference category consisted of workers in blue-collar positions.

Some analysts claim that men's jobs require greater skills and more specialized training than women's jobs, and this determines job rewards rather than the demographic composition of the occupation (Tam, 1997). To control for this argument, an index tapping the skill and training requirements of the occupation was created. The fourth edition of the *Dictionary of Occupational Titles* (Institute for Social Research, 1983) provided information on job requisites. Several measures were recorded, including the skill requirements (work with data, reasoning skills, language skills, math skills, numerical aptitude, and

general intelligence) and length of specific vocational preparation for a job. The items chosen to create the index were selected in a manner consistent with England et al. (1994), and the index was created by summing item z scores. After aggregating across jobs, the composite score for the occupation's cognitive skill requirements was matched to the occupation of the PSID respondent.

Analysts have also shown that industrial structure affects the creation of promotion ladders (Baron, Davis-Blake, & Bielby, 1986). The model estimated below includes controls for employment in government or in the manufacturing sector. Government employment is often associated with placement in an internal labor market. Moreover, government hires and promotes with affirmative action guidelines in mind, possibly benefiting women (Collins, 1983; but see Steinberg et al., 1990). Firms in the manufacturing sector create job ladders that promote wage mobility but maintain a rigid distinction between line and staff positions (Sennett & Cobb, 1972) that may slow the rate of movement into supervisory positions.[5] In addition, unions assist in the creation of promotion ladders, which increase salaries, but they also may observe the distinction between line and staff positions (Baron et al., 1986). Thus, a binary control for union membership will be included in the analysis.

The model also includes controls for events occurring over time that may affect promotion chances. For example, workers may experience a birth in their families; these workers received a score of 1 on a binary predictor. In addition, Felmlee (1982) found that women increased their economic standing by changing employers, suggesting the need to control for changing employers during the year (coded as 1). The calendar year in which a case contributes to the pooled data set was also controlled to allow for the possibility that promotions to management vary with economic conditions. During the observation period, the economy improved from a deep recession (1981–1982) to a period of mild but sustained growth (1985–1987). Finally, the models include a predictor—the number of years a person appears in the pooled risk set—as a control for unobserved heterogeneity (Teachman, 1983).

Findings

Table 20.1 presents descriptive statistics on variables in the analysis. Table 20.2 presents the determinants of moving from a nonmanagerial to a managerial occupation. Logit coefficients can be interpreted as the change in the log odds of moving into management given a unit increase in a predictor. The bottom of Table 20.2 shows the number of men and women who actually moved into managerial occupations and provides information on the fit of the model to the data.

In many instances, the determinants of mobility are the same for men and women. For example, job attachment (i.e., annual hours worked) and higher pay both increase the chances of attaining a supervisory position. In addition, although the manufacturing sector creates internal labor markets that foster wage mobility (Baron et al., 1986), employment in manufacturing reduces the chances of receiving a managerial promotion as does membership in a union. Similarly, there is some evidence that unobserved heterogeneity is present in this sample: The more years workers remain in the risk set, the lower their chances of receiving a managerial promotion.

Table 20.2 shows some gender differences in the promotion process. First, age is positive and significant for women but not men. Either older women are better able than younger women to demonstrate their skills in the workplace (Reskin, 1988), or age is no barrier to men's promotion chances (Krecker, 1994). In addition, employer tenure negatively influences women's promotion chances but not men's. This suggests that unlike women, men with long record of service to their employers are still candidates for a managerial promotion (Krecker, 1994). Finally, men use clerical and sales positions as a stepping stone into management, whereas women do not, and men's movements into management are more responsive to economic conditions (i.e., the year variable) than is the case for women.

Turning to the variables of interest, occupational segregation interacts with gender in determining managerial promotions.[6] In support of Hypothesis 1, men are more likely to move into management as the percentage of females in the origin occupation increases; for women, the effect is the opposite. Among men, each 10% increase in the percentage of female workers in the occupation increases the chances of attaining a managerial position by 11.06%, $(e^{.011}-1) x 100 x 10 = 11.06$. The positive effect of gender composition provides strong support for the argument that men working in female-typed occupations enjoy the benefits of a glass escalator. According to Williams (1992, 1995), men in female-dominated occupations are mismatched to the gender-stereotypical expectations of their occupations. Tensions resulting from this arrangement are relieved by promoting men into management. On the other hand, women in female-dominated occupations are subject to the devaluing effects of segregation. Once placed in female-typed occupations, women are less likely to receive the training and job assignments that enhance career mobility (Baron & Newman, 1990; Reskin, 1988). Table 20.2 shows that among women, each 10% increase in the percentage of females in an occupation slows the rate of entry into management by 6%, $(e^{-.006} - 1) x 100 x 10 = -5.98$. These results are the first from a national sample supporting the contention that the effect of gender segregation on managerial promotions differs for men and women.[7]

Hypothesis 2 receives partial support in that percentage of Blacks in the origin occupation reduces women's chances of receiving a managerial promotion; for men, the impact is not significant. On the other hand, the race of the respondent has no impact on the likelihood of becoming a manager for women, but it has a strong negative effect for men. Black men are 52% less,

$(e^{-.732} - 1) \times 100 = -51.91$, likely than White men to attain a managerial position, once relevant personal and job-related factors are controlled. These findings clearly indi-

cate that ascriptive traits and segregation patterns combine to produce different mobility trajectories by race and gender.

Table 20.1

Descriptive Statistics on Predictor Variables in Analysis, Workers Ages 18 to 62, Panel Study of Income Dynamics, 1981 to 1987

Variable	White		Black	
	Mean	SD	Mean	SD
Men				
Age in years	35.13	10.91	34.38	10.56
Married (coded 1)	.85	.36	.74	.44
Preschool–age child (coded 1)	.34	.34	.42	.49
Had a birth during year (coded 1)	.07	.26	.09	.28
College educated (coded 1)	.16	.36	.03	.18
Hours worked in year (in hundreds)	20.98	5.71	19.695.57	5.57
Hourly wage (1980 dollars)	10.00	5.15	7.42	3.31
Years tenure in job	5.36	6.42	6.15	6.81
Employed in manufacturing (coded 1)	.36	.48	.37	.48
Public sector employment (coded 1)	.14	.35	.22	.41
Union presence at work (coded 1)	.36	.48	.41	.49
Professional occupation (coded 1)	.19	.39	.05	.23
Clerical/sales occupation (coded 1)	.13	.34	.09	.29
Number of years in pooled data set	2.34	1.34	2.40	1.36
Calendar year	82.55	1.43	82.58	1.41
Changed employers during year (coded 1)	.13	.33	.09	.29
Cognitive skills index	−.11	6.43	−4.39	5.18
Percentage of female workers in occupation	18.59	22.48	20.54	23.94
Percentage of Black workers in occupation	9.61	6.78	14.78	9.23
Number of person years	5,635		2,899	
Women				
Age in years	34.42	10.90	34.64	10.94
Married (coded 1)	.75	.43	.52	.50
Preschool–age child (coded 1)	.26	.44	.37	.48
Had a birth during year (coded 1)	.05	.22	.07	.25
College educated (coded 1)	.15	.36	.05	.22
Hours worked in year (in hundreds)	16.35	5.81	16.86	5.49
Hourly wage (1980 dollars)	6.37	3.26	5.35	5.35
Years tenure in job	3.82	4.64	4.77	5.13
Employed in manufacturing (coded 1)	.20	.40	.23	.42
Public sector employment (coded 1)	.19	.39	.26	.44
Union presence at work (coded 1)	.16	.37	.23	.42
Professional occupation (coded 1)	.20	.40	.09	.28
Clerical/sales occupation (coded 1)	.42	.49	.29	.45
Number of years in pooled data set	2.18	1.31	2.30	1.35
Calendar year	82.80	1.58	82.76	1.52
Changed employers during year (coded 1)	.14	.35	.09	.29
Cognitive skills index	−.60	5.79	−3.99	5.49
Percentage of female workers in occupation	72.66	26.37	70.96	25.49
Percentage of Black workers in occupation	11.75	7.85	18.95	12.72
Number of person years	4,643		3,135	

The results above suggest that women are crowded into female-typed occupations, which hampers career development. Because Black and White women are equally harmed by prevailing patterns of segregation in the labor force, racial identity is inconsequential in determining mobility chances for women. That is, the ill effects of crowding and devaluation are experienced by White and Black women alike, such that race matters little in differentiating the promotion chances of women. Black men, on the other hand, are more evenly distributed across occupations than women are. Thus, the mobility impact of the racial composition of occupations is negligible for men. Yet, Black men must be concerned with interpersonal dynamics and forming alliances in the workplace to ensure their success (Jones, 1986). Because they do not share the background and outlooks of current management (i.e., White men), Black men are less likely to be promoted into their ranks, which many attribute to racial discrimination.

There is some empirical support for these arguments. First, occupational segregation is higher for women than Black men. In their analysis of census data, Reskin and Cassirer (1996) compared segregation by race, gender, and ethnicity. They found that the index of dissimilarity (the number of people that would have to change jobs to integrate the occupational

Table 20.2

Logistic Regression Model of Entry Into Management, Workers Ages 18 to 62, Panel Study of Income Dynamics, 1981 to 1987

Predictor Variable	Men		Women	
	Logit Coefficient	Standard Error	Logit Coefficient	Standard Error
Black (coded 1)	−.732**	.202	−.142	.186
Age in years	−.004	.008	.020**	.008
Married (coded 1)	−.066	.195	.209	.171
Preschool-age child (coded 1)	.250	.158	.114	.188
Had a birth during year (coded 1)	−.412	.272	−.236	.403
College educated (coded 1)	.138	.187	.134	.251
Hours worked in year (in hundreds)	.035****	.011	.107****	.014
Hourly wage (1980 dollars)	.044****	.010	.069****	.020
Years tenure in job	.005	.015	−.061**	.021
Employed in manufacturing (coded 1)	−.340**	.169	−1.113****	.279
Public sector employment (coded 1)	−.181	.801	−.186	.207
Union presence at work (coded 1)	−1.032****	.207	−.686**	.285
Professional occupation (coded 1)	−.100	.309	−.528	.399
Clerical/sales occupation (coded 1)	.478**	.216	.462	.239
Number years in pooled data set	−.669****	.078	−.380****	.084
Calendar year	.210***	.050	.059	.055
Changed employers (coded 1)	.313	.183	.321	.202
Cognitive Skills Index	.039	.022	.023	.027
% female in occupation	.011****	.003	−.006**	.003
% Black in occupation	−.006	.014	−.054****	.015
Intercept	−20.297****		−9.617**	
Model chi–square	346.573****		251.697****	
df	20		20	
Number of person years	8,534		7,778	
Number entering management	254		195	
% of cases correctly classified	80.8		80.4	

**p<.05.   ***p<.01.   ****p <.001.

hierarchy) between White men and White women was 54.9 and was 62.7 for White men and Black women. For Black men, however, the index was only 31.5.

Despite lower levels of occupational segregation, Black men often suffer discrimination in seeking managerial positions. The latest research contends that particularistic criteria are used in promotion decisions. That is, subjective evaluations of a candidate's ambition and loyalty (among other things) are important determinants of receiving a managerial promotion. Black men received lower ratings on these dimensions after controlling for measures of human capital and job performance (Braddock & McPartland, 1987; Mueller, Parcel, & Tanaka, 1989; Wilson, 1997). These findings lead to claims that Black men are unable to reach the pinnacle of their organizations because of the presence of a glass ceiling (Collins, 1993; Jones, 1986).

To summarize the argument thus far, women (both Black and White) are crowded into sex-typical occupations, in which their work efforts are devalued and ignored, causing their careers to lag behind White men's. Compared with women, Black men and White men are more likely to work in the same general occupation. But Black men are also more likely than White men to receive low evaluations from their supervisors and suffer from blocked mobility opportunities. The slower rate at which Black men, Black women, and White women advance to managerial positions is what many mean by the term *glass ceiling*. By contrast, White men are not only spared the frustrations of contending with the glass ceiling but enjoy the benefits of enhanced mobility chances (the *glass escalator*) as the percentage of females in the origin occupation rises.

The existence of a glass escalator for White men and a glass ceiling for everyone else can be illustrated by examining race and gender differences in the speed of ascendance to managerial status. This is accomplished by substituting the race- and sex-specific means on predictor variables (from Table 20.1) into the models in Table 20.2. By allowing tenure to vary, the models

predict the log odds of promotion at each year of tenure. In addition, the gender composition of the occupation is set at 90 to approximate employment in a female-dominated occupation. After transforming the predicted log odds to predicted probabilities, the cumulative product of 1 minus the duration-specific promotion probabilities yields a survival curve (Teachman, 1983). Plotting the survival curve against duration in the job will show how long the typical respondent waits for a managerial promotion when employed in female-dominated occupations. Figure 20.1 presents these plots.

Working in a female-dominated origin occupation enhances mobility for White men. Figure 20.1 predicts that after 12 years, 56% of White men will be waiting for a promotion, meaning that 44% will have been promoted and exited the risk set. By contrast, after 12 years, 83% of Black men, 85% of White women, and 93% of Black women remain in the risk set waiting for a promotion. Moreover, these curves should be viewed in light of Rosenbaum's (1979) finding that an early promotion (in the first 3 to 5 years) is essential for receiving promotions later in the career. In this sample, 21% of White men had received a managerial promotion by the end of the fifth year, compared with less than 10% of Black men, Black women, and White women. Figure 20.1 affirms the argument above: White men who work in female-typed occupations receive the benefits of a glass escalator into management, whereas Black men and women are victimized by the glass ceiling.

The Declining Significance of Race

William Wilson criticizes empirical tests of race differences in rewards because they fail to eliminate past discrimination from current comparisons. That is, older Blacks suffered discrimination in the past, the effects from which are reflected in their lower rewards relative to Whites. Wilson (1989) insists that younger Blacks entering the labor market after the passage of civil rights legislation should enjoy parity with Whites in career rewards (but see Cancio et al., 1996). This should especially be true for educated Blacks, with valuable skills to offer to employers.

Wilson's argument is tested by limiting the sample to those who fit the age and educational profiles of those for whom the significance of race should be declining. First, the sample is restricted to those who were between the ages of 18 and 39 years of age when they were at risk of receiving a managerial promotion between 1981 and 1987. The oldest of this group (39-year-olds in 1981) would have entered the labor market in 1960 if they began their careers at age 18. The majority of respondents, however, began their careers after the passage of the 1964 Civil Rights Act. Then, in Panels 2 through 4, increasingly restrictive educational criteria are imposed on these young workers; because respondents in Panels 2 through 4 are subsets of those included in Panel 1, the number of person years declines.

Table 20.3 shows the net effect of being Black on the log odds of receiving a managerial promotion after imposing various age and educational restrictions. In the first panel, the sample is restricted to younger respondents. Among those between the ages of 18 and 39, the effect of race is marginally significant in the pooled analysis, insignificant for women, but significant for men. These findings mirror closely those shown in Table 20.2, which included older workers. Thus, the race gap in managerial promotions cannot be explained away by including in the main sample those who may have suffered discrimination in the past.

Panels 2, 3, and 4 in Table 20.3 impose successively higher educational restrictions on the age group shown in panel 1. Panel 2 includes young workers with at least a high school diploma. In this subset, being Black significantly reduces men's chances of attaining a management position in the pooled model and among men. Panel 3 further restricts the sample to young workers with some college training; we see that Black men still lag behind White men in reaching management. Among college graduates, however, the effect of race on promotion chances is eliminated (Panel 4). Only by limiting the sample to young college graduates can we find evidence that race is declining in signifi-

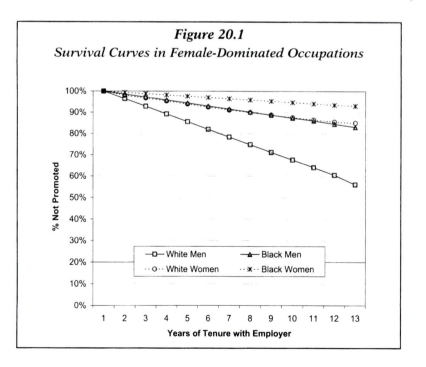

Figure 20.1

Survival Curves in Female-Dominated Occupations

Table 20.3

Effect of Race on the Log Odds of Entry in Management, Selected Samples,
Panel Study of Income Dynamics, 1981 to 1987

	All	Men	Women
Ages 18 to 39			
Slope effect for race (1 = Black)	−.268*	−.572***	−.034
Number of person years	11,485	6,081	5,404
Number entering management	329	194	135
Twelve or more years of schooling, ages 18 to 39			
Slope effect for race (1 = Black)	−.300**	−.527**	−.151
Number of person years	9,315	4,797	4,518
Number entering management	310	184	126
Thirteen or more years of schooling, ages 18 to 39			
Slope effect for race (1 = Black)	−.222	−.530**	−.010
Number of person years	3,730	1,946	1,784
Number entering management	182	121	61
Sixteen or more years of schooling, ages 18 to 39			
Slope effect for race (1 = Black)	.270	.166	.313
Number of person years	1,413	725	688
Number entering management	78	57	21

Note: Effect of race is net of the variables shown in Table 20.2.
*$p<.10$.   **$p<.05$.   ***$p<.01$.

cance. Given that young college graduates constitute less than 10% of the African American population (Farley & Allen, 1987), this article concludes that skin color continues to inhibit the career development of large numbers of Blacks.

Summary and Suggestions for Future Research

This article began by noting the increasing representation of White women, Black women, and Black men among the ranks of managers. It is estimated that women's entry into management accounts for one fourth of the decline in occupational segregation since 1970 (Jacobs, 1992). Although still underrepresented among the ranks of managers, Blacks' rate of entry into management exceeded that of Whites in the 1970s (Nkomo & Cox, 1990). From these trends, some may be tempted to argue that White women, Black women, and Black men are reaching parity with White men in their career development.

The findings of this article suggest otherwise. Examining work histories between 1981 and 1987 from the PSID, this article assessed the likelihood of reaching managerial status. The extent of gender and racial segregation in the origin occupation significantly slowed women's progress in reaching supervisory positions. This stands in stark contrast to the experiences of men who enjoyed enhanced mobility opportunities as the percentage of females in the origin occupation increases (i.e., the glass escalator). However, the effectiveness of this glass escalator is much lower for Black men, who receive fewer managerial promotions than do White men. Finally, consistent with the image of a glass ceiling, women and minorities wait longer for promotions they do receive than is the case for White men. Unlike past studies, these findings on the impacts of occupational segregation on managerial promotions come from a large representative sample of the U.S. labor force.

This study does have some limitations, however, that suggest the need for additional research. First, it is possible that women and Blacks promoted to management are really "glorified clerks" with little authority or influence (Jacobs, 1992; Reskin & Roos, 1990). By using the census definition of manager (given to those in professional jobs), this article measured the likelihood of mobility to the top of the occupational hierarchy. Even so, data limitations precluded an examination of authority mobility or control of the firm's resources. If White women, Black women, and Black men are achieving parity with White men, they should be taking positions with numerous subordinates and affecting the profitability of the firm. Hachen (1990) examined authority mobility with retrospective data, but he did not explicitly include segregation in the origin occupation as a predictor. Other studies have examined women's and Blacks' exclusion from authority hierarchies in a cross-sectional design (Mueller et al., 1989; Steinberg et al., 1990; Wilson, 1997), but research examining transitions into authority-conferring positions is lacking. Clearly, this is a topic in need of further research.

Second, this article examined work histories in the early 1980s for Blacks and Whites. As such, new forms of inequality emerging in the 1990s could not be detected in this study. For example, White women have made progress in entering traditionally male jobs. In doing so, African Americans and Latinas take traditionally female jobs vacated by White women (Reskin, 1999). Changing patterns of segregation are partly responsible for the growing wage gap between White women and other disadvantaged groups (Browne, 1999). But, in addition, the growing presence of White women in the labor force (who are better educated than other groups of women) is also partly responsible for wage inequality among women (England, Christopher, & Reid, 1999). Examining how ethnicity, human capital, and occupational segregation affect the process of reaching managerial positions in more recent samples of women should also be a priority of future research.

Finally, research is needed on whether women and minority men stay in management once they have reached these positions. Because White men regard managerial positions as their turf, there is ample documentation of their rejection of minority coworkers, resulting in lower commitment for women and Blacks (e.g., see Jackson, Thoits, & Taylor, 1995; Jacobs, 1989; Kanter, 1977). With regard to gender, Jacobs (1989) argues that opportunities for employment in male-dominated occupations have increased, but men's resistance to women's presence has resulted in nearly as many women leaving these jobs. This pattern of revolving doors for women has resulted in only a slight decline in occupational segregation since 1970. Studies that examine exit rates from management positions are also needed to determine whether the career profiles of Black men, Black women, and White women resemble those of White men.

Discussion Questions

1. Compare the concept of "glass ceiling" with that of "glass elevator." Which phenomenon do you think is more pervasive in workplaces?

2. Have you ever experienced the effects of either in a job?

3. Do you think the chapter on soft skills (Chapter 19) is relevant to this chapter?

Endnotes

1. The Panel Study of Income Dynamics (PSID) rectified this situation in later years by adding a Hispanic subsample in 1990. The study begins observing workers in 1981 because the PSID began recording occupation at the three-digit Standard Occupational Classification level of detail in that year. The more detailed occupational coding is needed for accurately assessing the degree of segregation in a person's occupation. The presence of older workers in the sam-

ple is important because inequality in career dynamics may occur at later ages (Olson & Frieze, 1987; Rosenfeld, 1980). Finally, sample members were either household heads or spouses; other adult household members were excluded because the PSID failed to ask extensive questions about their labor force situations.

2. To verify this point in the data, the hourly wage in year$_{t+1}$ was compared to the wage in year$_t$. When workers entered management, their real wage increased by 20.2% compared with only a 10.7% increase for those who changed jobs but did not enter management (data not shown).

3. Included in the measure of hourly wage are earnings, bonuses, and paid overtime; excluded from the measure are income from investments, monetary gifts from family and friends, and transfer income. A handful of observations had values of less than $2 or more than $75 an hour. Rather than deleting these cases, they were recoded to these values. Wages were indexed to 1980 prices to adjust for inflation during the period.

4. To test for nonlinear associations with promotions, squared terms for age, tenure, and wage were entered into the models. These squared terms were insignificant predictors of movement into managerial positions. In addition, controls for region, metropolitan residence, and the educational attainment of parents were insignificant predictors of managerial mobility. All of these variables were dropped from the analysis.

5. Several different levels of detail in capturing industry effects on career mobility were examined. For example, in the manufacturing sector, durable goods production was distinguished from nondurable goods. In addition, several service-sector dummy variables were entered in the model (keeping personal services as a reference group). In all cases, these supplemental analyses produced similar results to those shown in Table 20.2 (available to readers on request).

6. Gender differences in the effect of gender composition of the occupation on managerial mobility were verified in a pooled model that included an interaction term (Gender x Percentage of Females in the Origin Occupation). Similarly, gender differences in the effect of racial segregation on mobility chances were verified in a pooled model including an interaction term. Results from these analyses are available on request.

7. The results in Table 20.2 may be questioned because the sample includes part-time workers. If men are more likely than women to work full-time, this could affect the determinants of attaining a supervisory position. To examine this possibility, the models were reanalyzed after excluding part-time workers. First, the sample was restricted to respondents who worked

2,000 hours during a given year (i.e., an average of 40 hours per week for 50 weeks). At this threshold, the results were similar to those presented in Table 20.2 for men, but the number of women entering management relative to sample size was too small to provide reliable results. Alternative thresholds for full-time work were tried at 1,750, 1,500, and 1,000 hours worked per year. At these thresholds, the results were similar to those shown in Table 20.2 (available on request).

References

Acker, J. (1990). Hierarchies, jobs and bodies: A theory of gendered organizations. *Gender and Society, 4,* 139–158.

Allison, P. D. (1984). *Event history analysis: Regression/or longitudinal event data.* Newbury Park, CA: Sage.

Baron, J. N., Davis-Blake, A., & Bielby, W. T. (1986). The structure of opportunity: How promotion ladders vary within and among organizations. *Administrative Science Quarterly, 31,* 248–273.

Baron, J. N., & Newman, A. E. (1990). For what its worth: Organizations, occupations and the value of work done by women and non Whites. *American Sociological Review 55,* 155–175.

Bielby, W. T., & Baron, J. N. (1986). Men and women at work: Sex segregation and statistical discrimination. *American Journal of Sociology, 91,* 759–799.

Blau, P. M., & Duncan, O. D. (1967). *The American occupational structure.* New York: Academic Press.

Braddock, J. H., & McPartland, J. M. (1987). How minorities continue to be excluded from equal employment opportunities: Research on labor market and institutional barriers. *Journal of Social Issues, 43,* 5–39.

Browne, I. (1999). Latinas and African American women in the U.S. labor market. In I. Brown (Ed.), *Latinas and African American women at work* (pp. 1–31). New York: Russell Sage.

Cancio, S. A., Evans, T. D., & Maume, D. J., Jr. (1996). Reconsidering the declining significance of race: Racial differences in early career wages. *American Sociological Review, 61,* 541–556.

Cockburn, C. (1991). *In the way of women: Men's resistance to sex equality in organizations.* Ithaca, NY: ILR Press.

Collins, S. (1983). The making of the Black middle class. *Social Problems, 30,* 369–382.

——. (1993). Blacks on the bubble: The vulnerability of Black executives in White corporations. *Sociological Quarterly, 34,* 29–47.

Cordtz, D. (1994, August 16). The glass ceiling. *Financial World,* p. 64.

DiPrete, T. A., & Soule, W. T. (1988). Gender and promotion in segmented job ladder systems. *American Sociological Review, 53,* 26–40.

England, P., Christopher, K., & Reid, L. (1999). Gender, race, ethnicity, and wages. In I. Brown (Ed.), *Latinos and African American women at work* (pp. 139–182). New York: Russell Sage.

England, P., Farkas, G., Kilbourne, B. S., & Dou, T. (1988). Explaining occupational sex segregation and wages: Findings from a model with fixed effects. *American Sociological Review, 55*, 544–558.

England, P., Herbert, M., Kilbourne, B., Reid, L., & Megdal, L. (1994). The gendered valuation of occupations and skills: Earnings in 1980 census occupations. *Social Forces, 73*, 65–99.

Farley, R., & Allen, W. R. (1987). *The color line and the quality of life in America*. New York: Oxford University Press.

Felmlee, D. H. (1982). Women's job mobility processes within and between employers. *American Sociological Review, 47*, 142–151.

Filer, R. K. (1990). Compensating differentials and the male-female wage gap: A comment. *Social Forces, 69*, 469–473.

Greenhaus, J. H., Parasuraman, S., & Wormley, W. (1990). Effects of race on organizational experiences, job performance evaluations, and career outcomes. *Academy of Management Journal, 33*, 64–86.

Hachen, D. S. (1988). The competing risks model: A method for analyzing processes with multiple types of events. *Sociological Methods and Research, 17*, 93–116.

——. (1990). Three models of job mobility in labor markets. *Work and Occupations, 17*, 320–354.

Harlan, S. L. (1989). Opportunity and attitudes toward job advancement in a manufacturing firm. *Social Forces, 67*, 766–788.

Hartmann, H. I. (1987). Internal labor markets and gender: A case study of promotion. In C. Brown & J. A. Pechman (Eds.), *Gender in the workplace* (pp. 59–92). Washington, DC: Brookings Institute.

Institute for Social Research. (1982). Current population survey: Annual demographic file, 1981 [MRDF] (ICPSR Study No. 7863). Ann Arbor, MI: Survey Research Center.

——. (1983). Dictionary of occupational titles [MRDF] (4th ed.) (ICPSR Study No. 7845). Ann Arbor, MI: Survey Research Center.

——. (1992). A Panel Study of Income Dynamics: Procedures and tape codes [MRDF] (various years) (ICPSR Study No. 7439). Ann Arbor, MI: Survey Research Center.

Jackson, P. B., Thoits, P. A., & Taylor, H. F. (1995). Composition of the workplace and psychological well-being: The effects of tokenism on America's Black elite. *Social Forces, 74*, 543–558.

Jacobs, J. A. (1989). *Revolving doors: Sex segregation and women's careers*. Stanford, CA: Stanford University Press.

——. (1992). Women's entry into management: Trends in earnings, authority, and values among salaried managers. *Administrative Science Quarterly, 372*, 282–301.

Jacobs, J. A., & Lim, S. T. (1995). Trends in occupational and industrial segregation in 56 countries, 1960–1980. In J. A. Jacobs (Ed.), *Gender inequality at work* (pp. 259–293). Thousand Oaks, CA: Sage.

Jacobs, J. A., & Steinberg, R. (1990). Compensating differentials and the male-female wage gap: Evidence from the New York State comparable worth study. *Social Forces, 69*, 439–468.

Jaynes, G. D., & Williams, R., Jr. (1989). *A common destiny: Blacks and American society*. Washington, DC: National Academy Press.

Jones, E. W., Jr. (1986). Black managers: The dream deferred. *Harvard Business Review, 64*, 84–93.

Kanter, R. M. (1977). *Men and women of the corporation*. New York: Basic Books.

Kilbourne, B. S., England, P., Farkas, G., Beron, K., & Weir, D. (1994). Returns to skill, compensating differentials, and gender bias: Effects of occupational characteristics on the wages of White women and men. *American Journal of Sociology, 100*, 689–719.

Kluegel, J. (1978). The causes and costs of racial exclusion from job authority. *American Sociological Review, 43*, 285–301.

Krecker, M. (1994). Work careers and organizational careers: The effects of age and tenure on attachment to the employment relationship. *Work and Occupations, 21*, 251–283.

Maume, D. J. (1999). Occupational segregation and the career mobility of White men and women. *Social Forces, 77*, 1433–1459.

Mueller, C. W., Parcel, T. L., & Tanaka, K. (1989). Particularism in authority outcomes of Black and White supervisors. *Social Science Research, 18*, 1–20.

Nkomo, S. M., & Cox, T. (1990). Factors affecting the upward mobility of Black mangers in private sector organizations. *Review of Black Political Economy, 19*, 39–57.

Olson, J. E., & Frieze, I. H. (1987). Income determinants for women in business. In A. H Stromberg, L. Larwood, & B. A. Guteck (Eds.), *Women and work: An annual review* (Vol. 2, pp. 173–206). Newbury Park, CA: Sage.

Paulin, E. A., & Mellor, J. M. (1996). Gender, race, and promotions in a private-sector firm. *Industrial Relations, 55*, 276–295.

Reskin, B. (1988). Bringing the men back in: Sex differentiation and the devaluation of women's work. *Gender and Society, 2*, 58–81.

——. (1999). Occupational segregation by race and ethnicity among women workers. In I. Brown (Ed.), *Latinos and African American women at work* (pp. 183–204). New York: Russell Sage.

Reskin, B., & Cassirer, N. (1996). Occupational segregation by gender, race, and ethnicity. *Sociological Focus, 29*, 231–243.

Reskin, B., & Roos, P. (1990). *Job queues, gender queues: Explaining women's inroads into male occupations*. Philadelphia: Temple University Press.

Reskin, B., & Ross, C. E. (1995). Jobs, authority and earnings among managers: The continuing significance of sex. In J. A. Jacobs (Ed.), *Gender inequality at work*. Thousand Oaks, CA: Sage.

Rosenbaum, J. E. (1979). Tournament mobility: Career patterns in a corporation. *Administrative Science Quarterly, 24*, 220–241.

Rosenfeld, R. (1980). Race and sex differences in career dynamics. *American Sociological Review, 45*, 583–609.

Sennett, R., & Cobb, J. (1972). *The hidden injuries of class*. New York: Random House.

Sorenson, E. (1989). Measuring the effect of occupational sex and race composition on earnings. In R. T. Michael, H. I. Hartmann, & B. O'Farrell (Eds.), *Pay equity: Empirical inquiries* (pp. 49–70). Washington, DC: National Academy Press.

Steinberg, R. J. (1990). The social construction of skill. *Work and Occupations, 17*, 449–482.

Steinberg, R. J., Haignere, L., & Chertos, C. H. (1990). Managerial promotions in the public sector. *Work and Occupations, 17*, 284–301.

Stone, P. (1995). Assessing gender at work: Evidence and issues. In J. A. Jacobs (Ed.), *Gender inequality at work* (pp. 408–423). Thousand Oaks, CA: Sage.

Tam, T. (1997). Sex segregation and occupational inequality in the United States: Devaluation or specialized training? *American Journal of Sociology, 102*, 1652–1692.

Teachman, J. D. (1983). Analyzing social processes: Life tables and proportional hazards models. *Social Science Research, 12*, 263–301.

Tomaskovic-Devey, D. (1993). *Gender and racial inequality at work*. Ithaca, NY: ILR Press.

U.S. Bureau of the Census. (1980). *1980 census of the population: Alphabetical index of industries and occupations* (1st ed.). Washington, DC: Government Printing Office.

Williams, C. L. (1992). The glass escalator: Hidden advantages for men in the "female" professions. *Social Problems, 39*, 253–267.

——, C. L. (1995). *Still a man's world: Men who do "women's work."* Berkeley: University of California Press.

Wilson, G. (1997). Pathways to power: Racial differences in the determinants of job authority. *Social Problems, 44*, 38–54.

Wilson, W. J. (1980). *The declining significance of race: Blacks and changing American institutions* (2nd ed.). Chicago: University of Chicago Press.

——. (1989). The declining significance of race: Revisited but not revised. In C. V. Willie (Ed.), *Caste and class controversy on race and poverty* (2nd ed., pp. 22–36). Dix Hills, NY: General Hall.

Wolf, W., & Fligstein, N. D. (1979). Sex and authority in the workplace: The causes of sexual inequality. *American Sociological Review, 44*, 235–252. ◆

21

The Organization of Mass Production Law

Jerry L. Van Hoy

In this chapter, the author discusses the deprofessionalization of an important segment of the legal profession. His case study materials describe the development of franchise law firms, in which some attorneys work under centralized control in their provision of standardized services. He maintains that the franchise law firms are chains of local offices, conveniently located for clients and staffed by a small number of employees, including attorneys, who offer a limited "menu" of services in a standardized format. Typically, a branch office is staffed by a managing attorney, who is contracted by the firm; one or more low-paid staff attorneys, often recent law-school graduates, who consult with clients and sell services; and several secretaries who have a general office management role, aided by an elaborate computer system. The author contends that whether the managing attorney is working on a contract basis or is a local owner, the firm maintains tight control over the operation of the branch offices.

Concepts such as franchising and mass production conjure up images of young (or now increasingly elderly) workers occupying positions which require little more than a warm body. Garson (1988, p. 20) quotes a young McDonald's employee to show the bleak work environment:

> Don't worry, you don't have to understand. You follow the beepers, you follow the buzzers and you turn your meat as fast as you can. It's like I told you, to work at McDonald's you don't need a face, you don't need a brain. You need to have two hands and two legs and move 'em as fast as you can. That's the whole system. I wouldn't go back there again for anything.

Clearly, we do not have the same image in mind when we speak of attorneys. Even the most exploited attorneys, offering the most basic of services, acquire a level of knowledge and skill far superior to the unskilled worker. Therefore, it is necessary to define what is meant when the concepts of mass production and franchises are applied to the work of lawyers. Franchise law firms can be best understood as part of a process in American society Ritzer (1996) has called "McDonaldization." McDonaldization combines the principles of franchises, bureaucracies, scientific management and assembly lines to achieve a maximum level of rationalization in the creation and delivery of products and services. Within the context of law this means organizing the law firm and legal work to minimize the efforts of lawyers as experts and put more responsibility into the hands of support staff. In this chapter I discuss how franchise law firms have developed rational organizations that make the delivery of legal services efficient.

The Basic Model

Franchise law firms are chains of local law offices located in shopping malls, strip malls or other retail business districts. Despite my calling these firms "franchises," not all law firms which fit this model are truly franchised. Beck & Daniels currently requires that attorneys buy into the firm and pay royalties on their earnings. Arthur & Nelson offices remain entirely owned by its founding partners. Indeed, Beck & Daniels' transformation to the franchise format happened during the course of this study. Previous to reorganizing the firm, Beck & Daniels' structure was similar to traditional bureaucracies found in many corporations. I have chosen to call these firms "franchises" for a number of reasons. First, despite issues of ownership, Arthur & Nelson and Beck & Daniels share a number of "McDonaldized" qualities with modern franchises. For example, only a limited "menu" of services is offered and each service that is offered has been standardized. This standardization makes the same services obtained at any local or branch office quite similar. In addition, as we shall see, each local office employee has a specific and limited set of roles and responsibilities. Second, Arthur & Nelson and Beck & Daniels have been moving toward "McDonaldized" (or highly rationalized) organizational structures, the end result of which appears to be franchiselike (where attorneys are subjected to centralized control over the work they perform). And finally, throughout the course of the study, many office managers and employees referred to the firms as "franchises," suggesting that the concept serves as a commonly accepted description of branch office manager and employee experiences.

The typical branch office includes a managing attorney (who may also be an owner), one or more staff attorneys and a number of secretaries. Arthur & Nelson offices may be as small as a managing attorney and one secretary, with no staff attorneys, while Beck & Daniels offices usually include at least one staff attorney and two secretaries under the managing attorney. Between the branch offices and each firm's founding partners are two or three levels of management, including district, regional and, at Beck & Daniels, national managers. However, in the 1990s the trend at both firms has been to subject local office man-

aging attorneys to less direct supervision and to cut the middle management ranks where possible. Thus, Arthur & Nelson rewards successful managing attorneys by promoting them to managing partners. The only difference between managing attorney and managing partner positions is the level of supervision. Managing partners report directly to the founding partners, bypassing middle management. Local partners at Beck & Daniels (managing attorneys who buy into the firm) are assessed monthly based on revenue generated, but have little supervision of day-to-day affairs.

Positions and Roles

Managing Attorneys

Managing attorneys are contracted by the firms to operate each local or branch office. Experienced attorneys may be hired directly into managing attorney positions or staff attorneys may be promoted to fill such positions. Arthur & Nelson provides a minimal training session for the managing attorney position. During a two- to five-day orientation, managing attorneys are introduced to the firm's administrative forms and office procedures.

Beck & Daniels' policy is to hire even experienced attorneys as staff attorneys for a period of one month to one year to introduce them to the firm's procedures and production system. For example, Beck & Daniels managing attorneys must learn how to use the firm's "operation manual" which details everything from the responsibilities of each branch office employee, the hours each office must be open and how accounting and paperwork is to be handled, to what types of legal cases an attorney may work on, how a client should be treated, how to organize case files (including where staples are to be placed in file folders) and the number of times a telephone may ring before it must be answered. Firm management often presents such procedures as a road map to success. For example, a Beck & Daniels national manager explains that attorneys are often bad businessmen, so we do everything for them. We tell them what to do, when to do it and how to do it. Our system frees them to just practice law and serve the client. If they can do that, they can make money for us.

Some managing attorneys, such as Frank, accept the view of management that the rigid procedures in the operations manual ensure success:

We've got a huge operations manual that standardizes operations here and [at] every other Beck & Daniels office. . . . To give you an example, for accounting there are procedures for handling the receipt of fees and cost . . . that sort of thing. It's the same here as with any Beck & Daniels office. There is no guesswork involved. There aren't 50 million ways to do things. That makes it easy. Office functions, for example, you know what our mission is, what our goal is in terms of client satisfaction, in terms of revenues, in terms of getting the work done, in terms of hiring legal assistants or attorneys—what to look for. All that is pretty much standardized. They tell us this is what we should look for, this is what we should expect, this is how it should be handled. And, as I said, it makes it very easy because if you follow the instructions, if you only deviate within accepted limits, then all this has been worked out for us, all this has been tested, and all this has been successful here and elsewhere. If we utilize it, then it makes our job a lot easier.

Other attorneys, however, are less enthusiastic. Sam's comments are typical.

We have very definitive operating procedures. We have an extremely complicated office manual that outlines almost everything that you might want to know about how to do—including how to order a light bulb when it burns out in your office. So we have procedures on how to do everything. They are pretty uniform and they are right here for anyone who wants to see them.

Managing attorneys earn a percentage of their office's profit as compensation. Ar-

thur & Nelson takes a 35–40 percent cut of total branch office revenue "off the top" each month. Beck & Daniels managing attorneys in offices owned by the firm receive 20 percent of their local office's profit as their compensation. At other local offices managing attorneys (called local partners) buy a 92 percent stake in their office. Local partners must pay Beck & Daniels 8 percent of gross revenues each month and pay into regional advertising pools. In any case, managing attorneys are responsible for covering all office overhead, including the salaries of staff attorneys and secretaries, rental to the firms for furniture and equipment (including computers and their servicing), supplies (paper, pens, forms, etc.), office rental and utility costs and health and malpractice insurance.

Although both firms have similar compensation systems for managing attorneys, they package them quite differently. Arthur & Nelson managing attorneys are encouraged to view their position as negotiated with management and as relatively independent. They see themselves as earning profits for both themselves and the firm. Thus, Phil explains the compensation system as

work[ing] on the idea that a percentage of your profits goes to the law firm and a percentage stays with you. From that percentage you subtract your expenses and that's it. So for example, let's just say the office made $30,000 for the month, OK? So, if they took 35 percent of $30,000 what are we looking at, $10,500? That would leave you $19,000. If you subtracted your office expenses— let's say they ran $10,000—that would leave you a *profit* of $9,000 for the month. . . . So it's based on a percentage of what they take. *The percentages vary on the various managing attorneys that have come aboard in the various stages. So, they're all structured differently.* (emphasis added)

Beck & Daniels, on the other hand, encourages a view of managing attorneys as salaried employees. Managing attorneys are provided a minimum monthly income guarantee. In months when the office is not profitable enough to cover the guarantee, the managing attorney is provided with a steady income. In more profitable months the managing attorney is required to repay the "loan" forwarded by the firm. Beck & Daniels call the managing attorney's guarantee a "salary." The amount of the managing attorney's 20 percent of office profit that exceeds the guarantee is referred to as "bonus." In addition, bonuses are only paid on a quarterly basis. Thus managing attorneys at Beck & Daniels tend to view their guarantees as something they receive whether or not they earn it. Bonus is seen as a reward for high productivity rather than as part of the 20 percent of office profit they are entitled to in their contracts.[1]

> Beck & Daniels attorneys are salaried; however, they do get a bonus. . . . You get your salary no matter how well or how poorly you do in any given month.

> If you have a month where your revenues are low or your profits are low, depending on the situation, and you have a month where they are high—your profits are high, your revenues are high—the two months are going to be taken into consideration in determining whether or not you are entitled to a bonus. However, in no instance would they ask you to return any of your salary.

Both Arthur & Nelson's profit-based incentive system and Beck & Daniels' "salary" and "bonus" incentive system encourage managing attorneys to see their main role as creators of profits or revenue, not as attorneys serving client needs. Firm policies for evaluating local office performance reinforce this view. Like Carl, Arthur & Nelson managing attorneys find that branch offices are evaluated with

> statistics on how many people you've seen, how many people you've retained, what kind of money you are earning, that kind of thing. . . . I never get any feedback other than statistics that they send me comparing this office . . . to other offices.

Client service is evaluated with periodic file audits and evaluation cards clients are asked to fill out and return by mail after they have bought a service. As Adam remarked, there is no real evaluation process "but there is an oversight process there."

> My office as a whole gets reviewed on several different levels. My own work, not really. My office gets reviewed from an accounting point of view—they'll do an audit. From a trust point of view—they'll do a trust reconciliation audit. And, they will send down people to see if I'm using the right [administrative and accounting] forms. But my legal work qua legal work doesn't [get evaluated], not really. Sometimes I wish it was. I do have a superior, a district manager. . . . She does a file review. It's not so much to review my work, but to make sure no files are falling through the cracks. She does a file review probably two, three times a year. For the most part her suggestions are innocuous; send another letter, remind the clients they owe X amount of money.

When local offices earn high profits for the firm even the minimal file audits seem to disappear.

> The district manager is supposed to do a yearly file audit. I saw [him] the other day and said, "so when are you coming by to audit my files?" He said, "in a couple of weeks probably." That was two months ago and he hasn't been by yet. File reviews don't always get done, especially if an office is doing well.

> They keep their eye on the numbers.

> *That's all?*

> As far as I know. I had the supervisor's job for a while and I know what he has time to do. As long as the office is making money I'm the last guy he wants to look at. Although lately I haven't been making enough money, so maybe he is looking at me. I don't know.

The managing attorney's main role at franchise law firms is to operate a profitable office. Firm policies, incentive systems and evaluative systems all emphasize this main goal over the quality of client service. As we shall see, an important part of the managing attorney's job is to negotiate with management over the hiring and firing of support staff to create an environment where people work together as efficiently as possible.

Staff Attorneys

While the managing attorney's role is to ensure that the office is productive and profitable, staff attorneys are hired to consult with clients and sell services. In addition, staff attorneys often perform the legal tasks which are not directly revenue generating, such as going to court and conducting plaintiff's personal injury consultations (which generate fees only if a favorable settlement is reached through negotiations or the courts). Although staff attorneys may be delegated tasks by managing attorneys, most of their work is accomplished individually. Renee, a Beck & Daniels managing attorney, compares staff attorneys at her firm to associate attorneys at traditional law firms:

> Unlike in a traditional law firm where you might have an owner or manager who basically takes in the cases and then farms the work out to his associates or to the nonpartners—he can call upon any of the nonpartners or associates to take his case or cover this or do that—here every Beck & Daniels attorney is responsible for his or her own cases. You don't have that option. You take a case on, it's your case and you handle it from start to finish.

Staff attorneys describe their responsibilities in a similar, though somewhat more harried, fashion. Rick and Jeff are staff attorneys at Arthur & Nelson and Beck & Daniels, respectively:

> [I] just handle very large case loads. I don't know exactly how many but I'd say about 50, 60 files, and mainly divorce, bankruptcies—consumer bankruptcies— and other general, you know, wills, deeds, general practice, other things. Some litigation, civil litigation. Some

> criminal, but a majority of it's divorce and bankruptcies.

> I do the intakes. When people come off the street and they want to see an attorney they see me or my boss. . . . Basically I get the less desirable cases to handle. So my job is to interview people and to figure out what their problem is and to make some kind of recommendation and to make a sale or just tell them that we can't help them.

Although staff attorneys have similar responsibilities at both Arthur & Nelson and Beck & Daniels, each firm has a distinct strategy for using staff attorneys. At Arthur & Nelson staff attorneys are extra help hired when managing attorneys believe they have more work than they (or secretaries) can handle. For managing attorneys the decision to hire a staff attorney is based on a cost-benefit equation. Will another attorney in the office increase revenue and profit? From the perspective of management, adding another attorney to an already successful office is a good way to increase gross revenues and the firm's take from that branch office. But for managing attorneys the decision is more complicated. Phil explains the dilemma as follows:

> [Management] would love it for one reason: the more gross [revenues] you get, the more it helps the firm. But the more gross you do, if your expenses exceed what you're grossing, well, now your net is a little less than what you had and you have more work and more files. For example, if I take [an] attorney on who makes another $10,000 [in gross revenues], the firm gets its share off the top. But if my expenses are $10,000, what did I just do? I took on more work, more of a headache, and I'm not making the net. So you have to be careful.

Because the firm takes its cut of revenues off the top each month, managing attorneys remain responsible for the costs involved with staff attorney compensation and benefits. It is possible for Arthur & Nelson management to benefit from the hiring of staff attorneys while managing attorneys suffer.

While Arthur & Nelson managing attorneys find the hiring of staff attorneys to be a risky proposition, Beck & Daniels generally mandates at least one staff attorney to be present in each local office. To help ensure that an attorney is always available for client consultations, most Beck & Daniels offices have two or three staff attorneys. Traditionally, managing attorneys have had little control over the number of staff attorneys employed at their offices. Staffing policies have been mandated by upper management as part of the production system local offices must follow.[2]

Managing attorneys at both firms view staff attorney costs as overhead which may hurt branch office profits if not managed correctly. From the managing attorney's perspective it is necessary to have staff attorneys generate as much revenue as possible at a low cost to the office. This is accomplished in a number of ways. First, staff attorneys tend to be young, recent law school graduates who are entering an overcrowded labor market. For example, the average age of the staff attorneys I interviewed at Arthur & Nelson is 30; at Beck & Daniels the average age is 29.[3]

Second, staff attorneys begin to develop and service their own clients immediately upon being hired. Staff attorneys learn the practice of law through direct experience with virtually no formal training by the firm. As Rick put it,

> you're given primary responsibility for case files the second you walk in the door. And that could mean taking a divorce from the initial stages and pleadings all the way through to a contested trial. Or it could mean writing up a couple of real estate contracts. It varies in the general practice area from that degree of basically office work to large strings of court appearances. And you do all that right away. It's not like a regular large firm where you'll be writing pleadings for your first few weeks, and then maybe they'll let you take some depositions, and then maybe some motion practice, and you won't go near a trial for at least two years into your experience with the firm.

Third, as is evident from virtually all of the quotations in this section, staff attorneys are constantly working: seeing clients, drafting court motions and other documents for their managing attorneys, and going to court. Arthur & Nelson staff attorneys report working an average of 57 hours each week. Beck & Daniels requires staff attorneys to work a minimum of 45 hours each week. Yet firm requirements that branch office attorneys remain available to clients during specific hours each day means that staff attorneys such as Jeff often put in another ten hours each week.

> I put in anywhere from 50 to 60 [hours] each week. I think I put in more than I'm required to. . . . If I have something to do I'm going to come in and do it. I never take lunch either, which is kind of a bad habit. I kind of eat while I'm doing work and its not real healthy. I need to start taking some time off—just getting out of the office for half an hour or whatever.

Finally, while being kept busy for relatively long hours, staff attorney salaries are kept low. For example, my sample of Arthur & Nelson staff attorneys have an average annual income of $29,000. At Beck & Daniels the salaries are kept even lower, averaging $21,250. Beck & Daniels staff attorneys are told that while the salary is low, they may earn bonuses based on the revenue they generate each month. During the period of the study, staff attorneys earned 27 percent of all revenues in excess of $8,700 they brought into the firm each month. However, combining bonus and salary, staff attorneys still only report average annual incomes of $23,000. Staff attorneys at both firms feel as though they are thrown into a lion's den without proper compensation for their efforts. Mike, a staff attorney employed by Beck & Daniels, focuses upon the low salary in his assessment of the firm:

> The salary is terrible. It's very aggravating. I mean, I'm just way overworked, and the hours I work—that's my main complaint about the job in addition to the salary—there are just too many cases to really do a good job.

At Arthur & Nelson (where salaries are slightly higher), Josh is more concerned about the long hours he works:

> It's one thing to say that you can expect to periodically put in some time, but just consistently long hours! I think once, a while back, I was just trying to add up all the hours that I put in—not in a week, but in a month's period of time— and then say, the return here, is it really worth it?

This intense exploitation of staff attorneys would not be possible without an overcrowded labor market. Phil, who is particularly clear on this topic, explains the role of the legal labor market in his successful practice with Arthur & Nelson:

> There's a great resource out there of young attorneys. Every year the law schools are turning them out. Huge amounts, right? This year we're going to have maybe 4,000–5,000 passing the bar, being admitted and looking for jobs. They're willing—we started [my staff attorney] at the salary of $24,000. They're willing to work for $24,000 for the experience alone! Law school has been 50 percent of what they're doing. Now it's actual practice. It's dealing with people. It's all the guidelines that they can't do alone. We're almost at a point where, if we wanted to, we could be like the medical profession and drive them down to an intern's fee of $15,000 or $10,000 because of the need for experience. And it's getting to be that way because there is a huge surplus of young attorneys out there. I don't actually need an expert attorney. In one year he becomes pretty good. I need him to do all the work that's necessary for fill-ins. If it's a serious case, I'll handle it. I could turn over an attorney every two years, and that's the way it works.

Perhaps the most telling comparison is the relative worth of secretaries versus staff attorneys at franchise law firms. Secretarial salaries range from $16,000 to $36,000 while staff attorney compensation ranges include a low of $14,000 to a high of $36,000. Staff attorney compensation is comparable to, and in some cases lower than, secretarial compensation. Indeed, most managing attorneys admit that secretaries are more important to branch office productivity and profits than are staff attorneys.

Secretaries

Secretaries are instrumental to operating successful branch offices. Secretaries wear many hats, providing services wherever they are needed. The different tasks performed by secretaries include dealing with incoming cash and accounting procedures, ordering office supplies, updating clients on the current disposition of their cases, motivating potential clients who telephone to make appointments, screening out undesirable potential clients, creating and copying documents, writing letters to clients and producing wills and other legal forms. As one managing attorney put it, a secretary is

> a jack of all trades. Obviously, the initial client contact is through her; she sets up appointments. She has them [clients] fill out the initial consultation sheet that we have them do. She handles all the money coming into the firm in terms of payment of retainers and ongoing payments on cases. And she handles a lot of the administrative red tape, for example, submitting petty cash requests, keeping track of the trust fund information and the general disbursements fund, the business account, things of that nature.

In addition to the tasks mentioned above, secretaries at Beck & Daniels branch offices also control an elaborate computer system that is used for producing legal documents and letters, tracking clients, and keeping contact with the home office. The two roles of operating the computer system and dealing with clients are considered distinct enough that most Beck & Daniels branch offices have two full-time secretaries who switch between answering the telephone and dealing with clients in the office and producing legal forms and documents on the computer system. Managing attorneys learn to view secretaries as essential partners in operating branch offices. For example, Carl at Arthur & Nelson has found that

> a secretary plays a big role if you've got a good one. She can make your job a lot easier and a lot more enjoyable. . . . She can play a role to screen clients and taking questions as opposed to just putting questions through [to the attorney]. I think that's important. It's very easy to say, "Well, he's not here can I take a message?" and come back with a big stack of messages. Whereas my secretary will say, "He's not here, is there something I can help you with?" to try to alleviate a lot of the messages. The secretary plays a big role.

It is important to point out that while secretaries perform many "paralegal" duties, neither Beck & Daniels nor Arthur & Nelson employ certified paralegals. Management at each firm regards paralegals to be too expensive and too narrowly trained to serve the needs of local offices. Franchise law firms create "legal assistants" suited to the requirements of franchise practice through on-the-job training of novice secretaries.

Despite their lack of legal training, it does not take long for secretaries to realize their importance to branch office success. Secretaries describe their responsibilities as "doing everything" necessary to keep the branch office operating. Many refer to their role as being the unofficial "office manager." Sarah (Beck & Daniels) and Sandy (Arthur & Nelson) provide typical examples of secretary experiences at franchise law firms:

> Oh my, I do everything. I type, I file, book appointments. I handle all the cash flow. I greet clients. I meet clients. I do financial affidavits for divorce clients. I do everything. I copy, I file, I order supplies, I maintain supplies. . . . I do everything except for go[ing] to court.

> I run the office, let's put it that way. My boss would be lost without me. I do almost everything in the office except interview the clients. All the paperwork is done by me. Everything is done by me and I run the office. I order supplies, I take care of petty cash. I take care of a lot of things that the managing attorney does not take care of.

The compensation systems reflect the critical role of secretaries in office production. Secretaries are salaried rather than hourly employees. This serves to insulate the secretaries somewhat from the peaks and valleys of income that managing attorneys may experience. To help motivate secretaries, both firms require managing attorneys to pay bonuses based on each office's monthly revenues. Yet the compensation system also serves another purpose. It allows managing attorneys to work secretaries for long hours without increasing their pay. This helps managing attorneys to minimize labor costs while exploiting secretaries to the fullest possible extent. Phil at Arthur & Nelson relates how secretaries are best utilized as he explains why he is not burdened by administrative work:

> We have very good assistants who eliminate a lot of that [administrative] work. The secretary is able to give [the administrative office] the information they need about what clients are coming in, who is retained. And that sheet she fills out with the retainer [paid by the client] and the [balance due] statement practically shows everything. . . . The point that the managing attorney has is, number one, to be here, to constantly see people, to work his files and his clients, *and to make sure the secretaries are constantly busy. . . . The idea is we have that constant flow of work.* (emphasis added)

For their average annual incomes of $26,000 and $18,000 at Arthur & Nelson and Beck & Daniels, respectively, secretaries are required to work 37.5 hours each week. However, branch office secretaries generally give beyond the call of duty. Secretaries at Arthur & Nelson (the only firm I have this data for) report working a minimum of 40 hours and an average of 50 hours each week. Given the volume of work and diversity of tasks completed by secretaries as part of their regular duties, it is no wonder that managing attorneys prefer to lose staff attorneys rather than experienced secretaries from their offices.

The Evolving Mass Production Model

In this chapter I have described the basic organizational model franchise law firms have developed. It is clear that secretaries aided by computer boilerplate are the essential element in office productivity. Staff attorneys are neither essential nor considered to be legal experts. They are extra help to facilitate selling services to clients. Managing attorneys also engage in the sales process through consultations with clients. But the main role of managing attorneys is to supervise secretaries and staff attorneys, and take the economic risks inherent in operating branch offices.

Managing attorneys and firm management rely upon one another to help assure the smooth operation of the law firm and the earning of profits. For example, Arthur & Nelson and Beck & Daniels managements develop nationally or regionally disseminated advertising campaigns. Managing attorneys have virtually no input with advertising strategy. Managing attorneys expect that firm owners and managers will develop campaigns which will bring clients to their local offices to buy services provided at those offices. In return, management expects local offices to adhere to firm policies and production standards when dealing with clients. However, during the course of this study both Beck & Daniels and Arthur & Nelson sought to rationalize client services beyond the basic franchise models described earlier in the chapter. The changes instituted at each law firm are quite different—Beck & Daniels franchised its offices; Arthur & Nelson developed special units which circumvent branch offices. Despite these differences, both firms were reacting to disgruntled local office employees and the 1990s economic downturn in the legal services industry.

By the 1990s the legal services industry began to stagnate. Large law firms that had prospered in the 1980s began to fail (Brill 1989; Nelson and Trubek 1992). The legal press carried stories reporting layoffs at law firms (Brill 1991a; Clarke 1991) and announcing the end of the legal services boom of the 1980s (Brill 1991b; Rutman 1991). Arthur & Nelson was stagnating. By 1993 the firm was closing as many branch offices as it opened. Beck & Daniels was in decline and had closed more than half of its local offices by 1993.

Arthur & Nelson

The basic franchise model involves local offices which offer services to clients based on production systems and criteria determined by law firm management. As long as the law firm successfully and responsibly advertises for services available at the local offices, both management and branch offices potentially benefit. Prior to reorganizing, Arthur & Nelson focused its advertising and branch office production on the area of family law, particularly divorce. During the recession, however, family law ceased to be as lucrative as it had been. Arthur & Nelson management chose to change the direction of emphasis of the law firm to other areas of personal legal services. Specifically, it decided to develop personal bankruptcy and personal injury emphases. But rather than "retool" and retrain branch office attorneys and secretaries for these new areas of legal practice, Arthur & Nelson developed a system of special units to process case files which initiated at branch offices.[4]

Similar to branch offices in organization, special units rely upon support staff to perform many of the routine tasks. Generally, a few attorneys supervise a large cohort of secretaries. Kent, a former personal injury unit staff attorney explains that

> the unit actually gets run by mirrors. There are a heck of a lot of support staff and not a lot of attorneys. There is one managing attorney. When I left I was one of two attorneys who actually handled files. The bulk of the files were in

the hands of the paralegals. . . . Each attorney had a handful of paralegals and each paralegal held close to 100 files. So while I had my own case load that I would handle in a normal fashion—just trying to negotiate, try and settle, or . . . do the litigation, arbitration or whatever—there were a lot of responsibilities for supervising the paralegals and the files they had. They would handle the files for the first six months to a year. I had to make sure that they were doing that properly because they were only trained on the job as paralegals. They certainly did not have a law degree! Most of them did not even have paralegal degrees, for what good that does.

From the time a file would come in—it would come into the branch office, it would get transferred to us, the file would be open—it would be assigned to an attorney and paralegal. At that point the attorney would review the file [and] tell the paralegal what had to be done up front. The paralegal would have to make sure the client was going to the doctor, resolve the property damage, order the investigation, [and] set up the claims with the insurance company on both sides. Basically, the paralegal would run the file until the person was either done treating or it was, for statute reasons or whatever, to be put into [a law] suit.

To increase productivity further, Arthur & Nelson invested in computer systems and developed software for the specific needs of the bankruptcy and personal injury units. For example, the firm has "internally developed" "a series of bankruptcy programs where there's a tracking system to keep track of all the bankruptcy clients." In addition to these programs, the "staff has three or four word processors" with specific programs that are used to produce standardized forms and letters.

By focusing more of its resources on the personal bankruptcy and personal injury units, Arthur & Nelson expanded its clientele and centralized its case file processing. Centralizing production offers a number of benefits. First, by centralizing negotiations with creditors (for bankruptcy) and insurance companies (for personal injury) the

firm is able to develop ongoing contacts and become a "repeat player" (Galanter 1974) in those arenas. Repeat players have more success in legal arenas because their continuing contact allows them to develop specific knowledge and personal ties related to obtaining the desired outcome. "One-shotters" or less frequent players may not be able to develop the same level of knowledge or resources simply because they are not involved in the process on a regular basis (Galanter 1974). Branch office attorneys tend to become repeat players for divorce negotiations (though not at centralized locations). Special units allow the firm to develop similar relationships for personal injury (PI) and bankruptcy cases.

Second, centralized production offers management greater control over the work process. For example, attorneys working in personal injury units complain that Arthur & Nelson management limits the number of cases they may litigate and sets quotas for settling cases. Bill, another former personal injury unit staff attorney, explains the limits imposed on his practice:

> The system only works if the attorneys are in the office at almost all times. So our job was to make sure that we stayed in the office. To do that you couldn't litigate a lot of cases. So there were, for a large part of the time I was there, there were imposed caps in the number of cases that could be put into suit for any one attorney at any one time. They'd push the paralegals to get people to finish treating and wrap up getting their medicals. Then they would push us to try and settle cases. They'd push the accounting people to get the money in the door. . . . As far as trying to settle cases, settlement was stressed a lot more there than it is in most PI [personal injury] firms. It was my major function as far as they were concerned. Their viewpoint was, "Well for those few cases that you can't settle, you'll have to put them into suit and do [litigate] those."

As the above quote suggests, special units emphasize processing routine (e.g., non-litigated) cases as quickly and efficiently as possible. By using support staff and computers to process the large number of cases channeled to them from branch offices, special units take advantage of increased productivity and better control over the work force.

The third benefit of centralizing production in special units is lower overhead costs. By processing bankruptcy and PI cases at centralized locations, management need not supply all branch offices with the necessary staff, computers and software. Branch office attorneys and secretaries complain that the firm is "stuck in the dark ages" of technology, while special units are "made nicer, better offices."

Finally, centralized production makes it possible to develop new clients, more efficient production techniques and lower overhead costs in a manner that benefits firm management more than branch offices. Arthur & Nelson's network of branch offices provides clients with convenient access to all available services. But by removing the processing of lucrative cases to special units, management deprives branch offices of most of the revenues and profits generated by those cases. Although branch offices are required to perform initial consultations for clients whose case files are sent to special units, their only compensation is a small referral fee which is determined by management.

Beck & Daniels

Beck & Daniels' reorganization, called the local partner initiative, follows from the premise that better, more dedicated branch office managing attorneys are necessary to make the existing production system function in a profitable manner. As the managing partner of the law firm explains it, the local partner initiative

> involves the installation of equity partners at our [branch] offices. Historically, the local office managing attorney has been an employee of the firm with some profit participation, but not ownership. Our local partners will be owners of their offices and the profits from their operations will belong to them.

With local partnership, successful managing attorneys, regional managers and national managers are offered the opportunity to buy a "controlling" interest (92 percent) in one or more branch offices. Unprofitable offices and offices for which there are no buyers are closed. In buying their offices managing attorneys gain more responsibility for office operations. Local partners take over staff hiring and salary decisions. In addition, payroll and other disbursements are also handled locally. For most managing attorneys who become local partners the change in status from employee to owner is very important. Eric is a typical example.

> I guess, very simply, you become an owner-operator, for want of a better term, of an office and you pretty much take over an office lock, stock and barrel. The employees work for you. You pay them. You give them benefits. You maintain independent malpractice insurance. You run the office as if it was yours. There is contact with Beck & Daniel . . . but for all practical purposes, from a business standpoint, it really is my office.

It is interesting to note that, with the exception of hiring and firing decisions, managing attorneys have always been responsible for fulfilling the duties mentioned in the above quote. As discussed earlier in this chapter, all managing attorneys have to generate sufficient revenues to pay employees and other overhead costs—including insurance. Local partners simply accept responsibility for paying the bills directly from their offices. In addition, Beck & Daniels retains an 8 percent stake in each office as well as control over television advertising, production systems, technology and revenue goals. Local partners must service the debt from their equity buy-in (which is often financed by the firm); they must pay 8 percent of monthly gross revenues and an additional monthly advertising fee to the firm. Failure to fulfill any number of responsibilities may result in the loss of partnership. Matt explains:

What happened is . . . they asked me if I wanted to become a partner, and really, you know, it was very expensive to buy a partnership. I mean, I paid a hundred and something thousand dollars for this office. . . . And basically, I pay quite a lot of money for the advertising, plus I pay 8 percent of my revenues to them. Every Tuesday they electronically transfer from my bank account—because I gave them limited power of attorney to do so—8 percent of my revenues plus an advertising fee. The advertising fee is fixed based on the number of offices [in an advertising district]. Like we have nine offices in this area. But the 8 percent is not fixed. You have a minimum, a minimum [revenue] requirement that you have to meet, and I think that's $16,000 a month. Eight percent of $16,000 a month or they can pull your partnership agreement away.

In addition to the economic issues, partnership agreements ensure that the nature or character of branch offices, including production and computer systems, services provided and the hours each office remains open, remains unchanged. Beck & Daniels' managing partner emphasizes that

how we provide affordable and convenient access to the legal system to middle-income people will not change. The local partner does not take down the sign, destroy the letterhead, and become a personal injury firm or a litigation firm or a firm that specializes in employment discrimination and complex litigation. He operates a Beck & Daniels office consistent with the standards set forth in the partnership agreement, all of which require him to maintain the essential character of the office. So . . . I think our local partners believe that they have more autonomy, more freedom, greater control of their office operations, but understand pretty clearly that the nature of the practice has not changed.

Local partners confirm that the operations manual has not been discarded:

Oh yeah, yeah, it's still the same standard system for all the Beck & Daniels offices, and, you know, we also have to remain open 9:00 to 8:00 Monday through Thursday, 9:00 to 6:00 on Fridays, and 9:00 to 4:00 on Saturdays.

As far as hours of operation, case types that we have to offer, representation, yeah, there is an office procedures manual as far as file management, accounting, what not, sure.

To help assure that the Beck & Daniels production system will remain in use, management requires each local office to purchase a new computer system that links the corporate headquarters to each office. The computer system provides branch offices with the forms and programs previously developed by the firm and allows management to check up on branch offices on a daily basis. Management can use the computer network to check branch office revenues as well as case types that the office has recently performed work on. Management also uses the computer system to calculate and collect its royalties and advertising fees each week. Many local partners view the computer system as a symbol of their lack of control over their legal work—past and present. Frank's complaints are typical among local partners and managing attorneys:

We had no input on the computer system that we got. Right now, in the different regions, there are three computer systems being used. The original, the one that I was brought in with, is a ten-year-old or a twelve-year-old Wang system which makes a God-awful noise when it goes off and is very slow. And it's very expensive to keep up. Then there's the LINDA [computer system] which I happen to love. I thought I'd go through life being computer illiterate and I fought tooth and nail when they insisted that I be trained on the LINDA system. But I got trained on it and I became good at it and I really enjoyed it. I thought it was just fine.

Now the local partnership offices, for the most part, have been put onto what they call the LOIS system. That's where we are now. [Management] knows quite well I hate it. I truly hate it. . . . We had no say at all, none whatsoever. This is what we are getting. If we are going to get the offices we're obligated to purchase [the LOIS system]. As a managing attorney I could have accepted that. . . . [But now] it is important for them to ask us. And it is important to us that they hear what we have to say, because, still, *with partnership we don't have the unrestricted authority to go ahead and just do things the way we want to if we don't think that what [management] is suggesting is the best way to do it.* (emphasis added)

Despite buying a controlling interest in branch offices, partnership agreements allow Beck & Daniels to maintain tight control over the operation of branch offices. Beck & Daniels local partner initiative assumes, as the firm's managing partner put it, that "we've always had great systems to represent . . . clients efficiently, competently and profitably." Because management retains control over advertising, production techniques and technology and revenue standards, many local partners refer to Beck & Daniels as a franchise. For example, Lorna argues that her position is "set up basically like a franchise . . . but they claim it's a partnership." Such a view is not unwarranted. Local partners contract to use the Beck & Daniels name, production and technology systems to provide legal services to consumers targeted by the firm. In return, local partners agree to pay management a royalty of 8 percent of gross revenues and to operate local offices to Beck & Daniels' specifications. Even Beck & Daniels' managing partner admits that the "economic parallels between . . . a franchise and our new partnership structure are pretty obvious."

For the founding partners of the law firm the local partnership initiative has been a way to raise capital quickly and begin expanding the law firm again while local partners burden the risk. As a national manager explains, local partnership is

a really great method of raising capital. It also is an opportunity to expand the law firm using other people's capital to do so. In the history of our firm [the founding partners] have been brilliant in being able at every point where there has been an expansion of the firm to do it basically without any of their own money. And this is another opportunity to do that.

But to the local partners it appears that there is no longer a "law firm." Instead the founding partners are now profiting by selling production and technology systems for processing specific legal case types. In Matt's estimation management has used the reorganization of the law firm as "an opportunity to alleviate a lot of the headache . . . from a centralized management type of organization" as well as "an opportunity to drastically reduce their overhead. Those people are pretty damn smart . . . for better or for worse."

* * *

Beck & Daniels and Arthur & Nelson have developed networks of branch offices based on concepts of rational organization to deliver legal services to consumers. The organization of work and incentives at these firms assigns specific responsibilities and duties to each of the three positions found in branch offices. Managing attorneys are responsible for the day-to-day operation of local offices. They are clearly focused on productivity and profits. Staff attorneys are not essential staff. Rather, they are extra help for managing attorneys to ensure that clients meet with an attorney without a long wait for an appointment. Staff attorneys are not required or expected to be legal experts. They tend to be young, new law school graduates who have encountered a difficult job market. Secretaries at franchise law firms have the broadest range of tasks and responsibilities. They are acknowledged by all attorneys to be essential to the operation of branch offices. Although managing attorneys assume the economic risks of operating branch offices, secretaries make them run smoothly, efficiently and profitably. One of the most telling indicators of the relative importance of secretaries versus staff attorneys is their levels of compensation. Secretarial compensation is comparable to, and in some cases exceeds, staff attorney compensation levels.

Local offices are organized around task-oriented production systems and are capable of processing a large number of clients on a regular basis. Nonetheless, Arthur & Nelson and Beck & Daniels have sought to further increase productivity and lower costs. Arthur & Nelson has created special units to process personal bankruptcy and personal injury claims. Special units centralize production, offering greater managerial control, higher rates of productivity and lower overhead costs. Special units pose a dilemma for branch offices because they have the potential to remove all skilled work from branch offices and reduce attorneys to nothing more than intake workers.

Beck & Daniels has followed a different path, selling local offices to managing attorneys. The local partner initiative does not significantly alter the work performed at branch offices. In fact, Beck & Daniels management has gone to lengths to make sure that the character of branch office work remains unchanged. Rather than giving branch offices more autonomy, local partnership asks managing attorneys to pay for the privilege of continuing to use Beck & Daniels' name and highly specified production systems. Nonetheless, local partnership appears to elicit greater satisfaction from managing attorneys who are taking greater economic risks while accomplishing the same tasks as managing attorneys who have no equity investment. . . .

Discussion Questions

1. Select an occupation with which you have some familiarity and discuss the ways in which it does and does not measure up to the ideal of a profession.

2. Have you ever had an occasion to obtain legal assistance from a franchise law firm?

3. Develop an argument that skilled manual occupations, like electrician or carpenter, are also professions.

Reprinted from Jerry L. Van Hoy, "The Organization of Mass Production Law," in *Franchise Law Firms and the Transformation of Personal Legal Services* (Westport, CT: Quorum Books, 1997, pp. 27–50). Used by permission.

Endnotes

1. Arthur & Nelson also provides its managing attorneys with a guaranteed income to cover unprofitable months. However, Arthur & Nelson managing attorneys are encouraged by firm management to view the guarantee as a loan, not a salary.
2. Staffing policies are discussed in more detail in Chapters 5 and 6.
3. These ages exclude one 50-year-old and one 44-year-old staff attorney at Arthur & Nelson and Beck & Daniels, respectively. Despite his age, the 50-year-old staff attorney was a recent law school graduate. The 44-year-old was more experienced but was in training for a Beck & Daniels managing attorney position.
4. Arthur & Nelson currently has three special units: personal bankruptcy, personal injury and criminal. Most of my discussion in this book is limited to the personal bankruptcy and personal injury units.

References

Brill, S. 1991a. "Headnotes." *American Lawyer* (June): 3, 56.
——. 1991b. "Short-Term Pain, Long-Term Gain." *American Lawyer* (January): 5–6, 55–59.
——. 1989. "The Law Business in the Year 2000." *American Lawyer* (June): 10.
Clarke, C. V. 1991. "Shattered Dreams." *American Lawyer* (June): 5–63.
Galanter, M. 1974. "Why the 'Haves' Come Out Ahead: Speculations on the Limits of Legal Change." *Law and Society Review* 9: 96–160.
Garson, B. 1988. *The Electronic Sweatshop.* New York: Penguin Books.
Hall, R. H. 1968. "Professionalization and Bureaucratization." *American Sociological Review* 33: 92–104.
Nelson, R. L. and D. Trubek. 1992. "Arenas of Professionalism: The Professional Ideologies of Lawyers in Collective and Workplace Contexts." In *Lawyers' Ideals and Lawyers' Practices,* edited

by R. Nelson, R. Solomon and D. Trubek. Ithaca, NY: Cornell University Press.

Ritzer, G. 1996. *The McDonaldization of Society* (revised edition). Thousand Oaks, CA: Pine Forge Press.

Rutman, K. 1991. "The Boom Abates." *National Law Journal* (September): S2–S4. ✦

22
Unlikely Rebels

Stephen R. Barley and
Gideon Kunda

Stephen Barley and Gideon Kunda examine the change in the 1980s and 1990s whereby workers in the occupation of college-educated technical professionals became contingently employed "itinerant experts" with no benefits who move from firm to firm for short-term contract work. Two main perspectives by which to understand the growth of contingent work in the United States in general are presented, along with the authors' more comprehensive perspective.

Itinerant Experts

Clothed in a light blue T-shirt and chinos, Kent Cox revealed nothing to suggest that he was in the vanguard of an employment revolt that was spreading quietly across America's industrial landscape. Kent had no obvious tattoos or piercing. He carried no union card. He was not out to change the world. His passions were for code, ballroom dancing, and science fiction, not for politics—especially not for politics of the organizational sort. His short, dusty blond hair was only slightly rumpled, and his wire-rims suggested nothing more than intelligence. Had you seen him that day sitting across from us in a Chinese restaurant in downtown Mountain View in the heart of Silicon Valley, you might not have given him a second glance, so well did he blend in with the other techies who frequent the establishment in search of noonday egg rolls and sweet-and-sour soup. If you had no-

ticed a difference between Kent and the rest, it would have been in the minutiae: he entered the restaurant alone, not as a member of a pack, and his T-shirt bore no company logo.

On the other hand, if you were a programmer who had been in the Silicon Valley long enough, you might have recognized Kent, at least by name, as a guru of sorts. Firms on the cutting edge of high technology eagerly sought Kent's expertise as a software developer. At thirty-six, he had already worked for a "who's who" of companies, some of which are household names across America; others are famous only among the technogensia. Kent's six-figure income was testimony to his talent. Yet, by some people's measure, he had not been gainfully employed in nearly a decade, if being gainfully employed means being permanently employed. Since 1989 Kent had worked only as an independent contractor, a "hired gun" as they are sometimes called, moving from firm to firm every six to eight months in search of another challenge.

At sixteen, when most of his peers were still entranced by the dancing phosphorescence of Space Invaders, Kent began programming. He enrolled in Cal Poly a year later, where he majored in computer science. Hearing no scholarly calling, Kent took several years off to write code. "I was an indifferent student," he admitted. "I was only motivated to program." After eventually graduating in the mid-1980s, he programmed for his father's start-up for several years, and in 1989 he went to work as a full-time developer for Sun Microsystems. After a year of eighty-hour weeks, Kent "burned out," left Sun, and took an eight-month vacation to, as he put it, "put my head back together." He realized he didn't want another full-time job. Indeed, he was ambivalent about work in general. But in 1990 a friend convinced him to join a software project as a contractor. From then on Kent was never permanently employed, yet he had worked continuously on a stream of projects that ranged from building device drivers for printers and digital cameras to developing applications for the Web. He attributed his success not only to his skills but also to his reputation in the technical community. "My career," he explained, "has been not so much getting hired to do the same thing, but getting hired by people I know who can't find someone they need to fill a particular niche, so they hire someone they think can learn to do it."

Like many experienced contractors, Kent found work through colleagues, friends, and acquaintances. "When you want to get work," he explained, "the key is to make sure everybody you know knows you're looking. Just call all of your friends and say, 'Hey, I'm looking and one of 'em will say, 'Oh we need somebody to do IO [input-output].' NEC came through somebody I danced with.[1] Her husband was doing contracting for them. You get contracts anywhere. Anyone you know is a potential contract. One of my friends gets a lot of his jobs through church." Kent was currently charging $90 an hour for his services and working thirty hours a week. He could have worked more, but he preferred to use the rest of his time to surf, read, and write his own software.

At the time we met Kent, he had just run up against one of the catch-22s of being a hired gun. He had contracted to provide guidance to a project team supposedly composed of "crack engineers." But, he explained, "I have not meshed well with this team. Most of them are on their first or second project. I'm more like on my twenty-fifth, and that gives you a very different perspective. I did some egregious political blundering in the beginning when I pointed out things that were going to be problems in three months. They did become problems, but I was asking for trouble because they couldn't see what was coming. I've gotten back into everybody's good graces, but it's been a strain. This is the first time I've really had this problem because I'd been working for a long time with people who have a similar level of experience as me."

Kent's only regret about having worked so long as a contractor was the proverbial Silicon Valley story of opportunity lost: "One of the hardest things is watching people regularly get rich. I turned down a job at Netscape because I wanted to contract.[2] I mean, I turned down a job offer from Netscape the month before they went public! I decided not to apply when they moved to Mountain View even though I was doing Web development at the time. That's the one that hurts. Of course, I had no idea at the time that Netscape was going to do that. I keep reminding myself of that when I start feeling really stupid.". . .

If Kent Cox was an unlikely foot soldier in an employment revolt, Yolanda Turner, a well-dressed, fifty-two-year-old African-American woman with three grown children and an infectious laugh, was even less likely. Yolanda had lived her entire life in and around Los Angeles. In 1982, at the age of thirty-six, Yolanda decided to pursue a bachelor's degree in film at Pomona College after raising her children as a single mother. Four years later, she graduated and worked a number of temporary clerical jobs before landing a full-time job, first at UCLA and then at Rockdyne, as an administrative assistant. Had Yolanda's story ended here, she might have served as a classic example of how difficult it is for older African-American women to rise above socioeconomic and racial barriers, even with a degree from a prestigious college. But Yolanda's supervisor at Rockdyne noticed her interest in PCs and paid for her to take courses in hardware and software. Before long, she became an in-house expert who informally assisted and coached her co-workers when their computers went out of whack. Gradually, Yolanda began to spend most of her time fixing workstations and tweaking software, even though she was still employed as a secretary. Six years later in 1995, and still employed as an administrative assistant, Yolanda submitted her resume to an online job board and landed a contract as a workstation technician at an IBM subsidiary. Since then Yolanda had worked exclusively as a contractor, moving over time from workstation maintenance to systems administration and then on to quality assurance and testing.

Unlike Kent Cox, who relied on his extensive network, Yolanda secured her positions solely through staffing agencies that served as brokers between her and the clients who bought her services. These agencies had sprung up in the 1980s and 1990s to take advantage of firms' lack of information about contractors and contractors' lack of information about job openings. Most, but not all, modeled themselves after temporary help agencies. In return for locating positions, deducting payroll taxes, and occasionally offering access to health insurance, agencies added a markup of approximately 30 percent to 40 percent to Yolanda's hourly pay of $35 per hour. Yolanda didn't much like the markup, which she considered excessive, but she accepted it as the way the game was played. When we met Yolanda in 1998, she was working forty- to fifty-hour weeks for an annual income of about $87,000. Being a morning person, Yolanda typically arrived at work at 6:00 A.M. and left at 2:30 in the afternoon. Often, she worked part of Saturday or Sunday as well. Yolanda's contracts typically lasted between three and six months, and since 1995 her total "downtime"—the time in between contracts—amounted to less than two weeks. When asked why she had forsaken permanent employment, Yolanda left no doubt about her motives: "Significantly more pay! Significantly more independence! And, you don't get immersed in the political environment that goes on in companies. I like the independence. I like being able to move around and see how different companies do things. In most cases you make a significantly higher salary than you do as a full-timer." Yolanda estimated that she typically made $10 to $15 more an hour than permanent employees doing the same work. When she first started contracting, however, this was not the case: "I used to do work on the side fixing people's computers and I was charging $15 an hour and I thought, 'I'm doing pretty good.' Then, I met a girl who was charging $65 an hour and I said, 'Wait a minute. What's wrong with this picture?' So, I started charging more and getting it. To make it as a contractor," she advised, "you need to know what the market is and what your skills are worth." Yolanda did this, in part, by talking with other contrac-

tors and, in part, by subscribing to *Contract Professional*, a monthly magazine targeted at contractors.

Yolanda had mastered the art of staying current. At the time we spoke with her, she was learning SAP with the goal of becoming an SAP consultant within three years.[3] She had chosen SAP because "it's very lucrative, and that's what I'm focusing on: money." In addition to buying and reading technical books and surfing the Web for more up-to-date information, Yolanda maintained her own home computer lab. "I have a full system at home. I've got two computer systems and two different types of modems. I've got a scanner and two printers and a little digital camera. So, I have all the equipment I need to learn something, if I need to know it." Yolanda chose her contracts for their learning potential. "I don't have a lot of time to read," she reported, "so while I'm working on this product—and it's a product that's in SAP—I'm learning as I go along. I'm pretty familiar with about three of the modules right now. And in some cases," she added, laughing, "more familiar than some of the people who are the SAP consultants there."

At first glance Julian Stoke could not have been more different from Yolanda Turner. Julian was a corpulent white man with thinning hair and horn-rims. To call him disheveled would have been an understatement. He wore wrinkled chinos, running shoes, and a short-sleeved plaid shirt whose tails had sneaked out on both sides of his pants, revealing twin triangles of pale white skin. A devout Mormon, Julian was the father of seven children ranging from seven to twenty-four years of age. Although Julian was part of the same movement in which Kent and Yolanda had enlisted, his story was different.

After graduating from Brigham Young University in 1974 with a self-designed bachelor's degree in computational linguistics, Julian moved with his wife and first child to the Silicon Valley to be near his parents. Within a year he was working full-time for The Gap, where he climbed the ladder over the next five years from programmer to third-level technical manager.

He was working fifty- to sixty-hour weeks and like Kent Cox finally reached the point where he burned out. But rather than take time off, Julian wended his way through three more permanent positions in rapid succession until he finally landed at Citicorp in 1981 as a systems programmer. Before his probationary period ended, however, he was fired.

"They quit me!" Julian explained as if still reeling from incredulity twenty years later. "The irony was that the manager of the group was a contractor. He came to me one day and said, 'You don't fit in with our group.' I said, 'Right, I agree with you. You are not the same kind of people that I am.' He said, 'We will have to let you go.' I said, 'Well, have I done something wrong? You don't like my work?' and he said, 'No, you just don't fit in.'"

After looking for work unsuccessfully for "quite a while," Julian cast his lot in with a friend, an independent contractor with whom he had worked at The Gap. Like Yolanda and Kent, Julian found the lure of money and autonomy hard to resist. "I am not ordinarily a 'live-on-the-edge' sort of guy, but I was really intrigued by several aspects of contracting: the money, the mobility, and the professionalism." For most of the 1980s, Julian sold his services as a VM system programmer to an array of clients in the Bay Area through his friend's business.[4] But in 1988 the business collapsed and his friend absconded with three thousand of Julian's dollars. Julian then took his first contract through a broker and had since worked exclusively through staffing agencies. "Once burned, twice shy," he explained.

Over the years, Julian had become savvy about dealing with agencies. "Every broker tells you, 'You have a career with us, and when we are done with this assignment, we'll find you another. You're a valued member of our team.' But what it really comes down to is that if they have no openings, there is no commitment to you." To cope with uncertainty and the lack of commitment, and to increase his chances of finding work when he needed it, Julian had learned to work with many agencies simul-

taneously. Although he did not like it, he accepted their markup—usually around 40 percent, he told us—as an unavoidable fact of the contracting life. Several years earlier, Julian had gone through a trying period without health insurance. At one point he was even forced to fall back on the charity of the Mormon Church to help cover steep medical bills incurred after his son was injured in a road accident. Julian subsequently took a permanent job for a year, largely to qualify for the HMO, which he was able to retain at his own expense once he returned to contracting.

Unlike Kent and Yolanda, Julian's career as a "warm body" had been rocky. Since 1988, he had moved between contracting and permanent employment on four occasions. Although he had seen little downtime, he had been fired on three occasions, once from two separate contracts simultaneously. When we met Julian, he was making $55 an hour, working over sixty hours a week (not including the time he spent keeping his skills up-to-date), and having difficulty making ends meet. He blamed his financial difficulties on old debts, on a wife who was unable to work, and on being "bad with money," especially credit cards. Julian had not taken a vacation in years. With such wages, "It's a huge temptation to work every hour of the day," he admitted.

Julian, like Kent, was involved in a professional community. But whereas Kent's was formally organized, Julian's existed loosely on the Web. "Do you know about the IRC?" Julian asked in response to our question about professional relationships. "That's one of the major types of chat rooms, where you get online to talk and make friends. I have one group of professional people I get on with every once in a while. That is one of the tools of problem solving. When you can't find the answer to a technical problem in the manuals, the next best thing is use a bulletin board. I subscribe to about ten of them. I go on and put out my question, 'Why is this happening? How do I get around this?' I get answers all the time. Chat has changed the face of contracting in recent years, because when people in a company have problems they ask the contractor, whom they see as a guru, their mentor."

Although Julian's wife had misgivings about contracting and periodically urged him to "get a real job," Julian was reluctant to do so. His last few contracts had gone well, and he had doubts about his ability to hold down a permanent job. The opportunities to learn new technologies were plentiful. And, like Kent, Julian saw himself as an expert, a systems programmer who saved his clients from themselves. "We contractors have a superiority, a superciliousness," he confided. "We sometimes get the impression that we are doing the real work, that we are going the distance. These other guys go home at five and we stay until eight. But we always know that there will come a day when we sign our project over to somebody and it is no longer our problem. It's theirs."

Despite their many differences, Julian, Yolanda, and Kent had one thing in common: all had made a conscious decision to step outside the mainstream of employment. They had questioned and then jettisoned, at least for the time being, the vision to which their parents and society had taught them to aspire: the safe haven of a permanent job. Like most of us, they had been told that with a college education they could get a "good job," a code word for going to work full-time for a reputable employer. In the absence of a major recession and in return for loyalty and hard work, employers would reward them with a good salary, health insurance, promotions, and perhaps most important, reasonable expectations for long-term security. In the end, they'd retire at sixty-five with a pension, a gold watch, and some savings.

At least initially, like most Americans their age, all three had reason to believe in the bargain. They were, after all, technical professionals whom employers historically valued more highly than most other kinds of employees. But for reasons ranging from being laid off to longing for a less hectic lifestyle, each had decided to bet on his or her skills and forgo full-time work, even though all believed they could have secured a permanent job had they so desired. Each

knowingly entered a world of work that demanded they change employers two to three times a year and adopt a notion of security based on their continued ability to market their expertise to a portfolio of buyers. In short, they had left behind the familiarity of traditional employment for the uncertainty of a more fluid labor market. None seemed to regret their choice.

Kent, Yolanda, and Julian are what we call technical contractors. They sometimes even called themselves contractors (or consultants), although they usually introduced themselves by their occupation: software developer, technical writer, multimedia developer, systems programmer, and so on. As contractors, they possessed skills and knowledge similar to those of the full-time engineers, software developers, and technical writers with whom they worked. They performed similar tasks and worked in the same firms as the full-timers. Yet, even though they worked at the cutting edge of the postindustrial revolution, the mode of their employment resembled that of craftsmen in the Middle Ages, especially the stonemasons who built the great cathedrals of Europe.[5]

Stonemasonry was, and still is, the queen of the crafts. Although we don't think of stonemasons as high-tech workers, in medieval Europe they were. Shaping artful and well-engineered Gothic cathedrals from hand-hewn stone was a significant technical achievement requiring expertise that took years to master. For this reason, stonemasons were in short supply and great demand. Building a cathedral was an expensive, multiyear project commissioned by the clergy and royalty of a city. Since most medieval cities were small, they needed and could only afford one cathedral. Accordingly, masons could expect to be gainfully employed in one place for no more than a few years. Because of this constraint, stonemasons worked as itinerant craftsmen, traveling from city to city throughout Europe, joining projects and leaving cathedrals in their wake. Like these artisans of old, technical contractors also ply their trade as "itinerant experts." Some, known in contracting circles as "nomads" or "road warriors," even move from city to city in search of projects, just as stone-masons did five centuries ago. Firms substitute for cities and projects for cathedrals.

In late 1997 when we set out to study technical contracting, we didn't think of ourselves as entering a world of itinerant experts. We certainly didn't think of contractors as social pioneers. Our goal was simply to understand how employment relations were changing at the dawn of the twenty-first century. We hoped to document the social dynamics of skilled "contingent labor," a term economists and sociologists now use for an array of short-term arrangements including part-time work, temporary employment, self-employment, contracting, outsourcing, and home-based work. To be honest, if anything, we saw contingent work, in general, and possibly even contracting, as social problems indicative of corporate America's willingness to abdicate its responsibility to employees in return for greater profits. Contingent employment seemed to bear a troubling resemblance to the laissez-faire capitalism of the late nineteenth century, which, in the name of individualism and the free market, spawned a plethora of exploitative practices.[6] In our concern we were hardly alone. . . .

Making Sense of Contingent Work

In the early 1990s, contingent work began to attract the attention of sociologists, labor economists, and journalists. Most commentators focused on the reasons firms employed contingent workers and on the costs and benefits of doing so.[7] Analysts who took the workers' perspective were fewer in number and fell into two opposing camps: the "institutionalists" and the advocates of "free agency."

The Institutional Perspective

The institutionalists were economists or sociologists who interpreted contingent work through a historical and social lens.[8]

They told a cautionary tale. From an institutional perspective, contingent work's expansion threatened the security of the workforce and the American system of social welfare, which was based on full-time employment. The institutionalists framed the threat from the perspective of dual labor market theory, the notion that industrial economies are composed of two sectors: "primary" and "secondary."[9]

Primary labor markets provide stable employment, career ladders, job security, high wages, and attractive benefit plans. Secondary labor markets are, by comparison, less stable and offer lower wages. Classic examples of secondary labor markets include farm labor, food service, and hospitality work. Research has shown that participants in secondary markets are more likely to be members of minority groups and to work for employers who provide meager benefits. Because scholars saw secondary markets as peripheral, they had historically treated them as a social problem to be addressed using existing institutions (for example, minimum wage laws), rather than as a fundamental threat to the system of employment.

Institutionalists warned that the growth of contingent work represented the spread of secondary labor into the economy's core. Many feared that this development would undermine the well-being of American workers and their families.[10] Others warned that contingent work's spread would increase demand for government assistance in a downturn and facilitate the oppression of minorities. Indeed, demographic studies consistently showed that most contingent workers made less money than full-time employees in the same occupation, that they were less likely to have access to health insurance and pension plans, and that in comparison to the full-time workers, women, African-Americans, and Hispanics comprised a larger percentage of the contingent work force.[11] Finally, some critics charged that the shift to contingent labor signaled an attempt to undermine unions.[12] In short, institutionalists saw the spread of contingent labor as an unraveling of the New Deal, and they urged policy makers to bolster existing institutions or search for new ones that would enhance security.

Anthropologists and sociologists who had done ethnographies of contingent work generally confirmed the institutionalists' fears.[13] Their studies depicted the difficulties that clerical and light industrial "temps" encountered in a world geared to full-time employment. Informants in these studies reported being forced into temporary employment by downsizing and other circumstances that made it difficult to find full-time jobs.[14] Most complained of poor working conditions, low wages, and high work-related expenses. They spoke of disputes with clients and agencies over payment and hours, antagonism with permanent employees, continual insecurity and uncertainty, and a sense of exclusion, estrangement, and dissatisfaction with work.

The ethnographies reported few compensating advantages. Some temps claimed to enjoy the flexibility of scheduling their own work and the freedom to reject particularly unpleasant jobs. Others said they preferred to receive their compensation as "fast cash" rather than wait for a monthly paycheck. Still others reported obtaining satisfaction from knowing that their services were "really needed" by companies in crisis. But, in general, the ethnographic evidence indicated that at least among low-skilled workers, the disadvantages of "temping" outweighed its advantages.[15] It is significant that the institutionalists built their interpretation of contingent work without examining highly skilled workers.[16] In sharp contrast, commentators who wrote for the popular press largely built their interpretations by ignoring the low end. Unsurprisingly, they painted a considerably different picture of contracting.

The Free Agent Perspective

At the height of dot-com mania, "new economy" magazines like *Fast Company* and *Wired* began to lionize highly skilled contractors as "free agents," the heroes and heroines of postindustrialism. Most of free agency's advocates were (and continue to

be) futurists, human resource consultants, and staffing industry experts who wrote for the general public.[17] The "free agenteers" agreed with the institutionalists on one point: employment security and its supporting institutions were unraveling and their demise represented a breach of faith. Corporations had reneged on their part of a culturally well-understood bargain. But, unlike the institutionalists, free agency's spokespersons sang contracting's praises while advocating a kind of libertarian, anticorporate rebellion.

Authors of this ilk portrayed corporate life as stifling and petty. The corporate world, they claimed, forced people to play "politics" and subject themselves to the whims of incompetent managers for inadequate pay. Besides, they added, "jobs" and "careers" were outmoded inventions of the industrial revolution, designed for the benefit of employers. Daniel Pink, a former speechwriter for Secretary of Labor Robert Reich and the best-known advocate of free agency, wrote:

> The old social contract didn't have a clause for introspection. It was much simpler than that. You gave loyalty. You got security. But now that the old contract has been repealed, people are examining both its basic terms and its implicit conditions. Free agents quickly realized that in the traditional world, they were silently accepting an architecture of work customs and social mores that should have crumbled long ago under the weight of its own absurdity. From infighting and office politics to bosses pitting employees against one another to colleagues who don't pull their weight, most workplaces are in dysfunction. Most people do want to work; they don't want to put up with brain-dead distractions.[18]

Sometimes bordering on demagoguery, free agency's antiorganizational rhetoric reframed employment history. Firms had not simply broken the contract; the contract was terrible in the first place because it lulled employees into dependency. Traditional employment and the careers it offered were relics of corporate "paternalism" that encouraged employees to play the role of children and firms, the role of parent. Simon Caulkin, a journalist writing for the San Francisco Examiner, explained:

> At the bottom, the trade of loyalty for security was unsustainable and exploitative. By tying their career and skills to one employer, employees sacrificed mobility and market value in return for a promise that couldn't be kept. By contrast, in the emerging new deal, the very mobility of career-independent employees provides a powerful incentive to companies to keep their promises—the most important of which . . . is to provide interesting, motivating work. Otherwise, those valuable staff members will leave. So the death of the security-loyalty contract has made room for a more durable and satisfying employment relationship—this time based on independence rather than the employer paternalism of the past.[19]

Faced with the demise of traditional employment and the potential for firms to renege on their part of the bargain, advocates of free agency recommended that people turn the tables on companies by refusing to give loyalty and by embracing the shift to a skills-for-hire economy. The trick, they proposed, was to use the demise of traditional employment as an opportunity to set oneself free. They encouraged people to view themselves as free agents, to develop and market their own skills to the highest bidder, and to view themselves as a business, even when in a full-time job. Free agenteers, in short, promoted a postindustrial vision of economic individualism in which entrepreneurial workers would regain independence and recapture a portion of their surplus value.

To support their claims, free agenteers offered readers stories of contractors who vacationed when and where they chose, who telecommuted to work from exotic places, and who successfully integrated the demands of work and family. Although the heroes and heroines of these tales were usually professional and technical workers,

proponents contended that all people could benefit by adopting a similar attitude to work. The central icon of the movement was the hero of the movie *Jerry Maguire*, who rejected a world of greed and unethical behavior for independence, wealth, and self-respect. Caught up in the revolutionary spirit, Pink and Warsaw even penned what they called a "Free Agent Declaration of Independence."[20]

The vehicle of the free agent's independence was the market. In *Job Shift*, William Bridges promised, "In a market . . . people don't have bosses. . . . There are no orders, no translation of signals from on high, no one sorting out the work into parcels. In a market one has customers, and the relationship between a supplier and a customer is fundamentally non-organizational. . . . One's boss is really a major customer rather than an authority in the old sense."[21] Of course, the irony that Bridges and others had trouble seeing was that freeing oneself from the chains of traditional employment meant catering to the same employers against whom one was rebelling.

Despite such inconsistencies, the advocates of free agency sketched an optimistic picture of contingent labor based on a rhetoric of free markets that challenged the institutionalists point by point. Free agenteers argued that contingency was a choice rather than a constraint; that it represented liberation rather than isolation; that it minimized uncertainty about employment while enhancing flexibility and personal control; that contractors made more money than permanent employees because they were paid at rates that reflected the real value of their skills; and that relying on one's skills led to self-actualization rather than estrangement.

Who to Believe?

As sociologists with a background in industrial relations and a taste for left-of-center politics, our initial response was to side with the institutionalists and to treat the rhetoric of market freedom with a healthy dose of disbelief, if not suspicion.[22] But as ethnographers, we believed that data should be allowed to speak for itself. No a priori formulations, no matter how elegant or consistent with their proponents' worldview, should be exempt from the requirement that they rest on solid empirical evidence. For us, evidence meant an empathetic and rich description of the perspectives and practices of the people about whose lives social scientists made claims.[23] From this perspective we found both sides of the debate wanting.

How could anyone tell whether the institutionalists or the free agenteers offered a more viable image of contracting when neither had systematically examined the lives of technical contractors? With the exception of the ethnographers of temporary work and Daniel Pink's book, *Free Agent Nation*, analysts on both sides of the debate had given no voice to contingent workers themselves. Most advocates of free agency based their claims, at best, on well-chosen anecdotes. The institutionalists were much better empiricists, but their data were heavily weighted toward the experiences of low-skilled temps. This bias was especially troubling because students of work have long known that the worlds of low- and high-skilled occupations substantially differ. Permanent professional, technical, and managerial jobs are usually more secure, more remunerative, more varied, and more involving than clerical and industrial jobs. It stands to reason that low- and high-skilled contingent work should vary in similar ways. By ignoring highly skilled contingent work, institutionalists conflated the effects of contingent employment with correlates of low-skilled work. Conversely, advocates of free agency peddled images of contracting built solely on the experiences of an elite. In the absence of adequate data, the institutionalists' and the free agenteers' claims about the everyday realities of contracting, and the theoretical edifices they erected on these claims, rang hollow.

We had substantive concerns as well. These rested on our reading of the existing literature, on our experience as researchers of technical work, and on our anecdotal familiarity with technical contracting. Meeting contractors like Kent, Yolanda, and Julian reinforced our concerns. Three issues, in particular, troubled us.

First the discourse on contracting seemed too rigid, too black and white, to be believable. For institutionalists, contingent work was a clear and unambiguous social problem. Temps and contractors were victims of systemic changes promulgated by exploitative employers acting entirely in their self-interest without regard for the common good in the face of a government that was unable or unwilling to protect them. For the advocates of free agency, contingent employment represented no less than a path for escaping a decaying system that had subjugated the many to the whims of the few. If ethnographers have learned anything about social life it is that reality rarely comes so neatly packaged.

Which camp's box, for instance, could comfortably hold Kent Cox, Yolanda Turner, and Julian Stoke? The institutionalists could easily argue that Julian's experience supported their contentions. He became a contractor after being laid off. He had clearly lived on the edge of financial solvency. He had difficulty making ends meet, he had trouble keeping a job, his wife was anxious about their future, and he vacillated between contracting and permanent employment. Even protecting his family's health had been a serious problem. But, to the institutionalist's consternation, Julian didn't seem to mind his troubles! Worse yet, he considered himself to be a success, at least in his own terms, and he planned to continue contracting.

Kent Cox would give the institutionalists an even bigger headache. Other than missing the opportunity to cash in on the fantasy of becoming rich through stock options, Kent seemed in no way disadvantaged. In fact, by all indications, and certainly in his own view, contracting had been good to him. But it would be Yolanda Turner who most violated the institutionalist's worldview. Here was an African-American woman who, despite her efforts, had been unable to flourish until she took her career, her skills, and her wages into her own hands as a contractor.

On the face of it, Yolanda's and Kent's tales should have brought great cheer to free agency's camp. Either could have easily been a sidebar in one of the slick "new economy" manifestos on free agency. Yet, on closer scrutiny, their stories posed problems. At least in Yolanda's case, free agency's promise of freedom, flexibility, and leisure seemed elusive. In fact, Yolanda worked long and hard, at least as much and maybe more than she had as a full-timer. Her employability depended uncomfortably on staffing agencies, and her potential earnings were hijacked by their markups.

But Julian would have been free agency's real embarrassment. Even *Wired* would have had to struggle to find glamour in an overweight, balding middle-aged man with credit card problems and a penchant for being fired. Moreover, Julian lived hand to mouth and suffered seriously from the lack of health care benefits. From an ethnographer's perspective, a satisfying analysis of contracting has to account for all three stories.

Second, except for the ethnographers of clerical work, most analysts on both sides of the debate spoke as if contingent labor markets were dyadic: composed simply of employing organizations and contingent workers. Although this is sometimes the case when a contractor is incorporated or works as an independent, in most instances, contingent labor markets are triadic. In addition to buyers and sellers there are brokers, the staffing agencies that mediate between the two to arrange and close deals. Contractors, like Yolanda and Julian, regularly rely on staffing agencies to find work. An accurate analysis of contracting must, therefore, take the agency's role into account regardless of whether the goal is to portray the structure of the market or describe contractors' experience more fully. Leaving out such an important group of actors guarantees misrepresentation.

Finally, the debate on contingent work was framed as if it were an argument between proponents of organizations and advocates of free markets. Institutionalists set their vision of employment against the backdrop of an organizational society, its laws, and its regulations. When institutionalists recommended reform, they inevitably turned to legal and bureaucratic remedies for the social costs of unfettered markets. They believed that full permanent employment was the foundation of an equitable system. Conversely, advocates of free agency preferred the market as a model for organizing the world of employment. For them releasing the forces of a free market would remedy the ills of an overly bureaucratic society. While organizations and markets are clearly important for framing an understanding of and prescriptions for the world of employment, they do not exhaust the possibilities. Occupations, which both institutionalists and advocates of free agency ignore, are just as important.

Sociologists of work have repeatedly shown that lawyers, scientists, police, carpenters, machinists, accountants, and members of other skilled occupations construct their identities and organize their practice not only around their employer or the market for their services, but also around their occupational affiliations.[24] Ask a doctor what she does for a living and she'll first tell you her specialty, not that she works for Kaiser Permanente. This was precisely what Kent, Yolanda, and Julian appeared to be saying when they highlighted the importance of their networks and their involvement in professional communities, regardless of whether they found those communities at a users' group, through a professional organization, or in a chat room.

Professionals' closest contacts are usually other practitioners of their craft. Professional associations, occupational unions, and communities of practice provide experts with critical support, knowledge, and information. In fact, the more esoterically skilled the practitioner, the more an occupational community is likely to be important. Since technical contractors were highly skilled, it seemed to us that their occupational affiliations had to be at least as relevant as markets and organizations for understanding contracting and interpreting its significance....

Discussion Questions

1. According to the authors, one perspective for understanding the growth of contingent work maintains that this growth is no less than an "unraveling of the New Deal." Do you agree with this perspective or not? Why?

2. Have you or someone you know been a contingent worker? In what occupation?

3. Several of the "unlikely rebels" seem to like the freedom of being contract workers. Would you like it?

Barley, Stephen R. and Gideon Kunda, *Gurus, Hired Guns, and Warm Bodies*. Princeton University Press. Reprinted by permission of Princeton University Press.

Endnotes

1. NEC was a company for whom Kent had contracted.
2. From today's perspective, Kent's decision not to go to work for Netscape does not appear as bad as it did at the time.
3. SAP is the most widely used inter-enterprise software program developed and marketed by the German firm of the same name. Inter-enterprise software is a class of programs that integrate data across a variety of application areas including finance, human resources, customer relationships, supply chain management, forecasting, and so on. It is a kind of one-stop software platform for firms.
4. VM (virtual machine) is an operating system for IBM mainframes.
5. Knoop and Jones (1967), Gimpel (1980), and Applebaum (1992) describe the work of medieval stonemasons and the organization of cathedral building in medieval Europe.
6. Laissez-faire capitalism refers to the doctrine that economic systems function best when they are free of governmental interference. Having first been articulated by French scholars, John Stuart Mill, Adam Smith, and Jeremy Bentham took the doctrine of laissez-faire as the central tenet of classical economics and fused it with a doctrine of radical individualism. In the early twentieth century, laissez-faire practices were associated with the rise of monopolies and cycles of boom and bust. Laissez-faire principles still underwrite conservative economic doctrine in the United States and Great Britain. For a superb discussion of laissez-faire capitalism in the United States and Great Britain, see Bendix (1956).
7. The research literature on firms' strategic reasons for employing contractors includes Abraham (1988), Abraham and Taylor (1996), Davis-Blake and Uzzi (1993), Harrison and Kelley (1993), Kalleberg and Schmidt (1996), Matusik and Hill (1998), Nollen and Axel (1998), Pfeffer and Baron (1988), and Rubin (1996).
8. "Institutional" and "institutionalist" are words with rich and thick meaning in the social sciences. We use the term "institutionalist" to refer to analysts who view markets as "socially embedded" and who ask how institutions shape labor markets. By "institutions" they typically mean not only laws and established organizations but also cultural norms and practices. Economists who study how social structures affect markets have historically been called "institutional economists." Osterman (1988), Parker (1994), Barker and Christiansen (1998), Cappelli et al. (1997), Carre and Joshi (1997), Kalleberg et al. (1997), and Smith (1998) are institutionalists who have written about contingent labor.
9. For extended discussions of dual labor market theory, see Berger and Piore (1980), Piore and Sabel (1984), Osterman (1984), and Baron and Bielby (1984).
10. For discussions of the negative social consequences of an expanding contingent workforce, see Dillon (1987), Osterman (1988), Martella (1991), Cohen and Haberfeld (1993), Hipple and Stewart (1996), Polivka (1996b), Christensen (1998), Barker (1998), Spalter-Roth and Hartmann (1998), Banigin (1998), and Houseman and Polivka (1999).
11. See Spalter-Roth et al. (1997), Kalleberg et al. (1997), and Kalleberg, Reskin, and Hudson (2000) for demographic data on the contingent workforce.
12. Aronowitz and DeFazio (1994) and Rifkin (1995) level charges of union busting.
13. An ethnography is a study of a group of people in which the data are collected by some combination of participant observation and interviews. The ethnographer's objective is usually to describe and depict the "native's point of view," the perspective of the people studied. Parker (1994), McAllister (1998), Rogers (1995, 2000), Henson (1996), and Smith (1998) have written important ethnographies of contingent work in clerical and industrial settings.
14. Jurik (1998) is a notable exception in that only 20 percent of her self-employed home workers felt forced into their home businesses. Nevertheless, Jurik fixes on the perceptions of those 20 percent in assessing how home workers feel about their work arrangements.
15. For exceptions, see Barker and Christensen (1998), Jurik (1998), Smith (2001), and Rogers (2000).

16. Some institutionalists have suggested that the situation may be different for highly skilled contractors, but their data do not allow much exploration. This is largely because economists and industrial relations researchers have relied on aggregate data and random samples that are heavily weighted toward the responses of traditional temporary employees.

17. Free agency's spokespersons include Bridges (1994, 1995), Pink (1998, 2001), Beck (1992), Caulkin (1997), Darby (1997), Reinhold (2001), and McGovern and Russell (2001). Although Bridges was the first to market with the idea, Pink coined the name and gained notoriety. Pink runs a Web page called "Free Agent Nation" (<http://www.freeagentnation.com>).

18. Pink (1998, 132).

19. Caulkin (1997, 2).

20. The "truths" that Pink and Warsaw (1997) claim to be "self-evident" are: "Who we are and what we do should not stand on opposite sides of a psychological divide. . . . Nothing is permanent. Security is an illusion. . . . The power to choose is the power to say no. . . . Fear has no place in Free Agent Nation. . . . The fun in work is the reason for work. . . . We're on our own, but we're not alone."

21. Bridges (1994, 64–65).

22. In fact, we had already written a critical historical analysis of how American managerial rhetorics have repeatedly vacillated since the 1870s between rhetorics of rational and normative control (Barley and Kunda 1992).

23. The ethnographer's creed is that all interpretations of a social system must rest on "the native point of view," or what anthropologists have called an "emic" perspective. The distinction between emic and etic is the anthropologist's way of distinguishing concepts used by the people being studied and those used by the people doing the studying. The terms come from linguistic anthropology. "Etic" is a term derived from the word "phonetic." It contrasts with "emic," which comes from "phonemic." "Phonetics" is the study of the sounds that people can physically produce. "Phonemics" is the study of the sounds that people distinguish as meaningful. Others have used the terms first-order and second-order or experience near and experience far to make the same distinction.

24. We offer an extensive argument to support the importance of an occupational perspective in organizational analysis in Barley and Kunda (2001).

References

Abraham, Katharine G. 1988. "Flexible Staffing Arrangements and Employers' Short-Term Adjustment Strategies." In *Employment, Unemployment, and Labour Utilization*, pp. 288–311. Ed. Robert A. Hart. London: Unwin Hyman.

Abraham, Katharine G., and S. K. Taylor. 1996. "Firms' Use of Outside Contractors: Theory and Evidence." *Journal of Labor Economics* 14: 394–424.

Applebaum, Herbert. 1992. *The Concept of Work: Ancient, Medieval, and Modern*. Albany, NY: State University of New York Press.

Aronowitz, Stanley, and William DeFazio. 1994. *The Jobless Future: Sci-Tech and the Dogma of Work*. Minneapolis: University of Minnesota Press.

Banigin, William. 1998. "Visa Program, High-Tech Workers Exploited, Critics Say." *Washington Post*, July 26, sec. 1, p. 1.

Barker, Kathleen. 1998. "Toiling for Piece-Rates and Accumulating Deficits: Contingent Work in Higher Education." In *Contingent Work: American Employment in Transition*, pp. 195–220. Ed. Kathleen Barker and Kathleen Christensen. Ithaca, NY: ILR Press.

Barker, Kathleen, and Kathleen Christensen. 1998. "Controversy and Challenges Raised by Contingent Work Arrangements." In *Contingent Work: American Employment in Transition*, pp. 1–20. Ed. Kathleen Barker and Kathleen Christensen. Ithaca, NY: ILR Press.

Barley, Stephen R., and Gideon Kunda. 2001. "Bringing Work Back In." *Organization Science* 12: 75–94.

——. 1992. "Design and Devotion: Surges of Rational and Normative Ideologies of Control in Managerial Discourse." *Administrative Science Quarterly* 37 363–99.

Baron, James N., and William T. Bielby. 1984. "The Organization of Work in a Segmented Economy." *American Sociological Review* 49: 454–73.

Beck, Nuala. 1992. *Shifting Gears: Thriving in the New Economy*. Toronto: Harper Collins.

Bendix, Reinhard. 1956. *Work and Authority in Industry: Ideologies of Management in the Course of Industrialization*. New York: Harper and Row.

Berger, Suzanne, and Michael J. Piore. 1980. *Dualism and Discontinuity in Industrial Societies*. New York: Cambridge University Press.

Bridges, William. 1995. "A Nation of Owners." *INC* 17: 89–91.

——. 1994. *Job Shift: How to Prosper in a Workplace without Jobs*. Reading, MA: Addison-Wesley.

Cappelli, Peter. 1999. *The New Deal at Work: Managing the Market Driven Workforce*. Boston, MA: Harvard Business School Press.

Cappelli, Peter, Laurie Bassi, Harry Katz, David Knoke, Paul Osterman, and Michael Useem. 1997. *Change at Work*. New York: Oxford University Press.

Carre, Francoise J., and Pamela Joshi. 1997. *Building Stability for Transient Workforces: Exploring the Possibilities of Intermediary Institutions Helping Workers Cope with Labor Market Instability*. Cambridge, MA: Radcliffe College.

Caulkin, Simon. 1997. "Skills, Not Loyalty, Now Are Key If You Want Job Security." *San Fran-*

cisco *Sunday Examiner and Chronicle*, September 7, sec. 4, p. 2.

Christensen, Kathleen. 1998. "Countervailing Human Resource Trends in Family-Sensitive Firms." In *Contingent Work: American Employment in Transition*, pp. 103–26. Ed. Kathleen Barker and Kathleen Christensen. Ithaca, NY: ILR Press.

Cohen, Yinon, and Yitchak Haberfeld. 1993. "Temporary Help Service Workers: Employment Characteristics and Wage Determinants." *Industrial Relations* 32: 272–87.

Darby, Joseph B. 1997. "The Ultimate Contractor: Lessons from a Parallel Universe." *Contract Professional* 2: 27–32.

Davis-Blake, Allison, and Brian Uzzi. 1993. "Determinants of Employment Externalization: A Study of Temporary Workers and Independent Contractors." *Administrative Science Quarterly* 38: 195–223.

Dillon, Rodger L. 1987. *The Changing Labor Market: Contingent Workers and the Self-Employed in California*. Sacramento, CA: Senate Office of Research.

Gimpel, Jean. 1980. *The Cathedral Builders*. New York: Harper and Row.

Harrison, Bennett, and Mary E. Kelley. 1993. "Outsourcing and the Search for 'Flexibility'." *Work, Employment, and Society* 7: 213–35.

Henson, Kevin D. 1996. *Just a Temp*. Philadelphia, PA: Temple University Press.

Hipple, Steven E, and Jay Stewart. 1996. "Earnings and Benefits of Workers in Alternative Work Arrangements." *Monthly Labor Review* 119: 46–54.

Houseman, Susan K., and Anne E. Polivka. 1999. "The Implications of Flexible Staffing Arrangements for Job Stability." *Working paper 99-056*, W. E. Upjohn Institute for Employment Research, Kalamazoo, MI.

Jurik, Nancy J. 1998. "Getting Away and Getting By: The Experiences of Self-Employed Homeworkers." *Work and Occupations* 25: 7–35.

Kalleberg, Arne L., Edith Rasell, Ken Hudson, David Webster, Barbara F. Reskin, Cassirer Naoi, and Eileen Appelbaum. 1997. *Nonstandard Work, Substandard Jobs: Flexible Work Arrangements in the U.S.* Washington, DC: Economic Policy Institute.

Kalleberg, Arne L., Barbara F. Reskin, and Ken Hudson. 2000. "Bad Jobs in America: Standard and Nonstandard Employment Relations and Job Quality in the United States." *American Sociological Review* 65: 256–79.

Kalleberg, Arne L., and Kathryn Schmidt. 1996. "Contingent Employment in Organizations." In *Organizations in America: Analyzing Their Structures and Human Resource Practices*, pp. 253–75. Ed. Arne L. Kalleberg, David Knoke, Peter V. Marsden, and Joel L. Spaeth. Thousand Oaks, CA: Sage.

Knoop, Douglas, and G. P. Jones. 1967. *The Medieval Mason: An Economic History of English Stone Building in the Later Middle Ages and Modern Times*. New York: Barnes and Noble.

Kochan, Thomas A., Harry C. Katz, and Robert B. McKersie. 1986. *The Transformation of American Industrial Relations*. New York: Basic Books.

Martella, Maureen. 1991. *Just a Temp: Expectations and Experiences of Women Clerical Temporary Workers*. Washington, DC: U.S. Department of Labor, Women's Bureau.

Matusik, Sharon F., and Charles W. L. Hill. 1998. "The Utilization of Contingent Work: Knowledge Creation and Competitive Advantage." *Academy of Management Review* 23: 680–97.

McAllister, Jean. 1998. "Sisyphus at Work in the Warehouse: Temporary Employment in Greenville, South Carolina." In *Contingent Work: American Employment in Transition*, pp. 221–42. Ed. Kathleen Barker and Kathleen Christensen. Ithaca, NY: ILR Press.

McGovern, Marion, and Dennis Russell. 2001. *The New Brand of Expertise: How Independent Contractors, Free Agents, and Interim Managers Are Transforming the World of Work*. Woburn, MA: Butterworth-Heinemann.

Nollen, Stanley D., and Helen Axel. 1998. "Benefits and Costs to Employers." In *Contingent Work: American Employment in Transition*, pp. 126–43. Ed. Kathleen Barker and Kathleen Christensen. Ithaca, NY: ILR Press.

Osterman, Paul. 1999. *Securing Prosperity: The American Labor Market: How It Has Changed and What to Do About It*. Princeton, NJ: Princeton University Press.

——. 1996. *Broken Ladders: Managerial Careers in the New Economy*. New York: Oxford University Press.

——. 1988. *Employment Futures: Reorganization, Dislocation, and Public Policy*. New York: Oxford University Press.

——. 1984. *Internal Labor Markets*. Cambridge: MIT Press.

Osterman, Paul, Thomas A. Kochan, Richard M. Locke, and Michael J. Piore. 2001. *Working in America: Blueprint for the New Labor Market*. Cambridge: MIT Press.

Parker, Robert E. 1994. *Flesh Peddlers and Warm Bodies: The Temporary Help Industry and Its Workers*. New Brunswick, NJ: Rutgers University Press.

Perrucci, Robert. 1971. "Engineering: Professional Servant of Power." *American Behavioral Scientist* 14: 492–505.

Perrucci, Robert, and Joel E. Gerstl. 1969a. *Engineers and the Social System*. New York: Wiley.

——. 1969b. *Profession without Community*. New York: Random House.

Pfeffer, Jeffrey, and James N. Baron. 1988. "Taking the Workers Back Out: Recent Trends in the Structuring of Employment." In *Research in Organizational Behavior*, vol. 10, pp. 257–303. Ed. Barry Staw and Lawrence Cummings. Greenwich, CT: JAI Press.

Pink, Daniel H. 2001. *Free Agent Nation: How America's New Independent Workers Are Transforming the Way We Live.* New York: Warner Business Books.

——. 1998. "Free Agent Nation." *Fast Company,* December/January: 131–47.

Pink, Daniel H., and Michael Warsaw. 1997. "The Free Agent Declaration of Independence." *Fast Company* 12: 182.

Piore, Michael J., and Charles F. Sabel. 1984. *The Second Industrial Divide: Possibilities for Prosperity.* New York: Basic Books.

Polivka, Anne E. 1996. "A Profile of Contingent Workers." *Monthly Labor Review* 119: 10–21.

Reinhold, Barbara B. 2001. *Free to Succeed: Designing the Life You Want in the Free Agent Economy.* New York: Plume.

Rifkin, Jeremy. 1995. *The End of Work.* New York: Putnam.

Rogers, Jackie K. 1995. "Just a Temp: Experience and Structure of Alienation in Temporary Clerical Employment." *Work and Occupation* 22: 137–66.

——. 2000. *Temps: The Many Faces of the Changing Workplace.* Ithaca, NY: Cornell University Press.

Rubin, B. 1996. *Shifts in the Social Contract: Understanding Change in American Society.* Thousand Oaks, CA: Pine Forge Press.

Smith, Vicki. 2001. *Crossing the Great Divide: Worker Risk and Opportunity in the New Economy.* Ithaca, NY: Cornell University Press.

——. 1998. "The Fractured World of the Temporary Worker: Power, Participation, and Fragmentation in the Contemporary Workplace." *Social Problems* 45: 1–20.

Spalter-Roth, Roberta, and Heidi I. Hartmann. 1998. "Gauging the Consequences for Gender Relations, Pay Equity, and the Public Purse." In *Contingent Work: American Employment in Transition,* pp. 69–102. Ed. Kathleen Barker and Kathleen Christensen. Ithaca, NY: ILR Press.

Spalter-Roth, Roberta M., Arne L. Kalleberg, Edith Rasell, Naomi Cassirer, Barbara F. Reskin, Ken Hudson, David Webster, Eileen Appelbaum, and Betty F. Dooley. 1997. *Managing Work and Family: Nonstandard Work Arrangements Among Managers and Professionals.* Washington, DC: Economic Policy Institute. ✦

23

Professionalization and Work Intensification

Robert L. Brannon

Robert Brannon contends that the reorganization of nursing tasks and consequent creation of an unmediated relationship between the professional registered nurses (RNs) and clients (patients) run counter to theories of professional practice. He also indicates that the relatively low level of credentialing and gender-segregation of nursing is thought to limit RNs' professionalization. He notes that when faced with less support staff and sicker patients, RNs manage the increased work responsibility by not doing some tasks or by shifting some tasks to patients and their families while becoming more accountable to physicians and management. Overall, moreover, the author finds that the changes did not increase RNs' standing vis-à-vis physicians, who remained the most powerful actors in the health-care system.

During the past two decades, the health care industry has experienced a period of social change that may be aptly referred to as the cost containment era. Although further reforms in health care policy and administration are pending, the 1970s and 1980s brought changes that ensure there will be no return to the system of prior decades in which hospitals and physicians enjoyed greater autonomy in the provision of services. Not only have large capitalist corporations entered into the production of health care services, but with the growing economic burden of rising health care expenditures, corporate and state purchasers of services have pressured providers to control costs and have begun to intervene in institutional spheres that had previously been regarded as the domain of the health care establishment.

Sociologists have examined the changing political economy of the industry, the corporation of hospitals, and the reorganization of elites as state administrators, and corporate managers have introduced more rationalized systems of bureaucratic control and state regulation (Bergthold, 1990; Immershein, Rond, & Mathis, 1992; Ruggie, 1992; Starr, 1982). Much of the discussion has focused on the medical profession and the effects of change on its power in the health care system. An extensive debate has taken place on whether physicians are experiencing professional decline; that is, deprofessionalization or even proletarianization (see bibliography and overview of debate in Light & Levine, 1988). Meanwhile, less esteemed allied professions, semiprofessions, and paraprofessions have been neglected (Fox, 1985). The majority of these workers are women in gender-segregated occupations, who produce the bulk of patient care and whose occupational status, including aspirations for professional colleagueship with physicians, may be more seriously affected by changes in the industry.

In this article I focus on nursing, the most important of the allied professions, and examine pivotal changes in the organization of nurses' work in the cost containment era. During the decades of the 1970s and 1980s, nursing work on hospital wards was reorganized from a division of labor that emphasized stratification—registered nurses (RNs), licensed practical nurses (LPNs), and nurses' aides performing differentiated tasks—to one in which a majority of RNs perform reunified tasks in an unmediated relationship with their patients (Brannon, 1988, in press). This change and its effects on workers have received relatively little attention, either from medical sociologists or sociologists of work and occupations.[1]

Throughout the post-World War II era until the late 1970s, the stratified form of nursing labor called "team nursing" dominated on hospital wards. Auxiliaries, as LPNs and aides were labeled by nursing administrators, worked in teams supervised by RNs, who were responsible for overall nursing care and for the performance of more skilled tasks that were believed to be appropriately assigned to the professional nurse. LPNs and nurses' aides were delegated the routine tasks that required a greater presence at the bedside (Hughes, Hughes, & Deutscher, 1958, chap. 6).

Beginning in the 1970s and continuing throughout most of the 1980s, team nursing was replaced by a reunification of nursing tasks and a trend toward an all-RN workforce. Although there were a variety of adaptations and modifications, task reunification and the displacement of auxiliaries was associated with what nursing leaders[2] called "primary nursing" and "total patient care" (Joiner & van Servellen, 1984).

Few hospitals completely replaced auxiliaries, but the effect of reunifying nursing tasks and returning RNs to the bedside reversed the composition of nursing workers on hospital wards. Until the mid-1970s, the conventional mode of hospital staffing consisted of approximately two-thirds auxiliaries and one-third RNs (Christman, 1978). By the late 1980s, RN-predominant forms of practice had supplanted team nursing nationwide and the proportion of professional workers was nearly the opposite. Thus, whereas RNs comprised only 33% of all hospital nursing personnel in the early 1970s, by the late 1980s, RN staffing had increased to 63%, whereas auxiliaries' presence on hospital wards had declined to 37% (American Hospital Association, 1991, Fig. 18). Auxiliaries were displaced through attrition and by shifting their employment to work sites on the periphery of hospitals, in nursing homes, clinics, and home health care (Brannon, 1988; Glazer, 1988).[3]

In recent years a highly publicized RN shortage has led hospitals to retain rather than displace LPNs and aides. The American Medical Association has even campaigned for a new category of auxiliary nurse. In this environment, nursing leaders are less likely to advocate primary nursing with an all-RN workforce (Manthey, 1988). Nevertheless, the reorganization of the division of labor in hospitals has been sustained. The majority of hospital nursing personnel now consists of RNs, and auxiliary nurses are being used in far fewer numbers than in prior decades, when team nursing was the principal form of practice.

This major organizational change was initiated by nursing's elite, who, during the team-nursing period, had become increasingly dissatisfied with the large number of nonprofessional nurses on hospital wards and the failure of RNs to attain full professional status. The vast majority of RNs were still being trained by hospital-based nursing schools that provided less than a professional education. Moreover, nursing leaders claimed that team nursing with a stratified workforce was based on a task-oriented method that fragmented care and deprofessionalized nursing practice (Joiner & van Servellen, 1984; Manthey, 1980; Marram, Schlegel, & Bevis, 1974).

In the 1970s and 1980s, nursing educators and administrators promoted the development of collegiate credentialing programs and the reunification of nursing tasks, viewing both as consistent with the professionalization of the occupation. According to this elite, primary nursing would establish the most important features of professional practice: RNs' complete responsibility for nursing care through reunified tasks and an unmediated relationship with the patient. As primary nursing and "total patient care" were implemented, the integrity of RNs' professional practice would be restored and the occupation would finally attain its goal of colleagueship with physicians. Just as patients refer to a physician as "my doctor," without auxiliaries at the bedside, patients would now recognize only the RN as "my nurse" (Manthey, 1980; Manthey, Ciske, Robertson, & Harris, 1970). Furthermore, physicians themselves would validate the RN's new status, coordinating medical care with the primary nurse and seeking out the nurse's professional opinion.

In contrast to the interpretation prevailing in the nursing literature, I will argue that, although the reorganization of the division of labor on hospital wards was initiated as an occupational strategy to upgrade nursing practice, the change actually contradicts sociological theories of professionalization and serves managerial interests. Rather than upgrade RNs' work, reunified tasks and an unmediated relationship with patients reversed the professionalization process. RNs were not deskilled; that is, "technically proletarianized" (Derber, 1982); however, task reunification intensified their work and forced them to seek ways to limit an overextended work jurisdiction.[4] At the same time, the reorganization of work failed to elevate RNs to professional colleagueship with physicians. Not only did RNs remain subject to physicians' professional dominance and to administrators' bureaucratic control, but the elimination of the paranursing hierarchy increased their accountability.

Theoretical Issues and Constraints on Professionalization

Sociological theories of proletarianization largely support nursing leaders' assertions that team nursing and the subdivision of labor had deprofessionalized RNs. For example, Braverman (1974), in his study of the degradation of work in advanced capitalism, argued that semiprofessional and technical occupations were subject to the same process that deskilled craft workers with the development of factory production. And, in a sociological treatment specifically of nursing, Wagner (1980) has argued that the subdivision of nursing labor and the hiring of a cheaper workforce to perform deskilled tasks did in fact proletarianize RNs.

I have indicated that team nursing was more complex (Brannon, 1992, in press). It is true that this form of labor was based on a differentiation of work and the employment of cheaper workers to perform routine tasks. In addition, task differentiation was facilitated by the application of scientific management principles, a managerial strategy emphasized by Braverman (Reverby, 1979). Nevertheless, RNs were not deskilled through this process. Hospital employment and the rationalization of work in the postwar period actually increased RNs' skills and claims to professional status.[5]

Because team nursing with auxiliaries did not deskill RNs, it may be more accurate to argue, as did Hughes (1971, chap. 31) and Hughes et al. (1958, chap. 6), that the differentiation of nursing tasks and the delegation of routine and "dirty work" to auxiliary workers was characteristic of the professional upgrading of the occupation. Theories of professionalization continue to be based on the principle that core tasks are upgraded at the same time that routine tasks are delegated to paraprofessional and nonprofessional workers, creating a more extensive division of labor (Abbott, 1988; Rueschemeyer, 1986). Yet it is also the case that the differentiation of nursing tasks and the delegation of work to auxiliary nurses did not fully professionalize RNs. As Freidson (1970/1988) indicated during the team-nursing period, RNs were subordinated to physicians' professional dominance. Rather than provide a means of attaining professional status, the differentiation of nursing tasks created a "paranursing hierarchy within the paramedical hierarchy" (p. 65). In addition, administrators' bureaucratic control of nursing work limited RNs to a semiprofessional status (Etzioni, 1969).

Nevertheless, because RNs' tasks were upgraded rather than degraded, team nursing more closely approximates prevailing sociological theories of professionalization than does primary nursing. Although nursing leaders have promoted the reunification of tasks as professional upgrading, clearly primary nursing contradicts theories of professionalization in that RNs resume tasks that were formerly delegated to nonprofessional workers.

In addition, the creation of an unmediated relationship between the professional and the client contravenes rather than exemplifies theories of professional practice. As Abbott (1981, 1988) has pointed out, professional status is typically advanced through "professional regression," by moving away from direct and routine client involvement. This continues to be the case in nursing in that RNs in the most professionalized segments of the occupation acquire higher credentials and typically leave patient care behind for careers in education and administration (Brannon, in press).

Furthermore, the labor force that made the conversion to primary nursing possible for the most part lacked a level of credentialing that would sustain a collective claim to professional status. Although the American Nurses' Association has advocated the baccalaureate degree as the professional credential since 1965, nursing has remained class stratified, and throughout the 1970s and 1980s the majority of staff nurses continued to lack this credential. With the decline of hospital training schools, the education of RNs did shift from hospitals to collegiate settings. However, community college programs prevailed over baccalaureate programs, so that RNs with 2-year associate degrees provided the major supply of primary nurses.[6] Community colleges are more likely to be attended by students from working-class rather than middle-class backgrounds, and the credentials acquired are intended for technical rather than professional occupations (Brint & Karabel, 1989; Karabel, 1972). Because the majority of primary nurses lacked more advanced degrees, it would appear that a higher level of credentialing is not necessary for adequate performance as a primary nurse. In fact, RNs with community college, hospital diplomas, and university degrees have all qualified for licensure and worked as primary nurses, demonstrating a weak linkage between educational credentialing and the reality of work on hospital wards.

Finally, the gender characteristics of nursing may also continue to limit RNs' professionalization. Although there has been a slight increase in male participation among RNs in the last decade, nursing remains a gender-segregated occupation in which women constitute the vast majority (94%) of RNs (Williams, 1992). Nursing's association with caring roles, which are undervalued both in paid and unpaid forms of work (Hochschild, 1989; Reverby, 1987), may contribute to occupational and organizational constraints on nursing's professionalization.[7] Nonetheless, in explaining the reorganization of nursing labor and its effects, gender is not the critical factor. Rather, I have emphasized the work process; that is, tensions between RNs and nonprofessional nurses (the majority of whom were also women), and RNs' inability to monopolize an exclusive work jurisdiction on hospital wards. Ironically, primary nursing overcame these problems at the same time that it created new dilemmas and failed to professionalize RNs.

Research Setting and Method

The topic of this article is part of a larger research project that combines historical-comparative research on the changing patterns of nursing labor with participant observation of contemporary changes (Brannon, in press). The findings that follow are based principally on an extended case study at "Pacific" Hospital, a pseudonym for a California hospital recognized in the industry for its advanced nursing practice. The case study was conducted between 1979 and 1988, when I worked for several periods as a ward clerk, the only nonnursing worker continuously on hospital wards. I interacted with nurses, doctors, and patients while participating in the work process and observing the effect of recent changes on RNs and support workers.

The findings are based on a case study, but I believe that the major points of the argument are generalizable to changes occurring at hospitals nationwide. Related studies do not document the effects of reorganizing nursing labor through observations on hospital wards; however, evidence does exist that broadly similar changes have taken place at hospitals throughout the country (American Hospital Association, 1991; Glazer, 1988; Sacks, 1988, chap. 8).

Like other leading hospitals, Pacific Hospital began implementing primary nursing in the early 1970s and in the 1980s received an award for its professional nursing practice with a high proportion of RNs. Throughout this period, LPNs and nurses' aides were reduced through attrition and by shifting their employment to peripheral work sites (nursing homes, outpatient clinics, home health care) that the hospital acquired or established as it responded to external cost containment pressures by reorganizing into a diversified health care corporation. By the mid-1980s, the hospital workforce was composed overwhelmingly of RNs: approximately 85% RNs and 15% auxiliaries. The last group of nurses' aides was shifted to employment in a rehabilitation hospital that the corporation opened in the early 1980s. Although Pacific Hospital continued to employ some LPNs, they typically worked the evening or night shift, and before an RN shortage in the late 1980s, nurses believed that LPNs would eventually be replaced as well. Meanwhile, LPNs were assigned their own patients and did not compete with RNs. From my position in the production process I was fortunate to be able to observe nursing work at a hospital that claimed to have made the transition to professional practice.

Findings

Overcoming the Problems of Team Nursing

Although nursing leaders promoted primary nursing as professional upgrading, staff RNs themselves were ambivalent about their professional status. RNs did not believe that primary nursing necessarily professionalized their work, yet they considered the new organization of labor on the wards to have clear advantages over team nursing. Reunifying tasks facilitated their exercise of responsibility for nursing care without the problems they had experi-

enced when auxiliaries mediated between RNs and patients.

Team nursing had not deprofessionalized or deskilled RNs (Brannon, 1992), but subdividing tasks had created difficulties between RNs and auxiliaries. Differentiated work jurisdictions were supposed to correspond to clear distinctions in credentialing and skill levels, with RNs officially assigned what were believed to be the more skilled and professional tasks and auxiliaries the less skilled, routine tasks. However, in daily life on the wards tasks overlapped extensively (Hughes et al., 1958, chap. 6). The demands of the work process often required RNs to delegate unauthorized tasks to LPNs and aides, and at the same time RNs were vulnerable to substitution by these workers. During the team-nursing period, RNs were unable to monopolize a core set of technical tasks, and auxiliaries assimilated a practical knowledge of procedures that were formally reserved for the professional nurse.[8] Furthermore, LPNs' and nurses' aides' more continuous presence at the bedside resulted in a greater familiarity with patients and empowered auxiliaries by creating a competing experience of responsibility. (For a detailed discussion of these difficulties, see Brannon, in press.) RNs at Pacific Hospital recalled the problems vividly: "Before Pacific switched to primary nursing we had what was called team nursing. It was terrible. Some of my worst nursing experiences were with team nursing."

Primary nursing overcame the disadvantages of team nursing. For staff RNs, the critical difference was not the prospect of professionalization, but a reunification of tasks that eliminated the predominance of auxiliaries at the bedside. RNs were no longer threatened by auxiliaries' ability to substitute and were no longer forced to delegate unauthorized work or to violate formal rules while doing so. Primary nursing was viewed as an advance because RNs now had complete control over the work for which they were accountable. An RN summarized the advantages in the following comments:

Team nursing was difficult because the LPNs and nurses' aides were at the bedside, but we had responsibility for the care they gave the patients. When we told them what to do, they resented it. We're still responsible for nursing care, but we're no longer responsible for auxiliaries' work.

Furthermore, although primary nursing eliminated RNs' supervisory position over auxiliary nurses, it maintained RNs' autonomy within the nursing hierarchy. RNs were no longer team leaders, but neither did they experience direct supervision by ward head nurses or shift charge nurses. With corporation and greater responsibility for cost containment, the head nurse role became more removed from the production of nursing care. Ward head nurses were now referred to as "unit managers" and were preoccupied with utilization review, costing by "diagnostically related groups" (DRGs), the budget, and administrative meetings. In addition, although the shift charge nurse might be considered a first-line supervisor, this role was clearly distinct from the supervisory relationship that RN team leaders had with LPNs and nurses' aides. The charge nurse worked at the nursing station to coordinate activities and to process doctors' orders, but the primary nurse was the indispensable figure on the wards. Charge nurses depended on the knowledge and skills of primary nurses, who planned, organized, and performed "total patient care" for all their patients.

Intensifying Work

Although primary nursing elicited RNs' cooperation in the reorganization of work by facilitating their exercise of responsibility and control over nursing work, this new form of labor served managerial interests and created new problems for rank-and-file RNs. Rather than job enrichment (Joiner & van Servellen, 1984), the reunification of tasks constituted job enlargement and an intensification of work. Thus, although primary nursing was initiated by nursing's elite as an occupational strategy to professionalize nursing, hospitals were under external pressure to contain health care costs, and the change was successfully implemented because it converged with managerial interests in increasing labor productivity (Brannon, in press). RNs' unit labor cost was of course greater than that of auxiliaries, but hospital administrators believed staffing with RNs was more productive in that RNs could perform a wider range of nursing tasks (Aiken, 1982, 1987; Aiken, Blendon, & Rogers, 1981). The "professional" work jurisdiction now encompassed the routine tasks that were formerly delegated to auxiliaries as well as the conceptual and skilled tasks assigned RNs. In other words, RNs had to organize the work to be done and then perform it all.

The burden of reunified tasks began in report, which took place at the beginning of each shift on wards throughout the hospital when off-going nurses passed on responsibility for their patients. Although report was the most sedentary activity RNs engaged in and could seem uneventful when compared to patient care out on the floors, the work done in report was quite important. With the displacement of auxiliaries, RNs' conceptual work had changed significantly. Rather than plan patients' overall nursing care and delegate tasks to auxiliaries on their team, RNs now planned how they themselves would individually perform the complete range of nursing tasks for each of the patients in their assignment.

As off-going nurses communicated information about patients' current condition, oncoming RNs associated doctors' orders and patients' needs with nursing tasks, each making a complex assessment of the work to be done during their shift. Because RNs were now faced with a much larger work jurisdiction, effectively organizing one's work was critical to meeting the greater demands of patient care.[9] In the words of an experienced nurse,

> By the time you leave report you know how heavy your assignment is going to be. You know which patients have the greater needs. You've thought about what you have to do and how you're going to go about it. You know whether

you have time to talk with your patients or whether it's just going to be getting the basic care done.

The burden of primary nursing weighed heavily once RNs engaged in labor on the wards. With auxiliaries gone, RNs now passed the meal trays and took routine vital signs on all their patients at appropriate intervals throughout the shift. They performed the dirty work of helping patients use bedpans, urinals, and bedside commodes; they changed patients' gowns and bed linens and cleaned patients who had vomited or been incontinent. RNs were responsible for giving the daily bath and for routinely turning patients to avoid skin breakdown or respiratory complications. RNs also engaged in more of the emotional work that had been previously performed by auxiliaries because of their presence at the bedside. "Tender loving care" or "TLC," as it was called, included such tasks as listening and talking to patients, or simply holding a patient's hand for reassurance. Although of low status medically, these services were important to patients, their personal comfort, and to their hopes for recovery. Finally, RNs absorbed many of the custodial tasks that resulted from patients' dependency during their hospitalization. They assisted with phone calls, adjusted television sets, turned lights on and off, and opened and closed doors.

Of course, RNs continued to perform the more skilled tasks that had been assigned to them in team nursing even though experienced LPNs and competent nurses' aides had often assisted or substituted (Hughes et al., 1958, chap. 6; Levi, 1980). This included the administering of all medications, a demanding activity as patients were frequently on many medications that were given at different times and in different doses. "Giving meds" for five or six patients over the course of the shift required attention to detail and organization so that errors were not made. Many medications were administered orally, but others required other means of administration, including injection or intravenous delivery. RNs started IVs, performed various dress-ing changes, tube feedings, suctioning, irrigations, blood transfusions, and assisted physicians with special procedures. Furthermore, there was always "charting" to do in each patient's medical record. Although auxiliaries had formerly been excluded from documenting nursing care in the patient's chart, the prestige of charting had disappeared along with the auxiliaries. It was now a tiresome clerical task that frequently kept RNs from going home on time as they rushed at the end of shift to complete the required entries.

The intensification of RNs' work was magnified by state changes in reimbursement for hospital services (Bergthold, 1990; Ruggie, 1992) and the subsequent effect on patient care. With the tightening of Medicare reimbursement and the growth of outpatient services and treatment at facilities providing lower levels of care, nurses felt keenly that when patients were hospitalized they were more likely to be seriously ill. Patients' nursing needs or "acuities," as they were called, were rising. In addition, once admitted to the hospital and treated, patients were frequently discharged as soon as feasible so that the costs of their hospitalization would fall under DRG reimbursement ceilings, realizing a profit for the hospital. Nurses believed that some of these patients were soon readmitted and then required more intense nursing care.

At the same time, Pacific Hospital's administrators were taking steps to reduce labor costs in support departments. Cutbacks in support services contributed to intensifying RNs' labor, because nurses relied on prompt and competent service from a variety of paraprofessional and nonprofessional workers whose tasks must be coordinated with nursing care. The RN might need a lab tech to draw blood cultures on a feverish patient, a supply room clerk to bring an infusion pump to the floor before the nurse could begin an IV medication, or a respiratory therapist to administer treatment to a patient short of breath. When services or supplies needed for patient care were slow coming to the wards, when meal trays were missing or in error, or when housekeeping workers were unavailable to clean a room promptly, RNs were forced to produce care under more difficult conditions, many times performing the tasks themselves.

RNs became increasingly dissatisfied with the intensified work process. An RN who had worked under both team and primary nursing remarked,

> Sometimes when I am tired from running to keep up with the patients and the doctors, I think it was better for RNs when we were team leaders supervising auxiliary nurses. The trouble now is, they keep including more tasks and heavier assignments in which you have to do everything! I don't think we can take on much more.

Despite such reservations, RNs were caught between the contradictions of primary nursing and the difficulties of team nursing, and seemed to prefer the newer system. One RN's comments captured the sentiments of many when she stated, "Primary nursing keeps you running and it's getting worse. We need some help but we don't want team nursing back."

Omitting Work, Shifting Work, and Controlling Patients' Participation

With reunified tasks and unmediated relations with patients, primary nursing could require virtually the continuous presence of the RN at the bedside. Frustrated by the incongruity between an elite ideology of professional practice and the reality of work intensification, nurses struggled for solutions. RNs on one ward suggested the administration provide a notice in the patient's admission packet explaining that RNs could no longer perform nonessential services that had been customary in the past. RNs discovered that openly raising such issues with administrators was fruitless, as the hospital, in dealing with an increasingly competitive market, continued to trade on Pacific Hospital's reputation for total quality care by professional nurses. RNs confided that when they continued to complain about the additional burden on

the wards they were told to improve their organizational skills, that *"professional nurses should be able to get all their work done."*

To keep pace with the demands of work, RNs were forced to engage in informal strategies to shrink an overextended work jurisdiction. RNs believed that nurses who attempted to consistently perform the full range of services were unlikely to get the essential work done within the time constraints of the shift and were vulnerable to the occupational hazard of burnout, a term used on the wards during this period to describe nurses' emotional exhaustion and loss of interest in the care of their patients. To ensure their completion of higher priority work, RNs omitted some of the tasks formerly performed by auxiliaries, shifted other tasks onto patients and their families, and structured work at the bedside to limit excessive patient demands.

A common strategy was simply to omit lower level tasks when RNs found it necessary to do so. Thus a former team leader with many years of experience conveyed that "patients got more personal care, more TLC under team nursing. They got more back rubs, baths, the personal care tasks, including more opportunities to talk with someone." Other RNs who had worked under both team and primary nursing agreed. "In team nursing LPNs and aides were available to do this work. There are fewer nurses now, and we have to limit more of the personal service."[10]

RNs also attempted to shift tasks that were formerly performed by auxiliaries onto patients and their families.[11] They did so by encouraging patients to increase participation in their own care. Patients had contributed from the beginning of their hospitalization by providing personal information, donning a hospital gown, and cooperating in the production of care. However, with the displacement of auxiliaries, RNs informally redefined the boundary between the production and consumption of services by urging patients to produce their personal care at a level RNs considered appropriate to a patient's medical condition. Requests to perform tasks that RNs believed patients were capable of doing themselves were considered unwarranted. Shifting this work onto patients was legitimized by an ideology that it was therapeutic for patients to take a more active role in their care. Family members were also encouraged to invest in the patient's recovery by performing lower level tasks that could consume a great deal of the RN's time.

RNs viewed patients' requests as appropriate when their medical condition justified the concentration of the RN's time and energy. However, with less support staff and sicker patients, nurses viewed patients who persistently demanded "nonessential" services as "problem patients," particularly if they interfered with RNs' performance of work that was considered to have higher priority. Lorber (1975) documented similar findings even before the transition to primary nursing, arguing that "ease of management was the basic criterion for a label of good patient, and that patients who took time and attention felt to be unwarranted by their illness tended to be labeled problem patients" (p. 220). The intensification of work on nursing wards in the 1980s accentuated this tendency.

At the same time that RNs shifted tasks onto patients and their families, there were definite limits to doing so as this strategy could undermine RNs' control over their work. On the one hand, with reunified tasks and an unmediated relationship between the RN and the patient, dependency often led patients to demand services at a level that could overwhelm RNs' capacity to get their work accomplished. On the other hand, the patient's dependence facilitated RNs' command of the work to be done. Because stress could result not simply from the intensity of work but from RNs' fear of falling behind, RNs balanced encouraging greater participation with retaining control over the work.

RNs limited patients' demands and controlled their participation by structuring the performance of work at the bedside. While patients were preoccupied with their own needs, the RN addressed what had to be done for all assigned patients within the

time available, and this overview provided the context for assessing each patient's claims on their time and labor. Although patients and family members were encouraged to perform more of the lower level tasks, questioning the nurse's priorities or attempting to participate in core tasks that RNs considered clearly within their occupational jurisdiction were unwelcome. RNs commonly believed that the patients and family members most knowledgeable about their illness, medical orders, and hospital procedures were more difficult to take care of because they tended to question the nurse excessively and to interfere with the management of work.

Although alert patients technically had the capacity to affect their care to the point of refusing it altogether, patients' power was limited. They were sick and participated within the context of subordination to doctors' orders, hospital rules and procedures, and nurses' knowledge and organization of the care produced. In structuring production at the bedside, RNs made themselves readily available when it suited their priorities and relatively unavailable at other times. With varying degrees of subtlety, RNs educated patients to appropriate demands on their time and labor. Tacit agreements were often made, with RNs frequently negotiating the timing of tasks and accommodating patients' preferences when the costs of doing so were not excessive. For uncooperative patients, a range of sanctions existed that led to compliance or the intervention of medical or administrative authority, which could lead to an exit from the hospital in extreme cases. With most patients, RNs were able to effectively exercise their power to both enlist and limit patient participation. Yet they did so while they themselves remained subordinate both to physicians and administrators.

Physicians' Continued Professional Dominance

Although nursing advocates claimed that primary nursing would elevate RNs to colleagueship with physicians, the reorganization of work occurred within a subordinate work jurisdiction that physicians continued to dominate through their position over the medical division of labor. Physicians controlled the critical decisions of admitting and discharging patients, determining the medical diagnosis, and conceptualizing the overall plan of care. RNs were at the top of the paraprofessional hierarchy, but they did not decide on the medical problems to be addressed or the means of doing so. Their observation, discretion, and continuous presence on the hospital's wards were essential to meeting physicians' medical objectives, but RNs were more likely to facilitate the production of care rather than to define what that care should be. Furthermore, whereas reunified tasks provided RNs immediate control over nursing work, the displacement of auxiliaries flattened the nursing hierarchy, reinforcing RNs' accountability.

Both doctors and nurses talked of "admitting patients," but only physicians had the power to actually do so. In seeking medical help, the patient consulted a physician, who then decided if hospitalization was required. Only after the patient was admitted to a bed on a specific ward was an RN assigned responsibility for nursing care.

In admitting the patient, the doctor determined the diagnosis and conceptualized what Strauss, Fagerhaugh, Suczek, and Wiener (1985, pp. 8–39) refer to as the "illness trajectory" and "the arc of work." Whereas RNs and paraprofessional workers had secondary spheres of responsibility, the physician was responsible "for ordering, evaluating, and acting on diagnostic tests; for laying out the lines of work that need to be done; for utilizing the ward's organizational machinery" (p. 26). Physicians did so by defining the overall plan for medical treatment and by specifying detailed medical orders that mobilized and largely defined the labor of RNs and ancillary workers. This included orders for all medications, lab tests, diagnostic tests of the body's functioning and condition, vital sign checks, therapies, various nursing treatments, skin care, procedures for the care of the body's systems of elimination, intake and output measurements of fluids, and

even whether the patient could engage in such simple activities as get out of bed, drink fluids, or eat. The physician's orders determined whether the patient would be seen by a medical specialist, receive the services of a variety of paraprofessionals, or be set up for surgery or for any special procedures in which RNs assisted. Physicians also prioritized RNs' and paraprofessionals' work by specifying the execution of particular orders as "ROUTINE," "ASAP," or "STAT."

While the physician left the ward to see other patients in the hospital or return to their office practice, the RN proceeded to carry out the medical orders, which, as I have indicated, delineated the product to be produced and dictated many of the primary nurse's work activities. Some tasks were not stipulated by medical orders but derived from the RN's responsibility for work that, although important to the patient, was of secondary consideration to the physician. This included tasks involving body functions considered dirty work as well as many of the routine and custodial tasks I discussed earlier. The RN also informally assumed responsibility for coordinating and integrating diverse services ordered by the physician and produced by workers lower in the occupational division of labor.

Doctors monitored and directed patient care through brief daily visits to the wards to examine their patients. They checked for laboratory results and for technical information documented by the nurse: vital signs, weights, input and output measurements, blood sugar results. They wrote new orders if necessary and updated their assessment of the patient's condition in the "doctors' progress notes," which followed doctors' order sheets in the front of the patient's chart. RNs and paraprofessional technicians documented their care in sections behind the doctors' orders, reflecting the occupational division of labor and the hierarchy of professional responsibility.

Throughout the shift the primary nurse frequently referred to the physician's orders, which were carefully transcribed and placed in a Kardex file for easy referral.

Also filed in the Kardex was the nursing care plan, which was supposed to be written and maintained by the primary nurse. In an attempt to establish nursing's expertise as comparable to that of physicians, nursing educators had followed the medical model and required that a "nursing diagnosis" and "nursing orders" be specified in each patient's care plan. Although nurses had spent many hours devising care plans as part of their training, on the wards new RNs quickly learned that these innovations were not taken seriously. Of course, doctors never consulted the nursing care plan, but nurses seldom did either. With the intensity of work, RNs considered writing detailed nursing orders a low priority and care plans were usually incomplete.[12] In practice, nurses maintained continuity of care through shift report and informal personal interaction.

Primary nurses carried out doctors' orders and coordinated patient care. However, they acted not simply as physicians' "hands," but also as physicians' eyes, ears, and brains, in the sense that they observed the patients, interpreted the effects of medical treatment, and sometimes suggested what was needed. Because nurses were continuously on the wards, doctors relied on RNs for keeping them informed of changes in the patient's condition, which could range from the serious, such as an impending respiratory insufficiency, to the more frequent and routine, such as the need for a pain medication or a change in a patient's diet order. Many interactions with doctors were not problematic, but orders required that RNs actively engage in negotiating changes in medical orders that doctors might not readily agree to, but that RNs believed necessary due to their greater proximity to the patient (more continuous observation), the risk involved (an impending respiratory or cardiac arrest), or a greater familiarity with a patient's needs (the dosage of a pain med). There was always the possibility for differing interpretations and misunderstandings, but in most cases RNs were prohibited from acting on their own judgment without a doctor's order. For this reason and because RNs were required to keep physicians informed, nurses found it irritating when doctors seemed to take advantage of their dominant position by acting rude or annoyed by nurses' phone calls to report changes or to seek alterations in medical orders.

As the patient moved through the "illness trajectory," if the conditions that led to their hospitalization were eliminated or controlled at a level acceptable to the physician, the doctor ordered the patient to be discharged home or to a convalescent facility. The patient's hospitalization ended with the same division of labor that structured the admission. The physician ordered the discharge, the medications and treatments the patient was to continue at home, and any follow-up office visits. The doctor might ask the primary nurse how the patient was feeling but certainly did not ask for the RN's participation in the decision to discharge the patient. Once the physician had written the discharge order, the primary nurse discontinued the medical orders and coordinated the patient's departure, making sure the take-home medications were procured from the pharmacy and that the patient was ready when the transportation aide arrived to escort the patient to the entrance of the hospital.

As essential as RNs were to patient care, doctors did not treat them as professional colleagues. Nursing educators and administrators had argued that "without auxiliaries at the bedside, physicians would consult the professional nurse about the care of the patient as physicians do with their medical colleagues (Manthey, 1980; Manthey et al., 1970). RNs did function with considerable autonomy in performing their duties, but as I have described, their work remained within a subordinate work jurisdiction over which physicians maintained professional dominance through critical decisions and the formulation of medical orders. When there was a problem with their orders being carried out, doctors did seek out the primary nurse; however, they did not usually discuss the case in great detail. Furthermore, the nurse who wished to communicate with the doctor often found it difficult to do so. In day-to-day activity on the wards, it was not unusual for nurses to leave notes on the front of patients' charts as physicians typically visited patients briefly and sometimes left medical orders without communicating with the primary nurse at all. Doctors also gave verbal orders to the charge nurse and occasionally to the ward clerk to be communicated to the patient's nurse. And, although doctors did read the technical data documented in the patient's chart, nurses believed that physicians routinely skipped the "nurses' notes" section; that is, the nurse's ongoing assessment of the patient's condition.

Moreover, rather than elevate RNs to colleagueship with physicians, primary nursing actually reinforced RNs' accountability. If medical orders were not properly carried out, physicians could exercise their authority to initiate an administrative investigation of RNs' work performance. Without auxiliaries, there was no longer any ambiguity as to who was responsible for nursing care and for carrying out specific tasks. RNs were individually accountable for the complete care of patients. Thus, despite an elite occupational ideology of professional upgrading, primary nursing was never a threat to physicians' professional dominance, and consequently, physicians never initiated a campaign to defeat its implementation.

Bureaucratic Control

Throughout the post-World War II period, RNs have been subject to two lines of authority—medical and administrative—(Smith, 1958), and with the onset of the cost containment era, they were subject to greater bureaucratic control. Even physicians' sphere of power was more limited by the growth of managerial functions (Light & Levine, 1988). However, as I have indicated, physicians continued to dominate the medical division of labor within hospitals, and the flattening of the nursing hierarchy augmented RNs' accountability. The reorganization of nursing labor had similar effects on managers' administrative control.

Unlike physicians, RNs were employed by the hospital. Bureaucratic control of nurses began prior to their engagement in labor, as RNs were subject to managerial policies dictating the terms of employment: the hours, wages, shift, and job requirements. In accepting a position, the professional nurse formally agreed to follow hospital directives specifying scheduling, rest and meal breaks, the nurse's uniform, documenting time cards, norms for conduct while on duty, and a detailed job description of the RN's tasks and responsibilities.

An extensive web of hospital rules and procedures also guided the performance of RNs' labor on the wards. Policies existed for the admission and discharge of the patient, the performance of many nursing tasks, the documentation of care, and even the sequential placement of forms in the patient's chart. There were rules for answering the patient's call light, taking vital signs, calling the doctor, and a variety of other tasks, including the ordering of services from support departments. RNs also followed hospital protocols for transfusing blood, administering medications, performing postoperative care, "coding" the patient who arrested, and many other procedures.

Ironically, although bureaucratic rules continued to proliferate, administrative control of RNs' labor was strengthened by the *elimination* of rules that had been established in team nursing to order the labor of stratified workers. With the reunification of tasks, a plethora of formal rules differentiating the work of RNs, LPNs, and nurses' aides was no longer needed. In fact, the complexity of these rules and their frequent violation had compromised the effectiveness of bureaucratic control (Brannon, in press). As tasks were reunified and the nursing hierarchy flattened, RNs were now clearly answerable for violations of hospital protocols and procedures. RNs had gained control over the work they were responsible for, but in doing so, they were now more accountable to management as well as to physicians.[13]

Conclusion

The reorganization of nursing on hospital wards was initiated by nursing leaders as an occupational strategy to overcome nursing's failure to attain a full professional status. Although reunified tasks and an unmediated relationship with patients were promoted as the upgrading of RNs' practice, I have argued that the reorganization of work actually contradicted sociological theories of professionalization and served managerial interests. In reunifying nursing tasks, primary nursing did give RNs control over the work they were accountable for, but at a high cost. Rather than professionalize their practice, primary nursing enlarged RNs' work to encompass the complete range of nursing tasks, including the routine tasks formerly delegated to less credentialed workers. Nursing leaders trumpeted the change as professional upgrading, but practicing RNs endured work intensification. Burdened with an overextended work jurisdiction, staff RNs were forced to limit their workload by omitting lower level tasks or shifting such tasks onto patients and families while carefully managing the production of care to ensure RNs' continued control at the bedside. Furthermore, despite an ideology of professionalism in which RNs supposedly attained colleagueship with doctors, the flattening of the nursing hierarchy actually increased their accountability to both physicians and administrators.

Because the reunification of nursing tasks serves managerial interests and contradicts theories of professionalization, it may be tempting to interpret the reorganization of nursing as simply the proletarianization of the occupation. As I have suggested, the difficulty with this interpretation is that the reunification of tasks contradicts a major theory of proletarianization as well. RNs are not deskilled and managers no longer rely on a detailed labor process in which nonprofessional workers perform the bulk of routine bedside care (Braverman, 1974; Glazer, 1988).

Rather than fit the reorganization of nursing into prevailing theories of either professionalization or proletarianization, I think it is more accurate to conclude that the case of nursing demonstrates the complexity of these processes, which may occur simultaneously rather than be mutually exclusive (Brannon, in press; Coburn, 1988). Thus throughout the post-World War II period, nursing leaders have pursued occupational features that we associate with professionalization (mandatory registration and licensing, a stronger theoretical base rooted in higher credentials acquired in colleges and universities) at the same time that the organization of work has changed dramatically, both differentiating and reunifying nursing tasks. Although both task differentiation and reunification (dedifferentiation) have been linked with claims of professionalization in different historical periods, neither fully professionalizes RNs, who remain subordinate to physicians and administrators in forms of domination and exploitation that do not require deskilling (Derber, 1982; Sarfatti-Larson, 1980).

Discussion Questions

1. Nursing is often considered a semi-profession. To what extent do you think its failure to fully professionalize may be connected to the fact that it is a female-dominated occupation?

2. Some say that physicians are becoming deprofessionalized. Why might that be true?

Robert L. Brannon, "Professionalization and Work Intensification: Nursing in the Cost Containment Era" (*Work and Occupations* May 1994), pp. 157–178. Copyright © 1994 by Sage Publications, Inc. Reprinted by permission of Sage Publications, Inc.

Endnotes

1. For exceptions that do not necessarily fall within these areas of specialization, see Glazer (1988) and Sacks (1988, chap. 8). My own work has focused extensively on the reorganization of nursing work on hospital wards, the central work site in the industry. Anthropologist Karen Sacks briefly discusses the reorganization of nursing labor in hospitals in an interesting

study of nonprofessional workers engaged in a unionization drive at Duke Medical Center. Glazer has focused primarily on the shift from wage labor to unpaid work in the home.

2. Nursing's elite of educators and administrators is internally divided on various issues but I shall use the term *nursing leaders* to refer to a dominant segment of the elite that successfully promoted the replacement of team nursing with primary nursing and its variants.

3. This worked to the particular disadvantage of Black women, who were overrepresented in auxiliary occupations. Whereas only 8.5% of RNs are Black, 19% of LPNs and 34% of nurses' aides, orderlies, and attendants are Black (Hodson & Sullivan, 1990, Appendix Table 1).

4. See Abbott (1988) for a theoretical discussion of occupational and work jurisdictions.

5. Before the postwar period, RNs worked principally in private duty practice in patients' homes. Hospital wards were staffed with nursing apprentices undergoing training in hospital-based schools. The transition from private duty to hospital employment began with the collapse of the private duty market during the 1930s. For discussion of nursing in the prewar period, see Melosh (1982).

6. In the 1982–1983 academic year, during the peak years of the transition to RN-predominant staffing, 15% of RN graduates received degrees from hospital diploma programs, 31% from baccalaureate programs, and 54% from associate degree programs (American Nurses' Association, 1985, Table 2.6). In contrast, during the 1965–1966 academic year, at the height of team nursing, 75% received degrees from hospital diploma programs, 15.5% from baccalaureate programs, and only 9.5% from community colleges (calculated from data in McClure & Nelson, 1982, Table 4-3).

7. In contrast to physicians, nursing's greater emphasis on the socioemotional aspects of patient care may result not only from gender socialization but from physicians' superordinate work jurisdiction and dominance over the most technical aspects of patient care. Thus when RNs' work does emphasize technical tasks, RNs are limited to the role of subordinate technician. For a discussion of this dilemma in intensive care units, see Zussman (1992, chap. 5).

8. For a discussion of workplace knowledge assimilation, see Abbott (1988, chap. 3).

9. New RNs often found it difficult to develop the required organizational skills, which were learned informally on the job rather than in credentialing programs.

10. At the same time, restricting such work could be personally difficult as RNs often felt an obligation to care for patients, regardless of whether the tasks involved were associated with technical skills. An experienced RN acknowledged, "nursing emphasizes the technical tasks, but what is important to the patient is TLC." In addition, although mundane tasks might provide the opportunity to assess the patient's medical condition while attending to intangible psychosocial needs, nurses found it difficult to turn low-level tasks into professional tasks. As another RN confided, "How many times can you empty the bedpan and still convince yourself that this work contributes to your professional knowledge and practice?"

11. Glazer (1988) emphasizes a shift between work performed by paid nurses in hospitals to work performed by unpaid women in the home, viewing this as a strategy developed by capitalists and managers to reduce labor costs. In contrast, I argue that the shift within the hospital was initiated by workers informally in response to intensified work and an overextended work jurisdiction as well. I have also argued (Brannon, 1988, in press) that the external shift of work from the hospital to the periphery of the health care delivery system, including home care, was as much a managerial strategy to "commodify" the periphery, as an effort to "decommodify" services or "dewage" labor. Consequently, health care costs have continued to rise and health care employment has continued to expand.

12. Unit managers may have surreptitiously shared staff RNs' opinion, as they usually overlooked incomplete care plans. The one time unit managers stressed their completion was just before the annual inspection by the Joint Commission on the Accreditation of Hospitals. With respect to the nursing diagnosis, Abbott (1988) insightfully notes that the "current concept of 'nursing diagnosis' embraces nearly every aspect of well-being. It will for that reason be untenable" (p. 347, N. 38).

13. Of course, this does not mean that RNs simply abided by bureaucratic rules. As I have discussed elsewhere (Brannon, in press), RNs violated certain rules to get their work accomplished. In some cases management ignored the violations, for example, RNs' failure to take routine rest breaks or to fully document overtime, because it facilitated getting the work done. At other times, higher levels of management were unaware of rule violations, as when shift charge nurses attempted to regulate the ward's workload by delaying admissions or encouraging patient transfers to other wards and when staff nurses omitted tasks or intentionally passed work on to the next shift.

References

Abbott, A. (1981). Status and status strain in the professions. *American Journal of Sociology*, 86(4), 819–835.

Abbott, A. (1988). *The system of professions*. Chicago: University of Chicago Press.

Aiken, L. H. (1982). The nurse labor market. *Health Affairs*, 7(4), 30–40.

Aiken, L. H. (1987, December). Breaking the shortage cycles. *American Journal of Nursing*, 87(12), 1616–1620.

Aiken, L. H., Blendon, R. J., & Rogers, D. E. (1981, September). The shortage of hospital nurses: A new perspective. *American Journal of Nursing*, 81(9), 1612–1618.

American Hospital Association. (1991). *Hospital nursing in the '90s: The effect on patient care.* Chicago: American Nurses' Association.

American Nurses' Association. (1985). *Facts about nursing, 84–85.* Kansas City: American Nurses' Association.

Bergthold, L. A. (1990). *Purchasing power in health.* New Brunswick, NJ: Rutgers University Press.

Brannon, R. L. (1988). *The production of care: The hospital industry and the nursing labor process.* Ann Arbor, MI: University Microfilm International.

Brannon, R. L. (1992, April). Professionalization or proletarianization: Team nursing reexamined. Paper presented at the meeting of the Southern Sociological Society, New Orleans, LA.

Brannon, R. L. (in press). *Intensifying care: The hospital industry, professionalization, and the reorganization of the nursing labor process.* Amityville, NY: Baywood.

Braverman, H. (1974). *Labor and monopoly capital.* New York: Monthly Review Press.

Brint, S., & Karabel, J. (1989). *The diverted dream.* New York: Oxford University Press.

Christman, L. (1978). A micro-analysis of the nursing division of one medical center. In M. L. Millman (Ed.), *Nursing personnel and the changing health care system* (pp. 143–152). Cambridge, MA: Ballinger.

Coburn, D. (1988). The development of Canadian nursing: Professionalization and proletarianization. *International Journal of Health Services*, 18(3), 437–456.

Derber, C. (1982). Toward a new theory of professionals as workers: Advanced capitalism and postindustrial labor. In C. Derber (Ed.), *Professionals as workers: Mental labor in advanced capitalism* (pp. 193–208). Boston: G. K. Hall.

Etzioni, A. (Ed.). (1969). *The semi-professions and their organization.* New York: Free Press.

Fox, R. C. (1985). Reflections and opportunities in the sociology of medicine. *Journal of Health and Social Behavior*, 26, 6–14.

Freidson, E. (1988). *Profession of medicine.* Chicago: University of Chicago Press. (Original work published 1970)

Glazer, N. Y. (1988). Overlooked, overworked: Women's unpaid and paid work in the health services' "cost crisis." *International Journal of Health Services*, 18(1), 119–137.

Hochschild, A. (1989). *The second shift.* New York: Avon.

Hodson, R., & Sullivan, T. A. (1990). *The social organization of work.* Belmont, CA: Wadsworth.

Hughes, E. C. (1971). *The sociological eye.* Chicago: Aldine.

Hughes, E. C., Hughes, H. M., & Deutscher, I. (1958). *Twenty thousand nurses tell their story.* Philadelphia: J. B. Lippincott.

Immershein, A. W., Rond, P. C, & Mathis, M. P. (1992). Restructuring patterns of elite dominance and the formation of state policy in health care. *American Journal of Sociology*, 97(4), 970–993.

Joiner, C., & van Servellen, G. M. (1984). *Job enrichment in nursing.* Rockville, MD: Aspen.

Karabel, J. (1972). Community colleges and social stratification. *Harvard Educational Review*, 42(6), 521–562.

Levi, M. (1980). Functional redundancy and the process of professionalization: The case of registered nurses in the United States. *Journal of Health Politics, Policy, and Law*, 5(2), 333–353.

Light, D., & Levine, S. (1988). The changing character of the medical profession: A theoretical overview. *Milbank Quarterly*, 66(Suppl. 2), 10–32.

Lorber, J. (1975). Good patients and problem patients: Conformity and deviance in a general hospital. *Journal of Health and Social Behavior*, 16(2), 213–225.

Manthey, M. (1980). *The practice of primary nursing.* Boston: Blackwell.

Manthey, M. (1988, May). Can primary nursing survive? *American Journal of Nursing*, 88(5), 644–647.

Manthey, M., Ciske, K., Robertson, P., & Harris, I. (1970). Primary nursing: A return to the concept of "my nurse" and "my patient." *Nursing Forum*, 9(1), 64–83.

Marram, G. D., Schlegel, M. W., & Bevis, E. O. (1974). *Primary nursing: A model for individualized care.* St. Louis: C. V. Mosby.

McClure, M., & Nelson, M. (1982). Trends in hospital nursing. In L. H. Aiken (Ed.), *Nursing in the 1980s* (pp. 59–73). Philadelphia: J. B. Lippincott.

Melosh, B. (1982). *The physician's hand: Work culture and conflict in American nursing.* Philadelphia: Temple University Press.

Reverby, S. (1979). The search for the hospital yardstick: Nursing and rationalization of hospital work. In S. Reverby & D. Rosner (Eds.), *Health care in America* (pp. 206–225). Philadelphia: Temple University Press.

Reverby, S. (1987). *Ordered to care.* Cambridge: Cambridge University Press.

Rueschemeyer, D. (1986). *Power and the division of labour.* Stanford, CA: Stanford University Press.

Ruggie, M. (1992). The paradox of liberal intervention: Health policy and the American welfare state. *American Journal of Sociology*, 97(4), 919–944.

Sacks, K. B. (1988). *Caring by the hour.* Urbana: University of Illinois Press.

Sarfatti-Larson, M. (1980). Proletarianization and educated labor. *Theory and Society*, 9, 131–175.

Smith, H. (1958). Two lines of authority: The hospital's dilemma. In E. G. Jaco (Ed.), *Patients, physicians, and illness* (pp. 468–477). Glencoe, IL: Free Press.

Starr, P. (1982). *The social transformation of American medicine.* New York: Basic Books.

Strauss, A., Fagerhaugh, S., Suczek, B., & Wiener, C. (1985). *Social organization of medical work.* Chicago: University of Chicago Press.

Wagner, D. (1980). The proletarianization of nursing in the United States, 1932–1946. *International Journal of Health Services,* 10(2), 271–290.

Williams, C. L. (1992). The glass escalator: Hidden advantages for men in the "female" professions. *Social Problems,* 39(3), 253–267.

Zussman, R. (1992). *Intensive care.* Chicago: University of Chicago Press. ✦

24

Why Teamwork Fails: Obstacles to Workplace Change in Four Manufacturing Plants

Steven P. Vallas

One of the central ideas associated with the new economy is that work organizations are changing from hierarchical, bureaucratic structures to flatter, less-centralized structures. With the reduction in the number of layers in the organization, authority and the autonomy to act are supposed to move down the organizational structure until the people at the "point of production"—those who produce and deliver the goods and services—have more to say about day-to-day decisions. One example of this change is the creation of work teams, in which people participate in sharing ideas about how to solve problems and improve productivity and the quality of work. It is believed that such teams are more flexible than hierarchical structures and that they can respond to the needs of customers more easily. In the old hierarchical structure, one has to wait for questions to move up the structure and for answers to come down the structure. This not only takes time but can lead to distortions of messages and miscommunication.

This chapter reports the results of a study of workplace change in four manufacturing plants. The author defines the success of workplace change initiatives (like work teams) in terms of whether they change the antagonism and division between management and workers. The main conclusion of the study is that successful workplace change must be based on shared normative commitments that bring workers and management together to recognize and reward work-related achievements. The greatest barrier to success was the desire to measure results in terms of productivity.

Organization theorists commonly argue that centralized, bureaucratic organizational structures are increasingly giving way to more "flexible" and participative arrangements that are better suited to contemporary economic conditions (for reviews see V. Smith 1997; Vallas 1999). Some theorists celebrate these developments as heralding an era of increased worker autonomy (Adler 1992; Heckscher 1988,1994; Kern and Schumann 1992). Others warn of heightened managerial influence (Barker 1993, 1999; Berggren 1992; Graham 1995; Grenier 1988). Few dispute the notion that U.S. firms are undergoing historically significant patterns of change that promise to redefine the nature of managerial authority and the structure of organizational control (Cappelli 1995; Kalleberg 2001; Powell 2001).

Yet the further one moves past such abstract generalities, the more ambiguities and uncertainties one seems to confront. One such uncertainty stems from a disturbing gap between theoretical models of the new work practices and the empirical evidence concerning their actual implementation. Claims made on behalf of the "lean" system of production, for example (Adler 1992; Hackman and Wageman 1995; Kenney and Florida 1993; Womack, Jones, and Roos 1990), have often found little support in empirical case studies, suggesting that the promise of the "quality movement" may be limited to a handful of "celebrity" organizations such as Saturn or the New United Motor Manufacturing, Inc. plant (NUMMI), jointly run by Toyota and General Motors (Berggren 1992; Dohse, Jurgens, and Malsch 1985; Lawler, Mohrman, and Ledford 1992, 1995; Milkman 1997; Prechel 1994; Rubinstein 2000). A second source of uncertainty concerns a development that Pil and MacDuffie (1996: 423) have dubbed a "striking paradox." Although a substantial body of evidence now indicates that new work practices make possible significant performance advantages over their Fordist equivalents (e.g., Appelbaum et al. 2000; Cappelli and Neumark 2001; Ichniowski et al. 1996; Levine and Tyson 1990; Shaiken, Lopez, and Mankita 1997), the proportion of establishments that can genuinely be called "transformed" remains quite small (cf. Osterman 2000). The question, then, is why firms that purport to be rationally acting organizations appear to resist the very methods that would best equip them to achieve their stated goals. A third source of uncertainty arguably underlies the previous two and stems from the tendency of researchers to focus on the outcomes of workplace change without examining the social and organizational processes that arise during the introduction of the new work practices. Among students of industrial relations, for example, the tendency has been to gather data on the performance of particular types of work systems typically using either cross-sectional survey data or (less commonly) panel data on productivity. Although some studies have incorporated a broader set of outcome measures such as wages, stress, or job attitudes (see Appelbaum et al. 2000; Berggren 1992; Kuhlmann and Schumann 2001), the prevailing research designs make it difficult to capture the social relations that unfold during the course of workplace change. As a result, little is known about the ways in which nominally similar work practices are shaped by particular organizational conditions. Nor do we have a clear understanding of how actors at different levels within organizations tend to respond to organizational changes of various sorts.

Here I take aim at these sources of uncertainty, using qualitative methods to study workplace transformation initiatives at four unionized, brownfield manufacturing sites. My goals are both interpretive and explanatory. First, I seek to provide a deeper understanding of the changes that have unfolded within U.S. manufacturing plants during the 1990s, when interest in new production concepts significantly increased. Second, I aim to identify some of the most salient obstacles to the pursuit of workplace change, accounting for the relatively limited success of new structures in displacing traditional, hierarchical work structures. The plants studied here are all drawn from a single, fairly traditional branch of production: the pulp and paper industry, a largely unionized and capital-intensive branch of production that has often lagged in the introduction of new process technologies and work practices (Vallas 2001; Vallas and Beck 1996). Because this industry has recently sought to adopt many forms of innovation suggested by the quality movement, it provides an especially opportune site for research on the obstacles to workplace change. My analysis is not framed as an exercise in hypothesis testing; instead, it aims to reconstruct existing theory by drawing attention to important tendencies that have previously been ignored (Burawoy 1998).

I begin by reviewing previous lines of analysis concerning the nature and impact of nontraditional work systems and by sketching the theoretical orientation that guides the present analysis. I describe the research strategy employed and the contexts in which the data were collected. Then I present findings bearing on two important forms of workplace change—"team" initiatives and "continuous improvement" programs—neither of which succeeded in transcending the traditional boundary between salaried and hourly employees. I argue that the reason for such limited gains lay in the managerial orientation toward production that informed the workplace restructuring initiatives. This orientation, which privileged scientific and technical rationality, had a double effect on the outcome of workplace change. First, it sharply limited the firm's ability to provide any overarching normative or moral framework within which workplace change might unfold. Second, the predominance of a technical, expert-centered orientation toward production introduced salient contradictions into the new work regimes, which were often torn between two conflicting organizational logics. Workplace change progressed furthest, and was relatively contradiction-free, at the one plant that enjoyed a significant measure of freedom from corporate control, suggesting that centralized corporate dominance over the process of workplace change acts to reproduce workplace hierarchy. I conclude by drawing out the theoretical and practical implications of my findings and by suggesting future lines of analysis for research on the limits of workplace change.

Teams, Tradition, and Workplace Transformation

Much of the initial ferment concerning new managerial practices in the United States emerged during the 1980s, when international competition from Europe and Japan exposed important vulnerabilities within U.S. production systems, in effect delegitimating the organizational orthodoxy that firms had inherited from the past (Appelbaum and Batt 1994; Cappelli and Neumark 2001; Heckscher 1988, 1994). Initially, the focus for change was on employee involvement and quality circles. By the end of the 1980s, however, two more fully articulated models had appeared.

One model drew inspiration from economic developments in Western Europe (Berggren 1992; Kern and Schumann 1992; Piore and Sabel 1984), arguing that because consumer tastes increasingly demanded diversified, high-end consumer goods, production required much greater skill and flexibility than the routinized, Fordist production systems could provide. Theorists in this genre advocated the abandonment of mass production models in favor of neo-craft systems that employed highly skilled workers organized into autonomous production teams (Appelbaum and Batt 1994; Berggren 1992; Hirst and Zeitlin 1991; Sabel et al. 1989; Vallas 1999). A second and ultimately more influential approach was spawned by the quality movement emanating from Japan. Although formulations varied, what has come to be called "lean" production involves three principal characteristics: First, it calls for elimination of the unproductive bureaucratic hierarchies previously used to oversee production workers and to maintain quality control. Second, it advocates redistributing the latter tasks to front-line employees themselves. And third, it stresses the need for the continuous improvement of the firm's operations (e.g., through the practice of *kaizeri*), with production workers expected to place their knowledge at the disposal of the firm. Because it presupposes the ongoing consent of its production workers, the lean system not only claims to enhance efficiency and product quality but also promises to free workers from the long-established dictates of centralized control (Adler 1992; Hackman and Wageman 1995; Kenney and Florida 1993; Womack et al. 1990; cf. Berggren 1992; Dohse et al. 1985).

Regardless of their differences, theories of neo-craft or lean work regimes imply a significant challenge to the Weberian theory of bureaucracy, in that both foresee a historical transcendence of the "iron cage" of imperative coordination. To be sure, lean production, in particular, places a strong emphasis on quantitative analysis and rational calculation: "Total Quality Management" and "Statistical Process Control" both make abundant use of probability theory and mathematical modeling as bases for process control (Hackman and Wageman 1995; Hill 1991; Klein 1994; Rothschild and Ollilainen 1999). Yet the lean approach *also* stresses the *normative* or moral aspects of organizational control in lieu of the traditional reliance on managerial imperatives. Indeed, Barley and Kunda (1992) go so far as to characterize/the current era of workplace change in terms of a shift from "rational" to "normative" managerial rhetoric, that is, a movement *away* from reliance on scientific and technical rationality (such as Taylorism or operations management), and *toward* a normatively grounded pattern that seeks to elicit a shared commitment to the firm.[1]

Others see team systems in somewhat different terms. Rather than speaking of a shift from one rhetorical system to another, for example, Adler (1992) views lean theory as making possible a *synthesis* of the rational and the normative components of the firm. Studying the now-famous NUMMI assembly plant at Fremont, California, Adler sees the plant's success as stemming precisely from its ability *to fuse* the normative aspects of team systems with the rational emphasis of Taylorism, thus enabling management to elicit workers' commitment to the rationalization of their own jobs. Key to this plant's success was its dramatic reduction in the size of its engineering staff—a shift made possible by transferring the work of job design and analysis to front-line production workers themselves (cf. Kern and Schumann 1992).

Critics of lean theory have questioned the nature of any such syntheses under conditions of advanced capitalism (Berggren 1992; Graham 1995; Grenier 1988). The argument that critics have advanced is that lean production serves powerful ideological functions, encouraging workers to internalize managerial definitions of their work situation, thus actually reducing the residues of autonomy that workers retained under the Fordist regime (Barker 1993, 1999). Although this line of analysis is theoretically suggestive, the evidence presented on its behalf has often seemed weak. For example, in Graham's (1995) study of a Japanese-managed auto plant, workers only rarely seemed to internalize the norms their employer favored. Instead, they engaged in various forms of resistance, even in the absence of union organization (cf. Grenier 1988).[2] In light of such

findings, it seems useful to pursue a different, more empirically rooted investigation that seeks to explain the gap between lean theory's claims and the actual work practices it has inspired. Why have the theoretical virtues of workplace transformation so rarely been achieved in practice? What processes and conditions seem to encourage the reproduction of Fordist authority relations? What changes *have* firms sought to adopt, and why?

Previous research in this direction has tended to divide into three discrete lines of analysis. One points toward the phenomenon of structural inertia, suggesting that organizations are "imprinted" with the conditions under which they were born, thereafter tending to cling to long-established routines, production methods, and identities (Hannan and Freeman 1984; Pettigrew 1979; Schoenberger 1997; Stinchcombe 1965). A second approach fastens on resistance to change among middle managers, who are said to view new work practices as threats to their traditional status and authority (Taplin 2001; Zuboff 1988; cf. V. Smith 1990). A third approach has been influential among labor relations specialists, who stress the characteristics of the innovations that firms introduce. Because firms have tended to adopt innovations singly, rather than in the clusters or "bundles" that team systems are said to require, they often fail to achieve the structural complementarities needed to accomplish far-reaching organizational change (Ichniowski, Shaw, and Prennushi 1997; MacDuffie 1995; Pil and MacDuffie 1996. . . .

Departing from these approaches, I appeal to developments within industrial sociology—especially Thomas's (1994) "power-process" theory of organizational change (cf. Kelley 1990; Wilkinson 1983). As applied here, the notion is that the outcome of workplace change initiatives is in large part shaped by the social and organizational processes that unfold during the implementation of the new work practices. In other words, workplace change is not akin to a surgical procedure performed under anesthesia. Rather, it constitutes a negotiated phenomenon in which the language, rhetoric, and strategies that particular occupational groups employ can either blur or heighten the boundaries that exist within the firm (Thomas 1994; Vallas 2001; cf. Fine 1984, 1996; Strauss 1978). As Thomas further suggests, workplace change often provides occupational groups with an opportunity to realign their positions within the firm, setting in motion processes that can have autonomous effects on the outcomes that emerge. Where workplace change fails to transform existing organizational patterns, the reasons may stem less from the nature of the innovations than from the processes that surround and shape their introduction.

By anchoring his analysis within a general theory of social reproduction, Thomas (1994:225–28) relies on Gidden's theory of structuration. By contrast, I suggest that critical theory—in particular, the work of Habermas (1971, 1979, 1987)—may hold important advantages, in that it helps identify the competing logics that can inform particular institutional domains. Thus, in his critique of Max Weber's theory of rationalization, Habermas (1987) suggests that the proliferation of instrumental rationality represents but one side of a complex and often contradictory process of historical evolution. The neglected side of the rationalization process involves the growth of communicative rationality oriented toward shared understandings and collective debate. Although the spread of industrial capitalism has allowed instrumental action systems to dominate, or even to "colonize," communicatively oriented ones, for Habermas the relationship between the two constitutes an ongoing tension, as various social groups struggle over the legitimate application of instrumental and communicative rationality (Agger 1991; Habermas 1987).

Although Habermas's reasoning is couched at a high level of abstraction, his thinking holds value for the study of formal organizations and workplace change (Burrell 1994). First, it sensitizes us to the ways in which the growth of scientific and technical rationality can obstruct the pursuit of workplace change. Where management favors such a form of rationality without recourse to communicative processes, it seems reasonable to expect that workplace transformation will assume a distorted or contradictory form, with workers viewing the resulting innovations as tending to foreclose the possibility of genuine dialogue and debate. Second, this approach begins to identify conditions that may be necessary for the success of workplace change. Key for Habermas, and for some theorists of the "post-bureaucratic organization" (Heckscher 1994), is the effort to develop institutional supports for communicative processes, ensuring that the new forms of authority rest on debate and discursive legitimation rather than on systemic regulation alone.

However disparate they may seem, these theoretical orientations complement one another in important ways. Both Thomas and Habermas address themes relevant to Weberian analysis of work organizations (cf. Halaby 1986). Both are attuned to the symbolic contexts in which practical activity takes place. And where one focuses on the intraorganizational processes that accompany workplace change, the other situates such processes within the larger context of modernity and the tensions the latter often entails. Taken together, they provide a useful set of orienting assumptions with which to approach the cases at hand.

The Paper Industry as a Strategic Research Site

Until recently, the pulp and paper industry was a highly traditional, regionally focused branch of the economy with a strong pattern of family ownership (McGaw 1987; M. Smith 1997). Firms in this heavily capital intensive industry have generally adopted a conservative approach toward their mill operations, favoring incremental changes in production to preserve the value of their existing fixed capital investments (Cohen 1984; M. Smith 1997). Interviews with former managers and executives of mills at different parts of the country suggest that until the early 1970s, many aspects of production continued to rely on a quasi-craft form of work organization in which strategic aspects of the production process rested on traditionally acquired knowledge held by supervisors and hourly employees (cf. Vallas and Beck 1996; Zuboff 1988). To ensure the availability of, such local knowledge, companies typically made elaborate provisions for internal labor markets, thus providing incentives for the acquisition of asset-specific skills (Althauser and Kalleberg 1981; Doeringer and Piore 1971). Under these conditions, workers often sustained a rich occupational community among their own ranks, especially among workers holding the most highly skilled jobs (cf. Dudley 1994; Vallas 2001).

Always a highly cyclical industry marked by wide swings in both prices and profits, by the early 1980s the paper industry began to suffer sustained bouts of overproduction and weak economic returns. These problems intensified with the rise of international competition and tightened environmental regulation, prompting many large firms to seek ways of reducing their operating costs and achieving greater operational flexibility. As a result, company after company in the United States began to perceive the traditional system of work rules they inherited as an impediment to their organizational performance (Birecree 1993; Holmes 1997; Walton, Cusher-Gerschenfeld, and McKersie 1994). Three fundamental changes ensued.

First, corporations sought dramatic changes in their labor relations, with many large firms engaging in sharp confrontations with the major unions in the industry. These conflicts, which sometimes involved the use of permanent replacement workers, cast a pall over labor relations and led to a decided shift in the balance of power between labor and management (Beck 1989; Eaton and Kriesky 1994; Getman 1998).

Second, firms began to recast the character of the production process itself. Although the industry had long relied on continuous process production methods, firms now began to introduce an entirely new generation of production machinery and process control systems that promised to achieve greater economies of scale, more consistent quality, reduced crew sizes, and greater stability and throughput. With the introduction of these technologies (and growth in the number of engineering employees as well), many managers began to speak of the need to move papermaking "from an art to a science"—an oft-repeated phrase in many mills (Vallas 2001; Vallas and Beck 1996).

Third, firms searched for newer and more effective work systems that might provide an optimal fit with the new production processes. Especially within more consumer-oriented firms, management energetically sought to transform the structure of mill operations, transcending inherited hierarchies—especially the traditional boundary between salaried and hourly employees. Toward this end, most large firms have introduced a variety of nontraditional work systems (most notably, self-directed teams, high-performance work systems, and employee involvement initiatives) in place of the traditional bureaucratic model. The fate of these initiatives—their success in transcending deeply established organizational forms—is of central importance for my analysis.[3]

Research Strategy and Methods

This study originated as part of a wider effort to understand the social processes that underlie the outcome of technological and organizational change. To capture such processes, I invoke qualitative methods, drawing especially on recent developments in workplace ethnography (see Barley 1996; Burawoy 1998; Hodson 1999, 2001; Morrill and Fine 1997).[4] Mindful of the limits of single-site ethnographic research, I combine the depth and richness of such fieldwork with the analytic breadth that multisite research allows. This strategy—essentially that of comparative ethnography—allows me to identify salient variations in the outcome of workplace change and to seek the social and organizational processes that account for such differences (cf. Burawoy 1990, 1998).

My study was jointly sponsored by the company (which I shall call U.S. Paper) and the major union in the industry (PACE International Union, AFL-CIO). Although the original research design allowed for fieldwork at three different mills (chosen to provide variation in the age, history, and product line of the industry's mills), consultation with union staff identified a fourth site that expanded the range of comparisons on which the study could draw. The resulting sample provides for sharp contrasts in plant size (from 400 to 2,000 employees) and complexity (ranging from relatively simple, single-product mills to massive, highly differentiated industrial complexes). All of these mills are unionized, reflecting the industry's high union density, but labor relations are sharply varied, ranging from adversarial to cooperative.

Because all four mills are owned and managed by U.S. Paper, a leading manufacturer of forest products, company ownership has been held constant. Like many of the largest firms in the industry, U.S. Paper has grown largely through acquisitions and now has establishments in many major industrialized nations. Several other firms were approached but declined to provide access for this study, raising the possibility that these data are biased in the direction of a greater openness toward change than is typical in the industry. Data collected from other firms—from an earlier stage of fieldwork conducted at a separate company (Vallas and Beck 1996), as well as oral history interviews and site visits at various mills—indicate that, while such selection biases do exist, they are not highly pronounced.

Data collection began in November 1999 and continued until August 2001. I conducted the great bulk of the fieldwork myself, but two graduate researchers joined in the research, providing additional sources of insight and observation. With management's permission, we were free to select departments for particular attention, to join production crews during their shifts, to sit in on various production and team meetings of both salaried and hourly personnel, and generally immerse ourselves in the culture of the mills. Although data were collected in both traditional and nontraditional production areas, I focused particular attention on the nontraditional departments, which included 10 discrete instances of "team" initiatives.[5] In addition, data were collected on the nature of the firm's "continuous improvement process," a company-wide program to involve salaried and hourly workers in project-oriented teams that aimed to enhance mill operations in concretely measurable ways.

In all, roughly 1,700 hours were spent collecting observational data in these mills, with observations conducted during varying times of day. To supplement the ethnographic data, semistructured interviews were conducted with a purposive sample of roughly 75 salaried employees (mainly managers, supervisors, and process engineers) on matters involving new technology and team systems. To grasp temporal processes, a considerable proportion of these interviews (as well as conversations during the fieldwork generally) was oriented toward reconstructing the evolution of workplace change initiatives. These data, combined with documentary sources (memoranda, correspondence, and reports), provided a reasonably full picture of the processes involved in the transformation of work. Key features of the four mills (which I call Bordermill, Pinetown, Mountainmill, and NewTown) are outlined in Table 24.1.

Following the claims that many theorists have made (Adler 1992; Heckscher 1988, 1994; Kern and Schumann 1992; Womack et al. 1990; Zuboff 1988), I define the success of workplace change initiatives not on the basis of their performance but instead on their ability to transcend the long-standing antagonism between salaried and hourly workers—that is, the division between the manager and the "managed." I therefore define "successful" efforts at workplace transformation as involving formally-initiated changes in workplace governance that expand hourly workers' autonomy, foster a heightened level of commitment to the firm, and in so doing blur the boundary between hourly and salaried employees. "Failed" initiatives are those that generate ongoing conflict and distrust, or demands for a return to a traditional work system. Initiatives that attain an intermediate or transitional state—some measure of success, but with conflicts and resentments still apparent—are defined as having achieved "mixed success."

Findings

U.S. Paper began to undertake workplace change initiatives in the early 1990s. These initiatives, which were loosely drawn from the quality movement, fell into two broad categories. One centered on the introduction of *nontraditional work systems*, which managers generally referred to in terms of "team concept," self-directed teams, and high-performance work systems. Although these initiatives vary, workers involved in them are typically expected to assume responsibilities previously assigned to supervisors. Team members hold meetings at the outset of each shift, planning key activities and tasks on their own (thus allowing for sharp reductions in the number of first-line supervisors). Typically, workers are employed in the context of simplified or flexible job classifications (often

---

Table 24.1
Elements of Workplace Transformation in Four Pulp and Paper Mills

	Mill			
Elements	Bordermill	Pinetown	Mountainmill	NewTown
Size (number of employees)	Large (>1,000)	Large (>1,000)	Medium (<500)	Medium (<800)
Character of labor relations	Generally cooperative	Sharply adversarial since 1980s	Adversarial	Sharply adversarial until late 1980s, then increasingly cooperative
Team Initiatives[a]				
Where applied (number of workers and outcome in parentheses)	*Case 1.* New converting machine (32; failure)	*Case 5.* New converting machine (32; mixed)	*Case 7.* New paper machine (45; failure)	*Case 10.* Recycled pulping operation (28; mixed)
	Case 2. New paper machine (40; mixed)	*Case 6.* Woodyard (45; success)	*Case 8.* Pulp mill (12; success)	
	Case 3. New cutting and wrapping machine (16; success)		*Case 9.* Maintenance (50; failure)	
	Case 4. Woodyard (32; success)			
Continuous Improvement (PIP)[b]				
When and how adopted	1996, in compliance with headquarters provisions	1997, in compliance with headquarters provisions	1997, in compliance with headquarters provisions	1991, as local initiative
Provisions for union involvement	None	None	None	Extensive
Extent of hourly worker participation	Occasional	Rare	Rare	Extensive

[a] "Successful" team initiatives involve formally-initiated changes in workplace governance that expand hourly workers' autonomy, foster a heightened level of commitment to the firm, and blur the boundaries between hourly and salaried employees. "Failed" initiatives are those that generate conflict and distrust, or create demands, for a return to traditional work systems. "Mixed-success" initiatives attain some measure of success, but conflicts and resentments remain.

[b] The Plant Improvement Process (PIP) involves employees in project teams charged with improving mill operations in specific and measurable ways. Teams are commissioned by a Leadership Team, to which they are accountable.

requiring workers to rotate jobs as the situation requires) and pay-for-knowledge systems of compensation (that reward the accumulation of new skill sets). Most team members have responsibility for a functional area (such as production, quality, or safety), which requires frequent reporting to and consultation with team members. The 10 team initiatives I studied are described in Table 24.1, which enumerates each and provides data summarizing the outcome and number of workers involved as well.

A second category of workplace transformation involved a *continuous improvement initiative*. This effort, which I call Plant Improvement Process (PIP), for the most part began in 1994 when a leading management consulting firm introduced it on a trial basis at two of the firm's mills. Informed by lean theory, the principle underlying PIP was the effort to enhance mill performance in measurable ways without requiring increased capital investments. To achieve this goal, managers were instructed to seek the commitment of all employees, both hourly *and* salaried, encouraging them to share their production knowledge and expertise across organizational boundaries and ranks. By the time my fieldwork began in 1999, these two forms of workplace change had been underway for a minimum of four years, and in one mill for nearly a decade. Table 24.1 also provides data summarizing each mill's experience with PIP.

Viewed as a whole, my fieldwork gives rise to five important observations concerning U.S. Paper's efforts to break with traditional hierarchical work structures. First, even using relatively generous estimates (counting both "mixed" and "successful" cases as favorable outcomes), the data in Table 24.1 suggest that the aggregate impact of these nontraditional team initiatives has been quite limited. Even at Bordermill, the plant where labor relations have been the most cooperative, viable team systems have encompassed only 88 workers, or just under 10 percent of the mill's workforce. In none of the other mills has the penetration of workplace transformation exceeded this percentage—in most,

the number is considerably smaller. In short, efforts to transform the work systems in these mills have remained exceptional initiatives encompassing a small minority of workers. Moreover, these initiatives show little sign of expanding their reach.

Second, "successful" initiatives are confined to the smaller, traditional, cases where workers have invoked customary patterns . . . of machine control rather than the more elaborate systems that human resource managers have preferred. In these smaller, traditional initiatives—Cases 3, 4, 6, and 8—highly skilled workers have in effect used management's wish to cut supervisory layers to gain de facto rights of self-management over their own production areas. As one manager told me (referring to the workers in Case 3), "They run that machine the way they like, and they don't call us unless the place is burning up." Likewise, in Case 8 at Mountainmill, when the human resource manager proposed a high-performance work system for a small pulping department, the operators rejected his proposal in favor of their own, preferred arrangement. In the larger production areas, by contrast, where human resource managers *have* introduced the more highly formalized systems (Cases 2, 5, and 10), the results have been significantly less favorable, achieving only "mixed" success at best. In these latter cases, team initiatives have gained a measure of acceptance, and workers do welcome the reduced closeness of supervision they entail. But there is little evidence of a sharp change in workers' attitudes toward their jobs or in their perceptions of salaried employees. Substantial residues of conflict and resistance toward management persist in these instances, with workers often refusing to participate in key features of the new work systems (such as job rotation).

Third, even these limited gains have been offset by instances (Cases 1 and 7, and to a lesser extent Case 9) in which team initiatives have quite dramatically and visibly collapsed amid accusations of deception and betrayal running in both directions.[6] These instances of failure are especially important, not only because of the heightened distrust toward management they produce among the workers who were directly involved but also because such experiences typically ripple outward into the adjoining production areas, reaffirming the traditional boundaries that exist among other workers as well.

Fourth, although the company has invested thousands of hours in PIP, and has derived significant cost savings, steering committees and PIP teams at three of the mills have remained almost entirely the domain of salaried employees (especially process engineers), with participation by hourly workers remaining extremely rare.[7] Moreover, very little connection has been formed between PIP and the efforts to introduce team systems: The two categories of workplace change have essentially run in parallel, with few if any points of interaction between them. This has reinforced the relative isolation of existing team initiatives, while depriving PIP of any strong normative or moral component that might engage the energies of hourly employees.

Fifth, Table 24.1 also reveals an important exception to the prevailing pattern of limited organizational change. At New-Town, PIP has developed much more fruitfully than elsewhere, engaging hourly workers to a far greater extent than at the other three mills, despite the inauspicious labor relations in place when it was first introduced. Indeed, NewTown's version of PIP has achieved a far-reaching change in authority relations not evident elsewhere in the firm. This disparity in the development of PIP warrants careful discussion and analysis below.

Thus, despite the resources the company has invested, the overall pattern is one in which new production concepts have registered only limited success. Nontraditional team systems have in effect remained islands in a sea of adversarial work relations. Although the company has invested energy and resources in PIP, and has in fact reaped some economic benefits, the predominant pattern has been one in which the boundary between salaried and hourly workers has been largely reproduced and in some cases apparently inflamed (cf. Milkman 1997; Prechel 1994).

The issue to be addressed, then, centers on the conditions that account for the tenacity of the Fordist regime. What social and organizational processes have inhibited workplace change, forestalling the spread of new work practices and confining them within particular departmental boundaries? Why have efforts to adopt innovative work systems remained relatively undeveloped and isolated phenomena within particular production areas? Why have three of the company's mills shown so little movement toward "transformed" work practices, while one mill has so clearly surpassed them in this regard? And why has the continuous improvement process been so starkly dominated by salaried employees?

Normative Deficiencies Within Team Systems

Both advocates and critics of team systems contend that the new work practices hinge on the articulation of a normative pattern of control that encourages employees to internalize a sense of commitment or moral obligation to the organization's goals (Graham 1995; Kunda 1992; Zuboff 1988). I found little evidence of such a trend. To be sure, managers did take some steps in this direction. At the start-up of Mountainmill's new paper machine (Case 7), production crews were trained in numerous "soft skills," whose content (e.g., conflict resolution and team leadership) was oriented toward generating worker commitment to the team initiative and to the success of the new machine. During the course of my fieldwork, the company also adopted new "leadership development" workshops as well as a new "Core Values" policy that outlined the company's moral commitments, in these ways signaling management's aim of engaging the allegiances of its employees.

Yet overall, such efforts played a decidedly minor role in the everyday operations of these mills. Indeed, when my fieldwork began, symbolic gestures (such as the hosting of dinners honoring the achievements of particular production crews) had been dramatically curtailed, usually on budgetary grounds. Moreover, many workers on team systems felt frustrated at the company's reluctance to provide sufficient facilitators on shift to support their team initiatives. It was hard to escape the conclusion that managers tended to view the normative or cultural elements of the new work practices as holding only secondary importance, instead focusing the bulk of their attention on the technical and financial aspects of production. As a result, the social and cultural aspects of workplace change went largely unaddressed, placing sharp limitations on the team initiatives U.S. Paper introduced.

I observed three distinct ways in which such limitations arose. The first developed where workplace rules grew weak, inconsistent, or ill-defined—conditions that approximate what Hodson (1999, 2001) has termed the "anomic workplace." A second emerged where status distinctions among hourly workers were imported into the new team systems, undermining the possibility of cooperation and coordination within production crews. A third arose where managers were compelled to rely on their personal resources—most notably, charismatic authority—in ways that proved highly volatile or unstable, sometimes leading to the collapse of nontraditional initiatives in highly public ways. Although these conditions are analytically distinct, empirically they often combined, not only with one another but also with other factors to be discussed below.

Workplace anomie. Although U.S. Paper's executives had made a commitment to reconfigure the firm's internal operations, the precise contours of their efforts in some ways remained highly ambiguous. Most notably, their obvious commitment to the ideal of continuous improvement coexisted uneasily with their support for worker self-direction, without ever specifying precisely how these elements would combine in actuality. Not surprisingly, given such inconsistencies at the corporate level, efforts to develop team systems sometimes developed abiding ambiguities and inconsistencies at the point of production itself. Such anomic conditions in the work rules governing particular initiatives often provided the basis for conflicting interpretations that in turn generated substantial discord, suspicion, and distrust. This was the case at Bordermill and Mountainmill (Cases 1 and 7), where team initiatives ultimately resulted in bitter and highly public failures.

The events that unfolded at Bordermill occurred on a new converting (rewinding and packaging) machine that was introduced in the mid-1990s. Although both plant and corporate management hoped that this team system would spread outward into the surrounding production areas, the initiative instead rapidly escalated into bitterness and accusations on either side. Within a year, management concluded that workers had used the team system merely to gain higher wages, without offering any increased work effort in return. For their part, workers felt that management was using the team system to undercut key provisions of their collective bargaining contract, thereby reducing the local union's strength. Such discord stemmed partly from two ambiguities in the work rules that governed the new team system. One involved the role of workers' seniority rights; the second centered on the distribution of pay-for-skill wage increments.

The first of these issues emerged in the selection of workers for assignment to the team system. Although the collective bargaining agreement was unclear on this point, managers believed that when vacancies occurred on the team system, they had the right to fill such openings without being encumbered by the contract's seniority provisions. Hourly workers interpreted the agreement quite differently and reacted with sharp resentment when workers hired off the street began to earn much higher pay (owing to the pay-for-skill system used in this case) than did the workers who had been at Bordermill for years. Senior workers saw this as a slap in the face and began to view the team system as a means of pitting young workers against old.

Magnifying the intensity of this seniority conflict was an ambiguity in the pay-for-skill system both parties had devised: When pay increments were delayed for months while a certification system was established, workers began to suspect that the department's manager was intentionally dragging his feet in order to minimize his production costs. Effort levels began to fall off noticeably—workers stopped rotating jobs, and production quotas went unmet for months at a time—in turn redoubling management's determination to sidestep the traditional seniority system. This production area has been shrouded in conflict and acrimony for several years now, with many workers now viewing it as "a joke."

Equally anomic conditions, although in a different form, arose when the new paper machine was installed at Mountainmill (Case 7). As a very old mill, Mountainmill had accumulated a complex melange of work rules, many of which were poorly documented.[8] Adding a new team system only complicated the situation, as it gave rise to an elaborate array of rules based alternately on custom, the collective bargaining contract, and the new cooperative agreement, with each side resorting to one or another set of rules in accordance with its needs.

During the start-up of the new machine at Mountainmill, a spirit of cooperation persisted until disputes arose over the rules surrounding holiday and funeral pay, which eventually escalated into a major battle concerning the distribution of overtime among maintenance workers in traditional and non-traditional areas of the mill. These disputes prompted management to shift its understanding of the team concept, retreating from its commitment to self-directed work teams in ways that left the coordinates of the new initiative that much more ambiguous. When an arbitrator ruled in favor of the workers on the overtime grievance, management refused to pay, and the cooperative relationship management had sought with its hourly employees gave way to intense discord. As one worker put

if, with only a little exaggeration: "The only thing that keeps [the mill manager] alive is the company's 'no-weapons' policy."

The cases briefly described here involve situations in which managers and workers reached what they thought was a clear understanding of the rules that would govern the transition from traditional to nontraditional work systems. Yet, despite the apparent clarity, the process of change brought forward highly charged events and situations that revealed such understandings to be fraught with ambiguities. Such anomic conditions created the space for sharply conflicting definitions of the situation and of the motives each party attributed to the other, leading to the collapse of both team initiatives. When my fieldwork concluded, few workers continued to comply with the expectations of these two team systems, and the initiatives were widely viewed as deeply troubled efforts at best. Many managers acknowledged that their planning for the team initiatives was much too hastily completed, especially when compared with the careful planning and the abundant resources devoted to the technical aspects of the new machine systems.

Status distinctions among hourly employees. Normative deficiencies in the new team systems found a second form of expression in demographically based status distinctions, especially across gender and racial lines. Analysts of workplace change have neglected these factors until quite recently (Ollilainen and Rothschild 2001; Townsend and Scott 2001), but my evidence suggests that such distinctions warrant much more attention than they have received.

On many converting machines, jobs are embedded within "lines of progression" (job ladders) that reach upward from highly routinized jobs at the sealing and wrapping ends of the machine to more highly skilled and better paying jobs at the winding end. Because work at the winders has strategic effects on the quality of subsequent operations, winder operators enjoy considerable informal authority. And because the winder's job is a heavy and arduous one, entailing the lifting of heavy metal chucks (spools), the work has historically been defined as a "man's job." Fearing both the physical and social consequences that might flow from their performance of such jobs, women have been loathe to move upward in the line of progression. As a result, a sexual division of labor is apparent within traditionally organized converting areas, with men generally controlling the winder's jobs and women clustered at the sealing and wrapping ends of the machines. Moreover, because the men have taken decades to work their way upward in the line of progression, they tend to develop a strong identification with their jobs and grow highly reluctant to perform less skilled tasks at the other end of their machines. My data suggest that *these gender boundaries are often imported into the new team systems,* establishing powerful impediments to the flexibility and job rotation that the new systems presuppose.

This pattern was most clearly apparent at Pinetown's new converting machine (Case 5). This machine was installed in the mid-1990s using a team system that has had mixed effects. The new production area was more heavily mechanized than the older converting machines at Pinetown, easing the physical burdens of the work considerably. The machine was designed to encourage a cooperative and flexible deployment of labor, and workers were expected to develop operational proficiency at both ends of the machine (winding *and* wrapping). In theory, this obligated the operators to work "flexibly"—to provide cooperation and mutual support across traditional job boundaries and to accept rotating job assignments, whether during a given shift or from one shift to the next. But in practice, things have not worked out this way.

Although women workers did tend to participate in job rotation, working either end of the machine as circumstances required, the same cannot be said for the men. The great majority of men steadfastly clung to the winding end of the machines, resisting suggestions that they take their turns at the wrapping end. Moreover, most of the men I observed were reluctant to

help women workers at the wrapper except under the most urgent conditions. The women resented having to nag the men for help—the domestic parallels are obvious here—but little change has been forthcoming. The situation is described in the following excerpt from my field notes, taken at Pinetown's new converting department.

> I stroll over to talk with Kiner and Gun. . . . They're on the #10 winder, sitting for a bit as the machine seems to do well. We talk a little about the work system, and both Gun and Kiner say they don't see any reason to rotate. The reasons they give are several—they don't feel really proficient on the wrapper, they are more comfortable running the winder—but they simply seem more attached to the winders, and don't want to be bothered with other parts of the machines. Kiner mentions that there is tension among crew members—"people get the red ass for whatever reason"—and he allows that most of the conflict does seem to happen across the winder and wrapper end of the machines. Asked why, he says it's because "you know what women are like—they tend to fight more when they're put together. You know what I mean?" From the wrapper end, the argument is one of resentment at the winder operators' refusal to pitch in and help their fellow crew members. But from the perspective of the men, it's really just a question of women who fight and nag too much, as women are "prone" to do. (Pinetown, March 24, 2000)

A similar pattern emerged again a few days later:

> Larry's got his hands full right now—his winder is repeatedly jamming and needs careful coaxing. So I move over to talk with Ernie for a while. He's over by one of the winders, as usual. I ask him whether there's ever much conflict among team members. Laughing at the question, he says "My Lord, yes!"—especially between the men and the women. He explains: "You got the women going 'yap yap yap' [motions with his hands to indicate flapping jaws]. You know how

women are? They want everything like they want it. But we took care of that." He means that, as shop steward, he was able to find ways of reducing the obligation of senior workers to participate in job rotation. (Pinetown, March 26, 2000)

All of the evidence indicates that *gender boundaries run like an implicit seam across this converting machine,* defining one side of it as a man's territory and the other side of it as women's—constraining its functioning in various ways.

Racial boundaries sometimes played a similar role, as was especially apparent in Bordermill. Although work relations at this mill were generally, but not entirely, amicable, and the local union has elected an African American to an important position in the recent past, there are sharp racial disparities in the composition of its various departments. For example, the overwhelming majority of workers in the converting department (in which Case 1 was embedded) were African Americans—a situation that stands in sharp contrast with the racial composition of the mill's other production areas and with the make-up of the supervisory force. Senior black workers believe that such racial disparities stem from discriminatory practices during the 1960s and 1970s, when converting was "a man-killer's job" (as one worker put it) and came to be race-typed. Although there was little evidence of present discrimination, a sharp boundary was evident between the white supervisory force and the department's largely black workforce, introducing important elements of distrust into the department's team system (Case 1) and multiplying the intensity of the conflicts engendered by the organizational ambiguities discussed above.

This fact was apparent in the selection of employees for assignment to the new converting machine, as suspicion arose among some minority workers that management would try to favor whites for these higher-paying jobs. At least one African American worker chose to apply for the team system only when he and his friends concluded

that whites would otherwise be preferred. Later, when the pay-for-skill system was delayed, a group of minority workers felt that neither the company nor the local union was acting in good faith and circulated a petition alleging discrimination on the part of management and their union. The minority workers in this production area were relatively senior, and most could recall the dirty and undesirable jobs black workers were initially assigned. Many felt that they had already paid their dues in multiple ways and saw little reason to provide the intense work effort their white supervisors demand.[9]

The limits of charismatic authority. Given the relative lack of organizational attention to the normative aspects of workplace change, some managers felt compelled to resort to an extraordinary, person-centered form of authority as a means of establishing a common bond across the class divide. Such charismatic forms of authority did for a time inspire in team members the feeling that they were embarking on an especially significant mission that warranted sacrifices and a selfless orientation they would not ordinarily embrace. However, such charismatic bonds ultimately proved highly volatile. In the absence of structural supports, the establishment of charismatic authority tended to displace social conflicts in a lateral direction, fostering disputes among production crews. These conflicts, coupled with the "shocks" of managerial succession, rendered team systems based on charismatic authority impossible to sustain:[10]

The use of charismatic authority was especially apparent in the case of a business manager who oversaw the installation of Mountainmill's new paper machine (Case 7). This man, an experienced manager I will call Joseph, positioned himself as a visionary leader of the start-up of the new machine and its team initiative. Once the workforce was selected, training in both "hard" and "soft" skills was provided in a schoolhouse adjacent to the mill. Workers recall feeling part of an inspiring endeavor that was opening up new paths in the industry's history. This perception even found expression in the technical training that workers received, which was often provided by Joseph himself. Under his tutelage, workers who gained formal knowledge (replete with "diplomas" and graduation ceremonies) were encouraged to think of themselves as a distinguished group of employees, apart from and above their counterparts in the older, traditional parts of the mill. By establishing sharp distinctions between "his" team members and the hourly workers they had left behind, Joseph succeeded in blurring the boundary between salaried and hourly workers in the new area of the mill.

This aspect of the start-up is remembered quite vividly by workers in all areas of this mill. One member of the start-up crew recalled Joseph encouraging his workers to believe that *"we* walk up *here* [gestures with one hand] while other workers walk down *here* [other hand, lower]."* Said a worker in the traditional production area of this mill: "It was like they were the special child. Here we were, running the mill and keeping things afloat, and *they* were off *studying* things." Another worker recalls coworkers whom he'd known since grade school snubbing him in the supermarket, as if he were no longer worthy of attention. Such divisions established sharp limits on the possible application of team systems, which the older parts of Mountainmill came to view with disdain. They also jeopardized the cooperation needed across different parts of the production complex, with information sharing across the mill sometimes becoming strained. When I asked one worker in the new production area whether he'd ever think about going back to the older department from which he came, he immediately said no. When I took this as a measure of support for the team system, he quickly corrected my interpretation: "You have to understand—if I went back over there, *those guys would kick my ass!"*

Eventually, even as anomic conditions took their toll on the team system, Joseph was promoted to general manager of the Mountainmill plant, a position that required him to adopt a new relation toward the workers he had previously managed. As he sought to cope with the needs of multiple departments within the mill, and as his successors proved unable to sustain the charismatic bonds he had established, team members increasingly felt betrayed and manipulated, and they eventually played leading roles in the effort to discredit Joseph in the eyes of corporate executives. His person-centered work regime in effect produced his own downfall. When "his" workers brought particularly damning information to light, he eventually had to resign.

The Thrust for Efficiency: Continuous Improvement, Contradiction, and Corporate Control

Thus far I have suggested that management's orientation toward the production process led it to neglect the *normative* components of the very team systems the company sought to introduce. This deficiency left the new team systems vulnerable to dislocations in varying forms. Related to this tendency was a second source of weakness in the company's new work practices, as was especially apparent in the Plant Improvement Process (PIP), its continuous improvement program. Here what occurred was a tendency to stress the *rational* components of production so heavily as to introduce significant tensions and contradictions into the process of workplace change. Because of the value that management attached to scientific and technical rationality, PIP evolved into an expert-centered initiative that eventually stood at odds with the notion of worker participation itself.

Management's emphasis on scientific and technical rationality imposed two distinct limitations upon PIP. First, it often brought two distinct and incompatible logics to bear on the new team initiatives, eventually giving rise to inherently contradictory regimes on the new paper machines. Second, as part of the firm's commitment to strengthening the technical basis of its internal operations, management adopted a centralized, corporate-wide system governing PIP, lending this program a rigidity that limited its ability to engage hourly workers or to respond to local needs.

Conflicting logics. My fieldwork provides data on social relations at three newly installed paper machines. Two of these had incorporated nontraditional work systems (Case 2 at Bordermill and Case 7 at Mountainmill). A third machine, installed at Pinetown, relied on a traditional work system and is thus not shown in Table 24.1.

It is vital to understand that a new paper machine often requires the investment of massive amounts of capital (sometimes in excess of $500 million) and time. Once installed, a new machine commonly generates the bulk of a mill's daily tonnage, which means that any downtime has a major financial impact on both the plant and the corporate division to which it belongs. Such accumulation pressures provide corporate executives with a powerful incentive to ensure that local production managers leave very little to either chance or to the discretion of their hourly employees. For these reasons, executives in each corporate division pursued multiple strategies for reducing the uncertainties that accompanied the operation of their new paper machines. The most obvious result was an effort, beginning in the early 1990s, to impose a system of "best practices" throughout the company's operations.

This effort, which involved the application of detailed grade recipes (directives governing machine operations), took particular force where new paper machines had been introduced. Reinforced by corporate audits of each production area, the system encouraged plant-level business managers and superintendents to "drive out the variation" within the production process— that is, to ensure that operators applied company-defined process settings rather than basing machine operations on their own idiosyncratic ideas. Managers and process engineers wholeheartedly embraced the best practices initiative, seeing it as a way of optimizing the production process. Operators responded differently, seeing the best practices as an ill-defined

and often counterproductive system that infringed on their own knowledge and proper sphere of authority.

Such conflicts, common on many of the paper machines I observed, were especially heated on the new paper machines where team systems had been introduced. In these cases, production crews that were recruited on the promise of greater autonomy confronted managerial practices that instead limited their control over machine operation. Here, management's effort to quantify and standardize machine operations came into conflict with its effort to foster self-direction, giving rise to inherently contradictory regimes that were torn between two distinct logics.[11] On one side stood a logic of *standardization* that flowed from corporate management's attachment to a high-volume conception of production (as evident in the system of best practices). Yet on the other side was a logic of *participation*, arising from the effort to establish self-directed teams of autonomous production crews. Such contradictory pressures generated substantial levels of discord and disillusionment, with workers commonly complaining of being made to feel "handcuffed" or "like puppets on a string."

Resentment was especially apparent on the new paper machines at Bordermill and Mountainmill (Cases 2 and 8). At Bordermill, the company had introduced a new, state-of-the-art paper machine in the early 1990s and introduced a self-directed team system that most operators had embraced. Yet shortly after the start-up, severe technical problems developed with the machine's head box (a key component that initiates the formation of the sheet), leading to significant amounts of downtime. Seeking to maintain the confidence of the corporate executives, the plant's production manager (appropriately nicknamed "T-Rex") insisted on applying the firm's best practices as fervently as possible, denying operators the authority to change critical process settings regardless of the situation. This approach led to lingering resentment and widespread perceptions of managerial hypocrisy. . . .

Similar developments unfolded at Mountainmill's new paper machine (Case 7), where decisions concerning the selection of important equipment and materials began to be made over the heads of the production teams, compounding the workers' suspicions about management's motives. While working the graveyard tour, for example, the D shift discovered that a large tear had opened up in their machine's wire (an expensive plastic mesh needed to drain water from liquid pulp). Contrary to customary procedures, the crew was forced to wait several hours until a manager authorized the obvious repair—and even then, the workers were told that only *the vendor* could install a new wire (a decision they found insulting). In another case, a highly skilled worker was chastised for using a greater amount of defoaming agent than the grade recipe allowed—a trivial intervention, about which his manager knew far less than did the worker himself. In still another case, a production crew on this machine encountered a major spillage, but was unable to reach their superintendent. Forced to take action, they responded by shutting down their machine—a reasonable decision, in the eyes of a maintenance supervisor at least, but one that infuriated their superintendent, who nearly broke the hinges on their control room door when he was told of their decision. Workers took this as yet another sign that management viewed the language of self-direction as empty rhetoric.

The result of these contradictions was a pervasive sense of frustration and betrayal among hourly workers. Some workers accepted the standardization of their jobs, despite their previous aspirations ("making broke don't pay the bills"). Other workers voiced a sense of indignation and resignation ("You begin to wonder why they keep you on the payroll if they think so little of your ability. Wouldn't you feel that way?"). Ironically, the newly installed paper machine that used a traditional work system— the one located at Pinetown—manifested substantially fewer contradictions, resulting in a markedly lower incidence of conflict and discontent, despite the generally adversarial character of labor relations at this mill.

Centralized corporate control. Reflecting the emphasis that U.S. Paper has placed on the achievement of technical efficiency, all four of its mills employed PIP, the company's continuous improvement program. Yet beneath the apparent identity of this effort can be found substantial variations in the nature and evolution of the PIP initiative across the different plants: Three mills—Pinetown, Bordermill, and Mountainmill—adopted variants of PIP that were a direct outgrowth of the corporate-mandated program, while at NewTown, PIP evolved earlier and proceeded down a different and much more locally defined path. These divergent patterns had enormous consequences and warrant careful scrutiny.

The dominant variant of PIP first emerged during the mid-1990s, when a group of senior executives and consultants designed and introduced an elaborate continuous improvement program. Implementation of this program was delegated to a cadre of 20 corporate staff members, who conducted extended site visits at each mill, training plant managers and process engineers in the system they were expected to adopt. At each initial site visit, the corporate staff conducted a "diagnostic analysis" that specified the cost reductions, broken down by business unit, that each mill would be expected to achieve. Formal evaluations (innocuously called "10,000 Mile Check Ups") were later conducted to determine each mill's relative success. Salaried employees were made to understand that their career development would hinge to a considerable extent on their enthusiastic compliance with PIP.

Implementation of PIP in this manner imposed three significant characteristics on the initiative, which were apparent at all of the mills except NewTown. First, PIP's focus was centered narrowly on mill performance and production costs. Second, PIP operated under the authority of business unit managers and process engineers, with only weak provisions made for the inclusion of hourly employees. Third, the program had few if any connective links to team initiatives, instead operating as a specialized province dedicated above all to generating enhanced economic returns.

The development of these features can most easily be seen at Pinetown, which was one of the first mills to adopt the corporate variant of PIP. In keeping with corporate directives, the plant established a steering committee composed of the mill's senior business managers. "Breakthrough" teams were commissioned on a variety of tasks, and were led by salaried personnel (mainly superintendents and engineers). Initially, the program met with some enthusiasm; a few teams succeeded in recruiting hourly workers alongside salaried employees. After the initial waves of activity, however, difficulties began to emerge. Salaried employees began to feel overwhelmed by the sheer demands on their time, and the program began to show diminishing returns. Hourly worker participation fell off dramatically. When corporate executives grew dissatisfied with the results, key members of the plant's management were replaced. Their successors managed to infuse the program with a heightened sense of urgency, but also reinforced PIP's hierarchical character, imbuing the program with an efficiency imperative that placed even greater limitations on the involvement of hourly employees. . . .

Yet the limits on worker involvement clearly lay far beyond the reach of any "breakthrough" team and reached deep into the very way PIP had been conceived and introduced. By vesting control over the program within the mill's senior business managers and process engineers, focusing its work single-mindedly on efficiency improvements, and pressuring engineers to deliver performance gains timed to coincide with quarterly business reviews, corporate managers had set in motion a set of organizational processes that inevitably reproduced the boundary between salaried and hourly employees. Not surprisingly, even when operators *did* attend PIP meetings, they often came away shaking their heads and resolving never to return!

One instructive example emerged in Mountainmill, where a PIP team was established to reduce the use of starch on the mill's new paper machine. The team leader, a process engineer, began by taking some technical readings and modeling the expected variation in starch consumption on the basis of theoretical assumptions that seemed plausible to him and the other salaried employees on this team. The work unfolded with little involvement from hourly workers until one dissenting engineer made an effort to consult with production crews, eliciting a number of suggestions he felt were highly promising. His counterparts were loathe to pursue the new ideas, however, fearing that a change of direction might delay their progress report. Eventually, the team submitted a favorable report on time, but completely ignored the hourly workers' ideas. Although the team leaders claimed to have achieved significant cost savings, the report was later found to have used erroneous process readings. Although the hourly workers felt vindicated, none of the operators on this machine bothered to participate in PIP from that point on.[12] . . .

Conclusion

I have set out to achieve two goals: To characterize the process of workplace change at four manufacturing plants during the 1990s; and to identify the major social and organizational conditions that have affected the course of workplace transformation. Using qualitative methods, this study contributes a number of findings that hold significance for both the theory and the practice of workplace change.

First, and at the most general level, the study provides an image of workplace change that is at odds with the idealized conception of team systems found among both advocates and critics of the new work systems alike. Rather than articulating a heavily normative or moral rhetoric, the firm studied here generally exhibited little inclination to develop an overarching normative orientation that might elicit the commitment of its hourly employees. Indeed it was precisely management's inattention to such normative matters that left the firm's work systems vulnerable to both anomic tendencies and to inherited status distinctions among hourly workers, both of which limited the functioning of team initiatives. Such normative deficiencies also compelled plant managers to rely on their own personal resources, invoking charismatic patterns of authority in lieu of broader organizational symbols and ideals. Such person-centered efforts ultimately proved highly volatile and unstable, inviting conflicts that proved difficult for management to contain.

A second set of obstacles to workplace transformation stemmed from the rhetorical constructs that were apparent in these mills. Most salient in this respect was a heavily rationalist, quantitatively based conception of production that was favored by process engineers at various levels within the firm. This approach was especially manifest in the company's implementation of best practices and continuous improvement processes, both of which emphasized the need to standardize machine operations, using scientific expertise as the basis for process control. Although this expert-centered orientation enabled engineers to claim positions of increased centrality within most of these mills, it imposed sharp constraints on the discursive legitimation of the new work practices. The result introduced salient contradictions into the company's production areas, limiting the degree to which workplace change might effectively proceed.

These findings hold a number of implications for previous efforts to explain the limits of workplace change. Labor relations researchers might argue that these findings stem from the inherent character of lean production itself. From this point of view, the firm's stress on best practices and the standardization of production methods, coupled with its relatively weak emphasis on the normative or integrative aspects of organizational life, represent signature expressions of the quality movement and its overly quantitative, Deming-based outlook. Although this interpretation has some merit—studies of Total Quality Manage-

ment in particular do resonate with the present study's results (cf. Klein 1994; Prechel 1994; Vallas and Beck 1996)—such an approach overlooks the variations that emerged even where the same form of workplace change was involved.

Recall that all four of the mills in this study made a determined effort to introduce continuous improvement initiatives throughout their production areas, and they did so with an eye toward enhancing the performance of mill operations. Yet, as this study has shown, *the same initiative unfolded in very different ways:* Under conditions of centralized corporate control, plant managers had little capacity to adapt the program so to suit local needs, generating a palpably hierarchical outcome that only reproduced the boundary between salaried and hourly employees. By contrast, under conditions of local autonomy, the same initiative seemed far more malleable, evolving in ways that generated significantly higher levels of normative integration across the salaried/hourly divide. Thus, rather than viewing the outcome of particular work practices as unmediated reflections of their essential traits (Hunter et al. 2002), we need to acknowledge that even similar managerial practices are likely to manifest highly variable features, in keeping with the conditions under which they are introduced (Katz 1985). . . .

Discussion Questions

1. Put yourself in the position of a plant manager or a union leader, and consider how you would try to develop self-directed work teams.

2. What incentives can be used to get workers and supervisors to make continuous improvements in their work?

3. What do you think of working in teams? Would you like it, or are you more of a "lone ranger"?

4. How does a focus on productivity work against the development of a strong

normative climate of cooperation in the workplace?

Steven P. Vallas, "Why Teamwork Fails: Obstacles to Workplace Change in Four Manufacturing Plants," in *American Sociological Review* Vol. 68, No. 2 (Apr. 2003), pp. 223–250. Reprinted with permission of the American Sociological Association.

Endnotes

1. Throughout the following analysis, I rely on Barley and Kunda's (1992) distinction between these two forms of organizational rhetoric and control (cf. Kunda 1992). By "rational" controls I mean an orientation toward production based primarily on the efficacy of scientific and technical expertise. By "normative" controls, I mean an orientation that seeks to cultivate a sense of moral obligation or allegiance to collectively defined goals.

2. Elsewhere, I have argued that the "hegemony" view of team systems exaggerates management's ability to reshape workers' orientations toward the firm (Vallas forthcoming a). Even in plants that are not unionized, I found that team systems actually increase worker solidarity over against their managers (cf. Hodson et al. 1993).

3. Zuboff's (1988) research is particularly important here. The firm she studied is known throughout the industry for its exceptional human resource practices. Although these practices have gained widespread prestige, they have generally failed to inspire substantial emulation within the industry as a whole. One question I pose is why Zuboff's "post-hierarchical workplace" has made such limited headway in recent years.

4. Of particular relevance are the efforts of Burawoy (1990, 1998), whose "extended case method" develops a strong program linking qualitative research with theory reconstruction (also see Barley 1996).

5. These 10 initiatives represent the population of such efforts in these mills, with one exception—a small production area in one mill, employing roughly 20 utility workers—where I was unable to gather sufficient data for inclusion in the analysis.

6. Case 7, discussed further below, is typical. The operators on this paper machine were once enthusiastic participants in their team system, but now bitterly refuse to comply with its dictates. They view plant management's behavior as utter manipulation through which a cohort of managers sought career advantages at the workers' expense.

7. Company data from Pinetown are illustrative. Of the 140 salaried employees who were potentially involved in PIP during the third wave of 2000, 132 participated (or 94.3 percent). By contrast, only 50 hourly employees (less than 5 percent) are listed as participants. My observations suggest that even these figures overestimate hourly worker participation. Pressured by managers to increase worker involvement, supervisors often report higher levels of worker participation than actually exist.

8. A flood had wiped out many of management's files, forcing them to rely on local union documentation. This fact, coupled with the mill's tendency to rely on customary agreements, left the status of many work rules chronically unclear, especially when shifts occurred in key management positions.

9. Interestingly, the successful team initiative in Bordermill's converting department (Case 3) was composed entirely of white employees, who enjoyed a greater sense of kinship with the department's managers (Townsend and Scott 2001; Vallas forthcoming b).

10. Surprisingly, despite the purported trend toward the dismantling of bureaucracies, there have been few recent studies of charismatic authority by sociologists of work and organizations. The bulk of the research on charismatic leadership has been driven by organizational psychologists (e.g., House, Spangler, and Woycke 1991; Shamir, House, and Arthur 1993). For an exception, see Biggart (1989).

11. For discussion of the concept of organizational logics, see DiMaggio (2001:230–36) and Stark (2001).

12. Similar patterns obtained at both Pinetown and Bordermill, with some hourly workers simply standing up in team meetings and declaring the meetings to be a waste of their time.

References

Adler, Paul S. 1992. "The 'Learning Bureaucracy': New United Motor Manufacturing, Inc." *Research in Organizational Behavior* 15:111–94.

Agger, Ben. 1991. "Critical Theory, Poststructuralism, Postmodernism: Their Sociological Relevance." *Annual Review of Sociology* 17:105–31.

Althauser, Robert and Arne Kelleberg. 1981. "Firms, Occupations, and the STructure of Labor Markets: A Conceptual Analysis." Pp. 119–49 in *Sociological Perspectives on Labor Markets*, edited by I. Berg. New York: Plenum.

Barker, James R. 1993. "Tightening the Iron Cage: Concertive Control in Self-Managing Teams," *Administrative Science Quarterly* 38:408–37.

——. 1999. *The Discipline of Teamwork: Participation and Concertive Control*. Thousand Oaks, CA: Sage.

Berggren, Christian. 1992. *Alternatives to Lean Production: Lessons From the Swedish Automobile Industry*. Ithaca, NY: ILR/Cornell University Press.

Cappelli, Peter. 1995. "Rethinking Employment." *British Journal of Industrial Relations* 33:563–602.

Graham, Laurie. 1995. *On the Line at Subaru-Isuzu*. Ithaca, NY: ILR/Cornell University Press.

Grenier, Guillermo. 1988. *Inhuman Relations*. Philadelphia, PA: Temple University Press.

Hannan, Michael T. and John Freeman. 1984. "Structural Inertia and Organizational Change." *American Sociological Review* 49:149–64.

Heckscher, Charles. 1988. *The New Unionism: Employee Involvement in the Changing Corporation*. New York: Basic.

——. 1994. "Defining the Post-Bureaucratic Type." Pp. 14–63 in *The Post-Bureaucratic Organization*, edited by C. Heckscher and A. Donnelloa. Thousand Oaks, CA: Sage.

Hodson, Randy. 1999. "Organizational Anomie and Worker Consent." *Work and Occupations* 26:292–323.

——. 2001. *Working With Dignity*. London, England: Cambridge University Press.

Hunter, Larry, John Paul MacDuffie, and Lorna Doucet. 2002. "What Makes Teams Take? Employee Reactions to Work Reforms." *Industrial and Labor Relations Review* 55:448–72.

Kalleberg, Arne. 2001. "The Advent of the Flexible Workplace: Implications for Theory and Research." Pp. 437–53 in *Working in Restructured Workplaces: Challenges and New Directions for the Sociology of Work*, edited by D. Cornfield, K. B. Campbell, and H. J. McCammon. Thousand Oaks, CA: Sage.

Kern, Horst and Michael Schumann. 1992. "New Concepts of Production and the Emergence of the Systems Controller." Pp. 111–48 in *Technology and the Future of Work*, edited by P. Adler. New York: Oxford University Press.

Klein, Janice. 1994. "The Paradox of Quality Management: Commitment, Ownership, and Control." Pp. 178–94 in *The Post-Bureaucratic Organization: New Perspectives on Organizational Change*, edited by C. Heckscher and A. Donnellon. Thousand Oaks, CA: Sage.

Kuhlmann, Martin and Michael Schumann. 2001. "What's Left? Workplace Innovation and Workers' Attitudes Toward the Firm." *Research in the Sociology of Work* 10:189–215.

Kunda, Gideon. 1992. *Engineering Culture*. Cambridge, MA: MIT Press.

Milkman, Ruth. 1997. *Farewell to the Factory*. Berkeley, CA: University of California Press.

Ollilainen, Marjukka and Joyce Rothschild. 2001. "Can Self-Managing Teams Be Truly Cross-Functional? Gender Barriers to a 'New' Division of Labor." *Research in the Sociology of Work* 10:141–64.

Powell, Walter W. 2001. "The Capitalist Firm in the Twenty-First Century: Emerging Patterns in Western Enterprise." Pp. 33–68 in *The Twenty-First Century Firm*, edited by P. DiMaggio. Princeton, NJ: Princeton University Press.

Prechel, Harland. 1994. "Economic Crisis and the Centralization of Control Over the Managerial Process: Corporate Restructuring and Neo-Fordist Decision-Making." *American Sociological Review* 59:723–45.

Smith, Vicki. 1997. "New Forms of Work Organization." *Annual Review of Sociology* 23:315–39.

——. 2001. *Crossing the Great Divide: Worker Risk and Opportunity in the New Economy*. Ithaca, NY: ILR/Comell University Press.

Townsend, Anthony and K. Dow Scott. 2001. "Team Racial Composition, Member Attitudes, and Performance: A Field Study." *Industrial Relations* 40:317–37.

Vallas, Steven P. 1999. "Rethinking Post-Fordism: The Meanings of Workplace Flexibility." *Sociological Theory* 17:68–101.

Vallas, Steven P. and John Beck. 1996. "The Transformation of Work Revisited: The Limits of Flexibility in American Manufacturing." *Social Problems* 43:339–61.

Zuboff, Shoshana. 1988. *In the Age of the Smart Machine*. New York: Basic. ✦

25

Inside a Japanese Transplant

Laurie Graham

The introduction of the so-called Japanese style of management into U.S. companies began in the 1980s and spread rapidly in the corporate world. A video describing the type of workers ("associates") sought by companies that embraced Japanese-style management lists the following eight qualities: (1) Team approach. Help out others. Teams frequently meet on their own time. (2) Quality is the top priority. All associates take part in quality discussion groups. (3) *Kaizen* means searching for a better way. (4) We must eliminate waste throughout the company. Working weekends or overtime when needed. Work tempo is fast and consistent. (5) Work flexibility. Multi-talented workers. (6) Job security is important to all of us. Continuous training leads to security. Security means safety. (7) Our spirit is enthusiastic involvement. Come to work every day on time. (8) Open communication builds mutual trust.

The author of this chapter worked in a Japanese automobile plant in the United States. She describes the reactions of workers to some of the eight principles listed above, including patterns of cooperation and resistance.

Since the 1970s, researchers have suggested that modern Japanese management provides a new cooperative, managerial model based on work force participation (Cole, 1979; Dore, 1973). Theorists argue that participation programs are potentially a winning situation for both parties (Piore & Sabel, 1984; Zwerdling, 1980), that "they engage workers' minds with the managerial aspects of their jobs" (Safizadeh, 1991, p. 61), and that they provide greater employee involvement in decision making thus improving worker satisfaction (Brown & Reich, 1989).

A different approach to the theme of participation suggests that it has the potential to expand worker control at the expense of management. It assumes that participation schemes give workers a level of control over their work, which will increase their expectations and cause them to seek even greater control (Derber & Schwartz, 1988; Edwards, 1979; Kornbluh, 1984). Both approaches share a common assumption that participation schemes potentially increase workers' control on the shop floor, one from a technical perspective, the other from a political perspective.

The automobile industry has become a focus of the debate about the transferability of participative schemes based on the Japanese approach (Brown & Reich, 1989). Research by Florida and Kenney (1991) concerning Japanese transplants suggests that management has been successful in transferring the Japanese model to the United States. However, their analysis measures success by the mere existence of structures. Worker response to those structures was not assessed.

Distinctive features of Japanese management are the extraordinary commitment, identification, and loyalty employees exhibit toward their firms (Lincoln & Kalleberg, 1985, p. 738). Theorists argue that participation schemes and, more specifically, the "Japanese experience rejects the assumption that technological advance occurs only at the expense of employees . . . [instead] Japanese managers have succeeded in blending technological improvements with good human relations" (Hull & Azumi, 1988, p. 427). The assumption behind this body of work is a belief in the fundamental compatibility of the interests of workers and management (Blauner, 1964).

Research has challenged this compatibility and the assumption that participatory methods lead to greater worker control (Fantasia, Clawson, & Graham, 1988; Graham, 1985). Participation is viewed as a conscious attempt to undermine current union organization (Parker, 1985; Parker & Slaughter, 1988; Slaughter, 1983) and to defeat future organizational drives (Grenier, 1988).

Two general questions emerge from these findings. The first is whether worker control is enhanced by the Japanese model; the second is if the intraorganizational components of Japanese management can be successfully transferred without a high level of cooperation and commitment from its employees.

The present research, involving a direct participant/observation in a Japanese automobile transplant, challenges the assumption that worker control is enhanced by this participatory scheme. In fact, these findings suggest the opposite. Ironically, *kaizening*[1] and decision making by consensus served to reinforce the unequal power relation between workers and management. During kaizening, management tightly controlled the topics that could be raised for consideration and decision making by consensus was simply a mirage. A legitimate consensus between management and workers, who are vulnerable to discipline or job loss, was simply impossible. Management controlled which decisions were reached because of the unequal relationship. Concerning the assumption that worker autonomy is increased through decentralized management structures, in the present case study, decentralized authority created a situation where workers had virtually no autonomy.

In addition to challenging the promises of enhanced worker control, the present findings challenge the successfulness of management's ability to transfer a Japanese intraorganizational environment to the United States. Emergent patterns of shop floor behavior indicate that Japanese management practices can result in a range of individual and collective resistance among U.S. workers. These findings provide additional insight concerning the nature and effectiveness of worker resistance. Workers participated in both spontaneous and planned resistance. Whether spontaneous or planned, only collective resistance pro-

duced the strength necessary to effectively challenge management's control on the shop floor. Two methods of resistance effectively upset the balance of power: collective, sustained resistance and collective, spontaneous resistance.

These findings support Fucini and Fucini's (1990) conclusion concerning adaptation problems with a different Japanese company (Mazda). When a political dimension, measured through shop floor behavior, is included in an examination of intraorganizational transference, these findings suggest that even though the structures of Japanese management are present, the way in which those structures are mediated by the work force does not indicate the successful transference assumed by Florida and Kenney (1991).

In the present analysis, seven components within the Japanese management structure are identified and each is examined in relation to worker compliance and resistance. The findings are evaluated in light of the labor process literature that addresses the nature of control at the point of production.

Theoretical Background

A clear definition of control at the point of production is difficult to pin down, because it involves a complex process of struggle between workers and management. Two aspects of control stand out in the literature. First, control is identified as possessing the technical knowledge of work, from conception through execution (Braverman, 1974). Management systems aimed at gaining control over the technical aspects of work have been identified as Taylorism (Braverman, 1974), despotic (Burawoy, 1985), direct (Friedman, 1977), and the technical component of hierarchical control (Edwards, 1979).

The second aspect of production control is the social aspect, located in workers' culture and reflected in their behavior toward the boss and each other at the point of production. The essence of this social aspect of control is described by Montgomery (1979) in the craft workers' ethos of brotherhood: a collective code in which the skilled worker was expected to assume a "manly posture" toward the boss, to control his or her own output through working a certain stint each day, to control the use of his or her time, and to enforce the quota by stopping "rate busters" (Montgomery, 1979). Theorists have categorized management systems that attempt to interfere with workers' social behavior as bureaucratic (Edwards, 1979), responsible autonomy (Friedman, 1977), and hegemonic (Burawoy, 1985).

For the purposes of this study, control is multidimensional, grounded in the context of the production process, possessing both technical and social aspects. The struggle for control over the technical aspect emerges as a worker attains special knowledge about each job. Even management's fragmenting the most technical task will not necessarily uncover the tricks that workers learn from each other or from the act of doing a particular process, tricks that often save the worker time and effort. According to labor process theory, this time becomes the focus of management's control. The social aspect of worker control is found in the workers' culture, which is reflected in behavior and the day-to-day relationships at the point of production. Management focuses on controlling shop floor culture in order to win a worker's total allegiance in its competitive struggle.

Research Setting and Data

The research focuses on the work experience within a single Japanese automobile transplant. From July 1989 through January 1990, I worked as a hidden participant/observer at Subaru-Isuzu Automotive (SIA) located near Lafayette, Indiana.[2] Both management and workers were unaware that they were under observation.

The intent of this research is to identify patterns of behavior that reflect the relationship among workers and between workers and management in their day-to-day work experience. The analysis is based on extensive field notes involving informal discussions with numerous co-workers and team members,[3] on day-to-day observations of co-worker and worker/management interactions, and on formal documents distributed by the company.

The analysis has many limitations, the greatest of which is that evidence concerning the nature and effectiveness of management's control strategies are deduced from the position of a worker. There is no way of knowing management's intentions; they can only be inferred from observations and documents. Another limitation concerns the time period of the study. It is unique because it is during the company's initial months of production. People working in the plant today are experiencing a faster assembly line, a second shift now exists, and temporary workers work side by side with regular employees. Another unique aspect of the start-up period is that a certain amount of excitement over beginning production existed among many workers; this excitement may dissipate as the newness wears off. On the other hand, the start-up also provides an ideal setting for management to take advantage of workers' optimism and to attempt to induce a spirit of cooperation and "pulling together" to beat the competition. Therefore, patterns that emerge contrary to this goal will serve as evidence of management's inability to gain control through cooperation and effectively transfer its intraorganizational environment.

A definite advantage of working during plant start-up was that it often allowed me free access to other areas within the plant. During start-up, there were problems getting the paint department up and running on a continuous basis. On several occasions, the line would be down for an entire day or, at least, for several hours at a time. When this occurred, we would find excuses to leave our area and investigate other parts of the plant. This enabled me to informally question workers from other areas and observe them at work. This was fortuitous, for when Chinoy (1955) worked on an assembly line as a participant/observer in an auto plant, he found that he was so tied to the line, that it was difficult to talk to other workers (Chinoy, 1955).

The setting for the bulk of the observations is the trim and final department of the plant. Trim and final is the most labor-intensive area of the plant, where Subaru cars and Isuzu trucks are assembled. The car and truck bodies entered our department as empty shells and were driven off the line ready to be sold.

I worked on Team 1 in car assembly. There were 12 team members plus a team leader. Team 1 was part of a group of four teams under one group leader. The group leader was the lowest-level salaried employee. A total of about 14 teams assembled the cars. Each worker was responsible for one station that, at that time, involved about 5 minutes of work on every car. We worked at a constant pace as the cars moved along the line, repeating the same set of tasks every 5 minutes.

Team 1 was the first team to work on the cars after they came out of paint (workers referred to the various departments, such as the paint department, simply as "paint"). When the cars were finished in paint, they were held in one of the overhead conveyer systems. Once on our conveyer, the bodies (cars were referred to as "bodies") were spaced about 3 or 4 feet apart.

There were a total of 67 workstations on both sides of the assembly line for assembling the cars. Team 1 was divided into 12 stations, 6 to a side. The stations and the people working them were referred to by their location on the line. In other words, when people referred to the work I performed, it was "one left." However, workers did not refer to one another by station location when away from the line.

The Japanese trainer organized Team 1 so that each person stayed on one side of the car and worked across from another team member. There was one exception. "One right" finished the work at that station, before "one left" began working, and each worked both sides of the car. Some of the parts were installed by two people, working across from one another, but most were installed by only one person.

On the line, each station (or person) had control of the car for a predetermined distance. Workers walked next to the moving car, installing parts as it moved through their area. Although the distance did not vary, the speed of the line could be changed so that the amount of time the team had to work on the car was increased or decreased. The tact time[4] was not supposed to vary from station to station; however, many of the processes did not work as smoothly as anticipated by the Team 1 trainer, so some stations took more time than others. In addition, most people simply did not work at exactly the same speed, so some workers just barely kept up. Also, after the start of production, the team was plagued by hand and wrist injuries (at one point, 7 out of the 12 team members had hand or wrist problems), which forced a change in the way certain parts were installed, usually involving more time. Finally, due to injuries, many workers were forced to work in wrist splints, which also slowed team members down.

When designing the Team 1 stations, the Japanese trainer used standardized times based on how long it took workers in Japan to install each part. The times were recorded to the tenth of a second, and the timing for the installation of each part was broken down step by step. From this, he calculated the number of stations necessary for installing all of the parts designated for our area within a tact time of 3 minutes and 40 seconds (the goal time for full production). He jokingly told team members, "We could each have an armchair at our station for resting between cars." The 5-minute tact time was a hectic pace for some and a reasonable pace for others.

"One left" was the station I became most familiar with, as it was the last station I was assigned. The following is a step-by-step account of that process.

1. Go to the car and take the token card (a metal plate that contained specific information for each vehicle) off a wire on the front of the car.

2. Pick up the 2 VIN (vehicle identification number) plates from the embosser and check the plates to see that they have the same number.

3. Insert the token card into the token card reader. This will cause the specifications for that car to be printed out on a broadcast sheet and a "spec" sheet.

4. While waiting for the computer output, break down the key kit for the car by pulling the three lock cylinders and the lock code from the bag.

5. Copy the vehicle control number (this number is the computer system number, which keeps track of the location of the car) and color number on to the appearance check sheet.

6. Inspect the car for damage sustained while in the paint department. Look over the outside of the car and open each door and inspect all areas that are not later covered up by some part. Mark down any scratches, chips, dents, or any other damage on a sketch of the car, which is located on the appearance check sheet.

7. Go to a rack and pick up a hood stay, the work basket (which contains plugs and grease), the hood jig (which holds up the hood while you install the hood stay), and lay them in the empty engine compartment.

8. Lift the hood and put the hood jig in place so it will remain open while installing the hood stay.

9. Insert the rubber hood stay grommet.

10. Insert the hood stay into the grommet, lift the hood, and prop it open with the hood stay. Insert a rubber hose at the top of the hood stay to insure that the hood will not fall while people work in the engine compartment.

11. Go to the printer and get the broadcast sheet (this alerts everyone down the line as to what options that particular vehicle will need). Check the VIN numbers on the sheet to the plates and ver-

ify that the plates match the coding for front- or four-wheel drive.

12. Attach the broadcast sheet to the front edge of the hood with masking tape.

13. Check the VIN number from the broadcast sheet to the number engraved on the car body at the back of the engine compartment.

14. From the work basket, pick up two rubber hood buffers and slide them onto the two hooks on either side of the engine compartment, so that the hood will rest on them when closed.

15. Pick up a right-side fender cover from the right side of the line and attach it over the right fender.

16. Pick up two screw grommets and the fender top grommet from the basket and insert them in the proper holes under the left front fender.

17. Attach the front left fender cover (located on the left side of the line) and remove the hood jig and the basket from the car.

18. Tear off the specification sheet from the second printer, attach it to the clip board with the appearance sheet, and put the key lock code on the specification sheet.

19. Collect the clipboard, the trunk lock cylinder, the token card, and the black VIN plate. Put everything except the clipboard in the box on the car carrier and insert the clipboard into the slot underneath the car on the carrier.

20. Get the riveter, the two door lock cylinders, pick up two rivets and the large VIN plate. Carry them to the car.

21. Toss the yellow cylinder to the passenger side, and place the white cylinder on the floor of the driver's side.

22. Rivet the large VIN plate to the left-hand center.

23. Begin with Step 1 on the next car.

In addition to the duties directly related to working on the line, each worker was responsible for keeping the stations neat and clean, recording the level of the "oilers" and pressure gauges on the air lines located above the stations, recording each car number, and keeping tools in good condition. The number of tasks that "one left" performed was typical of that at other stations. At the goal tact time, these tasks were to be completed in 3 minutes and 40 seconds.

Before "one left" finished with the car, "two left" and "two right" would have already begun. Whenever possible, each person tried to work ahead by beginning his or her station before the car actually crossed the line to enter his or her area. This gave the team an edge against breakdowns and parts shortages—the things that brought great emotional and physical stress because they caused the team to fall behind. Once behind, the team had to work intensely to catch up. Once the line speed began to increase toward goal tact time, the opportunity to work ahead steadily decreased and the Team 1 trainer ordered us to stop working ahead. Eventually, it became a moot point; there was no extra time. If someone on the team could see that another worker needed help, he or she would help if possible. It was, however, clearly a matter of pride to keep one's station under control and operating at the goal time.

As both the truck and car lines ran the length of trim and final and then back again in a "U" shape, Team 1 was located between the final line on the truck side and the final line on the car side. Team 1 was the first team to work on the cars and, at the same time, could see the finished product driven off the line.

In trim and final, a typical day began at 6:25 a.m. (5 minutes before the scheduled start of work) when music was played over the loudspeaker signaling morning exercises. After 5 minutes of exercises, the team members would stand in a circle for a meeting. When the paint department worked out its problems, and the line was moving throughout the day, the team meeting lasted no longer than 5 minutes, because the line started moving at 6:35 a.m. At the

end of the meeting, the team performed a daily ritual. Each person extended his or her left arm into the center of the circle, with the hand clenched into a fist. The team leader then called on one of the members to deliver an inspirational message to the team. The usual message was, "Let's have a safe and productive day." A few of the team members sometimes told a good-natured joke, making light of the ritual. After the message, all of the team members brought their right arms around into the circle with everyone's hands meeting in the center in clenched fists. While doing this, the members shouted "Yosh!" (a long "o" sound) and then broke up and went to work.[5]

At exactly 6:35 a.m. a buzzer sounded, and the assembly line began to move. At 8:30 a.m. it stopped for a 10-minute break. At 10:30 a.m. the line stopped for a half-hour, unpaid lunch. At 1:00 p.m. it stopped for another 10-minute break and at 3:00 p.m. the work day was over.

The type of work each team member performed varied as to its physical demands, its potential for injury, the speed in which it could be performed, and whether or not he or she was able to speak to other team members. For the most part, however, working on the line required a worker's undivided attention. During plant start-up, workers had time for conversation between each car and even while working the stations. As line speed increased, time for interactions between workers and periods of rest continually decreased. Increased line speed was also accompanied by the emergence of injuries. Once the speedup began, the workers experienced constant pressure from the assembly line. Everyone was forced to work at a continuous, rapid pace.

Findings

Of primary significance in the Japanese management scheme is its multidimensional structure. This multidimensional approach is most consistent with Burawoy's (1979) concept of hegemonic control, providing the qualification that Burawoy misses the resistance that is present in workers' adaptations in production (Thompson, 1989). Its goal is to gain workers' total cooperation in the company's competitive struggle.

Each component in this system of control does not seem very powerful when examined separately. When combined, however, they form a formidable obstacle to the individual worker. When workers failed to resist collectively, practices such as speedup and working off the clock were common. Some workers could be seen working during their breaks to get caught up, and others came in early to set up their stations. At the same time, however, this system of control gave rise to resistance by many workers. In general, it was only through collective action that workers were able to effect any balance in control on the shop floor.

To describe the full range of worker response and the dynamic nature of worker reaction to this system, the findings are divided into two sections: compliance and resistance. The first section connects examples of worker compliance to each component in the management's scheme. For this analysis, the management scheme at SIA is separated into seven components. Five components focused on controlling the social aspects of production:

1. Preemployment selection process.

2. Orientation and training for new workers.

3. The team concept.

4. A philosophy of kaizen.

5. Attempts at shaping shop floor culture.

Two components comprised the technical aspects of control:

6. The computerized assembly line.

7. Just-in-time production.

The second section analyzes the range and effectiveness of resistance to this management scheme.

Compliance to Management's Scheme

Selection process. The first component in SIA's system of control began before a worker was hired with a preemployment selection process. All applicants underwent a battery of tests and observed exercises. I began my attempt to gain employment at the company in February 1989, and 6 months later I was finally hired.

The selection process focused on eliminating potential workers. Applicants were evaluated after each step of the process and, if successful, were invited to participate in the next level of testing. The first step involved a 4-hour General Aptitude Test (GAT). Anyone who scored a certain percentile (when I applied it was above 85%) was invited to participate in Phase 1, a 4-hour exercise involving 20 applicants.

During Phase 1, the participants were divided into groups of five and each group participated in team scenarios involving problem-solving exercises. If an applicant passed the Phase 1 evaluation, then he or she would be invited to participate in Phase 2. Phase 2 involved approximately 8 hours of written attitude tests and timed exercises assembling parts. Following Phase 2, the successful applicants were scheduled for a physical examination and drug screening at a local clinic. The final step in the hiring process was an interview with three team leaders at the plant. Even though team leaders were hourly workers, they made the ultimate decision on hiring.

After I was hired, I discussed the selection process with other workers. The more cynical view was that most people had succeeded in being selected because they were smart and had figured out the process, not because they were team players. There was a general sentiment that SIA used the selection process to get rid of anyone the company considered undesirable. One person thought the process was an effort to screen out anyone who was not willing to be cooperative. Another said that the GAT was given to cut out anyone who was not fairly intelligent. One worker was pretty certain the whole selection process was aimed at exposing any union supporters.

Two workers responded positively when asked about the selection process. One person, in particular, believed that the selection process was fantastic. When describing how he felt, he said that, for once, it gave him the chance to be fairly evaluated because the process involved much more than simply filling out an application and hoping for an interview. "It gave guys like me, who didn't know the right people, a chance." He felt that SIA had actually "tapped into his potential," that the examiners had "really gotten to know him through the tests."

Based on their statements, it appears that many workers complied with the perceived terms and conditions of employment at SIA by involving themselves in a kind of charade. Even those who expressed apprehension about working in a team setting said that they had made an effort to appear cooperative and enthusiastic when interacting with other applicants during team scenarios. When questioned, several people stated that they really were not team players, that they would rather work alone if given the choice. Other workers stated that, right from the start, they knew what type of behavior the company was looking for. There were many sources from which potential employees could deduce the requisite qualities of the successful SIA worker. A booklet explaining the company's team philosophy was made available when applicants first filled out applications. Area newspapers ran several articles focusing on the company's "new style" of management based on a team concept that stressed cooperation and quality.

In addition to giving the company ample time for selecting what it perceived as the most qualified workers, the selection process has the potential to affect behavior on the shop floor. Because it was not necessary that an inherent liking for team participation be part of one's personality, the goal of the process is to select workers who outwardly adapt to management's efforts at structuring behavior. To get the job in the first place, one had to be willing to play by the rules.

Orientation and training. Management's second mechanism aimed at social control on the shop floor emerged through the company's orientation and training program. Every worker underwent 1 week of orientation and a minimum of 2 weeks of classroom training. The instruction fell into three general areas. The first area included "nuts and bolts" information concerning such items as benefits, pay schedules, work rules, uniform fittings, and tours of the plant. Within this area were basic lessons in reading blueprints, using statistical process control, and structuring time studies. The second area involved lessons on the company's history and philosophy including testimonials from instructors and management. Also within this category were instructions in the concept of kaizening (a philosophy of continuous improvement) and lectures designed to demonstrate SIA's egalitarian nature. The third area of instruction involved an attempt to socialize workers as to their expected behavior at SIA. This took place through formal, video-driven behavior training sessions and also through facilitating informal interactions with other classmates. Generally, the nuts-and-bolt area of instruction involved practical training, whereas the second and third components worked toward shaping attitudes and values.

If the amount of time spent within an area of instruction is any indication of its value to the company, then practical training was not the priority of the orientation and training process. Out of 127.5 hours of orientation and trainings approximately 56 hours were actually spent in practical training. The remaining 71.5 hours were concentrated on attitude and behavior.

The weeks in orientation and training worked as part of the company's overall scheme by providing a bridge between the worker's experience in the selection process and working in the plant. Workers at SIA often formed stronger bonds with their orientation and training class members than they did with their team members. For example, even though classmates were scattered in different departments throughout the plant, they often met for lunch on a daily basis and socially after work. This continued for at least several months after workers were separated in the plant.

The bond of friendship that formed between classmates was a useful tool in the company's overall attempt at shaping a co-operative work force. First, it laid the groundwork for a smooth transition into the plant. As a new worker in a factory environment, I experienced less alienation and fear than I had when beginning work in previous factory jobs. A primary reason for this was that I had already formed connections with other workers; the training experience was often the first topic of conversation when a new worker joined the team.

Team concept. Perhaps the most powerful aspects of SIA's scheme was located in the team concept and its reorganization of work. Organizing work around the team could control workers in three ways. First, a form of self-discipline emerged from the responsibilities of team membership. Workers often pushed themselves to the limit in order to keep up their "end of the bargain." Second, peer pressure "clicked in" if self-discipline failed. For example, when a worker fell behind or made mistakes, others on the team suffered because they were forced to correct those errors before the vehicle left the area. It was highly likely that, if the team member did not solve the problem, he or she would experience resentment from the others. For example, a worker from another team told me that he was training one of his team members on a station and that the team member was very slow. In reference to that worker's speed he said, "You know, it kind of makes me mad." A third level of direct control was exerted through the team leader and the Japanese trainers.

Self-discipline emerged as a part of the team structure. I found that I quickly internalized the responsibilities of team membership. I went to extreme measures to "hold up my end of the bargain." An example of this occurred during a period of time when management began altering my station. Each change increased the time it took to complete my series of tasks, forcing me to change other areas of the station in order to keep up. At one point, it simply became impossible to do the amount of work required, and I kept falling behind. Even though I knew the team leader had set unrealistic goals for my station, I felt guilty and feared the other team members would resent me for falling behind.

The following example illustrates the type of peer pressure that could be exerted by team mates. One member of our team, "Joe," regularly made mistakes and fell behind. We were understaffed, and each of us was working at least two and sometimes three stations. Joe was covering two stations. Because he was having problems, the rest of us observed him and found that he was not following any prescribed order when doing his stations. One simply could not predict which part he would pick up first. In turn, this meant that we never knew which part or parts he might forget. Because our responsibilities included checking the work already completed and correcting any mistakes, Joe's unpredictability increased the level of stress for the team members that followed him. The team leader and team members tried to get Joe to use a system, but he refused.

The team leader decided that Joe was simply pretending to be slow and confused in order to get out of working those particular stations. Finally, the team leader devised a scheme to correct the situation. The team leader informed the rest of the team of the plan. None of the team members told Joe of the potentially humiliating plan. Team members cooperated with the team leader in an attempt to put pressure on another team member concerning his job performance.

Direct control was exerted through the team concept by the team leader. There was a team leader for about every seven workers, so a worker's behavior was constantly monitored. Workers' actions were under close scrutiny, and, if inappropriate behavior occurred, workers were pressured to change. At times this meant a "friendly" visit from the group leader. At other times, the attention of a department manager was engaged.

Additional pressure came from our Japanese trainer. He inspected each car as it left our team and reported on our defects (any missed or improperly attached parts). In some cases, he found as many as 30 defects. Even though the majority could be attributed to Joe, the problem worker, the other team members were upset. It was important to each one to gain and keep the respect of the Japanese trainer, not only because he was the boss, but because team members liked him and had great respect for his knowledge of work and assembling the car.

Another aspect of the team structure was that it gave the company technical control over job assignments. Team members were cross-trained to perform one another's jobs, so management was able to move workers around freely within the team or between similar teams. This not only increased flexibility, it allowed the company to hire fewer workers, because covering for absent or injured workers was handled by other team members.

Philosophy of kaizen. The fourth element of SIA's system of control was epitomized in the phrase, "Always searching for a better way." This was how one vice president described the philosophy of kaizen during orientation and training. What it meant was that everyone was expected to continually make his or her job more efficient, striving to work to maximum capacity. Kaizening could be directly enforced through periodically decreasing the task time by speeding up the line. This forced workers to find ways of shaving additional seconds from work tasks. Indirectly, it had a "domino effect" on the work force. Making one person's job more efficient often meant shifting part of that process to another worker or team, thereby intensifying someone else's job.

A large part of kaizening involved time study. During training, workers were taught to perform time studies on each other and to check against the established standard for each task. This practice continued on the shop floor and was used to speed up each person's work process. If any time was left after the completion of a process, other tasks or subassemblies could be added, intensifying the job. For example, when "two right" got his station under control and was able to work ahead, he was given additional duties. He performed rework such as taping wiring harnesses. The goal was for workers to be working every second of every minute.[6]

Although the Japanese system is most consistent with the concept of hegemonic control, not every aspect of Burawoy's theory is applicable. "Making out"—the idea that workers play games to create spare time and still make quotas, and by doing so, develop a consensual relationship within production—took on a different form in the present case. Instead of a consensual relationship developing through workers' games, kaizening attempted to block workers from making out in two ways. First, it threatened a worker with constant disruption by suddenly introducing changes in the workstation, directly interfering with the making out process. Just when a worker had a station under control, with a few seconds to spare, he or she ran the risk of having it kaizened—intensifying the job. Second, through the kaizen philosophy of continual improvement, management attempts to gain control over workers' creative knowledge and to use it to its own advantage. Kaizening is not only designed to capture a worker's secrets for gaining spare time; once management appropriates that knowledge, it controls when, where, and how those ideas are implemented. Kaizening, therefore, is an extremely effective procedure. It essentially convolutes the making out process, which under other management systems benefits the worker, into a process that puts continuous stress on the worker and forces workers' compliance.

Shop floor culture. The fifth element, cultural control, was two-tiered. First, at the level of the shop floor, there was an attempt to shape workers' culture through the team structure. Organizing work around the team circumvented the natural formation of small informal work groups, a traditional mechanism of worker solidarity and support (Roy, 1983). By formalizing work groups, management created a structure in which team members worked together to meet company goals. If the company could successfully appropriate workers' solidarity and support, then they would identify their interests with the company's. Daily quotas and speedup placed increased demands on workers and created resentment toward management. The culture of the team was one mechanism of dissipating resistance to those demands. Quite simply, when helping other team members keep up, workers supported the speedup.

The second level of cultural control was the organizational level. There was an active campaign to create a companywide team culture at SIA, premised on the concept of egalitarianism. This was an attempt to elevate the responsibilities of team membership and identification to the level of the company.

Attempts to create an egalitarian culture occurred through specialized symbols, ideology, language, and rituals. For example, everyone from the company president on down wore the same uniforms, parked in the same parking lot, and used the same cafeteria. Workers were never referred to as employees or workers. Instead everyone, including management, was an associate. In addition, the company president and vice presidents were often seen on the shop floor.

The team metaphor was used at all levels of the company. Company documents compared team leaders to basketball captains and group leaders to coaches (*Subaru-Isuzu Automotive, Inc.—Facts and Information*, 1989, p. 2). The team metaphor was further extended to embrace the company's struggle in the market place. When defining its corporate character in the *Associate Handbook*, the second principle was, "Together, we must beat the competition." The company song was "Team Up for Tomorrow." At one department meeting right before the start of official production (when we began building cars that would be sold in this country), the trim and final manager gave a speech that was reminiscent of a coach's "go get 'em" right before the big game. In a very solemn tone he told the workers that "we are finally entering into the competition. The company has done everything to prepare us for this moment. Now it is up to us to beat the competition."

Company rituals included morning exercises, team meetings, department meet-ings, and company celebrations. These rituals brought workers in contact with management in a relaxed and casual atmosphere. At department meetings the teams sat together in the cafeteria, smoking and drinking pop while the trim and final manager delivered a "pep talk."

Company celebrations not only included workers but workers were often the focus of the celebration. At the ceremony commemorating the official start of production, state dignitaries, community leaders, and top management from Fuji Heavy and Isuzu were present. The ceremony was laden with images of nationalism, the marching band from the local university played, and baton twirlers performed. The climax of the celebration occurred when all of the employees from the plant marched across the stage through a haze of smoke as the company song "Team Up for Tomorrow" played over the speaker system. An associate from Team 2 said, "It seems kind of like graduation." One might argue that it is odd for a Japanese company to appropriate all of these American symbols; however, if the company's goal is control through enlisting workers' cooperation as team members, then appropriating American symbols seems quite natural.

Computerized assembly line. The most direct form of control at SIA was the computerized assembly line. It not only set the pace of work; the mainframe computer system had the ability to focus everyone's attention on any team that fell behind. For example, when a worker fell behind, he or she pulled a yellow cord located above the line. At that instant, the team's music (each team was assigned a few bars of music) would be heard throughout the area occupied by the 14 teams that assembled the cars in trim and final via the loudspeaker system. The computerized music was played repeatedly until the cord was pulled again by the team leader, signaling that things were under control. If the line actually stopped, the music continued until the line began moving again. This had the effect of focusing department-wide attention on the team with the problem.

In addition to playing music, the computer system kept track of the number of times each team pulled the cord and how long the line was stopped. Such a system of "bookkeeping" allowed management to put tremendous pressure on specific team and group leaders. This pressure was passed on to team members. For example, at the morning team meetings, in addition to receiving a defect report, other teams' problems were often topics of discussion. Problems arising within the team were a definite focus of conversation. During start-up, our group leader attended one morning meeting to inform us that we were "the only team in trim and final that was still having trouble making tact time."

Just-in-time production. The final mechanism of control that had the effect of directly intensifying and speeding up our work was just-in-time production. This is a method of inventory control in which the company keeps parts stocked on the line for only a few hours of work. This put severe time constraints on the material handlers who stocked the line and on the workers assembling the cars and trucks. Because the line was only stopped when absolutely necessary, the vehicles often continued moving, even when parts were missing. This meant that when the missing part arrived, the team had to work down the line installing that part after other parts had been attached, a difficult and time-consuming job. Even if the missing part arrived only a few seconds late, it was often enough to put that worker behind. Once behind, a worker often could not catch up and, therefore, the rest of his or her day was affected. No one wanted to fall behind and experience this pressure, thus workers often made extreme efforts to see that their parts were stocked. Sometimes workers left the moving line and, literally, ran down the aisle in search of a material handler to warn him or her that the line was becoming dangerously low on a part. Such actions could also put workers behind and increased the intensity of the jobs.

Summary: The points outlined above indicate that the combination of these components of control was quite powerful in controlling the individual worker. Only through collective action were workers able to affect any balance of power on the shop floor. The next section analyzes the nature and success of worker resistance.

The Nature of Resistance

Evidence of worker resistance to SIA's system of management emerged in various collective and individual forms. Collective resistance emerged as sabotage when workers surreptitiously stopped the assembly line. Collective resistance emerged when workers collectively protested and refused to participate in company rituals. Collective resistance emerged in the form of direct confrontation when workers refused management requests, and in the form of organized agitation at team and department meetings. Individual resistance was expressed through silent protest when workers, on an individual basis, refused to participate in company rituals and in the form of complaints through anonymous letters written to the company as part of the company's program of rumor control.

Collective resistance. Sabotage occurred when workers on one of the trim and final teams discovered how to stop the assembly line without management tracing their location. Whenever one of their team members fell behind and the "coast was clear," they stopped the line. This not only allowed people on their team to catch up, it gave everyone time away from the line. In addition, it provided entertainment as workers watched management scramble around trying to find the source of the line stoppage. At one morning team meeting, our team leader reported that the line had stopped for a total of 20 minutes the day before, and the company was unable to account for the time. Clearly, that team was taking a chance; however, the workers who were aware of the sabotage never told management. Whether the reason for the complicity was selfish, because of the appreciated breaks, or was loyalty to other workers, their silence was a direct act of resistance and evidence of a lack of commitment to the company.

Collective resistance also emerged in the form of protest. For example, in response to what they considered an unfair action by the company, Team 1 refused to participate in company rituals such as exercises and team meetings. This occurred in response to the company unilaterally taking away a 5-minute cleanup period at the end of the day.

Collective resistance emerged in the form of direct confrontation with management. When the cleanup period was no longer allowed, workers refused management's request to work "after the buzzer" (the end of the shift) in order to clean up and put away tools. For example, even when management directly requested workers' assistance in this matter, they were met with direct resistance at meetings and on the line. The group leader for our area called a special meeting of Team 1 and Team 2 to enlist help in cleaning up after the buzzer. At the meeting, several workers from both teams directly confronted the group leader. A worker from Team 1 said, "This is the kind of b____ s____ that brings in a union." A second remarked, "This place is getting too Japanese around here, pretty soon you will be asking us to donate our Saturdays." A worker from Team 2 assured the group leader that he was "not a volunteer." As a group, they were adamant that they would not work after the buzzer. On the following day, the line continued moving until the buzzer sounded, and as it happened, I was so far behind that when the line stopped, I did not realize the buzzer had sounded and I kept working. As two teammates walked by, they called to me, "Laurie, don't do it!" I put down my tools. As I was leaving, I overheard our team leader ask another team member a question concerning work. He replied, "Look, it's after 3:00. I don't know" and he walked on by. From that day on, whenever the line ran up to quitting time, everyone on the team dropped whatever they were doing and immediately walked out, leaving the team leader to lock up the tools and clean the area. At a team meeting, the team leader complained that she had stayed almost an hour after work cleaning up and putting

away our tools. One team member said, "She was crazy to do it, and we weren't going to."

Another form of collective resistance that emerged was jokes. Workers made light of company rituals and the philosophy of kaizen. For example, as mentioned above, some workers told jokes at the team meeting when called on for an inspirational message during the "yosh" ritual. They were making light of what was presented to us as a fairly solemn ritual. Another example of making light of rituals occurred at morning exercises when workers would jump around and act silly. Kaizening, the company's philosophy of continuous improvement, was also the brunt of workers' jokes. When the line stopped, someone would say, "Let's kaizen that chair," or if something really went wrong, they would say, "I guess they kaizened that."

Several examples of resistance emerged in response to management's unilateral scheduling and unscheduling of overtime. Resistance to overtime became resistance to the company's philosophy of cooperation. In December, both Isuzu and Subaru were trying to meet the end of the year production quota. Within 1 week the following happened. On a Tuesday we were told that we would work Saturday. The following morning the car manager informed us that we would work 9 hours that day and the next 2 days, so we would not have to work Saturday. At the same time, however, he assured us that if there were too many unscheduled line stoppages, we would end up working Saturday after all. One team member said the company was "just trying to screw us out of 8 hours of overtime." Then Friday morning they informed us that we would only work our regular 8-hour shift. However, when the 3:00 bell sounded, the line continued to move. Instead of staying with the line, nearly everyone on the car line put down their tools and walked out. As it turned out, the line only moved for another minute or so, but no one in trim and final knew this. To leave a moving line was a direct act of resistance and just cause for firing.

On the truck line, overtime scheduling was an even bigger issue because they had to meet larger monthly production quotas (ours were reduced because of the problems in paint). In the middle of December, I talked to a truck line worker I knew from my training class. Overtime scheduling was the subject of our conversation. On the previous day, her group leader told her team at 2:50 that the truck line would work until 4:00. At 3:00 they were given no break (even though stated company policy provided for a 5-minute break at 3:00 when working overtime), so they were unable to call home. She was particularly upset because her young son came home from school to an empty house. At 4:00 the line was not stopped. It did not stop until 4:50. She said that several members of her team started leaving at 4:00, even though the line was still moving. The group leader literally chased them down and got them back to work by threatening them with their jobs.

Another act of resistance, triggered by overtime scheduling and the company's response to workers exercising their rights according to company policy, occurred on Team 1. Two days before December vacation, the car manager decided to work the team overtime without sufficient notice. Our team leader asked us individually whether or not we were willing to stay over. I declined and so did another woman on my team. Previously, the company had handed down a policy concerning overtime that stated that "scheduled" and "emergency" overtime were mandatory, but "unscheduled" was not. Scheduled was defined as having been announced by the end of the shift on the previous day. Therefore, in this case, the overtime was unscheduled, and we had the right to refuse.

That afternoon, the group leader approached me and asked why I was not willing to work. I, of course, had not expected to work and had a medical appointment I wanted to keep. Shortly after that, our team leader informed us that, "According to human resources, if we left at 3:00, it would be an unexcused absence." The company was instituting this policy on the spot. This caused a third woman on our team to also refuse the overtime. She said that it was obvious to her that the company was simply fabricating the policy to force us to work. On principle, she decided to leave with us to protest the company's method of assigning unexcused absences. Now three team members were leaving. When the group leader learned this, he informed the car manager that there would not be enough people to keep the line moving. At this point, the car manager approached me with the group leader by his side. He said, "Look, here at SIA we are trying to be different. If this was any other place, I wouldn't bother to talk to you. I'd just tell the group leader to tell you to work or else. I don't want to get into a position where I am talking discipline with an employee, because I know you are a good worker. I've seen you work." I replied, "This wasn't scheduled overtime and he himself had said it wasn't an emergency, so how could he discipline me?" He said, "Anyone who leaves the line while it is moving is in jeopardy of being fired."

At this juncture, our team leader made a surprising announcement; she told the car manager that she was also leaving. He put immediate pressure on her, in front of the team, informing her that she was putting her job in jeopardy if she left. Finally, when faced with the intended departure of 4 team members, and the fact that this would shut the line down, management backed down. I suggested to the manager that if he agreed that no one would get an unexcused absence for leaving, both the team leader and the other protester would agree to stay. They accepted those terms; the other worker who needed to leave and I left. The next day, our teammates informed us that only three cars were built after we left. They described the demands made on us as a "power play by management."

Finally, collective resistance emerged through organized agitation at team and department meetings. This occurred as workers attempted to stop the company from instituting a policy of shift rotation. Management announced the policy and stated that it was "not up for discussion." All workers would have to rotate when the second shift was added. This infuriated many workers. Several people stated that it was typical of the kinds of decisions workers were not allowed to participate in. Many things that had a direct effect on workers' lives, such as overtime, line speed, and shift rotation were not up for discussion. The essence of the participation workers were granted involved at best, improving quality, at worst, and more commonly, speeding up the job. Workers informally passed the word around the plant to "keep the pressure on by bringing it up at meetings." After that, the issue of shift rotation was brought up almost daily at the morning team meetings. Department meetings were regularly disrupted when various workers would state how "unfair" it was that we had no input into the shift rotation decision. The issue continued to surface. Eventually, management changed its ruling, and an announcement was made that there would be no shift rotation.

Individual resistance. Silent protest was a common form of individual resistance and an easy target was morning exercises. For example, workers arrived late for work in order to avoid morning exercises or else they remained sitting while others participated. The exercises were a relatively safe target of protest because they occurred before the start of the shift. Legally, workers had the right to refuse. A second form of individual resistance emerged in anonymous letters to the company.

The anonymous letter was a weak form of resistance because it involved little risk to the individual and it used a formal procedure instituted by the company. As part of their "fair treatment policy," the company distributed prestamped, self-addressed envelopes for people to write in anonymously with questions or comments. The comments were posted throughout the plant on special bulletin boards with both the worker's comment and the company's reply. Between October 26, when the first batch was posted, and January 5, 150 comments, questions, and complaints were aired. At first they were optimistic, containing questions concerning the future. For example, people asked if there would be a credit

union, a car purchase program, daycare facility, or a fitness gym. Later it became a sounding board for complaints and dissatisfaction. Concerns emerged over scheduling overtime without notification. Parents complained that scheduling meetings after work and long hours of overtime conflicted with their children's hours at the day-care center. Workers also expressed concern that favoritism existed in parking, lunch hours, bonus plans, scheduling of overtime, and the loaning out of company cars. Repeated complaints emerged that group leaders and team leaders were being chosen without any job postings. Trim and final associates wanted to know why maintenance associates were paid $2 more per hour. There were repeated concerns that quality was being sacrificed in order to meet daily quotas. Workers questioned why seniority was used for some things such as enrollment in the pension plan but not for transfers and promotions. One worker wanted to know why security checks were unequally applied as people with lunch boxes were searched when leaving through the front door, whereas those with briefcases were not checked. Another worker quoted state law concerning overtime pay, stressing that it was illegal for the company to require workers to clean their areas and put their tools away after the shift had ended. There were also the more predictable complaints concerning the food and long lines in the cafeteria, uniforms, gloves, and plant temperature. Many complaints revealed that the company was not totally successful in instituting a spirit of cooperation and a culture of egalitarianism.

Figure 25.1 provides a summary of the forms of worker resistance. Strength of resistance is measured by workers' success at gaining a desired change in company policy or action. In general, the weakest forms of resistance were individual and called for no action by the company. The most effective forms tended to be collective, involved some risk to the individuals involved, were goal directed, and challenged the company's claim to fairness and equality. Planned, collective action was not necessarily more effective for achieving desired

Figure 25.1
Dimensions of Worker Resistance

Weak ⟵⟶ Strong

	1. Veiled Protest	2. Symbolic Protest	3. Dispersed Agitation	4. Direct Confrontation
Examples of individual resistance:	Refusal to exercise	Anonymous letters		
	Sabotage			
Examples of collective resistance:	Jokes that made light of company philosophy or rituals	Not exercising as a team protest	Conflict over shift rotation	Leaving a moving line
	Sabotage with group knowledge and approval			Refusal to cooperate and work without pay
				Overtime confrontation

1. Evidence of a "spirit" of resistance with no direct request for change, resulting in no apparent change by management.
2. Acts of resistance with a low level of risk that had a goal of changing a specific management policy or action but resulted in no apparent change by management.
3. Actions that were organized, sustained over a period of time, dispersed throughout the company, and directed at a specific goal. This resistance resulted in management changing its policy after a period of time.
4. Actions that involved a threat to the job security of the individual worker. They tended to be spontaneous, collective, and goal oriented. Workers usually expressed that they were acting on "principle," and invoked management's policy of fairness. This type of resistance resulted in immediate capitulation from management.

results than was spontaneous, collective action. Possibly this was because spontaneous action could be interpreted as a direct indication of the importance that workers placed on a particular issue. Spontaneous, collective action was not only a show of worker solidarity, it indicated a certain level of militancy, as it reflected a worker's willingness to engage in risky behavior without knowing if others would join in. In either case, both planned and spontaneous actions expressed a collective will in direct opposition to management's authority.

Conclusion

Data collected from this case study do not support the contention that the participation scheme found in modern Japanese management increases worker control. This was true technically and politically.

First, although deskilling and task fragmentation are traditional means of gaining greater technical control, they do not address the case at hand. Job enrichment or enlargement more accurately described the assignment of tasks. The number of tasks tended to be expanded rather than narrowed, as expected in a deskilling process. However, even though workers performed a wider range of tasks, they were not "reskilled." Jobs were fragmented and rationalized to the tenth of a second. Additionally, even though workers were trained to perform others' stations, this cross-training did not increase worker control over the technical aspects of work. The opposite was true. Flexibility increased management's control by making workers more vulnerable to job intensification and speedup. When a worker was absent or fell behind, the others were forced to pick up the extra load.

Second, these findings do not support the contention that participation schemes engage workers' minds in managerial aspects of their jobs. The kaizen process had the opposite effect. Management controlled the parameters of what was within the realm of consideration and also how, when, and where a job was altered. Kaizening provided a mechanism for keeping decisions under the tight control of management. Workers were seldom allowed to make even the most inconsequential decision on their own. Additionally, the company's use of consensus in decision making strengthened management's control over the outcomes. The unequal relationship between worker and management made it nearly impossible to reach a consensus involving little more than token input from workers.

Finally, at SIA control was decentralized through the team leader and the management structure was flat, not the hierarchical structure found in bureaucratic control. The lack of a burdensome bureaucracy may, on the surface, seem to be a reason for arguing that the team structure is a winning situation for both parties. However, decentralized authority within the plant created a situation where workers had very little autonomy. On the average, every seven workers were under the direct supervision and close scrutiny of the team leader. The concept of team participation in a decentralized structure hid the capitalist-worker relationship through an ideology of egalitarianism. This calls into question Edwards's (1979) contention that bureaucratic structures are required to mask the capitalist-worker relationship. Although bureaucratic structures can do what Edwards says, so can other structures.

Concerning the issue of transference, the resistance by workers at SIA provides additional evidence that intraorganizational transference of Japanese management practices may not be as successful as research has indicated. This is particularly the case when including a political dimension of analysis, shop floor control. This research, with its emphasis on patterns of worker behavior, suggests that successful transference at one level of measurement is not synonymous with successful adaptation of worker behavior on the shop floor. This raises the question of whether the existence of formal structures is a reliable mea-

sure for determining the successfulness of intraorganizational transference, particularly when a distinctive feature of that organization is employee commitment, identification, and loyalty.

Discussion Questions

1. What is your reaction to the eight principles of Japanese-style management listed in the introduction to this chapter?

2. Which principles do you think would develop the most support or resistance from workers?

3. Describe examples of Japanese-style management that you may have experienced or heard about.

Laurie Graham, "Inside a Japanese Transplant: A Critical Perspective" (*Work and Occupations* 20 [May 1993]), pp. 147–173. Copyright © 1993 by Sage Publications, Inc. Reprinted by permission of Sage Publications, Inc.

Endnotes

1. *Kaizening* is a philosophy of continuous improvement. It is instituted by asking workers to continually find faster or more efficient ways of performing their jobs.

2. Gaining employment and working in the plant as a hidden participant/observer is the method of choice for this particular study for several reasons. First, entry could not be gained with management's knowledge. Second, it has been used by other researchers when attempting to understand shop floor culture and experience (Cavendish, 1982; Kamata, 1982; Linhart, 1981; Pfeffer, 1979). Third, entering the plant without the knowledge of management or worker speeds up the process of gaining acceptance and is least disruptive to the natural course of events—as people may attempt to modify their behavior if aware that they are under observation. Finally, this type of methodology allows questions to be asked and observations to be made as events occur (Bollens & Marshall, 1973).

3. Through the course of the preemployment selection process and the 6 months working at SIA, I talked with 150 employees; 46 were women, 3 were Black.

4. Tact time is the amount of time a worker is given to complete a station; it was the same throughout the entire plant.

5. It was our understanding that "Yosh!" was a cheer, meaning something similar to "Let's go!" Every team in trim and final performed this daily ritual.

6. In a typical American auto plant, workers maintain a 40- to 50-second-a-minute work pace, whereas Japanese auto plants tend to run close to 60 seconds a minute (Fucini & Fucini, 1990, p. 37).

References

Blauner, R. (1964). *Alienation and freedom: The factory worker and his industry.* Chicago: University of Chicago Press.

Bollens, J., & Marshall, D. (1973). *Guide to participation.* Englewood Cliffs, NJ: Prentice-Hall.

Brown, C., & Reich, M. (1989). When does union-management cooperation work? A look at NUMMI and GM-Van Nuys. *California Management Review*, Summer, pp. 26–44.

Braverman, H. (1974). *Labor and monopoly capital.* New York: Monthly Review Press.

Burawoy, M. (1979). *Manufacturing consent: Changes in the labour process under monopoly capitalism.* Chicago: University of Chicago Press.

———. (1985). *The politics of production.* New York: Verso.

Cavendish, R. (1982). *Women on the line.* London: Routledge and Kegan Paul.

Chinoy, E. (1955). *The automobile workers and the American dream.* Garden City, NY: Doubleday.

Cole, R. (1979). *Work, mobility, and participation: A comparative study of American and Japanese industry.* Berkeley: University of California Press.

Derber, C., & Schwartz, W. (1988). Toward a theory of worker participation. In F. Hearn & R. Belmont (Eds.), *The transformation of industrial organization.* Belmont, CA: Wadsworth.

Dore, R. (1973). *Japanese factory, British factory.* Berkeley: University of California Press.

Edwards, R. (1979). *Contested terrain.* New York: Basic Books.

Fantasia, R., Clawson, D., & Graham, G. (1988). A critical view of worker participation in American industry. *Work and Occupations*, 15, 468–488.

Florida, R., & Kenney, M. (1991). Transplanted organizations: The transfer of Japanese industrial organization to the U.S. *American Sociological Review*, 56, 381–398.

Friedman, A. (1977). *Industry and labor: Class struggle at work and monopoly capitalism.* London: Macmillan.

Fucini, J., & Fucini, S. (1990). *Working for the Japanese: Inside Mazda's American auto plant.* New York: Free Press, Macmillan.

Graham, G. (1985). Bureaucratic capitalism and the potential for democratic control. *Humanity and Society*, 9, 443–457.

Grenier, G. (1988). *Inhumane relations: Quality circles and anti-unionism in American industry.* Philadelphia: Temple University Press.

Hull, F., & Azumi, K. (1988). Technology and participation in Japanese factories: The consequences for morale and productivity. *Work and Occupations*, 15, 423–448.

Kamata, S. (1982). *Japan in the passing lane.* New York: Pantheon.

Kornbluh, H. (1984). Workplace democracy and quality of work life: Problems and prospects. *Annals of the American Academy of Political and Social Science*, 473, 88–95.

Lincoln, J., & Kalleberg, A. (1985). Work organizations and work force commitment: A study of plants and employment in the U.S. and Japan. *American Sociological Review*, 30, 738–760.

Linhart, R. (1981). *The assembly line.* Amherst: University of Massachusetts Press.

Montgomery, D. (1979). *Worker's control in America: Studies in the history of work, technology, and labor struggles.* Cambridge: Cambridge University Press.

Parker, M. (1985). *Inside the circle: A union guide to QWL.* Boston: South End.

Parker, M., & Slaughter, J. (1988). *Choosing sides: Unions and the team concept.* Boston: South End.

Pfeffer, R. (1979). *Working for capitalism.* New York: Columbia University Press.

Piore, M. J., & Sabel, C. F. (1984). *The second industrial divide.* New York: Basic Books.

Roy, D. F. (1983). "Banana time": Job satisfaction and informal interaction. In J. Hackman, E. Lawler, & L. Porter (Eds.), *Perspectives on behavior in organizations* (pp. 329–335). New York: McGraw-Hill.

Safizadeh, M. H. (1991). The case of workgroups in manufacturing operations. *California Management Review*, Summer, pp. 61–82.

Slaughter, J. (1983). *Concessions and how to beat them.* Detroit Labor Education and Research Project.

Subaru-Isuzu Automotive, Inc.—Facts and information. (1989). Produced in cooperation with Indiana Department of Employment and Training Services.

Thompson, P. (1989). *The nature of work: An introduction to debates on the labour process* (2nd ed.). Atlantic Highlands, NJ: Humanities Press International.

Zwerdling, P. (1980). *Workplace democracy.* New York: Harper Colophon. ◆

26

Being Broken In: The First Two Weeks

Richard M. Pfeffer

This chapter describes the experiences of a new worker in the first two weeks on the job. It is not necessarily about the new economy, but it describes the wide range of things that a worker must learn in order to be an effective employee. There are technical aspects of a job that entail learning to run machines, and there are social aspects of a job that require getting along with others who can help you do your job. One of the interesting things about this description of the first two weeks on the job is that much of what a worker needs to know cannot be put in a job description or a training manual. There may be no substitute for learning to do a job by actually doing it, but the new worker can benefit from a caring and helpful trainer-supervisor.

Being Broken In: The First Two Weeks

The first two weeks at Blancs primarily were spent learning the routine, trying frantically to catch up on missed years of working-class socialization and experiences with machines, coping with a variety of disruptive events, meeting fellow employees, and trying to manage the intense emotions generated in me by these phenomena.

I reported for my first day on the job after a nervous weekend during which I had indulged my fear of the unknown. Picking up my badge at the guardhouse, I went to Ron Merritt's office in the Service Department, where my superintendent introduced me to my foreman, Sam Leonard, who had me wait a few minutes and then, in turn, introduced me to the current trashman, Bryan Morton. Morton, as he was called, was to break me in. When Sam told him to teach me the routine, Morton asked if he should let me operate the fork on the first day. Sam answered yes. By so doing, Morton later confided to me, he shifted the responsibility for whatever damage I might do with the fork to Sam.

From that initial brief talk with Sam, the main message that stuck in my mind, which Morton reinforced by repeating several times during the morning, was, "Watch out for the rings." Piston rings in all sizes are what the plant daily produces by the thousands. The rings in process are simply piled up on the floor or stacked on racks of several sorts and deposited all over the plant's main production and inspection areas. Viewed from the vantage point of a fork driver's seat, these main areas look like a sea of stacked rings, crisscrossed by more open but crowded aisles as wide as 15 feet, and dotted with a variety of workbenches and one-person machines, the tops of which, along with the heads of workers, are visible at a distance over the rings.

Morton began breaking me in by showing me where to sign in and out each morning and afternoon. Then he took me to First Aid to get my own pair of safety glasses, which were to be worn at all times in the production and inspection areas of the plant. Finally, he led me to the fork I was to drive. The good fork, he explained, was broken, so we had to use the older, bigger one, which doesn't have an automatic clutch. That fork, number 116, like most, has one gear in forward and one in reverse, plus a low gear for going up inclines and carrying heavy loads. The other levers on the towmotor adjust the height and pitch of the two fork blades. After demonstrating how to operate it, Morton quickly got me up in

369

the operator's seat. For the rest of the day he continued to give me instructions, advice, and warnings on what to do and what not to do, as well as directions on where to go next. But from perhaps ten o'clock on I did much of the driving. In learning the routine I encountered four main difficulties, some of which were overcome with time but others of which persisted.

First, I had to learn to operate the fork, which was largely a matter of practice and experience. Although its operation could not be mastered in fifteen minutes, as the superintendent had seemed to suggest, the simple mechanics of operating it could be learned quickly and then routinized. The art of driving it could be acquired within a few months. In learning to operate the fork I had to cope with several problems. Compared to a car, the fork had an incredibly small turning radius; it could turn on a dime. That meant, however, that the back end of the fork, if not controlled, could swing out wildly while the five-foot blades in the front mowed down anything in their path. In addition, frontal vision was somewhat obstructed even when the blades were empty, and when I was carrying a hopper up front, vision could be badly obstructed. Consequently, it was often necessary to drive the fork backward when it was loaded, which not only improved vision but also increased maneuverability. Getting accustomed to driving backward took a while. Finally, clearances between the fork and its load, on the one hand, and walls, machines, employees, and goods waiting to be processed, on the other, were frequently only an inch or two on either side.

Second, I had to learn the route to be followed to get to each of my twenty or so Honda-Civic-sized hoppers. The hoppers were located both inside and outside of the various buildings that were joined together essentially into two elongated structures, set one on each side of an internal, outdoor 250-yard roadway that bisected the entire plant. The inside hoppers were located off one of a number of aisles, some set at open intersections, others perpendicular or parallel to walls, and still others tucked into quite inaccessible corners. On that first day,

as I followed Morton's directions, I completely lost any sense of where I was, feeling as if I were being directed in one overhead door and out another through a complicated maze of aisles. By lunch I felt I had been in and out of 15 separate buildings, and I knew at that moment that I would have been unable to find one-half of the hoppers I had dumped that morning. Sam had said it would take about a week to learn the route. Morton reassured me that I was doing OK and that by midweek I would get the route down.

Third, I had to learn how to dump the hoppers into the compactor and how to pack the 12-ton container so it could be taken out when full, dumped, and returned empty. Dumping the hoppers required driving the fork up the short, narrow compactor ramp while raising the blades with the hopper on them, then parking the fork, tilting the blades down toward the compactor bin, and finally getting off the fork and improvising with a two-by-four to lift the hopper's release lever so the hopper would dump. Often, because hoppers were unbalanced and would not dump, I had to push them over bodily. The dumping task was further complicated by the several sizes of hoppers, by the absence of an emergency brake on the fork I was operating (which meant it had to be left in gear), and by the absence of its ignition key so that the fork had to be started and turned off with a rasp inserted into the ignition, a makeshift that repeatedly fell out at crucial moments.

Fourth, I had to learn to avoid the omnipresent stacks of rings.

The stacks, I was told, toppled easily and the rings were easily nicked and damaged. If they became so damaged that they had to be melted down and reproduced, the cost, I was told, could run into thousands of dollars. On that first day, I remember vividly, the rings were what terrorized me most. The thought of smashing into a stack as I painfully maneuvered my fork to make a pickup or dropoff intimidated me every minute of the day. Compared to this newly inculcated and overwhelming concern for the rings, my concern for the safety of pedestrians seemed almost marginal. Just beep, I was told by several coworkers, and pedestrians will get out of your way.

The essence of the trashman's job is keeping the hoppers empty. In seven months on the job I dumped at least 3000 hoppers. The task of dumping is more complicated than it might sound. At the risk of belaboring it, let me describe the process. One hopper I had to dump early each day was located up front in a building on the opposite side of the road from the compactor building. To get to it, I followed Morton that first morning down the road toward the main gate, turned left around an outside ring-storage area, went down a narrower road, passed the company gas pump, made a left through another outside storage area, and then came to one of the seven or eight large overhead doors that were my means of ingress and egress from buildings. At that point, Morton had me get down while he demonstrated how to get the hopper. It required the following steps: turning the fork around; backing through the door with the empty hopper I had carried there; executing a 90-degree turn to the left, being careful to avoid the sides of the door and whatever else might be in the doorway area; backing about twenty yards down a narrow aisle dotted with stacks of rings that seemed to have been deposited along its length helter-skelter; raising the hopper to avoid hitting rings that could not be cleared; lowering the hopper to avoid hitting overhead fluorescent lights; backing down a ramp and into a tight corner to the left of the full hopper that was to be picked up; making a difficult turn into the aisle perpendicular to the one I backed down; dropping the empty hopper nearby in that second aisle; backing up carefully to avoid the pillar and stacks of rings on two sides in the aisle; making a sharp left turn to approach the full hopper; maneuvering the fork and lowering the blades to insert them into the bottom of the full hopper; tilting and lifting the blades to pick up the full hopper; backing up so as to position the fork to drive out forward, up the aisle by which I entered; driving up that aisle a few yards and dropping the full hopper; disengaging the fork from that hopper; backing

up and turning into the perpendicular aisle to approach the empty hopper; picking up that hopper; backing up to the position opposite where the hopper had to be deposited; turning and driving forward to get to the position to drop the empty hopper; dropping the hopper and disengaging; backing up to the corner opposite the hopper, still being very careful; turning left and going forward up the ramp and the entrance aisle; picking up the full hopper and continuing up the entrance aisle, raising and lowering the hopper to avoid both rings and ceiling lights, respectively; executing a very tight left turn out the overhead; and then driving the fork with the loaded hopper back to and halfway up the main road away from the front gate; making a left turn through another overhead into the building where the compactor is; driving down the main aisle through the Final Inspections Department; making a left near the end of that aisle; driving forward and through another internal overhead door; making a sharp right into the compactor room; driving up the ramp to the compactor; putting on my gloves; dumping the hopper; turning on the compactor until the materials were pressed into the outside container; switching off the compactor; throwing some chemical salts into the empty hopper to cover trash odors; taking off my gloves; starting the fork and backing it down the ramp; and then going off to dump another hopper.

That particular process, which might be considered challenging but hardly rewarding, had to be repeated, with variations, about twenty times a day. It could be done in an average of, say, 20 minutes. In those first days it took me more like 45. Although not all the other hoppers involved such an intricate routine, each hopper involved its own distinctive routine with its peculiar difficulties. Many hoppers, in their own way, were at least as difficult to manage as the one described.

During that first day, needless to say, I felt extremely harried. I hardly wanted to take the two 10-minute breaks allowed during the day, one at 9:20 A.M. and the other at 2:20 P.M. I wasn't hungry at lunch, for which we were allotted an unpaid half-hour between 12:20 and 12:50. By lunch time we had picked up and dumped seven or eight hoppers, but I knew we still had to clean out the two cafeterias after lunch and then dump the remaining hoppers. I had to force myself to take the entire lunch hour, spending the first 25 minutes in one of the crowded, blistering hot cafeterias eating and observing, and the last 5 minutes back in the Service Department, where a number of my co-workers were playing a few snatched minutes of cards; bid whist, I think it was.

After lunch, Morton and I began to clear out the empty cartons and to clean out the six or eight trashcans and garbage pails in each cafeteria. Although the cafeterias had not been serviced since Saturday, cleaning them in no sense was obnoxious. For the trashcans, the process involved lifting the outside of each trashcan up and off its inside container and removing the large plastic bag inside the container. All the trash-filled bags, cartons, and garbage pails were dumped in hoppers outside the cafeterias. Both cafeterias were to be cleaned out and their hoppers dumped by two o'clock or so, Morton told me, so that we could then return to finish off the rest of the plant's hoppers.

The afternoon seemed a bit easier than the morning, as I began to get the feel of it. Several men approached me to talk, one of whom had held the job before. He indicated it was a dead-end job, not easy to get off of. He also told me that to do the job I'd have to figure out my own pace and system. Soon after, Morton unantagonistically advised me not to talk much to other guys during working time unless I was ahead of schedule.

The last part of the afternoon passed fairly easily. It was very hot and humid, but for some reason it didn't bother me too much. I just kept drinking a lot of water and sweating. During the final hours of the first day I was mostly on my own, with Morton just telling me where to go and what hoppers to pick up or re-pick up. He'd meet me where I was supposed to go and then meet me again someplace else when I was done

dumping the hopper. About 4:00 we knocked off, and he began filling out our time cards. Work officially stopped at 4:20. But after 4:00 we just killed time, standing around near the compactor, talking a bit. Morton had been on the fork for about a year and, as soon as I was trained, would move up a grade to his new job as machine oiler. At the end of the day I thanked Morton, who didn't seem to want my thanks. He said he was just doing what Sam, our foreman, told him to do. At 4:20 we went back to Sam's office to ask for a locker for me. Sam told Morton to show me where the lockers were, which he did, and then we split. As my final act of the day, I went to First Aid to order a pair of safety shoes, the cost of which would be deducted from my wages and for which, I was told, I would have to wait about two weeks.

All in all, it had been a hard but decent first day. It certainly could have been much worse. Morton, I could see, got his job done reasonably efficiently and with as little effort and time spent on it as possible in order to have some time to hide when he got ahead of schedule.

I began work the next day at 6:00 A.M. My hours, I learned, would be 8:00 A.M. to 4:30 P.M. Monday, 6:00 A.M. to 4:30 P.M. Tuesday through Friday, and 6:00 A.M. to 2:30 P.M. Saturday. It was unlikely I would have to work more than those hours, Morton informed me, since additional hours would involve getting paid double-time, and "the company don't want to pay a trashman double-time." Thank God! Fifty-six hours a week was quite enough for me.

Beginning work at 6:00 A.M. was good, though it meant getting up five days a week at 4:40 and leaving the house without any contact with my wife and son. At that time of the morning it was cool, the plant was fairly empty, and it was easier to get around to do the job. Besides, getting in a couple of productive early morning hours made me feel like I had a jump on the day. By eight o'clock it was already hot as the devil. The fans inside the plant moved the hot air around some, and it wasn't at all bad while I was up on the fork moving. But, in any event, I was concentrating on the job too much to pay much attention to the heat. By eleven o'clock, five hours into the day's job, I was wishing it was lunch time, though I was coming along all right with the fork. Morton even complimented me. A stranger watching me move around in a tight spot spontaneously said to me, "Good work." That felt fine.

I still had to learn the maze, however. As I got a little time to think about the job, I wondered why we didn't pick up the hoppers in the tightest areas early in the morning before most machine operators, truckers, and other fork drivers get in. That thought, I realized somewhat later, was the beginning of working out my own system for doing the job.

I had lunch with one of the muscled, young, black guys who had undergone the physical exam with me. He was from Alabama and we talked about the differences between the North and the South, which he said was less violent. After lunch Marbles, a union official, who worked as a janitor in the plant, called me over to his table to say my shop steward would be contacting me by the twentieth of the month to sign me up for the union. I said OK, though my lunch mate had indicated he wasn't eager to give up the compulsory $25 union initiation fee and the $8.50 a month in checkoff dues.

By around three o'clock our container at the compactor was filled, so we couldn't dump any more trash in the compactor. Thereafter we just moved around for a while and then sat down outside on benches along the roadway with a bunch of other guys who also were waiting in the heat for the work day to end. For many, work simply stopped before time was up, and men sat, stood, and chatted, looking from time to time to see whether their foreman or superintendent was coming.

While we were sitting another stranger came over to me and in a friendly way told me I hadn't put my fork blades down right. I went to the fork and put them down, following another guy's directions about getting them flat so no one would trip on them. As Morton came by, one of the men told him he should have showed me how to leave the blades. Morton said he had

showed me, though I didn't recall, and later told him so. He repeated he had told me; I let it go, realizing that Morton doesn't make mistakes.

The next day was another scorcher, well into the 90s. That morning I began to write out the route and the routine of how to handle each hopper, no doubt an intellectual's response to a laborer's task. As I went through the routine, I got angry at myself for getting into jams with the fork and having to rely a few times on Morton to get me out, I also got angry at some undefined "others" for leaving rings in the aisle, swearing out loud to an unkind fate. At times I felt I wanted to throw up my hands in total frustration with the conditions of the work process. Morton seemed able to make the fork go anywhere. I could not. For myself, I realized that it frequently was worth the trouble and time to check out an area first before I came into it with the fork, moving what obstacles I could out of the way so I would have a relatively unobstructed ingress and egress. The problem was that moving stacks of rings myself was still nerve-wracking, and if I wanted the truckers to move them I had to ask them, which, having their own work to do, they didn't always appreciate.

That morning, like many others thereafter, just wasn't my morning. For the first time, I knocked down some rings. The rings shouldn't have been where they were, but Morton had just shouted, "Watch out," as my back wheel went over the bottom of the stand on which the rings were stacked. Morton was angry, but after my first feelings of deep apprehension, I was actually a bit relieved since I had expected the wrath of the gods to descend upon me, what with all the fuss everyone had made about hitting rings. We picked them up, apparently undamaged, and had the rest of the rings moved out of the way. I dutifully reported the incident to Sam, who was unperturbed.

Shortly thereafter, as I was passing through the overhead door leading toward the compactor area, the sliding, rippled metal door crashed down on the fork's protective frame above my seat. Apparently, unnoticed, one of the pull-chains hanging down on either side of the overhead had gotten caught in the fork frame, and my moving forward had jerked the chain, bringing the door down over me. Fortunately, the door didn't jam, and with some help from others I extricated the fork after the door had been raised. I considered putting a plastic covering over the fork frame to prevent a chain from getting caught again in the frame.

Just after that, as I was making a sharp swing outside on the road with a hopper on the front of the fork, the hopper flew off the blades. It scared the hell out of me since someone could have been seriously hurt or something badly damaged. I had neglected to tilt the blades back far enough to prevent the hopper from becoming dislodged as I swung around. I resolved to be more careful and alert after that.

By lunch time I was feeling better, less inadequate, as the routine went more smoothly. The afternoon passed quickly. I worked hard and more efficiently. I dumped about 22 hoppers in the compactor that day, about average. When I had 40 in the compactor I called Sam, who then called Robb Tyler, Inc., the container service company, which later sent a truck to pick up, dump, and return the empty container.

In those early days everything was new to me, the particular physical tasks, doing manual labor, being a trashman, everything. My reactions to these aspects of the job were intense. With each hopper I dumped efficiently, I felt a sharp sense of tangible accomplishment and, as hopper followed hopper, a growing capacity to handle the job. Far from bothering me, the physical work actually gave me pleasure and I felt joy in becoming aware of my body again after so many years. By contrast, I did not like hiding and standing around looking busy, and resolved to adjust Morton's schedule to cut the hiding time to enable me to do my job more cautiously. As one kind of experience in a lifetime, I was rather enjoying the job, notwithstanding the frustrations, anxieties, and demands on my time. But to have to do this for a lifetime, to know that one's life would be mea-

sured out in trash hoppers, seemed inconceivable to me in those first days on the job.

During that day I had learned a few very simple things about the fork: how much air to put in the tires, which deflated almost overnight; where and how to get gas for the fork, and where to put it. I looked forward to getting the regular fork back, since it was smaller, supposedly easier to handle, and had an emergency brake and an automatic clutch. But in retrospect I was not sorry to have been broken in on the clumsier, older fork, expecting that shifting from the 116 to the regular fork, like swinging a regular bat after swinging the heavier lead-weighted bat in baseball, would make the smaller fork seem that much more manageable.

By the fourth day I was relying more on my notes regarding the route and details for dumping each hopper than on Morton directly. I didn't need his help much that day, so we talked more about working for Blancs. Morton told me the union was lousy, a "company union," he called it. Union meetings, which are held once a month on Sunday mornings, are "bullshit," he said. There had been a short strike last November and might be another this year. The reason the union was after me to sign up fast, he declared, was so that if I got fired during my 60-day probationary period with the company, it could still get its cut out of me.

Some time later in the day Sam ordered us to take an empty hopper over to where several men were sweeping up street trash, to wait until it was filled and then to dump it. At first I resented the interruption in the routine, the performance of which I saw as my responsibility. Morton, however, did not seem to mind the interruption at all. For him, working time was working time. And he knew better than I that our foreman was, indeed, our boss: that what Sam said went, and that as long as we followed Sam's orders we were covered.

Friday, like the day before, passed rather smoothly. The only events of note were Morton's wanting to deliver the compactor key to me in front of Sam so the transfer of responsibility would be official, and my advising Sam that the big hopper from the Chrome Department was very difficult to dump. Morton had been having trouble dumping that hopper but had never complained. He said that when we got the regular forklift back the hopper would dump OK. But in the interim I was afraid of injuring myself while trying to push the hopper over to dump it. In response to my telling Sam the hopper didn't work right, Sam called Morton in alone and, according to Morton, chewed him out. Morton apparently didn't back me up, saying he had been able to dump it all right. As a consequence, Sam confronted me, asking how come Morton could dump the hopper and I couldn't. He said he wanted to see the hopper the following day I told Morton he should have backed me up, called him a "motherfucker," and was cool to him for the rest of the day.

On Saturday, I had to dump all the hoppers in eight hours instead of the usual ten. Fortunately Morton offered to help out with another fork. The five or six hoppers he leisurely dumped eased the burden considerably. He seemed to regret not having backed me up the day before, and we had a good day together. At lunchtime he introduced me formally to the heads of the two cafeterias. With him leaving, he said for the first time, I would get free snacks and free lunches there—trashman's perquisites. He also got a pickax and chopped out the quick-dry cement that had solidified in the bottom of the foul-smelling Chrome hopper, making it so difficult to dump.

Morton knew his job well. Although he didn't express ideas or even directions with any clarity, he was able to show me how to do various routine tasks and how to cope with whatever concrete problems came up during the week. He also gave me more general advice about not taking on work that wasn't my responsibility, since, he warned, if I started to do so everyone would take advantage of me. Morton was my only teacher on the job and he taught me well, almost exclusively through practical, on-the-job training. But whatever problems had not arisen while carrying out the routine during that first week, I realized even then,

would be problems that in the future I would not know how to deal with.

With this awareness, I encouraged Morton on Saturday to notify Sam that the fork seemed to be losing power. When I first noticed the loss, I wondered what it might be. I didn't know anything about machines, but I didn't want to advertise my total ignorance to my foreman. On the other hand, I also didn't want to simply wait for the fork to break down if there was something that could be done to revive it. I thought perhaps I had been operating the fork incorrectly, that I might have been driving it in low or something. On checking with Morton, however, that proved not to be the case. It worried me that I might come in on Monday, more or less on my own, and find the fork dead. So, shortly after Morton mentioned the problem to Sam, I stopped by the office and told Sam I thought we were going to have trouble with the fork. Sam responded, almost offhandedly, that we were having trouble with everything, as if he couldn't be bothered with the problems of my fork. From his perspective I'm sure he had other more pressing breakdowns and responsibilities, but from my perspective as a new and inexperienced worker nothing could have been more pressing than being assured of having a working forklift. My needs, however, were subordinated in the nature of things to my foreman's. That day I began to suspect repairs were not likely to be made on the fork until it actually broke down. I worried about that over the weekend.

The weekend didn't begin until three o'clock Saturday afternoon when I arrived home from work. It passed as if it had never existed, without giving me time to really relax, to feel away from the routine. This reinforced my dominant impression of the week. Working 56 hours a week on the job, plus 3 hours of unpaid lunch hours, plus about 50 minutes a day commuting, and another half hour every day cleaning up after work, I was putting *67 hours a week into work.* I had to get up about 2 hours before my wife on 5 days of the week and leave the house without seeing her or my son. And by the time I came home, cleaned up, and spent a half-hour typing up my notes for the day, I was too tired after supper to do anything but stare at the tube until eight-thirty or nine o'clock, when I often fell asleep.

It was no way to nourish a marriage, no way to raise a family, or for that matter, to do anything else. Except for shopping at supermarkets that are open all kinds of hours, I could hardly run errands, go see a doctor, or do anything in the community. I found myself unable or unwilling to read newspapers, though I had been accustomed for years to reading the *New York Times* every day. I found myself torn between spending those few precious hours of waking leisure with my son, with my wife, or by myself. I found myself, in short and with some important differences no doubt, trying to live with drastically curtailed and compressed free time, as millions of American workers have learned to live, snatching moments of personal satisfaction largely from time not sold to others. And my family found itself struggling to adjust to a situation that repeatedly threatened to effectively turn me into an absentee father and an absentee husband.

With the abbreviated weekend over, the second week on the job began as expected. The fork was "down," marking a poor beginning to what turned out to be one of my worst weeks at work. I killed time until the fork was repaired by the company mechanics, walking my route, checking the hoppers, and wondering when I could get back to work. At morning break I spoke to a middle-aged black worker who had been with the company for some years. He said the only way he could make ends meet was to work overtime, that he couldn't hack it on 40 hours. He was angry and dissatisfied with his lot, saying he had in the past voted for a strike every chance he had. He hoped we would have another strike this year.

By ten-thirty I was back at work. I worked entirely on my own all day. Despite the delay, the routine went fairly well. I dumped about seventeen hoppers, which is adequate for a Monday, the slowest day of the week on trash.

Tuesday began deceptively well, but as I was going through the overhead door near the compactor room, the pullchains must have caught again in the fork's top frame, and the overhead door crashed down on the frame, this time jamming badly. I tried to fix it, with the gracious help of the foreman in the area, but the door wouldn't unjam. I called Sam to report it, and he reacted like a sonofabitch. He asked me, "How come all these things have started to happen since you're here?" It was hardly a question I could answer, and I told him the problem with the door wasn't my fault. He hung up on me. I went over to the office to talk to him, where he had me sit and cool my heels, talking to me intermittently when he wasn't otherwise occupied, which was rare. We had a long, interrupted talk in which I said I tried to do my job and wasn't lazy or especially weak. "What about the Chrome hopper you complained about?" he retorted. Morton, he said, had been there for a year and had had no complaints. Then he put it to me: "If you don't like the job," he flatly stated, "now is the time to tell me." I felt abused and cornered, blamed for two things that weren't my fault, and responded angrily striking out at the absent Morton, which was stupid and unfair. Morton, I said, didn't know enough to come in from the rain. Sam got madder, saying Morton had done a good job for him. I apologized and indicated I thought Morton had done a good job training me, but that I was using the old, clumsy fork. Many of the hoppers in fact didn't dump well, I said, but I hadn't complained about them. The Chrome hopper really was too tough to dump and therefore a safety risk. Sam conceded that the hoppers were built in such a way that if loaded incorrectly they could be very hard to tilt. I said I understood, but that the Chrome hopper's problem was beyond that. Then he shifted the topic somewhat, asking me about the fork's having lost power, which turned out to be due to a slipped clutch. Again he appeared to blame me. I was incredulous and incensed. How, I asked, could I have done all that damage to that old machine in six days? He said the engine was idling too fast and I therefore probably had to play the clutch more than I should have. I should have told him, he said, about the idle. I replied that I'd never driven a fork before, and was concentrating on other things that first week. He said I had driven a motorcycle and a car and should have known. And so it went.

Sam ended the conversation indicating he was merely trying to find out why all these things had happened. He denied being sarcastic. I told him that asking someone why all these things are happening now that you're here is not exactly a question one can answer. I was pissed off, but only half showed it. Why, I wondered to myself, was he intent on blaming me for these mishaps? And was it really true that these breakdowns began when I took the job?

No matter, I was depressed for most of the remainder of the day. Sam sent a man over to fix the pullchains, who told me the fork I was using was higher than the one normally used, which is why the chain got caught in it. To try to prevent a reoccurrence, the man repaired and raised the chain. Later in the day the container was picked up, which cost me more time.

The daily mishaps, along with my foreman's disapproval, were getting me down. Nevertheless, I realized, despite such interruptions I could do the job adequately within the allotted time. So that wasn't the main problem. The hardest thing seemed to be adjusting emotionally to that endless series of disruptions in my routine, many of which were beyond my control. Breakdowns, added tasks, delays, obstructions and no one really to blame, including myself. That's the way the job is, I realized intellectually. No sooner did I think I had the routine knocked, then something else went wrong. And as often as not when I took a problem to my foreman, the man to whom I was supposed to take job problems, he seemed too busy to be bothered, though not too busy to note it for later use against me.

As the day passed, I tried to assess how many of my difficulties were of my own making. I might well have contributed marginally to the deterioration of the clutch, for example. I did tend to complain more

often than others. I probably did have an "I-rate-special-treatment," complaining approach to the job and life. I resolved to try to discipline myself, to lay low and cover myself. Talking about the problems with a fellow worker, I was reminded both that I had no rights while I was on probation, and, on the other hand, that my foreman had not as yet given me any warning slips. Still, I was skating on thin ice during this 60-day probation period and, Elinor and I agreed when I got home that evening, I might just get fired.

The following day was a relief. Few problems. The routine went well. By eleven o'clock I had nearly completed the morning routine and was trying to kill some time, which in those first weeks didn't come easy to me. Finishing up before lunch, I barely tapped a wall that looked like any other wall until a woman came out from behind it to explain that on the other side of that wall were rings hanging on nails in the wall. Again I was reminded that there is no telling when and from what sources trouble can come. Constant alertness is required, and yet the tasks must be routinized, making it difficult to keep alert.

During the day I spoke to two co-workers. One, a young movement type, warned me to watch out for certain workers like Marbles, the union committeeman who had earlier approached me. Those guys, he claimed, in effect spy for the company. The other, as we were talking about my problems with Sam, gave me advice subsequently heard over and over again on the job: generally avoid all foremen. Sam, this man claimed, liked to exercise his authority and power, whether a worker was at fault or not. Partly out of my own exasperation and partly to see the response, I asked, "But what do they want from us, blood?" "They want it all," he replied.

Them and us. Whatever the complexities of the relationship between workers and management, it was becoming clear to me, as never before, that indeed it was them against us. And by the middle of my second week on the job I could see that many of my coworkers almost unavoidably saw the work world as divided in the same way.

I came in to work the next day determined to work efficiently and to avoid calling my foreman's attention to me. After dumping three hoppers, I drove over to get the hopper outside the service shop. As I approached the hopper, one of the men taking an early break nearby informed me that there were no lug nuts on my front left wheel. I got down from the fork with a sinking feeling in my stomach. All six of the lug nuts were off. One man speculated they had been stolen; another that a mechanic who had fixed the tire at some point might have neglected to replace the nuts. A third thought it was sabotage, perhaps directed against me personally. In any event, the fork was unsafe to drive.

I dreaded telling Sam when he came in around 7:40. At the suggestion of one of the workers, I retraced the route looking for the lug nuts. I found two or three of them, where they had obviously rolled away from the moving fork. The company mechanic gave me another couple, though he doubted they would fit my wheel. They didn't. So there was no alternative.

When Sam came in, I went over and told him. He turned around without speaking and walked away. Later, in talking with one of the mechanics, I was told Sam had blamed me for this problem, too, saying I had probably been driving too fast, that I was working the old fork too hard, both of which were untrue and nothing short of ridiculous as explanations for the lug nuts coming off. Sam seemed to want to blame someone. The dominant fact, however, was that the fork hadn't been kept up decently and was in lousy shape.

But I knew, on the other hand, that I was not completely free of fault. Earlier that morning as I had been picking up my first hopper I had heard a sound as if something metal had hit the ground. I had ignored it, assuming the sound had been caused by my running over some piece of metal on the pavement. Then, as I was cleaning up around the hopper, I saw two large nuts and assuming they had produced the noise, but thinking nothing else about them, I threw them into the trash. If I had had more experience with machines, I probably would

have recognized them for what they were and checked my own wheels. Needless to say, I did not confess this to Sam or anyone else. And anyway, why had six lug nuts almost simultaneously come loose in the first place? No way I could be to blame for that.

But self-righteousness was no defense against the events of the day, which quickly went from bad to worse. The front wheel rim, it turned out, was damaged and could not be fixed, because the holes for the hub bolts had become elongated. One mechanic at the garage assured me that the problem was of long standing and the lug nuts had probably worked themselves loose over time. Regardless, I had to wait for an outside mechanic to come in to do the repair job. When he arrived, he casually informed me that there "wasn't much left of the tire either," a characterization that seemed more broadly descriptive of the state of most of our equipment. Shortly after my fork went, another fork in the department also broke down.

I had to spend the rest of the day killing time, loafing. It was very hard for me, not even being able to perform as a trashman. I moved around the plant from spot to spot, not knowing many workers, and at times feeling as out of place as a leper. I continued to worry, with new cause, that Sam might fire me. At one point when my super, Ron Merritt, called me over, I thought, "This is it," but it wasn't. He merely wanted to inquire whether a set of keys that had been found was mine. It was. I thanked him and simultaneously recognized the loss of the keys as symptomatic of my disorientation.

The only good thing about not being able to do my job that day was that it freed me to talk more to other employees. Feeling badly, I sometimes sought their sympathy and advice. Several assured me there was no way Sam could blame me for the loss of the lug nuts, but my impression was that he did, which really bothered me. The fact, hidden from my fellow workers, that I had somewhat contributed to the loss, also bothered me, making me feel incompetent. I feared my mistake being exposed, and relatedly and more profoundly I continued to fear being exposed myself as an imposter. I felt very vulnerable. In dealing with authority figures in the exercise of their power and authority over me in the past, I had relied heavily for protection upon my own capacity to perform competently and upon my related sense of independence. In this job, however, I was very dependent upon factors beyond my control and often beyond my understanding and competence.

My problems in dealing with power holders, however, obviously were not unique. One worker who had been at the plant for more than five years said he had had trouble with Sam for about three years until he decided to simply do whatever Sam told him to. "If Sam says jump off the roof, I'll do it," he says, "since I'm getting paid to obey Sam."

More than that, the demoralization I felt after only nine days on the job seemed to be widely felt. As several of us that day discussed working, one worker who had been with the company more than 20 years said that "that's 20 years too long, but it's too late to do anything else." In talking about the equipment, he said that in all the time he'd been there he'd seen the plant buy only a couple of brand-new forks. Instead, they bought second-hand forks, and the Service Department often got hand-me-down forks from other departments no longer willing to use them. About the very crowded conditions in the plant, he said that each time the plant was expanded, conditions quickly seemed to get more crowded than before.

The discussion tentatively confirmed a suspicion that had been growing day by day in me. Given the conditions, the trick in working is to not care about doing a good job. Do what you have to. Getting by is what counts, and practically speaking, that's all there is for most workers. By contrast, trying to do a good job is too frustrating and not rewarding. Put in your hours. Don't become too involved in your work. And try to leave the work world behind you as soon as you go out the gate.

Trouble is, the next day there it is again. And my next day began as the last one had ended, with my fork still out of commission and no way to know when it would be

operational again. I walked my route, planning which hoppers to dump first, while half expecting at any moment to get the ax from Sam.

About eight-thirty I was paged and told by Sam to use a rented forklift. When I asked for someone to show me how to operate it, Sam did. He then made a little joke about my having had to "hump the trash on my back" the day before, which made me feel a bit less tense about the job. I adjusted to the new fork fairly quickly. Using a different fork, however, interfered in small but tangible ways with my routine. Different forks have different specifications and personalities, different turning radii, different widths, different blade sizes, and different positioning and modes of operation of levers. Since routine is the heart of the trashman's job, such interference with the routine is not only mildly troublesome, it also increases the probability of accidents.

Moreover, the horn on the rental fork was out of order. I angrily drove it that way for a brief period, anxious all the while that someone would pop out of one of the blind aisle crossings and walk in front of my moving fork. But what could I do? No way I would bother Sam with the problem if I could help it. Concerned with my predicament, I asked advice from a savvy fellow worker, who said I definitely should tell Sam, to put the responsibility on him, not me, if something happened. I could see he was right, so I told Sam, who took it in stride and told me, perfunctorily, I thought, to use the fork but to be careful at cross aisles. I drove as carefully as I could, but driving without a horn down crowded factory aisles is dangerous per se. At lunch another worker I told about the situation said I had been right to lay it on Sam. Then he swore at the Union Safety Committee, which apparently was supposed to check equipment out before we used it. I got through the rest of the day without any other mishaps.

Saturday morning Elinor, who needed the car, got up early and drove me down to work. When I arrived, I learned from Sam that I hadn't been posted to work that Saturday. Then I understood why he had asked me to work two extra hours of overtime the evening before. Nevertheless, I was delighted to have the day off. As I left the plant, the guard at the gate asked me where I was going. I told him I had the day off, naively surprised that they checked up on employees leaving the plant at odd hours, like truant officers checking to see if kids are playing hookey.

That was how my first two weeks at Blancs ended. The plant was about to begin its two-week summer shutdown, during which it would be out of production and most employees would be taking their vacations. Those working were mostly either Service Department employees, who would be doing maintenance and cleanup and moving heavy machinery, or other workers who hadn't been on the job long enough to have earned vacations. Either way, I would work the next two weeks.

Would the coming weeks be significantly different from the first two? The experience of working those first weeks had reinforced the experience of looking for a job. The same fundamental message was hammered home in both processes: *what you think or care about is essentially irrelevant and ignored, because the basic purposes of the processes to which you are being subjected have been determined without your participation and are primarily for another's benefit. You are nobody—hands to be used.* As a worker, your principal responsibilities are: do your job; obey your foreman. On probation with

the company and not yet a member of the union, you as a new worker in particular are nearly as powerless and as lacking in substantial rights, autonomy and control as you were as a job seeker.

Under such conditions it is understandable that workers learn to respond in kind, in the shared spirit of expediency, trying to "get by," and trying in whatever small ways they can to assert some control over their lives as workers.

Discussion Questions

1. Think about the first two weeks of a job that you held. How did you learn about what the job entailed?

2. Have you ever been in a training program to prepare you for a job? How effective was the training? What was left out?

3. Consider the eight principles of Japanese-style management described in the introduction to Chapter 25. How would you train a worker to embrace these principles?

Reprinted from Richard M. Pfeffer, "Being Broken In: The First Two Weeks," in *Working for Capitalism* (New York: Columbia University Press, 1979, pp. 29–49). ✦

27

Gender and Service Delivery

Barbara A. Gutek, Bennett Cherry, and Markus Groth

Barbara Gutek, Bennett Cherry, and Markus Groth examine research on gender and service delivery by looking at the gender of provider and/or customer; the congruency between the provider and customer roles and gender of the provider and customer; the spillover of gender role to both the provider and customer roles; and the effects of having provider and customer of the same or different genders. They find that most research on service delivery ignores, or does not study, the gender of provider or gender of customer.

In his forecast about the postindustrial society, Daniel Bell (1976) provides a brief historical summary of the nature of work. When the United States was an agrarian society, farmers struggled against the physical environment. As manufacturing replaced farming in the industrial era, people wrestled with and mastered machines to produce goods. In the postindustrial (service) society that Bell predicted, he noted that people would simply have to deal with each other rather than with the land or with machines. That postindustrial society based on services rather than manufacturing or farming is now upon us.

Service is a broad category covering work that does not produce either a tangible durable product or foodstuffs. It ranges from professional activities such as law, medicine, and higher education to fast food, insurance, banking, and retail operations to domestic labor. In addition, many manufacturing firms and agribusiness ventures also have service components to them.

Over 70% of the U.S. labor force now works in service jobs (Appelbaum & Batt, 1994). Americans also spend more time than ever using (and purchasing) services. For example, consumers paid approximately $3.3 trillion for services in 1997 (U.S. Department of Commerce, 1998). The payroll for service industries is about 1.5 times the payroll for goods-producing industries (Bureau of Economic Analysis, 1998b), and although the United States has a trade deficit for goods, it has a trade surplus for services (Bureau of Economic Analysis, 1998a). Because the importance of services will probably not diminish anytime in the foreseeable future, much attention has been directed toward understanding this growing segment of the economy and how people experience service in the marketplace.

This chapter explores the topic of gender and service delivery. Both sexes work in service jobs, and both sexes purchase services. There is evidence, however, that a higher proportion of women than men work in service jobs (Hochschild, 1983) and that women do more buying than men (i.e., women purchase goods and services for their household, family, and spouse more than men do) (Katz & Katz, 1997). Prior to the introduction of equal opportunity legislation in the 1960s, part of the male sex role was to be the breadwinner for the family and part of the female sex role was to act as chief consumer for the household. As more women have moved into the labor force, these roles have blurred, with both sexes earning money and spending it. Furthermore, households are likely to consume more services than ever, purchasing some of the services formerly provided by the housewife/mother. In turn, many of those wives and mothers are today employees who are engaged in providing services to others for pay.

Our analysis of gender and service delivery is organized around the service provider, the customer, and the environment in which they interact. First, we review the key concepts for studying service delivery and the key concepts for studying the gendered nature of service. Then we discuss the research as it relates to gender and service providers, to gender and customers, and to gender and the service environment. Finally, we discuss the different ways in which this research is conducted and draw some conclusions. In this way, we expect to address two questions: (1) What do we know about gender and service delivery? and (2) What else do we need to know?

Key Concepts

We begin by discussing four concepts of interest: the service transaction, the service provider, the customer, and the service environment.

The Service Transaction

Service interactions constitute a subset of all human interactions that take place between two parties. In a typical service transaction, a customer (service seeker) desires a product (service) that is usually offered by multiple parties (service providers) in the marketplace. Often, the customer identifies the most desirable service provider, communicates the desire to receive some service, and the service provider responds. After receiving the service, the customer typically offers money in exchange for the service rendered and departs the service environment. Many variants exist, however. In the case of government services, there is typically only one agency providing service. Sometimes the customer pays a set periodic fee in exchange for an

unspecified amount of service (e.g., membership in a club, professional association, or health maintenance organization [HMO]). Service transactions may occur over the telephone rather than face-to-face, and they can even occur without a human provider. For instance, automatic teller machines (ATMs) and voice mail instructions are increasingly available to provide service to customers.

In purchasing a good (e.g., a car or a TV), a customer will usually determine its satisfaction and utility by assessing the purchased good itself. However, the customer's assessment of the utility of a service purchase is dependent on his or her experience in the interaction with the service provider. In fact, the social interaction between the recipient and the provider is to a large extent the service rendered. Those who study services often point out that services are produced and consumed simultaneously to separate them from goods in which production and consumption are separate processes (Gronroos, 1983, 1990; Schneider & Bowen, 1985, p. 423).

Service interactions can take place between two people who know each other or between two strangers (Gutek, 1995; Gutek, Bhappu, Liao-Troth, & Cherry, 1999). Service *relationships* occur when a customer has repeated contact with a particular provider. Customer and provider can get to know each other as role occupants and sometimes as acquaintances or even friends. *Encounters*, on the other hand, typically consist of a single interaction between a particular customer and provider; neither expects to interact with the other in the future. Most research on service providers focuses on encounters.

The Service Provider

Service providers deliver intangible goods to paying customers, usually face-to-face or over the phone. Employees who actually deliver the service and interact directly with customers are called frontline service personnel (Hochschild, 1983; Mac-Donald & Sirianni, 1996) because, in most cases, they are pseudo-ambassadors for the organization, living representations of the organization to the customer. According to Bulan, Erickson, and Wharton (1997), "The primary tasks of such [frontline] workers is not to produce material goods, but to produce speech, action, and emotion that symbolize one's willingness to 'do for' the client or customer" (p. 235). As organizations become more aware of the impact these representatives have on their customers' perception of the service interaction, they try to manage employees' behavior and emotions such that the service interaction is deemed satisfactory by the customers.

Customers who value expertise are likely to have relationships with providers they seek out based on reputation. This is true not only of highly educated professional service providers such as attorneys, physicians, and stockbrokers, but also of hairstylists, auto mechanics, nannies, and travel agents (Gutek, 1995). Providers who deliver service in encounters, on the other hand, are likely to be evaluated by their delivery style, especially if all providers deliver the same service (e.g., same quality hamburger and fries) or if the customer is not able to evaluate the provider's expertise (Gutek, 1995; Iacobucci, Grayson, & Ostrom, 1994).

The Customer

Customers purchase goods or services for which they or someone else typically pays, making them valuable assets because they ultimately assure profits and revenues that determine a service organization's success. Knowing who their customers are and understanding their customers is often viewed as a competitive advantage for service providers. Customers, who often witness the process of service delivery firsthand, usually measure the success of a service transaction by comparing the *actual* service quality with their *expected* service quality. Because customer satisfaction may determine the willingness to repeat a service delivery, service providers strive to know what does not satisfy people consuming their services. At times, when customers actively participate in the service transaction (e.g., using an ATM or filling out an order form before approaching a service counter), they are engaging in coproduction, so-called because of their participation in the production as well as the consumption of the service (Bowen & Jones, 1986; Mills, Chase, & Margulies, 1983).

Customers are typically treated differently in relationships and encounters. They may receive customized service from a provider they know and trust in a service relationship, whereas in an encounter, customers are typically subject to standardized treatment by a provider who is a stranger to them (including learning the provider's first name, e.g., "Hello, my name is Gary. I will be your server tonight!"). Although more frequent and better-paying customers may get priority over others in relationships, encounters usually are egalitarian (i.e., all customers are treated the same and are typically served on a first-come, first-served basis).

The Service Environment

The physical environment (Bitner, 1992) and the social environment (Baker, 1987) in which services are performed have long been the focus of research in the service literature. Bitner provides a framework that focuses on objective physical elements (the *servicescape*), such as ambient conditions, spatial layout and functionality, as well as signs, symbols, and artifacts. Bitner argues for the importance of considering the impact of physical surroundings on the behaviors of customers and employees. However, she excludes components of the social environment. Interpersonal issues between customers and service providers as well as gender issues have been considered by others (e.g., Baker, 1987) interested in either broadening the concept of servicescape or simply understanding the environment in which service interactions take place.

The Gendered Nature of Service

Because gender is a basic cognitive category by which we classify people (e.g., Bem, 1981; Laws, 1979) and because of its visibility, it is plausible to think that the gender of both participants will affect their experiences in service interactions and their evaluation of those experiences. Gender can affect the consumption and delivery of service in several ways. First, we can consider provider gender and/or customer gender. Because work is sex segregated, men are more likely to hold some provider jobs and women are more likely to hold other provider jobs. Although not as well documented or discussed, it is also probable that men are more likely to be customers in certain kinds of situations (e.g., buying tires, getting a haircut at a barber shop), whereas women are more likely to be customers in other situations (e.g., purchasing children's clothing or household items). Thus, we can consider the provider gender, customer gender, the gender role associated with the provider, and the gender role associated with the customer. A provider role is either congruent with (or "fits") one's gender or incongruent with gender. Similarly, a customer role is either congruent with (or "fits") one's gender or is incongruent with gender. Thus, one could be a female provider congruent with the provider role (e.g., a female waitperson), a female provider incongruent with the provider role (e.g., a female surgeon), a male provider congruent with the provider role (e.g., a male mechanic), or a male provider incongruent with the provider role (e.g., a male hairstylist). Similarly, one could be a female customer congruent with the customer role (e.g., getting a manicure), a female customer incongruent with the customer role (e.g., purchasing a tire for her motorcycle), a male customer congruent with customer role (e.g., purchasing sports equipment), or a male customer incongruent with customer role (e.g., getting a manicure). In this chapter, we use the term *congruency* or congruent to refer to the association between gender and role. We consider the term *fit* as a synonym for congruency.

Although we recognize that some provider roles and some customer roles may not be associated with one gender or the other, we expect that (1) these situations are relatively uncommon, (2) they are more common of the customer role than the provider role, and (3) whether a particular provider or customer role is associated with

one gender or the other changes over time. For example, the roles of residential real estate salesperson and bartender have relatively recently changed from being male dominated to female dominated (Reskin & Roos, 1990). The role of clinical psychologist, which today is relatively sex integrated, may in 10 or 20 years become female dominated, because jobs rarely stay sex integrated but tend to become either male dominated or female dominated over time. Today, both sexes do grocery shopping, whereas that was a customer role associated more with women in the past. In the past, men purchased cars much more often than women, but today both sexes do so.

Gender can affect service delivery in yet other ways. Regardless of the provider or customer role, gender can be expected to have an effect. Sex-role spillover operates in service delivery such that women are expected to exhibit certain kinds of behaviors (whether they are in a congruent role or not) and so are men (Gutek & Morasch, 1982; Nieva & Gutek, 1981). Sex-role spillover is the carryover of gender-role expectations to the provider role and/or the customer role. For example, women providers and customers, regardless of the sex composition of the occupation they hold, may be expected to smile more, to be nicer or more accommodating than men in the same position. More than women, men may be expected to act as an authority or be waited on quickly. Thus, sex-role stereotyping may affect both provider and customers and may influence how both respond to the service interaction. Furthermore, sex-role spillover may be stronger when providers are in jobs that are sex-role congruent, where the job itself takes on aspects of gender role (Gutek & Morasch, 1982; Sheffey & Tindale, 1992).

One aspect of sex-role spillover that has been examined in several studies is emotional labor. Hochschild (1983) defined emotional labor as the "management of feeling to create a publicly observable facial and bodily display" (p. 7). Women may be expected to engage in more emotional labor than men, that is, to create a publicly observable facial and bodily display more than men are expected to do so. In addition, men may be expected to engage in a different kind of emotional labor (e.g., to be demanding or authoritative when selling insurance or collecting debts) than women (who, more often, may be expected to create a friendly, ingratiating, or perky emotional display). Although the concept of emotional labor has generated considerable interest among researchers (e.g., James, 1989; Rafaeli, 1989a, 1989b; Sutton & Rafaeli, 1988), relatively little has focused on gender as our review below shows.

Gender can be considered in yet another way in the study of service delivery because service delivery takes place between two people, each of whom is either a man or a woman.[1] A study may focus on the gender of the provider but ignore (or not study) the gender of the customer. Alternately, a study may focus on the gender of the customer but ignore (or not study) the gender of the provider. A study may also focus on both the gender of the provider and the gender of the customer. Figure 27.1 shows a 2 x 2 matrix that allows one to classify research on service delivery into one of four cells. The majority of the research on service delivery falls into Cell I, in which the gender of provider and gender of customer are both ignored (or not studied). In contrast, as will be clear in our review of the literature that follows, relatively few studies fall into the other three cells.

Cell III is particularly relevant to researchers interested in the study of gender and services because they can consider not only whether both customer and provider are congruent or incongruent with gender role but also whether provider and customer are the same gender or a different gender. That is, we can consider the gender composition of the provider-customer dyad. We use the term *gender matching* to refer to those instances in which provider and customer are the same gender. Where customer and provider are different genders, gender is not "matched." Note that one can have gender matching (provider and cus-

tomer are same gender) but one or both parties may be incongruent with gender role. For example, there is a gender match when a female patient has a female surgeon although that female surgeon is gender incongruent because surgery is a male-dominated field. There is a gender match when a male customer sees a male loan officer at a bank; in addition, both customer and provider are congruent with their respective roles. Men are expected to seek bank loans more than women, and traditionally more loan officers are male than female (Kulik & Holbrook, 1998).

In sum, in examining gender and service delivery, one can examine the gender of provider and/or customer, the congruency between the provider and customer roles and gender of the provider and customer, the spillover of gender role to both the provider and customer role, and the effects of having provider and customer the same or different genders. Despite the myriad ways in which gender can affect service delivery, the available research, reviewed below, is scanty. It shows that very few of the many possibilities have been explored.

Gender and Service Providers

We now turn to a review of the research on gender and service delivery, starting with research on service providers.

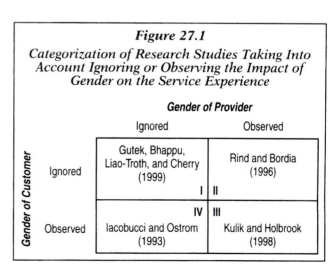

Figure 27.1

Categorization of Research Studies Taking Into Account Ignoring or Observing the Impact of Gender on the Service Experience

		Gender of Provider	
		Ignored	Observed
Gender of Customer	Ignored	Gutek, Bhappu, Liao-Troth, and Cherry (1999) I	Rind and Bordia (1996) II
	Observed	IV Iacobucci and Ostrom (1993)	III Kulik and Holbrook (1998)

Depending on the industry, the majority of service providers can be male or female or the work can be gender integrated. The traditional women's professions, nursing (94.5% female in 1990), elementary school teaching (85.2% female in 1990), librarianship (83.3% female in 1990), and social work (68.2% female in 1990, see Williams, 1995, p. 3), are all service jobs; not surprisingly, women occupy a majority of the service jobs in the United States (U.S. Bureau of the Census, 1996). Hochschild (1983, Table 4, pp. 240–241) estimated that in 1970 approximately 4.4 million women and 3.6 million men worked in service occupations excluding private household workers (a very high proportion of whom are women). According to Adkins (1995, p. 8), 81% of all employed women in Britain work in service occupations and more than 70% of women's employment in nine of the member states of the European Community is concentrated in the service sector. It is therefore not surprising that service jobs tend to be sex segregated, with women dominating some areas (e.g., manicurists, baby-sitters, flight attendants, and dental hygienists) and men dominating others (e.g., police officers, insurance salespersons, bill collectors, and physicians). As Leidner (1991) notes, the "gender segregation of service jobs contributes to the general perception that differences in men and women's social positions are straightforward reflections of differences in their natures and capabilities" (p. 175).

Research on service providers tends to focus on several service domains including industrial selling, banking, hospitals, restaurants, dental services, and insurance sales. In general, there is relatively little research on gender and service providers; what exists tends to focus on a somewhat disparate set of topics. We divide the research into two broad topics: the delivery of services by male and female providers and customers' reactions to male and female providers. Within each of these topics, we review research relevant to each of the gender concepts reviewed above. Much of the research focuses on sex-role spillover (i.e., the carryover of gender-based expectations to the workplace). This is discussed as

"doing gender" and as creating "gender scripts." In addition, there is some research on emotional labor, including the extent to which men versus women are expected to engage in emotional labor and how emotional labor affects them and their job satisfaction. Surprisingly little research focuses on the effects of being in a gender-incongruent job, but some research focuses on gender matching (i.e., differences in behavior when provider and customer are either the same sex or different sexes).

Delivery of Services by Male and Female Providers

Siguaw and Honeycutt (1995) investigated gender differences in selling behaviors and job attitudes of industrial salespersons who sell high-cost products, typically including high-quality service and expertise, to the buyer. Their results support previous findings that saleswomen have higher customer-oriented selling behaviors (Busch & Bush, 1978; Gibson & Swan, 1981) and are more considerate of their customers (Rhey, Rustogi, & Watson, 1992). Responses to a self-report questionnaire by members of a sales association yielded a response rate of only 16.4%, and of those responding, only 10.4% were women. Although the authors argue that the low representation of females is consistent with the male-dominated industrial sales industry, both the low response rate and the low representation of women raise concerns about the validity of the results.

Many other studies show that sex-role spillover is common in service delivery. For example, it has been posited that organizations create gendered scripts of behavior for employees to use while on the job, requiring workers to display their gender as an integral part of their job tasks and duties (Hall, 1993). A female provider is doing gender if she presents herself as a caring nurturer, a motherlike figure providing for her child, or a sex object (Hall, 1993). From the data yielded in the case study, Hall (1993) concluded that restaurants create gendering processes by embedding gender into prescribed work performance; specifically, they "frame service work as women's work . . . construct and legitimate a gendered image of a deferential servant . . . and structure interactions of women servers as sexual objects" (pp. 455–456). For example, restaurants tend to hire women who display social and domestic skills needed to perform good service. Hall also reveals that managers are sometimes "pleased when customers make sexual advances" toward their servers (p. 457).

In another case study, Leidner (1991) investigated two highly routinized interactive service jobs: fast food counter workers and insurance sales.

Leidner (1991) noted that both McDonald's counter workers and insurance salespersons have to "take on the role of interactive inferior, adjusting themselves to the styles and apparent preferences of their customers and paste on smiles when they did not feel like smiling and to behave cheerfully and deferentially to people of every status and with every attitude" (p. 171). However, managers, customers, and employees generally interpret these tasks in different ways depending on the structure of the environment, the incumbents, and the perception of control or subservience in the service context, which encourages sex-role spillover. The standardization of many service interactions encourages "repeat performances" of socially congruent gendered behaviors. As an example, trainers and agents view insurance sales jobs as demanding masculine attributes like determination, aggressiveness, and persistence. By continually reinforcing these attributes, through training and organizational literature, the "manly" nature of the sales job is understood.

It is not only jobs or organizational practices that encourage sex-role spillover but also service workers' behavior. In a sense, the service provider affirms his or her own gender identity when he or she works in a way that matches the socially constructed stereotype of male or female. As Leidner (1991) suggests, "Workers in all kinds of jobs need to consider how their work relates to their own identities, including their gender identities" (p. 157). Thus, service providers might be more comfortable in their jobs when they behave in a manner

consistent with gender-role expectations. If that were the case, one might expect that service providers in gender-incongruent jobs would experience more negative job outcomes than those who are in jobs that are traditionally held by their sex. But the scant research available suggests that this is not necessarily the case. For example, Siguaw and Honeycutt (1995) found that industrial saleswomen have lower levels of role conflict and role ambiguity than their male counterparts.

Because an important aspect of service work is attentiveness to customers' needs and expectations, many organizations are creating prescriptions of behavior for frontline employees to follow. For instance, some service personnel are expected to smile and greet each customer as if they were really glad to see them. These performance expectations create an additional type of employee cost (in excess of physical or mental work), which has been termed emotional labor (Hochschild, 1983). Albrecht and Zemke (1985) described the emotion management task: "The service person must deliberately involve his or her feelings in the situation. He or she may not particularly feel like being cordial and becoming a one-minute friend to the next customer who approaches, but that is indeed what frontline work entails" (p. 114). This presentation of self used to be a private issue; now it is often controlled by an organization (Hochschild, 1983; Wharton, 1993). Emotional labor may produce a workforce of people faking their feelings to increase profit share (Hochschild, 1983; Leidner, 1991).

In her pioneering study, Hochschild (1983) examined two service occupations, flight attendants and bill collectors. Although both are "frontline" service workers, they are expected to display very different emotions. Whereas flight attendants are expected to be cheerful, nurturing, and subservient, bill collectors are expected to be suspicious and sometimes exude bad will (Hochschild, 1983, p. 137).

Hochschild (1983) concluded that emotional labor has costs for workers. Workers can identify wholeheartedly with the job and risk burnout, or they can separate themselves from the job and feel they are "fakes, just acting" (p. 187). Although both sexes are expected to engage in emotional labor, Hochschild contends that men and women experience it differently. In particular, she argues that (1) women more than men are expected to be emotional managers and (2) men have a "status shield" that protects them against poorer treatment of their feelings. She notes that female flight attendants are "the company's main shock absorbers against 'mishandled' passengers" and that "their own feelings are more frequently subjected to rough treatment" (p. 175).

Although Hochschild's innovative notion of emotional labor has fostered a substantial amount of research, not everyone agrees that emotional labor is exclusively a cost. Being good at emotional labor might be a source of accomplishment and satisfaction. As Bulan et al. (1997) suggest and Wharton (1993, p. 218) states, "It may be that previous researchers have overstated the psychological costs and understated the psychological rewards of emotional labor, relative to other types of work."

Richmond (1997) explored Hochschild's suggestion that emotional labor is associated with negative job outcomes by studying 203 fast-food workers at one of 14 locations of a chain of stores in Tucson, Arizona. Contrary to expectations, she found that employees who engaged in more emotional labor reported greater job satisfaction, more job commitment, and less job stress than service providers who did not.

A number of researchers have extended Hochschild's (1983) work by doing in-depth case studies of service work, focusing specifically on gender and emotional labor. For examples, see Adkins (1995) on the tourism industry in Britain, Pierce (1995) on law firms in the San Francisco area, and Tyler and Taylor (1998) on the airline industry in the United Kingdom. Others have used survey research to study gender and emotional labor. For example, Wharton (1993) examined the social-psychological consequences, both positive and negative, of emotional labor for a sample of men and women service providers. She hypothesized that women are more likely to be involved in

emotional labor jobs than men and will suffer more negative effects of emotional labor because their feelings on the job are less protected than those of men.

Wharton found that men and women were equally unlikely to experience emotional exhaustion from emotional labor but, in direct contrast to the hypothesized relationship, the women who engaged in emotional labor were more satisfied with their jobs than their male counterparts (p. 225). Bulan et al. (1997) claim that women may be less negatively affected by emotional labor because of their satisfaction in interacting with other people.

Bulan et al. (1997) were interested in understanding the impact of organizationally imposed rules of facial and bodily display on employees' feelings of inauthenticity at work. They operationalized inauthenticity as the employees' inability to be themselves at work and how often they had to "fake how they really felt when they were at work" (p. 240). Results showed that service providers who spent more time interacting with other employees had lower levels of inauthenticity, whereas "handling people" was related to higher levels of inauthenticity:

> Most [women] experience the most inauthenticity when they were highly involved in their jobs and did not spend much time interacting with other workers. In contrast, men felt most inauthentic when they were *not* very involved in their jobs and did not spend much time interacting with others. (Bulan et al., 1997, p. 252)

Most of the research on emotional labor focuses on service encounters where providers are interacting with customers whom they have neither previously met nor expect to meet again in the future. Because the customer is a stranger, the provider typically has no prior feelings about him or her and therefore manufactures the appropriate emotion as part of the job. The effects of service relationships on emotional labor, however, may be quite different (Gutek, 1995, pp. 80–83). In relationships, the provider not only displays appropriate emotions but also, over time, develops real feelings about the customer, and vice versa. Although in some cases the emotions may be strong, both customer and provider are expected to refrain from displaying their felt emotions. For them, emotional labor means putting aside real feelings and displaying less intense, blander emotions, whether positive or negative. Service providers cannot let a client know they think he or she is boring or obnoxious. Repeated interaction can lead to one person developing strong bonds of affection, physical attraction, or love, which may not be reciprocated by the other. At the very least, strong emotions can complicate the service relationship. In contrast to the burgeoning research on emotional labor and emotional expression in encounters, these phenomena have not been studied in service relationships.

Reactions to Male and Female Service Providers

It is probable that customers facilitate sex-role spillover when they react to male and female providers differently because of the gender stereotypes they hold. These gender stereotypes can affect a provider's behavior in a number of ways. One possibility is that some behavior may be more effective for a female than a male provider in the same job, and vice versa. An interesting example comes from a series of studies on tipping behavior in restaurants.

Research has shown that certain provider behaviors (e.g., smiling) can generate increased restaurant tips given by customers (Tidd & Lockard, 1978). Rind and Bordia (1995) found that writing "thank you" on the back of the check resulted in positive tipping behavior. In a later study, they examined the effect of drawing a happy face on the back of the check. Using both male and female servers allowed them to ascertain whether the gender of the server combined with the drawing had any effect on tipping behavior. To test this, two servers (one male, one female) provided service at an upscale restaurant during the lunch hour throughout a 3-day period. To achieve randomization, each server was given 50 3 x 5 cards, half with a happy face,

the other half blank. At the end of the meal, the server randomly selected a card. If a happy face was drawn, the server drew a happy face on the back of the meal check; if a card was blank, the server simply delivered the check.

Rind and Bordia (1996) hypothesized that drawing a happy face on the check would be effective for the female server but not for the male server (the happy face would be considered "perfectly natural" for a woman to draw, but not for a man). They thought that the drawing would create a negative impression of the man and would likely negate any positive "friendliness" effect of the drawing on tipping behavior. On the other hand, the woman would be responding to sex-role spillover or doing gender by drawing a happy face because women are believed to be more emotionally expressive than men (Allen & Haccoun, 1976; Broverman, Vogel, Broverman, Clarkson, & Rosenkrantz, 1972). A woman would engage in sex-role spillover when she drew a happy face, a man when he did not draw a happy face. Results show that the happy face significantly increased tips for women but not for men.

Under some circumstances, the gender of the service provider may be less important than whether the service dyad is same sex or other sex. For example, an other-sex customer might elicit different behavior in a provider than a same-sex customer. Hall (1993) found that food servers were friendlier to customers of the other gender (e.g., male servers were most apt to flirt with a party composed of women, and female servers were most likely to flirt with a male-dominated group). As well, she found that although flirting occurred at high-prestige restaurants, job flirts and sexual bantering by waitresses were more likely to occur at low-prestige restaurants than in elite restaurants. Finally, Hall found that control clashes were more likely to occur when the customer and provider were of the same gender. As one waiter remarked about his interactions with male customers, "[They] tend to talk a little harshly to the waiter . . . 'Hey, get me this' . . . and the waiter takes offense . . . 'I'm not a dog . . . I'm not below you' " (Hall, 1993, p. 463).

Gender and Customers

We all play the role of customer many times a week, but there is evidence that women play that role more often than men. In fact, the amount of goods and services purchased by American women is staggering. By one estimate, women in the United States have "more purchasing power than the total economic output of any other country, including Japan" (Katz & Katz, 1997, p. 4). Katz and Katz argue that women can put this purchasing power to work in a variety of ways by supporting companies that are woman-friendly. To help women in this endeavor, they rate companies, states, and countries on a variety of criteria, including number of women on the board, number of female top officers, the company's benefits program, and pay disparities. Although it is generally acknowledged that gender is important, there is a paucity of research on how gender affects the experiences or evaluation of customers. "Gender colors what we customers expect as good service" (Hall, 1993, p. 452). Our real-world experiences as customers of service establishments help to bolster our feelings that one gender often does a better job in one service area than in others.

We divide the research on gender and customers into two areas: treatment of male and female customers and male and female customers' evaluation of services. Within these two areas, we examine the extent to which gender congruency, sex-role spillover, and gender matching are studied. In the case of research on customers, gender matching sometimes assumes an in-group bias (i.e., that customers prefer a service provider of their own sex).

Treatment of Male and Female Customers

Although the effects of customers' gender during the delivery of services have not been subject to much research, speculations about gender differences naturally lead to the question of whether a customer's sex affects the service that the customer receives. Zinkhan and Stoiadin (1984) attempted to determine if men receive service priority over women in department stores. They defined priority as the order of service when two customers arrive at a department store counter simultaneously. Even though service priority does not directly measure service quality, service length, or interpersonal treatment, it is nevertheless considered to be an important service dimension.

In the study, pairs of one female and one male customer simultaneously approached a counter in various department stores; observers recorded which one (the male, the female, or neither) received service first. Results show that men receive service priority over women. Men were served first 63% of the time and women 23.5% of the time; 13.5% of the time service priority was considered neutral. The male advantage was homogeneous across several factors such as price of merchandise (high, moderate, low) and type of merchandise ("male," "female," "neutral"). Furthermore, the sex of the clerk also did not significantly affect the results. The only exception was that female customers who shopped in department stores offering primarily "male" products received especially poor service.

Beliefs about male and female customers appeared to influence the results in Zinkhan and Stoiadin's (1984) study. Qualitative data, obtained through interviews with clerks after observations of service priority, suggest that women are perceived to shop around more, that they need less help than men, that men are more serious buyers, and that men are easier to deal with.

In a similar field study, Stead and Zinkhan (1986) examined whether certain customer characteristics, such as sex and dress, affect service priority. Again, a male and a female customer arrived simultaneously at a counter in a department store and observations were made as to who received service first. Results were similar to Zinkhan and Stoiadin's (1984) study. Overall, men were served first 61% of the time and women 32% of the time; in 7% of the cases service priority was neutral. Customer dress also showed a significant effect. Men in business dress were served first

67.3% of the time, whereas those in casual dress were served first only 54.7% of the time. Service promptness was especially low, however, for women in business dress (29.3%) relative to those in casual dress (34.7%). No other main effects or interactions were observed. Neither the sex of the clerk nor the type of department store (selling either "female," "male," or "neutral" products) was significant.

Evaluation of Services by Male and Female Customers

Iacobucci and Ostrom (1993) studied the role of customers' sex in the delivery of services by drawing on the literature on gender differences in information processing as well as Fiedler's (1967) work on leadership, suggesting that some people are more task oriented and others are more relationship oriented. Iacobucci and Ostrom cite several studies (Eagly, Makhijani, & Klonsky, 1992; Inderlied & Powell, 1979) as further evidence that under certain circumstances, men may be more goal oriented and women more relationship oriented.

Applying these findings to the service setting, Iacobucci and Ostrom (1993) predicted that the two sexes will attend differently to two components of the service experience that have been identified in the marketing literature: the core service (e.g., a haircut or a dinner) and the relationship component (e.g., the interpersonal interaction between the service provider and the customer as well as the delivery of the service itself) (Berry, 1983). Using written scenarios describing hypothetical short-run and long-run service experiences, Iacobucci and Ostrom expected that in the short run, men will attend more to the core service and women to the relationship component. In the long run, one expects these differences to disappear because if one of the two components is not satisfactory in repeated interactions, the customer is likely to be dissatisfied with the service overall and is less likely to return to the provider in the future.

Overall, the results suggest that there are indeed differences between men and women in the evaluation of services. However, the data did not clearly support the initial hypotheses and are somewhat complicated and contradictory. For example, women seem to attend to both aspects (core service and relationship component) in the short run as well as in the long run. Men, on the other hand, attend more to the core service in the short run and attend to both components in the long run, suggesting that men and women attend to different aspects of service in service encounters but not in service relationships. More specifically, in service encounters women attend more than men to service delivery, whereas in relationships both sexes attend to both service and service delivery.

Mohr and Henson (1996) examined whether customers care about the gender of a service provider and whether there is a general bias in favor of one gender over the other. They explored congruency bias (i.e., customers preferring men in male-dominated jobs and women in female-dominated jobs) and in-group bias (i.e., customers preferring providers of their own sex).[2]

The results of responses to written scenarios of hypothetical service encounters in which one expects either mostly male or mostly female employees show that customers generally preferred employees whose gender is congruent with the gender type of the job (e.g., a male auto mechanic or a female nurse). Some evidence (though not very strong) of in-group bias existed in that male and female customers generally seemed to prefer same-sex providers.

Overall, it appears that the gender of providers had far less of an effect than service quality on the evaluation of customer satisfaction. Customers rate providers more favorably if their sex is congruent with their expectation, but overall service quality plays a more important role than the gender of the service provider.

Another study suggests that in the field of psychotherapy, there have been some changes in clients' expectations. Stamler, Christiansen, Staley, and Macagno-Shang (1991) cited an earlier study by Fuller (1964), who found that both male and female clients indicated a preference for male counselors, presumably because males were viewed as more competent. In their study of 495 clients who participated in an intake interview for individual therapy at a large university during 1987, Stamler et al. (1991) asked, "Do you have a preference for a male or female therapist?" They found that 57% of women and 37% of men expressed a preference; of those who did, a majority of both sexes (90% of women and 69% of men) said they preferred a female therapist. Perhaps women, or women therapists more specifically, were viewed in 1987 as more competent than they were in 1964 or perhaps factors other than competence influenced the choice of clients. Therapy has changed over the years from being a male-dominated field to being a gender-neutral or even female-dominated area. Thus, in 1964 male therapists were gender congruent, whereas by 1987 it was female therapists, at least in the minds of some clients.

Finally, in her in-depth interview study of 76 men working in the traditionally female professions of nursing, elementary school teaching, librarianship, and social work, Williams (1995) found that customers expected these service workers to be women. Men, she concludes, face discrimination and prejudice from "clients, who often react negatively to male nurses, teachers, and to a lesser extent, librarians. Many people assume that the men are sexually suspect if they are employed in these 'feminine' occupations either because they do or they do not conform to stereotypical masculine characteristics" (Williams, 1995, p. 108). Men who conform to masculine stereotypes are viewed as potential sexual predators who might exploit their access to vulnerable populations like children or patients, whereas those who do not are suspected of homosexuality.

Gender matching assumes that customers prefer a same-sex service provider. Kulik and Holbrook (1998) recently conducted an interesting study that examined the effects of gender and race matching between customers and service providers. Kulik and Holbrook surveyed 119 people who had applied for a loan from a large

bank. The respondent pool included multiple races and both sexes (57% were male). (For the purposes of this chapter, the race effects are not discussed.) The researchers expected that gender-matched customers would not respond any differently to unfavorable outcomes than would gender-unmatched customers; results, however, were contrary to the hypothesis. In fact, gender-matched customers responded most negatively to unfavorable outcomes. They reasoned that this result is based on the customers' trust in the service provider, citing organizational research that suggests that lower levels of trust are sometimes observed in female gender-matched relationships.

For this study in particular, the gender-matching effect suggests that female customers may respond negatively to unfavorable outcomes because they perceive that the female loan officer has limited ability to provide a more favorable outcome. Male gender typing of the loan officer job may fuel expectations by customers that female loan officers will provide inferior outcomes. Drawing conclusions from these results may be a bit premature, however, in that only one service area was investigated and results were not easily explained. Perhaps men and women prefer interacting with members of the other sex in applying for loans just as wait staff and their customers seem to (Hall, 1993). Additional research is needed to more fully understand gender matching between service provider and customer.

Gender and the Service Environment

A number of researchers have examined the way customers respond to the service environment. Building on Bitner's (1992) concept of the servicescape, Fischer, Gainer, and Bristor (1998) explore what makes servicescapes feel more or less gendered. Fischer et al. presented participants with hypothetical service scenarios (e.g., auto repair shops, hardware stores, fabric stores, and aerobic classes). They collected qualitative data by asking open-ended questions about reactions to particular service settings that were not clearly labeled as male or female, about elements that participants perceived as contributing to the gendering of the servicescape, and about suggestions of how a new hair studio or auto repair facility should be designed to target the other sex (e.g., layout and design). As one would expect, results suggest that people perceive some service settings to be gendered. However, the cues in the environment that seem to be responsible for these perceptions are not all physical. It appears that people perceive the sex of the provider, the sex of the people who will be in the service setting, and which sex will buy or use the product or service to be most important in influencing the perception of gendered servicescapes. Interestingly, people seem to "construct" servicescapes in their own minds. Even though they had never actually been in the hypothetical service settings that were described, the study's participants nevertheless formed a clear representation of what the service-scape would be like.

The most common reactions to gendered spaces by the "other gender" are confusion and mystery, as well as fear and feeling unwelcome and alien (Fischer et al., 1998). When they are in men's spaces, women report lack of information and lack of control as a common fear, whereas men in women's spaces fear a contamination of their masculinity. Schmidt and Sapsford (1995) reported similar findings in a study that examined females' reactions to being in public bars in the United Kingdom, a service environment that appears to be traditionally male. Focus groups and in-depth interviews with women between 26 and 47 years of age revealed that, from the moment they walk in the bar and feel the stares of male customers, to bartenders' behavior that appears to be preferential toward males, to sitting alone at a table and feeling vulnerable, female customers often feel uncomfortable and intimidated and perceive the servicescape to be highly gendered.

Fischer et al.'s (1998) conclusion that the sex of service providers and the sex of customers are the most salient in the perception of gendered servicescapes has also been supported by Stern, Gould, and Tewari (1993). Stern et al. found that service-related variables (those pertaining to service context) were more important in determining sex-typed service images than self-related variables (those pertaining to the customer). Although many services have sex-typed images based on masculinity or femininity ratings, the sex of the customer only partially influences the sex typing of services. Furthermore, study respondents tended to predict that the sex of the "typical customer" and the "typical provider" will be congruent with the sex-typed images (e.g., typical customers and providers of a feminine service [jewelry store] are likely to be women).

Methods of Studying Gender and Service Delivery

Research Design

In studying gender and service providers, researchers have mainly used self-report questionnaires and large-scale surveys directed toward frontline service providers (Bulan et al., 1997; Klose & Finkle, 1995; Siguaw & Honeycutt, 1995; Wharton, 1993) or their customers (Klose & Finkle), or they conduct case studies. In general, whereas questionnaires ask frontline service personnel about the requirements and the consequences of service work, the case studies investigate sex-role spillover or the "gendering" of jobs (Adkins, 1995; Hall, 1993; Leidner, 1991; Pierce, 1995; Tyler & Taylor, 1998; Williams, 1995) including the emotional requirements of frontline service employees (Hochschild, 1983; Pierce, 1995). Illustrative information about real employees in real service jobs has been obtained by conducting interviews with employees and engaging in participant observation of actual work. In many qualitative studies, researchers rely on multiple methods of obtaining information (e.g., participant observation, content analysis of documents, structured or unstructured interviews)

(Leidner, 1993; Tyler & Taylor, 1998). Multiple sites are frequently studied (Hall, 1993; Pierce, 1995). In some cases, researchers have attended training or worked in the job of service provider to gain information about the work (Adkins, 1995; Hochschild, 1983; Pierce, 1995). For example, to learn about service jobs at McDonald's, Leidner (1991, 1993) attended classes at Hamburger University (McDonald's training center), participated in orientation and "window crew" training, and actually worked as a food order taker. To learn about insurance sales jobs, she went through a two-week training program for life insurance agents, interviewed agents, and worked with a team in the field.

In studying gender issues from the customer's viewpoint, a common approach is to use written scenarios that describe a particular hypothetical service experience (Fischer, Gainer, & Bristor, 1997, 1998; Iacobucci & Ostrom, 1993; Mohr & Henson, 1996). Participants (students in most cases) read a hypothetical scenario and then rated the quality of service and service satisfaction, as well as other aspects regarding the service experience. Using written scenarios in the laboratory allows for tight control over independent variables such as characteristics of the customer and the provider, and the physical and social aspects of the service environment. In one study (Fischer et al., 1997), participants were shown black-and-white line drawings to elicit visual perceptions about the service environment. Although these methods are effective in controlling the environment being explored, they lack realism and may not be very effective in collecting data about actual reactions from real customers.

Despite some of the methodological challenges, field studies are very effective in overcoming some of the shortcomings of laboratory studies. Most important, actual behavior can be observed, rather than asking people how they would behave or feel in a hypothetical situation. A few researchers (Rind & Bordia, 1996; Stead & Zinkhan, 1986; Zinkhan & Stoiadin, 1984) have designed field studies to investigate gender effects in the real world. Even though most such studies are limited to service encounters within a particular domain (e.g., department stores), the results are nevertheless interesting and suggest the need for further research using field experiments.

Service Domains

Domains studied in the research on gender and the delivery of services have typically been service settings that are commonly perceived to be dominated by one gender—for example, beauty salons and barber shops (Fischer et al., 1998), auto repair (Mohr & Henson, 1996), banking (Bulan et al., 1997; Wharton, 1993), health care (Bulan et al., 1997; Mohr & Henson, 1996), and industrial selling (Siguaw & Honeycutt, 1995). Even though one would expect these service environments to differ in certain physical attributes, Fischer et al.'s (1998) hypothetical examples of hardware stores, fabric stores, auto repair shops, and aerobics studios suggest that gendered servicescapes are mainly socially constructed rather than physically constructed.

Service Usage and Duration

In the past, it appears that researchers limited their investigations to frequent customer usage environments (e.g., barber shops). Gutek et al. (in press), on the other hand, investigate both frequent and infrequent service interaction environments to gain a better understanding of the complexity of all types of service interactions. Extant research has mainly investigated service interactions that occur over a short duration or are one-time interactions (Gutek, 1995). In most cases, the service interaction took place between strangers (i.e., encounters), not between individuals known to each other (i.e., relationships). Additionally, most research conducted thus far on service and gender reflects occupations that are staffed by nonprofessionals (e.g., food servers), possibly because of researchers' accessibility to these occupations.

As researchers continue examining gender effects in service interactions, they should pay careful attention to the duration of the interaction, the type of interaction (encounter or relationship), and whether the service provider is considered a professional (e.g., lawyer, accountant, physician). We reason that the effects of gender will be different or maybe nonexistent in certain kinds of service interactions. Because some professional jobs are stereotyped as either male or female, gender may play a part in the customer's evaluation of service quality. Williams (1995) found, for example, that some customers are suspicious of the motives of men in the female-dominated professions of nursing, elementary school teaching, and social work. However, the certification or licensing of service providers may help to calm customers' fears about the expertise (of female providers) or the motivations (of male providers), thus making gender less important. On the other hand, the gender of the provider may be a ready attribution if the service outcome is unfavorable (e.g., "I knew I shouldn't have trusted a woman to sell industrial equipment"), but may be irrelevant for favorable outcomes (Kulik & Holbrook, 1998).

Similarly, gender effects might differ depending on whether the provider and customer have a service relationship or a one-time encounter (see Gutek, 1995, pp. 253–257). Encounters are universalistic and egalitarian in that everyone, at least in theory, is treated the same and given equal access to treatment; providers who discriminate against any class of customer could be charged with discrimination. The one-time nature of encounters invites stereotyping because neither customer nor provider has any prior experience with the other. Because gender is so noticeable, it is easy to attribute behavior to gender when it fits a gender stereotype (e.g., "She took forever to make up her mind" and "Men buy on impulse"). Although it is relatively difficult to discriminate in encounters, it is easier to do so in relationships where, generally, men and women can select same-sex providers if they choose. Thus, we might expect to see more gender matching in relationships

than in encounters. Relationships do not facilitate stereotyping, however, because customer and provider build up a history of interaction against which they can interpret any specific behavior (e.g., "She took a long time to make up her mind because she was distracted by family problems" and "He was late for work so he did the shopping quickly"). In short, we would expect to see more discriminatory treatment in relationships and more stereotyping in encounters.

Conclusions

Although it is clear that services are increasingly important and a dominant force in the United States and the global economy, we know relatively little about how gender affects the service delivery process. It appears that the old dichotomy of men earning money and women spending it is breaking down, yet we seem to have relatively little information in the research literature (perhaps much more in marketing research) about the extent to which men versus women provide and purchase services. (For an exception, see Katz & Katz, 1997.)

Service jobs, occupations, and industries seem to be as sex segregated as those in the non-service sector, and sex-role spillover appears to play a role in the delivery of service. Stereotypes appear to affect men and women who are in nontraditional service jobs, much as they affect any other nontraditional worker. Sex-role spillover occurs, however, as much or more in traditionally female jobs, where it appears that the job takes on some of the characteristics that are associated with being female (e.g., being patient and nurturing). Presumably, sex-role spillover occurs in traditionally male jobs as well, but most of the research focuses on women in traditional jobs (e.g., flight attendants, wait staff). Williams's (1995) research is an exception.

One difference between service jobs and other jobs is that providers are affected by stereotypes held by customers as well as those held by managers and coworkers.

Furthermore, service providers also engage in sex-role spillover; they seem to expect male customers in some situations and females in others, apparently based on history or institutionalization (i.e., whichever sex has filled the role in the past seems to be viewed as the appropriate one to fill the role in the present). Being stereotyped is a particular concern for encounter providers and customers. Because each interacts only once with the other in encounters, providers and customers do not even have the opportunity to counteract stereotyping the way a provider can with a coworker or manager, or the way both provider and customer can with the "regular" customers or provider in a service relationship.

Although there is some evidence that providers and customers of the "wrong" sex are penalized or punished (Williams, 1995), the results are not always consistent (Siguaw & Honeycutt, 1995), nor is it clear how they attempt to compensate, successfully or unsuccessfully, for their disadvantage. Finally, service environments are gendered to the extent that the people in them (providers and customers) are one sex or the other. People, not physical cues, make a service environment gendered.

In contrast to gender congruency and sex-role spillover, we find less support for gender matching. It is not clear that gender matching of customer and provider systematically yields either positive or negative results. In some situations, such as in restaurants, being waited on (or waiting on) someone of the other sex seems to be desirable, but there is little support for the notion that across the board people prefer to interact with either the same sex or the other sex. The relative paucity of research on gender matching gives us little on which to base a conclusion. Examining the differences between, for example, the therapy situation (where a majority of women clients seem to prefer a female therapist) and restaurant dining (where both sexes might prefer the other sex as a waitperson or customer) might provide some clues about how gender matching works. Finally, we think it is important to place gender effects in context. Research is insufficient to determine the magnitude of gender effects, but even where gender is significant, it is not clear that the effect is all that strong. As the amount of research grows, it is important to report effect sizes so that we can compare the effects of gender with other factors. After all, don't we really just want good service?

Discussion Questions

1. Why do you think that gender of provider or customer is seldom studied in research on service work?

2. Have you ever worked where your gender was an "issue"? In what way?

Endnotes

1. The exception occurs when a customer interacts with a machine (e.g., ATM, voice mail) rather than a human service provider (see Gutek, 1995, chaps. 3, 8, and 9).
2. Their study fits under the general concept of a service gap (as summarized by Klose & Finkle, 1995). A service quality gap occurs when the actual service received fails to meet the consumer's expectations of the service experience. A particular example of this failed expectation can come as a result of a customer expecting a service provider of one gender and receiving the other gender instead.

References

Adkins, L. (1995). *Gendered work: Sexuality, family, and the labour market.* Buckingham, UK: Open University Press.

Albrecht, K., & Zemke, R. (1985). *Service America! Doing business in the new economy.* Homewood, IL: Dow Jones-Irwin.

Allen, J. G., & Haccoun, D. M. (1976). Sex differences in emotionality: A multidimensional approach. *Human Relations, 29,* 711–722.

Appelbaum, E. & Batt, R. (1994). *The new American workplace: Transforming work systems in the United States.* Ithaca, NY: ILR.

Baker, J. (1987). The role of environment in marketing services: The consumer perspective. In J. Czepiel, C. Congram, & J. Shanahan (eds.), *The services challenge: Integrating for competitive advantage.* Chicago: American Marketing Association.

Bell, D. (1976). *The coming post-industrial society: A venture in social forecasting.* New York: Basic Books.

Bem, S. L. (1981). Gender schema theory: A cognitive account of sex-typing. *Psychological Review, 88,* 254–364.

Berry, J. W. (1983). Acculturation: A comparative analysis of alternative forms. In R. J. Samuda & A. L. Woods (Eds.), *Perspectives in immigrant and minority education* (pp. 66–77). Lanham, MD: University Press of America.

Bitner, M. J. (1992). Servicescapes: The impact of surroundings on customers and employees. *Journal of Marketing, 56,* 57–71.

Bowen, D. E., & Jones, G. R. (1986). Transaction cost analysis of organization-customer exchange. *Academy of Management Review, 11*(2), 428–441.

Broverman, I. K., Vogel, S. R., Broverman, D. M., Clarkson, F. E., & Rosenkrantz, P. S. (1972). Sex-role stereotypes: A current appraisal. *Journal of Social Issues, 28*(2), 59–78.

Bulan, H. E, Erickson, R. J., & Wharton, A. S. (1997). Doing for others on the job: The affective requirements of service work, gender, and emotional well-being. *Social Problems, 44*(2), 235–256.

Bureau of Economic Analysis. (1998a, September 24). [On-line]. Available: <http://www.bea.doc.gov/bea/dn/niptbl-d.htm>.

Bureau of Economic Analysis. (1998b, September 25). [On-line]. Available: <http://www.bea.doc.gov/bea/dn/pitbl.htm>.

Busch, E., & Bush, R. F. (1978). Women contrasted to men in the industrial sales force: Job satisfaction, values, role clarity, performance, and propensity to leave. *Journal of Marketing Research, 25,* 438–448.

Buss, D. M. (1995). Psychological sex differences: Origins through sexual selection. *American Psychologist, 50,* 164–168.

Eagly, A. H., Makhijani, M. G., & Klonsky, B. G. (1992). Gender and the evaluation of leaders: A meta-analysis. *Psychological Bulletin, 111,* 3–22.

Fiedler, F. E. (1967). *A theory of leadership effectiveness.* New York: McGraw-Hill.

Fischer, E., Gainer, B., & Bristor, J. (1997). The sex of the service provider: Does it influence perceptions of service quality? *Journal of Retailing, 73*(3), 361–382.

——. (1998). Beauty salon and barbershop: Gendered servicescapes. In J. F. Sherry (Ed.), *Servicescapes* (pp. 565–590). Chicago: American Marketing Association.

Fuller, F. F. (1964). Preferences for male and female counselors. *Personnel and Guidance Journal, 42,* 463–467.

Gibson, C. K., & Swan, J. E. (1981). Sex roles and the desirability of job rewards, expectations, and aspirations of male versus female salespeople.

Journal of Personal Selling & Sales Management, 2, 39–45.

Gronroos, C. (1983). *A service quality model and its management implications.* Helsinki, Finland: Swedish School of Economics.

——. (1990). *Service marketing and management.* Toronto, ON: Lexington Books.

Gutek, B. A. (1995). *The dynamics of service: Reflections on the changing nature of customer/provider interactions.* San Francisco: Jossey-Bass.

Gutek, B. A., Bhappu, A. D., Liao-Troth, M. A., & Cherry, B. (1999). Distinguishing between service relationships and encounters. *Journal of Applied Psychology, 84*(2).

Gutek, B. A., & Morasch, B. (1982). Sex-ratios, sex-role spillover, and sexual harassment at work. *Journal of Social Issues, 38,* 55–74.

Hall, E. J. (1993). Smiling, deferring, and flirting. *Work and Occupations, 20*(4), 452–471.

Hochschild, A. R. (1983). *The managed heart.* Berkeley: University of California Press.

Iacobucci, D., Grayson, K., & Ostrom, A. (1994). Opinion: Customer satisfaction fables. *Sloan Management Review, 35*(4), 93–96,

Iacobucci, D., & Ostrom, A. (1993). Gender differences in the impact of core and relational aspects of services on the evaluation of service encounters. *Journal of Consumer Psychology, 2,* 257–286.

Inderlied, S. D., & Powell, G. (1979). Sex-role identity and leadership style: Different labels for the same concept? *Sex Roles, 5,* 613–623.

James, N. (1989). Emotional labor: Skill and work in the social regulation of feelings. *Sociological Focus, 37*(1), 15–42.

Katz, P., & Katz, M. (1997). *The feminist dollar.* New York: Plenum.

Klose, A., & Finkle, T. (1995). Service quality and the congruency of employee perceptions and customer expectations: The case of an electric utility. *Psychology & Marketing, 12*(7), 637–646.

Kulik, C. T., & Holbrook, R. L., Jr. (1998). *Demographics in service encounters: Effects of racial and gender congruence on perceived fairness.* Paper presented at the annual meeting of the Academy of Management, San Diego, CA.

Laws, J. L. (1979). *The second X: Sex role and social role.* New York: Elsevier.

Leidner, R. (1991). Serving hamburgers and selling insurance: Gender, work, and identity in interactive service jobs. *Gender & Society, 5*(2), 154–177.

——. (1993). *Fast food, fast talk: Service work and the routinization of everyday life.* Berkeley: University of California.

MacDonald, C. L., & Sirianni, C. (1996). *Working in the service society.* Philadelphia: Temple University Press.

Mills, P. K., Chase, R. B., & Margulies, N. (1983). Motivating the client/employee system as a service production strategy. *Academy of Management Review, 8*(2), 301–310.

Mohr, L. A., & Henson, S. W. (1996). Impact of employee gender and job congruency on customer satisfaction. *Journal of Consumer Psychology, 5*(2), 161–187.

Nieva, V. F., & Gutek, B. A. (1981). *Women and work: A psychological perspective.* New York: Praeger.

Pierce, J. (1995). *Gender trials: Emotional lives in contemporary law firms.* Berkeley: University of California Press.

Rafaeli, A. (1989a). When cashiers meet customers: An analysis of the role of supermarket cashiers. *Academy of Management Journal, 32*(2), 245–273.

———. (1989b). When clerks and customers meet: A test of variables related to emotional expressions on the job. *Journal of Applied Psychology, 74*(3), 385–393.

Reskin, B. F., & Roos, R. A. (1990). *Job queues, gender queues: Explaining women's inroads into male occupations.* Philadelphia: Temple University Press.

Rhey, W. L., Rustogi, H., & Watson, M. A. (1992). Buyer's perceptions of automobile saleswomen: A field study. In *Proceedings of the Southwestern Marketing Association* (pp. 41–46). Baton Rouge: Louisiana State University & Southwestern Marketing Association.

Richmond, S. (1997). *The demands-control model in a fast-food organization: Effects of emotional labor, customer behavior, demands, controls, and support.* Unpublished doctoral dissertation, Department of Management and Policy, University of Arizona.

Rind, B., & Bordia, P. (1995). Effect of server's "thank you" and personalization on restaurant tipping. *Journal of Applied Social Psychology, 25,* 745–751.

———. (1996). Effect of restaurant tipping on male and female servers drawing a happy, smiling face on the backs of customers' checks. *Journal of Applied Social Psychology, 26*(3), 218–225.

Schmidt, R. A., & Sapsford, R. (1995). Issues of gender and servicescape: Marketing UK public houses to women. *International Journal of Retail & Distribution Management, 23,* 34–40.

Schneider, B., & Bowen, D. E. (1985). Employee and customer perceptions of service in banks: Replication and extension. *Journal of Applied Psychology, 70,* 423–433.

Sheffey, S., & Tindale, R. S. (1992). Perceptions of sexual harassment in the workplace. *Journal of Applied Social Psychology, 22,* 1502–1520.

Siguaw, J. A., & Honeycutt, E. D. (1995). An examination of gender differences in selling behaviors and job attitudes. *Industrial Marketing Management, 24,* 45–52.

Stamler, V. L., Christiansen, M. D., Staley, K. H., & Macagno-Shang, L. (1991). Client preference for counselor gender. *Psychology of Women Quarterly, 15,* 317–321.

Stead, B. A., & Zinkhan, G. M. (1986). Service priority in department stores: The effects of customer gender and dress. *Sex Roles, 15,* 601–611.

Stern, B. B., Gould, S. J., & Tewari, S. (1993). Sex-typed service images: An empirical investigation of self-service variables. *The Service Industry Journal, 13,* 74–96.

Sutton, R. I., & Rafaeli, A. (1988). Untangling the relationship between displayed emotions and organizational sales: The case of convenience stores. *Academy of Management Journal, 31*(3), 461–487.

Tidd, K., & Lockard, J. (1978). Monetary significance of the affiliative smile: A case for reciprocal altruism. *Bulletin of the Psychonomic Society, 11,* 344–346.

Tyler, M., & Taylor, S. (1998). The exchange of aesthetics: Women's work and "the gift." *Gender, Work and Organization, 5*(3), 165–171.

U.S. Bureau of the Census. (1996). *Statistical abstract of the United States: 1996.* Washington, DC: Bureau of Economic Analysis.

U.S. Department of Commerce. (1998). *National accounts data.* Washington, DC: Bureau of Economic Analysis.

Wharton, A. S. (1993). The affective consequences of service work. *Work and Occupations, 20,* 205–232.

Williams, C. L. (1995). *Still a man's world: Men who do women's work.* Berkeley: University of California Press.

Yoder, J. D. (1994). Looking beyond numbers: The effects of gender status, job prestige and occupational gender-typing on tokenism processes. *Social Psychology Quarterly, 57*(2), 150–159.

Zinkhan, G. M., & Stoiadin, L. F. (1984). Impact of sex role stereotypes on service priority in department stores. *Journal of Applied Psychology, 69,* 691–693. ✦

28

Over the Counter: McDonald's

Robin Leidner

Robin Leidner shows how the decentralized fast food franchises of McDonald's achieve success through uniformity and predictability. By actually working in an urban franchise, Leidner witnessed the interviewing, training, and daily work routines. She finds that most of the employees are part-time, working for minimum wage without benefits at the grill or at the counter. Managers, on the other hand, receive very different treatment in terms of salary, fringe benefits, training, and promotion opportunities.

Organizations have many ways of obtaining the cooperation of participants, ranging from persuasion and enticement to force and curtailment of options. All organizations "hope to make people want to do what the organization needs done" (Biggart 1989: 128), but when they cannot count on success in manipulating people's desires they can do their best to compel people to act in the organization's interests.

Organizations choose strategies that rely on socialization and social control in varying mixtures that are determined by the aims of the organization, the constraints set by the organizational environment and the nature of the work, and the interests and resources of the parties involved. In service-providing organizations, upper-level management must concern itself with the wishes and behavior of service-recipients and various groups of workers. For each group, service organizations try to find the most effective and least costly ways to get people to act in the organizations' interests, proffering various carrots and sticks, making efforts to win hearts and minds, closing off choices.

Organizations that routinize work exert control primarily by closing off choices. There is much room for variation, however, in what aspects of the work organizations will choose to routinize, how they go about it, and how much freedom of decision making remains. Moreover, even when routines radically constrain choice, organizations still must socialize participants and set up systems of incentives and disincentives to ensure the compliance of workers and customers.

McDonald's

No one ever walks into a McDonald's and asks, "So, what's good today?" except satirically. The heart of McDonald's success is its uniformity and predictability. Not only is the food supposed to taste the same every day everywhere in the world, but McDonald's promises that every meal will be served quickly, courteously, and with a smile. Delivering on that promise over 20 million times a day in 54 countries is the company's colossal challenge (*McDonald's Annual Report* for 1990: 2). Its strategy for meeting that challenge draws on scientific management's most basic tenets: find the One Best Way to do every task and see that the work is conducted accordingly. To insure that all McDonald's restaurants serve products of uniform quality, the company uses centralized planning, centrally designed training programs, centrally approved and supervised suppliers, automated machinery and other specially designed equipment, meticulous specifications, and systematic inspections. To provide its customers with a uniformly pleasant "McDonald's experience," the company also tries to mass-produce friendliness, deference, diligence, and good cheer through a variety of socialization and social control techniques. Despite sneers from those who equate uniformity with mediocrity, the success of McDonald's has been spectacular.

McFacts

By far the world's largest fast-food company, McDonald's has over 11,800 stores worldwide (*McDonald's Annual Report* for 1990: 1), and its 1990 international sales surpassed those of its three largest competitors combined (Berg 1991: sec. 3, 6). In the United States, consumer familiarity with McDonald's is virtually universal: the company estimates that 95 percent of U.S. consumers eat at a McDonald's at least once a year (Koepp 1987: 58). McDonald's 1990 profits were $802.3 million, the third highest profits of any retailing company in the world (*Fortune* 1991: 179). At a time when the ability of many U.S. businesses to compete on the world market is in question, McDonald's continues to expand around the globe—most recently to Morocco—everywhere remaking consumer demand in its own image.

As politicians, union leaders, and others concerned with the effects of the shift to a service economy are quick to point out, McDonald's is a major employer. McDonald's restaurants in the United States employ about half a million people (Bertagnoli 1989: 33), including one out of fifteen first-time job seekers (Wildavsky 1989: 30). The company claims that 7 percent of all current U.S. workers have worked for McDonald's at some time (Koepp 1987: 59). Not only has McDonald's directly influenced the lives of millions of workers, but its impact has also been extended by the efforts of many kinds of organizations, especially in the service sector, to imitate the organizational features they see as central to McDonald's success.

For a company committed to standardization, McDonald's inspires strikingly varied reactions, both as an employer and as a cultural icon. On one side, Barbara Garson (1988), for instance, presents work at McDonald's as so systematized, automated, and closely monitored that all opportunity for thought, initiative, and human contact, let alone self-development, has been removed. To other critics, the ubiquity and uniformity of McDonald's epitomize the homogenization of U.S. culture and its imperialist export. At McDonald's, they point out, local culture is invisible and irrelevant, personal interactions are flattened into standardized patterns, and individual preferences are subordinated to efficient production processes. Nutritionists scorn McDonald's menu, environmentalists its packaging.

However, McDonald's has been as widely admired as reviled. To its supporters, McDonald's represents efficiency, order, familiarity, good cheer, and good value. Many business writers hold McDonald's up as an example of excellence in service management (see, e.g., Heskett, Sasser, and Hart 1990; Peters and Austin 1985; Zemke with Schaaf 1989). A pioneer in the standardization and mass-production of food and service, the company is often represented as emblematic of American capitalist knowhow. It is a company whose phenomenal growth has resulted from steadfast commitment to its basic promise to customers of fast service, hot food, and clean restaurants.

The relentless standardization and infinite replication that inspire both horror and admiration are the legacy of Ray Kroc, a salesman who got into the hamburger business in 1954, when he was fifty-two years old, and created a worldwide phenomenon. His inspiration was a phenomenally successful hamburger stand owned by the McDonald brothers of San Bernardino, California. He believed that their success could be reproduced consistently through carefully controlled franchises, and his hamburger business succeeded on an unprecedented scale. The basic idea was to serve a very few items of strictly uniform quality at low prices. Over the years, the menu has expanded somewhat and prices have risen, but the emphasis on strict, detailed standardization has never varied.

Kroc set out to achieve the kind of tight control over work routines and product quality that centralized production in factories makes possible, although the fast-food business is necessarily highly decentralized. Not only are the stores geographically dispersed, but approximately 75 percent of McDonald's outlets are owned by individual franchisees rather than by the corporation (*McDonald's Annual Report* for 1989: i). In his autobiography, Kroc describes how he approached the problem of combining standardization with decentralization (Kroc with Anderson 1977: 86):

> Our aim, of course, was to insure repeat business based on the system's reputation rather than on the quality of a single store or operator. This would require a continuing program of educating and assisting operators and a constant review of their performance. It would also require a full-time program of research and development. I knew in my bones that the key to uniformity would be in our ability to provide techniques of preparation that operators would accept because they were superior to methods they could dream up for themselves. . . .

You Deserve a Break Today: Conditions of Employment

Although McDonald's does not want teenagers to hang out on its premises, it certainly does want them to work in the stores. Almost half of its U.S. employees are under twenty years old (Wildavsky 1989: 30). In recent years, as the McDonald's chain has grown faster than the supply of teenagers, the company has also tried to attract senior citizens and housewives as workers. What people in these groups have in common is a preference or need for part-time work, and therefore a dearth of alternative employment options. Because of this lack of good alternatives, and because they may have other means of support for themselves and their dependents, many people

in these groups are willing to accept jobs that provide less than subsistence wages.

Traditionally, McDonald's has paid most of its employees the minimum wage, although labor shortages have now forced wages up in some parts of the country, raising the average hourly pay of crew people to $4.60 by 1989 (Gibson and Johnson 1989: B1). Benefits such as health insurance and sick days are entirely lacking for crew people at most franchises. In fact, when the topic of employee benefits was introduced in a class lecture at McDonald's management training center, it turned out to refer to crew meetings, individual work-evaluation sessions, and similar programs to make McDonald's management seem accessible and fair.

The lack of more tangible benefits is linked to the organization of employment at McDonald's as part-time work. According to the manager of the franchise I studied, all McDonald's hourly employees are officially part-time workers, in that no one is guaranteed a full work week. The company's labor practices are designed to make workers bear the costs of uncertainty based on fluctuation in demand. McDonald's places great emphasis on having no more crew people at work at any time than are required by customer flow at that period, as measured in half-hour increments. Most workers therefore have fluctuating schedules, and they are expected to be flexible about working late or leaving early depending on the volume of business.

Not surprisingly, McDonald's employee-turnover rates are extremely high. Turnover averaged 153 percent in 1984, and 205 percent in 1985 (training center lecture). These high rates are partly attributable to the large percentage of teenage workers, many of whom took the job with the intention of working for only a short time. However, the limited job rewards, both financial and personal, of working at McDonald's are certainly crucial contributing factors.

Some argue that the conditions of employment at McDonald's are unproblematic to the workers who take them. If we assume that most McDonald's workers are teenagers who are in school and are not responsible for supporting themselves or others, then many of the features of McDonald's work do not seem so bad. Fringe benefits and employment security are relatively unimportant to them, and the limited and irregular hours of work may actually be attractive (see Greenberger and Steinberg 1986). These arguments are less persuasive when applied to other McDonald's employees, such as mothers of young children and retirees, although those workers might similarly appreciate the part-time hours, and access to other forms of income and benefits could make McDonald's employment conditions acceptable, if not desirable. Employment security would not be important to the many people who choose to work at McDonald's as a stopgap or for a limited period. Many of the workers at the franchise I studied had taken their jobs with the intention of holding them only temporarily, and many were being supported by their parents. However, other workers there were trying to support themselves and their dependents on earnings from McDonald's, sometimes in combination with other low-paying jobs.

The average McDonald's store employs about sixty-five workers (training center lecture), most of whom are hired as "crew people" and may be trained to do more than one job. The two main jobs for crew people are grill and window (counter service). Typically, most male crew members work on the grill and most female crew members work on the window, although the corporation now encourages gender-neutral work assignment. A smaller job category is that of "host" (a polite term for workers whose main functions are to empty the trash cans and keep the lobby, windows, bathrooms, and dining areas clean). A few other crew people work primarily on equipment maintenance. People trained to work on the grill or at the window may be "cross-trained" to do the other main job or such specialized tasks as making salads, making biscuits, setting up equipment, or unloading trucks of supplies. All crew people are expected to clean and to restock supplies.

A crew member can be promoted to crew trainer and (in some restaurants) to crew chief, and eventually—if the person is over eighteen and available to work enough hours—to "swing manager." Crew trainers and crew chiefs are responsible for showing new workers their jobs, and they are also required to check the work of other crew people against the "Station Operation Checklist" provided by McDonald's for each position. They are expected to set a good example and also to report other crew people who are not working responsibly. Swing managers are hourly workers who are qualified to run a shift by themselves: to distribute cash-register drawers full of money, to deal with customer complaints, and to make adjustments in the number and distribution of workers.

Each McDonald's unit also employs four or five salaried managers, ranging in rank from manager trainee through second and first assistant manager to store manager. Salaried managers are treated very differently from crew people. Although they tend to work very long and somewhat unpredictable hours, they have the kinds of employment conditions associated with primary labor markets, including greater employment security, benefits, and salaries ranging from $10,000 to $36,000 as of 1988 (Parcel and Sickmeier 1988: 39). Managers may continue to advance by moving beyond store-level operations to the corporate hierarchy, perhaps moving from market-, regional-, and zone-level positions to corporate headquarters. McDonald's is proud of its promote-from-within approach. More than 50 percent of its store managers and almost 40 percent of its corporate officers started as hourly workers (Wildavsky 1989: 30). . . .

Taking Hamburgers Seriously: Training Managers

McDonald's main management-training facility is located on eighty beautifully landscaped acres in Oak Brook, Illinois, a suburb of Chicago. Its name, Hamburger University, captures the thoroughness and intensity with which McDonald's approaches management training, and it also suggests the comic possibilities of immersion in McDonald's corporate worlds. The company tries to produce managers "with ketchup in their veins," a common McDonald's phrase for people who love their work, take pride in it, and are extraordinarily hard-working, competitive, and loyal to McDonald's. A line I heard frequently at Hamburger U. was, "We take hamburgers very seriously here." Nothing I saw called this fixity of purpose into doubt.

Ensuring uniformity of service and products in its far-flung empire is a major challenge for McDonald's. In each McDonald's store, in regional training centers, and at Hamburger University, crew people, managers, and franchisees learn that there is a McDonald's way to handle virtually every detail of the business, and that doing things differently means doing things wrong. Training begins in the stores, where crew people are instructed using materials provided by the corporation, and where managers prepare for more advanced training. Management trainees and managers seeking promotion work with their store managers to learn materials in manuals and workbooks provided by the corporation. When they have completed the manual for the appropriate level, they are eligible for courses taught in regional training centers and at Hamburger University: the Basic Operations Course, the Intermediate Operations Course, the Applied Equipment Course, and, finally, the Advanced Operations Course, taught only at Hamburger University. Altogether, the full training program requires approximately six hundred to one thousand hours of work. It is required of everyone who wishes to own a McDonald's store, and it is strongly recommended for all store managers. By the time trainees get to Hamburger University for the Advanced Operations Course, they have already put in considerable time working in a McDonald's store—two to three and a half years, on average—and have acquired much detailed knowledge about McDonald's workings.

Hamburger University sometimes offers special programs and seminars in addition to the regular training courses. For example, a group of McDonald's office workers attended Hamburger University during my visit; a training manager told me that they had been brought in to get "a little shot of ketchup and mustard."

The zeal and competence of franchisees and managers are of special concern to McDonald's, since they are the people responsible for daily enforcement of corporate standards. Their training therefore focuses as much on building commitment and motivation as on extending knowledge of company procedures. In teaching management skills, McDonald's also works on the personalities of its managers, encouraging both rigid adherence to routines and, somewhat paradoxically, personal flexibility. Flexibility is presented as a virtue both because the company wants to minimize resistance to adopting McDonald's ways of doing things and to frequent revision of procedures, and because managers must provide whatever responsiveness to special circumstances the system has, since crew people are allowed virtually no discretion. Hamburger University therefore provides a large dose of personal-growth cheerleading along with more prosaic skills-training....

About 3,500 students from all over the world attend classes at Hamburger University each year, most of them taking the Advanced Operations Course (Rosenthal 1989). Those who complete the course receive diplomas proclaiming them Doctors of Hamburgerology. As late as 1978 or 1979, a training manager told me, most classes included only one or two women, but women now comprise 40–60 percent of the students, and women and minorities now make up 54 percent of McDonald's franchisees (Bertagnoli 1989a: 33). In my homeroom, however, the proportion of women was much smaller, and there was just a handful of minority students.

The course lasts two weeks and is extremely rigorous. Class time is about evenly divided between work in the labs and lectures on store operations and personnel management. In the labs, trainees learn the mechanics of ensuring that McDonald's food is of consistent quality and its stores in good working order. They learn to check the equipment and maintain it properly so that fries cook at precisely the right temperature, shakes are mixed to just the right consistency, and ice cubes are uniform. "Taste of Quality" labs reinforce McDonald's standards for food quality. For instance, in a Condiments Lab, trainees are taught exactly how to store vegetables and sauces, what the shelf lives of these products are, and how they should look and taste. Samples of "McDonald's quality" Big Mac Special Sauce are contrasted with samples that have been left too long unrefrigerated and should be discarded. The importance of serving only food that meets McDonald's standards is constantly emphasized and, a trainer pointed out, "McDonald's has standards for everything, down to the width of the pickle slices."

The management classes deal with such matters as hiring and training crew people, delegating authority, building sales, managing personnel, and maintaining good community relations. Not surprisingly, the work of the professors is standardized. Most deliver their lectures in a spontaneous style with their own embellishments, but they work from scripts prepared by the curriculum-development department. If they stray too far from the script, their lectures will be out of synch with the fancy slide presentations that accompany most lectures and with the "programmed notes" that are distributed to students to help them follow along and take notes. . . .

In addition to lectures and labs, trainees participate in competitions designed to develop team-building skills and management know-how. The first of these is "Hot Hamburgers," a week-long team competition in a game-show format. Teams are tested on their knowledge of McDonald's history and policies and on the minutiae of McDonald's standards. Trainees took this competition very seriously. I had dinner with one team just before the first round of competition, and was astonished to find that the conversation at the table consisted almost exclusively of questions and answers being fired back and forth. At what temperature do frozen apple pies thaw?

What is the height of an English muffin? What is the warm-up time of a biscuit oven? What is the yield of a gallon of hotcake mix? The answers to these questions are contained in a small, green quality-standards booklet that managers are supposed to carry with them at all times. The actual competition featured a professional master of ceremonies, a panel of judges, a giant game board, and the bells and buzzers typical of television game shows. . . .

The training at Hamburger University combines a sense of fun with dead seriousness about keeping McDonald's on top in the hamburger business through relentless quality control and effective management of workers and customers. It is up to the owners and managers of individual McDonald's stores to make that happen.

One McDonald's Franchise

I was assigned to a McDonald's in the downtown area of a small city near Chicago. It was a new store, only about fifteen months old when I began my fieldwork, but an exemplary one; it had recently won a major McDonald's award. The store was far more elegant than the average McDonald's. Adjacent to an expensive hotel, the restaurant was designed to seem "high-class," not garish or tacky. The interior decor included marble walls, a mahogany dining counter, black Art Deco fixtures, and mauve draperies. Outside were window boxes filled with flowers or greenery, and a relatively small Golden Arches sign, since the city council would not permit a large one.

This McDonald's differed from most in that it had neither a parking lot nor a drive-thru [*sic*] service window. It depended on pedestrian traffic for business, and its clientele included business people, college students, senior citizens, and shoppers. Fewer families came in than is typical for a McDonald's, and more people ordered just coffee or ice cream rather than a full meal; the average check size was accordingly smaller than at most McDonald's stores. At the time of my research in 1986, the store served 1,700 customers on an average day. In the course of a year, those customers collectively spent about one and a half million dollars. (The average McDonald's store brought in $1.34 million in 1985, half of it in drive-thru sales [training center lecture].

The franchisee who owned the store owned three other McDonald's stores in the Chicago suburbs. The business had made him wealthy, and he proudly showed off a "new toy" to me, a Corvette convertible, complete with telephone. He also had a yacht. He, his wife, and some of their grown children were closely involved in running the store, coming in several times a week, planning improvements, and overseeing the operation. Such involvement is encouraged by the corporation, which wants all of its franchisees to be "owner/operators," not just investors.

This McDonald's store had five salaried managers, all male, three white and two black. The owner's son, another white, also worked as a manager on occasion. In addition, there were as many as five hourly swing managers at a time (all female; three black, one white, one Native American). During my fieldwork, two crew people, a black woman and an Asian man, were promoted to that level of management.

The store's crew fluctuated in size between sixty-five and about one hundred people in the course of six months; the store manager believed that eighty-five was optimal. There were about equal numbers of window workers and grill workers.

Personnel policies at McDonald's franchises, including pay scales, are determined by the franchise owners, not by the corporation. Many press reports have described fast-food franchises raising wages and offering benefits to compete for the declining number of teenage workers, but the crew at this franchise, both grill and window workers, started work at the federal minimum wage, $3.35 in 1986, and they received no benefits such as health insurance, paid holidays, or paid sick days. Merit raises of five or ten cents per hour were granted quarterly, when job performance reviews were made, and crew people promoted to crew trainer or crew chief re-

ceived raises of five to fifteen cents per hour as well. The pay remained quite low, however. One crew trainer who had worked at the franchise for about a year and a half was earning $3.75.

Most, though not all, male crew members worked on the grill and most female crew members worked on the window. This pattern was usually based on managers' decisions when hiring workers. Some crew people reported having been given a choice about where they would start out, but more than half said that they had been assigned to their job.[1] A couple of crew people reported that the first women to be crosstrained to work on the grill had to persuade managers that they should be allowed to do so. In my interview sample of window people, 75 percent of the workers were women; according to the store's manager, this proportion accurately approximated the actual gender composition of the job category.

Salaried managers were expected to work forty-six to fifty hours per week. Officially, all of McDonald's crew workers are part-time, but 25 percent of my interview sample of window crew said that they usually worked thirty-five hours or more per week. The number of hours worked by crew people varied greatly, since many of them were students who only wished to work a few hours per week. Those who did want longer hours were expected to compete for them, proving themselves deserving through conscientious job performance. In practice, a core group of about twenty steady workers was sure to get its preferred hours, but cutting back an employee's hours was a standard way the managers showed their displeasure over poor job performance or attitude. The usual strategy for getting rid of poor workers, the store manager told me, was to decrease the hours they were scheduled to work until they got the message.

Through its scheduling practices McDonald's attempted to minimize labor costs without sacrificing speedy service for customers. As in almost all restaurants, McDonald's business normally came in waves rather than in a steady stream, with big rushes at meal times. On the one hand, managers did not want to have to pay crew people for hours they were not needed, since crew labor productivity is one of the main criteria by which managers are judged (Garson 1988: 32). On the other hand, they wanted to be sure to have enough people to keep lines moving quickly when business was brisk. The computerized cash-register system analyzed sales by hour of the day and day of the week, and managers used these figures to schedule work crews.

Since, however, computer projections are never entirely accurate, the schedules at this McDonald's were designed so that workers bore much of the burden of uncertainty. On the work schedule, posted one week in advance, a line for each crew person showed the hours she or he was scheduled to work. A solid line indicated hours the employee could count on working, and a zigzag line marked an additional hour or so. If the store was busy when a worker's guaranteed hours were finished, she or he would be required to work that extra time; if it was not busy, she or he would be asked to leave. In addition, it was quite common at unexpectedly quiet times for managers to tell workers they could leave before their scheduled hours were completed or even to pressure them to leave when they would rather have kept on working. I heard one manager say, "Come on, can't I make a profit today?" when a crew person resisted being sent home fifteen minutes early. Conversely, when the store was busy, managers were reluctant to let workers go when their scheduled hours, including the optional time, were done. When lines of people were waiting to be served, workers—I was one of them—would often have to ask repeatedly to be "punched out" (off the time clock) at the end of their shift.

Workers' preferences for longer or shorter hours varied; some wanted to earn as much as possible, others preferred to have more time for other activities. Whatever their preferences, the scheduling practices made it difficult for workers to plan ahead. Arrangements for transportation, social activities, child care, and so on could be disrupted by unexpected changes in the schedule, and workers could not accurately predict how much money they would earn in a given week. Furthermore, one of the most common complaints among the workers was that they had been scheduled to work at times they had said they were not available. Once on the schedule, they were held responsible for finding a replacement (see Garson 1988: 32–33). Since the McDonald's schedule was made up of such small units of time, however, it was usually relatively easy for workers to arrange hours for their convenience, an advantage McDonald's emphasized in recruitment. For example, workers who played on a high school team could cut down their hours during the sports season, and workers who needed to take a particular day off could usually arrange it if they gave sufficient notice.

The Interview Sample

Thirty-five percent of my sample was of high school age. (It is possible that I undersampled high school students simply because, since they were less likely to work many hours, I had less opportunity to meet them.) Although the majority of my sample (65 percent) were eighteen years old or over, 60 percent of the crew people told me that this was their first job.

The great majority of the crew people in the store were black, although blacks are a minority, albeit a large one, of the city's population. In my interview sample, 80 percent were black (including three Caribbean immigrants), one person was Hispanic-American, one was an Asian immigrant, and the rest were American-born white. A sizable minority of the workers commuted long distances, from the South Side and the West Side of Chicago. A full 25 percent of my sample had one-way commutes that took at least an hour and required at least one change of train, and I knew of several other workers with commutes at least that long. Given that the crew people started work at McDonald's at minimum wage, this pattern strongly suggests that these workers had been unable to find work near their homes or better-paying jobs elsewhere.

About two-thirds of the store's crew people were trained to work at the window. My sample of twenty-six window workers was not completely representative of all of the employees who worked behind the counter during the months I was there. Since my sampling method depended on my meeting the worker in the crew room, I probably oversampled those who worked relatively long or relatively steady hours and missed both those who worked only a few hours per week and those who worked for only a short time before quitting. I oversampled crew trainers and crew chiefs—30 percent of my sample had been promoted to one of these jobs. However, according to the store's manager, my sample was fairly representative of the store's population of customer-service workers in its gender, race, and age distributions.

Learning the Job

. . . At the store level, it is the responsibility of the first assistant manager, the person directly below the store manager in the store hierarchy, to oversee training, but other managers, crew chiefs, and crew trainers all participate in training new workers.[2] McDonald's recommends that its managers use a four-step process to train crew people: prepare, present, try out, follow up. In this method trainees first watch the videotape and then watch an experienced worker, a crew trainer, do the job and ask questions of the trainer. Next, trainees try the job while the trainer watches and makes corrections. In the follow-up stage, trainees build speed and competence and the trainer checks on performance, using a Station Operations Checklist as a guide.

Before this task-oriented training begins, newly hired employees attend an orientation session at which they see a videotape about McDonald's, fill out employment forms, and learn the store's rules and regulations. New employees at the store I worked at were told to show up for this session wearing a white shirt or blouse and dark blue or black slacks. Since the orientation session was held in the basement crew room, out of sight of customers, the re-

quirement about dress was apparently intended primarily to see whether the new workers could follow directions. My orientation session was attended by three new workers, including myself, and was run by Jim, the first assistant manager. . . .

Much of the orientation session was spent reviewing the rules crew people were expected to follow. Jim started with the dress code and other rules about personal appearance. Some of these rules reflected concerns about safety and hygiene; others were intended to promote a uniform image of neatness and wholesomeness.[3] All workers had to wear a clean uniform complete with hat and name tag. Women had to wear white nonskid shoes, had to tuck their hair up under their hat, and could not wear heavy makeup, brightly colored nail polish, more than two rings, or dangling jewelry. Men had to wear black shinable shoes and could not have long sideburns, beards, or hair touching their collars.

Jim next went over "easy ways to get fired." These included arguing on the work floor, fighting, stealing (including giving away food), failing to show up for work, or coming to work drunk or on drugs. He explained the store's procedures for finding out one's work schedule, calling in sick, arranging for days off, and picking up paychecks, and he told us what benefits workers received: a fifteen-minute paid break for four hours of work (with an additional five minutes for every additional hour), and meals at half-price.

Finally, Jim scheduled job-training sessions for each of the new workers. The window crew, of which I was to be a member, was responsible for cooking french fries, so I was scheduled to be "trained on fries" and to work one shift at the french-fry station before attending a window training session where I would learn to work the cash register and deal with customers.

My french-fry training was not what I had been led to expect. I was sent down to the crew room to watch the videotape, which presented very detailed instructions on loading fries into their baskets, using the cooking equipment, salting and bagging the cooked fries, and making sure that only fresh, hot fries are served. My field notes record what happened when the video ended:

> I go back upstairs and find [the manager], who says, "OK, now you're on fries, go ahead." I say, "Are you serious? That's it for training?" She says, "Oh, no," but I'm not sure that she wouldn't have put me right on if I hadn't said anything. . . .

The training to work on the window was more formal. "Window class" was run by a swing manager, Charlene, and lasted a whole morning. My training group included two other newly hired window workers and a grill worker who was being cross-trained to work window. The training began, as usual, with a videotape. It emphasized the importance of the window crew's work, telling us that to guests (McDonald's word for customers), "You ARE McDonald's." Interactive work is only part of the window crew's job, though. In addition to learning about dealing with people, we had many details to learn about dealing with things. The videotape provided instructions on what the various-sized cups and bags were used for, how to stock the counter area, how to work the soda and shake machines, and how to load a bag and set up a tray properly.

Interactions with customers, we were taught, are governed by the Six Steps of Window Service: (1) greet the customer, (2) take the order, (3) assemble the order, (4) present the order, (5) receive payment, and (6) thank the customer and ask for repeat business. The videotape provided sample sentences for greeting the customers and asking for repeat business, but it encouraged the window crew to vary these phrases. According to a trainer at Hamburger University, management permits this discretion not to make the window crew's work less constraining but to minimize the customers' sense of depersonalization:

> "We don't want to create the atmosphere of an assembly line," Jack says. They want the crew people to provide a varied, personable greeting—"the thing that's standard is the smile." They prefer

the greetings to be varied so that, for instance, the third person in line won't get the exact same greeting that he's just heard the two people in front of him receive. . . .

The cash register was my biggest problem. Lights kept flashing for reasons I did not understand, it took me forever to find the right keys, and I kept botching up special orders. (In fact, Charlene had given us incorrect instructions on which keys to hit in what sequence for special orders.) Nonetheless:

> I start to get the hang of it fairly soon. The other crew people are quite nice and helpful, and the customers are all polite, too—I don't serve any nasty guests. One customer startles me by saying, "Thank you, Robin." It takes me a moment to realize that I'm clearly labeled. When I mess up, I send the customers off with, "Come back soon—I'll do better."

Unlike this relatively thorough and successful training, my preparation to work the window at breakfast time was completely inadequate and left me frustrated and angry as well as incompetent. No videotape was shown, and the four-step training procedure was also abandoned. Diana was my crew trainer again, but this time she did not explain procedures to me carefully. At the beginning of the shift, she had me take a few orders on her cash register, but soon I was given my own register:

> I start working, with Diana by my side, without being given any training. For a while she just points to the keys as people order things, since I don't know where they are, and can't figure out the abbreviations. Most of the time I take the orders and money and Diana goes to get the products—a good thing, since I still don't know what goes with what. . . . I am finding this extremely frustrating—I feel very unprepared and don't like having to do the job without being competent to do it.
>
> Eventually Diana goes through the keyboard with me, reciting what each key does. After reciting them, she names

a few items and has me point to the keys. When a customer comes in after we've gone through only a few keys, my "training" is abandoned. I find the keys confusing—there's an Egg McMuffin key and a Muffin and Egg key; a biscuit with sausage and egg, biscuit with sausage and no egg, muffin with sausage and egg, etc. Some of the biscuit sandwiches have cheese on them, some don't. Often I can't tell whether someone is ordering a special grill or a regular sandwich, because I don't know what's on those things. . . .

Whereas my field notes for the day I was trained to work on window ended, "I leave in a good mood—it was fun," I went through this breakfast shift in a state of suppressed rage. This object lesson in what happens when McDonald's training procedures are not followed made me appreciate the company's ceaseless efforts to see that its standards are enforced. It was also a good lesson in why workers do not necessarily resent routinization—clear, well-planned routines make them feel they can do at least an adequate job. But what is left of the job?

The Routine

McDonald's had routinized the work of its crews so thoroughly that decision making had practically been eliminated from the jobs. As one window worker told me, "They've tried to break it down so that it's almost idiot-proof." Most of the workers agreed that there was little call for them to use their own judgment on the job, since there were rules about everything. If an unusual problem arose, the workers were supposed to turn it over to a manager.

Many of the noninteractive parts of the window workers' job had been made idiot-proof through automation. The soda machines, for example, automatically dispensed the proper amount of beverage for regular, medium, and large cups. Computerized cash registers performed a variety of functions handled elsewhere by human waitresses, waiters, and cashiers, making some kinds of skill and knowledge unneces-

sary. As a customer gave an order, the window worker simply pressed the cash register button labeled with the name of the selected product. There was no need to write the orders down, because the buttons lit up to indicate which products had been selected. Nor was there any need to remember prices, because the prices were programmed into the machines. Like most new cash registers, these added the tax automatically and told workers how much change customers were owed, so the window crew did not need to know how to do those calculations. The cash registers also helped regulate some of the crew's interactive work by reminding them to try to increase the size of each sale. For example, when a customer ordered a Big Mac, large fries, and a regular Coke, the cash register buttons for cookies, hot apple pies, ice cream cones, and ice cream sundaes would light up, prompting the worker to suggest dessert. It took some skill to operate the relatively complicated cash register, as my difficulties during my first work shift made clear, but this organizationally specific skill could soon be acquired on the job. . . .

The interactive part of window work is routinized through the Six Steps of Window Service and also through rules aimed at standardizing attitudes and demeanors as well as words and actions. The window workers were taught that they represented McDonald's to the public and that their attitudes were therefore an important component of service quality. Crew people could be reprimanded for not smiling, and often were. The window workers were supposed to be cheerful and polite at all times, but they were also told to be themselves while on the job. McDonald's does not want its workers to seem like robots, so part of the emotion work asked of the window crew is that they act naturally. "Being yourself" in this situation meant behaving in a way that did not seem stilted. Although workers had some latitude to go beyond the script, the short, highly schematic routine obviously did not allow much room for genuine self-expression.

Workers were not the only ones constrained by McDonald's routines, of course. . . .

McDonald's ubiquitous advertising trains consumers at the same time that it tries to attract them to McDonald's. Television commercials demonstrate how the service system is supposed to work and familiarize customers with new products. Additional cues about expected customer behavior are provided by the design of the restaurants. For example, the entrances usually lead to the service counter, not to the dining area, making it unlikely that customers will fail to realize that they should get in line, and the placement of waste cans makes clear that customers are expected to throw out their own trash. Most important, the majority of customers have had years of experience with McDonald's, as well as with other fast-food restaurants that have similar arrangements. The company estimates that the average customer visits a McDonald's twenty times a year (Koepp 1987: 58), and it is not uncommon for a customer to come in several times per week. For many customers, then, ordering at McDonald's is as routine an interaction as it is for the window worker. Indeed, because employee turnover is so high, steady customers may be more familiar with the work routines than the workers serving them are. Customers who are new to McDonald's can take their cue from more experienced customers.

Not surprisingly, then, most customers at the McDonald's I studied knew what was expected of them and tried to play their part well. They sorted themselves into lines and gazed up at the menu boards while waiting to be served. They usually gave their orders in the conventional sequence: burgers or other entrees, french fries or other side orders, drinks, and desserts. Hurried customers with savvy might order an item "only if it's in the bin," that is, ready to be served. Many customers prepared carefully so that they could give their orders promptly when they got to the counter. This preparation sometimes became apparent when a worker interrupted to ask, "What kind of dressing?" or "Cream and sugar?," flustering customers who could not deliver their orders as planned.

McDonald's routines, like those of other interactive service businesses, depend on the predictability of customers, but these businesses must not grind to a halt if customers are not completely cooperative. Some types of deviations from standard customer behavior are so common that they become routine themselves, and these can be handled through subroutines (Stinchcombe 1990: 39). McDonald's routines work most efficiently when all customers accept their products exactly as they are usually prepared; indeed, the whole business is based on this premise. Since, however, some people give special instructions for customized products, such as "no onions," the routine allows for these exceptions. At the franchise I studied, workers could key the special requests into their cash registers, which automatically printed out "grill slips" with the instructions for the grill workers to follow. Under this system, the customer making the special order had to wait for it to be prepared, but the smooth flow of service for other customers was not interrupted. Another type of routine difficulty was customer dissatisfaction with food quality. Whenever a customer had a complaint about the food—cold fries, dried-out burger—window workers were authorized to supply a new product immediately without consulting a supervisor.[4]

These two kinds of difficulties—special orders and complaints about food—were the only irregularities window workers were authorized to handle. The subroutines increased the flexibility of the service system, but they did not increase the workers' discretion, since procedures were in place for dealing with both situations. All other kinds of demands fell outside the window crew's purview. If they were faced with a dispute about money, an extraordinary request, or a furious customer, workers were instructed to call a manager; the crew had no authority to handle such problems.

Given the almost complete regimentation of tasks and preemption of decision making, does McDonald's need the flexibility and thoughtfulness of human workers?

As the declining supply of teenagers and legislated increases in the minimum wage drive up labor costs, it is not surprising that McDonald's is experimenting with electronic replacements. So far, the only robot in use handles behind-the-scenes work rather than customer interactions. ARCH (Automated Restaurant Crew Helper) works in a Minnesota McDonald's where it does all the frying and lets workers know when to prepare sandwich buns, when supplies are running low, and when fries are no longer fresh enough to sell. Other McDonald's stores (along with Arby's and Burger King units) are experimenting with a touch-screen computer system that lets customers order their meals themselves, further curtailing the role of the window worker. Although it requires increased customer socialization and cooperation, early reports are that the system cuts service time by thirty seconds and increases sales per window worker 10–20 percent (Chaudhry 1989: F61).

Getting Workers to Work

The extreme routinization does not mean that McDonald's work is undemanding. I found that the company asked a lot of its workers, and the stresses of the job could be considerable. Especially when the store was busy, window work was extraordinarily hectic. From the grill area came the sounds of buzzers buzzing and people shouting instructions. Workers dashed from side to side behind the counter to pick up the various products they needed. Just getting around was extremely difficult. There might be six window workers, a manager or two overseeing the flow of food from the grill and backing up window workers, and another worker in charge of french fries, all trying to maneuver in a very small area, all hurrying, often carrying drinks, ice cream cones, stacks of burgers. Workers with pails of soapy water would frequently come to mop up the greasy floor, leaving it slippery and treacherous even for workers in the regulation nonskid shoes. Traffic jams formed around the soda machines and the salad cases. In the course of

a shift various supplies would run out, and there would be no lids for the large cups, no clean trays, no Italian dressing, no ice, until someone found a moment to replenish the stock. Food products were frequently not ready when needed, frustrating window workers' efforts to gather their orders speedily—the supply of Big Macs in the food bin could be wiped out at any moment by a worker with an order for four of them, forcing several other workers to explain to their customers that they would have to wait for their food. The customers, of course, could be a major source of stress themselves. All in all, McDonald's work may be regarded as unskilled, but it was by no means easy to do well. Window workers had to be able to keep many things in mind at once, to keep calm under fire, and to exhibit considerable physical and emotional stamina.

Even when the store was not crowded, workers were expected to keep busy, in accordance with the McDonald's slogan "If there's time to lean, there's time to clean." I was struck by how hard-working most of the crew people were:

> Matthew moves very fast, sweeps up whenever he has a spare moment. In fact, all of the crew people work like beavers—backing each other up, cleaning, etc.

Considering workers' low wages and limited stake in the success of the enterprise, why did they work so hard? Their intensity of effort was produced by several kinds of pressures. First, it seemed to me that most workers did conceive of the work as a team effort and were loath to be seen by their peers as making extra work for other people by not doing their share. Even workers who had what managers would define as a "bad attitude"—resentment about low wages, disrespectful treatment, or any other issue—might work hard in order to keep the respect of their peers.

Naturally, managers played a major role in keeping crew people hard at work. At this store, managers were virtually always present behind the counter and in the grill area. During busy periods several managers would be there at once, working side by side with the crew as well as issuing instructions. Any slacking off by a worker was thus very likely to be noticed. Managers insisted on constant effort; they clearly did not want to pay workers for a moment of nonproductive time. For instance, I heard a manager reprimand a grill worker for looking at the work schedule: "Are you off work? No? You look at the schedule on your time, not on my time." A handwritten sign was posted recommending that window workers come in fifteen minutes early to count out the money in their cash-register drawers on their own time so that, if the amount was wrong, they would not later be held responsible for a shortage. Crew trainers and crew chiefs were encouraged to let managers know about any workers who were shirking or causing problems.

The presence of customers on the scene was another major factor in intensifying workers' efforts. When long lines of people were waiting to be served, few workers had to be told to work as swiftly as possible. The sea of expectant faces provided a great deal of pressure to keep moving. Window workers in particular were anxious to avoid antagonizing customers, who were likely to take out any dissatisfactions on them. The surest way to keep people happy was to keep the lines moving quickly. The arrangement of the workplace, which made window workers clearly visible to the waiting customers as they went about their duties, and customers clearly visible to workers, was important in keeping crew people hard at work. This pressure could have an effect even if customers did not complain. For example, on the day I was to be trained to work window during breakfast, I spent quite a while standing behind the counter, in uniform, waiting to be given instructions and put to work. I was acutely aware that customers were likely to wonder why I did not take their orders, and I tried to adopt an air of attentive expectancy rather than one of casual loitering, in the hope that the customers would assume there was a good reason for my idleness.

These sorts of pressures were not the only reasons crew people worked hard and enthusiastically, however. Managers also tried to motivate them to strenuous efforts through positive means. The managers' constant presence meant that good work would not go unnoticed. McDonald's Corporation stresses the importance of acknowledging workers' efforts, and several workers mentioned that they appreciated such recognition. Indeed, I was surprised at how much it cheered me when a manager complimented me on my "good eye contact" with customers. Various incentive systems were in place as well, to make workers feel that it was in their individual interest to work hard. Free McDonald's meals (instead of the usual half-priced ones) and free record albums were some of the rewards available to good workers. Contests for the highest sales totals or most special raspberry milk shakes sold in a given hour encouraged window workers to compete in speed and pushiness. The possibility of promotion to crew trainer, crew chief, or swing manager also motivated some workers to work as hard as possible.

Group incentives seemed to be especially effective in motivating the crew. As part of a national advertising effort stressing service, all of the stores in McDonald's Chicago region competed to improve their speed. The owner of the store where I worked promised that if one of his stores came out near the top in this competition, the entire crew would be treated to a day at a large amusement park and the crew trainers would be invited for a day's outing on his yacht. The crew trainers and many other workers were very excited about this possibility and were willing to try to achieve unprecedented standards of speed. (They did not win the prize, but the crew of one of the owner's other stores did.) Some workers, though, especially the more disaffected ones, had no desire for either promotions or the low-cost rewards available and spoke derisively of them.

Managers also tried to make workers identify with the interests of the store, even when it clearly resulted in harder work for the same pay. At a monthly meeting for crew trainers, a manager acknowledged that workers were always asking why the store would not pay someone for an extra fifteen minutes to sweep up or do other such tasks not directly related to production, instead of making workers squeeze these tasks in around their main duties. He explained the importance to management of keeping labor costs down:

> "Say we use four extra hours a day—we keep extra people to [wash] the brown trays" or some other tasks. He reels off some calculations—"that's 120 hours a month, times—let's pay them the minimum wage—times twelve months. So that's 1,440 hours times $3.35, equals $4,825." There are oohs and ahs from the trainers—this sounds like a lot of money to them. I don't think it sounds like that much out of $1.5 million (which he had just said the store brought in annually). The manager went on, "So how do we get extra labor? By watching how we schedule. A $200 hour [an hour with $200 in sales], for instance, will go smoother with four window people, but three good people could do it. We save money, and then we can use it on other things, like training, for instance."

The crew trainers were willing to agree that it was only reasonable for the store to extract as much labor from them as possible, though resentments about overwork certainly did not disappear. The manager was also successful enough in getting the crew trainers to identify with management that they were willing to give the names of crew people who were uncooperative. . . .

All of these factors affected store morale and presumably had an impact on crew efficiency, turnover rates, and customer satisfaction, just as Hamburger University preaches. For the most part, it seemed that sticking to corporate directives on proper management produced good results, while, predictably, more authoritarian and arbitrary interactions with staff produced resentment. The apparently respectful, even-handed, psychologistic management style that McDonald's encourages helped make the repetitive, fast-paced, low-autonomy, low-paid jobs tolerable to workers.[5] Workers learned to accept even rules that were quite disadvantageous to them when they perceived those rules to be fairly administered by people who regarded them as human beings. The official McDonald's stance was likely to anger workers, however, when, faced with customers who did not treat the crew as human beings, managers felt it was more important to satisfy the paying public than to defend the workers' dignity. . . .

Overview

. . . Most McDonald's work is organized as low-paying, low-status, part-time jobs that give workers little autonomy. Almost every decision about how to do crew people's tasks has been made in advance by the corporation, and many of the decisions have been built into the stores' technology. Why use human workers at all, if not to take advantage of the human capacity to respond to circumstances flexibly? McDonald's does want to provide at least a simulacrum of the human attributes of warmth, friendliness, and recognition. For that reason, not only workers' movements but also their words, demeanor, and attitudes are subject to managerial control.

Although predictability is McDonald's hallmark, not all factors can be controlled by management. One of the most serious irregularities that store management must deal with is fluctuation in the flow of customers, both expected and unexpected. Since personnel costs are the most manipulable variable affecting a store's profitability, managers want to match labor power to consumer demand as exactly as possible. They do so by paying all crew people by the hour, giving them highly irregular hours based on expected sales—sometimes including split shifts—and sending workers home early or keeping them late as conditions require. In other words, the costs of uneven demand are shifted to workers whenever possible. Since most McDonald's crew people cannot count on working a particular number of hours at precisely scheduled times, it is hard for them to make plans based on how much money they will earn or exactly what times they will be free. Workers are pressured to be flexible in order to maximize the organization's own flexibility in staffing levels. In contrast, of course, flexibility in the work process itself is minimized.

Routinization has not made the crew people's work easy. Their jobs, although highly structured and repetitive, are often demanding and stressful. Under these working conditions, the organization's limited commitment to workers, as reflected in job security, wages and benefits, makes the task of maintaining worker motivation and discipline even more challenging. A variety of factors, many orchestrated by the corporation, keeps McDonald's crew people hard at work despite the limited rewards. Socialization into McDonald's norms, extremely close supervision (both human and electronic), individual and group incentives, peer pressure, and pressure from customers all play their part in getting workers to do things the McDonald's way. . . .

Obtaining the cooperation of workers and managers is not enough to ensure the smooth functioning of McDonald's relatively inflexible routines. Customers must be routinized as well. Not only do customers have to understand the service routine and accept the limited range of choices the company offers, they also must be willing to do some kinds of work that are done for them in conventional restaurants, including carrying food to the table and throwing out their trash. Experience, advertising, the example set by other customers, and clear environmental cues familiarize customers with McDonald's routines, and most want to cooperate in order to speed service. For these reasons, McDonald's interactive service workers do not have to direct most customers, and window workers' routines are therefore not designed to give them power over customers. . . .

Discussion Questions

1. Describe how the work of a counter clerk in McDonald's is emotion work.

2. Why do you think that customers like their food prepared the McDonald's way?

Reprinted from Robin Leidner, "Over the Counter: McDonalds," in *Fast Food, Fast Talk: Service Work and the Routinization of Everyday Life* (Berkeley and Los Angeles: University of California Press, 1993, pp. 44–85).

Endnotes

1. This group included three men who had been assigned to window work, so gender was not the only criterion considered.
2. The store manager is responsible for overseeing the training of other managers, working with them as they go through the series of manuals issued by the corporation and helping them prepare for intensive courses at the regional training centers and Hamburger University.
3. I assumed for weeks that one window worker who always had a piece of adhesive tape on his ear must have some sort of injury, and was amused to learn that the tape hid a small, gold pierced earring. The tape was much more noticeable than the earring (the worker was black, the tape white), but apparently the managers considered it less offensive.
4. The defective food or its container was put into a special waste bin. Each shift, one worker or manager had the unenviable task of counting the items in the waste bin so that the inventory could be reconciled with the cash intake.
5. On the use of "human relations" managerial techniques to accommodate workers to Taylorist work regimes, see Braverman (1974: 139–51) and Howard (1985).

References

Acker, Joan. 1990. "Hierarchies, Jobs, Bodies: A Theory of Gendered Organizations." *Gender & Society* 4: 139–58.

Berg, Eric N. 1991. "An American Icon Wrestles with a Troubled Future." *New York Times* (May 12): sec. 3, 1.

Berk, Sarah Fenstermaker. 1985a. *The Gender Factory: The Apportionment of Work in American Households.* New York: Plenum.

——. 1985b. "Women's Work and the Production of Gender: A Reciprocal Relation." Paper presented at the annual meeting of the American Sociological Association, Washington, D.C.

Bertagnoli, Lisa. 1989. "Mcdonald's: Company of the Quarter Century." *Restaurants and Institutions* (July 10): 32–60.

Biggart, Nicole Woolsey. 1983."Rationality, Meaning, and Self-Management: Success Manuals, 1050–1980." *Social Problems* 30: 298–311.

——. 1989. *Charismatic Capitalism: Direct Selling Organizations in America*. Chicago: University of Chicago Press.

Braverman, Harry. 1974. *Labor and Monopoly Capital: The Degradation of Work in the Twentieth Century*. New York: Monthly Review Press.

Chaudhry, Rajan. 1989. "Burger Giants Singed by Battle." *Nation's Restaurant News* (August 7): F36.

Fortune. 1991. "Fortune Global Service 500: The 50 Largest Retailing Companies." (August 26): 179.

Garson, Barbara. 1988. *The Electronic Sweatshop: How Computers Are Transforming the Office of the Future Into the Factory of the Past*. New York: Simon and Schuster.

Gibson, Richard, and Robert Johnson. 1989. "Big Mac Plots Strategy to Regain Sizzle." *Wall Street Journal* (September 29): B1.

Greenberger, Ellen, and Laurence Steinberg. 1986. *When Teenagers Work: The Psychological and Social Costs of Adolescent Employment*. New York: Basic Books.

Heskett, James L., W. Earl Sasser, Jr., and Christopher W. L. Hart. 1990. *Service Breakthroughs: Changing the Rules of the Game*. New York: Free Press.

Howard, Robert. 1985. *Brave New Workplace*. New York: Viking.

Koepp, Stephen. 1987. "Big Mac Strikes Back." *Time* (April 13): 58–60.

Kroc, Ray, with Robert Anderson. 1977. *Grinding It Out: The Making of McDonald's*. Chicago: Contemporary Books.

McDonald's Annual Report. Various years. Oak Brook, Ill.

Parcel, Toby L., and Marie B. Sickmeier. 1988. "One Firm, Two Labor Markets: The Case of McDonald's in the Fast-Food Industry." *Sociological Quarterly* 29: 29–46.

Peters, Tom, and Nancy Austin. 1985. *A Passion for Excellence: The Leadership Difference*. New York: Random House.

Rosenthal, Herma M. 1989. "Inside Big Mac's World." *Newsday* (June 4): magazine section, 8–12, 16, 19, 24–25.

Stinchcombe, Arthur L. 1990. *Information and Organizations*. Berkeley: University of California Press.

Wildavsky, Ben. 1989. "McJobs: Inside America's Largest Youth Training Program." *Policy Review* 49: 30–37.

Zemke, Ron, with Dick Schaaf. 1989. *The Service Edge: 101 Companies That Profit From Customer Care*. New York: NAL Books. ✦

29
Wal-Mart

Barbara Ehrenreich

In this chapter, Barbara Ehrenreich details her work in an entry-level job in ladies' wear at Wal-Mart. Her main tasks every day are to put away carts full of clothes and keep them organized in a certain way on the racks. She does this for $7 a day, too little to allow her to live with other low-income tenants in other than a motel and too little even to permit her to work at Wal-Mart for very long.

I go forth on Monday to begin my life as a Wal-Martian. After the rigors of orientation, I am expecting a highly structured welcome, perhaps a ceremonial donning of my bright blue Wal-Mart vest and a forty-five-minute training on the operation of the vending machines in the break room. But when I arrive in the morning for the ten-to-six shift, no one seems to be expecting me. I'm in "softlines," which has a wonderful, sinuous sound to it, but I have no idea what it means. Someone in personnel tells me I'm in ladies' wear (a division of softlines, I learn) and sends me to the counter next to the fitting rooms, where I am passed around from one person to the next—finally ending up with Ellie, whose lack of a vest signals that she is management. She sets me to work "zoning" the Bobbie Brooks knit summer dresses, a task that could serve as an IQ test for the severely cognitively challenged. First the dresses must be grouped by color—olive, peach, or lavender, in this case—then by decorative pattern—the leafy design on the bodice, the single flower, or the grouped flowers—and within each pattern by size. When I am fin-

ished, though hardly exhausted by the effort, I meet Melissa, who is, with only a couple of weeks on the job, pretty much my equivalent. She asks me to help her consolidate the Kathie Lee knit dresses so the Kathie Lee silky ones can take their place at the "image," the high-traffic corner area. I learn, in a couple of hours of scattered exchanges, that Melissa was a waitress before this job, that her husband works in construction and her children are grown. There have been some disorganized patches in her life—an out-of-wedlock child, a problem with alcohol and drugs—but that's all over now that she has given her life to Christ.

Our job, it emerges in fragments throughout the day, is to keep ladies' wear "shoppable." Sure, we help customers (who are increasingly called "guests" here as well), if they want any help. At first I go around practicing the "aggressive hospitality" demanded by our training videos: as soon as anyone comes within ten feet of a sales associate, that associate is supposed to smile warmly and offer assistance. But I never see a more experienced associate do this—first, because the customers are often annoyed to have their shopping dazes interrupted and, second, because we have far more pressing things to do. In ladies' wear, the big task, which has no real equivalent in, say, housewares or lawn and garden, is to put away the "returns"—clothes that have been tried on and rejected or, more rarely, purchased and then returned to the store. There are also the many items that have been scattered by customers, dropped on the floor, removed from their hangers and strewn over the racks, or secreted in locations far from their natural homes. Each of these items, too, must be returned to its precise place, matched by color, pattern, price, and size. Any leftover time is to be devoted to zoning. When I relate this to Caroline on the phone, she commiserates, "Ugh, a no-brainer."

But no job is as easy as it looks to the uninitiated. I have to put clothes away—the question is, Where? Much of my first few days is devoted to trying to memorize the layout of ladies' wear, one thousand (two thousand?) square feet of space bordered by men's wear, children's wear, greeting cards, and underwear. Standing at the fitting rooms and facing toward the main store entrance, we are looking directly at the tentlike, utilitarian plus sizes, also known as "woman" sizes. These are flanked on the left by our dressiest and costliest line (going up to $29 and change), the all-polyester Kathie Lee collection, suitable for dates and subprofessional levels of office work. Moving clockwise, we encounter the determinedly sexless Russ and Bobbie Brooks lines, seemingly aimed at pudgy fourth-grade teachers with important barbecues to attend. Then, after the sturdy White Stag, come the breezy, revealing Faded Glory, No Boundaries, and Jordache collections, designed for the younger and thinner crowd. Tucked throughout are nests of the lesser brands, such as Athletic Works, Basic Equipment, and the whimsical Looney Tunes, Pooh, and Mickey lines, generally decorated with images of their eponymous characters. Within each brand-name area, there are of course dozens of items, even dozens of each *kind* of item. This summer, for example, pants may be capri, classic, carpenter, clam-digger, boot, or flood, depending on their length and cut, and I'm probably leaving a few categories out. So my characteristic stance is one of rotating slowly on one foot, eyes wide, garment in hand, asking myself, "Where have I seen the $9.96 Athletic Works knit overalls?" or similar query. Inevitably there are mystery items requiring extra time and inquiry: clothes that have wandered over from girls' or men's, clearanced items whose tags haven't been changed to reflect their new prices, the occasional one-of-a-kind.

Then, when I have the layout memorized, it suddenly changes. On my third morning I find, after a few futile searches, that the Russ shirt-and-short combinations have edged Kathie Lee out of her image. When I groaningly accuse Ellie of trying to trick me into thinking I'm getting Alzheimer's, she's genuinely apologetic, explaining that the average customer shops the store three times a week, so you need to

have the element of surprise. Besides, the layout is about the only thing she *can* control, since the clothes and at least the starting prices are all determined by the home office in Arkansas. So as fast as I can memorize, she furiously rearranges.

My first response to the work is disappointment and a kind of sexist contempt. I could have been in plumbing, mastering the vocabulary of valves, dangling tools from my belt, joshing around with Steve and Walt, and instead the mission of the moment is to return a pink bikini top to its place on the Bermuda swimwear rack. Nothing is heavy or, as far as I can see, very urgent. No one will go hungry or die or be hurt if I screw up; in fact, how would anyone ever know if I screwed up, given the customers' constant depredations? I feel oppressed, too, by the mandatory gentility of Wal-Mart culture. This is ladies' and we are all "ladies" here, forbidden, by store-wide rule, to raise our voices or cuss. Give me a few weeks of this and I'll femme out entirely, my stride will be reduced to a mince, I'll start tucking my head down to one side.

My job is not, however, as genteel as it at first appears, thanks to the sheer volume of clothing in motion. At Wal-Mart, as opposed to say Lord & Taylor, customers shop with supermarket-style shopping carts, which they can fill to the brim before proceeding to the fitting room. There the rejected items, which are about 90 percent of try-ons, are folded and put on hangers by whoever is staffing the fitting room, then placed in fresh shopping carts for Melissa and me. So this is how we measure our workload—in carts. When I get in, Melissa, whose shift begins earlier than mine, will tell me how things have been going—"Can you believe, eight carts this morning!"—and how many carts are awaiting me. At first a cart takes me an average of forty-five minutes and there may still be three or four mystery items left at the bottom. I get this down to half an hour, and still the carts keep coming.

Most of the time, the work requires minimal human interaction, of either the collegial or the supervisory sort, largely because it's so self-defining. I arrive at the start of a shift or the end of a break, assess the damage wrought by the guests in my absence, count the full carts that await me, and plunge in. I could be a deaf-mute as far as most of this goes, and despite all the orientation directives to smile and exude personal warmth, autism might be a definite advantage. Sometimes, if things are slow, Melissa and I will invent a task we can do together—zoning swimsuits, for example, a nightmarish tangle of straps—and giggle, she in her Christian way, me from a more feminist perspective, about the useless little see-through wraps meant to accompany the more revealing among them. Or sometimes Ellie will give me something special to do, like putting all the Basic Equipment T-shirts on hangers, because things on hangers sell faster, and then arranging them neatly on racks. I like Ellie. Gray-faced and fiftyish, she must be the apotheosis of "servant leadership" or, in more secular terms, the vaunted "feminine" style of management. She says "please" and "thank you"; she doesn't order, she asks. Not so though, with young Howard—*assistant manager* Howard, as he is uniformly called—who rules over all of softlines, including infants', children's, men's, accessories, and underwear. On my first day, I am called off the floor to an associates' meeting, where he spends ten minutes taking attendance, fixing each of us with his unnerving Tom Cruise-style smile, in which the brows come together as the corners of the mouth turn up, then reveals (where have I heard this before?) his "pet peeve": associates standing around talking to one another, which is, of course, a prime example of time theft.

A few days into my career at Wal-Mart, I return home to the Clearview to find the door to my room open and the motel owner waiting outside. There's been a "problem"—the sewage has backed up and is all over the floor, though fortunately my suitcase is OK. I am to move into Room 127, which will be better because it has a screen. But the screen turns out to be in tatters, not even fastened at the bottom, just flapping uselessly in the breeze. I ask for a real

screen, and he tells me he doesn't have any that fit. I ask for a fan and he doesn't have any that work. I ask why—I mean, this is supposedly a working motel—and he rolls his eyes, apparently indicating my fellow residents: "I could tell you stories. . . ."

So I lug my possessions down to 127 and start trying to reconstruct my little domestic life. Since I don't have a kitchen, I have what I call my food bag, a supermarket bag containing my tea bags, a few pieces of fruit, various condiment packets salvaged from fast-food places, and a half dozen string cheeses, which their labels say are supposed to be refrigerated but I figure are safe in their plastic wraps. I have my laptop computer, the essential link to my normal profession, and it has become a matter of increasing concern. I figure it's probably the costliest portable item in the entire Clearview Inn, so I hesitate to leave it in my room for the nine or so hours while I'm away at work. During the first couple of days at Wal-Mart, the weather was cool and I kept it in the trunk of my car. But now, with the temperature rising to the nineties at midday, I worry that it'll cook in the trunk. More to the point at the moment is the state of my clothing, most of which is now residing in the other brown paper bag, the one that serves as a hamper. My khakis have a day or two left in them and two clean T-shirts remain until the next trip to a Laundromat, but a question has been raised about the T-shirts. That afternoon Alyssa, one of my co-orientees, now in sporting goods, had come by ladies' to inquire about a polo shirt that had been clearanced at $7. Was there any chance it might fall still further? Of course I had no idea—Ellie decides about clearancing—but why was Alyssa so fixated on this particular shirt? Because one of the rules is that our shirts have to have collars, so they have to be polos, not tees. Somehow I'd missed this during orientation, and now I'm wondering how long I have before my stark-naked neck catches Howard's attention. At $7 an hour, a $7 shirt is just not going to make it to my shopping list.

Now it's after seven and time to resume my daily routine at the evening food-gathering phase. The town of Clearview presents only two low-priced options (there are no high-priced options) to its kitchenless residents—a Chinese all-you-can-eat buffet or Kentucky Fried Chicken—each with its own entertainment possibilities. If I eat out at the buffet I can watch the large Mexican families or the even larger, in total body mass terms, families of Minnesota Anglos. If I eat KFC in my room, I can watch TV on one of the half dozen available channels. The latter option seems somehow less lonely, especially if I can find one of my favorite programs—*Titus* or *Third Rock From the Sun*. Eating is tricky without a table. I put the food on the chest of drawers and place a plastic supermarket bag over my lap, since spills are hard to avoid when you eat on a slant and spills mean time and money at the Laundromat. Tonight I find the new sensation, *Survivor*, on CBS, where "real people" are struggling to light a fire on their desert island. Who are these nutcases who would volunteer for an artificially daunting situation in order to entertain millions of strangers with their harassed efforts to survive? Then I remember where I am and why I am here.

Dinner over, I put the remains in the plastic bag that served as a tablecloth and tie it up tightly to discourage the flies that have free access to my essentially screenless abode. I do my evening things—writing in my journal and reading a novel—then turn out the lights and sit for a while by the open door for some air. The two African American men who live in the room next door have theirs open too, and since it's sometimes open in the daytime as well, I've noticed that their room, like mine, has only one bed. This is no gay tryst, though, because they seem to take turns in the bed, one sleeping in the room and the other one napping in their van outside. I shut the door, put the window down, and undress in the dark so I can't be seen through the window. I still haven't found out much about my fellow Clearview dwellers—it's bad enough being a woman alone, especially a woman rich enough to have a bed of her own, without being nosy on top of that. As far as I can tell, the place isn't a nest of drug dealers and prostitutes; these are just working people who don't have the capital to rent a normal apartment. Even the teenagers who worried me at first seem to have mother figures attached to them, probably single mothers I hadn't seen before because they were at work.

Finally I lie down and breathe against the weight of unmoving air on my chest. I wake up a few hours later to hear a sound not generated by anyone's TV: a woman's clear alto singing two lines of the world's saddest song, lyrics indecipherable, to the accompaniment of trucks on the highway.

Morning begins with a trip, by car, to the Holiday gas station's convenience store, where I buy a pop container full of ice and a packet of two hard-boiled eggs. The ice, a commodity unavailable at the motel, is for iced tea, which I brew by letting tea bags soak in a plastic cup of water overnight. After breakfast I tidy up my room, making the bed, wiping the sink with a wad of toilet paper, and taking the garbage out to the dumpster. True, the owner's wife (or maybe she's the co-owner) goes around from room to room every morning with a cleaning cart, but her efforts show signs of deep depression or possibly attention deficit disorder. Usually she remembers to replace the thin little towels, which, even when clean, contain embedded hairs and smell like cooking grease, but there's nothing else, except maybe an abandoned rag or bottle of air freshener, to suggest that she's been through on her rounds. I picture an ad for a "traditional-minded, hardworking wife," a wedding in her natal village, then—plop—she's in Clearview, Minnesota, with an Indian American husband who may not even speak her language, thousands of miles from family, a temple, a sari shop. So I clean up myself, then do my hair with enough bobby pins to last through the shift, and head off for work. The idea is to make myself look like someone who's spent the night in a regular home with kitchen and washer and dryer, not like someone who's borderline homeless.

The other point of my domestic rituals and arrangements is to get through the time when I can't be at work, when it would look weird to be hanging around in the Wal-Mart parking lot or break room. Because home life is more stressful than I have consciously acknowledged, and I would be dreading my upcoming day off if I weren't confident of spending it on the move to better quarters at the Hopkins Park Plaza. Little nervous symptoms have arisen. Sometimes I get a tummy ache after breakfast, which makes lunch dicey, and there's no way to get through the shift without at least one major refueling. More disturbing is the new habit of plucking away at my shirt or my khakis with whichever hand can be freed up for the task. I have to stop this. My maternal grandmother, who still lives on, in a fashion, at the age of a hundred and one, was a perfect model of stoicism, but she used to pick at her face and her wrist, creating dark red circular sores, and claimed not to know she was doing it. Maybe it's an inheritable twitch and I will soon be moving on from fabric to flesh.

I arrive at work full of bounce, pausing at the fitting room to jolly up the lady on duty—usually the bossy, self-satisfied Rhoda—because the fitting room lady bears the same kind of relation to me as a cook to a server: she can screw me up if she wants, giving me carts contaminated with foreign, nonladies' items and items not properly folded or hangered. "Here I am," I announce grandiosely, spreading out my arms. "The day can begin!" For this I get a wrinkled nose from Rhoda and a one-sided grin from Lynne, the gaunt blonde who's working bras. I search out Ellie, whom I find shooting out new labels from the pricing gun, and ask if there's anything special I need to be doing. No, just whatever needs to be done. Next I find Melissa to get a report on the cartage so far. Today she seems embarrassed when she sees me: "I probably shouldn't have done this and you're going to think it's really silly . . ." but she's brought me a sandwich for lunch. This is because I'd told her I was living in a motel almost entirely on fast food, and she felt sorry for me. Now *I'm* embarrassed, and beyond that overwhelmed to discover a covert stream of generosity running counter to the dominant corporate miserliness. Melissa proba-

bly wouldn't think of herself as poor, but I know she calculates in very small units of currency, twice reminding me, for example, that you can get sixty-eight cents off the specials at the Radio Grill every Tuesday, so a sandwich is something to consider. I set off with my cart, muttering contentedly, "Bobbie Brooks turquoise elastic-waist shorts" and "Faded Glory V-neck red tank top."

Then, in my second week, two things change. My shift changes from 10:00–6:00 to 2:00–11:00, the so-called closing shift, although the store remains open 24/7. No one tells me this; I find it out by studying the schedules that are posted, under glass, on the wall outside the break room. Now I have nine hours instead of eight, and although one of them is an unpaid dinner hour, I have a net half an hour a day more on my feet. My two fifteen-minute breaks, which seemed almost superfluous on the 10:00–6:00 shift, now become a matter of urgent calculation. Do I take both before dinner, which is usually about 7:30, leaving an unbroken two-and-a-half-hour stretch when I'm weariest, between 8:30 and 11:00? Or do I try to go two and a half hours without a break in the afternoon, followed by a nearly three-hour marathon before I can get away for dinner? Then there's the question of how to make the best use of a fifteen-minute break when you have three or more urgent, simultaneous needs—to pee, to drink something, to get outside the neon and into the natural light, and most of all, to sit down. I save about a minute by engaging in a little time theft and stopping at the rest room before I punch out for the break (and, yes, we have to punch out even for breaks, so there's no padding them with a few stolen minutes). From the time clock it's a seventy-five-second walk to the store exit; if I stop at the Radio Grill, I could end up wasting a full four minutes waiting in line, not to mention the fifty-nine cents for a small-sized iced tea. So if I treat myself to an outing in the tiny fenced-off area beside the store, the only place where employees are allowed to smoke, I get about nine minutes off my feet.

The other thing that happens is that the post-Memorial Day weekend lull definitely comes to an end. Now there are always a dozen or more shoppers rooting around in ladies', reinforced in the evening by a wave of multigenerational gangs—Grandma, Mom, a baby in the shopping cart, and a gaggle of sullen children in tow. New tasks arise, such as bunching up the carts left behind by customers and steering them to their place in the front of the store every half hour or so. Now I am picking up not only dropped clothes but all the odd items customers carry off from foreign departments and decide to leave with us in ladies'—pillows, upholstery hooks, Pokemon cards, earrings, sunglasses, stuffed animals, even a package of cinnamon buns. And always there are the returns, augmented now by the huge volume of items that have been tossed on the floor or carried fecklessly to inappropriate sites. Sometimes I am lucky to achieve a steady state between replacing the returns and picking up items strewn on the racks and the floor. If I pick up misplaced items as quickly as I replace the returns, my cart never empties and things back up dangerously at the fitting room, where Rhoda or her nighttime replacement is likely to hiss: "You've got three carts waiting, Barb. What's the *problem*?" Think Sisyphus here or the sorcerer's apprentice.

Still, for the first half of my shift, I am the very picture of good-natured helpfulness, fascinated by the multiethnic array of our shoppers—Middle Eastern, Asian, African American, Russian, former Yugoslavian, old-fashioned Minnesota white—and calmly accepting of the second law of thermodynamics, the one that says entropy always wins. Amazingly, I get praised by Isabelle, the thin little seventyish lady who seems to be Ellie's adjutant: I am doing "wonderfully," she tells me, and—even better—am "great to work with." I prance from rack to rack, I preen. But then, somewhere around 6:00 or 7:00, when the desire to sit down becomes a serious craving, a Dr. Jekyll/Mr. Hyde transformation sets in. I cannot ignore the fact that it's the customers' sloppiness and idle whims that make me bend and crouch and run. They are the shoppers, I am the antishopper, whose goal is to make it look as if they'd never been in the store. At this point, "aggressive hospitality" gives way to aggressive hostility. Their carts bang into mine, their children run amok. Once I stand and watch helplessly while some rug rat pulls everything he can reach off the racks, and the thought that abortion is wasted on the unborn must show on my face, because his mother finally tells him to stop.

I even start hating the customers for extraneous reasons, such as, in the case of the native Caucasians, their size. I don't mean just bellies and butts, but huge bulges in completely exotic locations, like the backs of the neck and the knees. This summer, Wendy's, where I often buy lunch, has introduced the verb *biggiesize*, as in "Would you like to biggiesize that combo?" meaning double the fries and pop, and something like biggiesizing seems to have happened to the female guest population. All right, everyone knows that midwesterners, and especially those in the lower middle class, are tragically burdened by the residues of decades of potato chips and French toast sticks, and I probably shouldn't even bring this up. In my early-shift, Dr. Jekyll form, I feel sorry for the obese, who must choose from among our hideous woman-size offerings, our drawstring shorts, and huge horizontally striped tees, which are obviously designed to mock them. But compassion fades as the shift wears on. Those of us who work in ladies' are for obvious reasons a pretty lean lot—probably, by Minnesota standards, candidates for emergency IV nutritional supplementation—and we live with the fear of being crushed by some wide-body as she hurtles through the narrow passage from Faded Glory to woman size, lost in fantasies involving svelte Kathie Lee sheaths.

It's the clothes I relate to, though, not the customers. And now a funny thing happens to me here on my new shift: I start thinking they're mine, not mine to take home and wear, because I have no such designs on them, just mine to organize and rule over. Same with ladies' wear as a whole. After

6:00, when Melissa and Ellie go home, and especially after 9:00, when Isabelle leaves, I start to *own* the place. Out of the way, Sam, this is Bar-Mart now. I patrol the perimeter with my cart, darting in to pick up misplaced and fallen items, making everything look spiffy from the outside. I don't fondle the clothes, the way customers do; I slap them into place, commanding them to hang straight, at attention, or lie subdued on the shelves in perfect order. In this frame of mind, the last thing I want to see is a customer riffling around, disturbing the place. In fact, I hate the idea of things being sold—uprooted from their natural homes, whisked off to some closet that's in God-knows-what state of disorder. I want ladies' wear sealed off in a plastic bubble and trucked away to some place of safety, some museum of retail history.

One night I come back bone-tired from my last break and am distressed to find a new person, an Asian American or possibly Hispanic woman who can't be more than four and a half feet tall, folding T-shirts in the White Stag area, *my* White Stag area. It's already been a vexing evening. Earlier, when I'd returned from dinner, the evening fitting room lady upbraided me for being late—which I actually wasn't—and said that if Howard knew, he probably wouldn't yell at me this time because I'm still pretty new, but if it happened again. . . . And I'd snapped back that I could care less if Howard yelled at me, which is a difficult sentiment to fully convey without access to the forbidden four-letter words. So I'm a little wary with this intruder in White Stag and, sure enough, after our minimal introductions, she turns on me.

"Did you put anything away here today?" she demands.

"Well, yes, sure." In fact I've put something away everywhere today, as I do on every other day.

"Because this is not in the right place. See the fabric—it's different," and she thrusts the errant item up toward my chest.

True, I can see that this olive-green shirt is slightly ribbed while the others are smooth. "You've *got* to put them in their right places," she continues. "Are you checking the UPC numbers?"

Of course I am not checking the ten or more digit UPC numbers, which lie just under the bar codes—nobody does. What does she think this is, the National Academy of Sciences? I'm not sure what kind of deference, if any, is due here: Is she my supervisor now? Or are we involved in some kind of test to see who will dominate the 9:00–11:00 time period? But I don't care, she's pissing me off, messing with my stuff. So I say, only without the numerals or the forbidden curse word, that (1) plenty of other people work here during the day, not to mention all the customers coming through, so why is she blaming me? (2) it's after 10:00 and I've got another cart full of returns to go, and wouldn't it make more sense if we both worked on the carts, instead of zoning the goddamn T-shirts?

To which she responds huffily, "I don't *do* returns. My job is to *fold*."

A few minutes later I see why she doesn't do returns—she can't reach the racks. In fact, she has to use a ladder even to get to the higher shelves. And you know what I feel when I see the poor little mite pushing that ladder around? A surge of evil mirth. I peer around from where I am working in Jordache, hoping to see her go splat.

I leave that night shaken by my response to the intruder. If she's a supervisor, I could be written up for what I said, but even worse is what I thought. Am I turning mean here, and is that a normal response to the end of a nine-hour shift? There was another outbreak of mental wickedness that night. I'd gone back to the counter by the fitting room to pick up the next cart full of returns and found the guy who answers the phone at the counter at night, a pensive young fellow in a wheelchair, staring into space, looking even sadder than usual. And my uncensored thought was, At least you get to sit down.

This is not me, at least not any version of me I'd like to spend much time with, just as my tiny coworker is probably not usually a bitch. She's someone who works all night and naps during the day when her baby does, I find out later, along with the information that she's not anyone's supervisor and is in fact subject to constant criticism by Isabelle when the two overlap. What I have to face is that "Barb," the name on my ID tag, is not exactly the same person as Barbara. "Barb" is what I was called as a child, and still am by my siblings, and I sense that at some level I'm regressing. Take away the career and the higher education, and maybe what you're left with is this original Barb, the one who might have ended up working at Wal-Mart for real if her father hadn't managed to climb out of the mines. So it's interesting, and more than a little disturbing, to see how Barb turned out—that she's meaner and slyer than I am, more cherishing of grudges, and not quite as smart as I'd hoped.

* * *

On the day of my move to the Hopkins Park Plaza, I wake up savoring the thought of the perishables I'm going to stock my refrigerator with: mayonnaise, mustard, chicken breasts. But when I get there Hildy is gone and the woman in the towering black beehive who has taken her place says I didn't understand, the room won't be available until *next* week and I should call first to be sure. Had I really been so befogged by wishful thinking that I'd "misunderstood" what had seemed to be a fairly detailed arrangement (bring your money down at nine on Saturday, you can move in at four, etc.)? Or had someone else just beat me to it? Never mind, I've been clearheaded enough to know all along that the Park Plaza apartment with kitchenette, at $179 a week, was not a long-term option on Wal-Mart's $7 an hour. My plan had been to add a weekend job, which I have been tentatively offered at a Rainbow supermarket near the apartment where I originally stayed, at close to $8 an hour. Between the two jobs, I would be making about $320 a week after taxes, so that the $179 in rent would have amounted to about 55 percent of my income, which is beginning to look "affordable."[1] But Rainbow also falls through; they decide they want me to work part-time five days a week, not just on weekends. Furthermore, I have no control

at the moment over what my days off will be. Howard has scheduled me to have Friday off one week, Tuesday and Wednesday the next, and I would have to do some serious sucking up to arrive at a more stable and congenial schedule.

Ergo, I either need to find a husband, like Melissa, or a second job, like some of my other coworkers. In the long run everything will work out if I devote my mornings to job hunting, while holding out for a Park Plaza opening or, better yet, a legitimate apartment at $400 a month or $100 a week. But to paraphrase Keynes: in the long run, we'll all be broke, at least those of us who work for low wages and live in exorbitantly overpriced motels. I call the YWCA to see whether they have any rooms, and they refer me to a place called Budget Lodging, which doesn't have any rooms either, although they do have dorm beds for $19 a night. I can have my own locker and there's no "lockout" in the morning—you can hang out in your dorm bed all day if you want. Even with these enticements, I have to admit I'm relieved when the guy at Budget Lodging tells me they're located on the other side of Minneapolis, so I can rule out the dorm on account of the drive and the gas costs, at least as long as I'm working at Wal-Mart. Maybe I should have just dumped Wal-Mart, moved into the dorm, and relaunched my job search from there. But the truth is I'm not ready to leave Wal-Mart yet; it's my connection to the world, my source of identity, my *place*.

The Budget Lodging clerk, who seems to have some familiarity with the housing nightmares of low-wage workers, suggests I keep trying motels. He's sure there must be some that cost less than $240 a week. In the meantime, the Clearview Inn wants an unconscionable $55 for any additional nights there, which means that, for a couple of nights, almost any motel would be preferable. I call Caroline to ask for her insights into the housing situation and—I should have guessed this was coming—she calls back in a few minutes to invite me to move in with her and her family. I say no, I've already had a stint of free lodging and now I have to take my chances with the market like anyone else. But for a moment I get this touched-by-an-angel feeling I'd gotten from Melissa's sandwich: I am not really entirely alone. I start calling around to motels again, now ranging even farther out from the city, into the northern towns, the western towns, St. Paul. But most have no rooms at all, at any price, either now or for the coming weeks—because of the season, I'm told, although it's hard to see why a place like, say, Clearview, Minnesota, would be a destination at any time of the year. Only the Comfort Inn has a room available, at $49.95 a night, so I make a reservation there for a couple of days. The relief I should feel about leaving the Worst Motel in the Country is canceled by an overwhelming sense of defeat.

Could I have done better? The *St. Paul Pioneer Press* of June 13, which I eagerly snatch out of the box in front of Wal-Mart, provides an overdue reality check. "Apartment rents skyrocket," the front-page headline declares; they've leaped 20.5 percent in Minneapolis in the first three months of 2000 alone, an unprecedented increase, according to local real estate experts. Even more pertinent to my condition, the Twin Cities region "is posting one of the lowest vacancy rates in the nation—possibly the lowest." Who knew? My cursory pre-trip research had revealed nothing about a record absence of housing. In fact, I'd come across articles bemoaning the absence of a Twin Cities dot-com industry, and these had led me to believe that the region had been spared the wild real estate inflation afflicting, for example, California's Bay Area. But apparently you don't need dot-com wealth to ruin an area for its low-income residents. The *Pioneer Press* quotes Secretary of HUD Andrew Cuomo ruing the "cruel irony" that prosperity is shrinking the stock of affordable housing nationwide: "The stronger the economy, the stronger the upward pressure on rents." So I'm a victim not of poverty but of prosperity. The rich and the poor, who are generally thought to live in a state of harmonious interdependence—the one providing cheap labor, the other providing low-wage jobs—can no longer coexist.

I check in at the Comfort Inn in the firm expectation that this will be only for a night or two, before something, somewhere, opens up to me. What I cannot know is that this is, in some sense, my moment of final defeat. Game over. End of story—at least if it's a story about attempting to match earnings to rent. In almost three weeks, I've spent over $500 and earned only $42—from Wal-Mart, for orientation night. There's more coming eventually—Wal-Mart, like so many other low-wage employers, holds back your first week's pay—but eventually will be too late.

I never do find an apartment or affordable motel, although I do make one last attempt, seeking help one morning at a charitable agency. I found the place by calling United Way of Minneapolis, which directed me to another agency, which in turn directed me to something called the Community Emergency Assistance Program, located a convenient fifteen-minute drive from Wal-Mart. Inside the office suite housing CEAP, a disturbing scene is unfolding: two rail-thin black men—Somalis, I guess, from their accents and since there are a lot of them in the Twin Cities area—are saying, "Bread? Bread?" and being told, "No bread, no bread." They flutter out and a fiftyish white woman comes in and goes through the same routine, leaving with the smile of supplication still frozen awkwardly on her face. For some reason, though—perhaps because I have an appointment and haven't worn out my welcome yet—I get taken to an inner office where a young woman interviews me absentmindedly. Do I have a car? Yes, I have a car. And a couple of minutes later: "So you don't have a car?" and so forth.

When I tell her I'm working at Wal-Mart and what I earn, she suggests I move into a shelter so I can save up enough money for a first month's rent and deposit, then she sends me to another office where she says I can apply for a housing subsidy and get help finding an apartment. But this other office offers only a photocopied list of affordable apartments, which is updated weekly and is already out of date. Back at the first office, my interviewer asks if I can use some emergency food aid and I explain, once again, that I don't have a refrigerator. She'll find something, she says, and comes back with a box containing a bar of soap, a deodorant, and a bunch of fairly useless food items, from my point of view—lots of candy and cookies and a one-pound can of ham, which, without a refrigerator, I would have to eat all in one sitting.[2] (The next day I take the whole box, untouched, to another agency serving the poor, so I won't appear ungrateful and the food won't be wasted.)

Only when I'm driving away with my sugary loot do I realize the importance of what I've learned in this encounter. At one point toward the end of the interview, the CEAP lady had apologized for forgetting almost everything I said about myself—that I had a car, lived in a motel, etc. She was mixing me up with someone else who worked at Wal-Mart, she explained, someone who had been in just a few days ago. Now, of course I've noticed that many of my co-workers are poor in all the hard-to-miss, stereotypical ways. Crooked yellow teeth are one sign, inadequate footwear is another. My feet hurt after four hours of work, and I wear my comfortable old Reeboks, but a lot of women run around all day in thin-soled moccasins. Hair provides another class cue. Ponytails are common or, for that characteristic Wal-Martian beat-up and hopeless look, straight shoulder-length hair, parted in the middle and kept out of the face by two bobby pins.

But now I know something else. In orientation, we learned that the store's success depends entirely on us, the associates; in fact, our bright blue vests bear the statement "At Wal-Mart, our people make the difference." Underneath those vests, though, there are real-life charity cases, maybe even shelter dwellers.[3]

*   *   *

So, anyway, begins my surreal existence at the Comfort Inn. I live in luxury with AC, a door that bolts, a large window protected by an intact screen—just like a tourist or a business traveler. But from there I go out every day to a life that most business travelers would find shabby and dispiriting—

lunch at Wendy's, dinner at Sbarro (the Italian-flavored fast-food place), and work at Wal-Mart, where I would be embarrassed to be discovered in my vest, should some member of the Comfort staff happen to wander in. Of course, I expect to leave any day, when the Hopkins Park Plaza opens up. For the time being, though, I revel in the splendor of my accommodations, amazed that they cost $5.05 less, on a daily basis, than what I was paying for that rat hole in Clearview. I stop worrying about my computer being stolen or cooked, I sleep through the night, the sick little plucking habit loses its grip. I feel like the man in the commercials for the Holiday Inn Express who's so refreshed by his overnight stay that he can perform surgery the next day or instruct people in how to use a parachute. At Wal-Mart, I get better at what I do, much better than I could ever have imagined at the beginning.

The breakthrough comes on a Saturday, one of your heavier shopping days. There are two carts waiting for me when I arrive at two, and tossed items inches deep on major patches of the floor. The place hasn't been shopped, it's been looted. In this situation, all I can do is everything at once—stoop, reach, bend, lift, run from rack to rack with my cart. And then it happens—a magical flow state in which the clothes start putting *themselves away*. Oh, I play a part in this, but not in any conscious way. Instead of thinking, "White Stag navy twill skort," and doggedly searching out similar skorts, all I have to do is form an image of the item in my mind, transpose this image onto the visual field, and move to wherever the image finds its match in the outer world. I don't know how this works. Maybe my mind just gets so busy processing the incoming visual data that it has to bypass the left brain's verbal centers, with their cumbersome instructions: "Proceed to White Stag area in the northwest corner of ladies', try bottom racks near khaki shorts. . . ." Or maybe the trick lies in understanding that each item *wants* to be reunited with its sibs and its clan members and that, within each clan, the item *wants* to occupy its proper place in the color/size hierarchy. Once I let the clothes take charge, once I understand that I am only the means of their reunification, they just fly out of the cart to their natural homes.

On the same day, perhaps because the new speediness frees me to think more clearly, I make my peace with the customers and discover the purpose of life, or at least of my life at Wal-Mart. Management may think that the purpose is to sell things, but this is an overly reductionist, narrowly capitalist view. As a matter of fact, I never see anything sold, since sales take place out of my sight, at the cash registers at the front of the store. All I see is customers unfolding carefully folded T-shirts, taking dresses and pants off their hangers, holding them up for a moment's idle inspection, then dropping them somewhere for us associates to pick up. For me, the way out of resentment begins with a clue provided by a poster near the break room, in the back of the store where only associates go: "Your mother doesn't work here," it says. "Please pick up after yourself." I've passed it many times, thinking, "Ha, that's all I do—pick up after people." Then it hits me: most of the people I pick up after are mothers themselves, meaning that what I do at work is what *they* do at home—pick up the toys and the clothes and the spills. So the great thing about shopping, for most of these women, is that here *they* get to behave like brats, ignoring the bawling babies in their carts, tossing things around for someone else to pick up. And it wouldn't be any fun—would it?—unless the clothes were all reasonably orderly to begin with, which is where I come in, constantly re-creating orderliness for the customers to maliciously destroy. It's appalling, but it's in their nature: only pristine and virginal displays truly excite them.

I test this theory out on Isabelle: that our job is to constantly re-create the stage setting in which women can act out. That without us, rates of child abuse would suddenly soar. That we function, in a way, as therapists and should probably be paid accordingly, at $50 to $100 an hour. "You just go on thinking that," she says, shaking her head. But she smiles her canny little smile in a way that makes me think it's not a bad notion.

With competence comes a new impatience: *Why does anybody put up with the wages we're paid?* True, most of my fellow workers are better cushioned than I am; they live with spouses or grown children or they have other jobs in addition to this one. I sit with Lynne in the break room one night and find out this is only a part-time job for her—six hours a day—with the other eight hours spent at a factory for $9 an hour. Doesn't she get awfully tired? Nah, it's what she's always done. The cook at the Radio Grill has two other jobs. You might expect a bit of grumbling, some signs here and there of unrest—graffiti on the hortatory posters in the break room, muffled guffaws during our associate meetings—but I can detect none of that. Maybe this is what you get when you weed out all the rebels with drug tests and personality "surveys"—a uniformly servile and denatured workforce, content to dream of the distant day when they'll be vested in the company's profit-sharing plan. They even join in the "Wal-Mart cheer" when required to do so at meetings, I'm told by the evening fitting room lady, though I am fortunate enough never to witness this final abasement.[4]

But if it's hard to think "out of the box," it may be almost impossible to think out of the Big Box. Wal-Mart, when you're in it, is total—a closed system, a world unto itself. I get a chill when I'm watching TV in the break room one afternoon and see . . . *a commercial for Wal-Mart*. When a Wal-Mart shows up within a television within a Wal-Mart, you have to question the existence of an outer world. Sure, you can drive for five minutes and get somewhere else—to Kmart, that is, or Home Depot, or Target, or Burger King, or Wendy's, or KFC. Wherever you look, there is no alternative to the megascale corporate order, from which every form of local creativity and initiative has been abolished by distant home offices. Even the woods and the meadows have been stripped of disorderly life forms and forced into a uniform made of concrete. What you see—highways, parking lots, stores—is all there is, or all that's left to us here in the reign of globalized, totalized, paved-over, corporatized everything. I like to read the labels to find out where the clothing we sell is made—Indonesia, Mexico, Turkey, the Philippines, South Korea, Sri Lanka, Brazil—but the labels serve only to remind me that none of these places is "exotic" anymore, that they've all been eaten by the great blind profit-making global machine.

The only thing to do is ask: Why do you—why do *we*—work here? Why do you stay? So when Isabelle praises my work a second time (!), I take the opportunity to say I really appreciate her encouragement, but I can't afford to live on $7 an hour, and how does she do it? The answer is that she lives with her grown daughter, who also works, plus the fact that she's worked here two years, during which her pay has shot up to $7.75 an hour. She counsels patience: it could happen to me. Melissa, who has the advantage of a working husband, says, "Well, it's a job." Yes, she made twice as much when she was a waitress but that place closed down and at her age she's never going to be hired at a high-tip place. I recognize the inertia, the unwillingness to start up with the apps and the interviews and the drug tests again. She thinks she should give it a year. *A year?* I tell her I'm wondering whether I should give it another week.

A few days later something happens to make kindly, sweet-natured Melissa mad. She gets banished to bras, which is terra incognita for us—huge banks of shelves bearing barely distinguishable bi-coned objects—for a three-hour stretch. I know how she feels, because I was once sent over to work for a couple of hours in men's wear, where I wandered uselessly through the strange thickets of racks, numbed by the sameness of colors and styles.[5] It's the difference between working and pretending to work. You push your cart a few feet, pause significantly with item in hand, frown at the ambient racks, then push on and repeat the process. "I just don't like wasting their money," Melissa says when she's allowed back. "I mean they're *paying* me and I just wasn't accomplishing anything over there."

To me, this anger seems badly mis-aimed. What does she think, that the Walton family is living in some hidden room in the back of the store, in the utmost frugality, and likely to be ruined by $21 worth of wasted labor? I'm starting in on that theme when she suddenly dives behind the rack that separates the place where we're standing, in the Jordache/No Boundaries section, from the Faded Glory region. Worried that I may have offended her somehow, I follow right behind. "*Howard,*" she whispers. "Didn't you see him come by? We're not allowed to talk to each other, you know."

"The point is our time is so cheap they don't care if we waste it," I continue, aware even as I speak that this isn't true, otherwise why would they be constantly monitoring us for "time theft"? But I sputter on: "That's what's so insulting." Of course, in this outburst of militance I am completely not noticing the context—two women of mature years, two very hardworking women, as it happens, dodging behind a clothing rack to avoid a twenty-six-year-old management twerp. That's not even worth commenting on.

Alyssa is another target for my crusade. When she returns to check yet again on that $7 polo, she finds a stain on it. What could she get off for that? I think 10 percent, and if you add in the 10 percent employee discount, we'd be down to $5.60. I'm trying to negotiate a 20 percent price reduction with the fitting room lady when—rotten luck!—Howard shows up and announces that there are no reductions and no employee discounts on clearanced items. Those are the rules. Alyssa looks crushed, and I tell her, when Howard's out of sight, that there's something wrong when you're not paid enough to buy a Wal-Mart shirt, a *clearanced* Wal-Mart shirt with a stain on it. "I hear you," she says, and admits Wal-Mart isn't working for her either, if the goal is to make a living.

Then I get a little reckless. When an associate meeting is announced over the loudspeaker that afternoon, I decide to go, although most of my coworkers stay put. I don't understand the purpose of these meetings, which occur every three days or so and consist largely of attendance taking, unless it's Howard's way of showing us that there's only one of him compared to so many of us. I'm just happy to have a few minutes to sit down or, in this case, perch on some fertilizer bags since we're meeting in lawn and garden today, and chat with whoever shows up, today a gal from the optical department. She's better coifed and made up than most of us female associates—forced to take the job because of a recent divorce, she tells me, and sorry now that she's found out how crummy the health insurance is. There follows a long story about preexisting conditions and deductibles and her COBRA, running out. I listen vacantly because, like most of the other people in my orientation group, I hadn't opted for the health insurance—the employee contribution seemed too high. "You know what we need here?" I finally respond. "We need a union." There it is, the word is out. Maybe if I hadn't been feeling so footsore I wouldn't have said it, and I probably wouldn't have said it either if we were allowed to say "hell" and "damn" now and then or, better yet, "shit." But no one has outright banned the word *union* and right now it's the most potent couple of syllables at hand. "We need *something*," she responds.

After that, there's nothing to stop me. I'm on a mission now: *Raise the questions! Plant the seeds!* Breaks finally have a purpose beyond getting off my feet. There are hundreds of workers here—I never do find out how many—and sooner or later I'll meet them all. I reject the break room for this purpose because the TV inhibits conversation, and for all I know that's what it's supposed to do. Better to go outdoors to the fenced-in smoking area in front of the store. Smokers, in smoke-free America, are more likely to be rebels; at least that was true at The Maids, where the nonsmokers waited silently in the office for work to begin, while the smokers out on the sidewalk would be having a raucous old time. Besides, you can always start the ball rolling by asking for a light, which I have to do anyway when the wind is up. The next ques-

tion is, "What department are you in?" followed by, "How long have you worked here?"—from which it's an obvious segue to the business at hand. Almost everyone is eager to talk, and I soon become a walking repository of complaints. No one gets paid overtime at Wal-Mart, I'm told, though there's often pressure to work it.[6] Many feel the health insurance isn't worth paying for. There's a lot of frustration over schedules, especially in the case of the evangelical lady who can never get Sunday morning off, no matter how much she pleads. And always there are the gripes about managers: the one who is known for sending new hires home in tears, the one who takes a ruler and knocks everything off what he regards as a messy shelf, so you have to pick it up off the floor and start over.

Sometimes, I discover, my favorite subject, which is the abysmal rate of pay, seems to be a painful one. Stan, for example, a twenty-something fellow with wildly misaligned teeth, is so eager to talk that he fairly pounces on the seat next to mine on a bench in the smoking area. But when the subject arrives at wages, his face falls. The idea, see, was that he would go to school (he names a two-year technical school) while he worked, but the work cut into studying too much, so he had to drop out and now. . . . He stares at the butt-strewed ground, perhaps seeing an eternity in appliances unfold before him. I suggest that what we need is a union, but from the look on his face I might as well have said gumballs or Prozac. Yeah, maybe he'll go over and apply at Media One, where a friend works and the wages are higher. . . . Try school again, umm. . . .

At the other extreme, there are people like Marlene. I am sitting out there talking to a doll-like blonde whom I had taken for a high school student but who, it turns out, has been working full-time since November and is fretting over whether she can afford to buy a car. Marlene comes out for her break, lights a cigarette, and emphatically seconds my opinion of Wal-Mart wages. "They talk about having spirit," she says, referring to management, "but they don't give us any reason to have any spirit." In her view, Wal-Mart would rather just keep hiring new people than treating the ones it has decently. You can see for yourself there's a dozen new people coming in for orientation every day—which is true. Wal-Mart's appetite for human flesh is insatiable; we've even been urged to recruit any Kmart employees we may happen to know. They don't care that they've trained you or anything, Marlene goes on, they can always get someone else if you complain. Emboldened by her vehemence, I risk the red-hot word again. "I know this goes against the whole Wal-Mart philosophy, but we could use a union here." She grins, so I push on: "It's not just about money, it's about dignity." She nods fiercely, lighting a second cigarette from her first. *Put that woman on the organizing committee at once*, I direct my imaginary coconspirators as I leave.

All right, I'm not a union organizer anymore than I'm Wal-Mart "management material," as Isabelle has hinted. In fact, I don't share the belief, held by many union staffers, that unionization would be a panacea. Sure, almost any old union would boost wages and straighten out some backbones here, but I know that even the most energetic and democratic unions bear careful watching by their members. The truth, which I can't avoid acknowledging when I'm in those vast, desertlike stretches between afternoon breaks, is that I'm just amusing myself, and in what seems like a pretty harmless way. Someone has to puncture the prevailing fiction that we're a "family" here, we "associates" and our "servant leaders," held together solely by our commitment to the "guests." After all, you'd need a lot stronger word than *dysfunctional* to describe a family where a few people get to eat at the table while the rest—the "associates" and all the dark-skinned seamstresses and factory workers worldwide who make the things we sell—lick up the drippings from the floor: *psychotic* would be closer to the mark.[7] And someone has to flush out the mysterious "we" lurking in the "our" in the "Our people make the difference" statement we wear on our backs. It might as well be me because I have nothing to lose, less than nothing, in fact. For each

day that I fail to find cheaper quarters, which is every day now, I am spending $49.95 for the privilege of putting clothes away at Wal-Mart. At this rate, I'll have burned through the rest of the $1,200 I've allotted for my life in Minneapolis in less than a week.

I could use some amusement. I have been discovering a great truth about low-wage work and probably a lot of medium-wage work, too—that nothing happens, or rather the same thing always happens, which amounts, day after day, to nothing. This law doesn't apply so strictly to the service jobs I've held so far. In waitressing, you always have new customers to study; even housecleaning offers the day's parade of houses to explore. But here—well, you know what I do and how it gets undone and how I just start all over and do it again. How did I think I was going to survive in a factory, where each *minute* is identical to the next one, and not just each day? There will be no crises here, except perhaps in the pre-Christmas rush. There will be no "Code M," meaning "hostage situation," and probably no Code F or T (I'm guessing on these letters, which I didn't write down during my note taking at orientation and which may be a company secret anyway), meaning fire or tornado—no opportunities for courage or extraordinary achievement or sudden evacuations of the store. Those breaking-news moments when a disgruntled former employee shoots up the place or a bunch of people get crushed in an avalanche of piled-up stock are one-in-a-million events. What my life holds is carts—full ones, then empty ones, then full ones again.

You could get old pretty fast here. In fact, time does funny things when there are no little surprises to mark it off into memorable chunks, and I sense that I'm already several years older than I was when I started. In the one full-length mirror in ladies' wear, a medium-tall figure is hunched over a cart, her face pinched in absurd concentration—surely not me. How long before I'm as gray as Ellie, as cranky as Rhoda, as shriveled as Isabelle? When even a high-sodium fast-food diet can't keep me from needing to pee every hour, and my feet are putting some podiatrist's kid through college? Yes, I know that any day now I'm going to return to the variety and drama of my real, Barbara Ehrenreich life. But this fact sustains me only in the way that, say, the prospect of heaven cheers a terminally ill person: it's nice to know, but it isn't much help from moment to moment. What you don't necessarily realize when you start selling your time by the hour is that what you're actually selling is your *life*.

Then something happens, not to me and not at Wal-Mart but with dazzling implications nonetheless. It's a banner headline in the *Star Tribune*: 1,450 hotel workers, members of the Hotel Employees and Restaurant Employees Union, strike nine local hotels. A business writer in the *Pioneer Press*, commenting on this plus a Teamsters' strike at the Pepsi-Cola bottling plant and a march by workers demanding union recognition at a St. Paul meatpacking plant, rubs his eyes and asks, "What's going on here?" When I arrive for work that day I salvage the newspaper from the trash can just outside the store entrance—which isn't difficult because the trash can is overflowing as usual and I don't have to dig down very far. Then I march that newspaper back to the break room, where I leave it face up on a table, in case anyone's missed the headline. This new role—bearer of really big news!—makes me feel busy and important. At ladies', I relate the news to Melissa, adding that the hotel workers already earn over a dollar an hour more than we do and that that hasn't stopped them from striking for more. She blinks a few times, considering, then Isabelle comes up and announces that the regional manager will be visiting our store tomorrow, so everything has to be "zoned to the nth degree." The day is upon us.

I have a lot more on my mind than the challenge of organizing the Faded Glory jeans shelves. At about six I'm supposed to call two motels charging only $40 a day, where something may have opened up, but I realize I've left the phone numbers in the car. I don't want to use up any breaks fetching them—not today, with the strike news

to talk about. Do I dare engage in some major time theft? And how can I get out without Isabelle noticing? She's already caught me folding the jeans the wrong way—you do them in thirds, with the ankles on the inside, not on the outside—and has come by to check a second time. It is, of all people, Howard who provides me with an out, suddenly appearing at my side to inform me that I'm way behind in my CBLs. New employees are supposed to make their way through the CBL training modules by leaving the floor with the permission of their supervisors, and I had been doing so in a halfhearted way—getting through cardboard-box opening, pallet loading, and trash compacting—until the program jammed. Now it's been fixed, he says, and I'm to get back to the computer immediately. This gets me out of ladies' but puts me a lot farther from the store exit. I apply myself to a module in which Sam Walton waxes manic about the perpetual inventory system, then I cautiously get up from the computer to see if Howard is anywhere around. Good, the way is clear. I am walking purposefully toward the front of the store when I catch sight of him walking in the same direction, about one hundred feet to my left. I dart into shoes, emerging to see him still moving in a path parallel to mine. I dodge him again by going into bras, then tacking right to the far side of ladies'. I've seen this kind of thing in the movies, where the good guy eludes the bad one in some kind of complicated public space, but I never imagined doing it myself.

Back in the store with the numbers in my vest pocket, I decide to steal a few more minutes and make my calls on company time from the pay phone near layaway. The first motel doesn't answer, which is not uncommon in your low-rate places. On a whim I call Caroline to see if she's on strike: no, not her hotel. But she laughs as she tells me that last night on the TV news she saw a manager from the hotel where she used to work. He's a white guy who'd enjoyed reminding her that she was the first African American to be hired for anything above a housekeeping job and here he was on TV, reduced to pushing a broom while the regular broom pushers walked the picket line. I'm dialing the second motel when Howard reappears. Why aren't I at the computer? he wants to know, giving me his signature hate smile. "Break," I say, flashing him what is known to primatologists as a "fear grin"—half teeth baring and half grimace. If you're going to steal, you better be prepared to lie. He can find out in a minute, of course, by checking to see if I'm actually punched out. I could be written up, banished to bras, called in for a talking-to by a deeply disappointed Roberta. But the second motel has no room for another few days, which means that, for purely financial reasons, my career at Wal-Mart is about to come to a sudden end anyway.

When Melissa is getting ready to leave work at six, I tell her I'm quitting, possibly the next day. Well then, she thinks she'll be going too, because she doesn't want to work here without me. We both look at the floor. I understand that this is not a confession of love, just a practical consideration. You don't want to work with people who can't hold up their end or whom you don't like being with, and you don't want to keep readjusting to new ones. We exchange addresses, including my real and permanent one. I tell her about the book I'm working on and she nods, not particularly surprised, and says she hopes she hasn't said "too many bad things about Wal-Mart." I assure her that she hasn't and that she'll be well disguised anyway. Then she tells me she's been thinking about it, and $7 an hour isn't enough for how hard we work after all, and she's going to apply at a plastics factory where she hopes she can get $9.

At ten that night I go to the break room for my final break, too footsore to walk out to the smoking area, and sit down with my feet up on the bench. My earlier break, the one I'd committed so many crimes to preserve, had been a complete bust, with no other human around but a management-level woman from accounting. I have that late-shift shut-in feeling that there's no world beyond the doors, no problem greater than the mystery items remaining at the bottom of my cart. There's only one other person in the break room anyway, a

white woman of maybe thirty, watching TV, and I don't have the energy to start a conversation, even with the rich topic of the strike at hand.

And then, by the grace of the God who dictated the Sermon on the Mount to Jesus, who watches over Melissa and sparrows everywhere, the TV picks up on the local news and the news is about the strike. A picketer with a little boy tells the camera, "This is for my son. I'm doing this for my son." Senator Paul Wellstone is standing there too. He shakes the boy's hand, and says, "You should be proud of your father." At this my sole companion jumps up, grinning, and waves a fist in the air at the TV set. I give her the rapid two-index-fingers-pointing-down signal that means "Here! Us! We could do that too!" She bounds over to where I'm sitting—if I were feeling peppier I would have gone over to her—leans into my face, and says, "Damn right!" I don't know whether it's my feet or the fact that she said "damn," or what, but I find myself tearing up. She talks well past my legal break time and possibly hers—about her daughter, how she's sick of working long hours and never getting enough time with her, and what does this lead to anyway, when you can't make enough to save?

I still think we could have done something, she and I, if I could have afforded to work at Wal-Mart a little longer.

Discussion Questions

1. To what extent do you think that unionization would be possible and would be a panacea for the entry-level workers at Wal-Mart?

2. Television advertisements about working for Wal-Mart always stress the opportunities for promotion. How can you do research to see if this is true?

Reprinted from Barbara Ehrenreich, "Wal-Mart," in *Nickle and Dimed: On (Not) Getting By in America* (New York: Owl Books, 2001, pp. 153–191).

Endnotes

1. Actually, rents usually have to be less than 30 percent of one's income to be considered "affordable." Housing analyst Peter Dreier reports that 59 percent of poor renters, amounting to a total of 4.4 million households, spend more than 50 percent of their income on shelter ("Why America's Workers Can't Pay the Rent," *Dissent*, Summer 2000, pp. 38–44). A 1996–97 survey of 44,461 households found that 28 percent of parents with incomes less than 200 percent of the poverty level—i.e., less than about $30,000 a year—reported problems paying their rent, mortgage, or utility bills (*Welfare Reform Network News* 1:2 [March 1999], Institute for Women's Policy Research, Washington, D.C.). In the Twin Cities, at the time of my stay, about 46,000 working families were paying more than 50 percent of their income for housing, and, surprisingly, 73 percent of these families were home owners hard-pressed by rising property taxes ("Affordable Housing Problem Hits Moderate-Income Earners," *Minneapolis Star Tribune*, July 12, 2000).

2. Middle-class people often criticize the poor for their eating habits, but this charitable agency seemed to be promoting a reliance on "empty calories." The complete inventory of the box of free food I received is as follows: 21 ounces of General Mills Honey Nut Chex cereal; 24 ounces of Post Grape-Nuts cereal; 20 ounces of Mississippi Barbecue Sauce; several small plastic bags of candy, including Tootsie Rolls, Smarties fruit snacks, Sweet Tarts, and two bars of Ghirardelli chocolate; one bubble gum; a 13-ounce package of iced sugar cookies; hamburger buns; six 6-ounce Minute Maid juice coolers; one loaf of Vienna bread; Star Wars fruit snacks; one loaf of cinnamon bread; 18 ounces of peanut butter; 18 ounces of jojoba shampoo; 16 ounces of canned ham; one bar of Dial soap; four Kellogg Rice Krispies Treats bars; two Ritz cracker packages; one 5-ounce Swanson canned chicken breast; 2 ounces of a Kool-Aid-like drink mix; two Lady Speed Stick deodorants.

3. In 1988, Arkansas state senator Jay Bradford attacked Wal-Mart for paying its employees so little that they had to turn to the state for welfare. He was, however, unable to prove his point by getting the company to open its payroll records (Bob Ortega, *In Sam We Trust: The Untold Story of Sam Walton and Wal-Mart, the World's Most Powerful Retailer* [Times Books, 2000], p. 193).

4. According to Wal-Mart expert Bob Ortega, Sam Walton got the idea for the cheer on a 1975 trip to Japan, "where he was deeply impressed by factory workers doing group calisthenics and company cheers." Ortega describes Walton conducting a cheer: " 'Gimme a W!' he'd shout. 'W!' the workers would shout back, and on through the Wal-Mart name. At the hyphen, Walton would shout 'Gimme a squiggly!' and squat and twist his hips at the same time; the workers would squiggle right back" (*In Sam We Trust*, p. 91).

5. "During your career with Wal-Mart, you may be cross-trained in other departments in your facility. This will challenge you in new areas, and help you be a well-rounded Associate" ("Wal-Mart Associate Handbook," p. 18).

6. Wal-Mart employees have sued the retail chain for unpaid overtime in four states—West Virginia, New Mexico, Oregon, and Colorado. The plaintiffs allege that they were pressured to work overtime and that the company then erased the overtime hours from their time records. Two of the West Virginia plaintiffs, who had been promoted to management positions before leaving Wal-Mart, said they had participated in altering time records to conceal overtime work. Instead of paying time and a half for overtime work, the company would reward workers with "desired schedule changes, promotions and other benefits," while workers who refused the unpaid overtime were "threatened with write-ups, demotions, reduced work schedules or docked pay" (Lawrence Messina, "Former Wal-Mart Workers File Overtime Suit in Harrison County," *Charleston Gazette*, January 24,1999). In New Mexico, a suit by 110 Wal-Mart employees was settled in 1998 when the company agreed to pay for the overtime ("Wal-Mart Agrees to Resolve Pay Dispute," *Albuquerque Journal*, July 16, 1998). In an e-mail to me, Wal-Mart spokesman William Wertz stated that "it is Wal-Mart's policy to compensate its employees fairly for their work and to comply fully with all federal and state wage and hour requirements."

7. In 1996, the National Labor Committee Education Fund in Support of Worker and Human Rights in Central America revealed that some Kathie Lee clothes were being sewn by children as young as twelve in a sweatshop in Honduras. TV personality Kathie Lee Gifford, the owner of the Kathie Lee line, tearfully denied the charges on the air but later promised to give up her dependence on sweatshops. ✦

Part IV

Work and Family Connections

Tension and Conflict

Prior to advanced industrialization, work and family were integrated, with the nuclear family being the work unit, first in the home and then in early factories. With the development of technology within the factory system, husbands, wives, and children were separated from one another and under the supervision of others, often strangers. This led to considerable social concern, the shortening of the workday, and work restrictions on women and children, who were relegated to educational institutions. With the growing labor force participation of women, including married women with children in the latter half of the twentieth century, came social concern once again, this time to reintegrate work and family.

In the first chapter in this part, Jennifer Glass describes how paid work and family care became incompatible in the United States, and proposes ways in which this incompatibility could be lessened. She traces how the change from an agrarian economy in which the household is the central economic unit to a capitalist market structure made family care-giving problematic, as it ended worker autonomy and control over the incompatibility between home work and market production. Children increasingly became economic and social costs that mothers especially, not communities or employers, bore. At the same time that demands on families to raise well-rounded children were increasing, demands and rewards for market work were similarly increasing. As automation eliminated human labor and globalization made labor cheap, workers were encouraged to invest even more in a 24/7 economy. A major response was the development of market substitutes for family care, such as for-profit child care centers, for which families, once again, must bear the cost.

Glass envisions a solution to the paid work/family care crisis in which everyone has a responsibility for family care and community building and no one gets differentially rewarded (with increased skill, responsibility, and authority) for increased investment in market work. Demands on workers would be modified, whereby shorter hours would represent full-time work and there would be flexibility in both the time (e.g., partially overlapping work shifts for spouses) and the location (e.g., telecommuting) of those hours. Additionally, new forms of worker protection would lessen pressure on caregivers to find substitutes for themselves. Demands would be modified on parents, whereby a normative climate would be created in which all adults contribute to caregiving and community building. Glass proposes five public policy changes to further this process while acknowledging probable obstacles to change in cynicism about the government as a solution, the heterogeneity of families, and resistance of the business community.

In the second chapter in this part, Jerry Jacobs and Kathleen Gerson approach divergent views about how much time Americans spend at work by refocusing the problem on the amount of time dual-earner couples jointly work instead of the individual earner's time. Analyzing U.S. census data from 1970 to 1997, they show that a family transformation from single (male) earner to dual-earner couples in which wives work accounts for most of the growth in working time. The increase in working time in 1997 for these dual-earner couples is due largely to the fact that such couples were older, more likely to have college degrees and hold managerial positions, and had fewer children younger than 18 years of age. Also, there is an increasing segment of the population working extremely long hours, namely, couples who are highly educated and in high-profile professional and managerial occupations. Importantly, women's increased work was not accompanied by a corresponding increase in fathers' work, thus producing a time squeeze. Jacobs and Gerson argue that both single and dual-earner parents face increasing pressures at work and at home and need more flexibility on the job as well as options to reduce working time.

Moving beyond the strain model of work-family conflict, Penny Becker and Phyllis Moen use interviews with 117 people in white, middle-class, dual-career couples in upstate New York to examine their combined strategies for balancing family with demanding work. They identify three specific couple-level strategies of scaling back work commitments, namely, placing limits, distinguishing between a job and a career, and trading off. Additionally, couples used scaling back in other areas of their lives—specifically, limiting the number of children they had, reducing social commitments and service work, enjoying less leisure time, and lowering expectations for housework.

In the fourth chapter, Sue Mennino, Beth Rubin, and April Brayfield examine the effect of supportive workplace cultures and availability of two family-related benefits on work-family conflict when workers are trying to balance work and family. They ask: "To what extent do the causes and consequences of spillover differ for women and men?" More specifically, they ask to what extent family-friendly policies reduce negative spillover for either women or men. Do certain workplace cultures increase the extent of negative job-to-home spillover? Do workers with a spouse and/or children have higher levels of home-to-job spillover?

They find that usually the workplace is not supportive of employees with family responsibilities. Both women and men experience greater job-to-home spillover than home-to-job spillover. Women experience higher levels of job-to-home spillover than do men, and having a partner and children increases negative spillover for women but usually not for men. Family-friendly policies alone do not reduce negative spillover in either direction for either women or men. Rather, a supportive workplace culture, regardless of availability of family-friendly policies, is most important to managing both kinds of spillover. In addition, time pressure on the job and long work hours have the most job-to-home spillover for both women and men. ✦

30

Envisioning the Integration of Family and Work

Jennifer L. Glass

Jennifer Glass depicts change in the United States from an agricultural to an industrial economy and how this made problematic the care of family members. She then proposes steps that would reduce this compatibility, including public policies to further the process of reintegration.

In trying to uncover just what it is about women's jobs and career profiles that creates a stubbornly persistent wage gap, I—like most other scholars of gender stratification—have been forced to look at the fundamental incompatibility between succeeding in a capitalist labor market and raising reasonably well-adjusted children. This incompatibility is experienced as an individual problem for the millions of parents, especially mothers, who must struggle to carve out time for adequate family care while holding down jobs. But the real culprit is the institutionalization of job structures unresponsive to workers' care-giving responsibilities and household/community structures that excessively privatize child-rearing responsibilities. The economic and social cost to children and families is staggering in the United States, although it is somewhat blunted in the welfare states of Western Europe that have developed family policies to ameliorate the harsher aspects of a wage labor economy (Bergmann 1996;

Kamerman 1996). In this essay, I sketch out a historically grounded understanding of how we got where we are, and therefore how we can best extricate ourselves from this situation.

The Incarnation of the Problem

Before we can begin to craft even a reasonably useful utopian solution to a problem, we must understand its historical and sociological origins, and the dynamics that have prevented successful resolution in earlier incarnations. In reading historical accounts of the transition from an agrarian household economy to a capitalist market structure, hastened by the Industrial Revolution in Western Europe and the United States, one can't help but be struck by the extent to which reproduction and child rearing become problematic as the household ceases to be the site of market production. As long as the central economic unit remains a large and flexible household, reproduction can be accommodated easily. The level of productive activity in the household, particularly the pace and timing of work tasks, is determined largely by weather and season, but also by the limitations facing members of the household (illness, injury, childbearing, stress and fatigue, and so on). No external authority determined work rules and regulations, and parents had little material incentive to avoid the bearing and rearing of children who would then become active participants in the household economy.[1]

Moving production out of the household, however, created entirely new "relations of production" and an entirely new class of workers: those who operated under the rules and regulations of factory owners, and later under the bureaucratic procedures of large organizations. While maximally efficient for mass production and the creation of market profits, the factory system eliminated the autonomy and control that workers exercised when care-giving responsibilities interfered with market production in the household. While many scholars have made the point that moving

435

to the factory system dramatically increased control over workers for the expropriation of profit (Edwards 1979, for example), they have usually missed the fact that a major component of this strategy was to prevent workers from losing any time to care giving. As industrial employment spread throughout the populace, the negative consequences of this for reproduction and childbearing became clearer.[2]

Ever since the Industrial Revolution, Western nations have engaged a series of stopgap solutions to the problem of combining production and reproduction. However, these have never satisfactorily resolved the fundamental incompatibility between wage labor and reproductive labor (some earlier solutions included industrial homework, taking in boarders and lodgers in private households, and employing children along with their parents). The attempt to exclude married women from wage labor and to create a family wage for male workers—popularly known as the system of "separate spheres"—is but one of the more persistent solutions crafted during the nineteenth century. In theory, at least, the productivity gains of industrialization were to be used to free women, children, and the elderly from wage labor and into homemaking, schooling, or leisure, respectively.

As others have shown, however, the "separate spheres" solution was doomed to failure (Bernard 1981; Davis 1989; Ehrenreich 1984). It was too expensive for capital ever to extend to all working-class men; and it proved to be an inefficient method for subsidizing the women and their children now purposely excluded from wage labor or relegated to its periphery (since not all men were married, stayed married, stayed employed, stayed alive, or generously shared their wages with their families). In retrospect, the state programs later designed to ameliorate the failings of the family wage system (primarily ADC and Social Security) were in fact much more successful at shifting income to the elderly nonpoor than protecting families from poverty (Preston 1984; Blakeley and Voss 1995). The instability of the family wage system, coupled with the decline in strength requirements

and the rise in educational requirements for most jobs in the labor market, has given us the twin pillars of modern family life: postponed and lower rates of childbearing, and children raised predominantly by either a single employed parent or two employed parents.

Escalating Demands on Parents

Our current concerns with the gender wage gap, the rise in divorce and single parenthood, the second shift of domestic labor, the feminization of poverty, welfare reform, the "epidemic" of infertility, the high price and low quality of U.S. child care, failing public schools, and the escalating costs of higher education are but the modern incarnation of this far earlier historical struggle about who should bear the costs of reproduction in a market system in which the direct economic and social benefits of such work have disappeared. Children have ceased to be sources of income and security for parents, and require longer and longer periods of dependence to receive the education and training necessary to become productive workers (Zelizer 1985).[3] Yet the psychological and material costs of bearing and rearing children remain firmly rooted in the family household, even as the rewards have diminished. Perhaps as a result, parenthood (unlike marriage and employment) is the only major adult social role that does not increase either the material or psychological well-being of the adults who undertake it (McLanahan and Adams 1987). As Nancy Folbre writes, "childbearing in the United States today stands out as an activity that is conducted despite, rather than because of, economic self-interest. The decision to raise a child imposes truly phenomenal economic costs upon parents and provides virtually no economic benefits" (1983: 279).

I argue here that the costs of reproduction for parents have been escalating over the course of the twentieth century partly because childbearing has become an increasingly private rather than community obligation, not just because children require longer periods of education before they are productive and self-sustaining; and that the result has been a decrease in the number of adults, particularly men, who co-reside with children. Increasingly, the costs of reproduction have been privatized and feminized (Sprague 1996), while the benefits of reproductive labor have become socialized. More and more functions of communities have been transferred to parents, who often want no part of the increased pressures for involvement and economic support brought to bear on them. Yet successful child rearing produces law-abiding, tax-paying, trained and productive citizens, and thus clearly and directly benefits employers, communities, and the state. These social institutions have a strong stake in retaining these benefits, while resisting their costs. Again, Folbre writes, "the great fear that women may reject their traditional childbearing responsibilities . . . grows at least in part out of the recognition that no other persons and no other institutions are apparently willing to assume these responsibilities" (1983: 279).

One of the most striking features of most social commentary on the state of families today is the extent to which parents alone are held accountable for the moral, intellectual, and financial preparation of children for adulthood, without much (if any) institutional support. Parents are now responsible for an exhausting number of functions in their children's lives. They must provide enough income to support their children without assistance, preferably by buying safe housing in neighborhoods with good schools, even if that means working very long hours away from the children. Mothers should breastfeed for at least a year, despite the failure of employers to accommodate breastfeeding in any reasonable way (Blum 1999). If parents cannot garner enough income to live in a "good" neighborhood (and sometimes even if they can), they are to volunteer in their children's schools to monitor and improve them, and monitor their neighborhood (and their neighbors) for the availability of guns, pornography, or drugs. When children are young, parents must exhaustively search for and interview child care provid-

ers, and then continuously monitor the performance of those providers, given the failure of any decent regulatory system to emerge.[4] They must read and play music daily to encourage the brain development of their children, and must attune themselves to their children's needs in a pattern that Sharon Hays terms "intensive mothering" (1996). Children can no longer be left to play in public parks, neighborhood streets, or schoolyards without constant parental supervision. Parents are supposed to provide healthy, well-balanced meals and opportunities for exercise, and protect their children from the dangers of unsafe water, food, or exposure to the sun. Parents must sit with their children when they watch TV or go to movies, to protect them from exposure to excessive media violence or sexually explicit content, and monitor their internet use to avoid exposure to adult web sites or pedophiles in chat rooms. Parents are to teach their children moral values and prosocial behavior, and are held accountable when children succumb to the myriad temptations to engage in inappropriate or antisocial behavior in the community. When children are older, parents must get to know their friends and their friends' parents and watch for precocious sexual activity, bulimia in their daughters, and aggression in their sons.

While I can find little in historical accounts with which to compare the modern economic, physical, and social costs of childbearing,[5] care giving has indeed become risky and dangerous work in the modern economy. Performing this work, either paid or unpaid, increases an individual's risk of poverty (Arendell 1987), lowers their wages, status, and authority at work (Bonnar 1991; Kilbourne, England, Farkas, Beron, and Weir 1994; Waldfogel 1997), subjects them to closer scrutiny by the state (Monson 1997), and increases mental distress (Kessler and McLeod 1984; Simon 1995). Certainly the direct monetary expenditures that parents make to care for their children have increased over the twentieth century—the latest government estimate was $150,000 to raise a single child born in 1997 to adulthood in the United States (not including the cost of higher education). Higher education—once a luxury, but now a virtual requirement if children are to find secure and self-sustaining employment in adulthood—has become increasingly expensive and stubbornly resistant to public subsidy. This represents just another escalating cost (training) that has been silently passed from communities and employers to private households.

The clear failure of communities, employers, or the state to provide good schools, safe neighborhoods, food and water, involved neighbors, and decent health care for children leaves parents with the impossible task of creating "safe havens" around their children in an otherwise hostile world at the same time that they must provide enough income to meet their children's material needs. Yet both demands—that parents shoulder the cost of child rearing alone, and that parents monitor and control their children's physical and social environment at all times—come from the same historical process of privatizing the costs of reproduction. As reproductive labor ceases to confer any direct material or social benefit to the adults who perform it, fewer and fewer adults have children or actively parent the children they have. This is especially true for men (Eggebeen and Uhlenberg 1989; King 1999), but increasingly true for women as well. As more and more of the population become child free, the temptation to organize social institutions around the interests of adults, regardless of the consequences for children or their parents, becomes stronger. Hence, attempts to regulate the internet, ban pornography, place warning labels on CDs, or publicize the whereabouts of released sex offenders are attacked by liberals as infringements on the individual rights of adults. Proponents are dismissed as puritanical zealots. Similarly, pleas for comprehensive sex education in the schools and gun control legislation are derided by conservatives as excuses for parents to get out of their responsibilities for monitoring and controlling their own children.

I do not believe that the costs of reproduction are gendered, *per se*. The social and material handicapping of those who rear children, care for the disabled and elderly, and support community institutions through their volunteer efforts comes from the time and energy spent in the unpaid or poorly paid care giving itself. What is truly gendered is the extent to which women as a group are willing to bear these costs, relative to men, or have too little economic or social power to transfer these costs to others. I don't mean to romanticize women's moral sensibilities here. We know that many privileged women have "downloaded" their domestic labor and child care responsibilities to immigrants and women of color too disenfranchised in the labor market to refuse. We know that some women, particularly those who are still young and economically dependent, are so overwhelmed by their care-giving responsibility that they abandon, harm, or even kill their children. Yet women, as a demographic group, continue to bear the brunt of the costs of care giving even as those costs continue to escalate. Their primary form of resistance seems to be a continuing, dramatic postponement and reduction in childbearing (Bachu 1997) to our current below-replacement fertility level. While the Census Bureau touts the growing number of childless women as a visible sign of women's empowerment, one has to wonder about the future of a society in which the ability to avoid reproduction is "empowering."

Escalating Demands on Workers

The escalating demands on parents represent only half of the equation that makes combining achievement in the labor market and successful parenting so difficult. The other half comes from the accelerating tendency of employers to provide either overemployment or underemployment for their workers, neither of which accommodates the needs of privatized child rearing. The rising postindustrial economy has exacerbated the problems families face, most acutely in the United States but also in the more supportive European welfare states. What is postindustrial about the postindustrial economy? As far as I can tell from my own reading, it consists of two major trends: an acceleration in the substitution of automated machinery for human labor and the globalization of the wage labor force. The first process eliminates millions of jobs in the production of goods (and increasingly services as well—note the automated teller and the cashier-free grocery stores) and makes labor cheap. The second process expands the pool of available labor by setting capital investment free of national boundaries and constraints, also making labor cheap because capital is now free to flow to wherever labor costs are lowest worldwide. Real male wages have fallen as automation and offshore production shrink the demand for manufacturing jobs, while service sector jobs continue to proliferate precisely because they pay poorly. Divorce and out-of-wedlock childbearing rise partly because of the difficulty couples face in maintaining long-term economic solvency, and their disillusionment with the patriarchal bargain of traditional marriage which fewer men can keep and fewer women want. Thus, the postindustrial economies of Western nations hasten an economic decline for families with dependents, both by destabilizing family relationships and destabilizing employment contracts.

Several scholars have recently published books in which the dominant thesis is both that jobs are eroding in number as technology increasingly replaces human labor, and that the remaining jobs will be bifurcated into (1) long-hour jobs with high wages and benefits and (2) part-time, temporary or contract jobs with lower wages and/or far fewer benefits and worker protections— (see, for example, Aronowitz and DeFazio 1994; Rifkin 1994; Schor 1991; Hunnicutt 1988). The former jobs will provide the money but not the time necessary for rearing children, and the latter will provide the time (in some instances) but not the money. Perhaps the most readable account of how this historical process has unfolded can be found in Wolman (1997). Empirical evidence of the rise in work hours for managers and professionals and the increasing variance in work hours across jobs can be found in Jacobs and Gerson (1998). Virtually all these scholars note the decreasing power of labor relative to global capital, and the resulting pressure for workers to acquiesce to eroding conditions at work. Success in the labor market now requires increased effort, longer hours at work, and continuous training—conditions that discourage family and community involvement and encourage diminished fertility and the purchase of market substitutes for family care.

For purposes of this discussion, the important point is that the same social processes that diminish fertility and devalue parenting simultaneously elevate the material and social rewards of waged work. Some scholars have even gone so far as to suggest that the rewards of paid work have replaced the comforts of home (Hochschild 1997) and that employment has become the "master status" in industrial societies (Hunnicutt 1988). Regardless of whether most individuals obtain their primary identities from paid work, it is indisputably true that adults are materially and socially rewarded by concentrating their energy and efforts on achievement in the labor market rather than childbearing and community building. Coupled with the institutional pressures to replace human labor with technology which erode the number of well-paying jobs available in postindustrial economies, this means that workers are goaded by both demand—and supply-side factors to increase their investment in market activity. And the nature of the information technology that has been transforming work encourages workers to be even more available to respond to productivity demands outside the "normal" work day. E-mail, fax machines, cell phones, and beepers encourage the continuous availability of workers in a 24-hour economy.

Countervailing pressure to diminish work demands to accommodate dual-earner families or spread work around more equitably to increase employment is weak and poorly institutionalized by comparison (Kelly and Dobbin 1999; Glass and Estes 1997). Many workers are too scared they will lose pay or promotions (or even lose their jobs) if they ask for family accommodations. Those employed in organizations with work/life programs designed to help dual-earner or single-parent families are often loath to use the assistance offered because it brands them as less committed or dedicated workers (Hochschild 1997; Fried 1998).

While the observation that success in the labor market requires single-minded pursuit of career goals to the exclusion of family responsibilities is not new in industrial capitalism, the consequence of that reality in a nation of predominantly dual-income households and single-parent families is. Those parents cannot single-mindedly pursue career success, but must increasingly compete with other workers who can. The result is the relative impoverishment of households with children on both an average and per capita basis. But perhaps an even more serious consequence is that successful careerists, those who ascend to the most powerful positions in business, government, and politics, tend to be those who do not have and perhaps never had ongoing daily care-giving responsibilities for children.[6] The most important and consequential decisions for all of us collectively get made predominantly by people who have never worried about the pesticides on the food their children eat, have never gotten up five times in the night to nurse a child with an ear infection and then dragged themselves into work the next day, have never worried about whether their day care provider was attending to their child's needs, nor have made the agonizing decision of whether to leave a child home alone in an emergency or call in sick and risk their job. They have never sent their children to inadequate schools, or been forced to keep their children indoors in crime-ridden neighborhoods.

This collision course between success at work and success at child rearing has not gone unnoticed by either scholars or policy makers. Hunt and Hunt (1982) argued that the dual-career family, then much in vogue as an object of study, would be merely a transient phase as families with children would devolve into dual-earner families while only voluntarily childless marriages could truthfully be called "dual-career." The Hunts argued that de-gendering caregiving work would only ensure that both male and female caregivers were disadvantaged in comparison to their child-free peers in demanding careers. In a new book, Deutsch (1999) writes that even in truly egalitarian marriages where both husbands and wives actively share child rearing and breadwinning, both spouses acknowledge the career sacrifices this pattern entails. Yet the book's conclusion seems to be that you can't have it all after all, and that as long as the costs of parenthood are equitably distributed across parents, mothers and fathers and children are better off. Rarely, if ever, do scholars question the taken-for-granted assumption that those who responsibly parent their children should expect diminished career success.

What have been the predominant responses to this crisis of reproduction in our market-driven economy? The responses from different institutions have varied, of course, but the dominant (and I would add dystopian) response seems to be the increased marketization of care-giving functions. As family members cease to be able to provide care themselves, or are increasingly punished economically and socially for doing so, the market has taken over. Either those functions are transferred directly to the capitalist market and performed by workers as market substitutes for family care, or capital invades the public or civic institutions formerly run by volunteers or public servants. The former process can be seen in the proliferation of for-profit child care centers, nursing homes, cleaning services, and take-out restaurants. Sometimes these marketable services are taken to laughable extremes—in Japan, for example, an overworked executive can hire an attractive young couple to visit his elderly parents for him. The latter process can be seen in the for-profit takeover of public hospitals, schools, and voluntary associations. Technology-poor schools hard pressed for cash have become increasingly receptive to private capitalist bailouts—witness the growth in exclusive vendor contracts with Pepsi or Coke with a promised profit sharing or flat fee paid to schools, as well as the infamous Channel 1, in which middle school children are forced to watch 15 minutes of commercial television programming daily in their classrooms so that their schools can receive donated equipment and cash (for a good recent analysis, see Manning 1999).

The purchase of market substitutes for family care does not empower parents or solve the crisis of reproduction. Market substitutes, especially for-profit substitutes, erode rather than enhance familial control of care giving[7] and expropriate for profit a portion of the capital and labor supposed to be expended on care. We all know the nutritional content of the average fast food meal is far from optimal, and that for-profit nursing homes and child care centers vary wildly in their standards of care. Most importantly, however, the marketization of care leaves the payment for such services solidly in the family household once again. And such services are by no means cheap, spurring workers again to work longer and harder to earn enough to pay for them, or accept low-quality substitutes (or no substitutes—witness the growing number of latchkey children) in return. In the 1970s social critic Christopher Lasch (1977) was worried that the functions of the family would be taken over by the modern state—I worry much more today that the functions of the family and the state will be taken over by a triumphant capitalist market.

Crafting a Utopian Solution

The lesson from history is that the ability to segregate workers' responsibilities for reproduction led to a dramatic decline in the visibility and value associated with this work in the family and the rise of cheap market substitutes. This suggests that any solution must begin with a reintegration of workers' responsibilities for production and reproduction. It is far easier for me to imagine this utopian solution to the crisis of reproduction than to imagine its implementation. Yet I am persuaded by Erik Wright's (2000) notion that practical utopias are of far more value than radical utopian visions. So I will try to craft a practical utopian solution that reintegrates family care giving and paid work.

The cornerstone of my utopian solution is that all jobs must be crafted around the notion that everyone has a responsibility for familial care and community building. No one is expected to live a life totally devoted to paid work, *and nobody gets differentially rewarded for doing so.* As long as some workers are exempted from the work of reproduction and community building, they will remain subjected to strong incentives to invest in longer work hours and greater productivity in employment instead. This extra involvement in market work will be rewarded through increased skill, responsibility, and authority in the workplace, and subsequently higher wages and faster ascension up promotional ladders in return. These material incentives are so strong that simply offering better public policy supports for parenting—bigger tax deductions for dependents, subsidized and higher quality child care, for example—won't either stem the fertility decline in developed economies or end the opportunity costs of parenting in the workplace that punish those workers who most need income and authority at work.

This central idea—that all jobs should assume an incumbent with care-giving responsibilities—requires a modification of the employment contract so that workplaces pay a greater share of the cost of reproduction, not just through wages but through working conditions and worker protections. But it also requires the creation of normative responsibilities among adults to participate in the support of community and neighborhood institutions that form a "protective web" for children (Louv 1990). In this way, the costs of caring, not just the rewards, get socialized. This solution is achieved through complementary modifications in the contemporary demands on parents and demands on workers. I deal with each in turn.

Modifying Demands on Workers

The central features of a new employment contract between employers and employees must be (1) the elimination of involuntary and higher waged overtime and the enforcement of shorter work hours, and (2) the creation of new forms of worker protections that lessen pressure on parents and other care-giving adults to find substitute providers for the care that they do not have time to provide. Many scholars have written about the twin benefits of shortening standard work hours: Parents and other adults have time to engage in care giving and community building, while employment gets spread around to a larger number of people as jobs become scarce in a postindustrial economy (Hunnicutt 1988; Rifkin 1994). A 30-hour week benchmark for full-time employment would dramatically reduce the number of hours children spend in substitute care in two-parent households, while lessening the fatigue and stress parents often experience in their interactions with family members at the end of a long workday. Just as important, a 30-hour work week would level the playing field for involved parents and nonparents in the employment arena: Comparative availability for work assignments and productivity on the job would be enhanced for those caregiving parents now hampered by their family responsibilities. Such a reduction in hours may not actually reduce worker productivity dramatically, since employees are not maximally productive at the end of a long work shift, according to Juliet Schor (1991). If so, wages should not fall appreciably during the transition to a shorter work week.

But shorter hours must be combined with flexibility in both the time and location of those hours to maximize their effectiveness in reducing job-family incompatibility. Conceivably, a two-parent dual-earner family could consist of one parent working eight-hour days Monday through Thursday and a second working eight-hour

days Wednesday through Saturday, leaving only two or three days per week without a parent at home. Partially overlapping work shifts on those days could minimize the use of substitute care even further without creating a family structure in which parents never jointly spend time with their children. Flexibility in both time and place could be extended to a large number of jobs in the economy, especially those not dealing with customer service. But granting such flexibility requires a shift away from seeing continual availability and physical presence in the workplace as markers of productivity. Instead, measures of productivity will have to be based on assessments of work accomplished, which will require better communication between employees and their managers.

Allowing workers to telecommute or work from home also offers some workers greater freedom to interweave paid work and domestic labor, as in the nineteenth century household economy. Some home tasks (waiting for plumbers and furniture deliveries, watching a soup simmer or a baby nap) can coexist with work tasks that require immediate attention. However, child care and the sustained attention needed for some work tasks don't coexist well; for that reason, most home-based workers report needing some form of child care while they work. Nevertheless, having a parent work from home at least some of the time reduces commuting time, increases parental availability to children, and allows greater parental participation in children's scheduled activities, such as after-school lessons and sports. It wrests control over the pace and timing of work tasks from employers to employees, and for this reason alone empowers parents.

Changes in the "normal" schedules of employees are but one facet of a new employment contract between employers and employees. The other linchpin of this new employment contract must be new forms of worker protection for the unusual and extraordinary circumstances that parents face in caring for family members. Chief among them are guarantees that leaves for sick child care and family emergencies (as when child care providers are ill) can be taken without fear of reprisal. Others include the ability to refuse travel and relocation that interferes with family responsibilities, without serious repercussions in future performance evaluations. And another must be the abolition of discrimination against parents in training and assignments, based on stereotypical assumptions about the commitment or capabilities of employed mothers in particular. With the assumption that all adult workers have care-giving responsibilities outside the workplace, this form of discrimination should naturally wither away. But formal legal prohibition of discrimination against caregiving workers would address any residual statistical discrimination in the interim.

These new worker protections require supervisor or managerial support to become commonplace practices. Numerous studies document the failure of corporate work-life programs when managers and supervisors tacitly communicate the negative consequences for workers using leave or flexible work arrangements (Fried 1998; Hochschild 1997). The prohibition of discrimination against parents must extend to any worker using the work-life policies designed to facilitate family care. But managers and supervisors must increasingly come from the ranks of employees who have used such policies in the past as well. Successful job performance after returning from a leave or while telecommuting should be noted as extraordinary accomplishments indicating potential for advancement.

I have studiously avoided listing the incorporation of direct services to families in the new workplace contract between employers and employees. I am not certain that the provision of health care, child care, prepared meals, and sick child care by employers does more than cement the dependence of workers on employers and, hence, augment employer control. Most employer-provided services are designed to increase the hours of work employees can contribute to the organization, not to increase the autonomy of parents and others to care for their families and communities themselves. As well, the cost containment pressures that employers face in a competitive market do not work toward the continued provision of high-quality services to employee families, but instead encourage third-party vendor contracts with for-profit child and health care chains. While I have clearly outlined a whole host of benefits that I think workplaces can reasonably provide, I don't believe that the outsourcing of family care should be one of them.

Modifying Demands on Parents

The next step toward a utopian solution concerns the obligations now sustained only by parents that could be shared more widely and reorganized more effectively. The most general goal here is to create a normative climate in which all adults contribute effectively to the well-being of children and elderly and disabled individuals as part of the obligations of citizenship. Many creative experiments could lead us to a normative climate in which larger numbers of people have incentives to build community and share the costs of reproduction. I will describe five promising public policy changes that might hasten this process.

1. *Linking Volunteerism to Employment.* Many older middle-class adults can still remember a time when employees were evaluated partly on their volunteer efforts and level of community involvement. This service work was considered an essential investment in the community in which employers, especially large ones, existed. The public good created by such involvement generated positive feelings and name recognition for the company, made recruitment and retention easier because the community was a more desirable place to live, and connected employees to larger support and information networks within the community.

Although the global movement of capital has eroded ties between employers and communities as labor becomes a more fluid and transient component of production, public policy can still encourage good citizenship among employees. Corporations are currently allowed large tax write-offs for monetary contributions to charitable organizations. Why can't organizations be given similar tax breaks for the cost of releasing workers for four hours each week to perform volunteer service in the communities where they reside? Rather than giving large charitable organizations corporate money, why not give smaller and more local community groups the time and talents of employees? Imagine unleashing all workers for one afternoon per week into the community to engage in neighborhood cleanups, tutoring in elementary or secondary schools, mentoring programs for youth, planting community gardens, coaching sports, and participating in cooperative day care. This is different from the modern corporate practice of using the workplace to recruit volunteers for a company-sponsored charitable cause. That form of workplace volunteerism does not give workers choice in how and for which purposes their talents can be used, nor does it give workers time off for their efforts in behalf of their community. And it encourages the development of solidarity around workplaces rather than neighborhoods or communities where people live.

The type of voluntary activity could be left unbounded, or employers could develop screens to make sure that voluntary efforts are indeed directed toward areas of greatest need. Parents of young children and caregivers of disabled or elderly family members could simply use the extra time as compensation for their care-giving efforts. Parents of older children could be encouraged to partner with their children in volunteer efforts—helping with school functions, working to clean up parks, provide care at animal shelters, or tutoring younger children, and the like. This both brings parents and children together in shared activities, and provides children with adult role models who incorporate community service into their everyday practices.

One practical problem with this scenario is how to instill in people the desire and expectation of community service throughout the life cycle, and how to help people understand their particular talents and where they may best serve the needs of their community. This is a gradual learning process best begun earlier in life, perhaps in adolescence when idealism is high and firsthand understanding of the problems in communities would form a lasting impression. Many school districts already have either mandatory or voluntary service learning programs, but these are not connected to any practical incentives to continue service in adulthood. If service learning programs were to become part of the general educational curriculum, and linked to apprenticeship programs in service organizations, larger numbers of people would be able to test their interests and volunteer skills as youth. With employer support for community involvement as described above, more workers would be prepared and motivated to continue their community building efforts across the life cycle.

2. Stemming the Marketization of Care Giving. Because the contemporary problems of parents have been "solved" by pushing more and more familial functions into the for-profit market sector, steps must be taken to stem the further erosion of familial time and the replacement of parents and family caregivers with market substitutes. But most conservative attempts to do so have involved token payments to family members (mostly women) who care for children and elderly parents, and this may simply strengthen a gendered division of labor and encourage women to take more time out of the market, despite the long-term disadvantages of doing so. Extending the Child Care Tax Credit to at-home parents (most of whom are mothers) is a good example of this strategy. A gender-neutral policy must encourage fathers and sons to do more care giving, rather than just better rewarding mothers and daughters for what they already disproportionately do. As well, some consensus must be achieved about what exactly can be "marketized" without threat to families or children's autonomy and well-being, and what should be preserved as a familial function that cannot be outsourced under ordinary circumstances.

Arguably, infant care might be the best place to first start this process. The emerging consensus among parents, child development experts, and care providers themselves is that full-time substitute infant care (40+ hours per week) is difficult to find, difficult to provide by one consistent trained caregiver, extremely expensive, and probably not optimal for the emotional and social needs of either infants or parents in the earliest months of life. Parents overwhelmingly prefer parental care for their infants and toddlers, and go to great lengths to avoid overreliance on nonparental care (Sonenstein 1991; Glass 1998). Extending parental leaves and discouraging full-time infant care, while providing subsidized high-quality part-time options beginning at six months of age, preserves both parental choice (not all parents can or want to be full-time caregivers for an extended period of time, and not all parents are at their best when providing care full-time) and the early extensive parental involvement in which infants thrive. The normative expectations for new parents should be that they contribute concentrated time and energy to their infants and toddlers, while receiving support and assistance from their community for doing so. Six-month paid parental leaves to each of the child's parents, combined with the flexible and shorter-hour employment schedules advocated above, would ensure that even single parents do not have to place their infants or young children in substitute care for more than 30 hours per week. Paternal involvement should increase if families lose a six-month paid leave unless the father takes his. Fines or losses of public subsidies for leaving children in substitute care for more than 35 hours a week, for example, might be a draconian but effective way to encourage parents to provide most of their children's care before age 3 rather than invest more heavily in paid work.

Care for preschoolers could become incorporated effectively within the public school system. Many skills needed for school success must be developed much earlier, and are particularly critical for preschoolers living in disadvantaged families or neighborhoods. Some school districts, notably in Georgia and California, already have preschool programs for children age 4 and above. This ensures that child care becomes a public responsibility, fosters closer ties between families and neighborhood institutions, and encourages developmentally appropriate cognitive and emotional stimulation for all children in these crucial years. As day care centers or preschools become "homes away from home" for increasing numbers of children, and care providers become confidants and partners for parents in their child rearing, it makes tremendous sense to root those institutions in existing neighborhoods where transportation costs are minimal and children develop a sense of community and safe boundaries. Schools often already have the infrastructure (accreditation and training procedures) to hire and monitor teachers, and procedures in place to ensure the physical safety of children. They may need to consider retrofitting spaces for very small children, reconfigure classrooms and curriculum for the developmental needs of young children, and separate play spaces for older and younger children. And schools may require site councils that include parents and neighborhood residents to ensure their accountability to the community as they take on additional functions.

The drawback of this plan is that it requires adequate public expenditures on schools to be successful, a problem that already plagues public school funding in many places. But socializing the costs of public schooling (now extended down to age 3) might be less difficult if those institutions had a repository of adult volunteers from the community already committed to them, and if those institutions made themselves more accessible and useful to child-free adults. Schools could become community centers, whose facilities (such as libraries, computers, gyms, and playgrounds) could be used by community members after hours and on weekends. Frequent public meetings held on school grounds remind adults that they own the schools and are responsible for their operational effectiveness. Turning schools into multipurpose centers also allows schools to respond flexibly to changes in the demographic composition of their neighborhoods, rather than shutting down.

Public preschools will not appeal to all parents and will not serve the needs of all children. Private and specialized schooling will no doubt continue to exist alongside these "community schools." But the presence of expanded schools will link families to each other, connect care providers, teachers, and parents more easily and effectively, and provide spaces and places for neighborhood members to organize and congregate.

The marketing of other forms of domestic labor, such as cleaning, laundry, and cooking, seems less problematic when divorced from an employment contract in which pressure to work additional hours exists. Families can then more freely choose between providing those services for themselves and paying someone else to do them. These services are now dramatically expanding because workers feel such pressure to work additional hours and neglect domestic care. However, even in less coercive circumstances, it is worth examining the costs of marketized cooking and cleaning services. I'd be the last person on earth to suggest eliminating takeout restaurants and laundromats. Yet cleaning services are not likely to have much incentive to reduce their use of chemical pollutants in your home and on your clothes—environmental problems that children will inherit either through their own health problems or the cumulative future effect on water and soil. And the increasing proportion of the American families' food budget spent on restaurant and fast food meals is partly responsible for the rise in childhood obesity and the proliferation of food produced by corporations for other corporations. The market for organic food and nutrient-rich heirloom vegetables does not come from chain restaurants. Control over the types of food and the ways in which food gets produced is enhanced when families do their own grocery shopping and food preparation. This does not have to mean the end of collective food service, however, or the end of collective living arrangements that redistribute the costs of reproduction more generally.

3. *Supporting Co-housing and Other Forms of Shared Living Arrangements.* Co-housing and other forms of urban communities are new patterns of housing in which neighborhoods become more closely linked through the provision and use of shared services. In some co-housing projects, individual families own their own homes, yet share a community center that provides daily meals, a laundry center, child care services, and a reading/game room. Some have community vegetable gardens, shared lawn and home maintenance equipment, and requirements for contributed labor from each resident to the common good. Decisions about community expenditures, dues, and services provided are made collectively by a co-housing association. Many retirement communities are based on a similar concept—the ability to live independently as long as one has the energy and ability to do so, but support services (including communal dining and home health care) as these become necessary. Why not extend this same concept to families with children?

Whatever their ultimate form, shared living arrangements tend to increase the ratio of adults to children per household, provide a greater number of eyes and ears to monitor and protect children's well-being, and involve a greater number of adults in the lives of children. This both lessens the strain on parents and increases the connections of children to other adult confidants and role models (although potentially exposing them to negative role models as well). These shared living arrangements should strengthen the voting base supportive of children's interests in public policy, as more adults live in households with children and have some stake in how they are treated by civic institutions. Right now, zoning laws and development preferences often exclude shared housing arrangements or make them more difficult to pursue. Tax incentives for co-housing projects might very well pay for themselves if the enhanced quality of life reduces the need for police and social services in these communities.

4. *Requiring Family Impact Statements for Proposed Legislation.* Because caregiving parents represent a diminishing share of all voters and shoulder a disproportionate financial obligation for children, they deserve to have a family impact statement attached to all forms of state and national legislation that clearly spells out the consequences of the proposed laws for families and children. We now require environmental impact statements on both private and government projects that might degrade our natural environment or violate federal standards. But we share another environment as well—our childbearing environment. Surely children and families deserve similar oversight against corporate greed and short-sighted solutions to long-term problems. Legislation that shifts the burden of protection from the state or community to parents or caregivers, or shifts costs from the state or community to individual parents (either intentionally or unintentionally), should require special legislative review. Perhaps evidence of negative effects on children could even become grounds for challenging or blocking enactment of new laws. Such changes have the negative effect of increasing litigation, and possibly increasing bureaucracy without creating additional resources for families. But such a system might force politicians, lobbyists, and the special interests they serve to notice and address the needs of families, and consider the rights of children to adequate care and future opportunities for growth and development.

A process of judicial review that considers the rights of families and dependent children, not just the rights of adult citizens, might help us achieve several public goods that diminish demands on parents to monitor and control their children's environments. Gun control, environmental health and safety laws, drug treatment rather than incarceration, and widespread community policing might be easier to implement with such a system in place. Controversies such as the censorship of the Internet, television, and advertising might

be easier to resolve if the issues were reframed around how to provide adult services without exposing children to them or expecting parents to be vigilant about their child's everyday activities.

Current law requires private-sector, not just public, initiatives to undergo environmental review. Perhaps private housing developments, such as those with restrictive covenants against children, should be forced to justify their existence with evidence that their presence will not alter the housing market for families with children, discourage the growth of families in the community, or alter the tax base for services to children.

A more radical alternative to Family Impact Statements would be to allow children to have a vote in all electoral processes. Of course, they could not vote for themselves until they reach the age of reason, somewhere between ages 12 and 15, when they could vote with a parental consent attached to their vote. Upon turning 18, children would get full control of their vote (this might also socialize children into voting as a civic obligation, perhaps increasing young voter participation). Before children reach age 12, parents would be allowed to vote for them, just as parents serve as surrogates for children's rights in such matters as informed consent for health care procedures, research studies, and sports participation. We would have to decide collectively how to allocate votes between mothers and fathers in two-parent households, but single custodial parents would pose less of a problem. This simple step might make a dramatic difference in the rhetoric and content of political campaigns, without clearly advantaging either the traditional political left or right.

5. *Synchronizing School Schedules and Work Schedules.* Another important facet of any plan to increase the compatibility between families and workplaces has to be synchronization of children's school schedules and work schedules. A system of shared holidays would be a good start—for example, by reducing the number of days in which parents must locate ad hoc child care arrangements for a single day at a

time. But most discussions about synchronization begin with the premise that children should be in school more, not that workers should work less. The rhetoric goes something like this: There is more to learn, children in the United States are falling behind their peers elsewhere, and schooling should therefore be tougher and more intense. I begin with the assumption that perhaps both need to occur: We need both more holidays for workers and fewer for children. We need slightly shorter work days for adults and slightly longer school days for children. Somewhere in the middle they will meet. While summer vacations pose big challenges to employed parents at present, particularly parents of pre-adolescents and middle-schoolers, schools could incorporate fine arts, foreign language, sports, and computer workshops into comprehensive summer programs for these children. This would enable a break from "regular" schooling while still developing skills and abilities in students over the summer months which get short shrift in the regular curriculum.

Rather than assuming that longer days in school can be equated with greater learning, let's examine particular proposals for what would be done with the extra time at school. The educational model provided by Japan, with its extra "juko" schooling, does not achieve the kind of independent thinking and creativity desired in American education. It makes sense to extend the school day, perhaps to seven hours, but also to re-think how those seven hours are spent. A longer day might allow for more integrative projects, creative and entrepreneurial activities (fine and performing arts, craft and service businesses, etc.), and foreign language/communication training.

We also need to think about how those hours in school are distributed across the day. Some evidence suggests that adolescents need more sleep, particularly in the early morning hours. A start time of 9:00 and an end at 4:00 or 4:30 might dovetail better with their developmental needs in middle and high schools, as well as matching some parents' work schedules. Or perhaps schools as well as workplaces can

work around "flex time"—a class schedule in which everyone attends for some core hours, but that early morning or late afternoon schedules are available for those students and teachers who prefer them. Since parents often work nonstandard work hours, including early morning and late afternoon shifts, parental contact time with older children could be maximized this way. It may even be possible to extend this model down to the elementary school level in moderately sized schools, so that parents on nonstandard work shifts can avoid the use of either before- or after-school programs. Clearly, no one plan for extending the school day or scheduling it more flexibly will meet the needs of all families in a 4-hour economy, yet significant improvements that create more family time for many families can be implemented.

Overcoming Obstacles to Change

There are three primary political and cultural barriers to the implementation of the interlocking changes I believe are necessary to lessen the incompatibility between parenting and waged work. First, we must overcome resistance to a proactive role for government in solving families' problems. Current political rhetoric portrays government as the problem rather than the solution, although individual political initiatives to support families and children often receive strong popular support. Cynicism about the government's being able effectively to sponsor social change in ways that respect pluralism and family choice is rampant. Yet without crucial public policy changes enforced by government edict to level the playing field for all workers, new forms of worker protection and new reproductive responsibilities for both schools and communities will be difficult to achieve. It is true that government intervention invariably favors certain family structures over others, sets certain priorities as more important than others, and will fail without some consensus among the governed that these changes, on balance, are beneficial rather than harmful. My utopian vision places gender equality, children's well-being, and parents' workplace empowerment as central priorities over, say, maximizing economic efficiency, increasing adult autonomy, or reducing the size of government. My vision also asks parents to yield their almost complete control (and responsibility) over children in favor of a more communal approach to child rearing that involves nonparents and community institutions in the welfare of their children. I believe most parents hunger for this involvement, but it may be resisted by some.

The second challenge will be to find support for programs that ensure fairness and justice for families in diverse circumstances—immigrants, single parents, nonheterosexual families, families of varying cultural and ethnic backgrounds, and the like. The heterogeneity of American families is surely one cause of our collective failure to invest more in programs for families and children, despite our sympathy and support for "family values" in general. Convincing people to care for other people's children with their own time and money is difficult to do when those children appear so different and even threatening to one's own cultural beliefs. Finding the resolve to do so requires overcoming racism, religious intolerance, and fear. One way to hasten this process might be to more tightly link the fate of today's children with tomorrow's aging population in public discourse, and make clear how dependent older generations will be on the productivity and good citizenship of today's youth as they mature.

The third, and perhaps most difficult obstacle to overcome will be the resistance from the business community to any policy change that shifts the costs of reproduction from the private family household to the public economy of business and government. Their successful ability to resist much encroachment in the past must be countered by a broad-based social movement united around a common goal of reconfiguring social institutions so that they support families and children. The "separate spheres" solution to the problem of combining production and reproduction

became institutionalized partly because it was supported by such broad segments of the population—unionists, working-class women, middle-class reformers, clergy, and health care professionals, to name but a few. A similar meeting of the minds across a broad panoply of soccer moms, conservative family traditionalists, liberal social reformers, religious leaders, unions, and professional educators might be able to pull off a similar challenge to the power of international capital to set working conditions, wages, and taxation at unpalatable minimums. It's worth a try.

Discussion Questions

1. Which of Glass' proposed public policy initiatives do you think is most plausible, given the nature of American society today? Why?

2. How do you feel about state-supported full-day kindergarten? What are the pros and cons? ◆

Reprinted from Jennifer L. Glass, "Envisioning the Integration of Family and Work: Toward a Kinder, Gentler Workplace." *Contemporary Sociology, Vol. 29, No. 1, Utopian Visions: Engaged Sociologies for the 21st Century.* (Jan., 2000), pp. 129–143. Reprinted with permission of the American Sociological Association.

Endnotes

1. Of course, there were also large classes of people, indentured servants and slaves for example, for whom reproduction was either compromised or severely controlled.
2. Brenner and Ramas (1984) demonstrate how the conditions of early industrial capitalism threatened the ability of mothers and infants to survive, and encouraged the adoption of the "family wage" system.
3. Although research shows adult children provide substantial companionship and assistance to their aging parents, the flow of resources continues to go from parents to children well into adulthood (Hogan, Eggebeen, and Clogg 1993).
4. As an assistant professor, I was once told by a university administrator that if I didn't like the low-quality child care options available to me in the community, I should just "start my own child care center."

5. While the physical dangers of childbearing were certainly much greater before the twentieth century, it does not appear that the social and economic costs of caring for children were considered significant brakes on fertility (Juster and Vinovskis 1987).

6. Much is currently being made of "sequencing"—the value of women, in particular, dropping out of the market to concentrate on childbearing for a while, and later returning to the market to build powerful careers. Sandra Day O'Connor and Madeline Albright are often held up as exemplars of this pattern. But the very exceptional number of women who have been able to do this points out how much more common it is for women to drop out of the market only to find it is extremely difficult ever to make up for lost time and opportunities

7. In no way am I trying to claim that familial care is always superior to paid substitutes, or that there should be no role for market substitution in solving the incompatibility between work and family. Yet the current trend takes this tendency toward marketization to an unbalanced and impoverishing extreme.

References

Arendell, Terry. 1987. *Mothers and Divorce*. Berkeley: University of California Press.

Aronowitz, Stanley and William DiFazio. 1994. *The Jobless Future: Sci-Tech and the Dogma of Work*. Minneapolis: University of Minnesota Press.

Bachu, Amara. 1997. *Fertility of American Women, June 1995*. Current Population Reports P20-499. Washington, DC: U.S. Bureau of the Census.

Bergmann, Barbara. 1996. Saving *Our Children From Poverty: What the United States Can Learn From France*. New York: Russell Sage Foundation.

Bernard, Jessie. 1981. "The Good-Provider Role: Its Rise and Fall." *American Psychologist* 36: 1–12.

Blakely, Robin M. and Paul R. Voss. 1995. "Indicators of Child Well-Being in the United States, 1985–1992: An Analysis of Related Factors." Madison: Applied Population Laboratory of the University of Wisconsin.

Blum, Linda. 1999. *At the Breast: Ideologies of Breastfeeding and Motherhood in the Contemporary United States*. Boston: Beacon Press.

Bonnar, Deanne. 1991. "The Place of Caregiving Work in Industrial Societies." Pp. 192–207 in *Parental Leave and Child Care*, edited by J. Hyde and M. Essex. Philadelphia: Temple University Press.

Brenner, Joanna and Maria Ramas. 1984. "Rethinking Women's Oppression." *New Left Review* 144: 33–71.

Davis, Kingsley. 1989. "Wives and Work: A Theory of the Sex-Role Revolution and Its Consequences." In *Feminism, Children, and the New Families*, edited by S. Dornbusch and M. Strober. New York: Guilford Press.

Deutsch, Francine. 1999. *Halving It All: How Equally Shared Parenting Works*. Cambridge, MA: Harvard University Press.

Eggebeen, David and Uhlenberg, Peter. 1989. "Changes in the Organization of Men's Lives, 1960–1980." *Family Relations* 34: 251–57.

Ehrenreich, Barbara. 1984. *The Hearts of Men: American Dreams and the Flight From Commitment*. Garden City, NY: Anchor Press/Doubleday.

Folbre, Nancy. 1983. "Of Patriarchy Born: The Political Economy of Fertility Decisions." *Feminist Studies* 9: 261–84.

Fried, Mindy. 1998. *Taking Time: Parental Leave Policy and Corporate Culture*. Philadelphia: Temple University Press.

Glass, Jennifer. 1998. "Gender Liberation, Economic Squeeze, or Fear of Strangers: Why Fathers Care for Infants in Dual Earner Households." *Journal of Marriage and the Family* 60: 821–34.

Glass, Jennifer and Sarah Beth Estes. 1997. "The Family Responsive Workplace." *Annual Review of Sociology* 23: 289–313.

Hays, Sharon. 1996. *The Cultural Contradictions of Motherhood*. New Haven, CT: Yale University Press.

Hochschild, Arlie. 1997. *The Time Bind: When Work Becomes Home and Home Becomes Work*. New York: Metropolitan Books.

Hogan, Dennis, David Eggebeen, and Clifford Clogg. 1993. "The Structure of Intergenerational Exchanges in American Families." *American Journal of Sociology* 98: 1428–58.

Hunnicutt, Benjamin. 1988. *Work Without End: Abandoning Shorter Hours for the Right to Work*. Philadelphia: Temple University Press.

Hunt, Janet and Larry Hunt. 1982. "The Dualities of Careers and Families: New Integrations or New Polarizations?" *Social Problems* 29: 499–510.

Jacobs, Jerry and Kathleen Gerson. 1998. "The Endless Day or the Flexible Office." Paper presented at the 1998 meetings of the American Sociological Association, August, San Francisco, CA.

Juster, Susan and Maris Vinovskis. 1987. "Changing Perspectives on the American Family in the Past." *Annual Review of Sociology* 13: 193–216.

Kamerman, Sheila. 1996. "Child and Family Policies: An International Overview." Pp. 31–48 in *Children, Families, and Government*, edited by E. Zigler, J. Kagan, and E. Hall. Cambridge: Cambridge University Press.

Kelly, Erin and Frank Dobbin. 1999. "Civil Rights Law at Work: Sex Discrimination and the Rise of Maternity Leave Policies." *American Journal of Sociology*.

Kessler, Ronald and Jane McLeod. 1984. "Sex Differences in Vulnerability to Undesirable Life

Events." *American Sociological Review* 49: 620–31.

Kilbourne, Barbara, Paula England, George Farkas, Kurt Beron, and Dorothea Weir. 1994. "Returns to Skill, Compensating Differentials, and Gender Bias: Effects of Occupational Characteristics on the Wages of White Women and Men." *American Journal of Sociology* 100: 689–719.

King, Rosalind B. 1999. "Time Spent in Parenthood Status Among Adults in the United States." *Demography* 36: 377–85.

Lasch, Christopher. 1977. *Haven in a Heartless World: The Family Besieged.* New York: Basic Books.

Louv, Richard. 1990. *Childhood's Future.* Boston: Houghton Mifflin.

Manning, Steven. 1999. "Students for Sale: How Corporations Are Buying Their Way Into America's Classrooms." *The Nation,* September 27: 11–18.

McLanahan, S. and J. Adams. 1987. "Parenthood and Psychological Well-Being." *Annual Review of Sociology* 13: 237–57.

Monson, Rene. 1997. "State-in Sex and Gender: Collecting Information From Mothers and Fathers in Paternity Cases." *Gender and Society* 11: 279–95.

Preston, Samuel. 1984. "Children and the Elderly: Divergent Paths for America's Dependents." *Demography* 21: 435–57.

Rifkin, Jeremy. 1994. *The End of Work.* New York: Putnam.

Schor, J. (1991). *The Overworked American.* New York: Basic Books.

Simon, Robin W. 1995. "Gender, Multiple Roles, Role Meaning, and Mental Health." *Journal of Health and Social Behavior* 36:182–94.

Sonenstein, Freda L. 1991. "The Child Care Preferences of Parents With Young Children: How Little Is Known." Pp. 337–53 in *Parental Leave and Child Care,* edited by J. S. Hyde and M. J. Essex. Philadelphia: Temple University Press.

Sprague, Joey. 1996. "Seeing Gender as Social Structure." Paper presented at the annual meeting of the American Sociological Association, New York.

Waldfogel, Jane. 1997. "The Effect of Children on Women's Wages." *American Sociological Review* 62: 209–17.

Wolman, William. 1997. *The Judas Economy: The Triumph of Capital and the Betrayal of Work.* Reading, MA: Addison-Wesley.

Wright, Erik Olin. 2000. "Reducing Income and Wealth Inequality: Real Utopian Proposals." *Contemporary Sociology* 29:143–56.

Zelizer, Vivian. 1985. *Pricing the Priceless Child.* New York: Basic Books. ✦

31

Overworked Individuals or Overworked Families?

Jerry A. Jacobs and Kathleen Gerson

Jerry Jacobs and Kathleen Gerson trace the increase in American's working time to the increase in dual-career families and the amount of time these couples jointly work. They also indicate that there is one segment of the population that works extremely long hours—namely, highly educated, professional and managerial couples.

The challenge of balancing work and family has drawn increasing attention in public debate, policy analysis, and academic research. Indeed, this topic has spawned a rapidly growing interdisciplinary field, complete with research and policy discussions (Parcel & Cornfield, 2000; Pitt-Catsouphes & Googins, 1999), academic conferences,[1] journals (e.g., *Community, Work and Family*), research centers,[2] and electronic databases.[3] Because time spent at work sets an upper boundary on the time left to spend in other pursuits, working time constitutes a starting point for understanding the shifting balance between work and family in American households.[4] Working time also sets limits on how much economic support a worker can provide and thus is closely linked to earnings and

income. Too much time at work can undermine personal and family welfare, whereas too little time can endanger a family's economic security and lower its standard of living.

Despite the importance of working time, recent studies have produced sharply divergent views on the question of how much time Americans are devoting to paid work. One perspective, first articulated by Juliet Schor (1991) and since echoed by many others (Bond, Galinsky, & Swanberg, 1997; Hochschild, 1997, pp. 268–269, Endnote 3; Mishel, Bernstein, & Schmitt, 1999), contends that American workers are logging more time at the workplace than their parents or grandparents, thus producing an "unexpected decline of leisure" in American society. Schor argues that time on the job, which declined steadily from the early days of the factory system until 1940, when 40 hours became the standard schedule, has risen in recent decades. For Schor, the decline in union strength has made it difficult for organized labor to counter employers' power to increase work time demands. Yet Schor (1998) also suggests that American workers' preferences have also contributed to the growth of time on the job. From this perspective, workers are trapped in a "squirrel cage" of competitive materialism that causes families to focus unduly on consumer purchases and feeds the need to work long hours.

Extending the focus on cultural shifts, Hochschild (1997) posits a cultural transformation in which "home has become work and work has become home." Rather than stressing the role of employer demands, this perspective contends that a shift in the relative values attached to home and work has led many workers to place more emphasis on the rewards of work and to view the workplace as a respite from the difficulties of contemporary family life.

Accounts that point to a shift in time or loyalty to paid work, whether due to rising employer demands or shifting employee preferences, suggest that work commitments are encroaching on the needs of family life. Yet others have argued that this picture of growing work commitments is misleading. Relying on time-diary studies, Robinson and Godbey (1997) maintain that leisure time, not working time, is increasing. Still others argue that, although leisure may not be increasing, the length of the average workweek has changed very little in recent decades and thus cannot account for the growing perception that families are being squeezed (Jacobs & Gerson, 1998; Rones, Ilg, & Gardner, 1997).

In place of these contradictory arguments, we propose a reformulation of the problem and a synthesis of the opposing views about how workers are balancing paid work and family life. In the debate over the growth of work versus leisure, we offer a perspective that incorporates important aspects of both views. Indeed, we argue that increasing work and increasing leisure are not mutually exclusive propositions. To resolve these apparent contradictions, we focus on diversity and variability among workers and their families.

Focusing on changes in the distribution of time on the job, we have found growth in the proportion of workers concentrated at both the high and low ends of the spectrum. One segment of the labor market contains workers who are putting in more hours at work than ever before, whereas another segment consists of workers who are unable to find jobs that provide enough hours of work (see also Bluestone & Rose, 1997). We thus maintain that working time is increasingly bifurcated, with one group of workers putting in long hours and another working constricted hours. We contend, moreover, that it is vital to attend to the shape of the distribution among workers rather than to the experience of the "average" worker.

In addition to focusing on variation among workers, we also propose to redirect the analysis of working time from individuals to families. The perception of an increase in working time is part of a larger social shift from male-breadwinner families to dual-earner couples and single-parent households. We suggest that a decline in support at home rather than an increase in the working time of individuals underlies the growing sense that families are squeezed for time and that work and family life are in conflict.

The Overworked-American Thesis

According to Schor (1991), an increase in working time can be found by estimating the annual hours worked by the average man and woman in the labor force (see also Leete & Schor, 1994).[5] Her results suggest that women's annual hours of paid work increased 305 hours between 1969 and 1987, while men's annual total increased by 98 hours during this period.

The argument that women and men are working longer today than was typical several decades earlier has touched a resonant chord in the popular imagination.[6] Despite the appeal of this thesis, there are several problems with this conclusion. First, the changes observed during the period are principally due to changes in the number of weeks worked per year, not the number of hours worked per week. The evidence clearly indicates remarkable stability in the length of the average workweek. Schor's (1991) own figures indicate an increase of 0.8 hours per week for men and 1.8 hours per week for women.[7] Indeed, if one compares 1970 with 1997, the length of the average workweek remained virtually unchanged (Jacobs & Gerson, 1998). Thus, during this time span, the only increase in annual hours would have to come from changes in the number of weeks worked per year.

Second, the Current Population Survey (CPS) data are not ideal for measuring annual hours on the job. The CPS questionnaire does not elicit information on vacations and holidays. Respondents are specifically instructed to include paid vacation time when reporting on the number of weeks worked last year. Thus, one key issue—whether employers are squeezing more days per year out of workers—is difficult to ascertain with this data source.

Third, and most important, Schor makes too much of the changes in weeks worked per year. Greater continuity in labor force attachment on the part of women will inevitably produce increases in the number of weeks worked per year as measured by the CPS. Whereas the CPS focuses on employment in the previous calendar year, it does not attempt to discern whether the respondent intends to work for a short interval or is instead in the middle of a sustained spell in the labor force. Many who are measured as part-year workers were, in fact, beginning a long spell of employment but just happened to start that spell at some point in the middle of the previous calendar year. For the 1997 CPS data (discussed in more detail below), we found that more than 60% of those who worked part-year (less than 50 weeks) in 1996 were still employed in March 1997. Part-year work is thus principally a measure of the extent of churning associated with labor market entries and exits. As women's labor force participation climbs, labor market interruptions decrease, and the number of employment spells that begin in the middle of the calendar year decline as well, thus producing an increase in the number of weeks worked per year.[8] To verify this assertion, we correlated women's labor force participation over the period 1950 through 1998 with the proportion of employed women who worked full-time, full-year. We found that these two trends moved together over time in lock step (the serial correlation was .965). Because the number of weeks worked per year reflects continuous versus discontinuous employment, combined with occasional or seasonal work, changes in this measure are more closely connected to the demography of the labor force than to the behavior of employers or the structure of work.

An Increase in Leisure Time?

In bold contrast to the overworked-American thesis, Robinson and Godbey (1997) argue that the period between 1965 and 1995 has witnessed a surprising increase in leisure time. In contrast to most national labor force surveys, including the CPS on which Schor's results are based, Robinson and Godbey rely on time-diary data, which asks respondents to record their activities in half-hour intervals that span a 24-hour day.

Time diaries are certainly valuable for assessing the way Americans spend their time while not at work, but Robinson and Godbey (1997) claim that time diaries provide more accurate and less biased measures of working time as well. They argue that people are not likely to know the amount of time they spend working in a given week and, given only a few seconds to think about the question, many are likely to give a very rough estimate of their workweek. Respondents may overstate their working time by forgetting about non-work-related errands and appointments conducted during the workday, or they may understate their workweek by forgetting about work brought home. If self-reports about the workweek are error prone, they will produce more unexplained variation.

Because random errors do not change the mean or result in biased estimates of the effect of independent variables, they are not the gravest concern for statistical analysis. The question of bias is more troubling. Robinson and Godbey (1997) maintain that those working long hours exaggerate the time they spend working because being busy has some caché, and it is easy for respondents who work long hours to tack another 5 or 10 hours onto their reports. They also argue that this tendency to exaggerate has increased over time. If true, this claim would mean that our estimates of the workweek are overstated. It would also require us to revise our understanding of the wage distribution, because wages are calculated from earnings and hours worked.[9]

In a companion article, Jacobs (1998) has shown that the claims about the superiority of time-diary data have not been substantiated. When error and exaggeration are tested for a wide variety of demographic groups working in a wide variety of job settings, self-reports of working time hold up remarkably well. There is, therefore, little evidence of systematic bias.

Time-diary data are quite useful, but they do not readily offer answers to some important questions about the labor force. For example, a standard daily diary does not provide the length of the workweek for a given individual or a married couple. Instead, the weekdays and weekends of different individuals must be combined to create a synthetic workweek.[10] For many purposes, such as translating weekly earnings into hourly wage rates, a daily time diary will not suffice.

Overwork, Growing Leisure, or Both?

Setting aside the issue of differences in the quality of data, the most important question remains: Has working time increased or declined? On the surface, the overworked-American thesis and the increase in leisure thesis seem irreconcilable. After all, time is a metric with a fixed upper limit, and changes in work and leisure should involve a zero-sum trade-off: Any increase in work time should decrease leisure time. However, a closer examination reveals that once the diversity among workers is taken into account, there can be a kernel of truth in each account. From this perspective, leisure could increase if the share of the working population were declining or the share of the population with lower levels of housework were increasing. The first means of reconciling the two arguments fails, whereas the second succeeds.

Although Schor's (1991) arguments apply to the employed population, Robinson and Godbey (1997) point to the growth of certain segments of the nonworking population, including demographic groups that are relatively high in leisure time. Specifically, increasing proportions of men are retiring at younger ages, thus increasing the share of the population that enjoys significant amounts of leisure time. At the other end of the age distribution, a growing group of individuals in their 20s are remaining in school for a longer period of time. Because students and retired men have more apparent leisure than does the average worker, the growth of these groups would point to an increase in leisure time in the general population, even with no change in the average workweek.

The growth in women's labor force participation has more than offset these changes, however. In fact, a larger fraction of the adult population is in the labor force today than at any time since the Second World War. For example, the ratio of employed individuals to the population (age 16 and above) rose from 56.1% in 1950 to 63.8% in 1997. Similarly, the percentage of the population in the civilian labor force rose from 59.2% to 67.1% during the same period (U.S. Department of Commerce, Bureau of the Census [USDOC-BOC], 1998, Table 644). If we removed the growing fraction of the population aged 65 or above from these calculations, the growth in the employed population would appear even steeper. Thus, any observed changes in working time pertain to a growing, not a shrinking, share of the population.

A decline in time spent in housework provides another, sounder way to reconcile discrepant claims regarding work and leisure. Robinson and Godbey (1997) note that the amount of housework performed by some segments of the population is lower than among others. Single women, for example, spend less time doing housework than do married women, and those without children do less housework than do parents. Over the past 30 years, the average age of marriage has increased, the age at first birth of children has increased, and the number of children per household has declined. All these demographic trends give people more leisure time without reducing their time on the job.[11] It is thus possible for the workweek to remain stable (or even grow slightly) while an increase in leisure time in the population also occurs.

A more serious problem with the debate about leisure versus work is that it focuses on the average experience of the average American. Instead of focusing on averages, which depend on the size of various groups and their experience of work or leisure, it is more informative to explore the distribution of working time. We find that, although the average workweek has not changed significantly, notable shifts in the distribution of working time across groups of workers have occurred.

Furthermore, it is important to focus on the family's workweek rather than on the individual earner's. Because dual-earner couples are becoming more common and male breadwinners less common, husbands and wives may experience a sharp increase in the shared workweek even if the average individual working time shows little change. Single mothers, who also cannot rely on an unpaid worker at home, may undergo a similar time crunch. Again, we will see that single mothers, as a group, are not significantly more pressed for time than they were 30 years ago. Instead, this long-standing problem has diffused to a much larger number of families as the number of single mothers has grown.

Presser 1994, 1995) examined the distribution of shift work among dual-earner couples but did not explore the length of the workweek per se.[12] Nock and Kingston (1988) found that long workweeks do take away time that parents could otherwise spend with children, but they also found this primarily reduced activities in which children were peripherally involved rather than activities in which children were the center of attention. Moreover, they did not explore historical trends in the length of the workweek for working spouses. Thus, despite the importance of overall trends and variations in how dual-earner couples jointly allocate time between work and other activities, scant attention has been given to these matters. We turn our attention, then, to trends in working time among dual-earner couples and seek to determine how many hours these couples jointly devote to paid employment.

Working Time for Individuals or Families?

Although the experiences of individual workers are important, focusing on families provides another way of approaching the question of working hours. Dual-earner couples and single-parent families are the groups most likely to feel squeezed between the demands and rewards of work and the needs of family life. Indeed, single parents, who are predominantly mothers, are likely to experience an even greater time burden than are dual-earner couples. It is not the amount of working time but rather the loss of someone to take care of domestic needs that links single mothers with dual-earner couples. The debate over the causes and consequences of work-family conflict thus pertain most acutely to the experiences of these groups.

Although numerous studies have offered detailed examinations of the time couples allocate to housework and related domestic tasks, relatively few have focused on the amount of time dual-earner couples jointly devote to paid work. In a series of articles,

The Growth of Dual-Earner Families

Although most analysts argue that the rise of work-family conflict reflects an increase in the amount of time people are working, a focus on the combined hours of employed couples, rather than on changes in the behavior of individual workers, points to a different explanation. If more members of a family are in the labor force, each is more likely to feel squeezed between home and work. A rise in the proportion of households with either two earners or one parent is likely to produce the perception of a growing time squeeze, even if the average amount of time individuals spend working has not increased substantially. Contemporary dual-earner couples may feel time pressures quite similar to those experienced by their predecessors in 1970. It is not the amount of time workers are devoting to work that has increased but rather the proportion of workers who experience the conflicts associated with a dual-earner (or single-parent) situation. Because most married couples now depend on two incomes, this experience has become typical rather than unusual.

Demographic Shifts in Working Time

Does the growing sense of time pressures stem from changes in working hours or from a basic demographic shift in family structure? Because recent studies have failed to document dramatic changes in the length of the average workweek, the widespread transformation in how households are organized has likely played a larger role than has increased working time for individual workers. Nevertheless, we know little about the relative importance of each of these factors or how they vary across the labor force. Even if the average length of the individual workweek has remained fairly constant, has the combined working time for couples increased? How does the distribution of working time for couples vary, and how has it changed? What are the contours of the shift in family composition, and what does this shift imply for the shape of the labor force?

Although economists, demographers, and sociologists have studied the determinants of labor supply for decades, most have focused only on whether women are employed, with much less concern for how many hours men and women work. Our goal is to account for changes in working time between 1970 and 1997 by examining the factors most likely to account for shifts over time in the working time of couples. Previous studies have found that demographic factors, such as education, age, and the number of children, help explain working time. For example, studies have shown that those with more education are likely to work longer hours (Coleman & Pencavel, 1993a, 1993b; Jacobs & Gerson, 1998). We thus expect that a general increase in educational levels in the labor force would account for a portion of the increasing working time.

The aging of the workforce may also have spurred a longer workweek. The aging of the baby-boom generation has created a labor force in which a smaller fraction of workers were younger than age 30 in 1997 than in 1970. Because men and women in their 20s tend to work less than those between age 30 and 55, this shift may account for some of the changes occurring in this period.

The number of children in a worker's family also influences a family's working time. The presence of children depresses the number of hours that women work while having relatively little effect on men's working time. The decline in family size may thus also have contributed to an increase in the time that women spend at work. Our analysis estimates the significance of these demographic factors in accounting for changes over time in the joint paid working time of married couples.

Data and Method

To answer these questions, we analyzed the March Annual Demographic Files of the CPS from 1970 and 1997 (USDOC-BOC, 1970,1997) and created data files organized by household rather than by individual working time. We sorted individuals by household, and within household, by family type. We then matched married individuals within families. In 99.5% of households, there were no more than two married individuals in the family: the householder and the householder's spouse. In 0.5% of households, however, there were two additional married individuals. In these more problematic cases, we sorted individuals by family within the household and then matched husbands and wives within each. We restricted the sample to married couples in which both spouses were aged 18 to 64. This procedure produced a sample of 32,676 married couples in 1997 and 27,494 married couples in 1970. We weighted the data using the March supplement person-weight so that the weighted sample would reflect the characteristics of married couples in the United States at these two points in time.

Although many studies of working time restrict the focus to wage and salary workers employed in the nonagricultural labor force, we decided to include self-employed individuals.

Because our focus is on working time per se and not on the employer-employee relationship, there was no reason to exclude self-employed workers. We did, however, exclude agriculture workers because the organization of working time on farms differs in fundamental ways from the structure of work in other employment settings. It would be misleading to allow the historical decline in the size of the agricultural sector to overshadow other, more significant trends.

The CPS provides several measures of working time, including a measure of average weekly working time for the job (or jobs) held last week and a measure of average time spent at work last year. To ascertain time commitments based on a worker's current job, we analyzed responses to the question "How many hours did you usually work per week in the job (or jobs) held last week?" To determine if a measure based on all jobs held in a year would yield appreciably different results, we also conducted analyses of the question on time spent at work last year.[13]

Couples were categorized into four exhaustive and mutually exclusive categories: (a) dual-earner couples, (b) male-breadwinner couples, (c) female-breadwinner couples, and (d) couples with neither spouse employed. Couples were apportioned among these four groups according to whether each spouse had worked at least 1 hour in the previous week. For each spouse, we then culled data on his or her education and age. For the household, we obtained several measures of the number and ages of children in the family. We also present results for working parents and single mothers.

The education measures for 1970 and 1997 are not strictly comparable. In 1970, the CPS solicited information on the number of years of schooling completed, but, in 1997, respondents were asked to report the highest degree attained. To make these

measures more comparable, we grouped the 1970 measure into four categories: (a) less than high school, (b) high school graduate (i.e., 12 years of schooling completed), (c) some college (13 to 15 years of schooling completed), and (4) college graduate (16 or more years of schooling). To see how much difference resulted from the change in the educational measure, we replicated our analysis with data from the 1990 CPS (USDOC-BOC, 1990), which coded education in the same manner as in 1970. This set of analyses produced results that are entirely consistent with those reported below.

Results

Working Time in Dual-Earner Families, 1970 and 1997

Table 31.1 compares the distribution of couples in 1970 and 1997 by presenting the proportion of couples in each of the four types of families—dual earner, male breadwinner, female breadwinner, and neither employed. These results indicate a marked shift from the male-breadwinner family to the dual-earner couple. In 1970, the male breadwinner remained the modal type among couples, with 51.4% of couples falling into this category. In contrast, husbands and wives were both employed in just greater than one third (35.9%) of married couples younger than age 65. By 1997, however, the dual-earner couple represented a solid majority (59.5%) of married couples. In this context of family transformation, it is not surprising that there has been growing social concern about balancing work and family.

Table 31.1 also compares the number of hours devoted to paid employment in 1970 and 1997 for each type of couple. Among all couples, working time performed by both husband and wife increased from 52.5 hours per week to 62.8 hours per week. In addition, the proportion working very long hours, that is, 100 hours per week or more, more than doubled from 3.1% to 8.6% of all couples. As a group, married individuals have less time to spend at home, because they devote more joint time to work.

The growth of working time among married couples, however, does not result from significant increases in working time for each household type. Rather, it is principally due to the growth in the overall proportion of couples that fit the dual-earner pattern. The smallest changes occurred among male-breadwinner couples. By 1997, male breadwinners were working 44.7 hours per week on average, a very slight increase from the 44.4 hours these husbands averaged in 1970. Working time for female breadwinners in intact marriages also grew only slightly, rising from an average of 35.5 hours per week in 1970 to a weekly average of 36.9 hours in 1997. More important, over this same period, female breadwinners in married-couple

households remained an unusual group. The influx of wives into the labor force has not induced husbands to stay home.

The largest increase in working time occurred among dual-earner couples, who also constitute the fastest growing group. Husbands and wives in these marriages jointly devoted 81.3 hours per week in paid employment, up just more than 3 hours per week from the 78.0 hours per week reported in 1970. In addition, the proportion reporting very long workweeks rose sharply, from 8.7% to 14.4%. Notably, it is wives' working time that provides the major cause of the growth in combined working time for these couples. Whereas husbands' mean hours at work rose by only 0.8 hours during this period, wives' time at paid work rose by 2.5 hours. The relative balance in working time between husbands

Table 31.1
Trends In Joint Hours of Paid Work by Husbands and Wives, 1970–1997, (nonfarm) Married Couples Aged 18–64

Group (% of overall total)	Mean Hours Last Week All Jobs (SD)	% Working Less Than 70 Hours per Week	% Working 100+ Hours per Week	Husband's Hours	Wife's Hours
1997					
Total, all couples	62.8 (29.6)	51.0	8.6	38.4	24.4
Both work (59.5)	81.3 (18.4)	20.3	14.4	44.9	36.4
Only husband works (25.9)	44.7 (12.9)	95.2	0.0	44.7	0.0
Only wife works (7.2)	36.9 (12.9)	98.4	0.0	0.0	36.9
Neither works (7.4)	0.0 (0.0)	100.0	0.0	0.0	0.0
1970					
Total, all couples	52.5 (25.7)	63.4	3.1	38.9	33.6
Both work (35.9)	78.0 (16.9)	24.9	8.7	44.1	33.9
Only husband works (51.4)	44.4 (11.0)	96.0	0.0	44.4	0.0
Only wife works (4.6)	35.5 (10.7)	99.6	0.0	0.0	35.5
Neither works (8.2)	0.0 (0.0)	100.0	0.0	0.0	0.0

Source: U.S. Department of Commerce, Bureau of the Census (1970, 1997).

and wives thus also shifted during this period, as wives became more strongly committed to work outside the home.

The changes that occurred between 1970 and 1997 can be divided into two components: (a) changes in the distribution of marriages across various family types and (b) changes in the working time of individuals in the same marriage types. If we hold joint working time constant at 1970 levels for each marriage type and substitute the 1997 distribution of marriage types, the total working time for married individuals would have risen from 52.5 to 60.5 hours. In other words, 8.0 of the 10.3 additional hours worked can be attributed to the shift in the economic arrangements of married couples. In percentage terms, more than three quarters (77.7%) of the growth in working time among married couples is due to the growth of dual-earner households. The remaining quarter (22.3%) results from an increase in working time, particularly among dual-earner couples. Although there has been a slight increase in the total amount of time dual-earner couples devote to work, the principal source of change has been the rise in the proportion of couples who fit the dual-earner pattern. Changes in working time have been modest compared to the sharp growth in the size of this group.

A growing segment of the population appears to be working extremely long hours. Whereas couples working 100 hours or more per week are likely to feel squeezed for time, this group of "overworked" couples does not represent the average. Some dual-earner couples may be working longer hours than their historical predecessors, but dual-earner couples have always been stretched thin in balancing work and family time.

The major change of the last generation has not been a fundamental shift in the working time of individuals but rather a dramatic growth in the number of people whose families depend on two incomes. Moreover, there is scant evidence of a general shift in the relative importance of work and family among couples in which both partners work. Instead, the rise of family time deficits has a more straightforward explanation: the rise of women's employment and the demographic transformation of family life, with little in the way of a countervailing shift in men's nonworking time.

The Distribution of Working Time Across Couples

Despite the small increase in the average working time of dual-earner couples as a group, we have found growth in the number of couples whose joint work hours are quite high. Who are the couples putting in these very long hours, and how do they compare to others? Are members of this "overworked" group attracting disproportionate attention because their numbers are growing or because they occupy socially prominent positions in society? Moreover, do they face acutely more difficult circumstances because they are juggling child rearing with very long work hours, or are they more likely to be working long hours because children are less likely to be present in the home? To answer these questions, we examine the distribution of couples' combined working time across important social dimensions, such as education, occupation, and child situation.

Table 31.2 presents trends in working hours, with couples classified by the educational level of the wife. This table makes it clear that the growth in working time has been concentrated among couples with the most education. Couples in which the husband had completed 4 years of college were working 2.1 hours more than in 1970, whereas couples in which the husband had not completed high school were working 0.6 hours less than in 1970.[14] A 3.4-hour difference in favor of the most educated couples in 1970 grew to become a 6.1-hour differential by 1997.[15]

These changes principally reflect the growing hours on the job of working women: Working wives with at least some college education increased their working time by more than 2 hours per week during this period.

Table 31.2
Trends In Joint Hours of Paid Work by Husbands and Wives, 1970–1997, by Wife's Educational Level, Nonfarm Dual-Earn Couples

Wife's Educational Level (% of overall total)	Mean Hours Last Week All Jobs (SD)	% Working Less Than 70 Hours per Week	% Working 100+ Hours per Week	Husband's Hours	Wife's Hours
1997					
College graduate (29.4)	83.3 (19.8)	18.9	16.3	45.7	37.7
Some college (29.6)	80.0 (17.7)	22.3	10.6	44.4	35.5
High school graduate (33.8)	79.5 (17.8)	22.7	9.2	43.9	35.6
Less than high school (7.2)	77.2 (17.0)	25.9	8.2	42.4	34.8
1970					
College graduate (27.6)	81.2 (20.2)	23.2	18.4	45.8	35.4
Some college (49.5)	77.0 (18.1)	27.3	8.2	44.5	32.6
High school graduate (12.0)	77.6 (16.4)	24.9	7.5	44.0	33.6
Less than high school (11.0)	77.8 (15.9)	24.6	7.1	43.5	34.3

Source: U.S. Department of Commerce, Bureau of the Census (1970, 1997).

To examine the importance of education for both marital partners more directly, we considered trends in paid working time among couples where both the husband and wife were college graduates (results available from authors). Among this group, a 3.8-hour-per-week increase in working time occurred between 1970 and 1997. Significantly, this increase results almost entirely from an increase in working time among wives. These wives worked 3.5 hours per week more than they did in 1970, whereas the husbands worked only 0.3 more hours per week.

Although some working families are putting in more time at work than did their counterparts several decades ago, this trend appears to be modest. It is sharpest among one group: couples in which the combined working time of both workers adds up to very long workweeks. Because these couples are more likely to be highly educated, they occupy a disproportionate share of high-profile occupational positions in the professional and managerial sector. The high visibility of this segment of the labor force has probably enhanced the national attention given to the problem of overwork.

The underlying reason for observed changes in the working time of married couples appears to be the rise of employment among married women. The growing work commitment of wives is the major cause of change in married couples' working time, whether measured as a rise in the proportion of couples who have two earners or a rise in the amount of time such couples are devoting to paid work. Because married men's working time has remained fairly stable or grown modestly, women's movement out of the home has not been offset by a comparable shift toward greater family time among men. In this context, it is easy to understand why families feel squeezed.

Explaining Trends Among Dual-Earner Couples

Although there has been an increase of roughly 3 hours per week in the paid working time of dual-earner couples, it is unclear to what extent this change is due to changes in workers' attributes or to shifts in the nature of jobs. To untangle these forces, we estimated a series of regression equations predicting the total number of hours in paid employment of husbands and wives in dual-earner couples. Pooling data from 1970 and 1997, we sought to account for the 3-hour increase that occurred during this period. To measure the influence of demographic changes, we included four individual measures—(a) age, (b) age squared, (c) education (three dummy measures of degree attainment, with college graduates serving as the reference group), and (d) occupation (three dummy measures: managerial, professional, sales, and all others as a reference group)—and one family measure: the number of children younger than 18. These individual variables were measured for both husbands and wives.

This very simplified model of working time for dual-earner couples explains two thirds of the increase in working time among this group. In other words, the growth of 3 hours is due largely to the fact that dual-earner couples in 1997 were slightly older than their counterparts in 1970, were more likely to have a college degree, were more likely to be in managerial occupations, and had fewer children younger than age 18. Once these factors were taken into account, the growth in time on the job was reduced to just more than 1 hour per week. This simple model does not account for a great deal of the variance in time on the job, but it does account for the preponderance of change during this period of time.

Dual-Earner Parents and Working Time

Because the greatest concern about increased working time centers on the potentially negative consequences for children, it is important to ascertain to what extent working couples with very long workweeks are juggling these work demands with child rearing. Have couples with children at home increased their combined working time, or are they more likely to be cutting back from work to meet their child rearing obligations?

To answer this question, Table 31.3 presents trends in the hours of paid employment for working couples with and without children. In 1997, working parents worked for pay 2.1 hours less per week than did couples without children. In addition, working hours declined slightly as the number of children increased. For those with one child younger than 18, couples worked an average of 81.2 hours per week; those with three or more children worked 79.0 hours. The difference principally reflects reduced working time among mothers. For husbands, working hours actually increased slightly with the presence of children and as the number of children rose. Those fathers with three or more children worked 1.5 hours per week more than did husbands without children. In contrast, mothers with three or more children worked 5 hours less per week than married women without children.

To examine this distribution, Figure 31.1 presents trends in the hours of paid employment among working parents. The distribution shows increased dispersion in 1997 compared with 1970, with fewer couples concentrated around the 80-hour central tendency and more couples at both the high and low end of the spectrum.

Despite the transformation from male-breadwinner to dual-earner marriages, gender differences in the work consequences of parenthood persist. The arrival of children still tends to push men toward stronger work participation while pulling women toward somewhat less involvement, creating a larger gender gap in their levels of work commitment compared to childless couples. These differences are nonetheless greatly attenuated compared to the once dominant pattern in which women withdrew from paid work altogether when children arrived.

Table 31.3

Trends in Joint Hours of Paid Work by Husbands and Wives, 1970–1997, by Parental Status, Nonfarm Dual-Earner Couples

Parental Status (% of overall total)	Mean Hours Last Week All Jobs (SD)	% Working Less Than 70 Hours per Week	% Working 100+ Hours per Week	Husband's Hours	Wife's Hours
1997					
No children ≤ 18 (41.9)	82.5 (19.4)	18.1	16.5	44.4	38.1
Some children ≤ 18 (58.1)	80.4 (17.6)	21.9	12.8	45.2	35.1
1 child ≤ 18 (23.1)	81.2 (17.4)	19.0	13.2	44.9	36.4
2 children ≤ 18 (24.2)	80.1 (17.6)	22.7	12.5	45.3	34.8
3+ children ≤ 18 (10.7)	79.0 (18.0)	26.6	12.7	45.9	33.1
1970					
No children ≤ 18 (33.4)	79.5 (16.6)	19.5	9.5	43.2	36.4
Some children ≤ 18 (66.6)	76.9 (17.2)	28.7	8.2	44.8	32.1
1 child ≤ 18 (23.6)	78.3 (17.4)	24.4	8.8	44.3	34.0
2 children ≤ 18 (21.0)	76.5 (16.7)	30.6	8.1	45.1	31.4
3+ children ≤ 18 (22.0)	75.9 (17.3)	31.8	7.7	45.1	30.8

Source: U.S. Department of Commerce, Bureau of the Census (1970, 1997).

Although the combined working time of dual-earner parents is slightly less than that of childless couples, the degree of change over time is slightly larger. Thus, between 1970 and 1997, the joint hours in paid employment of working couples increased by roughly 3 hours for those without children and by about 3.5 hours for those with children. The percentage of couples putting in very long workweeks (of 100 hours or more) rose for both groups, but the rise was less pronounced for parents in both absolute and percentage terms. The percentage of childless couples working at least 100 hours a week rose from 9.5% to 16.5%, whereas the percentage of working couples with children rose from 8.2% to 12.8%.

Again, the trend toward more time at work holds for parents as well as for couples without children at home, but it appears to be less pronounced for those workers with the largest family obligations. Whatever may be fueling these widespread social changes, they are not concentrated among parents and thus do not appear to stem from parents' preferences for work over family time.

Another important group of parents is represented by single mothers. Single parents are truly caught in a time bind, because they need to work as much as possible to support their families, while needing all the free time possible to supervise and care for their children. How do single mothers balance these competing time demands? Figure 31.2 displays the trends in working time among this growing group. The story here is one of dispersion rather than a shift toward a longer workweek. The fraction working the modal time on the job, 40 hours, has declined by nearly 10% (from 45.3% to 37.4%), with increases observed at both the high and low ends of the distribution. The average workweek for this group actually declined slightly, from 38.5 hours per week in 1970 to 36.0 hours in 1997.

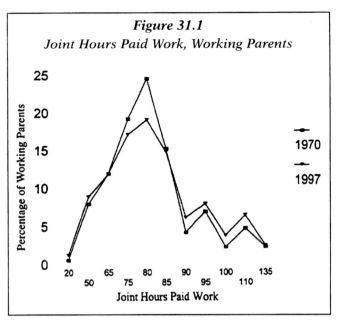

Figure 31.1

Joint Hours Paid Work, Working Parents

Conclusion

We have endeavored to clarify the causes and contours of changes in working time by focusing not on individual workers but rather on the combined work commitments of households, whether headed by couples or single mothers. We have discovered that the bulk of the change is not the result of increased working time within particular types of families but is instead a reflection of changes in family composition, and especially the growth of dual-earner couples. In addition, although overall changes in working time are modest, the past several decades have witnessed the emergence of a segment of employed couples who are putting in very long workweeks of 100 hours or more. These couples are especially likely to be concentrated among highly educated workers, who tend to occupy the most prestigious jobs and occupations. Finally, although parents do not appear to be putting in more time at work than are other groups, a disparity persists between fathers, who tend to work more than their childless counterparts, and mothers, who tend to work less.

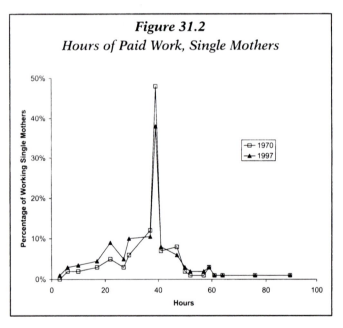

Figure 31.2

Hours of Paid Work, Single Mothers

These findings have important implications for family welfare and gender equality. First, they show that changes in the working time of individual workers cannot explain the rise of family time deficits. Rather, these changes stem from a transformation in family composition and gender relations. This widespread demographic transformation reflects basic social-structural and economic changes, including the erosion of the single-income "family wage" and the growth of women's commitment to an adulthood not confined to the home. These developments are deeply rooted and apparently irreversible, but they do not indicate that parents prefer work to family life. They suggest, instead, that adults, and especially women, are seeking a balance between home and work that may be increasingly elusive.

The central problem caused by this family transformation can be better understood by comparing the large changes in women's lives with the more intransigent situation for men, whose work commitments have remained comparatively stable and whose domestic involvement has not increased sufficiently to offset women's rising work commitment. This situation has left dual-earning families to cope with persisting family demands in the context of rising work obligations for the couple, and it has left employed, single mothers facing even greater time squeezes.

Our analysis suggests that the future of family and child well-being will depend on developing policies that accept the irreversibility of this demographic transition. Unfortunately, the full incorporation of women, and especially mothers, into the labor force continues to evoke ambivalence. Whereas welfare mothers are criticized for not working enough, middle-class women are castigated for spending too much time in paid employment.

We have focused on time in paid employment, but it is certainly not the whole story. Highly competitive workplaces may have created rising pressures, even for those workers putting in the same number of hours. Consequently, the amount of flexibility on the job, and not just the total number of hours, needs to be considered (Gerson & Jacobs, in press). The organization of time, and not just the duration of jobs, needs to be taken into account. Presser (1999) reminds us of the disruptive effects of evening, night, and weekend shifts on family life. Despite families' rising work pressures, cultural pressures for "in-

tensive mothering" have intensified (Hays, 1997). Thus, single parents and parents in dual-earner couples face not only a shortage of time but also increasing expectations during that limited time, both on the job and at home.

These crosscutting ideals lend credence to the argument that the problems currently facing American families stem not from too much change but from too little. Despite women's growing need and desire to work outside the home, there remains widespread resistance to providing women with equal opportunities at work and to overcoming the "stalled revolution" that has left men shouldering less than an equal share at home (Hochschild, 1989). Ultimately, however, the problem of family time deficits cannot be solved by chastising parents for working too much. Instead, the time has come to create a more flexible and family-supportive workplace, including more options for reducing working time (Jacobs & Gerson, 1998), commensurate with the family transformation that has already taken place.

Discussion Questions

1. Is the distinction that Jacobs and Gerson make between increases in joint time versus increases in individuals' time spent in paid work convincing to you? Why or why not?

2. Do you think people might spend more time at work in order to escape the problems of family life?

Endnotes

1. Recent conferences include "Work and Family: Today's Realities, Tomorrow's Visions," Alfred P. Sloan Foundation, Business and Professional Women's Foundation, and The Wellesley College Center for Research On Women, November 6 and 7, 1998, Boston; "A Time of Transition:

Work, Family and Community After 2001," Families and Work Institute Forum, February 25 and 26, Tarrytown, New York; "No Time to Care—Whose Business Is It Anyway?" Radcliffe Public Policy Institute Conference, May 5, 1999, New York City.

2. These include the Boston College Center for Work and Family, the Cornell Employment and Family Careers Institute, and the Families and Work Institute (New York City).

3. The Sloan E-Network for Work-Family researchers, url address: <http://www.bc.edu/bc_org/avp/csom/cwf/wfhetwork.html>.

4. Does excessive time on the job cause stress? Many questions on stress are defined in terms of not having enough time to meet all of one's obligations. For example, see Bond, Galinsky, and Swanberg (1997, p. 65).

5. This figure is obtained from the March Current Population Survey (CPS) by multiplying the usual number of weeks worked during the previous calendar year by the number of hours usually worked per week during that same period.

6. Schor's (1991) book spent numerous weeks on *The New York Times* Best Sellers list.

7. Because Schor excludes those involuntarily employed part-time from her analysis, this small increase is itself overstated. Because this group of underworked individuals grew in size during her period of study, including it would reduce the growth of time on the job.

8. The same is true for men as well. Labor force participation varies over the life course, with somewhat lower levels of labor force participation among young men (under age 25) and older men (over 55 or 60). In those life stages with lower labor force participation, there are also fewer weeks worked per year. Small changes in weeks worked per year for men and women reflect cyclical changes in the labor market and changes in workers' demographic attributes, such as age and education.

9. Hourly wages are typically computed by dividing earnings by hours worked. If the true working time is less than reported working time, the hourly wage would be higher. The potential concentration of this effect among high earners would inflate estimates of inequality and the returns to education, and would affect analyses of other behavior that is associated with wages.

10. A weekly diary may avoid this problem, but it is even more expensive to collect. Moreover, the accuracy of time-diary data over the period of a week has yet to be determined. It may be that respondents would tire of filling out diaries after a few days and would become increasingly sloppy in their reporting, forgetting activities in which they engaged.

11. It is possible that some families are postponing parenthood because work is so demanding, as Robinson and Godbey (1997, p. 9) note. The extra time available to young adults without chil-

dren may itself reflect a concession to the voracious demands of paid work.

12. Presser also noted the rise of "nonstandard" work shifts, which take place at night, on weekends, and during other periods formerly considered private time. These shifting work schedules, coupled with the rise of new technologies such as e-mail and cell phones, may also have contributed to the sense that family life is being disrupted by work demands.

13. Jacobs (1998) noted that there is less dispersion in an annual, compared with a weekly, measure of working time. Unfortunately, we were unable to use hours typically worked at the respondent's job in the previous year because this measure was not available in the 1970 CPS. We reestimated the results presented below over the period 1976 to 1997 with data on the longest job held last year and obtained results similar to those reported here.

14. This finding is consistent with that of Coleman and Pencavel (1993a, 1993b) on educational differentials in working time and Jacobs and Gerson (1998) on the growing bifurcation of time spent at work.

15. When changes over time are displayed by husbands' education, the changes are similar (results available from authors).

References

Bluestone, B., & Rose, S. (1997, March-April). Overworked and underemployed: Unraveling an economic enigma. *The American Prospect, 31*, 58–69.

Bond, J. T, Galinsky, E., & Swanberg, J. E. (1997). *The 1997 national study of the changing workforce*. New York: Families and Work Institute.

Coleman, M. T., & Pencavel, J. (1993a). Changes in work hours of male employees, 1940–1988. *Industrial and Labor Relations Review, 46*, 262–283.

——. (1993b). Trends in market work behavior of women since 1940. *Industrial and Labor Relations Review, 46*, 653–676.

Gerson, K., & Jacobs, J. A. (in press). Work-family conflict, work flexibility and gender equity in the modem workplace. In R. Hertz & N. Marshall (Eds.), *Work and family*. Berkeley: University of California Press.

Hays, S. (1997). *The cultural contradictions of motherhood*. New Haven, CT: Yale University Press.

Hochschild, A. R. (1989). *The second shift*. New York: Avon.

——. (1997). *The time bind: When work becomes home and home becomes work*. New York: Metropolitan.

Jacobs, J. A. (1998). Measuring time at work: An assessment of the accuracy of self reports. *Monthly Labor Review, 121*, 42–53.

Jacobs, J. A., & Gerson, K. (1998). Who are the overworked Americans? *Review of Social Economy, 56*, 442–459.

Leete, L., & Schor, J. B. (1994). Assessing the time-squeeze hypothesis: Hours worked in the United States, 1969–1989. *Industrial Relations, 33*, 25–43.

Mishel, L., Bernstein, J., & Schmitt, J. (1999). *The state of working America 1998–99*. Washington, DC: Economic Policy Institute.

Nock, S. L., & Kingston, P. W. (1988). Time with children: The impact of couples' work-time commitments. *Social Forces, 67*, 59–85.

Parcel, T., & Cornfield, D. B. (Eds.). (2000). *Work and family: Research informing policy*. Thousand Oaks, CA: Sage.

Pitt-Catsouphes, M. & Googins, B. (Eds.). (1999). The evolving world of work and family: New stakeholders, new voices [Special issue]. *Annals of the American Academy of Political and Social Science, 562*.

Presser, H. B. (1994). Employment schedules among dual-earner spouses and the division of household labor by gender. *American Sociological Review, 59*, 348–364.

——. (1995). Job, family, and gender: Determinants of non-standard work schedules among employed Americans in 1991. *Demography, 32*, 577–598.

——. (1999, June 11). Toward a 24-hour economy. *Science, 284*, 1778–1779.

Robinson, J. P., & Godbey, G. (1997). *Time for life: The surprising ways Americans use their time*. University Park: Pennsylvania State University Press.

Rones, P. L., Ilg, R. E., & Gardner, J. M. (1997, April). Trends in hours of work since the mid-1970s. *Monthly Labor Review*, 3–14.

Schor, J. (1991). *The overworked American*. New York: Basic Books.

——. (1998). *The overspent American*. New York: Basic Books.

U.S. Department of Commerce, Bureau of the Census. (1970). *Current population survey, annual demographic file*. Washington, DC: Author.

——. (1990). *Current population survey, annual demographic file*. Washington, DC: Author.

——. (1997). *Current population survey, annual demographic file*. Washington, DC: Author.

——. (1998). *Statistical abstract of the United States*. Washington, DC: Author. ✦

32

Scaling Back: Dual-Earner Couples' Work-Family Strategies

Penny Edgell Becker and Phyllis Moen

Drawing on interview data from white, middle-class, dual-earner couples in New York, Penny Becker and Phyllis Moen document three of their combined strategies for balancing family and work demands, although they find that these strategies are used especially by women and at different stages of the life cycle.

In a recent review of the literature on dual-earner couples, Spain and Bianchi (1996) note that the "problem" of the dual-earner couple typically has been framed as a woman's problem of balancing work and family. Some studies of dual-earner couples have focused on the second shift because women retain the primary responsibility for housework and child-care (Brines, 1994; Gerson, 1985; Hertz, 1986; Hochschild, 1989). Other studies emphasize the higher stress and reduced occupational advancement for women in dual-earner marriages or, conversely, examine the positive effects of employment for such women's emotional and physical health (Barnett, 1994; Barnett & Rivers, 1996; Wethington & Kessler, 1989; and see reviews by Moen, 1992; Spain & Bianchi, 1996).

Another body of theory and research has focused on adaptive strategies in managing the experiences of family life for both men and women. Building on Hill (1970), this work emphasizes the processes through which family members actively construct and modify their roles, resources, and relationships (cf. Goode, 1960; Moen & Wethington, 1992). Researchers in the 1980s and early 1990s identified a broad range of coping strategies and repertoires, including gender and life-stage differences in individual coping styles (e.g., Gilbert, 1988; Schnittger & Bird, 1990; Skinner & McCubbin, 1991). How do these insights apply to couple-level strategies used to manage the work-family interface?

Recent studies paint conflicting pictures of work-family strategies in dual-earner couples. *The Time Bind* (Hochschild, 1997) is an ethnographic account of couples with one partner working at Amerco, a "greedy workplace" that demands long hours of work and "face time" (Coser, 1974; Nippert-Eng, 1996). Hochschild finds employees identifying home as a place of stress and unending demands, and identifying work as a pleasant place of friendships and support (cf. Nippert-Eng). Hochschild finds that, instead of resisting the time bind, some people use a couple-level strategy of overcommitment to work that reproduces it (cf. Robinson & Godbey, 1997; Schor, 1992). Hochschild examines the strategic choices of some dual-earner couples, but cannot identify the entire range of strategies that working couples employ.

Barnett and Rivers' (1996) work seems to indicate that the strategy of working more to avoid stress at home is not a typical one. In their study of Boston-area two-earner couples in which both spouses work full-time, they find that respondents have warm and loving relationships with their children, satisfaction in their marriage and parenting, and more stability in their incomes due to the buffering that two jobs provides in an uncertain economy (cf. Schwartz, 1994). They attribute much of society's concern over dual-earner couples to a thinly disguised discomfort with the rapid change in women's roles, and they urge the development of policies that help dual-earner couples find the flexibility they need to have successful careers and rewarding family lives.

High-profile books like *The Time Bind* and *She Works, He Works* (Barnett & Rivers, 1996) not only influence a generation of new academics but also generate a great deal of popular interest and carry weight with business and policy elites. They move beyond a focus on the strain model of work-family conflict to examine the strategies of action that dual-earner couples use to manage their work and family responsibilities (cf. Moen & Wethington, 1992; Swidler, 1986). Together they voice two sides of the contemporary social problem framing of research on dual-earner couples (cf. Furstenberg, 1998).

We draw on data from in-depth interviews with members of middle-class dual-earner couples in up-state New York to build on the idea of the family as a locus of strategic actions that may shift and change at different points during the life course. We focus on neither the problems nor the benefits of the dual-earner arrangement, but, rather, on understanding how couples describe their adaptations, and how this varies by gender and life stage (cf. Schnittger & Bird, 1990). We find that couples are using a variety of adaptive strategies to manage day-to-day aspects of their work and family lives, most designed to achieve what we call scaling back, or buffering their family lives from the ever-increasing demands of work. These strategies vary by career stage and the presence or absence of young children in the home and are influenced by prevailing gender norms.

Our findings build on and extend an existing body of literature that documents how families actively construct their own environments through strategic action (Moen & Wethington, 1992.) Our evidence challenges the overgeneralizations about all dual-earner couples based on the experiences of a small group of privileged couples in which both spouses are pursuing high-powered careers.

Studying the Adaptive Strategies of Middle-Class Dual-Earner Couples

The Cornell Couples and Careers Study draws on data from focus groups and in-depth interviews conducted in 1997 and 1998 with members of dual-earner couples in upstate New York. We focus on middle-class couples. Our goal is to understand how those with the most resources—middle-class managers and professionals and their spouses—think about and strategize their lives. Lamont (1992) notes that college-educated managers, professionals, and business persons are likely to be gatekeepers in organizations and professions, controlling valuable resources and setting a general style through the perpetuation of their values via the mass media (See Lamont pp. 1–14 for discussion.) This is true not only for professionals and policy elites in places like New York City and Washington, DC but also for the middle-class professionals who comprise the elite in the majority of occupational and residential settings, including small towns and mid-sized, regional cities. The work-family strategies of the kinds of dual-earner couples whom we study may have a social impact beyond their own lives.

We use couples as the unit of analysis and we examine their combined strategies and subjective definitions regarding the meshing of work and family in their lives (cf. Hochschild, 1997). We attempt to understand how work-family strategies of couples differ or remain the same at various stages of the life course (Moen & Wethington, 1992; Moen & Yu, in press). Our goal is to conceptualize dual-earner couples as decision-making units, to understand couples' patterns of and plans for meshing work and family across the life course as they interweave work and family careers (cf. Han & Moen, 1997, 1999).

Respondents are employees from seven up-state New York companies that are participating in the Cornell Couples and Careers Study—two educational institutions, three private industry firms, two healthcare organizations. At each company, exempt employees (salaried workers) received letters from their human resources vice-president and from the director of the Cornell study inviting their participation. Those willing to participate replied directly to the Cornell Careers Institute. This procedure, designed to respect the confidentiality of company employee lists, does not permit us to calculate a response rate. Our respondents, however, reflect the range of occupations in the companies polled and include both men and women from a wide range of life stages.

From this pool, respondents were randomly chosen for interviews. For over half the couples profiled (56%), both spouses were interviewed (each singly, not in a pair). In the rest of the couples, either the man or the woman was interviewed. Most interviews were conducted by telephone. The exception is that two couples were interviewed in person, together, due to their strong preference. Interviews were taped and transcribed; transcriptions included an initial summary and for each question a paraphrased answer, along with extended verbatim quotations for most questions.

The analysis reported here is based on 117 interviews with working men and women at various life-course stages who are members of dual-earner couples. Our interviewees range in age from 21 to 67 years of age. Most were in the 25-54 age range. (See Table 32.1.) About two thirds have children, and one third do not.

We used an open-ended semi-structured interview schedule. Interviews averaged around an hour in length. After ascertaining the respondent's age, marital status, number of children, and current job title, interviewers asked a series of questions about the respondent's employment background and characteristics and how the couple manages work and family responsibilities. In each case follow-up questions that are not included here might have been asked for clarification, and interviewers were instructed to skip a question if the respondent had answered it in a previous response. In addition, some respondents were asked focus questions at the end of the core questions, if time permitted. These included questions about how they use free time, how they use technologies like cell phones and email to manage their work and family lives, and how they use support networks and other resources.

Answers are the primary data used in this analysis. Answers were coded inductively to identify couple-level work-family strategies using Strauss' (1987) guide-lines for developing codes that capture the relationship between structural conditions, actors' perceptions, and actors' interactions. The codes were inductive but also shaped by the structure of the interview questions, which asked specifically about both partners' work commitments and whether there had been any change in expectations about work and family over the life course. A small group of interviews (15) was used to develop an initial coding scheme. The three broad categories of strategies used here were developed based on this set of interviews, and then the rest of the interviews were coded with this initial scheme. This kind of stepwise coding increases internal validity (Bailey, 1994).

External validity was achieved by having one author code all interviews and the second author code a sample of interviews. Disagreements were adjudicated, and ultimately complete intercoder reliability was achieved. External validity was also achieved by comparing the themes that emerged in the interviews with the themes in the six focus groups (Bailey, 1994). Participants in focus groups were recruited from the same pool as interview respondents; no respondent participated in both an interview and a focus group. Gamson (1992) argues that focus groups reveal the polite social discourse in a given social group on a given issue. The fact that the same themes emerged in focus groups indicates that the work-family strategies that people were willing to talk to us about are the same ones they talk about with each other, and in the same terms. We view this as an indication that these are both articulate and institutionalized strategies.

Table 32.1
In-Depth Interviews by Life Stage

	Anticipatory	Launching	Establishment	Shifting Gears	Total Sample
Age					
Age range (years)	21–30	27–39	35–54	50–62	21–67
Number of interviews	23	26	43	14	117[a]
Average age (years)	27.6	34.5	43.7	54.1	38.9
Marital status					
Single	8 (34.8%)				14 (12%)
Married or living with partner	15 (65.2%)	26 (100%)	43 (100%)	14 (100%)	103 (88%)
Children					
No children	23 (100%)				40 (34.2%)
Expecting		4 (15.4%)			4 (3.4%)
Children		22 (84.6%)	43 (100%)	14 (100%)	73 (62.4%)
Gender					
Female	14 (60.9%)	16 (61.5%)	20 (46.5%)	10 (71.4%)	68 (58.6%)
Male	9 (39.1%)	10 (38.5%)	23 (53.5%)	4 (28.6%)	48 (414%)[b]

Note: *Anticipatory* includes married or single persons aged 21–30 year with no children. *Launching* includes married persons aged 27–39 years with children or expecting children. *Establishment* includes persons aged 35–49 years who are married and have children. *Shifting gears* includes married persons 50–62 years with older children. These life stages are meant to capture meaningful transitions in both career and family formation. For this study, long-term singles and long-term childless persons were not included. A few young singles were asked about their plans for family-formation and career. N = 117.

[a]Includes 10 interviews for which we do not have exact age information and one couple interview. [b]Does not include couple interview.

Our research design is grounded in recent advances in the sociology of culture and in family studies that underscore the importance of subjective meanings in understanding how couples mesh the various aspects of their lives and the role of strategic adaptation to structural constraints. Do couples employ taken-for-granted responses in managing work and family, or do they engage in conscious, reflexive action? Moen and Wethington (1992) argue that adaptive strategies of households play a creative role in shaping social change. Some of the working definitions of a good family life or a good career that emerge in couples' repertoires of work-family strategies in a period of social change become institutionalized and shape the subsequent repertoire of strategies available for future generations (cf. Swidler, 1986, Wuthnow, 1989). Employees, employers, policyma-

kers and scholars both build on and revise this conventional wisdom about the problems and the appropriate solutions associated with dual-earner family life.

Findings

Scaling Back

The conventional depiction of middle-class working couples, especially those in professional or managerial jobs, is of two people heavily invested in climbing their respective career ladders (Hochschild, 1997; Kanter, 1977; Pleck, 1985; Pleck & Staines, 1985; Schor, 1992). But only a few couples in our study fit this stereotypical picture, forging ahead with two demanding careers. They were almost all childless couples in their 20s and 30s or those in their 50s and 60s whose young adult children no longer lived at home. There were several couples with preschoolers who were aggressively pursuing two careers and who relied on full-time paid child-care and other paid household services. Their strategy of hiring a "wife" underscores the difficulty of managing two absorbing careers while simultaneously raising young children.

Most of the couples we interviewed, especially those raising children, were involved in scaling back one or both set[s] of career expectations and activities. Our analysis reveals three specific couple-level strategies of scaling back designed to limit work involvement: placing limits, distinguishing between a job and a career, and trading off (see Table 32.2). Our data underscore the processes by which dual-earner couples strive to keep home bounded and protected from work encroachments (Nippert-Eng, 1996).

The decision to scale back appears to be reflexive and conscious. The couples we interviewed recognized the demanding nature of contemporary careers and were consciously trying to buffer family life from too many work demands, while at the same time maintaining two ties to the workforce. One woman in her 30s, without children and on the staff of a major university, gave a good summary of the tensions that most of the people we talked to expressed when she told us that her biggest challenge is:

> balancing the commitment I feel to both [my husband and my work]. Successfully doing my job to the point I feel it can be done, without being a workaholic, spending enough time with my husband. Getting out of work at a reasonable hour so that we can sit down every night and have a meal together and

Table 32.2
Scaling Back: Three Work-Family Strategies

Strategy	Behavioral Correlates	Status Correlates
Placing Limits	Limiting work encroachments on home time Limiting number of hours worked Refusing to put in "face time" or overtime Turning down jobs with more travel Turning down promotions requiring relocation	Both couple strategy and individual spouse's strategy (typically wives). For women, occurs in all life stages but especially associated with birth of first child; for men, triggered by parenting experiences and career establishment.

Job versus Career	One primary breadwinner (career), one job
	Person with job:
	  is primary caregiver or primarily responsible for home
	  often moves to follow spouse's career opportunities
	  can reduce time worked or while children are small
	Often a traditionally gendered strategy (male career, female job), but there are exceptions
		Individual strategy (66% wives)—but see trading off below. Life stage: launching and shifting gears. For men, career-to-job switch triggered by chance events.

Trading off	Job versus career Placing limits or who has the job and who has the career changes over time, due to career opportunities or life-course-related events; accompanied by a shift in childrearing and home responsibilities	Couple strategy Life stage: throughout the life course, couples trade off job and career statuses.

talk, see where we both are for the day. That's important to me, . . . but it's hard. . . . *The work drives my ability to get out of the office and spend time with family* [italics added].

It was this sense of resisting the demands of a greedy workplace that caused us to label these strategies as scaling back. Respondents were resisting the expectations of a 60—or more—hour work week inherent in many professional careers.

With varying degrees of success, the couples we interviewed were beginning to question—explicitly and in practice—the hierarchy of values that places the demands of work over those of family. The specific strategies they employed—placing limits, having a one-job-one-career marriage, and trading off—for the most part emerged as pragmatic responses to specific decision points that varied over the life course. If the decision to scale back was often a conscious one, the specific manner in which scaling back was achieved was pragmatic and often unremarked.

About 75% of the people that we interviewed reported using at least one of these three scaling-back strategies. Some employed more than one. Typically these strategies operated in tandem with an egalitarian gender ideology and a companionate model of marriage, although in practice these strategies often led to traditionally gendered roles for men and women. Scaling back was also linked to life-course stages and transitions, particularly the bearing and raising of children. Although not everyone who was scaling back had children, virtually everyone raising children was engaged in at least one strategy to scale back the couple's combined commitment to work.

Moreover, these strategies for scaling back the couple's total work commitments tended to be deployed along with a bundle of other strategies for scaling back or lowering expectations in other areas of life. These included limiting the number of children, reducing social commitments and service work, having less leisure time, and reducing expectations for housework. As one woman said during the first focus group, "You can't eat off my floors, but that's not what they're for." This scaling-back of housework often is interpreted as a problem in popular media accounts, but a feminist analysis might applaud any indication of a reversal of the 20th-century trend in the expansion of women's household labor, despite the invention of labor-saving technologies (cf. Brines, 1994; Collins, 1992; Hoy, 1995).

Placing Limits

In general, people manage multiple and contradictory roles and obligations by placing what they see as reasonable limits on the demands that drive them (cf. Goode, 1960). Just over a third of those we spoke with told us about placing limits on the number of hours they work and reducing long-term expectations for career advancement in order to spend more time with family. Others, particularly those with young children, refused to take a new job or a promotion because it would involve too much travel or a relocation that would disrupt their children's lives or their spouse's career. Some talked about refusing to engage in the materialism that they associated with a fast-paced life where career comes first.

Some specifically relocated to (or remained in) upstate New York, deliberately foregoing the style of life they associated with larger cities like New York or Washington, DC. We interpret this to mean that scaling-back may be a regional or context-dependent set of work-family strategies. These forms of placing limits were, for the most part, couple strategies, not just individual strategies. Both partners placed limits on work over the course of their lives, or both partners agreed that one spouse would limit his or her work-time investment.

For example, a few have dropped out of fast-track jobs to be more family centered, like this man who is a software engineer in a small start-up company:

> I was a high-riser at RCA and gave it up to try an entrepreneurial thing that had

lower pay, much higher risk. I wasn't thinking money, just career freedom, and a different lifestyle than living in central New Jersey. So I voted with my feet, I came here, chose a less-stressful lifestyle, work 45 hours a week at most, focus more on stuff outside of work than many of my friends.

Although this engineer did not yet have children, it was in part the anticipation of raising a family that drove his strategic choices. He described himself as more family centered than his wife, ready to start having children and to be an equal co-parent in raising them. For this man, both getting out of a large company and moving to a small town were key to his ability to actually live according to his values—with family and friends as important as work. His wife, quoted above on the importance of getting out of work "at a reasonable hour," described herself as more career focused than her husband, in part because she had not reached the point in her career where she had the respect and autonomy she desired. Nevertheless, she agreed that living in a smaller town and spending their evenings and weekends with friends and family or working together to rehabilitate the old house they bought were more important than trying a fast-track, large-city-centered, career-oriented life, especially because they planned to have children in the next few years.

Others reported reducing their working hours due to family demands. Two women in their 40s, both managers in large companies, talked about strategies for cutting back hours. One told us that, despite the pressure to put in face time, she had refused to work weekends when her two children were younger, instead putting in more time only when her children entered high school. The other manager said, "I believe very strongly that you don't have to put [in] sixty hours to do a good job. I refuse to do this. I don't believe in staying if I don't have work to do."

This woman said that she patterned her choices on those of a former boss, a man who "put his family ahead of his job and still continued to do well." She tried for efficiency and would come in early or work during lunch if need be, but she would not "play the game of staying later than my boss." She felt that her performance spoke for itself and that resisting the overtime pressure in her department and living by her own values about working "reasonable, efficient hours" had not hurt her. She had received five promotions in five years.

Only a third of those who talked about placing limits were men. This was almost always associated with their experiences of fathering and a desire to spend more time with their children. Most of the men who were placing limits were in their 40s, and many contrasted their experiences of spending time with their children with their own experiences growing up. When a manager in a large company, who had two school-aged children, told us he really wanted to "be there for the special things" like recitals, school plays, and baseball games because his father never was for him, he echoed a common theme.

Two thirds of those placing limits were women. Not surprisingly, women were more likely to turn down a job that required a move or more travel or were more likely to reduce working hours while their children were at home (cf. Bielby & Bielby, 1992). For women, placing limits was most typically associated with having young children at home. However, unlike male respondents, a significant portion of the women we spoke with placed limits on paid employment across all ages and life-course stages, even when there were no children in the home.

Placing limits is similar to the work-family strategies that Hertz (1986) noted. Our study suggests that this strategy has become institutionalized among dual-earner professional and managerial couples. Despite being a common strategy, it is not an easy one to implement. It requires more flexibility and autonomy than even many managers and professionals have and years of concerted, coordinated effort. One of our respondents managed a child-care center at a large organization and was married to a man who worked for the federal government. In their late 40s, they had school-aged children. They both worked 40–45 hours a week, and both reported finding their jobs challenging and interesting. Between them they worked one weekend and three to four evenings a month. She described this as "a great life," and she told us that it allowed her to meet her life-long goals to have both children and a "great job."

But in her description of both her own and her husband's career trajectories, it is possible to see just how much effort went into achieving this great life, with enough time for all the important things. Along the way, she suffered serious depression after going back to work when her daughter was born. They have had several career-related moves, have gone through periods of greatly reduced income and underemployment, and have experienced their own time-bind, like the year when both she and her husband were working full-time and had two preschoolers at home, and he was finishing the written work for his doctorate. She described their present life as the consequence of both "perseverance and luck" in finally finding jobs that are good for each of them yet compatible with their goal of having a rich and rewarding family life.

Job Versus Career

The people we interviewed typically found it difficult to articulate an ideal family life. But if what it means to have an ideal family is variable or pluralistic (Skolnick, 1991), most of those we interviewed did have some sense that, in their working lives, what is ideal is more than just a job—it is a career. Not everyone saw themselves as having a career, and some said that they preferred not to pursue a career for family reasons. But virtually everyone in this sample of middle-class dual-earner couples seemed to understand the distinction between careers and jobs. Jobs were understood to be ad hoc and flexible, more about making money than intrinsic satisfaction. Careers progress in a straight line, and

change less often, and are rewarding in themselves.

In almost 40% of the couples we interviewed, one person had what was perceived by both as a job and the other person had what was perceived by both parties as a career. One woman in her 20s who was planning to start a family soon said of her husband's work, "He has more heart into his career. Mine's just a job. I feel this is a job, just to pay the bills." She went on to say that "I like what I do, but I don't really consider it . . . what I was born to do." Her husband, however, did feel that he was born to do his work as a research scientist. One woman who had recently become a mother and was working part-time in a large private company said she "had had a career in the past but now had a job, but would have a career again" when her daughter was older. When asked what distinguished the job from the career, she said, "Nothing. I'm doing the same thing. It's my attitude." Her husband was involved in his own career. She was the one scaling back by negotiating to work part-time, but she saw this as a couple strategy, a choice they made together.

This strategy allowed for flexible timing in at least two important ways. First, it reduced the strain of a job search and relocation on a marriage because it was generally understood that the person with the career would take advantage of career opportunities when they arose, but the person with the job would follow or accommodate (Bielby & Bielby, 1992). There were variations on this, of course. As one woman said, "I refuse to move without a job; I've seen too many women do that." Even though her husband's career determined where they moved, she would have veto power if she could not find at least a job of her own. The one-job, one-career strategy also allowed one person to drop in and out of work or to rearrange work for short periods in order to raise young children or to respond to specific family crises.

Like placing limits, the job versus career strategy tended to be gendered. In over two-thirds of the couples in our sample who used a one-job, one-career strategy, the woman had the job and the man the career.

This strategy was especially prevalent among the older couples we interviewed, those in their 50s and 60s. Older women would tell us that having a job and not a career made it easier for them to fulfill a modified form of the traditional female caretaker role (Hays, 1996), taking time off when they had children, something they perceived as valuable for both their families and themselves.

Although more older couples followed this pattern, this does not simply reflect a cohort difference in women's commitment to paid work. Having a one-job, one-career strategy was common in all life-course stages. Younger women talked about starting out with an egalitarian ideology and major career expectations but confronting situations early in marriage that placed them on a job track, not a career trajectory, often without any planning of this shift in goals. Usually, this was the result of their accommodating the birth of a child. Sometimes, it was as a result of an early career opportunity for the husband, who was already better established or who had a firmer idea of what he wanted his career trajectory to be.

This strategy need not always mean that traditional gender roles are perpetuated. In one third of the cases in which couples adapted in this way, the husband had the job and the wife pursued a career. One woman told us:

> We began to realize . . . that my job was going to be the primary job. He tried to work at other jobs during the year, but he wasn't at all happy. So I told him at that point that he had to try to make a go at a career in coaching. Fortunately, he found a part-time job at a college 40 miles away. He hardly earned anything. It was probably less than our babysitting costs. In the meantime, my job was going very well.

The flexibility associated with a job paid off in terms of childcare, as well, for this couple.

> My husband spent a lot of time with our son, and that made it easier for me to pursue my work. Between our wonder-

ful nanny and my husband, I felt very supported in my career. If my husband had had a job like mine, it would have bothered me terribly.

The men we interviewed who opted for a job had done so because of specific circumstances that were somewhat exceptional. For example, several in their 30s and 40s found that their own careers foundered when their wives had come across good career opportunities. This kind of chance occurrence, more than any commitment to reversing traditional gender roles, pushed men into the job role and its accompanying responsibilities. For a few older couples, the man's retirement from his primary management job coincided with his wife's spending more time on her own small business or restarting her career. In one or two young couples, this strategy was a response to the woman's opportunity to pursue graduate study in a top-quality program, while the man had not yet decided on his own career path.

In our sample, men who had jobs also took over many of the primary caretaking responsibilities for the children and the household, although they also got help from their wives and sometimes from paid house cleaners and providers of child-care services. This is in contrast to Brines' (1994) finding that, when men's employment is reduced or eliminated, they often do less housework in order to symbolically bolster their gender identity as males. The difference between our findings and Brines's could reflect the degree of control or choice experienced. The men and women pursuing a one-job, one-career strategy in our sample were doing so as a conscious choice, and they felt good about using this strategy to manage the complexities of his work, her work, and their family. Both men and women who had a job and not a career tended to speak of this as a conscious choice and to say that they were happy about having the flexibility to spend more time with their children. In addition, satisfaction with the job role for both men and women may be linked to the perception of this status as temporary. Most told us that they planned to resume a more typical career orientation later. The experiences of other couples in our sample suggest that these expectations are realistic. Many couples did trade who had the job and who had the career over the life course.

Trading Off

For some couples, trading off was part of a larger ideal of egalitarian sharing. It was also a life-course strategy. Couples traded other strategies (such as placing limits and one-job, one-career) over the course of their lives. Just over a third of the couples we spoke with used a strategy of trading off, either between who has the job and who has the career or between who placed limits on work hours to spend more time at home and who did not.

One woman, who followed her husband to graduate school and supported him early in his artistic career, found a challenging and exciting career for herself as assistant controller of a large corporation, just at the point when her husband began to run into career roadblocks. He began doing some freelance art work but focused on home and children while she had the primary career. Her recent promotion caused her to reflect:

> He has picked up the slack at home. I don't know what I would have done if he continued with his career and I took on this greater responsibility. We would have figured something out. . . . He has cut back a lot. He is the one who picks up the children and takes them to all their events. He has become involved in the community. He is now a soccer coach for our son's team. He could not have done this.... He's cut back on his hours a lot. Right now, he has a few things in the works and eventually will take a new job. His career situation has eased this situation immensely.

This man planned to pick up his career again, not stay in a job as a permanent strategy.

Trading off was also a strategy that allowed couples to readjust from a one-job, one-career marriage to a two-career marriage. In effect, this allowed the couples to have it all, to scale back as needed and yet to manage over the life course to invest in two careers at different life stages. In many cases, a man in his late 40s, 50s, or early 60s had reached a stage in his own career when he had more discretion and was able to place limits on his own work hours without hurting his career. Tenured professors and upper-middle managers told us about coming home early to meet the kids after school or doing more child care and cooking while their wives put in longer hours again, emphasizing their own career after a period when they had been invested more heavily in home and children.

Discussion and Conclusions

Dual-earner couples are increasingly the focus of scholarly attention, and the emphasis, especially in recent work, has been on the full-speed-ahead dual-career couple. Our findings point to a wider range of strategies, even in a sample of managers and professionals who could have been expected to follow a high-powered, two-career lifestyle. Our analysis highlights the importance of incorporating a life-course perspective and a critical analysis of gender into the study of the experiences and strategies of dual-earner couples and suggests a different way to think about the relationship between greedy work and home life for middle-class dual-earner couples.

Gender, the Life Course, and Scaling Back

Our research suggests that people employ specific scaling-back strategies at various life stages and that men and women do so differently. The initial impetus in adopting a one-job, one-career strategy is often the birth of a first child. This strategy is mostly enacted by women. Women's definition of their employment as a job or a career, particularly, is linked to the ages of their children. In contrast, a strategy of placing limits is used by our female respondents at all life-course stages.

For men, placing limits is often triggered by life-stage transitions, particularly parenting experiences or entering a more established phase of their careers. Most of the men using a strategy of placing limits began doing so after they had established themselves in their careers and had achieved an acceptable level of flexibility and autonomy. This reverses the pattern found in the 1970s (Scanzoni, 1980) in which men accrued and retained privileges in marriage as a result of their occupational prestige. But this reversal occurs only for some of the men in our study. In contrast, having a job, for men, seems less linked to a particular life-course stage and more to chance events and turning points in their working lives or their wives' careers (Abbott, 1997). Unlike Brines (1994), we found that men in jobs were willing to pick up the slack at home. The evolving links between life-course stage, gender, and work-family strategies appear to be both complicated and in flux.

Our data underscore the key role that early expectations and chance events—turning points—play in gendering the management of work and family responsibilities over the life course. For example, an important turning point seems to be the discovery by one person early in their career trajectory (roughly in their 20s to early 30s) of an exceptionally good career opportunity. The person whose career takes off first may be the one who subsequently has the primary career during a significant proportion of the life course. Differential gender socialization shapes this process. A few of the women we interviewed reported always knowing that they would have a high-powered career and arranging their family lives accordingly, but most did not. By contrast, it was more common for men to be career-oriented and on a career track earlier in their lives. (One woman told us her husband knew what his career would be "since he was 3 years old.") More generally, men were less prone than women to a lengthy process of casting about to find the right job or a satisfying career. Despite the egalitarian gender ideology that underlies the strategy of scaling back (Schwartz,

1994), uneven gender outcomes often result.

Work Constraints and Spillover

We found in these interviews an unquestioned primacy of paid work. When we asked people about their ideal careers, they did not usually mention family. But when we asked about their ideal families, most people mentioned work spontaneously. The career that people in our sample envision is the consuming career of the high-powered manager or professional—long hours spent at something seen as demanding and rewarding with linear advancement and domestic life arranged around its demands for mobility. Even if people cannot always attain this, it is the goal for most, and usually at least one person in the couple achieves it.

We also found, as did Hochschild (1997), that a language of time management is being applied to the home. There is a professionalization of the discourse surrounding family life. The ideal family, respondents told us, is one of teamwork, partnership, and fairness where both partners can be challenged and fulfilled. This is remarkably similar to the way in which these managers and professionals talk about their work, emphasizing many of the same aspects that they value in their careers.

Sometimes, this way of managing home life in relationship to overarching occupational demands works out well for all concerned. One man told us laughingly of "Wegman's day," his strategy for making the weekly grocery shopping into fun time with his son, a strategy that arose out of his realization that otherwise there simply is not enough time in a given week for him and his wife to go to work, take care of household needs, and spend time with their children. Wegman's day is a fun and creative solution to time-consuming demands and need not be disparaged simply because it is different from past work-family strategies.

But other examples show the limits of managing the home in the same way that one would manage a problem at work. One woman told us despairingly of the sadness her young son felt when they moved to a new area where both she and her husband were working long hours. She was extremely frustrated because she could not justify taking time off to comfort her son—he was not ill, he was "just sad." There is no policy for taking time off when children are sad. And her son was not just blue for a little while; he was sad for months. His parents were disturbed, but neither of them seriously felt that they could take a leave to spend time with him to help him adjust to the move. More generally, we found that other patterns, like dropping out of the labor force entirely for long periods while children are young, are either not envisioned or are seldom utilized by our respondents, as is evident in this woman's remark:

> I'd like to not work, to raise my kids, just up until they're in school, then work part-time while they're in school, but that's not going to happen. That's my dream, but that's not going to happen.

We did not find in our sample the transfer of emotional allegiance from home to work that Hochschild (1997) found at Amerco. Our respondents are enjoying their work, but they are not spending time there at the expense of home, and they do not enjoy work more than home, nor have they transferred their emotional commitment from family relationships to work friendships. But they do feel that their family time and personal lives are being squeezed by the demands of long working hours. And although the strategies that couples use for the most part reduce the intrusion of work into the home, they also involve some of the time-management aspects of home life that Hochschild finds troubling.

Our evidence suggests the strategy of scaling back has two faces. While some respondents have made a conscious decision to put family first and make serious career sacrifices to accommodate a more holistic sense of their family's needs, others are scaling back in order to carve out enough time from an encroaching workload to maintain any sense of family relationship at all. Both represent pragmatic choices (cf. Breiger, 1995) in the face of the structural imperatives of the organization of work and the situational imperatives of personal and family relations. Scaling back represents a private, family-level response to what is too often depicted as a private, family-level trouble, rather than a public issue (Mills, 1959).

Private Strategies Versus Public Solutions

Scaling-back strategies are privatized in the sense that they take for granted that the solutions to work-family problems must be provided by individuals and families. As such, the dominant theme in talking about family life in these interviews was the value of flexibility. Rather than an ideal family being a specific bundle of roles, relationships, and decisions made by a pre-set routine, an ideal family for these respondents involves flexibility, mutual support, trading off, caring—a certain way of doing things and making decisions that is adaptable and can be applied across a complicated and changing set of conditions and situations. Some respondents said that an ideal family would include children. Others were less in accord even on this point.

Flexibility is what most of these managers and professionals want in the workplace, as well. On the whole, the managers and professionals we spoke with reject the idea that the government should mandate policies to help members of dual-earner couples care for their children or require companies to adopt such family-oriented programs as flex-time and job sharing. Although some younger respondents did call for such reforms, others were more likely to favor on-site day care and extended family leave instead of more radical kinds of changes in the structure of work or careers. These attitudes provide little impetus for policy change. A professional who works in a small office, voicing a typical theme, told us about why he did not like the Family Leave Act:

Everybody is different. The player is different, the workplace is different. If you are sick, you go home. If not, you go to work. . . . [In my group] it's like 15 or 20 people who are very close and make decisions among themselves, nothing in writing, nothing in contract. If something goes wrong, we are here to back you up. I like that because it goes on faith, as opposed to some piece of paper.

This man has found a supportive environment. Flexibility works for him, with everyone in his office covering for each other when the children are sick or when there is some other home-related emergency.

Yet many of the people in our sample in lower-level managerial jobs told us that they do not have the kind of flexibility that this man had found. These respondents provide an important counter-theme in our interviews: instead of informal workplace understandings that give flexibility, this group of respondents strongly prefer formal policies that guarantee them rights. Being able to approach one's manager for time off with a sick child puts one in the position of having to request (or even beg for) something that ought to be taken for granted.

Over 10 years ago Hertz (1986) found privatization of work-family strategies among the dual-earner couples she studied. Our study suggests that privatization has become widely institutionalized among middle-class dual-earner couples. Rather than challenging established social hierarchies, privatization is rooted in them. Women reduce their work commitment when they bear and raise children. Even if they resume a more career-oriented focus later, they often have damaged their long-term occupational attainment and have reproduced gender stratification. Privatization is rooted in other forms of social hierarchy, as well. It is a good fit with the interests of businesses because it places the costs of adapting to social change on families instead of employers. It is a good fit with the assumptions of independence and autonomy with which managers and professionals are comfortable, while leaving the needs and preferences [of] lower-level employees unaddressed.

Context and Limitations

Small-scale studies are highly contextual, and one crucial context is the workplace environment. We draw our couples from a variety of company settings in upstate New York, and find a subsequently wider range of work-family strategies than does Hochschild (1997), who draws her sample from just one workplace.

Region is an important aspect of context, as well. Several of our respondents explicitly linked their scaling-back strategies to their decision to live in upstate New York, foregoing the fast-track lifestyle they associated with large metropolises. More people actually live and work in medium-sized cities and small towns like those in upstate New York than live in the large urban centers of Boston, Chicago, Los Angeles, New York, and Washington, DC. This may be a context that is systematically overlooked by the media and academicians who focus on large urban centers in their analysis of work and family life.

The dual-earner couple is an evolving social form that spans social class, regional, and ethnic boundaries. We have documented a diversity of work-family strategies in one sample of White, middle-class couples, but more study is needed to document the diversity in work-family strategies across other lines of social division. Scaling back may presuppose a middle-class set of educational and work opportunities. It is common for managers and professionals to put in 60 hours a week or more, and it is this expectation from which our respondents are scaling back.

Small-scale qualitative studies like this one, based on in-depth interviews and observations, generate good accounts of couples' practices and their understandings of those practices. For example, we find couples who are quite conscious and articulate about resisting the demands of workplaces they perceive as greedy. But they are unable to articulate possibilities for a family life not organized around at least one career.

They talk about their commitment to egalitarian marriage, but they remain unaware of or silent about the fact that women do more scaling back than men, or that this has long-term adverse consequences for women's careers. It is important to understand the perceptions and the silences of this group of couples because of their social location and the influence they have on myriad institutional and organizational settings. Even here, we found more diversity than expected based on the two-career stereotype, but this is only the beginning of understanding the complexities of the experiences of dual-earner couples.

Discussion Questions

1. To what extent are the strategies used by the couples in the Becker and Moen study compatible with those proposed earlier (in Chapter 30) by Jennifer Glass?

2. Do the Becker and Moen findings support those who believe that "you can have it all"—that is, a career and a family?

Penney E. Becker and Phyllis Moen, "Scaling Back: Dual Earner Couples' Work-Family Strategies," in *Journal of Marriage and the Family*, Nov. 1999: 995–1007. Copyrighted 1999 by the National Council on Family Relations, 3989 Central Ave. NE, Suite 550, Minneapolis, MN 55421. Reprinted by permission.

References

Abbott, A. (1997). On the concept of turning point. *Comparative Social Research, l6*, 85–105.

Bailey, K. (1994). *Methods of social research*, (4th ed.). New York: Free Press.

Barnett, R. (1994). Home-to-work spillover revisited: A study of full-time employed women in dual-earner couples. *Journal of Marriage and the Family, 56*, 647–656.

Barnett R., & Rivers, C. (1996). *She works, he works*. New York: Harper Collins.

Bielby, W. T., & Bielby, D. D. (1992). I will follow him: Family ties, gender-role beliefs, and reluctance to re-locate for a better job. *American Journal of Sociology, 97*, 1241–1267.

Breiger, R. (1995). Social structure and the phenomenology of attainment. *Annual Review of Sociology 21*, 155–236.

Brines, J. (1994). Economic dependency, gender, and the division of labor at home. *American Journal of Sociology 100*, 652–688.

Collins, R. (1992). Women and the production of status cultures. In M. Lamont & M. Fournier (Eds.) *Cultivating differences* (pp. 213–231). Chicago: University of Chicago Press.

Coser, L. (1974). *Greedy institutions: Patterns of undivided commitment*. New York: Free Press.

Furstenberg, E. (1998). Review of the book *A Generation at Risk*, by P. Amato & A. Booth. *Contemporary Sociology, 27*, 223–226.

Gamson, W. (1992). *Talking politics*. New York: Cambridge University Press.

Gerson, K. (1985). *Hard choices: How women decide about work, career and motherhood*. Berkeley: University of California Press.

Gilbert, L. A. (1988). *Sharing it all: The rewards and struggles of two-career families*. New York: Plenum Press.

Goode, W. J. (1960). A theory of role strain. *American Sociological Review, 25*, 483–496.

Han, S.-K., & Moen, P. (1997). Coupled careers: Men's and women's pathways through work and marriage in the United States. Paper presented at Conference on Couples' Careers in a Dynamic Perspective, Bremen, Germany, June 21.

——. (1999). Work and family over time: A life-course approach. *The Annals of the American Academy of Political and Social Science, 562*, 98–110.

Hays, S. (1996). *The cultural contradictions of motherhood*. New Haven, CT: Yale University Press.

Hertz, R. (1986). *More equal than others: Women and men in dual-career marriages*. Berkeley: University of California Press.

Hill, R. (1970). *Family development in three stages*. Cambridge, England: Schenkman.

Hochschild, A. (1997). *The time bind: When work becomes home and home becomes work*. New York: Metropolitan Books.

Hochschild, A. (with Machung, A.). (1989). *The second shift*. New York: Avon Books.

Hoy, S. (1995). *Chasing dirt: The American pursuit of cleanliness*. New York: Oxford University Press.

Kanter, R. M. (1977). *Work and family in the United States: A critical review and agenda for research and policy*. New York: Russell Sage.

Lamont, M. (1992). *Money, morals, and manners*. Chicago: University of Chicago Press.

Mills, C. W. (1959). *The sociological imagination*. New York: Oxford University Press.

Moen. B, & Wethington, E. (1992). The concept of family adaptive strategies. *Annual Review of Sociology, 18*, 233–251.

Moen, P. (1992). *Women's two roles*. New York: Auburn House.

Moen, P., & Yu, Y. (in press). Having it all: Workers who successfully manage their work and family roles. In T. L. Parcel (Ed.) *Research in the sociology of work*, Vol. 7. Greenwich, CT: JAI Press.

Nippert-Eng, C. (1996). *Home and work: Negotiating boundaries through everyday life.* Chicago: University of Chicago Press.

Pleck, J. H. (1985). *Working wives/working husbands.* Beverly Hills, CA: Sage.

Pleck, J. H., & Staines, G. (1985). Work schedules and family life in two-earner couples. *Journal of Family Issues, 6,* 61–82.

Robinson, J. P., & Godbey, G. (1997). *Time for Life: The surprising ways Americans use their time.* University Park: Pennsylvania State University Press.

Scanzoni, J. H. (1980). *Family decision-making.* Beverly Hills, CA: Sage.

Schnittger, M. H., & Bird, G. W. (1990). Coping among dual-career men and women across the family life-cycle. *Family Relations, 39,* 199–205.

Schor, J. (1992). *The overworked American: The unexpected decline of leisure.* New York: Basic Books.

Schwartz, P. (1994). *Peer marriage: How love between equals really works.* New York: Free Press.

Skinner, D. A., & McCubbin, H. I. (1991). Coping in dual-employed families: Gender differences. *Family Perspective, 25,* 119–134.

Skolnick, A. (1991). *Embattled paradise: The American family in an age of uncertainty.* New York: Basic Books.

Spain, D., & Bianchi, S. (1996). *Balancing act.* New York: Russell Sage Foundation.

Strauss, A. (1987). *Qualitative analysis for the social sciences.* New York: Cambridge University Press.

Swidler, A. (1986). Culture in action: Symbols and strategies. *American Sociological Review, 51,* 273–286.

Wethington, E., & Kessler, R. (1989). Employment, parental responsibility and psychological distress. *Journal of Family Issues, 10,* 527–546.

Wuthnow, R. (1989). *Communities of discourse.* Cambridge, MA: Harvard University Press. ✦

33

Home-to-Job and Job-to-Home Spillover: The Impact of Company Policies and Workplace Culture

*Sue Falter Mennino,
Beth A. Rubin, and
April Brayfield*

In this chapter, Sue Mennino, Beth Rubin, and April Brayfield use data from a national cross-sectional probability sample to examine the effect of availability of two family-friendly policies on work-family conflict. Neither dependent-care benefits nor flextime lessens the negative job-to-home or home-to-job spillover. On the other hand, demanding workplace culture and time pressure on the job increase negative job-to-home spillover.

Ever since Kanter (1977) debunked the myth of separate spheres for work[1] and family, researchers have been examining the nature and extent of the job-family interface. One facet of this interface is the spillover from one domain to the other, whereby experiences in one domain moderate the experiences in the other (Barnett 1994). Spillover conceptually represents the process whereby behaviors, moods, stress, and emotions from one realm of social life affect those in another and vice versa (Williams and Alliger 1994; Frone, Yardley, and Markel 1997).

Spillover can be positive, but our concern is with the negative spillover, or work-family conflict, people experience while trying to balance a job and family in contemporary society (Greenhaus and Parasuraman 1999; Grzywacz, Almeida, and McDonald 2002; Schieman, McBrier, and Van Gundy 2003). Negative spillover occurs when demands from the two domains of job and home compete for an individual's time, energy, and attention (Small and Riley 1990). For example, a worker whose child or elderly parent is ill may be less able to concentrate on the job. Similarly, a worker who is facing a tight deadline at work might have less time to help a child with homework or tend to a leaky roof. This balancing act is likely to become increasingly difficult as businesses attempt to maintain their profitability in the competitive 24/7 global economy, and as the workplace becomes more of a "greedy institution" (Coser 1974; Epstein et al. 1999). Workplaces impinge further and further into peoples' lives, but offer less financial and occupational stability. In so doing, they aggravate employment-related problems such as stress, turnover, and lowered commitment as employees struggle to reconcile increased demands with diminishing resources of time (Rubin 1996; Rubin and Brody 2002).

We use gender theory to guide our analysis of the spillover between job and home life. This theory defines gender as a structure, with established patterns of expected behaviors that constrain individuals (Connell 1987; Lorber 1994; Risman 1998; Martin 2003). The roots of the gender structure lie in the gendered division of labor in society. With the advent of industrialization, work not only became divided into the separate spheres of market work for men and domestic work for women, it also became hierarchically arranged, with (male) market work taking precedence over (female) domestic work (Acker 1990; Ferree 1990; Kelly 1999; Glass 2000). We will argue that, despite some advances in gender equity during the past few decades, the ideology of gendered separate spheres sustains inequalities in two ways. First, the preponderance of this ideology maintains an inequality between women and men, who do not share equally in the work of household maintenance and childrearing in the domestic sphere, nor do they share equally in the responsibilities and rewards in the public sphere. Second, this ideology also maintains the primacy of market work over domestic work—for both women and men—by rewarding employees who seem most committed to their jobs and who do not appear to allow family obligations to infringe on that commitment.

Gender theory illustrates how the public and private spheres of work are gendered in the sense that they are ideologically separate and unequal *regardless of the gender of the role incumbents*. Because market work is masculinized (Acker 1990; Collinson and Hearn 1994; Martin 2003) and because masculinity holds greater value than femininity (Scott 1986; Foster 1999; Kelly 1999), market work is valued over domestic work. For example, those who achieve the highest workplace success are those who practice masculinity (Wajcman 1999) not only by engaging in practices and behaviors culturally associated with masculinity but more so by prioritizing market work over domestic work (Martin 2003). Achieving job-family integration thus requires a collective ideological shift away from gendered separate spheres (Greenhaus and Parasuraman 1999; Kelly 1999; Boweri 2000; Gerson 2000; Glass 2000); understanding the mechanisms that affect job-to-home spillover is a step in that direction.

Gender theory allows us to study the social structure of gender by separating the gender of specific social roles from the gender of the occupants of those roles (Ferree 1990) and by separating the gender of each work sphere from the gender of the participants in those spheres.

Gender theory, however, does not adequately explain why the availability of formal family-friendly policies does not reduce negative spillover. Companies have implemented a host of such policies that should gradually degender the workplace by facilitating the integration of job and home life for both women and men. As competitive pressures put increasing demands on companies to retain highly productive workers, companies can ill afford the decreased commitment and increased stress that chronic negative spillover can create, both of which research shows decrease overall productivity (Kirchmeyer 1993; Meyer and Allen 1997). Likewise, employers can ill afford the loss of talented labor that the absence of family-friendly policies might cause. Hence, employers often establish formal company policies, particularly flexible working arrangements, to alleviate these problems (Allen 2001). Child care benefits and flextime, in particular, have emerged as cost-effective ways to attract and keep valuable employees, especially women (Goodstein 1994; Osterman 1995; Witkowski 1999).

While the existence of such policies may increase the attractiveness of the employer to potential and incumbent employees, the usefulness of these policies in reducing negative spillover is questionable. Employees often assume that despite a formal structure of family-friendly policies, actually invoking them will result in curtailed career trajectories (Kossek, Barber, and Winters 1999; Thompson, Beauvais, and Lyness 1999). There is mounting evidence that the *culture* of a workplace, more so than the availability of work-family policies, is more likely to affect an employee's ability to effectively manage a job and a family (Galinsky, Bond, and Friedman 1996; Thompson et al. 1999; Allen 2001). Family-friendly cultures are found in work organizations with environments that are universally supportive of job-family integration. Since cultures carry taken-for-granted assumptions and normative expectations for behavior, we also use neo-institutional theory to examine the effects of both the formal policies and the informal norms of workplace organizations on negative spillover since this theory addresses such issues directly.

Neo-institutional theory is particularly useful for understanding such slippage between organizational policies and practices. This theory has a variety of goals (DiMaggio and Powell 1991)[2] but most generally examine the relationship between organizations and their environments to make sense of socially constructed organizational practices. For example, within neo-institutional theory, the presence of family-friendly policies can be explained not only in the aforementioned economic terms, that is, preserving and in recruiting talented labor, but also as a response to mimetic pressures to maintain legitimacy within organizational fields in which incorporating family-friendly policies is normative. The particular project of neo-institutional analysis that is of relevance here is the examination and explanation of the gap between organizational reality and the formal accounts of that reality (Meyer and Rowan 1977; DiMaggio and Powell 1991). For these insights, we turn to the more microcomponents of neo-institutional theory that focus on the interactive and cultural components of organizational life.

These aspects of neo-institutional theory point us to the basic observation that social relations, both within and outside of organizations, are reproduced through everyday interaction, and these interactions, in conjunction with formal rules and procedures, shape the behavior of individuals in organizations (Meyer and Rowen 1977; DiMaggio and Powell 1991; Zucker 1991). A key insight of neo-institutionalism is that institutions, such as gendered separate spheres, are associated with standardized behaviors, activities, and expectations containing taken-for-granted rationales (Jepperson 1991). Thus, inasmuch as separate spheres ideology has been institutionalized in organizational structures and practices, simply creating "family-friendly" policies is insufficient for reducing spillover. In order for family-friendly policies to have that outcome, they would need to become part of the taken-for-grantedness of organizational life.

In other words, if the strict separation of home and the workplace is the normalized interactional pattern within a workplace, formal company policies that challenge that assumption will be ineffective. In addition, the success of such policies depends on two prerequisites: they must be equally available to male as well as female workers, and those who use the policies must not suffer any deleterious consequences.

Neo-institutional theory, combined with gender theory, improves on the more frequently used role theory in prior spillover research (e.g., Gutek, Searle, and Klepa 1991; Duxbury, Higgins, and Lee 1994; Schieman et al. 2003). Although gendered social roles are a vital piece of the work-family puzzle, role theory alone offers an incomplete explanation of negative spillover between the job and home because it relies primarily on biological differences and childhood socialization to explain gender differences. Similarly, it ignores the power differential inherent in the gender structure (Connell 1987; Ferree 1990; Risman 1998). Our study focuses on the social roles of paid worker and family member, but goes beyond much of the previous research. We do so by combining gender theory with neo-institutional theory. We examine the relationships among the formal structures of work organizations and the taken-for-granted expectations about work and family to explain the persistence of negative spillover even in the presence of family-friendly policies. We contend, along with others (e.g., Barnett 1999; Greenhaus and Parasuraman 1999), that a sociological understanding of the job-family interface entails a multidimensional analytic lens that examines not only individuals and organizations, but also includes ideologies about work and family that are the deeply held beliefs of individuals and components of organizational culture. Toward these objectives, we use data from the *1997 National Study of the Changing Workforce* (NSCW) (Bond, Galinsky, and Swanberg 1998) to investigate how company policies and cultures, along with job characteristics and family configurations, together influence negative home-to-job and job-to-home spillover.

Determinants of Negative Spillover

Gender theory treats gender as a social structure that is concurrently part of our individual identity and part of the organizational schema of institutions that are maintained by daily interactions between individuals (Lorber 1994; Ridgeway 1997; Risman 1998). Neoinstitutional theory explains why it is quite difficult to challenge the gender system with formal company policies once that system has become part of normative interactional patterns in workplaces. We argue that job-to-home and home-to-job spillover for women and men is determined dynamically and simultaneously not only by a person's sex, individual household, and job circumstances, but more so by the larger gender system that is institutionalized within the family, the workplace, and the economy. In this section we develop research hypotheses about these relationships.

Gender of the Individual

Perhaps the first question about spillover is: To what degree do the causes and consequences of spillover differ for women and men? Despite a trend toward more egalitarian attitudes about gender behavior (Thornton 1989), both women and men gravitate toward a traditional division of labor in the home, especially if they have children (Sanchez and Thomson 1997; Kaufman and Uhlenberg 2000). Even though most women contribute to the family income and many men help out with the housework and child care, women and men strive to maintain the traditional identities

of women as primary family caregivers and men as breadwinners, for themselves as well as for their partners (Potuchek 1997; Deutsch and Saxon 1998). These behavioral patterns, in turn, contribute to the maintenance of traditional gender ideology whereby women often are more involved than men in the home sphere (Thompson and Walker 1989; Risman 1998). As a result, women and men may very well experience and report spillover differently.

The findings on the spillover differences between women and men are inconsistent in this regard. Some researchers find that women and men experience similar levels of spillover (Frone, Russell, and Cooper 1992; Barnett 1994; Eagle, Miles, and Icenogle 1997), and a few find differences between women and men either only in one direction or only under certain conditions (Gutek et al. 1991; Duxbury et al. 1994; Gignac, Kelloway, and Gottlieb 1996). Nevertheless, several researchers find that women report higher levels of spillover than do men, especially home-to-job spillover (Duxbury and Higgins 1994; Kirchmeyer 1995). Because of the preponderance of traditional gender ideology, women may take more responsibility for work in the home and be more aware of the ways in which employment encroaches on family life. Accordingly, we expect that women will experience higher levels of spillover in both directions than will men.

Family-Friendly Company Policies

Many companies today are striving to appear more family friendly, usually to increase employee productivity and to reduce employee turnover costs (Witkowski 1999). Toward this end, employers have developed a variety of policies that include such things as support for dependent care in the form of referral services for child or elder care, cash subsidies, pretax salary set-asides, and, less frequently, on-site or near-site child care centers (Galinsky and Stein 1990; Ferber, O'Farrell, and Allen 1991; Kelly 1999). In addition, the temporal and spatial structures of work reflect a company's potential family-friendliness. Flexible working arrangements such as flextime, job-sharing, and work-at-home policies are some of the initiatives that both employees and employers consider to be family-friendly (Wiatrowski 1990; Kelly 1999). Of course, flexible employment policies are often as much about facilitating employers' flexible deployment of labor as they are about facilitating employee's flexible use of time (Harrison 1994; Rubin 1995; Vallas 1999). Thus, companies use temporary or part-time employment to increase their competitiveness and create flexibility regardless of employees' preferences.[3] When flexibility takes this form, it often increases the problems of resolving the tensions between the demands of home and family since irregular schedules can make resolving the pressures between home and work even more difficult.

Despite these caveats, research points to the family-friendly policies as mutually beneficial for employers and employees. Employees in companies that offer dependent benefits and flexible working options report lower absenteeism and tardiness rates, higher morale, higher job satisfaction, higher employer loyalty, and lower turnover rates (Galinsky and Stein 1990; Thompson et al. 1999; Roehling, Roehling, and Moen 2001). While beneficial in a number of ways, it is unclear whether these specific policies reduce negative spillover. Some studies show that the availability of family benefits (Thompson et al. 1999) and flexible scheduling (Thomas and Ganster 1995) reduce job-to-home spillover; other studies provide evidence that they do not (Warren and Johnson 1995; Galinsky et al. 1996).

Part of the inconsistency in results may reflect the gender-specific impact of the effects. The persistence of gendered expectations for women's versus men's homemaking responsibilities, as well as women's increased participation at all levels of the labor market, suggests that family-friendly policies are often geared toward attracting and retaining desirable female workers rather than reflecting employers' genuine efforts to alleviate tension between home

and job responsibilities (Wiatrowski 1990; Kelly 1999; Witkowski 1999).

Consistent with these gendered status expectations (Ridgeway 1997), empirical evidence demonstrates that both women and men in the workplace perceive family-friendly policies as women's policies and women are, in fact, more likely than men to use such policies (Sandberg 1999; Thompson et al. 1999; Gerstel and Clawson 2001). Moreover, companies who have more female employees are more likely than other companies to offer such policies (Goodstein 1994; Osterman 1995). There is little empirical support, however, to demonstrate that the availability of family-friendly policies successfully reduces spillover for either women or men. Accordingly, because of the prevalence and persistence of the separate spheres ideology with its integral valorization of work over the domestic sphere, and the power of normative expectations to shape behaviors in the workplace, we expect that the availability of family-friendly policies will have *no* effect on negative spillover for either women or men.

Workplace Environment

Neo-institutional theory suggests that workplace culture encompasses far more than employment practices. It includes the informal rules about how relationships "should be structured" (Fligstein 2001). The shared set of beliefs about the norms, values, and goals of an organization comprise workplace culture and its informal structure (Gherardi 1994). The norms about interactions, including, we argue, those surrounding workplace and family roles, lead to routinized and stable outcomes (Meyer and Rowan 1977; DiMaggio and Powell 1983). The assumptions about the relationship of family to the workplace, then, are an integral component of workplace culture.

Inasmuch as workplace practices become embedded in the normative expectations associated with the employing organization, they become taken for granted; the informal environment of an organization reflects that culture. For example, the unspoken assumption in an organization that employees leave their family at the door reflects the family-unfriendly norm of separate spheres. Conversely, an organization where most of the employees routinely take time during regular work hours to tend to family or personal matters with no fear of reprisal demonstrates a more family-friendly workplace culture.

Only a few researchers have evaluated the relationship between workplace culture and spillover and these have tested spillover in only one direction. These studies consistently demonstrate that a supportive workplace culture reduces job-to-home spillover (Warren and Johnson 1995; Galinsky et al. 1996; Thompson et al. 1999). These results are consistent with the neo-institutional arguments that cultures "carry" rules, procedures, and goals that are institutionalized, but not necessarily represented in the policies of a formal organization (Jepperson 1991:150). Accordingly, we test the hypothesis that the culture of a workplace, despite the existence of formal company policies, is the strongest influence on an individual's ability to successfully balance job and home responsibilities.

Workplace environment also includes the conditions of the job itself. Research demonstrates that particular job characteristics also affect spillover. Workers in high-pressure jobs, whether the pressure stems from long hours, a professional position, or unrelenting demands from employers, often experience greater job-to-home spillover than do other workers (Gutek et al. 1991; Frone et al. 1992; Duxbury and Higgins 1994). Well-paid professional jobs are often the most stressful, requiring not only additional time but also a priority commitment from the worker (Perlow 1997; Rones, Ilg, and Garner 1997; Perlow 1998). Job pressures are not restricted to professional jobs; most employees who feel that they must work hard, work fast, and constantly learn new things also feel enormous job pressures (Rubin 1996; Vallas 1999). Generally, employees in many occupations are working longer hours than ever before (Rones et al. 1997). There is growing evi-

dence, however, that these long hours are not always a result of increased job demands, but rather emerge out of "time-demanding" organizational cultures that valorize long hours and reward those workers who are willing to sustain them (Perlow 1997; Epstein et al. 1999; Rubin and Brody 2002). This tendency is likely to increase the extent of negative spillover.

The pressures of demanding jobs are accompanied and reinforced by gendered beliefs about the appropriate priorities of the occupants of such positions. That is, given the persistent ideology of gendered separate spheres, all workers, especially those who fill the highly compensated professional positions, are expected to behave as traditional male breadwinners and prioritize workplace demands over family demands, regardless of their actual sex or family situation (Collinson and Collinson 1997; Epstein et al. 1999). We therefore expect that both women and men with demanding jobs will experience the highest levels of negative spillover.

Family Characteristics

Researchers generally find that greater family demands cause higher levels of home-to-job spillover (Crouter 1984; Gignac et al. 1996). Workers with greater household responsibilities carry over more of those responsibilities into the workplace (Gutek et al. 1991). For example, workers can be distracted by family concerns while on the job, be too tired from doing things for the family to concentrate on the job, or spend time at work taking care of family duties. Not surprisingly, having a spouse or partner and/or children at home adds complexity to a worker's family life, especially for women. Although women and men may share household responsibilities more today than in the past, people tend to exhibit the more traditional behavior of male-breadwinner and female-caregiver in the context of couples and/or parenting relationships (South and Spitze 1994; Sanchez and Thomson 1997). Thus, because coupling and parenting seem to invoke gendered status expectations, we anticipate that workers with a partner and/or children, especially women in those situations, will experience higher levels of home-to-job spillover than will other workers.

Methods

Data and Sample

We use data from the *1997 National Study of the Changing Workforce* (NSCW) (Bond et al. 1998). The NSCW surveyed 3,718 respondents, a national cross-sectional probability sample of 3,381 employed women and men ages 18 through 64 and 337 women who had dependent children who were not in the labor force. For this analysis, we selected only wage and salaried workers (N = 2,877); we eliminated respondents who reported being self-employed because of our interest in the influence of company policies and supervisors on job-to-home spillover. We assume that those who are self-employed do not have supervisors and may also have more influence on the type of company policies available to them. We also deleted respondents with missing data on any of the independent or dependent variables, resulting in a final sample size of 2,334: 1,245 women (53.3 percent) and 1,089 men (46.7 percent).[4]

Measures

Appendix A summarizes the measurement details for all variables in the analysis. We examine two dependent variables: home-to-job spillover and job-to-home spillover. For the items that comprise both of these additive indices, the response categories range from 1 *never* to 5 *very often*; higher scores indicate higher levels of negative home-to-job and job-to-home spillover.[5]

For the independent variables, we focus primarily on workplace characteristics, both the formal policies offered by the employer and the culture of the workplace. We include two measures of formal employer policies: an index of dependent care benefits available to the respondent from the

employer and an indicator of flextime availability.

We use several variables to measure workplace culture. First, we use a variable that indicates whether the respondent's supervisor is supportive about family matters. Studies consistently find that workers with supervisors who are sympathetic about family and personal matters report lower levels of spillover (Thomas and Ganster 1995; Warren and Johnson 1995; Galinsky et al. 1996; Frone et al. 1997; Kossek and Ozeki 1998). Second, we use an index measuring the employee's perception of the family-friendliness of the workplace environment. A family-supportive workplace environment, that is, one with normative expectations that allow employees to balance job and family responsibilities, also reduces job-home conflict (Galinsky and Stein 1990; Warren and Johnson 1995; Thompson et al. 1999).

Several facets of a workplace environment can negatively affect its family-friendliness, for example, expectations regarding work priority over family, perceived damaging career consequences, and employer insensitivity to employee's family responsibilities (Thompson et al. 1999). As another measure of the workplace culture, we include an indicator of how easy it is for employees to take time during the day to attend to family matters at the respondent's workplace. Finally, in this era of economic uncertainty and tenuous job security, many may fear losing their jobs and anxiety may be part of the climate or culture of a workplace (Rubin and Smith 2001; Rubin and Brody 2002). Thus, we also use an indicator of the respondent's feeling of job security.

Workplace culture is one facet of the employee's workplace experience; another is the employee's job itself. We include several variables that measure aspects of the respondent's job. These are the respondent's occupational group, an indicator of the job's exempt status, an indicator of the respondent's perception of time demands on the job, and an index of the amount of autonomy reported by the respondent.

Previous research suggests that there is a difference in spillover levels between workers in different occupational groups. For example, white-collar workers experience higher levels of job-to-home spillover but lower levels of home-to-job spillover than do blue-collar workers (Frone et al. 1992). Similarly, workers in managerial or professional positions report higher levels of job-to-family spillover than do workers in other occupations (Duxbury and Higgins 1994). Whether an employee's job is exempt or nonexempt, however, may also have important implications for spillover. Because exempt employees are not limited by labor legislation as to the amount of time their employers can require them to work, the boundary between employment and home is often less defined for exempt employees than for nonexempt employees (Perlow 1997; Jacobs and Gerson 1998). Thus, we categorize occupations in two ways: by occupational group (executive, administrative, managerial, and professional; technical; sales; administrative support; service; and production, operation, and repair) and by exempt status.

We include a measure of employees' subjective assessment of the time pressures associated with their job. Time pressure on the job, or the feeling of not having enough time to get everything done, is associated with increased feelings of job-family stress (Perlow 1997).

The amount of control people have in their jobs also influences negative spillover. Having the ability to choose when and how a task is completed is an important factor in controlling job-family stress (Duxbury et al. 1994; Edwards and Rothbard 1999). In addition, we use the calculated total weekly hours worked by the respondent, which is the sum of the number of paid hours respondents usually work at their main job, the number of paid and unpaid overtime hours at their main job, and the number of hours respondents usually work at other jobs, if any.

Finally, we include a measure of the respondent's job satisfaction because satisfaction with one's job can mitigate negative job-family spillover (Kossek and Ozeki 1998) and dissatisfaction can increase job-to-home spillover (Gignac et al. 1996).

In addition to workplace and job characteristics, an employee's household configuration can also affect negative spillover. We include in our models three variables that measure different characteristics of the respondent's household. These variables are the respondent's household income, whether the respondent is part of a couple, and the total number of children in the household classified into three age groups (under 6, 6 through 12, and 13 through 17). We classify as part of a couple if the respondent is either married or reports living with a partner in a committed relationship.[6] We also control for respondent's age and level of education.

Findings

Consistent with gender theory, we find that, overall, negative job-to-home spillover ($\bar{x} = 14.7$) is more extensive than negative home-to-job spillover ($\bar{x} = 9.7$; $t = -51.832$, p .000).[7] This finding illustrates the primacy society gives to the workplace over the family (Daniels 1987; Kelly 1999; Ciscel, Sharp, and Heath 2000; Glass 2000). Home-to-job spillover occurs less often than job-to-home spillover because, as gender theory predicts, workers as well as the workplace itself allow fewer intrusions from the home into the workplace; workers adjust their family lives around their jobs rather than vice versa.

Table 33.1 reveals several noteworthy sample characteristics. Not surprisingly, since women typically take on more of the family caregiving responsibilities than do men, women report slightly higher levels of both types of spillover than do men. Interestingly, there are no differences between women and men on several important employment characteristics, including particular occupational categories, time pressure, job satisfaction, and job security. Women and men are equally likely to have dependent benefits available and a supportive supervisor. Men, however, work longer hours and have more job autonomy and flextime availability while women have more supportive workplace cultures. Women and men differ in ways other than employment characteristics. Male respondents are more likely than are female respondents to live with a partner and to have more children under age 6. Male respondents also live in households with higher incomes and have more education than do women.

We use Ordinary Least Squares (OLS) regression to examine the influence of the independent variables on job-to-home and home-to-job spillover. Although some of our variables are moderately correlated, multicollinearity is not a problem. To control for any difference between respondents who were missing income data, we include a missing-data indicator for household income.

The multivariate results present a somewhat different picture of the estimated relationships than do the bivariate results, especially the differences between women and men, and thus we focus our discussion on the regression equations. Overall, our findings show that time pressure on the job is the greatest cause of negative spillover in both directions, as indicated by the standardized coefficients. Moreover, job-to-home spillover is aggravated by the sheer number of hours people spend on the job. Having a domestic partner at home also increases job-to-home spillover, as does having more children in each age group, but to a much lesser extent than time pressure and time commitment. Conversely, being satisfied with one's job strongly decreases spillover in both directions. Moreover, the findings illustrate the powerful effect that an authentically family-friendly workplace culture has on negative spillover. A supportive environment and being able to take time during the day to attend to family matters are vital factors in reducing spillover from job to home.

Net of other effects, women experience far greater levels of job-to-home spillover than do men, and this net gender difference (Table 33.2) is notably much greater than the initial baseline difference (Table 33.1) after other factors, including workplace controls, are taken into account. Yet there is no significant difference between women and men in home-to-job spillover. This finding may be attributed to the limited occurrence of home-to-job spillover and, as we will clarify, may be better explained by factors other than individual sex.

As predicted, family policies have no effect on spillover in either direction.[8] Therefore, the availability of such policies alone does not matter as much as other workplace factors, such as the ability to take advantage of the policies without fear of reprisals.[9]

The results generally support our prediction about workplace culture. Having a supervisor who is supportive about family issues lowers job-to-home spillover. Working in an organization with a supportive environment and one in which it is easy to take time during the day to attend to family matters lowers spillover in both directions. In contrast, the possibility of frequent layoffs increases job-to-home spillover, but has no net effect on home-to-job spillover.

As others have argued, and we concur, making job-family issues visible in the workplace by acknowledging that they are not individual problems but rather social issues that affect workplaces is a necessary facet of a workplace culture that alleviates negative spillover (Barnett 1999; Gerson 2000; Glass 2000). Similarly, our findings demonstrate the supremacy of *informal* over formal attributes of the organization in affecting the negative spillover between home and workplace.

Just as workplace characteristics affect spillover, so do job characteristics. As mentioned earlier, the evidence about the effect of job demands relative to other job characteristics on the two types of spillover is partially supportive of our hypotheses. Working long hours, feeling time pressure on the job, and having little autonomy all contribute to job-to-home spillover, but only feeling time pressure on the job increases the negative spillover from home to job. Being satisfied with one's job decreases both types of spillover.

Contrary to our prediction, however, the type of occupation only affects job-to-home spillover. Executives and managers experience more job-to-home spillover than do service workers. There are no other differ-

Table 33.1
Means and Standard Deviations of the Dependent and Independent Variables by Sex of Respondent

Variables	Women (N = 1,245) Mean	SD	Men (N = 1,089) Mean	SD	t-ratio[a]
Home-to-job spillover	9.83	3.32	9.55	3.44	-1.99*
Job-to-home spillover	14.84	4.88	14.45	4.83	-1.95*
Controls					
Age	40.87	11.94	39.01	11.17	-3.87***
Education					
High school or less	.34	.47	.36	.48	.99
Some college	.36	.48	.29	.45	-3.58***
Four-year degree or higher	.30	.46	.35	.48	2.58**
Job characteristics					
Occupation					
Executive/administrative/ managerial	.16	.36	.17	.37	.67
Professional	.21	.41	.16	.37	-2.70**
Technical	.06	.23	.04	.20	-1.39
Sales	.12	.32	.11	.31	-.89
Administrative support	.25	.43	.06	.23	-13.54***
Service	.12	.32	.09	.29	-2.07*
Production/operation/repair	.09	.30	.37	.48	16.22***
Exempt job position	.38	.48	.37	.48	-.19
Hours worked per week	43.04	12.68	49.56	13.66	11.95***
Never enough time	2.77	1.16	2.79	1.10	.50
Job autonomy	2.96	.74	3.09	.73	4.08***
Job satisfaction	3.36	.70	3.23	.70	1.17
Family characteristics					
Household income	51,113.61	51,688.17	59,772.32	65,571.46	3.51***
Couple	.57	.50	.67	.47	4.82***
Children under 6	.20	.50	.32	.64	4.79***
Children 6–12	.33	.65	.35	.68	.90
Children 13–17	.27	.59	.23	.55	-1.53
Company policies					
Dependent care benefits	1.20	.26	1.20	.27	-.04
Flextime available	.42	.49	.46	.50	1.97*
Workplace culture					
Supervisor support regarding family	3.35	.72	3.31	.69	-1.54
Family supportive environment	3.02	.78	2.95	.75	-2.48**
Easy to take time for family	2.82	1.01	2.90	1.00	-1.82
Frequent layoffs	.10	.30	.10	.30	.01

[a]Difference between women's and men's means.
*p ≤ .05, **p ≤ .01, ***p ≤ .001.

Table 33.2
Ordinary Least Squares Regression Equations for Spillover Models

Variable	Home-to-Job Spillover			Job-to Home Spillover		
	b	S.E.	β	b	S.E.	β
Woman	.254	(.151)	.038	.963	(.191)***	.099
Controls						
Age	−.016	(.006)*	−.054	−.031	(.008)***	−.074
Education (High school or less)						
Some college	.012	(.169)	.002	−.094	(.214)	−.009
Four-year degree or more	.476	(.208)*	.066	.550	(.263)*	.053
Job characteristics						
Occupation (Executive/managerial)						
Professional	.337	(.233)	.039	−.406	(.295)	−.033
Technical	−.410	(.355)	−.026	.044	(.450)	.002
Sales	−.004	(.272)	−.004	−.227	(.344)	−.015
Administrative support	.216	(.258)	.023	−.027	(.326)	−.002
Service	−.234	(.292)	−.021	−.750	(.370)*	−.047
Production/operation/repair	−.289	(.261)	−.036	−.141	(.330)	−.012
Exempt job position	.133	(.166)	.019	.400	(.211)	.040
Hours worked per week	−.005	(.005)	−.021	.059	(.007)***	.165
Never enough time	.536	(.063)***	.180	.922	(.080)***	.216
Job autonomy	.112	(.105)	.025	−.335	(.133)*	−.051
Job satisfaction	−.218	(.092)*	−.056	−.726	(.116)***	−.130
Family characteristics						
Household income[a]	.021	(.120)	.036	−.007	(.150)	−.008
Missing income	−.207	(.306)	−.013	−.327	(.388)	−.015
Couple	−.254	(.150)	−.037	.509	(.190)**	.051
Children under 6	.517	(.125)***	.088	.397	(.159)**	.047
Children 6–12	.306	(.104)**	.060	.424	(.131)***	.058
Children 13–17	.355	(.119)**	.060	.468	(.151)**	.055
Company policies						
Dependent care benefits availability	.019	(.259)	.002	−.344	(.327)	−.019
Flextime available	.024	(.147)	.003	.010	(.186)	.001
Workplace culture						
Supervisor support regarding family	−.088	(.118)	−.018	−.423	(.149)**	−.061
Family supportive environment	−.473	(.103)***	−.107	−.667	(.131)***	−.105
Easy to take time for family	−.247	(.077)**	−.073	−.941	(.097)***	−.195
Frequent layoffs	.410	(.229)	.037	1.768	(.288)**	.048
Intercept		10.474***			16.815***	
Adjusted R^2		.108***			.303***	

Note: N = 2,334. For polytomous categorical variables, the reference category is in parentheses.
[a]Income coefficients multiplied by 10,000.
*p ≤ .05, **p ≤ .01, ***p ≤ .001.

ences in spillover between executives and managers and other occupational groups.

We find mixed support for our predictions about the demands of family circumstances. Not surprisingly, workers with more children in all age groups experience higher levels of both home-to-job and job-to-home spillover than do other workers. Having a partner at home, however, affects only job-to-home spillover.

Both of our control variables achieved statistical significance. Older people experience higher levels of job-to-home spillover than do younger people, perhaps because they may have more responsibilities in both the workplace and at home than younger people. Finally, having at least a four-year college degree increases spillover in both directions.

Taken together, the model explains a much greater percentage of the variance in job-to-home spillover (30 percent) than the variance in home-to-job spillover (11 percent). Undoubtedly, family characteristics other than couple status and number of children, such as the health of family members and care responsibilities for family members residing outside the household, are far more important than these particular workplace characteristics in determining how family life may spill over into the job domain. Several of the variables, however, approach statistical significance in the home-to-job spillover model. These are being female, fear of layoffs, and being single.

Because the models fail to fully explain why women experience higher levels of negative spillover between the workplace and home than do men, we estimated separate models for women and men to further investigate the effect of individual sex on spillover.[10] Table 33.3 presents models for home-to-job spillover; Table 33.4 presents models for job-to-home spillover.

Table 33.3 reveals that most of the same characteristics affect home-to-job spillover in the same ways for women and men, as illustrated by the Z scores. Time pressure on the job is the leading cause of negative home-to-job spillover for both women and men. Having more children under age 6

and more children ages 6 through 12 also increases home-to-job spillover for women and for men. A supportive environment and satisfaction with one's job both help to alleviate home-to-job spillover for both women and men. None of the following variables affect home-to-job spillover for either women or men: occupation type, having an exempt job, working long hours, household income, the availability of dependent care benefits or flextime, level of supervisor support, and fear of layoffs.

Table 33.3 also reveals some differences between women and men in their experience of negative spillover. For women but not for men, having more teenagers and being younger increases home-to-job spillover but being more satisfied with their jobs decreases it. For men only, those with at least a college degree experience higher levels of spillover. Interestingly, having a job in a workplace where it is easy to take time during the day to attend to family helps to lower home-to-job spillover for men but not for women.

We compared the male and female coefficients to determine if there is a statistically significant difference between them (Clogg, Petkova, and Haritou 1995). As the Z scores in Table 33.3 indicate, only job autonomy affects women and men in different ways. Having more job autonomy increases negative home-to-job spillover for men whereas it decreases it for women, although this effect is not significant for women. This unexpected finding illustrates the discrepancy between having more job autonomy, as the men in this study do, and increasing demands on men to be more involved in domestic responsibilities. These combined pressures can only lead to more spillover between home and the workplace unless institutional support is present (Gerson 2002). The separate models explain a similar but small amount of the variance in home-to-job spillover, 11 percent for women and 10 percent for men. In addition, the Chow test F[11] indicates that the predictors have a similar influence on home-to-job spillover women and men.

Table 33.4 reveals many similarities between women and men in the variables that

Table 33.3
Ordinary Least Squares Standardized Regression Coefficients Predicting Negative Job-to-Home Spillover, by Sex of Respondent

Variable	Women (N= 1,245)			Men (N = 1,089)			
	b	S.E.	β	b	S.E.	β	Z
Controls							
Age	−.020	(.008)*	−.071	−.006	(.010)	−.020	1.09
Education (High school or less)							
Some college	−.060	(.226)	−.009	.080	(.258)	.011	−.06
Four–year degree or more	.211	(.287)	.029	.746	(.310)*	.103	1.27
Job characteristics							
Occupation (Executive/managerial)							
Professional	.347	(.315)	.042	.373	(.354)	.040	.05
Technical	−.405	(.462)	−.027	−.322	(.564)	−.019	.11
Sales	−.216	(.373)	−.021	.088	(.402)	.008	.23
Administrative support	.099	(.313)	.013	.613	(.515)	.041	1.18
Service	−.401	(.386)	−.039	.011	(.457)	.001	.65
Production/operation/repair	−.111	(.406)	−.010	−.204	(.371)	−.029	−.17
Exempt job position	.322	(.224)	.047	−.051	(.254)	−.007	−1.10
Hours worked per week	−.004	(.008)	−.017	−.005	(.008)	−.020	−.09
Never enough time	.540	(.086)***	.188	.538	(.095)***	.173	−.02
Job autonomy	−.081	(.138)	−.018	.361	(.165)*	.076	2.05***
Job satisfaction	−.279	(.122)*	−.073	−.176	(.142)	−.044	.55
Family characteristics							
Household income[a]	.119	(.160)	.039	.247	(.190)	.023	.52
Missing income	−.170	(.395)	−.012	−.384	(.489)	−.023	−.34
Couple	−.074	(.195)	−.011	−.450	(.248)	−.062	−1.19
Children under 6	.488	(.191)*	.074	.549	(.173)**	.102	.24
Children 6–12	.352	(.143)*	.069	.297	(.154)*	.059	−.26
Children 13–17	.546	(.156)***	.096	.109	(.190)	.018	−1.78
Company policies							
Dependent care benefits availability	−.162	(.357)	−.013	.190	(.380)	.015	.68
Flextime available	−.136	(.198)	−.020	.230	(.223)	.033	1.23
Workplace culture							
Supervisor support regarding family	−.005	(.158)	−.001	−.203	(.178)	−.040	−.83
Family supportive environment	−.388	(.140)**	−.091	−.565	(.155)***	−.123	−.85
Easy to take time for family	−.171	(.106)	−.052	−.310	(.113)**	−.090	−.90
Frequent layoffs	.552	(.312)	.051	.258	(.338)	.023	−.64
Intercept	10.841***			9.963***			
Adjusted R^2	.108***			.103***			
Chow test F–ratio				.960			

Note: For polytomous categorical variables, the reference category is in parentheses.
[a]Income coefficients multiplied by 10,000.
*p ≤ .05, **p ≤ .01, ***p ≤ .001.

predict job-to-home spillover. Time pressure on the job and working long hours have the greatest effect on job-to-home spillover for both women and men; younger people experience more job-to-home spillover than do older people. Being able to take time during the day for family eases negative job-to-home spillover for both women and men, although this effect is greater for men, as shown by its Z score in Table 33.4. Several variables have no effect on either women's or men's experience of negative spillover. These are occupation type, household income and the availability of family-friendly company policies of dependent care benefits and flextime.

Family characteristics affect only women's experience of negative spillover, as illustrated by the Z scores. Being part of a couple and having more children in all age groups increases job-to-home spillover for women. In addition, fear of layoffs and having at least a college education increases job-to-home spillover for women only. For men but not for women, having an exempt job increases job-to-home spillover whereas having a supportive supervisor decreases it. With the exception noted above, the effects of all of the variables on job-to-home spillover are the same for women and men. The separate models explain a substantial portion of spillover from the job to the home, although the model is a slightly better predictor of job-to-home spillover for women (31.1 percent), than for men (29.3 percent). The Chow test F-ratio indicates that the predictors of job-to-home spillover influence women and men differently, which supports the analytical decision to estimate the model separately.

Discussion and Conclusion

This study provides compelling evidence that a family-friend workplace culture rather than the availability of formal company policies reduces negative spillover. In family-friendly workplace climates, men as well as women find it easier to balance their jobs and family lives because their employing organizations acknowledge nonwork-place demands and do not penalize employees who attend to their lives of the workplace.

We empirically assessed the independent impact of workplace culture, company policies, job characteristics, and household characteristics on women's and men's experiences of negative spillover between home and job. Our study fills a gap in previous research by focusing on whether *the availability* (not use) of family-friendly benefits actually reduces negative spillover. Generally, our findings are consistent with our expectations, with some exceptions that reflect the complexities of the interrelationships among gender as a social structure, work organizations, and the larger society.

Gender theory predicts that, on an individual level, women experience greater negative spillover than do men. Our findings show that, overall, women report slightly higher levels of negative spillover in both directions than do men. The multidimensional effect of gender on negative spillover becomes clearer once workplace and family characteristics are taken into account; women experience much higher levels of job-to-home spillover than do men, and having a domestic partner and children aggravates negative spillover for women but generally not for men. These data show how differences in work and family responsibilities between women and men persist on an individual level. Gender theory also posits that gender is not merely a characteristic of individuals; it is also a social structure that modifies the experience of negative spillover for both women and men. Our findings illuminate how the workplace is gendered male in two ways.

First, our findings point to an ongoing set of expectations that still privilege employment responsibilities over family responsibilities. They do this by consistently demonstrating the greater existence of job-to-home spillover than home-to-job spillover for both women and men. Furthermore, the gross differences between women and men in home-to-job spillover (Table 33.1) disappear once we account for the unique effects of respondent's sex, employment, and family characteristics. Em-

Table 33.4
Ordinary Least Squares Standardized Regression Coefficients Predicting Negative Job-to-Home Spillover, by Sex of Respondent

Variable	Women (N= 1,245)			Men (N = 1,089)			
	b	S.E.	β	b	S.E.	β	Z
Controls							
Age	−.024	(.011)*	−.058	−.027	(.012)*	−.063	−.18
Education (High school or less)							
Some college	−.005	(.290)	.000	−.164	(.321)	−.015	−.39
Four–year degree or more	.734	(.368)*	.069	.448	(.386)	.044	−.54
Job characteristics							
Occupation (Executive/managerial)							
Professional	−.620	(.405)	−.052	−.044	(.440)	−.003	.96
Technical	−.019	(.594)	−.001	.281	(.702)	.012	.33
Sales	.012	(.479)	.001	−.404	(.500)	−.026	−.60
Administrative support	−.093	(.402)	−.008	.191	(.641)	.009	.38
Service	−.684	(.496)	−.045	−.696	(.569)	−.042	−.02
Production/operation/repair	−.197	(.521)	−.012	.117	(.462)	.012	.45
Exempt job position	.072	(.288)	.007	.848	(.316)**	.085	1.81
Hours worked per week	.075	(.010)***	.197	.050	(.010)***	.142	−1.77
Never enough time	.974	(.111)***	.232	.833	(.119)***	.191	−.87
Job autonomy	−.370	(.178)*	−.057	−.232	(.205)	−.035	.51
Job satisfaction	−.687	(.156)***	−.123	−.781	(.177)***	−.139	−.40
Family characteristic							
Household income[a]	−.132	(.250)	−.014	−.025	(.200)	−.003	.33
Missing income	−.327	(.508)	−.016	−.277	(.608)	−.012	.06
Couple	.791	(.251)**	.081	.280	(.308)	.027	−1.29
Children under 6	.621	(.246)**	.064	.314	(.216)	.042	−.94
Children 6–12	.681	(.184)***	.091	.200	(.191)	.028	−1.81
Children 13–17	.656	(.201)***	.079	.303	(.236)	.035	−1.14
Company policies							
Dependent care benefits availability	−.569	(.458)	−.031	−.212	(.473)	−.012	.54
Flextime available	−.203	(.254)	−.021	.157	(.277)	.016	.96
Workplace culture							
Supervisor support regarding family	−.341	(.203)	−.051	−.541	(.221)*	−.077	−.67
Family supportive environment	−.708	(.180)***	−.114	−.663	(.193)***	−.103	.17
Easy to take time for family	−.749	(.136)***	−.156	−1.157	(.141)**	−.240	−2.08***
Frequent layoffs	1.007	(.401)**	.063	.490	(.420)	.031	−.89
Intercept	16.137***			17.823***			
Adjusted R^2	.311***			.293***			
Chow test F–ratio				1.99***			

Note: For polytomous categorical variables, the reference category is in parentheses.
[a]Income coefficients multiplied by 10,000.
*p ≤ .05, **p ≤ .01, ***p ≤ .001.

ployment, still ideologically male, warrants more attention, concern, and importance for most people than does the ideologically female domain of family life. Not only individuals, but the structural spaces, or spheres, are gendered and these gendered social spaces maintain inequalities independent of the sex of the participant. Work and family must be viewed as an interrelated *system* characterized by these gendering processes. These data support the claim that individuals do not hop back and forth between the unique and distinct social spheres of home and workplace. Rather, they are always workers, mothers, fathers, managers, daughters, administrators, sons, and laborers. As Stryker and Serpe (1983) have shown, different settings may invoke one identity over another, rendering one more salient *in that context* than others, but it does not alter the reality of coexisting multiple identities. This phenomenon occurs regardless of whether one is male or female.

Second, despite some workplaces where the culture is overtly family friendly, the workplace environment is typically *not* supportive of employees with family responsibilities. Company policies, in the absence of changed normative expectations, do not lower home-to-job spillover for either women or men, regardless of their family circumstances. A company culture that is not explicitly family friendly increases home-to-job spillover for *all* of its employees, in effect, treating them as "traditional" men who have no domestic obligations. We argue that the persistence of cultural assumptions in which the male model is the workplace model is consistent with gender theory. In other words, if we had found that family-friendly policies reduce spillover, we could conclude that while the spheres of home and work might well be viewed as separate, they are not gendered since *employee-based* policies reduced *employee* negative spillover.

Families, however, still require someone to do a variety of activities, especially caregiving. In the traditional gendered separate spheres model, women performed most of the private sphere tasks, especially

the everyday chores such as meal preparation, laundry, and housecleaning, although men typically took responsibility for occasional tasks such as home repairs and automobile maintenance. In contemporary society, the vast majority of women and men participate in both spheres, albeit unequally. They both enact traditional male behavior by participating in the labor force, the work sphere. Similarly; both women and men enact traditional female behavior by being involved in home life, the private sphere. Most organizations and their incumbents, however, continue to adhere to the hierarchical separate spheres model, as demonstrated by our findings that not only actual time spent working but also time pressure increases spillover.

Ideologically, market work is still separate from and takes priority over domestic work. Rather than moving toward an egalitarian breadwinner-caregiver model, workplace organizations, perhaps in an effort to retain that ideological advantage, seem to be clinging to a breadwinner-only model for both women and men, which leaves the caregiver role inadequately filled (Hochschild 1989). The latter is certainly an empirical question that emerges from our research here. Thus, while there is evidence of reduced gender inequality in some dimensions of social life in the form of the sex of breadwinners and caregivers, negative spillover remains in the form of the persistent gendering of market work as male and caregiving as female. This trajectory suggests a sort of perverted gender equality in which women and men experience equivalent levels of negative spillover between their jobs and their homes instead of contentedly sharing market work and caregiving.

Gender theory alone, however, does not explain another major finding—the failure of family-friendly policy to decrease negative spillover. Combining the insights of neoinstitutional theory with gender theory, however, does explain our results. Scholars have repeatedly demonstrated, as neo-institutional theory suggests, the disjuncture between official policies and implicit normative orders surrounding job-family boundaries (Perin 1991; Bailyn 1993; Perlow 1997). Our findings reaffirm the observation that the superimposition of family-friendly policies in the absence of genuine supervisor support and commitment to a family-friendly workplace environment not only fails to benefit the worker, but also could be to the worker's detriment.

Workplace cultures reflect and reinforce the culture of the wider society. The institutionalization of the separation between market work and domestic work, between job and home exemplifies this relationship. This firmly entrenched ideology is difficult to change since individuals enter workplaces with these normative expectations well institutionalized. Additionally, the notion of separate spheres is more than just an institutionalized informal practice. It was at one time strongly supported by formal policies such as legal sex discrimination, the family wage, sex-biased parental leave, and divorce settlements that automatically awarded custody to mothers and mandated financial, but not caregiving, support from fathers.

In sum, our research has made two contributions to the extant understanding of job-to-home and home-to-job spillover. Guided by both gender theory and neo-institutional theory, this study demonstrates that reducing negative job-to-home spillover in the absence of deinstitutionalizing the habituated understandings about separate spheres, family-friendly policies alone will not make an organization family friendly. A supportive workplace culture, regardless of the availability of family-friendly policies, is paramount to the successful management of job-to-home and home-to-job spillover. A second contribution is demonstrating the utility of combining gender and neo-institutional theory to understand these dynamics.

Our study also demonstrates that time pressure is a considerable obstacle to successfully managing home-to-job and especially job-to-home spillover. Time commitment to a job is a norm that reinforces both the separate spheres ideology and gender inequity (see Epstein et al. 1999). All employees have trouble finding enough time to balance a job and a family. Yet, when women decide to do so by taking time away from the job, they conform to and thus reinforce the legitimacy of the gendered status expectations that view women as less competent employees (Ridgeway and Erickson 2000). A genuine family-friendly workplace culture and relaxed time pressure on the job are fundamental to achieving the dual objectives of job-family balance and gender equity in contemporary society.

Appendix A

Variables and Measurement

Variables	Measurement
Dependent variables	
Home-to-job spillover index	5 (never) to 25 (very often) Cronbach's alpha: .79
	How often has your family or personal life:
	• kept you from getting work done on time at your job?
	• kept you from taking on extra work at your job?
	• kept you from doing as good a job at work as you could?
	• drained you of the energy you needed to do your job?
	• kept you from concentrating on your job?
Job-to-home spillover index	5 (never) to 25 (very often) Cronbach's alpha: .86
	In the past three months, how often have you _____ because of your job?
	• not had enough time for yourself

Variables	Measurement
Job-to-home spillover index, cont.	• not had enough time for your family or other important people in your life • not had the energy to do things with your family or other important people in your life • not been able to get everything done at home each day • not been in as good a mood as you would like to be at home

Independent variables
Controls

Age	Age, in years
Education	Education level • High school or less • Some college • Four-year college degree or more

Job Characteristics

Occupation	Category of occupation • Executive, administrators, managers • Professionals • Sales • Administrative support • Service • Production, operations, repair
Exempt job position	0 nonexempt, 1 exempt
Hours worked per week	Number of paid hours usually worked per week at main, job, number of paid and unpaid overtime hours usually worked per week at main job, and number of paid hours worked at all other jobs
Never enough time	1 (strongly disagree) to 4 (strongly agree) I never seem to have enough time to get everything done on my job
Job autonomy index	1 (low autonomy) to 4 (high autonomy) Cronbach's alpha: .67 • I have the freedom to decide what I do on my job. • It is basically my own responsibility to decide how my job gets done. • I have a lot of say about what happens on my job.
Job satisfaction indicator	1 (not satisfied at all) to 4 (very satisfied)

Family Characteristics

Couple	0 not a member of a couple, 1 member of a couple
Household income	Total household income in 1996
Children under 6	Number of children under 6 years of age in the household
Children 6–12	Number of children ages 6 through 12 in the household
Children 13–17	Number of children ages 13 through 17 in the household

Company Policies

Dependent care benefits index	0 (no benefits) to 1 (all benefits) Cronbach's alpha: .70 *Does your employer:* • have a program or service that helps employees find child care if they need it, or not? • have a program that helps employees get information about elder care or find services for elderly relatives if they need them, or not?

Variables	Measurement
Dependent care benefits index, cont.	• operate or sponsor a child care center for the children of employees at or near your location, or not? • provide employees with any direct financial assistance for child care—that is, vouchers, cash, or scholarships, or not? • have a program that allows employees to put part of their income BEFORE TAXES in an account that can be used to pay for child care or other dependent care? These programs are sometimes called "cafeteria plans" or "dependent care assistance plans."
Flextime available	0 no, 1 yes
Workplace Culture Supervisor support re: family index	1 (strongly disagree) to 4 (strongly agree) Cronbach's alpha: .86 • My supervisor is fair and doesn't show favoritism in responding to employees' personal or family needs. • My supervisor accommodates me when I have family or personal business to take care of—for example, medical appointments, meeting with child's teacher, etc. • My supervisor is understanding when I talk about personal or family issues that affect my work. • I feel comfortable bringing up personal or family issues with my supervisor. • My supervisor really cares about the effects that work demands have on my personal and family life.
Family supportive environment index	1 (strongly agree) to 4 (strongly disagree) Cronbach's alpha: .74. • There is an unwritten rule at my place of employment that you can't take care of family needs on company time. • At my place of employment, employees who put their family or personal needs ahead of their jobs are not looked on favorably. • If you have a problem managing your work and family responsibilities, the attitude at my place of employment is "You made your bed, now lie in it!" • At my place of employment, employees have to choose between advancing in their jobs or devoting attention to their family or personal lives.
Easy to take time during workday for family matters	0 (not very easy) to 4 (very easy)
Frequent layoffs when work slow	0 no , 1 yes

Source: Reprinted from *The Sociological Quarterly* 46 (2005) 107–135 © 2005 Midwest Sociological Society.

Discussion Questions

1. The authors focus on negative effects of work-family conflicts. In what ways do you think there could be positive spillover from job to home? From home to job?

2. Why do you think that family-friendly policies do not lessen work-family conflict?

Sue Falter Mennino, Beth A. Rubin, and April Brayfield, "Home-to-Job and Job-to-Home Spillover: The Impact of Company Policies and Workplace Culture," in *Sociological Quarterly* 46 (2005), 107–136. Copyright © 2005, Midwest Sociological Society. Reprinted with permission from Blackwell Publishing Ltd.

Endnotes

1. The term "work" in the job-family literature invariably represents wage labor, even though researchers acknowledge that there is much soci-

etal work besides paid labor, such as housework, child care, volunteer work, and emotion work (Daniels 1987; Tilly and Tilly 1998).

2. Just as there are many variants of gender theory, there are many variants of neo-institutional theory (Powell and DiMaggio 1991).

3. The point is that "flexibility" is complex in its meaning and it is not always clear for whom the flexibility is arranged.

4. Employers often implement family-friendly policies to attract and/or retain critical constituencies of employees (Goodstein 1994; Ingram and Simons 1995), in particular parents or, more commonly, women. Because caregiving activity is not restricted to either parents or women, we do not restrict our sample to those constituencies.

5. Each spillover index is highly reliable; Cronbach's alpha coefficients were .79 for home-to-job spillover and .86 for job-to-home spillover. Factor analysis confirms that the items in each index cluster into meaningful measures of spillover. Items in each index loaded above .69 on the single factor. Nevertheless, as a reviewer pointed out, some of the items in the indices are more subjective than others and thus might be more sensitive to interpretation by the respondents. The ubiquitous doctrine of gendered separate spheres may differentially impact not only men's and women's answers to spillover questions but might also influence the wording of the questions themselves.

6. Ideally we would include other measures of household characteristics, demands, and pressures; the data simply do not allow it.

7. Job-to-home spillover is also more extensive than home-to-job spillover for both women ($t = -38.917$, $p < .000$) and men ($t = -34.311$, $p < .000$) as separate groups.

8. We also estimated the model with a subsample that included only parents (respondents with any children under 18). The benefits variables were not significant (results not shown).

9. As pointed out by a reviewer, dependent care policies may not be equivalent in terms of their helpfulness. We therefore tested models that included the five dependent care policies as separate items rather than as an index. None of the separate dependent care benefit variables was significant (results not shown).

10. We began investigating the observed differences between women and men by estimating models that included multiplicative terms for the interaction of sex with each of the workplace variables (supervisor support, frequent layoffs, family supportive environment, and ease of taking time for family) and each of the family variables (couple and the three age groups of children). None of these interaction terms was significant, although the interaction between sex and ease of taking time for family

during the day approached significance ($p = .059$). We then estimated each model by sex so that we could further explore the observed sex difference.

11. We used the Chow test (Chow 1960) to examine whether the covariance of Y and X is distributed differently for women than for men.

References

Acker, Joan. 1990. "Hierarchies, Jobs, Bodies: A Theory of Gendered Organizations." *Gender & Society* 4: 139–158.

Allen, Taminy D. 2001. "Family-Supportive Work Environments: The Role of Organizational Perceptions." *Journal of Vocational Behavior* 58: 414–435.

Bailyn, Lotte. 1993. *Breaking the Mold: Women, Men, and Time in the New Corporate Culture*. New York: Free Press.

Barnett, Rosalind C. 1994. "Home-to-Work Spillover Revisited: A Study of Full-Time Employed Women in Dual-Earner Couples." *Journal of Marriage and the Family* 56: 647–656.

——. 1999. "A New Work-Life Model for the Twenty-First Century." *Annals of the American Academy of Political and Social Science* 562: 143–158.

Bond, James T., Ellen Galinsky, and Jennifer E. Swanberg. 1998. *The 1997 National Study of the Changing Workforce*. New York: Families and Work Institute.

Bowen, Gary L. 2000. "Workplace Programs and Policies That Address Work-Family and Gender Equity Issues in the United States." Pp. 79–98 in *Organizational Change and Gender Equity: International Perspectives on Fathers and Mothers at the Workplace*, edited by Linda L. Haas, Philip Hwang, and Graeme Russell. Thousand Oaks, CA: Sage.

Chow, Gregory C. 1960. "Tests of Equality Between Sets of Coefficients in Two Linear Regressions." *Economica* 28: 591–606.

Ciscel, David H., David C. Sharp, and Julia A. Heath. 2000. "Family Work Trends and Practices: 1971 to 1991." *Journal of Family and Economic Issues* 21(l): 23–36.

Clogg, Clifford, Eva Petkova, and Adamantios Haritou. 1995. "Statistical Methods for Comparing Regression Coefficients Between Models." *American Journal of Sociology* 100(5): 1261–1293.

Collinson, David L. and Margaret Collinson. 1997. "Delayering Managers: Time-Space Surveillance and Its Gendered Effects." *Organization* 4(3): 375–407.

Collinson, David and Jeff Hearn. 1994. "Naming Men as Men: Implications for Work, Organization, and Management." *Gender, Work, and Organization* 1: 2–22.

Connell, Robert. 1987. *Gender and Power: Society, the Person, and Sexual Politics*. Stanford, CA: Stanford University Press.

Coser, Lewis A. 1974. *Greedy Institutions*. New York: Free Press.

Crouter, Ann C. 1984. "Spillover From Family to Work: The Neglected Side of the Work-Family Interface." *Human Relations* 37: 425–442.

Daniels, Arlene Kaplan. 1987. "Invisible Work." *Social Problems* 35(5): 403–415.

Deutsch, Francine M. and Susan E. Saxon. 1998. "Traditional Ideologies, Nontraditional Lives." *Sex Roles* 38(5/6): 331–362.

DiMaggio, Paul J. and Walter W. Powell. 1983. "The Iron Cage Revisited: Institutional Isomorphism and Collective Rationality in Organizational Fields." *American Sociological Review* 48: 147–160.

——. 1991. "Introduction." Pp. 1–38 in *The New Institutionalism in Organizational Analysis*, edited by Walter W. Powell and Paul J. DiMaggio. Chicago: University of Chicago Press.

Duxbury, Linda and Christopher Higgins. 1994. "Interference Between Employment and Family: A Status Report on Dual-Career and Dual-Earner Mothers and Fathers." *Employee Assistance Quarterly* 9: 55–80.

Duxbury, Linda, Christopher Higgins, and Catherine Lee. 1994. "Work-Family Conflict: A Comparison by Gender, Family Type, and Perceived Control." *Journal of Family Issues* 15(3): 449–466.

Eagle, Bruce W., Edward W. Miles, and Marjorie L. Icenogle. 1997. "Interrole Conflicts and the Permeability of Work and Family Domains: Are There Gender Differences?" *Journal of Vocational Behavior* 50: 168–184.

Edwards, Jeffrey R. and Nancy P. Rothbard. 1999. "Work and Family Stress and Well-Being: An Examination of Person-Environment Fit in the Work and Family Domains." *Organizational Behavior and Human Decision Processes* 77: 85–129.

Epstein, Cynthia Fuchs, Carroll Seron, Bonnie Oglensky, and Robert Saute. 1999. *The Part-Time Paradox: Time Norms, Professional Life, Family and Gender*. New York: Routledge.

Ferber, Marianne A., Brigid O'Farrell, and La Rue Allen. 1991. *Work and Family: Policies for a Changing Work Force*. Washington, DC: National Academy Press.

Ferree, Myra Marx. 1990. "Beyond Separate Spheres: Feminism and Family Research." *Journal of Marriage and the Family* 52: 866–884.

Fligstein, Neil. 2001. "Social Skill and the Theory of Fields." *Sociological Theory* 19(2): 105–125.

Foster, Johanna. 1999. "An Invitation to Dialogue: Clarifying the Position of Feminist Gender Theory in Relation to Sexual Difference Theory." *Gender & Society* 13(4): 431–456.

Frone, Michael R, Marcia Russell, and Lynne M. Cooper. 1992. "Antecedents and Outcomes of Work-Family Conflict: Testing a Model of the Work-Family Interface." *Journal of Applied Psychology* 77(1): 65–78.

Frone, Michael R., John K. Yardley, and Karen S. Markel. 1997. "Developing and Testing an Integrative Model of the Work-Family Interface." *Journal of Vocational Behavior* 50: 145–167.

Galinsky, Ellen, James T. Bond, and Dana E. Friedman. 1996. "The Role of Employers in Addressing the Needs of Employed Parents." *Journal of Social Issues* 52(3): 111–136.

Galinsky, Ellen and Peter J. Stein. 1990. "The Impact of Human Resource Policies on Employees: Balancing Work/Family Life." *Journal of Family Issues* 11(4): 368–383.

Gerson, Kathleen. 2000. "Gender and the Future of the Family: Implications for the Postindustrial Workplace." Pp. 11–21 in *Challenges for Work and Family in the Twenty-First Century*, edited by Dana Vannoy and Paula J. Dubeck. New York: Aldine de Gruyter.

——. 2002. "Moral Dilemmas, Moral Strategies, and the Transformation of Gender: Lessons for Two Generations of Work and Family Change." *Gender & Society* 16: 8–28.

Gerstel, Naomi and Dan Clawson. 2001. "Unions' Responses to Family Concerns." *Social Problems* 48(2): 277–297.

Gherardi, Silvia. 1994. "The Gender We Think, the Gender We Do in Our Everyday Organizational Lives." *Human Relations* 47: 591–608.

Gignac, Monique A. M., E. Kevin Kelloway, and Benjamin H. Gottlieb. 1996. "The Impact of Caregiving on Employment: A Mediational Model of Work-Family Conflict." *Canadian Journal on Aging* 15(4): 525–542.

Glass, Jennifer. 2000. "Envisioning the Integration of Family and Work: Toward a Kinder, Gentler Workplace." *Contemporary Sociology* 29: 129–143.

Goodstein, Jerry D. 1994. "Institutional Pressures and Strategic Responsiveness: Employer Involvement in Work-Family Issues." *Academy of Management Journal* 37(2): 350–382.

Greenhaus, Jeffrey H. and Saroj Parasuraman. 1999. "Research on Work, Family, and Gender: Current Status and Future Directions." Pp. 391–412 in *Handbook of Gender and Work*, edited by G. N. Powell. Thousand Oaks, CA: Sage.

Grzywacz, Joseph G., David M. Almeida, and Daniel A. McDonald. 2002. "Work-Family Spillover and Daily Reports of Work and Family Stress in the Adult Labor Force." *Family Relations* 51: 28–36.

Gutek, Barbara A., Sabrina Searle, and Lilian Klepa. 1991. "Rational Versus Gender Role Expectations for Work-Family Conflict." *Journal of Applied Psychology* 76(4): 560–568.

Harrison, Bennett. 1994. *Lean and Mean: The Changing Landscape of Corporate Power in the Age of Flexibility*. New York: Basic.

Hochschild, Arlie Russell. 1989. *The Second Shift: Working Parents and the Revolution at Home*. New York: Viking.

Ingram, Paul, and Tal Simons. 1995. "Institutional and Resource Dependence Determinants of Responsiveness Work-Family Issues." *Academy of Management Journal* 38(5): 1466–1482.

Jacobs, Jerry A. and Kathleen Gerson. 1998. "Toward a Family-Friendly, Gender-Equitable Work Week." *University of Pennsylvania Journal of Labor and Employment Law* 1(2): 457–472.

Jepperson, Ronald L. 1991. "Institutions, Institutional Effects, and Institutionalism." Pp. 143–63 in *The New Institutionalism in Organizational Analysis*, edited by Walter W. Powell and Paul J. DiMaggio. Chicago: University of Chicago Press.

Kanter, Rosabeth Moss. 1977. *Work and Family in the United States: A Critical Review and Agenda for Research and Policy*. New York: Russell Sage Foundation.

Kaufman, Gayle and Peter Uhlenberg. 2000. "The Influence of Parenthood on the Work Effort of Married Men and Women." *Social Force* 78(3): 931–949.

Kelly, Erin L. 1999. "Theorizing Corporate Family Policies: How Advocates Built 'the Business Case' for 'Family-Friendly' Policies." *Research in the Sociology of Work* 7: 169–202.

Kirchmeyer, Catherine. 1993. "Nonwork-to-Work Spillover: A More Balanced View of the Experiences and Coping of Professional Women and Men." *Sex Roles* 28: 531–552.

——. 1995. "Managing the Work-Nonwork Boundary: An Assessment of Organizational Responses." *Human Relations* 48: 515–536.

Kossek, Ellen Ernst, Alison E. Barber, and Deborah Winters. 1999. "Using Flexible Schedules in the Managerial World: The Power of Peers." *Human Resources Management* 38: 33–46.

Kossek, Ellen Ernst and Cynthia Ozeki. 1998. "Work-Family Conflict, Policies, and the Job-Life Satisfaction Relationship: A Review and Directions for Organizational Behavior-Human Resources Research." *Journal of Applied Psychology* 83(2): 139–149.

Lorber, Judith. 1994. *Paradoxes of Gender*. New Haven, CT: Yale University Press.

Martin, Patricia Yancey. 2003. " 'Said and Done' versus 'Saying and Doing': Gendering Practices, Practicing Gender at Work." *Gender & Society* 17(3): 342–366.

Meyer, John P. and Natalie Allen. 1997. *Commitment in the Workplace: Theory, Research, and Applications*. Thousand Oaks, CA: Sage.

Meyer, John W. and Brian Rowan. 1977. "Institutionalized Organizations: Formal Structure as Myth and Ceremony." *American Journal of Sociology* 83(2): 340–363.

Osterman, Paul. 1995. "Work/Family Programs and the Employment Relationship." *Administrative Science Quarterly* 40(4): 681–700.

Perin, Constance. 1991. "The Moral Fabric of the Office: Panopticon Discourse and Schedule Flexibilities." *Research in the Sociology of Organizations* 8: 241–268.

Perlow, Leslie A. 1997. *Finding Time: How Corporations, Individuals, and Families Can Benefit From New Work Practices*. Ithaca, NY: ILR Press.

——. 1998. "Boundary Control: The Social Ordering of Work and Family in a High-Tech Corporation." *Administrative Science Quarterly* 43: 328–357.

Potuchek, Jean L. 1997. *Who Supports the Family? Gender and Breadwinning in Dual-Earner Marriages*. Stanford, CA: Stanford University Press.

Powell, Walter W. and Paul J. DiMaggio. 1991. "Introduction." Pp. 1–38 in *The New Institutionalism in Organizational Analysis*, edited by Walter W. Powell and Paul J. DiMaggio. Chicago: University of Chicago Press.

Ridgeway, Cynthia L. 1997. "Interaction and the Conservation of Gender Inequality: Considering Employment." *American Sociological Review* 62: 218–235.

Ridgeway, Cynthia L. and Kristan Glasgow Erickson. 2000. "Creating and Spreading Status Beliefs." *American Journal of Sociology* 106(3): 579–615.

Risman, Barbara J. 1998. *Gender Vertigo: American Families in Transition*. New Haven, CT: Yale University Press.

Roehling, Patricia V., Mark V. Roehling, and Phyllis Moen. 2001. "The Relationship Between Work-Life Policies and Practices and Employee Loyalty: A Life Course Perspective." *Journal of Family and Economic Issues* 22(2): 141–170.

Rones, Philip L., Randy E. Ilg, and Jennifer M. Garner. 1997. "Trends in Hours of Work Since the Mid-1970s." *Monthly Labor Review* 120(4): 3–14.

Rubin, Beth A. 1995. "Flexible Accumulation: The Decline of Contract and Social Transformation." *Research in Social Stratification and Mobility* 1: 297–323.

——. 1996. *Shifts in the Social Contract: Understanding Change in American Society*. Thousand Oaks, CA: Pine Forge Press.

Rubin, Beth A. and Charles J. Brody. 2002. "Insecurity, Time and Technology: Coercing Commitment in the New Economy." Paper presented at the 97th Annual Meetings of the American Sociological Association, Chicago, August 16–19.

Rubin, Beth A. and Brian T. Smith. 2001. "Re-Employment in the Restructured Economy: Surviving Change, Displacement, and Gales of Creative Destruction." Pp. 323–342 in *Working in Restructured Workplaces: Challenges and New Directions for the Sociology of Work*, edited by Daniel Cornfield, Karen E. Campbell, and Holly J. McCammon. Thousand Oaks, CA: Sage.

Sanchez, Laura and Elizabeth Thomson. 1997. "Becoming Mothers and Fathers: Parenthood, Gender, and the Division of Labor." *Gender & Society* 11(6): 747–772.

Sandberg, Joanne C. 1999. "The Effects of Family Obligations and Workplace Resources on Men's and Women's Use of Family Leaves." *Research in the Sociology of Work*, 261–281.

Schieman, Scott, Debra Branch McBrier, and Karen Van Gundy. 2003. "Home-to-Work Conflict, Work Qualities, and Emotional Distress." *Sociological Forum* 18: 137–164.

Scott, Joan W. 1986. "Gender: A Useful Category of Historical Analysis." *The American Historical Review* 91(5): 1053–1075.

Small, Stephen A. and Dave Riley. 1990. "Toward a Multidimensional Assessment of Work Spillover Into Family Life." *Journal of Marriage and the Family* 52: 51–61.

South, Scott J. and Glenna Spitze. 1994. "Housework in Marital and Non-Marital Households." *American Sociological Review* 39: 327–347.

Stryker, Sheldon and Richard T. Serpe. 1983. "Toward a Theory of Family Influence in the Socialization of Children." *Research in Sociology of Education and Socialization* 4: 47–71.

Thomas, Linda Thiede and Daniel C. Ganster. 1995. "Impact of Family-Supportive Work Variables on Work-Family Conflict and Strain: A Control Perspective." *Journal of Applied Psychology* 80: 9–15.

Thompson, Cynthia A., Laura L. Beauvais, and Karen S. Lyness. 1999. "When Work-Family Benefits Are Not Enough: The Influence of Work-Family Culture on Benefit Utilization, Organizational Attachment, and Work-Family Conflict." *Journal of Vocational Behavior* 54: 392–415.

Thompson, Linda and Alexis J. Walker. 1989. "Gender in Families: Women and Men in Marriage, Work, and Parenthood." *Journal of Marriage and the Family* 51: 845–871.

Thornton, Arland. 1989. "Changing Attitudes Toward Family Issues in the United States." *Journal of Marriage and the Family* 51: 873–893.

Tilly, Chris and Charles Tilly. 1998. *Work and Capitalism.* Boulder, CO: Westview Press.

Vallas, Steven P. 1999. "Rethinking Post-Fordism: The Meaning of Workplace Flexibility." *Sociological Theory* 1: 68–101.

Wajcman, Judy. 1999. *Managing Like a Man: Women and Men in Corporate Management.* Cambridge, UK: Polity.

Warren, Jennifer A. and Phyllis J. Johnson. 1995. "The Impact of Workplace Support on Work-Family Role Strain." *Family Relations* 44: 163–169.

Wiatrowski, William J. 1990. "Family-Related Benefits in the Workplace." *Monthly Labor Review* 113(3): 28–33.

Williams, Kevin and George M. Alliger. 1994. "Role Stressors, Mood Spillover, and Perceptions of Work-Family Conflict in Employed Parents." *Academy of Management Journal* 37: 837–868.

Witkowski, Kristine M. 1999. "Becoming Family-Friendly: Work-Family Program Innovation Among the Largest U.S. Corporations." *Research in the Sociology of Work* 7: 203–232.

Zucker, Lynne G. 1991. "The Role of Institutionalization in Cultural Persistence." Pp. 83–107 in *The New Institutionalism in Organizational Analysis,* edited by Walter W. Powell and Paul J. DiMaggio. Chicago: University of Chicago Press. ✦

Part V

Emerging Issues

A. Policies for Work and Family

The successful integration of work and family obligations depends on policies and practices that reflect a number of interests, including individual worker's preferences, employers, labor unions, and the state. With respect to the state, Janet Gornick and Marcia Meyers compare the United States with several other industrialized countries in Europe in terms of the development of welfare state programs and collective-bargaining agreements that shift some part of the cost of caregiving from the family to the larger society.

Because the United States has lagged behind Europe, families in the former have devised private solutions, including reducing the employment of only one parent, usually the mother; arranging "split shift" parenting so that one parent takes care of children while the other is employed; shifting portions of child care outside the home, such as child care centers; or use of self-care by children. There are problems with such solutions, however, including mothers' penalties in wages and promotion opportunities, sometimes resulting in family economic instability and poverty; and mothers' lack of time to participate in public citizenship and almost anything else, including housework and personal care. Fur-thermore, child care is relatively low-paid work and of varying quality, penalizing children when they are young.

As we have seen in previous chapters, the contract between employers and employees has been changing in numerous ways. It is less and less the case that employees can expect long-term job security, rapid advancement, and regular increases in pay and benefits. It is in this context that P. V. Roehling, M. V. Roehling and P. Moen explore the relationships among work-family policies for the provision of child care and flexible time, supervisor support of work-life needs, and employee loyalty to their current employer, current position, and supervisor.

In the final chapter in this section, Jennifer Glass and Sarah Estes note that both the needs and power of parents and employers differ such that, for the most-needed family policies, the federal government eventually may have to put political pressure on employers. Otherwise, to deal with the ups and downs of labor demand, existing employer strategies of downsizing and subcontracting could be replaced with family-responsive work options. Additionally, to cut payroll and physical plant costs to maintain profitability, employers could use job-sharing, voluntarily reduced work hours, and work-at-home options. And, instead of early retirements or layoffs, employers could offer part-time work with prorated benefits. The authors contend that better research on the human and financial consequences of specific work-family policies would facilitate the development of political agreement on policy-making.

Section B. Revitalizing the Workplace

This final section of the book examines some labor, political, and employer strategies to revitalize the American workplace. The first chapter focuses on possibilities for unionization of workers in apparel production in Los Angeles. Edna Bonacich analyzes the system of contracting out and the need for organizing workers. She contends that for manufacturers, who are mostly white European in origin, the contract system allows them to avoid maintaining a stable labor force year round; serves as a labor-control mechanism by pitting contractors, typically Asian immigrant entrepreneurs without much capital, against each other in bidding to get the work, and inhibiting unionization; and easily evades state inspection of working conditions in the "independent" businesses that are widely dispersed in Los Angeles and offshore.

Bonacich depicts the contingent workers, Latina immigrants, as low paid by the piecework system, seldom receiving any fringe benefits, and working under sweatshop conditions. Finally, she compares the strengths and weaknesses of five approaches to organizing garment workers in Los Angeles while recognizing that any organizing effort may result in more rapid flight of the industry to Mexico. She contends that the city and state can support contractors' efforts to upgrade their factories and that corporate campaigns and consumer pressure can hold accountable firms that move to Mexico.

The second chapter also focuses on unionization for improving the working condition of workers. Stephanie Luce discusses some labor victories that have resulted from the movement for living-wage ordinances and suggests some lessons about organizing for the labor movement that come from the success of ten years of the living-wage movement.

Some unions have been successful in organizing new workers, getting raises for already unionized workers, and retaining union jobs. The lessons for labor are that labor needs to develop allies and work on issues that appeal to union members and community partners; to develop and assert its own moral vision; to not fear breaking from mainstream political parties; to work through outside pressure and protest politics, as well as through internal channels, to implement stronger enforcement; to welcome campaigns that are conflictual because they have a better chance of enforcement if passed; and to find ways to mobilize the rank-and-file members of labor unions.

In the third chapter, Donald Bartlett and James Steele discuss the inadequacies that characterize the present "market system" of health care for underinsured as well as insured Americans, and propose a cost-effective remedy. The authors contend that the United States should provide universal comprehensive health-care coverage and create a single payer system in which there is one agency, free from politics, to collect medical fees and pay claims. They predict that change will come from both workers, who face increasing costs and shrinking care, and from U.S. corporations, which refuse to incur the added costs.

A final chapter, by Stacy Kim, Marta Lopez and James Bond, describes a variety of employer-sponsored work-life and work-family programs and policies that are aimed at assisting lower-wage, low-income families who most need assistance while also furthering business objectives. The practices pertain to a range of employer needs and different levels of effort on the part of employers, as well as a range of employee needs. ✦

34

The Reluctant American Welfare State: Opting Out of Public Responsibility

Janet C. Gornick and
Marcia K. Meyers

Janet Gornick and Marcia Meyers document that there is reluctance in the United States to having government take on a larger role in easing family-work conflicts. In their comparison of the United States with other western and northern industrialized countries, it is striking how much the United States lags behind in welfare state development and industrial relations. It spends only 0.5 percent of gross domestic product (GDP), compared with 1.5–2.2 percent of GDP in European welfare states, on expenditures on family-related benefits, including family allowances, family-support benefits, lone-parent allowances, paid family leave, and refundable tax credits for families. Not surprisingly, perhaps, when pay is not a factor, a higher percentage of Americans than their counterparts in other industrialized countries are dissatisfied with the time they have available for their families.

Economic, social, and demographic changes in the latter half of the twentieth century combined to destabilize the traditional model of family organization. However, the economic and social arrangements of families have been only partially transformed. The new model of partial specialization allows women to join men in the economic sphere; but it is also creating a time crunch for many families, increasing demands on employed mothers, and perpetuating gender inequalities.

To understand the implications for American families, it is necessary to review another chapter of American history. The demise of the traditional family, the competing demands on parents, and continued gender inequality are problems not unique to the United States. The economic and social transformations of the past two centuries have created unprecedented opportunities and expectations for women and new challenges for families in all of the industrialized countries. In many countries that industrialized at about the same time as the United States, however, particularly the countries of western and northern Europe, these transformations have been accompanied by the development of welfare state programs and collective-bargaining arrangements that shift a portion of the cost of caregiving from the family to the larger society. The United States has lagged behind its European counterparts in welfare state development and industrial relations for more than a century, creating a legacy that defines caregiving in exceptionally private terms.

Between 1880 and 1930, the first large-scale welfare state programs were enacted in Europe, largely in response to new and heightened forms of economic insecurity resulting from industrialization and urbanization. By the early 1930s, when an economic downturn swept through Europe, nearly all countries had enacted most of the four broad programs that would become the core of the European welfare state: old-age, disability, and survivors' pensions; workers' compensation; unemployment compensation; and health, sickness, and maternity benefits. In the 1930s and 1940s, the later-developing European welfare states established the rest of these programs, and nearly all countries added a fifth—family allowances. By 1960, the last of the major European welfare states had enacted a family allowance program (Hicks 1999).

In comparison with most of the European countries, the United States has been characterized as having a reluctant, residual, or only partial welfare state (Katz 1986, 1989; Patterson 1986; Trattner 1994). While most European countries were developing universal social protections for their citizens, the United States continued its colonial tradition of localized, charity-based assistance for the "deserving poor" and forced work—or destitution—for those considered able-bodied and undeserving of charity. During the first two decades of the twentieth century, several of the American states established public income supports, including workers' compensation and mothers' pensions, but the national government took no substantial responsibility for protecting Americans from economic hardship. In 1935, largely as a response to the Great Depression, the United States became one of the last Western countries to establish a national program of old-age, disability, and survivors' pensions, along with unemployment insurance. When the architects of the New Deal initiated the American welfare state, however, they opted out of crucial elements of the European policy package—including national health insurance, sickness pay, and maternity benefits. In subsequent years, when family allowances were established across Europe, policy makers in the United States once again chose not to follow suit.

The divergent histories of welfare state development in Europe and the United States reflect fundamentally different conceptions of the role of the state. The institutional histories of the United States and most of Europe also differ on the important dimension of unionization. Most of the European countries combine legislated programs with benefits and job protections that are collectively bargained. In many countries, organized labor is inseparable from government; employer-employee negotiations over working conditions and social benefits are regulated, and the state often participates directly in negotiations. When the needs of European workers and their families are not met through public programs, large numbers have access to employer-based options, negotiated through representative bodies that have substantial bargaining power.

The United States has predicated its social protection system on a far more limited role for the state, a greater reliance on employer-based provisions, and much weaker institutions for worker representation. Entire programs that are wholly or primarily public in many other countries, including health insurance, sickness pay, and maternity benefits, are largely privately provided—by employers—in the United States. The majority of working-age Americans who have access to these benefits obtain coverage through employment, sometimes as part of a standard employee-benefit package, sometimes through individualized negotiation.

Where the United States does provide public social benefits, it often restricts eligibility or benefits (or both) to an exceptional degree in comparative terms. The United States' national Old-Age, Survivors, and Disability Insurance program is the most universal of our programs, providing pensions to most aged and disabled workers and their surviving spouses and children. Most other U.S. social-welfare programs are highly restricted categorically, or pay low benefits, or both. In place of universal health-insurance coverage, for example, the United States grants public insurance only to elderly, disabled, and low-income citizens. The American unemployment-compensation system is also unusually meager; it was ranked seventeenth out of nineteen industrialized countries in a recent study of benefit generosity (see Gornick 1999).

Americans also obtain far fewer social benefits through collective bargaining than their European counterparts. As the United States developed a residual rather than a comprehensive welfare state, it also crafted public institutions that limit the role of unions and collective bargaining. The role of collective bargaining is limited partly because only a small fraction of the workforce is either unionized or represented by unions—about 15 percent overall, 10 percent in the private sector—and partly because bargaining is highly decentralized, generally affecting only one employer at a time. In most European countries, collective bargaining is both more widespread and much more centralized; agreements often affect whole industries—and sometimes nearly all workers in the country.

Unions are less developed in the United States than in many other industrialized countries for a number of historical, geographic, institutional, and cultural reasons. Although cultural preferences may play a role, the legal rules that govern collective bargaining in the United States effectively reduce both union coverage and union power. Furthermore, some nonunion forms of worker representation that are widespread in Europe are essentially disallowed by U.S. labor law. For example, Richard Freeman (1994) notes that the so-called works councils—bodies of workers that consult with employers at the enterprise level—would violate the terms of the primary U.S. labor law, the National Labor Relations Act. Although the causes underlying the limited development of unionization in the United States are subject to debate, the consequences are clear: when American parents turn to their employers for work-family benefits, they have a weak collective voice and little bargaining power.

Welfare state and collective-bargaining institutions have had particularly important consequences for families with children, in both Europe and the United States. Throughout western and northern Europe, the reorganization of the family in the twentieth century has been accompanied by the growth of social policies for parents and children. In most countries, the major welfare state programs—pensions, workers' compensation, unemployment, health, maternity, and family allowances—have been supplemented by housing assistance, lone-parent allowances, "sick-child days," paid parental leaves for mothers and fathers, and substantial public provisions for early childhood education and care starting at the age of three or even younger. This comprehensive package of programs protects working families from income shocks associated with bearing and caring for children. In addition, family leave and child care programs facilitate maternal employment, potentially reducing gender inequalities in the labor market and the home. All of the major family policies also have important redistributive effects. Because family policy benefits are financed largely by general revenues or contributory social insurance funds, they redistribute a portion of the costs of child rearing—across the life span, across generations, between more- and less-affluent households, and between families with and those without children.

The American state has taken a much more confined role in supporting families, especially families with children below school age. Outside of public education, the public sector in the United States has largely resisted redistributing the costs of child rearing. While the European countries were adding universal family allowances, the United States pieced together means-tested (and now time-limited) cash assistance for poor families, supplemented by modest child credits for families with tax liabilities and (later) a refundable Earned Income Tax Credit (EITC) for low-income employed parents. While many of the countries of Europe were establishing child- or parent-based entitlements to public child care, the United States developed a child care market for parents who could afford to purchase substitute care and limited public programs for poor families. While our European counterparts were enacting paid family leave schemes, the United States left the vast majority of workers to negotiate with their employers for wage replacement following childbirth.

The extent to which the United States lags behind the social-welfare states of Europe in using the power of government to socialize some of the costs of caregiving is neatly summarized in a comparison of expenditures on family-related benefits, including family allowances, family-support benefits, lone-parent allowances, paid family leave, and refundable tax credits for families (see Table 34.1). Most of the European welfare states spend in the range of 1.5 to 2.2 percent of gross domestic product (GDP) on these family cash programs; that translates to about $1,400 to $2,300 for each child under the age of 18. The United States, in contrast, spends only 0.5 percent of GDP (including the EITC), and average spending for each child is: just $650.

Table 34.1
Cash Benefits for Families, 1998

Country	Expenditures as Share of GDP (Percentage)	Expenditures per Child Under the Age of Eighteen
Nordic Countries		
Denmark	1.5	$1,822
Finland	1.9	$1,883
Norway	2.2	$2,249
Sweden	1.6	$1,417
Continental Countries		
Belgium	2.1	$2,265
France	1.5	$1,390
Germany	2.0	$2,247
Luxembourg	2.4	$4,270
Netherlands	0.8	$884
English-Speaking Countries		
Canada	0.8	$793
United Kingdom	1.7	$1,557
United States	0.5	$650

Sources: Expenditures data from OECD (2001b); population data from Bureau of the Census (2002a).
Note: Expenditures include cash benefits for families, that is, programs targeted on families (family allowances for children, family support benefits, and lone-parent cash benefits) as well as paid family leave and refundable tax credits for families. Approximately 60 percent of the expenditures in the United States is accounted for by the EITC. Expenditures are in $U.S. 2000, ppp-adjusted.

The Response of Families: Private Solutions

The reluctant American welfare state, combined with the weak collective-bargaining strength of American workers, does little to redistribute the costs of caring for children or to support families who are combining employment and caregiving. In the United States, far more than in most European countries, families have been left to their own devices to craft solutions to the demands of balancing work in the home and in the labor market. More parents work for pay than a generation ago, and many are at work for more hours, yet their responsibilities in the home remain largely unchanged. Parents (mostly mothers) are expected to provide care for children and other family members without compensation and generally without adjustments in employment schedules. They are expected to find alternative care and supervision for children while they themselves are at work, largely without assistance from government. Families are left to craft private solutions when paid work and child rearing create competing demands on their resources.

Contemporary families have demonstrated considerable resourcefulness in crafting these private solutions. One solution chosen by many families is to reduce the employment of one parent. As reported earlier, it is still overwhelmingly women who make this accommodation by reducing hours of work or withdrawing from employment altogether. Although the labor force participation of mothers has risen steeply in recent years, women with young children are still less likely to be employed, and they are likely to work fewer hours (for pay), than either women without children or men. When children are young, most mothers continue to resolve the competing demands of employment and home by limiting their time in the labor market.

Other families balance competing demands by arranging "split-shift" parenting. A substantial share of two-parent families organizes their schedules so that one parent is employed while the other cares for their children; the second parent goes to work after the first returns home. Many single mothers arrange their employment hours similarly, sharing caregiving shifts with another adult, usually their own mothers; Harriet Presser (forthcoming) reports that one-third of grandmothers who provide child care for their grandchildren have other jobs themselves.

Presser (forthcoming) estimates that one in five employed Americans now works nonstandard hours (evenings, nights, or on rotating shifts), and one in three works Saturdays or Sundays, or both. Why is there so much employment during nonstandard hours? The growth in nonstandard-hour work is usually explained by changes in employer demand (Presser forthcoming; Kimmel and Powell 2001). The majority of workers with nonstandard hours are employed in the rapidly expanding and relatively low-skilled, low-paying service sector. Moreover, in the modern twenty-four-hour economy, the services provided by these workers—cashiers, waiters and waitresses, janitors and cleaners, nurses, orderlies, and nursing attendants—are demanded at all hours.

Although demand-side factors seem to drive the overall prevalence of round-the-clock employment, many workers seek nonstandard hours to accommodate their caregiving needs. Parents with young children are the most likely to work nonstandard hours: in 35 percent of couples with a child under the age of five, and in 31 percent of dual-earning couples with a child under the age of fourteen, at least one adult works nonstandard hours or weekends (or both) (Presser forthcoming). This accommodation is extensive: Presser (1995) estimates that the presence of a preschool-age child increases mothers' likelihood of working non-day hours by 46 percent. When asked directly, more than one-third

(35 percent) of mothers reported that child care is the primary reason for working nonstandard hours; another 9 percent indicated care for another family member as their primary reason (Presser forthcoming). This proportion may be even higher if the majority of women who indicate "job-related reasons" as the primary reason for nonstandard hours have elected to work in occupations that allow or require them to work during hours when other family members are available for child care.

Finally, many families also accommodate competing market and caregiving demands by shifting a portion of child care out of the home. More than three-quarters of preschool-age children with employed mothers are now cared for in nonparental child care settings; one-half of these children are in care for thirty-five or more hours a week (Capizzano, Adams, and Sonenstein 2000). Some of this care is provided by relatives, but nearly half of preschool-age children are cared for in child care centers or family child care homes. The use of child care has increased steadily with maternal employment, and recent increases have been particularly steep for very young children. Two-thirds of children with employed mothers are in nonparental care before their first birthday, as are three-quarters of two- and three-year-old children (Ehrle, Adams, and Tout 2001).

School-age children also spend a considerable number of their out-of-school hours in nonparental care. Among children between the ages of six and twelve with employed mothers, nearly half spend an average of 12.5 hours a week in nonparental care arrangements other than school (Capizzano, Tout, and Adams 2000). Parents of school-age children are also much more likely than parents of younger children to leave children without supervision (in "self-care") for at least some portion of their employment hours. According to parents' reports, about 5 percent of six-to-nine-year-old children are in self-care for some hours of the week; by the age of ten, about 23 percent are in some hours of self-care; and by the age of twelve, nearly half spend some time on their own (Capizzano, Tout, and Adams 2000). Because parents may be reluctant to report that they leave children, particularly young children, on their own, these survey-based estimates are likely to be conservative.

The Problem of Private Solutions

Reductions in maternal employment, split-shift parenting, and the extensive use of nonparental care and self-care for children are some of the most significant private responses to the competing demands of the home and the workplace. In the absence of assistance provided by the state or negotiated through collective bargaining, however, these and other accommodations can do little to resolve the fundamental contradiction that arises from society's willingness to benefit from families' caregiving work and its unwillingness to share the costs. Families' solutions are often adaptive in the short term; but they are also creating new financial, time, and social problems for families while exacerbating longstanding problems of gender inequality.

Gender Inequalities in the Labor Market

One of the most significant problems associated with private solutions to work-family dilemmas is that women's withdrawal from employment to care for children (and to perform other domestic work) reinforces deep and costly gender inequalities in employment. Table 34.2 compares the average employment hours of American mothers and fathers as of 2000. (These averages include parents employed for zero hours—that is, they conflate gender differences in both employment rates and hours.) What is perhaps most striking is the constancy of fathers' hours with respect to the ages of their children. Fathers in two-parent families work for pay an average of forty-four hours a week, regardless of the ages of their children. In sharp contrast, partnered mothers' hours fall steadily with their children's ages and, presumably, the

children's needs for care and supervision. As a result, fathers' weekly hours in the labor market exceed those of mothers across all children's age groups—and by as much as twenty hours a week for those with the youngest children.

Anecdotal evidence often attributes gender gaps in employment only to the most advantaged families (because women can afford to opt out of employment) or to those who are less advantaged (because women have fewer incentives to enter employment). A disaggregation of the data suggests otherwise. Gender gaps are similar when we compare women and men in families at different income levels (Table 34.2). In every income group, fathers' hours are largely invariant across the stages of childhood, whereas mothers adjust their labor force attachments to the demands of parenthood. Similar patterns emerge when the data are disaggregated by education (Table 34.3); fathers at every educational level spend substantially more time in the labor market than do their female partners.

These care-related reductions in employment have far-reaching consequences for women. When women weaken their labor force ties to provide care work at home, they incur penalties in wages and opportunities for advancement that last well beyond the early child-rearing years. These employment reductions are the primary factor underlying gender inequality in both employment and earnings. Ann Crittenden (2001) has labeled the reduction in earnings owing to women's disproportionate caregiving responsibilities the "mommy tax" (Crittenden 2001). A number of researchers have estimated the magnitude of this tax. One approach examines the hourly wage penalty associated with motherhood. Jane Waldfogel (1998), for example, finds that after controlling for various individual characteristics, young childless women earned 90 percent as much as men, but mothers earned only 70 percent as much as men. Using longitudinal data and a research design that rules out capturing spurious effects, Michelle Budig and Paula England (2001) estimate that mothers pay a wage penalty of about 5 percent an hour for each child.

Other researchers have estimated the mommy tax as the total reduction in earnings over a woman's entire working life.

Crittenden (2001) estimates that the total lost earnings over the working life of a college-educated woman can easily top $1,000,000. In a middle-income family— for example, one in which a father earns

---

Table 34.2
Average Weekly Hours Spent in Market Work by Mothers and Fathers in Two-Parent Families, by Income Quartile, 2000

Age of Youngest Child (Years)	Mothers (A)	Fathers (B)	Total (A + B)	Difference (B–A)
All two-parent families				
Birth to two	24	44	68	20
Three to five	24	44	68	20
Six to twelve	28	44	72	16
Thirteen to seventeen	31	44	75	13
Low-income families (bottom quartile)				
Birth to two	16	40	56	24
Three to five	19	39	58	20
Six to twelve	21	38	59	17
Thirteen to seventeen	22	35	57	13
Middle-income families (middle two quartiles)				
Birth to two	26	45	71	19
Three to five	26	44	70	18
Six to twelve	30	44	74	14
Thirteen to seventeen	32	43	75	11
High-income families (top quartile)				
Birth to two	27	47	74	20
Three to five	27	47	74	20
Six to twelve	30	47	77	17
Thirteen to seventeen	34	48	82	14

Source: Authors' calculations, based on data from CPS.
Note: Data refer to parents aged twenty-five to fifty. Hours refer to "usual hours worked per week," exclusive of commuting time and lunch breaks. Average hours include persons spending zero hours in market work.

Table 34.3
Average Weekly Hours Spent in Market Work, Mothers and Fathers in Two-Parent Families, by Educational Level, 2000

	Mothers (A)	Fathers (B)	Total (A + B)	Difference (B–A)
Less than high school	21	39	60	18
High school graduate	27	42	69	15
Some college	28	43	71	15
College graduate	27	45	72	18
Postgraduate degree	30	47	77	17

Source: Authors' calculations, based on data from CPS.
Note: Data refer to parents aged twenty-five to fifty. Hours refer to "usual hours worked per week," exclusive of commuting time and lunch breaks. Average hours include persons spending zero hours in market work.

$30,000 a year in full-time work and a mother $15,000 in part-time work—the mommy tax will still exceed $600,000. Although the mommy tax is highest for highly educated women, who can command high market wages, it exacerbates gender inequality in the labor market at all levels of income. For families at the bottom of the skills and earnings distributions, particularly single-mother families, it greatly heightens the risk of economic instability and poverty. As Crittenden suggests, "There is increasing evidence in the United States and worldwide that mothers' differential responsibility for children, rather than classic sex discrimination, is the most important factor disposing women to poverty" (Crittenden 2001, 88).

In sharp contrast, men's lesser engagement in care work advantages them in the labor market. A recent study by Hyunbae Chun and Injae Lee (2001), for example, finds that having a wife raises a married man's hourly wage by about 12 percent on average and by more than 30 percent if the wife is a stay-at-home partner. They conclude that wage gains for men are explained by the degree of specialization within marriage. In other words, it is not the selection of high-ability (and potentially high-earning) men into marriage that explains the marriage wage premium; rather, it is the likelihood that wives shoulder a significant share of household tasks.

The resulting differences in mothers' and fathers' earnings are immense. Among working-age adults with no children, American women take home 41 percent of all labor market earnings each year; among married parents with children, however, women command only 28 percent of total labor market earnings (authors' calculations, based on CPS 2000). This means that among families with children, fathers earn almost three dollars for every one earned by mothers. In families headed by couples, this inequality translates into wives' economic dependency and unequal power in the home. In single-parent families, which are overwhelmingly headed by women, it translates into lower incomes and higher poverty rates. For older women, who have

contributed less to public and private retirement pensions during their working years, it heightens the risk of economic insecurity.

The concentration of women's work in the home has other, noneconomic consequences as well. Men's lesser engagement in the home not only advantages them in the labor market; it also invests them with disproportionate power in the family and positions them to engage more fully in civic and political activities. As the British sociologist Ruth Lister observes, "Women's caring and domestic responsibilities in the private sphere make it very difficult for many of them to participate as citizens in the public sphere" (Lister 1990, 457). Women without strong ties to paid work are less likely to participate in civic activities such as arts and cultural groups, neighborhood or civic groups, and volunteer work (Caiazza and Hartmann 2001). Robert Putnam (2000) finds, similarly, that working inside the home reduces women's participation in public forms of civic engagement.

Gender Inequalities in the Home

Private solutions to work-family demands that rest on women's disproportionate assumption of household and caregiving work have other problematic consequences. Although women's hours of unpaid work have declined with rising employment, their hours in domestic work and caregiving at home continue to exceed men's by a large margin. This leaves many mothers with more total work time and less leisure time than either childless women or men. Moreover, though the cost of gender specialization in the home appears to be steepest for women, men also pay a price, in the form of absences from their children's lives.

Women's disproportionate assumption of caregiving work leaves them little time for other activities when they have dependent children. As described earlier in this chapter, many mothers adjust to the presence of children by reducing their hours in market work. Mothers who are employed also appear to manage the time demands of the workplace and their children by reducing hours devoted to everything else (Robinson and Godbey 1997; Bianchi 2000). Employed mothers spend more than seven fewer hours each week on housework than their nonemployed counterparts. Employed mothers also spend less time sleeping (fifty-five compared to sixty-one hours a week), less time on personal care (sixty-nine compared to seventy-four hours), and much less time in leisure activities (twenty-nine compared to forty-one hours) (Bianchi 2000).

Women spend more time on housework and family caregiving than their male counterparts; and the quality of this time also differs. As of the mid-1990s, women spent about twice as many hours on housework as men. Among married women, 81 to 89 percent of these hours (depending on the data source) were spent on core housework tasks such as cooking, cleaning, and laundry. Among married men, in contrast, 50 to 64 percent of the hours were spent on discretionary tasks such as repairs, paying bills, and car maintenance (Bianchi et al. 2000). Men and women also differ in how they spend their time with children—and when. Mothers, for example, devote an average of nearly thirty-five hours a week to direct child care, in contrast to less than twenty hours a week for men. Of the hours spent in direct care, married mothers are one-and-a-half times as likely as fathers to spend those hours during weekdays, when conflicts with employment are most intense. During those weekdays, one-third of the time women spend in direct care are devoted to children's personal-care activities (for example, bathing, dressing, changing diapers, or feeding) or having meals with children—twice the share of men's hours devoted to these tasks (Fuligni and Brooks-Gunn 2001).

Gender gaps are also evident with respect to "free time"—the time that remains after paid work, housework, child care, and self-care are all completed. Time-diary data suggest that American men and women do not differ greatly in their total hours of free time each day. In their study of the gender gap' in free time, Marybeth Mattingly and

Suzanne Bianchi (forthcoming) report that men have an average of about five and a half hours' free time each day, while women have about a half hour less—a small but significant difference. On the other hand, though this difference is minimal on a daily basis, Mattingly and Bianchi point out that, if extended throughout the year, men's additional free time adds up to 164 hours a year—the equivalent of more than four weeks of vacation (at forty hours a week). In addition to having somewhat less total free time, women have significantly fewer hours of both "pure" free time (time that is not contaminated by nonleisure secondary activities) and "adult" free time (time with no children present).

Women appear to pay the steepest economic and personal costs when families solve work-family dilemmas by allocating a disproportionate share of the care work to women. However, gender inequalities, particularly in the care of children, may have costs for men as well. Most important, the gendered divisions of labor in unpaid work have marginalized men's engagement in the home, including the care and nurturing of their children. The "absent father" problem is most extreme in the growing number of families headed by a divorced, separated, or never married mother. Yet in a substantial number of two-parent homes, resident fathers are nearly as absent from their children's lives as fathers who live elsewhere.

Working Nonstandard Hours: Split-Shift Parenting and Disrupted Family Life

Many of the one-quarter to one-third of couples in which one parent works nonstandard hours rely on what Presser (forthcoming) calls "split-shift" or "tag team" parenting to provide child care for their young children. Split-shift and tag-team parenting, like other aspects of the work-family balancing act, have a gendered cast. Adapting work schedules to respond to caregiving needs remains the domain of women. Mothers are four times as likely as fathers to cite caregiving responsibilities as the primary reason for working nonstandard hours (Presser forthcoming). In addition, though men's likelihood of working evenings, nights, and weekends is unaffected by the presence or ages of children in the home, women are much more likely to work nonstandard hours when they have a preschool child (Presser 1995). As Presser observes, "Women generally are the adapters who arrange their work hours around those of their husbands rather than vice versa. . . . Men are acceptors: they are willing to care for children when mothers are employed" (Presser 1989, 531).

Is split-shift parenting a viable solution to the problem of balancing work and family obligations? Is it just one more symptom of the problem? In terms of gender equality, split-shift parenting has the potential advantage of engaging men more fully in the care of their children. Whether by choice or necessity, fathers are more likely to care for preschool children if their work hours are different from those of mothers (Presser 1989; Brayfield 1995). For example, among dual-earner couples with preschool-age children, two-thirds of families in which the mother is at her job for ten hours or more when the father is not at his job rely primarily on the father to provide child care during those hours (Presser forthcoming).

Although split-shift parenting may help reduce gender inequalities in the provision of care for children, it does so at a high cost to workers and their families. A large body of research from Europe and the United States finds that working nonstandard hours—especially night work and rotating shifts—is associated with workers' likelihood of suffering coronary disease, sleep disturbances, gastrointestinal disorders, and chronic malaise (ILO 1995; Presser 1999); round-the-clock employment also raises the likelihood of workplace accidents (Kauppinen 2001).

What Presser (forthcoming) calls the "social consequences" of nonstandard work schedules are also troublesome for families. She finds that non-day employment is associated with lower marital quality, especially when there are children, and

more-limited interactions between parent and child. Nonstandard schedules are associated with increased likelihood of marital separation or divorce, even controlling for couples' total employment time and time spent together. Married fathers who work fixed night shifts are six times more likely than their counterparts who work days to face marital dissolution; for married mothers, fixed nights increase the odds by a factor of three (Presser 1999).

There is also disturbing evidence that children whose parents work night and weekend shifts fare much worse than other children. Mothers who work nonstandard hours with infants have higher levels of depression, which may diminish the quality of the attention and care they provide to children; preschool-age children whose parents work nonstandard hours are also less likely to be cared for in formal child care settings that may provide important school-readiness experiences (Han 2002). Parents who work nonstandard hours, particularly those working evenings and weekends, have less time to spend with their school-age children (Heymann 2000; Presser 1986), and this may translate into less supervision, help with homework, and other positive inputs. In a study of the effects of nonstandard employment on the cognitive development of infants, Wen-Jui Han (2002) concludes that children whose mothers have ever worked nonstandard hours—and particularly those who work more than thirty hours a week in evening, night, or variable shifts—perform significantly worse on cognitive outcomes at one, two, and three years of age. Examining the effects of nonstandard work on older children, Jody Heymann (2000) finds that, after controlling for other family and parental characteristics, each hour that a parent works between six and nine in the evening corresponds with a 16 percent increase in the likelihood that their children score low in mathematics at school. Children of parents who work nights are also nearly three times as likely to get suspended from school.

Child Care Costs for Parents, Children, and Providers

Many families solve the competing demands of the workplace and the family by shifting a portion of children's care from the family to the market. The movement of women from the home to the labor market when their children are young has greatly increased both the demand for and the supply of nonparental child care. Like other private solutions, however, extensive use of child care has created as many problems as it has solved.

Most nonparental care arrangements in the United States are market based in both provision and financing, and the use of private child care imposes steep financial costs on families. Among working families with children under the age of thirteen, about half pay for child care during their working hours. Across all families, these costs average $286, or 9 percent of family earnings, each month; the share of family income devoted to child care is much higher among families with lower earnings (Giannarelli and Barsimantov 2000). Child care costs are as high as or higher than tuition at public colleges in many states. Unlike the parents of college-age children, however, parents of young children are unlikely to have accumulated savings to pay these expenses.

Reliance on consumer markets for child care has other consequences for the quality of care that children receive. A number of observational studies conclude that the quality of most child care in the United States is low; most estimate that more than half of settings provide care that is "adequate" to "poor" and only about one in ten provide developmentally enriching care (Helburn et al. 1995; Galinsky et al. 1994; NICHD 1997). The generally poor quality of care received by American children reflects the inability or unwillingness of parents to pay the full cost of high-quality care by well-trained professionals. This creates another, often overlooked problem in the American child care market: the impoverishment of a large, low-wage child care workforce dominated by women. Ironically, though market care is costly relative to family budgets, child care professionals are among the most poorly paid of all workers in the United States. Most also work without either employment benefits or realistic opportunities for career advancement. By way of comparison, the average earnings of workers in child care centers are about the same as—and those of family child care providers are barely half of—the wages earned by parking-lot attendants (Whitebook 1999).

Economic Insecurity and Poverty

The movement of many more women into the labor market during recent decades has created new time demands and other social pressures. We would surely expect that this increase in household labor supply was good for families' economic well-being. Indeed, throughout most of the 1990s, the United States experienced one of the longest sustained periods of economic growth in recent history. For a period of several years, the standard economic indicators seemed to convey only better and better news: the economy was growing, stock prices were climbing, unemployment rates were low, and inflation was minimal.

Although many families fared well during the 1990s, many others experienced a different economic reality. The percentage of children living in poverty decreased slightly starting in the late 1990s, but this drop only succeeded in returning the United States to the poverty rates of the 1970s. At the end of the decade, more than 18 percent of children between the ages of six and seventeen, and 22 percent of those under the age of six, were living in families officially defined as poor (Shirk, Bennett, and Aber 1999).

That nearly one in five children lives in poverty is sobering enough. It is even more troubling when we consider just how poor these children are. The formula for setting the poverty threshold in the United States has been under fire for many years. Critics point out that the underlying formula, adopted in the 1950s, was never designed to set the threshold for a reasonable standard of living and has not been updated to reflect nearly a half century of changing household-consumption patterns. The current poverty-line formula also fails to take into account several forms of government assistance—such as food stamps and the EITC—and to account for necessary expenses such as out-of-pocket payment for child care and health insurance. Updating the poverty line to respond to these criticisms suggests that poverty is an even more pervasive problem. For example, applying a "family budget" methodology to estimate the income needed to avoid economic hardship, researchers Heather Boushey and her colleagues of the Economic Policy Institute estimate that whereas 10 percent of families with children were "officially" poor in the late 1990s, nearly 30 percent had incomes below the level required for a safe and decent standard of living (Boushey et al. 2001).

The causes of persistent poverty and economic insecurity in the United States are complex. Like gender inequality, they have roots in both the economic transformations of the industrial and postindustrial eras and the resolutely private American conception of responsibility for children, especially children below school age. Of particular importance for the issues in this book, economic insecurity is heightened for many families with children by the loss of earnings associated with childbirth and early caregiving. Although some workers have the right to unpaid leave at the time of childbirth under the Family and Medical Leave Act (FMLA), the limited availability of paid leave means that many parents cannot take advantage of their right to withdraw from employment to care for infants. Nearly 80 percent of employees who do not take FMLA leave when needed report that the reason is that they could not afford to lose their pay for the period of leave ([U.S.] DOL 2000). The relatively small share of women estimated to have some paid maternity benefits under state temporary-disability insurance programs receive, on average, only $140 to $270 a week in benefits

(Wisensale 2001), well less than enough to keep a family out of poverty. Others, lacking even these protections, rely on public-assistance benefits while on leave ([U.S.] DOL 2000). Once mothers are able to return to paid work, many face losing a substantial portion of their earnings to child care. Despite recent expansions in public child care programs, as few as 10 to 15 percent of income-eligible families are estimated to be receiving child care subsidies ([U.S.] DHHS 2000). In the absence of assistance, child care costs keep some mothers out of employment and push many near-poor families deeper into poverty.

Private Solutions and Child Well-Being

American parents are struggling to resolve competing demands from employment and caregiving, and the evidence is strong that their private solutions impose a variety of economic and social costs. For many, these solutions also fail to provide reasonable economic security. The costs for families are not solely economic, however, another body of scholarship suggests that these private solutions may be compromising children's well-being as well.

Chronic poverty, material hardship, and related problems pose some of the most direct threats to children's well-being. Persistent income poverty places children at risk for problems ranging from poor health to compromised cognitive development, poor school achievement, and early childbearing (Danziger and Waldfogel 2000; Brooks-Gunn, Duncan, and Aber 1997; Kamerman et al. forthcoming.)

Reduced parental availability during children's earliest years may pose another, more subtle risk. Inflexibility in working hours, lack of paid parental leaves, and economic necessity combine to create a limited set of choices for many parents: full-time paid work or no paid work. During the first three years after childbirth, for example, Christopher Ruhm notes that most women either do not hold jobs or work for many hours (Ruhm forthcoming). For many children, this means many hours of each day are spent without the direct care and attention of either, or the sole, parent during their earliest and most developmentally sensitive years. Although parental employment is generally good for children, providing both income and role models, some research suggests that long hours of parental employment during a child's first year of life may be associated with worse developmental outcomes (see Ruhm forthcoming for a review). Lack of parental (or other) supervision owing to employment schedules may be a risk factor for older children as well. Rates of juvenile crime triple during afternoon hours, when many young adolescents are unsupervised, and research suggests that juveniles are especially likely to experiment with drugs, sex, and other risky behaviors during these unsupervised hours (David and Lucile Packard Foundation 1999).

Although still inconclusive, research is suggesting what many parents understand intuitively: children do better when they have sufficient time with their parents, and that is especially true during the first year of life. This is precisely the input into child development that is compromised by many families' private solutions to work-family demands.

Conclusion

American families are struggling to resolve tensions arising from new economic and social arrangements in the family and the labor market. Women expect, and are expected, to participate with men in the labor market; they are also expected to provide most care work in the home. Most parents are employed, but workplaces and social policies are still designed for workers with minimal family responsibilities. Families have increased their labor supply, but many have experienced little real economic progress or have even fallen further behind. Many parents are working nonstandard hours as a child care strategy. Others are purchasing child care in the market and, despite spending an appreciable share of their earnings, are leaving their children in care of mediocre or poor quality. Families

are being forced to make compromises, and these compromises have a distinctly gendered cast: women continue to pay steep wage penalties for motherhood, to experience high rates of poverty, and to care for children for either no or for miserably low wages. These compromises may be imposing still other penalties on children, who get too little of their parents' time when they are very young and care of uncertain quality when their parents are at work.

Although families are facing the challenges of work-family balance in all industrialized countries, families in the United States are doing so in a context of limited public responsibility for the private costs of rearing children. Problems of income and time poverty, gender inequality, questionable child care arrangements, and poor outcomes for children may not be inevitable, however.

Discussion Questions

1. How can you account for the fact that the United States lags far behind other industrialized countries in terms of family-friendly family-work policies?

2. How would you rank order (from easiest to most difficult to achieve) the different family-friendly policies discussed in this chapter?

Janet C. Gornick and Marcia K. Meyers, "The Changing American Family and the Problem of Private Solutions." In *Families That Work: Policies for Reconciling Parenthood and Employment.* © 2003 Russell Sage Foundation, 112 East 64th Street, New York, NY 10021. Reprinted with permission.

References

Bianchi, Suzanne M. 2000. "Maternal Employment and Time With Children: Dramatic Change or Surprising Continuity?" *Demography* 37(4): 401–414.

Bianchi, Suzanne M., Melissa A. Milkie, Liana C. Sayer, and John P. Robinson. 2000. "Is Anyone Doing the Housework? Trends in the Gender Division of Household Labor." *Social Forces* 79(1): 191–228.

Boushey, Heather, Chauna Brocht, Betheny Gunderson, and Jared Bernstein. 2001. *Hardships in*

America: The Real Story of Working Families. Washington, D.C.: Economic Policy Institute.

Brayfield, April. 1995. "Juggling Jobs and Kids: The Impact of Employment Schedules on Fathers: Caring for Children." *Journal of Marriage and the Family* 57(2): 321–332.

Brooks-Gunn, Jeanne, Greg J, Duncan, and Lawrence J. Aber, eds. 1997. *Neighborhood Poverty: Context and Consequences for Children*. New York: Russell Sage Foundation.

Budig, Michelle J., and Paula England. 2001. "The Wage Penalty for Motherhood." *American Sociological Review* 66(2): 205–25.

Caiazza, Amy B., and Heidi I. Hartmann. 2001. "Gender and Civic Participation." Paper presented at the Work, Family, and Democracy Conference. Racine, Wisconsin (June 11–13).

Capizzano, Jeffrey, Gina Adams, and Freya Sonenstein. 2000. "Child Care Arrangements for Children Under Five: Variation Across States." Washington, D.C.: Urban Institute.

Capizzano, Jeffrey, Kathryn Tout, and Gina Adams. 2000. "Child Care Patterns of School-Age Children With Employed Mothers." Washington, D.C.: Urban Institute.

Chun, Hyunbae, and Injae Lee. 2001. "Why Do Married Men Earn More: Productivity or Marriage Selection?" *Economic Inquiry* 39(2): 307–319.

Crittenden, Ann. 2001. *The Price of Motherhood: Why the Most Important Job in the World Is Still the Least Valued*. New York: Metropolitan Books.

Danziger, Sheldon, and Jane Waldfogel, eds. 2000. *Securing the Future: Investing in Children From Birth to College*. New York: Russell Sage Foundation.

David and Lucile Packard Foundation. 1999. "When School Is Out." *Future of Children* 9(2): 4–20.

Ehrle, Jennifer, Gina Adams, and Kathryn Tout. 2001. "Who's Caring for Our Youngest Children? Child Care Patterns of Infants and Toddlers." Washington, D.C.: Urban Institute.

Freeman, Richard B., ed. 1994. *Working Under Different Rules*. New York: Russell Sage Foundation.

Fuligni, Allison Sidle, and Jeanne Brooks-Gunn. 2001. "What Is Shared in Caring for Young Children? Parental Perceptions and Time Use in Two-Parent Families." Paper presented at the Biennial Meetings of the Society for Research in Child Development, Minneapolis, Minn. (April 9).

Galinsky, Ellen, Carollee Howes, Susan Kontos, and Marybeth Shinn. 1994. *The Study of Children in Family Child Care and Relative Care: Highlights of Findings*. New York: Families and Work Institute.

Giannarelli, Linda, and James Barsimantov. 2000. "Child Care Expenses of America's Families." Washington, D.C.: Urban Institute, Human Development Report Office.

Gornick, Janet C. 1999. "Income Maintenance and Employment Supports for Former Welfare Recipients: The United States in Cross-National Perspective." In *Rethinking Income Support for the Working Poor: Perspectives on Unemployment Insurance, Welfare, and Work*, edited by Evelyn Ganzglass and Karen Glass. Washington, D.C.: National Governors' Association Center for Best Practices.

Han, Wen-Jui. 2002. "Nonstandard Work Schedules and Child Cognitive Outcomes." Paper prepared for the Family and Work Policies Committee of the National Research Council and the Institute of Medicine's Board on Children, Youth, and Families.

Helburn, Suzanne, Mary L. Culkin, Carollee Howes, Donna Bryant, Richard Clifford, Debby Cryer, Ellen Peisner-Feinsberg, and Sharon Lynn Kagan, eds. 1995. *Cost Quality and Child Outcomes in Child Care Centers*. Denver: Department of Economics, Center for Research in Economic and Social Policy, University of Colorado at Denver.

Heymann, Jody. 2000. *The Widening Gap: Why America's Working Families Are in Jeopardy—and What Can Be Done About It*. New York: Basic Books.

Hicks, Alexander. 1999. *Social Democracy and Welfare Capitalism: A Century of Income Security Politics*. Ithaca, New York: Cornell University Press.

International Labour Organization (ILO). 1995. *Conditions of Work Digest: Working Time Around the World*. Geneva: International Labour Office.

Kamerman, Sheila B., Michelle J. Neuman, Jane Waldfogel, and Jeanne Brooks-Gunn. Forthcoming. *Social Policies, Family Types, and Child Outcomes in Selected OECD Countries*. Paris: Organisation for Economic Co-operation and Development.

Katz, Michael B. 1986. *In the Shadow of the Poorhouse: A Social History of Welfare in America*. New York: Basic Books.

——. 1989. *The Undeserving Poor: From the War on Poverty to the War on Welfare*. New York: Pantheon Books.

Kauppinen, Timo. 2001. "The 24-hour Society and Industrial Relations Strategies." Accessed April 20, 2003, at: <www.eurofound.ie/industrial/24hr.doc>.

Kimmel, Jean, and Lisa M. Powell. 2001. "Nonstandard Work and Child Care Choice: Implications for Welfare Reform." Paper presented at the conference, From Welfare to Child Care: What Happens to Infants and Toddlers When Single Mothers Exchange Welfare for Work? Washington, D.C. (May 17–18).

Lister, Ruth. 1990. "Women, Economic Dependency, and Citizenship." *Journal of Social Policy* 19(4): 445–467.

Mattingly, Marybeth J., and Suzanne M. Bianchi. Forthcoming. "Gender Differences in the Quantity and Quality of Free Time: The U.S. Experience." *Social Forces* 81(3).

National Institute of Child Health and Human Development (NICHD) Early Child Care Research Network. 1997b. "Poverty and Patterns of Child Care." In *Consequences of Growing Up Poor*, edited by Gary J. Duncan and Jeanne Brooks-Gunn. New York: Russell Sage Foundation.

Patterson, James T. 1986. *America's Struggle Against Poverty: 1900–1985*. Cambridge: Harvard University Press.

Presser, Harriet B. 1986. "Shift Work Among American Women and Child Care." *Journal of Marriage and the Family* 48(3): 551–63.

——. 1989. "Can We Make Time for Children? The Economy, Work Schedules, and Child Care: Population of America, 1989 Presidential Address." *Demography* 26(4): 523–543.

——. 1995. "Job, Family, and Gender: Determinants of Nonstandard Work Schedules Among Employed Americans in 1991." *Demography* 32(4): 577–598.

——. 1999. "Toward a 24-Hour Economy." *Science* 284(541): 1778–1779.

——. Forthcoming. *Working in a 24/7 Economy: Challenges for American Families*. New York: Russell Sage Foundation.

Putnam, Robert D. 2000. *Bowling Alone: The Collapse and Revival of American Community*. New York: Simon & Schuster.

Robinson, John P., and Geoffrey Godbey. 1997. *Time for Life: The Surprising Ways Americans Use Their Time*. University Park: Pennsylvania State University Press.

Ruhm, Christopher J. Forthcoming. "Parental Employment and Child Cognitive Development." *Journal of Human Resources*.

Shirk, Martha, Neil G. Bennett, and J. Lawrence Aber. 1999. *Lives on the Line: American Families and the Struggle to Make Ends Meet*. Boulder, CO: Westview Press.

Trattner, Walter I. 1994. *From Poor Law to Welfare State: A History of Social Welfare in America*. New York: The Free Press.

U.S. Department of Health and Human Services (DHHS). 2000. "Access to Childcare for Low-Income Working Families." Accessed October 21, 2002, at: <www.acf.dhhs.gov/news/press/1999/ccreport.html>.

U.S. Department of Labor (DOL). 2000. "Balancing the Needs of Families and Employers: The Family and Medical Leave Surveys, 2000 Update." Accessed July 9, 2000, at: <www.dol.gov/asp/fmla/main2000.htm>.

Waldfogel, Jane. 1998. "Understanding the 'Family Gap' in Pay for Women With Children." *Journal of Economic Perspectives* 12(1): 137–156.

Whitebook, Marcy. 1999. "Child Care Workers: High Demand, Low Wages." *Annals of the American Academy of Political and Social Science* 563(May): 146–161.

Wisensale, Steven K. 2001. *Family Leave Policy: The Political Economy of Work and Family in America*. London: M. E. Sharpe. ✦

35

The Relationship Between Work-Life Policies and Practices and Employee Loyalty

Patricia V. Roehling,
Mark V. Roehling, and
Phyllis Moen

As seen through previous chapters, the contract between employers and employees has been changing in numerous ways. It is less and less the case that employees can expect long-term job security, rapid advancement, and regular increases in pay and benefits. It is in this context that in this chapter, P. V. Roehling, M. V. Roehling, and Phyllis Moen explore the relationships among work-family policies for the provision of child care and flextime, supervisor support of work/life needs and employee loyalty to their employer, current position, and supervisor. Based on data from a national sample of U.S. workers, they find that employee child care policies are related to employee loyalty, varying for women and men at different stages of parenthood. Also, flextime policies are positively related to employee loyalty, with some variation by lifestyle. Most significant is the positive relationship between perceived informal support from supervisors and coworkers and employee loyalty.

Employee loyalty has long been a concern of employers because of its link to behaviors such as attendance, turnover, and organizational citizenship (Schalk & Freese, 1997). Two recent developments, however, have dramatically increased the value of a loyal work force. First, increased competition for employee talent and greater investment in employee development have made turnover more costly, making the retention of employees an acute human resource concern (Cliffe, 1998). Second, the growing transition from the hierarchical organization of work to an empowerment model, thought to be necessary to successfully compete in many business environments (Pfeffer, 1994), involves a loss of employers' formal control structures over their employees. Loyalty becomes a central concern as employers seek assurance that empowered employees will exercise their discretion in the organization's interests (Tsui, Pearce, Porter, & Hite, 1995).

While the importance of employee loyalty has become increasingly salient, there has been a concurrent decrease in the availability of traditional approaches to promote it; long term job security, rapid advancement, and regular increases in compensation have become the exception rather than the rule. Employers are, consequently, searching for different approaches to promote loyalty (Hiltrop, 1995). Many human resource experts argue that the adoption of "work/life policies" will result in a more loyal, committed workforce (e.g., Finney, 1996; Lawlor, 1996). Work/life policies include flexible work scheduling, child care assistance, family-leave policies, and other policies aimed at ameliorating conflicting work and non-work (i.e., off-job) demands. Survey findings indicate that a primary motive for adopting work/life policies is the expectation that they will lead to higher loyalty (e.g., Hochgraf, 1995).

Thus far, however, there has been only modest empirical support for the broad claims that are being made about the link between family responsive policies and employee loyalty. For example, one study of working parents of preschool children found satisfaction with work/life benefits to be positively correlated with organizational commitment (Goldberg et al., 1989), but a companion study using the same sample reported that level of use (number of family benefits actually used) was not a significant predictor of organizational commitment (Greenberger et al., 1989). Grover and Crooker (1995) directly assess the impact of both child care and flexibility policies on the organizational commitment of both parents and non-parents. They found that employees who had access to flexible hour policies had greater affective commitment, and that a policy of providing child care information had a significant impact on the commitment of employees eligible for that benefit. However, a policy of providing assistance with the cost of day care was not associated with higher levels of commitment among any group. Finally, using the 1997 National Study of the Changing Workforce, Bond, Galinsky and Swanberg (1998) found that fringe benefits, including dependent care benefits, explained very little of the variance in employee loyalty, while a supportive work environment explained a great deal of variance.

Although these and other existing research studies (e.g., Aryee, Luk, & Stone, 1998) have contributed to the understanding of the policy-loyalty relationship, based on our review, at least two of the four following limitations apply to most relevant existing studies: (a) no attempt is made to assess the role of supportive or unsupportive environments (e.g., level of supervisor support; Goldberg et al., 1989; Grover & Crooker, 1995); (b) no attempt is made to assess more complex (three-way) theoretically supportable interactions involving policy, gender, *and* other relevant variables (e.g., age, parental status) (Aryee, Luk & Stone, 1998; Bond, Galinsky & Swanberg, 1998; Greenberger et al., 1989; Goldberg et al., 1989); (c) a limited sample is used (e.g., employees from single a organization, only employees with children; Aryee, Luk & Stone, 1998; Goldberg et al., 1989; Green-

berger et al., 1989); or (d) a relatively small amount of variance is explained (Grover & Crooker, 1995). The Bond, Galinsky and Swanberg study addresses all but one of these limitations. They do not assess the interactions between gender and life stage variables as they relate to employee loyalty. We seek to extend their study by examining those complex interactions and by focusing specifically on benefits and workplace support which are specific to work-family issues.

Purpose

This study investigates the impact of family responsive policies on employee loyalty taking into account theoretically identified non-work and work contextual variables thought to influence the policy-loyalty relationship. Similar to Grover and Crooker (1995), the impact of child care and flexible-time policies on the workplace loyalty of both parent and non-parent employees is assessed. More importantly, however, this study extends the important contribution of Grover and Crooker (1995) by: (a) investigating the interaction of policies with relevant life course variables (age, parental status, marital status); (b) assessing the role of informal support for work/life policies; and (c) investigating the ways in which gender is related to policies and life course variables as they influence employee loyalty.

Relationship Between Family Responsive Policies and Employee Loyalty

Several theories that provide complementary insights inform our understanding of the relationship between family responsive policies and employee loyalty: social exchange theory, role theory, and social justice theory. We begin by briefly discussing these theories. Next, the life course perspective is described and its contribution is linked to the theoretical perspectives. Gender differences in the nature of the life course experience and the likely impact of those differences on employee loyalty are also discussed. Finally, we address the likely connections among family responsive policies, informal workplace support, and employee loyalty.

Primary Theoretical Perspectives

Social exchange theory. According to social exchange models of the employment relationship, employees seek a balance in their exchange relationships with organizations by having attitudes and behaviors commensurate with the degree of employer commitment to them (Wayne, Shore, & Liden, 1997). When an employer acts in a manner that is beneficial to employees, and when those actions go beyond the demands of the social role, the generalized norm of reciprocity (Gouldner, 1960) creates feelings of obligation whereby the employees feel they are obligated to be committed to their employers (Wayne, Shore & Liden, 1997). In general, research findings suggest that positive, beneficial actions directed at employees by an organization and/or its representatives create feelings of obligation for employees to reciprocate in positive, beneficial ways, including greater feelings of loyalty/commitment (Eisenberger et al., 1986; Hutchinson, 1997; Wayne, Shore & Liden, 1997).

Theories of social justice. The social exchange perspective provides a theoretical basis for expecting that family responsive policies would lead to higher loyalty *among employees who benefit from the policies.* That perspective also predicts that employees who do *not* receive the benefits of a policy may view the receipt of benefits by others as violating equity and equality norms (Greenberg, 1981; Grover, 1991), which, it is argued, tend to govern the allocation of rewards in business and economic exchange situations (Rothhausen et al., 1998). Perceived violations of justice in organizations are expected to lead to lower loyalty and withdrawal for those employees who perceive the violation (Adams, 1963;

Grover & Crooker, 1995; Rothausen et al., 1998). In this study we examine whether child care policies result in a "backlash" (lower levels of loyalty) among employees who do not directly benefit from those policies. Since flexible time policies potentially benefit all employees, we do not anticipate that backlash will be associated with flexible-time policies.

Role theory. The belief that work and family loyalties involve tradeoffs or require a "balancing" is frequently expressed in the literature (e.g., Bielby, 1992; Becker & Moen, 1999; Cannon, 1998). According to role theory (Cooke & Rousseau, 1984; Goode, 1960), expectations associated with work and family roles can lead to physical and psychological strain in at least two ways. First, expectations associated with the two roles may compete with each other for attention and energy, resulting in interrole conflict. Second, the dual role expectations can lead to an increase in overall workload and to feelings of overload within the work or family domain (Cooke & Rousseau, 1984). The feelings of strain resulting from interrole conflict and/or work overload, in turn, lead to a range of negative affective reactions, including lower job satisfaction, life satisfaction, and commitment to the organization (O'Driscoll, Ilgen, & Hildreth, 1992). This relationship is moderated by role quality. Greater role quality dampens the negative impact of interrole conflict on well-being (Helson, Elliot, & Leigh, 1990; Vandewater, Ostrove, & Stewart, 1997). Research to date finds that work-family conflict can have a negative impact on employee attitudes, including commitment (Kossek, 1990; O'Driscoll, Ilgen, & Hildreth, 1992), and that loyalty in one domain may be negatively related to loyalty in the other (e.g., Jans, 1989). Thus, it might be expected that those with greater role demands will report lower loyalty to work. Further, to the extent that family responsive policies assist employees in managing work and family demands, reducing role strain, employee loyalty should be enhanced.

The Life Course Perspective and Its Contribution to the Primary Theoretical Perspectives

Overview of life course perspective. Researchers have recognized, at least to some degree, that depending on one's life stage, different factors or issues take on differing degrees of importance, and that these varying factors and issues may affect attitudes and behaviors (Giele & Elder, 1998). To date, most of these studies defined life stages by age, parental status, or length of employment in an occupation or organization (occupational and organizational tenure) (e.g., Allen & Meyer, 1993; Morrow & McElroy, 1987; Ornstein, Cron, & Slocum, 1989). Generally researchers have found only a modest, positive relationship between career stage and loyalty. In this study we build on this research by adopting a broader life course perspective which takes into account both the age norm context of the individual and the connecting roles and relationships in a person's life. We operationalize life stage as the intersection of biological age and family configuration, capturing the dynamic movement across both career and family trajectories. Respondents are located in one of six life stages based upon their age, parental status, and age of the youngest child. There are four non-parent stages: young non-parents (ages 18–29), mid-age non-parents (ages 30–39), older non-parents (ages 40–50), and shifting gears (ages 50 +), and two parental stages: parents of preschool aged children (youngest child is 0–5) and parents of school-aged children (youngest child is 6–17).These life stages are a modification of the ten stage model developed by Moen and Yu (1999). This typology allows us to examine the potentially nonlinear relationship between employee age and loyalty, especially as we look at the interaction between, age, gender and employer policies. We also distinguish between parents of preschool children and parents of school-aged children. The potential role strain and the use of flexible-time and child care policies changes as children age. By distinguishing

between parents of preschool or school-aged range, we are able to examine whether these stages have a differential impact on the policy-loyalty relationship. Marital status is an element of one's family configuration that provides another level of social context which spans the life course stages. Marriage may influence the extent of one's obligations to family and work, the support and/or role conflict one experiences, and the nature of the role(s) that assume prominence in ones' life—important considerations from a life course perspective (Goldberg et al., 1989).

Gender differences in life course experiences. Research suggests that employment may take on a different meaning for women than for men. In contrast to men, women's work is more strongly influenced by experiences in other (nonwork) life domains, such as the timing and nature of family transitions (Krecker, 1994; Moen, Dempster-McClain, & Williams, 1992). Thus, women workers tend to confront more work-family role juggling than do their male counterparts (Cox & Harquail, 1991; Hochschild, 1989), and women are more apt to use family-related benefits (Greenberger et al., 1989). Differences in the way that women and men tend to experience and relate to work and nonwork, and the implications of those differences for employee loyalty, have only relatively recently received significant attention in the management literature. As researchers began to address gender differences, the pattern typically found among male samples was not consistently found among females. For example, Lynn, Cao, and Horn (1996) found that commitment to career varied across career stage for men, but not for women.

Hypotheses Involving Life Course Stages

According to social exchange theory, when an employer acts in a manner that benefits their employees the employees will reciprocate through increased levels of loyalty. The concerns, values, needs, and roles that assume prominence at different life course stages also have implications for the extent to which particular employer policies, such as providing child care benefits and flexible-time benefits, are likely to be viewed as beneficial. Recent employee surveys indicate that flexible-time policies are the most popular and most widely used work/life policies (e.g., Gregg, 1998). There appears to be widespread employee appreciation of the symbolism and/or potential practical advantages of being allowed some control over one's work hours. In contrast to child care assistance policies, flexible-hours are expected to be viewed as beneficial by employees across life stages, among both men and women. Therefore, the social exchange perspective would predict that flexible-time will engender greater employee loyalty across all life course stages.

Hypothesis 1a: The presence of flexible-time policies will be positively related to employee loyalty.

While we expect flexible-time policies to be generally related to employee loyalty, across life stage and gender, we also expect that the positive relationship will be stronger among women and employees with children. Because these groups of employees tend to experience greater role strain than their respective counterparts (men, and employees without children), we expect that they will have a greater appreciation for flexible-time policies, and as a result, will be more likely to reciprocate with higher levels of loyalty. Thus, in addition to the general (main) effect predicted in Hypothesis 1a, we predict the following:

Hypothesis 1b: The positive relationship between flexible-time policies and loyalty will be stronger for women and employees with children (employees in the preschool or school-aged children stages).

Employees with children are expected to be more likely to view child care assistance as beneficial than employees without children. Further, because women typically assume primary responsibility for child care, among employees with children, women are expected to place a higher value on

child care assistance provided by their employer, and as a result, feel greater obligation to reciprocate. These considerations, which reflect the social exchange perspective that family responsive policies lead to higher loyalty *among employees who benefit from the policies*, are the basis for following hypothesis.

Hypothesis 2: The relationship between child care policies and employee loyalty will be moderated by life stage and gender. There will be a positive relationship for employees with children (employees in the preschool or school-aged children stages), and that positive relationship will be stronger among women.

We note that Hypothesis 2 does not incorporate the social justice theory argument that employees who do *not* receive the benefits of a policy may view the receipt of benefits by others as violating equity and equality norms, leading to lower loyalty among employees who perceive a violation (Adams, 1963; Grover & Crooker, 1995; Rothausen et al., 1998). If this did occur, it would be evidence of backlash among those employees who do not benefit from child care policies. While this is a plausible argument, it has also been argued that child care policies may lead to a general perception that an employer treats its employees with fairness and concern, resulting in positive affective reactions among employees with and without children (Grover & Crooker, 1995). Because we have no rationale for favoring one of these arguments over the other, we chose to examine whether child care policies result in a "backlash" (lower levels of loyalty) among employees who do not directly benefit from such policies without making a specific prediction.

The Role of Informal Work Environments

Formal *policies* do not necessarily equate with corresponding *practices*. Policy use may be left to supervisor discretion and/or it may be counteracted by negative attitudes and nonsupportive informal work environments (Galinsky, Bond & Friedman, 1996; Raabe, 1990). Although informal support variables have been identified as important in the assessment of the impact of work/life policies (Galinsky, 1988, 1989; Grover & Crooker, 1995), based on our review of the literature, only one study has assessed the relative contribution of work/life policies and the informal work environment. Bond, Galinsky and Swanberg (1998) using the data from the National Study of the Changing Workforce found that a supportive work environment was a more powerful determinant of employee loyalty than fringe benefits. However, Bond et al. used a broad definition of workplace support (including flexible time policies, gender and race discrimination, and respect) and of fringe benefits (including earnings, medical coverage and other traditional benefits). We will examine the workplace-loyalty relationship focusing only on work-family related benefits and support.

In this study we investigate the relationship between employee loyalty and two variables that assess informal support for work/life policies in the workplace. "Supervisor support of work/life needs" (Support) assesses supervisors' affirmative support of employees in their attempt to address work-off work conflicts. For example, allowing an employee to take time off during the day to care for personal or family business (e.g., medical appointments or meeting with a child's parent) or allowing an employee to talk about personal or family issues that affect their work. The second informal support variable, "workplace intolerance of family-to-work interference" (Intolerance), differs from the Support variable in two ways. First, Intolerance refers to the environment of one's workplace (which may include co-workers, upper management and supervisors), while Support focuses on the behaviors of one's supervisor. Second, Intolerance assesses hostile reactions to work-off work conflicts, while Support focuses exclusively on the extent to which the respondent's immediate supervisor engages in affirmative reactions

to such conflicts. Support and Intolerance are conceptualized as related variables that capture distinct aspects of the respondent's work environment.

Supervisor support has been found to reduce work-family role conflict (Goff, Mount, & Jamison, 1990), and to increase loyalty (Bond, Galinsky & Swanberg, 1998), which is consistent with the role theory perspective. The social exchange perspective would also predict that supervisor support involves the kind of social exchange that creates feelings of obligation to reciprocate with increased loyalty (Wayne, Shore & Liden, 1997). In contrast, Intolerance is likely to increase role conflict and create a negative reaction to the work environment that undermines employee loyalty. Because Support and Intolerance are viewed as more proximal influences on employee behavior and attitudes than the organization's policies, and consistent with claims regarding the critical role of work environment support of work-life policies (Grover & Crooker, 1995), we expect that Support and Intolerance will explain variance in employee loyalty above and beyond that accounted for by childcare policies and flexible-time policies.

Hypothesis 3: Informal support for employees with work-family conflict will be positively related to employee loyalty even after controlling for life stage and work/life policy variables.

Method

Participants and Procedures

Respondents for the study were drawn from the 1992 National Study of the Changing Workforce (NSCW), a randomly selected, nationally representative survey of American workers between the ages of 18 and 64. The telephone survey took approximately an hour to complete. The sample included 3,381 respondents (53.2% male), with a mean age of 38.7 (ranging from 17 to 62). Seventy percent of the sample was married or living with a partner, and 42% had a child living at home at the time of the survey. Seventy-nine percent of the sample was White, 11% Black, 8% Hispanic, 1% Asian or Pacific Islander, and 1% Native American (for a further description of the sample see Galinsky, Bond, & Friedman, 1996). Because the employee loyalty construct is not applicable to self-employed individuals, respondents that were self-employed were excluded from the analyses. This reduced the sample from 3,381 to 2,958 participants.

Measures

Life stage. We operationalize "life stage" based on age, marital status,[1] and parental status. We collapsed the ten life stages used by Moen and Yu (1999) into the following six life stages (preliminary analyses of variance demonstrated that the collapsed stages did not differ from each other on employee loyalty): *Young non-parents*[2]—29 years of age and younger with no children living in the home; *Preschool-aged children*—parents whose youngest child is five or younger; *Mid-age non-parents*—respondents aged 30 through 39 with no children living in the home; *School-aged children*—parents whose youngest child having in the home is between 6 and 17 (inclusive); *Older Non-parents*—respondents aged 40 through 49 with no children living in the home; *Shifting gears*—respondents with no children having in the home, aged 50 and older, who are presumably preparing for retirement. We were unable to distinguish between respondents with grown children and childless respondents, so, by necessity, employees with grown children were included in one of the childless categories, the shifting gears category.

Employee loyalty. Employee loyalty was assessed using three items that asked respondents to report how loyal they felt to their employer, current position and supervisor. Each item was scored on a five-point Likert scale ranging from 1 (not loyal) to 5 (extremely). The alpha coefficient for the scale was .81.[3]

Child care policies. A child care policy index score was created by computing the mean of five items assessing whether the

participant's employer provided six child care related benefits (e.g., pay for child care expenses, on site or near site child care centers sponsored by the employer, child care reference and referral source).

Flexible-time policies. A summary score for policies regarding flexible-time was created by computing the mean response to five questions related to the ability of the employee to alter their work schedule to meet the demands of their personal life. The alpha coefficient for this scale was .58.

Supervisor support of work/life needs (Support). This measure assesses the supervisor's affirmative support of employees in their attempt to address work-off work conflicts. Each of three items was scored on a four-point Likert scale ranging from 1 (strongly disagree) to 4 (strongly agree). The alpha coefficient for the scale was .83.

Workplace intolerance of family-to-work interference (Intolerance). Intolerance assesses the work environment's intolerance to interference of family needs in the workplace. Intolerance was assessed by three items, each scored on a four-point Likert scale ranging from 1 (strongly disagree) to 4 (strongly agree). The alpha coefficient for Intolerance was .77. A principal component factor analysis performed on the items from the Support and Intolerance scales indicated two distinct factors representing the above two variables, providing evidence of discriminant validity.

Results

Sample by Life-Stage

Table 35.1 provides a breakdown of number of respondents by life stage, gender and marital status and for mean loyalty scores. There were more respondents in the stage involving school-age children in the home than any other stage. Consistent with other evidence of women's continued role as primary child care providers, there were many more unmarried women in this stage than unmarried men.

Table 35.1
Mean Loyalty Scores for Life Stage, Occupation, and Race Broken Down by Gender and Marital Status

	Men				Women			
	Married[a]		Not married[b]		Married[c]		Not married[d]	
	N	M	N	M	N	M	N	M
Life Stages								
Young non-parents	83	3.8	181	3.6	80	3.8	173	3.7
Mid-age non-parents	59	3.6	126	3.6	67	3.9	93	3.8
Older non-parents	93	3.8	87	3.6	106	4.1	104	3.7
Preschool children	254	3.9	12	3.7	209	3.9	74	3.8
School-aged children	220	3.8	18	3.9	265	3.9	142	3.9
Shifting gears	139	4.0	40	3.7	130	4.1	124	3.9
Occupation								
Professional	386	3.9	178	3.7	394	4.0	290	3.9
Non-professional	463	3.8	286	3.5	465	3.9	423	3.8
Race								
White	665	3.9	316	3.6	684	4.0	479	3.9
Non-white	187	3.8	142	3.7	176	3.9	235	3.7

[a]$n = 849$ [b]$n = 464$ [c]$n = 859$ [d]$n = 713$

Primary Analyses

To investigate the expected complex relationships among gender, marital status, policy, and life course variables on employee loyalty, we performed a hierarchical multiple regression equation, using listwise deletion of missing data, in which we tested for the main effects, two-way interactions, and three-way interactions of the variables of interest. The significance (or non-significance) of all of the interactions that were tested will be noted in the text. However, because of the large number of possible interactions that were tested, the final regression equation did not include all of the interactions that were not significant.

There were a number of missing values for four of our key independent variables: workplace flexibility (240 missing), child care policies (315 missing), supervisor support (343 missing) and intolerance (141 missing). We did two things to correct for this problem. First, we created a dummy variable for each of the four independent variables identifying whether the data for that variable were either present (1) or missing (0). The dummy coded variables were entered into the regression equation on the same step as the corresponding independent variable, controlling for bias associated with those who chose not to answer the questions. Second, for each item used to construct the above four independent variables we substituted the mean score for the missing values, allowing us to retain these subjects for our analyses.

Control variables. To control for the effects of demographic and workplace variables, race (white vs. non-white), occupation (professional vs. non-professional), size of workplace, hours worked per week, and organizational tenure were entered into the regression equation first (see Table 35.2 for a correlation matrix of the criterion and predictor variables). The demographic variables explained a small but significant portion of the variance in employee loyalty (see Table 35.3). Specifically, a higher level of loyalty was associated with longer tenure with an organization, being a professional/manager, being white, working for a relatively small organization, and working relatively long hours per week.

Table 35.2
Correlations Between Dependent and Independent Variables

	2	3	4	5	6	7	8	9	10	11	12	13	14	15	16
1. Loyalty	.06**	−.07**	−.09**	.08**	−.06**	.10**	.19**	.39**	−.27**	−.08**	−.04*	.00	.03	.03	.06**
2. Job tenure	1.00	−.04*	−.10**	.10**	.20**	.05*	−.04	−.01	.02	−.28**	−.07**	.12**	−.14**	.03	.36**
3. Race		1.00	.09**	−.02	.04	.00	−.07**	−.07**	.07**	.02	.02	−.02	.01	.00	−.03
4. Occupation			1.00	−.20**	−.16**	−.18**	−.19**	−.06**	.12**	.06**	−.05**	.00	.00	.00	.00
5. Hours per week				1.00	.10**	.02	.04	−.05*	.02	−.09*	.06**	.07**	.01	−.02	−.01
6. Size of org					1.00	.23**	−.04	−.04	.05**	−.06**	.01	.02	.01	.00	.02
7. Policies—child care						1.00	.27**	.20**	−.20**	.01	.04*	−.01	.01	.01	−.06**
8. Policies—flexibility							1.00	.28**	−.28**	.06**	.03	.00	−.01	−.04	−.05*
9. Support								1.00	−.46**	.10	−.03	−.01	.02	.00	.00
10. Intolerance									1.00	−.05**	.01	.03	.01	.01	.02
11. Young non-parents										1.00	−.17**	−.19**	−.23**	−.25**	−.20**
12. Midage non-parents											1.00	−.15**	−.18**	−.20**	−.16**
13. Older non-parents												1.00	−.19**	−.21**	−.17**
14. Preschoolers													1.00	−.26**	−.20**
15. School-aged														1.00	−.23**
16. Shifting gears															1.00

$**p < .01; *p < .05; N = 2894.$

Gender and marital status. Gender and marital status were entered into the second step of the multiple regression equation (see Table 35.3). These variables explained a significant amount of variance in the equation, raising the multiple R from .16 to .21. Women and married respondents reported higher levels of loyalty than did men and unmarried employees. The marital × gender interaction was not significant. Nor were any other marital status interactions significant (marital status × life stage, marital status × gender × life stage). Therefore, the marital status interactions were dropped from the model, and are not reported here.

Life stage. Dummy coded variables representing five of the six life stages (the shifting gears stage was selected as the omitted category against which the other stages would be compared) were entered in the third step of the multiple regression equation. Entering these variables as a separate group allows for the examination of the potential main effect of life stage on employee loyalty. This step explained a small amount of additional variance (F = 1.96, p = .08) in the loyalty scores (see Table 35.3). In general, employee loyalty tends to increase across life stage (even when controlling for organizational tenure), and parenthood is associated with higher levels of employee loyalty among men, but not women (see Figure 35.1).

Work-life policies: Main effects. Flexible-time policies and child care policies were entered as step 4. These policies explained a significant amount of variance, raising the multiple R from .22 to .29, almost doubling the amount of variance explained (from 4.6% to 8.4%; see Table 35.3). The presence of both flexible-time policies and child care policies were related to higher levels of employee loyalty. The significant beta coefficient for flexible-time policies supports Hypothesis 1a. However, the significant beta coefficient for child care policies was not predicted. The flexible policy dummy code for the missing data was significant at the .07 level. Respondents who did not answer questions regarding flexible-time policies had lower loyalty scores.

Work-life policies: Moderating influences of gender and life stage. To test the predictions that the relationship between flexible-time policies and child care policies are moderated by life stage and gender (Hypotheses 1b and 2), we entered three sets of interaction terms for flexible-time policies and also for child care policies. The

Table 35.3
Hierarchical Multiple Regression Among Unmarried Women Using Loyalty as the Criterion Variable

	R^2 change F^1	Standardized Beta								
		Step								
		1	2	3	4	5	6	7	8	9
Control variables	13.04**									
Hours per week		.07**	.10**	.10**	.10**	.10**	.10**	.10**	.10**	.11**
Race (0 = nonwhite, 1 = white)		−.05*	−.04	−.04*	−.03	−.03	−.03	−.03	−.03	.00
Job tenure		.06*	.06**	.04	.04	.04	.04	.04	.04	.04*
Employer size		−.09**	−.09**	−.09**	−.10**	−.10**	−.10**	−.10**	−.10**	−.07*
Occupation (0 = prof, 1 = non-prof)		−.08**	−.07**	−.07**	−.02	−.02	−.02	−.02	−.02	−.01
Demographic variables	25.86**									
Gender (0 = male, 1 = female)			.12**	.11**	.11**	.11**	.10**	.10**	.12**	.13**
Marital status (0 = single, 1 = married)			.09**	.07**	.07**	.07**	.07**	.07**	.07**	.07**
Life Stage	1.96									
Young non-parents				−.07*	−.10**	−.19**	−.19**	−.24*	−.23*	−.18*
Mid non-parents				−.06*	−.07**	−.13*	−.14*	−.16*	−.16*	−.11
Older non-parents				−.05	−.06*	−.13*	−.13*	−.14*	−.14*	−.06
Preschoolers				−.02	−.03	−.13*	−.13*	−.16*	−.15*	−.05
School-aged				−.03	−.03	−.20**	−.20**	−.22**	−.22**	−.16*
Shifting gears (omitted category)										
Work-life Policies	27.14**									
Flexible-time					.17**	.05	.06	.06	.06	−.01
Child care					.08**	.08**	.08**	.05	.05	.01
Flexible-time missing dummy code					−.03	−.03	−.03	−.03	−.03	−.03
Child care missing dummy code					−.02	−.02	−.02	−.02	−.02	−.01
Policy Interactions										
Flexible-time policies × Life stage interactions	2.22*									
Flex-time × Young non-parents						.12	.13*	.12	.11	.07
Flex-time × Mid non-parents						.00−	.07	.05	.04	.01
Flex-time × Older non-parents						.08	.07	.06	.08	.06
Flex-time × Preschoolers						.12*	.13*	.12	.05	−.01
Flex-time × School-aged						.19**	.19**	.18**	.23**	.19**
Flexibile-time × Gender × Life stage interactions[2]	0.88							—	—	—	—
Child policies × Life stage interactions[2]	0.21							—	—	—	—
Three-way Child care interactions	1.89										
Gender × Child care × Young non-parents										−.03	−.05
Gender × Child care × Mid non-parents										−.07	−.07
Gender × Child care × Older non-parents										.01	−.01
Gender × Child care × Preschoolers										−.13**	−.14**
Gender × Child care × School-aged										.08	.07
Informal support/Intolerance	106.67**										
Supervisor support											.33**
Intolerance of spillover											−.09**
Support missing dummy code											.00
Intolerance missing dummy code											.01
Multiple R		.155	.207	.215	.290	.296	.299	.300	.305	.469
Adjusted R^2		.022	.040	.042	.078	.081	.080	.079	.081	.208

$N = 2652$.
[1] F value for the change in R^2 that occurs when the variables are first entered in the equation.
[2] Step was not significant, therefore individual beta coefficients were not included in the table.
*$p < .05$; **$p < .01$; italics $p < .10$.

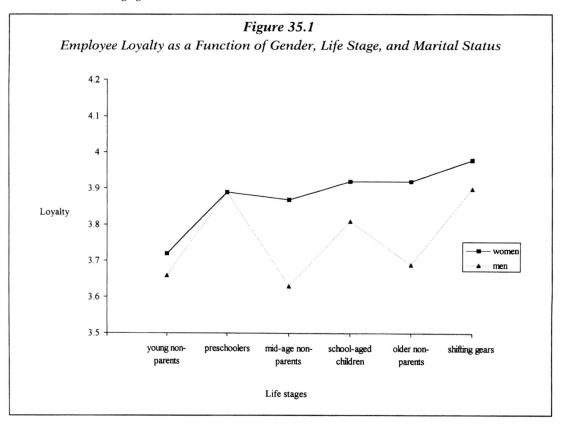

Figure 35.1

Employee Loyalty as a Function of Gender, Life Stage, and Marital Status

first set of interactions entered were the policy × life stage interaction terms. Next we entered the policy × gender interaction term. Finally, we entered the three way policy × gender × life stage interaction terms. The results of each set of interaction analyses will be reported separately for flexible-time and for child care policies. The policy × gender interaction terms did not explain a significant amount of variance for either flexible-time policies or child care policies, so they were excluded from the present analyses. We also tested the two- and three-way interaction terms involving marital status with gender, policies and life stage. None of the interactions were significant, and therefore were not included in the final regression equation.

The flexible-time policy × life stage interaction terms were entered as step 5 in the model. These interactions explained a significant amount of variance (see Table 35.3). To illustrate this interaction, mean loyalty scores across life stages were plotted separately for those with high levels of flexible-time policies and those with low levels of flexible-time (a median split was used to assign values of high and low levels of flexible-time). As Figure 35.2 reveals, flexible-time policies are related to higher levels of employee loyalty across all life stages. However, the relationship is greatest among employees who are of the traditional childbearing ages and particularly among parents of school-aged children. The relationship is the lowest among young non-parents, and employees who are over 50 with no children in the home.

The flexible-time × gender × life stage three way interactions were entered as step 6 in our model. This step did not explain any additional variance (see Table 35.3). Thus, hypothesis 1b received only limited support. The relationship between flexible-time policies and employee loyalty is moderated by life stage but not by gender.

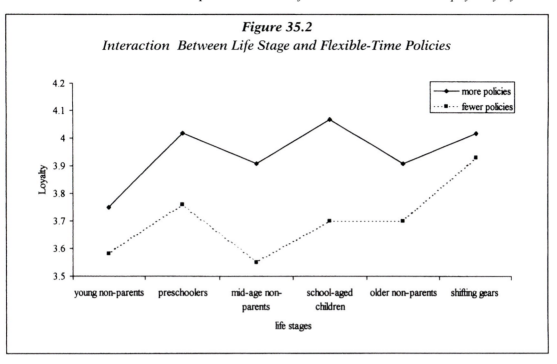

Figure 35.2
Interaction Between Life Stage and Flexible-Time Policies

The child care policy × life stage interaction terms were entered as step 7. This step did not add any significant information to our model (see Table 35.3).

On step 8 we entered the policy × life stage × gender three-way interaction terms. There was a trend toward these variables adding significantly to the regression equation (see Table 35.3). The only three-way interaction term found to have a significant beta coefficient was the one involving preschool-age children stage. To investigate the specific nature of the gender × child care × school aged interaction we plotted mean loyalty scores for each life stage, dividing subjects into groups with a relatively high or low number of child care policies (a median split was used to assign to high or low child care groups). Separate plots were created for women and men (Figures 35.3 and 35.4). The significant three-way interaction suggests that the relationship between child care policy and life stage differs for men and women. As Figure 35.3 demonstrates, for women, child care policies are related to higher levels of loyalty among mothers of school-aged children. However,

contrary to our prediction, the presence of child care policies was not related to higher levels of loyalty among mothers of pre school-aged children.

A closer examination of the individual child care policies examined in our child care policy scale, revealed that most of the increase in loyalty scores among mothers of school-aged children can be attributed to the availability of a child care resource and referral service.

Among men, there was a general positive effect of child care policies on employee loyally, which, contrary to our hypothesis did not appear to be greater for those with school-aged children or preschool-aged children (see Figure 35.4). In partial support of our hypothesis, the policy loyalty relationship was greater among women with school-aged children than it was for men with school-aged children. However, we did not find this to also be true of parents with preschool-aged children. We were surprised to find that child care policies had a generally overall positive relationship with loyalty among men (except in the shifting

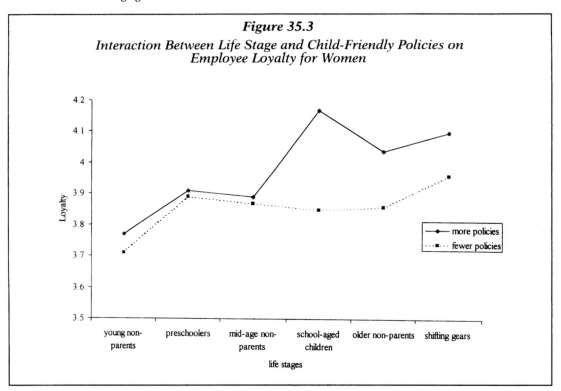

Figure 35.3

Interaction Between Life Stage and Child-Friendly Policies on Employee Loyalty for Women

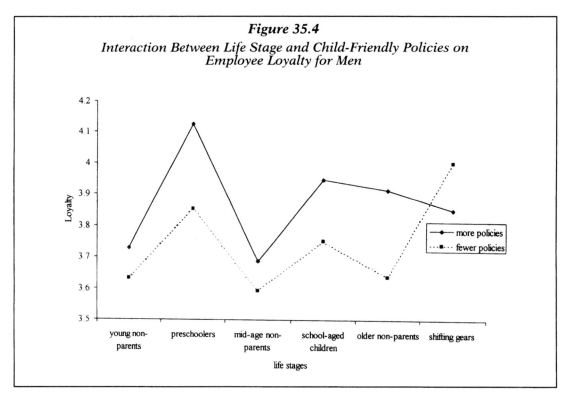

Figure 35.4

Interaction Between Life Stage and Child-Friendly Policies on Employee Loyalty for Men

gears stage) but had more stage-specific positive effects for women.

As Figure 35.4 also illustrates, for men over 50, with no children in the home, the presence of child care policies is related to lower levels of employee loyalty, which may indicate a backlash against child care policies. To test whether this difference was significant we recomputed the regression equation using young non-parents as the omitted category, rather than the shifting gears stage. This allowed us to test the significance of the shifting gears × child care policy interaction. This interaction term was not significant. Therefore we did not find support for a backlash against child care policies by older men with no children in the home.

Unique contribution of informal support/intolerance. In the final step we tested hypothesis 3, that informal support/intolerance would explain a significant amount of variance in employee loyalty after controlling for life stage and work-life policies. Our hypothesis was supported. Informal workplace support variables added significant predictive power for each group of respondents, explaining 13% of the variance beyond that explained by family-responsive policies and the other life course and demographic variables (see Table 35.3). As expected, higher levels of supervisor support and lower levels of intolerance were both associated with higher levels of loyalty.

Discussion

This study draws on survey data from a 1992 national sample of over 3,000 employed respondents to investigate the impact of work/ life policies and practices on employee loyalty taking into account theoretically identified potential moderators of the policy-loyalty relationship. Using a model that combines gender, life course variables, formal policies, informal practices, and relevant interactions, we are able to account for a little less than one quarter of the variance in employee loyalty (compared to the 2%–13% of the variance in organizational commitment that was ex-plained by Grover and Crooker, 1995). We extend previous research by: (1) providing evidence that, although work/life policies tend to be related to higher levels of loyalty for most employees, the strength of the work/life policy-loyalty relationship varies somewhat as a function of employee gender and life stage; (2) highlighting the differential relationships between two distinct types of policies and employee loyalty, policies that benefit employees with children and "employee-responsive" policies which benefit employees in general (i.e., flexible-time) and; (3) demonstrating that workplace tolerance and support for work-family conflict is more strongly related to employee loyalty than actual work-family policies.

Relationship Between Life-Stage and Loyalty (Independent of Work-Life Policies)

While this study focuses on the predicted interaction of life stage and work-life policies in their relationship to employee loyalty, the findings indicate that, independent of work-life policy, life stage is related to employee loyalty (see Figure 35.1). This independent or "main" relationship between life stage and loyalty varies somewhat by gender. Among the men in our sample, loyalty was lowest when there were no children in the home. Arguably, this finding is counter to role theory's suggestion that the fewer roles that one occupies, the more commitment one can give to each role. Rather, it appears that for men the additional role of parenthood is related to greater job commitment. When men become a parent their role as a provider may take on increased salience, thereby increasing their loyalty to their employer.

In contrast, the loyalty scores of married women (who have the highest levels of employee loyalty) are relatively unrelated to the role of parenthood. This also runs counter to what role theory would predict. The additional role of care taker that women traditionally assume with motherhood does not appear to adversely affect employee loyalty among women who remained in the workforce. For these women, rather than producing role strain, parenthood appears to result in role expansion. According to Marks (1977), a proponent of role expansion theory, the addition of a new role need not siphon energy and commitment from preexisting roles. Rather, Marks proposes, commitment can expand to meet the demands of additional roles as long as both roles are valued. Our findings suggest that for most employees, commitment and energy expand to encompass both parental and work roles. In some instances, particularly among men, parenthood may be associated with greater employee loyalty.

Flexible-Time Policies

The findings indicate that flexible-time benefits are associated with increased loyalty for men and women at all life stages, providing strong support for Hypothesis la. In contrast, there was little support for the prediction that the positive relationship between flexible-time benefits and loyalty found among employees in general would be stronger among employees expected to have the highest levels of role strain—women and particularly women with children (Hypothesis lb). Although women typically bear the brunt of care taking responsibilities and household chores (Presser, 1994), and report higher levels of role strain, flexible-time policies, which are widely believed to assist in the management of work-family conflict, are not more likely to be rewarded by women with increased loyalty than they are by men.

There was some evidence that the relationship between flexible-time policies and loyalty varied by life stage. However, the pattern of that relationship was not as expected. We predicted that employees with children (presumably those with the highest levels of role strain) would show the greatest relationship between flexibility and loyalty. While parents did display a strong relationship between flexible-time policies and loyalty, an equally strong relationship was also displayed by middle-aged employees without children.

In summary, using a highly generalizable sample and a multiple item measure of flexible-time benefits, the present findings suggest that flexible-time benefits have wide ranging positive loyalty consequences, with only slight variations associated with life stage. Work-life conflicts are ubiquitous, and it appears that even employees with relatively few role demands value flexible-time benefits and reciprocate with increased loyalty. Of course, these findings are only suggestive. A limitation of this study is that the extent to which employees appreciate or value flexible-time benefits is not directly assessed, and as a result, the role of employee appreciation in mediating the relationship between flexible-time benefits and employee loyalty is not specifically tested.

Child Care Policies

The relationship between child care policies, life stage and loyalty differed for men and women, but, again, not exactly as we hypothesized. We predicted that, consistent with social exchange theory, those who benefited the most from the child care policies would reciprocate with higher levels of loyalty. The expected relationship was found among women with school-aged children. For these women, the presence of child care policies was related to higher levels of loyalty to their employer. However, this was not true of women with preschool-age children, who presumably also have significant day care needs. For these women and for women without children, child care policies are not related to employee loyalty. There was no evidence of backlash associated with child care policies for women without children.

We propose two possible explanations for the relative lack of a relationship between child care policies and loyalty among mothers of preschool-aged children. First, child care policies may have a delayed positive effect on working mothers with young children. Women, compared to men, are typically more stretched by the dual roles of parenthood and work. For women, loyalty may be a finite resource during the taxing preschool years. Child care benefits, while appreciated, may not transmute into higher loyalty until these women are in a position to invest more of their psychological resources into their career, when their children are school-aged.

A second explanation for the relative lack of relationship between child care policies and loyalty among mothers of preschool-aged children may lie in the differing day care needs of preschool versus school-aged children. The day care needs of preschool-aged children are relatively invariant from week-to-week. In contrast, day care needs for school-aged children are variable. Summer vacations, school holidays, teacher conference days, and inclement weather days all require a shift in day care needs. It is difficult to find day care which will accommodate these weekly schedule changes. The availability of a child care resource and referral service was the child care policy that explained most of the increase in the loyalty scores of women with school-aged children. This resource may be particularly helpful to women who are coping with the fluctuating day care needs of school-aged children.

We were surprised to find a strong relationship between child care policies and loyalty among older women with no children in the home. Many of these women may have grown children who no longer live with them. If so, these women may have benefited from child care policies in the past.

We also only found partial support for our hypothesis regarding the relationship between child care policies and life stage among men. We predicted that the child care policy-loyalty relationship would be stronger for women than for men. This was true for men and women with school-aged children but not for those with preschool-aged children. Overall, for men life stage appeared to have little impact on the relationship between child care policies and employee loyalty. Social exchange theory would predict that the relationship between policies and loyalty would have been strongest for men who personally benefit from the policy. Rather, for most men (with

the exception of men over the age of 50 with no children in the home) child care policies were related to higher levels of loyalty. It may be that these men expect to have children, and therefore eventually benefit from child care policies. It may also be that the positive child care policy-loyalty relationship reflects a more general relationship between workplace climate and employee loyalty. Lambert (1995) found that many workers, particularly low income workers, are appreciative of workplace supports, even if they do not plan to use them. The availability of child care benefits may reflect the overall climate of the organization. Employers who offer generous child care benefits may be more supportive of employees in general.

The differences in how flexible-time and child care assistance policies relate to employee loyalty suggest the theoretical importance of distinguishing between policies that benefit employees in general versus those that benefit a narrower subset of employees. It may be a misnomer to call flexible-time policies "family-friendly." Regardless of family configuration these "employee-friendly" policies are associated with higher employee loyalty. In contrast, child care policies, are generally associated with higher employee loyalty but their positive impact is not as broad or predictable.

Informal Support/Intolerance

As hypothesized, supervisor support and intolerance of family-to-work interference are strong predictors of employee loyalty. Workplace environment variables doubled the amount of variance explained by policy and life course variables. Supervisor support was positively related to employee loyalty and an atmosphere of intolerance of family-to-work interference was negatively related to loyalty. This finding suggests that it is not enough to merely espouse employee-friendly policies. Employee loyalty is more strongly tied to the perceived flexibility and tolerance of the work environment than to workplace policies. Thus, the implementation of those policies is crucial to whether they will translate into a loyal workforce.

Limitations and Future Research

Our findings should be appropriately qualified by limitations intrinsic to the design. First, the cross-sectional nature of the data constrain our ability to make causal inferences. Second, the data for both criterion and predictor variables were collected with a survey and may suffer common method variance. This threat primarily applies to the assessment of the relationship between informal support/intolerance variables and loyalty. The other predictors involve factual questions (e.g., existence of specific employer policy, age, gender, etc.) which research has shown are less susceptible to individual perceptual bias as a source of common method variance (Wagner & Crampton, 1994). Third, the study provides a relative lack of data concerning the exact processes by which child care and flexible-time policies affect employee loyalty. Future research should assess the existence of micro-level processes that, according to the various applicable theories, mediate the relationship between policy and employee loyalty. For example, do beneficial policies lead to employee feelings of obligation, as predicted by social exchange theories?

Finally, the finding of a positive relationship between child care policies and employee loyalty among women with school-aged children in the home, but not among women with preschool-aged children, suggests the need for future research to give greater consideration to the potential differential impact of work-life policies over meaningfully distinct stages of parenthood. Much of the existing research focuses on a single stage of parenthood, most commonly on the parenting of young, preschool children (e.g., Greenberger et al., 1989; Goldberg et al., 1989; Grover & Crooker, 1995). Our results suggest that studies focusing on a single stage of parenting may have limited generalizability. For example, Grover and Crooker (1995) focused on the parents of children under the age of six, comparing those parents with all other employees in the sample (parents of children over six and non-parents). Their finding that providing assistance with the cost of day care for children was not associated with higher levels of commitment among parents of young children (nor among employees in general) is consistent with the lack of a positive relationship between child care policies and employee loyalty among women with *preschool-aged* children in the present study. However, the present study's finding that child care benefits were positively related to employee loyalty among women with *school-aged* children clearly suggest that it would be inappropriate to generalize Grover and Crookers' finding to all parents.

Implications for Employers

Several recommendations can be made to employers who are genuinely concerned about promoting or maintaining the level of loyalty in their work force. First, where feasible, employers should consider adopting flexible-time policies. Such policies appear to have an almost universal "employee loyalty pay-off." Second, child care policies, for the most part, are associated with increased employee loyalty, with little evidence of "backlash" among those who do not benefit from them, and should therefore be encouraged. Third, even more important than the presence of employee-friendly policies is the implementation of those policies. Supervisors should be trained to provide an environment in which employees feel that they will not be penalized for work-family conflicts, and that they will receive reasonable, affirmative support in their attempts to address work-nonwork life issues. To promote these practices, supervisor support for work/life issues should be assessed in the performance appraisal process and linked to the reward structure for supervisors.

Discussion Questions

1. To what extent are the empirical findings of this study consistent with the

earlier theoretical and somewhat utopian proposal by Glass (Chapter 30)?

2. Is it possible that employers no longer care about loyalty?

Springer and *Journal of Family and Economic Issues* 22(2001): 141–170, "The Relationship Between Work-Life Policies and Practices and Employee Loyalty," P. V. Roehling, M. V. Roehling, and P. Moen, copyright © 2001. Reprinted with kind permission from Springer Science and Business Media.

Endnotes

1. Includes both married and those partnered who are living together.

2. For the purposes of this study, those without children living in their home are considered non-parents.

3. The 1997 National Study of the Changing Workforce has a one-item measure of employee loyalty. We use the 1992 version because of the greater reliability of the three-item measure of loyalty.

References

Adams J. S. (1963). Towards an understanding of inequity. *Journal of Abnormal and Social Psychology, 67,* 422–436.

Allen, N. J., & Meyer, J. P. (1993). Organizational commitment: Evidence of career stage effects? *Journal of Business Research, 26,* 49–61.

Aryee, S., Luk, V., & Stone, R. (1998). Family responsive variables and retention-relevant outcomes among employed parents. *Human Relations, 51,* 73–87.

Becker, P. E., & Moen, P. (1999). Scaling back: Dual-earner couples' work-family strategies. *Journal of Marriage and the Family, 61,* 995–1007.

Bielby, D. D. (1992). Commitment to work and family. *Annual Review of Sociology, 18,* 281–302.

Bond, J. T., Galinsky, E., & Swanberg, J. E. (1998). *The national study of the changing workforce.* New York: The Families and Work Institute.

Cannon, D. F. (1998). Better understanding the impact of work interferences on organizational commitment. *Marriage & Family Review, 28,* 153–166.

Cliffe, S. (1998). Human resources: Winning the war for talent. *Harvard Business Review, 76,* 18–19.

Cooke, R. A., & Rousseau, D. M. (1984). Stress and strain from family roles and work-role expectations. *Journal of Applied Psychology, 69,* 252–260.

Cox, T. H., & Harquail, C. V. (1991). Career paths and career success in the early career stages of male and female MBAs. *Journal of Vocational Behavior, 39,* 54–75.

Eisenberger, R., Huntington, R., Hutchinson, S., & Sowa, D. (1986). Perceived organizational support. *Journal of Applied Psychology, 71,* 500–507.

Finney, M. I. (1996). Companies help employees manage personal business. *HR Magazine, 41,* 59–63.

Galinsky, E. (1988, August). *The impact of supervisors' attitudes and company culture on work-family adjustment.* Paper presented at the Annual Convention of the American Psychological Association, Atlanta.

——. (1989). The implementation of flexible time and leave policies: Observations from European employers. Unpublished manuscript commissioned by the Panel on Employer Policies and Working Families, National Academy of Sciences.

Galinsky, E., Bond, J. T., & Friedman, D. E. (1996). The role of employers in addressing the needs of employed parents. *Journal of Social Issues, 52,* 111–136.

Giele, J. Z., & Elder, G. H. (1998). The life course mode of inquiry. In J. Z. Giele and G. H. Elder (Eds.), *Methods of life course research: Qualitative and quantitative approaches* (pp. 5–27). Thousand Oaks, CA: Sage Publications.

Goff, S. J., Mount, M. K., & Jamison, R. M. L. (1990). Employer supported child care, work/family conflict, and absenteeism: A field study. *Personnel Psychology, 43,* 793–809.

Goldberg, W. A., Greenberger, E., Koch-Jones, J., O'Neil, R., & Hamill, S. (1989). Attractiveness of child care and related employer-supported benefits and policies to married and single parents. *Child and Youth Care Quarterly, 18,* 23–37.

Goode, W. J. (1960). A theory of role strain. *American Sociological Review, 25,* 483–496.

Gouldner, A. W. (1960). Cosmopolitans and locals: Toward an analysis of latent social roles–II. *Administrative Science Quarterly, 5,* 444–479.

Greenberg, J. (1981). The justice of distributing scarce and abundant resources. In M. J. Lerner and S. C. Lerner (Eds.), *The justice motive in social behavior* (pp. 289–316). New York: Plenum.

Greenberger, E., Goldberg, W. A., Hamill, S., O'Neil, R., & Payne, R. (1989). Contributions of a supportive work environment to parents' well-being and orientation to work. *American Journal of Community Psychology, 17,* 755–783.

Gregg, L. (1998). Humanity in the workplace: When work/family becomes an HR issue. *Credit Union Executive, 38,* 32–38.

Grover, S. L. (1991). Predicting the perceived fairness of parental leave policies. *Journal of Applied Psychology, 76,* 247–255.

Grover, S. L., & Crooker, K. J. (1995). Who appreciates family-responsive human resource policies: The impact of family-friendly policies on the organizational attachment of parents and nonparents. *Personnel Psychology, 48,* 271–288.

Helson, R., Elliot, T., & Leigh, J. (1990). Number and quality of roles: A longitudinal personality view. *Psychology of Women Quarterly, 14,* 83–101.

Hiltrop, J. M. (1995). The changing psychological contract: The human resource challenge of the 1990s. *European Management Journal, 13,* 286–294.

Hochgraf, L. (1995). Why are we putting families first? *Credit Union Management, 18,* 46.

Hochschild, A. R. (1989). *The second shift: Working parents and the revolution at home.* New York: Viking.

Hutchinson, S. (1997). Perceived organizational support: Further evidence of construct validity. *Educational and Psychological Measurement, 57,* 1025–1034.

Jans, N. A. (1989). Organizational commitment, career factors and career/life stage. *Journal of Organizational Behavior, 10,* 247–267.

Kossek, E. E. (1990). Diversity in child care assistance needs: Employee problems, preferences, and work-related outcomes. *Personnel Psychology, 43,* 769–791.

Krecker, M. L. (1994). Work careers and organizational careers: The effects of age and tenure on worker attachment to the employment relationship. *Work and Occupations, 21,* 251–283.

Lambert, S. J. (1995). An investigation of workers' use and appreciation of supportive workplace policies. *Academy of Management Journal Best Paper Proceedings,* 136-140.

Lawlor, J. (1996). The bottom line on work-family programs. *Working Woman, 21,* 54–59.

Lynn, S. A., Cao, L. T. T., & Horn, B. C. (1996). The influence of career stage on the work attitudes of male and female accounting professionals. *Journal of Organizational Behavior, 17,* 135–149.

Marks, S. R. (1977). Multiple roles and role strain: Some notes on human energy, time and commitment. *American Sociological Review, 42,* 921–936.

Moen, P., Dempster-McClain, D., & Williams, R. M. (1992). Successful aging: A life-course perspective on women's multiple roles and health. *American Journal of Sociology, 97,* 1612–1638.

Moen, P., & Yu, Y. (1999). Having it all: Overall work/life success in two-earner families. Forthcoming in T. Parcel (Ed.), *Research in the Sociology of work: Vol. 7.* Greenwich, CT: JAI Press.

Morrow, P. C., & McElroy, J. C. (1987). Work commitment and job satisfaction over three career stages. *Journal of Vocational Behavior, 30,* 330–346.

O'Driscoll, M. P., Ilgen, D. R., & Hildreth, K. (1992). Time devoted to job and off-job activities, interrole conflict, and affective experiences. *Journal of Applied Psychology, 77,* 272–279.

Ornstein, S., Cron, W. L., & Slocum, J. W., Jr. (1989). Life stage versus career stage: A comparative test of the theories of Levinson and Super. *Journal of Organizational Behavior, 10,* 117–133.

Pfeffer, J. (1994). *Competitive advantage through people: Unleashing the power of the work force.* Boston, MA: Harvard Business School Press.

Presser, H. B. (1994) Employment schedules among dual-earner spouses and the division of household labor by gender. *American Sociological Review, 59,* 348–364.

Raabe, P. H. (1990). The organizational effects of workplace family policies. *Journal of Family Issues, 11,* 477–491.

Rothausen, T. J., Gonzales, J. A., Clarke, N. E., & O'Dell, L. L. (1998). Family-friendly backlash—Fact or fiction: The case of organizations' on-site child care centers. *Personnel Psychology, 51,* 685–706.

Schalk, R., & Freese, C. (1997). New facets of commitment in response to organizational change: Research trends and the Dutch experience. *Journal of Organizational Behavior, 4,* 107–123.

Tsui, A. S., Pearce, J. L., Porter, L. W., & Hite, J. P. (1995). Choice of employee-organization relationship: Influence of external and internal organizational factors. In G. R. Ferris (Ed.), *Research in personnel and human resource management, vol. 13*(pp. 117–151). Greenwich, CT: JAI Press.

Vandewater, E. A., Ostrove, J. M., & Stewart, A. J. (1997). Predicting women's wellbeing in midlife: The importance of personality development and social role involvements. *Journal of Personality and Social Psychology, 72,* 1147–1160.

Wagner, J. A., III, & Crampton, S. M. (1994). Percept-percept inflation in micro-organizational research: An investigation of prevalence and effect. *Journal of Applied Psychology, 79,* 67–77.

Wayne, S. J., Shore, L. M., & Liden, R. C. (1997). Perceived organizational support and leader-member exchange: A social exchange perspective. *Academy of Management Journal, 40,* 82–111. ◆

36

The Family Responsive Workplace

Jennifer L. Glass and
Sarah Beth Estes

Jennifer Glass and Sarah Estes review the extant research literature on the current prevalence of various policies within work organizations and their effectiveness on organizational and family functioning. They focus specifically on work hours, flextime policies, and workplace support. They conclude that workers with greater market power may get concessions from employers while low-income workers, young and single parents at the early stage of their work careers, will continue to be least served by policies, in the absence of external, notably federal political pressure on the business community.

Introduction

As the number of dual-earner and single-parent households raising children continues to grow, pressure on organizations to attend to the family responsibilities of employees has been increasing (Families and Work Institute 1991, Goodstein 1994). The sexual division of labor spawned by the development of industrial capitalism in the nineteenth century has given way to a new demographic reality—one in which the responsibilities of workers to provide primary physical care to their dependents are no longer segregated from their responsi-

bilities to provide financially for their families. The US Census Bureau reported that 52% of mothers of infants under one year of age were in the labor force as of 1991 (US Bureau of the Census 1992), while projections indicate that over 85% of employed women can expect to become pregnant at some point during their work life. Indeed, some demographers argue that 90% of women aged 18–49 should be considered active members of the labor force, since even those not currently employed will soon be again (Stipp 1988).

These high rates of female labor-force participation affect men as well, since men are increasingly partnered to women who are likely to be lifetime labor force participants. Without housewives at home to attend to the organization and provision of care to children, fathers are also experiencing tensions between their work and family obligations, although not necessarily the same kind nor to the same degree as mothers (Gerson 1993). Judging from the increased proportion of employed men reporting child-care problems in 1988 compared to 1984, a trend toward greater paternal involvement in family management may be emerging (Fernandez 1990).

Historical Solutions

The problem of reconciling family caregiving with paid employment is not new in the history of industrial capitalism. In the nineteenth century, factories were sometimes filled with entire families working at the same location but at different tasks, justified in part by the need to adequately supervise and monitor children (Hareven 1982). But this pattern did not persist into the twentieth century as the supply of male labor increased and the effects of harsh working conditions on the health of mothers and children became a concern (Brenner & Ramas 1984). The family responsibilities of those women still compelled to work outside the home were addressed through protective labor legislation in the early twentieth century (Kessler-Harris 1982).

Throughout this period, men's roles as husbands and fathers were not ignored by unions and industrialists but were mostly redefined as only breadwinning responsibilities. Thus, some large companies in the early decades of the twentieth century competed for the loyalties of their predominantly male workers by offering a smorgasbord of benefits such as health, life, accident insurance, and pensions in a system that has become known as "welfare capitalism" (Edwards 1979). Because welfare capitalism proved to be expensive and failed to stop union activity, however, most programs did not survive the Great Depression (Edwards 1979).

World War II brought with it a resurgence of interest in work/family issues as the number of women workers in crucial defense industries dramatically increased. Federally funded child-care centers were opened near defense-related factories, temporarily setting aside the ideology of separate spheres for men and women. Although those child-care centers were closed soon after the war ended, some scholars have argued that the war nevertheless ushered in an era in which unions pushed for and corporations increasingly provided social welfare benefits (Cornfield 1990), mirroring many of the benefits offered under welfare capitalism—health and life insurance, pension plans, and disability protection. Importantly, however, this postwar expansion included federally mandated employer participation in such areas as workers' compensation and Social Security, institutionalizing the notion that employers had at least some obligation to provide for the security of the families of their employees.

Yet the degree to which employers rather than the state should be held responsible for the social welfare of families would continue to be contested. In the United States, to a far greater extent than in Western Europe's social democracies, employers have been allowed to vary in the degree of responsiveness they show to workers' family obligations. Strong welfare states in Western Europe assumed much greater responsibility for ensuring that employers contributed to the well-being of families,

through legislative and tax policies that provide paid leaves and reduced work hours for parents of young children and that redistribute income to families with children. The early dependence of European economies on female labor after World War II resulted in explicitly fashioned "family policies" that were designed to protect birth rates while simultaneously incorporating mothers into the labor force (Haas 1991).

In the United States, by contrast, dependence on married women's labor has come relatively late, and employers have mostly avoided regulatory policies that assist parents. Instead, the US welfare state has been fashioned around direct provision of services to families with heads unable to secure employment, financed through general tax revenues. As of this writing, even that minimal guarantee of government assistance to families with children was being decisively limited by federal welfare reform legislation. Yet, legislation that would force employers to accommodate childbearing and family caregiving, or even to sponsor affordable high-quality substitute care while parents work has not been swiftly forthcoming. For instance, the Family and Medical Leave Act of 1993 was twice vetoed by Republican administrations. The version of federally mandated parental leave that ultimately was signed into law shortened the originally proposed leave and contained provisions that exempted small businesses and employees in any business whose job duties were considered essential to the organization's operation.

Some scholars believe nevertheless that the tide is slowly turning in favor of government intervention in the work/family relationship, pointing to the proliferation of bills in the US Congress dealing with work/family issues in recent years (Burstein et al 1995). Although few have yet been passed, the degree of interest certainly suggests possible expansion of the state's interest in regulating the employment of parents of minor children. And the state's abandonment of guaranteed support to parents of minor children might paradoxically increase pressure on lawmakers to legislate solutions to job/family conflict. At present, however, neither government nor employers in the free market have institutionalized policies or procedures for dealing with the influx of workers with caregiving responsibilities into the labor force. No new model has emerged of a relationship between labor, management, and the state that would loosen managerial control over the hours and scheduling of work, allow time for childbearing, and guarantee adequate substitute care for young children.

Part of the problem stems from the fact that children need different types of parental care and supervision at different ages. This problem of heterogeneity in parents' needs is exacerbated by continued ideological debate over the appropriate approach to solving job/family conflicts—while some feel that employers should free workers' time and energy to care for their own children, others promote the transfer of caregiving functions from workers to other institutions such as schools, child-care providers, hospitals, and nursing homes, etc. These divergent perspectives suggest different policy alternatives—extended parental leave for newborns versus infant day care, paid sick days for family illness versus sick-child care, reduced or part-time work hours for parents versus extension of the school day and school year.

Another reason that employers and government have been slow to respond to the needs of parents has been the lack of information about the most efficacious and cost-effective policies to implement. Rigorous evaluation of various workplace policy initiatives designed to reduce job/family stress has, in our opinion, been conspicuously missing. The effects of family responsive policies on parental behavior and children's well-being have not yet received direct attention, although child development experts contributed heavily to the debate on mandated parental leave by summarizing the effects of mothers' early returns to work on the physical and emotional well-being of mothers and infants (Brazelton 1986, Hopper & Zigler 1989).

The remainder of this essay will *(a)* attempt to develop a conceptualization of "family responsiveness" that is rooted in an analysis of the problems employed parents face as well as the organizational problems that ensue from parents' caregiving responsibilities, *(b)* review the prevalence of policies designed to assist employed parents and the determinants of organizational adoption of workplace family policies, and *(c)* evaluate the extent to which various policy initiatives achieve their objectives, whether those relate to family well-being, worker satisfaction, or organizational productivity. We then conclude by discussing the disjuncture between policies that are most likely to solve the dilemmas faced by employed parents and the solutions that employers are likely to adopt strategically without legislative coercion.

The Changing American Worker

Ten years ago, in their review of literature in the then-burgeoning field of work/family conflict, Greenhaus & Beutell (1985) defined work/family conflict as "a form of interrole conflict in which the role pressures from the work and family domains are mutually incompatible in some respect" (p. 77). We look to the survey data on employed parents to determine the sources of job/family conflict as well as the working conditions and policies most desired by parents to ameliorate those conflicts.

What Do Parents Want

It is difficult to state definitively what employees desire in terms of family accommodations. Some studies assessing employees' preferences for workplace initiatives toward reducing work/family conflict sample all employees, while others sample only those with current child-rearing responsibilities. Importantly, the family needs of employees are not homogenous or static. While childbearing employees need leave for childbirth and infant care, parents of preschoolers need high-quality affordable child care and reduced work hours to meet the emotional needs of young children. Parents of school-aged children need after-school, vacation, and summer care, while parents of teens and caregivers of elderly parents need schedule flexibility and leave for emergencies. In a study on the utility of child-care programs, Kossak (1990) showed that these different family and work factors mean that the policies that are optimal for one class of employees at one point in time may have little to no effect on reducing work/family conflict for another class, or even for the same employees at another point in time.

Keeping these methodological caveats in mind, we can draw a general picture of parents' preferences. In a *USA Today* poll (cited in Vanderkolk & Young 1991) in which employed parents were asked what job benefits they considered to be most important, 40% of mothers and 21% of fathers replied that family benefits were the most important job benefits. Another 10% of mothers replied that flexible hours were most important, while 5% of fathers responded in this way. Together, this means that 50% of mothers and 26% of fathers valued family responsive policies in their jobs more than they valued pay (64% of fathers and 42% of mothers considered pay to be most important).

The National Study of the Changing Workforce, utilizing a nationally representative sample of 2958 employees, revealed that close to one fourth of employees lacking flexible schedules or the ability to work at home would change jobs to gain these benefits. Additionally, 47% of those lacking leave time to tend to family illness said they would sacrifice pay or benefits to gain leave for sick family members. Finally, day-to-day family responsibilities were claimed by 87% not just of parents but of all surveyed. The study says this suggests that employee pressure on businesses to become more family-responsive is indicative not simply of special interests, but of widespread need in the labor force *(Social Science and the Citizen 1993/94)*.

In another nationally representative study, respondents indicated that their quality of family life would be improved if, first, they were to receive merit raises, and second, they were provided with trained, family-accommodating supervisors (Galinsky & Stein 1990). In a sample of business and university employees, most indicated that some form of schedule flexibility or work reduction, such as flextime, part-time work, or parental leave, was their top choice toward improving the work/family balance. Rogers (1992) reported that his data from 20 *Fortune* 500 companies showed the work/family policy most consistently highly rated and desired by workers was full-time flexible scheduling; most employees with family responsibilities said they did not want to, or could not afford to, work less.

The types of family needs addressed through workplace initiatives fall into three general categories: *(a)* policies and benefits that reduce work hours to provide time for family caregiving through the provision of leave for vacation, illness, childbearing, and emergency child care or through reductions in average hours worked per week, *(b)* policies designed to give workers greater flexibility in the scheduling of work hours and the location of work hours while not decreasing average work hours, and *(c)* policies designed to provide workplace social support for parents, including forms of child-care assistance so that they work without concern for the care of dependents in their absence (for a similar categorization, see Silver & Goldscheider 1994). This categorization provides a useful heuristic for organizing the vast findings concerning individual-level and family outcomes of work/family conflict as well as for evaluating the effectiveness of organizational work/family policies.

Evidence of job/family conflict can be found both at the workplace and at home. Spillover from work to family affects the family by impairing both individual and family functioning. Spillover from the family to work often takes the form of lower productivity, higher absenteeism, and greater turnover. This family-to-work spillover can result in lowered career achievement for the employee. In the next section we investigate research on work-to-family spillover and its effects on family functioning and individual well-being. Then we review the available research on family-to-work spillover, focusing on the consequences for individual achievement and organizational functioning.

The Effects of Work/Family Spillover

Research has demonstrated fairly consistent links between work/family conflict and physical and mental health as well as to some aspects of family functioning such as marital satisfaction and parenting behaviors. However, measures of work/family conflict often rely on parents' self-reports of conflict levels (Bohen & Viveros-Long 1981, Bedeian et al 1988, Voydanoff 1988, Frone et al 1992) and generally fail to distinguish among different sources of job/family conflict. Because these measures combine conflict stemming from overwork, schedule inflexibility, and unsupportive work environments, it is hard to tell how particular sources of conflict affect various work and family outcomes. For example, Hughes and associates (1992) showed that nonspecific job/family incompatibility decreased marital companionship and increased marital tension. Studies using other measures, such as overtime hours or difficulties arranging child care (Kossak 1990), provide insight into the effects of specific types of work/family conflict. The individual and family outcomes we discuss are organized around the categorization of work/family issues outlined above—extended work hours, inflexibility, and unsupportive work environments.

Work hours. Extended work hours have been linked to work/family conflict (Piotrkowski et al 1987). Frone et al (1994) also demonstrated a link between lack of family time and compulsive drinking and smoking in employed mothers. While the relationship between lack of time and marital solidarity/satisfaction remains unclear (Piotrkowski et al 1987), some evidence suggests that parents' lack of time serves to diminish children's well-being. The increase in time spent in work results in a decrease in time spent with children (Nock & Kingston 1988) and an increase in the time children spend in substitute care, much of which is of relatively low quality in the United States (Cost, Quality & Child Outcomes Study Team 1995). Although decreased quantity of time spent with children does not necessarily indicate that the quality of interactions with children is decreased (Piotrkowski et al 1987), some scholars wonder whether there are upper limits to work hours above which even "quality time" suffers (Louv 1990, Hewlett 1991). Parents are aware of their sacrifice of time with their children to engage in paid employment. Schor (1996), for example, reported an increase in parents' interest in limiting their work time in recent surveys. Although we know that the lack of sensitive, responsive, and consistent care from overworked parents or substitute providers can lead to decreased cognitive and social skills (Parcel & Menaghan 1994) and can promote attachment insecurity in children (Belsky 1990), research is still unclear about the effects this time sacrifice may have on children.

Flexibility. Lack of workplace flexibility has been linked to depression in both women and men (Googins 1991), and to increased physical distress such as difficulty in falling asleep and in staying asleep, changes in appetite, tension-related aches and pains, etc. in men (Guelzow et al 1991). Ralston (1990) demonstrated that the proportion of employed women with rigid work schedules reporting difficulties in child-care arrangements and inadequacies in family time was much higher than the proportion of women with more flexible schedules who reported these problems, although significance levels were not reported.

Workplace social support. Finally, conflict arising from the lack of workplace social support, including child-care assistance, is manifested in the mental health of employees. Ross & Mirowsky (1988) demonstrated that employed mothers who had difficulty making child-care arrangements suffered increased depression. In a national survey, breakdowns in child-care arrangements served to decrease well-being for both mothers and fathers (Galinsky 1994). This study also revealed that workers in unsupportive work environments—

those characterized by discrimination or favoritism—experienced more negative family consequences.

The Effects of Family/Work Spillover

Family-to-work spillover also impairs organizational effectiveness, primarily by affecting absenteeism, productivity at work, and turnover. Child-care difficulties in particular commonly result in these problems. Parents report difficulty with several aspects of child care, such as "lack of time to deal with the very unpredictable nature of child care" (Fernandez 1990: 21), the availability of adequate care, and the affordability of such care (Fernandez 1990). Children who are barred when sick from attending their regular day care must have other arrangements made for them or stay home by themselves; breakdowns in regular child-care arrangements require unexpected time commitments to finding alternative care. Although parents may be able to find such care, their search often results in time lost from work or decreased productivity. Of the approximately 2300 employed mothers in the National Child Care Survey, 15% said they had either been late for work, left early from work, or missed a day of work in the month prior to being surveyed due to failure in their child-care arrangement (Hofferth et al 1991). Thirty-five percent of employed mothers reported that a child was sick on a work day during the past month, and 51% of these mothers stayed home to care for their child, resulting in an average of 2.2 days missed during the month for a sick child. Fernandez (1990) reported that in a 1987/88 survey of over 26,000 employees in diverse companies, 42% of women and 28% of men had missed work in the previous year due to personal/family problems.

Worker productivity is also impaired in other ways by family obligations. Fernandez (1986) reported that parents face work interruptions due to family responsibilities. These interruptions, like absenteeism, decrease as children grow older. Still, these interruptions were reported by 39% of mothers and 17% of fathers with children between ages 15 and 18 (Fernandez 1986). Fernandez (1990) intimated that interruptions probably occur more than parents report, but that parents make up for the infringement of family on work-time by working overtime or taking work home. Further, parental worry over sick children left alone at home, latchkey children who travel on their own from school to home to spend the afternoon alone, or the inadequacy of limited child-care choices has productivity consequences. One study showed that worry over children resulted in wasted time and mistakes in 53% of participants (Perry 1982). When asked if work/family stress affected their ability to concentrate at work, 28% of men and 53% of women sampled from 20 *Fortune* 500 companies replied positively (Rogers 1992). Evidence from experimental studies also supports the idea that the family affects worker productivity. In a sample of mothers, the incompatibility of family and work life decreased concentration and alertness, which resulted in the decreased effectiveness of task-oriented work (Barling & MacEwen 1991).

Another potential workplace outcome of family/work conflict is turnover. Felmlee (1995) found that among women, having preschool-age children was associated with greater rates of job changing and, in particular, job changing that resulted in downward mobility. Collins & Hofferth (1996) showed that the termination of child-care arrangements significantly increased the probability of employment exits among women with high per capita incomes. Other research reveals that women's disproportionate responsibility in the home results in significantly more turnover because of family illness, household duties, and changes in residence (Spilerman & Schrank 1991). Glass & Riley (1996) found that women in jobs requiring excessive time commitments were significantly more likely to change jobs or exit the labor force within one year of giving birth. The evidence supporting the link between family/work conflict and turnover is substantial, although Burke (1989) failed to find a link between work/family conflict and turnover.

The decreased productivity and increased absenteeism and turnover resulting from work/family conflict have serious consequences for the occupational attainment of workers and thus the financial stability of families. The experiences of women in the labor market are instructive. When family responsibilities expand, mothers are more likely than fathers to change jobs, to work part time, or exit the labor force for a spell because families cannot afford to lose father's wages. The result is often a decrease in mothers' financial and occupational attainment (Felmlee 1995, Corcoran et al 1984). Because the sex gap in wages is increasingly explained by differences in the effects of marriage and children on men's and women's wages, Waldfogel (forthcoming) has suggested that we view work/family conflict as the culprit, either through the mechanism of employer discrimination against mothers or employee behavioral adjustments that often result in curbed occupational attainment.

Organizational Interests in Family Responsive Policy

Organizations also suffer when employed parents experience absenteeism, turnover, and lower productivity (Spilerman & Schrank 1991, Goff et al 1990, Raabe 1990, Fernandez 1986). Capowski (1996) reported that over 35% of departing management associates at AT&T cited inability to balance work and family in their exit interviews; significant administrative and training costs were created when these employees had to be replaced. Increasingly, however, organizations are reporting difficulty recruiting employees, particularly managers and professionals, in the absence of family responsive policies (Scott 1992). Indeed, one report indicated that over two thirds of the Fortune 500 companies have instituted some type of family responsive program in order to remain competitive in the skilled labor market (Families and Work Institute 1991).

Prevalence of Family Responsive Policies in Work Organizations

How prevalent are work/family programs at the present time? Organizational surveys differ in their sampling frames and definition of family responsive policy, but they generally agree on two points: (a) tremendous growth has occurred in the number of formal work/family programs in the past 15 years, and (b) most large companies have by now instituted some type of initiative designed to address the family needs of workers for greater schedule flexibility, child-care services, and/or work hours reduction (Families and Work Institute 1991, Friedman 1990, Hewitt Associates 1991). A distinction needs to be drawn, however, between those surveys conducted by the US Bureau of Labor Statistics on firms with over 100 employees and those conducted on very large organizations by private consulting firms, with the former finding far lower rates of family assistance than the latter. For example, in the hours reduction category, the Bureau of Labor Statistics 1989 Employee Benefits Survey shows that 40% of employees held jobs covered by paid or unpaid maternity leave, while the 1991 Hewitt Associates survey of large employers found 56% of employing establishments offering (paid or unpaid) parental leave. Similarly the BLS notes that 11% of workers had flexible schedules available to them, while the Hewitt Associates survey reports that 53% of establishments offered flexible schedules [a figure that rose to 71% in a 1995 Hewitt Associates survey of 681 large firms (Capowski 1996)]. Under the heading of social support, the BLS reported dependent-care reimbursement accounts, (in which employees can set aside pre-tax earnings to pay for child or elder care) covered 23% of employees (Cooley 1990), while Hewitt Associates found 91% of firms offering dependent-care accounts.

Work/family policies are strongly associated with firm size, a finding confirmed by combined BLS statistics on benefit coverage from surveys of both large and small firms (small is defined as fewer than 100 employees). Grossman (1992) showed that maternity leave coverage dropped from 40% to 32% when small firms were included in the calculations; reimbursement accounts dropped from 23% to 18%. Using an earlier 1987 BLS special survey on child-care benefits, Hayghe (1988) reported a clear association between firm size and the proportion of establishments offering any type of direct child-care assistance (defined as financial assistance in paying for care, on-site child care, or information and referral services). Eleven percent of establishments provided some type of child-care assistance overall, but that figure ranged from 9% for firms with under 50 employees to 32% for firms with over 250 employees. Using a broader definition of flexible scheduling (flextime, flexible leave, and voluntary part-time schedules), the BLS survey on child care reported that 61% of establishments with over 10 employees provided some type of flexible work arrangement in 1987, but in contrast to other forms of assistance, there was no relationship between firm size and flexible scheduling (Hayghe 1988).

While these figures overall suggest impressive progress in the organizational adoption of work/family benefits, these benefits are far less institutionalized than others designed to protect traditionally male breadwinning responsibilities. For instance, while 40% of workers in the 1989 BLS survey received maternity leave in their jobs, 53% received leave for military service, 94% received life insurance, and 81% received some type of employer provided pension. Moreover, the extent and coverage of employer-reported family policies remain poorly understood. Survey questions on flextime, child-care assistance, and leave policies rarely explore the degree of employer commitment to the policy. Hyland (1990) showed, for example, wide variation in the duration of unpaid parental leaves for employees covered by leave policies in the 1989 BLS survey. Hayghe (1988) and Hewitt Associates (1991) both showed that flextime, which alters the start and end times of the workday while maintaining an eight hour day/40 hour week, was far more common than

more innovative scheduling policies such as compressed work weeks, job-sharing, and work-at-home arrangements. Child-care assistance is similarly diverse, with the most common forms of assistance being the cheapest and least helpful—dependent-care spending accounts and information and referral services, rather than on- or near-site child care or a direct employer subsidy to pay for care. Even within categories, employer commitment can vary. Some information and referral services simply provide employees with lists of licensed care providers, while others utilize human resource staff to assist parents directly in screening caregivers and locating openings. Direct employer subsidies for child—care expenses vary in the amounts committed, sometimes requiring the sacrifice of other benefits in "cafeteria style" benefit plans.

Furthermore, the degree to which access to family responsive policies is formalized and extended to all employees in organizations remains suspect. In the BLS surveys, individual employees were not surveyed; instead, all employees were assumed to be covered if any employees were covered, an assumption that has been challenged by various researchers. Kush & Stroh (1994) report that in their survey of Chicago firms, most flextime programs were temporary ad hoc arrangements, often restricted to certain classes of employees and/or certain times of the year. Rather than having a permanent formal policy, many organizations implemented flextime in response to specific requests by individual employees. Capowski (1996) quotes one consultant as follows, "When companies say, 'Oh we have flextime, we have telecommuting,' what they mean is, 'We have an individual working here who does this.' They don't mean they have an integrated system. . . . The difference is that in a flexible company these options would be available to everyone, instead of employees having to cut deals." Miller (1992) reports that women in professional and managerial positions are much more likely to receive family friendly benefits such as funded maternity leave, schedule flexibility, and child-care assistance than are women in less skilled jobs. It may be that more highly skilled workers are concentrated in more responsive organizations or have access to formal benefits from which other classes of workers are excluded, but it is also possible that skilled workers are better able to individually negotiate special concessions from their employers because of their greater market power. Given the associations between fertility, education, and occupational status, this means that the mothers most in need of family accommodations (e.g. young single mothers with low earnings and little human capital) are least likely to receive them from their employers.

Even the most optimistic observers of corporate climate admit that very few employers have moved beyond token acknowledgment of the family needs of employees (Galinsky & Stein 1990, Raabe & Gessner 1988). Moreover, the policies and practices of small firms, which employ over one third of the total US labor force and represent the strongest sources of future employment growth, show far less cause for optimism. The available information suggests that small employers offer less generous leave policies and benefits, and poorer working conditions in general, although they compensate for these deficiencies somewhat by offering a broader array of work hours and work schedules than do larger employers (Miller 1992, Wiatrowski 1994).

Most human resource specialists agree that, to be effective, companies must combine various initiatives into comprehensive programs to meet the family needs of workers (Galinsky & Stein 1990, Smith 1992, Capowski 1996). Adoption of a single policy such as flextime is unlikely to yield great benefits to an organization in the absence of other types of organizational assistance. Raabe (1990) reports several studies that have shown earlier returns to work following childbirth among mothers when maternity leave is combined with some form of child-care assistance. In an effort to rate systematically the extent to which companies provided a comprehensive program of family responsive policies, Galinsky et al (Families and Work Institute 1991) developed a typology of stages, with stage 1 indicating no overall strategy and an emphasis on child care, stage 2 indicating an integrated approach with several experimental initiatives, and stage 3 representing integration of family responsive policy into overall business strategy and organizational culture. Using this typology with their survey of 188 large firms, they found that 79% of sampled firms had not moved beyond stage 1, with 33% falling below even stage 1 criteria. Using a comprehensive list of 22 possible types of family assistance among a regional sample of 178 companies with more than 50 employees, Seyler et al (1995) found that 80% had three or fewer types of assistance, with the modal category being only one type of assistance (30%).

Researchers also agree that policies must be combined with supervisor support and advocacy from upper management to close the gap between company policy and practice (Smith 1992, Galinsky 1988, Raabe & Gessner 1988, Capowski 1996). Qualitative evidence has repeatedly revealed that employees will not take advantage of family responsive policies, particularly leave, work reduction, and work schedule policies, if they feel that doing so will jeopardize their job security, work assignments, or promotional possibilities. In some reported cases, employees had to receive supervisor permission before altering work schedules or taking leave, giving managers room to subvert formal company policy. For these reasons, consultants now routinely recommend management training as part of the implementation of work/family programs (Smith 1992).

Determinants of Organizational Adoption of Family Responsive Policies

Because the data on prevalence reveal great diversity in the extent to which employers have adopted family responsive policies, we turn now to the available literature on the organizational innovation and diffusion of work/family programs. Some scholars have used a rational choice perspective in which efficiency considerations either compel or retard organizational solutions to work/family conflict (Glass & Fujimoto 1995, Osterman 1995, Seyler et al 1995, Auerbach 1990). Others have explored the application of institutional theory to explain why employers implement work/family programs, focusing on isomorphism within organizational fields and the effects of professional personnel administration on employee benefits (Osterman 1995, Goodstein 1994, Glass & Fujimoto 1995, Auerbach 1990). Both perspectives suggest that organizations with predominantly female workforces and large firms in general should adopt policies earlier and more comprehensively than others, while institutional theory predicts quicker adoption of work/family policies in firms with formal personnel administration and among firms with frequent interactions with other organizations that have implemented work/family policies. Both perspectives also emphasize the importance of search and replacement costs in the instigation of efforts to reduce turnover—from an efficiency perspective this suggests that organizations with large training costs or greater reliance on skilled labor should more quickly implement family responsive programs, while an institutional perspective emphasizes the role of well-developed internal labor markets and high-commitment work systems (involving self-managed work teams and worker involvement in managerial decision-making) in the adoption of work/family programs.

The literature on this topic is just beginning to substantiate certain empirical regularities in the organizational characteristics of firms implementing family responsive policy. Using the total number of policies adopted by an organization (a rather crude measure given the variation in cost and employer commitment required by different policies), both Seyler et al (1995) and Osterman (1995) found that female concentration within firms and firm size were important determinants of the number of policies offered, although Osterman's results showed that the effect of female concentration disappeared after occupational controls were introduced. Using a categori-

zation scheme that emphasized the comprehensiveness of coverage as well as the number of policies offered, Goodstein (1994) also showed dominant effects of female concentration and firm size. However, Glass & Fujimoto (1995), using a sample of employed women, found that firm size was positively related only to formal benefits, while informal leave policies and schedule policies that depended on supervisor cooperation (working at home or using sick leave for children's illnesses) were more likely to occur in small firms.

Regarding formal personnel management and the need to remain isomorphic with the organization's environment (key components of institutional theory), Osterman (1995) found that the presence of human resource departments increased the number of policies offered, while Goodstein (1994) found large effects of prior diffusion of work/family programs in the organization's industry group. But the conception of "institutional isomorphism" used to explore diffusion of family responsive policy may need to be broadened. Friedman (1990), Auerbach (1990), and others have noted that firms whose product markets target families or have family-sensitive constituents (government or nonprofit social welfare organizations) are often more likely to be committed to workplace family responsive policies in principle and to see the implementation of family responsive policy as good for improving their public image.

The results of studies designed to test the effects of search and replacement costs on the adoption of work/family policies have been mixed. Seyler et al (1995) did not find effects of training costs on the number of work/family policies offered, although they did find that larger recruiting budgets predicted greater financial aid policies for workers with dependent care responsibilities. Osterman (1995) found large effects of high-commitment work systems on the number of family responsive policies offered, as well as strong indications that firms relying on professional and technical workers were more likely to adopt policies, but did not find any effect of the presence of an internal labor market. Glass & Fujimoto (1995) also found that professional and managerial workers were more likely to be covered by formal leave policies and to be able to work regular hours at home.

The empirical work in this area, as in others, would be greatly improved by a more uniform and adequate conceptualization of family responsive policy, one that accounts for both the different types of assistance offered and the intensity of employer commitment to policies (including training of managers and organizational support for employees using these benefits). Another difficulty plaguing investigation of organizational responses to family needs of employees is the inadequate measurement of work/family policies—some studies look only at formally institutionalized policies while others include informal work arrangements negotiated by individual employees. Perhaps part of the strong empirical association between firm size and work/family policies comes from the failure of small firms to have formal personnel policies in general, although they may actually be more receptive to individually negotiated arrangements than are more bureaucratic workplaces. It is also possible that large firms by their size alone are more likely to have at least a few employees on informally negotiated work schedules, and hence they are more likely to report the existence of family responsive policies when in fact those policies are only weakly institutionalized.

Evaluation of Family Responsive Policies

Organizational Effects of Family Responsive Policies

Evaluations of the effects of work/family initiatives focus primarily on employee recruitment, turnover, absenteeism, and productivity. While the literature suggests that organizations sometimes adopt family responsive policies in response to other concerns—the desire to avoid unionization,

forestall government regulation, create a positive public image with important constituents, etc (Friedman 1990, Auerbach 1990)—the available literature centers on the cost effectiveness of various family responsive policies. Though some work/family policies are praised as productivity-enhancers and money-savers, the empirical evidence is rife with problems that impede firm conclusions.

The main impediments to good evaluation research on the productivity effects of family responsive policy have been summarized by Auerbach (1990: 395) as: "a) defining and measuring productivity, b) imputing causality between the [family responsive] benefit and outcomes, and c) determining whether impacts . . . are worth the program's cost to the employer." The few studies that exist often use perceptual measures of work/family policy outcomes rather than behavioral measures of these effects. The lack of longitudinal and comparative data poses another problem in assessing the organizational effectiveness of family responsive policies (Raabe 1990). Without such information, we really do not know how organizational outcomes differ given a different mix of work/family policies. Family responsive policies and their organizational effects will be evaluated in light of these methodological concerns.

Work hours. Policies that address employees' needs for reduced work hours have been linked to both increased organizational productivity and decreased turnover. In one study, 62% of permanent part-time employees attributed increased productivity to part-time employment. Further, for workers in experimental part-time programs who were doing their previously full-time jobs in part-time hours, productivity appears to have been increased (Rogers 1992). However, because these studies rely on soft data in the form of self-reports, the link between reduced work hours and individual productivity is not well established. Findings relating part-time work to turnover suffer from similar problems. Rogers (1992) reported that nearly all of the 30 respondents in a part-time employment program said that, in the absence of the ability to reduce their work hours, they would have left the labor force. However, the link between reduced work hours and turnover was not directly tested.

Schedule flexibility. Flextime is the most widespread and time-tested of work/family policies. In their review of research on the organizational and individual-level effectiveness of flextime programs, Christensen & Staines (1990) found that these policies decreased tardiness, absenteeism, and turnover. Another study utilizing an experimental design demonstrated significant reductions in absenteeism with the implementation of flexible scheduling in the experimental group, although this study failed to find a link between flexible scheduling and turnover (Dalton & Mesch 1990). Further evidence of the efficacy of flexibility for organizations is offered by Rogers (1992). His research shows employees ranked the importance of the flexibility to balance work and family fourth out of sixteen factors in their decision to stay with the company. In the subsample of employees rated as high performers, flexibility ranked second only to compensation (Rogers 1992). Finally, other research has demonstrated a positive association between flextime policies and job satisfaction (Thomas & Ganster 1995, Christensen & Staines 1990). Given the documented link between job satisfaction and turnover (Mueller & Price 1990), policies that increase job satisfaction should be indirectly and negatively related to turnover.

Workplace social support. Formal social support policies, particularly on-site or employer assistance with child care, have shown limited organizational effects. In a study relying on supervisors' perceptions of job performance and child-care related absences, no link between on-site child care and absenteeism was found (Kossek & Nichol 1992). However, on-site child care positively affected employees' decisions to remain employed at the company and increased the extent to which they used the on-site child-care policy as a recruitment tool (Kossek & Nichol 1992). Youngblood & Chambers-Cook (1984) reported similar findings concerning on-site child care and

turnover, and they also failed to find a link between on-site child care and absenteeism. Additionally, Goff et al (1990) failed to find support for the linkage between on-site child care and absenteeism. It appears that on-site child care may be more important for recruitment and retention than dealing with actual day-to-day productivity concerns such as absenteeism. If there is no provision for sick children at the on-site child-care center, parents still have few options for child care when their children are sick, and thus they may provide care themselves.

Effects of Family Responsive Policies on Families

Individual workers and their families also benefit from the implementation of work/family policies, although few studies directly assess parenting behaviors or child outcomes. In this section, we evaluate the effects of flextime policies, reduced work hours, and both formal and informal social support on parents and their families.

Reduced work hours. Reduced work hours have been linked to increased mental health. Hyde et al (1995) showed that the combination of short maternity leave and marital concerns increased depression in women, while the combination of short maternity leave and low levels of job rewards resulted in increased anger in women. Longer time off work postpartum, in combination with other factors, served to decrease depression and anger. Similarly, full-time employment has been linked to increased anxiety levels in mothers. Homemakers and mothers working part-time displayed lower levels of anxiety than mothers who were employed full-time (Hyde et al 1995).

Schedule flexibility. Some research has failed to find a link between formal flextime policies and reduced work/family conflict (Shinn et al 1989), while other research shows associations between flextime and many individual and family outcomes. In a study of nurses (99% of whom were mothers), flextime was linked to decreased work/family conflict, decreased depression, fewer somatic complaints, and lower blood cholesterol (Thomas & Ganster 1995). Other studies reveal that flextime policies can increase time spent with family (Winnet et al 1982) and time spent on family needs (Christensen & Staines 1990). Flextime has also been linked to decreases in employee perceptions of work/family conflict, although it appears to have the least beneficial effects for employed women with husband and children present. Decreases in work/family conflict due to flextime policies are most enhanced for those employees without primary child-care responsibilities (Christensen & Staines 1990).

Social support. Finally, workplace social support also serves to enhance families' well-being. Supportive supervisors have been linked to decreased symptoms of health problems in married men (Greenberger et al 1989), as well as decreased work/family conflict for parents of preschoolers (Warren & Johnson 1995, Goff et al 1990). However, in a sample of parents of preschoolers, on-site child care was unrelated to work/family conflict. On-site child care may not be as helpful to parents as diffuse policies such as flextime, reduced work hours, and supervisory support, which allow parents to take care of their family responsibilities on their own time.

Summary

Although well-designed evaluative studies are still lacking in many areas, some general conclusions can be drawn about the effects of work/family policies on organizational and family functioning. Decreased work hours serve business by increasing employee productivity and decreasing turnover, and they serve families by decreasing depression in employees. Flextime policies increase employee productivity by decreasing absenteeism and turnover, and they positively influence family functioning by decreasing employee depression and work/family conflict while increasing the time families spend together. Importantly, most research conceptualizes schedule flexibility rather narrowly. This focus leaves unexamined policies that allow employees more autonomy in structuring their work hours.

The effects of workplace social support are mixed. On-site child care appears to have little effect on either family or organizational functioning, although a link between employer-provided child care and decreased turnover has been demonstrated. That employer-provided child care does not affect absenteeism, depression, or work/family conflict is somewhat surprising. The clearest advantage of on-site child care is the increase in the availability of child care; but the quality, hours of operation, and cost of on-site child care may not be substantially different than for off-site care. Further, even slots in on-site child-care centers may be limited, meaning spaces may not be available for all employees seeking care. These problems likely limit the effectiveness of on-site child care. However, evidence suggests that informal social support, in the form of sympathetic supervisors, does have positive effects on employees, decreasing symptoms of health problems and work/family conflict.

Barriers to Further Institutionalization of Family Responsive Policy

Scholars are still debating whether organizational recruitment, retention, and productivity problems are sufficient in themselves to prompt widespread adoption of family responsive policies. Effective family responsive policies cost work organizations, particularly in the early stages of development and implementation. In general, the economic motivations to institute family responsive policies remain unclear at best. While work/family programs have generated enormous interest within professional human resource management and are the subject of numerous publications and books, solid research evidence showing economic benefits to corporations instituting work/family programs has been difficult to document. Several scholars doubt that work/family programs can ever be viewed as economically preferable to the simple exclusion of workers with dependent care responsibilities (Hunt & Hunt 1982, Kingston 1990). Tactically, employers may find that statistical discrimination against workers planning or having childcare responsibilities (mostly young women) may be economically rational, particularly for positions involving employer-provided training or entailing large search and replacement costs. For other positions, employers may be willing to hire those with actual or expected caregiving needs because they choose to tolerate greater turnover and ensuing search and replacement costs rather than expend resources on work/family policies.

While evidence suggests that employee demand for family responsive policy is increasing, it is nevertheless the case that most workers only need intensive employer accommodation to family needs for the short period in their life cycle when they have young children at home. Most employees may eventually need family responsive accommodations but not continuously over their life course, thus muting employee pressure on employers at any given time. Unions have expressed increased interest in negotiating family responsive policy as part of their interest in employment sectors predominantly employing women. However, whether unions will be successful in achieving family responsive benefits remains unknown, particularly in this era of declining union membership.

Given the current economic climate in the United States, workers may face even bigger obstacles to family responsive policy in the coming years. While both employers and employees want a "flexible workforce," that term means vastly different things to those two groups. Pressured by shareholders demanding strong economic performance and international competitors seeking to undermine domestic producers, many companies are downsizing their labor force, extracting longer work hours from those that remain, and encouraging the use of temporary and part-time workers paid lower wages and few if any benefits

(Smith 1993, Schor 1992). To employers, this represents a new "flexible workforce." In contrast, employees use the term to indicate greater willingness to prorate benefits for part-time workers or job-sharing partners, allow work at home, and encourage creative scheduling such as fewer work days or staggered work hours to accommodate family schedules. Clearly, the forces of globalization and domestic economic restructuring are encouraging employers to increase productivity and exert more control over labor costs, goals that are often at odds with workers' attempts to increase their family time and preserve their families' well-being.

There may be cause for at least cautious optimism. Some human resource specialists are promoting the use of family responsive work options instead of the existing corporate tools of downsizing and subcontracting to deal with the ebb and flow of labor demand. Offering part-time work with prorated benefits instead of early retirement or layoffs, and using job-sharing, voluntarily reduced work hours, and work-at-home arrangements to cut payroll and physical plant costs are ways that companies can offer true flexibility while still maintaining profitability under intense competitive pressures (Scott 1992, Capowski 1996). Yet this win-win scenario assumes that the timing of workers' family needs will coincide with employers' needs to trim costs; moreover, it assumes that employers can cut costs and still meet caregivers' needs for adequate income (a questionable assumption given the costs of supporting dependents).

Future Research and Policy Directions

This essay has focused on the needs of parents and organizations for accommodations to employees' family obligations, the prevalence and organizational diffusion of specific types of assistance, and the evaluation of those types of assistance on both organizational effectiveness and employee family functioning. However, the motivations of parents and employers are not the same, nor are employees and employers equally powerful in determining the initiatives that achieve widespread adoption. For example, some scholars have castigated the corporate consultants who promote work/family programs for their neglect of the most compelling needs expressed by employed parents—for higher wages and job security (Kingston 1990, Raabe 1990). A more radical view of family responsiveness would promote workplace policies that raise wages while avoiding both excessive work hours and frequent layoffs or downsizing.

In contrast, employers' motivation is to ensure an adequate, trained supply of labor to the firm at the lowest possible cost. That translates into policies that help employees cope with their childrearing or elder care responsibilities without actually increasing the time or money employees have to fulfill those responsibilities themselves. Family responsive policies that free workers to care for their own dependents cut into the unfettered supply of labor to the firm and thus are less likely to be institutionalized in the business community without considerable external pressure (Glass & Fujimoto 1995). While some classes of workers, particularly those with greater market power, may get concessions that limit their employer's ability to schedule work at will, such concessions are unlikely to be extended to the labor force as a whole.

Some examples of the most popular work/family initiatives succinctly illustrate this problem. Flextime has become a commonplace, low-cost policy among employers. Yet flextime typically requires work throughout the "core" hours of 10 am to 3 pm. Moreover, most employees must obtain supervisor consent before they change their specific start and end times of work. These restrictions prevent the kind of flexibility parents require to attend school events, consult with teachers or health care workers, and stagger work hours with a cooperating spouse to increase parental time with children. The really flexible scheduling options for parents—work at home,

compressed work-weeks, freedom to schedule particular days or hours at work, freedom to leave work for emergencies, etc.—are far more rare. Work reduction options, such as job-sharing, and reduced-hour work weeks are even more difficult to find (Russell 1988).

The most popular child-care initiatives, such as information and referral services and flexible spending accounts, are equally problematic. Information and referral services often only provide employees with lists of licensed or registered care providers in the local community. In themselves, these services do nothing to improve the supply, quality, or cost of child care in the community. Just as importantly, they provide no guarantees to parents that the listed childcare providers are adequately trained, have spaces available, or will stay in business. Flexible spending accounts permit employees to use pre-tax earnings to pay for dependent care, substantially lowering the cost of care for earners in higher earnings brackets. However, tax codes already enable most employed parents to save the same amount through the child and dependent care tax credit. Moreover, low-income workers who owe no federal income tax obtain no benefit at all from these spending accounts.

The available evidence suggests collective failure to provide policies to those most in need—low income workers, young and/or single parents at the early stages of their work careers. A more realistic assumption may be that federal intervention will be required to level the playing field for all employers and employees with caregiving responsibilities, in much the same way the minimum wage ensures that labor exploitation does not allow some employers to prosper at the expense of family and community well-being. This has been the path followed by the welfare states of Europe, with accompanying increases in taxation in return (Kamerman & Kahn 1987). However, the United States is moving toward decreased federal and increased state responsibility for social welfare. Without federal minimum safeguards, it seems unlikely that caregivers will be able to advance in the labor market as well as those without caregiving obligations, exacerbating existing problems with child welfare (Spilerman & Schrank 1991).

To develop any type of political consensus on how public policy should assist employed parents, more and better research is needed on the consequences of specific work/family initiatives. In particular, the lack of research directly linking employer policies to parental functioning and child well-being represents a formidable obstacle to policy-making. Moreover, the existing research on costs and benefits to employers needs to be supplemented with research using more rigorous and clearly defined measures of organizational outcomes, as well as more representative samples of employers (including small firms). Finally, we advocate closer attention to the measurement of family responsiveness itself, focusing on three central dimensions: the type of policy (hours reduction, schedule flexibility, or social support), the intensity of the policy (the degree of employer commitment to the policy objective), and the formalization of the policy (the extent to which the policy is available to all employees). With better measurement, the comparative impact of leaves and hours reduction, schedule flexibility, and social support on the functioning of families and organizations can be assessed, as well as the effects of different policy combinations. This remains the research agenda for the future.

Discussion Questions

1. In general, why are companies reluctant to initiate family-friendly policies and programs?

2. If you were a single employee, how would you feel about company policies that provide no benefit to you?

References

Auerbach JD. 1990. Employer-supported child care as a woman-responsive policy. *J. Fam. Issues* 11:384-400

Barling J, MacEwen KE. 1991. Maternal employment experiences, attention problems and behavioral performance: a mediational model. *J. Org. Behav.* 12:495-505

Bedeian AG, Burke BG, Moffett RG. 1988. Outcomes of work-family conflict among married male and female professionals. *J. Mgmt.* 14:475-91

Belsky J. 1990. Parental and nonparental child care and children's socioemotional development: a decade in review. *J. Marriage Fam.* 52:885-903

Bohen H, Viveros-Long A. 1981. *Balancing Jobs and Family Life.* Philadelphia: Temple Univ. Press

Brazelton TB. 1986. Issues for working parents. *Am. J. Orthopsychiatry* 56:14-25

Brenner J, Ramas M. 1984. Rethinking women's oppression. *New Left Rev.* 144:33-71

Burke RJ. 1989. Some antecedents and consequences of work-family conflict. In *Work and Family: Theory, Research, and Applications,* ed. EB Goldsmith, pp. 287-302. Newbury Park, CA: Sage

Burstein P, Bricher MR, Einwohner R. 1995. Policy alternatives and political change: work, family and gender on the congressional agenda. *Am. J. Sociol.* 60:67-83

Capowski G. 1996. The joy of flex. *Mgmt. Rev.* March:14-18

Christensen KE, Staines GL. 1990. Flextime: a viable solution to work/family conflict? *J. Fam. Issues* 11:455-76

Collins N, Hofferth S. 1996. *Child care and employment turnover.* Presented at Annu. Meet. Pop. Assoc. Am., New Orleans

Cooley CA. 1990. 1989 employee benefits address families concerns. *Monthly Labor Rev.* June:60-63

Corcoran M, Duncan GJ, Ponza M. 1984. Work experience, job segregation, and wages. In *Sex Segregation in the Workplace,* ed. B Reskin, pp. 171-91. Washington, DC: Natl. Acad. Sci.

Cornfield D. 1990. Labor unions, corporations, and families: institutional isomorphism and collective rationality in organizational fields. *Marriage Fam. Rev.* 15:37-57

Cost, Quality, and Child Outcomes Study Team. 1995. *Cost, Quality, and Child Outcomes in Child Care Centers, Public Report.* Denver: Dep. Econ., Univ. Colorado, Denver. 2nd ed.

Dalton DR, Mesch DJ. 1990. The impact of flexible scheduling on employee attendance and turnover. *Admin. Sci. Q.* 35:370-87

Edwards R. 1979. *Contested Terrain.* NY: Basic Books

Families and Work Institute. 1991. *Corporate Reference Guide to Work Family Programs.* New York

Felmlee DH. 1995. Causes and consequences of women's employment discontinuity, 1967-1973. *Work Occup.* 22:167-87

Fernandez JP. 1986. *Child Care and Corporate Productivity.* Lexington, MA: DC Heath

——. 1990. *The Politics and Reality of Family Care in Corporate America.* Lexington, MA: Lexington Books

Friedman DE. 1990. Corporate responses to family needs. *Marriage Fam Rev.* 15:77-98

Frone MR, Barnes GM, Farrell MP. 1994. Relationship of work-family conflict to substance use among employed mothers: the role of negative affect. *J. Marriage Fam.* 56:1019-30

Frone MR, Russell M, Cooper ML. 1992. Antecedents and outcomes of work-family conflict: testing a model of the work-family interface. *J. Appl. Psychol.* 77:65-78

Galinsky E. 1988. *The impact of supervisors' attitudes and company culture on work family adjustment.* Presented at Annu. Meet. Am. Psychol. Assoc, Atlanta

——. 1994. Families and work: the importance of the quality of the work environment. In *Putting Families First,* ed. SL Kagan, B Weissbound, pp. 112-36. San Francisco: Jossey Bass

Galinsky E, Stein PJ. 1990. The impact of human resource policies on employees. *J. Fam. Issues* 11:368-83

Gerson K. 1993. *No Man's Land.* New York: Basic Books

Glass JL, Fujimoto T. 1995. Employer characteristics and the provision of family responsive policies. *Work Occup.* 22:380-411

Glass JL, Riley L. 1996. "Family friendly" policies and employee retention following childbirth. Unpublished manuscript, Univ. Iowa

Goff SJ, Mount MK, Jamison RL. 1990. Employer supported child care: work/family conflict and absenteeism: a field study. *Personnel Psychol.* 43:793-809

Goodstein JD. 1994. Institutional pressures and strategic responsiveness: employer involvement in work-family issues. *Acad. Mgmt. J.* 37:350-82

Googins BK. 1991. *Work/Family Conflicts: Private Lives-Public Responses.* New York: Auburn House

Greenhaus JH, Beutell NJ. 1985. Sources of conflict between work and family roles. *Acad. Mgmt. J.* 10:76-88

Grossman GM. 1992. U.S. workers receive a wide range of employee benefits. *Monthly Labor Rev.* Sept:36-39

Guelzow MG, Bird GW, Koball EH. 1991. An exploratory path analysis of the stress process for dual-career men and women. *J. Marriage Fam.* 53:151-64

Haas L. 1991. Equal parenthood and social policy: lessons from a study of parental leave in Sweden. In *Parental Leave and Child Care.* ed. JS Hyde, MJ Essex, pp. 375-405. Philadelphia: Temple Univ. Press

Hareven TK. 1982. *Family Time and Industrial Time: The Relationship Between the Family and Work in a New England Industrial Community.* Cambridge: Cambridge Univ. Press

Hayghe HV. 1988. Employers and child care: What roles do they play? *Monthly Labor Rev.* Sept:38-44

Hewitt Associates. 1991. *Work and Family Benefits Provided by Major U.S. Employers in 1991.* Lincolnshire, IL: Hewitt Assoc.

Hewlett SA. 1991. *When the Bough Breaks.* New York: Basic Books

Hofferth SL, Brayfield A, Deich S, Holcomb P. 1991. *National Child Care Survey, 1990.* Washington, DC: Urban Inst.

Hopper P, Zigler E. 1989. The medical and social science basis for a national infant care leave policy. *Am. J. Orthopsychiatry,* 58:324-38

Hughes D, Galinsky E, Morris A. 1992. The effects of job characteristics on marital quality: specifying linking mechanisms. *J. Marriage Fam.* 54:31-42

Hunt JG, Hunt LL. 1982. Dual career families: vanguard of the future or residue of the past? In *Two Paychecks: Life in Dual-Earner Families,* ed. J Aldous, pp. 41-60. Beverly Hills: Sage

Hyde JS, Klein MH, Essex MJ, Clark R. 1995. Maternity leave and women's mental health. *Psychol. Women Q.* 19:257-85

Hyland SL. 1990. Helping employees with family care. *Monthly Labor Rev.* Sept:22-26

Kamerman SB, Kahn AJ. 1987. *The Responsive Workplace.* New York: Columbia Univ. Press

Kessler-Harris A. 1982. *Out to Work; A History of Wage-Earning Women in the United States.* New York: Oxford Univ. Press

Kingston P. 1990. Illusions and ignorance about the family responsive workplace. *J. Fam Issues* 11:438-54

Kossak N. 1990. Diversity in child care assistance needs: employee problems, preferences, and work-related outcomes. *Personnel Psychol.* 43:769-91

Kossek EE, Nichol V. 1992. The effects of on-site child care on employee attitudes and performance. *Personnel Psychol.* 45:485-509

Kush KS, Stroh LK. 1994. Flextime: myth or reality? *Business Horizons* Sept/Oct:51-55

Louv R. 1990. *Childhood's Future.* Boston, MA: Houghton Mifflin

Miller B. 1992. The distribution of family oriented benefits. *Issue Brief: Employee Benefits Res. Inst.* Oct:No. 130

Mueller CW, Price JL. 1990. Economic, psychological, and sociological determinants of voluntary turnover. *J. Behav. Econ.* 19:321-35

Nock SL, Kingston PW. 1988. Time with children: the impact of couples' work-time commitments. *Soc. Forces* 67:59-85

Osterman P. 1995. Work/family programs and the employment relationship. *Admin. Sci. Q.* 40:681-700

Parcel TL, Menaghan EG. 1994. *Parents' Jobs and Children's Lives.* New York: Aldine De Gruyter

Perry KS. 1982. Employers and Childcare: Establishing Services Through the Workplace. Washington, DC: US Dep. of Labor

Piotrkowski CS, Rapoport RN, Rapoport R. 1987. Families and work. In *Handbook of Marriage and the Family,* ed. MB Sussman, SK Steinmetz, pp. 251-79. New York: Plenum

Raabe P. 1990. The organizational effects of workplace family policies. *J. Fam. Issues,* 11:477-91

Raabe P, Gessner JC. 1988. Employer family-supportive policies: diverse variations on the theme. *Fam. Relations* 37:196-202

Ralston DA. 1990. How flextime eases work/family tensions. *Personnel* August:45-8

Rogers CS. 1992. The flexible workplace: What have we learned? *Hum. Resources Mgmt.* 31:183-99

Ross CE, Mirowsky J. 1988. Child care and emotional adjustment to wives' employment. *J. Health Soc. Behav.* 29:127-38

Russell C. 1988. Who gives and who gets. *Am. Demographics* May:16-18

Schor J. 1992. *The Overworked American.* New York: Basic Books

——. 1996. *Time, work, money: escaping the cycle of work and spend.* Paper presented at Our Time Famine Conference, Iowa City, IA. March 8

Scott M. 1992. Flexibility can be strategic in marketplace. *Employee Benefits Plan Rev.* March: 16-20

Seyler DL, Monroe PA, Garan JC. 1995. Balancing work and family: the role of employer-supported child care benefits. *J. Fam. Issues* 16:170-93

Shinn M, Wong NW, Simko PA, Ortiz-Torres B. 1989. Promoting the well-being of working parents: coping, social support, and flexible job schedules. *Am. J. Community Psychol.* 17:31-55

Silver H, Goldscheider F. 1994. *Flexible work, family constraints, and women's earnings: a test of the theory of compensating differentials.* Presented at Annu. Meet. Am. Sociol. Assoc, Los Angeles

Smith DM. 1992. Company benefits and policies are only a start to becoming "family friendly." *Employee Benefits Plan Rev.* March: 11-16

Smith V. 1993. Flexibility in work and employment: the impact on women. In *Research in the Sociology of Organizations,* ed. S Bacharach. pp. 195-217. Greenwich CT: JAI

Social Science and the Citizen. 1993-1994. Conflict in the workplace. *Society* 31:2-3

Spilerman S, Schrank H. 1991. Responses to the intrusion of family responsibilities in the workplace. In *Research In Social Stratification and Mobility,* ed. R Althauser, M Wallace, 10:27-61. Greenwich, CT: JAI

Stipp HH. 1988. What is a working woman? *Am. Demographics* 10:24-27

Thomas LT, Ganster DC. 1995. Impact of family-supportive work variables on work-family conflict and strain: a control perspective. *J. Appl. Psychol.* 80:6-15

US Bureau of the Census. 1992. *Current Population Reports, Ser. P-20, No. 458. Household and Family Characteristics: 1991.* Washington, DC: US Govt. Printing Off.

Vanderkolk BS, Young AA. 1991. *The Work and Family Revolution: How Companies Can Keep Employees Happy and Business Profitable.* New York: Facts on File

Voydanoff P. 1988. Work role characteristics, family structure demands, and work/family conflict. *Marriage Fam.* 50:749-61

Waldfogel J. 1997. Working mothers then and now: a cross-cohort analysis of the effects of maternity leave on women's pay. In *Gender and Family Issues in the Workplace,* ed. F Blau, R Ehrenberg. New York: Russell Sage. In press

Warren JA, Johnson PJ. 1995. The impact of workplace support on work-family role strain. *Family Relations* 44:163-69

Wiatrowski WJ. 1994. Small businesses and their employees. *Monthly Labor Rev.* Oct:29-35

Winnet RA, Neale MS, Williams KR. 1982. The effects of flexible work schedules on urban families with young children: quasi-experimental, ecological studies. *Am. J. Community Psychol.* 10:49-64

Youngblood SA, Chambers-Cook K. 1984. Child care assistance can improve employee attitudes and behavior. *Personnel Admin.,* 29:45-95 ✦

37

The Challenge of Organizing in a Globalized Flexible/ Industry: The Case of the Apparel Industry in Los Angeles

Edna Bonacich

Edna Bonacich details the characteristics of the apparel production of "contracting out" as an example of global/flexible production. She then compares strengths and weaknesses of five approaches to organizing the garment workers for better working conditions.

The apparel industry combines some of the most backward production methods with some of the most advanced techniques of labor control in the "new world order" of post-"monopoly capitalism."[1] While basic production still depends on a worker, usually a woman, sitting at a sewing machine, because of advances in computer technology and containerized shipping, the industry has been able to engage in global production to an unprecedented degree. "Globaloney" may apply to some industries, but not to apparel. Garment manufacturers (and retailers) are able to shift production from one region or country to the next in order to seek out the best deal, including, importantly, the lowest labor standards in the world. Since they usually engage in arm's-length transactions, such as contracting and licensing, the level of globalization in this industry cannot be captured by investment figures or data on subsidiary ownership. The lack of fixed capital investment in offshore production increases the ease of mobility of the industry.

Apparel firms contract out labor not only offshore but also locally. The contracting system enables them to maximize "flexibility." Because sectors of the industry, especially women's outerwear, are driven by fashion, they are very risky. Apparel manufacturers are able to externalize the risk by only employing labor as it is needed. Contracting out the labor pushes the risk of production fluctuations onto the contractors, and ultimately onto the garment workers. They are the ones who must bear the instabilities of a boom and bust industry.

In this Chapter I shall describe the system of apparel production in Los Angeles, considering it to be a paradigmatic example of global/flexible production. I shall then briefly ask whether the labor process, as it is found in this industry, represents a return to pre-monopoly capitalist production methods or a new type of post-monopoly capitalist labor regime. Finally, I shall turn to the challenge of organizing workers in this system of global/flexible production (Bonacich 2000, Bonacich and Appelbaum 2000).[2]

The Los Angeles Apparel Industry

The apparel industry in the United States is declining. Every month new reports come out enumerating the loss of jobs, while parallel numbers report the monthly rise in imports. In 1970 the United States only imported $1 billion of clothing. By 1996, of the $95 billion of clothing sold at the wholesale level in the United States, 57 percent was imports (American Apparel Manufacturers Association 1997, 4). Meanwhile U.S. apparel jobs declined from 1.4 million in 1973 to about 800,000 today.

Los Angeles is the one exception to this pattern. Between 1993 and 1997 the LA apparel industry added an estimated 26,000 new jobs (Kyser 1997) and is now the largest apparel employer in the United States. As of December 1997, the industry officially employed 120,600 people, up from 115,300 the previous December. Since there is a large underground economy, the real numbers may be as much as 25 percent higher, making the apparel industry the largest manufacturing employer in LA County.

Why is Los Angeles different from the rest of the country? There are a number of interrelated reasons. The LA apparel industry specializes in the fashion-sensitive women's outerwear sector. Indeed, about one-quarter of all the women's wear made in the United States is now produced in LA. Los Angeles is a fashion center in part because of the presence of the entertainment industry, and in part because of the climate and mystique of "California." As a consequence of the volatility and riskiness of fashion, garment production typically requires the quick sewing of small lots. Local production saves time, and enables greater quality control over constantly changing designs. Moreover, LA has a growing textile industry which enhances the ability to design and produce the clothes quickly.

The character of the local population also encourages garment production in Los Angeles. The city is a center of immigration. Some immigrants come with capital and experience, and they become entrepreneurs in the low-capital garment-contract-ing business. Others are impoverished and some lack legal documents, and they come to LA seeking work. Garment shops are eager to employ them as a low-wage workforce that the employers hope and expect will be docile. Although the low cost of labor in Los Angeles cannot compete head-on with the wages paid in Mexico or China, its low level relative to the rest of the United States, combined with the other features of the local industry, continue to make Los Angeles an attractive garment production site.

Not all LA apparel manufacturers do their production in Los Angeles. Some have almost all of their clothing produced off-shore, while others outsource part of their production. Even if they do produce their garments in Los Angeles, few manufacturers do their own production in-house. They instead make use of contractors, often a fair number of them. There are literally thousands of garment contractors in Los Angeles, spread out across the basin. Most contractors are small businesses, employing an average of 35 workers, but some have over 100 workers and a few range up to 1,000 employees. These firms are typically assembly plants where workers sit at sewing machines and stitch together the cut materials that make up garments.

The contracting system is also a critical aspect of the retention of the industry in Los Angeles. Some regions of the country, notably the South, have large factories that mass-produce standard items. These kinds of factories are not easily adaptable to the production of fashion. Small contracting shops are found in New York and San Francisco, which also produce fashion. But LA has more such shops than anywhere else. Indeed, one can claim that LA has the most advanced system of "flexible production" in apparel manufacturing in the country.

Even though LA garment employment has grown in recent years, there is no guarantee that growth will continue. Industry leaders keep threatening to move production to Mexico, and, since the passage of NAFTA in 1994, there are indications that many have moved at least part of their production there. So far Mexico does not have the capacity to make small lots of highly fashion-sensitive garments sufficiently quickly, but the day may come when Mexican firms can replicate LA firms and more of the industry moves there.

The Benefits of the Contracting System to Manufacturers

The contracting system is touted by manufacturers for the flexibility it provides. Apparel manufacturing is unstable, since it is affected both by seasons and by shifts in fashion. The contracting system enables manufacturers to have work done only when they need it, thereby avoiding the need to maintain a stable labor force that they do not need year-round. The contractors are able to absorb the changing demands of the industry, shifting their work among different manufacturers in an effort to keep their factories running at full capacity.

But there is another side to the contracting system: it also serves as a very effective labor-control mechanism. The contractors typically oversee the sewing or assembly. Some contractors specialize in cutting, laundering, or finishing, but the majority are assembly plants. By contracting out, the manufacturers externalize the labor. The manufacturers never lose title to the goods that the contractors sew; they do not *sell* the cut goods to the contractors. Instead, the contractors supply only the labor. They are essentially labor contractors.

As noted, most contractors are small businesses. They are typically run by immigrant entrepreneurs who do not have much capital. Manufacturers are able to pit contractors against one another as they underbid each other to get the work. Contractors are typically offered a price for the work on a "take it or leave it" basis, because the manufacturer can always find another contractor who would be willing to do the work for less.

The small size and dispersion of apparel contracting firms in Los Angeles also mean that they can fairly easily evade state inspection. The number of state inspectors does not remotely come close to the number that would be needed to police the industry systematically. Moreover, even when firms are caught with violations, they can go out of business and open again in a new location, under a new name.

The contracting system enables labor costs to be kept at rock-bottom levels. Meanwhile, manufacturers can deny any responsibility for conditions in their contractors' factories because they are "independent" businesses. They can place all the blame for conditions in these shops on the contractors, turning a blind eye to the fact that they set the low prices within which the contractors must operate. The fictional aspect of this claim is evident in the fact that manufacturers often send quality-control people to the contractors on a daily basis, and keep a tight control over every aspect of production *except* labor standards.

Another way that contracting serves as a labor control system is by inhibiting unionization. The work of a particular manufacturer is spread out over a number of factories. The workers in each of the factories do not even know of each other's existence. Indeed, since manufacturers are very secretive about the identity of their contractors, even the contractors may not know who else works for "their" manufacturers. The inability to identify and locate one's fellow workers makes organizing extremely difficult, a problem that is exacerbated by the manufacturer's ability to shift production from one contractor to the next. Thus, even if you can find your fellow workers, they may not remain your fellow workers for long. Or you may find that the labels you used to sew no longer are being made in your factory.

Another dilemma for workers is that, given the low margins in the contracting shops, even if they should win a union struggle, it would be very difficult to get the contractor to pay higher wages. Moreover, the very act of trying to organize a factory is likely to lead the manufacturer to shift production away from that factory, a fact that contractors do not hesitate to point out to their employees. Worker militancy at the contractor level ends up being self-defeating, because manufacturers will boycott that contractor, and the workers will lose their jobs. This situation leads contractors to be fiercely anti-union, and it serves as a major inhibitor of worker militancy. The mobility of the industry, not just offshore but, more importantly, within Los Angeles, is a deadly club that can be wielded against worker organizing.

Workers are more likely to be successful if all the workers employed by contractors who work for the same manufacturer are able to find common cause. In other words, workers need to organize the entire production system of a single manufacturer simultaneously if they are to have any chance of success. Only then can they demand that the *manufacturer* face the demands for higher wages and benefits, since it is the manufacturer who profits most from their labor and who has accumulated the surplus from which increases could be drawn. And only then can they insist that the manufacturer not shift production away from unionized shops. But the dispersion of the workforce into multiple, shifting, small factories makes coordination extremely difficult. The contracting system is a well-honed, anti-union device.

The Workforce

Los Angeles's garment workers are almost uniformly immigrants. The majority are Latino, from Mexico and Central America, especially El Salvador and Guatemala. About 10 percent are Asian, mainly from China and Southeast Asia, including Vietnam, Cambodia, and Thailand. The largest group is Mexican. There are clear linkages between the movement of capital offshore and the employment of immigrant workers in the United States. First, the penetration of foreign capital, accompanied by the imposition of neoliberal policies, creates a displaced population that finds it necessary to emigrate for sheer survival. Second, the low wages associated with global production create competition for U.S. producers,

who seek the lowest-wage local labor force they can find. Immigrants fit the bill, in part because of their desperation for work, and in part because of their legal status. The result is that garment workers tend to be of the same ethnicities: Mexican, Central American, Chinese, and the like, regardless of whether they are employed in their homelands or in the United States.

A large, unknown number of LA garment workers are undocumented, without papers that legitimize their right to work in the United States. Clearly there is an imbalance in a process of globalization that allows capital to scour the world for the lowest price of labor, but puts severe restrictions on the mobility of labor to seek out the best-paying jobs. Stacking the "free market" in favor of capital and against labor obviously serves as a damper on wages and working conditions everywhere. The garment industry, along with domestic service, construction, agriculture, and, to a lesser extent, the hotel and restaurant business, is a major employer of undocumented workers. Undocumented immigrants are obviously especially vulnerable to exploitation, and their vulnerability is exacerbated in times of public, anti-immigrant fervor. Not only do they not have any of the usual legal recourse of citizens and permanent residents, but they are threatened with the possibility of exposure and deportation.

The majority of garment workers in Los Angeles are women—about 70 percent, according to the 1990 Census. Unlike the workers in the *maquiladoras* of Mexico and the Caribbean, LA's female labor force is not composed of teenagers. They are mainly young women in their twenties and thirties. Many are mothers, and some are the sole supporters of their families. The number of men working at sewing machines has grown in the last decade, probably as a consequence of growing anti-immigrant sentiment and policies in California. As the crackdown on illegal immigration is stepped up, more immigrants are driven to take whatever jobs they can find. The garment industry remains a willing employer of the undocumented. The fact that most garment workers are women adds to the likelihood that they will face domination of various types by their employers.

Conditions in the Shops

There is some variation in the conditions in the garment contracting shops of Los Angeles, but overall conditions are remarkably similar. Garment workers typically work on piece rate, that is, they are paid for each procedure they complete. This is similar to the pay system in agriculture, where farmworkers are paid for the number of pounds they pick. Garment workers are *contingent* labor, which means that they are employed and paid only when their work is needed. If there is no work, they are sent home, or sit around without pay until work arrives. While this arrangement obviously maximizes efficiency and flexibility from the point of view of the manufacturers, it creates great insecurity among the workers. They have no job security from day to day. All the risks associated with fashion and seasons trickle down the system and settle on their shoulders.

Both California and federal laws require that workers be paid minimum wage and overtime, even if they are paid a piece rate. The employer needs to keep time cards and ensure that the hourly minimum wage is covered, and that, when employees work over forty hours a week they must be paid one-and-a-half times their base wage. These regulations are *routinely* violated. Contractors want to pay only the flat piece rate, and they devise every trick in the book to hide the fact that that is what they are doing. They falsify the records, they maintain double books, they use double time cards, they cook up schemes so that overtime is calculated after the fact, they clock out workers after eight hours and pay them in cash thereafter, they have them work off the books on Saturdays, they encourage off-the-books homework, they get workers to kick back excess earnings in cash, and so forth. Thus minimum wage and overtime violations are extremely common in this industry. Using the 1990 Census figures, we calculated that the average garment indus-

try operative in LA earned $7,200 a year, well below the minimum wage of $8,840 for a full-time, year-round worker at the time. Even when workers are paid the legal minimum, garment workers remain among the lowest-paid workers in Los Angeles, and make up an important segment of the working poor.

A baseline survey of sixty-nine California garment firms was conducted in 1994 by California and federal labor enforcement agencies. They found that 61 percent of Southern California garment firms failed to pay minimum wage and that 78 percent failed to pay overtime. In addition, 74 percent had recordkeeping violations and 41 percent paid workers in cash (Targeted Industries Partnership Program 1996, 18). While subsequent surveys have found some diminution in some of these statistics, other areas show an increase in violations. The fact is that violations of the law remain at an excessively high level.

The piece-work system encourages self-exploitation, as workers work very fast and for as many hours as possible in order to make a living. It creates the illusion that workers control their earnings by their own skill level, and makes it difficult for them to feel a sense of common exploitation. The illusion of control is occasionally shattered, when workers are shifted to new tasks and find that their earning levels collapse, or when the contractor lowers the piece rate in a cost-cutting move. These kinds of actions are likely to trigger angry reactions on the part of workers, who feel that the rug has been pulled out from under them.

Homework is a fairly common feature in the LA apparel industry. Some work at home full-time, while others only take work home after hours. While homework may sometimes be attractive to women, who combine work with child care, it is typically associated with the lowest pay when all the workers' costs are added in (Fregoso 1988). Furthermore, none of the usual protections of minimum wage and overtime pay can be ensured because of the underground character of the work.

Garment workers rarely receive any fringe benefits whatsoever. They are typically not given paid vacations or paid sick leave. Medical insurance is virtually nonexistent for the workers themselves and out of the question for their families. In other words, the system is geared toward paying workers their piece rate, and that is that. Thus by not paying for the health care coverage of the workers in their contracting shops, manufacturers, who can own a very profitable enterprise and be very rich themselves, force their workers to rely on the impoverished LA County health care system. Once again, the contracting system, by creating a false distance between the employer and the workers, enables the manufacturer to avoid taking responsibility and forces the taxpayers to pick up what should rightfully be a tab that the owner pays.

Apart from poverty-level wages, garment workers are also subject to other forms of abuse. Since garment-contracting shops are small businesses, they lack bureaucratic rules and are subject to the direct authority of the owner and supervisors. This authority can easily be conducted in an arbitrary fashion, with favoritism and discrimination. Workers who are not favored can be given older, less efficient machines, or can be denied work. They can also be subjected to personal abuse of all kinds, from yelling to sexual harassment. Workers will sometimes say that they can bear the harsh burden of low wages, but cannot endure being treated in an insulting and demeaning manner.

In addition, many garment factories in Los Angeles have serious health and safety violations. In a recent sweep it was found that 96 percent of factories violated the law and that 72 percent had serious violations that could result in injury or death (Targeted Industries Partnership Program 1996). The violations included such things as blocked fire exits, exposed wires, and machines without safety guards. Many of the garment shops of LA could turn into death traps in the event of a fire.

Although I have stressed the role of piece rate in the domination of garment workers, it is not clear that putting an end to this system would ameliorate conditions in the industry. Employers are skillful at developing

alternative ways to squeeze workers when they are highly motivated. Thus intense quotas can be introduced as another mechanism for extracting the maximum amount of labor from workers. Indeed, quotas take the place of piece rate in most *maquila* factories without alleviating the oppression of the workers.

The Return of Sweatshops

We are in an era in which many government officials and others speak of a return of the sweatshop (U.S. General Accounting Office 1988,1994; Ross 1997). In the United States, garment industry sweatshops were more or less eradicated by a combination of the development of powerful garment worker unions and the New Deal, which provided support for basic labor standards. However, since the 1970s, and especially during the 1980s and 1990s, we have seen an erosion of wages and working conditions in the U.S. apparel industry. In 1950, average weekly wages of U.S. garment workers were 76.5 percent of the average manufacturing wage. By 1996, this figure had dropped to 55.3 percent. In women's outerwear, the ratio dropped from 87.3 in 1950 to 50.6 in 1996 (American Apparel Manufacturing Association 1997, 19).

Why are we seeing the return of sweatshops now? There are many reasons. Globalization certainly plays a critical role. Since apparel manufacturers and retailers can move—or threaten to move—offshore, they force local workers to face the grim choice of accepting the jobs as they are or losing the jobs altogether. Manufacturers and retailers can argue that they can get the work done offshore for a fraction of the price that they pay in Los Angeles. Any improvement in wages and working conditions is interpreted as a threat to the continuation of the industry in LA.

Globalization can also be seen as part of a larger set of trends that have led to the return of sweatshops, including the decline of the welfare state and the attack on the labor movement. In general, we have been witnessing an effort on the part of big business to enhance its power and to undermine the power of labor. Workers in the United States (and in other industrial nations) have gradually been stripped of the protections they were able to win in the New Deal era. Various public programs and social assistance have eroded, and real wages have fallen. Meanwhile, business owners, along with the managers and professionals whom they employ, have grown richer and richer. The gap between rich and poor has grown wider. Los Angeles shows these trends even more starkly than the rest of the United States.

The first blast of attack against the labor movement occurred when Ronald Reagan became president and broke the air traffic controllers' strike. Since then, unions have faced the erosion of the legal environment that had been developed to protect workers' rights to organize during the New Deal. Unfair labor practices on the part of employers have become more flagrant as they have learned that the cost of union-busting is minor compared to the cost of having to negotiate a union contract.

Another factor in the growth of garment sweatshops has been the consolidation of retailing. Since the mid-1980s there has been a major merger movement in retailing, as giant retailers have bought each other out, assuming huge debt in the process. Some retailers have gone bankrupt. Others have become billion-dollar giants who can exercise tremendous power over the industry. The United States has far too many stores per consumer, resulting in vicious competition. The retailers now have the power to pressure manufacturers to cut costs, change styles more rapidly, and maintain more inventory (Bird and Bounds 1997). Many retailers themselves now have their own private (or store) label, for which they employ their own contractors directly, bypassing the manufacturers altogether. They undercut the major brands, putting price pressure on them. All of this puts pressure down the line of the garment food chain, and the people most affected are the workers, both in the United States and elsewhere.

Although firms claim they must cut costs to remain competitive, the cost-cutting knife is rarely applied to the owners, managers, and professionals. Executive salaries, advertising costs, profits, and similar rewards that go to the nonlabor part of apparel production are allowed to soar with no outcry that these costs must be kept in check. The largest apparel manufacturers in Los Angeles are multimillionaires. For example, six of the one hundred highest-paid executives in Los Angeles are in the apparel industry, and five of them work for one company: Guess? Inc. (Sullivan 1997). Maurice Marciano, CEO of Guess, received $3.4 million in salary and bonus in 1996. It is estimated that the three Marciano brothers, who own most of the company, personally took home over $400 million between 1992 and 1996, including salaries, bonuses, distributions to stockholders, and the results of an initial public offering.

Ethnicity

In Los Angeles, the apparel industry is structured along ethnic lines. The manufacturers are, for the most part, European in origin, although some are Middle Eastern and Asian. Jews play an important role at this level and, while some are immigrants, many are American-born. The contractors, in contrast, are almost all immigrants, as stated. They are from all over the world, but the plurality are Asian. Although Koreans are not numerically the most important, they run some of the largest shops and are very visible in the garment district.

The workers, as we have seen, are predominantly Latino immigrants. While there are some Latino contractors, the predominant pattern in the industry is for an Asian contractor to hire Latino workers. There are cases where contractor and workers are of the same ethnicity, and where there are paternalistic linkages between employer and employees. But this is the exception rather than the rule in Los Angeles, where the relationship between contractor and worker tends to be strictly business. Exploitation is rarely softened by the bonds of family or ethnicity.

This pattern of ethnic differentiation between contractors and workers makes Los Angeles different from other U.S. cities, and maybe from other garment centers in Europe too. In these places, although garment contractors and workers are also immigrants, they often come from the same country and share certain bonds of obligation. For example, South Asians in Britain employ South Asians, Chinese in New York and San Francisco employ Chinese, and so forth. Obviously, some of this occurs in LA as well, and even when it does occur, it does not prevent exploitation. The infamous Thai "slave shop" of El Monte, uncovered in August 1995, involved Thai contractors employing Thai women.

The pattern found in Los Angeles is increasingly found in Mexico, Central America, and the Caribbean, where Asian entrepreneurs from Korea and Taiwan are going to countries like Guatemala and the Dominican Republic and hiring indigenous workers. These firms serve as contractors for U.S. manufacturers and retailers. This pattern may also be spreading to other U.S. cities, such as New York.

The phenomenon of ethnic difference among the three layers of the LA industry—white manufacturers, Asian contractors, and Latino workers—creates an important dynamic that spills over into the general race relations of the city. Considerable tension is developing between the Asian and Latino communities, since they meet at the front lines of an exploitative system. Meanwhile, the real economic powers—the manufacturers, retailers, real estate owners, bankers, and the like, who are mainly native-born whites—do not have to deal with the antagonisms that arise in the workplace, even though they are primarily responsible for them. They can push the blame onto the immigrant entrepreneurs, making them out to be sleazy business operators who mistreat their workers, unlike the good old, decent, American businessman who would never dream of running a sweatshop. Thus is racism fueled and used

to maintain current relations of power and privilege.

Efforts to Eliminate Sweatshops

As the sweatshop scourge has grown, more government attention has been devoted to trying to eliminate it. Both the state of California and the federal government have stepped up enforcement efforts. Together, the California Division of Labor Standards Enforcement (DLSE) and the U.S. Department of Labor (DOL) formed the Targeted Industries Partnership Program (TIPP), which singled out agriculture and apparel as the two most egregious violators of labor standards law. Moreover, in a public hearing held by the Los Angeles Jewish Commission on Sweatshops in late 1997, officials from these agencies acknowledged that, while they were making progress in cleaning up agriculture, the apparel industry was proving much more difficult.

The dilemma for enforcement agents in this industry lies in the fact that catching a contractor often results in that particular firm going out of business, sometimes only to open up again in a new location under a different name. Given the large number of contractors, it is impossible to keep track of them all. In any case, since the manufacturers (and retailers) control the prices that set the conditions under which garment factories operate, the challenge has been to find a method to hold them responsible for what goes on in "their" factories.

The DOL has been especially innovative in trying to untangle this knot. They have used the "hot goods" principle to force manufacturers to pay attention to the conditions under which their clothes are produced. Based on a provision in the Fair Labor Standards Act, this principle states that goods made under illegal conditions cannot be shipped across state borders. In the highly time-sensitive fashion industry, invoking this provision made it imperative for manufacturers to be sure that their contractors were not engaging in illegal practices. The DOL was able to get a number of major manufacturers to sign agreements that have forced the industry to develop compliance programs under which they themselves or specialized private firms investigate their contractors to make sure that they are obeying the law.

Needless to say, questions are raised about the effectiveness of such an approach, which has been described as "the fox guarding the chicken coop." Even when manufacturers undertake the effort seriously, there are several problems. Workers are afraid to reveal violations for fear they will be fired by the contractor. Contractors are faced with the threat that the work will be taken away from them by the manufacturer, a club that they use to get workers not to speak candidly with the manufacturer's inspectors. While the threat of removing work may serve as an inducement for some contractors to clean up their act, given the unchanged economics of the situation, for some it just means being more careful in hiding their misdeeds. The truth is, the only real sanction the manufacturer can use against the contractor is the "death sentence"—to stop shipping work, which will probably drive the contractor out of business. Since neither the contractor nor the workers want that, they both "conspire" to hide illegal practices from manufacturer monitors. Moreover, manufacturers themselves may turn a blind eye to problems among their contractors, since they do not want to disturb their production schedules. After all, their prices and practices created the problem in the first place. Their main motivation is to look clean so that the DOL will get off their backs.

New proposals, from the White House Apparel Industry Partnership, for example, suggest the need for *independent* monitoring both within the United States and in the global apparel industry. There is a call to have NGOs and religious groups serve as monitors, so that the problems inherent in self-monitoring are avoided. However, given the years of experience contractors have had in hiding violations, one wonders whether independent organizations will be able to ferret out the problems. Moreover, even if legal violations are uncovered, the poverty and poor working conditions endured by the majority of garment workers would still remain, since the legal requirements are very minimal.

A New Form of Labor Process?

Many observers of the apparel industry speak of a "return" of sweatshops, as we have seen. The implication is that we are witnessing a throwback to an earlier phase of capitalism, one characterized by the coercive control of workers as the primary means of extracting surplus from their labor. During the "social contract" period (from the New Deal to around 1960), it has been argued that, at least in the "monopoly sector," bureaucratic controls took the place of direct coercion and, through a combination of internal labor markets and union-imposed rules, the labor regime depended much more on the consent of the workers (Burawoy 1979). Of course, a "competitive sector" still remained throughout this period, retaining pre-Fordist systems of coercive control.

The Los Angeles apparel industry raises an important question: is global/flexible capitalism producing a new type of labor regime, or is it merely replicating the earlier forms of coercive control? I propose that, while there are some old features in the current labor process, it also has some new elements.

The Old Regime

Paying garment workers a piece rate harks back to the earliest and most primitive forms of wage labor under capitalism. It manipulates workers in obvious ways such that they work rapidly, for long hours, in order to make as much as they can, given the low prices per piece. Piece rate encourages self-exploitation, so that supervisors do not need to motivate workers in a directly coercive way.

In addition, simple coercion is found in LA's garment factories. Workers sometimes face abusive employers who yell at them, insist that they not go to the bathroom, prevent them from talking to other workers, and so on. Direct coercion supplements the motivation provided by the piece-rate system.

Contracting out is also not a new concept. It has been used at least since the beginning of the century in the New York apparel industry. Still, as I shall argue below, contracting out is far more developed today than it was in the pre-New Deal (or monopoly capitalist) period.

Finally, the LA apparel industry has returned to its pre-New Deal extreme anti-unionism. From the 1940s to the 1960s, garment workers' unions played a critical role in the near-elimination of sweatshops. Their activism was supported by a government that endorsed and protected the rights of workers to organize. The new attacks on unionism in this industry represent a throwback of sorts.

The New Regime

There are important differences between the labor regimes of the pre-and post-monopoly capitalist eras. First, the nonproduction sectors of the industry, namely the roles played by manufacturers in designing, grading, pattern-making, sometimes cutting, and merchandising, have all become much more sophisticated. In this industry, the division between conception and execution, between mental and manual labor, is almost total. The mental aspects of the industry have been heavily computerized, and, with the help of such elements as bar coding, it has been able to organize and coordinate production systems that range all over the globe. The computerization of the headquarters means that the ability to disperse and shift production has grown immeasurably. Globalization and flexibility change the way business is conducted.

These new characteristics have had an impact on the labor process. Labor control and anti-unionism are built into the very structure of these dispersed production systems. The manufacturers do not need to be overtly anti-union—though, of course, they will be if it becomes necessary. They can rely on the contracting system itself to keep workers disorganized. As described above, workers are unable to locate their fellow workers for the same manufacturer even in Los Angeles, let alone around the world. The shifting around of work means that workers are unstably linked to a particular manufacturer. Meanwhile, workers know, and their contractors inform them repeatedly, in case they have not gotten the message, that demands for any improvements in their wages and work conditions will result in the manufacturer shifting work away from their contractors. The workers may win a skirmish, but will certainly lose their jobs.

As stated, contracting out is not a new feature of apparel production, but it is far more evolved today than it was before World War II. In Los Angeles today almost all sewing is contracted out. In New York, a distinction is still drawn between a manufacturer and a jobber, with the former producing at least partially in-house, and the latter contracting out all production. In LA this distinction does not exist, since all "manufacturers" contract out. Furthermore, the ability to shift production out of the local area to other states, regions, countries, and even continents makes the current contracting system qualitatively different.

In sum, the very system of global/flexible production creates a new kind of labor regime and labor discipline. Workers are kept under control by the mobility and dispersal of the industry. This system, which constantly threatens job loss and severely inhibits labor struggles, keeps workers toiling at rapid speeds for long hours and low wages. They do not require coercive oversight to achieve the desired effect.

In addition, another element of globalization plays into the "new" labor regime in the apparel industry in Los Angeles, and that is the employment of immigrants, most of whom are undocumented. Their political vulnerability as noncitizens, and the ability of employers to threaten exposure and deportation, add to the disciplining effects of global/flexible capitalism.

Approaches to Unionization

I have worked closely with the Organizing Department in the Union of Needletrades, Industrial, and Textile Employees (UNITE) for about 10 years. During that time I have had a chance to talk with union organizing leaders, and to observe and participate in their activities. I have witnessed periods of optimism and growth, and periods of difficulty and loss. I have also witnessed a major change in regime after the merger of the International Ladies Garment Workers Union (ILG) and the Amalgamated Clothing and Textile Workers Union (ACTWU) into UNITE. The merger brought different leadership to the LA organizing effort as well as some different ideas and approaches to the challenge of organizing the city's garment workers.

I would like to discuss five basic approaches to organizing garment workers in Los Angeles, assessing their strengths and weaknesses: National Labor Relations Board (NLRB) elections, jobbers' agreements, corporate campaigns, community organizing, and workers' centers. In practice, they are not mutually exclusive and, in fact, often overlap and are implemented together.

Elections Under the NLRB

NLRB elections would appear to be the ideal way to organize garment workers. The union would meet with workers to discuss the pros and cons of unionization, and they would decide democratically whether they wanted to be represented by the union. The NLRB would then hold the election, ensuring that democratic rules are followed, and garment workers would either become unionized or not.

As most people probably know by now, this approach is fraught with problems in a number of industries. I feel confident in saying that, in the Los Angeles apparel industry, it is worthless. First, assuming that the workers in a particular contracting factory did successfully vote for a union, what would happen? If they were able to sign a contract with their employer, they would

not win very much because the profits of the contractor are low. As stated, the real profit centers of the industry are the manufacturers and retailers. Thus the victory would bring few gains. But more importantly, the contractor with unionized workers would almost certainly be avoided by the manufacturers, who would not be willing to employ a contractor whose price was one penny higher than the others', let alone one known to have "labor problems" that might threaten work schedules. The union contractor would be boycotted by all manufacturers, would receive no work, and would go out of business. The workers would have won the election, but lost their jobs.

Second, knowing that they would be driven out of business if a union election were won in their shops, contractors are highly motivated to do everything they can, legal and illegal, to break the union. This is, in practice, the experience of the union in Los Angeles. Case after case of factories with clear pro-union majorities end up in bitter defeat as the employer fires pro-union workers, threatens the others, calls in the immigration authorities, and so on. While many of these actions are illegal, the machinery of justice is so slow and the sanctions so weak that the organizing drive will be dead and buried years before any kind of redress—usually exceedingly minimal—is proffered. The fired union leaders simply lose their jobs, adding to the fear and intimidation that dominate the industry.

Apparel employers will sometimes call for elections, claiming that this is the only fair and American thing to do, that workers should have a free choice, and that they support a secret ballot. But these calls are completely cynical, arising only after the company has engaged in every union-busting practice in the book, and feeling assured that the workers will vote against the union. I feel safe in saying that no apparel manufacturer or contractor in Los Angeles would simply allow a union election to occur, without interference, in their plant. And even if a contractor did allow such an election, he would end up going out of business, as described above.

Clearly legal and procedural reforms are needed in the NLRB process. However, such reforms would still not crack the nut of the contracting system, which enables manufacturers—the real employers—to shift work away from unionized workers, thereby destroying any organizing effort in the long run, if not at the time of the election.

Jobbers' Agreements

The idea of a jobber's agreement comes out of the ILG's long experiences of organizing in the women's apparel industry in New York. The term "jobber" is still used from the New York context, even though it does not apply to the LA industry. A jobber's agreement is the union's equivalent of joint liability. It holds the manufacturer responsible for conditions in its contracting shops by getting it to sign a contract that ensures that it will only use unionized contractors, and will pay them the union scale and benefits. Under such an agreement, the manufacturer cannot boycott union contractors, but on the contrary, is bound to use them. The result is that the interests of the contractors are completely altered. Now it is advantageous for them to have a unionized shop, because it gives them preferred access to that manufacturer. Indeed, jobbers' agreements tend to stabilize the otherwise highly mobile and fluid garment business, since they lead the manufacturers to stick with a particular group of union contractors.

The organizing challenge posed by a jobber's agreement is to organize the entire production system of a manufacturer at one time, namely, both the workers who are employed in its headquarters (maybe sample-makers or cutters), and the workers in the dispersed contracting shops. If the workers in these various locations can be brought together to unite around the issue of gaining a union contract across the entire system, then they may be able to succeed in getting the manufacturer and the contractors to sign.

The basic strategic approach that has been used to organize such a dispersed production system is to turn the manufacturer's benefits of contracting out into weaknesses. The fact that the manufacturer does not have strong and stable ties with its contractors means that the links between them can be severed. The physical dispersal of production also opens up the possibility of interfering with the flow of garments between various plants. Moreover, because of the time-sensitivity of the fashion business, even temporary interruptions in the flow of production can be very costly, especially if they happen at the peak of the season.

Breaking the ties between the manufacturer and its contractors can be accomplished by a number of means. The workers in key contracting shops may go out on strike. Workers may picket certain shops or the company's warehouse, and may be able to persuade truckers not to cross their picket lines. Contractors, who may work with other manufacturers apart from the one that the union is trying to organize, may decide to opt out of the latter relationship for the period of the labor dispute so as to avoid all the disruption; since the manufacturer has probably not been that loyal to them, the contractors have little reason to see it through these tough times. The union may also be able to get some contractors to sign "me too" agreements with the union such that, if they agree to cease working with the manufacturer temporarily, they will be able to sign the union contract on whatever terms are negotiated later—and thus obtain secure work.

Although the manufacturer may be able to move production to other shops in order to avoid those contractors where workers are organized and engaged in various forms of protest, the fact is that, in the height of a publicized labor dispute it is difficult for the manufacturer to find others who will work with it and risk have a picket line thrown at them. As soon as the union is able to trace the work to a new contractor, they can meet with the contractor and warn it of the consequences of working with a manufacturer that is fighting with the union. Thus the obvious advantage to the manufacturer of being able to shift production can be minimized during an organizing campaign.

The strength of this approach lies in tying the manufacturer to the contractors, so that workers can win significant gains. Moreover, such an organizing drive is usually combined with a corporate campaign and community organizing, so that other aspects of the company's functioning, apart from its production, are also under attack. The purpose of such a multifaceted attack is to drive a firm, which otherwise would fight unionization to the death, to negotiate with the union.

Some may feel that such a "coercive" approach should not be necessary in a democratic society, but given the anti-union animus of the employers, nothing short of forcing them to the bargaining table will succeed. The union has to practically drive them out of business in order to get them to accept the organization of their workers. Conditions in the garment industry are such that nothing else will work. Employers will say that, if the industry is unionized, they will leave the country. To prevent that "necessity," they simply must stop unionization. Needless to say, this state of affairs makes organizing in this industry far more confrontational than in most industries.

I want to only mention a few problems with the jobber's agreement approach. First, it is extremely difficult to coordinate all the parts of the dispersed production system so that they are ready to take action at the same time. The general who is coordinating such a battle has to deal with numerous fronts at one time. Second, the problem of secrecy is intense, since the employer is likely to deploy many resources to kill such an effort before it gets off the ground. The need for secrecy obviously impedes organizing, and it certainly weakens the development of democratic structures among workers as the union is building membership. Third, such an organizing drive is most likely to succeed right away or not at all. The longer the struggle is drawn out, the more is the employer able to engage in evasive action, including devising methods for moving work away from contractors with strong union support. The manufacturer may build up the work load for its core contractors, or it may move some of its production to Mexico, among other options. This ability to shift production is deadly to the morale of the workers, who find their factory closed, at least in the short run, and begin to fear whether they will ever be able to win back their jobs.

A fourth problem with a jobber's agreement is that it lends itself to top-down organizing. In other words, it is possible to put sufficient pressure on the manufacturer so that it agrees to sign with union contractors. As we said, this changes the motivation of the contractors, who now rush to join the union. The contractors may sign with the union, not because of pressure from their workers, but because they know that a union contract will guarantee them stable work. The workers thus become irrelevant to the signing of the union contract. The contractors are motivated to sign whether the workers want a union or not. In sum, the agreement becomes one between the union, the manufacturer, and the contractors, with the workers potentially treated as the mere objects of the agreement.

Now there is nothing inherent in a jobber's agreement that precludes workers' participation in the struggle to win it. Indeed, driving the manufacturer to the bargaining table may depend on strong worker activism of various sorts. Nevertheless, the situation lends itself to top-down agreements whereby workers find themselves as members of a union for which they did not fight. Moreover the fact that their bosses, the contractors, are now eager union members makes the dynamics between workers and contractors a bit weird. The antagonistic relationship between the workers and their immediate employers is muted by the union contract, and the union often ends up dealing directly with the contractor rather than with the workers.

Developing union agreements that deal with the tiers and loose ties of industries like apparel is clearly a major challenge for this period of "flexible" capitalism. Perhaps the old ILG jobber's agreement is no longer the appropriate instrument for tying manufacturers (and retailers) to the shops that actually sew their clothing. Clearly some mechanism is needed to force the manufacturers and retailers to cough up some of the excess surplus they expropriate from the garment workers.

As we pointed out above, the contracting network of a manufacturer need not be limited to a particular city, region, or country. Indeed, many LA manufacturers contract offshore as well. The idea of organizing the entire production system of a particular manufacturer thus lends itself to cross-border organizing. In other words, all the workers in all the contracting shops of a manufacturer, regardless of their geographic location, could, in principle, coordinate their efforts and their demands. This vision is not beyond possibility, although only the first steps have been taken in a few cases to bring it to fruition (Armbruster 1995,1998).

Corporate Campaigns

Since the use of corporate campaigns in the effort to organize workers is not unique to the apparel industry, I will only touch on it lightly. The labor movement as a whole has become much more sophisticated at researching the companies it is trying to organize, and in finding other points of vulnerability apart from their production systems. Such vulnerabilities lie in the various plans and relationships of a particular company. For example, its stockholders may be dismayed to learn about certain company practices, and may be willing to exert pressure on the company to settle quickly with the union. When unions themselves are among the stockholders, this can be a potent weapon.

The fashion industry would appear to be especially vulnerable to one form of this kind of pressure, namely, an attack on a company's image. Fashion has a kind of "postmodern" quality, since it depends very much on the selling of an image, rather than simply a product. The image-selling aspect of apparel has accelerated in recent years, as certain key brand names, spending millions of dollars in advertising, have managed to create identities with which their consumers relate (Klein, 1999). More people happily wear clothing with the brand name plastered on it, helping them to define themselves to the public. Having a strong brand enables a company to sell its clothing at inflated prices, as people spend much more on the items than they are worth as physical products. Of course, advertising "labor" goes into constructing as well as selling these images, so that the discrepancy between sales price and cost of production is not pure profit.

However, the strength of image in fashion is also its weakness. If an image is tarnished, it can quickly drop out of public favor, leading to plummeting sales. Even without any "outside" interference, most apparel brands have a limited life cycle. Hot brands that cool off usually have a hard time revitalizing themselves, although anything is possible. Unions (and other organizations concerned with labor abuses) can try to take advantage of the vulnerability of a brand's public image by developing negative associations with that name. For example, efforts have been made to link Nike and Disney with sweatshop conditions in their offshore contracting shops. I cannot say whether these efforts have directly affected sales or forced the companies to take actions to improve conditions among their contractors, but it seems likely that they do exert a real pressure on the firms.

Corporate campaigns often attack a firm's sales in some form—by encouraging a consumer boycott, by putting pressure on retailers to drop that brand, by getting consumers to question salespeople about production conditions, and so forth. The idea is that, if a company's sales are hurting, it is more likely to be willing to come to the bargaining table. These campaigns may also affect the value of a company's stock, in turn leading the owners to feel that action must be taken to end the damaging publicity—including possibly settling with the union.

A major weakness of this approach arises if it is not linked to a strong worker-organizing component. Corporate campaign pressure on a company may, indeed, hurt its sales or stock prices, which in turn may lead the company to cut prices, cut wages, and lay off workers. In other words, workers may suffer from the consequences of a boycott (for example), and if they are not actively involved in the campaign, will feel that these efforts by others to "help" them are very unwelcome. Without strong worker participation in the decision to boycott, without their informed consent, with full knowledge that they may suffer some immediate repercussions, the approach can backfire, leading to the alienation of the very workers the union is trying to organize.

Community Organizing

Community organizing can have at least two distinct meanings. First, it can refer to outreach to middle-class supporters and other allies, who can help put pressure on the industry in general or on a particular campaign target. These community supporters can become participants in the corporate campaign, helping to demonstrate against the company, publicize its labor abuses, and spread the word about a boycott. In other words, the community that is mobilized helps to provide the troops that exert community pressure on the company. It may include various left-leaning organizations, other trade unions, religious groups, women's groups, students, artists, politicians, and so forth.

The best community organizing of this type involves not just calling on the union's friends and allies in the face of a union-planned action, but also establishing somewhat independent organizations that plan actions themselves and use their creativity and initiative to contribute new and distinctive energy to the movement. This was the idea behind Common Threads, a group of women that formed in Los Angeles to support garment workers and that helped a little with the Guess campaign in its early phases. Common Threads was an independent organization that included an artists' collective. It developed its own projects

in support of garment workers in addition to cooperating with the union on a number of actions.

Semi-autonomous community organizations have their strengths and weaknesses. A weakness, from the union's point of view, is that they cannot be completely controlled. They do not simply do the union's bidding, and may thus not satisfy exactly what the union needs at a particular time. On the other hand, what is lost in control is gained in enthusiasm. People who "own" what they are doing obviously engage in it with a great deal more relish than if they were merely pawns in an organization's plans.

The second type of community organizing involves organizing within the workers' own community. This approach is especially relevant when the workers are part of an oppressed group. In the case of LA garment workers, the majority are Latino immigrants, and the remainder are Asian immigrants. As we have seen, many are undocumented, which opens them up to the special stigmatization of that status. Community organizing in this context involves organizing around the broader issues facing the Latino and Asian immigrant communities, including the political assaults on both legal and illegal immigrants. The goal is to link the exploitation faced by garment workers to the broader agenda of the immigrant communities. Similarly, because most garment workers are women, it is possible to organize around the special needs of immigrant women.

The fact that garment workers are so poorly paid and work under such oppressive conditions contributes to the general impoverishment of the immigrant community, while the political oppression of Latinos in particular makes it much harder for garment workers to protect themselves against economic exploitation. Their positions as workers, as women, and as immigrants under attack reinforce one another in the overall oppression of the group. Latino/a garment workers are oppressed simultaneously as workers, as women, and as immigrants. The struggle to improve their situation thus extends beyond winning a union contract to winning political power for their community in general, and to supporting the rights of women within that community and in the society at large. The various types of struggle are all connected. The union needs to align itself with the political aspirations of the Latino/a community, even as Latino/a leaders need to recognize that the labor struggle is an important part of winning rights and respect for the Latino community. (Similar statements can be made for segments of the Asian communities, although they are more heterogeneous in both class and ethnic terms.)[3]

Organizing around race-ethnicity, immigration status, and gender obviously occurs apart from the union. Each community has developed its own organizations to help oppressed workers and to try to organize them in self-defense. For example, Asian Immigrant Women's Advocates (AIWA) in Oakland tries to link race, class, and gender issues in helping oppressed immigrant women workers fight for their rights. The union and these community organizations overlap to some degree, but they also have different approaches. Although at times they have tried to work together, too often they see each other as opponents and criticize each other for their failings. While there is, no doubt, plenty to criticize on both sides, such criticisms are likely to flourish when the task is very difficult and when all the organizations feel frustrated at their lack of progress.

Regardless of the impediments to cooperation between community groups and the labor movement, it is clearly desirable to forge these coalitions, and to overcome the disputes and disagreements that arise between them. Perhaps I am being naive but, having heard criticisms from both sides, I feel they are overdrawn. The overarching desirability of union-community cooperation in both the economic and political struggles should be paramount.

Workers' Centers

The concept behind workers' centers is that the organizing of garment workers needs to proceed, irrespective of a particular organizing drive. A workers' center can help accomplish this in a number of ways. It can provide services to garment workers, who are generally in great need of help in dealing with wage claims or immigration problems. It can also help to educate workers not only about their rights but also about the political economy in which they find themselves. In other words, it can provide workers with the tools they need to understand their world and to begin to fight back. And it can provide an environment where workers can engage in lower-risk political struggles rather than those presented by a full-fledged organizing drive. The importance of political action cannot be overemphasized, since it is in the course of political struggle that workers are able to learn that victories can be won. The very act of participation is radicalizing because it undermines the strong beliefs that the employers are all-powerful and that change is impossible.[4] In sum, a workers' center can be the training ground for the building of a general movement of garment workers. It involves amassing an army of garment workers, regardless of where they work, who are ready to fight when necessary. It is a form of worker-centered organizing.

UNITE has developed a few workers' centers, called Justice Centers, in New York and Los Angeles. I cannot speak about the condition in New York, but I have seen the ups and downs of the Los Angeles center over the years. Too often it has sunk under the burden of providing basic services to a very needy population, and has been unable to pursue the more long-term goals of developing an educational and political program.

I personally believe that this kind of worker-centered organizing is essential for building a *long-term* garment workers' movement in Los Angeles. The Justice Center can work in tandem with particular organizing drives by helping to prepare workers for participation in such campaigns, by providing worker-supporters for them, and by giving the workers who are engaged in a particular drive a place to go and a support structure, even if their factory has been boycotted by the manufacturer. The Justice

Center can also provide a community for garment workers who, too often, live under conditions of social fragmentation (as the newest immigrants) and who need to build social support networks.

Needless to say, this approach has potential weaknesses. In particular, the effort to engage in low-risk political actions is fraught with problems. There is an inherent contradiction between taking low risks and winning struggles, especially when the enemy is so fierce and so determined to crush any resistance. Yet in order to build the courage to take greater risks, small victories must be achieved. Finding winning actions that do not jeopardize the livelihoods of very vulnerable workers is a difficult challenge. A couple of possible approaches are pressing demands with state agencies, and engaging in protests in support of workers at a factory that is not one's own and from which one cannot be fired. Building an arsenal of actions should obviously be done by workers themselves, with the aid of union staff. The very act of developing political actions would be educational in itself.

Efforts to Implement These Ideas

A group has now formed in Los Angeles that wants to work on the three-pronged goals of providing services, developing an educational program, and engaging in lower-risk political actions.[5] The group, tentatively called the Garment Workers Coalition, brings together a number of community groups and the union. The community groups include the Asian Pacific American Legal Center (APALC), the Coalition for Humane Immigrant Rights of Los Angeles (CHIRLA), the Korean Immigrant Worker Advocates (KIWA), the Mexican American Legal Defense and Education Fund (MALDEF), the Legal Aid Foundation of Los Angeles (LAFLA), Beit Tzedek (a Jewish group that offers free legal services), and UNITE. Each of the community groups has engaged in organizing and providing services, and has plenty of experience in working with garment workers. The group is engaged in outreach to garment workers, providing them with legal services (with the assistance of student interns), and will help encourage workers to participate in UNITE's Justice Center with a view to building it as a place where workers can develop a political movement. The coalition, we hope, can devise a division of labor so that the center will be freed of some of its responsibility for services, while all the organizations can help with the development of an educational and political program.

The Potential Flight of the Industry to Mexico

Of course any organizing effort on the part of LA's garment workers may simply speed up the process of the flight of the industry to Mexico. Indeed, although they will not admit it, I suspect that many LA apparel manufacturers are looking at shifting production there as a form of insurance against local organizing. What can be done about this?

First, it is possible that sectors of the LA industry will not leave, regardless of improvements in production methods in Mexico. Small lots in the most fashion-sensitive sectors as well as replenishment stock may always be produced in Los Angeles. The number of garment factory jobs may decline in the future, but may not be disappear totally.

Second, the city and state cannot afford to allow the industry simply to leave, since it is such a major employer. So far their primary strategy for keeping the industry in Los Angeles is to try to bribe firms to stay with tax write-offs. However, alternative approaches are possible, including efforts to provide capital for contractors to upgrade their facilities and improve productivity through technology, rather than by squeezing the workers. Ironically, unionization can actually foster this process by stabilizing the relationships between manufacturers and contractors. In the current environment, contractors will not invest in their factories because they cannot count on receiving work from one week to the next. If the relationships are stabilized under a jobber's agreement, the contractors can depend on steadier work, thus reducing the risk of investment. Of course, given the general riskiness of the fashion business, stability is only likely to be attained for those contractors with the strongest ties to their manufacturers.[6]

Third, in the face of industry flight, it is better for workers to be organized rather than unorganized. If they can win a contract in Los Angeles, for example, they may be able to put clauses into it that limit the movement of capital offshore, or that at least make it more costly. They can also set up severance agreements, such as that which was negotiated by UNITE with Levi's, so that local workers are not simply abandoned when the manufacturer shifts production.

Corporate campaigns and consumer pressure are especially suitable for holding accountable firms that move to Mexico. If an apparel firm has shifted production to escape unionization in Los Angeles, consumer groups can point to the even lower labor standards in Mexico and to the greed of the manufacturer in seeking even higher profits from the exploitation of impoverished workers. Of course, such an approach is much more likely to succeed if the Mexican workers join the struggle against the manufacturer, so that both groups of workers call for consumer support to end the abuses on both sides of the border.

Conclusion

The garment industry in Los Angeles poses a formidable challenge to organizing. This industry can be seen as the wave of the future for "globalized/flexible" organization It is an immensely efficient engine of exploitation. Numerous efforts to slow down the reemergence of sweatshops have been tried, most with only partial success, if that. To counter this, we need approaches that bring together community and union organizing, and that are centered on developing the workers' own understandings

and capacities to fight back. Moreover, we need to develop cross-border organizing programs, where workers in the various countries of production join together in attempting to prevent being pitted against one another. We should recognize that social change in this arena is not going to be won overnight, and that the ground must be laid thoroughly and democratically in order to build a workers' movement that can last through the long, hard fights that lie ahead.

Finally, this entire discussion has taken for granted the capitalist approach to the production of apparel. Obviously this approach can be severely criticized from numerous angles. Eliminating it will require much more than a reactivated labor movement. However, given the current power configurations, worker organizing is definitely a step in the right direction.

Discussion Questions

1. How would you estimate the relative economic well-being of the immigrant Latinas in Los Angeles in comparison with women who work in American factories across the border in Mexico?

2. Can you identify sweatshop conditions in companies unconnected to the global economy?

"The Challenge of Organizing in a Globalized Flexible Industry" by Edna Bonacich, from *The Critical Study of Work* edited by Rick Baldoz, Charles Koeber, and Philip Kraft. Used by permission of Temple University Press. ©2001 by Temple University. All Rights Reserved.

Endnotes

1. In acknowledgment of the work of Harry Braverman, I am using the term "monopoly capitalism" to denote the economic system that held force from the New Deal to late 1950s or early 1960s; this system has been given other names, including the "social contract" and "Keynsian economics." Post-monopoly capitalist has also been known by a number of different names, including "global capitalism," "flexible capitalism," "neoliberalism," and the "new

world order." I shall use these terms interchangeably.

2. My conclusions are based on about ten years of investigating the LA (and Pacific Rim) apparel industry, while simultaneously working as a volunteer with the Union of Needle-trades, Industrial and Textile Employees (UNITE) Organizing Department. The research has resulted in the book *Behind the Label: Inequality in the Los Angeles Apparel Industry* (2000), co-authored with Richard Appelbaum.

3. The fact that Asian immigrants are overrepresented in the contractor population makes defining the struggle of Asian garment workers as an Asian community issue somewhat more difficult because it raises more intracommunity contradictions. Nevertheless, Asian community activists have plunged ahead in this difficult arena.

4. The influence of Paulo Freire (1970) should be evident in these ideas.

5. There is always a risk in describing a new group, because one never knows whether it will last. Who knows whether this group will still be in existence by the time this volume is published, or whether it will have died along with so many other good ideas?

6. An underlying question is how much the present "flexible" production system is driven by the needs of manufacturers for flexibility, and how much by the desire to shave labor costs to the bone. To the degree that it is driven by the latter, there will be more room for reconfiguring the industry in a more stable, capital-intensive direction.

References

American Apparel Manufacturers Association. 1997. *Focus: An Economic Profile of the Apparel Industry.* Arlington: Author.

Armbruster, Ralph. 1995. "Cross-National Organizing Strategies." *Critical Sociology,* 21(3): 77–91.

——. 1998. "Globalization and Cross-Border Labor Organizing in the Garment and Automobile Industries." Ph.D. dissertation, Department of Sociology, University of California, Riverside.

Bird, Laura, and Wendy Bounds. 1997. "Stores' Demands Squeeze Apparel Companies." *Wall Street Journal,* July 15, p. B1.

Bonacich, Edna. 2000. "Intense Challenges, Tentative Possibilities: Organizing Immigrant Garment Workers in Los Angeles." Pp. 130–149 in *Organizing Immigrants: The Challenge for Unions in Contemporary California,* edited by Ruth Milkman. Ithaca: ILR Press.

Bonacich, Edna, and Richard Appelbaum. 2000. *Behind the Label: Inequality in the Los Angeles Apparel Industry.* Berkeley: University of California Press.

Braverman, Harry. 1974. *Labor and Monopoly Capital: The Degradation of Work in the Twentieth Century.* New York: Monthly Review Press.

Burawoy, Michael. 1979. *Manufacturing Consent: Changes in the Labor Process Under Monopoly Capitalism.* Chicago: University of Chicago Press.

Fregoso, Rosa Marta. 1988. "The Invisible Workforce: Immigrant Home Workers in the Garment Industry of Los Angeles." Master's thesis, University of California, Berkeley.

Freire, Paulo. 1970. *The Pedagogy of the Oppressed.* New York: Seabury Press.

Klein, Naomi. 1999. *No Logo: Taking Aim at the Brand Bullies.* New York: Picador.

Kyser, Jack. 1997. *Manufacturing in Los Angeles.* Los Angeles: Economic Development Corporation.

Moody, Kim. 1997. *Workers in a Lean World.* London: Verso.

Ross, Andrew, ed. 1997. *No Sweat: Fashion, Free Trade, and the Rights of Garment Workers.* London: Verso.

Sullivan, Ben. 1997. "Bankers, Financiers Dominate Ranks of L.A.'s Highest Paid." *Los Angeles Business Journal,* June 23, p. 1.

Targeted Industries Partnership Program (TIPP). 1996. *Fourth Annual Report, 1996.* Sacramento: Author.

U.S. General Accounting Office. 1988. *'Sweatshops' in the U.S.: Opinions on Their Extent and Possible Enforcement Options.* Washington, DC: U.S. Government Printing Office.

——. 1994. *The Garment Industry: Efforts to Address the Prevalence and Conditions of Sweatshops.* Washington, DC: U.S. Government Printing Office. ✦

38

Lessons From Living-Wage Campaigns

Stephanie Luce

This chapter attempts to provide very useful information about unionization of workers. Specifically, Luce discusses three concrete victories for unions as well as six lessons for labor that come from the movement for living-wage ordinances.

If there were any doubt that the labor movement was facing hard times, the 2004 presidential election confirmed it. Despite an all-out effort by the American Federation of Labor-Congress of Industrial Organizations (AFLCIO) and major unions, including unprecedented campaign contributions and immeasurable in-kind donations of staff time, phone-banking, and other resources, labor-backed John Kerry received a smaller share of the popular vote than Al Gore did in 2000. Although the number of voters from union household increased from 2000, it was not enough to sway the election. And approximately 35% of voters from union households still voted for George Bush, despite his aggressive antiunion actions throughout his first term.

In the meantime, the intense focus on the election suggests it is highly unlikely much new organizing happened in 2004. With major staff resources devoted to voter turnout, few were left behind to build la-

bor's ranks. Meanwhile, union jobs are being outsourced at a rate far surpassing their share of the workforce. According to research by Bronfenbrenner and Luce (2004), 39% of the jobs moved out of the United States in the first quarter of 2004 were union jobs. Adjusting to a yearly figure, this means that a minimum of 80,000 union jobs were outsourced in 2004—and a more realistic estimate suggests as many as 154,000 union jobs lost. When the union density figures are released in January, they are certain to show yet another drop.

Certainly, many within the labor movement have realized that they are in a crisis situation: This was true long before the 2004 election and would also be true even if Kerry had won. But the Bush victory was part of a wake-up call. The labor movement needs to take drastic measures to survive, and it needs to do much more to convince a larger share of the U.S. population that labor's issues should be their priorities.

At the same time that organized labor's fortunes have declined, other workers have seen modest victories in another arena during the past 10 years. The living-wage movement came onto the scene in 1994 and spread rapidly. Ten years later, we find that almost 130 living-wage ordinances have passed around the country, and there are campaigns in the United Kingdom, Canada, Australia, and New Zealand. Over time, the movement itself has charted new directions, pushing into new territory, such as citywide minimum-wage laws and community-benefits agreements. Although living-wage campaigns tend to face opponents such as the Chamber of Commerce, the National Restaurant Association, large retail chains, and most mayors and newspaper editorial staffs, these efforts have a high success rate.

Are there lessons to be learned from the living-wage movement? In the aftermath of the presidential election, as labor unions look for new strategies for revitalization, are there any insights we can draw from the fight for a living wage? This article examines these questions, beginning with a look at some of the concrete victories for labor that have resulted from the living-wage movement. I then turn to some lessons one might take from the success of the living-wage movement for the labor movement.

Living-Wage Movement Brings Concrete Gains for Labor

Opponents of the living-wage movement claim that the real purpose behind the campaigns is an attempt to protect unionized workers at the expense of nonunion workers or to force companies to unionize. For example, an op-ed in the Heartland Institute (Reed, 1999) says about the living-wage movement: "It is the cannibalization of fellow workers by greedy, self-interested union bosses." An editorial in the *San Francisco Examiner* titled "The Wages of Sin" (1999) stated that one of the "dirty little secrets of [the living wage proposal] is that it's aimed at fighting the nonprofits on behalf of city unions." In reality, unions are not always enthusiastic supporters of living-wage campaigns. Those union leaders that do get involved don't usually do so for direct gains: Most agree that the living-wage movement on its own is not the most effective way to directly build unions. However, it is clear that there have been some concrete short-term gains for the labor movement, including new organizing, winning raises for already unionized workers and holding onto union jobs.

New Organizing

The link between union organizing and the living wage is complex. Although some living-wage opponents claim that unionization efforts are the main motive behind the movement, not all union leaders are convinced of the opportunities for translating living-wage campaigns into new organizing. In fact, some assert that the campaigns hurt organizing efforts: If workers can get higher wages through legislation, why would they fight for a union?

The reality is somewhere in between. Ken Jacobs, head organizer for the San Francisco living-wage campaign, argues that where unions have been strategic about involvement in campaigns, they have seen positive results. Where unions are neutral or even skeptical of the campaigns and stay out of them, living-wage ordinances can in fact be a detriment to new organizing. Unfortunately for unions, Taft-Hartley states that city governments cannot require employers to have unions or even that employers abide by card-check and neutrality agreements to get a city contract (Sahu, 2001). However, unions have been able to get some language in living-wage ordinances that allows cities to deny contracts or subsidies to firms with poor labor relations history if the city can show its economic interests are at stake. Some ordinances also contain language that explicitly prohibits employers from disciplining or firing workers who exercise their rights under the living-wage law, which can aid union-organizing efforts because workers who speak out about their right to join a union will be protected from job loss if they are also speaking about their right to receive a living wage.

To date, there are a number of examples of unions that have used provisions in the ordinances to organize new workers. For example, the neutrality clause in the Santa Cruz ordinance led to a card-check agreement with an antiunion employer that held a contract to drive city buses and vans. Subsequently, the 150 workers won a contract with United Transportation Union Local 23. In addition, the campaign also won a card-check agreement with the city to cover its 550 nonunion temporary workers, who are now represented by Service Employees International Union (SEIU) Local 415. In a few cases (in Los Angeles and Berkeley, California), the Hotel and Restaurant Employees union (HERE) has been able to use the opt-out clause and the antiretaliation clause to assist organizing drives, some of which have resulted in victory.

Greater success has come in indirect organizing victories, where the campaign has in some way spurred a new drive or assisted an existing one. For example, nonunion city workers in Tucson, Arizona, heard about the city's living-wage law, and contacted the Communication Workers of America to see about getting their own wages raised. Eventually, 1,500 workers won recognition and a first contract with the city. Union of Needletrades, Textiles and Industrial Employees (UNITE) has used living-wage ordinances in their campaign to organize workers at the laundry company Cintas. For example, UNITE discovered that Cintas held contracts for laundry services in Hayward and Los Angeles, California, and Madison, Wisconsin, and that the company had violated the living-wage law. The union helped workers file complaints to get backwages, and in Hayward and Madison, public pressure resulted in the city's dropping the Cintas contracts.

Other successful efforts to link living-wage campaigns to unionization have occurred in cities such as Berkeley and San Jose, California; Alexandria, Virginia; and Miami-Dade, Florida. Gains have also been seen overseas in London, where the East London Communities Organization helped the Transport and General Workers Union (T & G) win union recognition for 150 janitorial workers. According to T & G General Secretary Tony Woodley, the living-wage campaign has helped spark an important step: "There are millions of unorganized workers in the UK and the T & G is determined to reach them. This recognition agreement represents a significant breakthrough in our campaign for modern fighting back trade unionism" ("Cleaners' Union Wins Canary Wharf Breakthrough," 2004).

University living-wage campaigns have been closely tied to efforts to create or strengthen campus unions. At Wesleyan University in Connecticut, the University Student Labor Action Coalition first worked on a solidarity campaign to help janitors on campus (working for a private contractor) organize with SEIU Local 531. The students then mounted a campus living-wage campaign, requiring the university to pay all its direct and contracted employees a living wage. After students took over the admissions building for 24 hours, the university president gave in and signed off on the ordinance, resulting in a union contract with living wages for the janitors.

Perhaps the most extensive connection between the living wage and union organizing has occurred in Los Angeles. After the Los Angeles ordinance was passed, the Los Angeles Alliance for a New Economy and the living-wage coalition worked closely with local unions and the County Federation of Labor to turn the passage of the living-wage ordinance into a union-organizing opportunity. This was most effective at the Los Angeles International airport (LAX). The living-wage coalition was able to get food concession contracts awarded to employers that agreed to remain neutral in union campaigns. It was also able to rely on the antiretaliation language in the ordinance that protects workers' rights to organize around living-wage issues. According to Larry Frank and Kent Wong (2004), activity around the living wage at LAX helped HERE and SEIU dramatically increase the number of members at the airport: HERE went from representing "roughly one out of every five airport workers in its bargaining to four out of five" (Frank & Wong, 2004, p. 174). In the same period, SEIU "has moved from representing one in ten workers within their jurisdiction to representing more than half" (Frank & Wong, 2004, p. 174–175).

Winning Raises for Unionized Workers

Beyond showing up for picket lines, some living-wage campaigns have furthered the cause of organized workers in other concrete ways. The Alexandria, Virginia, living-wage ordinance resulted in raises for parking lot attendants at city-owned lots, represented by HERE. Unionized home health care workers in Chicago saw a wage increase with the city's living-wage ordinance in place.

Some unions have used living-wage campaigns as part of their contract campaign. In Seattle, Washington, workers at the Seattle Seahawks football stadium worked with a local living-wage coalition to win a strong contract for food concession workers. The workers, members of HERE Local 8, was in bargaining with their Aramark for 11 months before winning a contract that included for the first time ever, fully paid family medical, dental, and optical coverage for workers who worked at least 1,040 hours per year. The contract also included raises of up to $2.08 per hour, paid lunch breaks, strong language for immigrant's rights protections, and a guarantee that tipped workers would earn at least the minimum wage. The stadium workers were supported in their contract campaign by a local living-wage coalition. Michael Ramos, a staff person with the Washington Association of Churches and active in the campaign, commented,

> The teamwork between Seattle's faith community and stadium workers in this campaign for a fair contract has been rewarding for all of us. When members of the community join with workers in struggle, the experience and understanding we gain makes us stronger than ever before. (Peace and Justice Action League of Spokane, 2002)

In Ithaca, New York, 220 teachers' aides and assistants represented by the National Education Association (NEA) worked with the local living-wage coalition to win a better contract in 2001 and 2002. The teachers got help from the community in raising public awareness about their wage levels and working conditions. The campaign organized public hearings, rallies, marches, and a forum with religious leaders to pressure the school board. In the end, according to the NEA magazine, the union "won a whopping 50% wage increase during 3 years and also increased membership in their bargaining unit to a perfect 100%" (National Education Association, 2004). The NEA notes that as a result of the Ithaca victory, public school employees in Atlanta; Denver; St. Louis County, Missouri; Seneca Valley, Pennsylvania; Oshkosh, Wisconsin; Montgomery and Birmingham, Alabama; and Fayette County, Kentucky, have pur-

sued living-wage campaigns to win better contracts (NEA, 2004).

Gains for the already organized can be won on campus as well. In fact, the Harvard living-wage campaigns included demands for raises for some workers currently represented by HERE and SEIU as well as a call to bring subcontracted service work back in-house and back into the union. Students at Stanford University, Vanderbilt University, and the University of Maryland have also been involved in campus campaigns designed to win raises for unionized workers.

Saving Union Jobs

Although opponents suggest that preventing privatization of public sector union jobs is the main motivation behind living-wage campaigns, unions have not commonly used them for this purpose. However, there are a few cases of this. For example, a number of ordinances have worker retention provisions. This means that when the city changes contractors, the workers at the initial contractor have the right to keep their job with the new contractor. In San Jose, California, the provision has meant that hundreds of unionized workers have kept their jobs when the city changed contractors. This includes

> parking attendants who are members of SEIU Local 1877, food service workers at the Mineta San Jose International Airport who are members of Hotel Employees and Restaurant Employees Local 19 and Operating Engineers Local 40 workers who handle recycling for the city. (Lazarovici, 2003)

Workers in other cities have also benefited from this provision, helping to improve job security and retain union jobs.

These stories suggest that the living-wage movement has had some success in helping revitalize labor—by organizing new workers, raising wages for already unionized workers, and maintaining union jobs. But what about broader lessons that we might learn from the movement?

Six Lessons for Labor

After 10 years of living-wage campaigns, more than 120 victories, and scores more ongoing campaigns, there are a number of conclusions we can draw about successful organizing. Although every living-wage coalition and campaign looks different and there are exceptions to every rule, the following are some basic findings

Labor Needs Allies and Needs to Think Long Term

The fact that labor needs allies to elect candidates should come as a surprise to no one. AFL-CIO president John Sweeney remarked in 1998, "We're finding that some of the most successful programs, whether on initiatives or policy, even organizing workers, are done together with allies that share our concern about working families" (Hukill, 1998). But the idea that unions need to work with community partners on a range of issues beyond those immediately beneficial to unions is not as readily accepted. Even many of those who do accept the idea in theory are not always successful in converting into practice. Although the Union City program advocates building labor-community coalitions, many central labor councils have struggled to make this happen. Many union locals are torn between putting the resources and hard work into developing relations with potential partners and pressures from members who don't feel dues should be spent on such activities. Developing lasting and solid relations can take years, but unions feeling the need to organize, organize, organize may see that time as a luxury they can't afford. According to Harriet Applegate of the AFL-CIO, when it comes to coalition building, "It's tough to find time to do it right. We all know you can't just rent a preacher to come to events. On the other hand, we don't know how to do it right."

The solution may lie in thinking long term and selecting issues that truly are overlap issues: ones that appeal to union members or potential union members as well as community partners. Dan Clawson points to these kinds of issues and their ability to potentially ignite a next upsurge in the labor movement (Clawson, 2003). Overlap issues can bring together different groups into a true coalition. One example is the intersection of work and family and the issues that arise from this nexus: child care, flextime, and forced overtime. These are clearly labor issues, as one of the earliest union demands was for a shorter workday. But they can also be framed as women's issues and pro-family issues, attracting new supporters to a larger coalition. Work and family issues can form the basis of a true coalition of partners with real material demands.

The living-wage movement has shown that higher wages can also be an overlap issue. Polls consistently show that support for higher minimum wages is popular among voters. In the 2004 election, two statewide ballot initiatives to establish state minimum wages in Florida and Nevada won overwhelmingly: 72% in favor in Florida, 68% in Nevada, and both measures won in every single county in both states. Although politicians from major parties are often lukewarm on wage standards, the idea has broad appeal not only with voters but with religious leaders, community organizations, social service agencies, women's groups, student activists, and environmentalists.

Inside the labor movement, views are somewhat mixed and some high-wage union members see campaigns for low-wage workers as unrelated to their interests. But the majority of union leaders seem to have embraced the idea that a higher minimum wage can benefit labor and that living-wage campaigns in particular can be a valuable tool for building coalitions and educating the public about wages and working conditions.

One example of how the campaigns can be used for coalition building can be found in Atlanta, Georgia. The living-wage coalition was formed in 2001 by four groups: the Georgia Citizens' Coalition on Hunger, Project South: Institute for the Elimination of Poverty and Genocide; 9to5; Atlanta Working Women; and the Atlanta Central

Labor Council. The groups worked together on education, research, strategy, and outreach. Eventually, 95 other organizations became members of the coalition, ranging from Concerned Black Clergy to the Georgia Abortion and Reproductive Rights Action League. The coalition also brought in active participation from gay and lesbian rights group Georgia Equality as the living-wage proposal included domestic partner benefits.

The Atlanta campaign built wide support in the community, which is not surprising given that an earlier poll showed between 80% and 90% of voters supported significant raises in the minimum wage. The campaign also made headway among city leaders (Hickey, 2003). Living-wage advocates supported Shirley Franklin for mayor, and when she came into office, she announced that an ordinance would be a high priority. Eventually, the opposition stepped up its efforts to stop the ordinance by taking its claims to the state legislature. In late 2004, the state passed a bill that prevents the city from passing a traditional living-wage ordinance. However, the coalition remains strong and is exploring other avenues for living wages, such as instituting a point preference system for city contractors that pay a living wage.

The campaign is also an example of how labor needs to think long term when entering coalitions. According to Cindia Cameron of 9to5, the groups that came together to form the coalition were very explicit about their goals "to build a lasting coalition around working poverty issues and to create public debate on these issues." Winning a city ordinance was just one piece of that. When the state passed the preemption law, Living-wage Coalition leaders were frustrated but kept up their struggle to fight for living wages on other fronts. "Some people were motivated to keep going because they were so angry at the state legislature for stepping in to take away our rights at the local level," said Cameron. "And others remained committed to the longer term goals of the coalition."

Building labor-community alliances can be challenging, particularly in the south where unionization is low to begin with. According to Cameron, even with limited resources, the Central Labor Council leadership played a critical role in the campaign: "His resources, showing up as 'labor' and his relationship with the Mayor's office are a big part of our success." At the same time, union locals in the Atlanta region were not very involved in the campaign. The building trades members tend to make much more than the proposed living-wage rate, so they didn't see the need to get involved. In other cases, unions such as UNITE represented workers making less than the living wage who would not be covered under the proposed ordinance. But even the unions that did represent workers that would be directly affected by the ordinance (such as American Federation of State, County, and Municipal Employees, which represents city workers, or SEIU that represents a unit of parking lot attendants at the airport) did not really get involved. Given the potential of living-wage campaigns to organize new workers, win raises for already organized workers, and build long-term worker's rights coalitions, union leaders would do well to consider investing the time to get involved with these kinds of efforts.

Labor Needs a Moral Vision of Its Own

A second lesson that some might draw from the living-wage movement (and the 2004 election) is that the labor movement needs to assert its own moral vision. The Republican Party has been willing to ally with Christian Right, promoting its vision of morality based on the Bible. The Democratic Party has shied away from presenting an alternative vision, although some of its stable base has provided the country with that moral vision in the past. For example, the Civil Rights Movement relied heavily on a morality based on social justice and human rights. The labor movement has also begun to assert a vision of justice by promoting freedom of association and the right to safe working conditions as a human right. Last year, the AFL-CIO sponsored events around the country on December 10, International Human Rights Day.

Living-wage campaigns have also been a place where labor has joined in this appeal to morality. This is driven in part by the heavy participation of clergy in the movement, who rely on scripture from various faiths to assert that the right to a living wage is a human right and moral imperative. For example, in 2000, the United Methodist Church (2000) passed the following resolution: "The United Methodist Church recognizes the responsibility of governments to develop and implement sound fiscal and monetary policies that provide for the economic life of individuals. Every person has the right to a job at a living wage" (p. 55). Catholics point to several teachings in their tradition that call for a living wage, such as Catechism of the Catholic Church 2434: "A just wage is the legitimate fruit of work. To refuse or withhold it can be a grave injustice. In determining fair pay, both the needs and the contributions of each person must be taken into account." There are numerous examples of campaigns where clergy members have played leading roles in the modern living-wage struggle. Chuck Campbell (Hickey, 2003), a seminary professor and a leader in the Atlanta Living-wage Campaign, states, "What brought me personally to get involved in the living-wage campaign is, quite simply, my Christian faith, my deep sense that scripture has a profound concern for poor people." He adds, "My concern for this is a huge concern about God's being against economic systems that exploit the poor and rely on cheap labor for the profit of a few" (Hickey, 2003). In Los Angeles, a group called Clergy and Laity United for Economic Justice formed out of the living-wage campaign and went on to play a large role in the Santa Monica campaign. For example, Clergy and Laity United for Economic Justice helped organize a rally with prominent Christian, Muslim, and Jewish religious leaders. Reverend Jim Conn of the United Methodist Church spoke at the rally, declaring, "This is about how God wants people to live. God doesn't want people to go hungry. God doesn't want people to work full time and not make enough money to buy food and put a roof over their head" (Schley, 2002).

The participation of religious leaders in the living-wage movement is not a new development: Labor has worked with clergy at many points in its history. In fact, some of the early advocates for minimum wage legislation were Catholic priests, such as Father John Ryan who published *A Living Wage* in 1906 (Ryan, 1906). During the 1960s, the civil rights movement intersected with the labor movement in a few key places, most notably perhaps the fight for a living wage and union recognition by sanitation workers in Memphis, Tennessee. Religious leaders, including Dr. Martin Luther King, Jr., played a large role in this campaign to win a union and higher wages for the workers.

Of course, this kind of collaboration can be extended beyond campaigns for a living wage. The AFL-CIO has realized this and some attempts have been made to foster these alliances (such as the AFL-CIO Seminary Summer program). But it is important to note that having a moral vision must be more than getting a religious leader to speak at a rally. Labor must develop a picture of a society that bases decision making on economic and social justice and that demands poverty eradication as a goal equally as important as wealth creation. The AFL-CIO should continue to pursue its efforts to build a strong, unified voice arguing that worker's rights are human rights. This kind of vision must serve as a counterbalance to those that argue that the Republican Party or the evangelical Christian churches have a lock on moral values.

Labor Can't Be Afraid to Break From the Mainstream Parties

Another lesson that labor should take from the living-wage movement, and perhaps the 2004 election, is that to make serious advances on worker's rights, unions must not be afraid to break from the mainstream political parties. For the most part, living-wage campaigns take place at the municipal level where the races are officially nonpartisan—however, people generally know which political party candidates belong to. Neither Democratic nor Republican mayors are enthusiastic supporters of living-wage ordinances, and neither party has taken up the cause. Instead, living-wage campaigns must pressure their city councilors to adopt the laws by demonstrating support among constituents.

Although living-wage ordinances are popular with voters and often pass with enthusiastic support from city council members, city administrators are operating within a particular economic development model that is at odds with the living-wage concept. On the whole, city managers make economic development decisions based on the notion that they are competing not only with other countries but with other cities even in their state for capital. With no national industrial policy to promote economic development, the easiest way to create jobs is to lure them from elsewhere. And because other places are offering tax breaks, subsidies, and other incentives, most city managers must enter the game as well.

Despite the plethora of research showing negative outcomes from this competition, and despite calls for an end to "the bidding war between the states," city managers still adhere to this philosophy. Economic development policy becomes a competition for the best business climate. City managers are pressured to institute structural adjustment at home, to make their cities look most favorable for growth. This involves privatizing public services, downsizing government payrolls, and reducing regulations and taxes on businesses. In this context, a living-wage ordinance—a regulation on business that raises wage and benefit costs makes it harder to outsource public services, requires city staff to monitor, and attaches strings to subsidies—is antithetical to city administrator goals.

This highlights the constraints that activists face when dealing with economic policy on the local level. Globalization itself is not necessarily the issue, as most of the firm relocation occurs within the United States. However, the process of globalization and the establishment of trade agreements such as North American Free Trade Agreement have allowed employers more flexibility in their movements and their threat of movement (Bronfenbrenner, 2000).

The result is that in many cities, living-wage advocates have had to be bold in breaking from their allies on the city council or in the mayor's seat and holding those representatives accountable for their votes. In Boston, local union leaders were surprised when only one city council member showed up for the initial living-wage rally. Angered by what they felt was a show of disrespect, union leaders responded by making a public announcement that the living wage would be a top-priority issue when making endorsements in the next election cycle. Soon, the city councilors were speaking out in favor of the living wage and eventually passed the ordinance with almost a unanimous vote.

However, it is often the community groups or faith-based groups in the living-wage coalitions that are more likely to hold elected officials up to public scrutiny on their living-wage stance. In many cities, labor unions have had some success in building up influence in local governments. Their approach of candidate endorsements and get-out-the-vote efforts have been more successful at the local than the state or federal level, and union leaders are wary of jeopardizing those connections by applying public pressure on the candidates they helped get into office. The living wage is only one example of an issue that appeals to most voters yet is not a priority of either political party. Many other labor issues are similar: They have broad support, but neither party is willing to take them on. This means that labor unions cannot be afraid to call attention to those places where the parties don't support a labor agenda.

Labor Needs to Work From the Inside and the Outside

Although city officials have been persuaded to vote for living-wage ordinances, they have not necessarily been persuaded to enforce the laws. The business climate model of economic development that pervades city administration leads to a lack of commitment to implement living wages. The result is that of the 82 ordinances that passed by the end of 2001, 52% were only being weakly implemented: City administrators were just doing the minimum requirements to comply with the law, putting language in request for bids and in the contracts. No city staff monitored worksites to make sure posters were put up informing workers of the law. No trainings were conducted with workers to make sure they understood their rights. No evaluations were conducted to see how many workers were getting the higher wage. In another 10%, implementation was blocked altogether when cities refused to enforce, filed lawsuits against the ordinance, or simply repealed.

At the same time, labor unions can influence living-wage implementation. In about 20% of the cases, living-wage coalitions have been active in enforcement efforts, and this has resulted in stronger outcomes. This has occurred through several ways. First, some coalitions have relied on outside pressure, or protest politics, to push the city into stronger enforcement. For example, recently in Baltimore, Maryland, a HERE local discovered that it had members working for Aramark at the city stadium who were not being paid overtime pay as required by the living-wage ordinance. HERE did the ground work and filed complaints on behalf of the workers. The city eventually ruled in favor of the workers, ordering Aramark to pay $131,000 in back wages.

Advocates have also worked through internal channels to improve enforcement. In a few cities, living-wage coalitions were able to win living-wage implementation advisory boards as part of the ordinance. This establishes a committee of government, business, unions, and community groups to oversee implementation. In cities such as Boston, this kind of advisory board has been instrumental in expanding coverage of the ordinance and raising the wage level.

In a lot of cities with weak enforcement, it is easy for a firm to apply for and receive a waiver from the ordinance. But in Boston, the advisory board has been strict about requiring all firms requesting a waiver to produce adequate documentation proving hardship. In some cases, Boston has turned down this request for waivers.

Finally, there are some cases where advocates have combined inside and outside tactics to improve implementation, using a formal implementation task force as well as protest politics. This in fact appears to be the most effective way to improve implementation for several reasons. First, an inside method, such as seats on an official advisory board, provides living-wage advocates with regular access to information, such as lists of contracts coming up for bid, or ability to look at employer payroll records. Working through formal channels also allows for systematic improvements in enforcement. For example, the Ventura County advisory board came up with the idea that the county should require employers to send notification of the ordinance inside payroll envelopes. In Los Angeles, advocates worked with the city to make sure it hired Spanish-speaking staff to answer calls from workers. Third, working from within allows advocates to become policy experts, putting them on equal footing with city administrators.

However, when advocates work only through official channels, they could lose their independence. Individuals serving on implementation task forces are subject to capture just as city staff are. Pressure from the outside will keep the advisory board accountable to their mandate. In addition, sympathetic city staff often need outside agitation to do their job effectively. In essence, visible public outcry about implementation can give city staff cover for enforcing the ordinance against an influential employer. These examples show that unions can have influence in enforcing local policy, even in a context of globalization and even against the desires of city managers.

Labor Can't Shy Away From Conflict

Related to the above two points, my research on the implementation of living-wage ordinances found an interesting and perhaps surprising pattern. Cases where the campaign was more conflictual—where there was active opposition from elected officials and groups such as the Chamber of Commerce—tended to have a better chance of successful enforcement if passed. There are several possible explanations for this. First, it is likely that a contentious campaign forces living-wage advocates to develop their argument and to convince more people of the merits of the proposal. Second, more opposition would push the coalition to take on a variety of strategies to win, including both the inside and outside tactics mentioned above. Jen Kern, director of Association of Community Organizations for Reform Now's (ACORN) Living Wage Resource Center, remarks, "You might think that a bigger fight would intimidate people, but it doesn't. When they have to fight harder, they get more energized" (Luce, 2004, p. 163). The campaigns work harder and develop more tools that can later be employed in struggles about implementation.

Table 38.1 presents the data on the relationship between contentious campaigns and implementation outcomes. I rated all campaigns passed through December 2001 on two dimensions. First, if there was active opposition to the ordinance, I rated it as contentious; otherwise, it was scored as not contentious. To measure implementation, I looked at 14 dimensions, ranging from whether there was a person assigned to monitor the ordinance, whether employers were required to submit records regarding compliance, and whether there were procedures in place to educate workers about the law. I then grouped the ordinances into four categories based on these scores: *expansive implementation, moderate, narrow,* and *blocked.* Expansive implementation is where the city is doing the most to enforce the law. Under narrow implementation, the city does the bare minimum required by law. A few cases have had implementation blocked altogether when the city simply refused to enforce the ordinance, repealed the law, or put it up to legal challenge. In Table 38.1, we see that only 5% of the noncontentious campaigns ended up with expansive implementation, whereas 22% of the contentious campaigns were in this category.

The lesson here for labor is that conflictual organizing can have positive results. Or, turning that around, legislation that is passed quietly—perhaps by negotiations between union leaders and city councilors or the mayor—may not be enforced in the end. This has been a hard lesson for some unionists to learn. In a number of living-wage campaigns, union leaders have pushed to get living-wage ordinances in this fashion, shying away from tactics such as rallies, marches, or civil disobedience. Some labor union leaders have said they don't

Table 38.1
Implementation Outcomes in Contentious Versus Noncontentious Campaigns

Implementation Outcome	Not Contentious (Did Not Face Organized Opposition)	Contentious (Faced Organized Opposition)	Total
% blocked	15	5	10
% narrow	70	34	52
% moderate	20	29	25
% expansive	5	22	14
% total	100	100	
Total	40	41	81

Source: Author's analysis based on ordinances, interviews, and review of relevant documents. Table includes ordinances passed through December 2001.

want to embarrass their friends in elected office by calling on them to do something they don't want to do.

Labor Must Do a Better Job Involving Rank-and-File Members

Finally, all of the above lessons highlight a crucial point: Labor unions must find ways to activate their rank-and-file members. This is true for several reasons. First, the most successful living-wage campaigns mobilize a lot of people for visits to council member's offices, marches, rallies, door-knocking, educational events, and more. In many cities, it is the community organizations that are best at this and sometimes help teach union leaders how to get their membership active. In Alexandria, Virginia, Gyula Nagy of the Tenant and Workers Support Committee actually borrowed some rank-and-file union members and trained them how to knock on doors and do turnout for rallies. Nagy has worked with other living-wage campaigns to teach unions how to do strategic planning; identify goals, allies, and resources; engage in escalating tactics; and build coalitions. Mobilizing members does not come naturally or easily to many unions, so it is something they can learn from their community organization allies.

Eva Bonime[1] of the Working Families Party (WFP) in New York notes that the WFP also worked with unions to mobilize their members to come to hearings, rallies, and delegation visits with legislators in the Westchester and Suffolk County living-wage campaigns. Bonime says that with some training, the unions were able to mobilize "union members who would be affected by the legislation as well as higher paid union members who got involved for solidarity."

Second, the more rank-and-file workers are involved in the campaign and follow-up, the more likely the ordinance will be implemented. As mentioned above, the or-dinances are most likely enforced when those who have a direct stake are involved. This is an important lesson for unions in different contexts. Whether it is about passing other kinds of legislation or winning union recognition and a union contract, implementation and enforcement are more likely the more that the workers themselves are involved. This may serve as an important lesson for unions that are attempting to organize new workers through legislative efforts or by organizing employers through large-scale card-check agreements. Although these kinds of strategies may end up getting new workers into unions, it may mean there is little chance that workers on the shop floor will be there to enforce the contract.

Rank-and-file involvement improves accountability in other ways. In 2002, a living-wage coalition in Syracuse, New York, came close to getting their city council to pass an ordinance. However, the mayor opposed the proposal and got a few council members to switch their votes at the last minute resulting in defeat. Councilors who changed their vote included some labor-backed council members who had promised their support. The coalition headed by the WFP and local unions, decided to use the living wage as an issue in the council elections the following year. They found a challenger to run against one of the incumbents and ran an aggressive campaign. With rank-and-file union involvement, the coalition won and the living wage is back on the table. According to Eva Bonime of the WFP, living-wage campaigns show that "labor actually can hold politicians more accountable to promises they make if they mobilize their members."[2]

Third, involving rank-and-file members in union activity means that labor must continue and expand efforts to organize at the local level. Although the Union City program called for Central Labor Councils to revitalize themselves, there are still only a handful of cities where labor is an active political force.[3] Yet mobilizing members must start at the local level: in the shop floor and in neighborhoods. Indeed, this has been one of the strengths of the living-wage movement: It has capitalized on the fact that citizens without a lot of resources have more power at the local level, where people power can be an effective counterweight to money. According to Jen Kern of ACORN's Living Wage Resource Center, most organizations—even national ones—have local manifestations. This includes groups such as ACORN, which has chapters in cities around the country as well as churches. It also includes unions—which may be national organizations, but members experience the union first and foremost in their worksite. Kern argues that national organizations such as these tend to organize nationally by starting with the local chapters and building from there. Former South Bay Central Labor Council President Amy Dean agrees. Speaking about the San Jose living-wage campaign, she argued, "It's the cumulative effect of regional movements around the country that is going to drive national political reform" (Hukill, 1998).

Conclusion

The living-wage movement is certainly not a panacea for stemming the tide of declining union membership. However, across the country, unions have found ways to use living-wage campaigns to organize new workers, maintain union jobs, and win raises for already-organized union members. But the real contribution of the living-wage movement for labor comes in the form of lessons learned from 10 years of organizing. Living-wage campaigns usually win, but the campaigns are often hard fought. The organizing that is required to get the ordinances passed and enforced is an amalgamation of the best practices of community, faith-based, and labor organizations. The lessons learned are useful for any groups looking to pass legislation at the local level but also offer insights for rebuilding the labor movement.

Discussion Questions

1. To what extent do you think that unionization of workers is a "solution" to the disparate power of labor versus management?

2. Do you think a community would be harmed by having a living wage policy?

Endnotes

1. Eva Bonime, personal communication, December 1, 2004.
2. Eva Bonime, personal communication, December 1, 2004.
3. See the December 2004 issue of *Working USA* (2004) for a discussion of some of these cities.

References

Bronfenbrenner, K. (2000). *Uneasy terrain: The impact of capital mobility on workers, wages and union organizing.* Ithaca, NY: Cornell University Press.

Bronfenbrenner, K., & Luce, S. (2004). *The changing nature of corporate global restructuring: The impact of production shifts on jobs in the U.S., China, and around the globe.* Ithaca, NY: Cornell University Press.

Clawson, D. (2003). *The next upsurge.* Ithaca, NY: Cornell University Press.

Cleaners' union wins Canary Wharf breakthrough. (2004, June 24). *T&C News.* Retrieved December 1, 2004, from <http://www.tgwu.org.uk/Templates/News.asp ?NodeID=90895>.

Frank, L., & Wong, K. (2004). Dynamic political mobilization: The Los Angeles County Federation of Labor. *Working USA,* 8, 155-181.

Hickey, J. (2003). Waging a fight. Retrieved September 24, 2004, from <http://www.tompaine.com/feature2.cfm/ID/8162>.

Hukill, T. (1998, October 15-21). Labor's new face. Metro Active. Retrieved November 29, 2004, from <http://www.metroactive.com/papersmetro/10.15.98/cover/sobaylaborl-9841.html>.

Lazarovici, L. (2003). This is America, where we have freedom . . . America@Work. Washington, DC: AFL-CIO. Retrieved November 29, 2004, from <http://www.aflcio.org/aboutaflcio/ magazine/0803_freedom.cfm>.

Luce, S. (2004). *Fighting for a living wage.* Ithaca, NY: Cornell University Press.

National Education Association. (2004). Ithaca teacher aide honored for winning living wage campaign. Retrieved November 28,2004, from <http://www.nea.org/members/minnick.html>.

Peace and Justice Action League of Spokane. (2002). Living wage news. *Handful of Salt*. Retrieved November 29, 2004 from <http://www.icehouse.net/pjals/handful/1202/lwage.html>.

Reed, L. W. (1999). "Living wage" law is public policy at its worst. Intellectual ammunition. Michigan: The Heartland Institute. Retrieved November 28, 2004, from <http://www.heartland.org/Article.cfm?art!d=288>.

Ryan, J. A. 1906. *A living wage: Its ethical and economic aspects.* New York: MacMillan.

Sahu, S. J. (2001). *Living up to the living wage: A primer on the legal issues surrounding the enactment and enforcement of living wage laws.* Detroit, MI: Guild Law Center.

Schley, R. T. (2002, October 16-22). Clergy holds rally for living wage ordinance. *Santa Monica Mirror.* Retrieved November 26,2004, from <http://www.laane.org/pressroom/stories/smart/sm021016_no3smmirror.html>.

United Methodist Church. (2000). Book of Resolutions. Washington, DC: United Methodist Church.

The wages of sin. (1999, March 15). *San Francisco Examiner.* Retrieved November 29, 2004 from <http://www.psrf.org/issues/living_wage.jsp>.

Working USA. (2004). S(2). ◆

39

Critical Condition: How Health Care in America Became Big Business and Bad Medicine

Donald L. Barlett and
James B. Steele

It is generally agreed that the cost of health care in America is getting out of control. Donald Barlett and James Steele provide a cogent critique of the present "market system" of health care in the United States and propose a cost-effective remedy that has the potential of garnering the support of both workers and corporations.

Without a Safety Net

. . . In the late 1940s and early 1950s, President Harry S. Truman advocated a universal health care system to cover everyone. The medical establishment—principally the American Medical Association (AMA)—opposed it with such intensity that the idea went nowhere. The AMA's position drew strong support from those groups who saw the Red Menace everywhere. It was the Cold War era, and any proposal for govern-ment involvement on such a large scale was thought surely to be part of a Communist plot, although oddly no one seemed to pin the label on the nation's mandatory and publicly financed education system. Truman's successor, President Dwight D. Eisenhower, also opposed universal coverage for much the same reason, even though he personally had received government-paid health care for most of his life through the military and the Veterans Administration. Nonetheless, President Eisenhower recognized the dilemma. "We know that the American people will not long be denied access to adequate medical facilities. And they should not be," Eisenhower said in 1954. "We cannot rest content knowing that modern health services are beyond the financial or physical reach of many millions of our fellow citizens. We must correct these defects."

But not too hurriedly. It wasn't until 1965 that President Lyndon B. Johnson pushed through legislation creating the two largest federal programs to deal with some of the uninsured: Medicare to cover everyone over the age of sixty-five and Medicaid for all those individuals and families living in poverty. Medicare was financed entirely by the federal government, with a payroll tax applied equally on all employers and employees. Medicaid's costs were shared by the federal government, out of general tax revenue, and the states.

For the first time, millions of Americans were protected by basic health insurance. The pressure was off, and the rest of the uninsured disappeared from view. It wasn't until 1980 that the country began to notice them again, in a study by the National Center for Health Services Research. Even the government agency was taken aback. "One surprise of this study was the large number of persons who reported being uninsured—26.6 million persons or about 12.6 percent of the civilian population," the center reported.

Still, Congress ignored the issue. By 1987, according to the Census Bureau, the ranks of the uninsured had swelled to "at least thirty-one million people and perhaps as many as thirty-seven million." Although the numbers bounced up and down through the years, the long-term trend moved in one direction only. By 2003, the uninsured population had grown to forty-four million.

Who are these people? For the most part, according to the Kaiser Commission on Medicaid and the Uninsured, they are between the ages of eighteen and sixty-five and come from—low-income working families. Two-thirds have incomes below $30,000, which makes them too "wealthy" to qualify for Medicaid and much too poor to buy their own insurance. "Nearly 70 percent come from families where at least one person works full time and another 12 percent from families with part-time employment."

In addition to the forty-four million without insurance, there are tens of millions of people who are underinsured. They have insurance, but it does not come close to covering the costs they may incur if they become sick. It's sort of like having homeowner's insurance only to discover after your house burns down that it will pay to rebuild just one-fourth of it.

The exact number of Americans who are uninsured or inadequately insured is unknown, but it certainly exceeds 100 million. Yet perhaps the most misleading statistic of all is the number of Americans who do have health insurance. America's Health Insurance Plans, the industry trade association, puts the figure at 200 million. But this statistic is nearly meaningless, because it includes thousands of insurance plans with mammoth disparities in coverage. They range from the blue-chip plan that covers members of Congress and takes care of all their medical needs to high-deductible policies for working families who must shell out thousands of dollars a year in medical expenses before their policies pay one cent.

Health insurers have written all sorts of restrictions into their policies—loopholes, caps, exclusions—to minimize their exposure. They may write you a policy but decline to cover any expenses for a preexisting illness, the kind of protection people need most. If you lose your job or must drop out of school because of illness, you may lose

your health insurance. While a government plan called COBRA allows workers whose jobs are terminated to buy an individual policy at the group rate of their former employers, in what often turns out to be the crudest Congressional hoax of all, even that rate is far more than the average worker can afford. If you are able to keep your policy during a major illness, you may find that it has a low cap that is exhausted in a matter of days of hospitalization. Moreover, according to The Commonwealth Fund, health insurers are implementing across-the-board plans to restrict coverage: "In addition to paying more for their care, many privately insured adults also report that their plans are cutting back or placing new limits on covered benefits."

Increasingly, the health-insurance industry is designed to shut out those who are perceived to be liabilities—or even potential liabilities. Corinne Cooper, professor emeritus of law at the University of Missouri-Kansas City, went into business for herself in Arizona after her academic career and struggled to obtain health coverage as the owner of a small business. She asks, "Is insurance only to protect the people who don't need it?"

Even those who have top-of-the-line health coverage find out belatedly that it's not enough when a major illness strikes. . . .

Spending More for Less

. . . Until the late 1990s, Americans with insurance through their employers were insulated from rising costs. For years, corporate America had picked up the full insurance tab for both its workers and retirees. As health care costs became a larger portion of corporate expenses, companies pushed some of the costs off on workers. The process began, as such potentially jarring trends often do, slowly. Companies paid 90 percent of the insurance cost, workers the other 10 percent. The plans became less generous in what they covered. Then the employee's share edged up to 20 percent or above. About the same time, companies began dumping their retiree plans, either slashing or terminating the health care coverage they once had promised for life. With some exceptions, only public employees and some union workers still receive fully paid health care as a fringe benefit.

The next stage in the evolving crisis will exact the heaviest toll of all. Many, if not most, companies plan to freeze their contribution at a fixed dollar level. Let's take a family policy in 2003, which cost an average $9,100. If the All-American Widget Company pays 75 percent—or $6,825—that will be it. If the policy goes up $ 1,000, the company will still pay $6,825. Employees will shoulder the entire increase, boosting their share of the bill from 25 percent to 32 percent. Total out-of-pocket expenditure: $3,275. In the era of modest wage increases, this means many workers will see their entire raise go to health care, and perhaps even part of their existing pay. Co-pays for visits to doctors' offices and deductibles will continue rising. Also, a new three-tier pricing system for prescription drugs has become the norm. In its annual survey of corporate health care policies, Mercer, the human resource consulting firm, found that co-pays in 2003 averaged $10 for generic drugs, $21 for brand names on a plan formulary, and $37 for those drugs not included on the formulary. Those numbers will continue upward.

Barring an unforeseen burst in job creation, the ranks of the under-insured and uninsured will continue to swell. As companies prune their payrolls and replace full-time employees with part-time workers and independent contractors, those people will be forced to fend for themselves in the health care insurance market. Because they have no buying leverage, they will be hit with the highest bills of all.

An unmarried self-employed person in Philadelphia, Pennsylvania, for example, paid $4,660 in 2004 for a limited health care plan offered by Independence Blue Cross and Pennsylvania Blue Shield, which control three-fourths of the southeast Pennsylvania market. That's up 71 percent from 1998—or five times more than the inflation rate. During that time, the nonprofit Blues squirreled away $2 billion in extra "profit."

So exactly what is propelling the runaway costs that make medical care unaffordable to ever-growing numbers of Americans? Let us count the culprits. Many people overuse the system. They check into ERs when there's no emergency, they visit their doctor without a serious medical reason to do so, they demand medication, especially antibiotics, that they don't need. Doctors, fearful of malpractice lawsuits, accede all too willingly to their patients' entreaties. They order needless lab work, X-rays, CT scans, and MRIs and write prescriptions as fast as they can. Too many hospitals insist on having all the latest technology. Too many want to have a surgical unit that performs as many complex procedures as possible—from heart valve operations to kidney transplants. The news media—especially television—churn out daily stories urging their viewers and readers to undergo assorted tests, from colonoscopies to full-body scans, without ever mentioning the cost in dollars or the real savings in lives across the entire population.

But the driving force behind these and all other factors is one that politicians refuse to recognize: Washington's blind obsession with market-based health care, the notion that competition is always good and can never have a bad result.

To be sure, the market approach is unbeatable in most segments of the economy. Competition among multiple producers that turn out goods and services leads to innovation, better products, and lower prices. The concept works flawlessly when the commodity is cars, furniture, cereal, doughnuts, computers, clothing, gasoline, or any other consumer item.

The glaring exception to the theory is health care. The very core principle of the market system, that companies will compete by selling more products to everyone, is actually the last thing the health care system needs. The goal should be to sell less, not more—that is, fewer doctor visits, fewer diagnostic tests, fewer hospitalizations, fewer consultations with specialists, and fewer prescription drugs.

But when was the last time you saw a newspaper headline or television newscast lauding Microsoft because it sold fewer software programs? Or that stock in General Motors soared because it sold fewer cars? Or that the Dow Jones Industrial Average surged on word that General Electrics revenue would go down—not up?

Nevertheless, that's exactly what an efficient health care system needs to provide a longer and better quality of life for everyone. This was the theory on which managed care through competition was sold. It didn't work.

Watchdog for the Drug Companies

Nowhere are the market's shortcomings clearer than where costs are spiraling the most—prescription drugs. In 1980, drug expenditures totaled $12 billion, according to the Centers for Disease Control and Prevention (CDC). By 2002, that figure had climbed 1,250 percent to $162 billion. That was eight times more than the increase in spending on national defense; nine times more than the growth in outlays for veteran services and benefits. In 1980, spending on drugs accounted for a scant 4.9 percent of total health care outlays. By 2002, it had doubled to 10.4 percent. It now is on its way to 15 percent.

Only part of the increase is due to inflation. The rest is because pharmaceutical companies are selling more drugs to more people for longer periods of time, another indicator of a dysfunctional model. The comedian Chris Rock drove this point home in one of his humorous sketches in the 1990s:

> They got AIDS out there. You think they gonna cure AIDS? No. . . . They ain't gonna cure AIDS. They ain't never curing AIDS. Ain't no money in curing it. The money's in the medicine. That's how you get paid. Sick people . . . coming back and back. . . .

Rock made his point quite eloquently by focusing on AIDS. But AIDS patients then and now make up a tiny slice of the U.S. drug market. Now there are conditions where the potential for consumers is counted in the tens of millions. Pharmaceutical companies offer multiple drugs for elevated cholesterol, which millions of patients are urged to take for years, if not a lifetime. Same with high blood pressure—more millions of patients, more millions of prescriptions for years. Also sexual dysfunction. Likewise depression. Always, the drug prescribed is the newest and most expensive on the market. And always, it works best if taken for years.

Whatever their purpose, prescription drugs in the United States cost from 30 percent to 60 percent more than the exact same medications sold anywhere else in the industrialized world. That's because governments elsewhere do not consider drugs to be just another consumer item, like cars and clothing, but rather products vital to the health of their people. Although the process differs, each country has a mechanism to restrain the sticker price of prescription drugs to levels considered fair and reasonable, and still allow pharmaceutical companies a profit. France, for example, permits companies to sell their drugs at any price. However, according to a congressional study, if pharmaceutical companies want "the national health care system to reimburse patients for the cost of the drugs, the companies must agree to a lower, negotiated price."

Congress, on the other hand, allows pharmaceutical companies to charge whatever they want, which ends up making the medication too costly for millions of Americans. Congress even prohibits Medicare, the largest buyer of prescription drugs, from negotiating a price, thereby sticking taxpayers with the inflated tab. This would be like permitting Boeing to put whatever price tag it wanted on the latest jet fighter it was selling to the Air Force.

The premium prices Americans pay have made the pharmaceutical companies the country's most profitable industry. In 2002, New York-based Pfizer Inc., the world's largest drug company, reported a return on sales of 28.4 percent. That was two and a half times better than the 10.7 percent return of General Electric Company, perennially ranked as America's best-managed business. It was nearly nine times better than the 3.3 percent return of Wal-Mart Stores, the country's largest and best-run retailer. And it was nearly thirty-two times better than the 0.9 percent of General Motors Corporation, America's largest car manufacturer. Of course, because most Americans receive their health insurance— and prescription drug plans—through their employers, corporate America was simply transferring its earnings to the pharmaceutical industry. As for all the millions of individuals who had to pay for their own drugs, or the government agencies that purchased them for the poor, they were on their own.

After several years of double-digit increases in prices during the 1990s, resourceful older Americans living on fixed incomes took the matter into their own hands by traveling to Canada and Mexico, where they could purchase the same medications for half or less their cost in the United States. Through word of mouth, their numbers grew. Eventually, senior citizens organized bus pilgrimages, especially to Canadian cities along the U.S. border. In 1998, stories that described the practice started popping up in newspapers. A typical article, which appeared in the Portland, Maine, *Press Herald*, summed up the distress:

> Filling their prescriptions in Canada could save participants hundreds of dollars on their medications. The trip also is intended to highlight the plight of the elderly in the United States, where drug companies overcharge them, critics say.
>
> There are people who worked in the mills and worked hard all their lives who now cannot afford medication," said Bob Goldman, president of the Maine Council of Senior Citizens, which is sponsoring the trip. "That is the great tragedy of this issue."

For older folks, a doctor's prescription was a double whammy. In addition to having little disposable income to pay for expensive drugs, seniors also were among those who were charged inflated prices. . . .

The Remedy

The D-Day invasion of June 6, 1944, which would turn the tide of World War II for the Allies, was the largest amphibious assault in the history of warfare. Altogether, 5,000 ships, 13,000 aircraft, and 180,000 men took part in the initial landing on the coast of France. While not everything went according to plan, D-Day was both an incredible military success and a spectacular triumph of organization.

But imagine what would have happened if the American, British, and Canadian military units each had gone its own way instead of following a coordinated master plan. Suppose that each of the U.S. Army's twenty divisions had assembled its own list of targets, with the 101st Airborne Division dropping into one part of France, the 82nd Airborne into another. Suppose that each company within each of those divisions had done likewise. Then imagine the same for the British and Canadians: 180,000 troops, each man marching to his own drummer.

That is precisely the picture of the U.S. health care system today, thousands of individual entities heading off in many directions on missions that frequently conflict. It's really no system at all. Rather, it's a stunningly fragmented collection of businesses, government agencies, health care facilities, educational institutions, and other special interests wasting tens of billions of dollars and turning the treatment of disease and sickness into a lottery where some losers pay with their lives.

The United States has 6,000 hospitals and tens of thousands more freestanding medical centers, nursing homes, kidney dialysis centers, laboratories, MRI facilities, pharmacies, and medical schools. Each maintains its own computer system. Some can talk to one another; most can't. Overlying these are hundreds of HMOs, private insurers, and government plans. There's

Medicaid for the very poor, Medicare for everyone over sixty-five years of age, TRICARE and the Veterans Administration for the military, and a hodgepodge for everyone else. Each insurer has its own system of co-pays, deductibles, and spending limits. Each produces thousands of pages of impenetrable language setting forth the medical expenses it will pay, the ones it won't, and those that fall somewhere in between.

Then there are thousands of special interests, from the American Cancer Society to the American Medical Association, from the Pharmaceutical Research and Manufacturers of America (PhRMA) to the American Organ Transplant Association, each with its own agenda. Each wages an individual campaign to shape health care policy by manipulating public opinion through TV, newspapers, magazines, and radio. Each seeks to grab a piece of the health care pie. Out of all these thousands of self-interested entities, not one speaks for what's best for American health care overall.

And that explains why U.S. health care is second-rate at the start of the twenty-first century and destined to get a lot worse and much more expensive. It's why some people must hold garage sales to pay their medical bills, why almost no one knows what their health insurance will pay for until it's too late. It's why many Americans are forced to make job choices based not on what they might like to do in life, or what's in their best interest, but on the health insurance packages offered by employers. It's why U.S. corporations are at a disadvantage in a global economy, forced to divert ever more revenue and resources to administering health care plans. It's why some diseases such as colon cancer or attention deficit disorder, which capture the media's attention, get a substantial share of government research and treatment dollars, while other diseases that receive less attention, such as amyotrophic lateral sclerosis (Lou Gehrig's disease) and cystic fibrosis, receive far fewer dollars. It's why millions of Americans are forced to agonize over how to care for aging parents with Alzheimer's disease, or how to pay the bills for children with a catastrophic illness—and do so without depriving siblings of their needs. It's why millions of Americans needlessly consume expensive medications that enrich pharmaceutical companies and Wall Street, but that contribute little or nothing to a longer, healthier life. Finally, it explains why Americans are the most overtreated, undertreated, and mistreated health care patients on earth.

It need not be this way.

The simplest and most cost-effective remedy would be to provide universal coverage and to create one agency to collect medical fees and pay claims. This would eliminate the staggering overlap, duplication, bureaucracy, and waste created by thousands of individual plans, the hidden costs that continue to drive health care out of reach for a steadily growing number of Americans.

Under a single-payer system, all health care providers—doctors, hospitals, clinics—would bill one agency for their services and would be reimbursed by the same agency. Every American would receive basic comprehensive health care, including essential prescription drugs and rehabilitative care. Anyone who needed to be treated or hospitalized could receive medical care without having to wrestle with referrals and without fear of financial ruin. Complex billing procedures and ambiguities over what is covered by insurance would be eliminated.

Radical? We already have universal health care and a single-payer system for everybody aged sixty-five and over: It's called Medicare. For years, researchers, think tanks, citizens' groups, and health care professionals have advocated a similar plan for the rest of the population. Study after study has concluded that the most practical and cost-effective way to provide quality health care and to restrain costs is a single-payer system, but no plan has ever come close to adoption because of fierce opposition by the powerful health care lobby.

To discredit the single-payer idea, insurers, HMOs, for-profit hospitals, and other private interests play on Americans' long-standing fears of big government. This view was summed up by Susan Pisano, a vice president of the American Association of Health Plans, who contended in 2002 that a single-payer system "would lead to the creation of a large federal bureaucracy that would be less responsive and actually raise issues of cost, access and quality more than it would solve them."

In truth, it is the private market that has created a massive bureaucracy, one that dwarfs the size and costs of Medicare, the most efficiently run health insurance program in America in terms of administrative costs. Medicare's overhead averages about 2 percent a year. In a 2002 study for Maine, Mathematica Policy Research Inc. concluded that administrative costs of private insurers in the state ranged from 12 percent to more than 30 percent. Studies of private carriers in other areas have reached similar conclusions. This isn't surprising, because unlike Medicare, which relies on economies of scale and standardized universal coverage, private insurance is built on bewilderingly complex layers of plans and providers that require a costly bureaucracy to administer, much of which is geared toward denying claims.

Some studies have put the price tag for administering the current system at nearly one out of every three health care dollars, much higher than that of any nation with single-payer health care. There is no way of knowing how much the United States could save by adopting such a system, but even with one that covered 100 percent of the population, the savings would be substantial.

What kind of an agency would administer it?

The idea of a single-payer plan run by the U.S. government carries with it far too much political baggage ever to get off the ground. What's needed is a fresh approach, a new organization that is independent and free from politics, one that can focus with laserlike precision on what needs to be done to further the health interests of everyone in a fair manner. For in addition to covering the basic costs of all Americans, a new system needs to institute programs that will improve America's overall health, that will focus on preventing illness and disease as well as treatment, and do so without breaking the bank.

How does the United States come up with such a mechanism?

One possible answer: Loosely copy and then amend and expand on what already exists in another setting—the Federal Reserve System, a quasigovernmental organization that oversees the nation's money and banking policies. The Fed is one of the nation's most ingenious creations, a public agency that is largely independent of politics. The Fed's board members are appointed to staggered fourteen-year terms by the President with the consent of the Senate, meaning that neither the White House nor Congress can substantively influence the Fed's policies.

Call this independent agency the U.S. Council on Health Care (USCHC). Like the Federal Reserve, the council would set an overall policy for health care and influence its direction by controlling federal spending—from managing research grants to providing basic and catastrophic medical coverage for all citizens. Unlike the Federal Reserve, it would be entirely funded by taxpayers. The, money could come from just two taxes, a gross-receipts levy on businesses and a flat tax, similar to the current Medicare tax, on all individual income, not just wages. This would not represent an additional cost to society, but rather replace existing taxes and write-offs. It would cut costs for corporations and raise taxes slightly on individuals at the top of the income ladder. Members of the USCHC board would include both health care professionals and citizens from all walks of life. Its mission: Implement policies that improve health care for everyone, not just those suffering from certain diseases. In short, make the unpopular decisions that the market cannot make.

The council could establish regions similar to those of the Federal Reserve System, which divides the nation into twelve areas. Whatever their number, the geographic subdivisions could take into account cultural and regional differences among

Americans. They would allow for health care delivery to be fine-tuned at the local level, and ensure that regulations could take into account the differences between metropolitan and community hospitals.

Although the USCHC could be set up to keep partisan politics out of hospitals and doctors' offices, health care politics, which can be every bit as divisive as the mainstream variety, would still present a challenge. If you have any doubt, just assemble surgeons, radiologists, and internists in a room to discuss the merits of their particular approaches to treatment of a specific disease. But those members of a USCHC board drawn from outside the health care community would at least introduce a moderating influence.

Curing the Ills

This is not to suggest that a single-payer system overseen by a Federal Reserve-like board or some other independent organization would instantly correct everything that's wrong with market-driven health care. What it would do is provide the framework to reach that goal. For starters, there are certain basic things it would do:

- Guarantee that all Americans receive a defined level of basic care, including a fixed number of visits to doctors, routine lab work, immunizations for children, coverage for all childhood illnesses, and all hospital charges.

- Establish flexible co-pays for basic care that would vary depending on income as well as usage. Those people who seldom seek medical attention could have their co-pays waived. So, too, could those at the bottom of the income ladder. Those who use the facilities repeatedly without any serious medical reason for doing so could be charged with escalating co-pays.

- Pay all costs to treat any catastrophic illness, such as cancer or any devastating disease. It would pay all doctor bills, hospital charges, and any related

costs. There would be no co-pays and no deductibles for the seriously ill.

- Restore freedom of choice by allowing patients to choose their doctors, rather than insurers limiting the selection through their approved lists. They also could choose their hospitals.

- Redirect health care spending by allocating money for disease prevention as well as treatment. It would curtail out-of-control prescription-drug costs. It would rein in those doctors who have never met an expensive drug they didn't like and who practice medicine by prescription.

- Provide critically important drug information to consumers to balance the promotional hype of advertising. The council could insist that the results of all clinical drug trials be made public, so consumers may better assess both the upside and the downside of certain medications.

- Concentrate health care spending on cost-effective areas, such as stemming the growth in diabetes among children, which if allowed to continue unchecked ultimately will cost society more than AIDS, cancer, or other diseases.

- Control costs by getting to the root causes of health care spending, which varies widely among the residents of different states. Even after taking into account disparities in living costs, there is no medical reason that Medicare should spend, as it has, 48 percent more money on seniors in Mississippi than seniors in South Dakota, or 43 percent more on seniors in Florida than seniors in Minnesota, or 31 percent more on seniors in the District of Columbia than seniors in California.

- Halt the existing practice by which insurers, to improve their own bottom lines, squeeze doctors through unrealistically low reimbursement rates. The same for hospitals and nursing homes that squeeze nursing salaries and staffing levels.

- Reverse the costly, but seldom discussed, health care trend of overdiagnosis and overtreatment—something no market system will ever do. While many Americans suffer from a lack of health care, a growing number get too much. They seek out the latest tests, the newest pills, and the most popular screenings regardless of whether they are at risk. The overtreated include middle-income folks with generous insurance, Medicare enrollees, and even lower-income people who qualify for Medicaid. Its the kind of irony that finds some people going to bed hungry while others eat so much they are obese.

Once in place, the scope of the basic care package could be expanded as the system realizes savings derived from standardization, more efficient computer technology, and the end of market-based medicine with its required profits, stock options, and generous executive-compensation deals.

The health council could save money by creating an enforcement agency that would pay for itself by ferreting out fraud, which may run as high as $200 billion a year. One possibility would be to decriminalize health care fraud and make it a civil offense. There would be no perp walk, but the economic penalties could be draconian: Steal from health care and you lose all your personal assets—home, car, savings, retirement accounts, everything—no exceptions.

Individuals could supplement their basic government-supported coverage through private insurance. Wealthier citizens could continue to obtain whatever care they wanted and pay for it. But they would be barred from dropping out of the USCHC and would still be required to pay the earmarked taxes, just as everyone must contribute to Medicare and Social Security. Also, insurers would be barred from offering coverage that competed with the government-backed plan. Similarly, hospitals would be free to accept a certain percent-

age of cash-paying patients from outside the USCHC.

A unified single-payer system could make it possible to deal with medicine's thorniest issues, ones that the market system has either aggravated or done little to resolve. Three of those are interrelated and have a direct impact on the quality of care patients receive: mistakes, malpractice, and prescription drugs.

To reduce medical errors dramatically, the council could oversee creation and operation of a single information technology system that links all health care players—hospitals, doctors' offices, pharmacies, and nursing homes. Deaths caused by an error in one hospital or nursing home could be identified and corrective steps initiated before the error recurs in other facilities. Patient records would be stored electronically. Prescriptions would be computer-generated. It would help ensure correct dosages and preclude the dispensing of drugs with harmful interactions. Deaths from lethal drug interactions that now go unnoticed could be detected. This will be especially important since such deaths will grow as the population ages and more people take ever more drugs for longer periods. Under the existing fragmented system, no one is assigned the specific task of looking for these deaths. The ones that turn up, in most cases, are discovered by serendipity.

A reduction in medical mistakes also would lead to a fall-off in serious malpractice claims, one of the most contentious aspects of health care. The situation has become so grim under the profit-driven system that many doctors view their patients as potential adversaries and practice medicine accordingly. This is not only bad medicine, but also incredibly expensive. Yet the proposed solution—placing a maximum cap of $250,000 on damage awards—is hardly equitable.

Do you believe it's fair that a woman receive no more than $23 a day over, say, thirty years if both her breasts are removed by mistake? Is it fair for a man to receive the same $23 if a leg is amputated by mistake? Is it fair for an infant with severe birth defects as a result of a delivery mistake to receive no more than $14 a day over fifty years? Would you consider those sums to be fair if the mistakes involved you or members of your family? Yet that's Congress's idea of malpractice equity.

Of course, most doctors also are treated unfairly, compelled to pay exorbitant insurance premiums because of the actions of a few. This has led doctors in some states to go on strike while other physicians uproot their practices and move to less litigious communities.

With fewer errors and thus fewer deaths, lawsuits would decline. Equally important, a national health care database would make it possible for the USCHC to identify, those hospitals and health care workers— doctors, nurses, and technicians—who continue to be involved in mistakes and deaths. The most egregious errors could be litigated. For less serious mistakes, a no-fault system could be tested.

In a less hostile environment, doctors could stop practicing defensive medicine. They would no longer feel compelled to order medically unnecessary MRIs, X-rays, laboratory tests, biopsies, stress tests, and specialty consultations, with additional savings the result.

The national patient data archives could provide a treasure trove of information to improve the quality of health care. Researchers would be able to determine with greater accuracy the procedures that work and the ones that don't; which drugs are most effective and which are not. For the first time, the data would allow for large-scale clinical studies that are never done under the existing system. For example, what really is the best treatment for prostate cancer? Is surgery cost-effective? Or is it better to do nothing? While limited studies offer a variety of answers, a unified data bank could provide more solid ones. Similar studies could be carried out for a range of other diseases and conditions: Are colonoscopies cost-effective? What about the Pap smear? The PSA test? The bone-density test? Genetic screening? Or could much of the money for these and other tests be more productively spent to prevent disease and add healthy years to the lifespan of the population at large?

As for prescription drugs, no other segment of health care better illustrates why profit-based medicine and cost containment are mutually exclusive. Drug companies flourish by selling more pills, never fewer. Yet a good health care system would strive to prescribe fewer pills, especially since the effectiveness of many drugs is questionable. Antidepressants, the top-selling category of prescription drugs in 2001, had retail sales of $12.5 billion. But studies show that about two out of every three people who take antidepressants would do equally well on a harmless sugar pill. Furthermore, they wouldn't suffer from, and be treated for, the side effects of many antidepressants, such as sexual dysfunction, anxiety, insomnia, sweating, and nausea.

The USCHC, or some other single payer, could negotiate the best possible drug prices, something that Medicare is forbidden to do by Congress. It also could establish rules for holding down prices in other ways. Barring overwhelming evidence of the effectiveness of a new medication, there would be no mad rush to pay for the latest—and most costly—drug.

The pharmaceutical industry, to be sure, would object strenuously. It would argue, as it always has, that the United States must charge the world's highest prices to fund research for new drugs. Don't believe it. To begin with, taxpayers already have contributed to some drug research through government programs. More significant, companies often do little more than rearrange molecules to create a new version of an existing drug, or promote new uses for old drugs, just to keep the revenue stream flowing. The number of breakthrough drugs introduced in any given year is negligible. During the twelve years from 1989 to 2000, 65 percent of the new-drug applications approved by the FDA involved "active ingredients that were already available in marketed products." Another 11 percent "were identical to products already available on the U.S. market."

Concluded one study: "The increased emphasis on incremental drug development is not surprising. Large brand manu-facturers have reached a scale at which they must generate several billion dollars in additional revenue each year in order to meet Wall Street growth targets. Yet only a handful of firms were able to bring ten or more drugs with new active ingredients to market over the past decade, or at least one per year on average."

In addition, pharmaceutical companies have long been sheltered by government policies that have fostered bloated market-ing efforts. One-third or more of drug-com-pany revenue is spent on advertising, ad-ministration, and marketing, with much of the money going to support the armies of sales representatives who call on doctors to persuade them to write prescriptions.

Policies of a unified health care system could reduce those sales forces, with their dubious medical justification. If you are a professional making life-and-death treat-ment decisions, do you really need a sales-person to explain why his or her drug is just right for your patients? And if you're a pa-tient, do you want to rely on a doctor who prescribes a pill based on sales pitches? Some physicians already have opted out of the practice by refusing to see drug-com-pany representatives. Of course, these doc-tors do not get free meals and "consulting" fees, both of which would disappear under a centralized system. Indeed, doctors who overprescribe or misprescribe medications could be identified and penalized.

Crisis and Opportunity

Creating a Federal Reserve-style council to deal with the crisis in health care would be controversial and bitterly opposed, be-cause it would disrupt the powerful health care industrial complex, and because it would challenge many medical myths. Re-sistance would come from health care pro-viders themselves; from insurers, some of whom would go out of business; from some in the U.S. government bureaucracy who would lose control; from the antitax com-munity; from some physicians and individ-uals who are content with their personal

situations, and most of all, from members of Congress who benefit so handsomely from free-market health care. Many, per-haps most, of these groups and individuals will push instead to solve the crisis by add-ing on to the existing labyrinth, by expand-ing coverage to the uninsured through pri-vate insurers. That would only delay the inevitable and cost more money, while maintaining all the inequities.

Americans who are skeptical of anything that smacks of big government fear that a universal health plan would restrict per-sonal freedom. But the market system al-ready has done that. Those with health in-surance often can go only to physicians or hospitals approved by their plans, unless they are wealthy enough to pay the fees out of their own pockets. Many Americans fear that it would cost too much, even though the market system already has given the United States the world s most expensive health care with little to show for it. They fear the long waits they have heard about in Canada and other countries, even though comparable waiting times for tests and pro-cedures are commonplace in many parts of the United States. Lastly, they fear govern-ment-decreed rationing, even though health care is already rationed in the most inequitable of ways, including forty-four million with none at all.

Despite all the fears, change will come. The market system is a devastating failure, and nearly every major public opinion poll finds health care at or near the top of Amer-icans' concerns. While some will always be-lieve that market-driven medicine will work as well as market-driven automobile manufacturing, that attitude is changing, even among those who have long opposed government intervention.

This was confirmed in a study by the Center for Studying Health System Change, a nonpartisan Washington, D.C., think tank. Every two years, the center's re-searchers survey doctors, insurers, and other professionals in twelve major cities on the state of health care. In its 2004 study, researchers noted a marked shift in opinion among groups that have traditionally op-posed a government role: "An insurance broker said, 'The delivery system is a mess. The sectors don't talk. No one wants to change. The government must do something.' A surprised benefit consultant reported: 'There is now a lack of resistance to government involvement.'" As quickly as many offered their opinions, they followed with the caveat, "But we can't say that out loud." The study concluded:

"What is palpable across the twelve communities we studied is the recognition that private market forces are limited in their ability to achieve social objectives in health care services, and a growing sense that a broader conversation about what to do next should begin soon. This conversation may find more willing participants than would have been possible four to six years ago."

Ultimately, the driving forces behind change will come from two sources: working Americans who are disenchanted with ever-rising costs and shrinking care, and U.S. corporations, which are increasingly refusing to pick up the added costs. They can't afford to, because America's privately funded system puts U.S. companies at a disadvantage with their competitors in the industrialized world, where universal health care is funded by government. General Motors says the cost of providing health care to its workers and retirees now totals $1,400 for each vehicle sold in the United States, more than the cost of steel. William Clay Ford Jr., the chairman and chief executive of Ford, says, "employers in this country, and particularly manufacturing employers, can't compete internationally with this burden around our collective necks."

This is why companies are cutting back, trimming, or eliminating health care for their retirees, and reneging on promises made to encourage workers to leave early. They are imposing higher co-pays and requiring employees to pick up an increasing share of annual premiums. In fact, many companies will require workers to pay for all future cost increases.

America's health care system is in critical condition, and we find ourselves at a turning point. But this crisis represents an exceptional opportunity to reconsider our values, our priorities, our budget, and our options. We can continue to hold garage sales to finance health care, or we can do what every other civilized nation on earth does—take care of our citizens.

Discussion Questions

1. How would you evaluate the efficacy of the health-care system proposed by Barlett and Steele?

2. Have you had any experience with submitting medical claim forms? ✦

40

Promising Practices: How Employers Improve Their Bottom Lines by Addressing the Needs of Lower-Wage Workers

Stacy S. Kim,
Marta Lopez, and
James T. Bond

In this final chapter, Stacey Kim, Marta Lopez, and James Bond focus on a range of needs of relatively low-wage, low-income employees and describe selected actual employer-sponsored work-life and work-family programs and policies to address these needs. The programs and policies also pertain to a range of employee needs and different levels of effort from employers.

The work-family challenges faced by low-wage workers from low-income families are enormous, as described in the companion reports to this volume: *Information for Employers About Low-Wage Workers From*

Low-Income Families and the Impact of Job and Workplace Conditions on Low-Wage and -Income Employees and Their Employers. It is not that their work-family problems are unique, rather their situations are exacerbated by having fewer resources to cope with what is often a multitude of these problems.

Although both lower-wage and higher-wage workers benefit from many work-life and work-family programs and policies, the needs of lower-wage workers are not always the same as their higher-wage counterparts who may have better education, more resources to purchase child care at market rates, more reliable transportation, greater access to health insurance coverage, and so forth. For this report, we have attempted to identify promising practices—programs and policies—that directly address the needs of lower-wage workers while also furthering business objectives. We believe that these practices represent potential "win-win" solutions for both employees and employers.

It is important to remember that employers are not able to identify who among their employees are in low-income families since they only know the individual employee's wage or salary. Moreover, although employers can identify who among their employees are in the lower tier of wage earners, the definition of lower wages varies somewhat across companies. Thus, a lower-wage worker in one company may earn significantly more than a lower-wage worker in another company. Both geography and industry influence wage levels.

Despite somewhat different definitions of target employees, employers in this report have found that by directing programs to hourly, entry-level, non-supervisory employees, or in some cases even to all employees within their organization, they are also able to specifically support the work-family situations of lower-wage employees who most need assistance.

Not meant to be a comprehensive compendium of promising practices, this report highlights programs and policies illustrating a wide range of employer responses. First, the promising practices in this report respond to a variety of business needs from recruiting employees to enhancing internal processes. Second, the selected promising practices also address a variety of specific worker needs, from providing child care to providing transportation options so employees can get to and from work. Third, the promising practices reported here illustrate a variety of approaches, from using technology to forming partnerships with other organizations. Finally, these practices illustrate differing levels of effort put forth by the employers from simply helping their employees gain access to already existing resources, to implementing new comprehensive programs.

While these promising practices are diverse in their scope, level of effort, and content, there is one area of common ground. All of the practices were initiated in response to business needs. In some cases, implementing the program or policy was seen as an unavoidable cost of doing business or an economic necessity. Company desires to contribute to the greater good appear to be of secondary concern, although all of these practices have positive implications for families and communities. Indeed, one could argue that these practices are examples of "doing well by doing good."

Brief descriptions of promising practices follow. The table of contents (preceding) directs readers to practices addressing particular objectives.

Providing Jobs and Income

Providing Jobs

Many low-income people, particularly those with a history of welfare dependence, must overcome multiple barriers in order to find work and remain employed. Some companies are making an extra effort to reach out to potential workers with considerable employment barriers and provide them with jobs and a way to support themselves and their families. By doing so, these employers not only find a stream of candidates for hard-to-fill jobs, but they also benefit from federal tax credits for their businesses.

Recent changes in welfare legislation require welfare recipients to find jobs. This has created a pool of candidates for businesses to hire from. In order to further encourage employers to hire job seekers who are moving from welfare to work or job seekers who have experienced certain barriers to employment, the federal government created two tax credits—the Work Opportunity Tax Credit (WOTC) and the Welfare to Work Credit (WTWC). The WOTC is a tax credit for employers who hire and employ short-term welfare recipients, certain veterans and persons with disabilities, and residents of certain targeted areas who may have had greater difficulty in the past finding employment. The WTWC is a tax credit for employers who hire and employ long-term welfare recipients. Both of these federal tax credits require that the employee remain with the employer for specified periods of time. These credits are further described in Table 40.1.

In addition to federal programs, some states also offer tax credits for employers who hire individuals in similarly targeted groups. Both federal and state tax credits can significantly reduce the initial costs associated with hiring while providing these workers opportunities to find jobs and sustained employment.

In the promising practice described below, Sears found that the tax credits did far more than simply reduce the initial costs of hiring. Hiring welfare-to-work and other disadvantaged job seekers not only helped to fill open positions with greater ease, but also filled those jobs with a steady stream of qualified candidates. In addition, Sears found that the tax credits helped individual stores add to their bottom lines.

Sears: Welfare to Work

Sears, Roebuck and Co. is a broad line retailer with significant service and credit businesses. In 2001, the company's annual revenue was more than $41 billion. Sears employs about 275,000 people, of which

Table 40.1

	WOTC	WTWC
Target	Short-term welfare recipients, certain veterans and disabled persons, and residents of certain targeted areas.	Long-term welfare recipients and individuals no longer eligible for assistance payments.
Credit amount	40 percent of the first $6,000 of wages (or 25% if employment is less than 400 hours).	35 percent of the first $10,000 of wages in the first year of employment and 50 percent of the first $10,000 of wages in the second year of employment.
Minimum tenure	120 hours	400 hours

the vast majority are in hourly front-line positions.

Impetus. Brian Eby, Manager, HR Compliance, believes that many employers may be hiring from the welfare-to-work population without even being aware of it. Sears, he says, chooses to "do it smarter." As he says, "A well-run tax credit program can both fill open positions and yield financial benefits as a bonus."

Details. In response to new changes in the welfare system, Sears began efforts to actively hire welfare recipients as well as other job seekers in disadvantaged groups in the fall of 1997. To assist its several thousand hiring managers, Sears organizes its efforts by partnering with several organizations:

- A private vendor helps administer the tax credit programs, the Work Opportunity Tax Credit (WOTC) and the Welfare to Work Credit (WTWC); new hires call this private vendor for a confidential interview that helps determine eligibility for any tax credits.

- The Welfare to Work Partnership, a group of employers who pledged to hire welfare recipients, provides Sears HR staff with information, technical assistance and support.

- Nationwide, organizations like Job Corps (a public-private partnership) prepare disadvantaged young people for employment at Sears and other

companies through retail training programs.

- At the local level, various outreach organizations help local units of Sears find eligible job candidates and sometimes provide training for these job candidates.

In order to educate its managers and HR staff about the benefits of welfare-to-work programs, Sears developed an intranet site and a welfare-to-work brochure explaining the financial incentives of the tax credits as well as the process for participating in the program.

In order to encourage individual units to take full advantage of the tax credits, all credits earned by each unit are returned to that unit. "This is highly motivating for our HR staff," Mr. Eby notes. "The unit managers really appreciate that, with the help of HR, this program can deliver thousands of dollars to their units' bottom lines."

Results. Since the program began in October 1997, Sears has hired more than 40,000 former welfare recipients and members of other disadvantaged groups and has earned more than $18 million in Work Opportunity and Welfare to Work Tax Credits. Mr. Eby states that, on average, each qualified individual represents tax credits equivalent to the profit realized from selling $15,000 worth of merchandise in a Sears store.

Even more importantly, Sears has found that the retention rate among those hired from the welfare-to-work population and other disadvantaged groups is higher than that of other employees.

Costs. While there is no cost for working with the Welfare to Work Partnership, Job Corps or other outreach programs, Sears does pay a percentage of the tax credits received to the private vendor that administers its tax credit program. Mr. Eby, however, believes that it is a relatively small price to pay given the significant amount of money the tax credits bring in to the organization.

Lessons. Mr. Eby notes three challenges encountered as Sears began implementing this program and what they did to address each challenge:

- In the beginning, people had to be convinced that candidates from the welfare-to-work and other disadvantaged populations were indeed good candidates. This problem was resolved on its own. "It was just a matter of experience. In time, people saw first hand that these were indeed qualified candidates."

- The second difficulty was convincing already busy HR staff at the local units to devote time toward this program. To accomplish this, Sears first got the private vendor to regularly fax each local outreach program a list of job openings at nearby Sears locations. This not only drove a steady stream of applicants to the store, but it also lifted the burden from the HR staff.

- The other challenge was to increase call-in rates, or the number of new applicants who call the private vendor for tax credit screening. Sears fixed this problem by tying the tax credit screening to compliance of form 1-9 requirements and having the private vendor screen for both the tax credits and employment eligibility verification. Since every new employee must verify their employment eligibility before they can begin working, each employee is automatically screened by the private vendor for WOTC and WTWC "We turned this from a 'nice-to-do' into a 'must-

do.'" This raised our monthly call-in rates from 46 percent in January 1998 to 94 percent in November 2000.

Next Steps. Sears continues to work to find more employees eligible for tax credits by actively searching for qualified candidates with the help of various outreach organizations.

The HR compliance staff also continues to communicate and reinforce efforts to keep unit managers and local HR staff involved and supportive of the program. "We remind them how much they can bring into their unit through these tax credits. We ask, 'How many washer-dryers do you need to sell to get the profits to equal the amount of money brought in by an eligible employee?'"

Increasing Take-Home Pay

Other employers have been able to help their lower-wage employees take advantage of federal tax credits that allow them to take home more pay. By doing so employees move closer to self-sufficiency while employers benefit from increased commitment.

In the previous example, federal tax credits helped employers help job candidates make the transition from welfare to work. A very different type of tax credit provides tax relief to low-income workers themselves, the Earned Income Credit (EIC). Designed to "make work pay," this fully refundable tax credit is primarily targeted toward low-income workers with children. In 2001, workers with a family income less than $32,121 and 2 or more children were eligible for $20 to $4,008 depending upon their earnings level. The IRS pays the full amount due following submission of appropriate tax returns. There is also an option to receive part of the credit in regular paychecks under the Advanced EIC plan. The advanced payment option puts additional dollars in employees' regular paychecks that can be used to cover child care, transportation, and other household expenses, which potentially improves productivity and retention.

As described earlier, employers generally do not know an employee's total family income, even though they know the wages or salary the employee receives. One employer, however, took some simple steps to ensure that eligible employees took advantage of the EIC. In the following promising practice, we describe how the hotel chain Hyatt helped its employees increase their disposable income by partnering with organizations that provide EIC assistance to employees.

Hyatt: Helping Employees File Tax Returns to Get Tax Credits

Hyatt Hotels Corporation and its affiliates operate, lease, and franchise 120 hotels and resorts with more than 55,000 rooms in the United States, Canada, and the Caribbean. Hyatt International Corporation, through its subsidiaries, operates 58 hotels and 22 resorts with more than 28,000 rooms in 37 countries.

Hyatt helps its eligible employees get tax credits by helping employees file their tax returns.

Impetus. Knowing that many of Hyatt's hotel employees are in low-income families, Patricia Corcoran, Director of Staffing Compliance, seeks to help employees get more take-home pay through the federal Earned Income Credit (EIC) and Advanced Earned Income Tax Credit (Advanced EIC). Ms. Corcoran believes that one of the main barriers to receiving these benefits is filing income tax returns. By encouraging and assisting employees to file their tax returns, more of Hyatt's employees are able to take advantage of these tax credits.

Details. In 1996, Hyatt began a pilot program in Chicago to help employees receive their EIC by tapping into many existing resources in Chicago that help people file their tax returns. "Right across the street from the hotel, for example, at the public library, people can get help with filing their EIC tax forms," says Ms. Corcoran. Learning that the tax assistance was provided by the Volunteer Income Tax Assistance (VITA), a community outreach program run by the IRS and staffed by volunteers, Hyatt teamed up with VITA to help Hyatt employees file their returns. "An important factor was the location of VITA sites. It really helped that there was one across the street."

Hyatt also worked with the Center on Budget and Policy Priorities, a nonprofit organization that develops a corporate implementation packet for employers and updates that packet each year to reflect current eligibility requirements and benefits. The packet includes materials that describe the EIC/Advanced EIC programs to managers as well as colorful posters and paycheck stuffers written in both English, Spanish, and other languages that can be distributed to employees. (Materials can be downloaded at no charge from <www.cbpp.org/eic2002>.)

By working with VITA and the Center on Budget and Policy Priorities, Hyatt finds it beneficial to help their employees file their income tax returns, enroll in these tax credit programs, and take advantage of EIC credits. Hyatt has since expanded the program beyond Chicago and now assists their employees nationwide.

Costs. Costs are minimal given that VITA provides services and the Center on Budget and Policy Priorities develops the education materials and employer packets.

Lessons. Hyatt finds that by teaming up with VITA and the Center on Budget and Policy Priorities helping eligible employees get their tax refunds is very easy and is accomplished with minimal costs.

Retirement Planning

Lower-wage workers have very limited disposable income to invest toward their retirements. Consequently, many employers report that retirement plan participation rates among their lower-wage workers are very low. In contrast, Home Depot has had considerable success encouraging its workforce to participate in its 401K plan and to purchase company stock at a discount as a means of building retirement assets.

Home Depot: 401K and Stock Purchase Plan

The Home Depot is the world's largest home improvement retailer, with over 900 stores and about 245,000 workers in the United States, Canada, Puerto Rico, and Chile. Unlike many retailers, the majority of Home Depot employees work full-time. About a quarter of their employees work part-time—usually as added support during peak periods. The vast majority of employees are hourly workers.

Impetus. To retain employees in this competitive environment, to build pride in the company and morale, to increase employee commitment to customer service, and to help employees save for retirement, Home Depot offers a 401K plan and stock purchase plan for all employees.

Details. *401K Plan:* Both part-time and full-time employees may participate in Home Depot's 401K plan after one year of service, with matching contributions from the company. Store managers meet individually with each employee to explain details of the plan and its tax advantages. The company matches employee contributions with $1.50 per $1.00 contributed up to 1 percent of gross earnings, and with $0.50 per $1.00 contributed from 2 percent to 5 percent of earnings. Undoubtedly, this employer match through profit sharing is a vital element of Home Depot's successful plan. Although the company match is made with Home Depot stock, employees may sell this stock immediately and shift the proceeds into other investments to ensure diversification of their portfolios.

As of March 2003, 62 percent of employees—most of whom are hourly workers who have modest earnings—participate in the 401K plan. Prior to the recent downturn in the economy and the equity markets, 401K participation rates were substantially higher, and management expects participation to increase to previous levels as the economy improves.

Stock Purchase Plan: All employees may purchase Home Depot stock at a 15 percent discount without commissions using after-tax payroll deductions. Employees may invest up to 20 percent of their pay in company stock. There are two 12-month investment cycles each year—spring to spring and fall to fall. Employees are allowed to reduce their contributions by any amount once during each investment cycle in which they are participating. Particularly innovative and attractive to employee-investors is the fact that actual stock purchases are made at the end of each 12-month investment cycle when they are allowed to purchase company stock, using their 15 percent discount, at either the market value of the stock at the beginning of the cycle or its value at the end of the cycle. This offers substantial protection against declines in the value of the stock as well as significant opportunities to profit from appreciation in the value of the stock. Once stock purchases have been executed, employees may sell their shares with no commissions.

As of March 2003, more than 25 percent of employees—most hourly employees with modest earnings—participate in the Stock Purchase Plan. As with the 401K plan, participation was significantly higher before the recent downturn in the economy and equity markets and is expected to increase as the economy improves.

Results. Large proportions of employees have taken advantage of these plans. Not only has participation contributed to the retirement security of employees, management also believes that it has helped keep turnover rates low in contrast with the retail industry in general and that it has contributed to higher morale and better customer service.

Helping Workers Meet Personal and Family Needs

The companion reports to this volume—*Information for Employers About Low-Wage Employees From Low-Income Families and the Impact of Job and Workplace Conditions on Low-Wage and -Income Employees and Their Employers*—reveal that low-wage employees have less access to traditional fringe benefits such as health insurance, to child care benefits, and to flexible work arrangements. Having greater access to any one of these three supports is associated with lower turnover among low-wage employees, according to our research. Although quantitative data from our survey research does not address issues of transportation, focus groups and interviews with low-wage workers revealed that many face substantial challenges getting to and from work on a day to day basis. Although medically certified illness may be an adequate excuse for missing work, transportation problems typically are not.

Flexibility

Analyses of data from Families and Work Institute's National Study of the Changing Workforce reveal that providing flexibility and control over work schedules can substantially improve outcomes such as job satisfaction and job retention for lower-wage employees and their employers. JCPenney found that its employees wanted to spend more time taking care of their children themselves and in their own homes. By providing flexible work schedules, JCPenney allowed many of its employees to do just that. The promising practice described below demonstrates how JCPenney was able to provide the flexibility that many of its employees wanted while reducing unnecessary paperwork for those employees' managers. This created an additional benefit by enabling supervisors to spend more time on management and customer service issues.

JCPenney: Scheduling System

JCPenney is one of America's largest department store, drugstore, catalog, and e-commerce retailers, employing approximately 250,000 associates. As of 2002, it operated 1,068 JCPenney department stores in all 50 states, Puerto Rico, and Mexico, and 54 Renner department stores in Brazil. Eckerd Corporation (a subsidiary) operated 2,642 drugstores throughout the Southeast, Sunbelt, and Northeast regions of the U.S. JCPenney Catalog, including e-commerce, is the nation's largest catalog merchant of general merchandise.

Impetus. Managers at JCPenney were spending a great deal of time and energy scheduling employees for 12-hour retail store operations and 18-hour catalog center operations seven days a week.

At the same time, JCPenney was exploring the possibility of on-site or near-site child care centers. But, through employee surveys, the company learned that employees would rather have more flexible work schedules that allowed them to spend more time caring for their children themselves than have a child care center.

Details. In the early 1980s, JCPenney began exploring ways to both automate scheduling systems to reduce the burden on supervisors, and provide flexible schedules to accommodate the work-family needs and preferences of employees. The first result of this effort began in the company's 14 catalog and telemarketing sites. The Online Schedule Changes and Availability Requests, or OSCAR, enabled associates to customize their work times, add or drop shifts, or make last-minute schedule changes to meet their family and personal needs. With the completion of one form, the company's software configured employees' schedules by juggling predetermined basic and preferred schedules. OSCAR also allowed associates to identify colleagues who could exchange shifts when unanticipated needs arose without a line manager's intervention.

Although OSCAR did help to cut managers' time spent on creating master schedules each week, it was still necessary to enter the information from the employee forms into the computer—a labor-intensive task subject to error.

Thus, staff at JCPenney's retail units saw the need to put a different kind of system in place. User-friendly Associate Kiosks were placed on-site so that employees can enter their "general" and "preferred" availability times themselves. While changes to associates' availability times can be made anytime, subject to manager approval, employees can request temporary schedule changes to accommodate unanticipated needs. The Kiosks also allow employees to make requests for Paid Time Off (PTO) and for their manager to approve their PTO requests. Using all of the information, the automated scheduling system creates a master schedule each Wednesday for the workweek that begins on the following Sunday. Associates also use the Kiosks to print out their weekly schedules.

Results. Bob Swan, Manager of Human Resource Systems at JCPenney, estimates that the Kiosks have helped to reduce administrative paperwork at retail stores by two-thirds. As a result, the computerized systems allow "managers to do what they are hired to do—focus on the core business of selling merchandise and providing customer service."

In addition, Mr. Swan believes that flexible scheduling has become a critical recruitment and retention tool among associates. "The associates like the kiosks because they can take control."

Next Steps. Mr. Swan is now working to put the scheduling system on the Internet to allow managers and associates to access the system from their home computers. In addition, he plans to integrate the scheduling system with the payroll and other HR systems to further streamline managers' time and to provide employees with more information about their benefits and give them an even greater degree of control.

Child Care

Good child care is expensive and often difficult to find. While all employed parents face child care challenges, those in low-income families often find child care particularly difficult to afford and the child care options in their neighborhoods particularly wanting. Because lower-wage workers are more likely than other employees to work odd hours or night shifts, child care can be even more difficult to find and even more expensive. Because of their own preferences to leave their children with people they know as well as the unavailability of affordable and more formal types of child care, many turn to informal arrangements with relatives and neighbors.

Some employers have found that helping employees meet their child care needs makes good business sense. The promising practice described below shows how ConAgra Foods partnered with other public and private organizations to create a child care center that was accommodating to employees' shifts and their budgets, allowing the company to recruit and retain employees in a tight labor market.

ConAgra Foods: Child Care Center

ConAgra Foods' Refrigerated Foods Group, a division of ConAgra Foods, Inc. is the second largest food company in the U.S. At its Huntsville, Arkansas, location in the nation's poultry belt, 900 employees slaughter, de-bone, smoke, bake and package turkeys sold under the Butterball brand.

Impetus. In the late 1980s, ConAgra Foods planned to expand its Huntsville plant. The company knew that filling the plant with more employees was going to be a challenge given a low unemployment rate of less than 3 percent in the area and given the difficult jobs at the plant, which already had high turnover rates.

At the same time, the company discovered through focus groups that its employees were struggling with their child care options. Many of the employees were legal workers from Mexico, Vietnam, and Central America, and others who were drawn to jobs in Huntsville from Texas and other states. Having relocated, these employees had little support from friends and family to help with child care. Furthermore, there was only one small licensed center in the community. The focus groups revealed that parents were dissatisfied with the care their children were receiving and were concerned about being able to pay for child care.

Details. To address these issues, plant management knew they had to be innovative. Having no experience in running a child care center, however, ConAgra began working with a private company specializing in dependent-care issues as well as with the region's economic development organization. The team worked together for more than three years to conceive and build the Madison County Child Development Center.

The team created a public-private financing structure:

- ConAgra donated the land for the building.

- The ConAgra Foundation made an initial $50,000 grant for the equipment.

- A 501(c)(3) nonprofit organization, Northwest Arkansas Child Care, was established to make the center eligible for state grants, federal Head Start funding, and a Federal Housing Administration (FHA) loan to build the $600,000 facility.

The Madison County Child Development Center (sometimes called "Paul's Place" after the Butterball plant manager who got it started) serves up to 150 children ages 6 weeks to 12 years, including children in center-based and home-based Head Start programs. Butterball subsidizes approximately half of the cost for 65 spaces at the center for its workers' children. If the company did not subsidize child care, the average costs to the employee would be over $80 per week per child, a considerable amount for those who make an average of $9.00/hour. The remaining slots are open to children of non-employees and those who are Head Start-eligible.

The center operates at a minimum Monday through Friday year-round from 5 a.m. to 10 p.m. The extended hours of normal operation allow parents to arrange for hard-to-find before- and after-school care. In addition, the center is flexible enough to accommodate Butterball employees' unanticipated needs arising from work demands, school closings, and personal circumstances. For example, the center extends its hours to accommodate employees who need to work overtime or on weekends. The center has staff on call and allows child care workers to split their shifts, helping them accommodate their own family's schedules.

Results. The Madison County Child Development Center has become an impor-

tant recruitment and retention tool for ConAgra's Huntsville facility. The child care center is featured in local print and radio recruiting ads to attract employees. Turnover rates of employees who use the center are low relative to the industry norm, at 50 percent.

The center has also helped to expand the availability of child care for the community at large and Head Start-eligible children in particular.

Costs. Company costs include an initial land donation and an annual budget of about $250,000. ConAgra Foods believes that the center has paid for itself by reducing turnover and absenteeism, helping to recruit new employees, and generating goodwill among employees and the community. For example, plant estimates show that it costs $5,000 to recruit, train and get a new employee up to speed. With reduced turnover rates, the company believes that the center has produced more stability among its workforce.

Transportation

Low-wage workers in low-income families face multiple transportation challenges. Transportation options are often limited, making it difficult for them to go to and from home, work, child care, and other destinations. They are less likely to own personal vehicles, and when they do, their vehicles may not provide reliable transportation. Many rely on fragile arrangements with friends and neighbors, or on public transportation. This is problematic given that many public transportation systems serving these populations are often inadequate, not providing service to areas where, or during hours when, they need service the most.

United Parcel Service (UPS) found that by listening to their employees and by partnering with existing organizations the company was able to convince the public transit authorities to extend and create new bus routes to service their new airport facility in Philadelphia. The effort, as described below, addressed transportation barriers for the company's employees, and at the same time helped to attract the many part-time workers it needed.

UPS: New Bus Routes in Philadelphia

United Parcel Service is the world's largest express carrier and package delivery company and a global provider of specialized transportation, logistics and distribution financial services. The company employs more than 330,000 people and serves 1.7 million regular daily shipping customers. Headquartered in Atlanta, the company serves more than 200 countries and territories.

Impetus. Prior to opening a new facility adjacent to Philadelphia's airport, Al Patano, the District Human Resource Manager, and his colleagues knew something dramatic had to be done if they were going to get 3,000 employees to show up at work each day. The new facility was remotely located with only one access road and no public transportation nearby. Mr. Patano and his colleagues knew this would be a problem for many potential employees since they did not own cars or have drivers' licenses.

Details. The regional UPS HR team turned to the Transportation Management Association (TMA), a nonprofit government-supported organization, for help. The TMA introduced those at UPS to key contacts with the Southeastern Pennsylvania Transportation Authority (SEPTA).

SEPTA did not want to establish new bus routes unless it was sure that there would be enough riders to allow it to cover costs. Working closely with TMA and SEPTA, UPS devised a subsidization plan. UPS agreed to pay part of SEPTA's costs for the bus routes until SEPTA broke even or until the 6-month or 1-year contract ran out.

Because UPS carefully researched where employees and potential employees lived, they were able to identify the bus routes they needed. UPS gave geographic and demographic information to TMA, and TMA then supplied SEPTA with maps plotting out the proposed bus routes. In cases where SEPTA was not convinced of the viability of a proposed route, UPS hired school buses to test out the route. Once SEPTA saw the

filled buses, it established its own routes. Because of careful planning, UPS filled the buses on proposed routes quickly, allowing SEPTA to break even and UPS to end subsidization of the routes even before the contract periods ended.

The success of the SEPTA bus routes led Mr. Patano and his colleagues to implement similar programs to serve neighboring areas for the Philadelphia airport facility and other nearby UPS airport facilities:

- In order to access a large pool of job seekers in Camden, New Jersey, many of whom were welfare-to-work job seekers, UPS worked with the Camden County Improvement Authority. Together they established bus lines to bring workers to the airport facility.

- In Horsham Pennsylvania, there were no buses serving the Willow Grove airport facility making it difficult to find the part-time workers UPS needed. Together with SEPTA, UPS was able to bring in employees on new buses from different areas of Pennsylvania. And, with New Jersey Transit, they were able to bring in employees from Trenton, New Jersey.

Results. The Philadelphia airport facility now has four bus routes with 81 buses serving UPS employees. The Willow Grove airport facility has 50 buses serving UPS employees.

Costs. While UPS subsidized the bus routes until public transit authorities broke even, the well-researched bus routes often allowed them to reach break-even points before the contract period was up. This meant that UPS spent less than anticipated.

Mr. Patano believes that the benefits far outweigh the costs, especially since, the investments were driven by necessity. "It's been out of need, pure and simple," he notes.

Lessons. If establishing routes is the first step, Mr. Patano and his colleagues have found that fine-tuning the routes is the second step. At the Philadelphia airport facility, UPS holds "focus meetings" so that UPS employees have the opportunity to not only learn about what is happening at the facility but also to express any of their concerns. At one of these meetings, employees expressed concerns about safety. The 24-hour operation at the airport facility meant that employees were riding buses late at night, when bus schedules become less frequent or more irregular. When Mr. Patano found out that some of his employees were walking up to 20 blocks from the bus stops to their homes late at night, he and his staff worked again with transit authorities to fine-tune the bus routes and ensure that service continued even after midnight and dropped employees closer to their homes.

Next Steps. Mr. Patano and his colleagues are currently working on trying to resolve transportation issues in their facility in suburban Westchester, New York, where there is a cluster of industrial parks. Given the area's low unemployment, they again will look to neighboring areas to find workers and bus them in.

The HR staff will also continue to monitor how employees are doing through their focus meetings to identify new issues and problems that may arise over the course of time.

Health

Lower-wage workers are less likely than other workers to have health insurance coverage for themselves and their children. Not having insurance coverage reduces the likelihood that lower-wage workers and their children will receive preventive health care to identify and treat minor health problems before they become more serious or receive the prenatal care that is so important to the health of mothers and babies. Poor health results in lost work time and significant costs to employers and society.

The promising practices described below illustrate two different ways in which employers can promote better health among employees and their families. ConAgra encouraged prenatal care to improve the health of expectant employees and their babies, while cutting overall medical costs to the company. Mississippi Valley Gas was able to increase enrollment among employees in their medical plan by encouraging eligible employees to enroll their children in the State Child Health Insurance Program (SCHIP). Similar publicly subsidized child health insurance plans for lower-income families exist in all states.

ConAgra: Prenatal Care

ConAgra is the umbrella company for more than 70 food brands (divisions). With 2001 sales of $27.6 billion, it has 90,000 employees in 35 countries. Monfort, ConAgra's division of beef and hog processing plants, employs 20,000 workers.

Impetus. It began as a puzzle: Employees appeared to be no sicker, but medical costs were rising sharply. Human Resources professionals at ConAgra took a closer look and found that annual medical costs for premature and low birth-weight babies had reached $5 million in 1994. Further investigation showed that many of Monfort's employees, especially those from Central America, were uncomfortable or unfamiliar with the U.S. health care system and did not seek prenatal care. In order to cut costs and promote healthy child development, the company had to find a way to break through this cultural barrier.

Details. Monfort created public-private initiatives in all of its sites aimed at improving pre-natal care. At its plant in Greeley, Colorado, the company formed a partnership with the Weld County Health Department, a logical partner given that it already had a prenatal clinic, provided other preventive health services geared to women, and, most important, was staffed with bilingual employees.

The health department provides Monfort families with preconception and family planning services, prenatal checkups, screening tests, and well-baby care. These services are provided to Monfort employees at no cost—no co-payments and no deductibles.

Clinic staff also encourages expectant employees to enroll in Monfort's prenatal program, Healthy Moms, Babies and Families (HMBF). Created by the March of Dimes, the program promotes maternal and child health starting before conception. Women who enroll in the program are contacted on a quarterly basis. Once a woman becomes pregnant, HMBF-trained clinical staff (which include Spanish-speaking health professionals) calls them at least once a month and follow their progress throughout their pregnancies. In addition, parenting supports and resources are available to new parents after birth.

As an added incentive, HMBF pays 100 percent of the baby's delivery costs for families who enroll in the program within the first 12 weeks of pregnancy and stay involved in the program. (Families who do not participate are paid for only 60 percent of the baby's delivery costs.) Additionally, after the baby's birth, the company awards mothers $100 to be spent on items that promote the newborn's health and well being (i.e., car seats, food, etc.).

HBMF also provides voluntary home visitation for any expectant mother whose pregnancy has been identified as high risk. Spanish-speaking nurses and social workers see them in their homes to ensure that they continue with their prenatal care. In addition, all families are offered two home visits within two weeks after delivery. This gives them the opportunity to ask questions ranging from, "Which diapers should I use?" to, "Why does my baby cry so much?" Visiting families in their homes provides an additional opportunity for staff to assess the children's health and families' well-being.

Results. Medical costs for low-birth-weight or at-risk babies declined from $5.5 million in 1994 to $2.3 million in 1996. Between 1994 and 1996, Monfort saved $2,427,495 on costs related to pregnancy and childbirth and $748,048 on costs related to neonatal care. The average hospital stay for premature babies dropped from 17 days in 1993 to 1 day in 1996. These data suggest that fewer babies were born with major medical complications.

Mississippi Valley Gas: SCHIP Enrollment

Mississippi Valley Gas (MVG) is a publicly regulated utility company with roughly 700 employees in 31 offices across Mississippi. MVG serves over 265,000 customers in 35 counties in the state delivering natural gas through a 5,000-mile plus pipeline system. Its employees have a wide range of jobs, from ditch-diggers to engineers. The average length of service for its employees is 12.5 years.

Impetus. Although Mississippi Valley Gas provides an affordable personal health insurance plan for employees, it found that many lower-wage workers did not enroll in the company's health plan because they could not afford the costs of premiums to cover their entire family.

Details. By teaming up with the Mississippi Children and Families Forum, Mississippi Valley Gas helped enroll lower-income employees who qualified for State Child Health Insurance Plan (SCHIP) benefits for their children.

The Mississippi Children and Families Forum created a simplified application process and enrolled employees on-site. The company only had to provide proof of employment for the application.

Results. This public-private partnership provides qualified workers with low or no cost health insurance coverage for their children. The company has found that employees can afford to enroll themselves in the company's health plan and enroll their children in SCHIP. "It fills the missing piece in the puzzle," says Phil Hardwick, Vice President of Community and Economic Development for MVG.

Education

Low-wage workers typically have less education than other workers. While providing education to employees is beneficial to them, employers can also benefit by developing a more talented workforce.

The two promising practices described below show how two companies used different approaches to help their employees advance their education. UPS attracts and retains students as part of their part-time labor force by providing various types of educational assistance. By providing new employees with the necessary education and training to become qualified early childhood teachers/caregivers, Bright Horizons Family Solutions is not only able to attract potential teachers but ensure high quality child care for their clients. Ensuring high quality care has been central to Bright Horizons' success.

UPS: Education Assistance Programs

United Parcel Service (UPS) is the world's largest express carrier and package delivery company and a global provider of specialized transportation, logistics and distribution financial services. The company employs more than 330,000 people and serves 1.7 million regular daily shipping customers. Headquartered in Atlanta, the company serves more than 200 countries and territories.

Impetus. The majority (65%) of UPS employees work part-time. Many of the jobs are difficult, such as carrying heavy packages in the middle of the night. Turnover tends to be high, with about 30 percent quitting within 30 days. One way UPS recruits and retains part-time employees is to target students. By helping them attain their educational goals while they work at UPS, UPS has found that they are able to attract and retain talented, motivated, and flexible workers.

Details. Given the large size and decentralized structure of the company, UPS has found that implementing company-wide policies and programs can be time consuming and ineffective. Therefore, UPS encourages and empowers its regional, district, and local offices to craft their own programs and policies to better suit the needs of those offices.

In several large cities such as Chicago, Dallas, Louisville, Philadelphia, and Washington DC, UPS created School to Work programs. Targeting high school students 17 years or older, UPS helps students gain on-the-job work experience while offering college-level courses on-site or near-site. These programs are coordinated with government agencies, nonprofit organizations, local school systems, and higher education institutions.

To attract college students, UPS has also created an Earn and Learn program. UPS employees in 40 cities are eligible for up to $21,000 in total education assistance in the form of tuition grants and low-cost student loans. From the day they are hired, part-time UPS employees qualify for $3,000 per calendar year and a maximum of $8,000 in educational grants as well as $2,000 per calendar year and a maximum of $13,000 in loans. To retain college students, UPS will repay or forgive up to 100 percent of the loan if the student continues to work for UPS while attending college.

Louisville, Kentucky is the site of a new cutting edge automated sorting facility. In order to attract new employees to this site, UPS launched Metropolitan College. Students enrolled in the college who also work part-time at UPS are given free tuition, housing, and books. Students take classes from the collaborating institutions: University of Louisville, Jefferson Community College, and Jefferson Technical College.

Results. Over 7,000 UPS employees take advantage of the Earn and Learn program. UPS managers believe that this program substantially improves retention.

Bright Horizons: Child Development Associate Certification Program

Bright Horizons Family Solutions is a provider of work-site child care, back-up care, early education, and work-life consulting services. Bright Horizons Family Solutions manages 320 Family Centers for over 220 employers.

Bright Horizons developed an in-house on-the-job training program so that entry-level child care providers could be certified. The Child Development Associate (CDA) credential allows these employees to advance from entry-level, lower-wage positions into better paying positions with opportunities to advance to head teachers, directors, and other positions within the corporate offices.

Impetus. Bright Horizons developed this program because they could not find qualified people to fill their teaching positions. This jeopardized their ability to provide high quality child care for their clients and to ensure that quality was consistent across all of their Family Centers.

Details. A consultant was hired to design the Bright Horizons CDA credential curriculum. The curriculum was developed to not only meet national standards but to exceed them in order to meet the more stringent standards Bright Horizons sets. This was to ensure that all customers would receive the same high quality at any Family Center—something their clients expect.

The program was piloted in 1999 and implemented differently depending on the needs of each Bright Horizons region/center. In areas where it was hard to find qualified teachers, it was used as a recruiting tool. Potential hires were told they would be trained to become Child Development Associates while they were working at the Family Centers and receiving pay and benefits.

The training program lasts 8 weeks during which student teachers work in the Center for half a day and receive training for the remainder of the day. During training, these workers receive pay for the full day. After the training period, they work full-time. After fulfilling the minimum classroom hour requirement, they can apply for the CDA Credential.

In other centers, existing employees at the associate teacher level are selected for the CDA training so that they can advance to become head teachers. Classes are offered one night a week with occasional Saturday sessions for nine months at the center. These teachers can apply for the CDA credential at the end of the program.

Results. Through the program, Bright Horizons is able to attract potential teachers and train them to become certified teachers who are then able to move up within their organization, if they so desire. They are also more confident in the quality of service they are providing to their customers.

Over 10,000 students have gone through the program in Bright Horizons' eight regions.

Costs. Prior to implementing this program in-house, training was provided at nearby community colleges. Bright Horizons paid for their employees' tuition and licensing fees. These credentialing programs varied in cost and in quality across different regions of Bright Horizons' business operations.

The cost of the program includes the initial development of the curriculum, costs of providing the training in-house, and the assessment fees to qualify CDA candidates.

While the cost of implementing the program in-house may or may not be less than contracting with community colleges, Ms. Russell and her colleagues feel that results achieved through the in-house training program outweigh its costs.

Lessons. The new program did pose some challenges. Making sure that there are enough teachers to cover all classrooms while the associate teachers are in training can be difficult, especially if a teacher calls in sick. However, Ms. Russell reports that center directors usually are able to figure out last-minute solutions.

Ms. Russell also states that she and her colleague have learned to account for a certain number of students dropping out of the CDA program. Given that the curriculum works best when there are at least 6 students in the evening nine-month program and at least 12 students in the eight-week program, they make sure they have more than the minimum number of students before starting the training program to account for any attrition.

Another challenge has been managing employees at the associate teacher level who are not receiving the training by choice or because they were not selected or were not able to attend the training session being offered at that time. Some of these associate teachers had more classroom experience than new hires and expressed their dissatisfaction that they were not able to receive the training. Ms. Russell feels that as the program is expanded, this is less likely to occur.

Helping Workers Advance on the Job

Many low-wage workers live in low-income families that do not have enough financial resources to make ends meet. Their only hope for participating in mainstream America is to increase their incomes over time by advancing to jobs that pay more and have better benefits. Advancement is very much dependent upon the acquisition of greater job-related knowledge and skills. Findings reported in the companion reports to this volume—*Information for Employers About Low-Wage Employees From Low-Income Families and the Impact of Job and Workplace Conditions on Low-Wage and -Income Employees and Their Employers*—indicate that the majority of low-wage employees want to advance in their jobs and think that they have pretty good opportunities to advance with their current employers. However, they have fewer learning opportunities than other workers, and this lack of learning opportunities is associated with lower job satisfaction and higher turnover.

Low-wage, entry-level positions are often characterized as "dead-end" jobs, leading nowhere. This is unfair to the people who have these jobs and to many of their employers. Such jobs provide entry points into the workforce for many people with little job experience and limited education, and are crucial stepping stones to advancement. Employers can play very important roles in developing the competence of their lower-wage workforces—at the same time, providing themselves with more capable and productive employees, improving customer service, creating an internal pipeline for promotion, and increasing retention among low-wage employees who are able to advance.

Retaining and Recruiting Employees Through Training

The promising practices described below illustrate the commitments that two companies have made to develop their lower-wage and entry-level employees for advancement into supervisory and management positions. Home Depot has made creative use of technology to educate, train, and promote its associates, while Marriott International employs more traditional training methods to achieve these same goals.

Home Depot: Job Preference Process

The Home Depot is the world's largest home improvement retailer, with over 900 stores and about 245,000 workers in the United States, Canada, Puerto Rico, and Chile. Unlike many retailers, the majority of Home Depot employees work full-time. About a quarter of their employees work part-time—usually as added support during peak periods.

Impetus. As a way of retaining talented employees, Home Depot has always been committed to promoting employees from within. Initially, employees were asked to create a development plan at annual performance reviews. However, these plans were often not implemented. Furthermore, training was not consistent across stores. This made it difficult to fill open positions in one store with qualified employees from another nearby store and put the company at risk of losing capable employees who sought career advancement.

Details. In order to provide associates with consistent training throughout Home Depot stores, booklets were developed to describe and list the specific qualifications for all of the various positions that exist at all Home Depot stores. Through these booklets, new hires can learn about open positions. Current associates can also learn about other positions within the store to either move laterally or advance to higher positions. For example, associates in operations, such as cashiers, can learn what they need to do to become a sales associate or a head cashier, or to work at the returns desk. Sales associates from one department can learn how to become sales associates in other departments. They can learn how to advance to merchandising department supervisor positions, positions that would make them eligible to later become an assistant store manager and later a store manager.

Home Depot is committed to continuous learning. Therefore, within each of the 10 store divisions there is a training center. For example, millwork, cashier, flooring, etc. all offer training classes specific to their division. In addition, each employee is given 4.2 paid hours per month for training. Associates must use this time to first take Product Knowledge (PK) classes to master information for their department as well as "sister" departments. For example, a sales associate in lumber would first take the PK class for lumber and then a PK class for nails. These classes are structured to be self-paced. Once PK class requirements are fulfilled for their department and sister departments, associates can take PK classes to gain information that will help them win a promotion or transfer to another department.

Employees who have received the appropriate training and received satisfactory ratings on their latest performance reviews are then eligible to take the test for desired positions. Because the test is administered through kiosks located in the break room, employees can take the test when they feel they are ready. This allows the employee the best possible chance to pass the test. If an employee does not pass the test, however, he/she can take the test again after a 60-day waiting period. The kiosk also prompts them to areas within the Associate Development Guide, which provides tips for things the associate can do on the job to develop the skills they need to pass the test.

Once the employee passes the appropriate test successfully, the employee can then register their job preferences through the kiosk in the break room or through an 800 number also set up for this purpose. Through this Job Preference Process (JPP), developed in 1998, store managers are also able to list open positions within their store. Employees use the kiosk or 800-number to both learn of open positions and apply for them. Managers looking to fill positions are given a pool of applicants to choose from. In order to encourage managers to hire from within the Home Depot company, they are required to interview at least three applicants from this pool.

Results. Home Depot is able to retain its employees by promoting from within the company.

Employees are able to advance according to their preferences and can move to positions at other store locations when positions open.

Marriott International: Career Advancement Training

Marriott International is a worldwide hospitality company with over 2,000 operating units in the U.S. and 58 other countries and territories. Marriott operates hotels, resorts, corporate housing, conference centers, senior living communities and services, food distribution and procurement services. The company has approximately 151,000 associates, 80 percent of whom are hourly employees.

Impetus. Marriott's Career Advancement Training program has multiple goals: to retain talented and committed entry-level employees, to promote experienced associates from within the company as an efficient means of filling supervisory and management positions, to enhance customer service, and to improve the well-being of associates and their families.

Details. With the help of Marriott's Career Advancement Training program associates learn the skills they need to enhance their career opportunities. Through a series of 11 classes, employees learn the importance of customer service; setting goals; being a team player; developing an effective resume; and maintaining a professional image and demeanor.

In the context of Marriott International's corporate culture, this training focuses primarily on satisfying every customer. The program instructs associates on key elements to achieving good customer service—hospitality, a smile and having a willingness to help. Before associates can carry out the company's mission, they learn the foundation of its culture. Employees gain insight into the organization's history and core values—care for its employees, focus on growth and displaying pride in the company name and its accomplishments.

Marriott's infrastructure focuses on its employees' roles as team players; training their associates to be dependable, flexible and cooperative. In learning to be a team player, the Marriott program spotlights balancing a career and a personal life through time-management. Associates learn to reflect Marriott's emphasis on a professional image and good communication skills by displaying a positive attitude, developing proper business etiquette and taking pride in their appearance.

Results. The program was piloted with hourly employees in 2002, and larger numbers will participate in 2003 and 2004.

Forty percent of Marriott associates currently advance into management positions and become eligible for various employee benefit programs in the areas of housing, healthcare, tax credits and child care. The target outcome from this program is to increase this promotable percentage.

Sharing Resources Through Partnerships and Advancing Employees Across Companies

Employers seeking to help their lower-wage employees have found that by working with partners, they do not have to "reinvent the wheel." They can instead tap into existing resources that other companies, nonprofit organizations and public agencies can provide. Or, they can share costs and resources with businesses like their own.

Many of the companies with promising practices in this report have made connections and worked together with partners to achieve their goals. United Parcel Service (UPS) has worked with the nonprofit organization Transportation Management Association as well as public transit authorities to establish bus routes near their Philadelphia airport facility so that employees would have a means to get to work each day. In other locations, UPS also partners with neighboring educational institu-

tions to provide employees with classes on or near their work facilities. ConAgra worked with a local health clinic in order to improve the health of expectant employees and their infants in one of their meat-packing companies. Sears, Marriott, Hyatt, and Mississippi Valley Gas have each partnered with different nonprofit organizations and public agencies to help with the administration of federal programs designed to help employees at no cost to the employer or to the employee. ConAgra Foods turned to a private company and a nonprofit organization to create a new child care center that was affordable and accommodating to the schedules of its employees.

Described below is a comprehensive partnership between several businesses and community organizations that aims to improve the lives of low-wage workers in Grand Rapids Michigan by supporting employees with little work experience and starting to put in place job-to-job promotion across several companies.

Grand Rapids, Michigan: Job Progression Initiative

Grand Rapids/Kent County has a population of approximately 500,000. By joining forces, business and community leaders have created an integrated workforce development system that provides job training, support on the job, as well as career ladders, or opportunities to advance, for lower-wage workers in the Grand Rapids area.

Impetus. In the late 1990s, employers in Grand Rapids found it was increasingly difficult to fill minimum-wage and lower-wage jobs. They also found it very difficult to retain lower-wage workers, and turnover was a growing expense. This was a particularly severe problem for businesses that relied most heavily upon the labor of low-wage, entry-level workers, but it was also a problem for other employers seeking to fill better-paying entry-level jobs with employees who had work experience and basic skills.

At the same time, changes in welfare laws requiring work participation created a new pool of potential workers, former welfare recipients. However, to achieve successful transitions from welfare to work, it became clear to both employers and community leaders that this pool of workers required special support and training. Finding jobs was one matter, being able to sustain employment was another. The very low wages earned by many of these workers were not enough to pull their families out of poverty or provide a sustainable level of family income. Further training was needed to help these workers eventually advance into better jobs.

Local employers were motivated to make investments in the community for simple business reasons. They needed qualified people to fill positions in the short-run; they knew they would also need to fill positions in the longer-run as their businesses grew; and for some, the community was their primary customer base—the higher family incomes were the better their sales would be.

Details. Initially, there were two main groups within the community charged with addressing the issues outlined above. In 1999, Tina Hartley-Malivuk, President of Goodwill Industries of Greater Grand Rapids and a member of both working groups, began building a cross-sector collaboration involving all interested parties. She teamed with people such as Penny Pestle, Director of The Delta Strategy, which had experience building public-private partnerships in the region, and convened interested parties from a variety of backgrounds and perspectives. As they all worked together, the members from various business, nonprofit, and government organizations started to shed their insular perspectives and began thinking about the challenges more holistically and looking for solutions that would benefit employers, workers, and the larger community. "Bringing all the parties together at one table was really the catalyst that took [our efforts] to a different place," explains Ms. Pestle.

Particular attention was given to finding ways to support people moving from welfare to work. Initially, the lead company in

this initiative Cascade Engineering provided worksite case-management support for entry-level workers who were moving from welfare to work coordinating with community agencies as necessary to provide the full range of support that employees needed. Although Cascade's management had strong commitments to the community, its primary motivations were business related—more effective recruitment, enhanced skills and productivity, improved retention, and employee development/advancement.

Over time, these partners created a new model in which employers and employees can turn to a community-based resource program—SOURCE (Southwest Organizations Unifying Resources for the Community and Employees)—to achieve these goals. This evolving initiative is funded by a growing group of employers and public/private agencies and addresses the needs of entry-level workers who lack work experience, job skills, education, and English language skills or need social service support in order to become and remain employed.

Another commitment of this initiative is to implement a Job Progression Model that helps workers to advance from a job at one company to a better paying job with more generous benefits at another company as they acquire work skills and continue their education. Employers who participate identify work opportunities within their company, determine the skills required for those jobs, and specify the skills employees will gain from these jobs. The hope is that employees will remain at their current jobs for a reasonable period of time with the promise of advancement opportunities, but also advance to better jobs as they acquire more skills. The Job Progression Model is now beginning to be implemented by Butterball Farms, an entry-level food industry employer, and Cascade Engineering, a plastics-injection molding company that offers higher-level manufacturing jobs.

Results. While it is still too early to assess the results of this initiative, there have already been some promising outcomes:

- For participating companies, there is a steady flow of workers joining their organizations who are better prepared, remain with companies for longer periods of time, and are more likely to advance in their jobs.

- Employers who hire these entry-level workers also benefit from federal tax credits, the Work Opportunity Tax Credit (WOTC) and the Welfare to Work Credit (WTWC). (More information about these tax credits can be found in the first example in this report.)

- For the community, this initiative creates a steady, dependable, and continuously advancing workforce, and increases the buying power of that workforce, thereby strengthening the overall economic well-being of the community.

Costs. While the benefit/cost ratio of this initiative has not been determined at this point, those involved believe that the benefits in the form of higher retention alone have outweighed the costs to business and government. If the recruitment and productivity gains for business are factored in, the likelihood that benefits outweigh costs would be even greater.

Lessons. Following are two major lessons that this group learned through their collaboration to help lower-wage workers and the businesses that employ them:

- Those who control important resources—public and private nonprofit agency heads and business leaders or key staff—must be actively and continuously involved in the planning and implementation of the initiative.

- There should be community organizations and project managers who are seen by all participants as having the competence and authority to move the agenda ahead. Most employers have limited patience for and limited resources to devote to the "process" necessary for developing community-based programs, however important the outcome might be. Rather, they rely upon "intermediaries" in the community—who understand employer needs, employee needs, and community resources—to make things work.

Next Steps. Grand Rapids is continuing to develop its initiative recruiting more employers over time. It is also documenting and evaluating the process.

Summary Note

The promising practices described here only begin to illustrate the full range of existing and potential practices for addressing the needs of low-wage employees. However, we hope that this brief review—together with information in the companion reports, *Information for Employers About Low-Wage Employees From Low-Income Families and the Impact of Job and Workplace Conditions on Low-Wage and -Income Employees and Their Employers*—will provoke creative thinking about business strategies that serve both the needs of employers and the needs of low-wage employees. We firmly believe that there are many "win-win" opportunities.

Discussion Questions

1. Thinking about what you have learned from previous chapters, which policy/program do you think is most likely to be adopted by other companies? By employees?

2. What would motivate employers to help their low-wage employees?

Reprinted from Stacy S. Kim, Marta Lopez, and James T. Bond, "Promising Practices: How Employers Improve Their Bottom Lines by Addressing the Needs of Lower-Wage Workers." Used by permission of Families and Work Institute <www.familiesandwork.org>. ✦

CPSIA information can be obtained at www.ICGtesting.com
Printed in the USA
BVOW060248041111

275186BV00004B/1/P